AN URBANIZING WORLD: GLOBAL REPORT ON HUMAN SETTLEMENTS, 1996

An Urbanizing World: Global Report on Human Settlements, 1996

**United Nations Centre for Human Settlements
(HABITAT)**

PUBLISHED BY

OXFORD UNIVERSITY PRESS

FOR THE

**UNITED NATIONS CENTRE FOR
HUMAN SETTLEMENTS
(HABITAT)
1996**

Oxford University Press, Walton Street, Oxford OX2 6DP

Oxford New York Toronto Madrid
Delhi Bombay Calcutta Madras Karachi
Kuala Lumpur Singapore Hong Kong Tokyo
Nairobi Dar es Salaam Cape Town
Melbourne Auckland
and associated companies in
Berlin Ibadan

Oxford and Oxford English are trade marks of Oxford University Press

British Library Cataloguing in Publication Data
Data available

Library of Congress Cataloging in Publication Data
An urbanizing world : global report on human settlements 1996 / [UN
Habitat].
1. Human settlements. 2. Human settlements—Developing countries.
3. Regional planning—Developing countries I. United Nations
Centre for Human Settlements.
HT65.U73 1996 96–1388
307.76—dc20
ISBN 0–19–823346–9 (Pbk)
ISBN 0–19–823347–7

Set by Wyvern Typesetting Ltd., Bristol.
Printed and bound in Great Britain
by The Bath Press, Avon

HS/382/95/E

Foreword

By the early decades of the next century, the overwhelming majority of men, women, and children in every country will, for the first time in history, be living in urban surroundings. Driven by demographics, accelerated by the globalization and liberalization of the world economy, as well as by profound and ongoing economic and social change within countries, rapid urban growth over the past decades, especially in developing countries, has literally transformed the face of our planet. A global urban civilization will have a profound impact on the patterns of national and international development and economic growth and will certainly change the content and focus of national and international policy. It is bound, indeed, to transform the style and content of politics in many countries, as cities gain more demographic and economic weight. Human settlements development and the management of urbanization have become priority challenges for the international community and the United Nations.

It is appropriate, therefore, to include a conference on human settlements in the unprecedented continuum of United Nations conferences of this decade, a continuum that is defining the environmental, social, and economic development agenda of the international community for our times. At the United Nations Conference on Human Settlements (Habitat II) to be held in Istanbul in June 1996, international organizations, national governments, local authorities, the private sector, and other non-governmental entities will come together to confront common urban problems and address development tasks that must be undertaken in partnership. At the first session of the Preparatory committee for the Habitat II Conference in Geneva in April 1994, I observed that in the coming decades urban settlements will become the primary places for the struggle for development and social and economic progress. The mass exodus to cities has already led to sharpened urban poverty, especially among women and dependent children; scarcity of housing and basic services; unemployment and underemployment; ethnic tensions and violence; substance abuse, crime and social disintegration. The emergence of giant mega-cities has brought with it land degradation, traffic congestion, and air, water, and land pollution.

And yet, at the same time, profound ongoing processes of global demographic, economic, social and technological change provide persuasive evidence that we will be looking more and more to cities and towns for economic growth and jobs for future generations. The world's cities must become sustainable, productive, safe, healthy, humane, and affordable. This demands answers to some very hard questions suggested by the Report. How do we improve the governance and financing of human settlements? Which policies are needed to improve the living and working conditions of the poor, of families and communities? How can economic growth and employment opportunities be greatly expanded in cities while avoiding long-term environmental damage and without wasting the planet's finite natural resources? How do we provide affordable housing and services to the world's growing population? And these are not just questions aimed at the developing South. Far-reaching economic and social change has cast a long shadow over many cities in the industrialized North as well, giving rise to common problems and providing the basis in this interdependent world for a common global agenda to address them. At the 'City Summit' in Istanbul, the international community will seek to shape a common global agenda to address the challenge of an urban world and to improve shelter and the living and working environment of people everywhere. All levels of society are challenged. All levels of society must act. We are in an era caught up in a historic and dramatic transition that has still to run its course.

An Urbanizing World: Global Report on Human Settlements, is the second edition in a series of United Nations publications on human settlements trends and conditions world-wide. The *Report*, first published in 1986, was undertaken at the request of the General Assembly to provide a complete review of Human Settlements conditions, including their development and continuing evolution. As this 1996 edition makes clear, however, it does much more. It provides a thought-provoking analysis that goes to the heart of the central dilemma now confronting all human settlements—large and small, rich and poor—as they stand on the threshold of a new urban world.

BOUTROS-BOUTROS GHALI
Secretary-General United Nations

Acknowledgements

In seeking to cover in detail conditions and trends worldwide, this *Report* has drawn on the knowledge of a wide range of specialists from both the North and the South. This includes a series of background papers commissioned for this *Report*, a process of peer review for chapters, a review of the whole draft by an expert meeting, and two international workshops to develop material for the *Global Report*—the first on urban poverty, the second on innovations in housing finance.

The *Report* was written under the direction of the Research and Development Division within the UN Centre for Human Settlements (UNCHS-Habitat). David Satterthwaite (International Institute for Environment and Development—IIED) was the principal consultant author. Sections of the report were also drafted by L. S. Bourne and Richard Stren (University of Toronto), Diana Mitlin (IIED), Peter Newman (Institute for Science and Technology Policy—ISTP—Murdoch University), Richard Kirkby (University of Liverpool) and Mathias Hundsalz, D. Okpala, Steven Wainaina, Franz Vanderschueren, Graham Alabaster, Kalyan Ray, Tomasz Sudra, Catelina Trujillo, Baris Der Petrossian, Naison Mutizwa-Mangiza, I. Moisseev, P. Nota, and P. Gachuki from UNCHS.

The following contributed background papers on which the text drew or on which particular sections are based: Tade Akin Aina (CODESRIA), Silvina Arrossi (IIED-América Latina, Argentina), Richard Bird (Canada), L. S. Bourne (University of Toronto), Frank Carter (University of London), Anthony Champion (University of Newcastle), S. K. Das with Manju Gupta (India), Julio Davila (Development Planning Unit, London), Alphonse Yapi-Diahou (ENS-ORSTOM, Côte d'Ivoire), Mamadou Diouf (CODESRIA), Gustavo Garza (El Colegio de Mexico), Michael Goldberg (University of British Columbia), Arif Hasan (Pakistan), Nazrul Islam (Centre for Urban Studies, Bangladesh), Pedro Jacobi (CEDEC, Brazil), Sylvy Jaglin (Institut Français d'Urbanisme, France), Virginia Jimenez-Diaz (Venezuela), Jos Jonkhof (Institute for Forestry and Nature Research, Netherlands), Richard Kirkby (University of Liverpool), Amitabh Kundu (Jawaharlal Nehru University, India), Elena Mikoulina (Moscow Institute of Architecture), Diana Mitlin (IIED), Naison Mutizwa-Mangiza (UNCHS), Peter Newman (ISTP, Murdoch University), D. Okpala (UNCHS), Enrique Ortiz (Habitat International Coalition, Mexico), Margarita Pacheco (Instituto de Estudios Ambientales—IDEA, Colombia), David Satterthwaite (IIED, London), Gabriel Scimeni (University of Padova), Denis J. B. Shaw (Birmingham University), Johan Silas (ITS, Surabaya), Fredj Stambouli (Tunisia), Richard Stren (Centre for Urban and Community Studies, University of Toronto), Franz Vanderschueren (UNCHS), Emiel Wegelin (UNCHS), Ellen Wratten (London School of Economics and Political Science), and Hiroyuki Yamada (Kyoto University) with Kazuyuki Tokuoka (Doshisha University).

The following reviewed the whole report with UNCHS staff in an expert meeting in Nairobi in May 1995: Kunle Adeniji (Nigerian Institute for Social and Economic Research), O. P. Mathur (India), Elena Mikoulina (Moscow Institute of Architecture), Peter Ondiege (University of Nairobi), John Oucho (University of Nairobi), Carol Rakodi (University of Wales), Yap Kioe Sheng (Asian Institute of Technology), Willem van Vliet (University of Colorado), and Alexander Zakharov (UN Commission for Africa).

The following reviewed parts of the manuscript: L. S. Bourne (University of Toronto), Anthony Champion (University of Newcastle), Julio Davila (Development Planning Unit, University of London), Arif Hasan (Pakistan), Greg Goldstein (World Health Organization), Richard Kirkby (University of Liverpool), Liz Mills (European Academy of the Urban Environment, Berlin), Gordon McGranahan (Stockholm Environment Institute), Diana Mitlin (IIED), Peter Newman (ISTP, Murdoch

University), Kim Kyung-Hwan (UNCHS), Richard Stren (University of Toronto) and Richard Wilkinson (University of Sussex).

The following contributed papers to a workshop on urban poverty that was organized by CROP and IIED to help develop the section of the *Global Report* on urban poverty: Graham Alder (Matrix, Nairobi), Philip Amis (Development Administration Group, University of Birmingham), Jonathan Baker (Scandinavian Institute of African Studies), Jenny Bryant-Tokalau (University of the South Pacific), Jolanta Grotowska-Leder (University of Lodz), Jan Hesselberg (University of Bergen), Shahnaz Huq-Hussain (University of Dhaka), Nazneen Kanji (Tanzania), J. M. Lusugga Kironde (Ardhi Institute, Dar es Salaam), Augustín Escobar Lapatí (CIESAS-Occidente, Guadalajara), G. C. Macoloo (University of Nairobi), Else Oyen (University of Bergen and CROP), Carole Rakodi (University of Wales), Mercedes González de la Rocha (CIESAS-Occidente, Guadalajara), Mariken Vaa (Institute of Social Research, Norway), Ries van der Wouden (Social and Cultural Planning Office, Netherlands) Wielislawa Warzywode-Kruszynska (University of Lodz) and Ellen Wratten (London School of Economics and Political Science).

The following contributed to the development of the *Report* at its earlier stages: Pietro Garau (UNCHS), Anil Agarwal (Centre for Science and Environment, India), J. H. Ansari (School of Planning) and Marcello Balbo (Instituto Universitario di Architettura di Venezia, Italy), Charles P. Boyce (Massachussets Institute of Technology, Cambridge, USA), Michael A. Cohen (The World Bank), John Cox (The Institute for Research on Public Policy, Canada), David E. Dowall (University of California, Berkeley), Alain Durand-Lasserve (Groupement INTERURBA, France), Nikolai Demin (Kiev VNIITAG), Susana Finquelevich (CEUR, Argentina), Peter Hall (University College, London), Jorge E. Hardoy (IIED-América Latina, Argentina), Otto H. Koenigserger (Habitat International, UK), H.D. Kopardekar (All-India Institute of Local Self-Government), Piotr Korcelli (Institute of Geography and Spatial Organization, Poland), Alexandr Koudriavtcev (Moscow Institute of Architecture), W. Kreisel (World Health Organization), Gustave Massiah (ACT, France), Om Prakash Mathur (National Institute of Urban Affairs, India), G. Mertins (University of Marburg, Germany), Amos Rapopport (University of Wisconsin), David Satterthwaite (IIED), Hidehiko Sazanami (UNCRD), Juraj Silvan (State Institute for Town and Country Planning, CSFR), Jyoti Shankar Singh (UNFPA), Sun Hua Sheng (China Academy of Urban Planning and Design), Peter N. Townroe (Sheffield City Polytechnic), and Yap Kio Sheng (Asian Institute of Technology).

The following helped develop the section on innovative approaches to housing finance: Yves Cabannes (GRET, France), Francisco Fernandez (Pagtambayayong Foundation, Cebu), Alejandro Florian (FEDEVIVIENDA, Colombia), Diana Mitlin (IIED), Enrique Ortiz (Habitat International Coalition), and Randy Sachs (Rooftops, Canada).

Secretarial, reproduction and collation support were provided by Mary Dibo, Helen Musoke, Anne Idukitta, and Joseph Ochola.

Special thanks are due to the Swedish International Development Cooperation Agency and to the Canadian International Development Agency for their help in funding some preparatory workshops and background papers. Special thanks are also due to Andrew Lockett and Mick Belson (Oxford University Press) and to Tom Chandler, Judi Barstow, and Colin Baldwin for their parts in the preparation and publishing of this *Report*.

Contents

Contents

List of Boxes

List of Tables

List of Figures

List of Maps

Introduction

As we approach the new millennium, the world stands at a veritable crossroads in history. Urbanization holds out both the bright promise of an unequalled future and the grave threat of unparalleled disaster, and which it will be depends on what we do today. In publishing *An Urbanizing World: Global Report on Human Settlements, 1996* we do so in the hope that it will serve as a road map in helping us decide the direction to take.

With the new century just a few years away, we have relatively little time in which to act. Already, more than 600 million people in cities and towns throughout the world are homeless or live in life- and health-threatening situations. Unless a revolution in urban problem solving takes place, this numbing statistic will triple by the time the next century passes its first quarter.

The problem is getting worse because an ageing, decaying and neglected urban environment cannot keep up with an exploding urban population, one-third of which, and perhaps more, live in sub-standard housing, with basic necessities such as safe water and sanitation at a premium. Overall, the urban population is growing between two and three times faster than the rural population, virtually all of it in the developing countries.

By the year 2000, almost 50 per cent of the world's total population will be living in urban areas, and a few years later, for the first time in history, urban dwellers will outnumber those in the traditionally rural areas as the global urban population doubles from 2.4 billion in 1995 to 5 billion in 2025. Looking ahead to the end of the twenty-first century, more people will be packed into the urban areas of the developing world than are alive on the planet today.

The broad brush strokes of statistics can hardly suggest the conditions now demanding attention in our cities; but they indicate the urgency of action. By the same token, statistics alone cannot adequately describe the plight of today's rural dweller. The spotlight may be on the city, but we dare not lose sight of the fact that the less viable habitat of village and farm is also facing a deepening crisis as resources dwindle, land becomes rarer, and rural peoples sink deeper into poverty.

We will ignore this dimension of change at our risk if we see it solely in terms of the millions who have already abandoned economically stagnant rural areas in search of a better life in the cities. Indeed, we cannot get a true picture of today's shelter crisis without counting the number of people in the rural areas who also live in life- and health-threatening situations. And when we do so, it adds another 600 million to the global total, even as millions more in the developing countries flee environmental disasters and wars, intensifying the problem the more so.

Put together, the exodus from the rural areas has been called the largest migration in human history, with the search for all too many, ending in an exchange of rural poverty for urban poverty, and shelter, or the lack of it, is the most visible evidence of what is happening to them. What compounds the situation, moreover, is that the bulk of those affected are women and dependent children, a feminization of poverty that is rapidly becoming one of the most urgent issues on the international agenda.

This, in essence, is the alarm being sounded in *An Urbanizing World: Global Report on Human Settlements, 1996* an alarm we had best respond to in rich and poor world alike. For questions of where we live and how we live affect us all. One of the great ironies here is that the signs of urbanization are now so evident, so much a part of our daily lives, that we have almost come to take them for granted as part of the 'normal' urban scene: the slums and ghettos, the homeless, the paralysing traffic, the poisoning of our urban air and water, drugs, crime, the alienation of our youth, the resurgence of old diseases, such as tuberculosis, and the spread of new ones, such as AIDS. Every city knows the signs; every city must fight them.

In short, every one of us has a stake in humanizing the face of the urban environment, and that is why this *Global Report* is intended for the expert and the layman alike. Its publication coincides with the preparations being made for Habitat II, the Second United Nations Conference on Human Settlements, in Istanbul, Turkey, in June 1996. In convening it, the United Nations General Assembly has demonstrated its determination to take a giant step forward both in assessing the current shelter crisis and in proposing realistic solutions. Habitat II, which Secretary-General Boutros Boutros-Ghali has called 'the City Summit', comes 20 years after the first Habitat conference was held in Vancouver, Canada. It is important to note here that it is not taking place in isolation, but rather as a unique and comprehensive approach to the economic, social, and environmental problems sure to spill over from the old century into the new one, among them some of the most serious and pressing issues of human security now confronting the world community of nations.

The road to Istanbul actually started in 1992 at the Rio Summit—the United Nations Conference on Environment and Development—which adopted Agenda 21, the historic blueprint for sustainable development and its stress on the need to improve the social, economic, and environmental quality of human settlements and the living and working environments of all people, in particular the urban and rural poor. From there, the road went to Vienna and the International Conference on Human Rights. Then came Cairo and the International Conference on Population and Development, Copenhagen and the World Summit on Social Development, and Beijing and the Fourth World Conference on Women, with the final stop being, appropriately enough, Istanbul and Habitat II.

Cumulatively, these conferences are delivering a more holistic and humane message about the cooperative, interlinked solutions our global problems require. That is why it is so logical that Istanbul wind up this remarkable series. For it is in the cities, towns, and hamlets of the new urban world that the majority of us will live and work in the new century, where the most pollution will be generated and natural resources consumed, where political and social conditions are most likely to boil over into conflict, and where, ultimately, the roots of real global security—true human security—will lie.

All these facts add to the relevance and urgency of this second edition of the *Global Report on Human Settlements*, which has also been compiled in keeping with one of the main objectives of Habitat II: To present to the Conference a State of Human Settlements Report containing an assessment of the main challenges of urbanization, identifying human settlements development constraints at local, national and international levels, and building upon the basis of all available knowledge a vision of sustainable human settlements and adequate shelter for all.

Reading *An Urbanizing World* is not easy. Nor is it meant to be. The problems of urbanization are staggering—deeply disturbing—and this *Report* tells us why. But its intent is not to bemoan the situation, but rather to tell us that we have the power, the knowledge, and yes, even the resources, to do something about it. What we need is the courage and the will. And as we look beyond Istanbul, our hope is that the publication of *An Urbanizing World* will help provide the foundation on which to construct a set of sober and practical recommendations for our cities in the coming century, especially in the areas of urban economic development, governance, and environment.

With all the crises that urbanization has touched off, it also has within it the seeds of hope and promise, and these are what we must build on. This *Report* is, in fact, one of the first—and few—global studies to tell us that cities have an affirmative and constructive role to play in world society. Paradoxically, even while highlighting the problems of urbanization, it also states that it will be in the urban areas where we may be able to best provide services to people, alleviate poverty, improve life expectancy, and more wisely manage our planet's massive population growth.

The *Report* suggests that urbanization actually contributes to a nation's wealth (and thereby the planet's wealth) by enriching a country's domestic markets and its international trade. In addition, it points out that an urban setting can create the nurturing environment for scientific experimentation and technological achievement. Cities are also engines of job creation, and not least of all, as we know from archaeological excavations of ancient civilizations, cities are the vital conveyors of human culture through the centuries. Moreover, cities can provide better services because they benefit from the economies of scale. In reaching large numbers of people, metropolitan centres are able to reduce energy costs, offer more efficient transportation systems, provide better educational facilities at lower unit costs, and construct more habitable space.

But how do we make sure that cities—and those who live in them—prosper? The 1996 *Global Report* offers two routes: The first is the concept of sustainable human settlements development. This idea requires that hard-headed choices be made about production and consumption patterns in urban areas—between the demands of regions and the demands of cities; between balanced use of resources and the misuse of resources; between consideration for the finite nature of ecosystems or wilful indifference to them; between wasteful living standards and carefully managed ones. In addition, it calls for social equity through improved governance and adequate habitation.

The second is the notion of an 'enabling' role for government, which requires governments to recognize that they can be the active agents in renewing urban centres through the creation of public/private partnerships; competitive but regulated markets in land, housing finance and building materials; restructuring of shelter production regulations; the enlistment of non-governmental organizations in common enterprises; and the recognition that helping to construct low-income housing has a stimulating impact on economies.

Taken as a whole, *An Urbanizing World* offers us an overview of the harsh conditions in our human settlements that urgently demand creative innovation and action. And here it provides us with invaluable insights into the new partnerships being forged in the human settlements sector and the increasing importance of civic engagement and community initiatives being undertaken to help meet the growing challenges and needs of today for achieving sustainable human settlements. They offer encouragement and evidence of an untapped, latent capacity.

In the final analysis, the task before us is as much about doing something to cure the malaise of inadequate housing and decaying infrastructures, dangerous streets and environmental neglect, as it is about the willingness of society to meet the needs of humanity, the needs we all share with our neighbours in the 'global village' that is now our world. One of the problems we face here is that so many of us know so very little about the forces that are shaping our cities and towns—indeed, some of us may know more about the distant planets of outer space than about the cities of our own planet Earth. We have to shift our focus, and do it now.

An Urbanizing World: Global Report on Human Settlements, 1996 is directed towards that end. It is the net result of a determined effort to enhance the knowledge and understanding of everyone caught up in today's historic and dramatic transformation of our world, a transformation that has still to run its course. But perhaps its greatest value will be the practical information it provides policy-makers with at all levels, private enterprise, community based organizations and other practitioners—official and unofficial, public and private, indeed, all of us—on which to base innovative policies and programmes for the action that must be taken to make our human settlements—from the smallest hamlet to the largest mega-city—safe and liveable.

That is the only way we will pass on to our children an urban world that can sustain them in harmony, an urban world rid of the shameful poverty, the inequality, the discrimination that still pervades its ghettoes, an urban world at peace with the environment and with itself.

Nairobi, Kenya
December 1995

WALLY N'DOW
Assistant Secretary-General and
Secretary-General Habitat II

Key Issues and Messages

This *Global Report* on *An Urbanizing World* assesses conditions and trends in the world's human settlements—cities, towns, and villages. The growth in urban poverty has been one of the most noticeable trends during the 1980s and early 1990s. Another has been the limited achievements of governments and international agencies in improving housing and living conditions, including expanding the provision of safe and sufficient water supplies and adequate sanitation and drainage. Recent estimates as to the scale of the health burden suffered by those living in poor quality housing also highlight how little progress has been made.

However, while global achievements in improving housing and living conditions have been limited, there are also many examples in this *Global Report* of success. Certain national or city governments have greatly increased the proportion of their population with piped water and good sanitation. Many government agencies and non-government organizations have worked with low income groups and their community based organizations to greatly improve housing conditions and basic services (water, sanitation, drainage, health care, and garbage removal) at low cost. There are new models for housing finance that can allow low-income households to acquire better quality housing and still achieve high levels of cost recovery. Perhaps most fundamentally, there are new examples of city authorities that are more democratic, accountable and responsive to the needs and priorities of their citizens. These emphasise how much **good governance** matters. Within low-income countries or cities, good governance can greatly improve housing and living conditions which in turn can produce a 10- to 15-year increase in average life expectancies, without compromising good economic performance through excessive public expenditure. Within higher income countries, good governance can reduce poverty and deprivation and also the problems so often associated with contemporary urban living—high levels of homelessness, crime, and violence, and the concentration of the unemployed and unskilled in declining city centres or other districts.

Below are highlighted the key issues and messages of this Report under six headings:

* The role of cities within development
* Urban trends
* The limited social achievements
* Housing conditions and trends
* Governance
* Towards sustainable development

The Role of Cities within Development

1 **The role of cities and urban systems in economic development.** Urbanization has been an essential part of most nations' development towards a stronger and more stable economy over the last few decades and it has helped underpin improvements in living standards for a considerable proportion of the world's population. The countries in the South that urbanized most rapidly in the last 10–20 years are generally also those with the most rapid economic growth. Most of the world's largest cities are in the world's largest economies which is further evidence of this link between economic wealth and cities. Cities and towns also have important roles in social transformation. They are centres of artistic, scientific, and technological inno-

vation, of culture and education. The history of cities and towns is inextricably linked to that of civilization in general. Although this *Report* documents the social, health and environmental problems concentrated in cities, it also gives many examples of successful city-initiatives that show how such problems can be successfully tackled.

2 Without competent and accountable urban governance, much of the potential contribution of cities to economic and social development is lost. A positive view of cities is now emerging. This emphasizes the central role of cities in strong, competitive, and adaptable economies. Cities also have tremendous potential to combine safe and healthy living conditions *and* culturally rich and diverse lifestyles with remarkably low levels of energy consumption, resource-use and wastes. But realizing this potential depends on city authorities. Good urban governance also needs the appropriate legislative framework and support from national governments. This *Report* stresses the many opportunities and advantages which cities and towns offer, or could offer, if government policies changed. As the world approaches the 21st century with close to 6.0 billion inhabitants, and with close to half this number living in urban centres, it is now accepted that a predominantly urban population is not only an inevitable part of a wealthy economy but also one that brings many advantages. The challenge is how to manage cities and other human settlements within an increasingly urbanizing world. Such management must encourage cities to remain innovative and adaptable but also capitalize on their potential to provide high quality living conditions with much reduced resource use and environmental impact.

3 Promoting urban development does not mean neglecting rural development. This *Report* also describes the scale of rural poverty, and the inadequacies in provision for water supply and sanitation in rural areas. It emphasizes the problems that city-based demand for rural goods and city-generated wastes can bring for rural resources and livelihoods. However, it also stresses how rural–urban linkages can be positive and how governments can enhance these links. Few governments in the South appreciate the extent to which high-value crops can support rising prosperity in rural areas and encourage a more decentralized pattern of urban development. Few governments give sufficient support to developing the capacity and competence of local authorities in the market towns that should serve rural populations and improve their access to health care and education. It is even rarer to find governments acting on the factors that underlie impoverishment in rural areas and that often give poor rural households no alternative but to move to urban areas.

Urban Trends

4 Contrary to most predictions, population growth rates slowed for many cities in the South. The population growth rates of most of the South's largest cities during the 1980s were substantially lower than those for the 1960s and 1970s. During the 1980s, many of the world's largest cities in both the North and the South had more people moving out than in. In addition, in many nations, the proportion of the urban population living outside the largest city increased. However, there are countries where urbanization is more rapid than expected—especially in the relatively un-urbanized countries with high economic growth rates, such as China. There is also less evidence of large North–South contrasts during the 1980s, as several cities in the United States were among the fastest growing cities in the world.

5 The world is less dominated by mega-cities than predicted. Although there is a growing number of what has been termed 'mega-cities' with population concentrations of unprecedented size, these still contain a small proportion of the world's population. If mega-cities are considered to be cities with more than 10 million inhabitants, by 1990, only 3 per cent of the world's population lived in mega-cities. If the population threshold for a mega-city is reduced to 8 million inhabitants, less than 5 per cent of the world's population lived in mega-cities in 1990. The population size of some of these mega-cities is also exaggerated through boundaries being set for city-regions that include large numbers of people living outside the city's built-up area. The most recent censuses also found that many of the South's largest cities had several million people less than had been predicted—including São Paulo and Mexico City. The predictions that cities such as Calcutta and Mexico City will have 30–40 million inhabitants by the year 2000 are not coming true; Calcutta is likely to have less than 13 million while Mexico City is likely to have less than 18 million. This *Report* also documents how new kinds of urban systems are developing, in both the North and the South, often around the largest cities, where a dense network of smaller cities develop and prove more dynamic than the large city itself.

6 The links between urban change and economic, social, and political change. Although rapid population growth is often given as the reason for urban problems, what is apparent is not so much the speed with which cities are growing but the scale of the housing and environmental problems in cities and the deficits in the provision for piped water, sanitation, drains, roads, schools, health centres, and other forms of infrastructure and service provisions. The link between the scale of these problems and the speed with which the city grew are usually weak. As the *Report* describes, some of the largest and most rapidly growing cities also have some of the best records in improving infrastructure and service provision while some of the worst housing conditions are found in declining industrial centres and stagnant smaller towns.

The Limited Social Achievements

7 Rising poverty levels. Between one-fifth and a quarter of the world's population live in absolute poverty, lacking the income or assets to ensure they have sufficient food and to build, purchase or rent adequate shelter; more than 90 per cent of these live in the South. Although the number of people living in absolute poverty in rural areas is still higher than in urban areas, research during the late 1980s and early 1990s found that the scale of urban poverty had been greatly underestimated—largely because poverty lines were set too low in relation to the cost of living in cities. Such research also showed how many aspects of deprivation such as vulnerability and social exclusion had also grown. The number of urban dwellers living in absolute poverty grew rapidly during the 1980s, especially in Latin America and Africa and in the less successful Asian economies. Much of the growth in poverty was associated with deteriorating macro-economic conditions and structural adjustments. Changing labour markets also brought less job security and lower wages which increased the number of people with inadequate incomes. The number of urban dwellers living in absolute poverty also rose in much of the North, linked to higher levels of unemployment including rising levels of the long-term unemployed, lower wages for unskilled and casual workers and cutbacks in the scale and nature of welfare benefits. Poverty levels also rose in most countries in East and Central Europe, linked to the collapse of communism and the political disintegration of the former Soviet Union, although social progress had also slowed prior to these political changes. What remains uncertain is whether the major changes in East and Central Europe and the changes introduced in the South through structural adjustment will provide the basis for sustained economic growth during the 1990s and, if this happens, whether such growth will reduce the proportion of people living below the poverty line.

8 Long term social trends. Despite the setbacks during the 1980s, the long term trends in most nations were towards higher life expectancy, lower infant mortality, and higher literacy. There were also two developments that have important implications for human settlements in the future. The first was the much increased recognition of the discrimination faced by women in most aspects of employment, housing, and basic services and the greater efforts made by some governments and international agencies to reduce or remove this. The second was the growth in what might be termed the 'housing rights' movement as more governments recognized that citizens have a right to housing and as greater use was made of national and international law in demanding that this right be fulfilled and in opposing evictions. However, the exact nature of people's right to housing and the extent of a government's responsibility to ensure that this right is met remains much disputed.

Housing Conditions and Trends

9 Poverty and housing conditions. As real incomes decline, so individuals or households have to cut expenditure on housing. This often means moving to poorer quality housing. But one dramatic difference between the North and the South is the higher proportion of urban and rural dwellers in the South that live in very poor quality housing in relation to the proportion considered by official statistics to live in 'absolute poverty'. This reflects the low priority given by governments and aid agencies to improving housing and living conditions, especially provision for piped water and sanitation and measures to ensure sufficient land is available for new housing. At least 600 million urban dwellers in Africa, Asia, and Latin America live in housing that is so overcrowded and of such poor quality with such inadequate provision for water, sanitation, drainage, and garbage collection that their lives and their health are continually at risk. The same is true for more than one billion rural dwellers, largely because of inadequate provision for water and sanitation. In the North, while millions of low-income people may live in poor quality housing, most live in housing with piped water, toilets connected to sewers, drains, and bathrooms. This greatly reduces the health burden of being poor.

10 The enormous health burden of poor quality housing. The size of the health burden imposed on people living in poor quality and overcrowded dwellings with inadequate provision of water, sanitation and drainage has been greatly underestimated. So too has the extent to which improved housing and living conditions can improve health and alleviate poverty. For instance, the disease burden per person from diarrhoeal diseases caught in 1990 was around 200 times higher in sub-Saharan Africa than in the North. Disease burdens from tuberculosis, most respiratory infections (including pneumonia, one of the largest causes of death worldwide) and intestinal worms are generally much increased by overcrowding. Many accidental injuries arise from poor quality, overcrowded housing—not surprising when there are often four or more persons in each small room in shelters made of flammable materials and there is little chance of providing occupants (especially children) with protection from open fires or stoves. One of the greatest challenges for Habitat II is how governments can reduce this enormous health burden associated with poor quality housing. The means to achieve this are well known and as numerous examples given in this *Report* show, the costs are not high. Even in relatively poor countries, much can be done to reduce this health burden, especially through innovative partnerships between national government, local authorities, community organizations and local non-government organizations.

11 Poverty and insecure tenure. Several million urban dwellers are forcibly evicted from their homes and neighbourhoods each year, as a result of public works or government-approved redevelopment programmes. They are usually evicted without compensation and almost always without measures to consider how the public works or redevelopment could have been done while minimizing the scale of evictions and with relocation schemes that are acceptable to those relocated. Most low-income households are particularly vulnerable to evictions, as they have no legal tenure of the house they occupy. Over the last 20–30 years, most new housing in most cities of the South was built on illegally occupied or subdivided land as legal sites were too expensive or simply not available in sufficient quantities. Many illegal settlements developed on land ill-suited for housing—for instance on floodplains or steep hillsides—but housing conditions would have been much worse without them. Many 'shanty-towns' also develop over time into good quality residential areas with basic infrastructure and services either developed by the inhabitants or provided by the public authorities. However, even illegal land markets have become increasingly commercialized and it is rare for low-income households to be able to find land sites which they can occupy free of charge. This diminishes the housing options for low-income households and also increases insecurity for those living in illegal settlements.

12 The growing number of homeless people. An estimated 100 million people have no home and sleep outside or in public buildings (for instance railway or bus stations) or, where available, night shelters. There are many street-children among this homeless population. Far more people are homeless in the sense that their accommodation is very insecure or temporary—for instance squatters or those living in temporary shelters (for instance the 250,000 pavement dwellers in Bombay). Data on homelessness in the South is too sparse to know if this problem is growing, although the increasing commercialization of legal and illegal land markets probably means it is. Homelessness certainly grew considerably in most countries in the North during the 1980s and it also came to include a growing proportion of women and younger age groups.

13 Governments as enablers, not providers. In general, the wealthier the nation, the better the quality of housing. However, a well-conceived and implemented housing policy can ensure housing conditions become far above the norm for nations with comparable income levels per person. The government's main role is as an 'enabler' rather than as a provider of 'low-cost' housing. This requires actions to ensure a competitive but regulated market in land, housing finance, and building materials and to remove unnecessary bureaucratic constraints on the different stages of housing production. This includes ensuring that there is a ready supply of land for housing in urban areas with the price of legal housing plots with basic services kept as low as possible. Households will not develop housing on illegally occupied or subdivided land if they can afford legal plots. A competitive market for housing finance greatly increases the capacity of those with modest incomes to build, extend or buy housing. This *Report* also gives many examples of innovative ways in which governments have reached low-income groups with improved housing—for instance support for upgrading existing low-income settlements, working with and through their community organizations. This can also combine support for income generation with support for housing improvement. Or housing finance schemes for those whose incomes are too low or uncertain to allow them to obtain finance from the private sector. Government support for a wide range of non-profit social housing institutions has also greatly improved housing quality for lower income groups in many European countries.

Governance

14 The new institutional frameworks for urban authorities. One of the main reasons for the human settlements problems noted above has been the inadequacies in the institutions and the institutional framework for the development and management of human settlements. Local governments which have most of the responsibilities for managing urban change often lack the power and resources to fulfil these. Most urban authorities in the South have very little investment capacity, despite the (often) rapid growth in their populations and the need for infrastructure. However, decentralization policies of some kind have been implemented in most countries over the last 10–15 years. In many, this was associated with a move to democratic rule or a return to democracy. It has also been encouraged by citizen and community pressure for more effective and accountable local authorities. The extent to which power and resources (or the capacity to raise revenues) have been decentralized has varied. In some instances, it is largely only the tasks and responsibilities that have been decentralized. However, in some countries, decentralization is producing more effective responses to local problems.

15 Enhancing the role of citizen groups, community organizations, and NGOs. All cities are the result of an enormous range of investments of capital, expertise and time by individuals, households, communities, voluntary organizations, NGOs, private enterprises, investors, and government agencies. Many of the most effective and innovative initiatives to improve housing conditions among low income groups have come from local NGOs or community organizations, including women's groups. Yet in most cities in Africa, Asia and Latin America, the individual, household and community efforts that help build cities and develop services have long been ignored by governments, banks, and aid agencies, and often constrained by unnecessary government regulations. If governments and donor agencies can find ways to support these processes that build and develop cities— which is what an enabling strategy is all about—what appear as insurmountable problems begin to appear more manageable. What can be achieved by supporting the efforts of several hundred community organizations in a single city can vastly outweigh what any single government agency can do by itself. New 'enabling' institutions are needed that complement the efforts of individuals, households, communities, and voluntary organizations and ensure more coherence between them all so they can all contribute towards city-wide improvements. They must work out how funding and technical advice can be made available in ways that match the diverse needs and priorities of different settlements—with accountability and transparency built into the disbursement of funding.

Towards Sustainable Development

16 From environmental protection to sustainable development. Cities concentrate production and population and this offers many potential advantages in regard to waste minimization, reduced resource use, and reduced automobile dependence. Without environmental management, this same concentration produces serious environmental problems such as high levels of air pollution, faecal contamination, flooding, and uncollected garbage. Cities usually have serious environmental impacts far beyond their boundaries through the ecological impacts of the demand they concentrate for natural resources and the wastes that they generate and dispose of outside their boundaries. As urban authorities progress from a commitment to environmental quality to a commitment to sustainable development, two further tasks have to be addressed. The first concerns minimizing the negative impacts of city-based production and consumption on the needs of all people, not just those within their jurisdiction. The second concerns implementing urban development and management strategies based on an understanding of the finite nature of many resources (or ecosystems from which they are drawn) and of the capacities of ecosystems in the wider regional, national and international context to absorb or break-down wastes. In the long term, no city can remain prosperous if the aggregate impact of the production of all cities and their inhabitants' consumption draws on global resources at unsustainable rates and deposits wastes in global sinks at levels that undermine health and disrupt the functioning of ecosystems. Establishing sustainable patterns of urban production and consumption has many implications for citizens, businesses and city authorities. But certain city authorities have begun to act, as can be seen in their innovative local Agenda 21 plans.

17 The social components of sustainable development. While the economic dimensions of sustainable development are much debated and increasingly well understood, this is not the case for the social dimensions. Social equity, social justice, social integration, and social stability are central to a well-functioning urban society. Their absence leads not only to social tensions and unrest but also, ultimately, to civil wars and violent ethnic conflicts. Unless society is at peace, all development gains are under threat. One of the greatest challenges facing governments and international agencies at Habitat II is how human settlements policies can help increase social equity, social integration, and social stability. This obviously includes reducing poverty and other forms of deprivation, including reducing social exclusion. It also includes improving governance so that all localities have public authorities that can address local problems and remain entirely accountable to their citizens as they do so.

18 New approaches to planning. Many of the problems summarized above and described in more detail in this *Report* arise from inadequate and inappropriate planning and provisioning for settlements. But the need for planning becomes ever more necessary in the light of the increased social, economic, and environmental impacts of urbanization, growing consumption levels and renewed concerns for sustainable development since the adoption of Agenda 21. Environmentally sound land-use planning is central to the achievement of healthy, productive, and socially accountable human settlements within societies whose draw on natural resources and ecosystems are sustainable. The challenge is not only how to direct and contain urban growth, but also how to mobilize human, financial, and technical resources to ensure that social, economic and environmental needs are adequately addressed. Considering the limited effectiveness of current methods and approaches to settlements planning, new processes and approaches have to be devised that can be adapted to each society's conditions and circumstances. These must also support the trend towards increased accountability and participation.

Editor's Note

An Urbanizing World: *Global Report on Human Settlements*, is the second edition in the series, the first having been published in 1986, as called for by the United Nations General Assembly in its Resolution 34/114 of 14 December 1979. It mandated UNCHS (Habitat) to prepare, on a periodic basis, a 'Global Report on Human Settlements', presenting a comprehensive review of human settlements conditions, including an analysis of major issues and trends.

The specific objectives of this present Report are:

(*a*) To provide a statement on the global and regional conditions of human settlements useful to individual countries and international agencies concerned with improving their respective human settlements policies and programmes;

(*b*) To promote general interest in, and make contributions towards an informed understanding of the evolving nature of settlements, the interrelationships of their parts, and of the significance of settlements systems in providing setting for human, social, economic, and environmental development.

(*c*) To provide an update on global policy matters addressed by the United Nations as well as a synthesis of information available to the United Nations from other sources.

This *Report* realizes these objectives by incorporating key issues which have emerged since the first edition of the *Global Report on Human Settlements (1986)*. The earlier edition emphasized issues of shelter, settlements management, institutions, financing, land, infrastructure, and human settlements development strategies. Many of these remain of crucial importance today. However, since its publication, human settlements have also encountered environmental degradation, socio-economic polarization, social impacts of economic structural adjustment programmes, increasing and deepening poverty, social and political upheavals leading to the destruction of human settlements, and forced migrations of refugee populations and homelessness.

Global restructuring of economic production processes also have influenced the character of human settlements systems, altering the flow of capital and labour, prioritizing information services over manufacturing as the pre-eminent form of employment. Concurrently, decentralization and democratization have transformed the role of governments and communities in providing improvements for human settlements, necessitating new strategies for reducing poverty which involve more directly the capacities of the private sectors and communities.

In addition to large-scale trends since 1986, the *Global Report* is also presented in the context of a growing concern in the international community, which has served to highlight increased awareness of the state of human settlements and its interaction with economic and social development. The International Year of Shelter for the Homeless (IYSH, 1987) to a significant degree raised global community awareness of the continuing distressed living conditions of the world's urban and rural poor, and consequently made conditions of homelessness a focus of world public concern.

In a subsequent initiative soon after, the Global Strategy of Shelter to the Year 2000 adopted by the General Assembly in 1988, emphasized an enabling approach to shelter provision and improvement with a view to mobilizing, utilizing and coordinating the resources of community organizations, non-governmental organizations (NGOs), the private sector, and governments at different levels working together to improve the living conditions of people everywhere.

Part I of this report reviews the various trends that in one way or the other shape the conditions of human settlements development management, to which policies need to be directed. They include a review of economic, social, spatial, environmental, and institutional trends. The reviews provide a broad framework, context and setting for specific human settlements issues and topics, including trends in population growth and urbanization in various national, regional, and other spatial contexts, and the ramifications for human settlements development and management. Part I also considers among pertinent social issues, trends, inequality, gender, crime and violence, as well as pressing institutional concerns such as public financing of human settlements development, land adjudication, and the changing roles of central governments, local authorities and communities in an era of democratization and decentralization. In short, this section of the *Global Report* documents changes in settlements—their physical size, population, and internal organization in the context of larger economic, social, and political trends.

Part II assesses the state of the various sectoral components of human settlements and the factors that condition them. They include housing conditions, shelter supply and demand, and homelessness. This section focuses on the crucial issue of housing finance, highlighting the importance of access to credit, employment generation in housing production, and innovative mechanism used to finance low-income shelter. Part II also reviews the issue of land, which is a major factor in human settlements. The discussion considers the problem of access to land, the complex needs of squatter populations, and the role of government in making land available for development. This part also examines the state of infrastructure and services in human settlements: the state of water supply, sanitation, solid waste and related public health management, transportation, communication, etc.

Part III of the Report outlines the responses by governments, NGOs, community groups, the private sector and by the international community to human settlements conditions and trends identified in Parts I and II.

In light of the lessons and inferences drawn from Parts I, II and earlier chapters of Part III, the concluding chapter of this latter Part suggests, largely in the context of Agenda 21, new directions for human settlements. New directions have to give greater recognition to the positive role and contributions of cities to economic and social development. They involve improving the governance of municipal and rural settlements through approaches which encourage governments to enable neighbourhoods to manage, in the widest sense, local settlements improvements, facilities, and services. In addition, this concluding chapter highlights recent innovations in more effective partnerships among governments, the private sector, community-based organizations and NGOs in the planning development and management of cities, towns, and villages.

Part IV presents statistical annexes on various human settlements topics for reference and further studies. The annexes are designed to assist practitioners and scholars to build upon existing strategies for human settlements improvements, enabling innovative programming and applied social research.

Finally, the second edition of the *Global Report on Human Settlements*, together with the first edition published in 1986, provides what is in essence a history of the urbanization process that is literally reshaping the face of the planet in these closing decades of the century.

PART I

Conditions and Trends

1 The Global Context

1.1 Current Trends in Global Economic Conditions

Recent world economic trends

An understanding of economic change worldwide and within nations is needed to make sense of urbanization trends and of other changes in the spatial distribution of the world's population over the last 15–20 years. An understanding of economic change is also important for understanding the changing scale and nature of international and internal migration flows. Without such an understanding, it is difficult to make sense of the very rapid growth of many cities in China, the increasing concentration of the world's urban population in Asia, the slowing in growth of most major cities in Latin America (at least up to the early 1990s), the radical restructuring of the urban system in the United States and the revival of certain major cities in Europe. There are also important changes in the physical structure of cities and their wider metropolitan areas that are much influenced by economic trends. This brief review of economic change in the last two decades is to provide the broad context for considering changes in the scale and nature of urbanization in the second part of this chapter and the more detailed considerations of population and urban change within each of the world's regions in Chapter 2. It is also important for understanding the changes in the scale and nature of poverty in both rural and urban areas (described in Chapter 3) and the changes in the scale and nature of urban environmental problems (described in Chapter 4).

Although in aggregate, the world economy has expanded considerably over the last two decades, it has experienced a fluctuating growth pattern over this period. The 1980s began with the fear of a return to high inflation, following the 1979–80 oil price increase of around 150 per cent. When coupled with the structural problems facing the major economies, there was a fear among OECD nations that this would herald another period of recession comparable to that following the first oil-shock in 1973/4. However, the leading economies were better prepared and were able to use firmer monetary and fiscal policies that not only contained inflation but improved their economic performance. By 1984, the average inflation level within OECD stood at around 5 per cent compared with nearly 13 per cent in 1980. However, the recovery remained weak. Average real GDP growth rates for OECD countries fell from 3–4 per cent during the 1970s to less than 2 per cent in 1980 and 1981 and zero in 1982—see Table 1.1. Between 1983 and 1990, average real growth rates rose once more to between 2 to 4.5 per cent a year across the OECD countries. By the early 1990s, growth rates had fallen once more and real growth rates did not exceed 2 per cent between 1991 and 1993.

These aggregate figures conceal significant differences between countries.[1] The Japanese economy, for instance, grew strongly throughout the period except in 1992 and 1993. The US economy contracted sharply in 1982 (by 2.2 per cent) and rose strongly immediately afterwards, and managed to maintain real growth levels between 1991 and 1993, against the general trend. Economic growth in Northern, Southern and Western Europe has, in general, been lower than in Japan and more stable than in the US. In the early 1990s, the downturn was sharp, with negative growth in 1993 in 11 European countries (see Table 1.1). For the years 1991–93, certain nations had declines in their real GDP, the largest decline being in Finland but with declines also in Sweden, Switzerland and the United Kingdom.

The economic declines in East and Central Europe and in the republics that were formerly part of the Soviet Union in the early 1990s were considerably larger. After years of poor economic performance, attempts were made to introduce reforms in most of these countries—but it was the political revolutions of 1989 that brought abrupt changes in both political and economic organization. This included the collapse of existing trade patterns following the collapse of the Council for Mutual Economic Assistance (CMEA). As different countries sought to reduce the role of the state in production and to introduce other economic changes, they came to be labelled as 'transition' economies. There has been a sharp decline in output in most of East and Central Europe since 1989—and for the region as a whole, output diminished in each year from 1990 to 1993.[2] In 1992, output in the republics that were formerly part of the Soviet Union fell by 20 per cent.[3] Exports to the OECD began to provide some stimulus for growth for some of the transition economies from 1992.

For most countries in the South, the period 1975–95 has meant little growth in per capita

TABLE 1.1 Real GDP: Percentage changes from previous period

	Average 1970–77	1978	1979	1980	1981	1982	1983	1984	1985	1986	1987	1988	1989	1990	1991	1992	1993	Estimates & Projections 1994	1995	1996
United States	3.0	4.8	2.5	−0.5	1.8	−2.2	3.9	6.2	3.2	2.9	3.1	3.9	2.5	1.2	−0.6	2.3	3.1	3.9	3.1	2.0
Japan	4.4	4.9	5.5	3.6	3.6	3.2	2.7	4.3	5.0	2.6	4.1	6.2	4.7	4.8	4.3	1.1	0.1	1.0	2.5	3.4
Germany	2.7	3.0	4.2	1.0	0.1	−0.9	1.8	2.8	2.0	2.3	1.5	3.7	3.6	5.7	5.0	2.2	−1.1	2.8	2.8	3.5
France	3.5	3.4	3.2	1.6	1.2	2.5	0.7	1.3	1.9	2.5	2.3	4.5	4.3	2.5	0.8	1.2	−1.0	2.2	3.1	3.2
Italy	3.4	3.6	5.8	4.1	0.6	0.2	1.0	2.7	2.6	2.9	3.1	4.1	2.9	2.1	1.2	0.7	−0.7	2.2	2.7	2.9
United Kingdom	2.2	3.5	2.8	−2.2	−1.3	1.7	3.7	2.3	3.8	4.3	4.8	5.0	2.2	0.4	−2.0	−0.5	2.0	3.5	3.4	3.0
Canada	5.1	4.6	3.9	1.5	3.7	−3.2	3.2	6.3	4.7	3.3	4.2	5.0	2.4	−0.2	−1.8	0.6	2.2	4.1	4.2	3.9
Total of above countries	3.3	4.3	3.6	0.9	1.7	−0.3	2.9	4.6	3.3	2.9	3.2	4.5	3.2	2.4	1.0	1.6	1.4	3.0	3.0	2.7
Australia	3.3	4.0	4.0	2.5	3.4	−0.1	0.7	7.5	4.7	2.0	4.7	4.1	4.5	1.3	−1.3	2.1	3.8	4.3	4.3	4.0
Austria	4.1	0.1	4.7	2.9	−0.3	1.1	2.0	1.4	2.5	1.2	1.7	4.1	3.8	4.2	2.7	1.6	−0.3	2.6	3.0	3.1
Belgium	3.3	2.7	2.1	4.3	−0.9	1.5	−1.7	4.5	0.8	1.4	2.0	4.9	3.5	3.2	2.3	1.9	−1.7	2.3	3.0	3.1
Denmark	2.5	1.5	3.5	−0.4	−0.9	3.0	2.5	4.4	4.3	3.6	0.3	1.2	0.6	1.4	1.0	1.2	1.4	4.7	3.3	2.9
Finland	2.9	2.2	7.3	5.3	1.6	3.6	3.0	3.1	3.3	2.4	4.1	4.9	5.7	0	−7.1	−3.6	−2.0	3.5	4.8	3.9
Greece	5.0	6.7	3.7	1.8	0.1	0.4	0.4	2.8	3.1	1.6	−0.5	4.4	4.0	01.0	3.2	0.8	−0.5	1.0	1.5	2.3
Iceland	6.6	7.0	5.5	7.0	4.3	2.0	−2.0	4.1	3.6	6.5	8.8	−0.3	0.2	0.5	1.0	−3.7	0.9	1.9	1.6	2.0
Ireland	4.9	7.2	3.1	3.1	3.3	2.3	−0.2	4.4	3.1	−1.4	5.7	4.3	7.4	8.6	2.9	5.0	4.0	5.0	5.0	4.6
Luxembourg	2.7	4.1	2.3	0.8	−0.6	1.1	3.0	6.2	2.9	4.8	2.9	5.7	6.7	3.2	3.1	1.9	0.3	2.6	3.2	3.5
Mexico	5.8	8.2	9.2	8.3	8.8	−0.6	−4.2	3.6	2.6	−3.8	1.9	1.2	3.3	4.4	3.6	2.1	0.6	2.9	4.0	4.3
Netherlands	3.3	2.5	2.4	0.9	−0.7	−1.5	1.4	3.1	2.6	2.7	1.2	2.6	4.7	4.1	2.1	1.4	0.4	2.5	2.9	3.2
New Zealand	2.9	−6.4	1.5	0.4	4.7	3.4	1.1	8.7	1.1	0.7	−1.7	3.0	1.0	−0.1	−4.2	0.4	4.4	5.0	3.6	2.9
Norway	4.8	4.7	5.1	4.2	0.9	0.3	4.6	5.7	5.3	4.2	2.1	−0.5	0.6	1.7	1.6	3.4	2.2	3.6	2.9	2.3
Portugal	4.9	2.8	5.6	4.6	1.6	2.1	−0.2	−1.9	2.8	4.1	5.3	3.9	5.2	4.4	2.1	1.1	−1.1	1.0	2.6	2.9
Spain	4.7	1.5	0	1.3	−0.2	1.6	2.2	1.5	2.6	3.2	5.6	5.2	4.7	3.6	2.2	0.8	−1.0	1.7	2.9	3.3
Sweden	1.8	1.8	3.8	1.7	0	1.0	1.8	4.0	1.9	2.3	3.1	2.3	2.4	1.4	−1.1	−1.9	−2.1	2.3	2.3	2.5
Switzerland	0.9	0.6	2.4	4.4	1.4	−0.9	1.0	1.8	3.7	2.9	2.0	2.9	3.9	2.3	0	−0.3	−0.9	1.7	2.2	2.7
Turkey	6.4	1.7	−0.7	−1.9	5.3	4.2	5.3	7.4	4.5	7.8	9.1	2.1	0.9	9.1	1.0	5.5	5.9	−3.9	3.6	4.8
Total of smaller countries	4.2	3.1	3.4	2.9	2.3	1.0	0.9	3.8	3.0	2.0	3.6	3.2	3.6	3.6	1.3	1.5	0.7	2.0	3.3	3.5
Total OECD	3.5	4.1	3.6	1.2	1.8	0	2.6	4.4	3.3	2.7	3.3	4.3	3.3	2.6	1.0	1.6	1.3	2.8	3.0	2.9
OECD North America	3.3	5.0	3.1	0.2	2.4	−2.1	3.3	6.0	3.2	2.5	3.1	3.8	2.6	1.3	−0.4	2.1	2.9	3.9	3.2	2.3
OECD Europe	3.3	2.9	3.4	1.4	0.4	1.0	1.8	2.6	2.7	3.1	3.1	4.0	3.4	3.2	1.5	1.2	−0.1	2.3	3.0	3.2
EC	3.2	3.2	3.5	1.3	0.1	0.8	1.6	2.3	2.5	2.9	2.9	4.2	3.5	3.0	1.7	1.1	−0.3	2.5	3.0	3.2
Total OECD less the United States	3.8	3.7	4.2	2.3	1.8	1.2	1.8	3.4	3.4	2.6	3.4	4.5	3.7	3.4	2.0	1.2	0.2	2.2	3.0	3.4

Source: Annex Table 1, OECD Economic Outlook Issue no. 56, December 1994, OECD Publications, Paris.

income, especially from the early 1980s. Between 1980 and 1991, annual average growth in per capita income was negative for three regions: sub-Saharan Africa, the Middle East and North Africa, and Latin America and the Caribbean. Serious debt problems were evident in many countries from the beginning of the decade, as global recession and rising real interest rates meant many countries could not afford to repay their foreign debts. The 1980s thus came to be known as 'the lost decade' in Latin America and this description is applicable to most of Africa and many countries in Asia too.

The main exceptions are the leading Asian economies such as China and what have been termed the Dynamic Asian Economies (the Republic of Korea, Taiwan, Hong Kong, Singapore, Thailand, Indonesia and Malaysia) which sustained high economic growth rates for most or all of the 1980s and early 1990s. The region in which these nations are concentrated—East Asia and the Pacific—had much the highest economic growth rate of any of the world's regions during the 1980s and early

1990s. China had among the world's most rapidly growing economies between 1980 and 1993, including being the fastest growing economy in the region (and indeed in the world) for 1992 and 1993.[4] This is all the more remarkable, given that China has around one-fifth of the world's population. As will be described in more detail later, the growing role of East Asia within the world economy is also reflected in the fact that this region contains a growing proportion of the world's urban population and of its largest cities.

Most other countries in the South suffered from one or more of the following problems: economic stagnation, high inflation, poor terms of trade, severe external debt problems plus other domestic problems, such as rising unemployment, high interest rates, unstable currencies and falling incomes for a large proportion of their population. These usually had a devastating impact on the overall development of these countries, particularly on housing and living conditions including the quality and availability of housing, water supply and provision for sanitation as well as on their political and social stability. The number of urban dwellers living in poverty increased sharply in many countries during the 1980s and early 1990s (see Chapter 3).

In recent years, there has been some turn-around for certain countries in Latin America and in South Asia. For instance, the growth in GDP in Latin America averaged 3.1 per cent a year between 1991 and 1993—although much of this growth was concentrated in Argentina, Chile, Colombia and, until late 1994, Mexico. The economic performance of most African countries, particularly those in sub-Saharan Africa, remained poor over the last two decades[5]—and this region did not share the more buoyant economic performance achieved by South Asia and Latin America for 1991 to 1993.[6] Some countries in the continent have suffered from drought which has sharply reduced food production—with serious problems of under-nutrition in large regions and of famine in some. In addition some countries have suffered from civil strife and military and ethnic conflicts over long periods. In the economic area they have suffered from poor terms of trade for their primary commodity exports, higher oil prices for the non-oil producers and increasing debt burdens for most or all of the last fifteen years. Overall debt stock for sub-Saharan Africa rose from $84 billion in 1980 to $199 billion in 1993.[7] Most of the export earnings these countries were generating over the period were used mainly for purposes of servicing debt, which is largely owed to other governments and official agencies.

Changes in nations' per capita incomes[8]

These economic reversals during the 1980s in most of Latin America and Africa and much of Asia represented a change from the previous two decades. In most countries, per capita incomes in the early 1990s were still much higher than in 1960—and this is reflected in the regional figures given in Table 1.2. However, there are countries where there has been very little growth in per capita income since 1960 and, in a few, per capita income in the early 1990s is actually lower than it was in 1960. The following summary uses purchasing power parity adjusted per capita income estimates.[9]

Global GDP, in real terms, increased more than fourfold between 1960 and 1991 with the world's average per capita income almost tripling in this period.[10] In aggregate, per capita income for OECD nations tripled in this period; in Austria and Spain it increased more than fourfold and in Japan more than sevenfold. Within the North, the region with the most rapid growth in its per capita income was Southern Europe.[11]

TABLE 1.2 Changes in real income per person, 1960–1991

Country or region	Real GDP per capita (ppp US$)	
	1960	1991
World		5,490
'The North'		14,860
'The South'	950	2,730
'Least developed countries'	580	880
Latin America and the Caribbean	2,140	5,360
Arab States	1,310	4,420
South Asia	700	1,260
East Asia	730	3,210
South-East Asia	1,000	3,420
Sub-Saharan Africa		1,250
North America	9,780	21,860
Europe		
European Community	5,050	16,760
Nordic countries	5,770	17,230
Southern Europe	3,390	14,100

Source: Statistics drawn from UNDP, *Human Development Report 1994*, Oxford University Press, New York and Oxford, 1994.

ppp = purchasing power parities

In aggregate, per capita income in the South almost tripled between 1960 and 1991, although there was far more variation between countries and regions than in the North. In many Asian nations, it expanded more than threefold. For instance, in China, Malaysia, Thailand and Indonesia, it expanded more than fourfold, in Singapore more than sixfold, in Hong Kong, eightfold, and in the Republic of Korea more than twelvefold. In Latin America as a whole, it expanded 2.5-fold with Brazil (3.7-fold) having the largest expansion within the region. In Africa, some nations had dramatic increases—for instance the per capita income of Botswana increased tenfold between 1960 and 1991 with that of Egypt increasing 6.5-fold and Kenya 3.7-fold.

Although there are prominent exceptions, in general, the nations with the lowest per capita incomes in 1960 also had among the lowest per capita incomes in 1991. Most of the countries with the smallest increase in per capita income and virtually all those that had a decline in this period were in sub-Saharan Africa. Perhaps not surprisingly, many of the nations with a decline in per capita income in this period were those in which there were prolonged wars. Among those with declining per capita incomes are Mozambique, Somalia, Liberia and Afghanistan, which experienced serious civil war and strife. Angola, Sudan and Ethiopia, which also suffered serious and prolonged civil wars, had among the lowest increases in per capita income during this 31-year period.

Changing macro-economic conditions and impacts on human settlements

The lower economic growth rates that most countries in the South experienced during the 1980s in comparison to the 1970s generally meant reduced rates of growth in regard to consumption and to gross fixed capital formation. The weakness in overall investment growth is explained by a number of factors including the decline in disposable income for households, lower expenditures by firms and governments and a low level of confidence in general economic improvements.

During the 1980s and early 1990s, international finance was dominated by two developments. The first was the emergence of very large current account deficits in the USA and the huge surplus incurred by Japan and to a lesser extent by Germany and the dynamic Asian economies. The second development was the international debt crises. The 1980s also brought the virtual elimination of the very large OPEC surpluses. Among the key policy responses which have had widespread effects are the World Bank and International Monetary Fund (IMF) programmes which came to emphasize the seeking of debt solutions on a case by case basis, while at the same time introducing conditionality for countries implementing the programmes.[12]

It is important to note that in the 1980s, property lending in the OECD area expanded rapidly, due to its good credit rating among the depository institutions. Various factors explain why lending in this area was favoured: the sector's enjoyment of limited competition from the securities market relative to commercial lending; government encouragement for investment in housing; and the fact that real estate seemed to provide solid security for loans, in the wake of rising prices. Towards the end of the decade, property values declined in many countries with the result that collateral values underlying bank loans also fell, leading to reduced borrowers' capacity, rises in interest rates on housing loans, relative to market rates and a slump in lending activity.[13] In some countries, falls in the value of property led to large numbers of people with 'negative equity' as the value of their property fell below the value of the loan they had used to purchase it.

For most countries in the South, the 'lost decade' in terms of their economic performance also brought very inadequate investment in infrastructure, housing and services related to shelter. Planned investments in expanding city infrastructure and services were often among the first to be cut during a recession. In most countries, there was also a serious deterioration in existing infrastructure and services—reflected in the deterioration of city bus and train services, garbage collection services, road repairs and maintenance to water mains, sewers, drains and public buildings.[14] To this deterioration was added that arising from home-owners, landlords and businesses who postponed investments in maintenance and repair, as their own incomes diminished.[15] The lack of investment funds was further aggravated by the prevailing debt situation. For the transition economies, there was in the period a lull in growth associated mainly with reforms and later transition to market-based production systems. The elimination of subsidies and the state withdrawal from production sectors targeted for reforms, such as housing development, has implied less investment in the built environment and in infrastructure and services, even in countries where overall economic growth has begun to improve.

The inflationary conditions in most countries in the South in the 1980s and 1990s and also in the transition economies in the early 1990s also had repercussions on human settlements; unlike the major economies in the North, they were unable to contain inflation, owing to structural economic problems as well as weak monetary and fiscal systems. Overall inflation levels in many transition economies grew rapidly. Some of the newly independent states such as the Ukraine have been suffering from hyper-inflation due to monetary conditions, energy-related price rises and also prevailing price-control regimes.

Inflation levels have also remained high in many countries in the South. In general, it is the fastest growing economies that have been most successful in keeping inflation to single-digit rates, such as the Republic of Korea, Singapore, Malaysia, Thailand and Hong Kong. The problem with high inflation levels is that they have encouraged capital flight, discouraged domestic savings in cases where real interest rates are negative, and discouraged foreign investments. This in turn has led to a lack of investment funds from domestic sources to undertake investments in basic infrastructure and other capital developments. High levels of inflation have also led to lower credit availability and lower demand. Most households have to reduce their level of investments as their disposable income falls which, coupled with higher interest rates, reduces demand for loans, including mortgages.

Inflationary conditions also reduce business confidence with the effect that short-term projects are preferred over long-term investments which require long pay-back periods. Since most large infrastructure projects have high returns but long pay-back periods, there was a decline in the number of such projects. This was even the case in cities with rapidly growing populations and a great need for a large expansion in roads, public transport, water supply, sanitation, drainage and power. Construction has further been constrained by shortages of foreign currency reserves, which has also partly been hampered by the tightening of global credit conditions.

One particular problem facing many Southern countries is the cost of importing building materials, as the import content of conventional building materials is very high, on average 20 per cent but up to 60 per cent in some countries.[16] Countries with limited export earnings have difficulties generating the needed foreign exchange. Poor terms of trade and in particular, currency devaluations raise import costs making it difficult to afford regular supplies. Supply is further curtailed by foreign exchange shortages and rationing. This imposes great constraints on all building and construction projects that use imported materials and rising costs for on-going projects where costs often escalate even faster due to shortages and poor deliveries.

Structural reforms and structural adjustments

Structural reforms have been very important in both North and South since the 1970s, but became even more crucial in the 1980s when major economies experienced large current imbalances as well as external imbalances. In both the North and South, structural reforms have had the same primary aim of building capacity for sustained economic development. The difference in policies used has arisen out of the differences in the economic structures of the economies and the kinds and degree of market distortions and rigidities that are in existence.

In the North, policies have covered four areas: taxation, financial markets, product markets, and labour markets and social policies. Reforms have sought to streamline personal income taxes, corporate taxation and consumption taxes. In both personal and corporate taxes, rates have been lowered but the bases broadened. The aim has been to improve incentives to work and for saving, while better corporate taxes are aimed at improving investment climate. Financial market reforms have involved extensive deregulation aimed at improving their efficiency, increasing flexibility, reducing distortions in savings flow to final uses, improving responses to customers, creating a more receptive environment for the adoption of new technologies, enhancing the countries' position in the international markets for financial services, and creating an enabling market for monetary policy implementation using market-oriented instruments. The deregulation has involved allowing foreign participation and creating greater scope for competition.

In product markets, a range of reforms have been directed at specific industries or group of industries. Actions taken have been designed to promote competition from both domestic and foreign sources through deregulation, reduction in protection levels and a critical review of industrial policies. The process has involved broad domestic measures such as the dismantling of general price controls and international trade policies such as regional agreements, international negotiations as in GATT, and deregulation of services traditionally provided by regulated networks—such as those in transport and communications.

In labour markets and social policies the goal has been to reduce impediments to lowering unemployment. Policies in this area have included the removal of regulatory controls in wages, job training and retraining and adjustments in social programmes. From the mid-1980s, there was increased privatization and strong pressure to reduce the role of the state in the economy particularly in certain Northern economies such as UK and USA.

In the South, some similar reforms, such as those in taxation and product markets, are being implemented under specific programmes introduced to address structural reforms. Structural adjustment programmes have been characterized by moves towards privatization and the adjustment of the economy towards market-oriented economic systems, reduction of the public sector, exchange rate adjustments—mainly through devaluation of national currencies—deregulation of the price system, removal of subsidies and also deregulation of the service sector and factor inputs.

The implementation of the programmes has had implications at both national and global level. The policy changes in the North also reduced the flow of aid and other capital flows to the South, adding to the slowing down of economic activities. In the labour market, the programmes led to a reduction in general and public sector employment levels and often to cuts in incomes.

One of the principal policies in the structural reform programmes in both North and South has been to cut public spending and to reduce budgetary deficits. The cuts made are usually in sectors not considered as priority or core productive sectors which, in many cases, includes human settlements.

The effects of structural programmes in the South have been of much concern, particularly due to their undesirable immediate effects. As Chapter 3 will describe, structural adjustment programmes were often associated with rising levels of urban poverty. In the long run, it is hoped that the programmes will lead to sustained economic growth. In the short-run, the impacts were very different. Structural adjustment policies have an impact on human settlements through several channels: the national economic growth rates; the size and allocation of government expenditure;

and the impacts of government policies on different sectors. The immediate impact on the economy is deflationary to reduce domestic consumption and encourage exports and, through reduced government expenditure, to encourage private sector expansion.

The measures adopted to achieve the immediate objectives have generally resulted in higher prices of essential commodities, including food and building materials, reduced employment, and reduced incomes owing to the fiscal and monetary contraction. There were also other effects such as lower access to health care or reduced effectiveness (for instance as needed medicines could not be imported), and declining quality and effectiveness of schools and other basic services as a result of less public expenditure.

International and national debt burdens

Debt burdens have constrained global economic development since the problem came to the fore in 1982. The effect of the crises has been that increasing proportions of national revenues are devoted to debt servicing, with little or no additional capital to investment. As the crises continued in the 1980s, debtor countries began to experience a reversal in capital resource flows, lower investment capacity and growth and also higher inflation. The expansionary policies of 1979–81 coupled with large fiscal deficits (particularly of the USA), rapid increase of world interest rates, falling commodity prices and the recessionary conditions in turn made it difficult to find a lasting solution to this problem. The policy solutions used have been varied and have met with differing success depending on the debtor country's circumstances and magnitude of debt. These policies have included debt-swaps, debt relief, particularly for low-income countries, debt rescheduling, debt buy-back schemes, debt for trade swaps and other schemes such as debt and equity issues. However, in spite of progress made in a number of countries and relief for the very poor, debt has continued to be a threat to economic development in the South.

In the OECD countries, domestic government indebtedness is estimated to have increased from 22 per cent in 1979 to 40 per cent in 1990.[17] This has restricted governments' ability to maintain appropriate expenditures and tax plans, as an increasing share of public expenditure has to be devoted to meeting debt service obligations. The strategies chosen to deal with these debts include: across the board reduction of the share of non-interest expenditures (such as pensions and unemployment benefits), raising taxation and reducing investments, subsidies and capital transfers. However, it is the current imbalances in trade deficits and current account deficits that are the major concerns of Northern governments.

In the South, the concern has been both with foreign debt and domestic policies. This situation arose out of the growth patterns in the 1970s and early 1980s, when these countries used foreign borrowing to maintain unsustainable levels of consumption in the wake of falling export earnings and shifting terms of trade. The emergence of debt problems, and the tightening of loans in the 1980s led to problems in servicing the existing debts as well as serious balance of payments problems.

The effects of debt problems are varied although there are some common impacts. In all the countries, both public and private investments declined and in some cases virtually collapsed as sources of credit became scarce. In particular, public spending on projects including those associated with human settlements, were reduced as debt servicing became a priority.[18] This often meant declines in investments in water supply, sanitation, drainage and roads. Budgetary stringencies often meant declining support for all forms of housing project, including many squatter upgrading programmes and housing credit programmes that, unlike most forms of government support for housing had reached lower income groups with improved conditions. The situation was made worse by reduced shelter investment by the private sector as a result of the adjustment policies.

Housing finance was also affected by inflation and international interest rates, which rose as debt problems set in, and by the effect of the debt on other mechanisms employed by governments to raise funds. Mortgage interest rates based on a combination of international rates and underlying domestic inflation considerations also remained high. The result was lack of long-term fixed lending. The overall effect of reduced housing finance and demand was lower levels of lending and hence lower levels of construction, improvement and renovation.

Human settlements development was further constrained by the effects of debt on households' income and borrowing capacity. The reduction in savings as disposable income fell (or grew less quickly) had the effect of cutting down on investments in private sector housing. In countries where corporate investment in the housing sector is significant, the reduction in the availability of credit in the finance markets and reduced government grants following budgetary reductions had the effect of further reducing investments in housing and related infrastructure and services.

Changes in the world economy

There are a series of complex structural changes in the world economy that are not apparent in the economic indicators outlined above. For example, there are at least four major changes in the relative importance of different economic sectors that have profound implications for human settlements:

- The rapid decline in the value of natural resources within the global economy and relative to the value of manufactures which means the relative impoverishment of countries and regions dependent on natural resource production.[19] This helps explain why the economies of certain parts of Latin America and Africa fared so poorly during the 1980s. It also helps explain why many of the OPEC countries were no longer among the most rapidly growing economies in the world, during the late 1980s and early 1990s.

- The rapid growth in international trade (the value of which multiplied twelvefold since 1945) and the transformation of trade from one dominated by goods to one dominated by finance and specialized services. One commentator has suggested that this forms the basis for a new urban economic order of banking and service activities that comes to replace the older, typically manufacturing oriented urban core.[20] The cities with important stock-markets and financial services have also benefited from the very large expansion in the financial industry; for instance, between 1974 and 1994, the total capitalization of the world's stock-markets expanded more than sixteenfold in real terms from $900 million to $15 trillion.[21] Producer services have become the most dynamic, fastest growing sector in many cities.[22] Insurance, banking, financial services, real estate, legal services, accounting and professional associations are central components—and most mix business and consumer markets.[23] But there are also other important producer services linked to management, innovation, research and development, personnel, wholesale distribution, advertising, transport and communications, and servicing the offices and equipment used by this wide range of businesses. The globalization of production is probably increasing overall demand for producer services but the location of the producer services can be entirely disassociated from the manufacturing plant. Thus, the producer services in London and New York are meeting demands most of which are not generated within their own region.[24]

- The rapid growth in the media business and its increasing internationalization with much of it controlled by transnationals—for instance major news services, television, film and video industries, major newspapers and publishing houses. There is also a globalization of advertising and marketing agencies. Their increased importance has also greatly boosted the economy of the cities where they have concentrated.

- Tourism—both international and within nations—has become of major significance to the economies of many nations and within them, many cities and smaller urban centres. The scale of international tourism when measured in terms of arrivals increased more than fifteenfold between 1970 and the late 1980s.[25] This too has greatly boosted the economy of many urban centres, including some that were facing serious economic decline as their manufacturing base or importance as a port declined. Many cities in Europe earn more from tourism than from manufacturing.

There are other important changes, some of which underlie the relative importance of different economic sectors and these too have fundamental implications for human settlements in both the North and the South. They include:[26]

- The much increased importance of transnational corporations within the global economy. Just 500 companies account for two thirds of world trade, and around 40 per cent of this occurs within these companies.[27] This has meant a great increase in the proportion of industries and some services worldwide that are organized and controlled on a world scale, through global corporate networks. These have brought and continue to bring significant changes in the international division of labour. Export processing zones or new financial centres or simply new centres of industry are being created or much changed—including some that are at a considerable distance from the major cities. This has transformed the economic and urban base of many cities and regions. National and city governments have increasingly sought to ensure their countries or cities remain competitive through developing export processing zones, free trade zones and technopoles—see Box 1.1. They also seek to attract the global or regional offices of the multinationals and to capture a larger share of the international tourism and business convention market.

- The transformation of production processes with the technological revolution that allows changes in production (for instance flexible specialization and increased automation) and in its organization. One important organizational change that influences urban systems within nations is the 'just-in-time' production system that can encourage a concentration of industries and service enterprises that are part of the production process—although with modern transport and communications systems, allowing these to be in different cities. Another

BOX 1.1
Technopoles and innovation

The term 'technopole' has been given to deliberate attempts to plan and promote within one location technically innovative, industrial-related production. Technopoles include industrial complexes of high technology firms that arose without deliberate planning, though governments and universities had a critical role in their development—for instance Silicon Valley in California as a new complex and Boston's route 128 that was the transformation of an older industrial region. They also include 'science cities' that are scientific research complexes which are spatially separate from manufacturing—for instance Tsukuba (Japan) and Taedok (Republic of Korea).

There have been many attempts to create technopoles that have failed to generate what can be termed the 'innovative milieu' that drives the innovation and synergy between different firms and that allows a technopole to achieve a self-generating development.

'. . . without an innovative milieu, the development of high technology industries will contribute to regional development only within the heavy constraints set by the business cycles of industries that are likely to be highly volatile, There will be no possibility of truly indigenous growth, and thus no escape from the state of dependency on another region, another region's companies and another region's innovative individuals.' (pp. 234–5).

In addition, there are also the old metropolises that keep their leading role as centres of high technology firms and research (for instance Paris and Tokyo) and certain newer metropolitan centres that developed as centres of high technology production (Los Angeles and Munich). There are also some notable differences between countries—for instance in the United States, the large US corporate laboratories fled from the old major cities while in Japan they have remained within metropolitan Tokyo. The Keihin region of Japan embracing metropolitan Tokyo and its surrounding prefectures of Kanagawa, Saitama and Chiba is the leading high technology industrial area in the world. And in contrast to its leading rival in Southern California, its primacy is based firmly on production for the consumer market. It concentrates just under a quarter of Japan's manufacturing output and is the largest industrial region in Japan.

Source: Manuel Castells and Peter Hall (1994), *Technopoles of the World: The Making of 21st Century Industrial Complexes*, Routledge, London and New York.

whose impact is more international is the 'global' capital good where different components are made in places where production costs are minimized with the final product bearing parts made in dozens of different countries.

- Advances in telecommunications and in computer networks that permit a progressively centralized control of production but a greater decentralization of the production itself, either within transnational companies as they manufacture different parts of a single product in different countries or cities, or through subcontracting, joint venture and strategic alliances. This can lead to an almost complete separation between management and production as head offices arrange for the whole

design, production, promotion and sales process without the good being produced and sold necessarily coming to the city or even the country from where this whole process is controlled. Many elements in this new organization of production no longer need to be in central cities or even in cities at all. They no longer benefit from agglomeration economies and can benefit from cheaper locations within countries (e.g. on the edge of metropolitan centres or outside them on greenfield sites) or in lower-wage countries. This development was dependent on better logistical management and sophisticated telecommunications and it also reduces the dependence on unskilled labour. There is also a growing number of service activities that can be moved to cheaper locations within nations or internationally because of advanced telecommunications. For instance, many major companies in the North have a large part of their routine administrative, accounting or sales tasks undertaken in countries in the South. Many more companies have a substantial part of their workforce in rural areas or small towns, including a growing proportion who work from home through teleworking (Chapter 8 considers this in more detail).

- The increasing mobility of capital at both national and transnational level. Direct foreign investment has grown much more rapidly than the export trade.[28] The scale of direct foreign investment flows to the South has increased very considerably, rising from only a few billion dollars in 1980 to some $10 billion in 1986 to $56 billion in 1993;[29] the scale of private loans and portfolio equity investments has also increased rapidly in the early 1990s.[30] Direct foreign investment was boosted by the privatization of many state-owned enterprises, especially in Latin America and Eastern Europe. However, most direct foreign investment remains between countries in the North and most direct foreign investment to the South is concentrated in a limited number of countries.[31] For instance, in 1993, China was much the largest recipient with over a quarter of the total; China with Mexico, Argentina, Malaysia and Thailand received 59 per cent of foreign direct investment flows to the South.[32]

- The emphasis of most government policies on free markets in finance and trade in goods and services and the removal of protectionist trade barriers (and the development of regional trading groups) which has resulted in governments with less power and private capital with more power.[33] This has also been interpreted by some to mean that cities have greater power,[34] although it is only cities that can successfully compete for international, national or local investments that have more power.

These are all changes whose direct and indirect implications are considered in the rest of this chapter, and also in Chapter 2.

1.2 Global Population Change and Urbanization

Changes in population and in households

The world's total population in 1995 was estimated at 5.7 billion.[35] The rate at which it is has been growing was essentially constant between 1975 and 1990 (at around 1.7 per cent a year) and it is projected to drop to an average of around 1.5 per cent a year during the 1990s.[36] Fertility rates have declined almost everywhere in recent years, although the pace of change differs greatly. For aggregate regional statistics, the exception is Africa, although fertility decline has started in a number of countries in East and Southern Africa.[37] However, the global picture is one of immense diversity.[38] Thus, the discussion of recent demographic changes and their implications for human settlements will be concentrated in Chapter 2, within sections that consider population and urban change in each of the world's regions.

In most societies in recent decades there have been rapid changes in the size of households and in their structure (including the proportion of households headed by women and the types of person within the household). One of the most dramatic has been the increase in the proportion of female-headed households which are now thought to comprise more than one fifth of all households worldwide—although with large variations between countries.[39] Box 1.2 gives more details and discusses the links between this growth and economic and urban change. It is also likely that in most societies there is or has been an increase in the proportion of nuclear families and a fall in the average size of households, which has accompanied (and is linked to) an increasingly monetized economy and increasing proportions of the labour force working in non-agricultural activities and living in urban areas. For the United States and for much of Europe, the average household size is now less than three persons. Another important change, recorded in many countries in the North, is a rapid increase in the proportion of single person households. In much of Europe, over a quarter of all households are one-person households; in the USA, over a fifth of all households are one-person households. These and other changes in the size and composition of households have important and often underrated influences on urban changes and housing markets. They bring major changes in the number of households which need accommodation; a rapid growth in the number of households can mean that housing demand rises, even as the overall population of a city falls. They also bring changes in the type of accommodation that is sought, in household income and in households' preferences as to where they want to live.[40]

However, the scale and nature of changes in household size and structure appear too varied from society to society or within a society over time (or perhaps even between income groups) to permit much detailed generalization. International comparisons are also hampered by the differences in definition or interpretation of 'household' between countries and the fact that there is no recent data on households in many countries. In addition, the assumption that economic changes always promote a change from a predominance of extended families to a predominance of nuclear families has been challenged both by historical studies which show that household composition has long been highly variable in rural areas and by contemporary studies which find extended households common in urban areas.[41] The relative proportion of nuclear or extended families depends on a great variety of macro and micro factors—for instance, in rural areas, they include local forms of agricultural production, land availability and inheritance, kinship patterns and demographic variables such as life expectancy.[42] There is also evidence of a rising proportion of extended families in many urban areas, largely as a response by households to falling real incomes.[43] Chapter 6 will describe one aspect of this—the number of young adults (single and married) who share the house of parents or other kin as they lack the income to afford their own accommodation. Chapter 3 will also give examples of the growth of extended families in urban areas as relatives come to live with nuclear families because they have lost their own livelihoods or as relatives are welcomed for the extra income and household work they can contribute—although there are also examples of extended families dividing, as the nuclear household can no longer support relatives. Thus, 'while there is little doubt that household composition usually undergoes some change in the course of urban development, these changes take different forms at different times and in different places and they can by no means be generalized.'[44]

An urbanizing world

The last few decades have brought enormous changes to the · world's settlements—cities, smaller urban centres and villages. They include new forms of city and metropolitan areas, some

BOX 1.2

Women-headed households and urbanization

Women-headed households form a rising proportion of households in most parts of the world. Worldwide, it is estimated that one-fifth of all households are women-headed households.[45] This is not a homogeneous category as it includes not only single parent women-headed households (headed by unmarried, divorced, separated or widowed women) but also households headed by grandmothers and women who live alone or with other women. Although such households are not a new phenomenon and in many societies they have a long history, what is new is their importance relative to other forms of household and the fact that they have become common in many more societies.[46]

There are large variations between regions and nations in the proportion of women-headed households and in the extent to which this proportion is changing. For instance, only an estimated 13 per cent of households in Asia and the Pacific are women-headed compared to 19.1 per cent in Africa and 18.2 in Latin America.[47] In some countries, the proportion of women-headed households can rise to more than a third of all households. In some countries such as India and the Philippines, female household headship does not seem to have risen much or at all since the 1960s while in others, especially in Latin America and the Caribbean it has grown quite substantially.

Although women-headed households are not unique to urban areas and in some regions such as South Asia and sub-Saharan Africa they are more characteristic of rural districts, many of the factors responsible for female-headed household formation arise through urbanization. Urbanization and its outcomes brings changes in gender roles and relations and in gender inequalities (although with great variety in the form and intensity from place to place). This can be seen through the transformation of household structure, the shifts in household survival strategies, and changing patterns of employment.

In addition, the urbanization process is itself frequently shaped by gender roles and relations—for instance through the scale and nature of female migration into urban areas (which is much influenced by decisions in rural households about who should migrate and for what reason) and the influence on the urban labour market arising from constraints placed on women's right to work outside the home by households and societies and by the extent of the demand for female labour. The degree and nature of gender selective movement to urban areas is often a major influence on both the frequency and the spatial distribution of women headed households within countries.[48] In general, where men dominate rural–urban migration streams as in South Asia, North Africa, the Middle East and many parts of sub-Saharan Africa, urban sex ratios show more men than women and women-headed households are usually more characteristic of rural than urban areas. In the towns and cities of East and South-East Asia, and Latin America and the Caribbean, rural out-migration is female selective, urban sex ratios usually show more women than men and levels of female household headship are higher in urban areas.

There is a tendency to equate the growth in female households with the growth in poor or disadvantaged households—but this growth has positive aspects in many societies. For instance, women-headed households are likely to be free of patriarchy at the domestic level— while other benefits may be greater self esteem, more personal freedom, higher degrees of flexibility in terms of taking paid work, enhanced control over finances, and a reduction or absence of physical and/or emotional abuse. Women-headed households are not always over-represented among the lowest income groups. In addition, when women decide to set up their own houses, it may be a positive and empowering step, especially if in doing so, they are able to further their personal interests and the well-being of their dependants. Various studies have shown that the expenditure patterns of female-headed households are more biased towards nutrition and education than those of male-headed households, with less spent on items that contribute little or nothing to the household's basic needs.[49] Where this is the case, women and children within a low income female-headed household will usually have better diets than those in male-headed households with the same income, and with less tendency for children or youth to be withdrawn prematurely from school. However, while female-headed households may be better off than they had previously been when male-headed, in most societies, they are still disadvantaged by the widespread discrimination against women and against single parent households. Women-headed households face greater difficulties than male-headed households because of the discrimination women face in, for instance, labour markets and in access to credit, housing and basic services. And single parent households, most of which are female headed, also face the difficulties of one adult having to combine income-earning with household management and child rearing and this generally means that the parent can only take on part time, informal jobs with low-earnings and few if any fringe benefits.[50]

Source: Sylvia Chant, 'Gender aspects of urban economic growth and development', Paper prepared for the UNU/WIDER Conference on 'Human Settlements in the Changing Global Political and Economic Processes', Helsinki, 1995.

of unprecedented size. The average population of the world's 100 largest cities was over 5 million inhabitants by 1990 compared to 2.1 million in 1950 and less than 200,000 in 1800.[51] The last few decades have also brought a world that is far more urbanized, and with a much higher proportion living in large cities and metropolitan areas. Soon after the year 2000, there will be more urban dwellers than rural dwellers worldwide. There are also tens of millions of 'rural-dwellers' who may live in settlements designated by censuses as 'rural' but who derive their livelihood from work in urban areas or who work in industries or service enterprises located in 'greenfield sites.' In the North, most of these 'rural dwellers' also have homes that enjoy the quality of infrastructure and service normally associated with urban locations—for instance piped water and water-borne sanitation and the regular collection of garbage.

Table 1.3 shows how the world's total, urban and rural populations were distributed among the regions in 1990.[52] The extent to which Asia dominates each of the categories is particularly notable—with three-fifths of the world's population and just under three-quarters of its rural population. Despite being predominantly rural, it still had more than two-fifths of the world's urban population and more than two-fifths of the world's population in cities with 1 million or more inhabitants (hereafter called 'million cities'). Table 1.3 also highlights the scale of Africa's rural population—which in this year was larger than the rural population of Europe, North America, Oceania, Latin America and the Caribbean put together.

TABLE 1.3 The distribution of the world's total, rural and urban populations and its largest cities, 1990

Region	Total population (millions of inhabitants)	Percent of the world's:				Number of the world's	
		Total population	Rural population	Urban population	Population in 'million cities'	'million cities'	'mega cities'
World	5,285	100.0	100.0	100.0	100.0	281	12
Africa	633	12.0	14.4	8.8	7.5	25	0
Asia	3,186	60.3	72.2	44.5	45.6	118	7
Europe	722	13.7	6.7	22.8	17.9	61	0
Latin America & the Caribbean	440	8.3	4.2	13.8	14.7	36	3
North America	278	5.3	2.3	9.2	13.1	36	2
Oceania	26	0.5	0.3	0.8	1.3	5	0

Notes: The figures for the number of 'million cities' and 'mega-cities' and the population in 'million cities' should be treated with caution, as the criteria used in setting boundaries for cities or metropolitan areas varies greatly between nations. Some cities with more than a million inhabitants within their urban agglomeration or metropolitan area do not become 'million-cities' as the population for their 'city' as reported by governments to the United Nations does not contain a million inhabitants. There are also cities whose population may have exceeded 1 million inhabitants by 1990 but which have not been recorded by the United Nations Population Division in their 1994 revisions.

Source: United Nations, *World Urbanization Prospects: the 1994 Revision*, Population Division, New York, 1995. The number of 'million cities' and their populations have been adjusted, where new data were available.

What underlies urbanization

Urbanization trends during the 1980s have to be understood within the longer term changes of a world population that has been urbanizing rapidly for several decades. Urban populations did grow rapidly in most parts of the world during the 1980s—but they actually grew faster during the 1950s.[53] Population growth rates for most major cities in both the North and the South were slower during the 1980s, compared to the 1970s and 1960s. And for many of the world's largest cities, including many in the South, more people moved out of the city than in during the last inter-census period.

Recent trends in urbanization reflect economic and political changes, some long-rooted, some of more recent origin. For instance, the steady increase in the level of urbanization worldwide since 1950 reflects the fact that the size of the world's economy has grown many times since then and has also changed from one dominated by relatively closed national economies or trading blocs to one where most countries have more open economies and where production and the services it needs (including financial services) are increasingly integrated internationally. In 1950, most of the world's workforce worked in agriculture; by 1990, most worked in services. The period since 1950 has brought not only enormous changes in the scale and nature of economic activity but also in the size and nature of house-holds, in the scale and distribution of incomes within and between nations and in the scale and nature of government. All, inevitably, influence settlements patterns.

Perhaps the most fundamental influences on the world's settlement system in recent decades have come from the unprecedented changes in economic and political conditions. Section 1.1 outlined the main economic changes that meant that many countries in both North and South had the value of their per capita income multiply several times since 1960. In general, as the final section in this chapter describes in more detail, the countries with the most rapidly growing economies since 1950 were generally those with the most rapid increase in their level of urbanization while the world's largest cities are heavily concentrated in the world's largest economies. On the political front, virtually all the former colonies of European powers gained independence since 1950 and the political changes of that decolonization also meant major changes to settlement systems—especially through the concentration of economic and political power in national capitals and, in some nations, the removal of migration controls on indigenous populations. The more recent economic, social and political changes in East and Central Europe and the former Soviet Union and in South Africa are also fundamentally changing settlement patterns, although these changes are too recent to have been captured by available census data.

Many countries also experienced an unprecedented growth in their national populations. Over twenty nations with 1 million or more inhabitants in 1990 had populations that had more than tripled since 1950—most of them in Eastern Africa, Western Asia and Central America. Although rapid population growth does not, of itself, increase the level of urbanization, in most nations in the South it is the most important factor in increasing urban populations.[54] Even in regions with much less dramatic population growth and political change such as Western Europe and North America, there have been major demographic changes—for instance in age structures and household sizes and types—and as Chapter 2 will describe, these have contributed to major changes in settlement patterns.

But amidst rapid economic, social, political and demographic change, there are some elements of continuity in settlements. The average size of the world's largest cities may have changed enormously but their location has changed much less. For instance, in most of the world's regions, there is a perhaps surprising continuity in the list of the largest cities and metropolitan areas; more than two-thirds of the world's 'million-cities' in 1990 were already important cities 200 years ago while around a quarter have been important cities for at least 500 years.[55] In Latin America, most of the region's largest cities today, including virtually all national and most provincial capitals were founded by the eighteenth century with most of the largest cities founded by the year 1580 AD.[56] In Asia, close to 90 per cent of all its cities that had a million or more inhabitants in 1990 had been founded by 1800 AD and around three-fifths were already important cities by that date. In countries or regions with long urban histories, there is often a comparable continuity, even for small market towns. For instance, studies of various regions of India have also found that most of the urban centres, even down to small administrative centres and market towns, have long histories.[57] In most countries, settlement patterns have changed much less than the degree of economic, social and demographic change might imply. One reason is that existing cities represent a considerable concentration of human and physical capital and it is difficult for new cities to arise that can compete with the old ones.[58] Another is that in most instances, cities adapt to changing circumstances. A third is that most major cities are also important administrative centres, and this generally provides some economic stability.

A predominantly urban world?

Perhaps too much emphasis is placed on the impending transition of the world to where the number of urban dwellers will exceed the number of rural dwellers. There are two reasons for caution. The first is the extent to which this transition could be hastened or delayed by changes in definitions. It would only take China, India or a few of the other most populous nations to change their definition of urban centres for there to be a significant increase or decrease in the proportion of the world's population living in urban centres.[59] The proportion of the world's population currently living in urban centres is best considered not as a precise percentage (i.e. 45.2 per cent in 1995) but as being between 40 and 55 per cent, depending on the criteria used to define what is an 'urban centre'. What is perhaps more significant than the fact that more than half of the world's population will soon be living in urban centres is the underlying economic and social changes it reveals—that a steadily declining proportion of the world's population make a living from agriculture, forestry, hunting and fishing.

The second reason for caution arises from the confusion between the terms 'urban centre' and 'city'. Many people have commented that more than half the world's population will soon be living in cities—but this is incorrect since a significant proportion of the world's urban population live in small market towns and administrative centres. Certainly, the proportion of the world's

population living in 'cities', however defined, is substantially smaller than the proportion living in urban centres of all sizes.[60]

The definition of city and metropolitan populations

Caution is also needed when considering the population of individual cities—or comparing populations between different cities—since the size of a city's population depends on the boundaries chosen. For instance, the current population of most of the world's largest urban areas including London, Los Angeles, Shanghai, Beijing, Jakarta, Dhaka and Bombay can vary by many million inhabitants in any year, depending on which boundaries are used to define their populations. Different boundaries also mean different population growth rates—so London, Los Angeles, Tokyo, Buenos Aires or Mexico City can be correctly stated as having populations that are declining and expanding in recent decades, depending on which boundaries are chosen for defining their populations.

Even the citizens of a city use its name in different senses, depending on context. A Parisian may at times think of Paris as the central département of that name—largely corresponding to the area of 19th-century Paris. At other times (especially if the Parisian in question is an inhabitant of, say, suburban Seine St Denis), the continuously urbanized area, including the surrounding départements, may be included in the implied definition. At yet others, the whole Paris region—the Ile de France—may be the intended sense.[61]

It is also difficult to compare the populations of major cities 'outside the central city' because of the different ways in which the areas outside the 'central city' can also be subdivided—for instance into inner suburbs and outer suburbs—and often into 'exurbs' or population living in the metropolitan area but outside the built up area of the city itself. In many countries, the boundaries of the metropolitan area may be extended further to include urban centres or other settlements from which a considerable proportion of the economically active population commute to work in the metropolitan area or whose work is tied into the economy of the metropolis. Boundaries may also be set for 'extended metropolitan regions' which provide a useful regional planning framework for public authorities but which often encompass significant numbers of rural inhabitants and have a significant proportion of the labour force working in agriculture. Comparing the size, population growth rate or density of the central city population of one city with the size, population growth rate or density of another city but for its metropolitan area or 'extended metropolitan region' will produce dramatic contrasts but this is not comparing like with like. Even comparisons between two cities in terms of their 'central cities' can be invalid as in one city the central city refers to a very small central 'historic city' while in the other, it refers to a much larger area.

This is why any international list of 'the world's largest cities' risks great inaccuracy as some city populations are for large urbanized regions with thousands of square kilometres while others are for older 'city boundaries' with a few hundred square kilometres. It only needs a few cities to change the basis by which their boundaries are defined for the list of the world's largest metropolises to be significantly altered. For instance, London has long dropped off the list of the world's largest cities since it had less than 7 million people in its metropolitan area in 1991—but it has a population of 12.53 million if considered as a metropolitan region.[62] One of main reasons that Shanghai's population appears so large—at over 13 million—is that this figure is the population in an area of over 6,000 square kilometres which includes large areas of highly productive agriculture and many villages and agricultural workers.[63] The

TABLE 1.4 Examples of how the populations of urban areas change with different boundaries

City or metropolitan area	Date	Population	Area (sq. km)	Notes
Beijing[a] (China)	1990	2,336,544	87	4 inner city districts including the historic old city
		c.5,400,000	158	'Core city'
		6,325,722	1,369	Inner city and inner suburban districts
		10,819,407	16,808	Inner city, inner and outer suburban districts and 8 counties
Dhaka (Bangladesh)	1991		6	Historic city
		c.4,000,000	363	Dhaka Metropolitan Area (Dhaka City Corporation and Dhaka Cantonment)
		6,400,000	780	Dhaka Statistical Metropolitan Area
		<8,000,000	1,530	Rajdhani Unnayan Kartripakhya (RAJUK)—the jurisdiction of Dhaka's planning authority
Katowice (Poland)	1991	367,000		The city
		2,250,000		The metropolitan area (Upper Silesian Industrial Region)
		c.4,000,000		Katowice governorate
Mexico City (Mexico)	1990	1,935,708	139	The central city
		8,261,951	1,489	The Federal District
		14,991,281	4,636	Mexico City Metropolitan Area
		c.18,000,000	8,163	Mexico City megalopolis[b]
Tokyo (Japan)	1990	8,164,000	598	The central city (23 wards)
		11,856,000	2,162	Tokyo prefecture (Tokyo-to)
		31,559,000	13,508	Greater Tokyo Metropolitan Area (including Yokohama)[c]
		39,158,000	36,834	National Capital Region.[d]
Toronto (Canada)	1991	620,000	97	City of Toronto
		2,200,000	630	Metropolitan Toronto
		3,893,000	5,583	Census Metropolitan Area
		4,100,000	7,061	Greater Toronto Area
		4,840,000	7,550	Toronto CMSA equivalent[e]
London (UK)	1991	4,230	3	The original 'city' of London
		2,343,133	321	Inner London
		6,393,568	1,579	Greater London (32 boroughs and the city of London)[f]
		12,530,000		London 'metropolitan region'[g]
Los Angeles (USA)	1990	3,485,398	1,211	Los Angeles City
		9,053,645	10,480	Los Angeles County
		8,863,000	2,038	Los Angeles–Long Beach Primary Metropolitan Statistical Area
		14,532,000	87,652	Los Angeles Consolidated Metropolitan Area

Notes:
[a] Information supplied by Richard Kirkby based on data from the 1990 Census, in *Zhongguo renkou tongji nianjian 1992* (Yearbook of Population Statistics, 1992), Beijing, Jingji guanli chubanshe (Economic Management Press), 1992, 448 and (for area) Beijing Municipal Statistics Bureau, *Beijing Statistics in Brief*, Beijing, China Statistical Publishing House, 1988, 1. Apart from the educational quarter in the Haidian District (northwest) and the steel works and heavy industrial area of Shijingshan (west), prior to the 1980s economic boom the city proper could be broadly defined as that area within the *san huan lu*—the Third Ringroad. This encircles an area of just 158 km² in a total municipality spanning almost 17,000 km². Its population comprises all of the four inner-city districts and parts of the four inner suburban districts. In total, this 'core city' comprises only around half of the 10.82 million official residents of the capital in 1990.
[b] Garza, Gustavo 'Dynamics of Mexican Urbanization', Background paper for the UN Global Report on Human Settlements 1996.
[c] This ensures the inclusion within Tokyo of the vast suburban areas and includes Tokyo-to (including the islands) and Chiba, Kanagawa and Saitama Prefectures.
[d] Includes Greater Tokyo Metropolitan Area plus Yamanashi, Gunma, Tochigi and Ibaraki Prefectures.
[e] This is what Toronto's population might be if it was defined with the methodology used in the United States for defining Consolidated Metropolitan Areas. This would include Toronto Metropolitan Area, the adjacent Hamilton CMA (0.6 million), Oshawa CMA (0.24 million) and the rest of York County.
[f] Note that these figures for the City of London, Inner London and Greater London are census figures; official estimates for 1991 for Inner London were 2,627,400 and for Greater London were 6,889,900.
[g] A. G. Champion—see Section 2.4.

TABLE 1.5 The world's largest urban agglomerations in 1990

Urban agglomeration	Population (thousands 1990)	Comments	A.A. increment in population 1980-1990	A.A. growth rate (thousand) 1980-1990 (%)
Tokyo	25,013	The population would be c.31.6 million if Greater Tokyo Metropolitan Area was taken — see Table 1.4[a]	316	1.4
New York	16,056	19.3 million in the CMSA in 1990[b]	46	0.3
Mexico City	15,085	Would be several million larger if considerd as a polynucleated metropolitan region[c]	120	0.8
Sao Paulo	14,847	The population is for a large metropolitan region	275	2.1
Shanghai	13,452	This is the population within a large metropolitan region[d]	171	1.4
Bombay	12,223	One reason for its relatively rapid growth 1980-90 was a considerable expansion of its boundaries	416	4.2
Los Angeles	11,456	14.53 million in the CMSA in 1990[e]	193	1.9
Beijing (Peking)	10,872	Population for a large metropolitan region; the core city has a muchsmaller population - see Section 2.6	184	1.9
Calcutta	10,741	Urban agglomeration	171	1.8
Buenos Aires	10,623	Urban agglomeration	72	0.7
Seoul	10,558		228	2.5
Osaka	10,482	The population would be larger if measured as a Standard Metropolitan Economic Area.[f]	49	0.5
Rio de Janeiro	9,515	Metropolitan area	73	0.8
Paris	9,334	Urban agglomeration	40	0.4

Source: United Nations, *World Urbanization Prospects: the 1994 Revision*, Population Division, New York, 1995
Notes:
[a] The figure for 25.0 million is for the contiguous densely inhabited districts of Tokyo-to (ku-bu) and 87 surrounding cities and towns including Yokohama, Kawasaki and Chiba, spreading through Tokyo, Kanagawa, Saitama and Chiba prefectures.
[b] This figure of 16.1 million is for the urban agglomeration that includes Jersey City, Newark and part of north-east New Jersey; the Consolidated Metropolitan Statistical Area (CMSA) has a larger area—see Chapter 2.
[c] This figure is based on the metropolitan area. A larger area could be considered as an emerging polycentric metropolitan region as different metropolitan areas fuse or overlap—for instance linking the metropolitan areas of Mexico City, Toluca, Puebla and Cuernavaca. See Garza, Gustavo, 'Dynamics of Mexican Urbanization', Background paper for the UN Global Report on Human Settlements, 1996; see also Box 2.3 in Chapter 2 that is drawn from this background paper.
[d] The population in the core city or the built up area is substantially smaller; in 1992, the urban core districts contained less than 8 million inhabitants; see Box 2.6 in Chapter 2.
[e] This population of 11.5 million is for the urban agglomeration that includes Long Beach; the CMSA is much larger and more populous—see Chapter 2.
[f] The figure of 10.5 million includes Osaka densely inhabited districts and 36 cities surrounding Osaka. See Yamada, Hiroyuki and Kazuyuki Tokuoka, 'The trends of the population and urbanization in Post-war Japan', Background Paper for the United Nations Global Report on Human Settlements, 1995.

same is true for Beijing and Dhaka—see Table 1.4. 'Metropolitan Toronto' in 1991 can have between 2.2 million and 4.8 million inhabitants, depending on the boundaries used. Figures for the population of Katowice in 1991 can vary from 367,000 to nearly 4 million for similar reasons—and Tokyo can have anywhere between 8 and 40 million inhabitants.

To address the large physical expansion of major cities and the fact that their labour market may be considerably larger than the size of the urban agglomeration (for instance with settlements outside the urban agglomeration having mostly daily commuters to the urban area) new concepts have been developed·as the basis for measuring urban populations. These include functional urban regions and statistical metropolitan areas.

These definitions seek to include in a city's total population all nearby settlements whose economies or residents can be considered too intricately related to the city core to be considered a separate settlement. The US definition of 'Standard Metropolitan Areas' delimits what can be called 'functional regions' that include suburbs and other settlements outside the core city's built up area if the proportion of residents commuting to work in the central core exceeds a certain level and if the settlement meets other criteria of metropolitan 'character' (e.g. population density). In Europe, the tendency seems to be more to view metropolitan areas as areas that conveniently encompass all the continuously built up area of a metropolis but that exclude large and small urban centres and rural settlements nearby, even though

TABLE 1.5 continued

Urban agglomeration	Population (thousands 1990)	Comments	A.A. increment in population 1980-1990	A.A. growth rate (thousand) 1980-1990 (%)
Tianjin	9,253	This is the population for a large metropolitan region; the core city has about half this population.[g]	199	2.4
Jakarta	9,250	The population of the wider metropolitan region is almost twice this[h]	327	4.4
Moscow	9,048	Urban agglomeration	91	1.1
Cairo	8,633	The population in the 'Greater Cairo Region' is several million larger than this.[i]	178	2.3
Delhi	8,171	Urban agglomeration	261	3.9
Manila	7,968	Urban agglomeration	201	3.0
Karachi	7,965	Some local estimates suggest this is rather low	294	4.7
Lagos	7,742	This appears high in comparison to the 1991 census[j]	336	5.8
London	7,335	The population could be 12.5 million within a metropolitan region boundary[k]	–41	–0.5
Chicago	6,792	8,240,000 in the wider CMSA[l]	1	0.0
Istanbul	6,507	Urban agglomeration	211	4.0
Lima	6,475	Lima-Callao metropolitan area	204	3.9
Essen	6,353	Urban agglomeration[m]	2	0.0
Teheran	6,351	Urban agglomeration	128	2.3
Bangkok	5,894	This is for Bangkok Metropolitan Area; Greater Bankok Area or the metropolitan region have several million more[n]	117	2.2
Dhaka	5,877	Statistical metropolitan area	267	6.2

[g] See Kirkby, Richard, Background Paper on China prepared for the United Nations Global Report on Human Settlements, 1995; more details are given in Chapter 2.
[h] Jakarta metropolitan area (also called Jabotabek) is estimated to have had nearly 17 million inhabitants in 1990 within an area of around 5,500 square kilometres; about half of this was in the central city (DKI Jakarta); see Hadiwinoto, Suhadi and Josef Leitmann, 'Jakarta: urban environmental profile', *Cities*, vol. 11, no. 3, 1994, 153–57.
[i] UNCHS (Habitat), *Metropolitan Planning and Management in the Developing World; Spatial Decentralization Policy in Bombay and Cairo*, Nairobi, 1993.
[j] The 1991 census suggested that the population of Lagos was around 5 million inhabitants; Aina, Tade Akin, 'Metropolitan Lagos: population growth and spatial expansion; city study', Background paper for the Global Report on Human Settlements, 1995, suggested that this was an undercount but that Lagos still had less than 6 million inhabitants in 1991.
[k] A. G. Champion, unpublished tabulation using 1991 census data. 'Main built-up area (core)', 'Urban region' and 'Metropolitan region' are definitions based on the CURDS Functional Regions framework; more details are given in Chapter 2, Table 2.12.
[l] The figure for 6.8 million is for the urban agglomeration that includes part of Illinois and parts of north-western Indiana.
[m] Includes Duisburg, Essen, Krefeld, Mülheim an der Ruhr, Oberhausen, Bottrop, Gelsenkirchen, Bochum, Dortmund, Hagen, Hamm and Herne.
[n] See Chapter 2.

their housing and labour markets are fully integrated into those of the metropolitan centre. Extending metropolitan definitions in Europe to encompass 'functional urban regions' would considerably increase the population of most major cities—and for some would include many small cities, urban centres and villages at distances of 50 or even 100 kilometres from a large city, especially those close to railway stations with rapid services to the city.

No definition of urban areas is necessarily superior; each serves a particular purpose. Without more-or-less standardized definitions, however, international comparisons of urbanization may be highly misleading.

The world's largest cities

Table 1.5 lists the world's 30 largest urban agglomerations in 1990, and it shows that the population of most of them actually grew quite slowly during the 1980s—in terms of the annual rate of growth. Only two among these 30 cities (Dhaka and Lagos) had annual average population growth rates that exceeded 5 per cent during the 1980s—and it may be that Lagos had a much slower population growth rate than that shown in Table 1.5.[64] Most of the 'million-cities' with the highest population growth rates during the 1980s were not among the world's largest cities. Many examples will also be given in Chapter 2 of relatively small cities that had much more rapid population growth rates than the cities listed in Table 1.5 during the 1980s.

But population growth rates can be misleading in that the larger the city population at the beginning of a period, the larger the increment in population has to be to produce a high population growth rate. Table 1.5 also includes figures for the annual average increment in the city's population which reveals that only one urban agglomeration, Bombay, had a population that had an annual increase of more than 400,000 during the 1980s—and a large part of this is the result of much-extended boundaries being used in the 1990 census compared to the 1980 census, with many people counted as part of its population in 1990 that had been excluded in 1980. Three urban agglomerations had populations that grew by more than 300,000 a year between 1980 and 1990: Tokyo, Jakarta and Lagos—although this may overstate the scale of population growth in Lagos.[65] Again, some caution is needed in interpreting these figures, as the population growth rate or the annual average increment in population will depend on which city or metropolitan boundary is chosen. For instance, if for Los Angeles it is the Consolidated Metropolitan Area that is taken, the average annual increment in population during the 1980s was also over 300,000.

If a much larger sample of the world's largest cities is considered—the 281 or so 'million-cities' that existed by 1990—Table 1.6 shows the much-increased proportion of each region's population that lives in million-cities. This Table also highlights some of the regional shifts in the concentration of the world's urban and large-city population. The much-increased role of Asia within the world economy since 1950 is reflected in the sharp increase in its concentration of the world's urban population, 'million-city' population and proportion of the world's largest cities between 1950 and 1990. The concentration of the world's million-cities in Asia can also be seen in Map 1.1. But this is not so much a new trend as a return to what had been the case in previous centuries. Historically, Asia has long had a high concentration of the world's urban population and has always had most of the world's largest cities.[66] As Table 1.6 shows, Asia had more than three-fifths of the world's largest 100 cities in 1800 AD. Many of Asia's largest cities in 1990 had long been among the world's largest cities—for instance Tokyo, Beijing (formerly Peking), Guangzhou (formerly Canton), Istanbul and Calcutta. Most of the others that grew to become among the largest cities in the region were also cities with long histories. Most were the major cities either in the most populous countries or in the most successful economies—for instance Kyoto in Japan, Seoul and Pusan in South Korea, Karachi and Lahore in Pakistan, Delhi, Bombay and Bangalore in India, Jakarta and Surabaya in Indonesia and many of China's major cities.

The Americas, as a region, increased its share of the world's urban population, and 'million-city' population and share of the world's largest cities between 1950 and 1990 but with an important intra-regional shift. In 1950, Northern America had most of the urban and 'million-city' population; by 1990 this was no longer so. This is also not a new trend but a return to what existed prior to rapid industrialization in Northern America in both pre-Columbian and colonial times when most of the urban population and major cities in the Americas were in Central and South America. There was also a strong contrast within the Americas between the major industrial centres of Northern America that had been among the world's largest cities in 1950 and were no longer so in 1990—and the growing prominence of the major cities in Latin America's two largest economies—Mexico and Brazil—especially their largest industrial concentrations, Mexico City and Sao Paulo. This does not imply a lack of rapid urban change in Northern America; as Chapter 2 describes, many of the relatively new cities in the South and West of the US have been among the world's most rapidly growing cities since 1950.

In Africa, there was a rapid increase in the proportion of the world's urban population and 'million-city' population between 1950 and 1990, although the speed of change appears particularly high in all but Northern Africa because it had such a small base in 1950. One reason why it began from such a small base is that colonial governments strictly controlled the right of Africans to live in urban centres.[67]

In Europe, the rapid decline in the region's share of the world's urban population, 'million-cities' population and share of the world's 100 largest cities between 1950 and 1990 is particularly striking. Part of the reason is the dramatic decline in the relative importance of what were among the world's largest industrial centres in 1950—such as Naples in Italy, Hamburg and Dusseldorf in Germany and Birmingham and Manchester in the United Kingdom. But another important reason is the much slower rate of natural increase. Europe was the first of the world's regions to begin a rapid and sustained increase in its population, as birth rates came to regularly exceed death rates but also the first region to undergo a rapid decrease in birth rates to the point where the total population is hardly growing or even declining in many European countries.

But once again, the problem of urban boundaries is evident here. For instance, the number of 'million-cities' in Europe is considerably increased—and the share of the total population

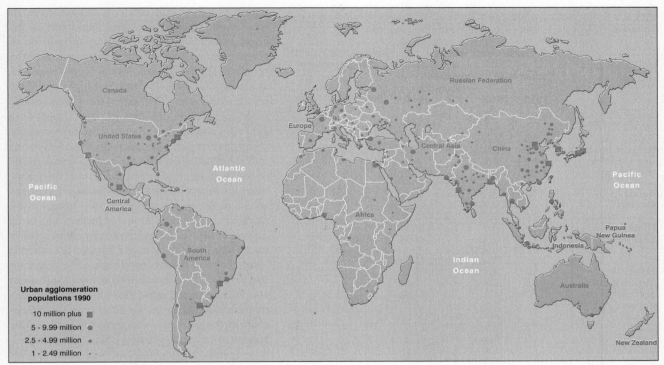

Urban agglomeration populations 1990

■ 10 million plus
● 5 - 9.99 million
• 2.5 - 4.99 million
· 1 - 2.49 million

MAP 1.1
The world's million-cities and 'mega-cities' in 1990

Notes: See Map 2.1 to 2.6 for more details for each region. This Map is based on populations in 'urban agglomerations' and drawn from the same source as Table 1.3 while Map 2.1 on North America is based on populations in metropolitan areas and Map 2.3 on West Europe is based on populations in functional urban regions. This means some slight differences in the list of 'million-cities'.

they concentrate considerably increased—if urban populations are defined by functional regions rather than by city cores. For instance, Glasgow in the United Kingdom is not included in the United Nations list of 'million-cities' but had more than a million in its functional urban region while Newcastle and Liverpool would both have more than a million in 1990, if their boundaries were for metropolitan regions (see Section 2.4 for more details)

Although most of the large cities in the North listed in Table 1.5 had very slow population growth rates during the 1980s, not all the world's most rapidly growing cities are in the South. This is especially the case if the growth of city populations is considered in this century—during which the United States has had many of the world's most rapidly growing large cities.[68] For instance, Nairobi is often held up as one of the world's most rapidly growing cities—but both Miami and Phoenix in the United States had larger populations than Nairobi in 1990, yet all were small settlements in 1900. The population of Los Angeles was around one tenth that of Calcutta in 1900 yet in 1990, it had about the same number of people in its metropolitan area (see Table 1.5). These and other examples of rapidly growing cities in the North do not alter the fact that most of the large cities in the world with the fastest population growth rates are in the South but it does suggest that the rate of growth of the largest cities in the South is not unprecedented.

Over the last few decades, there have also been important rearrangements of population and production within cities, metropolitan areas or wider 'city regions.' For many of the world's largest cities, part of the slow-down in their population growth is explained by a rapid growth in production and population just outside their boundaries—and with much of this production intimately connected to enterprises still within its boundaries. In general, all major cities or metropolitan centres experience a decentralization of population and of production, as they grow. This generally begins with suburban housing being developed at ever greater distances from the city centre and then a widening commuting field and an increasing concentration of enterprises in suburban locations or in belts around the metropolitan area. But the speed of this decentralization of people and enterprises and its spatial configuration seems to vary greatly from city to city and to change over time. There are also recent examples of city centres attracting new enterprises other than those that concentrate in central business districts and also new residents.[69]

This rearrangement of production within cities is perhaps best understood in terms of three sets of factors with different spatial implications:

- the factors that encourage a movement of enterprises out of major cities, metropolitan areas or even wider metropolitan regions, discourage new ones locating there, and cause a decline in the enterprises that are concentrated in central cities;

- the factors that still concentrate enterprises within or close to metropolitan areas (or urban regions) but outside the central city; and

TABLE 1.6 The regional distribution of the world's population in 'million-cities' and the location of the world's largest 100 cities, 1990, 1950 and 1800

| | Proportion of the world's | | | | Number of the world's 100 largest cities in | | |
| | urban popn | | population in million-cities | | | | |
	1950	1990	1950	1990	1800	1950	1990
Africa	4.5	8.8	1.8	7.5	4	3	7
Eastern Africa	0.5	1.7	–	0.8	–	–	-
Middle Africa	0.5	1.0	–	0.8	0	0	1
Northern Africa	1.8	2.8	1.8	3.2	3	2	5
Southern Africa	0.8	0.9	–	0.8	0	1	0
Western Africa	0.9	2.6	–	2.0	1	0	1
Americas	23.7	23.0	30.1	27.8	3	26	27
Caribbean	0.8	0.9	0.6	0.8	1	1	0
Central America	2.0	3.3	1.6	2.7	1	1	3
Northern America	14.4	9.2	21.2	13.1	0	18	13
South America	6.5	9.7	6.7	11.1	1	6	11
Asia	32.0	44.5	28.6	45.6	64	33	44
Eastern Asia	15.2	19.7	17.6	22.2	29	18	21
Southeastern Asia	3.7	5.8	3.4	5.6	5	5	8
South-central Asia	11.2	14.8	7.0	14.6	24	9	13
Western Asia	1.8	4.1	0.6	3.3	6	1	2
Europe	38.8	22.8	38.0	17.9	29	36	20
Eastern Europe	11.8	9.3	7.7	6.3	2	7	4
Northern Europe	7.7	3.4	9.0	2.1	6	6	2
Southern Europe	6.5	4.0	6.7	3.2	12	8	6
Western Europe	12.8	6.2	14.6	6.2	9	15	8
Oceania	1.1	0.8	1.6	1.3	0	2	2

Source: The statistics for for 1950 and 1990 were largely derived from data in United Nations, *World Urbanization Prospects: the 1994 Revision*, Population Division, New York, 1995, adjusted, when new census data is available. The calculations for 1800 were made, drawing on the IIED cities database that combines the data on city populations from 1950 to 1990 from United Nations 1995, *op. cit.* with recent and historic data drawn from around 250 censuses and from Chandler, Tertius and Gerald Fox, *3000 Years of Urban Growth*, Academic Press, New York and London, 1974.

- the factors that encourage enterprises back into central cities.

The scale and importance of the first of these sets of factors has long been evident and carefully documented. It includes advances in transport and communications and the fact that an increasing proportion of the national territory, including many smaller cities, had a skilled and literate workforce, good quality transport and communications and adequate quality infrastructure and services. In many countries in both the North and the South, large incentives were offered to attract manufacturing to smaller urban centres or poorer regions.

What is less well documented, especially in the South, is the fact that it has become common to have a decentralization of population and of production away from the central city (and even its inner suburbs) but with a continued or increased concentration of population and of production within the metropolitan area or wider region. Judged nationally, this remains an increasing concentration of population and economic activity within what might be termed 'core region' but a decreased concentration of population and eco-

nomic activity within the core region itself. In most major cities in the North and many in the South, there has been a declining proportion of the population living in the central city and the outward sprawl of the urban agglomeration, especially along major roads and highways. This has probably gone furthest in the United States where population densities in outer suburbs are generally much lower than in Europe and where many enterprises have also developed close to major highways outside the central areas. Some of the most innovative and successful concentrations of enterprises are not in cities but concentrated along major highways (for instance the firms along Route 128 in Massachusetts) or in Silicon Valley. This has led to new terms such as the '100-mile city' where there is no obvious 'central city'. This decentralization of production and of urban population within core regions can also be seen in the rapid growth of smaller cities that are close to the major cities or metropolitan areas as these attract both industrial and service enterprises that previously would tend to concentrate in major cities. Regions with good quality transport and communication networks encourage this, as does the 'just-in-time' system which needs some physical proximity.

One of the most remarkable examples of this is the region bounded by Sao Paulo, Belo Horizonte, Rio de Janeiro and Porto Alegre in Brazil which includes a great range of cities of different sizes, many of which have been successful in attracting new enterprises that previously would have concentrated in the major cities. Many such cities are within 200 km of Sao Paulo's central city and have many advantages and few disadvantages when compared to investment in Sao Paulo itself. Private investment in Greater Sao Paulo was discouraged by the well-organized trade union movement, pollution, transport problems and a lack of suitable land sites. Investment in cities nearby was encouraged by a whole range of factors including better roads and telecommunications, the availability of land and fiscal incentives in the smaller cities. The decentralization of production was also boosted by the promotion and support of the government in information technology in Campinas and in the aeronautics industry in Valle del Paraiba.[70] Motor vehicle companies such as General Motors, Volkswagen and Mercedes Benz have chosen different small cities within this region.[71] However, this model of a region with a diverse but highly integrated urban system and a declining importance for any dominant city depends on good transport and communications systems and good quality infrastructure and services available in different cities. Many of the largest cities in the South remain more concentrated, because of poorer transport and communications systems and as scarce infrastructure and skilled labour tend to be concentrated in large cities so modern economic activity clusters around them.[72]

There are also examples of successful cities once again attracting employment and residential populations back to central areas or to inner suburbs.[73] There are also examples of cities that have transformed their economic prospects, after facing economic decline—for instance Barcelona[74] and Baltimore.[75] One important reason why, as noted in a survey of cities in *The Economist* in 1995, is that financial markets like traditional cities in which enterprises are concentrated, even if advanced telecommunications allow many routine tasks to be located outside the financial district.[76] For banks and other financial services, 'face-to-face contact is irreplaceable, partly because it promotes the trust that is essential to make deals, and partly because the informal exchange of ideas in such businesses is unpredictable . . . serendipitous proximity cannot be reproduced by fax machine or video-conferencing'.[77] The concentration of banks in turn encourages a concentration of service enterprises associated with banks or their staff. In addition, many other service activities also find advantage in concentration, including design, marketing, advertising, film and television.[78]

The 'world cities'

The structural changes within the world economy described earlier have helped to reorder the relative importance of cities around the world and, for many cities, to reshape their physical form and the spatial distribution of enterprises and residents within them. Regions and cities have proved more flexible than nations in adapting to changing economic conditions—and certain key regions and cities have become successful locales of the new wave of innovation and investment—for instance Silicon Valley and Orange County in California, Arizona, Texas and Colorado in the western United States, Bavaria in Germany, the French Midi—from Sophia-Antipolis via Montpellier to Toulouse, certain cities in southern Europe, and, of course, many cities in the Asian Tigers[79] and in China. Meanwhile, most major port cities and traditional industrial centres in the North (and some in the South) that grew to become among the world's major cities during the second half of the nineteenth and first half of the twentieth century lost importance—and most had population declines during the 1980s.

The large and increasing share of the world's economy controlled by multinationals has led to certain cities becoming what are often termed 'global' or 'world' cities—as they are key command and control points of the world economy.[80] Some are unambiguously world cities as they are the 'commanding nodes' of the global system[81]—London, New York and Tokyo. New York and London are not only leading financial markets but also leading producers and exporters in accounting, advertising, management consulting, international legal services and other business services.[82] Tokyo—developing as an important centre for the international trade in services such as construction and engineering services, has developed beyond its initially restricted role of exporting only the services required by its larger international trading houses.[83] It is interesting to note that Tokyo also remains one of the world's major concentrations of industrial production whereas New York and London do not. It is a reminder of how advanced telecommunications systems and logistical management of production can separate almost completely in spatial terms the production process from those who manage and finance it and the 'producer services' that the managers and financiers need.

Another category of world cities consists of the cities that articulate large national economies into the system (Paris, Madrid, Sao Paulo) or subnational (regional) economies (Chicago) or simply have a commanding multinational role (Miami, Singapore).[84] Global cities are not necessarily the same as large cities—as many cities that are not among the world's largest have major international roles—for instance Singapore and Zurich. Several of the world's largest cities do not owe their size and economic base to their role within global production but to being national capitals in more populous nations with a high concentration of political power there—for instance Delhi and Cairo. Several other cities that are among the world's thirty largest listed in Table 1.5 derive their size more from their national role. It is interesting to note that the former national capitals of the most populous nation in Africa (Lagos in Nigeria) and Latin America (Rio de Janeiro in Brazil) are among the thirty largest cities in the world—and both owe much of their size and economic importance to the period when they were political capitals. Calcutta too grew to be much the largest city in India as the former capital; Delhi, to where the national capital was moved early in the twentieth century, has grown much faster than Calcutta in recent decades and may soon have a larger population than Calcutta.

A few of the world cities are capitals (London, Paris, Tokyo) but most are not, for instance New York, Frankfurt, Zurich, Amsterdam, Sydney, Los Angeles, Osaka and Toronto.[85] World cities have to adapt to changing circumstances to stay as world cities. For instance, Singapore's position could have been threatened by the rapid growth of the Thai and Malaysian economies but it chose to keep high wage jobs in dominant financial and producer services for itself while creating labour-intensive activities in manufacturing and tourism in regions just outside its boundaries.[86]

Internal and international migration

The scale, direction and nature of migration flows are so fundamental to understanding urbanization and, more generally, changes in the spatial distribution of population that it is surprising that internal migration receives so little attention. In most countries in the South, there has been relatively little recent research on the scale and nature of internal migration flows. There is much more work on the scale and nature of international migration flows, even though there is far more internal population movement than international population movement. The much increased volume of research on international migration is no doubt linked to political worries of governments in wealthy countries—for instance for countries close to areas of conflict or potential conflict that might create large flows of refugees and other emigrants and for wealthy countries that are close to low-income countries and with borders over which it is difficult to control population movements.

In most countries, there is very little idea of the scale and nature of internal migration flows, except that they are almost always diverse, complex, constantly changing and include rural to urban, urban to rural, urban to urban and rural to rural flows. It is often assumed that rural to urban migration is the dominant migration flow but rural to rural flows may be of a larger scale— and in many countries, urban to urban migration flows outnumber rural to urban flows. In virtually all nations, there are also large urban to rural migration flows, even in countries which are urbanizing; the fact that the nation is urbanizing merely reflects the fact that rural to urban migration flows outnumber migration flows in the opposite direction.

There is also considerable diversity between nations and regions in the migrants themselves— for instance in terms of age, level of education, extent to which the move is considered permanent or temporary and the extent to which this move is part of a complex and diverse household survival strategy. Recent studies have highlighted the extent to which migration patterns are also differentiated by gender.[87] Various studies have shown how female migration is of much greater volume and complexity than was previously believed and also how the migration of women differs in many ways from that of men in its form, composition, causes and consequences.[88]

There is also great diversity in the scale and nature of migration. There are around 30,000 urban centres in the South and each has its own unique pattern of in-migration and out-migra-tion that constantly changes, reflecting (among other things) changes in that centre's economic base, labour market and age structure. It also reflects social, economic and political changes within the region and nation and is influenced by such factors as crop prices, landowning structures and changes in agricultural technologies and crop mixes in surrounding areas and distant regions. Each detailed study of migrants in urban settings and of conditions in areas of out-migration reveals a long list of factors which influence migration, including: those relating to individuals or household structures and gender-relations within households; local social, economic and cultural factors; regional and national social and economic change; and international factors.[89] In each location, the relative importance of the different factors is subject to constant change. This cautions against seeking too many generalizations and general recommendations in regard to rural–urban migration.

One example of this diversity is the differences in the scale and nature of demand for female labour.[90] For instance, in South-East Asia, the demand for women workers in multinational industries and in unskilled and semi-skilled service occupations (domestic service, informal commerce, sex) is important in drawing young women to cities in Taiwan, Philippines, Thailand, Malaysia and South Korea.[91]

Although it is often assumed that the largest migration flows are in countries in the South, in fact, there is probably more migration in the United States in any one year in terms of the proportion of the population who move than in virtually all countries in the South. For instance, it is estimated that one person in five in the USA moves each year and as Chapter 2 will describe, the restructuring of the urban system there during the 1980s was more rapid and fundamental than that taking place in most countries in the South. This does not show up as rapid change in the level of urbanization as most migration is urban to urban. Chapter 2 will also describe the very rapid change in the urban system in China and here too, the change in the proportion of the population living in urban areas gives little indication of the scale of the change.

The scale of international migration has certainly increased over the last ten to fifteen years. Estimates for 1992 suggest that over 100 million people lived outside their own country of which 20 million were thought to be refugees and asylum seekers.[92] An estimate for 1990 suggested that around 15–20 million were in western Europe, around 15–20 million in North America, and 2–3 million were in the wealthiest nations in Asia including Japan, Taiwan and Singapore.[93] There are also large populations of foreigners within the wealthier countries in Africa and Latin America, most of them being from lower-income countries close-by. As in internal migration flows, there is great diversity in the types of international migrants and the forms that their movements take—contract labourers, students, professionals and skilled workers, immigrants joining their families through family reunification, people who retire to a foreign country—and asylum seekers and refugees.[94] Their scale and nature is greatly influenced by the attitude of the receiving country to immigrants and the provisions made to allow or control immigration.

Among these different categories of international migrants, the growth in the number of refugees has been most dramatic—by 1994, 23 million people qualified as refugees compared to about 2.5 million 20 years ago.[95] There has also been a considerable growth in international migration flows of highly qualified or skilled labour migrants, that include the professional and managerial staff transferred within the international labour markets of transnational corporations. For instance, in 1988, 83,000 Japanese were assigned to work in overseas branches of Japanese companies while a further 29,000 (not including students) went overseas to engage in scientific study and research.[96]

There is also great diversity in the scale of emigration out of and immigration into each nation—and also in who moves. A distinction can be drawn between countries where there is far more immigration than emigration—generally the wealthiest countries that also have relatively open policies to immigrants—and countries with high levels of emigration. There are also the exceptional cases of certain oil-exporting Middle East countries that have foreign workers making up more than half their workforce—for instance this was the case in 1990 in Bahrain, Kuwait, Saudi Arabia, Qatar and United Arab Emirates.[97] Other OPEC nations have generally been centres for immigration within their own region, although usually less so in the 1980s and early 1990s as the real price of oil fell. Singapore was also reported to have 11 per cent of its labour force made up of foreign workers—mainly from Malaysia, Thailand, Indonesia and the Philippines.[98] Although there is little recent data for most African countries, in nations such as Congo, Zaire and South Africa, immigrants made up more than 5 per cent of their population in the mid-1980s.[99]

Many countries have several per cent of their population or labour force living abroad—including Jordan, Russia, Burkina Faso and Egypt with more than 10 per cent of their population or labour force living abroad (although for Russia, most are in republics that were formerly part of the Soviet Union).[100] A considerable proportion of the population of Central America (excluding Mexico) live outside their country of origin.[101] In some instances, this is associated with war or civil strife—as in the huge emigration flows out of Afghanistan, Mozambique and most Central American countries, although in recent years, in all these countries, many emigrants (including refugees) have now returned. An increasing number of countries from which there were large emigration flows have changed to become major centres for immigrants—for instance most countries in Southern Europe, and several Central and East European states—particularly Hungary, Poland and the Czech Republic.[102] There are also many countries with large emigrant and immigrant flows—for instance with large emigration movements of skilled and professional emigrants and with unskilled immigrants coming in from lower income countries.

Many of the main migration flows have well-established historical roots.[103] A considerable part of them is also a consequence of an increasingly globalized economy. Between 25 and 30 million migrants are thought to be foreign workers, most of whom will return to their own countries.[104] An estimate for 1991 suggested that the total value of their remittances back to their own countries was $71 billion and if this is an accurate estimate, then it means that total remittance flows are larger than total aid flows and makes remittance flows one of the largest items in international trade.[105]

Below, are outlined some of the important changes in international migration during the last ten to fifteen years.[106] This is not a comprehensive list, but it does illustrate how international migration flows have to be understood within specific national and regional contexts.

- The removal of the Iron Curtain, the break-up of the former Soviet Union and the changes in international boundaries in East and Central Europe has changed the scale and nature of international migration in this region. Migration flows have been largest to Germany, although as Chapter 2 will describe, a large part of this is ethnic Germans moving to Germany and these are not considered by the German government as immigrants but citizens. There have also been large migration flows from the former Soviet Union to Israel and North America—and also from Hungary and Poland to North America.[107] Changing boundaries are also changing people's status from 'nationals' to 'immigrants' as in the splitting up of Czechoslovakia, Yugoslavia and the division of the former USSR into many independent republics.[108]

- The large-scale recruitment of foreign workers in the oil-rich Middle East. Most were admitted on strictly limited contract terms, were not allowed to bring dependants and were expected to return to their home country when their contract finished.[109] In the mid-1980s, with the drop in the real price of oil, hundreds of thousands of Arab, South and East Asian workers lost their jobs and returned home. Similarly, large numbers of foreign workers lost their jobs or were expelled during and after the Gulf War. However, most oil-rich Middle Eastern countries still rely heavily on foreign workers. There are considerable differences in the kinds of migrants coming from different countries—for instance, a higher proportion of skilled and professional migrants come from certain countries, while most unskilled women workers come from Philippines, Indonesia, Thailand, South Korea or Sri Lanka.[110]

- The very large increase in the number of refugees in Africa, associated with the wars and civil strife there—for instance the refugee flows from Rwanda, Burundi, the Sudan and Somalia. Mozambique was the single largest source of refugees in the early 1990s[111] but many have returned in the last few years. During the 1980s, there were also mass expulsions of foreign workers at particular times in countries such as Nigeria, Congo and Mauritania, linked to economic recession when in previously more prosperous periods, they had been tolerated.

- The changing nature of international migration in Asia as it grew rapidly and also became more concentrated within Asia, between the wealthier and the poorer nations, whereas previously it had been more oriented to nations outside Asia. Within Asia, it is possible to distinguish between labour importing countries (Japan, Singapore, Taiwan, Brunei), countries which import some types of labour but export others (Hong Kong, Thailand, Malaysia, Republic of Korea) and countries which are predominantly labour exporters (China, Philippines, India, Bangladesh, Pakistan, Sri Lanka, Indonesia).[112]

- In Latin America, there is uncertainty as to whether international migration increased during the 1980s and early 1990s. Certain factors led to a decrease—for instance, as the economic crisis lessened economic differences between countries and with the reduction in population displacements from war or civil strife in Central America.[113] The return to democracy in many countries encouraged or allowed the return of many hundreds of thousands of Latin Americans to their own countries.

- The changing nature of international migration to the North, with a growing importance within migration flows of high-skill workers, clandestine migrants and asylum seekers.[114] The growth in the number of asylum seekers is

perhaps the most dramatic in the last decade[115] with the number of asylum applications to Europe, North America and Australia multiplying around sevenfold between 1983 and 1991 to reach 715,000 in 1991.[116] It has grown considerably since then, reflecting the breakup of the former Yugoslavia; estimates for October 1993 suggest 5 million residents had been displaced from their home areas with 4.3 million moving to other places within the old borders and 700,000 having left for other countries.[117]

The relationship between economic growth and urbanization

Rising levels of urbanization and rapid population growth in large cities have often been considered problematic because governments and international agencies fail to ensure that infrastructure and service provision keeps up with the growth in population and governments often fail to enforce pollution control and other regulations needed to protect the quality of life in urban areas. Although the debate about the role of cities in development and in environmental problems continues, the key role that cities have in dynamic and competitive economies was increasingly acknowledged during the 1980s and early 1990s.[118] So too was the fact that major cities generally have a significantly higher concentration of the nation's economic output than of its population. In 1995, Singapore's information minister suggested that 'In the next century, the most relevant unit of economic production, social organization and knowledge generation will be the city.'[119]

One reason for this is that rising levels of urbanization are strongly associated with growing and diversifying economies—and most of the nations in the South whose economic performance over the last two decades is so envied by other nations are also the nations with the most rapid increase in their levels of urbanization. The nature of this relationship between the scale of the economy and the scale of the urban population is also illustrated by the fact that most of the world's largest cities are in the world's largest economies. Taking economic and population statistics for 1990, the world's 25 largest economies also had over 70 per cent of the world's 281 'million-cities'[120] and all but one of its 12 urban agglomerations with 10 million or more inhabitants.[121] The world's five largest economies on that date (United States of America, China, Japan, Germany and France) had between them half of the world's 10 million plus inhabitant urban agglomerations and a third of its 'million-cities'.[122]

Some argue that, whilst increases in the level of urbanization may be high, they are not abnormal when compared to other countries at a similar stage of their development.[123] For instance, there are examples of countries in the North which had increases in their levels of urbanization during the second half of the nineteenth century or first half of the twentieth century which were as or more rapid than most nations in the South over the last 30–40 years. There are also many examples of cities in the North that had population growth rates for several decades during the nineteenth or early twentieth centuries that were comparable to those of the most rapidly growing cities in the South over the last few decades. There are also instances of countries in the North where the overall growth rate of their urban populations was very rapid, even by contemporary standards—for instance in the United States, between 1820 and 1870, the estimated average annual growth rate for the urban population was 5.5 per cent.[124] The urban population in Japan grew at around 6 per cent a year during the 1930s. This can be compared to growth rates for the urban population in Africa of less than 5 per cent a year during the 1980s—and growth rates for the urban population of Asia of less than 4 per cent and for the urban population of Latin America and the Caribbean of close to 3 per cent.[125] What is unprecedented when comparing the last 3–4 decades to earlier periods is the number of countries undergoing rapid urbanization and the number of cities worldwide that are growing rapidly—although as noted earlier, the population growth rate of many cities slowed during the 1980s.

Many factors influence the scale of net rural to urban migration that in turn underlies increases in the level of urbanization. However, there is an evident relationship between changes in economic development in a country and the level of urbanization. The relationship can be seen by plotting countries' level of urbanization against per capita income—see Figure 1.1. The relationship is complex, with many factors at work—and whilst economic development may result in growing levels of urbanization, higher levels of urbanization in turn can stimulate more economic growth.[126]

It has also been argued that urban growth has been detrimental to economic growth and the term 'over-urbanization' has been used to describe countries where the level of urbanization relative to national income is considered to be high in comparison to reference countries. One reason put forward for this is that, with limited investment funds, high levels of investment in urban areas will reduce investment in other productive sectors of the economy including agriculture. Another argument is that economic growth or stability may be compromised by high levels of government investment in urban infrastructure and services.

One basis for the 'over-urbanization' thesis is that specific urbanization levels in the South have been achieved at lower levels of per capita income than those associated with similar levels of urbanization in the North. For example, the North was less urbanized than Asia or Africa when its per capita income was $US300.[127] In the case of Latin America, average levels of urbanization in 1980 were similar to those in the North but the level of per capita GNP was less than one-third that in the North. It has been argued that increases in the level of urbanization in the South have been achieved without economic growth, industrialization and increases in agricultural productivity.[128] However, there are a number of reasons why the 'over-urbanization' thesis might be questioned:

1. There are doubts about the quality and the comparability of the data for both urban populations and for per capita GNP. The margin of error for Northern urban data for 1800 and the South for 1930 is estimated to be about 6–8 per cent.[129] Another problem with such international comparisons noted already is that each country uses different criteria for measuring its urban population.

2. The accuracy of the GNP per capita estimates is questionable; many Southern countries have only recorded national income since 1950 and it is recognized that a considerable part of the economy may be unrecorded because of the extent of the informal economy and other unregistered activity. The accuracy of estimates for GNP may be particularly poor when a large proportion of production is for subsistence or traded outside of the money economy.

3. One important aspect of the relationship between level of urbanization and level of per capita income of particular interest is the extent to which levels of urbanization fall (or their rate of increase slows) with a stagnant or declining economy. Historic studies suggest that city populations may not respond as rapidly to economic decline as they do to economic growth and increases in the level of urbanization as income rises may not be matched by an equal reduction in the level of urbanization as income falls. The same can be said for countries in the Southern Cone of Latin America in recent decades where increases in the levels of urbanization have slowed, as have urban population growth rates—but they did not slow as abruptly as the economy. The results of an analysis of how urbanization levels change over time in response to economic change will show a strong correlation between the two—but while economic stagnation or decline may slow increases in the level of urbanization, they do not generally halt it. In

some countries in Africa, economic stagnation is reported to have encouraged some movement of city populations back to rural areas but the limited information available on this to date does not suggest a large scale movement. Even when incomes are falling, it seems to be rare that households perceive the advantages in rural areas to be sufficient to encourage them to move back on an equivalent scale. What appears more common, as will be described in Chapter 3, is household livelihood strategies that draw on both rural and urban resources.

4. In addition to an inertia to reverses in the level of urbanization, there may be other reasons to account for the high level of urbanization. One is that some economic activities such as mining increase urbanization by requiring a concentrated workforce (and usually an urban setting for their shelters) but do not necessarily increase national income by as much as had been the case in nineteenth-century Europe. National income may increase little because the profits from these activities are invested overseas (and much of the processing also takes place overseas). Another reason why levels of urbanization may be higher in recent decades for any given level of per capita income is that the role of government has expanded considerably during the twentieth century and state employees live mainly in urban centres.

5. Perhaps the main reason for doubting the validity of the 'over-urbanization' thesis is that it implies that the model of urban development undergone in the North represents a pattern that should be followed in the South and that any deviation from this model represents 'over-urbanization'. In this, it has similarities with the normative judgements made as to whether the distribution of population within urban centres in a country corresponds to particular mathematical distributions that are assumed to be 'correct' or 'balanced'. If, in general, Latin American countries are more urbanized today relative to per capita income than countries in the North, what should be sought are the reasons why. It would be surprising if urban trends in the South followed patterns in the North. The much weaker position of most countries in the South within world markets and the fundamental differences between the world in the nineteenth and the end of the twentieth centuries must affect the social, economic and political factors that influence levels of urbanization.

The level of urbanization in any country is influenced by many factors, both economic and social including:

- The proportion of the economy that is derived from manufacturing or service industries rather than agricultural activities.

- The nature of the economic activity within each sector. For example, the type of agriculture affects the scale of urban settlements. The extent to which agriculture stimulates or supports local urban development depends critically on the value of the crop, the extent to which there are local possibilities for adding value to the crop (for instance fruit juices and alcoholic beverages, jams and sweets) and the nature of land ownership.[130] High value crops that provide good incomes for farmers and agricultural workers within relatively intensive farming systems can support rapid growth of local urban centres to the point where agriculture supports a relatively urbanized population—and can also attract new enterprises from outside the area.[131]

- The influence of land-ownership patterns is important not only for its influence on what is produced but also in where the profits generated are spent or invested. In general, the larger the farm, the less likely the value generated by the production will be spent locally.[132] Plantations are an extreme example of agricultural production where it is usual for only a small proportion of the value generated by their production to be spent or invested nearby.

The relative importance of factors that influence levels of urbanization may change as countries become more urbanized. In advanced economies, many rural areas are urbanized as manufacturing and service enterprises can locate on 'greenfield' sites with many of the service and infrastructure benefits of urban locations but none of the congestion; and city-workers can live in rural areas and travel each day to work. In countries with a high population density, these criteria may apply to a large proportion of rural areas, as will be described in Section 2.6. This also helps explain why the relationship between per capita income and level of urbanization becomes much less obvious among the higher income countries—for instance there were large increases in per capita income for the United States and many European countries between 1970 and 1990 but relatively little increase in their level of urbanization.

To conclude, levels of urbanization for each country are likely to reflect not only the level of per capita GDP and the nature of the economy but a number of other factors including definitions used for urban areas, the nature of agriculture, physical factors such as the size and topography of the country, political factors including the relative degree of security in rural locations, and cultural preferences for types of lifestyle. In addition, government policies and state institutions are a major influence on the level of urbanization. This influence is felt in a number of different ways including:

- The share of national income spent by the public sector. This has clearly increased considerably in most countries during the last few decades, although much less so in the last decade or so. In part this is due to some areas that were previously provided by the private sector being drawn partially or wholly within the public sector, for example, health or transport services. Most state employees are urban residents (although not all are employed in the major cities). The importance of government employment within the urban labour force has been demonstrated by the impacts of redundancies arising from the implementation of structural adjustment programmes in the South. Assessments of the significance of this factor may take some time to emerge, in particular, because reduced employment opportunities in the public sector are likely to impact more on future rural to urban migration trends rather than result in urban to rural migration.

- Government macro-economic and regional policies also impact on the level of urbanization. Governments influence aggregate national income and the distribution between the different sectors of the economy. Subsidizes for agriculture or farmers in most countries in the North have helped to maintain farmers' income and investment capacity. Subsidized services in urban areas have encouraged industrial development. They also influence the relative cost of capital and labour in urban and rural areas and thereby affect employment opportunities. For example, countries in Eastern Europe have successfully kept levels of urbanization below what would have been expected relative to levels of income through a strategy of labour intensive agriculture.[133] Investments in infrastructure influence the costs associated with transportation and telecommunications. In the North, for example, improved transport links and home-based working using advanced telecommunications have also permitted a separation between of the location of residence and employment opportunities.

It is often suggested that governments have favoured urban rather than rural areas within their investment strategies and pricing policies and that this has encouraged the migration of people from rural to urban areas and therefore an increase in the level of urbanization, although within the Indian context public sector policies do not seem to have had a significant impact on the level of urbanization.[134] Instead, the evidence

suggests that the level of urbanization in India is relatively insensitive to public sector investment strategies.

These influences on the level of urbanization suggest that countries may have very country-specific components to the relations between levels of urbanization and economic variables, although the underlying nature of such relations may be broadly similar.

Recent census information has allowed a reconsideration of the trends and relationships discussed above.[135] The graphs in Figure 1.1 illustrate the relationship between urban and economic change for certain regions. For the countries included in this analysis from South America, the wide range in the levels of urbanization is immediately evident. The eight countries fall into three groups: high levels of urbanization for the Southern Cone countries that experienced economic growth during the first few decades of the twentieth century plus Venezuela (one of the OPEC countries); intermediate levels of urbanization (Peru and Colombia), and low levels of urbanization (Paraguay and Ecuador). Considering the graphical relationship between levels of urbanization and per capita income, two characteristics stand out. The first is the 'shock' to incomes during the late 1970s and early 1980s which took place with little reduction in the increase in the level of urbanization and second, the increase in urbanization in Venezuela despite a considerable reduction in per capita income.

Northern Europe (Scandinavia plus the UK and Eire) shows a very similar pattern between the two graphs indicating that most countries have succeeded in achieving small but continually rising per capita incomes (and at a similar level except Eire) during the period under consideration. The countries with high levels of urbanization show little increases in recent decades, despite the fact that incomes have continued to rise. These graphs suggest that urbanization levels will stabilize at different levels in different countries—although the different levels may simply reflect different definitions used for urban centres. There is also the fact noted earlier that in the wealthiest countries, an increasing proportion of the rural population are either urban workers (who commute to work) or work in manufacturing and service enterprises located in greenfield sites.

South-East and East Asia and Oceania also includes some of the wealthiest nations (Australia, Japan and New Zealand) for whom urbanization levels have shown little change in recent decades. Both South Korea and Indonesia have had increasing urbanization although this trend is less evident for Fiji and the Philippines. Considering incomes, two groups appear to emerge from the second graph: a high income group which has

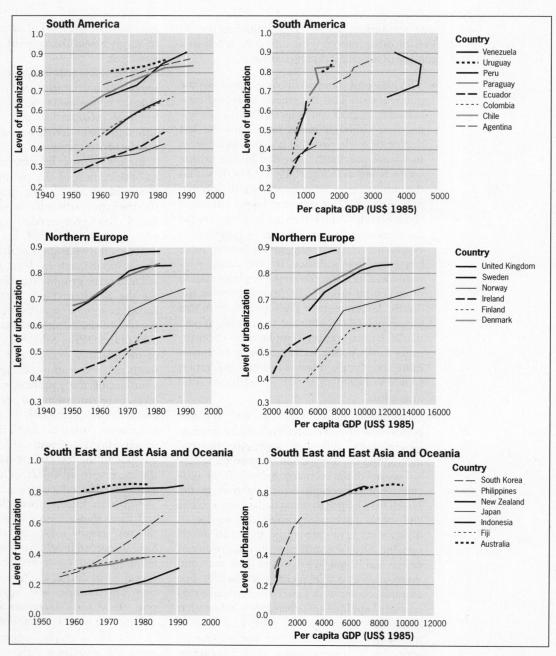

FIGURE 1.1
Urban and economic
changes in selected
countries

seen very little change in urbanization levels, and a low income group with increasing levels of urbanization and rising incomes. While South Korea's level of urbanization at first appears to have increased very rapidly, when considered with changes in per capita income (where the country has had one of the world's most rapid increases over the last 40 years), the trends are consistent with other countries.

In general, there is a close relationship between the level of urbanization and per capita income (measured here by GDP per capita). For the time period and countries considered here, there is also a correlation between the level of urbanization and the date (i.e. a time trend) in addition to the relationship with per capita GDP. This suggests that there may be other factors not specifically included in this model that are important in better understanding the process of urbanization and that have, in broad terms, been increasing over time. In this case, the time trend is acting as a proxy for a set of factors that are positively related to the level of urbanization and are correlated to the time trend but which have not been separately identified.

Notes and References

1. OECD, *OECD Economic Outlook*, Dec. 1994.

2. World Bank, *Annual Report 1994*, Washington DC, 1994.

3. World Bank, *Annual Report 1993*, Washington DC, 1993.

4. World Bank 1994, *op. cit.* and World Bank, *World Development Report 1994: Infrastructure for Development*, Oxford University Press, Oxford, 1994, Table 2.

5. World Bank, *World Development Report 1991*, Oxford University Press, Oxford, 1991.

6. World Bank 1994, *op. cit.*

7. Government of Kenya, *Economic Survey 1994*, Central Bureau of Statistics, Government Press, Kenya.

8. Per capita income is taken as per capita GDP in this section.

9. UNDP, *Human Development Report 1994*, Oxford University Press, Oxford, 1994.

10. UNDP 1994, *op. cit.*

11. *Ibid.*

12. OECD, *OECD Economic Outlook* (various issues) and World Bank, *World Development Report 1991*, Oxford University Press, Oxford, 1991.

13. OECD, *OECD Economic Outlook*, Dec. 1988.

14. Hardoy, Jorge E. and David Satterthwaite, *Squatter Citizen: Life in the Urban Third World*, Earthscan Publications, London, 1989.

15. *Ibid.*

16. United Nations, *Housing and Economic Adjustment*, United Nations Publication Sale No. 88.IV.1, DIESA, 1988.

17. *OECD Economic Outlook*, Dec. 1992.

18. World Bank 1991, *op. cit.*

19. See Table 2.5 in The World Bank, *Annual Report 1994*, Washington DC, 1994.

20. This section draws heavily on Sassen, Saskia, *Cities in a World Economy*, Pine Forge Press, Thousand Oaks, London, New Delhi, 1994. It also draws on Friedmann, John, 'Where we stand: a decade of world city research', Paper prepared for the Conference of World Cities in a World System, Center for Innovative Technology, April 1993, and Friedmann, John and G. Wolff, 'World city formation', *International Journal of Urban and Regional Research*, vol. 6, no. 3, 1983, 309–43.

21. Parker, John, 'Turn up the lights; a survey of cities', *The Economist*, 29 July 1995.

22. Sassen 1994, *op. cit.*

23. *Ibid.*

24. *Ibid.*

25. Harris, Nigel, *City, Class and Trade*, I. B. Tauris and Co. London and New York, 1991.

26. Amin, Ash and Nigel Thrift, 'Neo-Marshallian nodes in global networks', *International Journal of Urban and Regional Research*, vol. 16, no. 4, Dec. 1992, 571–87 and Hay, Dennis, 'On the development of cities', in David Cadman and Geoffrey Payne (eds.), *The Living City—Towards a Sustainable Future*, Routledge, London, 1990.

27. Korten, David C., *When Corporations Rule the World*, Earthscan, London, 1995.

28. *Ibid.*

29. Preliminary figure, from World Bank, *Annual Report 1994*, Washington DC, 1994.

30. World Bank 1994, *op. cit.*

31. Sassen 1994, *op. cit.*

32. World Bank 1994, *op. cit.*

33. Sassen 1994, *op. cit.*

34. Parker 1995, *op. cit.*

35. United Nations, *World Urbanization Prospects: the 1994 Revision*, Population Division, New York, 1995.

36. United Nations 1995, *op. cit.*; Cleland, John, 'Population growth in the 21st century; cause for crisis or celebration', Paper presented to the 21st Century Trust meeting on *Population Growth, Health and Development: Problems and Prospects for the 21st Century*, Oxford, 1995.

37. Cleland 1995, *op. cit.*

38. *Ibid.*

39. Varley, Ann, 'Women-heading households: some more equal than others?', *World Development* vol. 24, no. 3, 1996.

40. See Bourne, L. S., *Urban Growth and Population Redistribution in North America: A Diverse and Unequal Landscape*, Major Report 32, Centre for Urban and Community Studies, University of Toronto, Toronto, 1995.

41. Chant, Sylvia, 'Gender aspects of urban economic growth and development', Paper prepared for the UNU/WIDER Conference on 'Human Settlements in the Changing Global Political and Economic Processes', Helsinki, 1995.

42. Chant 1995, *op. cit.*, drawing from: Flandrin, Jean-Louis, *Families in Former Times: Kinship, Household and Sexuality*, Cambridge University Press, Cambridge, 1979; Laslett, Peter, 'Introduction: the history of the family', in Peter Laslett and Richard Wall (eds.), *Household and Family in Past Time*, Cambridge University Press, Cambridge, 1972, 1–89; Mitterauer, Michael and Reinhard Sieder, *The European Family*, Blackwell, Oxford, 1982; Peil, Margaret, with Pius O. Sada, *African Urban Society*, John Wiley and Sons, Chichester, 1984; Stivens, Maila, 'Family and state in Malaysian industrialization: the case of Rembau, Negeri Sambilan, Malaysia', in Haleh Afshar (ed.), *Women, State and Ideology: Studies from Africa and Asia*, Macmillan, Basingstoke, 1987, 89–110.

43. See Chant 1995, *op. cit.* for a review and a list of empirical studies on this; see also Gugler, Josef, 'Social organization in the city' in Alan Gilbert and Josef Gugler (eds.), *Cities, Poverty and Development: Urbanization in the Third World* (Second Edition), Oxford University Press, Oxford, 1992, 155–76.

44. Chant 1995, *op. cit.* 7.

45. Varley 1996, *op. cit.*

46. Chant 1995, *op. cit.*; Townsend, Janet and Janet Momsen, 'Toward a geography of gender in the Third World', in Janet Momsen and Janet Townsend (eds.), *Geography of Gender in the Third World*, Hutchinson, London, 1987, 27–81.

47. Varley 1996, *op. cit.*

48. Brydon, Lynne and Sylvia Chant, *Women in the Third World: Gender Issues in Rural and Urban Areas*, Edward Elgar, Aldershot, 1989; Chant, Sylvia and Sarah A. Radcliffe, 'Migration and development: the importance of gender', in Sylvia Chant (ed.), *Gender and Migration in Developing Countries*, Belhaven Press, London, 1992, 1–29.

49. Appleton, Simon, 'Gender dimensions of structural adjustment: the role of economic theory and quantitative analysis', *IDS Bulletin*, vol. 22, no. 1, 1991, 17–22; Chant, Sylvia, 'Single-parent families: choice or constraint? The formation of female-headed households in Mexican shanty towns', *Development and Change*, vol. 16, no. 4, 1985, 635–65; Chant, Sylvia and Cathy McIlwaine, *Women of a Lesser Cost; Female Labour, Foreign Exchange and Philippine Development*, Pluto, London, 1995 (chapters 3 and 7); Engle, Patrice, 'Father's money, mother's money and parental commitment: Guatemala and Nicaragua', in Rae Lesser Blumberg, Cathy Rakowski, Irene Tinker and Michael Montéon (eds.), *Engendering Wealth and Wellbeing: Empowerment for Global Change*, Westview, Boulder, 1995, 155–79; Hoddinot, John and Lawrence Haddad, *Household Expenditures, Child Anthropomorphic Status and the Intra-Household Division of Income*, Unit for the Study of African Economics, University of Oxford, 1991; Kanji, Nazneen, 'Structural adjustment policies: shifting the costs of social reproduction to women', *Critical Health*, vol. 34, 1991, 61–7; Kennedy, Eileen, 'Development policy, gender of head of household and nutrition', in Eileen Kennedy and Mercedes González de la Rocha, *Poverty and Wellbeing in the Household: Case Studies of the Developing World*, Centre for Iberian and Latin American Studies, UCLS, San Diego, 1994, 25–42; Weekes-Vagliani, Winifred, 'Structural adjustment and gender in the Côte d'Ivoire', in Haleh Afshar and Carolyne Dennis (eds.), *Women and Adjustment Policies in the Third World*, Macmillan, Basingstoke, 1992, 117–49.

50. Drawn from Chant, 1995, *op. cit.*, quoting Browner, C. H., 'Women,

household and health in Latin America', *Social Science and Medicine*, vol. 28, no. 5, 1989, pp. 461–473; Buvinic, Mayra, Juan Pablo Valenzuela, Temistocles Molina and Electra González, 'The fortunes of adolescent mothers and their children: the transmission of poverty in Santiago, Chile', *Population and Development Review*, vol. 18, no. 2, 1992, 169–97; Elson, Diane, 'The impact of structural adjustment on women: concepts and issues', in Bade Onimode (ed.), *The IMF, the World Bank and the African Dept Vol 2: The Social and Political Impact*, Zed, London, 1989; Haddad, Lawrence, 'Gender and poverty in Ghana: a descriptive analysis of selected outcomes and processes', *IDS Bulletin* vol. 22, no. 1, 1991, 5–16; Safa, Helen and Peggy Antrobus, 'Women and economic crisis in the Caribbean', in Lourdes Benería and Shelly Feldman (eds.), *Unequal Burden: Economic Crises, Persistent Poverty and Women's Work*, Westview, Boulder, 1992, 49–82.

51. Satterthwaite, David, 'Continuity and change in the world's largest cities', Background paper for the Global Report, 1995.

52. 1990 was chosen as the reference year in this section and also in Chapter 2 since the most recent census data in most nations is from censuses held between 1989 and 1991 and thus virtually all statistics for rural, urban or city populations for 1995 are simply estimates or projections based on earlier data.

53. See United Nations, *World Urbanization Prospects: the 1994 Revision*, Population Division, New York, 1995.

54. As Hardoy and Satterthwaite 1989 (*op. cit.*) note, it is still common for people to confuse 'growth in urban population' and 'growth in a nation's or region's level of urbanization'. Virtually all changes in the level of urbanization (i.e. in the proportion of population living in urban centres) are a result of population movements in or out of urban centres. Natural increase in population (ie the excess of births over deaths) does not contribute to increases in urbanization levels except where the rate of natural increase in urban centres is higher than that in rural areas. If this is the case, this may be the result of high proportions of migrants from rural to urban areas being of child-bearing age and their movement to urban centres changing urban centres' rate of natural increase. But rates of natural increase are generally lower in urban centres, compared to rural centres. Part of a change in a nation's level of urbanization is often due to rural settlements growing to the point where they are reclassified as urban (and thus are added to the urban population) or boundaries of cities or metropolitan areas being extended and including people that were previously classified as rural—and rapid rates of natural increase can increase this contribution. But in general, a nation's level of

urbanization is not influenced much by population increases for it is essentially the result of changes in economic structure; increased proportions of national populations in urban centres reflect an increase in the proportion of employment opportunities (or possibilities for survival) concentrated in urban centres.

55. This calculation is made from the Cities Database of the Human Settlements Programme of the International Institute for Environment and Development (IIED) and of IIED-América Latina. This combines the data on city populations from 1950 to 1990 from United Nations 1995, *op. cit.* with recent and historic data drawn from around 250 censuses and from Chandler, Tertius and Gerald Fox, *3000 Years of Urban Growth*, Academic Press, New York and London, 1974.

56. Hardoy and Satterthwaite 1989, *op. cit.*

57. Hardoy, Jorge E. and Satterthwaite, David (eds.), *Small and Intermediate Urban Centres; Their Role in National and Regional Development in the Third World*, Hodder and Stoughton (UK), 1986 and Westview (USA) 1986.

58. Harris 1991, *op. cit.*

59. Hardoy and Satterthwaite 1989, *op. cit.*

60. *Ibid.*

61. Cheshire P. C. and D. G. Hay, 'Background and the use of Functional Urban Regions', in P. C. Cheshire and D. G. Hay (editors), *Urban Problems in Western Europe*, Unwin Hyman, London.

62. See Section 2.4 for more details and the basis for this figure and its source.

63. Hawkins, J. N., 'Shanghai: an Exploratory Report on Food for a City', *GeoJournal* Supplementary issue, 1982.

64. See note j in Table 1.5; Aina, Tade Akin, 'Metropolitan Lagos: population growth and spatial expansion; city study', Background paper for the Global Report on Human Settlements, 1995.

65. The 1991 census figure for Lagos put its population at around 5 million.

66. Bairoch, Paul, *Cities and Economic Development: From the Dawn of History to the Present*, Mansell, London, 1988.

67. See chapter 8 of Hardoy and Satterthwaite 1989, *op. cit.*

68. Satterthwaite, David, 'Continuity and change in the world's largest cities', Background paper for the Global Report, 1995.

69. Parker 1995, *op. cit.*

70. Caride, Horacio E. and José A. Borello, *Industrial Location in Major Latin American Metropolitan Areas*, report prepared by IIED-América Latina for the Business Council on Sustainable Development, 1995.

71. Caride and Borello 1995, *op. cit.*

72. Harris, Nigel, 'Bombay in a global economy; structural adjustment and the role of cities', *Cities*, vol. 12, no. 3, June 1995, 175–84.

73. Parker 1995, *op. cit.*

74. Borja, J. and others, *Barcelona; un Modelo*

de Transformación, Urban Management Programme, Quito, 1995.

75. de Jong, Mark W. 'Revitalizing the urban core: waterfront development in Baltimore, Maryland', in Joanne Fox-Przeworski, John Goddard and Mark de Jong (eds.), *Urban Regeneration in a Changing Economy—an International Perspective*, Clarendon Press, Oxford, 1991, 185–98.

76. Parker 1995, *op. cit.*

77. *Ibid 7.*

78. *Ibid.*

79. Castells, Manuel and Peter Hall, *Technopoles of the World: The Making of 21st Century Industrial Complexes*, Routledge, London and New York, 1994.

80. Friedmann and Wolff 1983, Friedmann 1993, Sassen 1994, *op. cit.*

81. Friedmann 1993, *op. cit.*

82. Sassen 1994, *op. cit.*

83. *Ibid.*

84. Friedmann 1993, *op. cit.*

85. *Ibid.*

86. Parsonage, James, 'Southeast Asia's "Growth Triangle": a subregional response to global transformation', *International Journal of Urban and Regional Research*, vol. 16, no. 2, June 1992, 307–17.

87. See for instance Chant, Sylvia and Sarah A. Radcliffe, 'Migration and development: the importance of gender', Radcliffe, Sarah A., 'Mountains, maidens and migration: gender and mobility in Peru,' Pryer, Jane, 'Purdah, patriarchy and population movement; perspectives from Bangladesh', and Hugo, Graeme, 'Women on the move: changing patterns of population movement of women in Indonesia' in Sylvia Chant (ed.), *Gender and Migration in Developing Countries*, Belhaven Press, London, 1992.

88. See references in previous note; also Hugo, Graeme J., 'Migration as a survival strategy: the family dimension of migration' in United Nations, *Population Distribution and Migration*, ST/ESA/SER.R/133, New York, 1995.

89. See for instance references in the previous two notes; also Baker, Jonathan and Tade Akin Aina (eds.), *The Migration Experience in Africa*, Nordiska Africainstitutet, Uppsala, 1995; United Nations, *Population Distribution and Migration*, ST/ESA/SER.R/133, New York, 1995; Douglass, Mike, 'Thailand: territorial dissolution and alternative regional development for the Central Plains', in Walter B. Stohr and D. R. Fraser Taylor (eds.), *Development From Above or Below*, John Wiley and Sons, Chichester, UK, 1981, 183–208 and Saint, William S. and William D. Goldsmith, 'Cropping systems, structural change and rural-urban migration in Brazil', *World Development*, vol. 8, 1980, 259–72.

90. Chant and Radcliffe 1992, *op. cit.*

91. *Ibid.*

92. Castles, Stephen and Mark J. Miller, *The Age of Migration: International Population Movements in the Modern World*, MacMillan, London and Basingstoke, 1993.

93. Martin, P. L., 'Labour migration in Asia: conference report', *International Migration Review*, vol. 25, no. 1, 1991.

94. Champion, Tony and Russell King, 'New trends in international migration in Europe', *Geographical Viewpoint*, vol. 21, 1993, 45–56.

95. Kane, Hal, *The Hour of Departure: Forces that create Refugees and Migrants*, Worldwatch Paper 125, Worldwatch Institute, Washington DC, 1995. Note that this source also estimated that there were 27 million 'internal' refugees who have fled from persecution but have not crossed international boundaries.

96. Skeldon, R., 'International migration within and from the East and Southeast Asian regions: a review essay', *Asian and Pacific Migration Journal*, vol. 1, no. 1, 1992.

97. ILO, *Social and Labour Issues concerning Migrant Workers in the Construction Industry*, International Labour Organization, Sectoral Office Programme, TMMWCI, International Labour Office, Geneva, 1995.

98. Castles and Miller 1993, *op. cit.*

99. Russell, Sharon Stanton, 'Migration between developing countries in the African and Latin American regions and its likely future', in United Nations, *Population Distribution and Migration*, ST/ESA/SER.R/133, New York, 1995.

100. Stalker, Peter, *The World Of Strangers*, International Labour Organization, Geneva, 1994.

101. Russell 1995, *op. cit.*

102. Castles and Miller 1993, *op. cit.*

103. *Ibid.*

104. *Ibid.*

105. Russell 1995, *op. cit.*

106. The information presented about each region is largely drawn from Castles and Miller 1993, *op. cit.*

107. Castles and Miller 1993, *op. cit.*

108. Brubraker, W. R, 'Citizenship struggles in Soviet successor states', *International Migration Review*, vol. 26, 1992, 269–91; and Buttner, T. and C. Prinz, 'Structure and impact of German east-west migration', in W. Lutz (ed.), *Future Demographic Trends in Europe and North America: What Can we Assume Today?*, Academic Press, London, 1991, 379–98.

109. Castles and Miller 1993 and ILO 1995, *op. cit.*

110. Castles and Miller 1993, *op. cit.*

111. Russell 1995, *op. cit.*

112. Castles and Miller 1993, *op. cit.*

113. Russell 1995, *op. cit.*

114. Champion, A.G., 'International migration and demographic change in the Developed World', *Urban Studies*, vol. 31, nos. 4/5, 1994, 653–77; White, P., 'The social geography of immigrants in European cities: the geography of arrival', in R. King (ed.), *The New Geography of European Migrations*, Belhaven, London, 1993, 47–66.

115. Fernhout, R., 'Europe 1993 and its refugees', *Ethnic and Racial Studies*, vol. 16, 1993, 492–506; and Black, R., 'Refugees and asylum seekers in Western Europe: new challenges', in R. Black and V. Robinson (eds.), *Geography and Refugees*, Belhaven, London, 1993, 87–103.

116. Champion 1994, *op. cit.*

117. UNECE, *International Migration Bulletin no.3*, United Nations Economic Commission for Europe, Geneva, 1993.

118. See for instance Harris 1991 and Parker 1995, *op. cit.*; also World Bank, *Urban Policy and Economic Development: an Agenda for the 1990s*, The World Bank, Washington DC, 1991.

119. George Yeo, reported in Parker 1995, *op. cit.*

120. These statistics are drawn from the same sources listed in Table 1.6.

121. Satterthwaite 1995, *op. cit.*

122. *Ibid.*

123. Becker, Charles M., Jeffrey G. Williamson and Edwin S. Mills, *Indian Urbanization and Economic Growth since 1960*, The Johns Hopkins University Press, Baltimore and London, 1992.

124. Preston, Samuel H., 'Urban growth in developing countries: a demographic reappraisal', *Population and Development Review*, vol. 5, no. 2, 1979.

125. United Nations 1995, *op. cit.*

126. See Preston 1979, *op. cit.* and Kelley, Allen C. and Jeffrey G. Williamson, *What Drives Third World City Growth: A Dynamic General Equilibrium Approach*, Princeton University Press, Princeton, 1984.

127. Preston 1979, *op. cit.*

128. Bairoch 1988, *op. cit.*

129. *Ibid.*

130. Manzanal, Mabel and Cesar Vapnarsky, 'The Comahue Region, Argentina' in Hardoy, Jorge E. and Satterthwaite, David (eds.), *Small and Intermediate Urban Centres; Their Role in National and Regional Development in the Third World*, Hodder and Stoughton (UK), 1986 and Westview (USA) 1986; Hardoy and Satterthwaite 1989, *op. cit.*

131. Manzanal and Vapnarsky 1986, *op. cit.*

132. Hardoy and Satterthwaite 1986, *op. cit.*

133. Ofer, Gur, 'Industrial structure, urbanization and the growth strategy of socialist countries', *Quarterly Journal of Economics*, vol. 10, no. 2, 1976, 219–44.

134. Becker, Williamson and Mills 1992, *op. cit.*

135. Mitlin, Diana, *The Relationship between Economic Change and Level of Urbanisation*, Background paper for the Global Report on Human Settlements, 1995.

2 Regional Perspectives on Population and Urbanization

2.1 Introduction

Much attention has been given to the rapid growth in the world's urban population but rather less to the much larger and more fundamental economic, political and demographic changes that underlie it. Much of the attention has centred on cities in the South yet over the last ten to fifteen years, the scale and pace of urban change in parts of the North has also been rapid. Much attention has been given to the world's 'mega-cities', yet the vast majority of the world's urban population (in both the North and the South) do not live in mega-cities. It is also commonly stated that large cities are 'mushrooming' yet, as Chapter 1 described, most of the major cities in both the North and the South have long histories as cities.

There is also a tendency to generalize about cities as if they have many characteristics in common and to describe and compare them with economic and demographic statistics. But each metropolitan area, city and market town is so much more than these statistics can reveal. As John Friedmann points out:

> In the economist's language, particular cities are dissolved into market configurations, their history is replaced by something called the urban dynamic, where people disappear as citizens of the polis and are subsumed under the categories of abstract urbanization processes, while human concerns are reduced to property, profits and competitive advantage.[1]

Each urban centre has its own unique and complex ecological setting and political economy within which individuals, social groups, voluntary organizations, businesses and different government agencies coexist, collaborate or compete. Within this context, so often, historic and contemporary factors collide—and generally, also local, national and international interests. This is not only the case in large cities but also in thousands of small urban centres. These are aspects rarely covered in Global Reports because generalizations are less easily made. The complexity and diversity of urban centres are revealed in their histories—but only for the small proportion of the world's urban centres whose history has been recorded. Social and cultural aspects of cities that have importance for their inhabitants also receive little attention.

This Chapter aims to bring out this diversity and to base the description of population and urbanization in the specific social and economic context of each of the world's major regions. Separate sections look at North America, Latin America and the Caribbean, West Europe, East and Central Europe and the fifteen republics that were formerly the Soviet Union, Asia and the Pacific, and Africa. Each of these sections includes two primary focuses. The first is change in national populations—including their size, age structure and the role of international migration either in boosting or reducing populations. The second is changes in spatial distribution of population within national boundaries, including their distribution among metropolitan areas, cities, smaller urban centres and rural settlements. There is also a special interest in identifying trends during the 1980s and considering whether these represent continuations of trends evident in previous decades. There are certainly new urban trends that only become evident during the 1980s. There is also a special interest in considering what past and current trends imply for the future. Where possible, information is also given about trends in the early 1990s, although the fact that most data on population and urban change comes from censuses and most recent censuses were undertaken in 1990 and 1991 limits the amount of information available.

2.2 North America[2]

Introduction

Over the last few decades, both the United States and Canada experienced a much more rapid and fundamental reordering of their population and urban systems than Europe. They also had some of the world's most rapidly growing cities and metropolitan areas. Among the mature industrial economies, they have relatively new, fluid and malleable urban systems and in comparison to other industrialized countries (or continents), people, firms and jobs move with relative ease and surprising frequency, and over considerable distances. Between 1950 and 1990, there were major changes in the spatial distribution of population and in the relative importance of different cities and metropolitan areas. The dominance of the larger industrial cities and older eastern gateway ports were re-ordered and complex new urban hierarchies are emerging.

Between 1950 and 1990, the population of the US increased by 65 per cent to reach 248.7

million; in Canada, it increased almost 95 per cent, 1951–91, to reach 27.3 million. The proportion of the population living in urban centres in these same periods grew from 64 to over 82 per cent in the US and from 61 to 77 per cent in Canada.[3] The scale of economic growth was much greater during this period; the Gross National Product (GNP) of the US increased almost twenty-fold (from $288 billion to over $5,000 billion in constant 1982 US dollars), and from $1,900 to $23,000 per capita. The Canadian economy has shown somewhat higher long-term average growth rates, at least until the beginning of the latest recession in the late 1980s, and the level of per capita output is almost the same (allowing for variable currency exchange rates). This brought much expanded national production but also rapid technological changes in production, communication and transportation, dramatic revisions in occupational structures and in the spatial division of labour, continued income growth and markedly uneven wealth creation. The structure and relative importance of regional and urban economies shifted in response to both domestic needs and international competition. In response, massive metropolitan complexes are being created, often in formerly peripheral regions, and new and even more dispersed forms of urban agglomeration are evolving. In parallel, long-standing patterns of dominance and interdependence among cities, and between cities and suburbs, are being redefined. The North American continent and its cities are clearly in flux; its urban systems, metropolitan forms and suburban landscapes are still in the making.

Although the settlement systems of the US and Canada (as well as Mexico) are becoming increasingly interdependent, the two systems are considered separately here. Despite numerous common attributes, these two systems have rather different histories, differing regulatory environments and most recently varying growth trajectories.[4] They are also of vastly different size and political configuration. There were some 16,900 separate incorporated municipalities (both urban and rural) with over 10,000 inhabitants in the US in 1990, and only 759 in Canada. To discuss the two systems together would complicate the empirical analysis (since basic data sources and statistical definitions differ), obscure unique elements in both their structure and evolution, and otherwise swamp the Canadian urban experience.

Demographic change

The demographic basis of the post-World War II urban transformation in North America is the outcome of two principal components: immigration; and a series of socio-demographic waves (or transitions) and migration movements that swept across the continent. Both the US and Canada experienced a massive 'baby and marriage boom' beginning near the end of World War II, but especially during the years 1948 to 1963. Rates of natural increase rose significantly, and both birth rates and rates of natural increase were much higher than those prevailing in western Europe. The marriage rate also increased, and the average age of first-marriage and first-birth declined while in parallel, and over the same period, the death rate declined.[5] The resulting population boom contributed substantially to the rapid growth of the consumer economy, to increased aggregate housing demand and new residential construction, and to the evolution of new urban forms through widespread suburbanization.

The subsequent 'baby and marriage bust', when it did set in after 1963, was therefore even sharper than in most other western countries. Birth rates declined, and the age of first marriage increased.[6] The 'echo-baby boom', expected a generation later as the children of the first baby-boom reached child-bearing age, did not materialize. The result of these sharp demographic transitions is not simply large differentials in the size of individual age cohorts, but also wide variations in demand and supply pressures in the market—and thus a new 'market geography'. These variations continue to send ripples through housing and labour markets, and through the agencies responsible for public service delivery.[7] These, in turn, set the stage for significant shifts in the preferences, migration behaviours and economic well-being of age-specific household and family groups, and thus in the fortunes of the particular communities and regions where these groups reside.

Parallel to these demographic changes were equally dramatic changes in household and family composition, especially the proliferation and diversification of household types. Average household size declined over the study period from 4.0 persons to under 2.7 and is even lower in the metropolitan areas. Over 20 per cent of all households now have only one person, and in the US over 13 per cent are female-headed, single-parent households. Less than half of all households are now family households in the sense of having members related by blood or marriage. The impacts of these shifts in domestic living arrangement are often underrated as factors in metropolitan development. These include a substantially greater consumption of housing space, urban land and public resources per capita and per household than would otherwise have been the case.[8]

As rates of natural increase declined, they also became more uniform across the continent. As a result, internal migration flows assumed greater

TABLE 2.1 Comparisons between the United States and Canada in metropolitan populations

	United States 1990[a]	Canada 1991[b]
Total national population (millions)	248.7	27.3
% change in national population 1980/90;1981/91	9.8	12.1
Number of metropolitan areas	284[c]	28[d]
Total metropolitan population (million inhabitants)	192.7	16.4
% of national population in metropolitan areas	77.5	61.1
Average number of inhabitants in metropolitan areas (thousands)	678.5	653.8
Number of metropolitan areas with over one million inhabitants	39	3
% of metro. popn in metro. areas with over 1 million inhabitants	62.5	52.8
% change in metro. area populations 1980/90; 1981/91	11.6	20.4
% of national population in 3 largest metropolitan areas	16.3	31.6

Notes:
[a] Metropolitan Areas as defined April 1, 1990. Includes Consolidated Metropolitan Statistical Areas (CMSAs) and individual Metropolitan Statistical Areas (MSAs).
[b] Census Metropolitan Areas (CMAs) as defined in 1991.
[c] Includes 35 metropolitan areas with populations less than 100,000.
[d] Includes 3 census agglomerations with populations over 100,000, but not defined as census metropolitan areas in 1991.

Source: Bourne, L. S., 'Urban growth and population distribution in North America: A diverse and unfinished landscape', Major Report 32, Centre for Urban and Community Studies, University of Toronto, 1995.

importance as determinants of urban growth and population redistribution, and as the source of social change within localities. In any given year about 18 per cent of North Americans change their place of residence, and after five years, over 50 per cent have moved. With such high mobility levels, the potential for redistributing population and economic activity is obviously high. So too is the uncertainty with regard to future settlement trends.

Although the rate of immigration relative to national population and even the number of immigrants per year were much higher in the US earlier in the century (before World War I), both the number of immigrants and the overall rate have increased steadily (with wide fluctuations) since the 1950s. The rate of immigration averaged 1.9/1000 population during the 1960s and 1970s, rising to 2.5 in the 1980s, and then to 4.5 in the early 1990s. The historical rate of immigration into Canada has been considerably higher in relative terms (as has the rate of emigration), but with different cycles, depending on the needs of the economy, external pressures (e.g. wars and refugees), and public policy whims.[9] However, compared to the US, immigration to Canada peaked earlier and at much higher rates, at 9.7/1000 population in the 1950s. It then declined to 8.0 in the 1960s, to 4.1 during the 1970s and to 3.5 in the mid-1980s, before turning sharply upward in the early 1990s. As rates of natural increase have declined so much, immigration

comes to take on a larger role in population change. These immigration flows represented between 20 per cent (US) and 30 per cent (Canada) of total population growth over the 1970s and 1980s. By the early 1990s the two countries were officially admitting nearly 1.3 million immigrants (1.1 million in the US and over 200,000 in Canada) annually. In the last few years, as a result of a deliberate shift in policy, immigration to Canada has represented over half of total national population growth.

The origins of the immigrants have also shifted significantly away from long-established sources in Europe to countries in the South and especially Mexico and Latin America (for the US), and Asia. In Canada, for example, during the 1950s over 80 per cent of all immigrants were drawn from Europe and the US. By 1991 that proportion was down to below 30 per cent, while over 65 per cent were from Asian countries and the Caribbean.[10] In the US, over 80 per cent of immigrants now come from Asia, the Caribbean and Latin America. Many of these new populations are also visibly and culturally distinct from earlier European immigrants.

Regional change in total and urban populations

The spatial distribution of urban population and of economic activity has shifted even more sharply since 1950 than the national figures suggest. This is most evident in the differential growth of regional and state populations and in the expansion of the metropolitan urban system. The predominant regional movement in North America has always been from east to west, following the historical unfolding of European settlement.[11] In 1950, four of the five most populous American states were in the old manufacturing belt in the North-East and Great Lakes regions (New York, Pennsylvania, Illinois, Ohio; California was the exception). These two regions alone held 54 per cent of the national population in 1950, but only 44 per cent in 1990. By the Census of 1990 three of the four most populous states, California (29.7m), Texas (17.0m), and Florida (12.9m), were in the south and west (New York State had 18.0 million, roughly the same as in 1970). During the 1980s almost one-half of total US population growth was concentrated in these three states. This represents a considerable regional shift of population, economic activity and the distribution of political power.

In considering urban change, the more common yardstick of the urbanization process in the US is not the rural-urban balance but the distinction between metropolitan and non-metropolitan areas. The concept of a metropolitan area is

TABLE 2.2 US metropolitan area population rankings, 1990

Rank	Metropolitan Area	Population (in 1000s)	% change 1980–1990
1.	New York CMSA[a]	19,342	3.4
2.	Los Angeles CMSA	14,532	26.3
3.	Chicago CMSA	8,240	1.5
4.	Washington–Baltimore CMSA	6,727	16.1
5.	San Francisco–Oakland–San Jose CMSA	6,253	15.4
6.	Philadelphia CMSA	5,893	4.3
7.	Boston CMSA	5,187	–2.0
8.	Detroit CMSA	5,455	6.5
9.	Dallas–Fort Worth CMSA	4,037	32.5
10.	Houston CMSA	3,731	19.6
11.	Miami CMSA	3,193	20.7
12.	Seattle MSA	2,970	23.2
13.	Atlanta MSA	2,960	33.0
14.	Cleveland–Akron CMSA	2,860	–2.6
15.	Minneapolis–St. Paul MSA	2,539	15.5
16.	San Diego MSA	2,498	34.1
17.	St Louis MSA	2,493	3.2
18.	Pittsburgh MSA	2,395	–6.8
19.	Phoenix MSA	2,238	40.0
20.	Tampa–St. Petersburg MSA	2,068	28.1

Notes: [a] A consolidated metropolitan statistical area (CMSA) includes two or more primary metropolitan statistical areas (i.e. two or more large cities) while a metropolitan statistical area (MSA) is centred on one large city.

Source: US Bureau of the Census.

intended to delimit 'functional regions' not land uses or built environments. Metropolitan areas in the US are defined as including all incorporated urban places with populations of at least 50,000 within the central city, representing the 'urbanized core', plus those adjacent suburban areas (counties) that are closely integrated with that core through the operation of local housing and labour markets. The total combined population of central city (central county) and suburbs should be at least 100,000[12]. Typically, outlying areas are included within the metropolitan area if the proportion of their residents commuting to work in the central core exceeds a certain level, and if those areas meet certain other criteria of metropolitan 'character' (e.g. population density). Non-metropolitan areas, on the other hand, include every other form of settlement from small cities and towns to exurban and strictly rural areas.

In 1990, over 77.5 per cent of the entire US population was classified as metropolitan. In Canada, in 1991, 61 per cent of the population lived in census metropolitan areas (CMAs). The significant difference in these two proportions is in part attributable to the more restricted statistical definition of the minimum size and geographical extent of metropolitan areas used in the Census of Canada, and in part to the relatively greater importance of small towns and rural (non-farm) populations in Canada, especially in the country's vast resource periphery.[13] Table 2.1 compares the size and attributes of the two nations' national and metropolitan populations. Interestingly, and despite the differences in the numerical size of the two systems, the population of the 'average' metropolitan area was surprisingly similar in 1990/91 (654,000 in Canada to 679,000 in the US). What is not shown in this table, however, are the changing properties of individual places, the emerging relationships between these metropolitan areas and the increasing convergence of the two national urban systems into one North American system.

The system of metropolitan areas in the US has expanded and become much more complex. In 1950, for example, the US Census recorded 169 metropolitan statistical areas (MSAs), housing some 85 million people or 44.9 per cent of the national population. The US population had became predominantly metropolitan in the mid-1950s. By 1990 there were 284 metropolitan areas (some of which are defined as consolidated metropolitan areas, or CMSAs, created through the merger of several earlier and adjacent MSAs), with nearly 193 million residents, or 77.5 per cent of the total US population.[14] By 1990, just over half (50.2 per cent) of the US population resided not just in metropolitan areas but in large metropolises. Some—especially the consolidated metropolises formed by the aggregation of more than one MSA 'grew' into each other and are now of immense size: the New York–New Jersey–Connecticut CMSA has 19.0 million people while the Los Angeles–Anaheim–Riverside CMSA over 14.5 million (see Table 2.2) Even some of the relative latecomers to this size category are now of global proportions: for example, the CMSA which includes the capital, Washington, DC had over 4.0 million people in 1990.[15] Map 2.1 shows the largest metropolitan areas in Canada and the United States.

The United States is also unusual in having many relatively 'new' large metropolitan areas, unlike Europe, North Africa, Asia and Latin America where most of the largest metropolitan areas have long been important cities. By 1990, there were also CMSAs with between 2 and 4 million inhabitants that had not even been founded 150 years ago—including Miami, Seattle and Phoenix while Dallas–Fort Worth and Tampa were still not urban centres in 1850 and Los Angeles, Houston, San Diego and Atlanta had at most only a few thousand inhabitants. In

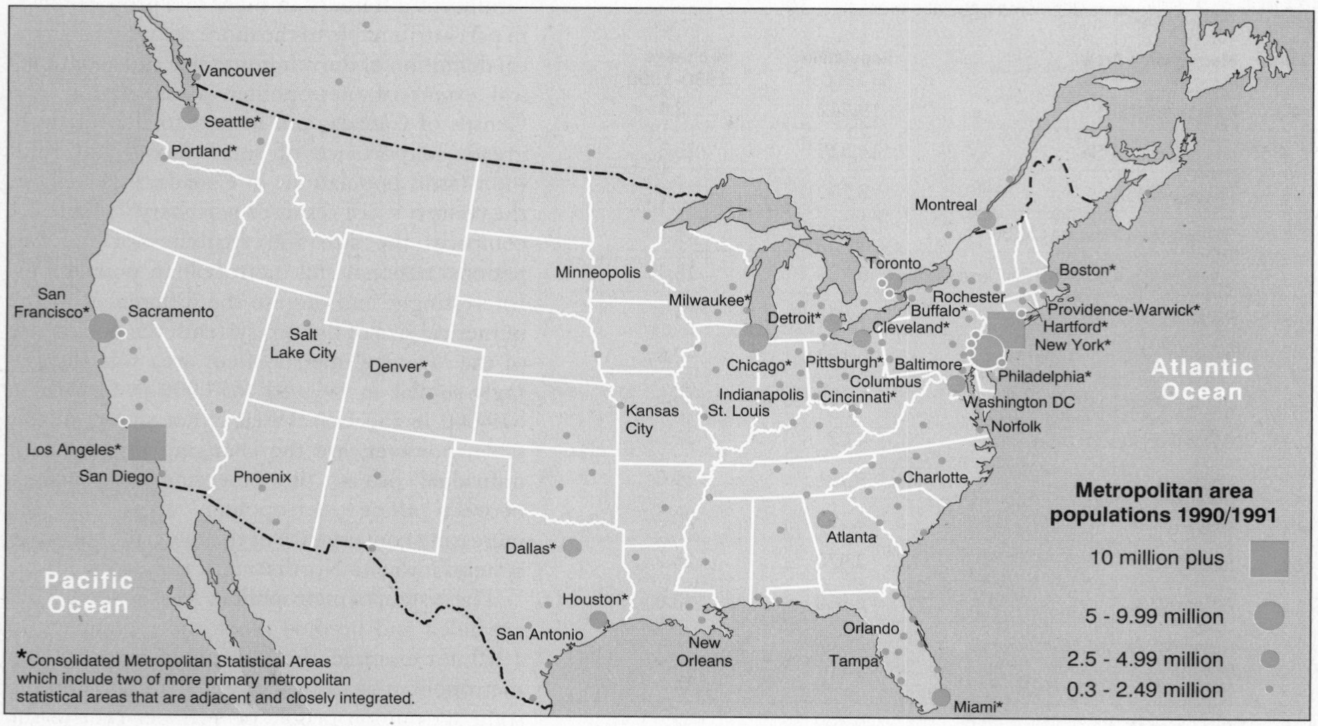

MAP 2.1
The largest metropolitan areas in North America, 1990–91

Notes: This map shows all the statistical metropolitan areas in the United States that had 300,000 or more inhabitants in the 1990 census—and all census metropolitan areas in Canada that had 300,000 or more inhabitants in the 1991 census. It highlights the relative concentration of the larger metropolitan regions in the northeast and southwest and the relative absence of large metropolitan areas in the mid-continent regions.

Source: Bourne L. S., 'Urban growth and population distribution in North America: A diverse and unfinished landscape', Major Report 32, Centre for Urban and Community Studies, University of Toronto, 1995, drawing on census data from the 1991 census in Canada and the 1990 census in the United States.

1850, many other 'million-cities' of the South and South-West were also very small or still to be incorporated as urban centres including Denver, Riverside, Orlando and Fort Lauderdale. The United States also has a considerable proportion of the world's fastest growing cities. Although it is common to stress the very rapid growth of large cities in Africa, Asia and Latin America, many of the US's larger metropolitan areas rank as among the world's fastest growing over the last few decades.

In Canada the historical rise in metropolitan concentration was somewhat slower, and started from a considerably lower base, as might be expected given the relatively small number of centres in the Canadian urban system (28 with over 100,000 population), the importance of the country's resource industries and the relatively low density and greater dispersion of the national population. The Canadian population became predominantly urban in the mid-1920s and predominantly metropolitan by the mid-1960s, roughly a decade later than the US. Prior to 1930, there were no metropolitan areas in Canada with over 1 million inhabitants. By the Census of 1991, however, the three largest metropolitan areas, Toronto (3.9 million), Montreal (3.2 million) and Vancouver (1.6 million), held nearly 32 per cent of the nation's population. If the more extensive metropolitan area definitions used in the US Census were applied to Canada, this level of concentration would be even higher.[16] The comparable figure for the largest three metropolitan areas in the US, as expected given the much larger number of places, was considerably lower, at 16.3 per cent. However, regardless of how they are measured, the living environments of the present generation of North Americans, and the policy problems associated with residing and working in these metropolitan environments, are very different from those of the previous generation.

Stimulated by a rapidly growing and relatively youthful population during the 1960s and 1970s, and by the reduction in real transportation costs, high levels of job creation and rising real incomes, migration flows increased and shifted direction. Certain regions and urban areas became prime destinations of those flows, and thus grew at impressively high rates. Others lost out. During the 1980s, for instance, the contribution of net migration (combining immigration and internal migration) to metropolitan population growth in the US varied widely, from a low of -8.9 per cent in Pittsburgh to +27.8 per cent in Phoenix—which helps explain why Phoenix was one of the world's most rapidly growing cities in this decade. For internal migrants only, the percentage contributions were equally varied, from -11.1 per cent for Chicago to +25.2 per cent in Tampa, but for different reasons. In comparison, rates of natural increase varied much less within the urban system. For the decade, they varied from a low of 0.3 per cent in Tampa (because this is a popular retirement centre), to 15.2 per cent in Houston. In Canada the corresponding differentials have been somewhat lower, varying in terms of rates of natural increase from 0.9 per cent in Victoria (a retirement centre) to 12.9 per cent in Calgary; and in internal migration from -9.8 per cent in Sudbury (a mining centre) to +9.4 per cent in Ottawa-Hull (the capital region). It should be noted that urban decline is seldom as rapid as growth.

Since migrants, on average, tend to be younger (excluding the elderly and retirement migrations) and better educated than non-migrants, these flows also transfer considerable wealth, market power and labour skills to the receiving regions. They also shift the locations of future generations of population growth. On the other hand, regions with high net out-migration rates tend to have lower consumption levels, lower rates of labour force participation and less potential (or demographic capacity) for future population growth. While the overall rate (or propensity) of migration has remained more-or-less constant over three decades or more, the destinations have not been constant. The net flows for any given city or region, as a result, are notoriously unstable and difficult to predict.

The contribution of immigrant flows to the growth of metropolitan populations also deserves consideration. Immigration is highly selective in its geographical destinations and impacts, even more so than for migration within the country. Most overseas immigrants, attracted by job opportunities and following the previous migration chains established by friends and kin, have gone to relatively few regions and the larger metropolitan areas. In Canada, nearly three-quarters of all recent immigrants have settled in the three largest metropolitan areas, Toronto, Montreal and Vancouver, with over 30 per cent of the total converging on Toronto. In the US, gateway cities such as New York, Miami, Los Angeles, San Francisco, and the border cities of Texas and the South-West, have captured most of these recent flows.

This concentration has substantially influenced patterns of national population and economic growth, although the effects are numerous and difficult to measure empirically. The larger the flows the more uneven the potential impacts. These flows are also rapidly transforming the social structure and ethno-cultural character of the recipient cities. Miami, Los Angeles, Vancouver and Toronto, among others, have been transformed into complex 'mosaics' of distinctive cultures, languages, races and ethnicities. In some of these cases the 'new minorities' will constitute a majority of the population in the central city by the turn of the century. The resulting pressures on local and state governments to provide services appropriate to these new and diverse populations, and the associated political tensions, have increased accordingly.

In contrast, the almost complete absence of immigration to most other urban areas has added to existing levels of social and economic differentiation among the cities in both countries.[17] Moreover, indices of income inequalities between growing and declining places, and among neighbourhoods within growing cities, are deepening and new sources of social inequality appear to be arising.[18]

Periodization of urban and regional growth

The scale and complexity of the changes in the economy, demography and life-styles in recent decades, unfolding over a vast and diverse continent, defy simple generalization and easy explanation. As a result most researchers offer some kind of periodization to illustrate the principal directions and patterns of change.[19] Here, three periods are suggested covering the 1950s to the 1980s with a fourth period launched by the recession of the early 1990s that remains to be defined. The differential growth rates of metropolitan areas in the US, by city-size category and by region (Table 2.3), illustrate the complex shifts between these three periods.

The first period covering the 1950s and 1960s, that can simply be titled *metropolitan growth and concentration*, was essentially a period of modest to rapid growth almost everywhere. In most regions, populations grew based on the waves of high natural increase, high rates of household formation and increased immigration. It was also a period of rapid economic growth with expansion in the industrial sector, in services and government activities, contrasting with the absolute decline of the workforce in agriculture and the resource industries. These, in turn, were mirrored in the continued concentration of economic power, employment and population in the larger metropolitan areas. At the same time, cheap mortgages, rising incomes and an expanding highway system opened the suburbs and adjacent rural areas to millions of new households. On average, the population of metropolitan areas grew faster than non-metropolitan areas, while that in peripheral rural areas in particular declined, often dramatically.

The second period, roughly from the early 1970s to the early 1980s, introduced the latest migration turnaround. It was a period defined

TABLE 2.3 Population change by region and metropolitan size category, US, 1960–90.

Region and Metropolitan Category	1990 Size (millions)	Per cent (10–year) Change		
		1960–70	1970–80	1980–90
North:				
Large Metro.	62.9	12.0	–0.9	2.8
Other Metro.	25.6	11.1	5.2	3.3
Non-Metro.	22.6	2.6	8.0	0.1
South:				
Large Metro.	28.2	30.9	23.4	22.3
Other Metro.	31.9	15.5	20.9	13.4
Non-Metro.	24.9	1.1	16.3	4.6
West:				
Large Metro.	33.8	29.1	20.0	24.2
Other Metro.	10.8	24.8	32.2	22.8
Non-Metro.	8.1	9.0	30.6	14.1
Region totals[a]:				
North	111.0	9.8	2.2	2.4
South	84.9	14.2	20.1	13.3
West	52.8	24.6	24.0	22.2
US totals:				
Large Metro.	124.8	18.5	8.1	12.1
Other Metro.	67.9	14.5	15.5	10.8
Non-Metro.	56.0	2.7	14.3	3.9

Notes:[a] The North region represents the combined Northeast and Midwest census regions. Where a metropolitan area overlaps regional boundaries it has been allocated to the region containing the principal central city.

Source: Bourne, L. S., 'Urban growth and population distribution in North America: A diverse and unfinished landscape', Major Report 32, Centre for Urban and Community Studies, University of Toronto, 1995. Data from US Bureau of the Census, 1960, 1970, 1980, 1990; and Frey, W. and A. Speare, Jr. 'The revival of metropolitan growth in the US', *Population and Development Review*, vol. 18, no. 1, 1992, 129–46.

by national *population deconcentration and a non-metropolitan revival*, incorporating renewed growth in smaller cities and towns and selected rural areas, and relatively slower metropolitan growth. For a short period at least, and for the first time this century, the growth rate of the population in non-metropolitan America exceeded that in the metropolitan areas. Metropolitan areas as a group experienced net out-migration, again for the first time, and for some areas (e.g. New York, Detroit, Chicago) the rates became overwhelmingly negative. Some of the older metropolitan areas in the North-East and Great Lakes regions of the US, particularly those with the misfortune to have economies specialized in the wrong sectors (such as Pittsburgh and Cleveland), experienced absolute population declines.

This non-metropolitan turnaround, often described as a process of de-urbanization or counter-urbanization, was the outcome of several forces acting simultaneously. These included declining rates of natural increase, an ageing population, and slower growth (if not decline) in the older manufacturing regions, in part due to widespread economic restructuring and deindustrialization, and in part to international competition.[20] At the same time, the oil price shock and increasing resource prices in the mid-1970s favoured non-manufacturing regions, such as Texas and the mountain states (and, in Canada, Alberta), and the expansion of retirement and life-style migrations continued to Florida, California, Nevada and Arizona (and British Columbia in Canada). Most of these tended to divert population, employment growth and new investment away from the large manufacturing cities and from the US North and North-East generally, to cities and rural areas in the South and South-West.

Although this process of national population deconcentration was real, the apparent migration turnaround and rural revival were partially a function of the statistical under-estimation (or under-bounding) of the physical extent—and thus the real size—of American metropolitan areas. Many of the most rapidly growing non-metropolitan counties in the US during this period were in fact immediately adjacent to existing metropolitan areas, as defined by the Census. As such, they very likely represented a further extension of the suburbanization process into the exurban fringe and beyond, rather than a rejection of urban living and a return to rural life styles and economic pursuits. Although much of what appeared to be counterurbanization can therefore be dismissed as a definitional problem, there was (and continues to be) a significant redistribution of population and industrial growth toward new regions and some non-metropolitan areas.

In Canada, during the 1970s, growth also shifted away from the older industrial heartland to the resource-based periphery in a parallel process of national population deconcentration. Indeed, and in direct response to higher resource prices (e.g. for oil, base metals, forest products and other primary commodities), growth was highly concentrated in the two western-most provinces—British Columbia and Alberta—and especially in those cities (Calgary, Edmonton and Vancouver) that serve as management and service centres for these resource sectors. Similarly, retirement migrations have stimulated localized growth in otherwise non-urbanized regions well outside the metropolitan areas.

Because few of the cities in the US South or South-West (excluding California), or in the Canadian west at this time were large, many observers concluded that this period signalled a revival of the fortunes of smaller urban centres and metropolitan areas and the subsequent 'death of the large metropolis'. This proved to be an over-statement since many middle-size urban areas have done well. Yet, it can be argued that rather than abandoning large cities, North Americans are simply building the next generation of large cities (or metropolises), and are doing so in different regions. This new generation of cities includes those noted earlier as being among the fastest growing cities in the world: the populations of Phoenix and Orlando have increased more than ninefold since 1950 while those of Houston, San Diego and Dallas–Fort Worth have increased around fivefold. Las Vegas should be added to the list; in 1950, it had less than 200,000 inhabitants and now has more than 1 million. The closest parallel in Canada was Calgary (an oil centre), which grew from under 200,000 in 1951 to over 750,000 in 1991.

This period of national deconcentration or counter-urbanization was relatively short-lived in both countries. The 1980s brought yet another— and an even more complex—pattern of growth. This period witnessed a modest level of national *concentration and metropolitan revival*, combined with a relative reduction in the growth rate of many peripheral and resource-based regions (e.g. Texas, Alberta). During much of this decade the growth rates of the larger metropolitan areas, on average, exceeded those of smaller metropolitan areas and of non-metropolitan regions, not unlike the pattern of the 1960s (see Table 2.3). But this was not the 1960s; the determinants and patterns of growth were not the same and overall growth rates were much lower. Retirement and life style (including recreational) migration flows continued, particularly to the South and South-West.

Even some northern metropolitan areas, such as New York City and Boston, also enjoyed a moderate degree of economic resurgence after 1975, as did selected parts of the traditional manufacturing belt. Often, however (as in the case of New York), there was very little if any associated population growth. Although there was minimum growth in employment in basic manufacturing, the major engines of metropolitan growth were the service sector, particularly producer services, finance, insurance and real estate, and in some instances high-tech industry.[21] The expansion of government employment and services, and the military, also played significant roles.

In Canada during the 1980s the pendulum of urban and regional growth shifted yet again.[22] While in the 1970s over half the nation's economic growth and population growth were in two western provinces (part of the traditional resource periphery), during the 1980s over one half was located in one region—central Canada— and most of that growth took place in the greater Toronto area. Since the Toronto region is both a manufacturing and service centre, and a provincial capital, as well as the command post for many national economic and cultural industries, it benefited from most of the sectoral reversals in the rest of the country. But this combination of growth inducements in the industrial heartland was not to last.

The differential in economic growth performance between cities also increased during this period. Those cities that were more closely linked to the new service economy and to the global economic system, either as global financial centres,[23] such as New York and Los Angeles, or as leaders in particular niche industries (e.g. Seattle) or leisure markets (e.g. Las Vegas, Orlando), or as government centres (e.g. Washington DC; Austin, Texas; Ottawa-Hull), did rather well. Even some of the formerly declining metropolitan areas, as noted above, exhibited a moderate resurgence, but for quite different and varied reasons. Some of these cities rediscovered and then built on (or marketed) their own comparative advantages, for example in terms of lower housing and labour costs, less environmental pollution, reduced traffic and congestion levels, new recreation and leisure facilities, and in some instances, lower taxes. For other older cities the deindustrialization process had simply run its course; there were few traditional manufacturing jobs left to lose.

This period, in turn, appears to have been brought to an abrupt halt by the recession of the early 1990s. That recession was particularly severe in terms of corporate downsizing and employment losses, notably full-time employment. Unlike earlier recessions the impacts were relatively strongest in the service and financial sectors. What the resulting economic dynamic of the post-recession decade will produce, in terms of urban growth and population redistribution, remains to be seen. Nevertheless, it is clear that the patterns will not be the same as those of the 1980s, or of any of the earlier periods.

Urban and regional contrasts

This brief summary of the components and patterns of population growth and change in North America can capture some of the shifts in the national urban systems, but it cannot do justice to the detailed patterns and determinants of growth that vary widely from region to region and from city to city. Rapid urban growth continues but in a more complex and 'punctuated' fashion, depending on the attributes of local places and regions, their position with respect to the urban system as a whole and increasingly with respect to the emerging continental and global economies. The tendency in the literature has been to characterize the urban growth patterns since 1950 in the vivid terms of polar extremes: in Canada as a polarization of heartland (or core) and periphery; and in the US as a contrast between sun-belt and frost-belt, or between the sun-and-gun (ie military) belt of the southern states and the northern rust-belt. These images are at times useful, but they are overly simplistic and potentially misleading. While it is true that southern regions and metropolitan areas in the US have been growing faster on average than the rest of the country, growth has been very uneven within both regions, and is often dominated by the performance of a few large states (Florida, Texas and California). It is also interesting to note that the four poorest states in the US are all in the booming sun-belt, while three of the four richest states are in the declining North-East.[24]

The overall pattern of growth in this period could be termed 'bi-coastal' (see Figure 2.1). Rapidly growing urban areas now dot both coasts from Maine to Miami on the east and from San Diego to Seattle and Vancouver on the west. The attraction here is not the coast *per se*, nor exclusively the climate (although that is obviously a positive feature) but also their position with respect to national and international urban systems. The traditional 'city-as-gateway' concept has become useful once again.

If metropolitan areas in North America are grouped according to their main economic bases, it reveals some interesting variations in population growth rates. The fastest growing urban areas in the US in the 1980s and early 1990s were typically smaller metropolitan areas whose economies were based on retirement and recreational pursuits (e.g. Ft. Pierce, Florida). The population of these communities grew by 46.9 per cent in the 1980s, compared to an average of 11.9 per cent for all metropolitan areas.[25] Most are in Florida, Arizona and Nevada. In Canada, most places similarly classified (but with lower growth rates) are in the westernmost province of

British Columbia on the east coast of Vancouver Island or in the lower mainland, and in the recreational areas of southern Ontario.

A second group, typically somewhat larger, included the finance and service centres identified above—those urban places serving as 'control and management' centres for the national economy. US metropolitan areas in this category grew by 14.5 per cent during the 1980s. Cities in a third group were involved primarily in public administration, often as national, state or provincial capitals, or as military centres (average growth rate 17.5 per cent). In contrast, manufacturing-based cities grew by only 1.5 per cent on average, and mining and resource communities declined on average by 2.0 per cent over the decade.

Canada showed similar patterns in terms of a nation-wide set of declining agricultural and resource-based communities, particularly in the east and northern regions. But without a comparable sun-belt or military complex, it showed somewhat less regional diversity in growth, but offers an even more prominent role for governments in urban and regional growth, particularly given the increasing economic and political power of the provincial governments. Of the eight fastest growing urban areas in Canada during the 1980s, five were provincial capital cities; another was the federal capital, Ottawa-Hull.[26]

Still other cities have found their fortunes as regional service centres in growing regions (e.g. Dallas, Atlanta), as military locations (e.g. San

FIGURE 2.1
Per cent change in state population within the United States, 1980–1990

Chart prepared by the US Bureau of the Census

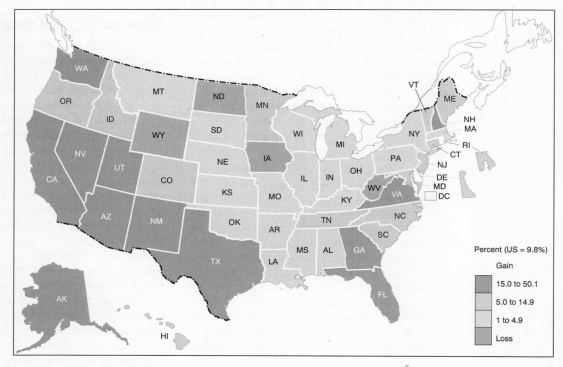

Diego), as hosts for expanding high-tech industries (e.g. Silicon Valley in San Jose; Software Valley near Salt Lake City, Utah; Kanata near Ottawa), and as centres for specialized services in such expanding fields as research and development, education and health care. Interestingly, many of these centres owe their growth stimulus to government policies, and to other public sector activities and decisions, rather than those of the market. In North America, as in most other regions, the state continues to play an important, but often under-rated part, in shaping the urban growth process.

Looking to the future

As both Canada and the US were emerging slowly from the recession of the early 1990s, the dynamics of population and urban economic growth remain as volatile as ever. It is unclear whether trends and patterns evident in the early 1990s will continue. With slower overall population growth, the redistribution of population and economic activity will assume greater importance. Among the more recent and significant factors that will contribute to this volatility in the future are immigration, an ageing population, life style shifts, the uncertain growth in income, revisions in welfare policies, technological innovations, trade liberalization and increased global competition. Here we examine the implication of an ageing population and of immigration to illustrate the potential sources of uncertainty.

Consider first the implications of an ageing population—this will be the most marked change as the baby-boom population moves through the life cycle. The proportion over 65 years will rise from 12.5 per cent (1989) to over 21 per cent by 2010. The question is: how will this relatively large group behave as consumers and where will they live? Will they tend to remain within their present and largely metropolitan environments, or will they migrate in large numbers, perhaps to small cities and towns and to environmentally attractive regions? The combination of ageing and a slower rate of population growth overall could have serious impacts on those older metropolitan areas that attract few migrants. Some of these areas could see their populations and economic base decline rather sharply in the near future.

Immigration is likely to continue having a major impact on population and urban change— all the more so as birth rates are likely to remain low and well below replacement level. The numbers of new immigrants in the future are unknown but potentially large. Whatever the size of the flows, the impacts of immigration—at least on particular regions and places—will continue to be large and uneven. In most instances the effects on urban life and economic growth will be positive, enriching and cumulative. But in some places and for specific groups, immigration will become a source of increased social tension and political conflict over urban space, jobs and scarce public resources. In some of the major gateway cities, over one-quarter of their populations are now foreign-born and often culturally and racially distinctive. As immigration continues, many inner cities could become dominated by such distinctive migrants. In the greater Toronto region, for example, 37 per cent of the population is currently foreign-born and one half of those are 'visible' minorities. By the turn of the century over 40 per cent of the population of the municipality of Metro Toronto will be classified as new minorities.

Even if we could anticipate the future components of national population increase over the next decade or two, this would tell us very little about where or how these people will live. In mobile societies such as the US and Canada, forecasts of population movements become qualitatively more complicated since they require an assessment of the combined effects on individual cities and regions of simultaneous revisions in national growth rates, demographic changes, economic restructuring, diverse life style choices about where and with whom to live, and changes in public policy (e.g. with regard to welfare, health-care, unemployment and social assistance, and taxation). Our best guesses for the 1990s and beyond must rest on a continuation, with variations, of trends evident during the 1980s and early 1990s.[27] On this basis we might expect continued growth of the coastal regions, the recipients of considerable economic investment, internal migration and immigration. In contrast, we might also expect widespread declines in the Great Lakes metropolitan regions, in parts of the industrial North-East and in the central and northern agricultural and mining interior (the Great Plains states). Yet the patterns will be much more complex than these generalizations suggest. Even within growing regions there will be decline (e.g. most of the state of Georgia outside of Atlanta-Athens and Savannah is declining), and in declining regions there will be growth (e.g. Minneapolis). In Canada, only the west coast (Vancouver, Victoria), Alberta (Calgary) and south-central Ontario (Toronto) are likely to witness significant urban population growth in the next decade.

Adding to this uncertainty are the potential impacts of heightened global competition, economic integration and further trade liberalization on urban growth and population distributions. The impacts, notably of the revised GATT Agreement (1993), the Canada–US Free Trade Agreement (FTA), signed in 1988, and its extension as the North American

Free Trade Agreement (NAFTA) to Mexico in 1993, are unclear.[28] Undoubtedly, they will in combination have differential effects by sector, by industry type, and by region, as well as among the three countries involved. As Section 2.3 describes, Mexico's urban system has also been reordered through increasing ties with the US economy. In the US and Canada, those places that will likely benefit most from NAFTA are the same cities and regions that have benefited from recent trends in national and global economies over the last two decades, notably those in the southern and western US and on the west coast of Canada. Cities with high-tech industries, or high-order service functions, as well as those with educational or health-based economies, should do well over the longer term, despite recent cutbacks in the public sector. Those with low-wage industries, as well as agricultural service centres and rust-belt manufacturing centres, will fare poorly under stiff competition from Mexico and lower-wage countries abroad. For Canada, as well as for Mexico, the effects of trade liberalization on urban and regional growth are likely to be very different, from each other and from the US, and in the case of Canada they are potentially more challenging, both economically and politically.

In both countries, as a result, the contrasts between places and regions that are winners and losers in this competition for growth will be larger and much more politically visible. Again, the challenge for policy makers is to minimize the uneven consequences of this highly differentiated urban growth.

2.3 Latin American and the Caribbean[29]

Introduction

Perhaps the three most notable aspects of population and urban change in the region since 1980 are the slower population growth (underpinned by lower fertility and in some instances by less immigration and more emigration), smaller increases in the levels of urbanization and the much slower rates of growth for many of the region's largest cities. In some countries, there were significant changes in the cities and regions where the most rapid urban growth took place. These represent important changes in long established trends since Latin America and the Caribbean have had among the world's most rapid growth rates in total and in urban populations for many decades. Prior to 1980, the region also had among the world's fastest growing large cities. It had the most rapid population growth rate of any of the world's regions for the period 1920–70[30], and during the 1970s its population growth rate was second only to Africa. By the mid-1990s, its total population was roughly the

same as that of Europe[31] whereas only 70 years ago, it was less than a third that of Europe's.[32]

The changes in the rate at which countries were urbanizing and the slower rate of growth for many of the largest cities became evident in the returns from censuses held between 1989 and 1991. For most nations, these are a response to abrupt economic changes. For the region as a whole, the period 1950 to 1980 can be characterized as one of economic expansion, rapid urbanization and increasing life expectancy. In most nations, it was also characterized by strong government support for industrialization largely based on import substitution—priorities that had been initiated in the 1930s and 1940s. By contrast, during the 1980s, most countries experienced a serious and prolonged economic recession. The 1980s was also a period of considerable political change as many countries in the region returned to democratic forms of government and as the scale and nature of government expenditure, investment and intervention changed, partly as a result of democratization, partly as a result of measures linked to the economic crisis and structural adjustment. In most nations, barriers protecting national industries were lowered or removed, many state enterprises were privatized and a greater priority was given to exports.

Care must be taken not to exaggerate the scale of the changes in demographic trends. For instance, many of the largest cities or metropolitan areas had had significantly slower rates of population growth prior to the 1980s. In addition, despite the slower population growth rates, most major cities still had larger annual increases in population during the 1980s than during the 1970s.[33] The economic and political changes of the 1980s are also likely to bring more fundamental changes to the spatial distribution of population during the 1990s but the form that these will take is not yet evident—rather as the spatial implications of the earlier concentration on import-substitution and industrialization also took time to become apparent, especially its concentration of urban and industrial development in a few major cities—most of them national capitals.

Demographic change

By 1990, the region's population totalled 440 million and had doubled in size since 1960. 71.4 per cent living in urban areas, a level of urbanization similar to that of Europe. Demographic statistics for the region are much influenced by Brazil and Mexico that between them have more than half the region's total and urban population. Just eight countries have more than four-fifths of the region's total population and around 87 per cent of its urban population.[34]

Perhaps the two most significant demographic

changes in recent decades have been the much increased life expectancy (from 56 to 68 years, 1960–92) and the declining rates of natural increase evident in most countries. By 1992, Cuba and Costa Rica had among the world's highest life expectancies (75.6 and 76.0) while in many other countries, life expectancies were above 70 years of age (Uruguay, Chile, Argentina and Venezuela) while figures for Mexico and Colombia were very close to 70. Several of these countries also had among the largest increases in life expectancy between 1960 and 1992 (see Chapter 3).

Most countries also underwent what is often termed the demographic transition from high mortality and fertility to low mortality and fertility between 1950 and 1990,[35] although for some, it had begun earlier. There is considerable diversity between countries in population growth rates, that can be illustrated by contrasting three groups of nations:

- Nations with relatively low population growth rates—for instance the three nations in the Southern Cone, Cuba and two of the wealthier Caribbean nations, Jamaica and Trinidad and Tobago. But for all but Trinidad and Tobago, these are countries whose population growth rates were already below 2.0 per cent a year in the 1950s with Jamaica and Uruguay having rates of 1.5 per cent a year or less.[36]

- Nations with population growth rates of between 1.8 and 2.5 per cent a year during the 1980s that includes many of the largest and wealthiest countries such as Venezuela, Mexico, Brazil and Colombia where population growth rates have fallen steadily from the 1950s or 1960s. The 1991 census in Brazil found that the average population growth rate for the country as a whole had fallen to 1.9 per cent a year between 1980 and 1991; for Mexico, it was down to 2.0 per cent a year between 1980 and 1990.

- Nations where population growth rates remained high during the 1980s—for instance Honduras and Paraguay with rates above 3.0 per cent a year and Guatemala with 2.9 per cent a year.[37]

At least since the 1960s, total fertility rates in large cities have been lower than the national averages although fertility rates are still above replacement levels in all but Havana.[38] In general, the larger the city, the lower the fertility rate although there are some medium size cities where fertility levels are even lower than those of the largest cities in their own countries.[39] The lower fertility rates in major cities is partly explained by the fact that desired fertility is lower there and health and contraceptive advice is more readily available; it is also linked to greater participation by women in city labour markets and the fact that

the education of children is more valued.[40]

Although fertility rates have generally been declining in most of the region's large cities, in some where total fertility was already low in the beginning of the 1980s—under three children per woman—there have been slight increases that are also evident at a national level. For instance, this is the case in Santiago de Chile and the postponement of births during the economic crisis, particularly between 1982 and 1985, may explain the fluctuations observed later in the decade.[41] In addition, the rate of natural increase in major cities may be closer to other urban centres and rural areas than the differences in fertility rates suggest because of higher than average numbers of women of child-bearing age[42] and because mortality rates are also lower. Infant mortality rates are generally lower in major cities compared to national averages—although the differences between the two are often smaller than might be expected, given the concentration of wealth and health services in the major cities.[43] Women generally had lower mortality rates in large cities, compared to those in other urban centres who in turn had lower mortality rates than women in rural areas.[44]

Large cities tend to have a lower proportion of children and a higher proportion of persons of working age than the national population. The population of large cities is also ageing more rapidly than their national populations, especially in countries where fertility declines began early. For instance, in Buenos Aires and Montevideo, continued lower fertility coupled with the arrival of sizeable numbers of international migrants during the 1940s and 1950s has given rise to older age structures than those found in other large cities in the region. Already by 1980, an estimated 13 per cent of the population of Buenos Aires was over 60 years of age.[45] There are often particular neighbourhoods in cities with a population that is ageing particularly rapidly, linked both to the concentration of older people (mostly women) and movement out of these neighbourhoods by younger age groups.[46]

In many countries in the region—especially the most urbanized—the number of rural inhabitants has been decreasing while in many more, population growth rates among the rural population is very slow—less than 0.4 per cent a year. In some countries, rural populations declined—for instance in Colombia between 1985 and 1993 and in Argentina for both the 1970–80 and the 1980–91 census periods. However, in several countries, notably Paraguay, Haiti and the countries in Central America, rural population growth rates remained at between 1.3 and 2.0 per cent a year during the 1980s.[47]

National and international migration

Detailed studies of migration processes for

particular individuals, households or those in particular settlements usually reveal a complexity and diversity that is not captured in national statistics. The scale and nature of population movements and of who moves also changes, influenced by broader economic and social change. As Alan Gilbert notes:

Better transportation, growing rural populations, more jobs in the cities and a greater awareness of the opportunities available in the cities are bound to have affected the kinds of people who move, their destinations and their motives. These interrelationships between migration and socio-economic change have become even more obvious since 1980 when severe economic problems began to hit most of Latin America's cities.[48]

Most countries in Latin America have had major changes in the regional distribution of their population. In many, this reflected changes in their economic orientation—for instance the rapid increase in the proportion of Ecuador's population in the coastal provinces as land there was developed for export agriculture and as Guayaquil, the chief commercial centre and port expanded and eventually grew larger than Quito, the national capital, located within the Sierras. In many countries, both formal and informal land colonization programmes in 'frontier' areas have also changed the distribution of populations, especially those with land in the Amazon that remained relatively unpopulated in the 1950s or 1960s. The proportion of the national population in Peru, Brazil, Colombia, Ecuador and Bolivia that is within the Amazon area has grown very considerably. Such regional shifts in population were generally largest in countries with large numbers of landless people or peasant farmers with very inadequate land holdings.

Rural to urban migration has come to have a much smaller role in urban population growth as countries become more urbanized.[49] Recent studies show a decline in migration to Mexico City,[50] Rio de Janeiro[51] and Santiago de Chile.[52] In Argentina, Chile and Peru, rural—urban migration accounts for a quarter or less of all internal migration.[53] In addition, urban to urban migration has come to have a much greater influence on population trends in many cities and has become increasingly important in reshaping urban systems in many countries. In Mexico, the growing weight of urban–urban migration has been documented along with the greater diversification of the urban system and increased migration from large to intermediate and small cities.[54] In the Dominican Republic, the proportion of migrants to Santo Domingo who originate in other urban centres has been increasing since 1970.[55] However, the removal or lowering of trade barriers that formerly protected small-scale farmers may in some countries lead to an increased importance of rural to urban migration.

For instance, there are some 2.4 million small-scale maize producers in Mexico whose livelihoods will be threatened if cheap maize can enter from the United States.[56] Cuba is an exception, since 75 per cent of its internal migration still consists of rural–urban or rural–rural movements, despite its high level of urbanization. In Cuba, most rural migrants originate in scattered rural areas and move to rural areas with a higher degree of concentration or to towns.[57]

It may be that migration movements, whether by individuals or by households, have become more diverse and more complex—in response to rapid and often unpredictable economic and social change.[58] For instance, Roberts has suggested that in contemporary Latin American cities, many people cope with unstable economic and political development through moving, seeking out new opportunities, at times returning to their original homes, at times shifting more or less permanently their base.[59]

There is often a preponderance of women in net migration flows to large cities[60]—although another reason for imbalanced sex ratios in some cities is the increasing proportion of people in older age groups in which women predominate. Men move in much greater numbers to mining towns and major new industrial cities where most available work is only open to men but women dominate migration flows to most large cities because of job opportunities there in domestic service, office cleaning, shop work, street selling and prostitution.[61] For instance, in Bogotá, there has been an increasing number of female migrants and by 1993, there were 93 males for each 100 females living in the city.[62] Social change and widespread poverty in rural areas have meant a disproportionate number of young women seeking employment in large cities, notably in domestic service but also in other services as well as manufacturing; since the late 1960s, the cut-flower export industry has been growing considerably in importance as a source of employment for young female labour, particularly in the municipalities close to Bogotá.[63] Many aspects of women's migration are distinct from men's migration but only recently has much attention been given to these aspects; as a recent review noted, the patterns of selectivity and rationality underlying gender-differentiated migration require more attention.[64]

For cities that attract fewer migrants, so natural increase comes to have a greater importance in city population growth, even if the rate of natural increase is relatively low compared to recent decades. For instance, Buenos Aires grew during most of this century mainly from internal and international migration but during the last two decades, natural increase has accounted for two-thirds of population growth.[65] Like many other cities in the region, Buenos Aires attracts fewer internal and international migrants and former migrants are moving from Buenos Aires to their places of origin or to other urban destinations and a growing number of native city residents have been moving to other parts of Argentina.[66]

International migration has always had an important role in population and urban change within many countries in Latin America and the Caribbean. The large flows of international migrants that converged on the region during the nineteenth and twentieth centuries are an important influence on population concentration between countries—and within countries since immigrants tended to settle in the larger cities. Immigrants attracted to the booming economies of Argentina, Uruguay and Southern Brazil in the late nineteenth and early twentieth century help explain the very rapid growth of many cities at that time although immigration became less important than rural to urban migration from around 1940.[67] Only eight countries received 95 per cent of the overseas migration that reached Latin America since the early nineteenth century and among them, seven are today among the most highly urbanized.[68] Among the largest countries, only Mexico and Peru received relatively few immi-

grants and in these countries it was the rural–urban migration of the indigenous population that underpinned urbanization.[69]

In recent decades, emigration has been on a scale to have significantly lowered population growth rates for particular countries for particular periods—often coinciding with military repression, civil strife and/or economic slump. El Salvador and Haiti had very low rates of population growth during the 1980s as a result of net international emigration and high mortality.[70] International emigration has also lowered population growth rates in Montevideo and Buenos Aires.[71]

Economic and spatial change

The economic and spatial changes during the 1980s represent a considerable break from prevailing trends in previous decades. Most countries in Latin America sustained an impressive economic performance for most of the period between 1945 and 1980.[72] For the region, per capita income grew at an annual average of 2.7 per cent during these 35 years, far above the historic rate. Manufacturing increased its share of GDP from 14 per cent in 1930 to 25 per cent in 1980 and imports share of GDP fell from 20 to 15 per cent in this same period.[73] Table 2.4 shows the dramatic contrast between economic performance in the 1970s compared to the 1980s. During the 1970s, only in Jamaica and in Nicaragua was there a decline in per capita income and in the case of Nicaragua, this was linked to the civil war that raged there for most of the decade. In many countries, the growth in per capita income was very rapid—especially in Brazil but also, among the other large population countries, in Mexico, Colombia and Ecuador. For most of these countries, this economic expansion built on a comparable or even higher economic expansion during the 1960s.

During the 1980s, only three countries listed within Table 2.4 (Jamaica, Colombia and Chile) avoided a decline in per capita income and their growth rates were very low in comparison to those achieved by most countries in the 1970s.[74] For many countries, there was a rapid decline and for several countries, their per capita income was 20 to 30 per cent lower in 1989 than it had been a decade earlier. The economic recession brought declines in income for those working in formal and informal sector enterprises (see Box 2.1) and a rapid growth in levels of unemployment. Social spending was also greatly reduced in most countries.[75]

The core of the industrial growth for most of the region since the 1930s had been import substitution industries that had usually been helped by large scale government support and protective barriers. There had been a strong

TABLE 2.4 Per capita GDP in 1992 and annual average changes in per capita GDP for the 1970s, 1980s and early 1990s (1988 US dollars)

Country	GDP per capita (1992)	Annual average change in per capita GDP		
		1970–79	1980–89	1990–92
Caribbean				
Cuba				
Dominican Republic	694	4.3	–0.5	1.3
Haiti	218	3.0	–2.9	–8.9
Jamaica	1,457	–2.9	0.9	–1.1
Trinidad & Tobago	4,188	4.4	–4.2	0.6
Central America				
Costa Rica	1,757	2.6	–0.6	2.0
El Salvador	1,102	0.2	–1.8	2.0
Guatemala	928	2.8	–2.0	1.0
Honduras	763	2.2	–1.0	0.4
Mexico	2,317	3.7	–0.7	1.0
Nicaragua	512	–3.2	–4.4	–2.7
Panama	2,257	2.2	–1.5	6.5
South America				
Bolivia	886	1.3	–2.5	1.5
Brazil	2,151	6.3	–0.7	–1.8
Colombia	1,490	3.3	1.5	1.2
Ecuador	1,298	5.6	–0.9	1.7
Paraguay	1,528	5.5	–0.0	–0.9
Peru	1,295	0.8	–3.3	–1.7
Venezuela	3,892	0.7	–1.8	6.9
Southern cone				
Argentina	4,327	0.9	–2.2	7.6
Chile	2,862	1.0	0.9	6.5
Uruguay	3,037	2.6	–0.3	4.5
Latin America	2,192	3.3	–1.1	1.4

Source: Inter-American Development Bank, Economic and Social Progress in Latin America: 1993 report, Johns Hopkins University Press, Washington DC, 1993.

economic rationale for import substitution from the 1930s, with the depression in Europe and North America both before and after World War II cutting export markets and with the war itself disrupting the possibilities of importing manufactured goods.[76] But from the 1960s onwards, a concentration on import-substitution meant that the region missed the opportunity to take part in the rapid expansion in international trade. High levels of inequality within most Latin American societies limited the expansion of the internal consumer market. During the 1980s, many industries developed on the basis of import-substitution declined or closed as local consumer markets shrunk with the recession and as protective barriers were removed and imports grew.

BOX 2.1

Declining incomes in Latin America during the 1980s

As the result of the recession, incomes have declined in both formal and informal activities. Between 1980 and 1991, real manufacturing wages fell by 23 per cent in Mexico and Argentina and average manual earnings fell by as much as 61 per cent in Lima. The value of the minimum wage fell even more dramatically: between 1980 and 1991 it fell 38 per cent in Brazilian cities, 53 per cent in urban Venezuela, 57 per cent in Mexico City and 83 per cent in Lima.

Incomes in informal sector work also fell in many countries; for instance during the 1980s, there was a rapid growth in the number of people working in the informal sector and income declines of between 24 and 39 percent in the informal sector in Costa Rica, Brazil, Argentina, and Peru.[77] Many of those working in informal occupations lost their income sources. In Mexico, the proportion of self-employed workers and family members working with remuneration increased from 16 to 21 per cent of the economically active population.[78]

Source: Gilbert, Alan, *The Latin American City*, Latin American Bureau, London, 1994.

In some countries, there was also a rapid shift in the orientation of the economies from industrialization based on import substitution to outward looking growth and from broad ranging state intervention to much greater reliance on market forces.[79] These changes brought major spatial changes. For instance, in Mexico City, the country's dominant centre for import substitution industries, 250,000 industrial jobs were lost as 6,000 companies closed down[80] while several of Mexico's cities on or close to the border with the United States grew rapidly because of the increase in employment linked to export production. Many other important centres of industrial production such as Buenos Aires (Argentina), Medellin (Colombia) and Monterrey (Mexico) also lost large numbers of manufacturing jobs.[81] Meanwhile, the concentration on exports stimu-

lated population growth in many urban centres that served export processing zones, zones with agricultural exports (especially those such as fruit with high value) and areas where fishing and forestry production were increased; in many countries, there was also rapid population growth among the more successful tourist centres.[82] There was a rapid growth in export processing zones in many countries, most of them located away from national capitals.[83]

Changes in employment

The economic crisis during the 1980s brought several important changes in the scale and nature of urban employment. One was the loss of industrial jobs noted above. Another was a cut in public employees or a cut in their real wages. In many countries, government budgets fell rapidly; for instance, in Mexico, the federal budget fell from 34 per cent of GDP to 20 per cent.[84] This also meant a large loss of jobs, given that around a fifth of all jobs in the region were in the public sector.[85] The recession during the 1980s also meant lower investment and dwindling resources in public works[86] which also meant fewer jobs.

Another notable change was the increasing proportion of the labour force working in services, although it is difficult to separate the influence of the economic crisis from long term economic trends that were already increasing the proportion of people working in services. For the region as a whole, by 1990, 48 per cent of the economically active population worked in services (including transport and commerce) compared to 26 per cent in 1950.[87] In 1990, 26 per cent of the region's population worked in industry—the same proportion as in 1980.[88] In most cities, commerce and services provide most jobs with industry rarely contributing more than 30 per cent.[89] In Argentina, industrial jobs had represented 37 per cent of all urban employment in 1974 but this fell to 24 per cent in 1991 with the proportion working in services rising from 44 to 54 per cent. By 1990, only 26 per cent worked in agriculture compared to 55 per cent in 1950.[90]

Two other changes were of particular importance to urban economies because they brought decreases in consumer demand. The first was the scale of open unemployment that grew steadily and in countries where it stabilized, it was at much higher levels than in previous decades.[91] The second was the increasing proportion of the workforce working in what is termed the 'informal sector' in most countries and this probably represents a change in a long-established historic trend towards increased proportions of the workforce working in formal sector enterprises.[92] Although many informal sector enterprises can generate incomes for those working in them that

TABLE 2.5 Latin America: total and urban populations for 1990 and urban change since 1950

Country in	Total popn 1990 ('000s)	Urban popn 1990 ('000s)	% urban 1950	% urban 1990	Change % urban 1950–90
Caribbean					
Cuba	10,598	7,801	49.4	73.6	24.2
Dominican Republic	7,110	4,293	23.7	60.4	36.7
Haiti	6,486	1,855	12.2	28.6	16.4
Jamaica	2,366	1,217	26.8	51.5	24.7
Puerto Rico	3,531	2,518	40.6	71.3	30.7
Trinidad & Tobago	1,236	854	63.9	69.1	5.2
Central America					
Costa Rica	3,035	1,429	33.5	47.1	13.6
El Salvador	5,172	2,269	36.5	43.9	7.4
Guatemala	9,197	3,628	29.5	39.4	9.9
Honduras	4,879	1,985	17.6	40.7	23.1
Mexico	84,511	61,335	42.7	72.6	29.9
Nicaragua	3,676	2,197	34.9	59.8	24.9
Panama	2,398	1,240	35.8	51.7	15.9
South America					
Argentina	32,547	28,158	65.3	86.5	21.2
Bolivia	6,573	3,665	37.8	55.8	18.0
Brazil	148,477	110,789	36.0	74.6	38.7
Chile	13,154	10,954	58.4	83.3	24.9
Colombia	32,300	22,604	37.1	70.0	32.9
Ecuador	10,264	5,625	28.3	54.8	26.5
Paraguay	4,317	2,109	34.6	48.9	14.3
Peru	21,588	15,068	35.5	69.8	34.3
Uruguay	3,094	2,751	78.0	88.9	10.9
Venezuela	19,502	17,636	53.2	90.4	37.2
Latin America and the Caribbean	439,716	314,161	41.6	71.4	29.8

Source: United Nations, *World Urbanization Prospects: the 1994 Revision*, Population Division, New York, 1995.

are comparable to or higher than in the formal sector, work in the informal economy is generally less stable and it also seems as if most of the growth in the informal economy was in what might be termed the 'survival informal sector' where incomes are very low.

There was also evidence of an increase in the proportion of people who are working less hours than they wished—what is sometimes called visible underemployment.[93] There was also a rapid growth in the number of people with incomes below national poverty lines (see Chapter 3 for more details). It is important to recall that a large proportion of those with below poverty line incomes are fully employed.

There is also evidence of a trend towards a loss of security and continuity in many jobs and also a decline in the proportion of the workforce with social security.[94] This was not only through an increasing proportion of the labour force working in the informal economy but also through ways in which formal sector enterprises can employ people on a temporary basis or in other ways to keep down wages or social security costs—for instance through part time jobs, the use of job-agencies for temporary workers,

the use of home-workers or simply employing but not registering workers.[95] Although there are no precise figures as to its scale, it is linked to the restructuring of enterprises that seek to remain competitive as national markets are opened up to international competition and to the weaker position of trade unions.

There is also a long term trend towards increased participation by women and decreased participation by men in the labour force. Between 1960 and 1985, female participation in the labour force increased in 21 out of 25 countries considered with male participation rates falling in all countries; among the reasons for lower male participation rates are expanding schools and an increased number of people with pensions.[96] In Argentina, the proportion of the labour force that was female grew from 32 to 36 per cent between 1980 and 1990 while the proportion in services grew from 55 to 60 per cent.[97] The contribution by women to the family's cash income also rose from 31 per cent in 1980 to 36 per cent in 1991.

Urban change

The region as a whole went from being predominantly rural to predominantly urban between 1950 and 1990 and also with a relatively high concentration of national and urban population in 'million-cities'. One measure of the scale of urbanization and its concentration in large cities is that by 1990, there were more people living in 'million-cities' in the region than living in rural areas.[98] By 1990, most countries with more than a million inhabitants had more than half their population in urban areas.

Table 2.5 includes the proportion of the population living in urban centres in 1950 and 1990 for all nations that had 1 million or more inhabitants in 1990. Many of these countries went from being predominantly rural to predominantly urban in these four decades. The scale of this transformation is particularly notable in Dominican Republic, Puerto Rico, Mexico, Brazil, Colombia, Peru and Venezuela. The scale of economic growth explains some of this; Brazil, Mexico, Dominican Republic and Colombia had among the region's most rapid economic growth and growth in manufacturing output.

Brazil's rapid economic growth and rapid urbanization also meant that its urban population came to have increasing weight within the region's urban population. In 1950, Brazil had 28 per cent of the region's urban population—little more than the three Southern Cone countries of Argentina, Chile and Uruguay with 24 per cent. Of the 'million-cities' in the region in 1950, the Southern Cone countries had three (one each, in their capitals) and Brazil two (Sao Paulo and Rio de Janeiro). By 1990, Brazil had 35 per cent of the region's urban population and twelve of its thirty-six 'million-cities'; the Southern Cone had just 13 per cent of the region's urban population and five of its million cities.

Table 2.5 also highlights the variety in the levels of urbanization between countries. Although the accuracy of comparisons between countries in their levels of urbanization are always limited by the differences in the criteria used to define urban centres, it is possible to identify three groups of nations.[99] The first, the most urbanized with more than 80 per cent of their population in urban areas includes the three nations in the Southern Cone and Venezuela. The second with between 50 and 80 per cent in urban areas includes most of the countries that had rapid urban and industrial development during the period 1950–90—Dominican Republic, Mexico, Brazil, Ecuador and Colombia—and also Cuba (that was already one of the most urbanized nations in the region in 1950), Bolivia, Peru and Nicaragua and Jamaica and Trinidad and Tobago. The third with less than 50 per cent of the population in urban areas includes only one in South America (Paraguay) and one in the Caribbean (Haiti) along with a group of countries in Central America (Costa Rica, El Salvador, Guatemala and Honduras); all are among the less populous countries in the region (all had less than 10 million inhabitants in 1990).

Care must be taken in making inter-country comparisons since what appears as a comparable level of urbanization may have behind it very different demographic dynamics.[100] For instance, the level of urbanization in Uruguay and Venezuela has converged but Venezuela has a much higher rate of population growth and of urban growth during the 1980s. As Lattes has noted, 'the exact path that a country follows towards high urbanization depends on the historical and structural processes that condition its demographic evolution.'[101] This can be illustrated by the factors that explain why the Southern Cone of Latin America has long had among the highest levels of urbanization.[102] The three countries in this region (Argentina, Chile and Uruguay) have among the highest proportion of their populations living in large cities of any of the world's regions; as a region, it has a higher proportion of its inhabitants in cities of 100,000 plus and one million plus inhabitants than East Europe, West Europe or North America. The three nations in the southern cone did not have rapid increases in their level of urbanization between 1950 and 1990; the proportion of Uruguay's population living in urban areas only grew from 78 to 89 per cent in these 40 years. But these three nations are unusual in that they have long been among the most urbanized nations in the world. In addition, they had among the slowest growing economies and slowest growth in

manufacturing output in Latin America, at least since the 1960s. Argentina and Chile also had a decrease in the proportion of their labour forces working in industry. The reasons for the high concentration of population in cities with one million plus inhabitants are rooted in their economic and demographic histories. These countries' populations were largely built up from rapid immigration from Europe in the late nineteenth and early twentieth centuries—but where landowning structures ensured little opportunity for the immigrants to acquire farmland. Most immigrants settled in the more prosperous cities.

Major cities

The scale of this region's urban population and its population in large cities has grown very rapidly. In 1900, it had less than 15 million urban inhabitants and no 'million-cities' although Rio de Janeiro had close to a million. By 1990, it had more than 300 million urban inhabitants, and 36 'million-cities', including three with more than 10 million (and one other, Rio de Janeiro, with close to 10 million)—see Map 2.2. The relative importance of its major cities within the world had also increased very considerably. In 1900, only two cities in the region were within the world's largest twenty cities (Rio de Janeiro and Buenos Aires) while only another two were within the largest fifty cities. By 1990, the region had two of the world's five largest cities (Sao Paulo and Mexico City), two more within the largest twenty cities (Rio de Janeiro and Buenos Aires) and, in total, eight of the world's fifty largest cities.

But despite the fact that the region's urban population increased more than twentyfold between 1900 and 1990, most of the major urban centres today were founded in the sixteenth century by the Spanish and Portuguese with some such as Mexico City, Cusco and Quito being much older pre-Columbian cities.[103] In addition, the most urbanized countries in 1950 are generally still the most urbanized countries while the least urbanized countries have remained as such.[104] What has changed is not so much the list of the region's most important cities but the relative size of these cities and the concentration of population in large cities. In 1990, some 29 per cent of the region's population lived in cities with one or more million inhabitants.

In reviewing changes in cities' relative size (in terms of number of inhabitants) and economic or political importance, not unsurprisingly, Sao Paulo has come to be the largest, reflecting its dominant economic role within the region's largest economy—although Sao Paulo was already one of the region's most important urban centres in 1900. Mexico City is the second largest, reflecting its dominant economic and

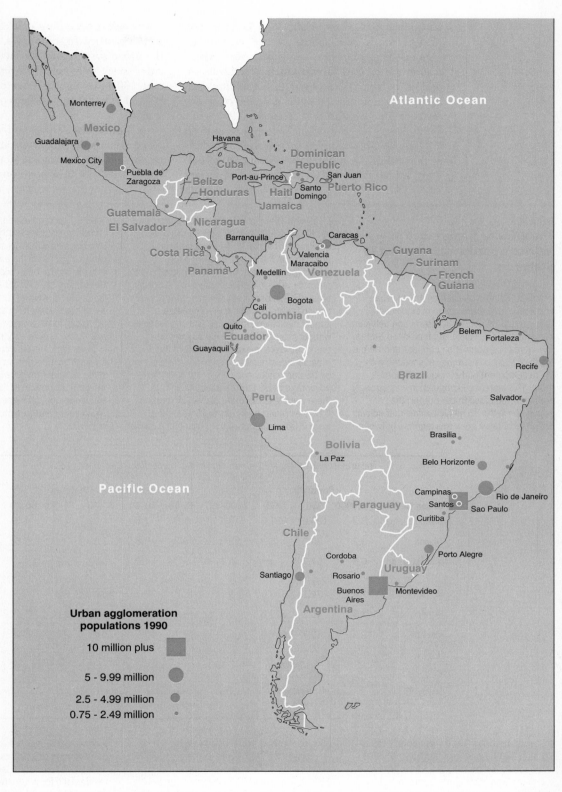

political role in the region's second largest economy.[105] Buenos Aires and Rio de Janeiro remain among the region's largest cities, although both have experienced some loss in their relative importance. Buenos Aires was the economic and political centre of Latin America's most prosperous economy in 1900. In this same year, Rio de Janeiro had been the economic and political centre of Brazil but it lost its role as political capital to Brasilia in the 1950s and Sao Paulo became the dominant economic centre. Most of the other major cities that rose up the list of the region's cities, if ordered by their population in 1990, were cities in the Southeast of Brazil where most of the rapid industrial development was concentrated: Belo Horizonte, Porto Alegre,

Curitiba and Campinas although Goiania and Brasilia (both new cities) in the centre and Manaus in Amazonia also grew to become among the region's largest cities. Brazil was also unusual in having so many of its largest cities that had not been important under colonial rule—for instance, Brasilia was only created in 1958 while Porto Alegre was only a small unimportant town in 1800. Belo Horizonte was created as a new city at the end of the nineteenth century while neither Fortaleza nor Curitiba were important towns before becoming state capitals in the nineteenth century. In some ways, this reordering of the urban system and the fact that many major cities today were relatively small and unimportant 100 years ago is more comparable to the United States than to other countries within the region.

In Mexico, the second and third largest cities, Guadalajara and Monterrey, also grew in importance—again reflecting the fact that Mexico is the region's second most populous country and sec-

---

BOX 2.2

The growing importance of Mexico's border with the United States

The distribution of population and of urban population in Mexico has been significantly changed by the economic interaction between settlements in its North and the United States. The increasing population concentration in the North of Mexico is strongly associated with the development of the *maquila* industries there. This increase in population was strongly concentrated close to the border; the population in the 36 municipalities that adjoin the United States grew fourteenfold between 1930 and 1990 from 0.28 million inhabitants in 1930 to 2.9 million by 1980 and close to 4 million by 1990.[106] These industries originated in the mid 1960s when the government of Mexico began a programme to promote industrial development in the border area.[107] This permitted Mexican and foreign owned factories within the border area to import machinery, materials and components without paying tariffs as long as the goods produced were re-exported. Most of the *maquila* industries that developed were owned by US companies and they could also take advantage of US tariff regulations. In 1967, there were less than 100 plants with around 4,000 workers; by the early 1990s, there were 2,000 employing more than half a million people. The devaluation of the Mexican currency against the US dollar in the 1980s also boosted industrial and agricultural exports.[108] Since the early 1970s, *maquila* industries have been allowed to set up in the interior and since 1989 to sell products in the domestic market. During the 1980s, some cities away from the frontier were attracting major investments—for instance new motor vehicle export plants were set up in Chihuahua, Hermosillo and Saltillo.[109] Table 2.6 lists the border towns that to date have attracted most *maquila* industries and the 'twin city' in the United States to which they are connected. Of these, Ciudad Juarez and Tijuana concentrated most *maquila* industries in 1990.

TABLE 2.6   The urban centres with the most *maquila* employment and their 'twin cities'

Urban Centre	Population			Compound Growth Rates						Partner Cities in USA
	c.1900	1950	1990	1900–30	30–50	50–60	60–70	70–80	80–90	
Ciudad Juarez	8.2	124.0	807.0	5.4	5.9	7.8	5.3	2.2	4.0	El Paso
Tijuana	0.2	60.0	755.0	12.6	10.3	9.8	8.3	2.4	5.8	San Diego
Nuevo Laredo	6.5	57.7		4.1	5.0	4.9	5.1	2.8		Laredo (and to San Antonio, Houston)
Reynosa	1.9	34.1	296.0	3.1	10.3	8.1	6.6	3.3	4.3	McAllen
Matamoros	8.3	45.8	319.0	0.5	8.1	7.3	4.3	3.0	5.4	Brownsville
Mexicali	0.0	65.7	637.0		7.7	10.6	4.4	2.1	6.4	Calexico
Nogales										Nogales (and up to Tucson and Phoenix)

Source: IIED and IIED-America Latina, *Poblacion y Cambio Urbano en America Latina y el Caribe, 1850–1989; Anexo Estadistico*, London and Buenos Aires, 1991, and more recent census data

---

It is worth recalling that it was not only the North of Mexico that was relatively poor and unurbanized before the *maquila* programme but so too was most of the border area in the United States; governments in both countries had neglected these areas.[110] With the exception of San Diego, some of the poorest US communities are on the US–Mexico border.[111] Before the *maquila* programme began, there was little industry in urban centres on either side of the border, although there had already been some economic developments in the North of Mexico associated with the United States from earlier in the century. For instance, Tijuana that in 1900 had only had 242 inhabitants grew rapidly during the 1920s from recreation and tourism during the prohibition period in the United States (when the fabrication and sale of alcoholic drinks was banned in the US). Tijuana has developed into an important metropolitan centre and may now have more than 1 million inhabitants. Mexicali which did not exist as an urban centre in 1900 received a considerable economic stimulus from the development of a large scale irrigation district during the 1940s and 1950s to respond to the demand for cotton during World War II and later conflicts such as the Korean War.[112] But by 1960, it still had only 174,500 inhabitants; by 1990 it had 637,000. Ciudad Juarez that had 8,200 inhabitants in 1900 and 124,000 in 1950 has also developed into an important metropolitan centre with around 1 million inhabitants.

ond largest economy. But in Mexico too, there has been a reordering of the urban system that is more recent than in Brazil but this too is creating major new cities away from the cities that are long-established centres of economic and political power—see Box 2.2.

Virtually all the cities in Latin America with a million or more inhabitants had much slower population growth rates during the 1980s than the average for the period 1950–90 and compared to the 1970s. Many had annual average population growth rates below 2 per cent a year during the 1980s including Mexico City, Buenos Aires, Sao Paulo and Rio de Janeiro; also, among the smaller metropolitan areas, Recife, Havana, Medellin, Cordoba, Rosario and Montevideo. The major cities in the Southern Cone had among the slowest rates of population increase during these four decades—a combination of low rates of natural increase for their populations and, generally, of slower economic growth. Montevideo had been the fifth largest city in the region in 1950; by 1990, it was no longer among the largest 20. Buenos Aires, Cordoba and Rosario in Argentina also grew relatively slowly in comparison to most other major cities.

Table 2.7 shows the proportion of the national population concentrated in four countries' capital cities (or, for Brazil, its two largest metropolitan areas) over time. It shows how Buenos Aires already had a fifth of Argentina's national population in 1895 and an increasing concentration up to 1970 with a decline since 1980. For Mexico City, the concentration of national population there was never on the same scale as in Argentina, but up to 1980, this concentration increased and has decreased since then. In Brazil, the concentration of national population within its wealthiest and largest metropolitan area, Sao Paulo, grew rapidly up to 1980 and declined between 1980 and 1991. For Rio de Janeiro, the decline began in the 1970s—although this was much influenced by the move-

ment of the Federal Capital from Rio de Janeiro to Brasilia in 1960.

In this table, Bogotá presents a completely different picture from the others since the concentration of Colombia's population in Bogotá increased very considerably between 1985 and 1993.[113] It is also interesting in that Colombia has long been noted as a country in which no one city is dominant with Medellin, Cali and Baranquilla all being cities which, although smaller than Bogotá, were of a comparable scale, at least up until 1973. However, since 1964, Bogotá's inter-census population growth rate has been higher than all three of these other cities with the differential particularly high for the period 1985–1993 when Bogotá's population grew at 5.1 per cent a year while the other three had average population growth rates of between 2.0 and 2.8 per cent a year.[114] Among other countries, the primacy of Santo Domingo within the Dominican Republic was also reported to increase during the 1980s.[115]

Decentralizing populations from metropolitan areas to core regions

One important urban trend which has recently become better understood is the heavy concentration of productive activities and of urban populations in a few 'core regions' which contain the largest cities or metropolitan areas but which cover a larger area than these. One of the most prominent examples of this was described in Chapter 1: the region in Brazil which centres on Sao Paulo metropolitan area and its surrounding belt but which also stretches to Belo Horizonte and Rio de Janeiro to its north and to Curitiba and Porto Alegre to the south. Two other important core regions are the La Plata–Buenos Aires–Campana Zarate–San Nicholas–Rosario–San Lorenzo region in Argentina and Mexico City–Toluca–Cuernavaca–Puebla–Queretaro in Mexico. While historically, the trend in most cities has been for much of the new (or expanding) industry to be within or close to the city's core area, in recent years or decades, industrial and commercial employment in many large cities has grown more rapidly outside the inner cities. There are examples both of central cities growing more slowly than suburban rings (or even losing population), of outer suburbs and 'commuting towns' growing more rapidly than inner suburbs and central cities—and finally of cities beyond the commuting range of the largest centres sustaining population growth rates higher than the metropolitan areas, a process termed polarization reversal.[116] For instance, in Buenos Aires, the central city (the Federal District) lost population between 1970 and 1980 while the population in the counties within the Greater Buenos Aires Metropolitan Area but outside the Federal District had a total

TABLE 2.7 Changes in the concentration of national populations in capital cities (or in Brazil, the largest two cities)

Per cent of national population in

	1895	1914	1947	1960	1970	1980	1991
Buenos Aires	20.6	26.9	30.1	34.4	36.0	36.0	34.5

	1900	1930	1940	1950	1960	1970	1980	1990
Mexico City	3.0	6.3	7.9	11.1	15.5	17.5	20.0	18.5

	1905	1918	1938	1951	1964	1973	1985	1993
Bogotá	2.7	2.8	4.2	5.8	9.7	12.8	14.7	18.4

	1900	1920	1940	1950	1960	1970	1980	1991
Sao Paulo	0.3	0.3	0.6	5.0	6.6	8.8	10.6	10.5
Rio de Janerio	5.5	4.7	5.6	6.3	7.2	7.7	7.4	6.5

Source: IIED and IIED-America Latina, *Poblacion y Cambio Urbano en America Latina y el Caribe, 1850–1989; Anexo Estadistico*, London and Buenos Aires, 1991, and more recent census data.

BOX 2.3
The spatial expansion of Mexico City

The spatial expansion of Mexico City can best be understood by considering its growth over time in relation to four boundaries:

—the central city (four delegations) with an area of 139 square kilometres;
—the Federal District (with 16 delegations, including the four central ones) with an area of 1,489 square kilometres;
—the Mexico City Metropolitan Area which combines the Federal District and 27 municipalities beyond the Federal District's boundaries in the State of Mexico—with an area of 4,636 square kilometres;
—the polynucleated metropolitan region (or megalopolis) that combines the metropolitan areas of Mexico City, Toluca, Cuernavaca and Puebla with an area of 8,163 square kilometres.

Based on these boundaries, the spatial expansion of Mexico City since 1900 can be considered in four stages:

1. The growth of the central nucleus, 1900–30. The population grew from 345,000 to one million in this period with all this growth within what is termed the

Federal District and 98 per cent of it in the central city.

2. Expansion of the periphery, 1930–50. The population grew from one million to 2.2 million; the central city's share in the total population fell from 98 to 71 per cent with all urban growth still within the Federal District. The population in the central city still grew but the population in the seven delegations around these (but still within the Federal District) grew more rapidly. The central city's share of the population declined from 98 per cent in 1930 to 71 per cent in 1950. This second stage marked the beginning of the decentralization of commerce, services and population towards what were then the peripheral delegations. Although this expansion took place only within the Federal District, by 1950, its northern boundaries had reached the neighbouring State of Mexico.

3. The metropolitan dynamic stage; 1950–80. The population grew from 3.1 to 14.4 million during these 30 years. During the 1950s, the urbanized area spilled beyond the northern limits of the Federal District, with very rapid population growth rates recorded by the three municipalities in the State of Mexico into which this occurred but with a population

growth rate of only 2.4 per cent a year in the central district. During the 1960s, seven new municipalities were added to the metropolitan area and these recorded an annual average population growth rate of 14.4 per cent during this period. During the 1970s, another eight municipalities were added so that by 1980, the Mexico City Metropolitan Area was composed of all 16 delegacions in the Federal District and 21 municipalities in the State of Mexico; by 1990, there were 27 municipal-ities. In 1950, the central city had 71.7 per cent of the population; by 1980 it had 18.6 per cent.

4. The emerging megalopolis. During the 1980s, there has been a rapid expansion of the urbanized area through the subur-banization of extensive areas and the rapid integration of previously isolated urban communities. This process had meant the emergence of a polycentric metropolitan region as different metropolitan areas fuse or overlap. By 1980, the metropolitan areas of Mexico City and Toluca had over-lapped while by 1990, this was also the case with the metropolitan areas of Toluca, Puebla and Cuernavaca.[117] The population of Mexico City Metropolitan Area was 15.0 million by 1990 with the total population of this wider 'megalopolis' of 18 million.

Source: Garza, Gustavo, 'Dynamics of Mexican Urbanization', Background paper for the UN Global Report on Human Settlements 1996.

population increase of 30 per cent.[118] Perhaps more significantly in the long term, Greater Buenos Aires did not increase its share of the national population during the 1970s and lost 1.5 per cent of its share during the 1980s.

Box 2.3 describes the spatial expansion of Mexico City. This illustrates the development of a metropolitan area and then of a wider core region with more than one metropolitan centre. The 1990 census figures certainly showed that the population in the metropolitan area was much smaller than that predicted by most people. With only 15.1 million people in 1990, it cannot possi-bly grow to 31 million inhabitants by the year 2000 as predicted by many in the 1970s[119] or even to 25 million as predicted in the 1980s; it will probably be substantially less than 20 million, and may only be 17 million or so. Although still one of the world's most populous metropolitan areas, none the less this is still little more than half the 31 million inhabitant projection that has been so widely used in the literature in discussions about 'exploding cities'. However, as Box 2.3 shows, the population within the wider urban agglomeration is significantly larger and this may come to have 25–30 million inhabitants within the next few decades, although over a much larger territory than the metropolitan area itself.

Bogotá reveals another pattern. A growing number of manufacturing establishments have developed around Bogotá since the 1950s, partic-ularly in a region within 250 square kilometres of the city, but the growth of such establishments has generally been much slower than in the capital city.[120] Bogotá's core has not experienced the regional dispersal of manufacturing industries; indeed, there has been a trend for manufacturing employment within the larger region to concen-trate no further than 50 km from Bogotá—although the dispersal of manufacturing jobs within the Bogotá metropolitan area away from the core observed in the 1970s continued throughout the 1980s although at a slower pace.[121]

Cuba's pattern of urban development does not bear much relation to that of other nations which experienced comparable rates of rapid economic growth during the 1960s and 1970s. Since the mid-Sixties, a declining proportion of its urban population has lived in Havana, the capital and much the largest city. The agrarian reform imple-mented shortly after the revolution in 1959 removed one of the main causes of rural to urban migration. Since then, a combination of eco-nomic and social development outside Havana (in rural and selected urban areas), the rationing system and a postponement of new housing and infrastructure investments in Havana reduced its dominance of the national urban system.[122]

Small and intermediate urban centres

In most Latin American countries, a considerable proportion of their urban population live in urban centres other than the large cities. For instance, the 1991 census in Argentina showed that 46.5 per cent of the national population lived in urban centres with less than 1 million inhabitants, including 18 per cent in urban centres with less than 100,000 inhabitants. In Mexico, the 1990 census showed that a third of the population live in urban centres with between 15,000 and 1 million inhabitants compared to 27 per cent in 1980—while the proportion of the national population in cities with one million plus had declined in this period.[123] In Colombia, more than half the urban population still lived outside the country's four 'million-cities' in 1993.

There are great contrasts in the size, growth rate and economic base among the urban centres in the region with less than one million inhabitants. They include thousands of small market towns and service centres with a few thousand inhabitants but also some of the region's most prosperous and rapidly growing cities over the last ten to twenty years. For instance, some of the most rapidly growing smaller cities in the region over the last few decades have been cities that served agricultural areas producing high value crops for export or cities that attracted substantial numbers of international tourists.[124] There are probably hundreds of urban centres in Latin America with between 20,000 and 300,000 inhabitants that grew rapidly and became prosperous because of high value agricultural export crops; the development of such centres has rarely been documented in detail. One example is the Upper Valley of Rio Negro and Neuquen in Argentina where, on a 700 square kilometre fertile river valley, the total population grew from around 5,000 inhabitants in 1900 to 400,000 in 1990 with more than 80 per cent of this population living in urban centres.[125] Another is the city of Zamora in Michoacan, Mexico whose rapid growth was linked to high value agricultural crops.[126] It is also worth recalling the importance of high value agricultural goods to the early development of some of the region's largest cities; Sao Paulo's early history was as a small frontier town that was well located to serve the production and export of coffee. However, there are also large numbers of small urban centres within agricultural areas that received little economic stimulus from agriculture or the demand gener-

ated by those who earned an income from agriculture. This included urban centres within prosperous farming areas where most of the producer and consumer demand for goods and services bypassed the local town and went direct to larger and more distant cities.[127] The pattern of landownership is often a major influence on the extent to which high value crop production stimulates urban development locally; a large number of small but prosperous farmers with intensive production can provide a large stimulus to local urban development whereas agricultural plantations or large landholdings steer most of the economic stimulus to more distant cities, including those overseas.[128]

There are other cities that have grown rapidly on the basis of tourism or where tourism has become increasingly important. For instance, Cuautla in Mexico grew from a small market town with 18,000 inhabitants in 1940 to a city with over 120,000 in 1991, with tourism becoming increasingly important, especially weekend tourism from those living in Mexico City.[129] Bariloche in Argentina had just 6,562 inhabitants in 1960 and 81,001 in 1991—and it received half a million visitors in 1992.[130] Other small or intermediate urban centres have had their size and importance boosted by major universities developing there—for instance Merida in Venezuela that was originally a small market town that grew to serve the production and export of coffee greatly increased its size to around 250,000; one of the main factors has been the development and expansion of the University of the Andes there that by 1987 had 37,616 students, 2,949 teachers and 3,268 employees and workers.[131]

There are also hundreds of smaller urban centres within the region that have lost importance, as the goods or services they provided were no longer in demand or because they were a market town and service centre for an agricultural area whose products were also in less demand or faced falling prices or competition from other areas. Latin America has many urban centres that originally grew as mining centres or to serve the production of coffee, bananas or sugar or that were centres of transport that are now bypassed (for instance old river ports with much less demand for their services as most goods move by road).[132]

Future prospects

Many countries have achieved relatively rapid rates of economic growth in the first few years of the 1990s and this may have increased once again the rate of increase in the level of urbanization. However, in some of the most urbanized countries, levels of urbanization are now so high that there is no longer great potential for substantial increases in urbanization levels, although there is considerable scope for changes in the spatial distribution of city and metropolitan centres that, as in the United States, are not reflected in changes in urbanization levels. For instance, profound changes will be brought to Mexico's urban system by a much smaller public sector and a more open economy (that may include millions of small farmers moving off the land because their maize production is undercut by cheap imports) and a continued shift of its modern industrial base to the border region. The drop in employment in manufacturing and in government that became evident in the 1980s may well continue through the 1990s; one estimate suggests that a further 10 million jobs may be lost in manufacturing in the region during the 1990s;[133] another suggests that between 5 and 10 per cent of the workforce may lose their jobs because of cutbacks in government and public sector enterprises.[134]

It is difficult to predict the scale and nature of urban change, given that it is so dependent on economic performance. For the countries that sustain rapid economic growth, urbanization is likely to continue. For countries that do not, levels of urbanization may not grow unless civil or political strife becomes important in forcing people off the land—as it did in Colombia during 'La Violencia' in the 1950s and 1960s, and in Peru during recent years because of the activities of the 'Shining Path' guerrillas. But whatever the economic performance, the dominance of the region's largest metropolitan areas both in their concentration of economic activities and their concentration of population is likely to lessen in most countries. In some, it will be in new cities; in others, still concentrated in core regions with the largest metropolitan centres at their core. Part of the reason is the change in economic orientation in which other cities have greater comparative advantage—the important centres for tourism and cities well located to attract new investment in export-oriented manufacturing or to benefit from forward and backward linkages from high value export agriculture. Part of the reason is the shrinking of government, that is likely to affect national capitals most. But there are also the factors that helped decentralize urban development in Europe and North America that are also operating in many of the higher income countries, including good quality inter-regional transport and communications systems.

2.4 West Europe[132]

Introduction

West Europe is now highly urbanized, with more than three-quarters of its population living in urban areas and only a few per cent of its labour force working in agriculture. As in North America, the most conventional measures regarding the scale of changes in population and urbanization—the growth in the total population and the increase in the level of urbanization—suggest little change in recent years. West Europe had the slowest growth in population of any of the world's regions between 1980 and 1995 and among the smallest increases in the level of urbanization. But as in North America, there were important changes in household size and composition and in age structure that in turn had important influences on housing markets and settlement patterns. The 1980s also brought important changes in trends for population movements in West Europe, with the 1980s being markedly different from the 1970s which in turn had been quite distinct from the previous two decades. As this section will describe, a considerable range of economic, social, demographic and political changes help explain the changes in population distribution, including the reordering of population within cities or wider metropolitan areas. Among the most notable economic changes were the rapid growth in the financial sector which helped revitalize the economy of certain key cities and the continued decline in most cities that had traditionally specialized in heavy industry and ports—although some such cities have managed to develop a new economic base.

Changes in the distribution of population also reflect political changes—for instance those reflecting the economic changes that resulted from the increasingly integrated and enlarged European Union. The widespread changes in the political and economic orientation of most governments in West Europe also influenced changes in the distribution of population—for instance as government support for poorer regions and for social programmes in general were cut back and as more attention was given to inner city regeneration. The sudden and dramatic political changes in East Europe and the former Soviet Union have also brought changes in the distribution of population, although it is only possible to highlight the short-term changes (for instance the massive wave of emigration from the former East Germany and many other parts of East Europe, principally to the former West Germany). In the absence of any unexpected political change, the longer term changes are dependent on the economic performance in the former Eastern Bloc and the scale and nature of economic linkages with West Europe. But there are also the uncertainties regarding the political stability of parts of East and Central Europe, as shown by the civil wars there and the political conflicts that underpinned the breaking up of various nation states.

Demographic change

Table 2.8 gives the national and urban populations of all the countries with more than a million inhabitants in 1990 in Northern, Southern and Western Europe. It includes countries that were formerly part of the Eastern Bloc, as these are now classified as part of these regions, after the political changes in East and Central Europe and the break-up of the former Soviet Union. However, the changes in population and urbanization in the countries that were previously part of this Eastern Bloc are considered in the next section because most of the data about such changes during the 1980s and early 1990s are from the years prior to the political changes. These must also be understood within longer-term trends that were evident during the 1960s and 1970s.

Within the nations in this region other than those that were formerly part of the Eastern Bloc, four basic developments are particularly relevant: the lowest population growth rates of any of the world's regions; the narrowing of inter-country differences for such growth rates, the waning of contrasts between Mediterranean Europe and the rest, and the reduction in the number of countries from which there was net emigration.

Northern, Southern and Western Europe have long had the slowest population growth rates of any of the world's regions and there has been a steady decline in annual average growth rates over the last few decades. For instance, the twelve countries that made up the European Union up to 1994 had their annual average growth rate of 0.96 per cent in 1960–65 fall to 0.71, 0.61, 0.37 and 0.27 per cent in the next four 5-year periods although it grew slightly to 0.34 per cent for the period 1985–90.[136] This recent upturn in growth rate is entirely due to a rise in net immigration, up from 0.5 per thousand in 1980–85 to 1.6 in 1985–90.[137] In much of Europe, the total fertility rate is well below replacement level. Very low population growth rates help explain why it is much more common for cities or regions to have a net loss of population—since a relatively low level of net out-migration can still exceed the rate of natural increase.[138]

The narrowing of inter-country differences in population growth rates is a long established trend but it has progressed particularly strongly since the 1970s. This is particularly noticeable between Southern Europe and the rest of the region—for instance, the population of Portugal, Spain, Italy and Greece between them grew in aggregate by only 3.5 per cent between 1980 and 1990, not much higher than the 2.9 per cent increase in the population of the central and northern member states of the Council of Europe in this same period. The differential had been much higher in the previous decade, reflecting Southern Europe's higher birth rate and, to some extent, return migration from North-West Europe following the 1973/4 economic recession and the breakdown of the guest-worker system.

The reduction in the number of countries recording net emigration is also particularly notable over the last 20 years. In 1970, nine of the larger Council of Europe members lost population through international movements; in 1980, the number had shrunk to five and by 1991, it was down to just one country—Portugal.

There have been important changes in household size and composition, in divorce and cohabitation and in the level and incidence of childbearing.[139] In much of Europe, the average household size is now below 3.0 persons and more women are starting their family later in life. In addition, over a quarter of all households contain only one person, at least 1 in 10 families is headed by a lone parent and around 1 in 3 marriages ends in divorce. These all affect migration but little is known about the geographic impacts. They certainly affect housing markets

TABLE 2.8 West Europe: total and urban populations and level of urbanization for 1990 (all countries with one million or more inhabitants in 1990)

Country	Population in 1990		Percent urban
	Total (thousands)	Urban (thousands)	
Northern Europe			
Denmark	5,140	4,357	84.8
Estonia*	1,575	1,131	71.8
Finland	4,986	3,063	61.4
Ireland	3,503	1,993	56.9
Latvia*	2,671	1,902	71.2
Lithuania*	3,711	2,552	68.8
Norway	4,241	3,068	72.3
Sweden	8,559	7,112	83.1
United Kingdom	57,411	51,136	89.1
Southern Europe			
Albania*	3,289	1,176	35.7
Bosnia/Hercegovina*	4,308	1,920	44.6
Croatia*	4,517	2,701	59.8
Greece	10,238	6,413	62.6
Italy	57,023	38,050	66.7
Portugal	9,868	3,303	33.5
Slovenia*	1,918	1,131	59.0
Spain	39,272	29,592	75.4
TFYR of Macedonia*	2,046	1,182	57.8
Yugoslavia*	10,156	5,392	53.1
Western Europe			
Austria	7,705	4,267	55.4
Belgium	9,951	9,606	96.5
France	56,718	41,218	72.7
Germany	79,365	67,699	85.3
Netherlands	14,952	13,262	88.7
Switzerland	6,834	4,070	59.5
Total; 3 regions (including all countries)	411,368	308,391	75.0

* These were part of East Europe or the former Soviet Union and the discussion of population and urbanization there is included in Section 2.5

Source: United Nations, *World Urbanization Prospects: the 1994 Revision*, Population Division, New York, 1995.

as they imply an increase in the number of households—especially the number of smaller, less wealthy households.

The influence of demographic changes can also be seen on cities and urban systems. For instance, the baby boom of the later 1950s and early 1960s was associated with strong suburbanization and deconcentration pressures as couples reaching the family-building stage sought affordable homes with gardens and a safe and pleasant environment within commuting distance of work. But it was followed by a period of low fertility when not only were the pressures for suburbanization reduced but also the large baby-boom cohort started reaching the age when they were drawn to larger cities to take advantage of their higher education facilities, better job-seeking networks, more varied social opportunities and cheaper rented housing. Meanwhile, as the population ages, so retirement migration becomes increasingly important. This generally takes the form of population movement away from larger metropolitan centres and more densely settled areas and down the urban and regional hierarchy, taking advantage of the lower house prices and the more congenial environments of smaller towns and more rural areas. However, the preferred locations for such migration has changed over time—for instance from seaside and spa towns in the 1950s to countryside areas in the 1960s and 1970s to the Mediterranean sunbelt zones in the 1980s.

Regional patterns of population change

The narrowing of differentials in birth rates across Europe has meant that the regional map of population change has become increasingly dominated by migration exchanges. However, levels of net inter-regional movement in Europe have been lower in recent years than they were in the 1960s and early 1970s, and the patterns are less clearcut than in the past.

Table 2.9 gives the range of population change between regions within fifteen Council of Europe members during the 1980s. The most notable feature is the very wide range of regional growth rates, despite the fact that the degree of inter-country variation was much lower in the 1980s than in previous decades. The highest range is found in Portugal with both the fastest growing and the fastest declining regions in Europe (apart from the case of Turkey) and even the country with the narrowest regional range (Belgium) exhibits a wider range than exists between the national growth rates. This is also a reminder as to how national averages for population change can be misleading in that they are often the aggregate of very diverse regional changes.

Table 2.9 also shows the regional range of crude birth rates and migratory change rates for each country. The range in the crude birth rates reflects the major changes that have occurred in southern Europe in recent years with some of the

TABLE 2.9 The range of population change indicators between regions within countries during the 1980s

Country	Statistical areas	Population Change			Birth Rate			Net Migration Rate		
		Min	Max	Diff	Min	Max	Diff	Min	Max	Diff
Austria	Bundesland (9)	−4.5	+7.3	11.8	10.1	13.7	3.6	−1.6	+2.7	4.3
Belgium	Province (11)	−3.3	+6.3	9.6	10.9	14.0	3.1	−3.8	+6.0	9.8
Denmark	Amt (14)	−8.3	+8.0	16.3	–	–	–	−1.7	+5.3	7.0
Finland	Province (12)	−3.1	+10.8	14.1	10.8	14.6	3.8	−3.4	+5.9	9.3
France	Region (22)	−1.0	+13.3	14.3	9.7	15.8	5.3	−6.3	+12.6	18.9
Germany (West)	RB (31)	−7.2	+8.6	15.8	9.0	12.0	3.0	−1.9	+15.2	17.1
Ireland	County (26)	−7.1	+23.1	30.2	–	–	–	−7.0	+5.0	12.0
Italy	Region (20)	−5.1	+7.2	12.3	6.5	14.2	7.7	−2.8	+4.6	7.4
Netherlands	Province (11)	+0.7	+13.8	13.1	11.3	14.0	2.7	−2.2	+6.8	9.0
Portugal	Distrito (20)	−8.6	+26.9	35.5	9.7	15.4	5.7	−7.0	+21.9	28.9
Spain	Comm. auto (16)	+0.8	+11.7	12.5	8.3	14.3	6.0	–	–	–
Sweden	County (24)	−3.7	+8.9	12.6	11.4	14.5	3.1	−4.1	+7.0	11.1
Switzerland	Canton (25)	−1.0	+14.6	15.6	8.7	17.5	8.8	−4.6	+8.5	13.1
Turkey	Province (67)	−7.7	+48.7	56.4	–	–	–	−23.0	+12.3	35.3
United Kingdom	County (69)	−7.0	+14.5	21.5	10.5	20.4	9.9	−8.0	+18.9	26.9

Note: All data are in annual rates per thousand.

Periods: Population change relates to 1980–8, except for France, Germany and Spain 1980–7; Ireland 1981–6; Turkey 1980–5; United Kingdom 1981–8. Birth rate is for 1988, except for Belgium, France, Germany, Spain, United Kingdom 1987. Net migration rate for 1980–8, except for Belgium, France, Germany, Italy, Spain 1980–7; Ireland 1981–6, Turkey 1980–5, United Kingdom 1981–8.

Areas: In Belgium, Brabant is subdivided into Brussels, Dutch-speaking, French-speaking. In Netherlands, Flevoland is grouped with Overijssel, In Switzerland, Basel-Stadt is grouped with Basel-Landschaft. In United Kingdom, local authority regions are used for Scotland, Boards for Northern Ireland.

Source: Calculated from data supplied by Eurostat and the national statistical agencies. Reprinted from Champion, A. G., 'Changes in the spatial distribution of the European population', In Council of Europe (eds.), *Seminar on Present Demographic Trends and Life styles in Europe: Proceedings*, Council of Europe, Strasbourg, 1991, 355–88.

regions in Spain, Italy and Portugal being characterized by the lowest birth rates of all the 385 regions included in the analysis.

However, migration is the dominant component of population redistribution between regions and as Figure 2.2 shows, the degree of variation in net migration changes for the 1980s within countries was much larger than any broader geographical variation across the continent—notably in Portugal, Turkey and the United Kingdom. Figure 2.2 suggests that there is no clear gravitation of migration flows towards the European core of North-West Europe and areas of migration gain and migration loss are scattered widely across the map.

Figure 2.2 also suggests that population shifts during the 1980s were very different from the dominant periphery-to-core population shifts that took place within countries in the 1950s and 1960s. The geographic patterns have generally become more difficult to interpret, appearing to owe more to special factors operated on a localized or short-term basis than any single all-important process. It can be seen as a complex and diverse mosaic of growth and decline, as the population of each individual place is affected by its inherited economic structure, its ability to take advantages of new sources of growth and its attractiveness as a destination for local urban decentralization.

There are however, two distinct groups of regions experiencing net out-migration:

- Heavily urbanized areas, mainly in North-West Europe and including most of the capital cities (London, Paris, Brussels, Copenhagen) with the most severe losses occurring where urban decentralization is reinforced by industrial decline and the decline of port activities.

- Less developed low-income rural areas, particularly in the rural hinterlands of the larger agglomerations in Southern Europe, but including the less heavily populated areas of Ireland and Scandinavia.

Net in-migration regions form a more disparate set but at least three types can be identified:

- The hinterlands of the major cities, mainly in Northern and Central Europe that are benefitting from the urban exodus, such as around London, Copenhagen and Randstad Holland.

- Many of the 'sunbelt' zones that are usually less urbanized areas with medium-sized and smaller cities, most notably southern areas of the UK, Germany, France and Portugal together with central and northeastern Italy.

- Some of the larger urban centres and/or their immediate hinterlands, particularly in Scandinavia, Mediterranean Europe and Ireland.

Regional change in urban populations

The 1980s brought important changes in trends for population movements in West Europe, with the 1980s being markedly different from the 1970s which in turn had been quite distinct from the previous two decades. The 1970s had brought major and largely unexpected changes in urban trends with what has been termed 'counterurbanization' and the waning of urbanization. Counterurbanization was not so much the movement of people from urban to rural areas but more the movement from major cities and metropolitan areas to smaller urban places and thus a deconcentration in the urban population. The 1980s also brought changes that were largely unexpected—as counterurbanization was expected to continue and to develop but this did not materialize or only took place in isolated cases.

The scale of the regional changes in the 1980s was also less than those in earlier periods with only small signs of the traditional rural–urban population shifts and rather limited evidence of the continuation of more recent counterurbanization tendencies and with no new form of geographical patterning coming strongly to the fore. However, as in North America, the scale of the increase in the proportion of the population living in urban centres ceases to be a useful measure of the scale of urban change since so much change is inter-urban, with most migration movements also inter-urban. When only a few per cent of the labour force work within agriculture and a high proportion of the rural workforce either commute to work in urban areas or work in non-agricultural activities (including in business parks or greenfield sites that remain classified as rural), the distinction between 'rural' and 'urban' has lost its meaning in terms of distinguishing between those who generally make a living from agriculture or forestry and those who do not. In addition, most rural households in West Europe now enjoy a level of service provision that was formerly only associated with urban areas—for instance water piped to the home, connection to sewage networks, regular collection of garbage. The rural-urban distinction based on access to urban-based cultural activities is also blurred as a considerable proportion of rural households can get to theatres, cinemas, discos and other urban-based cultural activities. In effect, rural areas have been urbanized—just as low density suburban and exurban residential areas for urban households display some rural characteristics.

The counterurbanization of the 1970s was unexpected, as it represented a significant departure from the pattern from 1945 to around 1970 that had been dominated by the movement of people from peripheral regions to national core regions, associated with widespread rural to urban migration and universal increases in the

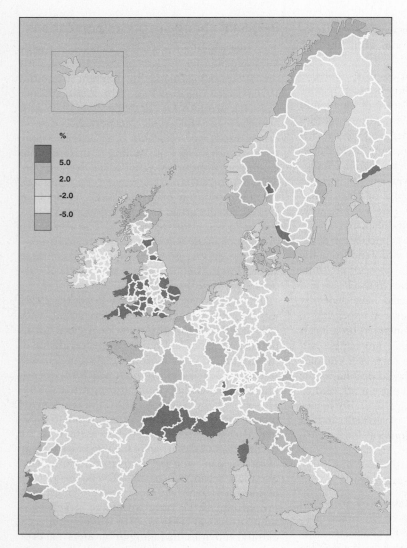

FIGURE 2.2
Regional map of net migration changes during the 1980s (annual average rate per 1000 people)

Source: Champion, A. G., 'Internal migration, counterurbanization and changing population distribution, in R. Hall and P. White (eds.), *Europe's Population: Towards the Next Century*, UCL Press, London, 1995.

pared to the first half. This table also suggests considerable diversity in trends between countries—and also highlights how trends in both Italy and Ireland moved against the general trend, switching from regional concentration to deconcentration and in the case of Italy, this process appears to have deepened during the 1980s. In France too, there was a constant trend towards deconcentration through the 1970s and 1980s. However, various studies have shown important differences in settlement system changes within European nations. For instance, the 1990 census results in France showed that the Paris agglomeration had matched the national rate of population growth in the 1980s but the highest rates of growth occurred in a broad zone stretching from the Alps through the centre–west part of the country.[140]

International migration

A 1990 estimate suggested that between 15 and 20 million people in West Europe are 'foreigners'. Most countries in the region have several per cent of their population who are 'foreigners' and a significant increase in the stocks of foreigners since 1980.[141] Table 2.11 gives some examples of the number of foreigners and of their increase since 1981. Germany has much the largest number with 6.5 million in 1993.

These figures understate the scale of international migration as they refer only to 'foreigners' and do not include international migrants who have been naturalized in the destination countries. For instance, in France, there are more than a million foreign-born people who have acquired French citizenship.[142] In the UK, there are some 4.5 million people of immigrant origin but 1.9 million foreign citizens in 1990.[143]

Not surprisingly, Germany has had the largest net influx of immigrants in recent years but most are not foreigners. The size of this influx peaked in 1989 at 977,000 persons with 344,000 from the former East Germany and around 377,000 ethnic Germans from Eastern Europe (especially from Poland, the former USSR and Romania); these are automatically deemed nationals because of their German ancestry and so are not considered 'foreigners'. There were also another 250,000 who were 'foreigners'.[144] The proportion of the population between 'East' and 'West' Germany also changed; in 1950, 'East' Germany had 26.5 per cent of their combined population; by 1993 it had 19.3 per cent.[145] Prior to 1989, there had been an even larger exodus of some 5 million people moving from East to West between 1949 and the erection of the Berlin Wall in 1961. In addition, the picture is complicated by other immigration flows.

A recent paper on international migration in

proportion of the population living in urban areas. In the 1970s, there was net migration out of many of the larger cities and more densely populated areas. The larger cities, notably those which began their rapid growth in the nineteenth century, were generally much less attractive for migrants in the 1970s than in the previous two decades; many such cities experienced substantial migratory losses. The scale of this exodus from the larger cities was sufficiently large to alter the traditional patterns of net migration from peripheral regions to national cores. During the 1980s, most countries have not seen any acceleration in this process but have instead a slowdown in such deconcentration or indeed a return to larger cities gaining from migration flows.

Table 2.10 shows trends in urbanization and counterurbanization for thirteen countries. A positive score means urbanization while a negative score means a shift towards counterurbanization. The table shows that more countries were experiencing urbanization in the 1980s than in the 1970s and that even more countries saw a shift in trend if the second half of the 1980s is com-

TABLE 2.10 Trends in urbanization and counterurbanization in the 1970s and 1980s for selected countries

Country (number of regions)	1970s	1980s	Shift	1980–84	1984–9	Shift
Austria (16, 8)	+0.38	+0.01	–	–0.25	+0.47	+
Belgium (9)	–0.36	–0.44	–	–0.49	+0.33	+
Denmark (11)	–0.79	–0.01	+	–0.04	–0.16	–
Finland (12)		+0.69	?	+0.51	+0.80	+
France (22)	–0.26	–0.36	–	–0.33	–0.31	nc
FRGermany (30, 12)	–0.29		?	–0.63	–0.08	+
Ireland (9)	+0.43	–0.35	–			
Italy (13, 20)	+0.12	–0.21	–	–0.16	–0.33	–
Netherlands (11)	–0.83	+0.12	+	–0.24	+0.46	+
Norway (8)	+0.21	+0.69	+			
Portugal (17)	+0.36	+0.52	+	+0.39	+0.53	+
Sweden (12, 24)	–0.26	+0.35	+	+0.14	+0.53	+
Switzerland (11)	–0.49*		?	–0.51	–0.06	+

Notes: Data are correlation coefficients of relationship between net migration rate and population density; 'Shift': + = shift towards 'urbanization'; – = shift towards 'counterurbanization'; * data for population change (not migration); nc = no change. Also note that the correlation coefficients should be interpreted with care because their significance level depends on the number of regions.

Source: Champion, A. G., 'Urban and regional demographic trends in the developed world', *Urban Studies*, vol. 29, 1992, 461–82. Compiled from Fielding, A. J., 'Counterurbanization in Western Europe', *Progress in Planning*, vol. 17, 1982, 1–52; Fielding, A. J., 'Counterurbanization in Western Europe' in A. Findlay and P. White (eds.), *West European Population Change*, Croom Helm, London, 35–49; and Fielding, A. J., 'Counterurbanization: threat or blessing?' in D. Pinder (ed.), *Western Europe: Challenge and Change*, Belhaven, London, 226–39 and calculations from data supplied to the author by national statistical agencies.

TABLE 2.11 The growth in the foreign population for selected European Countries, 1981–1994

Country	thousands of people	
	1981	**1994**
Austria	163	582 (1993)
Belgium	879	921
Denmark	100	189
Germany	4,453 (1980)	6,496 (1993)
Netherlands	521	779
Norway	83	154 (1993)
Spain	183	393 (1993)
Sweden	240	508
Switzerland	914	1,244 (1993)

Note: The United Kingdom and France also have large foreign populations—for the United Kingdom, it totalled 1.9 million in 1990 and for France some 3.6 million in this same year.

Source: Compiled from Council of Europe, *Recent Demographic Developments in Europe 1994*, Strasbourg, 1994.

Europe[146] suggested that there are at least five types of international migration that have grown in importance in the region since the early 1980s:

East-West migration within Europe: The political changes in East and Central Europe since the late 1980s has already led to major shifts of people from the former East Europe to West Europe, especially Germany and Austria. The unification of Germany removed one important barrier—and the scale of migration flows into Germany was noted above. Moves towards the integration of other East European countries into existing European networks are likely to reinforce the net flow to West Europe and overseas, particularly during the years of painful economic reconstruction in Eastern Europe. There are also the east-west migration flows driven by civil wars as in the disintegration of the former Yugoslavia and open confrontation with nationalist feelings and expulsion—as in the driving out of Turks formerly resident in Bulgaria.

Labour migrants from the South: Recent estimates suggest that there are at least 2 million and possibly 3 million immigrants in the countries in Southern Europe (Portugal, Spain, Italy, Greece), that only 20–30 years ago were countries of mass emigration.[147] The potential for continuing migration between the two are underpinned by the rapidly growing population in North Africa and the large and at present increasing economic differences between North Africa and Southern Europe.

Refugees: It is often difficult to distinguish refugees from labour migrants. The number of asylum applications in Europe rose sharply during the 1980s and early 1990s from an annual total of 75,000 in 1983 to more than 500,000 in 1991.[148] At the same time, the proportion of asylum-seekers granted refugee status decreased rapidly. The origins of asylum-seekers varied over time, reflecting crisis situations which provoke refugee movements. Between 1983 and 1990, Asian countries (chiefly Sri Lanka, India, Pakistan, Bangladesh, Iran, Iraq, Afghanistan) accounted for 50 per cent of all claims submitted to Europe with 31 per cent from other European countries and 16 per cent from Africa.[149] Pre-existing colonial or labour migration links often guide subsequent patterns of asylum migration.

Skilled international migration: The emergence of post-industrial society in Europe with associated restructuring of the global economy and the growth of information based services has led to a rapid increase in the size of the highly skilled labour force—especially in countries where the control functions of this new economic geography are located—notably the headquarters of multinational firms. Within Europe, there is a division of labour between the production facilities which are located in development regions of cheap and abundant low-skill labour such as Portugal or the West of Eire and office headquarters located in metropolitan cities such as London, Paris or Munich which tend to concentrate the high level personnel responsible for the control functions.

Retirement migration: Traditionally, retirement migration is within national boundaries. Where countries are large and have a variety of scenic and climatic environments, movements tend to take retirees to the seaside towns (e.g. along the South coast of England) to the sunnier warmer regions (e.g. Parisians migrating to the South of France) or attractive rural regions. In some instances, it is to where the retirees have roots. More recently, and aided by portable state or private pensions and by a general growth in wealth, increasing numbers of older people in Europe are moving on a temporary, seasonal or permanent basis to the Mediterranean sunbelt. They tend to cluster in purpose built tourist and residential complexes with many services (shops, leisure, medical) close by.

Europe's cities

West Europe is the only region in the world where considerable effort has been made to compare the population of cities in a great range of different countries, based on a consistent, common definition—what is termed the functional urban region. Functional urban regions seek to have boundaries that reflect 'the economic sphere of influence of a city with a core city defined in terms of concentrations of employment and a commuting hinterland composed of all those areas from which more people commute to the particular city in question than to some other city'.[150] Map 2.3 shows the largest urban centres in West Europe in 1991 based on the populations in functional urban regions.

Table 2.12 highlights this point by showing the population in 1991 of the six largest urban centres in the United Kingdom, using four different bases for calculating their populations. Not only does the population of each city vary enormously depending on which basis is chosen but the rank also changes. The example of Newcastle upon Tyne highlights just how much different criteria used to set city boundaries affect population size; this city has some 300,000 inhabitants when measured by its district population but becomes among the six largest cities in the UK when different criteria are used—and has over a million inhabitants, if considered as a metropolitan region.

Among the largest cities in the region, London and Paris remain much the largest, whether measured by populations in the urban agglomeration or the functional urban region. After that, the rankings become more ambiguous, depending on what boundaries are used. The city of Essen is sometimes listed as the third largest but this is for a highly urbanized and industrialized region more often referred to as the Ruhr region and it includes many cities going from Duisburg in the east to Dortmund in the West. Among the other largest urban agglomerations are Italy's three largest cities—Rome, Naples and Milan, Spain's largest two cities (Barcelona and Madrid), Athens, Birmingham, Amsterdam and several German cities (Stuttgart, Hamburg, Munich, Frankfurt and Berlin). Brussels also emerges as one of Europe's largest cities when considered as a functional urban region but not when considered within the city's administrative boundaries.

But comparing cities by their dominant characteristics rather than their population sizes gives more of a sense of current developments there. Table 2.13 presents eleven types of cities and their dominant characteristics, with examples of cities that can be placed within such functional types. This highlights the difference between the growing high-tech/services cities that include many cities that are not among the largest in Europe and the declining industrial and port cities, many of which still are among the largest cities but most with declining populations. Many experienced a large decrease in their employment base during the 1980s, although for many this decrease was also evident in the 1970s or even earlier.

Cities that are a country's point of entry and exit for goods or people have always had important roles. Two kinds can be distinguished: gateway cities of which historically port cities have been the most important but in the last three decades, international airports have taken on

TABLE 2.12 Four different lists for the six largest cities in the United Kingdom in 1991, using different bases for defining city boundaries (resident population, thousands)

Local Authority district		Main built-up area		Urban region		Metropolitan region	
Birmingham	961	London	6,699	London	7,380	London	12,530
Leeds	681	Birmingham	1,121	Birmingham	1,363	Birmingham	2,906
Glasgow	663	Manchester	915	Glasgow	1,071	Manchester	2,809
Sheffield	501	Glasgow	786	Manchester	1,044	Liverpool	2,096
Liverpool	453	Liverpool	621	Newcastle	901	Glasgow	1,705
Edinburgh	419	Newcastle	504	Liverpool	831	Newcastle	1,342

Note: London no longer has a local authority for the wider city as a whole, since the abolition of the Greater London Council, so it does not figure among the largest local authority districts. The population in 1991 for 'Greater London' was 6,679,700 but this is not comparable to the local authority districts used in this table. The 'urban region' includes the built-up area and the wider region based on commuting to the core. The 'metropolitan region' includes all the urban regions that are intertwined with the main region defined and is broadly equivalent to the CMSAs in the USA described in Section 2.2

Source: A. G. Champion, unpublished tabulation using 1991 census data. 'Main built-up area (core)', 'Urban region' and 'Metropolitan region' are definitions based on the CURDS Functional Regions framework.

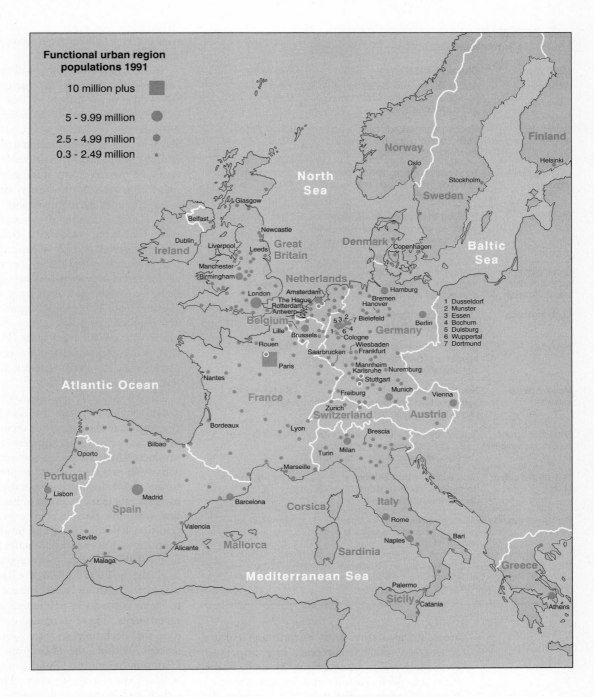

Functional urban region populations 1991

- 10 million plus
- 5 - 9.99 million
- 2.5 - 4.99 million
- 0.3 - 2.49 million

1 Dusseldorf
2 Munster
3 Essen
4 Bochum
5 Duisburg
6 Wuppertal
7 Dortmund

MAP 2.3
The largest urban centres in West Europe, 1991

Notes: This map is based on the list of functional urban regions developed by Hall, P. and D. Hay, *Growth Centres in the European Urban System*, Heinemann, London, 1980 with the population data for them developed by Paul Cheshire, drawing on the population censuses of 1990 and 1991. Where no population census was undertaken, registration data was used. The map includes all functional urban regions with one third of a million or more inhabitants in 1981; those with one million or more inhabitants are also named in the map.
Source: Functional Urban Region Database at the London School of Economics.

increasing importance; and border cities that have an important role as transport and administrative centres overseeing and often controlling the international exchanges between the two countries but often also international centres of trade, communication and information.[151] The fortunes of border cities fluctuate with changing political circumstances—for instance many inner European border cities within the European Community will lose some of their economic importance. Cities in or near to the borders of

Eastern Europe such as Frankfurt/Oder, Vienna, Trieste and Thessaloniki have taken over a new role as gateway cities. Most of the great traditional sea ports were gateway cities—such as Liverpool, Marseille, Genoa—and these three cities and many others have faced a decline in their employment base.

Tourism has become increasingly important as the economic base for large numbers of cities and smaller urban centres. This includes not only the Mediterranean 'sun-belt' areas and other tourist

TABLE 2.13 Functional types of cities

City Type	Characteristics	Examples
Global cities	Accumulation of financial, economic, political and cultural headquarters of global importance	London, Paris
Growing high-tech/services cities	Modern industrial base, national centre of R&D, production-oriented services of international importance	Bristol, Reading, Munich
Declining Industrial cities	Traditional (monostructured) industrial base, obsolete physical infrastructure, structural unemployment	Metz, Oberhausen, Mons, Sheffield
Port cities	Declining shipbuilding and ship repair industries, environmental legacies, in the South burdened by additional gateway functions	Liverpool, Genoa, Marseille
Growing cities without modern industrialization	Large informed economy and marginalized underclass, uncontrolled development and deteriorating environment	Palermo, Thessaloniki, Napoli
Company towns	Local economy depending to a high degree on a single corporation	Leverkusen, Eindhoven
New towns	New self-contained cities with overspill population in the hinterland of large urban agglomerations	Milton Keynes, Evry
Monofunctional satellites	New urban schemes within large agglomerations with focus on one function only (e.g. technopole, airport)	Sophia-Antipolis, Roissy
Small towns, rural centres, rurban belts	Smaller cities and semi-urbanized areas in rural regions, along coasts or transport corridors with weak economic potential	All over Europe
Tourism and culture cities	Local economic base depending on international tourism and cultural events of European importance	Saltzburg, Venice
Border and gateway cities	Hinterland divided by national border; gateways for economic migrants and political refugees	Aachen, Basel

Source: Kunzmann, Klaus R. and Michael Wegener, *The Pattern of Urbanization in Western Europe 1960–1990*, Report for the Directorate General XVI of the Commission of the European Communities, Institut für Raumplanung, Universitat Dortmund, Dortmund, 1991.

areas but also cities with historic and cultural attractions. Many major cities in Europe such as Paris, London, Amsterdam, Munich, Rome, Florence, Berlin, Seville and Copenhagen have long had major tourist industries but have also benefitted from the renewed interest in history, from the expansion of the international convention industry and from the growing mobility of an increasingly better-educated and affluent society.[152]

What underlies urban change

The marked differences in the scale and nature of urban change between the 1980s and the 1970s have led to a considerable debate about what caused these differences. One widely held view is that something anomalous has been occurring at some stage since the late 1960s but opinion is divided as to whether it is the counterurbaniza-tion of the 1970s or the waning of this trend in the 1980s that was unusual.

Several of the economic and demographic factors cited as explanations for the counterurbanization of the 1970s were unique to that decade. These include the mid-decade recession following the oil-price rise of 1973/4 which produced a major shock to the system, including disinvestment in manufacturing industries in traditional industrial areas and the run-down of the guestworker move-ment in north-west European cities. Population gains in some of the more peripheral and rural areas can be linked directly to an increase in oil and natural resource exploitation because of the oil price rise as well as a rise in expenditure in defence industries and related research establishments that are located in such areas. Higher education was also being expanded, also often away from the major existing population centres together with the gen-eral upgrading of public-sector infrastructure and private services in rural areas. However, certain studies have suggested that the changes that took place during the 1970s were a logical evolution of those in the 1950s and 1960s.[153]

The 1980s also had its share of particular eco-nomic changes. Perhaps the most important were the impacts of the worldwide recession, the slump in the real price of oil, minerals and agricultural products which meant less income and economic activity in many peripheral regions, the restruc-turing of manufacturing operations designed to increase efficiency in an era of immense competi-tion with new flexible approaches replacing the traditional Fordist model of production and the eclipsing of Keynsian approaches to the manage-ment of the economy. Shortage of public funds from the shrinkage of the tax base and also an ideological shift away from the welfare state led to major cutbacks in public sector infrastructure investments. There were also cutbacks in subsi-dies for declining and transforming industry (except within the European Community's Common Agricultural Policy) and in spending on regional development policy. There was also a switch within many governments from schemes for urban population dispersal towards policies for regenerating inner city areas, in response to the metropolitan problems of the previous decade. The late 1980s also brought the remark-able political events in East and Central Europe which by the end of the decade had brought reduced defence spending and large-scale immi-gration into Europe, especially to the former West Germany and Austria.

Given the fluctuations in the pace of deconcen-tration which occurred during the 1970s and the 1980s, these might be linked together in some form of cyclic relationship. For instance, an urban centre could proceed through a four-stage cycle:

- urbanization with fastest growth in its core;
- suburbanization with faster growth in the ring around the core;
- disurbanization with decline in the core and the ring, with the core performing worse than the ring; and finally
- reurbanization with the core again overtaking the ring.

This four-stage cycle can also be applied to wider (e.g. national) systems. Empirical studies of the changes in urban systems that occurred in the first three decades of the post-war period appear to bear out the changes predicted by the model. For instance:

In the 1950s, European population was concentrating remarkably into the metropolitan cores . . . But by the 1960s, a reversal had taken place: though metropolitan areas were still growing, they were decentralizing people from cores to rings. After 1970, this process accelerated, so that cores virtually ceased to grow.[154]

Further evidence of this interpretation came from early signs of *gentrification* in the older cores of some of the larger metropolitan centres during the 1970s, leading on to more significant levels of urban regeneration in the following decade.

Economic cycles play the dominant role in any identifiable cyclic behaviour affecting migration and population redistribution. Population and urban change can be explained by references to cycles as particular factors fluctuate in their strength and perhaps also their nature over time. These cycles include the relatively short-term business cycles that are associated with fluctuations in labour and housing markets and are related to employment opportunities and the availability and cost of credit. Of a rather longer periodicity are development cycles linked to the commercial property industry, notably retailing where developers find that the profitability of one type of building or location may fall after a decade or more and therefore switch their investment to competitive alternatives before returning later to redevelop the original site. There is also the suggestion of 50–60-year-long waves or Kondratieff cycles associated with major phases of innovation and technological development that are also a major influence on urban growth and change.

In seeking to account for the fluctuations over time in the degree of population concentration and deconcentration, there are three distinct sets of factors that influence the distribution of people and jobs:

- A number of forces operating over the longer term in favour of deconcentration—such as improvements in transport and communication, the increasing preference (in many countries) for owner-occupied housing, and the growth of tourism and outdoor recreation;
- Some factors encouraging concentration in large cities and more urbanized regions, particularly the growth of business services and corporate headquarters and other activities requiring a high level of national and international accessibility and a large supply of highly qualified personnel; and
- Factors which may have different geographic effects at different times, depending on prevailing circumstances, operating along cyclic lines as described above.[155]

The key to applying this perspective is to acknowledge that the two sets of concentrating and deconcentrating forces are both likely to vary in their relative strength over time, with an outcome that may reinforce or counter the effects of the third group of factors at any one time.

Overall, two separate processes can be held to be largely responsible for the swings in population redistribution trends away from and back to regional concentration that have been widely observed in Europe over the last 25 years. One is the regional restructuring process which tends to provide a major recasting of the macro-region map of economic activity at relatively long intervals—principally those of the long 50–60-year-waves. The other is the population deconcentration process which in its strict definition refers to a general shift towards lower density occupancy of urban space. This latter process is seen as long-established and deep-structural in nature, rooted in traditional suburbanization which still continues but which also includes the search by a significant number of residents and employers for smaller towns and more rural areas.

Looking towards the future

There is little agreement about the likely future pattern of growth—not least because of not knowing how the underlying factors which affect population distribution will themselves develop. The last 10–15 years have certainly brought great changes, resulting from changing markets, new methods of business organization and major political transformations. But there is little consensus as to whether these changes have run their course or will build on themselves cumulatively. The proponents of the long-wave theory believe that the main ingredients of the fifth Kondratieff are now in place, oriented around advanced telecommunications and new industries like biotechnology—but some large spatial readjustments can be expected during the 25-year growth phase of this new cycle. 'Flexible specialization' has already produced severe structural upheaval but institutional and political changes associated with the European Union and the removal of the Iron Curtain have the potential for a large scale redrawing of the economic map of Europe. The main argument centres on whether these changes will lead to the growth of a European core region at the expense of the continent's peripheral zones.

One group has suggested that growth in economic activity will be concentrated in a region stretching from south-east England through Benelux, south-west Germany and Switzerland to Lombardy and north-west Italy.[156] This is associated with the introduction of the single European Market at the end of 1992, with further steps towards European economic and political integration and by the expected enlargement of the Union and plans for the further development of the rapid rail system and telecommunications infrastructure. However, the experience in the past is that not all places within a favoured zone prosper while not all places outside a favoured zone are at a disadvantage. There is also the strong economic growth achieved by northern Italy, southern France and more recently by north-east Spain and these have led to suggestions that a Mediterranean sunbelt is emerging as a second major European growth zone. A third reason is the recognition that certain forces will counter the tendency towards ever greater concentration, including the costs of greater congestion, environmental damage in the fast-growing areas, the greater freedom of locational choice allowed by improved transport and communications and the necessity for effective government intervention to prevent increasing national and regional disparities that would threaten the European Union.

There is also the research which concludes that the economic fortunes of individual places have much more to do with their inherent characteristics and the way in which they position themselves with respect to the global economy and international capital than with their particular geographic location. Neighbouring places often develop in very different ways—and these can be linked to the quality of entrepreneurship and to their diverse range of inherited advantages and disadvantages.[157] This perspective sees Europe as made up of a large number of individual, largely urban-centred regions which compete for jobs, people and capital investment, sometimes in co-operation with their neighbours but as often as not in competition—while perhaps being linked to similar regions elsewhere through such networks as the Eurocities Group, POLIS, and the Commission des Villes.

One influence on changes in population distribution that is not easy to predict is the influence of quality of life considerations. Retirement migration is one clear example of this and the number of

people reaching retirement age will increase steadily after 2000 in response to higher post-1945 fertility and reach a peak in the 2020s. The preferences of these people in terms of their lifestyle and preferred location—and their purchasing power (which in turn is influenced by the nature of government provision for pensions) will obviously have an increasing influence on population distribution. As noted earlier, the locational preferences of retired people have changed over the last 30 years.

The reunification of Germany and the fall of the 'Iron Curtain' will bring important changes to the urban system of Europe and possibly to the distribution of population. For instance, the distribution of population within what was East Germany is also likely to change, perhaps most especially if Berlin does become the full capital of Germany.

Future changes in urban areas and urban systems will also be influenced by where employers choose to locate. The growth in business services has not only reinforced the position of the largest cities but also spawned a large volume of back-office jobs in suburban areas and more distant towns alongside decentralized factories and shopping complexes. In terms of residential implications, much depends on how far workers are prepared to commute and also on the extent to which telecommuting can substitute for daily physical presence in the main office. There is a complex mix of choice and constraint within the 'tug of war' between centralizing and decentralizing forces. Employers may make the main decisions about where to locate but location decisions are also based on the availability of certain types of labour. Both employers and employees make decisions about location within the context provided by planning authorities and the policies they pursue.

Predicting changes in population distribution up to the year 2000 and beyond also needs predictions or assumptions about the way in which policy attitudes will develop over time. Counterurbanization during the 1970s was certainly helped by government regional policies to support developments in more peripheral regions, just as the waning of counterurbanization also coincided with a much reduced regional development effort in the 1980s. The extent of European economic integration and the extent of any government and European Union support for a technopoles network and much improved transport and telecommunications infrastructure will have important influences. Increasingly stringent environmental policies may also have a major spatial impact—for instance as they close down some industries while others have to fundamentally reorganize their production to meet emission standards. There also remains the uncertainty as to when the civil wars and armed conflicts in various parts of East and Central Europe will be resolved and whether similar conflicts will spring up elsewhere.

2.5 East and Central Europe[158]

Introduction

The new political geography of the former Soviet Union and of what was previously called 'East Europe' suggests the need to no longer discuss this as one region. For instance, the three Baltic States (Estonia, Latvia and Lithuania) that were formerly part of the Soviet Union are, geographically, part of Northern Europe and best grouped with near neighbours such as Finland and Sweden.[159] Most East European countries and the former Soviet republics that are on their western borders might more appropriately be discussed as one region, since they share many demographic, economic and spatial characteristics. There is certainly a need to consider urban change in countries such as Hungary, the Czech and Slovak Republics and Poland within a broader European context as their major cities strengthen linkages with the German and Austrian urban systems—or rather renew such linkages since many of their major cities developed on the basis of their interactions with cities such as Vienna and Berlin. The four republics in Central Asia also share demographic, economic and spatial characteristics that suggest that these be considered as one group and, geographically, part of Asia.

However, if the interest is in population and urban change since 1980, the countries that were until recently considered as 'Eastern Europe' and the republics that were previously 'the Soviet Union' have to be considered together. Their economic systems and political structures had important characteristics in common—that were also distinct from those in the rest of Europe—and these were the major influence on population and urban change. Until 1989, they were demarcated from the rest of Europe by the so called 'Iron Curtain' and were subject to political and military control by the government of the Soviet Union. The whole region had a supra-national economic organization—the Council for Mutual Economic Assistance—and there were controls on population flows and trade with the West, although of varying strength, depending on the country and the decade. This brought major changes in their settlements, especially for cities and regions whose economies had previously developed through trading links with the West. This is why most of this section concentrates on East Europe as a group and on the former Soviet Union. Where possible, distinctions are drawn between the different republics in the former Soviet Union and between the countries formed by the break-up of Czechoslovakia and Yugoslavia. The only exception is the former East Germany that is considered within the section on West Europe. At the end of this section, some consideration is given to developments in the 1990s and what these may imply for population and urban change in the future.

Until the end of the 1980s, this varied group of 26 or more independent nations had economic and political characteristics quite distinct from those in West Europe that affected their settlement system and form that their cities took.[160] These include government decisions rather than market forces determining the nature and location of most productive investment. In general, priority was given to industry over services and in many instances, industries were located outside the major cities in places that differed from what a market economy would have produced. Industries were also kept in operation long after they would have been deemed unprofitable or too expensive in the West so at least up until the economic and political changes of the late 1980s, most industrial centres had not undergone the very rapid falls in industrial employment that had affected so many industrial centres in Europe. The abolition of a land market in cities, the limited role permitted to a private housing market and private enterprises and the large scale housing estates built by public enterprises brought a very different logic to the form and spatial distribution of residential areas and enterprises within cities.

East and Central Europe

The political revolutions of 1989 brought not only an abrupt change in economic and political organization but also the break-up of Yugoslavia, the division of Czechoslovakia into two Republics and the reunification of Germany. These combined with the ethnic conflicts and civil wars and the radical changes in economic policy are also likely to have set in motion new trends in population and urban change that are not revealed by existing statistics and will have to wait for a new round of censuses. This section will concentrate on population and urban change in the region from 1950 to 1992.

By 1992, the population in East Europe had reached 124 million with 56 per cent in urban areas—see Table 2.14. Half the total and the urban population was concentrated in Poland and Romania. This region had experienced the most rapid growth in total population and in urban population of any region in Europe—although in comparison to most of the world's regions, the scale of change was slow. The average for the region hides large differences—for instance, the slowest was in Hungary where population grew by only 11 per cent in this 42-year period while the two fastest were Poland (55 per cent) and Albania where the population nearly tripled.

Population density in the region lies between the higher densities found in West Europe and the lower densities of the Ukraine and the Russian Federation. The areas of high population density are generally around national capitals or the industrial and urban concentrations that often contain major metropolitan centres and these have gained from marked rural to urban migration since World War II.

In Bulgaria, Hungary and Romania, the high concentration of national population in and around the national capital is particularly notable. In 1990, 40 per cent of Bulgaria's population was concentrated in the south-west of the country with Sofia, its surrounding region and the neighbouring region of Plovdiv. In Hungary, a fifth of the national population was in Budapest with another 10 per cent in the surrounding county of Pest. In Romania, Bucharest and the south-east region of the country had almost 40 per cent of the national population in the early 1990s. The national capitals in the Czech and Slovak republics, Albania and Poland concentrate far lower proportions of their national populations.

In addition to the main urban centres and industrial agglomerations, there are also large areas of high population density, mostly in the southern states that correspond to industrial concentrations in small urban centres and denser rural tracts—for example of Croatia, north of Zagreb, in Serbia in the Morava valley and in Kosovo, in Romania in Wallachia, in Albania along the coastal plain and in the Maritsa valley in Bulgaria.

Demographic change

Population growth has slowed significantly over the last two decades; current estimates suggest an average annual growth rate of 1 per cent a year. Birth rates have fallen rapidly while death rates also fell until 1980, after which small increases were recorded. Over the last decade, rates of natural increase have been high in comparison to West Europe, especially in Poland, the former Yugoslavia and Romania. However, by the early 1990s, in several cases, rates of natural increase were very slow; in Bulgaria, birth and death rates were close to cancelling each other out. In Hungary, deaths already exceeded births in 1990. For Romania, some predictions suggest that the population will fall by a quarter over the next two decades as birth rates fall well below death rates.

Although it is difficult to compare age structures within East Europe because there is no agreed definition for the working population, countries such as Albania and Poland have a high proportion of children, reflecting religious and political policies in these states. There are considerable variations in the proportion of the 'aged' population. The smallest proportion is found in Albania with less than 10 per cent and the former Yugoslavia with 13 per cent—both probably attributable to poorer medical facilities. The highest proportions are found in Bulgaria, Hungary and the Czech and Slovak republics where the 'aged' population represent a fifth or more of total population. Overall, the age structure of the region over the next decade is likely to show a decreasing proportion of children and an increasing proportion of people aged over 64.

International migration

The removal of controls on people's movements and the greater possibilities of moving away from the region also brought changes in the settlement system. Prior to the changes in the late 1980s, the movement of people was regulated through registration formalities that allowed migration to be encouraged or discouraged in line with government priorities. In general, until the post-1989 changes, migration in Eastern Europe was only inter-regional within countries—apart from anomalies such as the repatriation of certain ethnic minorities or those people on temporary industrial and cultural appointments.[161] There was a steady flow of migrants to the West, sometimes involving significant numbers after such political upheavals as occurred in Hungary (1956), Czechoslovakia (1968) and Poland

TABLE 2.14 East Europe: total and urban populations in 1992 and urban change since the 1930s

Country	Population (millions) in 1992		Per cent of population in urban areas	
	Total	Urban	Pre-war	c.1992
Albania	3.3	1.2	15.4 (1938)	35.0
Bulgaria	9.0	5.9	21.4 (1934)	66.0
Czechoslovakia (old)	16.0	11.4	38.9 (1930)	72.2
Czech Republic	10.4	7.8		75.2
Slovakia	5.3	3.7		69.2
Hungary	10.4	6.1	33.2 (1930)	59.0
Poland	38.4	23.1	37.3 (1939)	60.9
Romania	23.2	12.3	21.4 (1930)	54.4
Yugoslavia (old)	23.9	11.0	13.2 (1931)	47.5
Bosnia/Hercegovina		1.5		34.2
Croatia	4.8	2.4		50.8
Macedonia	2.0	1.1		53.9
Slovenia	2.0	1.0		48.9
Montenegro		0.3		50.7
Serbia		4.6		46.5
Yugoslavia (new)		4.9		48.6
East Europe	123.7	71.1		56.4

Source: Carter, F. W., 'East Europe: population distribution, urban change, housing and environmental problems', background paper prepared for the Global Report on Human Settlements, 1995.

(1980/81) but in general, international migration out of the region was controlled. One exception was Yugoslavia and estimates for 1988 suggest that there were 870,000 Yugoslav economic migrants working abroad.

With the greater freedom to travel that is part of the post-1989 reforms, internal migration or emigration out of the region could have the most significant influence on population distribution in the immediate future. Two factors, one political, one economic, would underlie this. First, nationalist problems released with the political liberalization have encouraged ethnic and religious tension in East European states that in turn have contributed to conflict and oppression in certain areas. At present, the former Yugoslavia is the main source of such movement as the former federation's disintegration has resulted in a long and bitter civil war. Recent UN estimates suggest around 1.8 million displaced persons within the former Yugoslavia and over half a million refugees from outside the territory.[162] The split between the Czech and Slovak Republics could also lead to large-scale population movement, especially within the half million strong Hungarian minority in the new Slovakian state. The second reason is that emigration may be stimulated by economic adversity, resulting from rising unemployment, decreasing living standards and real incomes coupled with high inflation. Such factors, arising from the market reform, have encouraged people to search for better living conditions outside the region.

Economic and spatial change

Since 1989, there has been a distinct transformation in the economies of Eastern Europe towards more market-oriented growth. This is likely to bring major changes to settlement systems through changes in the scale, nature and spatial distribution of economic activities. The settlement changes are likely to be most dramatic in the countries with the most radical economic change. This change consists of initially macro-economic stabilization and a broad internal and external liberalization programme for the economy, followed by the launching of privatization. This describes the former Czechoslovakia in early 1991 and Albania 1992–3 and Poland 1989–91 while recent economic changes in Hungary may also place it in this category. In others, such as Romania, the economic (and spatial) transformation is likely to be more gradual. There are also those areas where economic reform has been halted while war-related expenditures and disorganization of the economy caused by armed conflict have led to hyper-inflation; this group includes Bosnia/Hercegovina, the 'new' Yugoslavia and to some extent Croatia.

Internal migration and urbanization

Internal migration has generally been from poorer to richer regions and from rural to urban areas. The scale of rural to urban migration in recent decades has been such that the number of people residing in rural areas fell in all but Albania. In the decade after 1965, more than half the increase in urban population was caused by rural to urban migration.[163]

Within the region, all but Albania and parts of the former Yugoslavia have more than half their population in urban centres while in the Czech and Slovak Republics and in Bulgaria, more than two-thirds live in urban centres. A significant part of the inter-regional migration trend pre-1989 was attributable to official government policies that promoted the growth of large towns and cities to provide the labour force for major plants and enterprises.

A very considerable proportion of the region's urban population lives in relatively small urban centres. In 1992, more than half the urban population lived in urban centres with less than 100,000 inhabitants and urban centres with 100,000 or more inhabitants contained a quarter of the region's population; for the European Union, by way of comparison, half the urban population live in cities of 100,000 or more inhabitants.

The proportion of the urban population living in cities with more than one million inhabitants also declined in most countries, due to the emphasis of communist planners on developing urban centres lower down the urban hierarchy. New-town development has been popular—usually connected to one economic function such as a town to house the population of a coal mine. In some instances, strong controls were placed on the growth of the largest cities. For instance, in Hungary, Budapest became so popular that a political decision was taken to discourage people from living there.

It has been noted already that many of the region's main population concentrations are around national capitals and major industrial centres. Upper Silesia near the Polish/Czech border is most characteristic of the industrial centres based on coal exploitation and this is the only industrial concentration similar in urban population density to those of Western Europe; in 1991, it had some 2.25 million inhabitants. Katowice county within which it is located covers just 2 per cent of Poland's territory but with around 4 million inhabitants, it has some 10 per cent of the national population.[164] There are also the large metropolitan centres that include state capitals such as Warsaw and Bucharest (each with over 2 million inhabitants) and Prague, Zagreb and Bratislava and regional agglomerations such as Brno, Kracow, Poznań, Lódz and

MAP 2.4
The largest urban centres in East and Central Europe

Notes and sources: This map shows all urban centres which were recorded as having 750,000 or more inhabitants in 1990 in United Nations, *World Urbanization Prospects: The 1994 Revision,* Population Division, Department of Economic and Social Information and Policy Analysis, New York, 1995 with additional cities added or reclassified where more recent census data was available. And as in the text of this section, it includes all countries that were part of the former USSR, even where these are now classified as being parts of Northern Europe, Southern Europe or Asia.

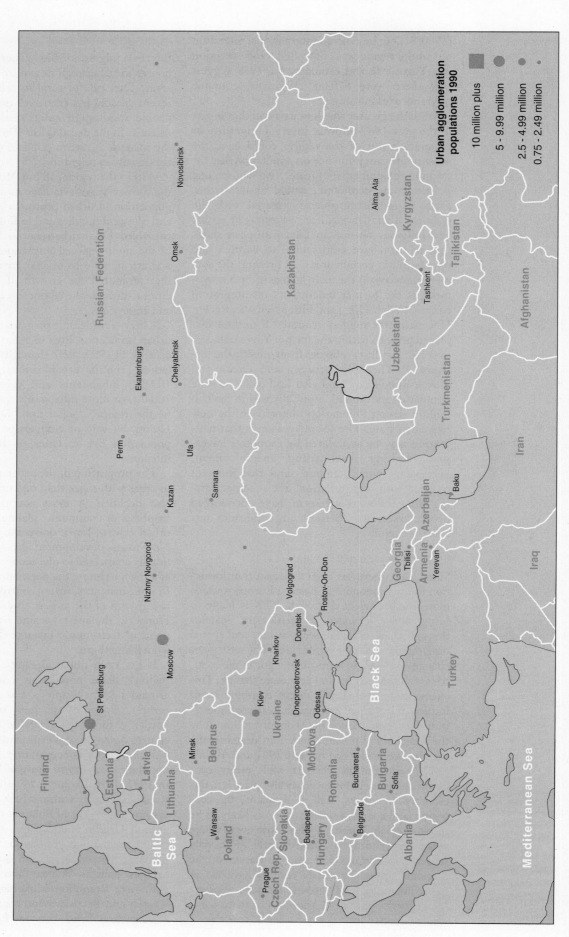

Wrocław. Unlike Katowice, most of these have been important urban centres for centuries and were part of an integrated system of Central European manufacturing and trading cities, prior to the industrial revolution.[165] For instance, Warsaw, Prague, Belgrade, Poznań, Budapest and Bucharest were among Europe's largest urban centres for parts of the late Middle Ages and/or sixteenth and seventeenth centuries.

There is considerable variation in the rate at which the region's major cities have grown in recent decades. Within the United Nations list of the 'million-cities' in the region shown in Table 2.15, Katowice appears as the largest and among the most rapidly growing in recent decades but this population of 3.5 million in 1990 refers to the county, not the town and Katowice County is perhaps better considered as a region rather than a city or metropolitan area. However, the Upper Silesian Industrial Region with around 2.25 million inhabitants in 1992 would be among three other metropolitan centres, each with over 2 million in 1990: Warsaw, Bucharest and Budapest. Map 2.4 shows the largest urban centres in East and Central Europe.

Table 2.15 also shows how Warsaw, Bucharest and Sofia have grown relatively rapidly since 1950 while Prague, Lodz and Gdansk have grown relatively slowly. Part of the reason for Warsaw's rapid growth since World War II has been the rebuilding of the city after most of it was destroyed by the Nazis; in addition, the communist policy of heavy industrial development attracted many rural to urban migrants while increased mechanization in agriculture lessened job opportunities in rural areas. Bucharest and Sofia grew rapidly as what were predominantly agricultural economies prior to World War II underwent rapid industrialization. Cities such as Prague, Budapest, Lodz and Gdansk were already established industrial centres prior to World War II; some experienced less war damage.

The Republics that formerly formed the Soviet Union[166]

In considering population and urban change in this region, most attention is given to the period 1959 to 1989, with a particular interest in the period 1979–89, because 1959, 1969, 1979 and 1989 were census years in the former Soviet Union and the census data permit a more detailed consideration of such change. During this period, the region's population grew from 209 million to 287 million—with a population growth rate relatively low by world standards; it was slightly lower than the population growth rate of North America. Aggregate statistics for the whole region are much influenced by what is taking place in the Russian Federation; with 147 million inhabitants in 1989, it concentrated just over half of the region's population on more than three quarters of its territory. Ten of the fifteen republics had less than 8 million inhabitants on that date; four had less than 4 million.

Table 2.16 shows the diversity in population and urban change for these three decades between what were to become the independent republics. The most rapidly growing republics more than doubled their population while the least rapidly growing had populations that increased by less than 30 per cent. There are clear contrasts between the small increases among the Russian Federation, the Baltic States to the north-west and the western republics that border Europe that have low birth and death rates and the southern—especially Central Asian—republics that have high birth rates and low death rates. Among the other republics, population growth rates fell between these two extremes.

This same geographic contrast is evident for levels of urbanization in 1989 and for the scale of increase in urbanization levels between 1959 and 1989. This same group of the Baltic States, the Russian Federation and the western republics bordering Europe are all among the most urbanized—all but Moldova had 65 per cent or more of their populations in urban areas by 1989—and were among the most rapidly urbanizing regions for this 30-year period. By contrast, the Central Asian republics are the least urbanized and urbanized much less rapidly—indeed in Tajikistan and Turkmenistan, the level of urbanization did not increase in these 30 years. The other republics, Kazakhstan, Armenia, Azerbaijan and Georgia, generally fall within these extremes. This reflects the general geography of development within the former USSR. Urbanization levels across the four Central Asian republics remained static or fell during the decade 1979–89 as rural populations grow more rapidly than urban populations.

Within the Russian Federation, there was considerable diversity in the level of urbanization among the eleven economic regions. The most

---

TABLE 2.15 Population growth among the 'million-cities' in Eastern Europe

Urban centre	1990	1970	1950	c.1930	c.1900	c.1850	c.1800
Katowice	3,449.0	2,767.0	1,689.0	126.0	32.0		3.0
Warsaw	2,235.0	1,723.0	1,014.0	1,172.0	756.0	164.1	75.0
Bucharest	2,201.0	1,667.0	1,111.0	639.0	276.0	104.0	34.0
Budapest	2,121.0	1,946.0	1,618.0	1,318.0	792.0	156.5	54.0
Sofia	1,313.0	881.0	547.0	213.0	68.0	43.0	46.0
Prague	1,216.0	1,078.0	1,002.0	848.0	202.0	118.4	77.4
Lodz	1,042.0	925.0	725.0	605.0	314.0	16.0	0.8
Gdansk	884.0	697.0 3	65.0	256.0	141.0	64.0	41.0
Krakow (also Cracow)	825.0	630.0 3	63.0	219.0	91.0	42.0	25.0

Source: Chandler, Tertius and Gerald Fox, *3000 Years of Urban Growth*, Academic Press, New York and London, 1974; United Nations, *World Urbanization Prospects 1992; Estimates and Projections of Urban and Rural Populations and of Urban Agglomerations*, Department of Economic and Social Information and Policy Analysis, ST/ESA/SER.A/136, United Nations, New York, 1993. Gdansk and Krakow are included as both had close to 1 million inhabitants by 1990.

TABLE 2.16 Total and urban populations and level of urbanization for the Republics, 1989, and scale of changes 1959–89

Republic	Total popn 1989 (thousands)	A.A. popn growth rate (1959–89)	Level of urbanization		Change in the level of urbanizn 1959–89
			1959	1989	
Baltic Republics					
Estonia	1,573	0.9	56.5	71.6	15
Latvia	2,680	0.8	56.1	71.1	15
Lithuania	3,690	1.0	38.6	68.0	29
Republics bordering Europe					
Belarus'	10,200	0.8	30.8	65.5	35
Ukraine	51,707	0.7	45.7	66.4	21
Moldova	4,338	1.4	22.3	47.0	25
Russian Federation	147,400	0.8	52.4	73.6	21
Caucasus					
Georgia	5,443	1.0	42.4	55.8	13
Azerbaijan	7,038	2.2	47.8	53.9	6
Armenia	3,288	2.1	50.0	67.8	18
Kazakhstan	16,536	1.9	43.7	57.2	14
Central Asia					
Uzbekistan	19,905	3.0	33.6	40.7	7
Kyrgyzstan	4,290	2.5	33.7	38.3	5
Tajikistan	5,109	3.2	32.6	32.6	0
Turkmenistan	3,534	2.9	46.2	45.4	–1
Total (former USSR)	286,731	1.1	47.9	65.9	18

Source: Shaw, Denis J. B., 'Settlement and urban change in the former Soviet Union', background paper for the Global Report, 1995, drawing from Census of Population, 1959 and 1989

urbanized were the Central region (83 per cent urban) with Moscow at its core and the North-West (87 per cent) with St Petersburg at its core; the least urbanized were the three more agricultural regions located in central and southern parts of the European territory—for instance the North Caucasus (57 per cent) and the Central Black Earth (60 per cent).[167]

Demographic change

There were major demographic changes in most parts of the region in the three decades up to 1989. Birth rates and rates of natural increase were high during the 1950s, partly as a result of the post-war 'baby boom' but both fell rapidly throughout the 1960s as the considerably reduced generation of wartime children entered its period of maximum fertility. An increased birth rate might have been expected in the 1970s when the larger post-war generation entered its twenties but this did not happen. A series of pro-natalist government measures sought to stimulate birth rates and may have contributed to a slight increase during the 1980s but by the end of the decade, birth rates were again in decline. Social and economic changes were important in helping explain such demographic change. Rising living standards and better health care combined with changing values help explain declining birth rates in the more wealthy

republics. However, some of the negative consequences of Soviet-style development have also been cited as helping to reduce fertility levels across the region including shortages of accommodation, poor health (linked to such factors as alcoholism, smoking, industrial pollution and inadequate expenditure on health protection) and low levels of service provision in cities (particularly affecting women who assume the larger share of domestic work).

This general picture of low birth rates, death rates and rates of natural increase applies much less to the more rural and traditional Central Asian republics. Although they also experienced a decline in birth rates during the 1960s, this decline began at a much higher level and also stopped at a higher level. While the average birth rate for the region in 1989 was 17.6 per 1000 population, it exceeded 30 in each of the Central Asian republics. Although Table 2.16 suggests that urban change is relatively slow in the four Central Asian republics, because of high natural growth rates, the rate of population growth in urban areas during this 30-year period exceeded that of many of the rapidly urbanizing republics. It is a reminder of how rapidly city populations can grow without large in-migration flows, when rates of natural increase are high.

Economic and urban change

Generalizations about urban change in this region are very difficult. First, there are an enormous number of urban centres—there were 6,216 urban centres in the 1989 census.[168] Second, there is the great economic, social and demographic diversity among the fifteen republics—and indeed the diversity within the larger ones, especially the Russian Federation. Third, there are the complex changes in national boundaries and in restrictions on international trade after the Second World War through which many major cities in the West lost economic and political importance—for instance Lvov and Riga.[169] But throughout the Soviet period, there was a strong relationship between urban and industrial growth, and the Soviet leadership's industrial development policies had a major impact upon population and urban change. The post-Stalin leadership (after 1953) broadened the goals of its economic policies to emphasize agriculture, consumer goods and services, without any absolute downgrading of the Stalinist accent on heavy industry and the military sector. A priority to industrial modernization and to introducing the plastics and chemical products that characterize modern industrial economies meant investment in oil and natural gas production. This new emphasis required increased output by the Volga–Urals oil and gas field, conveniently located in European USSR. This helps explain why several of the region's most rapidly growing cities both for the period 1959–1979 and for the period 1979 to 1989 were in the Volga–Urals regions.[170] And ultimately, as energy demands grew, this also meant drawing on the resources of various peripheral producers in the North, Siberia (especially West Siberia), Kazakhstan and Central Asia.

Patterns of urban growth during the 1980s still strongly reflect the industrial emphases of the post-Stalin years. Although the exploitation of oil and gas and other natural resources stimulated urban and industrial development in producing regions such as the Volga region and the southern part of Western Siberia, the growing network of oil and gas pipelines and electricity grids also permitted the continuing expansion of industrial output in the west, next to Europe where most of the population and industrial capacity were concentrated. Some industrial development was also stimulated in other territories that were further away but which had labour surpluses or other advantages—for instance Belarus', the Baltic republics and the Transcaucasus. Two other reasons help explain why urban development remain concentrated in the west. The first was that it had numerous environmental and social advantages over the east and a much higher standard in infrastructure provision. The second was the increasing importance of trade links with East Europe (through COMECON) and West Europe, especially after 1970.

Priority was also given to modernizing and diversifying the metallurgic industries, including iron and steel industries, most of which were located in the European territories. The most important development in European USSR was the Kursk Magnetic Anomaly and its associated metallurgical and supporting industries, in the Central Black Earth economic region in Russia. Its metal-demanding branches continued to develop in such traditional heavy industry regions as the Urals and Donets–Dnepr (Ukraine) but the less metal-intensive and often more skill-demanding industries were attracted to traditional engineering regions like those around Moscow, St Petersburg and the Baltic capitals. Similarly the motor vehicle industry developed around Moscow and in the newly industrializing Volga region.

As in Europe and North America, the location of defence-related industries and other military activities was an important influence on urban change. These were particularly important to the economies of the Centre, the Urals and the Far East. Both Moscow and St Petersburg have high concentrations of defence-related industry—especially St. Petersburg where by the late 1980s, around a quarter of the workforce were employed in the defence industry. Three of the other 13 'million-cities' in the Russian Federation, Ekaterinburg,[171] Perm and Chelyabinsk, were among the other cities with high concentrations of defence industries. A system of 'closed' towns also developed where military industry or research were concentrated whose existence was concealed.[173]

Many regions remained relatively untouched by the post-1953 industrial policies and their urban centres stagnated as a result. Others, such as parts of the Urals and the Donets–Dnepr with traditional iron and steel and heavy metallurgical industries or parts of the Centre with textile industries were too closely associated with Stalinist industrialization policies to benefit from the new economic directions. However, deindustrialization and the heavy unemployment associated with it were never features of the Soviet period, as many industries remained in production, long after the stage that they would have been deemed unprofitable in the West.

Large cities

An increasing proportion of the urban population came to live in large cities. By 1989, 61 per cent of the region's urban population lived in cities with 100,000 or more inhabitants compared to 49 per cent in 1959. This is much higher than in East Europe where only 46 per cent of the urban population lived in cities with 100,000 plus inhabitants. By this date, 22 per cent were living in 'million-cities' compared to 9 per cent in 1959.

TABLE 2.17 Distribution of urban population in different size categories of urban centres, 1989

Republic	Urban population (thousands)	% of the urban popn in urban centres with			
		up to 19,999	20,000–99,999	100,000–999,999	1 million plus
Baltic Republics					
Estonia	1,118	24.3	22.7	53.0	0.0
Latvia	1,889	20.1	19.1	60.9	0.0
Lithuania	2,487	22.2	18.7	59.1	0.0
Republics bordering Europe					
Belarus'	6,642	18.3	18.9	39.0	23.8
Ukraine	34,297	21.0	21.5	35.6	21.9
Moldova	2,020	27.2	16.9	55.9	0.0
Russian Federation	107,939	15.5	22.1	39.1	23.3
Caucasus					
Georgia	2,992	17.7	19.1	21.7	41.5
Azerbaijan	3,806	26.5	28.8	13.4	31.3
Armenia	2,222	12.8	22.7	13.8	50.7
Central Asia					
Kazakhstan	9,398	17.1	20.2	50.8	11.9
Uzbekistan	8,041	18.3	22.0	34.1	25.5
Kyrgyzstan	1,625	16.0	33.5	50.5	0.0
Tajikistan	1,655	25.7	28.8	45.4	0.0
Turkmenistan	1,591	31.2	26.8	42.0	0.0
Total (former USSR)	187,722	17.6	21.9	38.7	21.8

Source: Shaw, Denis J. B., 'Settlement and urban change in the former Soviet Union', background paper for the Global Report, 1995, drawing from Census of Population, 1959 and 1989.

Although official Soviet policy advocated controlling the growth of large cities, the elaborate government system for controlling migration to such cities established from the 1930s was never particularly effective. It was based on a system of residence permits, controls on employment and land use plans. The policy from the 1950s to persuade industry and other employers to locate in medium-size and small urban centres generally failed to counteract the attractions of the large cities. Most new or expanding enterprises located in larger cities. Large cities had an important role in the command economy for two reasons. First, they had the best quality infrastructure and skilled labour forces but also relatively low wages and other cost advantages that encouraged (or compelled) state and other enterprises to locate there. Unlike market economies, in the Soviet command economy, wage rates, taxes, the cost of land (or rent) and infrastructure costs were not necessarily higher in large and successful cities compared to smaller and less successful cities as they would be in West Europe or North America. Second, in a command economy, success depends as much on access to political and administrative decision-makers and government officials as economic performance and this enhanced the attraction of major administrative centres. Important ministries and enterprises wishing to locate in large cities had little difficulty in persuading local authorities to grant the necessary permissions (including resident permits) and/or persuading national party or government bodies to put pressure on local governments. This helps explain the increasing dominance of Union republic capitals and many regional administrative centres as they concentrated an increasing proportion of the urban population in their respective regions over the 1959–89 period.

An analysis of growth characteristics and socio-cultural development for the cities with 100,000 or more inhabitants for the 1970s permitted the 221 cities to be grouped into four types.[173] The first was a small group of 28 cities characterized by restricted industry-related growth and significant socio-cultural development; this favoured group included major urban centres such as Moscow and Kiev with high living standards. Next came a dynamic group of 42 cities with significant growth and development. This group included many cities towards the western and southern edges of the county that benefited from the post-Stalin policies of industrial modernization. The third group of 59 cities had significant growth but restricted socio-cultural development and included numerous resource centres and peripheral cities where rapid industrial growth, often under the aegis of only one or two dominant ministries was not matched by adequate provision of services. The fourth group of 92 cities had restricted growth and socio-

cultural development and these included the heavy industrial centres of the Stalinist era—for instance cities in the Donets–Dnepr region, the Urals and the Kuzbass coalfield.

This concentration of rapid urban development away from the old heavy industrial centres was also confirmed by a study of the fastest and slowest growing cities between 1979 and 1989.[174] Of the 35 fastest growing cities 1979–89, only two are in the older industrial regions. Most of these fast growing cities are close to Europe in Belarus', the south-west of the Ukraine and Moldova, along the Volga and Kama rivers (part at least due to the oil and chemical industries, part to new manufacturing enterprises) and in West Siberia, east of the Ural region where oil and gas development have given impetus to rapid city growth. The distribution of rapidly growing cities during 1959–79 is fairly similar, and again with few such cities being located in the older industrial areas—although the cities to the west experienced less growth than in the 1980s. Of the 36 cities with the slowest population growth 1979–89 (including six with a net decline in population), two thirds are the Central Region of Russia, the Donbas coalfield (mainly in Donets–Dnepr) or the Kuznetsk basin. Virtually all the slowest growing towns during 1959–79 were also in or adjoining the mature industrial regions of the country.[175]

By the 1970s, Soviet urban specialists became aware of a phenomenon that had previously been considered a characteristic of capitalism—the development of large urban agglomerations or clusters of functionally interrelated cities. The largest such agglomeration is the one with Moscow at its centre. There are also clusters of cities on the Donetsk mining centres, the Kuzbass coalfield (also known as the Kuznetsk basin), in the central Dnepr region, and the Urals group of metallurgic and mining cities. The development of such agglomerations or core regions highlighted the need for a more comprehensive system of land use planning working at a regional scale but until the end of the Soviet period, such a planning system had failed to emerge. Instead, systems of cities often developed because enterprises and agencies denied access to one city were able to choose a location in a neighbouring city. Similarly, many migrants unable to gain residence rights in one city found accommodation in another nearby and commuted into the city by train or bus. In many large cities, including Moscow and St Petersburg, 10 per cent or more of the labour force live outside their boundaries and commute. But unlike Europe and North America, it tends to be the poorer groups working in the less remunerative jobs and living in poor quality settlements that commute from 'suburban' locations while the inhabitants in privileged central cities enjoyed superior living standards and services. Central city residents also enjoy subsidized public transport while commuters travel on non-subsidized transport.

From the 1950s, with the drive to solve the housing crisis, Soviet cities also expanded their physical size. Despite land use controls, land was not always used efficiently and the inhabitants of new housing estates often had lengthy journeys to work. However, Soviet cities generally spread less than cities in the West. One reason was the state control of land and of much of the housing and the emphasis in public housing on apartment blocks rather than individual units within relatively low density suburban developments. A second reason was low levels of car ownership and the lack of development for roads, especially beyond city limits. However, growing cities made increasing land and resource demands on their wider region through, for instance, recreational demands (including *dachas* or second homes and collective gardens) and the rising demand for fresh water and for land for rubbish disposal. These often threatened the integrity of green belts and other valued resources and gave rise to severe disputes between neighbouring local authorities.

Rural settlements

Between 1959 and 1989, rural populations and the number of rural settlements declined in most regions. In the Russian Federation, the rural population declined by around a third and among its eleven economic regions, only those to the extreme east and the extreme south (North Caucasus) had population increases. The Ukraine, Belarus' and the three Baltic states also experienced declines in their rural population in this period. Most of the declines were the result of rural–urban migration and they left within many rural settlements the problems associated with an ageing population and labour scarcity. The number of rural settlements declined by more than half in this period to 332,000 in 1989. This particularly affected small settlements with less than 100 inhabitants that had housed 12.0 per cent of the rural population in 1959 but only 4.6 per cent in 1989. Such small settlements are characteristic of the landscapes of north Russia where the bleak natural environment restricts the opportunities for large villages to develop. The number of large rural settlements—those with over 1000 inhabitants—grew significantly in these three decades and they came to house 55.4 per cent of the rural population. Larger settlements are especially characteristic of the semi-arid and arid southern parts of the region.

The rapid decline in the proportion of people living in rural areas reflects the priority given to urban-based production and the limited success in improving economic and social conditions in rural areas. But it is also linked to conditions and trends that pre-date the 1950s. Rural and agricultural work had long been poorly rewarded with relatively low wages compared to cities and very inadequate provision of services. The radical changes in the form of agricultural production under Stalin with the effective abolition of peasant farming and its replacement with a system of state or collective farms offered minimum incentives to the rural labour force. Although, after 1953, many efforts were made to improve wage levels in rural areas, to make agriculture more efficient and to provide services, these did not stem rural to urban migration. In addition, some of the rural improvement policies such as the grouping of rural inhabitants into key settlements where services could be provided more efficiently may have hastened rather than slowed out-migration. Although the Soviet authorities also sought to control migration out of rural settlements by minimizing the issue of internal passports to collective and state farmers, this did not prove effective.

Recent developments

Recent political changes and the fundamental changes they have included in economic policies will have far reaching implications for all aspects of population and urban change. Some of these had begun prior to the break up of the USSR in 1991. The reforms known as *Perestroyka* launched by the government of President Gorbachov sought to decentralize the command economy by introducing market-like elements and implementing measures of democratization. These helped provoke the break up of the USSR and since 1991, all the newly independent republics have been promoting a more market-based economy (with varying degrees of enthusiasm) and many have moved towards some model of pluralist democracy.

Perhaps the most visible changes in settlement trends to date are the consequence of new political boundaries imposed across what was formerly a single political and economic space. One obvious change arises from each new republic having to reconstruct its independent political life around its capital city and inevitably, each capital city's significance will grow. A second change is the cutting of inter-republic linkages originally built up over many years to serve the interests of the Soviet command economy as a whole; when added onto market forces, these will have uncertain consequences for regional growth patterns. Transport routes are being reoriented—for example Russia's decision to build a new oil-exporting port near St. Petersburg to replace Ventspils in Latvia. Several southern republics are seeking alternative routes for their export of fuels and other products. If trade with West Europe and other world regions expands—as seems likely—cities that are well located, close to international frontiers and transport routes are likely to benefit. For instance cities like Vyborn near St. Petersburg or Nakhodka and Vladivostok in the Russian Far East stand to benefit from their Special Economic Zone status. Cities in general may benefit from an expansion of service activity that was long held back by Soviet development patterns. Some of the settlements on the various resource frontiers may also grow as a result of expanded foreign investment and resource extraction and with an enhanced ability (compared to the Soviet period) to keep some of the income in the locality.

On the negative side, regions and cities closely associated with the heavy industrialization of the Soviet era—most notably Donets-Dnepr in southern Ukraine, the Urals and the Kuzbass in West Siberia may well experience the deindustrialization and outmigration that has already hit so many similar regions in Europe and North America. The 'smokestack' industries were so widespread within the command economy that such processes will not be confined to a few regions and the effects are likely to be particularly devastating on 'company towns' that were dependent on one or two heavy industries or on the exploitation of a natural resource that is no longer required. Such urban centres are found everywhere but especially in eastern regions. Similarly, policies to reduce military expenditure and to restructure the military-industrial complex will have serious consequences both in established industrial regions and in some peripheral ones where military activity and employment has been significant. Some of these changes may be ameliorated by government subsidies and regional policy but the scope for such measures is restricted.

At least up to 1994, the transition to a market economy has had rather limited effects on regional development and settlement. Government subsidy has staved off the worst ravages of unemployment and the command economy is only now in the process of privatization. Where subsidies have been removed or government commitment reduced, the effects can be considerable. Many northern regions of the Russian Federation have lost population since 1989 as a result of the closure or reduction of some resource extraction activities and military reductions. For example, Magadan administrative region in the extreme northeast of Siberia, where gold and some other mineral resources are exploited is reported to have lost 43 per cent of its population between 1989 and 1994. Krasnoyarsk Territory in Siberia, also developed for its natural resources (timber, hydro-electric, minerals) lost 16 per cent of its population in this same period.

There are also the changes in population distribution that arise from mass migrations by people escaping political persecution or actual violence. In many parts of the former USSR and especially in its southern regions, the new political geography has precipitated disagreement, conflict and on occasion open warfare. One estimate for 1993 suggested that there were more than 2 million refugees and forced resettlers living in Russia. In the Transcaucasus, an exchange of populations of around half a million people accompanied the war between Armenia and Azerbaijan over Nagorno-Karabakh. Other regions have also produced large flows of refugees including parts of Georgia and the neighbouring North Caucasus and Tajikistan in Central Asia.

Finally, there are the changes taking place in rural settlements as state and collective farms are dismantled or restructured and land ownership or use privatized. Rural settlement patterns are likely to change in areas where agricultural production increasingly takes place within the private sector. For instance, the establishment of many new farms and small settlements linked to new market and agricultural service centres may replace the nucleated farm settlements of the large collectives.

But changes in the settlement (or urban) systems of the fifteen independent republics will depend much on the extent of their economic success. If the economic changes succeed in promoting a more widespread affluence, it may promote urban changes similar to those already described in West Europe and North America. The lifting of residence restrictions and of controls on migration suggests a much greater mobility than in the past. But there are large areas of the former Soviet Union that remained little changed by the post-1950s economic changes and have yet to be influenced greatly by the more recent economic and political changes.

2.6 Asia and the Pacific[176]

Introduction

Asia contains three-fifths of the world's population and also a large and increasing share of its economic activities and its urban population. It also contains many of the world's fastest-growing large cities, reflecting the fact that it also contains most of the nations with the highest economic growth rates since 1980. But few generalizations are valid for the region, given the number of countries that range from the richest to the poorest and the largest and most populous to among the smallest and least populous in the world. Although this remains a predominantly rural region, it also contains a high proportion of the world's largest cities—see Box 2.4.

BOX 2.4
The share of Asia's rural, urban and large city population within the world

In 1990, Asia contained:

● 72 per cent of the world's rural population. This included the five largest rural populations within nations: China, India, Indonesia, Bangladesh and Pakistan which between them had close to three-fifth's of the world's rural population. China and India alone had close to half the world's rural population.

● 44.5 per cent of the world's urban population. This includes the two largest urban populations within nations: China and India that between them had more than 500 million urban inhabitants. China's urban population was nearly as large as the total population of Latin America. Both China and India had urban populations that were larger than all of Africa and of all of North America.

● 42 per cent of the world's 'million-cities' including half of the world's ten largest urban agglomerations (Tokyo, Shanghai, Beijing, Bombay and Calcutta). See Map 2.5.

Notes: One reason for what appears to be a sudden increase in Asia's total, urban and rural population and in the number of 'million-cities' around 1990 was the breakup of the former Soviet Union, as several republics that were previously in the Soviet Union became part of Asia. They include Kazakhstan, Kyrgyzstan, Tajikistan, Turkmenistan and Uzbekistan (now part of South-Central Asia) and Armenia, Azerbaijan and Georgia (now part of Western Asia).

Demographic change

By 1990, the region's population totalled 3,186 million with 32 per cent living in urban areas. The region's total population doubled between 1955 and 1990 while the urban population more than tripled.[177] Most countries had populations that more than doubled between 1950 and 1990 while many had populations that more than tripled, especially in Western Asia. Demographic statistics for the region are much influenced by China and India; in this same year, between them they had more than three-fifths of the region's population and just over half its urban population. Table 2.18 gives statistics on population and urban change for Asian nations with 10 million or more inhabitants in 1990.

Population growth rates for the whole region have been declining since the late 1960s, although with an annual rate of change of 1.9 per cent a year during the 1980s, this remained second only to Africa among the world's regions. As in Latin America, there are countries with very low and very high rates of change. Some had growth rates below 1.0 per cent in the second half of the 1980s—including three of the wealthiest Asian countries—Japan (0.44 per cent a year), Hong Kong and Republic of Korea. Some had rates that were still above 3.0 per cent a year—including Yemen, Pakistan and Iran and many of the oil-rich states in Western Asia, although for

some of these, this was likely to be associated with immigration. Most countries fell between these two extremes. For the most populous countries, China's annual rate of change for the period 1985–90 was 1.5 per cent with India having 2.0 per cent and Indonesia having 1.8 per cent.[178] India's rate of population growth was reported to have declined to 1.9 per cent a year in 1991 and it is expected to fall further in coming years—one demographer suggested that it will fall to 1.6 per cent a year by the year 2000 and 1.3 per cent by the year 2005.[179]

Asia has had the largest increase in life expectancy of any of the world's regions since 1960—from around 45 years in the late 1950s to 62.5 years in the late 1980s. As Chapter 3 will discuss in more detail, most of the countries with the largest increase in life expectancy between 1960 and 1990 were in Asia.

There is also great variety in the age structure of national populations in Asia. Many countries still have predominantly young populations; projections for the year 2000 suggest that many countries in West Asia and several others (including Nepal, Lao and Cambodia) will have more than 40 per cent of their population under fifteen years of age. By contrast, Hong Kong and Japan are projected to have less than 20 per cent with Singapore and Republic of Korea having only just above 20 per cent. Japan is the only Asian country likely to have more than 20 per cent of its population over 60 years of age by this point. There is a comparable diversity in the age structures of city populations, although unlike national age structures, these reflect the extent to which the city attracts or fails to keep younger age groups. Industrial cities, long in decline, will often have relatively old age structures, unless a considerable proportion of those who leave the labour force retire to other locations.

Data on sex ratios in large Asian cities for 1990 show that most had more men than women—although not in Japanese or Australian cities.[180] In many countries, especially the higher-income and more industrialized and urbanized countries, there has been an increase in the proportion of women in the workforce. The same is true for Dhaka, although Bangladesh is among the lowest income countries in Asia. In Dhaka, in the past, much of the migration was single males but in recent years, there has been more family migration. There has also been a large in-migration of single females, linked to the rapid expansion of the export-oriented ready-garment industries there during the 1980s, and these employ over 700,000 women.[181]

Economic and spatial change

Table 2.19 shows the high economic growth rates that many Asian nations achieved during the period 1980–92—which is very much in contrast

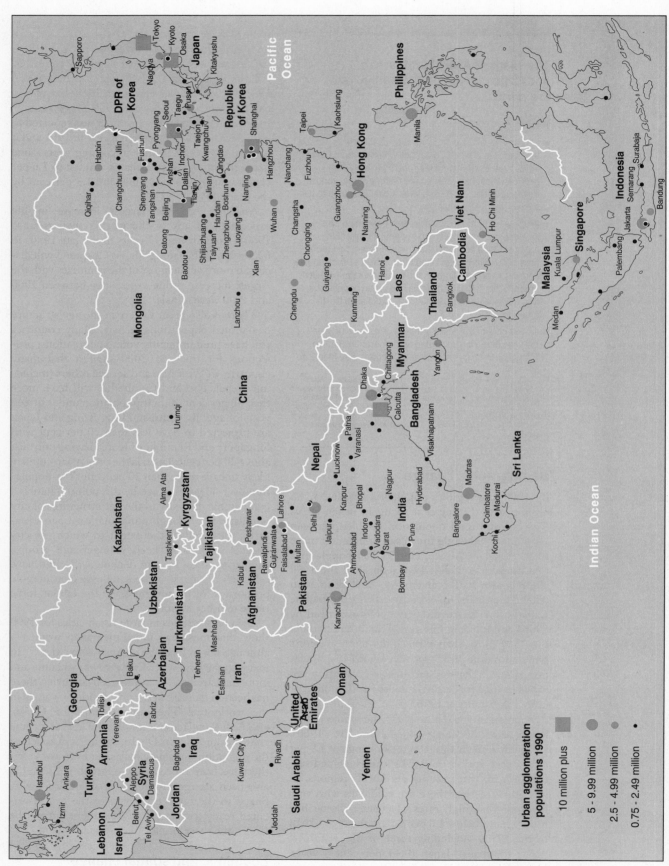

MAP 2.5
The largest urban centres in Asia

Source and notes: This map shows all urban centres which were recorded as having 750,000 or more inhabitants in 1990 in United Nations, *World Urbanization Prospects: The 1994 Revision.* Population Division, Department of Economic and Social Information and Policy Analysis, New York, 1995 with additional cities added or reclassified where more recent census data were available. Ulhasnagar is not included as a separate city within India as it is now part of Bombay urban agglomeration. The population figures for the cities in China are for administrative units that are larger than the built up areas. Their 'core populations' are generally substantially smaller—see for instance the difference between the population in 'Greater Shanghai' and in Shanghai's core urban districts described in Box 2.6.

Urban agglomeration populations 1990

10 million plus
5 - 9.99 million
2.5 - 4.99 million
0.75 - 2.49 million

TABLE 2.18 Population and urban change in Asian countries with 10 million or more inhabitants in 1990

Country	Population 1990 (000s)	Popn 1990/ popn 1950	Urban popn 1990 (000s)	% of popn, in urban areas (level of urbanization)		Level of urbanization in 1990 minus level of urbanization in 1950
				1950	1990	
Eastern Asia						
China	1,155,305	2.1	302,690	11.0	26.2	15.2
Dem. People's Rep of Korea	21,774	2.2	13,024	31.0	59.8	28.8
Japan	123,537	1.5	95,321	50.3	77.2	26.9
Republic of Korea	42,869	2.1	31,658	21.4	73.8	52.5
South-central Asia						
Afghanistan	15,045	1.7	2,745	5.8	18.2	12.4
Bangladesh	108,118	2.6	16,942	4.2	15.7	11.4
India	850,638	2.4	217,216	17.3	25.5	8.3
Iran, Islamic Rep. of	58,946	3.5	33,161	27.0	56.3	29.3
Kazakhstan	16,670	2.5	9,606	39.0	57.6	18.6
Nepal	19,253	2.4	2,104	2.3	10.9	8.6
Pakistan	121,933	3.1	39,029	17.5	32.0	14.5
Sri Lanka	17,225	2.2	3,680	14.4	21.4	7.0
Uzbekistan	20,421	3.2	8,285	31.4	40.6	9.1
South-eastern Asia						
Indonesia	182,812	2.3	55,923	12.4	30.6	18.2
Malaysia	17,891	2.9	8,909	20.4	49.8	29.4
Myanmar	41,813	2.3	10,350	16.2	24.8	8.6
Philippines	60,779	2.9	29,657	27.1	48.8	21.7
Thailand	55,583	2.8	10,408	10.5	18.7	8.2
Viet Nam	66,689	2.2	13,258	11.6	19.9	8.2
Western Asia						
Iraq	18,078	3.5	12,987	35.1	71.8	36.7
Saudi Arabia	16,048	5.0	12,405	15.9	77.3	61.4
Syrian Arab Republic	12,348	3.5	6,199	30.6	50.2	19.6
Turkey	56,098	2.7	34,179	21.3	60.9	39.6
Yemen	11,311	2.6	3,269	5.8	28.9	23.1

Source: United Nations, *World Urbanization Prospects: the 1994 Revision*, Population Division, New York, 1995.

Most of the Asian nations with among the fastest growths in their per capita GNP between 1980 and 1992 also had among the world's most rapid increases in per capita income between 1960 and 1980—especially China, Japan, Singapore, Hong Kong and the Republic of Korea. Indonesia, Malaysia and Thailand also sustained high growth rates per person in this earlier period—as did the oil-rich economies of Iraq and Saudi Arabia whose per capita incomes subsequently fell during the 1980s and early 1990s.

Urban change

Although with two-thirds of its population still living in rural areas in 1990, it is clear that Asia remains a predominantly rural continent, the extent of this 'ruralness' compared to other regions is partly explained by the criteria used by governments in defining their urban populations. For instance, it would only need India and

TABLE 2.19 Per capita GNP 1992 and annual average changes in per capita GNP for 1980–1992 and for 1960–1980 for Asian countries with 10 million or more inhabitants in 1990 and Hong Kong and Singapore

Country	GNP per capita		
	US dollars (1992)	Average annual growth rate (%)	
		1980–92	1960–80
Eastern Asia			
China	470	7.6	5.0*
Dem. People's Rep of Korea			
Hong Kong	15,360	5.5	6.8
Japan	28,190	3.6	7.1
Republic of Korea	6,790	8.5	7.0
South-central Asia			
Afghanistan			
Bangladesh	220	1.8	0.3*
India	310	3.1	1.4
Iran, Islamic Rep. of	2,200	–1.4	
Kazakhstan	1,680		
Nepal	170	2.0	0.2
Pakistan	420	3.1	2.8
Sri Lanka	540	2.6	2.4
Uzbekistan	850		
South-eastern Asia			
Indonesia	670	4.0	4.0
Malaysia	2,790	3.2	4.3
Myanmar			1.2
Philippines	770	–1.0	2.8
Singapore	15,730	5.3	7.5
Thailand	1,840	6.0	4.7
Viet Nam			
Western Asia			
Iraq			5.3
Saudi Arabia	7,510	–3.3	8.1
Syrian Arab Republic			3.7
Turkey	1,980	2.9	3.6
Yemen			

* For 1960–1982

Source: Drawn from World Development Indicators in the 1994, 1984 and 1982 *World Development Report*, Oxford University Press.

to most nations in Latin America and Africa. Perhaps the most remarkable is that of China with a fifth of the world's population and the second fastest growth in per capita income of any country in the world with 1 or more million inhabitants—the fastest growing being the Republic of Korea.

The nations with the most rapid economic growth include what are often called the 'Newly Industrialized Countries' of Hong Kong, Singapore, Taiwan (province of China) and the Republic of Korea—although it is many years since they could be called 'newly industrialized' and more than half of their GDP comes from services. Japan also sustained a relatively high growth rate per person, despite already being one of the world's most wealthy nations at the beginning of this period. Three of the 'ASEAN 4'—Indonesia, Malaysia and Thailand—also had among the world's fastest growths in per capita income in this period—while the growth in per capita income in this period in nations such as India, Pakistan and Malaysia compares favourably with most of the rest of the world.

China to change their definitions of 'urban centres' to definitions commonly used in many European or Latin American nations for Asia to become 50 to 60 per cent urban—as hundreds of millions of what are now classified as 'rural' dwellers become urban.[182] This is not to suggest that the definitions used in India and China are at fault but to demonstrate how the proportion of a country's or region's population that lives 'in urban areas' can be moved upwards or downwards, depending on the criteria used. Box 2.5 gives more details about the increase in urban population in China and notes how China's urban population might have been 169 million larger in 1990, had not new criteria been introduced for defining urban centres in the 1990 census. The proportion of Japan's population living in urban areas in 1990 can vary from 63.2 per cent to 77.4 per cent, depending on whether it is the population in city municipalities, densely inhabited districts or standard metropolitan employment areas that is being considered.[183]

The nations in Asia can be classified in three different groups, according to their level of urbanization, with the countries in such groups also having some economic characteristics in common.[184] The first, most urbanized group has Australia and New Zealand, Japan, Hong Kong, Singapore and the Republic of Korea. All are predominantly urban with agriculture having a minor role in their economy; agriculture represented between 0 and 4 per cent of GNP in 1990, except for New Zealand where it represented 8 per cent. In all these countries, more than half of their GDP in 1990 comes from services. A more recent estimate suggested that services account for close to 80 per cent of Hong Kong's GDP and around 60 per cent of that of Singapore.[185]

The second group is the 'ASEAN 4' (Thailand, Indonesia, Malaysia, Philippines) and Fiji and Pakistan where agriculture contributed less than a third to GDP and where, apart from in Thailand, between 30 and 50 per cent of their population is in urban areas. In most of these countries, the contribution of agriculture to GDP declined dramatically between 1960 and 1990 while that of industry and services tended to increase. Thailand appears very unurbanized within this group; it is reported to have only 19 per cent of its population in urban areas in 1990 and a total urban population of just 10.4 million[186] but this may be due to the urban definition used in Thailand excluding many settlements that would be classified as urban centres in other countries.

The third group contains China and all Southern Asian countries except Pakistan. These remain predominantly rural with agriculture having greater importance within their GDP and within their employment structure. However,

---

BOX 2.5
Urban population growth in China, 1978–1990

In 1990, China had 302 million urban inhabitants representing just over a quarter of its total population. The urban population had increased by almost 130 million between 1978 and 1990; estimates suggest that 35 per cent of this was due to net rural to urban migration, 25 per cent to natural increase and 40 per cent to various alterations in the urban administrative system. These alterations included a large increase in the number of settlements designated as towns (*zhen*) and municipalities (*shi*); in both instances, this large increase was associated with changes in the criteria by which a settlement became one of these. However, the scale of China's urban population would have been much larger if the new, more rigorous criteria had not been applied to its definition. China's urban population in 1990 based on the 1982 census criteria would have been 571 million, encompassing more than half the total population. The many different figures given for China's urban population at different points during the 1980s reflect the difficulties of the (then) current urban definitions in accommodating rapid economic change in both rural and urban areas.

Population counts for metropolitan centres underestimate the true numbers having *de facto* residence, as the economic reforms have created a growing pool of mobile labour. It is generally agreed that the larger the city, the larger this mobile or temporary population. Since 1984, Beijing has consistently reported over 1 million temporary residents or transients; in Shanghai, estimates for late 1988 suggest almost 2 million.[187]

Source: Kirkby, Richard 1994, 'Dilemmas of urbanization: review and prospects', in Denis Dwyer (ed.), *China: The Next Decades*, Longman Scientific and Technical, Harlow, 128–55.

China may soon be in the second group, given the speed of its economic growth, the declining proportion of its GDP in agriculture and its rapid urbanization. But again, China, like India, has such diversity in economic and urban trends within its boundaries that the use of aggregate national statistics is misleading. Certain parts of China and India have the economic and urban characteristics of Group 2 nations. There is also considerable diversity in the economic and urban characteristics of regions in countries such as Indonesia, Thailand and Bangladesh. It is also difficult to generalize about urban change in Asia when the region contains tens of thousands of urban centres. India alone had more than 4,000 urban centres in the 1991 census while there were nearly 500 urban centres in Bangladesh by 1990.[188]

The major cities

Table 1.5 in Chapter 1 listed the thirty largest urban centres in the world in 1990; half of them were Asian cities. But the list does not include two of the most dynamic cities—Hong Kong and

Singapore. For Singapore, the reason is simply the size of this city-state with just 600 square kilometres. Hong Kong's population is also restricted by its small size but when Hong Kong returns to China in 1997, it would only need a reclassification of its boundaries to reflect the new urban developments closeby for it to become one of the world's largest cities. During the 1970s and 1980s, the transformation of the city-landscape of Singapore and Hong Kong reflected the increasingly important role they came to have within the Asian (and world) economy.

Comparable transformations are also underway in many other Asian cities that are key centres in Asia's economic transformation—for instance Seoul, Kuala Lumpur, Taipei and Bangkok. In China too, there are cities that have undergone a remarkable transformation over the last ten to fifteen years—for instance Guangzhou—and cities that developed almost from scratch—for instance Shenzhen which by 1990 had an official population of 700,000 but whose real population was estimated at more than 2 million. More recently, Shanghai has begun such a transformation, especially in a new development to its east that is being developed as a high technology metropolis—see Box 2.6

Large flows of foreign investment in industry, tourism, land and business development are largely focused on major metropolitan centres such as Tokyo, Seoul, Beijing, Shanghai, Hong Kong, Taipei, Bangkok, Singapore and Jakarta and are leading to intense competition between the administrations of cities and the country of which they are part to capture a greater share of these investments and of tourism.[189] A report by the United Nations Economic and Social Commission for Asia and the Pacific noted that

Investment in convention centres, the rehabilitation of central cities and the growth of hotels are major features of these cities. Since these developments, while heavily reliant upon private capital, also need state investment particularly in ancillary infrastructure, there is intense competition for available capital for urban development.[190]

When comparing the populations of cities in China with those of other countries, one could use the populations of core cities which usually under-estimate the city populations since they exclude many of those living in suburban areas that are part of the city economy or the populations of city-regions which exaggerate their populations. In China, the process of annexation by large cities of surrounding areas tends to exaggerate the size of their populations and their relative importance. One extreme example is Chongqing that with annexed counties had some 12 million inhabitants by the mid-1980s, yet the urban agglomeration itself had less than 3 million inhabitants. Figures given for Shanghai's population have long been much larger than the population in the central urban agglomeration, although the rapid expansion of Shanghai's economy in recent years has lessened this difference. In China, there have been considerable incentives for local authorities to expand their boundaries since it offers them more direct control over rural resources.[191]

What is probably true for much of Asia is that the largest cities had slower rates of population growth during the 1980s than during the 1970s—although this is partly because as a city gets larger, it takes an ever increasing absolute increment in the population to maintain a city's growth rate. Thus, while most of the large cities in India had slower population growth rates during the 1980s, compared to the 1970s,[192] in fact most had larger

---

BOX 2.6
Shanghai

In 1949, Shanghai was the pre-eminent city with over half of China's modern industry. But after 1949, throughout the first phase of heavy industrialization, it was deprived of significant investment funds because of its location that was vulnerable to attack from the sea. Its population remained remarkably low, given that it had been the largest industrial centre in the world's most populous nation. In 1982, the city's urban core districts contained only 6.27 million inhabitants with the rest of its 11.8 million inhabitants distributed over what was then over 5000 square kilometres of mainly farming and small towns communities in neighbouring counties. It was not until the early 1980s that it was again given priority—

when it was designated one of the 14 'open cities' and with the establishment of the Shanghai Economic Zone in 1983—but it was still compared unfavourably with Guangzhou. In the early 1990s, a combination of strong local pressure and a concentration of ex-Shanghai leaders in the higher echelons of national politics led to a major programme of redevelopment, especially in its eastern hinterland—a large area of agricultural and marginal land generally referred to as Pudong (literally 'east of the Huangpu river'). Here, a new high technology metropolis is being developed, modelled on Singapore.

By 1992, greater Shanghai's population had risen to 12.87 million but the urban core districts now contained 7.86 million inhabitants. There was also a large floating population that was not included in this

figure—for instance in 1993, it had a registered temporary population of over 600,000. Migrants into Shanghai generally find employment in the suburban districts and the 6 counties annexed to the city and in almost every *zhen* and smaller town within Shanghai's orbit, there are established communities of migrants. Most are engaged in new small plants and off-farm enterprises.

Shanghai's official boundaries encompass more than 6,000 square kilometres and much of the remaining pockets of untouched farmland are being developed as housing estates, relocated factories and local enterprises, especially in ribbon developments along each highway. The development of rural industrialization in the city's attached counties has also introduced a new sense of urbanness into much of the peri-urban core.

Source: Kirkby, Richard, 'Country Report: China', Background Paper for the Global Report on Human Settlements, 1995.

annual increments in their population in the 1980s, compared to the 1970s.

Centralized deconcentration within urban systems?

There are too few detailed studies of changes in the spatial distribution of urban population within Asian nations to know whether urban populations are concentrating or deconcentrating within their urban system. In the largest and most populous countries, there are likely to be regions where there is increasing concentration of urban population in the major cities and also regions with increasing deconcentration—for instance, it would be surprising if all states in India and all

provinces in Indonesia were experiencing comparable trends in this. A detailed analysis of this has been undertaken in Japan[193] (see Box 2.7) which shows a continuous concentration of population in three metropolitan regions since 1945 and thus no 'counterurbanization' of the kind experienced in Europe during the 1970s—although as the Box notes, it may be that the trend to urban concentration in these three regions is ending. However, Japan's urban system is inevitably influenced by the role of Tokyo as one of the pre-eminent world cities—and it may be that an end to the urban concentration was delayed—or will continue to be delayed—by the expansion in economic activity within Tokyo.

In several of the large Asian countries, many

BOX 2.7
Urban concentration in Japan

Since 1945, the national population has been continuously concentrating in the three major metropolitan regions centred on Tokyo, Keihanshin (Kyoto-Osaka-Kobe) and Nagoya. By 1990, they contained half of the national population, compared to 38 per cent in 1950. As Table 2.20 shows, all three of these metropolitan regions had their most rapid population growth rates in the early 1960s and were growing relatively rapidly until 1975, after

which their population growth rate dropped considerably. It is also worth noting how the population growth in the other regions was very small or negative from 1955 to 1970 but more rapid for the 1970s and early 1980s, coming to almost equal that of the three major metropolitan regions in the later 1970s.

It may be that the long-term trend towards the increasing concentration of Japan's population in its three metropolitan regions—and especially that of Tokyo—has ended. Figure 2.3 shows the important changes in the number of net in-migrants to the three metropoli-

tan regions and 'other'. For Tokyo region, there was net in-migration for the whole period, except in early 1993 when the long term trend towards increasing concentration of the national population in Tokyo stopped. For the other two metropolitan regions, net in-migration continued until the early 1970s and then virtually stopped. For 'other regions', there was net out-migration until the mid 1970s when it stopped, then an increase in net out-migration, then a second halt in this in the early 1990s.

TABLE 2.20 Population growth in Japan's major metropolitan regions, 1955–89

Region	Population ('000s)		Compound Growth Rate (percentage)						
	Popn 1955	Popn 1990	55–59	60–64	65–69	70–74	75–79	80–84	85–89
3 Major Metro Regions	34,068	61,686	2.3	2.8	2.3	2.0	1.0	0.9	0.7
Tokyo Region	15,424	31,797	3.0	3.3	2.8	2.3	1.2	1.1	1.0
Nagoya Region	6,838	10,550	1.4	1.8	1.6	1.6	0.9	0.7	0.6
Keihanshin Region	11,805	19,340	2.0	2.5	2.1	1.7	0.7	0.6	0.4
Other regions	56,009	61,925	0.0	-0.2	0.0	0.8	0.8	0.5	0.1
National total	90,007	123,611	0.9	2.1	0.0	1.4	0.9	0.7	0.4

FIGURE 2.3
Changes in the number of net in-migrants for the three metropolitan regions and 'other'

Source: Yamada, Hiroyuki and Kazuyuki Tokuoka, 'The trends of the population and urbanization in Post-war Japan', Background Paper for the Global Report on Human Settlements, 1995. Figure 2.3 draws on the annual reports on internal migration in Japan.

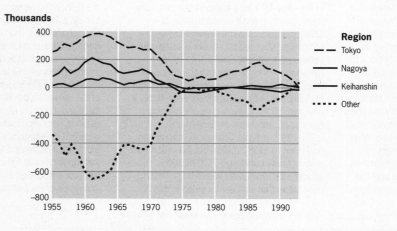

peripheral regions have urban populations that are growing well above the average for all urban centres. For instance in Indonesia, the provinces with the highest urban population growth rates during the 1980s were generally among the least populous and the top seven were all transmigration receiving provinces and all had annual average population growth rates of between 8.7 and 17.7 per cent a year.[194] In India, many of the states with the lowest per capita incomes and the lowest levels of urbanization had a more rapid growth in their urban population than wealthier, more urbanized states.[195] In China, the peripheral 'border region' had a more rapid increase in its population living in cities of 500,000 or more inhabitants than the much more developed and urbanized coastal and inland regions.[196]

Given the very rapid urban and industrial development in China since the early 1980s and the fact that so much of it is concentrated on the coast, this would be expected to show up in urban statistics. An analysis was made, comparing the growth in large city populations between 1981 and 1990 for the coastal region, the inland region and the border region—see Figure 2.4. However, the regional differences were not so dramatic. The growth in the aggregate population of the 46 cities that had more than 500,000 inhabitants in 1981 between 1981 and 1990 was 26 per cent for the coastal region, 24 per cent for the inland region and 15 per cent for the border region.[197] The difference between the coastal region and the inland region becomes greater—36 per cent compared to 31 per cent—if the inhabitants of outer suburban areas are added onto those of the core city populations.[198]

Metropolitan areas and extended metropolitan regions

Available data suggests a deconcentration of population within most of the large metropolitan centres with relatively slow population growth rates within the central city (or even population decline) and much higher population growth rates in the outer areas. For instance, the population within the metropolitan region of Jakarta appears to be deconcentrating quite rapidly. Central Jakarta had a relatively modest population growth rate during the 1980s—around 3.1 per cent a year—but the growth rates of the urban population in the three neighbouring districts that are part of 'Jakarta Greater Metropolitan Area' were 11.7, 20.9 and 19.8 per cent.[199] In the main cities within the more successful economies, there is also a major restructuring of central cities—as in office developments, convention centres, hotels and in the diverse range of service enterprises that develop to serve these and in the transport and communication facilities that have to be installed[200] and these will tend to expel population from central cities. As Chapter 7 will describe in more detail, millions of people are evicted from their homes each year to make way for new urban developments, and some of the largest evictions have taken place in the major cities of Asia.

In India, a process of urban and industrial dispersal can be seen within or around the largest metropolitan areas.[201] This can be seen first in the emergence of new towns and rapid growth of small towns within the metropolitan region and the slow population growth within the central city. In the 1991 census, there were 856 new urban centres i.e. settlements that met the criteria for being classified as urban centres—and most of the new urban centres in the more urbanized states were close to metropolitan cities and have strong links with them. Most of the new towns in the state of West Bengal are concentrated around Calcutta—that has long been India's largest city, although its population was surpassed by that of Bombay in the 1991 census. Other new urban centres have emerged around the other metropolitan cities of Bombay, Delhi, Madras, Bangalore, Ahmedabad, Hyderabad, Pune, Nagpur and Visakhapatnam.[202] The expanding physical area of major metropolitan centres such as Calcutta and Bombay has also absorbed what were previously physically separate urban centres.

There is also a tendency for the population in major cities to spread outwards even beyond the boundaries of metropolitan areas—and these are often referred to as Extended Metropolitan Regions.[203] The built-up area and labour market of cities such as Jakarta, Tokyo and Bangkok extend for great distances from their urban cores[204]—and this is often recognized by govern-

FIGURE 2.4
The coastal, inland and border regions of China

Source: Kirkby, Richard, 'Regional aspects of urban development during the post-Mao reform era', Background Paper for the United Nations Global Report on Human Settlements, 1995.

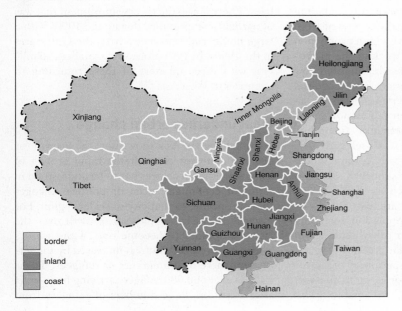

ments in defining new planning regions—for instance, in Thailand, the government has created an Extended Metropolitan region around Bangkok that stretches for some 100 kilometres from the central core.

It has also been suggested that extended metropolitan regions can be expanded to include corridors that run between them and thus to have interlocking extended metropolitan regions. This would apply to Tianjin and Beijing, Hong Kong and Guangzhou and Jakarta and Bandung and if these were defined as single metropolitan regions, it would bring considerable change to the list of the world's largest cities. There are similarities to the United States MSAs described in Section 2.2 although population densities in both the rural and the urban parts of these regions are typically much higher in Asia than in the United States.[205] However, a certain care is needed in defining such regions, if this is to establish a new base for comparing the population of city regions worldwide. For instance, new extended metropolitan regions could be defined in parts of Europe where major metropolitan areas are as close together as the cities noted above and these would increase the number of the world's largest cities from Europe.

There may be more diversity in this spatial reordering of population within metropolitan areas or extended metropolitan regions than the analyses to date have identified, in terms of the distance from the city centre of the areas with the most rapid population growth and in terms of their location—i.e. is there rapid population growth in virtually all peripheral areas or is it concentrated in certain peripheral areas or along particular transport axes?

There is also the difficulty of knowing where the metropolitan area or extended metropolitan region ends, both in terms of the urbanized area and in terms of the labour market (i.e. including settlements which are physically separated from the metropolitan area but have a high proportion of people who commute to work in the metropolitan area). T. G. McGee has highlighted how large areas of the countryside have acquired increasingly urban characteristics such as an increasing proportion of their population working in non-agricultural activities (including increased female participation in such activities) and a diverse mix of agriculture, cottage industries, industrial estates and suburban developments—but they are not part of any major city or metropolitan area.[206] They are also characterized by a fluid and mobile population, including those that commute to larger urban centres, but they are not simply suburban areas. These are often in areas adjacent to the periphery of metropolitan areas or other cities or along main roads that link cities that are reasonably close

together.[207] These are also areas where it is common for farmers and agricultural labourers to derive a significant part of their income from non-agricultural activities and for farm households to have household members working in non-agricultural activities.

There are also some interesting examples in Asia of urban agglomerations which cross national boundaries. For instance, Hong Kong can be regarded as the centre of the Hong Kong–Zhujiang Delta region, and also with the common pattern in large metropolitan areas of slow population growth in the central city (Hong Kong) with very rapid population growth in outer areas (Shenzen and Zhuhai).[208] A large proportion of Hong Kong's manufacturing production has been relocated in southern Guangdong and some three million workers in this part of China are employed in factories that were funded, designed and managed by Hong Kong entrepreneurs.[209]

Another example is the urban development around Singapore in Malaysia and Indonesia. In the late 1980s, Singapore sought to use its sophisticated financial, communications and management facilities to exploit relatively inexpensive labour and the rich land and other natural resources in the nearby industrial zones in the Johor state of Malaysia and Indonesia's Riau archipelago—notably Batam Island. There are good possibilities for this 'growth triangle' to be developed as a single investment area for industry and tourism.[210]

Another 'international' aspect of urbanization has been the large but fluctuating flows of foreign workers into the oil-producing countries in West Asia which obviously affects these nation's urban systems. But it has also had a considerable impact on the countries from where this emigration came as the emigrants channel back remittances to households and enterprises in their own countries. There is also the reverse movement that was of particular importance during the 1990s with a large number of 'returnees' from the Gulf states in the 1990s. In 1991 alone, they totalled 2.6 million with three quarters of these returning to countries in West Asia.[211]

What underlies urban change

Urban change in Asia shows how the growth (or decline) of major cities or the rapid growth of some small urban centres has to be understood in terms of economic, social or political changes that are specific to that city or wider region. For instance, Karachi's population growth over the last few decades to become one of the world's largest cities has been much increased by the settlement there of immigrants or refugees. These include over 600,000 refugees arriving from India after Partition, large numbers of refugees from

Bangladesh during the 1970s and large numbers of refugees from Afghanistan and Iran during the late 1970s and the 1980s.[212] An understanding of Karachi's economy also needs consideration of the role of remittances sent to families based there from Pakistani workers in the Middle East.[213] The very rapid growth of Dhaka in recent decades must also be understood in terms of its much expanded political role, first as part of East Pakistan, then as capital of Bangladesh—and more recently, linked to the rapid growth of garment industries there.

For Asia's largest cities, it is perhaps worth drawing distinctions between those where urban dynamics are strongly linked to the globalization of the world economy and those that are much more linked to political and economic functions of the nation-state. For instance, the size of Delhi and its rapid growth is far more linked to its role as capital of India than to its concentration of enterprises with roles within an increasingly globalized economy. By contrast, urban dynamics in Singapore and Hong Kong are much more shaped by their role within the global economic system than as political and administrative centres. Most of the other large cities in Asia come between these two extremes. For instance, Tokyo is the world's largest urban agglomeration because it is both the national capital of the world's second largest economy and one of the three pre-eminent global cities. It is also clear that Tokyo's role within the global economy has helped to counter a tendency towards decentralization out of the central city and during the 1980s, many enterprises opened their new offices in central Tokyo or moved their head offices to Tokyo. In addition, the deregulation and internationalization of Japanese financial markets helped to create a concentration of many profitable service activities in Tokyo.[214] For the cities that are strongly linked into the world economy, it is also worth stressing the distinction between those that serve as centres of production for the world market or those that are centres for international tourism—and those that are important 'command and control' centres and thus considered 'world cities'. It is to these latter cities that banks and other financial services, media and the regional headquarters of multinational companies are attracted and they in turn stimulate and support a large range of producer service enterprises while their employees also generate demand for consumer services.

The increasing importance of Asia within the world economy and of its 'world cities' was illustrated by a study of the locational behaviour and spatial organization of some major electronics firms between 1975 and 1991. Nine leading Japanese electronics firms expanded production much more rapidly outside Japan than inside,

especially in East Asia—but with research and development facilities continuing to concentrate in metropolitan areas such as Tokyo and Osaka.[215]

Urban trends in all Asian nations are also influenced by government actions and structures. Perhaps the most notable change during the 1980s was the relaxing or removal of government controls on urban growth in various countries and the scaling down or removal of special programmes encouraging or directing new investment to peripheral regions. The most dramatic change was in China where there was rapid rural to urban migration during the 1980s and the 1990s. This was made possible by changes in the household registration system that during the 1960s and 1970s had controlled rural to urban migration and by the growing private food and housing markets and employment opportunities that allowed people to find a livelihood and basic necessities outside of the official system; in 1994, the government announced the imminent demise of the household registration system.[216]

The spatial distribution of urban development in many other Asian countries is also likely to change, as their macro-economic policy orientation has changed. For instance, the size and spatial distribution of large cities in India has also been considerably influenced by government priorities to import substitution and heavy industry from the 1950s—and the new priority to export promotion and a lessening of protective barriers will favour different locations to those favoured under the previous policy. In Japan, the slowing in the concentration of population in the three main metropolitan regions during the 1970s was certainly helped by public investment—particularly by the fact that investment in transport facilities was relatively concentrated in non-metro regions—and public policies that restricted the building of such facilities as large factories in the major metropolitan areas and promoted their moving to the other regions. However, it was also helped by a buoyant economy and by structural changes that encouraged many activities to locate outside the three main metropolitan regions.

Small and intermediate urban centres

A very considerable proportion of Asia's urban population lives outside large cities. For instance, in India, despite the prominence given to its largest cities such as Bombay, Calcutta and Delhi in any discussion of its urban trends—or in general to its 23 'million-cities'—in 1991, there were still as many people living in urban centres with less than 100,000 inhabitants as living in 'million-cities'—although the proportion living in 'million-cities' is growing while that in urban centres with under 100,000 is decreasing.[217]

The economic and urban transformation of many cities in Asia noted above has also been matched by a less visible but perhaps as important transformation in many smaller urban centres and in particular rural areas. For instance, in China, there has also been a rapid transformation in the rural and 'township' economy:

The 1980s was a period of unprecedented transfer of China's farm population away from traditional agricultural pursuits. The proliferation of the rural enterprise sector (owned collectively at township and village levels and after 1984 complemented by millions of small privately run operations) has been the cornerstone of an urbanization policy emphasising small and intermediate settlements.[218]

Between 1983 and 1986, the number of rural enterprises increased by a factor of ten; some 90 per cent were privately owned. By 1988, the rural enterprise sector employed 95 million people, almost a quarter of the official rural workforce. In many industrial sectors such as building materials and garments, rural industries it now accounts for over half of national output. By 1987, the total value of rural enterprises's output had exceeded that of the agricultural sector[219] and by the end of the 1980s rural enterprises provided up to a quarter of China's export earnings.[220] This growth has helped to absorb the surplus rural labour that lost its means of livelihood with the abolition of collective agriculture. It also had the great advantage of being largely self-financing and of making only modest calls on the higher levels of government for infrastructural investment. The growth of the small-town economies was also a stimulus for agriculture.

But there are also thousands of small and intermediate size urban centres in Asia that do not have dynamic economies. Many became urban centres because they are a minor administrative centre or a market and centre of a local or regional road network.

2.7 Africa[221]

Introduction

Describing population and urban change in Africa over the last 10–15 years is particularly problematic because of large gaps in basic demographic data. Africa has certainly had among the most rapid population growth and urban change of any of the world's regions in recent decades yet for almost half of its nations, there is no census data available since the early 1980s.[222] For many nations, all figures for national, regional and city populations are estimates or projections based on census data from the 1970s or early 1980s so it is impossible to describe changes in national and urban populations. There are also many countries where war or civil strife make any estimates for city or regional populations questionable— for instance in Somalia, Rwanda, Burundi and Liberia. Map 2.6 shows the largest urban centres in Africa in 1990.

In the absence of census data, one becomes more reliant on studies of particular settlements or city neighbourhoods or sectors that give an insight into the scale and nature of change although it is never possible to know how representative this change is of other settlements or city neighbourhoods.

Demographic change

Most of the nations with the fastest growing populations are now in Africa, although this is a relatively recent phenomenon. It was only in the first half of the 1970s that the region's population came to grow more rapidly than that of Latin America and the Caribbean.[223] Table 2.21 shows how many countries had populations that grew more than threefold between 1950 and 1990—although some caution is needed in reading the statistics in this Table as many of the population figures for 1990 are based on estimates or projections.

Table 2.22 shows why the 1980s has been termed the 'lost decade' not only for Latin America but also for Africa. The table includes all countries with 5 or more million inhabitants in

MAP 2.6
The largest urban centres in Africa in 1990

Source and notes: This map shows all urban centres which were recorded as having 750,000 or more inhabitants in 1990 in United Nations, *World Urbanization Prospects: The 1994 Revision*, Population Division, Department of Economic and Social Information and Policy Analysis, New York, 1995 with additional cities added or cities reclassified where more recent census data were available.

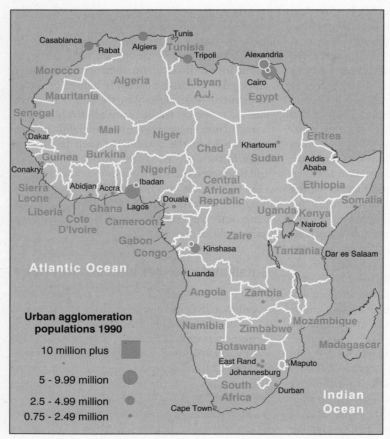

Urban agglomeration populations 1990

10 million plus
5 - 9.99 million
2.5 - 4.99 million
0.75 - 2.49 million

TABLE 2.21 Population and urban change in African countries with 1 million or more inhabitants in 1990, between 1950 and 1990

Country	Population 1990 (000s)	Popn 1990/ popn 1950	Urban popn 1990 (000s)	% of popn in urban areas (level of urbanization)	
				1950	1990
Eastern Africa					
Burundi	5,503	2.2	345	1.7	6.3
Eritrea	3,082	2.7	487	5.9	15.8
Ethiopia	47,423	2.6	5,815	4.6	12.3
Kenya	23,612	3.8	5,565	5.6	23.6
Madagascar	12,571	3.0	2,993	7.8	23.8
Malawi	9,367	3.3	1,106	3.5	11.8
Mauritius	1,057	2.1	428	28.8	40.5
Mozambique	14,187	2.3	3,795	2.4	26.8
Rwanda	6,986	3.3	391	1.8	5.6
Somalia	8,677	2.8	2,101	12.7	24.2
Uganda	17,949	3.8	2,003	3.1	11.2
United Rep. of Tanzania	25,600	3.2	5,325	3.8	20.8
Zambia	8,150	3.3	3,422	8.9	42.0
Zimbabwe	9,903	3.6	2,826	10.6	28.5
Middle Africa					
Angola	9,194	2.2	2,602	7.6	28.3
Cameroon	11,526	2.6	4,643	9.8	40.3
Central African Rep.	2,927	2.2	1,097	16.0	37.5
Chad	5,553	2.1	1,138	3.9	20.5
Congo	2,232	2.8	1,194	30.9	53.5
Gabon	1,146	2.4	523	11.4	45.7
Zaire	37,436	3.1	10,506	19.1	28.1
Northern Africa					
Algeria	24,935	2.8	12,899	22.3	51.7
Egypt	56,312	2.6	24,743	31.9	43.9
Libyan Arab Jamahiriya	4,545	4.4	3,744	18.6	82.4
Morocco	24,334	2.7	11,217	26.2	46.1
Sudan	24,585	2.7	5,544	6.3	22.5
Tunisia	8,080	2.3	4,438	31.2	54.9
Southern Africa					
Botswana	1,276	3.3	295	0.3	23.1
Lesotho	1,792	2.4	348	1.0	19.4
Namibia	1,349	2.6	430	9.4	31.9
South Africa	37,066	2.7	18,240	43.1	49.2
Western Africa					
Benin	4,633	2.3	1,345	5.3	29.0
Burkina Faso	8,987	2.5	1,605	3.8	17.9
Cote D'Ivoire	11,974	4.3	4,841	13.2	40.4
Ghana	15,020	3.1	5,107	14.5	34.0
Guinea	5,755	2.3	1,484	5.5	25.8
Liberia	2,575	3.1	1,084	13.0	42.1
Mali	9,212	2.6	2,193	8.5	23.8
Mauritania	2,003	2.4	937	2.3	46.8
Niger	7,731	3.2	1,177	4.9	15.2
Nigeria	96,154	2.9	33,808	10.1	35.2
Senegal	7,327	2.9	2,919	30.5	39.8
Sierra Leone	3,999	2.1	1,287	9.2	32.2
Togo	3,531	2.7	1,005	7.2	28.5

Source: United Nations, *World Urbanization Prospects: The 1994 Revision*, Population Division, New York, 1995.

1990—and Botswana and Mauritius are also included, because these were the exceptions in achieving high growth rates in per capita income during the period 1980–92. In Eastern and Middle Africa, for the eleven countries for which there is data, seven had declines in per capita income in this period with no growth in Tanzania and very small growth in Kenya. Western Africa presents a similar picture.

Although very few African countries had rapid and sustained economic growth prior to 1980, half the nations listed had per capita GNP that grew on average by 1.4 or more per cent between 1960 and 1980. Taking the whole period 1960 to 1992, Mauritius and Botswana were the only nations with spectacular economic growth, although all of the Northern African nations listed above except for the Sudan were substantially wealthier per person in 1992 compared to 1960. But per capita income in several nations such as Mozambique, Madagascar, Ghana and Niger was actually less in 1992 than in 1960. According to other sources,

TABLE 2.22 Per capita GNP 1992 and annual average changes in per capita GNP 1980–1992 and 1960–1980 for African countries with 5 million or more inhabitants in 1990 and for Mauritius and Botswana

Country	GNP per capita		
	US dollars (1992)	Average annual growth rate (%)	
		1980–92	1960–80
Eastern Africa			
Burundi	210	1.3	2.5
Ethiopia	110	−1.9	1.4
Kenya	310	0.2	2.7
Madagascar	230	−2.4	−0.5
Malawi	210	−0.1	2.9
Mauritius	2,700	5.6	2.3
Mozambique	60	−3.6	−0.1
Rwanda	250	−0.6	1.5
Somalia			
Tanzania, United Republic of	110	0.0	1.9
Uganda	170		−0.7
Zambia			0.2
Zimbabwe	570	−0.9	0.7
Middle Africa			
Angola			−2.3
Cameroon	820	−1.5	2.6
Chad	220		−1.8
Zaire			0.2
Northern Africa			
Algeria	1,840	−0.5	
Egypt	640	1.8	
Morocco	1,030	1.4	2.5
Sudan			−0.2
Tunisia	1,720		1.3
Southern Africa			
Botswana	2,790	6.1	9.2
South Africa	2,670	0.1	4.8
Western Africa			
Burkina Faso	300	1.0	0.1
Cote D'Ivoire	670	−4.7	2.5
Ghana	450	0.1	−1.0
Guinea	510		0.3
Mali	310	−2.7	1.4
Mauritania		1.6	
Niger	280	−4.3	−1.6
Nigeria	320	−0.4	4.1
Senegal	780	0.1	−0.3

Source: Drawn from World Development Indicators in the 1994, 1984 and 1982 *World Development Report*, Oxford University Press. Botswana and Mauritius are included to highlight their rapid economic growth during the 1980s.

this was also true for Somalia, Zambia, Mali and for some of the small population African nations not included in the above table such as Central African Republic and Liberia.[224]

African cities in the 1990s

Looking back over the period from the early 1960s, when most African countries obtained formal independence, to the mid-1990s, African cities have changed in at least four major ways: their size, their spatial organization or morphology, the quality and distribution of public services and infrastructure, and their employment base.

Size is the most obvious difference, since the population of most African cities have grown severalfold over the last few decades; some have grown more than tenfold during this period. Exact comparisons over the same time period are difficult to obtain because of differing intercensal periods; and for many countries whose recent censuses were in the late 1980s or early 1990s, the final results are still not available. Nevertheless, two clear trends are visible. First, the largest cities have continued to grow in population, although by the 1980s and 1990s their rates of growth have declined in comparison to the spectacular rates of growth during the 1960s and 1970s. And whereas the main component of the growth of the largest cities was rural–urban migration in the earlier post-independence period, natural increase is now the major element. Second, in many countries, many or most medium-sized cities have been growing more quickly than the largest cities. This may very well be partly a result of the more difficult economic situation facing urban dwellers as a whole during the last decade and a half; but it may also be reinforced by the steadily deteriorating condition of infrastructure and public services in the largest cities. These factors, in turn, reflect the determination of many African countries to favour smaller cities in investment and planning decisions, however much the implementation of these policies of spatial decentralization fall short of their original goals.

The deterioration of services and infrastructure is another common trend of the 1990s. This is to some extent an inevitable result of the fact that, as national (and urban) economies stagnate in absolute terms, at the same time as urban populations across the continent continue to grow (the United Nations estimates that for the whole region the growth rate is approximately 4.5 per cent per year)[225] the resources necessary for roads, sewers, water systems, schools and hospitals simply cannot keep up with the needs of the population. While there is a clear differentiation between the living conditions of the (relatively) small groups of upper-level managers, foreign diplomats, senior politicians and successful businessmen on the one hand, and the growing numbers of lower-income urban dwellers on the other hand, there is also a general deterioration in the public services and infrastructure available to everybody.

Changes in the labour market have been very dramatic since the 1960s. In the decade following independence, the educational system was expanding at every level, and African graduates had little difficulty finding good jobs in either the public service (and its parastatal arms) or the large-scale private sector. Now, the public service is contracting everywhere, parastatals are being disbanded or privatized to cut back on the numbers of employees they support, and even university-educated professionals have great difficulty in finding secure employment, if in fact they obtain suitable employment at all. Partly as a counterpart to the decline in well-paid, secure employment, more and more urban residents have found work in the burgeoning 'informal', or small-scale, unregulated sector where a bewildering variety of activities have developed to respond to the needs and financial capacity of the poor. These developments are reflected in the continued growth of spontaneous, popular housing areas; in the ever increasing numbers of ambulant hawkers and food-sellers on every corner of many downtown African cities; in the increase in the size and number of open-air markets; in the pervasiveness of small-scale, privately owned public-transport vehicles that have taken over the market from the monopoly state-regulated bus companies; and in a virtual explosion of small trades and services dealing with almost every facet of life in the city. From an overly regulated city which reflected the needs of the erstwhile colonial powers to control African urban life in every possible way, we are witnessing the birth of a new city form which reflects the new African reality. What could be called the 'self-help city' in the 1970s, might very well be called the 'informal city' in the 1990s.

All these changes have had a major effect on city form. Where once the central business district, with its clean, wide streets and high-quality shops and offices was the focus of urban life—in both the large capital cities and in secondary cities as well—the centre of gravity has shifted. Not only are central business districts more poorly maintained and more populated with small-scale hawkers and vendors than in the past, but more and more of the population is moving to the periphery of the larger cities, where land is cheaper and much more easily accessible, where shelter can be constructed economically using locally available materials, and where harassment from the police and restrictions of the formal planning system are rarely felt. This horizontal expansion of the African city into its rural hinterland not only attenuates major infrastructural elements such as piped water, electricity, sewerage and roads to a point where their efficacy is greatly reduced; but it also adds considerably to the costs of such services as education, health and social assistance. As these peripheral settlements expand, and the public resources to service them continue to contract, a new approach to the planning and management of African cities will have to emerge if they are going to survive as viable social and productive entities in the twenty-first century.

However, there were certain cities that fared better—especially in North Africa. For instance, the city of Tunis in Tunisia presents a different picture, especially in the city centre and the area around the international airport which has been transformed by national and international business corporations and international tourism.[226] Although Tunis also has serious housing and other urban problems,[227] these are not of the same scale and nature as those of most cities in sub-Saharan Africa.

Urban change

An understanding of urban change in the last 10–15 years requires some consideration of the colonial experience, since it is only three decades or so since most countries in the region achieved political independence. Although urban centres and urban civilizations had grown and flourished in many parts of Africa prior to colonial rule,[228] it was largely under colonial rule that the major cities and the urban systems that exist today were defined. In addition, it was the institutional structure left by colonial rule and initially little modified by newly independent governments that has proved so ineffective in managing urban change.

This was the case for three main reasons. In the first place, a great number of cities which became important during the colonial and post-colonial periods simply had not existed before colonial rule. Nairobi (now the capital of Kenya) was established on an open plain in 1899, in order to facilitate the building of the railway which was to run from Mombasa on the East African coast to Kampala in Uganda. Harare, the capital of Zimbabwe was originally built and administered by the British South Africa Company, beginning in 1890 when the Union Jack was first raised on the previously uninhabited site of (what was then) Fort Salisbury.[229] Abidjan, now the largest city in Côte d'Ivoire, was at best a small lagoon village before being chosen by a certain French Captain in 1891 as the terminus for a railway line which would link the Atlantic Coast with the vast Niger hinterland being developed by French military and commercial interests.[230] Finally, Johannesburg was established in the year 1886 on the site of a digger's village being developed on unclaimed farmland, in the immediate vicinity of a major gold mining complex.[231] All these new towns—and many others, such as Cotonou, Libreville, and Bangui (as capital cities); and large provincial towns such as Bouaké, Tamale, Enugu, Lubumbashi and Mwanza—developed as major centres of commerce and of administrative activity. Because their major purpose was to strengthen the ties between the metropolitan country and the colonial territory, they were often located on or near the coast or a major waterway. A new colonial urban system began to emerge, displacing internal networks of trade and influence which had developed over many centuries.

A second major urban effect of colonialism in Africa was the establishment of powerful currents of rural–urban migration. Although African populations had been moving around the continent for centuries in response to commercial opportunities, variations in environmental conditions, political upheavals, and the depredations resulting from the slave trade, colonial regimes and the economic activities which they promoted raised the level of migratory activity to a much higher level. As a cash economy was introduced, and goods and services could be obtained in exchange for wages, there were incentives for African labourers to migrate to work on mines, plantations, and urban employment. Most migration was rural–rural, but perhaps one-quarter of all migrants went to the towns.

By the mid-1950s, the 'winds of change' which nationalist movements brought to the African continent, combined with an increasing concern with African labour efficiency, led to a reassessment of the African role in towns—at least in the regions of eastern, central and southern Africa, where government control over African urban integration was the most marked. One of the main reasons for increasing administrative and political concern, near the end of the colonial period, was the very rapid increase in the population of many cities, largely the result of rapid in-migration. Annual average population growth rates of 5 to 7 per cent a year were common among the major cities in the 1950s and 1960s while some maintained even more rapid population growth rates for short periods. In general, these growth rates varied according to local political and economic circumstances. For example, most African cities grew quickly during the 1920s, slowed down during the 1930s, began to grow again during and after the Second World War, and slowed again during what were often political uncertainties during the 1950s. With Independence, they began to grow rapidly, a pattern which continued through to the 1980s.

The third major effect of colonial urbanization was the physical structure of cities that was bequeathed to the African governments that took over power from the late 1950s (for Ghana, Egypt, Tunisia and Morocco), through the 1960s (for almost all the rest of the Anglophone and Francophone countries) through to the 1980s. Looking at the totality of Francophone cities in thirteen West African countries at the end of the 1980s, a major study argues that

today's African cities were, for the most part, established by colonizers who applied urban planning principles appropriate to their country of origin. The most striking aspect of colonial urban planning is the partition of urban space into two zones, the 'European' city and the 'indigenous' city.[232]

The limited impact of conventional responses

After Independence, many African countries sought to respond to this colonial urban contradiction by major exercises in 'master planning', and by large-scale government-sponsored construction of residential dwellings. Neither proved adequate to the problems of urban management. For urban planning, typically, a major expatriate planning firm would produce a master plan for the future development of the capital city. The plan would contain an analysis of urban form and function, some analysis of likely future growth patterns, and a number of technical maps and plans such as a detailed land-use zoning map, plans for infrastructural development, and some proposals about procedures, regulations and even institutional reforms necessary to carry out the plan. These plans were the direct descendants of numerous plans produced during the colonial period, although successive documents tended to include more and more data of a sociological and economic nature. The city of Abidjan in Côte d'Ivoire had six major planning documents from 1928 to 1990; Dar es Salaam had three plans from 1949 to 1977; Nairobi had three from 1948 to the mid-1980s. While these plans often had an important influence on the overall approach to land-use planning in the central areas of the larger African cities, they failed to capture the speed and direction of growth in the peripheral areas, and in any case were almost never supported by the level of capital expenditure necessary to implement their infrastructural projections.

In the absence of major capital projects developed within the master plan framework, most urban planning decisions took place within the parameters of building and development regulations that were little more than copies of the existing legislation and bylaws in Britain, France and Portugal.[233] These usually ascribed a large and complex role in land-use management and other aspects of urban management to the public sector. Such European influence on African urban planning was reinforced by the fact that not only were virtually all urban planners working in Africa European in origin until at least the mid-1960s, but there were no schools of architecture or urban planning located on African soil (outside of South Africa) until the first decade after independence. Until at least the mid-1960s, virtually all the directors of urban planning in African countries were of European origin. Urban planning legislation was supplemented by building codes which, in many cases, were also very closely modelled on European regulations.

Within the terms of reference of the urban planners, but with a dynamic and importance of their own, were policies for the development of residential housing. Two of the hallmarks of the colonial approach to African urban housing in the 1950s were the redevelopment of decaying 'core' areas combined with the removal of 'slums' or squatter areas; and the construction of large rental (sometimes tenant-purchase) public housing estates. Once independence was accomplished, these policies were pursued by the successor governments. For instance, large scale 'slum clearance' programmes were implemented in many cities—including Dar es Salaam,[234] Nairobi,[235] Dakar,[236] Lomé,[237] and Abidjan.[238] And while in some instances, public housing was built for at least a proportion of those whose houses were destroyed, most of the displaced could not find alternative housing nearby to the areas where they had previously lived.

The public housing programmes were also rooted in colonial precedents. During the colonial period, large estate housing projects were undertaken in such countries as Southern Rhodesia (now Zimbabwe), Kenya, Senegal and the Ivory Coast, where the government (and parastatal agencies such as the railways and port authorities) needed to house their employees. After independence, this state-centred approach to housing developed more widely, with many countries establishing national housing agencies with an important mandate to improve housing for Africans. Behind this drive was the feeling of many urban Africans that their housing conditions should be upgraded in line with their changed political status.

However, very few of the public housing agencies produced enough housing units to make much impression on improving housing and living conditions and many of the units they produced went to middle or upper income groups. There were some exceptions—for instance the large construction programme in the Côte d'Ivoire of SICOGI (*Société Ivoirienne de Construction et de Gestion Immobilière*) and SOGE-

FIHA (*Société de Gestion Financière de l'Habitat*) and the very large land development programme within Abidjan undertaken by SETU (*Société d'Equipement du Terrain Urbain*). But the role of public agencies in supplying urban housing in Côte d'Ivoire was also drastically curtailed in the 1980s.

As public housing programmes remained relatively small and usually used up most of the government resources devoted to housing and as official norms, codes and standards made the cheapest 'legal' housing too expensive for most city households, so an increasing proportion of city inhabitants came to live in illegal or informal settlements. While there are many definitions of this type of housing, and many local variations around the main tendency, the central defining elements are usually twofold: (1) the housing in question is either illegally built (i.e. without formal permission from the authorities) or (and in many cases in addition) it sits on land which has not been properly purchased through the formal system and zoned for residential development; and (2) few, if any services—such as water, roads, sewerage and stormwater drainage, electricity, telephones, and community facilities (such as clinics and schools)—are built in the immediate neighbourhood. In general, there is a relationship between the formal illegality of a settlement and the quality of the housing stock within it, since owners (who are often landlords) will not invest in high quality building materials or in improvements if they cannot borrow against the property, or if there is a chance their dwelling will be demolished by the authorities. Thus, the more precarious a location from a legal point of view, normally the lower the quality of the dwellings within it. This general rule is modified in the case of neighbourhoods which, for political or other reasons, are relatively secure even if they are not legally sanctioned in a formal sense.

An urban crisis?

During the 1980s, the increase in the level of spontaneous, or informal housing in and around African cities reflected the almost total inability of most national or city authorities to provide adequate serviced land and infrastructure to their growing populations. The 1980s and early 1990s thus became, in common parlance, a period of 'urban crisis' across the continent. The crisis—which itself was a reflection of declining or stagnating economies in the face of continuous rural–urban migration—had three major components: a decline in levels of formal employment, and a corresponding rapid increase in 'informal sector' activities in many key areas of the urban economy; a deterioration in both the quality and distribution of basic services; and a decline in the quality of the urban environment, both built and natural. All these changes adversely affected the quality of urban life for everyone, but particularly for low income groups.

Employment

In the years immediately following independence in most African countries, Africanization of the public service and an expansion of parastatal agencies led to a high rate of new employment creation in urban areas, particularly in the capital cities and large regional centres. By the 1970s, these increases were paralleled by increases in both the quantity of manufacturing jobs available (most of them in the largest towns), and in average manufacturing wages. At the same time, agricultural wage employment fell, or stagnated in many countries, thus increasing the attractiveness of the larger towns to rural migrants who could not gain sufficient incomes by working in subsistence agriculture. As research has pointed out, those most likely to migrate from rural to urban areas were more educated than their non-migrating peers; more of them also tend to be male, young, and single.[239] Their numbers were increased after independence by a rapid expansion in primary and secondary schools in both rural and urban areas. But by the late 1960s and early 1970s, it became clear that the rate of rural–urban migration was greatly exceeding the rate of formal employment creation in Africa's cities. Total numbers of jobs created in the formal sectors (including government, the parastatal sector, manufacturing and the large-scale service sectors such as banking and tourism) were not keeping pace with the increase in the urban population, whether this was caused by rural–urban migration or by natural increase.

Figures on manufacturing employment in medium- and large-size establishments show the changes over time in one of the most important parts of the urban formal sector. In most countries, there was rapid growth in formal manufacturing employment between 1970 and 1975, followed by slower growth during 1975–80. With sharply increased oil prices after 1973, increasing foreign exchange needed to be allocated to oil (except in the few African countries which were net exporters of petroleum products), and lesser amounts were available for capital goods and the other intermediate inputs necessary for maintaining (let alone expanding) the manufacturing base. While the period from 1980 to 1985 (which included the second oil shock) saw renewed or accelerated manufacturing employment growth in some countries, others—particularly those with large manufacturing sectors such as Côte d'Ivoire, Ghana and Nigeria—reported negative employment growth rates, while such countries as Kenya, Senegal and Zambia had annual increases during this period of only 4, 3 and 1 per cent, respectively.[240]

African countries cannot afford to maintain publicly funded social security systems such as social assistance or unemployment insurance programmes that operate in most countries of Europe and North America. Thus, individuals in the labour force who cannot obtain well-paid, formal sector urban employment have a number of options. If they are migrants, they can return to rural areas to engage in subsistence agriculture (for refugees, or those who do not have access to land, this is not possible). Or they can attempt to obtain support from family members or friends living in the town; or they can engage themselves in small-scale, "informal" income earning activities in the town. For most Africans seeking urban employment, remaining in "open unemployment" is not a realistic option as few can afford to wait. As formal urban employment opportunities declined, the alternative of engaging in small-scale, less remunerative activities—now known collectively as the "informal sector"—became increasingly common. While there are differences of opinion over the use of this term,[241] it is used by many economists and other social scientists, and may be statistically delineated. Despite difficulties with certain aspects of the term, largely as a result of the fact that it represents a very diverse set of activities, an important recent study argues that:

the African informal sector can be fairly carefully defined. In the last twenty years, urban small-scale, artisanal, residual/casual, and home production have expanded considerably in African nations. Their relative importance varies considerably across countries, in accordance with economic structure and public policy. Nonetheless, the main informal activities include carpentry and furniture production, tailoring, trade, vehicle and other repairs, metal goods' fabrication, restaurants, construction, transport, textiles and apparel manufacturing, footwear, and miscellaneous services.[242]

Typically, enterprises with ten or more workers tend to function within the formal sector, while smaller enterprises (down to a single person) tend to function more informally. In any case, beginning in the 1970s, and gaining strength during the economic downturn of the 1980s and early 1990s, the urban informal sector has become a powerful force for employment creation in virtually all African cities.

Estimates made in the mid 1970s suggested that in the typical African country the informal sector employs 60 per cent of the urban labour force." The estimates for urban areas within individual countries were as follows: the Congo, 55%; Senegal, 50%; Upper Volta (now Burkina Faso) 73%; Benin, 95%; and Niger, 65%. For individual cities, the figures were also high: Abidjan, 44%; Nairobi, 44%; Kumasi, 65%; Lagos, 50%; Banjul (The Gambia) 42%; Lomé 50%; Brazzaville, 37%; and Djibouti 20%.[243]

Although good statistics are not available for the 1980s and 1990s, the proportion of the urban labour force in informal activities has almost certainly risen. A leading Ivoirian sociologist estimated that, between 1976 to 1985, the number of people "working on the street" in a variety of informal activities had risen from 25,000 to 53,850 in Abidjan alone. During the same period, the central government complement in Abidjan rose from 31,840 to 56,940. "Given the negligible difference between the two", he argues, "one could conclude that the street offers as much employment and provides a living to as many people as the public service."[244] One of the trends of the 1980s and 1990s has been the supplementation by informal activities of formal-sector jobs on the part of a large proportion of public-sector employees. Although many informal-sector workers are poor, this is by no means always the case as such activities as market trading, the operation of public-transport vehicles, or the renting out of housing in informal neighbourhoods may involve considerable income. Nevertheless, in general there is a marked gap between formal and informal wages.

The growth of the urban informal sector, reinforced by economic stagnation during the 1980s and concomitant structural adjustment programmes which had the effect of reducing employment in the formal public sector, has had a number of visible effects on African cities. As noted earlier, the areas of informal housing increased, most of them on the outskirts of cities, adding considerably to the horizontal growth of urban areas and spreading existing services and infrastructure even more thinly on the ground. A second consequence is the growth of large open-air (often informal) markets throughout cities, with a consequent decline in formal retail trade, even in main downtown areas. Around these markets are thousands of unregulated petty traders, who often occupy adjacent streets and sell goods and produce on the sidewalk in front of the established (and licensed) retail stores. A third area in which informal activity plays an important role is mass transit, with more and more private buses and vans operating throughout African cities. These vehicles often serve areas of the city—such as the peripheral extensions—that are not well served by the public transport system. Finally, rather substantial areas of African cities have developed into specialized quarters for informal activities, although there is also considerable dispersion of individual informal trades. The increasing physical presence of informal activities in African cities is having a major effect on the organization of space, as African cities distance themselves from their original colonial planning models.

Deterioration in services

As African cities continued to increase in size during the 1980s and 1990s, their declining economic situation led to a precipitous decline in the supply of basic infrastructure and urban services. In many African cities, most refuse is uncollected and piles of decaying waste are allowed to rot in streets and vacant lots. Schools are becoming so overcrowded that many students have only minimal contact with their teachers. A declining proportion of urban roads are tarmacked and drained, and many that are not, turn into virtual quagmires during the rainy season. Basic drugs—once given out freely—have disappeared from public clinics and professional medical care is extremely difficult to obtain, except for the rich. Public transport systems are seriously overburdened; and more and more people are obliged to live in unserviced plots in 'informal' housing, where clean drinking water must be directly purchased from water sellers at a prohibitive cost, and where telephones and electrical connections are scarcely available.

The lack of investment in urban infrastructure and services also inhibited economic expansion. This was demonstrated in a study of Lagos that found that

unreliable infrastructure services impose heavy costs on manufacturing enterprises. Virtually every manufacturing firm in Lagos has its own electric power generator to cope with the unreliable public power supply. These firms invest 10 to 35 percent of their capital in power generation alone and incur additional capital and operating expenses to substitute for other unreliable public services. The burden of investment in power generation, boreholes, vehicles, and radio equipment in lieu of working telephones is disproportionately higher for small firms. In Nigeria and many other low-income countries, manufacturers' high costs of operation prevent innovation and adoption of new technology and make it difficult for them to compete in international markets.[245]

Studies in other cities also show serious declines in public investment in infrastructure and services. For instance, in Togo, a study of urban investment levels in the four 5-year plans spanning the period from 1966 to 1985 shows a steady reduction from 17.9 per cent of total investment in the first plan, to 16.7 per cent in the second plan, to 10.6 per cent in the third plan and 6 per cent in the fourth plan.[246] This pattern, which appears to reflect a similar tendency in other French-speaking countries, may be connected to a decline in French overseas aid funds, both in absolute and relative magnitudes during

the same period.[247] In Dar es Salaam, there was a decline in expenditure on services and infrastructure of 8.5 per cent a year from 1978/9 through 1986/7, measured in constant currency units.[248] If Dar es Salaam's population growth is taken into account, the per capita decline in expenditures comes to 11 per cent per year over the period studied. While the Tanzanian economy as a whole was stagnating during much of this period, the decline of the urban infrastructural fabric was occurring at a much more rapid rate. To the north, Nairobi's services have also been deteriorating along with its revenue base. The capital expenditures of the Nairobi City Commission (in real US dollars per capita) for water and sewerage fell from $27.78 in 1981 to $2.47 in 1987; and per capita maintenance expenditures fell from $7.29 to $2.30 over the same period when calculated in a similar manner. Over a 6-year period, this represents an average annual decrease of approximately 28 per cent, compounded, when both capital and maintenance expenditures are added together. Similar calculations for expenditures on public works over the same period show an annual decrease of 19.5 per cent, compounded; and for social services an annual decrease of 20 per cent, compounded.[249] Such figures suggest an alarming decrease in the ability of a modern African city to service the needs of its population.

Two major urban services that have become increasingly overburdened in almost all African countries are waste management and public transport. For instance, in Nairobi, as the city grew both in population and spatially at a rate close to 5 per cent per year, the resources available to the municipal government to maintain its existing fleet of refuse removal vehicles—let alone to permit it to purchase additional vehicles—were severely limited. In 1989, officials felt 100 refuse collection trucks were needed to effectively serve the city of over a million people but only 10 trucks were functioning on a daily basis out of a total fleet of only 40 vehicles.[250] The number of functioning, operational vehicles fell steadily during the 1980s from a high of 86 in 1978.[251] In Dar es Salaam, a study of the city's garbage collection vehicles showed that in 1985, some 20 functioning trucks (of which only 6 were considered to be 'in good condition') were able to collect only about 22 per cent of the estimated 1,200 tonnes of garbage produced every day. The situation was remedied somewhat with the donation of a number of vehicles by the Japanese government, but a study in 1988 showed that with 33 functioning trucks now on the road, the city council was only able to increase its waste removal efficiency to 28 per cent of the estimated total of refuse produced daily.[252] While the proportion of wastes collected varies across the continent, it remains a severe problem in almost all countries.

Just as the urban poor, who tend increasingly to live in peripheral, unplanned settlements are only sporadically served by such services as water supply, refuse removal and electricity supply, their marginal location and low disposable incomes makes them more vulnerable to difficulties in public transport supply. The situation in most African cities in the 1960s and 1970s was one of monopoly supply, whereby a public (or publicly contracted) bus company organized the mass transport system throughout the whole of the municipality. Some of these companies were very large: for example, the SOTRA in Abidjan (a 'mixed' private company with both French and Ivorian shareholders) had a fleet of 1,179 vehicles, and a staff of 6,153 in 1989; the SOTRAC in Dakar (also a 'mixed' company) had a fleet of 461 vehicles and a staff of 2,871 in 1989.[253] While these and other large companies such as KBS in Nairobi and Zupco in Harare represent some of the larger and more successful companies, by the 1980s, the system was breaking down, as many city administrations could not afford to replace, let alone properly maintain their ageing bus fleets at the same time as the population was growing; and even the private companies (operating in many Francophone countries) were having difficulties maintaining an efficient service in the face of declining revenues. A more mixed service, involving large public or private companies on the one hand, and a variety of smaller operators offering service on routes not otherwise covered by the larger companies, emerged.[254] By 1989, informal privately operated cars, pickup trucks, minibuses or minivans had captured much of the public transport market in many cities.[255]

In spite of the considerable increase in market claimed by the small operators *vis-à-vis* the large transit companies, and the improved accessibility to the city which they have brought to many low-income groups, there are drawbacks that are constantly being discussed in the African press. Overcrowding is common; accidents appear to be much more frequent than in the public buses (particularly on peri-urban roads and highways), and the fare may even be higher than in the public system for the same, or similar routes.

The examples of waste disposal and public transport illustrate two dimensions of the current crisis of urban services in Africa. In the case of waste removal, in many cities, the inhabitants have been living through an absolute withdrawal in the level of public service provision, without alternatives being provided—even at a lower standard of performance—by the private sector. Private services are being provided in some cities, for a fee to the householder, and there is more

work for scavengers and small recyclers, but the absolute evidence of efficient garbage disposal in many cities has declined rather dramatically since the 1970s. In the case of public transport, a much greater variety of modes of service has quite clearly developed with the decline of the large public companies.

However, the potential for private investment to substitute for public investment in infrastructure and services varies considerably, according to the infrastructural or service component in question. Thus, while the decline in public support for piped sewerage and treatment, port and airport facilities, urban roads, and electrical transmission facilities cannot easily be compensated for by privatisation, the same is not—at least in principle—the case for urban transport, airport services, non-piped water services and waste collection (if not waste disposal).[256] As the state disengages from responsibility for providing a whole range of local services, and the urban population continues to grow, a new balance is emerging between private and public activity.

Deterioration in the built environment and environmental health

The deterioration in the built environment is sharply in evidence throughout most of urban Africa. As more of the urban population was forced into unplanned settlements on the outskirts of large cities, or into more crowded living space in an already deteriorating housing stock in the more established 'high density' areas; as a lower proportion of the population had direct access to clean, piped water, regular garbage disposal and good health services, the quality of life for the vast majority of the population deteriorated during the 1980s and 1990s. This trend seems to have been accentuated by the effects of structural adjustment in many countries, according to which urban workers lost more than rural smallholders. Some demographers have even suggested that the decline in mortality rates that was clearly evident during the 1960s and 1970s may have slowed down in the 1980s. For example, in 1978 the mortality rate for infants and children stood at 112 per thousand in Abidjan, and 197 in the rural areas; but the census of 1988 recorded a figure of 120 for Abidjan (an increase), as against 191 (a decrease) in the rural areas.[257] In general, in Abidjan as well as elsewhere, most indices of health show much higher levels in urban, as opposed to rural areas, although the differences may be declining with the economic downturn and a reduction in health and nutritional expenditures by both government and individuals.

Under these conditions it may not be surprising to learn that in the central districts of Brazzaville there is less than one infectious mosquito bite per person every three years; by contrast, the rate is more than 100 times higher in the new informal settlement areas with low population density. In Bobo-Dioulasso, the second largest city in Burkina Faso, the measured rate of malaria occurrence measured in a peripheral neighbourhood was almost twice as high as that measured in a central section of the town.[258]

Urban agriculture

Although urban agriculture has considerable importance in many Asian and Latin American countries—and also in certain cities in the North—it probably has the greatest importance in African urban centres as an important supplementary source of livelihood or of food and fuel for many more. Chapter 12 will return to its current and potential role; here, the aim is to illustrate its importance for urban populations in Africa.

A major study of six towns in Kenya (including the capital, Nairobi) was undertaken by a research NGO, the Mazingira Institute in the mid 1980s. The study sampled 1576 households on a wide range of economic activities and consumption habits. The data show that 29 per cent of all households grow food within the urban area where they live; and 17 per cent keep livestock. Extrapolating on their survey, the authors estimated that, in 1985, 25.2 million kg. of crops worth some $4 million were produced in urban areas in Kenya in one season. Most of the urban crop and livestock production was consumed as subsistence by the households themselves.[259] Reflecting similar findings to the Kenyan study, a survey of research on urban farming in Zambia finds that most urban farmers are poor women, who grow food because of the failure of incomes to keep up with prices.[260] A later study of Nairobi based on a different sampling strategy (the sample was chosen from those working on the land rather than randomly from urban households in the city) found that 64% of the respondents were female (very similar to the earlier Mazingira survey); that they tended to have only primary education, or no education at all; that most were born outside the city, in neighbouring districts; and that very few actually sold their crops.[261] The pattern of poor women practising urban agriculture in order to provide food for themselves and their families is also a major finding of a study of 150 urban farming households in Kampala, Uganda. While the study deals with households rather than individuals, most of those who worked in the fields were women; the households themselves were predominantly (73 per cent) at a 'low level of income'; 69 per cent were producing food primarily for household consumption and not sale; and the main crops grown were annual tuber crops (such as cassava, sweet potatoes, bananas and cocoyams) as well as maize and beans. Interviews with the producers in 1989 indicated that, on average they had been farming for 13 years and that the vast majority had begun the practice in the 1970s or early 1980s. This suggests very strongly that urban farming as a major activity developed in Kampala 'in response to the declining economic situation. The farmers had been living in the city a long time before they started their agricultural enterprises.'[262] Across the continent in Lomé, a study of the agricultural aspects of urban farming—while not comparable to work in East Africa—observes that most of the market gardeners are men, and that very large sections of public land reserves on the periphery of the city are under cultivation, with the tacit approval of the authorities. While market gardening increased in Lomé as a direct response to the economic difficulties beginning in the late 1970s and early 1980s, produce is sold commercially rather than consumed by the cultivators.[263] One of the effects of increasing urban agriculture in Africa is that the economic and cultural differences between city and rural areas have become blurred. This is particularly the case in peripheral, unplanned areas where formal infrastructure is scarce, and many households live in relatively large plots of land in a semi-rural environment.

Notes and References

1. Friedmann, John, 'The right to the city', in Richard M. Morse and Jorge E. Hardoy (eds.), *Rethinking the Latin American City*, Johns Hopkins University Press, Baltimore and London, 1992, 104–5.

2. This section on North America is a shortened version of the background paper prepared by Professor L. S. Bourne (University of Toronto) entitled 'Urban growth and population distribution in North America: diverse and unfinished landscape'. This has been published as Bourne, L. S., *Urban Growth and Population Redistribution in North America: A Diverse and Unequal Landscape*, Major Report 32, Centre for Urban and Community Studies, University of Toronto, Toronto, 1995.

3. In Canada the urban population is defined as that population living in incorporated places of 1,000 or more and at densities of over 1,000 per square kilometre. In the US the minimum threshold population for urban areas is 2,500.

4. Goldberg, M. and J. Mercer, *The Myth of the North American City: Continentalism Challenged*, University of British Columbia Press, Vancouver, 1986

5. There are numerous reasons for this differential in death rates, but in part at least it is attributable to relatively high infant mortality rates among Black Americans.

6. Miron, J., *Demographic Change, Household Formation and Housing Demand*, McGill-Queens University Press, Montreal, 1988.

7. Sternlieb, G. and J. W. Hughes (eds.), *America's New Market Geography*, Rutgers University Press, New Brunswick, 1986.

8. From 1970 to 1990, for example, the US population grew by 38% while the

number of households increased by 62%.

9. Beaujot, R., *Population Change in Canada*, McClelland and Stewart, Toronto, 1991.

10. Bourne, L. S. and D. Ley (eds.), *The Changing Social Geography of Canadian Cities*, McGill-Queens University Press. Montreal, 1993.

11. For example, the geographic centre (or centre of gravity) of the US population has moved continuously westward since the founding of the republic. In 1770 the centre was located on the coast just east of Baltimore, by 1850 it was in southern Ohio, by 1950 it had shifted west to the Indiana–Illinois border, and by 1990 it was almost exactly in the middle of the state of Missouri and thus near the mid-point of the country.

12. The minimum total population for defining a metropolitan statistical area in New England is 75,000.

13. The definitional difference arises because of two factors: one, the use of a higher size threshold for inclusion as a metropolitan area in the Canadian census; and second, the use of smaller geographical units as building blocks in defining the boundaries of metropolitan areas in Canada. In the US the basic building blocks in delimiting metropolitan areas are counties; that is the entire county is added to the metropolitan area even if only a small portion of it is developed. Some of these counties, especially in the west, are very large. As a result US metropolitan areas, on average, are much more geographically extensive than those in Canada.

14. As defined by the US Office of Management and Budget in 1980, and modified in 1990. CMSAs were defined only for metropolitan complexes of over 1 million in which two or more individual but adjacent metropolitan areas (MSAs) exhibited close economic and social integration.

15. The Washington DC and Baltimore MSAs, when combined, had a total population of 6.7 million in 1990.

16. For example, a consolidated metropolitan area definition for Toronto would include the Toronto CMA (3.9 million), the Hamilton CMA (600,000) and Oshawa CMA (240,000), and the rest of York County, for a total metropolitan population of 4.84 million in 1991.

17. As contrasting examples in Canada, the population of the Toronto metropolitan area in 1986 was about 36% foreign-born, compared to less than 3% in St. Johns, Newfoundland and only 2% in Quebec City.

18. Goldsmith, W. W. and E. J. Blakely, *Separate Societies: Poverty and Inequality in US Cities*, Temple University Press, Philadelphia, 1993; Bourne, L. S., 'Close together and worlds apart: an analysis of changes in the ecology of income in Canadian Metropolitan Areas', *Urban Studies* vol. 30, no. 8, 1993, 1293–317.

19. Borchert, J., 'Futures of American Cities', chapter 12 in J. F. Hart (ed.), *Our Changing Cities*, Johns Hopkins University Press, Baltimore, 1991, 218–50. Berry, B. J. L., *America's Utopian Experiments: Communal Havens from Long-run Crises*, University Press of New England, Hanover, NH, 1992.

20. Noyelle, T. and T. M. Stanback, Jr., *The Economic Transformation of American Cities*, Rowman, Totowa, NJ, 1984; and Mills, E. S. and J. F. McDonald (eds.), *Sources of Metropolitan Growth*, Rutgers University Press, 1992.

21. Markusen, A. and others, *High-Tech America*, Allen and Unwin, Boston, 1986.

22. Simmons, J. and L. S. Bourne, *Urban Growth Trends in Canada, 1981–86: A New Geography of Change*, Major Report No. 25, Centre for Urban and Community Studies, University of Toronto, 1989; and Coffey, W., *The Evolution of Canada's Metropolitan Economies*, Institute for Research on Public Policy, Montreal, 1994.

23. Sassen, S., *The Global City*, Princeton University Press, Princeton, 1991.

24. The four poorest states in per capita income are Mississippi, Arkansas, Alabama and Louisiana; the four highest income states are Connecticut, New Jersey, Maryland (these three include some of the higher income suburbs of New York and Washington DC) and Massachusetts.

25. Frey, W. and A. Speare, Jr., 'The revival of metropolitan growth in the U.S.', *Population and Development Review*, vol. 18, no. 1, 1992, 129–46.

26. The other two centres were Calgary, Alberta (oil, services) and Kitchener-Waterloo, Ontario (manufacturing, insurance, education).

27. Borchert 1991, *op. cit.*; Chinitz, B., 'A framework for speculating about future urban growth patterns in the US', *Urban Studies*, vol. 28, no. 6, 1991, 939–59; Bourne, L. S., 'Recycling urban systems and metropolitan areas: a geographical agenda for the 1990s and beyond', *Economic Geography*, vol. 67, no. 3, 1991, 185–209; and Hart, J. F. (ed.), *Our Changing Cities*, Johns Hopkins University Press, Baltimore, 1991.

28. Drache, D. and M. S. Gertler (eds.), *The New Era of Global Competition: State Policy and Market Power*, McGill-Queens University Press, Montreal, 1991; and Noponen, H., and others (eds.), *Trading Industries; Trading Regions: International Trade, American Industry and Regional Economic Development*, Guilford Press, 1993, New York.

29. This section drew on various background papers prepared for the Global Report: Davila, Julio D., 'Recent changes in production and population in Bogota, Colombia: a successful case of Clark's Law?'; Garcia-Guadilla, Maria Pilar and Virginia Jimenez-Diaz, 'Urban growth in the metropolitan area of Caracas;' Garza, Gustavo, 'Dynamics of Mexican urbanization: Mexico City emerging megolopolis and Metropolitan Monterrey'; and Jacobi, Pedro, 'Trends in Sao Paulo Metropolitan Area'.

30. For the period 1920–50—Hauser, Philip M. and Robert W. Gardner, *Urban Future: Trends and Prospects*, Paper presented at the International Conference of Population and the Urban Future, Rome, September 1980, with statistical annex which drew its data from United Nations, *The Growth of the World's Urban and Rural Population, 1920–2000*, Population Studies no. 44, United Nations, New York, 1969. For statistics from 1950 to the present, United Nations, *World Urbanization Prospects 1992; Estimates and Projections of Urban and Rural Populations and of Urban Agglomerations*, Department of Economic and Social Information and Policy Analysis, ST/ESA/SER.A/136, United Nations, New York, 1993, 164 pages.

31. Care should be taken in drawing too many inferences from this. The scale of population loss among the region's indigenous population after the conquest by European powers meant that only in the 1870s did the region's population return to what it had been prior to the conquest.

32. Statistics drawn from Hauser and Gardner 1980 and United Nations 1993, *op. cit.*

33. This is because they began from a much larger population base in 1980, compared to 1970. Some notable exceptions include Mexico City Metropolitan Area with a much reduced annual increment in its population during the 1980s compared to the 1970s—although this might be exaggerated by the 1980 census figure being too high—and the two other largest metropolitan areas in Mexico, Guadalajara and Monterrey. Caracas and Medellin also had smaller annual increments in their population during the 1980s compared to the 1970s while in Montevideo and in the three largest Argentine cities (Buenos Aires, Cordoba and Rosario) there was very little increase.

34. Lattes, Alfredo, 'Population distribution and development in Latin America', Proceedings of the United Nations Expert Meeting on Population Distribution and Migration, Santa Cruz, Bolivia, ST/ESA/SER.R/133, UN Population Division, New York, 1995.

35. *Ibid.*

36. Based on statistics drawn from UN 1993, *op. cit.*

37. United Nations 1993, *op. cit.*

38. Centro Latinoamericano de Demografia (CELADE), 'Population dynamics in the large cities of Latin America and the Caribbean', Proceedings of the United Nations Expert Meeting on Population Distribution and Migration, Santa Cruz, Bolivia, ST/ESA/SER.R/133, UN Population Division, New York, 1995.

39. CELADE, *Redistribución espacial de la población en América Latina: una visión sumaria del período 1950–1985*, CELADE, Santiago, 1988, quoted in CELADE 1995, *op. cit.*

40. CELADE 1995, *op. cit.*

41. *Ibid.*

42. Lattes 1995 and CELADE 1995, *op. cit.*

43. See CELADE 1995, *op. cit.* One exception was Haiti where in 1986, infant mortality rates in Port-au-Prince were 102 per 1000 live births compared to a national figure of 100.

44. Lattes 1995, *op. cit.* reporting on the World Fertility Survey

45. Recchini de Lattes, Zulma, 'Urbanization and demographic ageing: the case of a developing country, Argentina', in *Ageing and Urbanization*, Sales no. E.91.XIII.12, United Nations, New York, 1991, quoted in CELADE 1995, *op. cit.*

46. CELADE 1995, *op. cit.*

47. Lattes 1995 and United Nations 1993, *op. cit.*

48. Gilbert, Alan, *The Latin American City*, Latin American Bureau, London, 1994, 51.

49. This paragraph draws from Lattes 1995, *op. cit.*

50. Duhau, E., *Población y Economía de la Zona Metropolitana de la Ciudad de México: El Centro y la Periféria*, Universidad Autónoma Metropolitana, Mimeo, 1992, quoted in CELADE 1995, *op. cit.*

51. Valladares, Licia, 'Río de Janeiro: la visión de los estudiosos de lo urbano', in Mario Lombardi and Danilo Veiga (eds.), *Las Ciudades en Conflicto: una Perspectiva Latinoamericana*, Ediciones de la Banda Oriental, Montevideo, 1989, quoted in CELADE 1995, *op. cit.*

52. Rodríguez, J., *Dinámica Demográfica del Gran Santiago: Patrones Históricos, Tendencias Actuales, Perspectivas*, CELADE and Universidad de la Academia de Humanismo Cristiano (UAHC), Mimeo, 1992, quoted in CELADE 1995, *op. cit.*

53. Lattes 1995, *op. cit.*

54. CONAPO, *Sistema de Ciudades y Distribución Espacial de la Población de México*, vol. I, Consejo Nacional de Población, Mexico City, 1991.

55. Duarte, Isis, 'Población, migraciones internas y desarrollo en República Dominicana: 1950–1981', Paper presented at the seminar on Territorial Mobility of Populations: New Patterns in Latin America, Santo Domingo, 13–14 December 1991 quoted in Lattes 1995, *op. cit.*

56. Gilbert 1994, *op. cit.*

57. Comité Estatal de Estadísticas, 'Cuba: el crecimiento urbano y las migraciones internas en el contexto del desarrollo económico y social', Paper presented at the Conference on the Peopling of the Americas, International Union for the Scientific Study of Population, Veracruz, May 1992, quoted in Lattes 1995, *op. cit.*

58. Lattes 1995, *op. cit.*

59. Roberts, Bryan, 'Transitional cities', in Richard M. Morse and Jorge E. Hardoy (eds.), *Rethinking the Latin American City*, Johns Hopkins University Press, Baltimore and London, 1992, 50–65.

60. CELADE 1995, *op. cit.* drawing from Elton, Charlotte, *Migración Femenina en América Latina: Factores Determinantes*, Series E, No.26, CELADE, Santiago de Chile, 1978; Oliveira, Orlandina de and Brígida García, 'Urbanization, migration and the growth of large cities: trends and implications in some developing countries', in *Population Studies* No. 89, E.83.XIII.3, United Nations, New York, 1984; Recchini de Lattes, Zulma, 'Women in internal and international migration with special reference to Latin America', *Population Bulletin of the United Nations*, No. 27, 1989, 95–107; and Zasz, Ivonne, *Mujeres Inmigrantes y Mercado de Trabajo en Santiago*, CELADE, Santiago de Chile, 1994.

61. Gilbert 1994, *op. cit.*

62. DANE, *Información Censo 93*, Computer Diskette, DANE, Bogotá, 1994.

63. Davila, Julio D., 'Recent changes in production and population in Bogota, Colombia: a successful case of Clark's Law?', Background Paper for the United Nations Global Report on Human Settlements, 1995, plus appendices, 2–54.

64. Chant, Sylvia and Sarah A. Radcliffe, 'Migration and development: the importance of gender', in Sylvia Chant (ed.), *Gender and Migration in Developing Countries*, Belhaven Press, London, 1992, 1–29.

65. Lattes, Alfredo E. and Zulma Recchini de Lattes, 'Auge y declinación de las migraciones en Buenos Aires', in J. Jorrat and R. Sautu (eds.), *Después de Germani*, Editorial Paidos, Buenos Aires, 1992.

66. Lattes 1995, *op. cit.*

67. Gilbert 1994, *op. cit.*

68. Lattes, Alfredo E., 'Migraciones hacia América Latina y el Caribe desde principios del siglio XIX', *Cuaderno del CENEP*, No. 35, Buenos Aires, 1985.

69. Lattes 1995, *op. cit.*

70. *Ibid.*

71. *Ibid.*

72. Ramos, Joseph, 'Growth, crises and strategic turnarounds', *CEPAL Review*, no. 50, Aug. 1993, 63–79.

73. *Ibid.*

74. Figures for Cuba were not available

75. Gilbert 1994, *op. cit.*

76. Ramos 1993, *op. cit.*

77. Hakkert, R. and F. W. Goza, 'The demographic consequences of austerity in Latin America', in W. L. Canak (ed.), *Lost Promises: Debt, Austerity and Development in Latin America*, Westview Press, Boulder, 1989, 69–97.

78. Cordera Campos, R. and E. González Tiburcio, 'Crisis and transition in the Mexican economy', in M. González de la Rocha and A. Escobar (eds.), *Social Responses to Mexico's Economic Crisis of the 1980s*, Centre for US–Mexican Studies, University of California, La Jolla, 1990.

79. Ramos 1993, *op. cit.*

80. Garza, Gustavo, *Dinámica Industrial de la Ciudad de Mexico, 1940–1988*, Mimeo, 1991, quoted in Gilbert 1994, *op. cit.*

81. Clichevsky, Nora, Hilda Herzer, Pedro Pirez, David Satterthwaite and others, *Construccion y Administración de la Ciudad Latinoamericana*, Grupo Editor Latinoamericano, Buenos Aires, 1990; Gilbert 1994, *op. cit.*

82. See for instance Portes, Alejandro, 'Latin American urbanization during the years of the crisis', *Latin American Research Review*, vol. 24, no. 3, 1989, 7–44 on Uruguay and Chile.

83. Portes 1989, *op. cit.*

84. Tello, C., 'Combating poverty in Mexico', in M. González de la Rocha and A. Escobar (eds.), *Social Responses to Mexico's Economic Crisis of the 1980s*, Centre for US–Mexican Studies, University of California, La Jolla, 1990.

85. Iglesias, Enrique W., *Reflections on Economic Development: Towards a New Latin American Consensus*, Inter-American Development Bank, 1992, quoted in Gilbert 1994, *op. cit.*

86. CELADE 1995, *op. cit.*

87. Infante, Ricardo and Emilio Klein, 'The Latin American labour market, 1950–1990', *CEPAL Review*, no. 45, Dec. 1991, 121–35.

88. *Ibid.*

89. Gilbert 1994, *op. cit.*

90. Infante and Klein 1991, *op. cit.*

91. Clichevsky and others 1990, *op. cit.*

92. *Ibid.*

93. *Ibid.*

94. *Ibid.*

95. *Ibid.*

96. Arriagada, Irma, 'Unequal participation by women in the working world', *CEPAL Review* no. 40, April 1990, 83–98.

97. Based on figures drawn from INDEC's permanent household survey in Arrossi, Silvina, 'Latin America: Background paper for the Global Report on Human Settlements', IIED-América Latina, 1995.

98. CELADE 1995, *op. cit.*

99. This draws from chapter 2 of Clichevsky and others 1990 but using updated figures.

100. Lattes 1995, *op. cit.*

101. *Ibid.*

102. Hardoy, Jorge E. and David Satterthwaite, *Squatter Citizen: Life in the Urban Third World*, Earthscan Publications, London, 1989.

103. Hardoy, Jorge E., 'Two thousand years of Latin American urbanization', in J. E. Hardoy (ed.), *Urbanization in Latin America: Approaches and Issues*, Anchor Books, New York, 1975.

104. Lattes 1995, *op. cit.*

105. Mexico City's pre-colonial precursor,

Tenochitlan, was the region's largest city in 1500 and among the world's largest cities at that time.

106. Han-chande, Roberto, 'Demographic and urban aspects of Mexico's border with the United States', in Mutsuo Yamada (Co-ordinator), *Urbanization in Latin America: its Characteristics and Issues*, The University of Tsukuba, Tsukuba-shi, 1990, 31–42.

107. Sklair, Leslie, 'Global system, local problems: environmental impacts of transnational corporations along Mexico's northern border', in Hamish Main and Stephen Wyn Williams (eds.), *Environment and Housing in Third World Cities*, John Wiley and Sons, Chichester, 1994, pp. 85–105.

108. Gilbert 1994, *op. cit.*

109. *Ibid.*

110. Sklair 1994, *op. cit.*

111. *Ibid.*

112. Han-chande 1990, *op. cit.*

113. Davila 1995, *op. cit.*

114. *Ibid.*

115. Duarte 1991, *op. cit.*

116. Townroe, P. M. and D. Keen, 'Polarization reversal in the State of Sao Paulo', *Regional Studies*, vol. 18, no. 1, 1984, 45–54.

117. Negrete, María Eugenia and Héctor Salazar, 'Dinámica de crecimiento de la población de la ciudad de México: 1900–1980', in Gustavo Garza and others (eds.), *Atlas de la Ciudad de Mexico*, Departamento del Distrito Federal y El Colegio de México, Mexico DF, 1987.

118. Rofman, A. B., 'Argentina: a mature urban pattern', *Cities*, vol. 2, no. 1, Butterworth Press, 1985, 47–54.

119. See for instance United Nations, *Urban, Rural and City Population, 1950–2000, as assessed in 1978*, ESA/P/WP.66, New York, June 1980.

120. Davila 1995, *op. cit.*

121. *Ibid.*

122. Gugler, J., 'A Minimum of Urbanism and a Maximum of Ruralism: the Cuban Experience' in *International Journal of Urban and Regional Research*, vol. 4, 1980, 516–35 and Hardoy, Jorge E., *Urban and Agrarian Reform in Cuba*, SIAP/IDRC, Ediciones SIAP, 1979, Buenos Aires.

123. Garza, Gustavo, 'Dynamics of Mexican urbanization: Mexico City emerging megolopolis and Metropolitan Monterrey', Background Paper for the UN Global Report on Human Settlements, 1995. However, there are several Mexican cities that are growing rapidly and are close to 1 million inhabitants so the 2000 census may find an increased proportion in one million plus cities, as several cities have been added to the list of 'million-cities'.

124. Chapter 9 of Hardoy, Jorge E. and David Satterthwaite, *Squatter Citizen: Life in the Urban Third World*, Earthscan Publications, London, 1989.

125. Manzanal, Mabel and Cesar Vapnarsky, 'The development of the Upper Valley of Rio Negro and its periphery within the Comahue Region, Argentina', in Jorge E. Hardoy and David Satterthwaite (eds.), *Small and Intermediate Urban Centres; their role in Regional and National Development in the Third World*, Hodder and Stoughton (UK) and Westview (USA), London, 1986.

126. Verduzco, Gustavo, 'Crecimiento urbano y desarrollo regional: el caso de Zamora, Michoacan', *Revista Interamericana de Planificacion*, vol. 18, no. 71, September 1984, 67–80.

127. Chapter 9 of Hardoy, Jorge E. and David Satterthwaite, *Squatter Citizen: Life in the Urban Third World*, Earthscan Publications, London, 1989.

128. Hardoy and Satterthwaite 1989, *op. cit.*

129. del Olmo, Elvia, 'Case study: Cuautla, Mexico', in UNCHS (Habitat), *The Management of Secondary Cities in Latin America*, Nairobi, 1994.

130. Abaleron, Carlos Alberto, 'Marginal urban space and unsatisfied basic needs: the case of San Carlos de Bariloche, Argentina', *Environment and Urbanization*, vol. 7, no. 1, April 1995, 97–115.

131. Hernández de Padrón, Maria Inés, 'Case study: Merida, Venezuela', in UNCHS (Habitat), *The Management of Secondary Cities in Latin America*, Nairobi, 1994.

132. UNCHS (Habitat) 1994, *op. cit.*

133. Cline, W. R., 'Facilitating labor adjustment in Latin America', Unpublished document prepared for the Inter-American Development Bank, October 1991, quoted in Gilbert 1994, *op. cit.*

134. Iglesias 1992, *op. cit.*

135. This section draws heavily on Champion, A. G., 'Internal migration, counterurbanization and changing population distribution, in R. Hall and P. White (eds.), *Europe's Population: Towards the Next Century*, UCL Press, London, 1995 and on additional material supplied by A. G. Champion.

136. Eurostat, *Demographic Statistics 1991*, Luxembourg, 1991.

137. *Ibid.*

138. Champion 1995, *op. cit.*

139. See for instance Hopflinger, F., 'The future of household and family structures in Europe', in *Seminar on Present Demographic Trends and Lifestyles in Europe: Proceedings*, Council of Europe, Strasbourg, 1991, 289–338.

140. Jones, H., 'The French census 1990; the southward drift continues', *Geography* vol. 76, 1991, 358–61.

141. Champion, A. G., 'International migration and demographic change in the Developed World', *Urban Studies*, vol. 31, nos. 4/5, 1994, 653–77.

142. *Ibid.*

143. *Ibid.*

144. Kemper, Franz-Josef, 'New trends in mass migration in Germany', in R. King (ed.), *Mass Migrations in Europe*, Belhaven, London, 1993.

145. Council of Europe, *Recent Demograpic Developments in Europe*, Brussels, 1994.

146. Champion, Tony and Russell King, 'New trends in international migration in Europe', *Geographical Viewpoint*, vol. 21, 1993, 45–56.

147. King, R. and K. Rybaczuk, 'Southern Europe and the international division of labour: from emigration to immigration', in R. King (ed.), *The New Geography of European Migrations*, Belhaven, London, 1993, 175–206.

148. Hovy, B., 'Asylum migration in Europe: patterns, determinants and the role of East–West movements', in R. King (ed.), *The New Geography of European Migrations*, Belhaven, London, 1993, 207–27.

149. Hovy 1993, *op. cit.*

150. Cheshire, P. C. and D. G. Hay, 'Background and the use of Functional Urban Regions', in P. C. Cheshire and D. G. Hay (eds.), *Urban Problems in Western Europe*, Unwin Hyman, 1989, page 15.

151. Kunzmann, Klaus R. and Michael Wegener, *The Pattern of Urbanization in Western Europe 1960–1990*, Report for the Directorate General XVI of the Commission of the European Communities, Institut fur Raumplanung, Universitat Dortmund, Dortmund, 1991.

152. *Ibid.*

153. See for instance Fielding, A. J., 'Counterurbanization in Western Europe', *Progress in Planning*, vol. 17, 1982, 1–52; and Hall, P. and D. Hay, *Growth Centres in the European Urban System*, Heinemann, London, 1980.

154. Hall and Hay 1980, *op. cit.* 87.

155. Champion, Anthony G. and Sven Illeris, 'Population redistribution trends in Western Europe: a mosaic of dynamics and crisis', in Michael Hebbert and Jens Christian Hansen (eds.), *Unfamiliar Territory: The Reshaping of European Geography*, Avebury, Aldershot, 1990.

156. RECLUS, *Les Villes Européennes*, Rapport pour la DATA, La Documentation Francaise, Paris, 1989.

157. This approach has its roots in the 'localities' research tradition—see for instance Cooke, R., *Localities: The Changing Face of Urban Britain*, Unwin Hyman, London, 1989 quoted in Champion 1995, *op. cit.*

158. This section draws heavily on a background paper by F. W. Carter of the Dept of Social Studies, School of Slavonic and East European Studies at London University on 'East Europe: population distribution, urban change, housing and environmental problems'.

159. The United Nations now groups these three nations as part of Northern Europe.

160. This discussion draws on Musil, Jirí, 'Changing urban systems in post-communist societies in Central Europe: analysis and prediction', *Urban Studies*, vol. 30, no. 6, June 1993, 899–906.

161. These include people from abroad on contracts—for instance business people from the West, specialists on cultural assignments or foreign workers on limited, short-term contracts.

162. Carter, F. W., R. A. French and J. Salt, 'International migration between East and West in Europe', *Ethnic and Racial Studies*, vol. 16, no. 3, 1993, 467–91.

163. Carter, F. W., 'Bulgaria', Chapter 4 in A. H. Dawson (ed.), *Planning in Eastern Europe*, Croom Helm, London, 1987.

164. This should not be confused with Katowice city that had 360,000 inhabitants in 1992 or the Upper Silesian Industrial Region which is a metropolitan area within Katowice county within which Katowice city is located.

165. For instance, seven of them had populations of 20,000 or more inhabitants in 1500 AD.

166. This section draws heavily on a background paper by Denis J. B. Shaw of the University of Birmingham (UK) on 'Settlement and urban change in the former Soviet Union'.

167. Finansky i statistika 1990, 10–14.

168. Finansky i statistika 1990.

169. Both these cities were among the region's largest and most important during the 19th and early 20th centuries; Lvov lost part of its hinterland during the interwar period as it was in Poland and then lost its connections to the West after 1939; Riga suffered a loss of its hinterland during the interwar period when it was part of independent Latvia and then could not resume its overseas trading activities under Stalin's policies.

170. These include Naberezhnyye Chelny and Cheboksary, and Neftekamsk, Nizhnekamsk and Nochecheboksarsk that had not existed in 1959; see Cole, John P., 'Changes in the population of larger cities of the USSR, 1979–89', *Soviet Geography*, vol. 31, no. 3, March 1990, 160–72.

171. Formerly Sverdlovsk.

172. See for instance Cooper, Julian, *Soviet Defence Industry, Conversion and Reform*, Royal Institute of International Affairs/Pinter, London, 1991.

173. Medvedkov , O., *Soviet Urbanization*, Routledge, London, 1990.

174. Cole, 1990, *op cit*.

175. *Ibid.*

176. This section draws on a series of background papers commissioned for the Global Report. These include a series of background papers and boxes prepared by Richard Kirkby on China, Yamada, Hiroyuki and Kazuyuki Tokuoka, 'The trends of the population and urbanization in post-war Japan', Kundu, Amitabh, 'Population growth and regional pattern of urbanization in India: an analysis in the context of changing macro-economic perspective', Islam, Nazrul, Professor 'Dhaka; a profile' and 'Urbanization in Bangladesh'; and Hasan, Arif, 'Profiles of three Pakistani Cities: Karachi, Faisalabad and Thatta'.

177. United Nations 1995, *op. cit.*

178. *Ibid.*

179. K. Srinivasan, quoted in *The Economist*, 18 Feb. 1995, 76.

180. ESCAP, *State of Urbanization in Asia and the Pacific 1993*, Economic and Social Commission for Asia and the Pacific, ST/ESCAP/1300, United Nations, Bangkok, 1993.

181. Islam, Nazrul, 'Dhaka; a profile', Background Paper for the Global Report on Human Settlements, 1994.

182. Hardoy and Satterthwaite 1989, *op. cit.*

183. If the urban population is that in city municipalities, 77.4 per cent of the population lived in urban areas in 1990. If the urban population is that in what are termed Densely Inhabited Districts, which seek to exclude the rural populations that fall within city municipal boundaries, then 63.2 per cent of the population lived in urban areas in 1990. If Standard Metropolitan Employment Areas are used, 73.6 per cent of the population lived in urban areas in this year. See Yamada, Hiroyuki and Kazuyuki Tokuoka, 'The trends of the population and urbanization in Post-war Japan, Background Paper for the United Nations Global Report on Human Settlements, 1995.

184. This classification and analysis draws on McGee, Terence G. and C. J. Griffiths, 'Global urbanization: towards the twenty-first century', in United Nations, Population Distribution and Migration, Proceedings of the United Nations Expert Meeting, ST/ESA/SER.R/133, UN Population Division, New York, 1994.

185. Figures from Merrill Lynch for 1992 quoted in *The Economist*, 11 Feb. 1995.

186. United Nations 1995, *op. cit.*

187. *China City Planning Review*, vol. 2, 1988 and China Daily 12.8, 1988

188. Islam, Nazrul , 'Urban research in Bangladesh and Sri Lanka: Towards an agenda for the 1990s', in Richard Stren (ed.), *Urban Research in the Developing World: Volume I—Asia*, Centre for Urban and Community Studies, Toronto, 1994, 103–69.

189. ESCAP 1993, *op. cit.*

190. *Ibid.* 2–27.

191. Kirkby, Richard, 'Country Report: China', Background Paper for the United Nations Global Report on Human Settlements, 1995.

192. Bose, Ashish, 'Urbanization in India 1951–2001, in Bidyut Mohanty (ed.), *Urbanization in Developing Countries: Basic Services and Community Participation*, Concept Publishing Company, New Delhi, 1993, 107–24.

193. Yamada and Tokuoka 1995, *op. cit.*

194. Mboi, Nafsiah and Karen Houston Smith, 'Urban research in Indonesia: its evolution and its future', in Richard Stren (ed.), *Urban Research in the Developing World: Volume I—Asia*, Centre for Urban and Community Studies, Toronto, 1994, 173–251.

195. Kundu, Amitabh, 'Population growth and regional pattern of urbanization in India: an analysis in the context of changing macro-economic perspective', Background paper for the Global Report on Human Settlements, 1994.

196. Kirkby 1995, *op. cit.*

197. *Ibid.*

198. *Ibid.*

199. Mboi and Houston Smith 1994, *op. cit.*

200. McGee and Griffiths 1994, *op. cit.*

201. Kundu 1994, *op. cit.*

202. Along with 3 declassifications and 103 merging with other towns; see Kundu 1994, *op. cit.*

203. ESCAP 1993, *op. cit.*

204. McGee and Griffiths 1994, *op. cit.*, Kioe Sheng, Yap, personal communication.

205. Ginsberg, N., B. Koppel and T. G. McGee (eds.), *The Extended Metropolis Settlement Transition in Asia*, University of Hawaii Press, Honolulu, 1991.

206. McGee, T. G., 'Urbanization or Kotadesasi—the emergence of new regions of economic interaction in Asia', Working paper, Environment and Policy Institute, East West Center, Honolulu, June 1987.

207. McGee 1987, *op. cit.*

208. Lo, Fu-chen and Yue-man Yeung, *Global Restructuring and Emerging Urban Corridors in Pacific Asia*, United Nations University, Tokyo, 1995.

209. Lo and Yeung 1995, *op. cit.*

210. U. Myint, personal communication quoted in ESCAP 1993, *op. cit.*

211. United Nations, *Human Settlements Situation in the ESCWA Region: Development Trends in the Housing Sector during the last Two decades'*, Economic and Social Commission for Western Asia, E/ESCWA/HS/1993/1, 1993.

212. Hasan, Arif, 'Profiles of three Pakistani Cities: Karachi, Faisalabad and Thatta', background paper prepared for the Global Report on Human Settlements, 1994.

213. Hasan 1994, *op. cit.*

214. Yamada and Tokuoka 1995, *op. cit.*

215. Fujita, Masahisi and Ryoichi Ishii, 'Location behaviour and spatial organization of multinational firms and their impact on regional transformation in East Asia: a comparative study of Japanese, Korean and US electronics firms', *ISEAD Intermediate Research Report*, University of Pennsylvania, draft, quoted in Lo and Yeung 1995, *op. cit.*

216. Kirkby 1995, *op. cit.*

217. For more details, see census data in Prakash Mathur, Om, 'Responding to the urban challenge: a research agenda for India and Nepal', in Richard Stren (ed.), *Urban Research in the Developing World: Volume I—Asia*, Centre for Urban and Community Studies, Toronto, 1994, 49–100.

218. Kirkby, Richard (1994), 'Dilemmas of urbanization: review and prospects', in Denis Dwyer (ed.), *China: The Next*

Decades, Longman Scientific and Technical, Harlow, 140–1.

219. *Far Eastern Economic Review*, 24.3.1988

220. Zweig, D. (1991), 'Institutionalizing China's countryside: the political economy of exports from rural industry', *China Quarterly*, vol. 128, 716–41 quoted in Kirkby 1995, *op. cit.*

221. This is a condensed version of a paper by Stren, Professor Richard, 'Population and urban change in Africa' prepared for the Global Report on Human Settlements, 1995.

222. In United Nations 1995 (*op. cit.*), for half of all African nations, the latest census listed was 1983 or earlier while for 12 countries, there was no census listed since the early 1970s.

223. United Nations 1995, *op. cit.*

224. UNDP, *Human Development Report, 1994*, Oxford University Press, 1994.

225. For 1985–90, the United Nations estimates that the average rate of growth of Africa's urban population was 4.34% annually; for the period 1990–5, it was estimated at 4.38% and for 1995–2000, projected to be 4.29%—see United Nations 1995 *op. cit.*

226. Stambouli, Fredj, *The Urban Profile of Tunis City Today*, Background Paper for the Global Report, 1994.

227. *Ibid.*

228. At the height of their development, African cities rivalled in size and urban form both contemporary European and Middle Eastern cities. Thus, a Portuguese traveller, writing in 1694, described the town of Benin (in present day Nigeria) in glowing terms, '. . . as larger than Lisbon; the streets are aligned in a rectilinear pattern as far as the eye can see. The houses are large—particularly that of the King, which is elaborately decorated with fine columns. The town is rich and active. It is so well governed that theft is unknown, to the point that, because of a feeling of security, the people do not have gates for their houses.' (Quoted in Catherine Coquery-Vidrovitch, *Histoire des villes d'Afrique noire; Des origines à la colonisation*, Albin Michel, Paris, 1993, 181). Another traveller described the city of Djenné (near the town of Timbuktu in what is currently Mali) as 'great, flourishing and prosperous . . . one of the great markets of the Muslim world' (Abdurahman es Sa'di, as quoted in Basil Davidson (ed.), *The African Past*, New York, 1967, 94). Some of these settlements (such as Great Zimbabwe, Kano or Ife) began as spiritual centres, to evolve over time into secular towns. Others (such as Kampala or Kumasi) were originally the seat of a powerful king or ruling group.

229. Gervais-Lambony, Philippe, *De Lomé à Harare; Le fait citadin*, Karthala, Paris, 1994.

230. Attahi, Koffi 'Planning and Management in Large Cities. A Case Study of Abidjan, Côte d'Ivoire' in UNCHS (Habitat), *Metropolitan Planning and Management in the Developing World: Abidjan and Quito*, Nairobi, 1992, 35–6.

231. Mandy, Nigel, *A City Divided: Johannesburg and Soweto*, St. Martin's Press, New York, 1984, 1–3.

232. Poinsot, Jacqueline, Alain Sinou and Jaroslav Sternadel, *Les villes d'Afrique noire. Politiques et opérations d'urbanisme et d'habitat entre 1650 et 1960*, La Documentation Française, Paris, 1989, 11.

233. One of the most influential sources of colonial legislation was the British Town and Country Planning Act of 1932, which was the source of the urban planning legislation in Kenya, Tanzania and the Rhodesias and was behind the Nigeria Town and Country Planning Ordinance, proclaimed in 1948, which eventually became the model for post-independence planning in the various states of the federal union.

234. Kulaba, Saitiel, *Urban Management and the Delivery of Urban Services in Tanzania*, Ardhi Institute, Dar es Salaam, 1989, 226–7.

235. Stren, Richard 'Urban Policy', in Joel Barkan and John J. Okumu (eds.), *Politics and Public Policy in Kenya and Tanzania*, Praeger, New York, 1979, 186.

236. White, Rodney, 'The Impact of Policy Conflict on the Implementation of a Government-assisted Housing Project in Senegal', *Canadian Journal of African Studies*, vol. 19, no. 3, 1985, 512.

237. Adjavou, Akolly and others, *Economie de la construction à Lomé*, L'Harmattan, Paris, 1987, 20–1.

238. The estimate, which is accepted by other researchers, was offered by Heather Joshi, Harold Lubell and Jean Mouly, *Abidjan: Urban development and employment in the Ivory Coast*, ILO, Geneva, 1976, 66.

239. For a survey of this research see Charles M. Becker, Andrew M. Hamer and Andrew R. Morrison, *Beyond Urban Bias in Africa: Urbanization in an Era of Structural Adjustment*, James Currey, London and Portsmouth, NH: Heinemann, 1994, ch. 4.

240. *Ibid.* ch. 5.

241. See, for example, Alan Gilbert and Joseph Gugler, *Cities, Poverty and Development: Urbanization in the Third World*, Oxford University Press, New York, 1992, 94–100; and Lisa Peattie, 'An Approach to Urban Research in the 1990s', forthcoming in Richard Stren (ed.), *Urban Research in the Developing World*, vol. 4, Centre for Urban and Community Studies, Toronto.

242. Becker, Hamer and Morrison 1994, *op. cit.* 159–60.

243. International Labour Organization, *Informal Sector in Africa*, Jobs and Skills Programme for Africa, ILO, Addis Ababa, 1985, 13–15.

244. Touré, Abdou, *Les Petits métiers à Abidjan. L'imagination au secours de la 'conjoncture'*, Karthala, Paris, 1985, 18.

245. World Bank, *Urban Policy and Economic Development. An Agenda for the 1990s*, Washington DC, 1991, 38.

246. Dulucq, Sophie and Odile Goerg (eds.), *Les Investissements publics dans les villes africaines 1930–1985*, L'Harmattan, Paris, 1989, 149.

247. *Ibid.* 41–4.

248. Kulaba, Saitiel, *Urban Management and the Delivery of Urban Services in Tanzania*, Ardhi Institute, Dar es Salaam, 1989, 118.

249. DHS and Mazingira Institute, *Nairobi: The Urban Growth Challenge*, Mazingira Institute, Nairobi, 1988.

250. Stren, Richard, 'Large Cities in the Third World', in UNCHS, *Metropolitan Planning and Management in the Developing World: Abidjan and Quito*, Nairobi, 1992, 10–11.

251. Stren, Richard, 'The Administration of Urban Services', in Richard Stren and Rodney White (eds), *African Cities in Crisis. Managing Rapid Urban Growth*, Westview, Boulder, 1989, 47.

252. Kulaba 1989, *op. cit.* 133–41.

253. Godard, Xavier and Pierre Teurnier, *Les Transports urbaines en Afrique à l'heure de l'ajustement*, Karthala, Paris, 1992, 52.

254. See Chapter 8 for more details.

255. Godard and Teurnier 1992, *op. cit.*

256. World Bank, *World Development Report 1994: Infrastructure for Development*, Oxford University Press for the World Bank, New York, 1994, 115.

257. Antoine, Philippe and Amadou Ba, 'Mortalité et santé dans les villes africaines' in *Afrique contemporaine* (Numéro spécial, 'Villes d'Afrique') no. 168, Oct./Dec. 1993, 140.

258. Antoine and Ba 1993, *op. cit.* 144.

259. Lee-Smith, Diana, Mutsembi Manundu, Davinder Lamba and P. Kuria Gathuru, *Urban Food Production and the Cooking Fuel Situation in Urban Kenya*, Mazingira Institute, Nairobi, 1987.

260. Rakodi, Carole 'Urban agriculture: research questions and Zambian evidence' *Journal of Modern African Studies*, vol. 26, no.3, 1988, 495–515.

261. Freeman, Donald, *A City of Farmers: Informal Urban Agriculture in the Open Spaces of Nairobi, Kenya*, McGill-Queen's University Press, Montreal and Kingston, 1991.

262. Maxwell, Daniel and Samuel Zziwa, *Urban Farming in Africa: The case of Kampala, Uganda*, ACTS Press, Nairobi, 1992, 29.

263. Schilter, Christine, *L'agriculture urbaine à Lomé: Approches agronomique et socio-économique*, Karthala and IUED, Paris and Geneva, 1991.

3 Social Conditions and Trends

3.1 Assessing Progress

Introduction

Over the last 30–40 years, almost all countries have achieved considerable economic and social gains. The social gains can be seen in much increased life expectancy and the reduction in the proportion of the world's population facing hunger, life-threatening deprivation and easily preventable or curable diseases. They are also evident in the improvements in housing and living conditions and in the increased proportion of the world's population with access to piped water, sanitation, health care and education. But there is a growing body of data showing a slowing in social progress or even a halt and decline in some countries during the 1980s. In absolute terms, the proportion of the population living below the 'poverty line' increased during the 1980s. In the South, much of this is associated with economic stagnation and/or debt crises and with structural adjustment. In most of the transition countries, this is linked to the collapse of communism and the disintegration of the Soviet Union, although in many countries, social progress had also slowed in the years prior to these changes.

In several of the wealthiest countries, the slowing in social progress was less associated with economic stagnation and more associated with changes in the labour market, including a growth in long-term unemployment and with political changes that reduced expenditures on social welfare and gave a low priority to addressing such issues as structural unemployment and rising homelessness. In many such nations, inequalities in income distribution also grew. Changing labour markets also increased the number of people with inadequate incomes.

There are two great uncertainties about the long-term impact of structural adjustment in the South and the fundamental political and economic changes within the transition countries. The first is whether they provide the basis for a more stable and prosperous economy. The second is whether improved economic performance will then be translated into social progress. As Chapter 2 noted, the economic performance of many countries in Latin America during the early 1990s improved considerably, when compared to the 1980s, but there also remains a large backlog of social problems that need to be addressed, many of them considerably increased by the economic measures taken to provide more economic

stability and better prospects for economic growth. There are also doubts about the extent to which the renewed economic growth will be sustained, especially after the economic difficulties that Mexico faced from late 1994.

How best to assess social progress

Any review of social progress is faced with considerable difficulties in assessing conditions and how these changed. First, it is difficult to measure social progress or improvements in the quality of life. This is both in what should be measured and in what it is possible to measure (and whether it is measured for most countries). Ideally, a range of indicators should be measured that reflect two aspects of wellbeing: the *constituents* of well-being such as health, life expectancy, civil and political rights, and the main *determinants* of well-being— such as income, housing quality (that should include adequate provision for water, sanitation and drainage within neighbourhoods), and the quality and accessibility of schools, health care services and other social facilities.[1] But for most nations, there is very inadequate data available for most of these constituents and determinants of well-being to allow progress to be assessed. As Chapter 6 will describe, basic data on the quantity and quality of the housing stock is not available in most nations. In addition, the quality and accuracy of the little data that is available is open to question. Chapter 8 will describe the uncertainties as to whether the figures on the proportion of national populations with access to water and sanitation are accurate and question whether the statistics that show a considerable increase in the proportion of the world's population adequately served are valid. There is also a tendency for all international comparisons on social conditions and trends to fall back on a few indicators that are easily measured and for which there is data for most countries and use these as the basis for judging the extent of social progress—and perhaps too little critical consideration as to the quality of the data used or the extent to which the indicators chosen reflect social progress.

To give a broad overview of social progress worldwide, this chapter will mainly concentrate on a review of changes in *life expectancy at birth* which is probably the indicator that most accurately reflects the quality of housing and living conditions and provision for basic services. There will also be a brief review of progress in reducing infant mortality and increasing adult literacy, and a consideration of the Human Development Index that combines progress on per capita income, life expectancy and adult literacy.

The links between life expectancy and social progress

The life expectancy at birth in a country i.e. the average number of years a person will live from birth—is among the most valuable single indicators of social achievement. It is a measure of the extent to which economic, social and political factors within a country have made it possible for citizens to avoid premature death and, in general, lead a healthy life. A study of living standards in 48 low-income countries in 1980 developed an aggregate indicator based on four socio-economic indicators and one each for civil and political rights: among these six indicators, life expectancy at birth proved to have the strongest correlation with the aggregate indicator. The authors of this study suggested that 'if we had to choose a single, ordinal indicator of aggregate well-being, life expectancy at birth would seem to be the best'.[2]

Life expectancy at birth also has other advantages as a social indicator. Both the concept and the statistic itself is easily understood by all groups—unlike more sophisticated compound indicators.[3] It is sometimes possible to obtain figures for life expectancy disaggregated by income group, ethnic group or region—and in some instances for particular groups within nations, to see whether they are below or above the national average. For instance, a finding that the homeless in London have a life expectancy of over 25 years less than the national average gives some indication of their level of deprivation. Life expectancy figures can also be disaggregated by age groups; for instance, figures for the average life expectancy for a social group at a particular age—

TABLE 3.1 A summary of changes in social and economic indicators for regions and selected countries over the last few decades

Country or region	Real GDP per capita (ppp U$)		Life expectancy at birth (years)		Infant mortality rate		% of mal-nourished children		% of popn. with access to safe water		Adult literacy rate	
	1960	1991	1960	1992	1960	1992	1975	1990	1975/80	1988/91	1970	1992
World		5,490	53.4	65.6	128	60						
'The North'		14,860	69.0	74.5	35	13						
'The South'	950	2,730	46.2	63.0	149	69	40	35	36	70	46	69
'Least developed countries'	580	880	39.0	50.1	170	112	46	40	21	45	29	46
Latin America and the Caribbean	2,140	5,360	56.0	67.7	105	47	17	10	60	79	76	86
Arab States	1,310	4,420	46.7	64.3	165	54	25	20	71	79	30	57
South Asia	700	1,260	43.8	58.5	164	94	69	59	–	–	33	47
East Asia	730	3,210	47.5	70.5	146	27	26	21	–	–	–	–
South-East Asia	1,000	3,420	45.3	62.9	126	55	46	34	15	53	67	86
Sub-Saharan Africa	–	1,250	40.0	51.1	165	101	31	31	25	45	28	51
North America	9,780	21,860	70.0	75.8								
Europe												
European Community	5,050	16,760	69.7	76.3								
Nordic countries	5,770	17,230	71.9	76.5								
Southern Europe	3,390	14,100	67.6	76.9								
Countries with the largest increase in the human development index, 1960–92												
Malaysia	1,783	7,400	53.9	70.4	73	14	31	18	–	–	60	80
Botswana	474	4,690	45.5	60.3	116	61	37	27	–	–	41	75
Korea, Republic of	690	8,320	53.9	70.4	85	21	–	–	66	92	88	97
Tunisia	1,394	4,690	48.4	67.1	159	44	17	9	35	99	31	68
Thailand	985	5,720	52.3	68.7	103	26	36	13	25	76	79	94
Syrian Arab Republic	1,787	5,220	49.8	66.4	135	40	20	13	–	–	40	67
Turkey	1,669	4,840	50.1	66.7	190	57	15	11	68	92	52	82
China	723	2,946	47.1	70.5	150	27	26	21	–	–	–	–
Examples of countries with among the smallest increase in the human development index 1960–92												
Zambia	1,172	1,010	41.6	45.5	135	84	17	26	42	48	52	75
Uganda	371	1,036	43.0	42.6	133	104	28	26	35	15	41	51
Malawi	423	800	37.8	44.6	207	143	19	24	51	53	–	–
Ethiopia	262	370	36.0	46.4	175	123	45	40	8	28	–	–
Afghanistan	775	700	33.4	42.9	215	164	19	40	9	21	8	32

Source: Statistics drawn from UNDP, *Human Development Report 1994*, Oxford University Press, New York and Oxford, 1994.

rather than from birth—can highlight an above average mortality that demands attention.

The figure for a country's average life expectancy tells one much about the overall state of its human settlements. It is impossible for a country to achieve a high life expectancy without most of its inhabitants having good quality housing that includes safe and sufficient water supplies and adequate provision for sanitation. It is also impossible without a wide coverage by health care, including special provision for infants and children and women's reproductive health. The often very large differences in average life expectancy between countries with comparable levels of per capita income are closely linked to the quality of housing and the extent of basic service provision—although there is considerable controversy over the relative merits of improved housing, improved water and sanitation, improved health care and improved education—see Box 3.1. As Chapter 4 will describe, it tends to be the infectious and parasitic diseases and the very high maternal and peri-natal mortality rates that keep average life expectancies low—and much of the improvement in life expectancy at least up to 60–65 years or so arises from the improvements in health care and disease control, and in housing quality and the basic services associated with good quality housing.

Figures for a country's average life expectancy are also particularly sensitive to infant and child mortality rates and to maternal mortality rates since a high average life expectancy is impossible if there is a significant proportion of infants, children or young mothers dying. Even prosperous countries cannot become among the nations with the highest life expectancies, if a significant proportion of their population lack the income, living conditions and access to services that protect against premature death. However, among the more prosperous countries, increasing life expectancy also becomes a matter of encouraging healthy lifestyles and limiting the health costs of high consumption lifestyles, as well as ensuring all citizens have the basis for a healthy life.

Changes in life expectancy at birth

The world average for life expectancy increased by 12 years between 1960 and 1992 from 53.2 to 65.6 years. The average for the South increased by 17 years, although it began from a base of only 46.2 years in 1960. An average life expectancy of 46.2 years might seem very low but less than 100 years ago, this was also the life expectancy in the United States and in England and Wales.[4] Less than 100 years ago, in 1900, life expectancy at birth throughout Africa, Asia and Latin America was a mere 25–28 years.[5] Even the world average in 1992 of 65.6 years may seem low, yet the life

---

BOX 3.1
Does improved housing raise life expectancy?

There is considerable debate about which basic services and what aspects of health care are most cost-effective in terms of improving life expectancy. In recent years, relatively little consideration has been given to the role within this of good quality, adequate size and reasonably priced housing for which the inhabitants have secure tenure—although historic studies have sought to separate out the role of housing from other factors.[6] There is also a considerable debate about which basic services provide the greatest reductions in mortality—for instance the proponents of 'selective primary health care' argue for a concentration on a limited range of cheap interventions such as immunization against the many vaccine-preventable diseases and oral rehydration therapy for rapidly treating diarrhoeal diseases and give a lower priority to water supply and sanitation.[7]

It may be that there are few generalizable guidelines as the relative importance of the housing structure and size itself as distinct from housing-related infrastructure and services (piped water supply, provision for sanitation and drainage and, where needed, solid waste collection), education and health

care. Their relative importance is likely to vary from settlement to settlement. In very densely populated squatter settlements—with an average of four or more persons per room, in shacks made of temporary materials, with little room between shacks, and where people cook on open fires—the size and physical quality of the shelters—with high levels of indoor air pollution, ready transmission of communicable diseases linked to overcrowding (including acute respiratory infections, TB, influenza and meningitis), and the frequent burns, scalds and accidental fires associated with the overcrowding and temporary materials—may be a major factor in premature death. Certainly accidents and respiratory infections that are linked to high levels of indoor air pollution take a major toll in infant and child health in such settlements. In densely populated settlements with very inadequate provision for piped water and surface drainage and with provision for sanitation no more than pits or bucket latrines, shared by thirty or more persons, the inadequacy in provision for piped water, sanitation and drainage may be the main factor in premature death.

In urban centres, especially cities, the cost of housing becomes increasingly important as capacity to pay for housing influences housing quality and the amount of income available for

food and medicines. In addition, choices as to what should be the concentration of any government or donor agency should also consider what the inhabitants themselves regard as priorities and what they themselves would be prepared to contribute in both time and money. A water supply piped into the home of each squatter household might be considered 'too expensive' by the government or donor agency but might actually be very cheap where this is a high priority for the households who are themselves prepared to pay a high proportion of the costs. Perhaps the most important lesson is the difficulty of establishing general guidelines as to 'most effective intervention' to improve life expectancy since it is going to vary greatly from settlement to settlement, as is the contribution that the inhabitants themselves are able and/or willing to make towards each intervention. Identifying the most appropriate use of limited resources within each particular context will usually depend on greatly increasing the power of low income groups and their community organizations to influence priorities and how limited resources are used; the participatory tools and methods by which external agencies can do so are described in Chapter 9.

expectancy of the United States was around 66 years in 1950.[8] Thus, the world's average life expectancy at birth today is the same as that of the world's wealthiest country some 45 years ago. Table 3.1 presents statistics for the average life expectancy by region for 1960 and 1992.

Table 3.2 presents the increase in life expectancy for the five countries with the highest and the lowest increase in life expectancy at birth within eight country-categories. Countries were allocated to these categories according to their life expectancy in 1960. This is because it becomes increasingly difficult to increase life expectancy, as life expectancy increases.[9] It is easier for countries to achieve large increases in life expectancy, if they begin from a low base, since so much premature death is avoided through better nutrition, environmental health and health care. In commenting on these, note will also be made where a much increased life expectancy coincides with a much increased per capita income—and where it does not.

As might be expected, countries in the Group with the highest life expectancies in 1960 already had life expectancies of 70 or more years and had the smallest increase of any of the groups. What is also notable is the smaller range between the best and the worst performing countries, compared to other groups. Part of the reason for the relatively low levels of increase among countries such as Sweden, Netherlands and Norway is that they had already achieved life expectancies in excess of 73 years in 1960.

In Group 2, the five countries with the largest increase in life expectancy were also among the countries with the most rapid increase in their per capita income 1960–91. Not surprisingly they include Japan, which during this period became one of the world's wealthiest countries and also one of the major influences on the global economy. They also include Hong Kong, also with a leading role in the world economy (and among the countries with the most rapid growth in per capita income) and Greece and Spain from Southern Europe. Southern Europe had one of the most rapid growth rates for per capita income of any region during this period. The top-performing countries in this group had achieved levels of life expectancy comparable to those in the best-performing countries in Group 1. By contrast, most of the countries with the smallest growth in life expectancy in this period were from East Europe and Central Europe or from the former Soviet Union. Life expectancies fell in many countries in East Europe during the 1980s. In the countries that formerly made up the USSR, life expectancy at birth declined by nearly two years between 1970 and 1980 and by 1990, was back at around the same level that it had been in 1970.[10] Although Central and East European countries now have lower life expectancies than

countries in Western Europe, there was a period in the late 1940s and the mid-1960s when they converged.[11] There is considerable debate as to what underlies this. Explanations in the West have generally concentrated on bureaucratic inefficiencies in health services and in food production and distribution, on industrial pollution and on increased alcohol consumption.[12] However, an alternative explanation has been advanced that the young adult group in the Second World War suffered major deprivation and that a considerable proportion of healthy males were killed during the war—and so when this age group aged significantly in the mid-1960s, it was peculiarly vulnerable to mortality.[13] In addition, an analysis of the demographic impact of sudden impoverishment in Eastern Europe between 1989 and 1994 suggests that 'none of the traditional risk factors (environmental degradation, smoking, diet and alcohol consumption) appear to explain much of the recent increase in mortality, either because there is sufficient evidence that the variable in question has moved in a favourable direction (as in the case of industrial emissions and smoking) or because the existing information is either ambiguous or apparently un-correlated with the observed mortality outcomes'.[14] This study suggested instead that the drops in life expectancy were more related to economic stress and poorer quality health services—and also pointed out how in most countries, it was sharp increase in mortality among middle-aged males that was a major contributor to falling life expectancies.[15]

In Group 3, several of the countries with the largest increase in life expectancy were also the ones with the most rapid economic growth (for instance Portugal and Singapore). Others achieved large increases in life expectancy without rapid growth in per capita income—for instance Cuba and Costa Rica. As in Group 2, several of the countries in this Group with the largest increases in life expectancy had achieved among the world's highest levels of life expectancy by 1992. Three of the countries with the lowest increase in life expectancy were also those with among the smallest increases in per capita income (Sri Lanka, Argentina and Trinidad and Tobago). Paraguay had a relatively rapid increase in per capita income but much the lowest increase in life expectancy within this group.

In Group 4, the largest increases in life expectancy were achieved by three Latin American countries with among the highest increases in per capita income in their region and two wealthy oil-producing states. The two countries with the smallest increases also had among the lowest increases in per capita income and, in the case of Lebanon, extensive civil strife for much of the period under consideration.

TABLE 3.2 Countries with the highest and the lowest increases in life expectancy, 1960-1992

Countries with the highest increase in life expectancy 1960–1992			Countries with the lowest increase in life expectancy 1960–1992		
Country	Life Expectancy		Increase in life exp.	Country	Life Expectancy		Increase in life exp.
	1960	1992	1960–1992		1960	1992	1960–1992
1. Countries where life expectancy exceeded 70.0 years in 1960							
Switzerland	71.2	77.8	6.6	Sweden	73.1	77.7	4.6
France	70.3	76.6	6.3	New Zealand	70.9	75.3	4.4
Canada	71.0	77.2	6.2	Netherlands	73.2	77.2	4.0
Australia	70.7	76.7	6.0	Norway	73.4	76.9	3.5
Belgium	70.3	75.7	5.4	Denmark	72.1	75.3	3.2
2. Countries where life expectancy was between 65.0 and 69.9 in 1960							
Hong Kong	66.2	77.4	11.2	Bulgaria	68.5	71.9	3.4
Japan	67.9	78.6	10.7	Estonia	68.8	71.2	2.4
Greece	68.7	77.3	8.6	Czechoslovakia	69.9	72.1	2.2
Spain	69.0	77.4	8.4	Hungary	68.1	70.1	2.0
Cyprus	68.7	76.7	8.0	Latvia	69.6	71.0	1.4
3. Countries where life expectancy was between 60.0 and 64.9 in 1960							
Costa Rica	61.6	76.0	14.4	Sri Lanka	62.0	71.2	9.2
Panama	60.7	72.5	11.8	Bahamas	63.2	71.9	8.7
Cuba	63.8	75.6	11.8	Trinidad & Tobago	63.5	70.9	7.4
Brunei Darussalam	62.3	74.0	11.7	Argentina	64.9	71.1	6.2
Portugal	63.3	74.4	11.1	Paraguay	63.8	67.2	3.4
4. Countries where life expectancy was between 55.0 and 59.9 in 1960							
Bahrain	55.5	71.0	15.5	Fiji	59.0	71.1	12.1
Kuwait	59.6	74.6	15.0	Venezuela	59.6	70.1	10.5
Chile	57.1	71.9	14.8	Mauritius	59.2	69.6	10.4
Mexico	57.1	69.9	12.8	Lebanon	59.6	68.1	8.5
Colombia	56.6	69.0	12.4	Guyana	56.1	64.6	8.5
5. Countries where life expectancy was between 50.0 and 54.9 in 1960							
Solomon Islands	50.3	70.0	19.7	Dominican Repub.	51.8	67.0	15.2
United Arab Em.	53.0	70.8	17.8	El Salvador	50.5	65.2	14.7
Korea, Dem. Rep.	53.9	70.7	16.8	Ecuador	53.1	66.2	13.1
Turkey	50.1	66.7	16.6	Philippines	52.8	64.6	11.8
Qatar	53.0	69.6	16.6	Brazil	54.7	65.8	11.1
6. Countries where life expectancy was between 45.0 and 49.9 in 1960							
China	47.1	70.5	23.4	Botswana	45.5	60.3	14.8
Jordan	47.0	67.3	20.3	Egypt	46.2	60.9	14.7
Honduras	46.5	65.2	18.7	South Africa	49.0	62.2	13.2
Tunisia	48.4	67.1	18.7	Zimbabwe	45.3	56.1	10.8
Algeria	47.0	65.6	18.6	Ghana	45.0	55.4	10.4
7. Countries where life expectancy was between 40.0 and 44.9 in 1960							
Oman	40.1	69.1	29.0	Cambodia	42.4	50.4	8.0
Saudi Arabia	44.4	68.7	24.3	Burundi	41.3	48.2	6.9
Indonesia	41.2	62.0	20.8	Rwanda	42.3	46.5	4.2
Viet Nam	44.2	63.4	19.2	Zambia	41.6	45.5	3.9
Maldives	43.6	62.2	18.6	Uganda	43.0	42.6	−0.4
8. Countries where life expectancy was below 40.0 in 1960							
Cameroon	39.3	55.3	16.0	Afghanistan	33.4	42.9	9.5
Yemen	36.4	51.9	15.5	Mozambique	37.3	46.5	9.2
Togo	39.3	54.4	15.1	Guinea-Bissau	34.0	42.9	8.9
Nepal	38.4	52.7	14.3	Central Af. Rep.	38.5	47.2	8.7
Bangladesh	39.6	52.2	12.6	Malawi	37.8	44.6	6.8

Notes and Sources: Countries are grouped into eight categories, according to their life expectancy at birth in 1960, since in general, it is easier to achieve large increases in life expectancy if beginning from a low base. Statistics drawn from UNDP, *The Human Development Report 1994*. Oxford University Press, Oxford and New York, 1994.

Group 5 is interesting for the fact that South Korea, Thailand and Malaysia are in this group and had among the world's most rapid growth in per capita income but none of them figure among the five countries with the most rapid increase in life expectancy. However, in all three of these countries, life expectancy did increase by around 16.5 years. Brazil, which also had among the most rapid growths in per capita income of any country, is also the country with the smallest increase in life expectancy in this group.

In Group 6, China had among the largest increases in life expectancy of any country in the world between 1960 and 1992. The achievement is particularly notable, given that China contains around one-fifth of the world's entire population—and more people than Africa and North and South America combined. It is also worth recalling that China was certainly not free of social and political turmoil during this period—including the catastrophic famine of 1960/1 and the cultural revolution. Although Botswana, Egypt and South Africa all increased average life expectancy by between 13 and 15 years, this was a relatively small increase in relation to their economic performance. For South Africa, this is not surprising given that the apartheid policies of the (then) government limited greatly the possibilities for improvements in income and housing and living conditions for most of the population on the basis of their colour. For Ghana, with the lowest increase in life expectancy within this group, this is more associated with economic performance in that per capita income declined overall during these 32 years.

For Group 7, two of the countries with the largest increase in life expectancy were also among the world's most rapidly growing economies—Indonesia and Oman. The large increase in life expectancy in Indonesia might also be partially explained by the fact that inequality decreased during this period.[16] Four of the countries with the lowest increases in life expectancy were ones in which there were serious and prolonged wars (Cambodia) or civil wars (Rwanda, Burundi, Uganda) during these years while for the fifth (Zambia) there was an absolute decline in per capita income during this period.

The link between wars and relatively small increases in life expectancy can also be seen in Group 8 for Afghanistan and Mozambique. Group 8 is also notable in having none of the world's most rapidly growing economies; it contains none of the 20 countries with the largest overall increase in life expectancy during this period, even though, as noted earlier, the lower the average life expectancy in 1960, the more that social and economic progress is likely to be translated into large increases in life expectancy. Group 8 is also dominated by countries from sub-Saharan Africa. Twenty-three of the twenty-nine countries in this group are in sub-Saharan Africa—a reminder of how low life expectancies were in much of sub-Saharan Africa as most countries in the region gained independence in the late 1950s and the 1960s. Most countries in Group 8 began and finished the period under consideration (1960–92) with little or no

success within the world economy. A regional analysis of improvements in life expectancy between 1950 and 1990 found that sub-Saharan Africa was the region in the South showing the slowest improvement, although the rate of improvement still compares well with European experience in the nineteenth century.[17] The former socialist countries of Europe showed a rapid improvement during the 1950s and 1960s but the rise was much slower in the 1970s and 1980s.[18]

Life expectancy, human settlement policies and inequality

Two themes related to life expectancy are of particular relevance to human settlements. The first is the extent to which 'human settlement policies' in the widest sense (including policies on housing and the basic services associated with housing, especially water, sanitation and health care) can increase the average life expectancy of a country. The second is the extent to which it is the scale of inequality within nations in terms of income and assets that helps explain their national 'average life expectancy'.

The countries with the highest life expectancy are also generally the countries with the highest per capita income while the countries with the largest increases in life expectancy 1960–1992 are also those with the largest increases in per capita income. There are large variations in the life expectancy of countries with similar levels of per capita income—although beyond a certain level of per capita income, the variations become smaller. For instance, countries with per capita incomes of around $US500 in 1991 can have average life expectancies ranging from 43 to 53 years. At per capita incomes of $US1,000, average life expectancies can be under 45 years or close to 60 years. At per capita incomes of around $US2,000, the range is from 55 to over 65; at per capita incomes of around $US3,000, the range is from under 55 to over 70.

There are also large variations in the increase in life expectancy between 1960 and 1992 among countries with similar increases in per capita income who also had similar life expectancies in 1960. Among the two most important factors in explaining these variations in the proportion of the population with below poverty line incomes and the quality of housing and basic service provision. In general, countries that were well above and well below the average range for life expectancy in 1960 were also there in 1992. Among the countries that showed the greatest increase in life expectancy relative to increases in per capita income in these 32 years were Japan, Costa Rica, China, Cuba, Chile, Trinidad and Tobago, Barbados, Hong Kong and Jamaica.

A recent study highlighted how the extent of

inequality and of basic service provision are a major influence on the life expectancy achieved for any low income country.[19] This study looked at twenty-two low-income countries for which there was data on the proportion of people with below poverty-line incomes and public expenditure on social services, as well as on life expectancy and per capita income. This found that the significantly positive relationship between life expectancy and per capita income disappears in a regression of life expectancy against poverty incidence, public health spending and average income. The results also suggested that one-third of the increase in life expectancy was due to reduced poverty and two-thirds to increased spending on social services associated with higher incomes. As the study notes, 'this does not imply that economic growth is unimportant in expanding life expectancy but it says that the importance of growth lies in the way that its benefits are distributed between people and the extent to which growth supports public health services'.[20] The study noted that despite the small size of the sample and the lack of specificity in regard to health expenditures—it is clear that health expenditures concentrated on preventive rather than curative services are more effective in improving health and life expectancy in low income countries—'this cross-country evidence does offer some provisional support for the view that, at least for basic health, the main channels by which growth promotes human development in a typical developing country are through its impact on income poverty and the public provisioning of health services. Average income matters but only insofar as it reduces poverty and finances key social services'.[21]

The association between life expectancy and per capita income is also weak within the wealthiest countries but strongly associated with the level of inequality. The countries with the highest life expectancies are generally those with the smallest gap between the highest and the lowest income groups.[22] An examination of changes in income distribution in twelve European Union countries between 1975 and 1985 showed a more rapid improvement in life expectancy following a fall in the prevalence of relative poverty.[23] In the United States, mortality reduction to achieve a high level of life expectancy appropriate for its very high per capita income may be prevented by the fact that a sizeable segment of its population belong to groups who are severely disadvantaged.[24]

Progress in other social indicators

Infant mortality rates (the number of infants who die between birth and the age of 1) and child mortality rates (the number who die between birth and the age of 5) are also widely used as a measure of social progress. Given the vulnerability of infants and children to malnutrition and to many infectious and parasitic diseases, infant and child mortality rates are much influenced by levels of poverty and by the quality and extent of provision of health care (including special provision for infant, child and maternal health) and for water supply and sanitation. Infant and child mortality rates are the major influence on average life expectancy, for countries with a low life expectancy. The countries that had the largest increases in life expectancy between 1960 and 1992 are also generally those with the largest decreases in infant and child mortality. However, as reductions in poverty and improvements in health care and in housing and living conditions decrease these rates, so reductions in adult mortality become particularly important for achieving further increases in life expectancy. For instance, most of the recent gains in life expectancy in countries in the North have been the result of reduction in mortality among elderly people.[25] More than half the increase in life expectancy in Japan in the early 1980s was due to the reduction in mortality among elderly people.[26]

Worldwide, there were major improvements in both infant and child mortality rates over the last 30–40 years. As shown in Table 3.1, infant mortality rates in 1992 were less than half what they were in 1960 both as a world average (60 per 1,000 live births compared to 128 in 1960) and as an average for the South (69 compared to 149 in 1960).[27] Again, progress has been swift in the North and most of the South, especially in East Asia and the Arab states. But in 1992, there were still fifty countries with child mortality rates that exceeded 100 (i.e. with one child in ten who was born alive dying before their fifth birthday). In at least seven of these fifty countries, child mortality rates did not fall or increased between 1980 and 1992: Niger, Angola, Mozambique, Rwanda, Zambia, Uganda and Ghana. The statistics in Table 3.1 also show how progress in reducing infant mortality rates was least in Sub-Saharan Africa and South Asia and, in general, among countries designated as the 'least developed'.

A recent review of health and mortality within Europe noted that between 1980 and 1990, there was considerable progress in most European countries in lowering what were already among the lowest infant mortality rates in the world. In 1980, only eight among thirty-four European countries had infant mortality rates of 10 or less per 1,000 live births; by 1990, twenty-four countries had infant mortality rates of 10 or less. Only 30 years ago, infant mortality rates of 10 were considered the 'biological limit'.[28]

Among other indicators showing significant improvements worldwide or for the South are the proportion of the population with access to safe water (see Chapter 8). Adult literacy rates also increased significantly between 1970 and 1992 with the proportion of adults who are literate reaching 86 per cent in Latin America and the Caribbean and in South-East Asia by 1992. But worldwide, one adult in three is still illiterate.[29] Adult literacy rates remain lowest in South Asia and sub-Saharan Africa where only half the adult population was literate in 1992.

Significant increases were also achieved in the proportion of children enrolled in schools and immunized against common childhood diseases and in the proportion of the population with access to health care.[30] Primary school enrolment increased from less than 70 per cent to more than 80 per cent between the early 1970s and the early 1990s while secondary school enrolment grew from less than 25 per cent to 40 per cent.[31] However, what is uncertain in many instances is the quality of the schools and health care services—and whether the initial investment in extending these services is maintained. Most sub-Saharan African nations that managed large increases in the proportion of children in primary schools and the proportion of the population reached with primary health care services during the 1970s and early 1980s had great difficulties in maintaining coverage and quality during the late 1980s and early 1990s.

Various composite indicators of development have been developed over the last 30 years that seek to overcome the concentration on per capita income as the most widely used indicator of development. For instance, there was considerable debate in the late 1970s about the use of the 'Physical quality of life index' that was based on an average of life expectancy at age 1, infant mortality and literacy rates.[32] A recent review of composite development indicators also noted other indices developed in the late 1960s and early 1970s.[33] The most well known of these 'alternative' indicators that seek to ensure that social progress is monitored within development indicators is the human development index, developed by a team working with the United Nations Development Programme (UNDP). This index combines national statistics for life expectancy at birth, adult literacy rates and per capita income;[34] the index is also constructed in such a way as to diminish the influence of per capita income above a certain ceiling.

Table 3.1 includes a list of countries with the largest and among the smallest increase in their 'human development index' between 1960 and 1992. The influence of life expectancy on the human development index can be seen from the fact that among the countries that had the smallest increase in their human development index between 1960 and 1992 were also the countries with the smallest increases in life expectancy. The influence of increases in life expectancy is less strong among countries with the most successful economic performance. Thus, among the eight countries noted for the largest increase in their human development index between 1960 and 1992, only China had achieved an above average performance in increasing life expectancy relative to increases in per capita income. Among the other six, all but Botswana had been within the 'average' range for improving life expectancy relative to per capita income.

Inequality in social progress within countries

There are also major differences in social progress between population groups within national societies that reflect differences in their economic and political power and per capita incomes. They also reflect discrimination against particular groups—for instance by caste or ethnic group or by gender, as women face discrimination in labour markets and in access to services. The scale and nature of such inequality is often difficult to assess, as most statistics on social progress are not available, disaggregated by income-group. However, some are available by region or district within countries and these reveal the differences in social progress between those living in high quality, predominantly high-income areas and those living in poor quality, predominantly low-income areas. Some statistics on social progress are also available by ethnic group or (occasionally) by sex or age group.

Where statistics are available on life expectancy by region within a country, average life expectancies in the poorest regions can be many years less than the national average—or as much as 17–20 years less than the wealthiest regions (see Box 3.2). The same is true for cities—as in the example given in Box 3.2 where in 1988 there was a 22-year difference between average life expectancy in Fortaleza and Porto Alegre in Brazil. There are also differences in life expectancy between high-income and low-income regions in countries in the North, although the scale of the differences is much less—especially where there are effective measures to ensure that those with inadequate incomes can still obtain adequate food and access to adequate quality housing and basic services (including health care and education). Where statistics are available on life expectancy by 'ethnic group', where there are large differentials in income between such groups, there are usually large differentials in life expectancy—see Box 3.2.

Infant mortality rates can also vary greatly between districts or regions—sometimes by a factor of 10 or more when the poorest regions are compared to the wealthiest regions. They can also vary by this much or more between the wealthiest and poorest districts or municipalities

BOX 3.2
Examples of geographic, ethnic and gender-based inequalities in social progress

Differences in life expectancy. Within Brazil, life expectancy in the poor North-East is 17 years lower than in the much more wealthy South, while in Nigeria, there is a 20-year difference in life expectancy between Borno State and Bendel State.[35] Among cities, in 1988, average life expectancy in Fortaleza was just 51 years compared to 67 years in Sao Paulo, 68 years in Curitiba and 73 years in Porto Alegre.[36]

Differences between ethnic groups. In Canada, the aboriginal population (the Indians, Inuits and Metis) are reported to have a life expectancy 5.6 years lower than the rest of the population.[37] The legacy of apartheid in South Africa is even more dramatic where the life expectancy at birth for the small minority of whites is 9 years more than for the blacks.[38]

Differences in infant mortality rates. In China, the infant mortality rate in Beijing province is 11 per 1,000 live births; the national average is 35 and for some provinces, it is over 50 including Yunnan (74) and Guizhou (68).[39] Infant mortality rates in the different municipalities that make up Greater Sao Paulo in 1992 vary from 18 (in Sao Caetano do Sol) to 60 in Biritiba-Mirim—although these are much lower than the figures for 1980.[40] The infant mortality rate in the Easterhouse estate in the northeast of Glasgow, one of the poorest areas of Glasgow, was 46.7 per 1,000 births around 1990 compared to 10 for the middle-class suburb of Bishopbriggs.[41]

Differences in maternal mortality rates. In China, the maternal mortality rate per 100,000 live births in Beijing province is 40; the national average is 88 and in some provinces, it is 170 (Sichuan, Yunnan, Guizhou).[42] In South Africa, in 1989, the maternal mortality rate was 8 per 100,000 for whites and more than 58 per 100,000 for Africans.[43]

within cities. For instance, infant mortality rates in the municipalities that make up Greater Sao Paulo vary by a factor of three with the highest rate being 60 per 1,000 live births in 1992—although this represents great progress since 1980 when infant mortality rates between municipalities varied by a factor of 5 with the highest being 154.[44] Large differentials in infant mortality rates between the lower income, poor quality areas and city averages (or high income areas) have also been found in many other cities.[45] Again, differentials in infant mortality rates are generally less between districts within cities in the North—although around 1990, Easterhouse, one of the poorest areas within Glasgow (Scotland) had an infant mortality rate that was close to five times that of a middle class suburb[46] (see Box 3.2). New techniques have also been developed to document intra-urban differentials in mortality and morbidity, disaggregated by age, gender and geo-

graphic area, and these have confirmed that mortality rates are higher in areas with the poorest quality housing.[47]

Certain inequalities in social progress have less to do with income-inequality and more to do with political systems that determine priorities for social provision. The two examples given in Box 3.2 of large differences in maternal mortality rates are more about the scale and nature of government priority for women's reproductive health than about individual or household income.

The fact that most statistics on inequality are by geographic region or ethnic group has led to some confusion between social and spatial inequalities. Governments often react to what appear to be spatial inequalities with spatial programmes when it is the inequality in the distribution of income or of government resources for social programmes that underlies these inequalities. For instance, fiscal incentives to encourage new industrial investment in a 'low-income' region will do little to improve social indicators if the new investment does not bring increased incomes for a significant proportion of the lower income groups there. And the cost to the government in providing the incentives may have been far more effectively spent in working with the low-income population there in developing their livelihood opportunities and in improving infrastructure and service provision.

3.2 Poverty[48]

Introduction

Our knowledge about the nature of urban poverty and its causes increased considerably during the 1980s—linked perhaps to the rapid increase in urban poverty in many nations in the South and at least in several in the North. However, much of the recent research on urban (and rural) poverty is not so much on estimating its scale as on questioning the very basis on which such estimates are made. Poverty had come to mean what was measured and measurable[49] which may lead to a situation where the figures produced for the scale of poverty bear little relation to the number of people suffering serious deprivation.

Between a fifth and a quarter of the world's population live in absolute poverty, without adequate food, clothing and shelter.[50] More than 90 per cent of these live in the South. There is considerable debate about the exact number, and about how the number of people who are suffering from absolute poverty should be measured. This is especially so in urban areas where estimates range from under 200 million to at least 600 million. However, there is general agreement about the considerable growth in the number of urban dwellers living in absolute poverty during the 1980s. By 1990, at least 600 million people in the urban areas in Latin America, Asia and Africa were living in housing of such poor quality and with such inadequate provision for water, sanitation and drainage that their lives and health were under continuous threat.[51] United Nations estimates suggest that the urban population in the South will grow by more than 600 million during the 1990s and without major improvements in housing markets and in the expansion and improved provision of infrastructure and services, the number of people living in such conditions will expand very rapidly.

The definition of poverty

Poverty implies deprivation or human needs that are not met. It is generally understood to arise from a lack of income or assets. In all countries, it is possible to identify individuals or households who are poor because their income or asset base is too small to permit them to meet physical needs—for instance to obtain an adequate diet and to find (or build) adequate quality housing with basic services such as safe and sufficient water supplies and provision for sanitation. There is general agreement on other aspects of poverty—for instance those who cannot obtain health care when sick or injured and those who have no means of subsistence when unemployed, ill, disabled or too old to work are generally considered poor. There are other aspects about which there is less agreement—for instance should people who are denied basic civil and political rights or whose physical needs are met but who lack the resources that enable them to meet social obligations[52] or who in other ways are excluded from work or social activities be considered poor? Box 3.3 defines how the term poverty and also deprivation and vulnerability that are associated with poverty are understood within this section.

The measurement of 'poverty' both in the sense of how many people suffer deprivation as a result of poverty and the intensity of that deprivation is one of the most important means to monitor development and to assess the performance of public agencies both within nations and internationally. Simple and quantifiable definitions of 'poverty' are needed to permit its measurement. Definitions that set a 'poverty line' to divide the population into the 'poor' and the 'non-poor' are often the most inaccurate because they simplify and standardize what is highly complex and varied. 'What is measurable and measured then becomes what is real, standardizing the diverse, and excluding the divergent and different.'[53]

Most estimates as to the scale of poverty within

BOX 3.3
Some definitions

Poverty is more than low or inadequate income. It refers to lack of physical necessities, assets and income. A loss of assets is often what precipitates poverty. Assets include tangible assets (savings, stores, resources) and intangible assets (for instance claims that can be made for help or resources when in need).

Deprivation encompasses more than poverty as it includes other dimensions such as isolation, vulnerability, and powerlessness. In physical terms, people can be considered deprived if they lack the goods and services that are ordinarily available in their society—for instance the diet, clothing, housing, household facilities, and working and living conditions. In this sense, physical deprivation centres on the conditions experienced; poverty on the lack of income or other resources available that so often underpins deprivation. Powerlessness is important in that it weakens people's capacity to bargain for political and legal rights, access to services and goods allocated by governments.

Vulnerability means 'defencelessness, insecurity and exposure to risk, shocks and stress'.[54] Many low-income households have sufficient income to avoid deprivation until they have to cope with a sudden shock—for instance a sudden increase in the price of staple foods or in school fees or a serious injury or illness for an income-earner. Poor housing and living conditions and a lack of basic services makes people particularly vulnerable to illness and injury.

Source: Drawn largely from Chambers, Robert, 'Poverty and livelihoods; whose reality counts?', an overview paper prepared for the Stockholm Roundtable on Global Change, 22–4 July 1994, 40 pages; Townsend, Peter, *The International Analysis of Poverty*, Harvester/Wheatsheaf, New York, 1993.

---

nations and worldwide set an income level as the poverty line; those with per capita incomes below this line are considered to be poor. But the link between income level and level of deprivation is often weak as many with incomes above the poverty line income suffer serious deprivation and some below the poverty line do not. As a recent WHO report noted,

poverty defined solely by level of personal income cannot cover health, life expectancy, literacy or access to public goods or common property resources. Clean drinking water, for example, is essential for a reasonable standard of living but is not reflected in consumption or income as usually measured. Many poor households have lost access to common property resources which has meant a decline in the availability of fuel, fodder, food and building materials but this is not reflected in income statistics. Likewise, such aspects of a minimum quality of life as security against crime and physical violence and participation in the economic, cultural and political activities of the community are also not revealed in income-based poverty definitions.[55]

There are many people in both North and South that have above-poverty-line incomes but who are still exposed to unacceptable levels of environmental risk, crime and physical violence in their home but who cannot afford to move. There are also many individuals or households who have become poor because they lost assets, not income—for instance those evicted from their homes and lands to make way for 'development' projects and those who have lost access to common property resources that were previously important parts of their livelihood. Box 3.4 outlines some of the inadequacies in the use of income-based poverty lines.

In considering the extent of poverty worldwide and recent trends, this Global Report would prefer to concentrate on what has been termed 'housing-poverty'[56] rather than 'income-poverty' i.e. on the individuals and households who lack safe, secure and healthy shelter with basic infrastructure such as piped water and adequate provision for sanitation, drainage and the removal of household wastes. However, most data on the extent of poverty is on 'income-poverty' i.e. on the proportion of people with incomes below an income-based poverty line. There are obvious links between those with low incomes and those with poor quality housing in all locations where housing markets are monetized and where access to adequate quality housing is determined by a person's or a household's capacity to pay. However, as Chapter 6 will describe, the proportion of the population living in housing of inadequate quality is often much higher than the proportion with below-poverty-line incomes. Very poor housing conditions in many urban areas in the South are due as much to inadequacies in the capacity of city and municipal governments to expand infrastructure and service provision, constraints on land markets for housing and other institutional constraints as on the incomes of those in very poor quality housing.[57]

The extent of rural poverty

A study of rural poverty in 114 developing countries found close to one billion people had incomes and consumption levels that fell below nationally defined poverty lines (see Table 3.3).[58] Two-thirds are in Asia with just over a fifth in sub-Saharan Africa. In forty-two of the poorest countries, more than two-thirds of the rural population lived in poverty. Table 3.3 provides a profile of the rural poor and highlights how 52 per cent of them are in households with landholdings too small to provide them with an adequate income; 24 per cent of them are landless. Thus, for at least half of the rural poor, it is the lack of an adequate asset base—land—rather than a lack of income that underlies their poverty. The proportion of the rural poor that are nomadic/pastoralists is notable in sub-Saharan Africa and among

the 'least developed' countries. Latin America and the Caribbean is notable for having much the lowest proportion of smallholder farmers and much the highest proportion of landless among its poor rural population. This is likely to be related to among the world's most inequitable land-owning structures and a higher level of commercialization of agriculture and agricultural land markets.

The proportion of rural households headed by women is also notable, especially in sub-Saharan Africa. This is not a new phenomenon since under colonial rule, this separation was encouraged to provide cheap labour for mines, plantations or urban labour markets. But the proportion of split households may be increasing in many countries as more husbands migrate in search of work elsewhere, leaving their families behind in the rural areas and because of widowhood, divorce, separation and the disintegration of family bonds.[59]

In recent years, many countries have had an increase in the proportion of their rural population living below the poverty line. Among forty-one countries for which data exists to compare the percentage of the rural population below the poverty line for 1965 (or the closest year) and 1988, in twenty-three, the percentage increased. For all forty-one countries, the percentage decreased—from 35 per cent to 33 per cent of their rural population with incomes below the poverty line, but their number increased from 511 million to 712 million.

The extent of urban poverty

There are no accurate figures for the proportion of the world's population living in absolute poverty in urban areas. Estimates have been made for the number of 'poor' people living in urban areas in the South, based on per capita income. They vary from an estimate made in 1989 of 130 million of the South's 'poorest poor' living in urban areas to an estimate for 1988 made by the World Bank of 330 million people.[60] The first implies that 90 per cent of the South's urban population are not among the poorest while the second still implies that three quarters of the South's urban population are not living in poverty. Neither of these figures can be reconciled with the many national studies or studies of particular urban centres which show that a third to a half of a nation's urban population or a city's population have incomes too low to allow them to meet human needs. National studies in several of the poorest African, Asian and Latin American countries suggest that more than half the urban population are below the poverty line.[61]

There are two reasons why the above global estimates understate the scale of urban poverty.

BOX 3.4
The inadequacies of income-based poverty lines

Few economists would suggest that human welfare can be adequately described by income alone yet in practice, level of income (or consumption) is the most frequently used proxy for human welfare. People whose per capita income falls below an income-defined poverty line are defined as 'poor'. Income is defined as command over resources over time or as the level of consumption that can be afforded while retaining capital intact.[62]

Income-defined poverty lines are problematic for a number of reasons:

The obscuring of social and health dimensions of poverty: The deprivation caused by inadequate income is much reduced if those with low income have access to good quality housing (with adequate provision for water and sanitation) and health care. But income-based poverty lines obscure this. For instance, according to official Indian statistics, the Indian state of Kerala has virtually the same proportion of its urban population under the poverty line as the average for India but life expectancy in Kerala is 11–12 years higher than India as a whole.[63] In most countries in the South, the proportion of the urban population living in very poor quality, overcrowded dwellings with inadequate or no provision for water supply, sanitation, garbage collection and health care is considerably higher than the proportion officially recognized as living with below poverty-line-incomes.

Failure to allow for the very large variation in living costs within and between nations: National and international income-based 'poverty lines' usually fail to make allowances for the large differences in living costs between different locations. For instance, in most countries or regions in the South, the cost of housing, basic services and food for those whose livelihood is in the centre of a major city (whether they live there or have a long and expensive journey to and from work) is generally many times higher than those living in rural areas or small towns.

Failure to take into account intra-household differentials: Households that appear to be above the poverty line may have members who suffer deprivation because they face discrimination in the allocation of resources within the household. For instance, women often receive less than men and girls less than boys. Older people may receive less.

Failure to distinguish between different size households: Using per capita incomes as the poverty line fails to take account of the differences in incomes available to different size households. Given the economies of scale that benefit larger households in such things as shelter costs per person and food purchase and preparation, such households may be much better off than a person living alone, despite having the same per capita income. Small single-parent households and single elderly people with per capita incomes just above the 'poverty line' are likely to be among the 'poor' who are not counted as poor.

Failure to account for non-monetary income sources: The measurement of household income rarely takes into account or gives adequate attention to goods or services that are obtained free or far below their monetary value. For instance, in many rural settlements and small urban centres, a significant proportion of households obtain some foodstuffs, fuel and building materials from open access or common property resources. If they are denied access to this land—as has often been the case—their real incomes can decline very significantly although their monetary income does not. Many urban households engage in urban agriculture and the food so produced represents a significant part of their dietary needs; denying these people access to the land or water sources they need or limiting their right to cultivate foodcrops may not affect their monetary income.

Failure to understand the role of assets: Households with low incomes have often built up an asset base that allows them to avoid destitution when faced with a sudden economic shock (for instance a rise in food or fuel prices or school fees for their children) or an illness or injury to one of their income-earners. Programmes that help low-income households to build their asset base or that help them cope with shocks (for instance to pay for health care and provide a minimum income when income-earners are sick) may be more important for poverty reduction than conventional policy responses. The level of education and training of household members can also be understood as part of their asset base since it influences their capacity to find adequately paid work.

Ease with which income-based poverty lines can be manipulated: Changing the income level at which poverty lines are set or failing to increase the official poverty line to reflect a currency's decreasing purchasing power can decrease the number of people said to be 'poor'.

The way that income-based poverty lines obscure the underlying causes: Characterizing poverty as a 'lack of income' obscures the structural causes and processes that create or exacerbate poverty. In so doing, it helps encourage policy responses that do not address these structural causes. For instance, the more that poverty is equated only with insufficiency of income, the more easy it is to argue that economic growth should receive priority—rather than admit that addressing the root causes of poverty requires a complex combination of growth and redistribution and improved services and facilities.[64]

Source: This draws mainly from Wratten, Ellen, *Conceptualizing Urban Poverty*, Background paper for the Global Report on Human Settlements, 1994.

The first is the failure of income-based poverty lines to act as an accurate proxy for the resources needed to avoid deprivation. The second is that income-based poverty lines set for whole countries do not allow for the higher costs of living in cities. In some instances, income-based poverty lines are also set unrealistically low in relation to the cost of 'a minimum basket of goods and services' that people need to avoid deprivation. Box 3.5 outlines some differences between rural and urban populations in living costs and in their vulnerability to economic change and environmental hazards.

Poverty lines based on one single income level applied in both rural and urban areas will underestimate the scale of urban poverty, because in many urban locations, the costs of certain essential goods and services are substantially higher than in rural areas. No single poverty line can take into account the large differences in the availability and cost of the food, shelter, water, sanitation and health care services. For example, within nations in the South, the costs of fuel, food and shelter in central areas of major cities are generally much higher than in rural areas. In rural areas where subsistence production remains important, those with almost no income may be able to meet many of their nutritional, fuel and building material requirements from crops they grow and from drawing on 'wastelands', forests or woodlands which are open access or common

TABLE 3.3 The scale and nature of the rural poor in Africa, Asia and Latin America

	Asia	Sub-Saharan Africa	Near East & North Africa	Latin America & Car.	All 114 countries	'Least developed' countries
Total rural population (millions, 1988)	2,019	337	106	123	2,584	368
Total rural population below the poverty line	633	204	27	76	939	253
Percent of rural population below the poverty line	31	60	26	61	36	69
Percentage of rural population that are:						
- Smallholder farmers	49	73	42	38	52	67
- Landless	26	11	23	31	25	18
- Nomadic/pastoralists	2	13	5	–	6	16
- Ethnic/indigenous	4.5	0.9		27.1	7.3	1.1
- Small/artisanal fisherp.	4	3	2	5	4	5
- Internally displaced/refugee	5	6	13	1	6	7
Households headed by women as percentage of rural households	9	31	17	17	12	23

Source: Jazairy, Idriss, Mohiuddin Alamgir and Theresa Panuccio (1992), *The State of World Rural Poverty: an Inquiry into its Causes and Consequences*, IT Publications, London.

property resources. The inaccuracies in estimates for the scale of urban poverty are further increased where single poverty lines based on income levels are applied internationally. The income level needed for adequate food and a secure, uncrowded shelter in the centre of one of Latin America's largest cities is likely to be many times that needed for adequate food and a secure uncrowded shelter in most rural areas in sub-Saharan Africa and many rural areas in Asia. It would also be wrong to assume uniform living costs among different urban centres in a country—or even among different locations within a single large city.

BOX 3.5

Rural-urban differences that affect the scale and nature of poverty

Below are outlined some differences between rural and urban areas that will affect the scale and nature of rural and urban poverty. These highlight the disadvantaged position of urban dwellers, relative to rural dwellers. This is not meant to imply that rural dwellers have major advantages over urban dwellers since most urban dwellers have significant advantages over most rural dwellers in such aspects as access to health care, schools and literacy programmes and more diverse job markets. The disadvantages outlined below are also not universal; many are linked to markets for labour, land and commodities that are also influential in some rural areas. Thus, certain rural populations or those living in particular rural areas may face higher living costs than those in urban areas nearby.

Higher living costs: In most nations or regions in the South, urban dwellers generally face higher living costs than rural dwellers, as many items that have to be purchased in urban areas can be obtained free or cheaper in many rural areas as they are growing or produced locally—e.g. fuel, freshwater, traditional building materials (industrial building materials will usually be much more

expensive in rural areas), and housing itself. Urban areas are characterized by a greater degree of commercialization for goods, services and land than rural areas, with urban dwellers being more reliant on incomes or wages earned to obtain access to shelter, food, freshwater, fuel and other goods and services. Within the most urbanized societies, this distinction diminishes and may reverse itself as the costs of housing and basic foodstuffs becomes higher in some rural areas than in urban areas. There are also significant differences in living costs between different urban areas and, within cities, between different neighbourhoods. Urban households that work in or close to the centre of major cities perhaps face the highest costs either in housing or in transport to and from work.

Greater vulnerability to changes in income: The greater dependence of urban households on cash incomes noted above will usually mean a greater vulnerability to price rises and falls in income. In rural areas, there are greater possibilities for subsistence production or foraging, if prices rise or wage incomes fall—although commercialization of land markets in rural areas is often diminishing this. In addition, subsistence production is also important in many urban areas in the South—for instance through urban agriculture and livestock raising .[65]

In many rural areas, landless labourers may be as dependent as urban dwellers on cash incomes and also have limited or no means for subsistence production

'Intangible assets': The nature of support networks based on family, kinship and neighbourhood are generally different in urban areas and may be less effective in providing support or assistance, when needed. However, urban-based community organizations and mobilization may in certain circumstances obtain significant concessions for urban households from the state; in Latin America, urban social movements based on the recognition of collective class interests are important means by which the poor lobby for land rights and infrastructure.[66] Community based organizations also provide means of saving and arranging income earning opportunities.

Greater vulnerability of faecal contamination and certain other environmental hazards: In the absence of adequate provision for sanitation and drainage, urban populations face more serious environmental hazards than rural dwellers. Higher population densities and larger population concentrations mean that in the absence of piped water, drains, sewers and regular garbage collection, urban populations are more at risk from faecal contamination (see Chapter 4).

When allowance is made for differences in living costs between urban and rural areas, the scale of urban poverty increases. This is illustrated by a study of urban poverty for Latin America. The Economic Commission for Latin America estimated the magnitude of poverty in the region based on the number of people lacking the income to afford a minimum 'basket of goods'.[67] This meant poverty lines set for each nation which reflected the cost within that nation of this basket of goods. Some adjustments were also made to allow for differences in living costs between major cities, smaller urban centres and rural areas. This study suggested that 170 million people were living in poverty in urban areas in Latin America which is more than twice the number suggested by the World Bank estimates for 1985.

This and other studies suggest that poverty lines must be set within the context of each nation and that international estimates based on a single poverty line are inaccurate. It cautions against taking too aggregated a view of poverty; case studies of poverty reveal a complex set of causal and contributory factors—and show that the nature of poverty and who is poor or at risk of poverty and the relative importance of different causal or contributory factors vary for different individuals and social groups within nations. For some, poverty is seasonal or associated with particular circumstances—for instance poor rains or seasonal changes in food prices. Although seasonal variations in the number of poor people has long been understood in rural areas, there are also examples of similar variations in the scale of urban poverty as seasonal changes affect food prices and labour markets there.[68] The fact that a considerable proportion of the low-income population of many cities lives on floodplains or slopes vulnerable to land- or mudslides also means particular problems for these people during periods of high rain. For others, it is associated with an economic downturn which removed their source of livelihood or reduced their purchasing power. For others, it is associated with a particular point in their family cycle—for instance within households when children are young and not able to contribute to household income and where one parent (usually the mother) has few if any income-earning possibilities because of the need to care for the children and undertake household tasks. For many low-income people, poverty is the result of a sudden shock: a sudden or serious injury or death of an adult family member who was an income-earner; the confiscation of their street-trader's stock because they lacked a licence; the demolition of their home because it was on illegally occupied land; the loss of possessions and serious damage to their home from a flood; the depletion of any cash reserves spent on medicine and treatment for a family member that becomes ill. For a considerable proportion of the poor in sub-Saharan Africa, poverty is also associated with wars and civil strife, and the disruption they bring to their daily lives and livelihoods, as well as the threats to their lives.

National and regional statistics for urban and rural poverty

Table 3.4 provides estimates for the proportion of the rural, urban and national population that fall below a poverty line that was set, based on the income needed to satisfy basic 'minimum' needs. Virtually all the figures are derived from income-based poverty lines applied to data from household budget, income or expenditure surveys. The process used to define the income level at which the poverty line is set is rarely entirely objective and poverty lines often change as the criteria by which they are set are changed to exaggerate or deflate the number living 'below the poverty line'. Most of the figures are for the early 1980s and for the many countries that underwent economic decline during the late 1980s and early 1990s—often combined with structural adjustment—the proportion of the population below the poverty line would have increased. For reasons outlined already, many of the figures for the proportion of the urban population living below the poverty line are likely to be too low. However, note should be made of the many instances where some allowance was made for this by setting a higher poverty line for urban areas than for rural areas. This lessens the tendency to under-count the proportion of urban populations with below poverty-line incomes.

The figures in Table 3.4 are of interest for three reasons. The first is the extent of poverty in both rural and urban areas, even in relatively wealthy countries. In even the wealthiest countries, 10 per cent or more of the population is living in absolute poverty. In none of the countries listed in Europe and North America has the proportion of people living in 'absolute' poverty dropped below 10 per cent—and in many (France, Ireland, Spain and the UK) it was 18 per cent or more of the population. The proportion is much higher in some of the wealthier countries in the south such as in Venezuela and Mexico, compared to lower income countries. The second is the fact that it is not necessarily the wealthier countries that have a lower proportion of their rural and urban populations living below the poverty line. Although the figures for different countries are not directly comparable since different assumptions have been made when setting the poverty line—the very low proportion of the population of China and Tunisia with incomes below the poverty line are worth noting. This is consistent with these two countries'

TABLE 3.4 The extent of 'absolute' rural and urban poverty in selected countries.

Country or Region	Proportion of the population below the poverty line				Separate rural/urban poverty lines
	in urban areas	in rural areas	in whole nation	Date	
Africa	29.0	58.0	49.0	1985	
Botswana	30.0	64.0	55.0	1985/6	
Cote d'Ivoire	30.0	26.0	28.0	1980/86	
Egypt	34.0	33.7	33.8	1984	Yes
Gambia	63.8	57.7		1989	Yes
Ghana			59.5	1985	
Morocco	28.0	32.0		1985	
Mozambique	40.0	70.0	55.0	1980/89	
Swaziland	45.0	50.0	49.0	1980	Yes
Tunisia	7.3	5.7	6.7	1990	Yes
Uganda	25.0	33.0	32.0	1989/90	
Zambia	40.0		80.0	1993	
Asia (excluding China)	34.0	47.0	43.0	1985	
Bangladesh	58.2	72.3		1985/86	Yes
China	0.4	11.5	8.6	1990	Yes
India	37.1	38.7		1988	
Indonesia	20.1	16.4	17.4	1987	Yes
Korea, Republic of	4.6	4.4	4.5	1984	
Malaysia	8.3	22.4	17.3	1987!	
Nepal	19.2	43.1	42.6	1984/85	
Pakistan	25.0	31.0		1984/85	
Philippines	40.0	54.1	49.5	1988	
Sri Lanka	27.6	45.7	39.4	1985/86	Yes
Europe					
France			16.0	c.1990	
Germany			10.0	c.1990	
Hungary			15.4	1991	
Ireland			19.0	c.1990	
Italy			15.0	c.1990	
Poland			22.7	1987	
Spain			19.0	c.1990	
United Kingdom			18.0	c.1990	
Latin America	32.0	45.0		1985	
Argentina	14.6	19.7	15.5	1986	Yes
Brazil	37.7	65.9	45.3	1987	Yes
Colombia	40.2	44.5	41.6	1986	Yes
CostaRica	11.6	32.7	23.4	1990	
El Salvador	61.4			1990	
Guatemala	61.4	85.4	76.3	1989	
Haiti	65.0	80.0	76.0	1980–86	
Honduras	73.9	80.2	77.5	1990	
Mexico	30.2	50.5	29.9	1984	Yes
Panama	29.7	51.9	41.0	1986	Yes
Peru	44.5	63.8	51.8	1986	Yes
Uruguay	19.3	28.7	20.4	1986	Yes
Venezuela	24.8	42.2	26.6	1986	Yes
North America					
Canada			15.0	c.1990	
United States of America			13.0	c.1990	

Notes: These are all estimates based on data from a household budget, income or expenditure survey and are based on the concept of an 'absolute poverty line' expressed in monetary terms. The figures for different countries are not necessarily comparable since different assumptions will have been made for setting the poverty line. (NB comparisons between these countries should be avoided, as different criteria were used to set poverty lines).

Sources: For countries in Africa, Asia and Latin America, Tabatabai, Hamid with Manal Fouad, *The Incidence of Poverty in Developing Countries; an ILO Compendium of Data*, A World Employment Programme Study, International Labour Office, Geneva, 1993. India: Planning Commission, *Report of the Expert Group on the Estimation of Proportion and Number of Poor*, Government of India, New Delhi 1993. Zambia, Wratten, Ellen, *Zambia Peri-Urban Self-Help Project*, Report prepared for the Overseas Development Administration, London, October 1993. For countries in Europe and North America, Townsend, Peter, *The International Analysis of Poverty*, Harvester/Wheatsheaf, New York, 1993.

performance in terms of increased life expectancy since as noted earlier, these countries had among the highest increase in life expectancies of any nations between 1960 and 1992. These two countries also generally have above average provision for such aspects as health care, piped water provision and education, relative to their income per capita. However, it is difficult to accept the estimate that only 0.4 per cent of China's vast urban population live in absolute poverty.

The third point to note is that in many countries listed in Table 3.4, the proportion of the population with below-poverty-line incomes in urban areas is almost as high or higher than in rural areas. The countries where this takes place tend to be countries where different poverty lines were set for rural and urban areas to reflect the higher living costs in urban areas. This also suggests that the extent of urban poverty has been underestimated, although a certain caution is needed in that it is not clear whether a single poverty line set for all urban areas is realistic. Living costs for those engaged in poorly paid jobs or working in informal activities tied to central locations in major cities are likely to be much higher than for those living and working in small market towns—or in the less expensive areas within large cities.

Changes in the scale of poverty

There is great variation between countries in terms of recent trends in the scale and intensity of rural and urban poverty. There is also great variation between regions within countries, especially in the larger and larger-population countries. In some countries, there is evidence of a decline in the proportion of households with incomes below the poverty line during recent years. For instance, large falls in the proportion of the population living in absolute poverty during the 1980s were reported for many of most successful Asian economies—for instance China, Malaysia, South Korea and Indonesia.[69] In Indonesia, the proportion of the urban population living below the poverty line is reported to have fallen from 39 percent in 1976 to 15 per cent in 1990,[70] although the numbers of urban dwellers with below poverty line incomes fell much less because of the rapid growth in the urban population during this period.[71]

In other countries, there is evidence of an increase in the proportion below the poverty line—for instance in most of Latin America during the 1980s. For this region per capita income was reported to have fallen by 11 per cent and in many countries the income of low-income groups declined more than the average. Six out of seven countries for which there are comparable estimates (Argentina, Colombia, Costa Rica, Mexico, Panama, Uruguay, and Venezuela) showed higher indices of poverty in 1992 than around 1980.[72] In almost every country in Latin America, the rise of urban poverty was greater than in rural poverty; the number of poor people was estimated to have increased by more than 30 million in the urban centres compared to around 10 million in the rural areas.[73] In many countries, this increase in poverty during the 1980s was a reversal of trends, since there had been a decline in the proportion of people with below poverty line incomes. For instance, in Mexico, during the 1960s and the 1970s, there was a substantial decrease in the proportion of households considered poor; the percentage of such households fell from 81 per cent in 1963 to 53 per cent in 1981.[74] Most of the population had rising real incomes in this period—although the poorest ten percent of the population, most of them rural labourers, experienced little or no increase; their share of national income fell from 2.4 per cent in 1950 to 1.1 per cent in 1977.[75] The proportion of households considered poor increased significantly during the 1980s; from 53 per cent in 1981 to 63 per cent in 1988.[76] According to another source, by 1990, 41 million Mexicans were unable to satisfy their basic needs while 17 million lived in extreme poverty.[77] The average national minimum wage in 1990 had only 39.4 per cent of its 1978 value.[78] Official figures claim that there was a small fall in the number of households in extreme poverty between 1989 and 1992, although this has been questioned, because of bias in the 1992 survey.[79]

National statistics are less reliable for sub-Saharan Africa but the proportion of the population living below an absolute poverty line is likely to have grown significantly in most countries in this region. This is certainly borne out by studies of poverty for particular populations whose findings will be presented later in this chapter.

The extent of 'housing poverty'

In the absence of reliable statistics on poverty based on people's incomes and assets, one possible way of estimating the scale of poverty is to base it on how many people live in poor-quality homes or neighbourhoods that lack the basic infrastructure and services that are essential for good health. As noted earlier, at least 600 million urban dwellers in Africa, Asia and Latin America live in 'life- and health-threatening' homes and neighbourhoods because of the very poor housing and living conditions and the lack of adequate provision for safe, sufficient water supplies and provision for sanitation, drainage, the removal of garbage, and health care.[80] If these 600 million urban dwellers are considered 'poor'—for it is their lack of income and assets that makes them unable to afford better quality housing and basic services—it greatly increases the scale of urban poverty, when compared to conventional income-based poverty lines.

Of these 600 million people, most live in cramped, overcrowded dwellings with four or more persons to a room in tenements, cheap boarding houses or shelters built on illegally occupied or subdivided land. Tens of millions are homeless and they sleep in public or semi-public spaces—for instance pavement dwellers and those sleeping in bus shelters, streets, graveyards, train stations, parks or other public places.[81] Perhaps as many as 600 million also have inadequate or no access to effective health care which means that the economic impacts of disease or injury is much magnified. The same World Bank report that underestimated the scale of urban poverty also noted that

although urban incomes are generally higher and urban services and facilities more accessible, poor town-dwellers may suffer more than rural households from certain aspects of poverty. The urban poor, typically housed in slums and squatter settlements, often have to contend with appalling overcrowding, bad sanitation and contaminated water. The sites are often illegal and dangerous. Forcible eviction, floods and landslides and chemical pollution are constant threats.[82]

Although estimating levels of poverty based only on poor quality housing and an absence or basic infrastructure and services rather than levels of incomes and assets can be misleading,[83] this gives a more realistic estimate for the number of people living in poverty in urban areas of the South. It also emphasizes the fact that improving levels of infrastructure and service provision and support for housing improvement can reduce poverty. For a significant proportion of the 600 million people living in life- and health-threatening homes and neighbourhoods, this can be achieved at low cost and often with good possibilities of cost recovery. The reasons for the very poor housing and living conditions in which a sizeable proportion of these people live are not because they lack a capacity to pay for housing with basic services but that such housing is unnecessarily expensive or not available. Chapter 6 will describe how this is linked to the failure of governments to keep down land, housing and building material prices and to ensure efficient provision of infrastructure and services. Chapter 5 will also outline how national governments have consistently denied city and municipal authorities the financial base to permit them to improve infrastructure and service provision. Although increasing the supply and reducing the cost of good quality housing is not normally considered part of 'poverty reduction', government measures to increase the supply and reduce the cost of land for housing and to improve infrastructure and service provision can considerably reduce the number of people living in such poor conditions.

Data about the extent of 'housing poverty' in rural areas is more limited, except in relation to provision for infrastructure and services. Chapter 8 will describe the extent of provision for safe water supplies and provision for sanitation in rural areas—and this makes clear the extent to which rural populations are poorly served. For instance, in 1991, around one billion rural households lacked water supplies where some provision was made to ensure it was uncontaminated and of reasonable quality.[84] Around half the rural population in the South also lack hygienic means to dispose of excreta while several hundred million rely on simple latrines that do not necessarily ensure the users are guarded against the many diseases associated with inadequate provision for the disposal of excreta. And even though space is less of a constraint than in urban areas, a high proportion of rural households are too poor to build sufficient rooms to keep down overcrowding; the number of persons per room within the homes of poor rural households is often as high as within the homes of poor urban households.

Part of 'housing poverty' is a large burden of injury, disease and premature death, most of which disappears as housing conditions and levels of service provision improve. This in turn is linked not only to low incomes but also to the low priority given by governments and development assistance agencies to those measures that greatly reduce infectious and parasitic diseases. When low-income groups have the chance to present their views regarding poverty, good health or the avoidance of injury or disability is often given a high priority.[85] Weakness, sickness or disability are stressed as being bad in themselves and bad in their effects on others; having a household member who is physically weak, sick or handicapped, unable to contribute to household livelihood but needing to be fed and cared for is a common cause of income poverty and deprivation.[86]

Absolute and relative poverty

The inaccuracies inherent in a single income-based poverty line and the fact that it excludes all the non-monetary aspects of deprivation have led many governments to develop another poverty line that measures relative poverty. The absolute poverty line remains and seeks to identify people who are destitute—for instance lacking an income or asset base and the access to social services that mean that individuals or households cannot obtain sufficient food to eat, shelter and health care. In effect, their life is threatened by this level of deprivation.[87] The second poverty line, to identify those living in 'relative poverty', defines a minimum 'basket' of goods and services about which there is some agreement within a society that all citizens should have. 'People are relatively deprived if they cannot obtain . . . the conditions of life, that is the diets, amenities, standards and services, which allow them to play the roles, participate in the relationships and follow the customary behaviour which is expected of them by virtue of their membership of society.'[88] The range of goods and services within this socially determined level of need will vary greatly, not only related to the wealth and structure of a society but also to societal attitudes. There are usually major disagreements within any society as to what constitutes need and the income and level of service provision required to meet this need.

However, there is general agreement that poverty lines or other means to identify those suffering from deprivation have to be determined within each country so that the needs defined match the real needs in that particular society and culture. Poverty definitions also have to change as social and economic changes affect people's needs and their access to resources—for instance as people lose the use of common property resources that have long been central to their livelihoods as land and freshwater resources are appropriated by public agencies or private interests.[89] People's needs also change as they have to move in response to changing economic circumstances and this often means a deterioration in informal social support systems based on community and kinship that in the past helped to reduce poverty or alleviate its worst effects. Where such support systems are ineffective, there is a greater need for governments or other agencies to provide safety nets that allow individuals and households to eat and be adequately housed, and illnesses or injuries treated, when income earners are sick or lose their source of income.

One relatively new approach to considering the multiple dimensions of poverty which has some similarity to the concept of relative poverty is social exclusion.[90] The concept of social exclusion includes not only people's exclusion from basic needs because of a lack of income or assets but also their exclusion from labour markets and from civil and political rights. And because it seeks to identify the mechanisms by which they are 'excluded', it helps identify the social, economic and political underpinnings of poverty. It has proved particularly useful in Europe to describe what is sometimes called the 'new poverty' that is associated with technological change and economic restructuring—for instance, the rapid growth in the number of long-term unemployed and the inability of many young people to enter the labour market for the first time. It is also used to include the growing number of people in many countries in the North who can no longer obtain access to housing, education and health care, as they cannot afford these when purchased in private markets and as public provision has been cut back and is no longer available to them.

Economic decline, structural adjustment and poverty

Although there have long been serious problems with urban poverty in the South, it was only in the 1980s that it was given more attention as economic crises and the impacts of structural adjustment increased the number of households with incomes below the poverty line and increased the intensity of their deprivation. As Box 3.5 outlined, low-income groups in urban areas are generally hit more than those in rural areas by falling wages and rises in prices for food and other basic goods.

The international debt crisis forced many countries to agree to IMF conditions in order to secure the additional foreign currency then needed. Typical measures included both short-term stabilization policies and longer-term structural adjustment. By 1989, 64 countries had accepted adjustment loans from the World Bank.[91] Over thirty of these countries are in Africa.[92] A further twenty countries had accepted support from the IMF for adjustment programmes.[93] The fact that urban poverty grew with structural adjustment is well established[94]—although there are two reasons why it is not possible to separate the impacts of the structural adjustment from other economic, social and political forces. First, structural adjustment programmes have long-term objectives. Those arguing in favour of these programmes stress that short-term suffering will be replaced by long-term economic growth. Second, any measurement of the relative success of structural adjustment programmes has to consider—'what would otherwise have happened'. Some of the social and economic costs attributed to structural adjustment may have been there even if the policies associated with structural adjustment had not taken place—for instance, part of the growth in urban poverty in Africa arises from the general decline in urban wages that has been evident since the 1970s.[95]

The immediate impact of structural adjustment programmes is deflationary: scaling-down domestic demand to reduce inflation and encourage exports, and reducing government expenditure to encourage private-sector expansion. The urban population may be in a particularly difficult situation. As a recent World Bank publication notes, the poor in urban areas may 'bear the burden of relative price changes in the form of increasing prices of essential basic commodities, including food. They also may face severe unemployment and income loss as a result of fiscal and monetary contraction. They may also experience constraints on access to basic social services such as education and health because of contractions in public expenditure.'[96]

In most countries undergoing economic crisis and structural adjustment, large numbers of people lost what had been relatively stable jobs and very few received an income from social security or welfare systems. For instance, in Zimbabwe, between 1991, when the economic structural adjustment programme began and 1993, over

45,000 jobs were lost in the public and private sector.[97] There were retrenchments in the agriculture, textile, clothing, leather and construction industries and the number of people employed by the government in the civil service is set to fall by 25 per cent between 1991 and 1995.[98] Reductions in public expenditure have impacted directly on those employed by the public sector either through falling real wages for public sector employees and/or lower public sector employment. There have been substantial cuts in the civil service in most countries where structural adjustment programmes have been implemented including Bolivia (where the equivalent of 25 per cent of the public sector labour force was cut), Chile, Jamaica, Niger, Panama, Tanzania and Togo.[99] In most countries, wage levels for government employees also dropped significantly in the years after structural adjustment began.[100] Since most government employees live and work in urban centres, this will affect urban areas most with the greatest impact in urban centres with high concentrations of public employees. The impact will usually be greatest in national capitals, especially in centralized government systems and in poorer and less industrialized nations where public employees represent a substantial proportion of the urban employment base.

Most of those who lost their jobs had to compete for income sources or jobs within the 'informal economy' but falling incomes and declining production within the formal sector also meant declining demand for the goods and services supplied by many informal enterprises. Those who had to find new jobs or income sources also had to compete with women, youths and children who had previously not worked or had worked only part-time. Households had to send more members to seek new sources of income, however small, to avoid a drastic reduction in food consumption.[101]

The economic crisis also revealed the limited absorption capacity of the informal economy. A distinction should be drawn between informal activities that provide a reasonable income for those working there and those activities that are really 'survival' activities that people do when no other income source is available to them. For instance, the number of people who seek some income from waste picking and the number of children working on the street as part of their household's survival strategy often rises with economic recession. The limited absorption capacity of the informal economy became evident in most nations as entry into the more lucrative informal sector activities is often controlled and as increasing numbers working in the same 'survival' activities reduced returns.

The World Bank has suggested that the 'new poor' and the 'borderline poor' whose poverty is a direct consequence of macro adjustment should be distinguished from the chronic poor who were poor before the structural adjustment programme.[102] The new poor are those who fall below the poverty line as a result of losing their jobs as a direct consequence of structural adjustment. The borderline poor include those who became poor as their purchasing power fell in real terms—for instance public or private sector employees whose salaries fail to keep up with inflation and pensioners with fixed pensions which do not rise with inflation. The chronic poor may also find themselves even worse off after such adjustments.[103] Some studies have shown a dramatic increase in the number of poor individuals or households—for instance, a study in Buenos Aires suggested that the number of poor people tripled between 1980 and 1988 with a significant number of poorer groups coming from people who had previously had adequate incomes as professionals, public employees or salaried workers in small and medium-sized industries.[104] There is also evidence from Latin America not only of the poorest groups becoming even poorer during the 1980s but also for a very large downward mobility of middle-income groups.[105]

Household responses to the process of impoverishment during the 1980s

In countries with little or no provision for social security, poor households cannot afford not to respond to impoverishment. A review of *Urban Poverty in the Context of Structural Adjustment* in 1993 stressed that poor households are not passive and there is a need to consider how they respond to changes arising from structural adjustment programmes.

Evidence from cities as diverse as Manila, Dar es Salaam, Guayaquil, Mexico City and Guadalajara indicate that households modified their consumption and dietary patterns and adjusted household expenditures, in many instances in the direction of cheap and less nutritious substitutes. The cultivation of staples on 'family plots' has also been intensified. In addition, the participation of both women and children in the labour market has increased. At the community level, local authorities actively encouraged communities to bulk purchase staple food items.[106]

In some cities, there is evidence of decreasing unemployment with the economic recession as increasing numbers of people work as a response to the economic crisis. Unemployment can go down, while the number of people earning incomes below the poverty line increase, because incomes have become so low. This process was evident in many Latin American nations during the 1980s. For instance, one study of seven countries

BOX 3.6
The response of households to economic crisis in Guadalajara, Mexico

Households responded to the economic crisis in Mexico through a number of changes that cushioned the impact of lower wages and a stagnant formal economy.

- **Increase in the number of workers per household**. The groups that had the largest increase in labour participation were women over 15 years of age and young males (14 years old or younger) who left school to do so.[107]

- **Increasing reliance on informal employment.** For women this meant mostly domestic and other personal services while for men it usually meant self-employment.

- **Increased household sizes and increased presence of extended families**. The increase in household size was not simply through births but also daughters and sons-in-law staying in the parental houses. Although not new, this became more common as it saved money on housing expenses and in many other shared expenses and expanded the number of income earners within the house. Other relatives and non relatives also helped expand average household size. The increase in the number of extended families was also evident in many other Mexican cities.[108] When sons and daughters were married, it became important to keep them at home with their spouses instead of losing economically active members.

- **Lower expenditures on goods and services other than food**, especially clothes and services such as household maintenance. Food consumption did decline but not as severely as the decline in individual wages. Consumption of beef and milk decreased. Household work loads often increased as clothes had to last longer (and be continually mended) and many goods and services that had previously been purchased now had to be undertaken within the home.

- **Emigration to the USA.** The scale of such migration increased and became more heterogeneous since it now included male and female urban residents from working- and middle-class backgrounds as well as rural males who had previously been dominant in these emigration flows.

There were obvious differences between households in the extent to which they could respond. Among household members, women generally suffered most as they had to find jobs or earn incomes or increase the hours they worked while continuing to meet their responsibilities for household management and child-rearing. In many households, women and children were more vulnerable than men to falls in food intake—as working-class men generally received priority in the consumption of high-protein foodstuffs. The increased stress brought about by increased workloads and reduced real income is likely to have

Source: Escobar Latapí, Augustín and Mercedes González de la Rocha,'Crisis, restructuring and urban poverty in Mexico', *Environment and Urbanization* vol. 7, no. 1, April 1995, 57–75.

that contain most of the region's population found that the total number of employed persons increased faster than the population of working age between 1980 and 1989.[109] A household survey in Guadalajara that began to monitor changes in households in 1982 was among the first to document this[110] but other studies have since revealed comparable processes in other cities. Box 3.6 summarizes the changes made by households in Guadalajara in response to the economic crisis.

A study in Harare, Zimbabwe, also shows how households rearrange their activities to try to cope with economic crisis and the social impacts of structural adjustment. One of the most important points arising from the evidence presented in Box 3.7 is the range of impacts on households—from the drop in expenditures to changes in food intake, rises in rents, increases in costs for education, falls in income and in capacity to save and a rise in gender-based conflicts. It is this multiplicity of impacts on households and their social effects that is so difficult to understand and measure, without detailed studies.

The example in Box 3.7 also shows how some sectors of the informal economy had become saturated. Here, women could not increase their incomes from knitting, sewing and crocheting as they faced declining demand, increasing competition and rising input costs.[111] This situation of very limited possibilities of finding reasonable income-earning opportunities in the informal economy during a severe economic crisis is likely to have been common in most of the lower-income and less-urbanized economies during the 1980s.[112] It is also likely that those already working in the informal economy had to work longer hours to maintain their income.[113]

The processes that underlie impoverishment

Whether a household becomes temporarily or permanently poor is influenced by many factors.[114] They include the size and nature of any asset base to draw on, their capacity to send more household members to earn an income or to forage (for instance withdrawing a child from school to do so) and the extent of social relations and networks (for instance whether temporary help can be obtained from extended family, friends or through patron–client relations). For most of the world's urban population, it is the position of the individual or household in the labour market that is most influential in whether they can or cannot avoid poverty.[115] It is not only the income earned that affects the level of poverty but also the nature of employment-related social benefits such as health insurance—if any are provided. Thus, there are important distinctions between protected and unprotected wage labour—with the former having some security and often some provision for social security—and among unprotected wage labour, between regular workers and casual workers.[116]

For households, the capacity to avoid poverty also centres on the number of household members

BOX 3.7
The short-term impact of structural adjustment—the case of Kambuzuma, Harare

To obtain a detailed understanding of the short-term effects of structural adjustment, a study was made of 100 randomly selected households in Kambuzuma, Harare. Most were male-headed households (85 per cent in 1991, 84 per cent in 1992). Kambuzuma is a fairly typical low-income settlement in Harare—and not among the poorest—with considerable variation in incomes among its households. The households were interviewed in mid-1991 as the economic structural adjustment programme began and one year later in mid-1992 to see what changes had occurred. The changes that occurred between 1991 and 1992 are summarized below.

- **Expenditures**: Household expenditure rose by 34 per cent with expenditures on food, electricity, rent and money given to other family members all rising significantly. However, in real terms, expenditures fell as the cost of living rose by 45 per cent during this same period. Expenditure fell more sharply for the lower income groups than for the higher income groups.

- **Food intake**: Expenditure on food declined in real terms by 14 per cent with the greatest decline evident among lower-income households. Most households made some changes to their diet such as substituting food of higher bulk for high-protein foods, eating meat less frequently and buying cheaper cuts of meat.

- **Tenants**: Tenant households faced very large rent rises between 1991 and 1992 as their landlords tried to buffer themselves

from the increased cost of living. Many tenants felt that they no longer had any chance of owning their own land and developing their own house.

- **Transport**: Fewer households were able to pay for transport to work and a number of men and women had begun walking to work or had arranged lifts which cost less than the bus service.

- **Education**: In January 1992, fees for primary schools had been introduced for the first time and secondary school fees raised in urban areas. All the lower-income households and higher-income households with three or four children had difficulties paying for school fees and school uniforms.

- **Incomes and employment**: Incomes fell by 24 per cent in real terms and the decline in women's own income-earning activities such as petty commerce and sewing, knitting and crocheting was particularly notable. Women generally had to work longer hours and still received lower returns—for instance as demand fell for the goods or services they provided, input costs rose and competition increased. Women were much more dependent than men on non-wage income and had a greater decline in earnings and activities between 1991 and 1992. The proportion of households with monthly incomes below the official Poverty Datum Line increased from 23 per cent in 1991 to 43 per cent in 1992.

- **Savings and debt**: The proportion of households able to save on a regular basis dropped from 68 per cent in 1991 to 50 per cent in 1992. In 1991, no household was spending savings on consumption; in 1992, four were using savings for food and school fees. The proportion of households in debt rose from 8 to 12 per cent, with money borrowed to cover such consump-

tion items as food, school fees and rent. Families in 1992 expressed greater concern about their children being unable to find jobs when they finished school—aware that this implied taking financial responsibility for their children for longer periods and making it less likely that children could help look after their parents in their old age.

- **Expansion of household size but not of income-earners**: The main change in household structure was the increase in the number of dependants per paid worker from 3.2 to 3.8 per household. This was caused by an influx of dependent relatives from rural areas due to the drought and from other settlements in Harare.

- **Gender-based conflict at household level**: Women modified their lives more than men in response to economic difficulties. They took greater cuts in their own consumption, spent more time shopping to look for cheaper goods, worked longer and harder hours in informal sector activities for poorer returns and engaged in fewer leisure activities. It was seen as women's responsibility to ensure sufficient food was on the table and other household tasks met despite falling household incomes. The decline in women's earnings from informal sector activities also meant less control by the women of household budgets, lower self-esteem and increased conflict with husbands. Several of those interviewed felt that the men were not fulfilling their obligations as husbands and fathers.

- **Social dimensions of adjustment**: No household among the sample had benefited in any way from the special government programme to alleviate the negative short term impacts of adjustment on poverty and employment.

Source: Kanji, Nazneen, 'Gender, poverty and structural adjustment in Harare, Zimbabwe', *Environment and Urbanization* vol. 7, no. 1, April 1995, 37–55.

who can find some source of income. The higher the educational level of potential income-earners, the greater their income potential. Households with many dependants relative to income-earners will obviously be at a disadvantage—whether they have children, working-age adults who are sick, injured or disabled or elderly people also unable to work. Even if the children who are often sent out to work as a way of coping with impoverishment earn very little, it is often an important supplement to adult wages—just as it was for the tens of thousands of children also sent out to work in European cities during the nineteenth century.[117] Single-parent households will obviously be greatly disadvantaged, as the one parent has to combine income-earning with child-rearing and household management. If the single parent is a woman—as is usually the case—they are often further disadvan-

taged by the discrimination that women face within the labour market or the earlier discrimination within education that had limited the possibilities of obtaining qualifications. Any group that faces discrimination in labour markets will also be more at risk of poverty—for instance particular castes, immigrant groups or ethnic groups. It is thus not surprising to find in both the North and the South a great range of studies showing associations between households with inadequate incomes and households with unskilled workers, low educational attainment by adults there, households with many dependants and single-parent households with higher rates of poverty among particular ethnic or immigrant communities.[118]

The scale and nature of poverty within the world's wealthiest countries has also been underpinned by changes in labour markets and the fact that during the late 1970s and the 1980s, unemployment rose to levels that were unprecedented since the Second World War. In most countries, there was a considerable growth in the number of long-term unemployed people. In most countries, the scale and nature of welfare benefits for those who lost their jobs were cut substantially; what taxpayers proved willing to support in benefits to the unemployed when they represented only a few per cent of the workforce was rapidly revised downwards when changes in the labour market greatly increased the number of the unemployed. Here, as in most other instances, a variety of factors contributed to increased levels of poverty—for instance lower wages for unskilled and casual workers, fewer jobs, much reduced benefits for most of the unemployed, a decline in the services on which only those with low incomes depended and, as Chapter 6 will describe, a decline in the availability of cheap accommodation.[119] It has been suggested in Europe that the key economic divide in society is now much less that between the 'blue-collar' and 'white-collar' workers and more between those with relatively secure jobs and those with no jobs,[120] with those working in part-time or casual work located somewhere between these two.[121]

The influence of changes in the labour market on poverty levels can be seen in changes in Latin America, evident during the 1980s. First, open unemployment grew steadily and in countries where it stabilized, this stabilization took place at a much higher level than in previous years. For instance, open unemployment in Latin America's urban centres was 6.8 per cent in 1970 and 6.9 per cent in 1980; by 1985 it had reached 11.1 per cent and rose each year between 1980 and 1985.[122] Figures for open unemployment do not reflect the real scale of the problem. For instance, there are the large numbers of people who cannot afford to be unemployed since they are not covered by any social security or unemployment insurance scheme so receive no income at all if they cannot find work—and they have no assets or savings to fall back on. These people usually take on part time work although they want full time work (under-employment) or they work in jobs or become self-employed within the informal economy that provide very inadequate incomes. The data available for the period 1980–5 for selected urban centres in Argentina, Colombia, Peru and Costa Rica shows a growth in the number of people in both these categories.[123] There are also considerable numbers of people who are discouraged from seeking employment because of the unavailability of work opportunities.

The impact of the 1980s crisis in Latin America can also be seen in three processes within urban employment. The first is the growth in the relative importance of informal activities and this probably represents a change in that the historic trend before the crisis was a slow decrease in the proportion of the urban labour force working in informal activities. The second is the decline in the number of secure jobs—for instance through a growth in short-term contract work, part-time jobs, employment through job agencies, homework and greater use of casual labour. The third is the loss of social security previously achieved through labour legislation, although a large proportion of the workforce was generally outside such provision. In most countries, there was also a decline in industrial employment and a rise in the importance of tertiary activities—although the significance of this is much more in what tertiary activities grew most and the incomes they generated since term 'tertiary' covers such a wide range of jobs from among the most productive and highest paid to among the least productive and lowest paid.

Although most case studies of impoverishment are in economies that were stagnant or in crisis, there could also be a substantial increase in poverty within growing economies, linked to changes in the labour market. This was the case in the United States. During the 1980s, many of the jobs in manufacturing that had paid relatively high wages to people with relatively little formal education disappeared and the incomes of lower-income groups declined.[124] In many countries, there has also been a general trend towards lowering wages for many semi-skilled or unskilled jobs and the replacement of experienced industrial workers with cheaper, younger, often female labour. For instance, in Mexico, many manufacturing industries have turned to younger unmarried men and women with secondary schooling who are not skilled but are willing to work for lower wages than the previous skilled worker—and wages have dropped significantly.[125] In general, the level of job security has deteriorated in many countries around the world—both North and South.[126] Changes in the labour market underlie the growth of what has been termed the 'new urban poverty' in cities in the North—the growth in homelessness and begging, high rates of unemployment and low-paid insecure employment. It has also been cited as a major reason for rises in crime, drug and alcohol abuse and many other social problems.[127] Box 3.8 outlines some of the problems of youth unemployment in Africa, although much of what it says is relevant to youth in other regions of the world.

Gender and economic vulnerability

Poverty and vulnerability are not synonymous. For instance, within urban centres, inadequate incomes are the main cause of poverty but it is

BOX 3.8
Youth, cities, employment: a high-risk triad

There is a great need for concrete action on youth employment in African cities. The process of urban decay has been accelerating while at the same time the urban authorities have never seemed so unable to meet the expectations of the younger generations for social integration, especially through the job market. The scale of the problem has also greatly increased as urban populations have grown very rapidly. A high proportion of the urban population is made up of children and youth; about two-thirds of the urban population in Africa is made up of the 0–25 age group.

Young graduates are no longer guaranteed public sector jobs and they are in competition with the elderly for jobs within community-based systems. The informal sector is saturated to the point where its spirit of initiative has been perverted by the exploitation of child and youth labour. While people all around them have been made redundant by the implementation of adjustment policies, the young have not benefited from social-support programmes.

The urgent need to get out of the economic vicious cycle should not result in ignoring the social and political risks of having large numbers of unoccupied and very frustrated young people. Having sparked off the democratization process, the young now see themselves as the "moral generation" whose members are quick to denounce the abuses committed by the "rentier" state'. But these same young people are prone to plunge into any of a number of temptations: more or less politicised urban violence, fundamentalist or mafioso activities, the idealization of somewhere else considered as perfect, in spite of the evidence to the contrary. . . . But no other mobilizing utopia is offered to them, because even the most authentically democratic regimes have been forced, by a whole series of constraints to implement realistically stringent policies. As they are convinced that they legitimately have a major social role to play in the face of change, the young will not accept to behave as those who, in the beautiful words of the Senegalese singer Ismaël Lo 'push the broken down car of democracy only to be left by the wayside when it finally starts up again'.

Source: Emile Le Bris, 'Youth, Cities, Employment: a high risk triad', in *Villes en Développement*, No 18, Dec. 1992.

---

inadequate assets which underlie low-income groups' vulnerability to economic shocks or to the economic consequences of ill-health.[128] However, a low income means that it is harder for individuals and households to save and to build up some assets, to reduce their vulnerability to sudden changes in income or loss of income from illness. Low incomes also make it difficult for households to 'invest' in social assets such as education that can help reduce their vulnerability in future. Box 3.7 is a reminder of how much low-income parents will often sacrifice to keep their children in school, so their children have the education that is such an important asset within the labour market.

Women are generally more vulnerable than men because of the differentials between men and women in terms of access to income, resources and services. Such differentials may occur within households between men and women or between individuals (i.e. between single men and single women) or between households with women-headed households at a disadvantage to male-headed households. Women generally have fewer income-earning opportunities than men and they earn less.

Women may also face particular problems in the income-earning activities in which only (or mostly) women engage. For instance, most hawkers in Nairobi are women and thus suffer most from the harassment which usually involves the confiscation of their goods.[129] Low-income households are likely to be far more vulnerable in societies where there are major barriers that limit the possibilities of women to work.[130]

Women's income-earning activities cannot be considered in isolation from their roles within households and communities since each affects the other.[131] Within households, women usually take on most of the responsibilities for household management and, where there are children, it is almost always the women who take primary responsibility for looking after them. Women often contribute more than men to community organization and to initiatives to address the lack of provision by governments for infrastructure and services.[132] Meeting their responsibilities for childcare, household management and community action limits their capacity to earn an income. And the services that would help them combine these responsibilities with income-earning are also often deficient. For instance, crèches and child-care centres that can make it much easier for women with young children to earn incomes rarely receive government support and, where they do, their opening hours and locations are often inappropriate to low-income women's needs.[133] Public transport systems often overlook or misunderstand women's travel needs. Public transport systems are often oriented to meeting demand from main income-earners early in the morning and in the early evening. They do not serve the needs of secondary income earners (often women) who journey to and from work at different times and often to different destinations. They are rarely organized to help those responsible for shopping, taking children to and from school and visits to health centres.[134] Cost-cutting in public transport inevitably reduces off-peak services which means that the journeys that women make are often by foot or on extremely overcrowded public transport.[135]

Within low-income households, it is often women and older children who do most to absorb economic shocks—for instance through women having to increase the time devoted to income-earning. The increased time they have to devote to income-earning does not mean a lessening of their other responsibilities; men have not increased their role in caring for the children and household management to help women meet the extra demands on their time from income-earning.[136] There is also the issue of the division of work and income within households between men and women. Women often experience discrimination in the share of resources they receive, relative to the work they do—especially their responsibilities for child rearing and household management whose economic value is not considered. Women and children within households whose income is above 'the poverty line' may face deprivation because of the disproportionately small share of household income the woman controls from which she has to feed and clothe the family and meet health care needs.[137] In many societies, female children also experience discrimination in comparison to male children; in some countries in the South, child mortality rates are higher for female children than for male children; in the North, the reverse is true.

Among 'low-income households', those headed by women usually face particular problems in that the women experience discrimination in labour markets or in attempts to secure support for income generating activities or household improvement. To this is added the particular difficulties faced by all single-parent households in having to combine the triple role of child rearing, household (and community) maintenance and income generation.[138] In many low income settlements, 30 or more per cent of households are headed by women either because a male partner is temporarily absent or because of separation or death.[139] In many societies, widowed or abandoned women face particular problems in finding employment and studies of low-income communities often find a concentration of such women in the community.[140]

However, in many societies, cities may offer particular benefits to women. In Latin America, women find greater opportunities for work.[141] In parts of Africa, customary law excludes women from owning rural land in their own right and the city offers a means for their independent survival after marital separation.[142] In parts of Asia, widows or divorced women may face considerable prejudice in rural areas with urban areas offering them better possibilities for an independent livelihood.

Conclusions

This section has noted the inadequacy in the conventional means of measuring poverty and how a concern for quantification led to a considerable underestimation in the scale of urban poverty. It also helped contribute to an simplified understanding of both urban and rural poverty and the processes underlying impoverishment.

Here, as in many other subsections of this Report, our current state of knowledge does not permit accurate estimates as to the relative size of the urban and rural people living with unsatisfied basic needs or with incomes too low to permit them to meet such needs. Accurate global and regional estimates are only possible when they can be based on an aggregation from national studies that consider the scale and nature of urban and rural poverty within that particular national context. The many empirical studies on poverty on which this section has drawn suggests that far more attention should be paid by governments and international agencies to reducing urban poverty. But the fact that in most of the world's predominantly rural nations, so little has been achieved in reducing rural poverty also suggests a need, at the same time, for far more attention to reducing rural poverty. The empirical studies that look at rural–urban linkages also suggest that every national or sub-national programme on poverty reduction has to have both rural and urban components and these will vary greatly from place to place. In some areas, stimulating urban development and expanding urban employment may be an essential part of reducing rural poverty. In others, stimulating and supporting increased agricultural production and changes in the crops grown to those with higher value will be an essential part of reducing poverty in nearby market towns and service centres.

Low-income groups or groups suffering some form of deprivation often have their own criteria as to what constitutes well-being or deprivation. Their own conceptions of disadvantage and deprivation have often been found to differ markedly from those of 'experts'.[143] Great value is often placed on qualitative dimensions such as independence (including freedom from a need to rely on a patron's support), less powerlessness (and thus the possibility to organize and negotiate for, for instance, public services), security, health, self respect, identity, close and non-exploitative social relations, decision-making freedom and political and legal rights.[144] For them, the opposite of poverty may not be wealth but security—through command over sufficient assets and freedom from debt; both are linked to independence rather than dependence (on a landlord or patron) and self respect (through freedom from subservience and exploitation).[145] The importance to many low-income groups of both monetary and non-monetary assets as the best defence against poverty was also highlighted. The development of gender-aware planning during the 1980s highlighted the different needs and priorities of men and women within the same household. These led to new initiatives that involved 'low income' groups in defining what was deprivation and its underlying causes, and what resources are to hand from individuals, households and communities to address these (see Chapter 9).

3.3 Urban Crime and Violence[146]

The scale of crime in cities

At least once every five years, more than half the world's population living in cities with 100,000 or more inhabitants are victims of a crime of some kind—see Table 3.5. Among the world's regions, only in Asia does the proportion fall below 50 per cent and in Africa and the Americas, it is two-thirds or more. The overall rate fell in Asian cities but crimes against property, organized violent crime and drug-trafficking increased considerably. Even if criminal syndicates have an increasingly important role, most crime is not organized in this way.

Table 3.5 shows how most crime in these cities was against property—through the theft of vehicles, burglary or other thefts. Most theft is consumer items that are easily resold. The increase of crime against property is not only a phenomenon of the rich neighbourhoods but is also spread within many low-income areas, including tenements and illegal settlements.

Worldwide, urban violence is estimated to have grown by between 3 and 5 per cent a year over the last two decades, although there are large variations between nations and between different cities within nations in the scale of urban violence and in the extent of its growth. Violent crime has increased in most cities in recent years—and generally as a proportion of all crimes. It includes murder (or homicide), infanticide, assault, rape and sexual abuse and domestic violence and it now makes up between 25 and 30 per cent of urban crimes in many countries.[147] Violent crime is also growing in rural areas, though more slowly.

One aspect of the increase in violent crime is the increase in murders. This can be seen by considering the number of murders per 100,000 persons in the late 1980s in different countries and cities. These vary by a factor of 50 or more between countries. In most European countries and some wealthy Asian countries, using standardized death rates, there are less than 2 murders per year per 100,000 people with the rate falling below 1 for some countries.[148] In the United States, there were more than 8 in the late 1980s, in the former Soviet Union, more than 6—although the murder rate in Russia was reported to be twice that in the United States by the early 1990s.[149] In Latin America, the murder rate varied greatly from countries such as Uruguay with relatively low rates to countries such as Ecuador and Mexico with more than 12 murders per 100,000 persons per year. The murder rate in Colombia in 1992 was reported as being 86 per 100,000 inhabitants.[150]

The murder rates for particular cities can be much higher than those for the national averages. For instance, the murder rate in Rio de Janeiro in Brazil was reported to have reached 59 per 100,000 people in 1989[151] and over 60 in 1990 when 6,011 people were reported to have been murdered.[152] Sao Paulo had a murder rate of 35 per 100,000 inhabitants by the early 1990s.[153] The rate in Bogotá in 1993 was even higher than that in Rio de Janeiro with more than 5,000 murders in a city whose population stood at around 6 million. In the early 1990s, Cali, Colombia's third largest city had a murder rate of 87 per 100,000 people.[154] Several cities in the North also had high murder rates—for instance the murder rate in Washington DC was reported to be over 70 per 100,000 inhabitants in the early 1990s.[155] The combination of very large populations and high murder rates means that in several of the world's largest cities, more than 2,000 people are murdered each year, including Los Angeles, Rio de Janeiro, Bogotá and Sao Paulo.[156]

The murder rate for a whole country or for a city obscures the fact that it is particular groups who are most at risk from murder. For instance, murder rates are generally much higher for men than for women[157]—with the rate being particularly high among young men. Murders now figure as among the leading causes of death

TABLE 3.5 Per cent of the population who are victims of crime in urban areas with more than 100,000 inhabitants over a 5-year period

	Per cent of the population who over a 5-year period are victims of				
	Theft and damage of vehicles	Burglary	Other theft	Assault and other crimes of personal contact*	All crimes
West Europe	34%	16%	27%	15%	60%
North America	43%	24%	25%	20%	65%
South America	25%	20%	33%	31%	68%
East Europe	27%	18%	28%	17%	56%
Asia	12%	13%	25%	11%	44%
Africa	24%	38%	42%	33%	76%
TOTAL	29%	20%	29%	19%	61%

* Includes mugging, aggravated theft, grievous bodily harm, sexual assault.

Source: UNICRI (United Nations International Crime and Justice Research Institute) (1995), *Criminal victimisation of the developing world*, Rome, drawing from UNICRI and Ministry of Justice of the Netherlands, international survey of victims of crime (1988–1994), based on a sample of 74,000 persons in 39 countries.

for young males in certain countries or regions—and the leading cause for certain population groups, as in young African-American males in California in 1988 with a murder rate of 156 per 100,000.[158] But care is needed when making comparisons between different countries or cities, as the causes of murders and the perpetrators of the murders vary considerably. For instance, in Sao Paulo, one of the reasons for the very high murder rate was the fact that in the early 1990s, the military police were killing more than 1,000 suspects a year.[159] By contrast, one of the main causes of murder in Maharashtra, the Indian state in which Bombay is located, is young brides being burnt to death for not bringing enough dowry.[160] In Bangladesh, the murder of wives by husbands accounts for a high proportion of all murders.[161] In the United States, a large proportion of murders are young men being shot with firearms by other young men. This includes many murders by school-age children; in the decade from 1980 to 1989, an estimated 11,000 people were killed by high school aged youths, two-thirds of them by firearms.[162]

For every murder, there are many times more non-fatal assaults. In the United States, different estimates suggest there are seventy to a hundred times as many non-fatal assaults as murders.[163] The figures in Table 3.5 suggest that over a period of five years, around a third of the population in the cities in South America and Africa were victims of assault, mugging, rape or other crimes of personal contact. Asia had much the lowest rate of the regions shown with only one person in ten being a victim of these kinds of crimes over the five year period.

There is also a lot of crime that goes unreported, including vandalism or hooliganism. Although often considered 'petty' in the legal sense of the word, such incidents can make life very unpleasant for city dwellers.

The impact on urban centres

High levels of urban crime and perhaps especially of violent crime are bringing major changes in the spatial form of many cities and of their built up areas and public spaces. Violent crimes are more visible in cities, and they help create a sense of insecurity that generates distrust, intolerance, the withdrawal of individuals from community life, and in some instances, violent reactions.[164]

For instance, the increase in violence, insecurity and fear in Sao Paulo are changing the city's landscape and the patterns of daily life, people's movements and the use of public transport—as crime and violence discourages people from using the streets and public spaces altogether.[165] Streets where children used to play, where neighbours used to congregate and where it was common for people to stroll are now much less used. Increasingly, higher-income groups are living, working, shopping and taking their leisure in what are essentially fortified enclaves and are no longer making use of streets or public spaces which are abandoned to the homeless and the street children.[166] Similar developments are evident in many cities around the world as middle- and upper-income groups journey by private automobile between apartment complexes, shopping centres or malls and office complexes each with sophisticated security systems and their own secure car parks so there is little or no necessity to walk on the streets or to use open spaces. High levels of crime and fear of violence have helped to push shopping malls, office complexes and leisure activities to suburban areas and in some cities, this has reached the point where it is increasingly rare for middle- and upper-income groups to visit the city centre.

High levels of crime can have a very serious impact on the economy of a neighbourhood or city centre:

The abandonment of neighbourhoods by the most positive elements, the decrease in traffic and the risks of break-ins and armed robbery drive business out. House values drop, and buildings deteriorate. Urban services departments spend less and less to maintain and upgrade ageing and vandalized infrastructures. Industries opt for other sites because these areas no longer have the labour force they are looking for and the physical conditions they need to operate. Tourists are very careful to avoid venturing into these areas. The juxtaposition of these pockets of poverty and more affluent areas generates envy on one hand and fear on the other.[167]

Violence against women

The most common form of violence against women is domestic violence and in recent years, it has become acknowledged that in most countries, there are very serious problems with domestic violence. Surveys in a variety of countries in the South found that between a third and half (or more) of women surveyed report being beaten by their partner.[168] In the United States, battering is the leading cause of injury to women and accounts for nearly one-third of all emergency room visits by women.[169] It is also acknowledged that statistics collected from police records or from other official sources usually greatly underestimate the scale and the seriousness of the problem, as those who suffer domestic violence are reluctant to report the abuse.[170]

But it is not only in the domestic arena that violence against women is a serious and often growing problem. For instance, an estimate made by a US Senate Judiciary Committee suggested that at least one women in five in the United States will be sexually assaulted in her lifetime.[171] Rape and sexual abuse are now known to be far more common than was thought a few years ago—with generally a high proportion of those who perpetrate sexual abuse being known to their victims and often with a considerable proportion of victims being 15 years of age or under.[172]

Causes of urban violence

As one specialist on the study of violence commented:

It is not the city that generates violence: poverty, political and social exclusion, and economic deprivation are all working against the solidarity that would enable city inhabitants to live together peacefully despite their conflicts.[173]

There is a growing understanding that violence should be considered a public health problem for which there are prevention strategies. Many cities have very low levels of violence while others with high levels of violence have managed to reduce them by addressing some of the underlying causes.[174]

Urban violence is the result of many factors which affect each city depending on the specific local context—and there is considerable debate about the relative importance of different factors. Certain specialists stress the significance of inadequate incomes which are usually combined with very poor and overcrowded housing and living conditions, and often insecure tenure, as fertile ground for the development of violence. This view was stressed in the conclusions of the 1989 Montreal Conference of Mayors: 'the basic causes of violence increase: urban growth, with the marginalisation of the underprivileged and the isolation of groups at risk, qualitative and quantitative insufficiency of social housing programmes and community amenities, unemployment of young people.'[175] It is also more difficult for parents living in very poor quality housing and also usually working long hours to provide children with the social support they need both at school and at home. An unsupportive home life can lead to non-adaptation at school and to a lack of personal discipline and self-esteem which increase the risk of anti-social or criminal activity.[176]

Other explanations, while not contradicting those noted above, emphasize more the contemporary urban environment in which attractive goods are continuously on display and create targets for potential criminals. In cities, particularly in the South, the ostentatious display of luxury and prosperity (shops, cars) in certain areas, provokes those who have not accepted their unfavourable social situation, and engenders an attitude that legitimizes the 'distribution of wealth' through criminal activity. In addition,

police forces are usually unable to protect all individuals and businesses against theft and the police and the judicial system do not provide sufficient deterrent with low clear-up rates for most theft and violence. Meanwhile, insurance against theft, for those who can afford it, does not resolve the problem of prevention since it does not halt the theft itself (the breaking of the law) or its consequences.

Finally, oppression in all its forms, including the destruction of original cultural identities, together with racism and discrimination, is one of the root causes of many forms of violence.[177] It is difficult for any individual or household to identify with a culture if subjected to racism or discrimination in finding employment and in finding housing or obtaining access to social services—or for children, at school. This, in turn, inhibits their integration within schools, workplaces and neighbourhoods.

There are also many risk-factors associated with crime. There are the factors connected with the built environment itself and with the lack of a stable population within many residential areas. For instance, in many city areas such as those with a high proportion of short-term tenants or boarding houses, the constant movement of people in and out of the area inhibits the development of community actions and informal community surveillance that can deter crime or help identify the criminal. The nature and quality of street-life has a considerable influence on the incidence of crime and vandalism. So too does the physical design of housing areas, including the extent to which public areas are subject to informal supervision and the extent to which there is a clear visual definition as to who has the right to use it and is responsible for its maintenance.[178] The inadequate provision for or deterioration of public space and public facilities (parks, plazas, playgrounds, recreational centres, libraries, health centres, schools, bus, railway and metro stations) also discourages their use as well as the community-networks that they help reinforce.

Other risk-factors have been identified in the United States: the easy availability of guns; the level of violence on television and other media; the lack of priority in public policy to violence prevention; alcohol abuse; and the witnessing of acts of violence.[179] One factor in the increase in murders and violent crimes in many cities has been the growth in the drug traffic which has provided criminal syndicates with more financial power than ever. In many cities of Latin America, young people with very little prospect of employment in the formal labour markets have found considerably more profit in selling drugs. The struggle to control the drug trade is one factor behind the increase in violent crime in many cities.

Notes and References

1. This distinction between the constituents and the determinants of well-being is drawn from Dasgupta, Partha and Martin Weale, 'On measuring the quality of life', *World Development*, vol. 20, no. 1, 1992, 119–31.

2. *Ibid.* 124.

3. However, there is often some confusion in many people's minds between longevity and life expectancy.

4. Jones, Huw, *Population Geography*, 2nd edn, Paul Chapman Publishing, London, 1990.

5. Arriaga, E. and K. Davis, 'The pattern of mortality change in Latin America', *Demography*, vol. 6, 1969, 223–42, quoted in Jones 1990, *op. cit.*

6. Woods, R. J. and J. H. Woodward (eds.), *Urban Disease and Mortality in Nineteenth Century England*, Batsford, 1984.

7. See Briscoe, John, 'Selected primary health care revisited', in Joseph S. Tulchin (ed.), *Health, Habitat and Development*, Lynne Reinner, Boulder, 1986 for a robust defence of full primary health care.

8. World Bank, *World Development Report 1993*, Oxford University Press, 1993, 19.

9. Dasgupta and Weale 1992, *op. cit.*

10. Okolski, Marek, 'Health and mortality', chapter 2 in the Proceedings of the European Population Conference vol. 1, March, GV.E.94.0.15, United Nations, Geneva, 1994, 119–92.

11. Power, Chris, 'Health and social inequality in Europe', *British Medical Journal*, vol. 308, no. 6937, 30 April, 1994, 1153–56.

12. Feshbach, M., 'The Soviet Union: population trends and dilemmas', *Population Bulletin*, vol. 37, no. 3, 1982 quoted in Jones, 1990, *op. cit.*

13. Dinkel, R., 'The seeming paradox of increasing mortality in a highly industrialized nation: the example of the Soviet Union', *Population Studies*, vol. 39, 87–97' quoted in Jones 1990, *op. cit.*

14. Cornia, Giovanni Andrea, with Renato Paniccià, 'The demographic impact of sudden impoverishment: Eastern Europe during the 1989–94 transition', Paper presented at the Seminar on Demography and Poverty, IUSSP-UNICEF-University of Florence, Florence, 2–4 March 1995, 39.

15. *Ibid.*

16. Anand, S. and M. Ravallion, 'Human development in poor countries: on the role of private incomes and public services', *Journal of Economic Perspectives*, vol. 7, no. 1, Winter, 1993, 133–50.

17. World Bank 1993, *op. cit.*

18. *Ibid.*

19. Anand and Ravallion 1993, *op. cit.*

20. *Ibid.*

21. *Ibid.*

22. Power 1994, *op. cit.*

23. Wilkinson, R. G., 'Income distribution and life expectancy', *British Medical Journal*, vol. 304, 1992, 165–8, quoted in Power 1994, *op. cit.*

24. Jones 1990, *op. cit.*

25. World Health Organization, *World Health Statistics Annual, 1977–1989*, quoted in WHO, *Our Planet, Our Health*, Report of the Commission on Health and Environment, Geneva, 1992.

26. WHO, *Our Planet, Our Health*, Report of the Commission on Health and Environment, Geneva, 1992.

27. Statistics drawn from UNDP, *Human Development Report 1994*, United Nations Development Programme, Oxford University Press, Oxford and New York, 1994.

28. Okolski 1994, *op. cit.*

29. UNDP, *Human Development Report 1993*, Oxford University Press, 1993

30. UNDP, *Human Development Report 1992*, Oxford University Press, 1992.

31. UNDP 1993, *op. cit.*

32. McLaughlin, Martin M. and the staff of the Overseas Development Council, *The United States and World Development Agenda 1979*, Praeger Publishers, New York, 1979.

33. McGillivray, M., 'The human development index: yet another redundant composite development indicator?', *World Development*, vol. 19, no. 10, 1991, 1461–8.

34. UNDP 1994, *op. cit.*

35. UNDP 1994, *op. cit.*

36. Mueller, Charles C., 'Environmental problems of a development style: the degradation from urban poverty in Brazil', *Environment and Urbanization*, vol. 7, no. 2, Oct.1995, 68–84.

37. UNDP 1994, *op. cit.*

38. ANC, *A National Health Plan for South Africa*, Prepared by the ANC Health Department with the support and technical assistance of WHO and UNICEF, no date.

39. Unadjusted 1990 census (first 6 months' deaths and births data), quoted in *World Bank News*, vol. 13, no. 39, Oct. 1994.

40. EMPLASA 1994, *op. cit.*

41. ANC n.d. *op. cit.*

42. MMRs for 1989–91 derived from the National Surveillance System that produces regional averages; quoted in *World Bank News*, vol. 13, no. 39, Oct. 1994.

43. ANC n.d. *op. cit.*

44. EMPLASA, Plano Metropolitan da Grande Sao Paulo; 1993/2010, Empresa Metropolitana de Planejamento da Grande Sao Paulo SA, Sao Paulo, 1994.

45. These are summarized in Hardoy, Jorge E., Diana Mitlin and David Satterthwaite, *Environmental Problems in Third World Cities*, Earthscan Publications, London, 1992. See for instance Rodhe, J. E., 'Why the other half dies: the science and politics of child mortality in the Third World', *Assignment Children*, 1983, 35–67; Trudy Harpham, Tim Lusty and Patrick Vaughan (eds.), *In the Shadow of the City: Community Health and the Urban Poor*, Oxford University Press, 1988; Guimaraes, J. J. and A. Fischmann, 'Inequalities in 1980 infant mortality among shantytown residents and non-shanty town residents in the municipality of Porto Alegre, Rio Grande do Sul, Brazil', *Bulletin of the Pan American Health Organization*, 19, 1985, 235–51.

46. Pacione, Michael, 'The tale of two cities: the mitigation of the urban crisis in Glasgow', *Cities*, vol. 7, no. 4, Nov. 1990, 304–14.

47. See for instance Stephens, Carolyn, Ian Timaeus, Marco Akerman, Sebastian Avle, Paulo Borlina Maia, Paulo Campanerio, Ben Doe, Luisiana Lush, Doris Tetteh and Trudy Harpham, *Environment and Health in Development Countries: an Analysis of Intra-urban Differentials Using Existing Data*, London School of Hygiene and Tropical Medicine, London, 1994.

48. This section on poverty draws in particular on three sources. The first is a background paper prepared for the Global Report on *Conceptualizing Urban Poverty* by Ellen Wratten. The second is the work of Robert Chambers. The third is the CROP-IIED Workshop on *Urban Poverty* held in Bergen in October 1994 to review the scale and nature of urban poverty; this section draws to a considerable extent on the papers presented at this workshop and on the discussions during it.

49. Chambers, Robert, 'Poverty and livelihoods; whose reality counts?', an overview paper prepared for the Stockholm Roundtable on Global Change, 22–24 July 1994, subsequently published in *Environment and Urbanization*, vol. 7, no. 1, April 1995. See also Beck, Tony, *The Experience of Poverty: Fighting for Respect and Resource in Village India*, Intermediate Technology Publications, London, 1994, 4.

50. Different sources suggest different figures; these will be discussed later in this chapter.

51. Cairncross, Sandy, Jorge E. Hardoy and David Satterthwaite, 'The urban context', in Jorge E. Hardoy, Sandy Cairncross and David Satterthwaite (eds.), *The Poor Die Young: Housing and Health in Third World Cities*, Earthscan Publications, London, 1990.

52. For more details, see Wisner, Ben, *Power and Need in Africa: Basic Human Needs and Development Policies*, Earthscan, London, 1988; also Townsend, Peter, *The International Analysis of Poverty*, Harvester/Wheatsheaf, New York, 1993.

53. Chambers 1994, *op. cit.* 10

54. Chambers, Robert, 'Editorial introduc-

tion: vulnerability, coping and policy', in *Vulnerability: How the Poor Cope*, IDS Bulletin, vol. 20, no 2, April 1989, 1–7.

55. WHO 1992, *op. cit.*

56. Pugh, Cedric (1995), 'The role of the World Bank in housing' in B. Aldrich and R. Sandhu (eds.), *Housing the Poor: Policy and Practice in Developing Countries*, Zed, London, 1995.

57. See also Pugh 1995, *op. cit.*

58. Jazairy, Idriss, Mohiuddin Alamgir and Theresa Panuccio, *The State of World Rural Poverty: an Inquiry into its Causes and Consequences*, IT Publications, London, 1992.

59. *Ibid.*

60. The first figure comes from Leonard, H. Jeffrey, 'Environment and the poor: development strategies for a common agenda', in H. Jeffrey Leonard and contributors, *Environment and the Poor: Development Strategies for a Common Agenda*, Overseas Development Council, Transaction Books, New Brunswick (USA) and Oxford (UK), 1989, 3–45. The second comes from the World Bank, *Urban Policy and Economic Development: an Agenda for the 1990s*, The World Bank, Washington DC, 1991.

61. Tabatabai, Hamid with Manal Fouad, *The Incidence of Poverty in Developing Countries; an ILO Compendium of Data*, A World Employment Programme Study, International Labour Office, Geneva, 1993.

62. Piachaud, David, 'The Definition and Measurement of Poverty and Inequality', in Nicholas Barr and David Whynes (eds.), *Current Issues in the Economics of Welfare*, Macmillan, Basingstoke and London, 1993, 105–29.

63. The work of Amartya Sen develops this point about how certain societies with relatively low per capita incomes have social indicators that show much greater progress than others with comparable levels of per capita income. One of the examples he uses is the state of Kerala and the statistics about Kerala and India in this paragraph are drawn from Sen, Amartya, *Beyond Liberalization: Social Opportunity and Human Capability*, Development Economics Research Programme DEP no. 58, London School of Economics, London, 1994.

64. Townsend 1993, *op. cit.*

65. See for instance Egziabher, Axumite G., Diana Lee-Smith, Daniel G. Maxwell, Pyar Ali Memon, Luc J. A. Mougeot and Camillus J. Sawio, *Cities Feeding People: An Examination of Urban Agriculture in East Africa*, International Development Research Centre, Ottawa, 1994; Smit, Jac and Joe Nasr, 'Urban agriculture for sustainable cities: using wastes and idle land and water bodies as resources', *Environment and Urbanization*, vol. 4, no 2, Oct. 1992, 141–52; Lee-Smith, Diana, Mutsembi Manundu, Davinder Lamba and P. Kuria Gathuru, *Urban Food Production and the Cooking Fuel Situation in Urban Kenya—National Report: Results of a 1985 National Survey*,

Mazingira Institute, Nairobi, Kenya, 1987; and Mbiba, Beacon, *Urban Agriculture in Zimbabwe*, Avebury, Aldershot, 1995.

66. Castells, Manuel, *The City and Grass Roots: A Cross-Cultural Theory of Urban Social Movements*, Edward Arnold, London, 1983; and Friedmann, John, 'The Latin American *Barrio* movement as a social movement: contribution to a debate', *International Journal of Urban and Regional Research*, vol. 13, no. 3, 1989, 501–10.

67. Feres, Juan Carlos and Arturo Leon 'The magnitude of poverty in Latin America', *CEPAL Review*, no. 41, Aug. 1990, 133–51.

68. Amis, Philip, 'Making sense of urban poverty', *Environment and Urbanization*, vol. 7, no. 1, April 1995, 145–57; Harriss, John, 'Urban poverty and urban poverty alleviation', *Cities*, vol. 6, no. 3, Aug. 1989, 186–94.

69. The World Bank, *Implementing the World Bank's Strategy to Reduce Poverty: Progress and Challenges*, World Bank, Washington DC, 1993; World Bank, *World Development Report 1990: Poverty*, Oxford University Press, Oxford, 1990.

70. Central Bureau of Statistics, Jakarta quoted in ESCAP, *State of Urbanization in Asia and the Pacific 1993*, Economic and Social Commission for Asia and the Pacific, ST/ESCAP/1300, United Nations, 1993.

71. ESCAP 1993, *op. cit.*

72. Minujin, Alberto, 'Squeezed: the middle class in Latin America', *Environment and Urbanization*, vol. 7, no. 2, Oct. 1995, 153–66.

73. World Bank 1993, *op. cit.*

74. Escobar Latapí, Augustín and Mercedes González de la Rocha, 'Crisis, restructuring and urban poverty in Mexico', *Environment and Urbanization*, vol. 7, no. 1, April 1995, 57–75; Tuirán, Rodolfo, 'Estrategias familiares de vida en época de crisis: el caso de México', *Cambios en el Perfil de la Familia: La Experiencia Regional*, Naciones Unidas/Comisión Económica para América Latina y el Caribe, Santiago de Chile, 1993.

75. Escobar, Agustín and Bryan Roberts, 'Urban stratification, the middle classes, and economic change in Mexico', in González de la Rocha, Mercedes and Agustín Escobar Latapí (eds.), *Social Responses to Mexico's Economic Crisis of the 1980s*, Center for US-Mexican Studies, University of California at San Diego, La Jolla, 1991; and Reyes Heroles G.G., Jesús, 'Política económica y bienestar social: elementos de una estrategia para redistribuir el ingreso en México' in *Igualdad, Desigualdad y Equidad en España y México*, Instituto de Cooperación Económica, Madrid, 1985.

76. Hernández Laos, Enrique, *Crecimiento Económico y Pobreza en México; Una Agenda para la Investigación*, Universidad Autónoma de México, Centro de Investigaciones Interdisciplinarias en Humanidades, Mexico City, 1992,

quoted in Escobar Latapí and González de la Rocha 1995, *op. cit.*

77. Tello, Carlos, 'Combating poverty in Mexico', in González de la Rocha, Mercedes and Agustín Escobar Latapí (eds.), *Social Responses to Mexico's Economic Crisis of the 1980s*, Center for US-Mexican Studies, University of California at San Diego, La Jolla, 1991.

78. Tuirán 1993, *op. cit.*

79. Escobar Latapí and González de la Rocha 1995, *op. cit.*

80. Cairncross, Hardoy and Satterthwaite 1990, *op. cit.*

81. See Section 6.4 on homelessness for more details.

82. World Bank, *World Development Report 1990*, Oxford University Press, 1990.

83. Townsend 1993, *op. cit.*

84. More details are given in Chapter 8.

85. Chambers 1994, *op. cit.*

86. *Ibid.*

87. In some countries, those that fall well below the absolute poverty line are considered destitute or extremely poor—see Rakodi, Carole, 'Poverty lines or household strategies? a review of conceptual and methodological issues in the study of urban poverty', Paper presented to the CROP-IIED Workshop on Urban Poverty, October 1994. A revised version of this paper was subsequently published as Rakodi, Carole, 'Poverty lines or household strategies? A review of conceptual issues in the study of urban poverty', *Habitat International*, vol. 19, no. 4, 1995, 407–26.

88. Townsend 1993, *op. cit.* 36.

89. Ecologist, The, *Whose Common Future: Reclaiming the Commons*, Earthscan Publications, London, 1992.

90. This paragraph is drawn largely from Gore, Charles, 'Introduction: markets, citizenship and social exclusion', in Gerry Rodgers, Charles Gore and José B. Figueiredo, *Social Exclusion: Rhetoric, Reality, Responses*, International Labour Organization, Geneva, 1995, 1–40.

91. Grootaert, Christiaan and Ravi Kanbur, *Policy-Oriented Analysis of Poverty and the Social Dimensions of Structural Adjustment: A Methodology and Proposed Application to Cote d'Ivoire, 1985–88*, The World Bank, Washington DC, 1990.

92. World Bank 1990, *op. cit.*

93. Woodward, David, *Structural Adjustment Policies: What are they? Are they working?*, Catholic Institute for International Relations, London, 1993, 27 pages.

94. Moser, Caroline O. N., Alicia J. Herbert and Roza E. Makonnen, *Urban Poverty in the Context of Structural Adjustment; Recent Evidence and Policy Responses*, TWU Discussion Paper DP #4, the Urban Development Division, World Bank, Washington DC, May 1993.

95. Amis 1995, *op. cit.*

96. Moser, Herbert and Makonnen 1993, *op. cit.* 78. This in turn drew from World Bank 1991, *op. cit.*

97. The Zimbabwe Congress of Trade Unions puts the figure at 60,000; see Kanji, Nazneen, 'Gender, poverty and structural adjustment in Harare, Zimbabwe', *Environment and Urbanization*, vol. 7, no. 1, April 1995, 37–55.

98. Kanji 1995, *op. cit.* This paper also points to the droughts of 1990–1 and 1991–2 as also have a negative impact on macro-economic growth

99. Moser, Herbert and Makonnen 1993, *op. cit.*

100. See for instance: Hartmut, Schneider, in collaboration with Winifred Weekes-Vagliani, Paolo Groppo, Sylvie Lambert, Akiko Suwa, Nghia Nguyen Tinh, *Adjustment and Equity in Cote d'Ivoire*, OECD, Paris, 1992; and Grootaert and Kanbur 1990, and Moser, Herbert and Makonnen 1993, *op. cit.*

101. This point is made by Escobar Latapí and González de la Rocha 1995, *op. cit.* for Latin America but is also valid for other regions.

102. Moser, Herbert and Makonnen 1993, *op. cit.* drawing on World Bank, *Targeted Programs for the Poor During Structural Adjustment 1988: a Summary of a Symposium on Poverty and Adjustment*, World Bank, Washington DC, 1988.

103. Moser, Herbert and Makonnen 1993, *op. cit.*

104. Minujin, Alberto, 'En la rodada', in A. Minujin, E. Bustelo, M. del Carmen Feijoo, S. Feldman, A. Gershanik, H. Gonzales, J. Halperin, J.L. Karol, M. Murmis and E. Tenti Fanfini, *Cuesta Abajo; Los Nuevos Pobres—Efectos de la Crisis en la Sociedad Argentina*, UNICEF, Buenos Aires, 1992.

105. Minujin 1995, *op. cit.*

106. Moser, Herbert and Makonnen 1993, *op. cit.* 13.

107. González de la Rocha, Mercedes, 'Economic crisis, domestic reorganization and women's work in Guadalajara, Mexico', *Bulletin of Latin American Research*, vol. 7, no. 2, 1988, 207–23; and González de la Rocha, Mercedes, 'Family well-being, food consumption, and survival strategies during Mexico's economic crisis', in González de la Rocha, Mercedes and Agustín Escobar Latapí (eds.), *Social Responses to Mexico's Economic Crisis of the 1980s*, Center for US-Mexican Studies, University of California at San Diego, La Jolla, 1991.

108. Chant, Sylvia, *Women and Survival in Mexican Cities: Perspectives on Gender, Labour Markets and Low Income Households*, Manchester University Press, Manchester, 1991; and Selby, Henry, Arthur Murphy and Stephen Lorenzen, *The Mexican Urban Household; Organizing for Self-Defense*, University of Texas Press, Austin, 1990.

109. CEPAL, Serie A. no. 247, 1992, Table 4 in Escobar Latapí and González de la Rocha 1995, *op. cit.*

110. See for instance González de la Rocha, Mercedes and Agustín Escobar Latapí (1986), 'Crisis y adaptación: hogares de Guadalajara', paper presented at *III Encuentro de Investigación Demográfica*, SOMEDE, Mexico City, November; and González de la Rocha, Mercedes (1988), 'Economic crisis, domestic reorganization and women's work in Guadalajara, Mexico', *Bulletin of Latin American Research*, vol. 7, no. 2, 207–23. See Escobar Latapí and González de la Rocha 1995, *op. cit.* for a review of these and other studies.

111. Kanji 1995, *op. cit.*

112. *Ibid.* See also Brydon, L., 'Draft summary of findings on process and effects of SAPs in Ghana', mimeo for the ESRC, 1993, and Vandemoortele J., 'Labour market informalisation in sub-Saharan Africa', in G. Standing, and V. Tokman (eds.) *Towards Social Adjustment: Labour Market Issues in Structural Adjustment*, ILO, Geneva, 1991, 81–114.

113. Kanji 1995, *op. cit.*; see also Tibaijuka, A. K., 'The impact of structural adjustment programmes on women: the case of Tanzania's economic recovery programme', report prepared for the Canadian International Development Agency (CIDA), Dar-es-Salaam, Tanzania, 1988.

114. See Rakodi 1994, *op. cit.*

115. Harriss 1989, *op. cit.*

116. *Ibid.*

117. Hibbert, Christopher, *London: A Biography of a City*, Penguin Books, London, 1980.

118. For overview see Rakodi, Carole, 'Poverty lines or household strategies? A review of conceptual issues in the study of urban poverty', *Habitat International*, vol. 19, no. 4, 1995, 407–26.

119. See for instance Burt, Martha R., *Over the Edge; the Growth of Homelessness in the 1980s*, The Urban Institute Press, Washington DC, 1992.

120. See for instance Veenhoven, Rout, *Did the Crisis Really Hurt?* Rotterdam University Press, 1989.

121. Hutton, Will, *The State We're In*, Jonathan Cape, London, 1995.

122. Clichevsy, Nora and others, *Construccion y Administracion de la Ciudad Latinoamericana*, Grupo Editor Latinoamericano, Buenos Aires, 1990, drawing on PREALC data.

123. CEPAL, *Estudio económico de América Latina y el Caribe, 1986*, CEPAL, Santiago, 1986 and Clichevsky and others 1990, *op. cit.*

124. Burt 1992, *op. cit.*

125. Escobar Latapí and González de la Rocha 1995, *op. cit.*

126. Standing, G. 'Structural adjustment and labour market policies: towards social adjustment?' in G. Standing and V. Tokman (eds.), *Towards Social Adjustment: Labour Market Issues in Structural Adjustment*, ILO, Geneva, 1991, 5–52.

127. See Section 3.3

128. Chambers 1989 *op. cit.* pointed to this distinction; Pryer 1989 illustrated it through a case study—see Pryer, Jane, 'When breadwinners fall ill: preliminary findings from a case study in Bangladesh', in *Vulnerability: How the Poor Cope*, IDS Bulletin, vol. 20, no. 2, April 1989, 49–57.

129. Mitullah, Winnie, 'Hawking as a survival strategy for the urban poor in Nairobi: the case of women', *Environment and Urbanization*, vol. 3, no. 2, Oct. 1991, 13–22.

130. See for instance the detailed description of this in Pryer, Jane, 'The impact of adult ill-health on household income and nutrition in Khulna, Bangladesh', *Environment and Urbanization*, vol. 5, no. 2, Oct. 1993, 35–49.

131. Beall, Jo, *The Gender Dimensions of Urbanisation and Urban Poverty*, Paper prepared for the seminar on Women in Urban Areas, Division for the Advancement of Women, United Nations Office at Vienna, 8–12 Nov., Vienna, 1993.

132. See for instance Moser, Caroline O. N., 'Mobilization is women's work: struggles for infrastructure in Guayaquil, Ecuador', in Caroline O. N. Moser and Linda Peake (eds.), *Women, Housing and Human Settlements*, Tavistock Publications, London and New York, 1987, 166–94.

133. Moser, Caroline O. N., *Gender Planning and Development; Theory, Practice and Training*, Routledge, London and New York, 1993.

134. Moser, Caroline O. N., 'Women, human settlements and housing: a conceptual framework for analysis and policy-making', in Caroline O. N. Moser and Linda Peake (eds.), *Women, Housing and Human Settlements*, Tavistock Publications, London and New York, 1987, 12–32.

135. Levy, Caren, 'Gender and the environment: the challenge of cross-cutting issues in development policy and planning', *Environment and Urbanization*, vol. 4, no 1, April 1992, 120–35.

136. Moser, Herbert and Makonnen 1993, *op. cit.*

137. Oruwari, Yomi, 'The changing role of women in families and their housing needs: a case study of Port Harcourt, Nigeria', *Environment and Urbanization*, vol. 3, no. 2, Oct. 1991, 6–12.

138. Moser 1993, *op. cit.*

139. Moser 1987, *op. cit.*

140. See for instance Pryer 1993 *op. cit.* and Huysman, Marijk, 'Waste picking as a survival strategy for women in Indian cities', *Environment and Urbanization*, vol. 6, no. 2, Oct. 1994, 155–74.

141. Brydon, Lynne and Sylvia Chant, *Women in the Third World: Gender Issues in Rural and Urban Areas*, Edward Elgar, Aldershot, 1989.

142. Schlyter, Ann, *Women Householders and Housing Strategies: the case of George, Lusaka*, Social and Behavioural Sciences Series No. 14, National Swedish Institute for Building Research, Stockholm, 1988; and Schlyter, Ann, *Women Householders and Housing*

Strategies: The Case of Harare, Zimbabwe, The National Swedish Institute for Building Research, Stockholm, 1990.

143. See for instance Jodha, N. S., 'Poverty debate in India: a minority view', *Economic and Political Weekly*, Special Number, Nov. 1988, 2421–8.

144. *Ibid.*

145. Chambers 1994, *op. cit.*

146. This draws on a background paper by Franz Vanderschueren on 'From violence to justice and security', UNCHS, Nairobi, 1995. This will be published in *Environment and Urbanization*, vol. 8., no. 1, April 1996.

147. United Nations International Crime and Justice Research Institute (UNICRI), *Criminal Victimisation of the Developing World*, Rome, 1995.

148. Bourbeau, Robert, 'Analyse comparative de la mortalité violente dans les pays développés et dans quelques pays en développement durant la période 1985–89', *World Health Statistics Quarterly*, vol. 46, no. 1, 1993, 4–33.

149. *Urban Age*, vol. 1, no. 4, Summer 1993, 17.

150. Gilbert, Alan, *The Latin American City*, Latin American Bureau, London, 1994.

151. Zaluar, Alba, 'La drogua, el crimen, el diablo' and Sader, Emir, 'La violencia urbana en Brasil; El caso de Rio de Janeiro', in Concha, Albert, Fernando Carrion and German Cobo (eds.), *Ciudad y violencias en America Latina*, UMP Serie Gestión Urbana, Quito, 1995.

152. Carvalho de Noronha, José, 'Drug markets and urban violence in Rio de Janeiro: a call for action', *Urban Age*, vol. 1, no. 4, Summer 1993, 9.

153. Caldeira, Teresa, 'Building up walls: the new pattern of spatial segregation in Sao Paulo', *International Social Science Journal*, no. 147, March 1996.

154. Guerrero, Rodrigo, 'Cali's innovative approach to urban violence', *Urban Age*, vol. 1, no. 4, Summer 1993, 12–13.

155. Pinheiro, Paulo Sérgio, 'Reflections on urban violence', *Urban Age*, vol. 1, no. 4, Summer 1993, 3.

156. Los Angeles was reported in the *Urban Age*, vol. 1, no. 4, Summer 1993 to have had 2,062 homicides in 1991. See also Weiss, Billie, 'Violence prevention coalition', *World Health*, 46th Year, no.1, Jan.–Feb. 1993, 30–1.

157. See the tables in Bourbeau 1993, *op. cit.*

158. State of California Department of Health Services, 'Data summary: homicide among young males, by race/ethnicity', Dec. 1990, quoted in Cohen, Larry and Susan Swift, 'A public health approach to the violence epidemic in the United States', *Environment and Urbanization*, vol. 5, no. 2, Oct. 1993, 50–66.

159. Caldeira 1996, *op. cit.*

160. Rai, Usha, 'Escalating violence against adolescent girls in India', *Urban Age*, vol. 1, no. 4, Summer 1993, 10–11.

161. 'The Hidden problem' quoting Denise Stewart, 'The global injustice', *Viz-a-Viz*, Canadian Council on Social Development, 1989 in Davies, Miranda, (ed.), *Women and Violence: Realities and Responses Worldwide*, Zed Books, London and New Jersey, 1995.

162. 'Weapon carrying among high school students', *Morbidity and Mortality Weekly Report*, vol. 40, no. 40, 1991, 681–4, quoted in Jeanneret, Olivier and E.A. Sand, 'Intentional violence among adolescents and young adults: an epidemiological perspective', *World Health Statistics Quarterly*, vol. 46, no. 1, 1993, 34–51.

163. National Crime Survey cited in Jeanneret and Sand 1993, *op. cit.*

164. International Centre for the Prevention of Crime (ICPC), 'Urban policies and crime prevention', paper presented to the IX UN Congress for the Prevention of Crime, Montreal, 1995.

165. Caldeira 1996, *op. cit.*

166. *Ibid.*

167. International Centre for the Prevention of Crime (ICPC), Workshop on urban violence, 9th UN Congress on Crime Prevention, Cairo, Feb. 1995.

168. See Heise, Lori, 'Violence against women: the hidden health burden', *World Health Statistics Quarterly*, vol. 46, no. 1, 1993, 78–85 for a summary of the findings from many different studies.

169. Cohen and Swift 1993, *op. cit.*

170. 'The Hidden problem', *op. cit.*

171. US Senate Judiciary Committee, 'Violence against women: the increase of rape in America 1990', a majority staff report prepared for the use of the Committee on the Judiciary, United States Senate, 1990.

172. Heise 1993, *op. cit.*

173. Pinheiro 1993, *op. cit.*

174. For more details, see Vandeschueren 1996, Guerrero 1993 and Cohen and Swift 1993, *op. cit.* See also Banaynal-Fernandez, Tessie, 'Fighting violence against women: the Cebu Experience', *Environment and Urbanization*, vol. 6, no. 2, Oct. 1994, 31–56 for details of a programme in Cebu that is addressing the problem of violence against women, including sexual abuse and domestic violence.

175. Montreal meeting of Mayors.

176. Cohen and Swift 1993, *op. cit.*

177. *Ibid.*

178. Newman, Oscar, *Defensible Space: Crime Prevention through Urban Design*, MacMillan, New York, 1972; Coleman, Alice, *Utopia on Trial: Vision and Reality in Planned Housing*, Revised Edition, Hilary Shipman Ltd, London, 1990.

179. Cohen and Swift 1993, *op. cit.*

4 Environmental Conditions and Trends

4.1 Introduction

The environmental problems of the world's cities, towns and rural settlements are creeping up the political agenda of most governments and many international agencies. This is especially so for the major cities, where environmental problems are generally most visible. This has been helped by the Earth Summit (the United Nations Conference on Environment and Development) in 1992 whose recommendations point to the need for a renewed effort to address such problems. In many countries in Eastern Europe and the South, it has also been spurred by the return to democracy which often revealed a large legacy of environmental degradation that had been hidden under non-democratic regimes. Democracy also permitted environmental groups and citizen groups more space to demand a higher priority to environmental problems. The International Drinking Water Supply and Sanitation Decade and the international agencies involved in it helped promote a greater interest in improving water supply and sanitation and greatly increased the knowledge about the best ways and means of achieving this, even if, as Chapter 8 reports, ambitious targets for improved provision were not fully met. A greater attention to environmental problems in the South has also been encouraged by the increasingly detailed documentation of environmental problems and their impacts on the health and livelihoods of people and on the eco-systems within which settlements are located. This documentation has come from diverse sources—including the international agencies,[1] international research institutions[2] and national and local environmental groups in the South.[3]

The economic costs of poor environment

An increasing priority to environmental problems in settlements has also been spurred by unexpected recurrent disease epidemics—for instance, the return to Latin America in 1991 of cholera, when it had been assumed that this health threat had been eliminated from the region in the early twentieth century through improvements in water, sanitation, sewage treatment and food safety.[4] The scare regarding an apparent outbreak of plague in the Indian city of Surat in 1994 also heightened fears of what a lack of attention to water supply, sanitation, drainage and regular collection of solid wastes can cause. Although less dramatic diseases such as tuberculosis and diarrhoea continues to have a much more serious health impact, these sudden epidemics gained far more coverage from the media. These epidemics also made governments aware of the large sums of money they could lose, as the epidemics (or perhaps the sensational reporting about them) deterred tourists and private investments. The cholera epidemic in Peru not only caused over 320,000 cases and 2,600 deaths but an estimated $1 billion in losses from reduced agricultural and fisheries exports and tourism, less than the capital needed to radically improve water and sanitation in Peru's settlements.[5] The cost to India as a result of the 'plague scare' in terms of lost tourism revenues and the deterrence to foreign investment will also be very considerable and may outweigh the costs of greatly improving water and sanitation in cities like Surat. It is not even as if Surat is a particularly poor city; indeed, it has had a prosperous economy since the late 1960s and is regarded as a showcase of its State's economic upsurge—and it should have easily generated the capital needed to eliminate the conditions that permit large scale epidemics of infectious diseases.[6]

The most telling evidence of the inadequacy of response by governments and international agencies remains the scale of disease, injury and premature death that good environmental management and a basic health care system should eliminate. The scale of this easily preventable health burden is described in Section 4.2; it is certainly one of the most dramatic examples of inequality between the North and the South (for country level statistics) and between high income and low income groups (within countries). For instance, in 1990, the health burden per person from new cases of infectious and parasitic diseases caught in 1990 in sub-Saharan Africa was 50 times that in the North.[7]

However, it is difficult to assess environmental conditions and trends in the world's settlements when the term 'environment' encompasses so much, and means different things to different people. In addition, the scale and nature of environmental hazards in relation to human health and to the continued functioning and integrity of ecosystems varies enormously from country to country. There is also tremendous variation within nations as to the scale and nature of environmental hazards facing people depending on (for instance) occupation, income, sex, gender, age and, in some instances, race. This brief review of environmental conditions and trends in the worlds' cities, towns and villages concentrates on three aspects. The first is outlining the link between environment and health within settlements. The second is a summary of the health burden that arises from poor housing and living conditions. The third is summarizing the main environmental problems and their underlying causes at different geographic scales: the indoor environment, the workplace, the village or neighbourhood, the city, the region and the globe.

More attention is given to the environmental hazards that are responsible for or contribute most to ill health, injury and premature death worldwide. This limits coverage of many environmental hazards that are a major concern in wealthier nations but which, globally, are not among the main causes of death, disease or injury. In addition, because the focus is on settlements, little attention is given to environmental hazards that arise primarily from lifestyles and personal choices—for instance the enormous health impacts of tobacco smoking both for those who smoke and for those exposed to their smoke.

Urban management and health

The built environment within villages and urban areas of all sizes should be a safe environment—places where environmental hazards are minimized and where environmental factors do not figure as major causes of serious injuries or illnesses or premature death. The costs of achieving this are not very high and the social returns as well as the economic benefits are also very high.[8] However, to achieve this requires competent environmental management.

In all settlements, the health of the inhabitants has always depended on their ability to manage their environment. This can either be done cooperatively or through the delegation of this management to some city or village 'authority'. Some of the earliest co-operative 'management' schemes were to protect settlement's communal water sources and to control surface water—either for irrigation or for flood control. As the size of a settlement grows and as its economic base expands and demands increase on local resources, so does the need for a system to manage three environmental tasks:

—the safeguarding of basic resources—for instance to ensure that all inhabitants receive freshwater while the sources from which the freshwater is drawn is protected;
—to ensure wastes are removed; and
—to prevent any individual or enterprise dumping their environmental costs on others.

Officially, government agencies and local authorities have the main responsibilities for these three tasks. In practice, their failure or inability to do so in many settlements in the South have led to serious environmental health problems.

Although any person's state of health is the result of interactions between their human biology (including their genetic inheritance), lifestyle, the health-care system and the environment,[9] historically, the environment has always had a major role. In urban and rural settlements, environmental hazards, especially biological pathogens in the air, water, soil or food—have always been among the main causes of disease and death. A considerable part of the history of cities is the technical and managerial innovations that were developed in cities to address these three environmental tasks. There are many historical examples of ingenious ways through which cities solved their problems of freshwater supply and the removal and disposal of industrial, commercial and household wastes, although these were the exceptions and were implemented without any detailed knowledge of the processes by which diseases were transmitted.

What is unprecedented is the extent to which, over the last hundred years, the knowledge and resources have become available to make the environments of cities far less hazardous for their inhabitants. This has reached the point where, in a healthy city, environmental factors would have a relatively minor role in ill health and premature death. This can be seen in the decline in infant mortality rates. Today, infant mortality rates in healthy, well-served cities should be less than 10 per 1,000 live births and may be as low as 5. In a healthy city, it is very rare for an infant or child to die from an infectious or parasitic disease. Only 100 years ago, most prosperous European cities still had infant mortality rates that exceeded 100 per 1,000 live births; in Vienna, Berlin, Leipzig, Naples, St Petersburg and many of the large industrial towns in England, the figure exceeded 200 and in Moscow, it exceeded 300[10]—and infectious diseases were the main cause of such high infant mortality rates.[11]

In almost all cities, towns and villages in West Europe, North America, Australia and Japan, it is now very unusual for someone to die of acute respiratory infections, diarrhoeal diseases, tuberculosis, typhoid, typhus and yellow fever—yet all were major causes of death until relatively recently. The same is also true for measles, diphtheria and the other 'vaccine-preventable' childhood diseases that were major causes of infant and child death only a few decades ago in Europe and North America. What is also probably unprecedented over the last 100 years is the extent to which low-income groups have benefited in cities where this knowledge and capacity

BOX 4.1
Lessons from recent history on environmental health

Only in the second half of the nineteenth century did systematic action begin to be taken in the rapidly growing cities of North America and Europe to improve environmental health. Cities of unprecedented size were developing[a] where all the environmental hazards of rapid industrial growth and very poor housing and living conditions were added to more traditional concerns of freshwater supplies and the removal of household and commercial wastes. Then, as is often common now, city populations were doubling or tripling within two or three decades with very limited change in the form of government and thus in any capacity to manage the three environmental tasks. Manchester's population grew more than sixfold in less than sixty years (between 1774 and 1831) and 'many of its problems had been due to the fact that it had had to cope with mass immigration and dramatically rapid expansion, equipped with little more than the administrative powers of a village'.[14] New York City's population expanded more than ninefold between 1800 and 1850, also with few changes to its structure of government that still remained weak and very dependent on a (generally) hostile state government for funds.[15] The high population growth rates achieved in such cities were all the more dramatic, as health conditions were so poor that death rates often exceeded birth rates. Most or all city population growth was the result of net in-migration.[b]

During the late eighteenth and first half of the nineteenth centuries, the population of many cities in the nations undergoing the industrial revolution grew very rapidly. Densities were very high; in the absence of cheap mass transport, most people had to live within working distance of work. In the absence of effective governance to ensure safe and sufficient water supplies, the removal of waste and the control of industrial pollution and occupational hazards, health conditions for the majority were so poor than life expectancy in many cities was well below that of smaller towns or rural areas.[16] Average life expectancies in the industrial centres were often below 30—and below 18 years for the lowest income groups.[17]

The early development of what might be termed modern urban government and town planning has its roots in public health concerns that promoted much improved water supplies and public action to ensure the hygienic removal of excreta and other household wastes and commercial and industrial wastes. Such action was much stimulated by a series of cholera epidemics that swept through Europe and North America during the nineteenth century, often causing thousands to die in a single epidemic in one city. Although other diseases transmitted by contaminated water—for instance typhoid, typhus and diarrhoeal diseases—and certain air-borne diseases such as acute respiratory infections and tuberculosis probably had a more serious health impact, cholera's impact was all the greater as it was concentrated in sudden, large epidemics. In addition, the epidemics helped overcome the reluctance of city businesses and households to contribute towards the cost of improved water and sanitation since the epidemics threatened their health and also, increasingly, their business as wealthier groups fled from cities, as cholera epidemics approached.[18]

Notes: [a] Some of the capitals of large nations or empires had grown to more than a million before the industrial revolution —when few of the major industrial towns grew to this size during the 19th century—but what made the industrial centres unusual was the rapidity of their growth, their growing numbers and their concentration of industry and very poor housing and working conditions that much exacerbated the more traditional environmental problems.
[b] Cities in the South are often thought to have had unprecedented rates of in-migration but it may be that the main industrial centres in Europe and North America experienced a more rapid in-migration in the 19th century in terms of the number of in-migrants per year relative to total population as natural increase contributed little or nothing—or was even natural decrease.

has been applied. While low-income groups invariably have worse health and lower life expectancies than richer groups, as described in Chapter 3, the scale of these disparities have been greatly reduced in cities where environmental hazards have been much reduced. Ensuring that lower-income groups can obtain reasonable quality housing and are adequately served by water supplies, provision for sanitation and drainage and health care remain among the most effective means of reducing the disparities in health status between higher- and lower-income groups.

The speed of this transformation in the health of human populations and the means to protect against diseases that formerly thrived, especially in crowded cities, has been under-appreciated—as has the contemporary relevance of the means by which it occurred (see Box 4.1). However, this transformation has yet to take place for a large proportion of the world's urban centres and villages. In addition, in many cities the transformation has occurred, but only for a proportion of the population; in many Latin American and Asian cities, middle- and upper-income groups are as well protected against the diseases noted above as those in Europe and North America while up to half the population with low incomes lack such protection. An estimate in 1990 suggested that 600 million urban dwellers in the South lived in shelters and neighbourhoods in which their life and health was continually threatened because of the inadequacies in provision for safe, sufficient water supplies, sanitation, removal of solid and liquid wastes and health care and emergency services.[12] Probably twice this number living in rural settlements face comparable risks.[13]

Perhaps the most important contemporary lesson from this historic experience is the extent to which these changes were driven by increasingly well-articulated and organized demands from those who suffered most from the lack of water supply, sanitation and health care. The importance of increasingly more competent and accountable urban governments should also be stressed.

4.2 The health burden of poor housing

Any study of the health burden of poor housing has to consider the health burden arising not only within the home but also in the area around the home. It is difficult to separate out the health effects of poor quality housing from other important influences—especially the quality of health care and emergency services, the income level (which below a certain point has a crucial influence on nutritional levels) and the level of education. An individual's level of education is important not only because it affects their income-earning capacity but also because it improves knowledge about how to promote health, prevent disease and rapidly treat illness or injury and encourages greater use of health services. Infant and child mortality rates tend to be lower, the better educated the mother.[21] Within the house, there are also so many different factors that influence health that it is difficult to generalize about what promotes good health there. Box 4.2 gives more details of the nine features of the housing environment that the World Health Organization has singled out as having important direct or indirect effects on the health of their occupants.

A few studies have sought a more detailed understanding of the health costs faced by people living in very poor-quality housing. One such study in a low-income, poor quality settlement

---

BOX 4.2

Features of the housing environment that have important direct or indirect effects on the health of the occupants

- The structure of the shelter (which includes a consideration of the extent to which the shelter protects the occupants from extremes of heat or cold, insulation against noise and invasion by dust, rain, insects and rodents).

- The extent to which the provision for water supplies is adequate—both from a qualitative and a quantitative point of view.

- The effectiveness of provision for the disposal (and subsequent management) of excreta and liquid and solid wastes.

- The quality of the housing site, including the extent to which it is structurally safe for housing and provision is made to protect it from contamination (of which provision for drainage is among the most important aspects).

- The consequence of over-crowding—including household accidents and airborne infections whose transmission is increased: acute respiratory infectious diseases; pneumonia, tuberculosis.

- The presence of indoor air pollution associated with fuels used for cooking and/or heating.

- Food safety standards—including the extent to which the shelter has adequate provision for storing food to protect it against spoilage and contamination.

- Vectors and hosts of disease associated with the domestic and peri-domestic environment.

- The home as a workplace—where occupational health questions such as the use and storage of toxic or hazardous chemicals and health and safety aspects of equipment used need consideration.

Source: World Health Organization, *Shelter and Health*, WHO/EHE/RUN/87.1, Geneva, 1987.

---

in Khulna, Bangladesh's second largest city, documented the loss of income and nutritional problems in households where the main income earner was too sick to work.[20] In the case study settlement, the lower-income households not only lost more work days to illness or injury and more income than richer households but also a much higher proportion of their income. Most such households were heavily in debt. Many of their incapacitated income-earners had chronic illnesses that imply a continuous limitation on their capacity to work. Households with severely incapacitated earners were also much more likely to have severely undernourished children. In addition, among the households with severely undernourished children and incapacitated income-earners, most family members were undernourished. If the economic and nutritional consequences of sickness among poorer households in this settlement in Khulna are not untypical to those experienced by those living in illegal settlements in other urban centres in the South, the health burden associated with very poor housing conditions is greatly underestimated.

Most of the health costs for the lowest income group households in the settlement in Khulna could have been prevented or much reduced at low cost. A recent analysis of the global disease burden for each of the world's regions shows that much remains to be done.[21] Around half of the world's population still suffers from diseases or injuries that are easily prevented or cured. There are two underlying causes. The first is the low priority given by most governments and aid agencies to the measures that are most cost effective in preventing injury or disease or in limiting their health impact. This includes a failure to give priority to water and sanitation provision that is appropriate to the needs and purchasing powers of low-income groups. The second underlying cause is the considerable proportion of the world's population who lack the income (or assets) to afford a good quality house within a neighbourhood where basic services are provided.

In 1993, the World Health Organization and the World Bank produced the first detailed estimates of the 'global disease burden' and its main causes. These allow some estimation of the health costs associated with poor quality housing and living conditions and a lack of basic services. They also reveal the scale and nature of differences in health burdens between the poorer and richer regions of the world. When this is supplemented with health data from particular countries, or from particular regions within countries, it also shows the enormous differences in health burdens between countries with similar per capita incomes. This highlights how the distribution of income within a society and the extent and competence of measures to reduce the health burden for low-income groups has a major influence on the scale of any country's total disease burden.

Table 4.1 presents estimates for the number of life-days lost per person through disability or premature death as a result of new cases of diseases or injuries acquired in one year (1990). The data is presented for each of the world's regions. It allows inter-regional comparisons as to the scale of the total burden of disease and injury acquired in this one year and of the relative importance of different causes.[22]

The disease and injury burden for each person in sub-Saharan Africa was nearly five times that for each person in the wealthiest market economies—Western Europe, North America, Japan and Australasia.[23] The disease and injury burden per person for all other regions falls between these two extremes. The disease burden per person in China is notable for being so low, relative to the country's per capita income. It is lower than for Latin America and the Caribbean (where the average per capita income is higher than in China, even when adjusted for purchasing power parity) and almost as low as the countries in East and Central Europe.

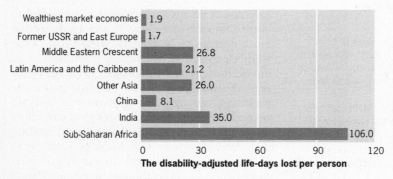

The disability-adjusted life-days lost per person

FIGURE 4.1
The disease burden per person from new cases of infectious and parasitic diseases acquired in one year (1990)

NB The figures for the disease burden in Figure 4.1 represent the average current and future disease burden per person in disability-adjusted life-days lost from new cases of infectious and parasitic diseases in one year (1990). Thus, they include the disability-adjusted life-days lost in later years that arose from an infectious or parasitic disease caught in 1990 but do not include the life-days lost in 1990 from diseases caught in years prior to, or subsequent to, 1990. For more details, see World Bank, *World Development Report 1993; Investing in Health*, Oxford University Press, 1993

Source: The original statistics on which this figure is based are drawn from tables B.2 and B.3 in the World Bank, *World Development Report 1993; Investing in Health*, Oxford University Press, 1993. Their conversion in disability-adjusted life-days and this figure is drawn from David Satterthwaite, Roger Hart, Caren Levy, Diana Mitlin, David Ross, Jac Smit and Carolyn Stephens, *The Environment for Children*, Earthscan Publications and UNICEF, London, 1996.

The differences in the health burden per person between regions are much larger for the infectious and parasitic diseases that are closely associated with poor quality housing and a lack of basic services. Most of the disease burdens arising from these can be considered as the health costs of this combination of low income and the incapacity or unwillingness of the government to install and maintain basic health care systems and to ensure widespread provision of water and sanitation and measures to keep down costs

and increase supplies of good quality housing. Figure 4.1 shows the regional differences in life-days lost per person to new cases of infectious and parasitic diseases acquired in 1990.

For the wealthy market economies, on average, less than two life-days are lost per person to the new cases of infectious and parasitic diseases caught in 1990. In Sub-Saharan Africa, 106 life-days are lost, more than 50 times the disease burden per person. For the other regions, except for China, the disease burden per person is between 11 and 18 times that in the wealthy market economies (Japan and the countries in West Europe, North America and Australasia). Again, the performance of China is notable in that the disease burden per person from infectious and parasitic diseases was much less than for other regions in the South.

The health burden from communicable diseases (which include infectious and parasitic diseases, respiratory diseases and maternal and perinatal diseases) becomes very low when a very high proportion of the population lives in good quality housing and has ready access to good quality health care. For instance, the number of infant deaths due to communicable diseases is as low as 0.4 per 1000 live births in Western Europe;[24] it is several hundred times higher among those living in the rural and urban settlements with the poorest quality housing and health care in Africa, Asia and Latin America. Communicable diseases contribute more to infant mortality in other parts of Europe—for instance to 4.7 infant deaths per 1000 live births in Central and Eastern Europe and 9.2 in the former Soviet Union. This can be attributed at least in part to poorer sanitary conditions in human settlements (e.g. lack of piped water supply at home).[25]

Table 4.1 also shows how the differences between regions are much smaller for the health burden per person from new cases of noncommunicable diseases—i.e. diseases that are not contagious and include heart diseases and cancers. However, this table does show that the health burden per person from this category of diseases is as high or higher per person in the lowest income continents as in the wealthiest regions. This demonstrates that these are not the 'diseases of affluence' as they are sometimes called, even if they may partly be associated with the lifestyles and hazards from urban and industrial development.

Among the infectious and parasitic diseases, worldwide, diarrhoeal diseases and the vaccine-preventable childhood infections cause the largest number of life-days lost. The differentials in life-days lost per person to diarrhoeal diseases between different regions of the world are also very large. For instance the disease burden per

TABLE 4.1 The number of life-days lost per person through disability or premature death by region and by cause, 1990

Cause	World	Sub-Saharan Africa	India	China	Other Asia and islands	Latin America & the Caribbean	Middle Eastern Crescent	Formerly socialist economies of Europe	Wealthy market economies
Proportion of									
- the world's population	100	9.7	16.1	21.5	13.0	8.4	9.6	6.6	15.2
- the world's disability adjusted life days	100	21.5	21.4	14.8	13.0	7.6	10.6	4.3	6.9
The number of life-days lost per person to different diseases or injuries									
Infectious and parasitic diseases	*25.8*	*106.0*	*35.0*	*8.1*	*26.0*	*21.2*	*26.8*	*1.7*	*1.9*
Tuberculosis	3.2	9.8	4.6	1.9	4.8	2.1	2.9	0.4	0.1
Human immunodeficiency virus (HIV)	2.1	13.1	1.7	0.0	0.7	3.6	0.2	0.2	0.7
Other sexually transmitted diseases	1.5	5.3	1.6	1.1	0.7	2.0	0.5	0.5	0.7
Diarrhoea	6.9	21.7	12.0	1.4	7.9	4.8	11.2	0.2	0.1
Vaccine-preventable childhood infections	4.7	20.1	8.4	0.6	4.3	1.3	6.2	0.0	0.0
(Measles)	2.4	11.5	4.0	0.1	2.2	0.3	2.8	0.0	0.0
(Tetanus)	1.1	4.1	2.2	0.2	1.1	0.2	1.8	0.0	0.0
Malaria	2.5	22.6	0.4	0.0	1.4	0.4	0.2	0.0	0.0
Tropical cluster	0.9	4.6	0.8	0.2	0.2	2.4	0.2	0.0	0.0
(Chagas' disease)	0.2	0.0	0.0	0.0	0.0	2.3	0.0	0.0	0.0
(Schistosomiasis)	0.3	2.5	0.1	0.1	0.1	0.1	0.1	0.0	0.0
(Leishmaniasis)	0.1	0.3	0.5	0.0	0.1	0.0	0.1	0.0	0.0
Trachoma	0.2	0.6	0.1	0.2	0.5	0.1	0.4	0.0	0.0
Worm infections	1.2	0.6	0.9	2.0	3.1	2.0	0.4	0.0	0.0
(Ascaris)	0.7	0.3	0.5	1.2	1.7	1.1	0.4	0.0	0.0
(Trichuris)	0.4	0.2	0.2	0.7	1.3	0.7	0.0	0.0	0.0
Pneumonia and other respiratory infections	*8.5*	*22.6*	*13.6*	*4.2*	*10.5*	*5.2*	*12.0*	*1.6*	*1.1*
Maternal causes	*2.1*	*5.7*	*3.4*	*0.8*	*2.3*	*1.5*	*3.1*	*0.5*	*0.3*
Perinatal causes	*6.9*	*14.9*	*11.5*	*3.4*	*7.0*	*7.7*	*11.4*	*1.5*	*0.9*
Non communicable diseases	*39.9*	*40.7*	*50.7*	*37.6*	*37.9*	*36.2*	*37.7*	*45.9*	*33.6*
Cancer	5.5	3.2	5.1	6.0	4.2	4.4	3.5	9.1	8.2
Nutritional deficiencies	3.7	5.9	7.8	2.1	4.4	3.9	3.8	0.8	0.7
Cardiovascular	10.2	8.7	12.2	9.1	9.2	7.8	9.2	18.1	10.0
Injuries	*11.3*	*19.6*	*11.5*	*10.8*	*10.7*	*12.7*	*13.6*	*10.2*	*5.1*
Motor vehicle	2.2	2.7	1.4	1.5	2.2	4.9	3.5	2.3	1.5
Falls	1.4	2.1	2.1	1.4	1.5	0.8	1.0	0.9	0.7
Intentional	3.5	8.8	1.5	3.3	3.0	3.6	5.4	2.9	1.7
(homicide and violence)	1.3	1.9	0.5	1.1	1.8	2.8	1.1	1.4	0.8
(war)	1.0	5.7	0.1	0.0	0.2	0.5	3.6	0.0	0.0
TOTAL: The average per person of life-days lost through disability or premature death*	94	210	126	65	94	85	105	61	43

* This is the sum of infectious and parasitic diseases, pneumonia and other respiratory infections, maternal and perinatal causes, non-communicable diseases and injuries.

** Western Europe, North America, Japan, Australia and New Zealand.

NB The original tables on which this is based list 109 different causes of disease and injury. In this table, the diseases associated with poor housing and living conditions and inadequate health care have been highlighted, with less detail given for other disease categories. The units have also been converted from hundreds of thousands of 'disability-adjusted life-years' to 'disability-adjusted life-days'.

person for new cases of diarrhoeal diseases caught in 1990 was around 200 times larger in Sub-Saharan Africa than in the wealthiest market economies. They are also particularly high in India and the Middle East—see Figure 4.2.

For diarrhoeal diseases, the links with the built environment are particularly strong as risk factors include overcrowding, poor sanitation, contaminated water and inadequate food hygiene.[26] A study of household environmental problems in Accra (Ghana) found that the environmental risk factors associated with a high prevalence of childhood diarrhoea were: overcrowded toilets (because each is shared by many households), fly infestation, interruptions to water supplies, questionable water-storage practices and children practising open defecation in the neighbourhood.[27] In the metropolitan areas of Southern Brazil, those without easy access to piped water were 4.8 times more likely to die from diarrhoea than those with water piped to their house. Those with water piped to their plot but not into their house were 1.5 times more likely to die from diarrhoea.[28] Many studies of poor urban districts have shown diarrhoeal diseases to be a major cause of premature death (especially among infants) and illness.[29] Where

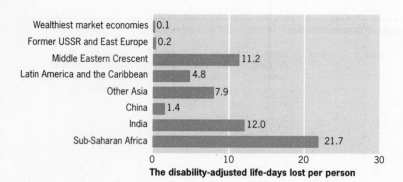

The disability-adjusted life-days lost per person

The disease burden per person from new cases of diarrhoeal diseases acquired in one year (1990)

NB The figures for the disease burden in Figure 4.2 represent the average current and future disease burden per person in disability-adjusted life-days lost from new cases of diarrhoeal diseases in one year (1990). Thus, they include the disability-adjusted life-days lost in later years that arose from a diarrhoeal disease caught in 1990 but do not include the life-days lost in 1990 from diseases caught in years prior to, or subsequent to, 1990. For more details, see World Bank, *World Development Report 1993; Investing in Health*, Oxford University Press, 1993

Source: The original statistics on which this figure is based are drawn from tables B.2 and B.3 in the World Bank, *World Development Report 1993; Investing in Health*, Oxford University Press, 1993. Their conversion in disability-adjusted life-days and this figure is drawn from Satterthwaite, David, Roger Hart, Caren Levy, Diana Mitlin, David Ross, Jac Smit and Carolyn Stephens, *The Environment for Children*, Earthscan Publications and UNICEF, London, 1996.

water supplies and provision for sanitation are inadequate for high proportions of the entire population, diarrhoeal diseases can remain one of the most serious health problems within city-wide averages.[30] More than 80 per cent of the life-days lost from diarrhoea were the result of infections in children under 5 years of age.[31] Safe and sufficient water supplies and adequate sanitation could reduce infant and child mortality by more than 50 per cent and prevent a quarter of all diarrhoeal episodes.[32] Reductions of between 40 and 50 per cent in morbidity from diarrhoeal diseases is possible through improved water and sanitation (see Box 4.3).

Box 4.3 also shows the dramatic reductions in morbidity from many other diseases that can be achieved through improvements in water supply

BOX 4.3

The potential reductions in morbidity for different diseases, as a result of improvements in water and sanitation

Diseases	Projected reduction in morbidity (per cent)
Cholera, typhoid, leptospirosis, scabies, guinea worm infection	80–100
Trachoma, conjunctivitis, yaws, schistosomiasis	60–70
Tularaemia, paratyphoid, bacillary dysentery, amoebic dysentery, gastro-enteritis, lice-borne diseases, diarrhoeal diseases,ascariasis, skin infections	40–50

Source: WHO, *Intersectoral Action for Health*, Geneva, 1986.

and sanitation. It shows how improved water supply and sanitation would greatly reduce morbidity from schistosomiasis (with its very considerable disease burden in Africa shown in Table 4.1) and trachoma and ascaris (with less dramatic disease burdens but ones that are evident in all regions in the South). Box 4.3 also highlights the extent to which increased water availability helps to control skin infections and infections carried by body-lice.[33] Various historical studies show how improvements in water and sanitation were major influences on improved life expectancy in Europe and even show that the timing of such improvements varies, according to when major investments were made in water and sanitation.[34]

Some of the diseases shown in Table 4.1 are related to inadequate provision for site drainage, garbage collection and the removal of household and human wastes since open water and household and human wastes provide opportunities for many disease vectors to live, breed or feed within or around houses and settlements. The diseases they cause or carry include malaria (*Anopheles* mosquitoes who breed in still, open water) and diarrhoeal diseases (cockroaches, blowflies and houseflies who often breed and/or feed in garbage).

Note should be made of the scale of the disease burden for malaria, especially in sub-Saharan Africa where it is estimated to cause a tenth of all life-days lost to illness or injury. Figure 4.3 shows its geographic scope. Malaria strikes as many as 300 million people a year (with over 100 million clinical cases).[35] Malaria is often considered as a predominantly rural problem but there are now severe problems with malaria in urban areas in large parts of Africa, Asia and Latin America. In many cities or poor peripheral city districts, malaria is one of the main causes of illness and death.[36] A community-focused programme that combines prevention (for instance draining sites where *anopheles* mosquitoes breed), improved protection against bites (including screens for houses or nets, especially to protect infants and children) and rapid and easily available treatment would greatly reduce this health burden.

The vaccine-preventable childhood infections show up in Table 4.1 as causing a very high health burden in sub-Saharan Africa and a high health burden for most Asian nations and for the Middle East. This is linked primarily to a lack of health care services that can implement effective immunization programmes. Table 4.1 highlights the role of measles and of tetanus in this; neither of these diseases should figure in statistics of health burdens as both can be avoided through immunization. Yet measles remains a major cause of infant and child morbidity and mortality in rural and urban areas.[37]

Tuberculosis is another vaccine-preventable

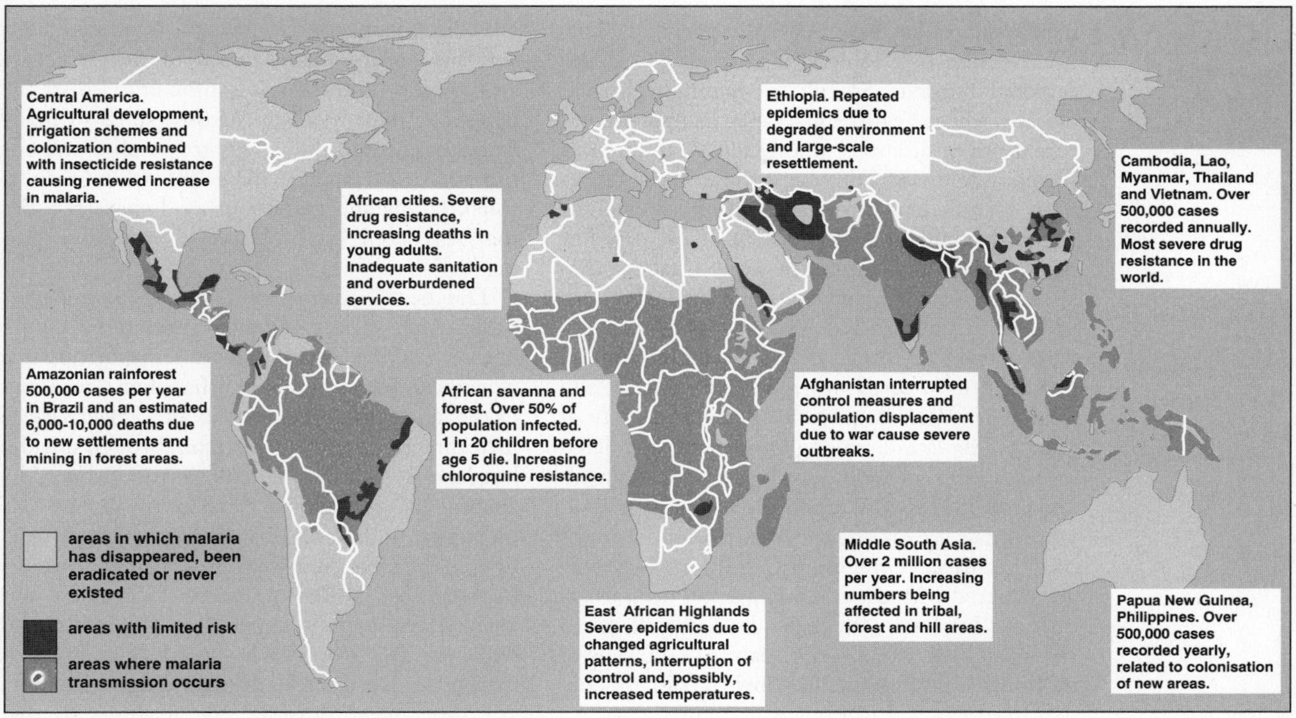
Central America. Agricultural development, irrigation schemes and colonization combined with insecticide resistance causing renewed increase in malaria.
African cities. Severe drug resistance, increasing deaths in young adults. Inadequate sanitation and overburdened services.
Ethiopia. Repeated epidemics due to degraded environment and large-scale resettlement.
Cambodia, Lao, Myanmar, Thailand and Vietnam. Over 500,000 cases recorded annually. Most severe drug resistance in the world.
Amazonian rainforest 500,000 cases per year in Brazil and an estimated 6,000-10,000 deaths due to new settlements and mining in forest areas.
African savanna and forest. Over 50% of population infected. 1 in 20 children before age 5 die. Increasing chloroquine resistance.
Afghanistan interrupted control measures and population displacement due to war cause severe outbreaks.
Middle South Asia. Over 2 million cases per year. Increasing numbers being affected in tribal, forest and hill areas.
East African Highlands Severe epidemics due to changed agricultural patterns, interruption of control and, possibly, increased temperatures.
Papua New Guinea, Philippines. Over 500,000 cases recorded yearly, related to colonisation of new areas.
areas in which malaria has disappeared, been eradicated or never existed
areas with limited risk
areas where malaria transmission occurs

FIGURE 4.3
The distribution of malaria world-wide, highlighting problem areas

disease that has a high health burden, especially in sub-Saharan Africa, but also in India and other Asian nations and in the Middle East (see Figure 4.4). The impact of Tuberculosis is all the greater, since it is the single largest cause of adult mortality worldwide, accounting for some 3 million deaths a year.[38] As noted earlier, the incidence of tuberculosis is also linked to overcrowded conditions.

Acute respiratory infections (that include pneumonia, influenza and bronchitis) show up in Table 4.1 as having one of the largest disease burdens, especially in sub-Saharan Africa, the Middle East, India and the rest of Asia (although the health burden in China is relatively low per person). These, especially pneumonia, are among the main causes of infant and child death and ill health in rural and urban areas in these regions.

The full extent of acute respiratory infections, their health impact and the risk factors associated with them remain poorly understood.[39] However, household surveys in many cities in the South have begun to reveal their health impact. For instance, a survey of a representative cross section of households in Jakarta found that of the 658 households with children under 6 who were interviewed, 27 per cent of the children had suffered from respiratory disease in the two weeks prior to the interview.[40] A comparable survey in Accra (Ghana) found that 12 per cent of children under six had suffered from acute respiratory infection in the two weeks prior to the interview.[41] A survey of households in Porto Alegre (Brazil) found that one-fifth of all infant deaths were caused by pneumonia. Mortality rates from pneumonia were six times higher in illegal settlements than in other areas (and the main cause of infant death there).[42] The quality of the indoor environment has an important influence on the incidence and severity of respiratory infections. Risk factors for respiratory infections probably include over-crowding, inadequate ventilation, dampness and indoor air pollution from coal or biomass combustion for cooking and/or heating.

It would be a mistake to assume that all the most serious health problems associated with poor-quality housing and living conditions and

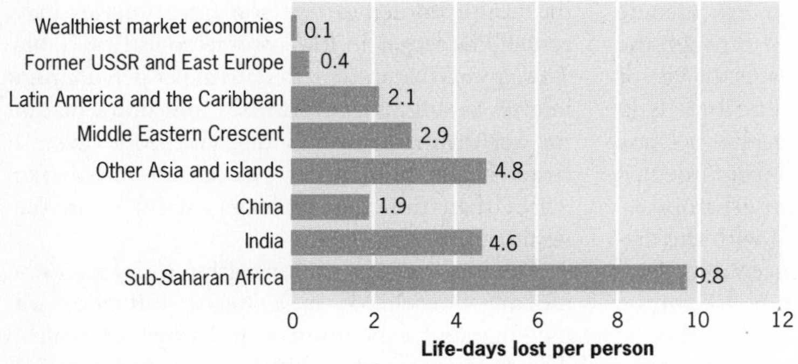
Wealthiest market economies 0.1
Former USSR and East Europe 0.4
Latin America and the Caribbean 2.1
Middle Eastern Crescent 2.9
Other Asia and islands 4.8
China 1.9
India 4.6
Sub-Saharan Africa 9.8
0 2 4 6 8 10 12
Life-days lost per person

FIGURE 4.4
The disease burden per person for new cases of tuberculosis acquired in 1990

NB The figures for the disease burden in Figure 4.4 represent the average current and future disease burden per person in disability-adjusted life-days lost from new cases of Tuberculosis in one year (1990). Thus, they include the disability-adjusted life-days lost in later years that arose from an infectious or parasitic disease caught in 1990 but do not include the life-days lost in 1990 from diseases caught in years prior to, or subsequent to, 1990. For more details, see World Bank, *World Development Report 1993; Investing in Health*, Oxford University Press, 1993.

Source: The original statistics on which this figure is based are drawn from tables B.2 and B.3 in the World Bank, *World Development Report 1993; Investing in Health*, Oxford University Press, 1993. Their conversion in disability-adjusted life-days and this figure is drawn from Satterthwaite, David, Roger Hart, Caren Levy, Diana Mitlin, David Ross, Jac Smit and Carolyn Stephens, *The Environment for Children*, Earthscan Publications and UNICEF, London, 1996.

inadequate or no basic services appear in Table 4.1. Because this Table is measuring global and regional burdens, it fails to highlight certain diseases whose health impact may include premature death or disability among tens of millions of people worldwide but where these never represent a sufficient proportion of the global or regional population to appear in Table 4.1. For instance, infection by guinea-worm (dracunculiasis) as a result of ingesting a small snail (Cyclops) present in unprotected water supplies causes a painful and debilitating disease—and ten million people are infected worldwide in Africa and South and West Asia with 100 million more at risk.[43] This is one among various water-related diseases that include schistosomiasis, filariasis and intestinal worms (especially ascariasis/roundworm) that are among the most common causes of ill health since hundreds of millions of people are infected with them. Only a small proportion of those infected with these diseases will die of them but they cause severe pain to hundreds of millions.[44] Table 4.1 shows how the disease burden from worm infections is particularly serious in China and much of Asia and in Latin America.

One disease strongly associated with housing conditions that shows up in Table 4.1 is Chagas' disease (American trypanosomiasis).[45] This is a debilitating parasitic disease that is widespread only in Latin America; Table 4.1 suggests that it accounts for close to 3 per cent of the region's total disease burden. An estimated 18 million people suffer from it and some 100 million are at risk. There is no effective treatment for this disease, although the risk of infection can be much reduced by preventive action (for instance plastering walls and regular spraying with insecticide) at relatively low cost. Most of those who are infected with Chagas' disease are low-income rural dwellers who become infected through the bites of the blood-sucking insect that is the vector for this disease. The insect rests and breeds in cracks in house walls. Some have also become infected through blood transfusion from infected donors. However, it has become an urban problem too as people who are infected with the disease move to urban areas; for instance the Federal District in Brasilia is considered to be free of the insect vector yet Chagas' disease was found to be responsible for around one death in ten among people of between 25 and 64 years of age.[46]

Many psycho-social disorders are associated with poor-quality housing—for instance depression, suicide, drug and alcohol abuse, and violence including child and spouse mistreatment and abuse, delinquency, rape and teacher assault.[47] Many physical characteristics of the housing and living environment can influence the incidence and severity of psycho-social disorders through stressors such as noise, over-crowding, inappropriate design, poor sanitation and inadequate maintenance of infrastructure and common areas. But it is difficult to isolate the particular impact of any stressor since so many factors influence the extent to which a stressor causes or contributes to ill health—including personal, family and neighbourhood characteristics that help people cope with stress, without becoming ill.[48]

The health impact of common mental disorders such as depression and anxiety have long been overlooked as attempts to set priorities on a world scale have been largely based on data about causes of death.[49] Depression and anxiety cause little direct mortality (other than through suicide) but have a considerable role in morbidity. The analysis of the global burden of disease, by including both mortality and morbidity, highlighted the large contribution of mental disorders to the global burden of disease. Depression and anxiety are mainly a problem in adults and women suffer from these disorders at approximately double the rate of men. These disorders are also concentrated in young adults so that among the population of between 15 and 44 years of age, depressive disorders are the fifth largest contributor to disease burdens in young adult women and the seventh for young adult men.[50]

Other health burdens associated with low incomes, poor quality housing and inadequate health care

Injuries are among the most serious health burdens in most countries. As with non-communicable diseases, injuries may contribute a much smaller proportion to the total disease burden in poorer countries than in richer countries but the scale of the health burden per person from injuries may actually be larger in low-income countries. Table 4.1 suggests that the health burden per person from injuries in sub-Saharan Africa is four times that in the wealthy market economies. War alone causes a larger health burden per person in sub-Saharan Africa than those of all forms of injury in the wealthy market economies.

The location of a shelter within a city for low-income households is a major influence on incomes and expenditures and thus on health. The best locations minimize time and costs of travel—to and from work (for primary and secondary income-earners), to school, health facilities and other services needed by urban households. For instance a shelter located on the outer periphery of a city far from income-earning possibilities means increased costs in time and fares for income-earners and this can restrict expenditures on food or health care. However, one important reason why health improvements among low income groups are often very considerable as their real incomes rise is that they choose to spend more on housing (either improving their existing shelter or moving to a better quality, better located shelter) and on health care.

There are also the health impacts of evictions. Chapter 7 will describe how several million people are forcibly evicted from their homes each year. The health impact of most such evictions is likely to be very considerable, especially on individuals, households and communities, most of whom had very low incomes prior to the evictions. The health impact arises not only because they lose their homes—in which they have often invested a considerable proportion of their income over the years. They usually lose their possessions, as no warning is given, before the bulldozers destroy their settlement. They also lose their friends and neighbours as they scatter to seek other accommodation, and so lose the often complex reciprocal relationships they had with many of them which provided a safety net to protect against the cost of ill health or income decline or losing a job and allowed many tasks to be shared.[51] They often lose one or more sources of livelihood as they are forced to move away from the area where they had jobs or sources of income. Where provision is made for resettling them, this is almost always a distant site where they are expected once again to build their homes but on land with little or no provision for infrastructure and services. They rarely receive any financial support for rebuilding. The land site on which they are relocated is also very often of poor quality.[52] Many evictions are also violent, with injuries and accidental deaths being part of the eviction process.

Gender and age differentials

In most regions, women have a higher disease burden than men for the infectious and parasitic diseases (although not in the sub-Saharan Africa and Latin America and the Caribbean) but a lower disease burden for non-communicable diseases and for injuries. Females lost fewer life-days from premature death than males but about the same as males from disability.[53] In the formerly socialist economies of East Europe, women's disease burden is 30 per cent less than that for men. In China and India, the health burden for women is higher than for men. In China, illegal female infanticide and in the recent past illegal sex-selective abortion are thought to be the main reason.[54]

The low priority given by most countries in the South to reducing maternal mortality would certainly be one of the most prominent examples of bias against women in the allocation of resources. Of the 500,000 women who die each year in childbirth, 99 per cent of them are in the South. Of every 100,000 women who give birth in Africa, from 200 to 1500 may die, compared to fewer than 10 among the world's wealthiest countries.

Table 4.2 illustrates how the health burdens of many diseases fall particularly on certain age groups. For instance more than 80 per cent of the health burden from diarrhoea is the result of infections in children under age 5 while the health burden of worm infections are concentrated among children of between 5 and 14 years of age. More than half the health burden from tuberculosis is borne by the 15–44 age group.[55]

4.3 The Indoor Environment[56]

Poor quality indoor environments bring high levels of environmental risk. Despite the many different forms that poor quality housing takes, from one room housing in rural areas to rooms rented in tenements or illegal settlements, beds rented in boarding houses and houses or shacks built on illegally occupied or subdivided land—almost all share three characteristics which contribute to poor environmental health: inadequate provision for water and sanitation; high levels of indoor air pollution; and overcrowding which increases the transmission of airborne infections and increases the risk of accidents. Each of these are considered below.

A lack of readily available drinking water, of sewage connections (or other systems to dispose of human wastes hygienically) and of basic measures to prevent disease can result in many debilitating and easily prevented diseases being endemic among poorer households—including diarrhoeal diseases, typhoid, many intestinal parasites and food poisoning.[57] Waterborne diseases account for more than 4 million infant and child deaths per year and hold back the physical and mental development of tens of millions more.

TABLE 4.2 The burden of five major diseases by age of incidence and sex, 1990 (millions of life-years lost through disability and premature death)

Disease and sex	Age (years)					
	0–4	5–14	15–44	45–59	60+	Total
Diarrhoea						
Male	42.1	4.6	2.8	0.4	0.2	50.2
Female	40.7	4.8	2.8	0.4	0.3	48.9
Worm infection						
Male	0.2	10.6	1.6	0.5	0.1	13.1
Female	0.1	9.2	0.9	0.5	0.1	10.9
Tuberculosis						
Male	1.2	3.1	13.4	6.2	2.6	26.5
Female	1.3	3.8	10.9	2.8	1.2	20.0
Ischemic heart disease						
Male	0.1	0.1	3.6	8.1	13.1	25.0
Female	**	**	1.2	3.2	13.0	17.5

** Less than 0.05 million

Source: World Bank, *World Development Report 1993; Investing in Health*, Oxford University Press, 1993

Most are caused by diarrhoeal diseases. Virtually all such deaths and much of the illness they cause would be stopped with adequate provision for water, sanitation and health care.[58]

There is also a large range of waterborne or waterwashed diseases that are only a serious cause of ill-health where provision for water and sanitation is inadequate. These include most intestinal worms, guinea worm (*dracunculiasis*) and filariasis, all of which cause severe pain to millions of people. They also include many infectious eye and skin diseases.

High levels of indoor air pollution arising from the use indoors of open fires or relatively inefficient stoves for cooking and/or heating probably represents the single most serious health impact from air pollution worldwide. The extent of exposure depends on many factors including provision for ventilation, how long is spent within the room with the fire or stove and even where in this room time is spent.[59] Box 4.4 gives more details of the health impacts that can arise.

The scale and nature of health problems associated with indoor air pollution are closely linked to household income as most households prefer cleaner, more healthy fuels, if they can afford them. The smoke, smell and dirt of the more polluting fuels are among the reasons why they are less preferred.[60] A study of cooking fuel use by households in Java in a large range of urban areas in 1988 found a general switch from wood (the dirtiest fuel) to kerosene to liquified petroleum gas (the cleanest fuel), the higher the household's income and the larger the urban centre.[61]

There is a considerable range of indoor air pollutants other than those associated with fuel combustion that are causing concern. The documentation about these is concentrated in the North, where there are far fewer problems with indoor air pollution from coal or biomass fuel. Among the most serious are asbestos fibres from asbestos used as insulation, various organic solvents used in building materials, wood preservatives and cleaning agents and radon gas.[62] A recent report on Europe's environment noted that some 2 million people in the region were at risk from ionizing radiation from naturally occurring radon and its decay products; miners and residents of particular areas where radon is emitted naturally from the soil were most at risk.[63] Recent studies from Finland, Norway and Sweden suggest that as many as 10–20 per cent of all lung cancer cases in these countries can be attributed to residential radon exposure.[64]

As with indoor air pollution from open fires and stoves, people's exposure to such indoor air pollutants depends on many factors including ventilation rates, building materials, the time spent indoors and aspects of personal behaviour (for instance smoking or living with others who smoke). This makes it difficult to quantify the health impacts of indoor air pollutants, even if the risks are relatively well known.[65] Pollution from traffic may also have important effects on the quality of indoor air in urban areas.[66]

BOX 4.4

The health impacts of indoor pollution from coal or biomass fuels

The combustion of raw biomass products produces hundreds of chemical compounds including suspended particulate matter, carbon monoxide, oxides of nitrogen and sulphur, hydrocarbons, aldehydes, acenaphthelene, benzene, phenol, cresol, toluene and more complex hydrocarbon compounds including polyaromatic hydrocarbons. Although indoor concentrations vary considerably, it is very common for health guidelines to be exceeded by several orders of magnitude.

The most serious health risks are from burns and smoke inhalation—with the severity of such risks dependent on the length and level of exposure. The principal adverse effects on health are respiratory but in poorly ventilated dwellings, especially when biomass fuels such as charcoal (and coal) are used to heat rooms in which people sleep, carbon monoxide poisoning is a serious hazard.

Exposure to carcinogens in emissions from biomass fuel combustion has been confirmed in studies in which exposed subjects wore personal monitoring equipment and women who spend two to four hours a day at the stove and have high exposure levels of total suspended particulates and Benzo-a-pyrene. This must be presumed to cause some risk of respiratory cancer.

Chronic effects include inflammation of the respiratory tract caused by continued exposure to irritant gases and fumes, which reduces resistance to acute respiratory infections; and infection in turn enhances susceptibility to inflammatory effects of smoke and fumes, establishing a vicious circle of pathological changes. These processes may lead to emphysema and chronic obstructive pulmonary disease which can progress to the stage where impaired lung function reduces the circulation of blood through the lungs, causing right-side heart failure (cor pulmonale). Cor pulmonale is a crippling killing disease, characterized by a prolonged period of distressing breathlessness preceding death.

Those people within the household who take responsibility for tending the fires and doing the cooking (generally women and girls) inhale larger concentrations of pollutants over longer periods of time. Infants and children may be heavily exposed because they remain with their mothers—for instance strapped to their backs, while fires are tended and cooking done. The added exposure to pollutants combined with malnutrition may retard growth, lead to smaller lungs and greater prevalence of chronic bronchitis. When infants and children are exposed to these irritant fumes and develop respiratory tract inflammation, their reduced resistance can lead to repeated episodes of acute respiratory infections, paving the way for early onset of chronic obstructive lung disease.

Another cluster of effects arises when the cook (with infants and small children) crouches close to the fire and sustains heat damage to the conjunctiva and cornea. These become chronically inflamed. Prolonged exposure can lead to keratitis, causing impaired vision and probably also increasing the risk of recurrent infection, cataract and ultimately blindness.

Source: WHO Commission on Health and the Environment, *Our Planet, Our Health*, WHO, Geneva, 1992.

Many health problems affecting poorer groups are associated with overcrowding, including household accidents, acute respiratory infections (of which pneumonia is perhaps the most serious), tuberculosis and other airborne infections. In the predominantly low income residential areas in cities in the South, there is often an average of four or more persons per room and in many instances less than one square metre of floor-space per person. A considerable proportion of the rural population in the South live in small one or two room shelters with an average of 2.5 or more persons per room. Infectious diseases are easily transmitted from one person to another. Their spread is often aided by low resistance among the inhabitants due to malnutrition.

Acute respiratory infections (especially pneumonia) are a major cause of infant and child death and ill health in rural and urban areas. An estimated 4–5 million infants and children die each year of these infections (mostly from pneumonia or influenza) while they are also a major cause of ill health among children and adults.[67] A child who contracts bronchitis or pneumonia in the South is 50 times more likely to die than a child in Europe or North America.[68] For those children who survive, their growth is often set back since a severe case of one of these infections will weaken their body and make them more susceptible to further infection and further malnutrition.[69] A WHO report summarized the problem:

Acute respiratory infections tend to be endemic rather than epidemic, affect younger groups, and are more prevalent in urban than in rural areas. The frequency of contact, the density of the population and the concentration and proximity of infective and susceptible people in an urban population promote the transmission of the infective organisms. Poorer groups . . . are much more at risk because of the greater proportion of younger age groups, limited health and financial resources, and over-crowded households in congested settlements with limited access to vaccines and antibacterial drugs. The constant influx of migrants susceptible to infection and possible carriers of new virulent strains of infective agents, together with the inevitable increase in household numbers fosters the transfer of nasopharyngeal microorganisms.[70]

The incidence of tuberculosis (the single largest source of premature death among adults worldwide) is also linked to overcrowded conditions in both rural and urban areas. The highest incidence tends to be among populations living in the poorest areas, with high levels of overcrowding and high numbers of social contacts.[71] In low-income areas in cities, a combination of overcrowding and poor ventilation often means that TB infection is transmitted to more than half the family members.[72]

A combination of overcrowded conditions and a lack of health-care services that can implement effective immunization programmes help ensure that the diseases spread by airborne infection or contact which are easily prevented by vaccines, such as measles, and pertussis (whooping cough) remain major causes of ill health and infant and child death. Measles is a major cause of infant and child morbidity and mortality in poor urban areas.[73] Rheumatic fever and meningococcal meningitis are also among other diseases transmitted by biological pathogens where overcrowded conditions increase the likelihood of transmission.[74] Both are common causes of death in many countries in the South yet good housing conditions and an adequate health-care system should greatly reduce their incidence. Crowded cramped conditions, inadequate water supplies and inadequate facilities for preparing and storing food also greatly exacerbate the risk of food contamination.[75]

The combination of overcrowding and poor quality housing also greatly increases the risk of accidents within the home. The true extent of accidental injuries is often grossly underestimated, especially in the South to the point where accident prevention and emergency services for rapid treatment receive little or no attention in environmental improvement programmes. An analysis of accidents in children in ten nations in the South found that they were the main cause of death for 5–9 year olds and 10–14 year olds.[76] For every accidental death, there are several hundred accidental injuries.[77]

Worldwide, domestic accidents represent about one third of all accidental deaths[78]—but probably a much higher proportion in countries where housing conditions are particularly poor. Many accidental injuries are linked to poor quality, overcrowded housing. Burns, scalds and accidental fires are more common in overcrowded shelters, especially when four or more persons often live in one room and there is little chance of providing occupants (especially children) with protection from open fires, stoves or kerosene heaters.[79] The risk of accidental fires is further increased in many urban dwellings because they are partially or wholly constructed with flammable materials (wood, cardboard, plastic, canvas, straw). Overcrowded dwellings and limited amounts of indoor space also make it difficult for parents to create a safe yet stimulating home environment for their children—including provisions to keep medicines and dangerous household chemicals (such as bleach) out of children's reach.[80] Here, as in many environmental problems, the level of risk is usually compounded by social factors such as a lack of adult supervision if most adults have to work. The health impact of accidents is also compounded by the lack of a health service that can rapidly provide emergency treatment, followed by longer-term treatment and care.[81]

In considering indoor environmental problems, those associated with the workplace are often forgotten. But environmental hazards arising in the workplace are among the most serious health problems in cities in the South and in many in the North. They are evident in workplaces from large and small factories and commercial institutions down to small 'backstreet' workshops and people working from home. They include dangerous concentrations of toxic chemicals and dust, inadequate lighting and ventilation, and inadequate protection for workers from machinery and noise. One global estimate suggests that there are 32.7 million occupational injuries each year with about 146,000 deaths.[82]

Many industries have long been associated with high levels of risk for their workforce—for instance in factories extracting, processing and milling asbestos, chemical industries, cement, glass and ceramics industries, iron and steel industries, factories making rubber and plastics products, metal and non-ferrous metal industries and textile and leather industries.[83] Some of the most common environment-related occupational diseases are silicosis, byssinosis, lead and mercury poisoning, pesticide poisoning, noise-induced hearing loss and occupational skin diseases.[84]

In most countries, the scale of occupational injuries and diseases is greatly under-reported. For example, in Mexico, official estimates reported an average of 2,000–3,000 cases of work-related illnesses across the country in 1988 but a study in just one large steel mill found 4,000–5,000 cases alone, with more than 80 per cent of the workers exposed to extreme heat, loud noise and toxic dust.[85] It is also rare for sufficient attention to be paid to occupational injuries and diseases in smaller enterprises and in all enterprises within the informal economy. In many countries, enterprises are only classified as a factory or workplace if they exceed a certain size—for instance, having more than 10 or 20 employees. Enterprises too small to be classified or enterprises that are not registered for other reasons are not subject to occupational health provisions or to factory pollution controls—even if a high proportion of a city's labour force work in such enterprises. New approaches need to be developed to promote occupational health and safety in small enterprises and within the informal economy.[86]

4.4 Environmental Hazards in the Neighbourhood

In villages or urban districts where inadequate or no attention is paid to environmental management, there are usually large health risks because of no collection of garbage and a lack of drainage and all-weather roads. These bring direct health risks such as more severe flooding and the health hazards posed by garbage and also more indirect health hazards as in the many disease vectors who breed or feed in garbage or waste water.

Many fatal or serious accidents occur within the roads, paths or open spaces within or around settlements. One of the most common is road accidents—responsible worldwide for some 885,000 deaths each year and many times this number of serious injuries.[87] There are also the physical hazards of the land sites on which housing develops. In most cities in the South, between a quarter and half the population live in illegal or informal settlements.[88] Many develop on dangerous sites. Tens of millions of urban inhabitants in Africa, Asia and Latin America are at risk and in nearly all cities in these regions, there are large clusters of illegal housing on dangerous sites (for instance steep hillsides, floodplains or desert land) or housing built on polluted sites (for instance around solid waste dumps, beside open drains and sewers or in industrial areas with high levels of air pollution). Most cities have large areas of unused and well-located land not subject to such hazards.[89] As Chapter 7 describes, the problem is rarely a shortage of the resource (safe land sites) but the fact that poorer groups have no means of getting access to such sites and governments do not intervene in their favour.

Without adequate provision for the collection of garbage and for draining waste water, a great range of disease vectors will live, breed or feed within or around houses and settlements. The diseases they cause or carry include some of the major causes of ill-health and premature death—especially malaria (*Anopheles* mosquitoes) and diarrhoeal diseases (cockroaches, blowflies and houseflies). There are many other diseases caused or carried by insects, spiders or mites, including bancroftian filariasis (*Culex* mosquitoes), Chagas' disease (triatomine bugs), dengue fever (*Aedes* mosquitoes), hepatitis A (houseflies, cockroaches), leishmaniasis (sandfly), plague (certain fleas), relapsing fever (body lice and soft ticks), scabies (scabies mites), trachoma (face flies), typhus (body lice and fleas), yaws (face flies), and yellow fever (*Aedes* mosquitoes).[90]

Many of these vectors thrive when there is poor drainage and inadequate provision for garbage collection, sanitation and piped water supply. *Anopheles* mosquitoes breed in standing water. The sandflies which transmit leishmaniasis can breed in piles of refuse or in pit latrines while the *Culex quinquefasciatus* mosquitoes that are one of the vectors for bancroftian filariasis can breed in open or cracked septic tanks, flooded pit latrines and drains.[91] Leptospirosis outbreaks have been associated with flooding in Sao Paulo and Rio de Janeiro—the disease passing to humans through water contaminated with the urine of infected rats or certain domestic animals.[92] Many of the diseases passed on by insect vectors have been considered predominantly rural problems but many are now serious problems in urban areas, as the expansion of urban areas can also change the local ecology in ways which favour the emergence or multiplication of particular disease vectors (see Box 4.5).[93]

4.5   The city environment

As the most serious communicable diseases described in the previous sections are tackled—through a combination of improved water supply and provision for sanitation, drainage, the collection of household wastes and health-care service—so other environmental hazards become important as they or the health impacts to which they contribute can be greatly reduced. Some such as exposure to chemical hazards are associated with more industrialized and urbanized economies, although the very rapid growth in the use of agrochemicals in the South has also greatly increased the number of rural people exposed to chemical hazards.[100] Increased urbanization and industrial development is also generally associated with a growth in physical hazards, road acci-

dents and with noise, although these are not only evident in urban areas.

Four of the most serious city-wide environmental problems are air pollution; water pollution; the collection and management of solid wastes (including toxic and hazardous wastes); and noise pollution. Many cities or city-districts are also at risk from natural hazards or hazards whose origin may be natural but where the level of risk and the number of people at risk is much increased by human actions. These will be considered below—although the inadequacies in the provision for the collection and management of solid wastes and water pollution are considered in more detail in Chapter 8.

Ambient air pollution[101]

In many cities, the mix and concentration of air pollutants are already high enough to cause illness in more susceptible individuals and premature death among the elderly, especially those with respiratory problems.[102] Studies in several cities in Europe and the United States have found that disease and death rates increase when air pollution levels increase.[103] A rise in the number of asthma attacks, especially for children, was associated with high levels of nitrogen dioxide while high ozone concentrations were associated with an increase in chronic breathing problems among

---

BOX 4.5
The adaptation of rural disease vectors to urban areas

Some diseases transmitted by insect vectors have long been an urban problem; for instance reports on malaria in Freetown (Sierra Leone) date from 1926,[94] while colonial town-planning regulations in Nigeria sought to protect the colonial populations from malaria by insisting on a building-free zone between European and non-European residential areas.[95] Other diseases remain concentrated in rural areas—especially those such as schistosomiasis that are associated with water reservoirs and irrigation canals and ditches—although even schistosomiasis is widespread in many cities.[96] One reason for this is the number of infected rural inhabitants who move to urban areas. Another is that some disease vectors have adapted to urban environments or the expanding urban areas have produced changes in the local ecology that favour the emergence or multiplication of a particular disease vector.

The expansion of the built-up area, the construction of roads, water reservoirs and drains together with land clearance and deforestation can effect drastic changes to the local ecology. Natural foci for disease

vectors may become entrapped within the suburban extension and new ecological niches for the animal reservoirs may be created. Within urban conurbations, disease vectors may adapt to new habitats and introduce new infections to spread among the urban population. For instance in India, where the vector of lymphatic filariasis is a peridomestic mosquito, there has been a rapid increase in the incidence of the disease and in the vector population associated with the steady increase in the growth of human populations in these endemic areas. Anopheline mosquitoes generally shun polluted water yet *A. stephensi*, the principal vector for urban malaria, is also reported in India and the eastern Mediterranean region to have adapted to survive in the urban environment and other species of anophelines have also adapted to breed in swamps and ditches surrounding urban areas in Nigeria and Turkey. *Aedes aegypti*, the vector of dengue and urban yellow fever proliferates in tropical urban settlements and has been frequently found to breed in polluted water sources such as soak-away pits, septic tanks and other breeding sites which have been found to contain a high amount of organic matter. *Aedes albopictus* was introduced to the Americas from Asia around 1986 and within

five years, it had spread in the United States to 160 counties in 17 states. It was also introduced into Brazil where is reported to be present in four states. This species is a peri-domestic species like *Ae. aegypti* and an excellent vector of dengue and other mosquito-borne viruses.

The diseases spread by the Aedes group of mosquitoes (which include dengue, dengue haemorrhagic fever and yellow fever) are serious health problems in many cities; pots and jars, small tanks, drums and cisterns used for storing water in houses lacking regular piped supplies can provide breeding habitats for these mosquitoes.[97] So too can small pools of clean water within residential areas in, for instance, discarded tin cans and rubber tyres.[98] Chagas' disease, with an estimated 18 million people infected in Latin America, primarily affects poor rural households, as the insect vector rests and breeds in cracks in house walls. But it is increasingly an urban problem too, both through the migration of infected persons to urban areas (there is no effective treatment for the disease) and through the peri-urban informal settlements where the insect vectors are evident.[99]

Source: Based on material drawn from WHO, *Our Planet, Our Health*, the report of the World Commission on Health and Environment, Geneva, 1992.

elderly people and in respiratory tract infections for children.[104] Air pollution is also causing or contributing to widespread ecological damage through, for instance, acid precipitation. This section will review conditions and trends in air pollution in cities, where the health problems are most serious while the impact of air pollution outside cities will be considered in a later section.

Most ambient air pollution in urban areas comes from the combustion of fossil fuels—in industrial processes, for heating and electricity generation, and by motor vehicles.[105] The use of fossil fuels in each of these tends to expand with economic growth; so too does air pollution unless measures are taken to promote efficient fuel use, the use of the least polluting fuels (for instance natural gas rather than coal with a high sulphur content for domestic and industrial use and unleaded petrol for motor vehicles) and the control of pollution at source.[106] In some cities, domestic heating is one of the major sources of air pollution as a considerable proportion of households use firewood or poor quality coal in open fires or inefficient house stoves—although this source of air pollution will tend to diminish with economic growth, just as it did in the North.

Cities have often been associated with air pollution, especially since the industrial revolution, although the burning of coal and biomass fuels in households probably made air pollution a serious problem in many cities prior to this. To what can be termed the 'traditional' pollutants that arise from the burning of coal, heavy oil or biomass were added the pollutants that come primarily from motor vehicle traffic: the photochemical pollutants, lead and carbon monoxide. There are also various toxic and carcinogenic chemicals that are increasingly found in urban air, although in low concentrations. These include selected heavy metals, trace organic chemicals and fibres (e.g. asbestos).[107]

In certain cities, industrial pollution can be so serious that it becomes a significant cause of above average infant and child mortality or reduced life expectancy.[108] This can be seen in statistics for Katowice, the industrial centre of the Upper Silesian Industrial Region. In Katowice Voivodeship, life expectancy is one year lower than the national average.[109] Urban male life expectancy has also fallen over the past 15–20 years. In Katowice city, the 1989 infant mortality rate was 25.5 per 1,000 live births which compares unfavourably with the national average of 16.1. A study undertaken in the sub-regions of the Voivodeship suggested that infant mortality is correlated with dust fall, ambient level of lead, tar, phenols, formaldehyde and benzo(a)pyrene. The Voivodeship also had the highest incidence of premature births, genetic defects and spontaneous miscarriages. Chronic bronchitis is reported in 35

per cent of children living in heavily polluted industrial areas.

Although most cities have some problem with air pollution, there are enormous variations in the scale of air pollution and in the relative importance of the different pollutants. Pollution levels often change dramatically from season to season. In most of the cities in the North, they have also changed over the last 20–30 years, reflecting changes in fuel use and economic structure (especially the much decreased importance of heavy industry) and, in some cases, tighter environmental regulations. For instance, in most cities in Europe and North America, it is no longer the traditional pollutants from the combustion of coal or heavy oil that are the main problem. Motor vehicles have become the major source of air pollution, as the number of motor vehicles in use has risen rapidly (and so too have conditions that exacerbate motor vehicle pollution such as congestion) while heavy industry has declined and major steps have been taken to limit the use of coal or heavy oil or to control the air pollutants associated with their combustion. Thus, cities such as Tokyo, New York and London have relatively low levels of sulphur dioxide and suspended particulates but all have problems with one or more of the pollutants from motor vehicles. Motor vehicle emissions also pose a serious problem for many larger cities in the South.

Sulphur dioxide and suspended particulates. An estimated 1.4 billion urban residents worldwide are exposed to annual averages for suspended particulate matter or sulphur dioxide (or both) that are higher than the minimum recommended WHO standards.[110] Based on exposure to suspended particulate matter alone, rough estimates indicate that if unhealthy levels of particulates were reduced to the average yearly level the World Health Organization considers safe, between 300,000 and 700,000 premature deaths a year would be avoided in the South. This is equivalent to 2–5 per cent of all deaths in those urban areas where levels of particulates are excessive.[111] The problem is not confined to the South. In Europe, as many as 15 per cent of asthma cases and 7 per cent of obstructive airways disease are estimated to be possibly related to prolonged exposure to high concentrations of particulates.[112]

In a study of air pollution in twenty of the world's largest cities (which between them have more than 200 million inhabitants), sulphur dioxide was not a major problem in twelve of them (see Table 4.3) although sulphur dioxide concentrations might exceed WHO guidelines in certain locations in these cities for certain parts of the year. The most serious problems were found in Beijing, Mexico City and Seoul where ambient levels exceeded WHO guidelines by a factor of

TABLE 4.3 Overview of air quality in 20 of the world's largest cities

City	Sulphur Dioxide	Suspended Partic.	Airborne Lead	Carbon Monoxide	Nitrogen Dioxide	Ozone
Bangkok	Low	Serious	Above guideline	Low	Low	Low
Beijing (Peking)	Serious	Serious	Low	(no data)	Low	Above guideline
Bombay	Low	Serious	Low	Low	Low	(no data)
Buenos Aires	(no data)	Above guideline	Low	(no data)	(no data)	(no data)
Cairo	(no data)	Serious	Serious	Above guideline	(no data)	(no data)
Calcutta	Low	Serious	Low	(no data)	Low	(no data)
Delhi	Low	Serious	Low	Low	Low	(no data)
Jakarta	Low	Serious	Above guideline	Above guideline	Low	Above guideline
Karachi	Low	Serious	Serious	(no data)	(no data)	(no data)
Manila	Low	Serious	Above guideline	(no data)	(no data)	(no data)
Mexico City	Serious	Serious	Above guideline	Serious	Above guideline	Serious
Rio de Janeiro	Above guideline	Above guideline	Low	Low	(no data)	(no data)
Sao Paulo	Low	Above guideline	Low	Above guideline	Above guideline	Serious
Seoul	Serious	Serious	Low	Low	Low	Low
Shanghai	Above guideline	Serious	(no data)	(no data)	(no data)	(no data)
Moscow	(no data)	Above guideline	Low	Above guideline	Above guideline	(no data)
London	Low	Low	Low	Above guideline	Low	Low
Los Angeles	Low	Above guideline	Low	Above guideline	Above guideline	Serious
New York	Low	Low	Low	Above guideline	Low	Above guideline
Tokyo	Low	Low	(no data)	Low	Low	Serious

Source: UNEP/WHO (1992), *Urban Air Pollution in Megacities of the World*, Blackwell, Oxford. Note that these are based on a subjective assessment of monitoring data and emissions inventories.

Notes:
Serious: WHO guidelines exceeded by more than a factor of 2.
Above guideline: WHO guidelines exceeded by up to a factor of two (short-term guidelines exceeded on a regular basis at certain locations).
Low: WHO guidelines normally met (short-term guidelines may be exceeded occasionally).
(no data): No data available or insufficient data for assessment.

nearly three for annual average concentrations. These three cities also had serious problems with suspended particulate matter with long term averages and peak concentrations many times that of WHO guidelines. Nine other cities also had comparable problems with suspended particulates, although for several of these and for Mexico City and Beijing, wind-blown dust was a major influence.

In Table 4.3, all the cities in the North had low levels of sulphur dioxide and significant reductions in sulphur dioxide levels in the air have been achieved in Northern and Western European cities and, to a lesser extent in Southern European cities.[113] But in many cities, this is a relatively recent achievement. Annual mean concentrations of sulphur dioxide in London up to the mid-1960s were still ten to twenty times those of today and many times what the World Health Organization now sets as its long-term guidelines.[114] New York and Tokyo also had much higher levels of sulphur dioxide in the 1960s and early 1970s.[115] However, in many cities in the North, WHO guidelines for air quality are exceeded for short periods during the year for sulphur dioxide and/or for total suspended particulates. In Eastern and Central Europe, air quality in cities has generally improved but still remains unacceptably high and several Central, Eastern and Southern European cities regularly exceed WHO guidelines for sulphur dioxide concentrations many times over. In general, concentrations of suspended particulate matter have also declined in Europe, although with considerable variation between cities.

Lead. Lead remains a particular concern, especially for children, since relatively low concentrations of lead in the blood may have a damaging and permanent effect on their mental development.[116] Children's exposure to lead comes not only from the exhausts of petrol-engined motor vehicles where lead additives are still used but also from lead water pipes (especially where water supplies are acidic), lead in paint, and lead in some industrial emissions. Airborne lead can also contaminate the soil and dust near busy roads[117]—affecting crops grown in gardens or other open spaces. A study in Bangkok which sought to rank urban environmental problems on the basis of their health risks suggested that lead should be ranked with airborne particulates and biological pathogens (primarily acute diarrhoea, dengue fever, dysentery and intestinal worms) as the highest risk environmental problems.[118]

Among the twenty major cities, airborne lead concentrations were well above the WHO guidelines in Cairo and Karachi; these cities also had among the highest concentrations of lead in petrol. Airborne lead was also above WHO guideline figures in Bangkok, Jakarta, Manila and Mexico City. In the other cities for which data was available, ambient levels of airborne lead were relatively low—in some instances because of the increasing use of lead-free petrol, in others because of relatively low traffic density. In general, in wealthy countries, airborne lead should not be a problem if lead levels in petrol are minimized and the use of lead-free petrol promoted—while industrial emissions are kept down. Countries with expanding economies and increasing numbers of motor vehicles can also take steps to keep down lead levels in petrol and to ensure that most or all new vehicles can use lead-free petrol. The problem is greatest in cities where there is already a high concentration of motor vehicles that cannot use lead-free petrol and where there is a slow turnover in replacing these with vehicles that can. However, high ambient levels of lead can also arise from industries—and this remains a problem in several Central and Eastern European cities where in certain locations, mainly around lead-emitting industries, the exposure to lead is still high, possibly resulting in impaired mental development of children and in behavioural problems. It is estimated that at least 400,000 children in eastern parts of Europe may be affected.[119]

Ozone. Ozone is formed by the reactions in the air between nitrogen dioxide, hydrocarbons and sunlight and it is present in photochemical smog along with other hazardous chemicals. The cities with the highest ozone concentrations tend to be the ones with the highest concentration of motor vehicles and a high degree of sunshine; among the twenty major cities, ozone pollution represented the most serious problems in Mexico City, Sao Paulo, Los Angeles and Tokyo. In Los Angeles, in 1988, national air quality standards for ozone were exceeded on half the days in the year; for Mexico City, they were exceeded on 70 per cent of days.[120] Ground-level ozone has recently attracted considerable attention because of the health problems with which it is associated and since it is a problem in some of the world's largest and wealthiest cities. However, in most urban centres around the world, it will not figure as among the most serious problems since they lack a concentration of motor vehicles and other sources of the chemicals from which ozone is formed that is in any way comparable to, say, Los Angeles.

Carbon Monoxide. Carbon monoxide is formed by the incomplete combustion of fossil fuels. The main danger in cities is high concentrations in particular areas, from motor vehicle emissions—for instance on or near major roads. Among the twenty cities, Mexico City had the most serious problems of carbon monoxide with London, Los Angeles and several other cities having less severe problems but with air quality standards being exceeded quite frequently.[121] High concentrations of carbon monoxide have also been recorded along busy roads or in central areas in many other cities[122] although too few cities monitor carbon monoxide levels to know how serious a problem this is.

Water pollution

Many cities in the North and virtually all cities in the South cause serious water pollution as local water bodies are used as a dumping ground for untreated or only partially treated sewage and storm and urban runoff and for industrial effluents. Most rivers in cities in the South are literally large open sewers.

The problems of controlling such pollution are much increased where much of the urban area has no drains and has no service to collect garbage—as in most urban centres of the South. In such instances, most of the liquid wastes from households and businesses (and often from industries) and a considerable proportion of the solid wastes end up washed into nearby streams, rivers or lakes, adding greatly to water pollution. Many cities face additional problems because of a shortage of freshwater which then adds greatly to the problem of disposing of liquid wastes, especially industrial effluents and sewage.

Solid wastes

An earlier section described the health problems that usually arise from a lack of a regular service to collect household wastes—while Chapter 8 describes in detail the inadequate provision for the collection and disposal of solid wastes in many cities in the South. To these problems must be added those connected to toxic or hazardous wastes—the industrial and institutional wastes that are categorized as 'hazardous' or 'toxic' because of the special care needed when handling, storing, transporting and disposing of them, to ensure they are isolated from contact with humans and the natural environment. Reports of health and environmental problems arising from the careless disposal of such wastes are increasingly frequent.[123]

There are many different kinds of hazardous wastes. Some are highly inflammable—as in many solvents used in the chemical industry. Some are highly reactive—and can explode or generate toxic gases when coming into contact with water or some other chemical. Some have disease-causing agents; sewage sludge or hospital wastes often contain bacteria, viruses and cysts from parasites. Some wastes are lethal poisons—for instance cyanide and arsenic and many heavy-metal compounds; many are carcinogenic (i.e. cancer inducing). Only in the last 20 years has the scale of the problem of hazardous wastes and the potential risk to people's health been recognized. Many countries in the North face a large and expensive backlog of clearing up toxic or otherwise hazardous wastes that were dumped on land sites with inadequate provision for their safe storage. The very high cost of safely storing or treating these was the main reason why many attempts were made to export such wastes to the South.

In many countries worldwide, especially in the South, a large proportion of the toxic or otherwise hazardous wastes are either disposed of as liquid wastes which run untreated into sewers or drains or direct into rivers, streams or other nearby water bodies, or are placed on land sites with few safeguards to protect those living nearby or nearby water sources from contamination.[124] Many nations still lack effective government systems to control the disposal of hazardous wastes. Many do not even have regulations dealing specifically with such wastes (or even the legal definition of toxic wastes), let alone the system to implement them.

Noise

Noise is a nuisance to increasingly large sections of the world's population. Within the wider urban environment, there are usually four principal sources of noise—aircraft, industrial operations, construction activities and highway traffic.[125] The proportion of a city's population adversely affected by noise depends on what level is considered acceptable. If a 70 dB(A) threshold is chosen that is well above the acceptable level of noise, 47 per cent of the urban population of Sofia is exposed to more than 70 dB(A) as are 25 per cent in Budapest, 20 per cent in St Petersburg and 19 per cent in Crakow; only 2 per cent of the population of Amsterdam and 4 per cent of Copenhagen's population are exposed to comparable noise levels.[126]

Current noise levels are probably posing a serious nuisance to hundreds of millions of people and a serious health threat to tens of millions, although the scale and nature of its precise health impacts are not known. Adverse effects include sleep disturbance (especially during night hours), poorer work performance and increased anxiety. High noise levels and repeated exposure can lead to hearing loss;[127] high noise levels are also known to be one of the critical stress factors which influence mental disorders and social pathologies.[128] The most intense, continuous and frequent exposure to high noise levels is generally within particular jobs in particular industries.

Those living in particular locations in cities experience above average noise levels. Large areas of many cities have high levels of noise from aircraft landing and taking off in nearby airports; for instance, in Latin America, many major airports are in the middle of densely populated areas (the international airport of Mexico City and airports in Lima, Bogota, Quito, Guayaquil, Buenos Aires, Port-au-Prince and Santiago de Chile).[129] Noise from major roads or highways is a major problem; in Shanghai, noise levels were reported to reach an average of 75 decibels at rush hour and 90 decibels in certain locations.[130] In Bangkok, noise from trucks, buses, motor-cycles and motorboats often mean noise levels greater than 70 decibels in many locations.[131] Perhaps not surprisingly, it tends to be low-income groups whose residential areas have the highest noise levels, especially those living in illegal or informal settlements that develop by major roadways or in and around major airports because high noise levels discourage their development for other uses.

Citizen pressures for governments to control noise probably increases as the more basic environmental problems are addressed. For instance, public opinion polls within the last ten years in the former West Germany found that between 22 and 33 per cent of the population of cities with 100,000 or more inhabitants were strongly/severely annoyed by street noise; in smaller urban centres, the proportion of people strongly/severely annoyed was considerably less.[132]

Natural and human-induced hazards[133]

Many cities are located on sites that are at risk from natural hazards. Others developed on sites that were safe but as their population expanded, so did the settlement of nearby sites that are on floodplains or slopes subject to landslides. The high concentration of population in major cities can also mean very large losses of life and property in the event of a disaster. For instance, the earthquakes that hit Mexico City in September 1985 and their aftershocks are estimated to have killed at least 10,000 people, injured 50,000 and made 250,000 homeless.[134] The October 1986 earthquake in San Salvador caused 2,000 deaths and 10,000 injuries.[135] But what is notable in both these earthquakes is the extent to which the injuries and losses of life were concentrated among the low income groups who either lived in the most dangerous areas (for instance on slopes subject to landslides) or in housing structures least able to stand the shocks.[136]

In most cities in the South, each year, there are less dramatic natural disasters. Earthquakes, floods, landslides or other forms of natural disaster do not kill or injure as many people but they still damage or destroy the homes of hundreds or even thousands of people. They also get less attention since they almost always fall most heavily on low-income groups. For instance, in Caracas, each year there are dozens of landslides, most of them affecting only low-income groups.[137]

There are also the large-scale industrial accidents such as the release of methyl iso-cyanate in Bhopal (India) that caused the death of over 3,000 with perhaps 100,000 or more seriously injured (and 200,000 people evacuated)[138] or the explosion in Islamabad (Pakistan) in 1988 (over 100 dead, some 3,000 injured)[139] or the 210 people killed, 1,500 injured and the vast damage to property in Guadalajara (Mexico) in 1992 as a result of explosions of gas which had accumulated in the sewers.[140] Among the accidents involving nuclear installations and facilities, the fire at the Chernobyl nuclear power plant in the Russian Federation is much the most serious to date; the full health impact of this accidental release of radioactive material is not known although it caused 31 immediate deaths, harmed over 1,000 people and necessitated the evacuation of 115,000 people from a 30 km zone around the power-plant where the worse contamination was measured.[141]

4.6 Cities' Regional Impact

Introduction

The growth and expansion of a city has various environmental impacts on the region within which it is located. Cities transform natural landscapes not only within the built-up area but also for considerable distances around them because of the demand they concentrate for the products of fertile land, watersheds and forests. There are also the massive changes wrought in the local ecology as a result of the mining or extraction of bulky, low-value materials that go into building materials, roads, foundations and other parts of the built environment, and the waste materials dumped as a result of excavations.[142]

The scale of this environmental impact rises, as the demand for resources grows from both industries and consumers and as levels of waste also grow. Liquid, gaseous and solid wastes generated by city-based enterprises and consumers often have significant environmental impacts on the region surrounding the city, even when these wastes are 'biodegradable'.

Regionally there are four impacts of particular concern:[143]

- *Unplanned and uncontrolled city expansion.* In the absence of any plan or development control, cities generally expand haphazardly—defined by where different residential areas and productive activities locate, legally and illegally. The result is what might be termed a 'patchwork' of different developments, including many high density residential settlements interspersed with vacant land (often held for speculative purposes). In cities where a significant proportion of the population can only find accommodation in illegal or informal settlements, city expansion will be much influenced by where illegal settlements develop. This whole process has serious social and environmental impacts. These include the segregation of the poor in the worst located and most dangerous areas and the greatly increased costs of providing basic infrastructure (such as roads and pavements, water mains and sewage pipes), public transport and social services.[144] Illegal or informal

settlements will also often grow on land sites subject to flooding or at risk from landslides or other natural hazards, especially where these offer the best located sites on which low income settlers can avoid eviction.

- *Disposal of liquid wastes.* Rivers, lakes or estuaries close to cities are also often polluted; many are also highly contaminated with heavy metals. River pollution from city-based industries and untreated sewage can lead to serious health problems in settlements downstream. Rivers that are heavily contaminated as they pass through cities may become unusable for agriculture downstream, or particular contaminants in the water may damage crops or pose risks to human health.

The possibilities for improvement vary greatly. In many of the largest cities in Europe and North America that are located on rivers or by lakes, great improvements have been achieved in reducing water pollution—mostly through stricter controls on industrial emissions and more sophisticated and comprehensive treatment of sewage and water run off collected in drains. Rather less success has been achieved in reducing polluting discharges to the sea. In most cities in the South, the problems are not so easily addressed as they have much more serious 'nonpoint' sources of water pollution than cities in the North because of the lack of sewers and drains and the inadequate services to collect solid wastes. A lack of solid waste collection adds to water pollution problems since many of the uncollected wastes are washed into streams, rivers or lakes, increasing the biochemical oxygen demand.

Fisheries are often damaged or destroyed by liquid effluents from city-based industries. Thousands of people may lose their livelihood as a result, as some of the largest cities are close to some of the world's most productive fishing grounds. Among the places where major declines in fish catches have been documented are many rivers and estuaries in India, China and Malaysia, Lake Maryut in Alexandria, the Gulf of Paria between Venezuela and Trinidad, Manila Bay, Rio de Janeiro's Guanabara Bay, the Bay of Dakar and the Indus delta near Karachi.[145] In cities on or close to coasts, untreated sewage and industrial effluents often flow into the sea with little or no provision for piping them far enough out to sea to protect the beaches and inshore waters. Most coastal cities have serious problems with dirty, contaminated beaches and the water there is a major health risk to bathers. Oil pollution often adds to existing problems of sewage and industrial effluents.

- *Solid waste disposal.* It is still common for most of the solid wastes that are collected within urban centres to be dumped on some site outside the city with no preparation of the site to minimize the threat of seepage and leaching contaminating local water resources and with no provision to cover the wastes to reduce the breeding of disease vectors and uncontrolled burning (as in sanitary landfill). Dump sites are often ecologically valuable wetlands. The inadequacies in provision for handling hazardous wastes was noted earlier; it is also common for hazardous wastes which require special handling, storage and treatment to ensure safe disposal to be dumped on the same land sites as conventional solid wastes, with few (if any) safeguards to protect those living nearby or nearby water sources from contamination.

- *Acid precipitation.* Sulphur and nitrogen oxides discharged by power stations burning high sulphur coal or oil, and from automobile exhausts can turn rain into acid rain which falls to earth a considerable distance from the emission source. The result can be declining or disappearing fish populations and damage to soils and vegetation. Toxic metals may also be leached from the soil into water used for animal or human consumption or copper, lead, cadmium or copper mobilized by acidic drinking water supplies from piped water systems. Acid precipitation is causing concern in the areas surrounding many cities in the North and South including the areas around the Rhine-Ruhr, many major industrial centres in Eastern and Central Europe, many cities in China, Petaling Jaya (Malaysia), several Indian cities and Cubatao, Brazil.[146]

The air pollutants that cause the most damage to forests, soils and agriculture are sulphur dioxide, oxides of nitrogen and ozone (and other photochemical oxidants) and, in certain instances, fluorides.[147] Sulphur dioxide and the oxides of nitrogen resulting from fossil fuel combustion in cities can be deposited directly from the air onto farmers' fields (dry deposition) or from rain, clouds/fog or snow acidified by these chemicals. Both can damage plants at high concentrations (causing acute damage, especially to certain species of plants that are particularly sensitive to exposure) although reaching the concentrations necessary to achieve this are rare, except in the immediate vicinity of intense sources of emission (for instance metal smelters with no pollution controls and lacking high chimneys). At lower concentrations, both sulphur dioxide and the oxides of nitrogen are associated with reductions in yields and growth for many crops, although there are many other factors which can influence

this.[148] Soils are also at risk since, in many tropical and subtropical countries, the soils are already acidic and are unable to buffer any further increases in acidity.

Cities' ecological footprints

A city's environmental impact on its region or on eco-systems beyond this region is principally the result of the demand it concentrates for renewable resources drawn from forests, rangelands, farmlands, watersheds or aquatic ecosystems from outside its boundaries. The concept developed by William Rees of cities' 'ecological footprints'[149] illustrates this phenomenon—see Box 4.6.

Wealthy and powerful cities have always had the capacity to draw resources from far beyond their immediate regions. For instance, imperial Rome drew timber, grain, ivory, stone and marble from North Africa.[150] But the scale of this capacity to draw on the productivity of distant eco-systems has been greatly increased in the last few decades as incomes have risen and transport costs declined. City-based consumers and industries in the wealthy nations have increasingly appropriated the carrying-capacity of rural regions in other nations. This separates the environmental impact of the demand the city concentrates for natural resources from the city itself—to the point where city inhabitants and businesses have no idea of the environmental impact for which they are responsible. One of the advantages of having this environmental impact in a city's own surrounds was the visible evidence of environmental damage that could spur actions to reduce it.

Certain natural resources are essential to the existence of any city—fresh water, food and fuel supplies. Many of the economic activities on which a city's prosperity depends require regular supplies of renewable resources; without a continuing supply of fresh water, agricultural goods and forest products, many cities would rapidly decline in size and have reduced employment opportunities for their residents. Many other formal and informal economic activities, although not directly linked to resource exploitation, depend on such exploitation to generate the income to support their own activities. In the past, the size and economic base of any city was constrained by the size and quality of the resource endowments of its surrounding region. The cost of transporting food, raw materials and fresh water always limited the extent to which a city could survive by drawing resources from outside its region. The high costs of transporting city-generated wastes away from the surrounding region promoted local solutions, and there was a need to ensure that such wastes did not damage the soils and water on which local agricultural production (and often fishing) depended. If local

BOX 4.6
The ecological footprint of cities

All cities draw on natural resources produced on land outside their built-up areas (e.g. agricultural crops, wood products, fuel) and the total area of land required to sustain a city (which can be termed its ecological footprint) is typically at least ten times or more greater than that contained within the city boundaries or the associated built-up area. In effect, through trade and natural flows of ecological goods and services, all cities appropriate the carrying-capacity of other areas. All cities draw on the material resources and productivity of a vast and scattered hinterland.

Ecologists define 'carrying-capacity' as the population of a given species that can be supported indefinitely in a given habitat without permanently damaging the ecosystem upon which it is dependent. For human beings, carrying-capacity can be interpreted as the maximum rate of resource consumption and waste discharge that can be sustained indefinitely in a given region without progressively impairing the functional integrity and productivity of relevant ecosystems.

Preliminary data for industrial cities suggest that per capita primary consumption of food, wood products, fuel, waste-processing

capacity, etc., co-opts on a continuous basis several hectares of productive ecosystem, the exact amount depending on individual material standards of living. This average per capita index can be used to estimate the land area functionally required to support any given population. The resultant aggregate area can be called the relevant community's total 'ecological footprint' on the Earth.

Regional ecological deficits do not necessarily pose a problem if import-dependent regions are drawing on true ecological surpluses in the exporting regions. A group of trading regions remains within net carrying-capacity as long as total consumption does not exceed aggregate sustainable production. The problem is that prevailing economic logic and trade agreements ignore carrying-capacity and sustainability considerations. In these circumstances, the terms of trade may actually accelerate the depletion of essential natural capital thereby undermining global carrying-capacity.

Because the products of nature can so readily be imported, the population of any given region can exceed its local carrying-capacity unknowingly and with apparent impunity. In the absence of negative feedback from the land on their economy or

life-styles, there is no direct incentive for such populations to maintain adequate local stocks of productive natural capital. For example, the ability to import food makes people less averse to the risks associated with urban growth spreading over locally limited agricultural land. Even without accelerated capital depletion, trade enables a region's population and material consumption to rise beyond levels to which they might otherwise be restricted by some locally limiting factor. Ironically then, the free exchange of ecological goods and services without constraints on population or consumption, ensures the absorption of global surpluses (the safety net) and encourages all regions to exceed local carrying-capacity. The net effect is increased long-range risk to all.

This situation applies not only to commercial trade but also to the unmonitored flows of goods and services provided by nature. For example, Northern urbanites, wherever they are, are now dependent on the carbon sink, global heat transfer, and climate stabilization functions of tropical forests. There are many variations on this theme, touching on everything from drift-net fishing to ozone depletion, each involving open access to, or shared dependency on, some form of threatened natural capital.

Source: Rees, William E., 'Ecological footprints and appropriated carrying capacity: what urban economics leaves out', *Environment and Urbanization* vol. 4, no. 2, October 1992, 121–30.

ecosystems were degraded, the prosperity of the city suffered—or in extreme cases, its viability as a city was threatened. A city's ecological footprint remained relatively local.

Motorized transport systems introduced the possibility of disassociating the scale of renewable resource-use in cities from the productivity of its region. Prosperous cities in the North now draw from the entire planet as their 'ecological hinterland' for food and raw materials. If consumers in (say) London or New York are drawing their fruit, vegetables, cereals, meat and fish from an enormous variety of countries, how can a link be established between this consumption and its ecological consequences?

Fresh water can also be drawn from distant watersheds and even pumped hundreds of metres up hills, as long as little consideration is given to the high energy costs that this entails (usually coming from thermal power stations that also mean high levels of greenhouse gas emissions). Such technology and its high energy requirements obscure the link between a city's renewable resource use and the impact of this use on the ecosystem where the resource is produced. Prosperous cities can also transport their wastes and dispose of them beyond their own region—in extreme cases, even shipping them abroad. Or they can 'export' their air pollution to surrounding regions through acid precipitation and urban pollution plumes with sufficiently

high concentrations of ozone to damage vegetation in large areas downwind of the city. Perhaps only when the cost of oil-based transport comes to reflect its true ecological cost in terms both of a depleting non-renewable resource and its contribution to greenhouse gas emissions will a stronger connection be re-established between resource use within cities and the productive capacity of the regions in which they are located.

Fresh water

One example of a scarce 'renewable resource' is fresh water. Many cities around the world are facing serious shortages of fresh water, and this is even the case in cities where half the population are not adequately served with safe, sufficient supplies. Many cities have outgrown the capacity of their locality to provide adequate, sustainable water supplies. For instance, in Dakar (Senegal), water supplies have to be drawn from ever more distant sources. This is both because local groundwater supplies are fully used (and polluted) and local aquifers over-pumped, resulting in saltwater intrusion; a substantial proportion of the city's water has to be brought in from the Lac de Guiers, 200 kilometres away (see Box 4.7).[151] Mexico City has to supplement its ground water supplies by bringing water from ever more distant river systems and pumping this water up several hundred metres to reach the Valley of Mexico where the city is located; the energy needed to pump this water represents a significant part of Mexico City's total energy consumption. Over-exploitation of underground water has also made the city sink—in some areas by up to 9 metres—with serious subsidence damage for many buildings and sewage and drainage pipes.[152] Ensuring sufficient water supplies for Los Angeles has meant that the water authorities have had to tap ever more distant watersheds and with considerable ecological damages caused to these watersheds by the freshwater supplies diverted to the metropolitan population. In Europe, the need to find clean water sources has led to the extraction of deep ground-water around cities; in Germany, this has caused irreversible changes of heathland around cities and in the Netherlands, to drying out of nature conservation areas.[153]

Hundreds of urban centres in relatively arid areas have also grown beyond the point where adequate water supplies can be drawn from local or even regional sources. Examples include many of the coastal cities in Peru (including Lima), La Rioja and Catamarca in Argentina and various cities in Northern Mexico. Many urban centres in Africa's dryland areas face particularly serious problems because of a combination of rapid growth in demand for water and unusually low rainfall in recent years, with the consequent dwindling of local freshwater resources. Many other cities face problems in financing the expansion of supplies to keep up with demand. Bangkok and Jakarta are among the many major coastal cities with serious subsidence problems as a result of drawing too much water from underground aquifers; they also face problems from saline intrusion into such groundwaters. In Jakarta, many shops, houses and offices can no longer drink the water from the wells they use because of saline intrusion.[154]

Rural–urban linkages

For most urban centres worldwide, an examination of their resource use reveals a scale and complexity of linkages with rural producers and ecosystems within their own region or nation which implies that 'sustainable urban development' and 'sustainable rural development' cannot be separated. The rural–urban linkages can be positive in both developmental and environmental terms. For instance, demand for rural produce from city-based enterprises and households can support prosperous farmers and prosperous rural settlements, where environmental capital is not being depleted. Few governments in the South appreciate the extent to which productive, intensive agriculture can support development goals in both rural and urban areas.[155] Increasing agricultural production can support rising prosperity for rural populations and rapid urban development within or close to the main farming areas—the two supporting each other. There are also many examples of organic solid and liquid wastes, that originate from city-based consumers or industries, being returned to soils.

These rural–urban links can also have negative aspects. For instance, agricultural land can be lost

---

BOX 4.7
Meeting Dakar's water needs

In 1961, on the eve of independence, Dakar was a city of approximately 250,000 people. It occupied a peninsular site, open to cooling winds and scoured by ocean currents. Most of the drinking water was drawn straight from the basalt aquifer on which the city was built. By 1988, the population of Dakar had reached 1.5 million.

As the city expanded it overran and polluted the local groundwater supplies, while overpumping of the aquifer resulted in saltwater intrusion. As the basalt aquifer became inadequate, supplies were drawn from sedimentary aquifers 80 kilometres distant. Later, as these were unable to keep up with demand, water was drawn from sedimentary strata further north. As these too were surpassed a pumping station was established in the Lac de Guiers, a shallow reservoir created in a fossil river valley, 200 kilometres from Dakar. By 1978 the Lac de Guiers was providing approximately 20 per cent of Dakar's water supply, although this figure varied greatly according to the amount of water in the lake. In the late 1970s plans were made for the doubling and tripling of the capacity of the water pipes from the Lac de Guiers to Dakar. The money was never found to finance these schemes. A much larger plan is now on the drawing board, to bring water from the southern end of the Lac de Guiers by an open canal, known as the Canal de Cayor. There is virtually no recycling of water; it is widely believed that there would be serious cultural objections to such a proposal.

An important effect of the overall lack of water is that the sewage and waste water canals and drains are inadequately flushed. To reduce the amount of household garbage dumped in the canals, some have been cemented over, hiding a growing problem. Sewage and semi-liquid waste are usually the first to have visible negative impacts on the urban system, resulting in increased coliform counts, beaches closed for swimming and reduced catches from the inshore fishery. In 1986 the Senegalese Department of the Environment put into operation its first (mobile) water quality laboratory. It carried out coliform counts for the beaches around the city and it presented the results in the annual (September) warning regarding storms and dangerous tides, which was published in the national newspaper. The results were appalling; for some samples the coliforms were too numerous to count. In the meantime the combination of household and industrial wastes has polluted the Baie de Hann so badly that algal growths have killed off the inshore fishery. Few local fishermen have the equipment to fish further from the shore. From simply being a nuisance, environmental decline has now begun to undermine the local economy beginning with fishery and tourism.

Source: White, Rodney R., 'The international transfer of urban technology: does the North have anything to offer for the global environmental crisis?', *Environment and Urbanization*, vol. 4, no. 2, 1992, 109–20.

as built-up areas expand without control and land speculation on urban fringes drives out cultivators; this appears more common in most Third World nations. Box 4.8 gives an example of some of the impacts of Rio de Janeiro on the wider region and also outlines the economic cost to the city of not paying attention to the control of environmental degradation.

4.7 Global Impacts

Introduction

This section concentrates on the global impact of settlements on the depletion of non-renewable resources, the emission of greenhouse gases and the emission of gases that are depleting the

stratospheric ozone layer. There are also the international dimensions of the concerns raised in the previous section on cities' regional impacts. Much of the 'ecological footprint' of the largest cities in the North is within the South, as most renewable resources are drawn from there.

In addition, the trade in environmental resources is not one way; the converse is pollution export from the North to the South. Attempts by businesses and municipal authorities in the North to export municipal or other wastes (including hazardous wastes) to the South, or by multinational corporations to move their dirtier industries there, are examples of the transfer of ecological costs from local sinks in the North to local sinks in the South. Certain dirty industries have been transferred from the North to the

---

BOX 4.8
Environmental problems in Rio de Janeiro

By 1990, Rio de Janeiro's population had grown to 9.6 million in a metropolitan area that covered almost 6,500 square kilometres. * Developing on a narrow piece of land between the sea and the mountains, the city developed within one of the world's most beautiful natural sites, beside Guanabara Bay; despite its name, there is no rio or river; the Portuguese navigators who named it had assumed that the entrance of the bay was the mouth of a river. This natural beauty is an important economic asset for residents and for tourists (the city alone has 80 kilometres of recreational beaches that can be enjoyed all year). The main problems include:

- Water pollution is a serious problem from both point and non-point sources. The main point sources are collected but inadequately treated domestic sewage and industrial effluent from chemicals, petrochemicals and petroleum refining, iron and steel production and other metal-refining industries. The main non-point sources are uncollected and untreated domestic wastes, agricultural run-off, storm water run-off and improperly disposed of solid waste. Water contaminated by untreated human excreta has a major role in the transmission of enteric and diarrhoeal diseases.

    The lack of control over water pollution also means widespread coastal pollution, especially around Guanabara and Sepetiba Bays, largely because of uncontrolled disposal of wastes from commercial and industrial activities.

- Increasing income disparities, high

unemployment and high and growing crime rates that have accompanied a growing distinction between the 'official' city and the 'non-official' city, much of it located on the periphery of the urban agglomeration.

- The incapacity of the municipal government to manage the vast quantity of solid and liquid wastes generated within Rio de Janeiro; much of this waste goes uncollected. In 1990, more than a quarter of households were not served with garbage collection. Most sewage is dumped untreated into rivers, bays and nearshore oceanic waters and ends up in Guanabara and Sepetiba bays; the only exception is sewage collected from approximately two million people in the Ipanema area that is disposed of through an outfall located some 3.5 km offshore.

- The rapid and uncontrolled expansion of urban settlements over land on the city's periphery sometimes on unsafe land in areas where local governments lack the capacity to guide the expansion of settlements, protect fragile slopes from settlements and provide basic services and infrastructure. By 1991, close to half of the population lived in peripheral municipalities, compared to 32 per cent in 1960. In 1990, 16 per cent of Rio's households still lacked piped water and 17 per cent lacked adequate sanitation. The annual expenditure per person on sanitation and health care in some of the poorest municipalities was US$8 or less per person 1988–91.

- Region-wide deforestation has led to severe erosion and degradation of water sources. The removal of vegetative cover from slopes combined with the development of lowland areas has led to very poor natural

drainage. Rainwater and earth from eroded soils pour down from the mountains during the summer rains, often causing stream channels to overflow and an inundation of floodplains.

One of the main constraints on effective action is the complex institutional structure, combined with a long-established reluctance of state and federal authorities to fund investments in Rio de Janeiro. Municipal authorities do not have total control over development decisions at local level much less at metropolitan level. Most local governments lack the staff and funds to administer urban and environmental planning. Many responsibilities for environmental control have been transferred to them from the state but without the resources to permit them to do so. Responsibilities for land use and zoning regulations rest with local governments but there are many problems of co-ordination between the different public agencies. Local governments have the authority to regulate commercial and residential use as long as their regulations do not conflict with federal and state laws; zoning at federal government level focusing on protection of forests and ecological reserves while at state level, it is meant to control the location of polluting firms. But overlapping jurisdictions often discourage co-ordination between different bodies and restrict effective action. To compound the problem, all municipalities other than the central Rio de Janeiro municipality have outdated property and other cadaster information, making it difficult to reach efficiency in implementing projects and enforcing law.

---

* This does not fully encompass the urban agglomeration. Different government agencies use different boundaries which can consist of anything between 12 and 17 municipalities. For instance, the population is sometimes set at 11.2 million in 1990 if larger boundaries are set on the metropolitan region that then encompasses 14 municipalities.

Source: Kreimer, Alcira, Thereza Lobo, Braz Menezes, Mohan Munasinghe, Ronald Parker and Martha Preece, 'Rio de Janeiro—in search of sustainability' and other papers in Alcira Kreimer, Thereza Lobo, Braz Menezes, Mohan Munasinghe and Ronald Parker (eds.), *Towards a Sustainable Urban Environment: The Rio de Janeiro Study*, World Bank Discussion Papers no. 195, World Bank, Washington DC, 1993.

South—for instance industries manufacturing asbestos and pesticides.[156] There is also the export of hazardous wastes to countries in the South, with minimal provision for their safe storage, and often to the poorest nations which lack the knowledge and the institutional capacity to manage them. While international action has sought to control this trade, the incentives to export hazardous wastes are considerable, given the high costs of storing or destroying them in the North.

Non-renewable resources

Per capita consumption of non-renewable resources such as metals and fossil fuels in the richest nations and cities of the world has reached unprecedented levels. In 1991, the average commercial energy consumption per capita in Africa was 12 gigajoules; in Canada, the United States, Australia and many of the richest European nations, it was between 15 and 30 times this figure with most of the more wealthy European nations and Australia having between 160 and 220 gigajoules and the United States and Canada having around 320.[157] Among the poorer African and Asian countries, the per capita average was between 1 and 10.

The average per capita consumption of steel within OECD nations is 450 kilograms compared to 43 kilograms in the South.[158] Per capita consumption of aluminium in the North is 20 times that in the South while that of copper is 17 times that in the South.[159] Comparable contrasts exist between per capita consumption in rich and poor nations for most other non-renewable resources.

There are fewer comparisons of city populations' non-renewable resource consumption but those that do exist also reveal an enormous disparity between North and South. By the late 1980s, the average waste generation for each urban citizen in North America was 826 kilograms a year compared to 394 kilograms for Japan and 336 for the European OECD nations; the average for low-income countries is between 150 and 200 kilograms a year and in many cities (or poor city districts) in the South the average can be as low as 50 per person per year.[160] Disparities in the quantities of non-renewable resources thrown away in the garbage (especially metals) are much higher because of the higher proportion of metals discarded in the wastes in cities in the North.

The highest levels of non-renewable resource use and waste generation by consumers tend to be in the wealthiest cities and among the wealthier groups within cities. Levels of resource use are generally much smaller in low-income countries or in small urban centres in poorer regions.[161] The main reason is simply the very

low incomes of most urban dwellers so they have too few capital goods to represent much of a drain on the world's finite non-renewable resource base. Low-income households in most cities in the South generate very little solid waste and much of the metal, glass, paper and other items in their wastes is reused or recycled. Many low-income households make widespread use of recycled or reclaimed materials when constructing their houses and little use of cement and other materials with a high energy input. Most rely on public transport (or walk or bicycle) which ensures low averages for oil consumption per person.

Thus, comparisons of per capita non-renewable resource consumption between nations or between cities are misleading. Worldwide, it is the middle- and upper-income groups which account for most resource use and most generation of household wastes; this only becomes a North–South issue because most of the world's middle- and upper-income people with high consumption lifestyles live in Europe, North America and Japan. High-income households in cities such as Lagos, Sao Paulo and Bangkok may have levels of non-renewable resource use comparable to high-income households in Los Angeles or Houston; it is the fact that there are many fewer of them within the city population which keeps city averages much lower.

But levels of household wealth alone are insufficient to explain the disparities between cities in terms of per capita resource use. For instance they do not explain why gasoline use per capita in cities such as Houston, Detroit and Los Angeles in 1980 was between four and eight times that in most European cities.[162] The study from which these figures were drawn suggested that larger vehicles, greater wealth and cheaper gasoline in the United States explain only between 40 and 50 per cent of the variation; other key factors are urban density and the pattern of land use which in turn are linked to public transport performance and level of traffic restraint.[163] The influence of density on per capita gasoline use can also be seen in the comparisons made between the core, inner suburbs and outer suburbs of Toronto; on average, each person in the outer suburbs had twice the gasoline consumption of each person in the core.[164] The disparities are even larger in New York, those in the outer area averaging five times the gasoline use per person of those in the central city (mainly Manhattan).

The dates when the price of non-renewable resources will begin to rise rapidly, reflecting depletion of their stocks, may have been overstated in the various reports produced during the 1970s, but the finite nature of non-renewable resource stocks is not in doubt. There may be sufficient non-renewable resources to ensure that 9–10 billion people on earth, late into the next century, have their needs met. But it is unlikely that the world's resources and ecosystems could sustain a world population of 9 or 10 billion with a per capita consumption of non-renewable resources similar to that enjoyed by the richest households today or even the average figure for cities such as Houston and Los Angeles.

Global environment

Discussions on the impact of human activities on global life-support systems centre on their contribution to atmospheric warming and to reducing the stratospheric ozone layer. There are also large disparities between countries or cities in the North and South in terms of greenhouse gas emissions and emissions of stratospheric ozone-depleting chemicals per person. Cities such as Canberra, Chicago and Los Angeles have carbon dioxide emissions 6–9 times greater per capita than the world's average and 25 times (or more) that of cities such as Dhaka.[165]

In regard to global warming, there is still much uncertainty about its possible scale in the future and its likely direct and indirect effects. But atmospheric concentrations of the most important greenhouse gases—carbon dioxide, halocarbons and methane—are increasing. There is evidence of an increase in the global average temperature over the last 120 years and many of the warmest years on record have been in the last 15 years. Glaciers in virtually all parts of the world are receding. These are consistent with global warming induced by greenhouse gases released by human activities but there are uncertainties as to the extent to which the increase in global temperature is the result of human activities and the extent (and rate) at which it will continue. For instance non-human induced factors such as volcanic eruptions are also important. The warming trend might be part of a natural variation that may reverse itself. But if global warming arising from human-induced releases of greenhouse gases does continue, it could bring major problems for a large part of the world's settlements. These can be divided into direct and indirect effects.

The main direct effects are higher global mean temperatures, sea level rises, changes in weather patterns (including those of rainfall and other forms of precipitation) and changes in the frequency and severity of extreme weather conditions (storms, sea surges).[166] Sea level rises will obviously be most disruptive to settlements on coastal and estuarine areas and this is where a considerable proportion of the world's population lives. Sea level rises will also bring rising groundwater levels in coastal areas that will threaten existing sewerage and drainage systems and may undermine buildings. Most of the world's largest cities are ports and the high cost of land in the central city and/or around ports has often encouraged major commercial developments on land reclaimed from the sea or the estuary and these will often be particularly vulnerable to sea level rises. So too will the many industries and thermal power stations that are concentrated on coasts because of their need for cooling water or as the sea becomes a convenient dumping ground for their waste.[167] Ports and other settlements on the coast or estuaries are also most at risk from any increase in the severity and frequency of floods and storms induced by global warming. For instance, in the unprotected river deltas of Bangladesh, Egypt and Vietnam, millions of people live within one metre of high tide in unprotected river deltas.[168] The lower reaches of many major rivers that also have high population concentrations present particular difficulties—for instance on the Mississippi (USA) and the Hwang Ho and Yangtze (China).[169] The Maldives, the Marshall coastal areas, archipelagos and island nations in the Pacific and Indian Oceans and the Caribbean are likely to lose their beaches and much of their arable land.[170] Global warming may also increase the incidence and severity of tropical cyclones and expand the areas at risk from them—bringing particular dangers to such places as the coastal areas of Bangladesh that are already subject to devastating cyclones.[171]

Global warming will also mean increased human exposure to exceptional heat waves. The elderly, the very young and those with incapacitating diseases are likely to suffer most.[172] Those living in cities that are already heat islands where temperatures remain significantly above those of the surrounding regions will also be particularly at risk. High relative humidity will considerably amplify heat stress.[173] Increased temperatures in cities can also increase the concentrations of ground-level ozone (whose health effects were discussed earlier), as it increases the reaction rates among the pollutants that form ozone.

Warmer average temperatures permit an expansion in the area in which 'tropical diseases' can occur—for instance global warming is likely to permit an expansion of the area in which mosquitoes that are the vectors for malaria, dengue fever and filariasis can survive and breed.[174] The areas in which the aquatic snail that is the vector for schistosomiasis may expand considerably.

The indirect effects of global warming will probably have as dramatic an impact on settlements as their direct effects. Increasing temperatures and changes in weather patterns will lead to changes in ecosystems that in turn impact on the livelihoods of those that exploit or rely on natural resources for their livelihoods. For instance, changes in the areas most favoured by rainfall and temperature for high value crops and for fresh water will change the pattern of settlements. Forests and fisheries may also be subject to rapid change. Both traditional and modern agricultural practices may be vulnerable to the relatively rapid changes in temperature, rainfall, flooding and storms that global warming can bring. The problems are likely to be most serious in the countries or areas where the inhabitants are already at the limits of their capacity to cope with climatic events—for instance populations in low-lying coastal areas and islands, subsistence farmers, and populations on semi-arid grasslands.[175]

One aspect of global warming is difficult to predict—the capacity and readiness of societies to respond to the changes that warming and its associated effects will bring. Societies have evolved a whole series of mechanisms to reduce risk from natural hazards—from those within traditional societies where house design and settlement layout often includes measures to limit loss of life and property from earthquakes or storms to those that have passed into law and statute books in industrial societies. These can be seen in the building and planning codes and in health and safety regulations, and the institutional measures developed to enforce them. Where these are appropriate to that particular society and its resources, and where they are enforced, they reduce risk and ensure that the built environment can cope with high winds, accidental fires or sudden heavy rainstorms. Their effectiveness can be seen in the great reductions achieved in accidental death and injury. For instance, even as late as the last century, it was common for accidental fires to destroy large areas of cities in the North. This complex set of institutional measures and the built environment that they have influenced will have to change to reflect new hazards or a much-increased scale of existing hazard. There is the vast stock of buildings, roads, public transport systems and basic urban infrastructure that was built without making allowance for the changes that global warming will bring.[176]

4.8 Solving the Most Serious Environmental Problems

This chapter has highlighted how the most serious environmental problems in the world's settlements still remain the biological disease-causing agents (pathogens) in the air, water, soil and food or the vectors that spread diseases.[177] The diseases they cause such as acute respiratory infections, diarrhoeal diseases, tuberculosis and malaria remain among the major causes of death and disease in most settlements in the South.

Most should not figure among the significant causes of death and most should also not be a significant cause of ill health.

Improving human settlements management. Adequate human settlements management becomes the most important way of addressing these environmental problems, both through reducing overcrowding and in ensuring that all households have adequate provision for water, sanitation, garbage collection and health care. Less crowded and better quality housing should also bring fewer household accidents. A prevention-oriented primary health-care system is an essential complement to this, not only because it can rapidly treat diseases but also for its capacity to ensure people are immunized against the many infectious diseases for which immunizations are cheap and effective.

But this chapter also made clear that urgent action is needed to reduce the chemical, physical and psychosocial hazards within homes and wider settlements or cities. These include reducing life- and health-threatening physical hazards from dangerous sites (for instance the cities or settlements within cities that are subject to floods/mudslides/rockfalls). They include provision for traffic management and ensuring adequate provision for play for children and recreation for the entire city population. They include the full range of measures needed to promote healthy and safe working practices in all forms of employment and to penalize employers that contravene them. They also include measures to control air and water pollution. As cities become larger, more industrialized and more wealthy, so too does the need for more comprehensive and effective control of emissions and wastes from industries and motor vehicles and the protection of workers from occupational exposures.

There are also the important regional dimensions. A considerable part of the 'solution' to rising levels of solid, liquid and gaseous wastes is to dispose of such wastes in the wider region. This chapter noted the ecological impacts that this can bring to the surrounding region. City populations and businesses also draw on regional resources and often with damaging environmental consequences—for instance the soils and gravels needed for buildings.

Finally, there are the global dimensions—ensuring that a city's ecological impact on global resources and systems is compatible with limits at a global level in terms of resource use, waste and the emission of stratospheric ozone-depleting chemicals and greenhouse gases. The world's wealthiest cities have, to a considerable degree, transferred the environmental costs that their concentration of production and consumption represents from their region to other regions and to global systems. While there is considerable disagreement as to where ecological limits exist and exactly where the limit is, it is clear that the level of waste and greenhouse gas emissions per capita created by the lifestyles of most middle- and upper-income households in the North (and South) could not be sustained if most of the world's population came to have a comparable level of consumption.

The great variety of different environmental problems evident in cities and the great differences between cities in their range and relative importance make it difficult to establish priorities. But there are certainly misplaced priorities within the growing interest in environmental problems in the South.[178]

Give consideration to settlements of all sizes. There is probably too much attention given to the environmental problems of the largest cities, relative to those in other settlements (both rural and urban) where the majority of the world's population lives. Reliable environmental data should be collected from these areas and resources for environmental protection should be allocated on an equitable basis.

Focus on the brown agenda: In the South, too little attention is given to the most basic of environmental problems—the provision of safe, sufficient supplies of water to households and enterprises and provision for the collection and disposal of faecal matter and other liquid and solid wastes—what the World Bank has dubbed the 'brown agenda' as distinct from the 'green agenda'.[179] Most aid agencies and development banks still give a low priority to water and sanitation—in both rural and urban areas—as Chapter 11 will describe. There is still a tendency for Northern and middle-class perceptions as to what is 'an environmental problem' to bias environmental priorities. Ambient air pollution in cities and the pollution of rivers, lakes and estuaries often receive more attention than the inadequacies in water supply, sanitation and drainage and the reduction of physical and chemical hazards within the home and workplace—although this latter group of problems usually takes a far greater toll on the health of citizens than the former.[180]

Build capacity for capacity. In addition, one of the lessons of the 1970s and 1980s is the limited impact of heavy investment in improved water-supply systems if no institutions exist to maintain and extend them and to fund their costs—and to ensure complementary investments in the collection and disposal of waste water. Many internationally funded water-supply and sanitation projects in the late 1980s and early 1990s were to rehabilitate or repair water and sanitation systems installed by these agencies not too many years earlier.[181] These are critical policy issues to which this Report will return in later Chapters.

Notes and References

1. For instance Bartone, Carl, Janis Bernstein, Josef Leitmann and Jochen Eigen, *Towards Environmental Strategies for Cities; Policy Considerations for Urban Environmental Management in Developing Countries*, UNDP/UNCHS/World Bank Urban Management Program, No. 18, World Bank, Washington DC, 1994; ESCAP, *State of Urbanization in Asia and the Pacific 1993*, Economic and Social Commission for Asia and the Pacific, ST/ESCAP/1300, United Nations, New York, 1993.

2. For instance, the results of the research by the Stockholm Environment Institute working with teams in Accra, Sao Paulo and Jakarta and published in Benneh, George, Jacob Songsore, John S. Nabila, A. T. Amuzu, K. A. Tutu, Yvon Yangyuoro and Gordon McGranahan, *Environmental Problems and the Urban Household in the Greater Accra Metropolitan Area (GAMA) Ghana*, Stockholm Environment Institute, Stockholm, 1993, and McGranahan, Gordon and Jacob Songsore, 'Wealth, health and the urban household; weighing environmental burdens in Accra, Jakarta and Sao Paulo', *Environment*, vol. 36, no. 6, July/Aug. 1994, 4–11 and 40–5; and the results of the research programme of the University of

Hawaii—see Douglass, Mike, 'The political economy of urban poverty and environmental management in Asia: access, empowerment and community-based alternatives', *Environment and Urbanization*, vol. 4, no. 2, Oct. 1992.

3. For instance in India the Centre for Science and Environment, *The State of India's Environment—a Citizen's Report*, Delhi, India, 1983; Centre for Science and Environment, *The State of India's Environment: a Second Citizens' Report*, Delhi, India, 1985; and the fortnightly journal published by CSE: *Down to Earth*.

4. WHO, *Our Planet, Our Health*, Report of the Commission on Health and Environment, Geneva, 1992.

5. World Bank, *Water Resources Management*, World Bank Policy Paper, Washington DC, 1993.

6. Shrivastava, Rahul, 'A plague on this country', *Down to Earth*, 31 Oct. 1994, 5–11.

7. The basis for this statistic and more details about it are given in Section 4.2.

8. Satterthwaite, David, Roger Hart, Caren Levy, Diana Mitlin, David Ross, Jac Smit and Carolyn Stephens, *The Environment for Children*, Earthscan Publications and UNICEF, London, 1996.

9. Foster, Harold D., *Health, Disease and the Environment*, John Wiley and Sons, Chichester, 1992; WHO 1992, *op. cit.*

10. Bairoch, Paul, *Cities and Economic Development: From the Dawn of History to the Present*, Mansell, London, 1988, 231, Wohl, Anthony S., *Endangered Lives: Public Health in Victorian Britain*, Methuen, London, 1983.

11. Undernutrition was also a major factor.

12. Cairncross, Sandy, Jorge E. Hardoy and David Satterthwaite, 'The urban context', in Jorge E. Hardoy, Sandy Cairncross and David Satterthwaite (eds.), *The Poor Die Young: Housing and Health in Third World Cities*, Earthscan Publications, London, 1990. The estimate was subsequently endorsed by WHO 1992, *op. cit.*

13. Water Supply and Sanitation Collaborative Council, *Water Supply and Sanitation Sector Monitoring Report 1993*, WHO and UNICEF, 1993.

14. Girouard, Mark, *Cities and People: A Social and Architectural History*, Yale University Press, New Haven and London, 1985, 268.

15. Pye, Michael, *Maximum City: the Biography of New York*, Picador, 1994.

16. Wohl, Anthony S., *Endangered Lives: Public Health in Victorian Britain*, Methuen, London, 1983, 440 pages;

Waller, P. J., *Town, City and Nation; England 1850–1914*, Oxford University Press, Oxford and New York, 1983.

17. Wohl 1983, *op. cit.*, and Woods, Robert and John Woodward, 'Mortality, poverty and the environment', in R. J. Woods and J. H. Woodward (eds.), *Urban Disease and Mortality in Nineteenth Century England*, Batsford, 1984, 19–36.

18. Rosenberg, Charles E., *The Cholera Years*, University of Chicago Press, Chicago, 1962.

19. Caldwell, John C. and Pat Caldwell, 'Education and literacy as factors in health', in Scott B. Halstead, Julia A. Walsh and Kenneth S. Warren (eds.), *Good Health at Low Cost*, Conference Report, The Rockefeller Foundation, New York, 1985, 181–5.

20. Pryer, Jane, 'The impact of adult ill-health on household income and nutrition in Khulna, Bangladesh', *Environment and Urbanization*, vol. 5, no. 2, Oct. 1993, 35–49.

21. World Bank, *World Development Report 1993; Investing in Health*, Oxford University Press, Oxford, 1993.

22. This table is based on the findings of a report prepared by WHO and the World Bank that sought to measure the global burden of disease for 1990 by combining losses from premature death and the loss of healthy life resulting from disability. See Tables B.2 and B.3 in World Bank, *World Development Report 1993; Investing in Health*, Oxford University Press, 1993.

23. The *World Development Report 1993; Investing in Health* termed these the 'established market economies'.

24. European Environment Agency, *Europe's Environment: the Dobris Assessment*, Copenhagen, 1995.

25. European Environment Agency 1995, *op. cit.*

26. Rossi-Espagnet, A., G. B. Goldstein and I. Tabizadeh, 'Urbanization and health in developing countries; a challenge for health for all', *World Health Statistical Quarterly*, vol. 44, no. 4, 1991, 186–244.

27. McGranahan and Songsore 1993, *op. cit.*

28. Victera, C. G., P. G. Smith, J. P. Vaughan and others, 'Water supply, sanitation and housing in relation to the risk of infant mortality from diarrhoea', *International Journal of Epidemiology*, vol. 17, no. 3, 1988, 651–4 quoted in Williams, Brian T., *The Health Burden of Urbanization*, Background Paper for WHO Expert Committee on Environmental Health in Developing Countries, RUD/WP/90.4, Geneva, 1990.

29. See for instance Songsore and McGranahan 1993, *op. cit.*; Misra, Harikesh, 'Housing and health problems in three squatter settlements in Allahabad, India' in Jorge E. Hardoy and others (eds.), *The Poor Die Young: Housing and Health in Third World Cities*, Earthscan Publications, London, 1990; and Adedoyin, M. and S. Watts, 'Child health and child care in Okele: an indigenous area of the city of Ilorin,

Nigeria', *Social Science and Medicine*, vol. 29, no. 12, 1989, 1333–41.

30. See for instance Songsore and McGranahan 1993, *op. cit.*, and Surjadi, Charles, *Health of the Urban Poor in Indonesia*, Urban Health Problems Study Group paper no. 29, Atma Jaya Research Centre, Jakarta, 1988.

31. World Bank, *World Development Report 1994; Infrastructure for Development*, Oxford University Press, Oxford and New York, 1994.

32. Esrey, Steven A., James B. Potash, Leslie Roberts and Clive Shiff, *Health Benefits from Improvements in Water Supply and Sanitation: Survey and Analysis of the Literature on Selected Diseases*, WASH Technical Report No. 66, US AID, Washington DC, 1990.

33. WHO 1992, *op. cit.*; Prost, A. and A. D. Negrel, 'Water, trachoma and conjunctivitis', *Bulletin of the World Health Organization*, vol. 67, no. 1, 1989, 9–18.

34. Preston, S. and E. van de Walle, 'Urban French mortality in the nineteenth century', *Population Studies*, vol. 32, 1978, 275–97 quoted in Jones, Huw, *Population Geography*, 2nd edn., Paul Chapman Publishing, London, 1990.

35. WHO 1992, *op. cit.*

36. Rossi-Espagnet, Goldstein and Tabizadeh 1991, *op. cit.*

37. Foster, S.O., 'Measles, the ultimate challenge in urban immunization', in *Universal Child Immunization—Reaching the Urban Poor*, Urban Examples 16, UNICEF, New York, 1990.

38. WHO 1992, *op. cit.*

39. Bradley, David, Carolyn Stephens, Sandy Cairncross and Trudy Harpham (1991), *A Review of Environmental Health Impacts in Developing Country Cities*, Urban Management Program Discussion Paper no. 6, The World Bank, UNDP and UNCHS (Habitat), Washington DC.

40. Surjadi, Charles, 'Respiratory diseases of mothers and children and environmental factors among households in Jakarta', *Environment and Urbanization*, vol. 5, no. 2, Oct. 1993, 78–86.

41. Songsore and McGranahan 1993, *op. cit.*

42. Guimaraes, J. J. and A. Fischmann, 'Inequalities in 1980 infant mortality among shantytown residents and non-shantytown residents in the municipality of Porto Alegre, Rio Grande do Sul, Brazil', *Bulletin of the Pan American Health Organization*, vol. 19, 1985, 235–51.

43. Warner, D. B. and L. Laugeri, 'Health for all: the legacy of the water decade', *Water International*, vol. 16, 1991, 135–41; and WHO, *Our Planet, Our Health*, Report of the Commission on Health and Environment, Geneva, 1992.

44. WHO 1992, *op. cit.* and WHO, *Global Estimates for Health Situation Assessments and Projections 1990*, Division of Epidemiological Surveillance and Health Situation and Trend Analysis, World Health Organization,

WHO/HST/90.2, Geneva, 1991.

45. The information about Chagas' disease in this paragraph is drawn from WHO, *Our Planet, Our Health*, Geneva, 1992; Briceno-Leon, Roberto, *La Case Enferma: Sociologia de la Enfermedad de Chagas*, Consorcio de Ediciones Capriles, Venezuela, 1990, and WHO Technical Report Series, no. 811, *Control of Chagas Disease: report of a WHO Expert Committee*, Geneva, 1991.

46. Gomes Pereira, Mauricio, 'Characteristics of urban mortality from Chagas' disease in Brazil's Federal District', *Bulletin of the Pan American Health Organization*, vol. 18, no. 1, 1984.

47. WHO 1992, *op. cit.*

48. Ekblad, Solvig, Chen Changhui, Li Shuran, Huang Yueqin, Li Ge, Li Yongtong, Zhang Weixi, Liu Mian, Xu Liang, Wang Qin, Shan Shuwen, Ran Wei and Zhang Suzhen, *Stressors, Chinese City Dwellings and Quality of Life*, Swedish Council for Building Research, Stockholm, 1991.

49. This and the following paragraph are largely drawn from Blue, Ilona and Trudy Harpham, 'The World Bank World Development Report: Investing in Health, reveals the burden of common mental disorders but ignores its implications', *British Journal of Psychiatry*, Editorial, vol. 165, 1994, 9–12 with the statistics drawn from World Bank 1993, *op. cit.*

50. Blue and Harpham 1994, *op. cit.*

51. Murphy, Denis and Ted Anana, 'Evictions and fear of evictions in the Philippines', *Environment and Urbanization*, vol. 6, no. 1, April 1994; Fernandes, Kenneth, 'Katchi abadis: living on the edge', *Environment and Urbanization*, vol. 6, no. 1, April 1994, 50–8.

52. Fernandes 1993, *op. cit.*; Hunsley Magebhula, Patrick, 'Evictions in the new South Africa: a narrative report from Durban', *Environment and Urbanization*, vol. 6, no. 1, April 1994, 59–62.

53. World Bank 1993, *op. cit.*

54. *Ibid.*

55. *Ibid.*

56. This consideration of environmental problems in settlements through considering their impact on human health at these different scales (indoor home/workplace, neighbourhood, city, city-region and globe) was first suggested in Hardoy, Jorge E. and David Satterthwaite, 'Third World Cities and the Environment of Poverty'—*Geoforum*, vol. 15, no. 3, July 1984, and elaborated in Hardoy, Jorge E., Diana Mitlin and David Satterthwaite, *Environmental Problems in Third World Cities*, Earthscan Publications, London, 1992. This section draws on this latter book .

57. Hardoy, Mitlin and Satterthwaite 1992, *op. cit.*

58. Satterthwaite, Hart, Levy and others 1996, *op. cit.*

59. McGranahan, Gordon, *Environmental Problems and the Urban Household in Third World Countries*, The Stockholm Environment Institute, Stockholm, 1991.

60. McGranahan 1991, *op. cit.*

61. World Bank, *Indonesia Urban Household Energy Strategy Study*, Energy Sector Management Assistance Programme, Report No. 1071/90, Washington DC, 1990, quoted in McGranahan 1991 *op. cit.*

62. WHO 1992, *op. cit.*

63. European Environment Agency 1995, *op. cit.*

64. Pershagen, G. and L. Simonato, 'Epidemiological evidence on indoor air pollution and cancer', in I. Tomatis (ed.), *Indoor and Outdoor Pollution and Cancer*, Springer-Verlag, Berlin, 1993, 119–34.

65. European Environment Agency 1995, *op. cit.*

66. *Ibid.*

67. Surjadi 1993, *op. cit.*; Songsore, Jacob and Gordon McGranahan, 'Environment, wealth and health; towards an analysis of intra-urban differentials within Greater Accra Metropolitan Area, Ghana', *Environment and Urbanization*, vol. 5, no. 2, Oct. 1993, 10–24.

68. Pio, A., 'Acute respiratory infections in children in developing countries: an international point of view', *Pediatric Infectious Disease Journal*, vol. 5, no. 2, 1986, 179–83.

69. UNICEF, *State of the World's Children 1986*, Oxford University Press, 1986.

70. WHO 1992, *op. cit.*

71. *Ibid.*

72. Cauthen, G. M., A. Pio and H. G. ten Dam, *Annual Risk of Tuberculosis Infection*, WHO, Geneva, 1988

73. Foster 1990, *op. cit.*

74. WHO 1992, *op. cit.*, and Schofield, C. J., R. Briceno-Leon, N. Kolstrup, D. J. T. Webb and G. B. White, 'The role of house design in limiting vector-borne disease', in Hardoy, Jorge E. and others (eds.) *The Poor Die Young: Housing and Health in Third World Cities*, Earthscan Publications, London, 1990.

75. McGranahan 1991, *op. cit.*

76. Manciaux, M. and C. J. Romer, 'Accidents in children, adolescents and young adults: a major public health problem', *World Health Statistical Quarterly*, vol. 39, no. 3, 1986, 227–31.

77. *Ibid.*

78. WHO 1991, *op. cit.*

79. Hardoy, Mitlin and Satterthwaite 1992, *op. cit.*

80. Satterthwaite, Hart, Levy and others 1996, *op. cit.*

81. Goldstein, Greg, 'Access to life saving services in urban areas', in Hardoy, Jorge E. and others (eds.), *The Poor Die Young: Housing and Health in Third World Cities*, Earthscan Publications, London, 1990.

82. WHO 1991, *op. cit.* Note that this includes occupational hazards for those working outdoors as well. In rural settlements, environmental hazards are often a significant health risk for farmers, pastoralists or foresters, those making a living from hunting and fishing, as well as those working indoors in related industries such as abattoir workers, tanners and furriers. 'Each group has its own particular occupational hazards but the first and second groups have most of their hazards specifically determined by environmental factors such as climate, close contact with animals and disease vectors and work with a variety of agrochemicals' (WHO 1992, *op. cit.* 77).

83. WHO, *Report of the Panel on Industry*, WHO Commission on Health and Environment, WHO/EHE/92.4 WHO Geneva, 1992.

84. WHO 1991, *op. cit.*

85. Castonguay, Gilles, 'Steeling themselves with knowledge' report on the work of Cristina Laurell, *IDRC Reports* vol. 20, No 1, April 1992, 10–12.

86. Greg Goldstein, WHO, personal communication.

87. WHO, *The World Health Report 1995: Bridging the Gaps*, Geneva, 1995.

88. Hardoy, Jorge E. and David Satterthwaite, *Squatter Citizen: Life in the Urban Third World*, Earthscan Publications, London, 1989.

89. *Ibid.*; Sarin, Mahdu, 'The rich, the poor and the land question', in Shlomo Angel, Raymon W. Archer, Sidhijai Tanphiphat and Emiel A. Wegelin (eds.), *Land for Housing the Poor*, Select Books, Singapore, 1983, 237–53.

90. Schofield, Briceno-Leon, Kolstrup and others 1990, *op. cit.*

91. Cairncross, Sandy and Richard G. Feachem, *Environmental Health Engineering in the Tropics; an Introductory Text* (2nd edn.), John Wiley and Sons, Chichester (UK), 1993.

92. Sapir, D., *Infectious Disease Epidemics and Urbanization: a Critical Review of the Issues*, Paper prepared for the WHO Commission on Health and Environment, Division of Environmental Health, WHO, Geneva, 1990.

93. WHO 1992, *op. cit.*

94. Blacklock, D. B. and A. M. Evans, 'Breeding places of Anopheline mosquitoes in and around Freetown, Sierra Leone', *Annals of Tropical Medicine and Parasitology*, vol. 20, 1926, 59–86, quoted in Rossi-Espagnet, Goldstein and Tabibzadeh 1991, *op. cit.*

95. Aradeon, David, Tade Akin Aina and Joe Umo, 'South-West Nigeria', in Jorge E. Hardoy and David Satterthwaite (eds.), *Small and Intermediate Urban Centres; their Role in Regional and National Development in the Third World*, Hodder and Stoughton (UK) and Westview (USA), 1986, 228–78.

96. Rossi-Espagnet, Goldstein and Tabibzadeh 1991, *op. cit.*

97. *Ibid.*

98. Cairncross and Feachem 1993, *op. cit.*

99. Gomes Pereira, M., 'Characteristics of urban mortality from Chagas' disease in Brazil's Federal District', *Bulletin of the Pan American Health Organization*, vol. 18, no. 1, 1989; Briceno-Leon, Roberto, *La Casa Enferma: Sociologia de la Enfermedad de Chagas*, Consorcio de Ediciones, Capriles C.A. Caracas, 1990.

100. Conway, Gordon R. and Jules N. Pretty, *Unwelcome Harvest*, Earthscan Publications, London, 1991.

101. This section draws to a considerable extent on UNEP and WHO, *Urban Air Pollution in Megacities of the World*, Blackwell, Oxford, 1992.

102. WHO 1992, *op. cit.*

103. See for instance Patel, Tara, 'Killer smog stalks the boulevards', *New Scientist* no. 1947, 15 Oct. 1994, 8.

104. *Ibid.*

105. WHO 1992, *op. cit.*

106. World Bank, *World Development Report 1992; Development and the Environment*, Oxford University Press, 1992.

107. UNEP and WHO 1992, *op. cit.*

108. This paragraph draws its information from Bartone and others 1994, *op. cit.*

109. Hertzmann, Clyde, *Environment and Health in Eastern Europe*, World Bank, 1994.

110. UNEP and WHO, *Assessment of Urban Air Quality*, Global Environment Monitoring Service, United Nations Environment Programme and World Health Organization, 1988.

111. World Bank, *World Development Report 1992*, Oxford University Press, 1992 quoted in Bartone and others 1994, *op. cit.*

112. In cities with the highest dust concentrations, the proportion of cases attributable to pollution reaches 23 per cent of asthma and 11 per cent of obstructive airways disease; see European Environment Agency 1995, *op. cit.*

113. This paragraph about Europe draws its information from European Environment Agency 1995, *op. cit.*

114. Annual mean concentrations of sulphur dioxide in London of between 300 and 400 µg per cubic metre were typical up to the mid 1960s and are now around 20–30, UNEP and WHO 1992, *op. cit.*

115. UNEP and WHO 1992, *op. cit.*

116. Needleman, Herbert L., Alan Schell, David Bellinger, Alan Leviton and Elizabeth N. Allred, 'The long-term effects of exposure to low doses on lead in childhood: an eleven year follow up report', *The New England Journal of Medicine*, vol. 322. no. 2, Jan. 1991, 83–8.

117. WHO 1992. *op. cit.*

118. US AID, *Ranking Environmental Health Risks in Bangkok*, Office of Housing and Urban Programs, Washington DC, 1990.

119. European Environment Agency 1995, *op. cit.*

120. UNEP and WHO 1992, *op. cit.*

121. *Ibid.*

122. Hardoy, Mitlin and Satterthwaite 1992, *op. cit.*; Sani, S., 'Urbanization and the atmospheric environment in Southeast Asia', in *Environment, Development, Natural Resource Crisis in Asia and the Pacific*, Sahabat Alam Malaysia, 1987.

123. Hardoy, Mitlin and Satterthwaite 1992, *op. cit.*

124. *Ibid.*

125. Lee, James A., *The Environment, Public Health and Human Ecology*, The World Bank, Johns Hopkins University Press, Baltimore and London, 1985

126. European Environment Agency 1995, *op. cit.*

127. WHO 1992, *op. cit.*

128. *Ibid.*

129. Hardoy, Mitlin and Satterthwaite 1992, *op. cit.*

130. Zhongmin, Yan, 'Shanghai: the growth and shifting emphasis of China's largest city', in Victor F. S. Sit (ed.), *Chinese Cities: the Growth of the Metropolis since 1949*, Oxford University Press, Hong Kong, 1988, 94–127.

131. Phantumvanit, Dhira and Wanai Liengcharernsit, 'Coming to terms with Bangkok's environmental problems', *Environment and Urbanization*, vol. 1, no. 1, April 1989, 31–9.

132. European Environment Agency 1995, *op. cit.*

133. It is obviously not only in cities that natural hazards take a large toll on human health. Some of largest losses of life have come in densely populated rural areas— as in the tens of thousands of people who lost their lives in floods and cyclones in Bangladesh in 1991 and the 24,000 or so people in Colombia who lost their lives in 1985 from the volcanic eruption in Nevado del Ruiz and the associated landslides—see UNEP, *Environment Data Report 1993–94*, prepared by GEMS Monitoring and Assessment Research Centre, Blackwell, Oxford, 1993. This section also draws from this document.

134. Davis, Ian, 'Safe shelter within unsafe cities: disaster vulnerability and raid urbanization', *Open House International*, vol. 12, no. 3, 1987, 5–15; Cuny, Frederick C. 'Sheltering the urban poor: lessons and strategies of the Mexico City and San Salvador earthquakes', *Open House International*, vol. 12, no. 3, 1987, 16–20; Degg, Martin R., 'Earthquake hazard assessment after Mexico', *Disasters* vol. 13, no. 3, 1989, 237–46.

135. Davis 1987, *op. cit.*; Barraza, Ernesto, 'Effectos del terremoto en la infraestructura de vivienda', and Lungo Ucles, Mario, 'El terremoto de octubre de 1986 y la situacion habitacional de los sectores populares', in 'El terremoto del 10 de octubre de 1986', a special issue of *La Universidad*, Nino CXII No 5, San Salvador, Jan.–March, 1987; Lungo Ucles, Mario, 'San Salvador: el habitat despues del terremoto', *Medio Ambiente y Urbanizacion*, no. 24, Sept. 1988, 46–52.

136. See references in previous two notes.

137. Jimenez Diaz, Virginia, 'Landslides in the squatter settlements of Caracas; towards a better understanding of causative factors', *Environment and Urbanization*, vol. 4, no. 2, Oct. 1992.

138. Centre for Science and Environment 1985, *op. cit.*

139. UNEP 1993, *op. cit.*

140. *Ibid.*

141. *Ibid.*

142. Douglas, Ian, 'Urban Geomorphology', in P. G. Fookes and P. R. Vaughan (eds.), *A Handbook of Engineering Geomorphology*, Surrey University Press (Blackie and Son), Glasgow, 1986, 270–83, and Douglas, Ian, *The Urban Environment*, Edward Arnold, London, 1983.

143. Hardoy, Mitlin and Satterthwaite 1992, *op. cit.*

144. Hardoy and Satterthwaite 1989, *op. cit.*

145. For India: Agarwal, Anil, 'The poverty of nature: environment, development, science and technology', *IDRC Report No. 12*, Ottawa, Canada, 1983, pp. 4–6. For China: Smil, Vaclav, *The Bad Earth: Environmental Degradation in China*, M. E. Sharpe, New York, and Zed Press, London, 1984. For Malaysia: Consumers Association of Penang, *Development and the Environment Crisis—A Malaysian Case*, 1982; and reports in *Environmental News Digest*, 1982. For Alexandria: Hamza, Ahmed, 'An appraisal of environmental consequences of urban development in Alexandria, Egypt', *Environment and Urbanization*, vol. 1, no. 1, April 1989, 22–30. For Gulf of Paria: Cover Story, *The Siren*, no. 38, UNEP, Nairobi, Oct. 1988. For Manila Bay: Jimenez, Rosario D. and Sister Aida Velasquez, 'Metropolitan Manila: a framework for its sustained development', *Environment and Urbanization*, vol. 1, no. 1, April 1989. For the Bay of Dakar: Kebe, Moctar, 'The West and Central African Action Plan', Interview in *The Siren*, No. 37, July 1988, 31–4. For Indus Delta: Sahil, 'Marine pollution and the Indus Delta', vol. 1 (House journal of National Institute of Oceanography, Karachi, Pakistan), 1988, 57–61; and Beg, M. Arshad Ali S. Naeem Mahmood, Sitwat Naeem and A. H. K. Yousufzai, 'Land based pollution and the marine environment of the Karachi coast', *Pakistan Journal of Science, Industry and Resources*, vol. 27, no. 4, Aug. 1984, 199–205.

146. For China: Smil 1984, *op. cit.* For Malaysia: Sahabat Alam Malaysia, *The State of Malaysian Environment 1983–4*—Towards Greater Environmental Awareness, 1983. For India: Centre for Science and Environment, *The State of India's Environment—a Citizen's Report*, Delhi, India, 1983. For Cubatao: Bo Landin, *Air Pollution*, film produced as part of the Television Series 'Battle for the Planet', Television Trust for the Environment, 1987.

147. This paragraph draws on Conway and Pretty 1991, *op. cit.*

148. Conway and Pretty 1991, *op. cit.*

149. Rees, William E., 'Ecological footprints and appropriated carrying capacity: what urban economics leaves out', *Environment and Urbanization*, vol. 4, no. 2, Oct. 1992.

150. Giradet, Herbert, *The Gaia Atlas of Cities*, Gaia Books, London, 1992.

151. White, Rodney R., 'The international transfer of urban technology: does the North have anything to offer for the global environmental crisis?', *Environment and Urbanization*, vol. 4, no. 2, Oct. 1992.

152. Damián, Araceli, 'Ciudad de México: servicios urbanos en los noventas', *Vivienda*, vol. 3, no. 1, Jan.–April 1992, 29–40; and Postel, Sandra, *The Last Oasis; Facing Water Scarcity*, Worldwatch Environmental Alert Series, Earthscan Publications, London, 1992.

153. European Environment Agency 1995, *op. cit.*

154. Douglass, Mike, 'The environmental sustainability of development—coordination, incentives and political will in land use planning for the Jakarta Metropolis', *Third World Planning Review*, vol. 11, no. 2, May 1989, 211–38.

155. Tiffen, Mary and Michael Mortimore, 'Environment, population growth and productivity in Kenya; a case study of Machakos District', *Development Policy Review*, vol. 10, 1992, 359–87; Manzanal, Mabel and Cesar Vapnarsky, 'The Comahue Region, Argentina' in Hardoy, Jorge E. and Satterthwaite, David (eds.), *Small and Intermediate Urban Centres; Their Role in National and Regional Development in the Third World*, Hodder and Stoughton (UK), 1986 and Westview (USA) 1986.

156. Castleman, Barry I., 'Workplace health standards and multinational corporations in developing countries' in Charles S. Pearson (ed.), *Multinational Corporation, the Environment and the Third World*, Duke University Press, Durham, USA, 1987, 149–72.

157. Table 21.2 in World Resources Institute, *World Resources 1994–95: a Guide to the Global Environment*, Oxford University Press, Oxford, 1994.

158. OECD, *The State of the Environment*, Organization for Economic Co-operation and Development, Paris, 1991.

159. World Resources Institute 1994, *op. cit.* 9.

160. OECD 1991, *op. cit.*

161. Hardoy, Jorge E., Diana Mitlin and David Satterthwaite, 'The future city', in Johan Holmberg (ed.), *Policies for a Small Planet*, Earthscan publications, London, 1992, 124–56.

162. Newman, Peter W. G and Jeffrey R. Kenworthy, *Cities and Automobile Dependence: An International Sourcebook*, Gower Technical, Aldershot, 1989.

163. *Ibid.*

164. Gilbert, Richard, 'Cities and global warming', in James McCulloch (ed.),

Cities and Global Climate Change, Climate Institute, Washington DC, 1990, 182–90.

165. Nishioka, Shuzo, Yuichi Noriguchi and Sombo Yamamura, 'Megalopolis and climate change: the case of Tokyo', in James McCulloch (ed.), *Cities and Global Climate Change*, Climate Institute, Washington DC, 1990, 108–33.

166. Scott, M. J., Draft paper on Human settlements—impacts/adaptation, IPCC Working Group II, WMO and UNEP, 1994.

167. Parry, Martin, 'The urban economy', presentation at *Cities and Climate Change*, a conference at the Royal Geographical Society, 31 March 1992.

168. Scott 1994, *op. cit.*

169. *Ibid.*

170. *Ibid.*

171. WHO 1992, *op. cit.*

172. *Ibid.*

173. *Ibid.*

174. *Ibid.*

175. Scott 1994, *op. cit.*

176. Satterthwaite, Hart, Levy and others 1996, *op. cit.*

177. WHO 1992, *op. cit.*

178. Hardoy, Mitlin and Satterthwaite 1992, *op. cit.*

179. Bartone and others 1994, *op. cit.*

180. Hardoy, Mitlin and Satterthwaite 1992. *op. cit.*

181. Hardoy, Jorge E. and David Satterthwaite, 'Environmental problems in Third World cities: a global issue ignored' *Public Administration and Development*, vol. 11, 1991, 341–61.

5 Institutional Trends and the Crisis of Governance

5.1 The Governance of Settlements[1]

Introduction

The governance of settlements has become a major issue over the last decade. The term 'governance' means more than government or management for it refers to the relationship not only between governments and state agencies but also between government and communities and social groups. 'Governance' is a broader and more inclusive term than 'government', just as 'local governance' is a more inclusive term than 'local government', in that it encompasses the activities of a range of groups—political, social and governmental—as well as their interrelationships. 'Local governance' thus subsumes the operations of local governments, their relationships with the societies within which they operate, and even the technical area of 'urban management', the term that has come to connote the actual management of local government services and infrastructure.

Three factors have helped 'local governance' emerge as a key issue in the discussion of policies for human settlements:

- The elaboration and implementation of decentralization policies in many countries including the emergence of the concept of subsidiarity.

- The introduction of or return to democratic principles of government in many countries during the 1980s and early 1990s, at both the national and local levels.

- The increased importance of citizen and community pressure—including urban social movements—combined with the growth worldwide of an environmental movement that have helped to place a greater emphasis on local control and involvement in decision making.

Decentralization

During the 1980s, concern grew about the inability of many governments to deliver development programmes to their people at the local level. In Africa, which was perhaps the most problematic region in terms of development over this decade, the World Bank stated that one of the continent's most urgent needs was to improve institutional capacity. This included a recommendation that local governments

could play a greater role if allowed more autonomy and regular, independent sources of revenue, especially in managing the expanding urban networks that link the towns to their hinterlands. In rural areas local services, such as water supply, could be better run at the communal level. This too requires genuine delegation of responsibilities.[2]

Another analysis put it more bluntly:

We will argue . . . that ethnic conflict, political inefficacy, administrative weaknesses, and economic stagnation can be understood in part as caused by attempts over the last two decades to impose a high level of centralization in contemporary African states, and that these explanations argue forcefully for changes in political structure and development strategy.[3]

It was not until the 1980s that a wide debate began in many countries about the balance of power and distribution of functions between national and local governments. Decentralization policies of different kind have been or are being implemented in most countries—including countries in Europe, North America and Africa, Asia and Latin America—and also in countries with centralized and decentralized structures.[4] Among the 75 countries in the South and in East and Central Europe that had 5 million or more inhabitants in the early 1990s, all but twelve were engaged in some form of transfer of power from national to local levels of government.[5]

There is great variety in the forms that decentralization takes. Assuming that decentralization involves the delegation of authority from a higher, or more general level of the state to a lower, or more specialized unit (or area),[6] four major variants have been identified:

- *Deconcentration*, or the transfer of functions, but not power, from a central unit to a local administrative office. This is one of the 'weakest' forms of decentralization and has become a common response by higher levels of government to deflect the blame for inadequate service provision from central to local authorities.

- *Delegation*, which involves, in most cases, the transfer of certain powers to parastatal agencies of the central state. While the parastatals have a certain autonomy in day-to-day management, they are usually controlled ultimately by government.

- *Devolution*, considered by some as 'real decentralization', since power and functions are actually transferred to sub-national political entities, who, in turn, have real autonomy in many important respects.

- *Privatization*, which involves the transfer of power and responsibility for certain state functions to private groups or companies.[7]

With so many cases of decentralization underway, and so many differences in the form that the decentralization takes, it is virtually impossible to generalize about either the reasons for any particular exercise, or the success or failure of the decentralization effort as a whole. However, a number of cogent arguments can be put forward to explain why so many countries have adopted decentralization strategies.[8] The first is because of the diversity between localities i.e. that the demand for public services varies from place to place both in quantity and quality, so that only decentralization of the provision for these services can ensure an efficient response to this variation in demand. A second argument is based on efficiency, in that locally financed and provided services can be produced at a lower cost—and with local government also able to work more easily with local community-based or voluntary sector organizations in ways that allow significant cost reductions. While this may be counterbalanced by the argument for larger units of service provision that achieve greater efficiency than smaller units at the lower level, it is still prevalent. A third argument is based on accountability—i.e. that a decentralized institution should in principle be more accountable to its constituents, who are more likely to have easy access to service providers and a better understanding of how institutions operate if services and institutions operate at a lower level than if they operate at a national, or centralized level. Finally, there is the argument for co-ordination. Many local services are interdependent. Improved water supply needs provision for sanitation and drainage, otherwise there are serious problems of waste water—and combining the installation of sewers, drains and street paving can considerably reduce costs. Street cleaning and solid waste collection are needed to keep drains unblocked, especially where open drains are used—and solid waste collection is often difficult or impossible without paved roads. The cost-savings from co-ordination can more easily be attained when it operates over a smaller, more local area.

All these arguments have merit, but they have been given particular relevance by the severe financial constraints in which most central governments have found themselves in recent years. In many countries in Latin America and Africa, structural adjustment programmes in effect since the 1980s, have increasingly reduced the resources from the centre to finance local services

and public administrations. If locally provided services are more likely to receive financial support from recipient populations (through taxes and fees) than if they were provided by the centre, this provides a good reason to decentralize the provision of such services. Even in wealthy Northern nations such as Canada and the United States, where an important range of functions are already in the hands of territorial and local authorities, there is a tendency to 'download' national support programmes such as social assistance and even medical care to local jurisdictions in order to reduce demands on central budgets. While decentralization has until recently been justified by arguments relating to efficiency and accountability, these arguments have been particularly attractive to central governments in recent years.

While there are good, or at least locally persuasive arguments for decentralization in the current economic climate—whether this decentralization involves privatization of services or localization of functions and responsibility—any shift of responsibility and financial power from one level of government to another level or agency brings both benefits and costs. Since arguments for central government provision of services include the presumption that they can be more equally distributed among the population as a whole, that they can be more effectively related to macroeconomic policy, and that they may benefit from higher levels of technology and information support, there can be costs when certain services are decentralized. One of these costs is the growth of disparities between local governments in terms of services provided, since some local governments have a greater ability to finance these services than others. The disparities can become very large, where many services are provided by local authorities from resources they raise within their own jurisdiction as local authorities in high income districts or municipalities have a much larger revenue base and capacity to pay among their populations than local authorities in low income districts. In many large cities, there are large disparities between neighbouring municipalities—for instance between the middle and upper income suburbs and the peripheral municipalities with high concentrations of illegal and informal settlements.

Another potential disadvantage of decentralization is central government's loss of control over fiscal policy, when some local and territorial governments spend or borrow disproportionately for their own needs and so contribute to inflation or increasing the debt service costs for the country as a whole. Finally, there is a question as to whether certain services—such as waste disposal, trunk sewers, public transportation, and secondary education—can and should be managed effectively by very local units, or whether they should not be managed by intermediate levels of government.

There are also the potential disadvantages related to privatization. One is the reduced transparency and accountability of infrastructure and service provision, when what was previously a government responsibility is privatized. Here, one particular worry is with the privatization of those forms of infrastructure and services that are 'natural monopolies'; once a piped-water system or electricity distribution network or sewage and storm drainage system is built and becomes the responsibility of one company, it is virtually impossible for another company to compete by building another water, sewage or electricity distribution system. Customers cannot turn to another supplier for water, drains or electricity, if the quality is poor and/or prices are too high. A second potential disadvantage of privatization is the loss of public assets if these are sold at below their real value. A third is the difficulty of ensuring that lower-income households and areas receive basic infrastructure and services. Privatization actually reinforces the need for competent, effective and accountable local government to act on behalf of the inhabitants in its jurisdiction to ensure that private companies maintain quality and coverage in infrastructure and service provision and do not abuse any natural monopoly position by raising prices. This is a point to which Chapter 10 will return in discussing public-private partnerships.

Democratization

The increased importance given to local governance is also related to a worldwide 'wave' of democratization from the late 1970s through the early 1990s. A 'democracy' in the twentieth century may be understood as a system in which the

most powerful collective decision makers are selected through fair, honest, and periodic elections in which candidates freely compete for votes and in which virtually all the adult population is eligible to vote.[9]

Thus, democracy implies the concurrent existence of freedoms to speak, publish, assemble and organize. It also implies the active functioning of more than one major political party in order to give voters a choice of alternative leadership groups. Beginning in 1974 in Portugal, and eventually spreading outward, a wave of democratization engulfed more than thirty countries in both the North and the South. Important changes in regime from authoritarian structures to democratic systems took place in 11 one-party systems, 7 regimes based on personal rulers, 16 regimes which had been under military control, and 1 regime (South Africa) which had been dominated by a racial oligarchy.[10] The years from 1973 to

1990 saw an increase in what could be classified as 'democratic states' from 30 to 59, and a decrease in 'non-democratic states' from 92 to 71.[11] While a few states slipped from democratic to non-democratic rule during this period, the overall democratic trend was particularly marked during the 1970s and 1980s in Latin America (with democratic transitions in such countries as Brazil, Peru, Ecuador, Chile, Argentina, Guatemala and Bolivia), and in the late 1980s and early 1990s in the former Soviet Union and in East and Central Europe.

In Africa, the overall direction of movement was more complex than in most major regions, perhaps because of the large number of countries, and the great variety of linguistic, cultural and historical traditions they represent. From a situation in the 1970s in which almost all regimes on the continent could have been considered 'authoritarian' by current standards, changes began to take place in party systems, electoral structures, and the application of the rule of law. By 1991, it was estimated that, of 54 countries for which reliable data was available to outside observers, 8 countries could be considered clearly 'democratic', 8 clearly 'authoritarian', and 3 more governed by a system which could best be described as 'directed democracy'. Apart from these, 35 countries were in various stages of 'transition' to more democratic government. A little more than three years later, based on the same criteria, 14 countries (including, by this time, South Africa) could be considered 'democratic', 3 'authoritarian', and 3 governed by 'directed democracy'. At this time, 7 countries were so unstable they could not be classified.[12] Thus, while more countries became thoroughly 'democratic' in this period, a number of countries became highly destabilized, and the level of commitment to democracy of many more was lower than it had been three years earlier. The consolidation of democracy on the continent, in spite of some hopeful trends over the last decade, is still an open-ended process in many countries.

The causes of this worldwide trend towards greater democracy are complex. But one of its important consequences is the strengthening of a 'political culture' in many countries which reinforces a closer relationship between, on the one hand, political leaders and governmental institutions, and on the other, major social and economic groups. Democratic governments, however competent or incompetent, are more likely to operate in response to public opinion, and—given the necessity of periodic and open elections—are less likely to take arbitrary and self-serving decisions than non-democratic governments. Governments which are democratic at the national level are also more likely to be democratic at the local level. Thus, a movement towards regular, open municipal elections instead of the selection of mayors and councillors by higher levels of government has paralleled the overall democratic trajectory in almost all cases. This has sharpened the debate in many countries on the appropriate division of powers between local and national governments, particularly as local politicians attempt to achieve more control over their jurisdictions. Given the economic stagnation and uncertainty which has faced many regions of the world over the last ten to fifteen years, combined with the growth of urban populations, it is not a foregone conclusion that recently elected municipal governments will be able effectively to cope with their new responsibilities and challenges. The debate on the appropriate role and functions for municipal governments will be a continuous one in all parts of the world.

Local social and environmental movements and NGOs

Starting in the 1970s, the larger and the more prosperous cities in most countries in the South became the focus of an increasingly intense conflict between the public authorities and large numbers of the urban poor. The conflict centred on the fact that a large part of each city's population had incomes that were too low to be able to afford the cost of shelter in areas that were planned and provided with basic infrastructure and services—including paved roads, piped water, drainage and provision for sanitation and electricity. Partly as a result, so-called 'squatter' or 'popular' settlements (variously named in different countries) developed on urban land that was unserviced, and where the land was occupied illegally—or if not illegally, at least without the approval of the urban authorities. However, the massive increase in the number of people living in the 'popular' settlements was not a challenge to the system of authority; they are much more an attempt by people with limited income or assets to gain a foothold in the urban economy which could serve as a first step toward integration into the labour market and integration within the institutions of the larger society. This helps explain why there have been so few radical challenges by these people to the established political order, despite this very large and usually growing number of people who are very poorly housed and serviced.

Following this logic, a number of policy innovations—such as sites and services schemes, and 'squatter upgrading' programmes—were developed in order to capitalize on the need for the urban poor to gain entry, at minimal cost, to the urban economy. As Chapter 11 will describe in more detail, these innovations, promoted by

such multilateral agencies as the World Bank, and a number of bilateral donor agencies, were the focus of urban policy innovation throughout the South during the 1970s and 1980s. Certain government institutions were also set up primarily to address the needs and priorities of those in illegal or informal settlements.[13]

The attempts by the urban poor to gain access to urban land and services were conceptualized—at least in Latin America—as an important component of what were called 'urban social movements'. A social movement was considered to reflect broad-based, often multi-class, co-ordinated activity at the local level; at the same time, while demands are made on the state, political parties and other specialized institutions are not the primary vehicles through which pressure is brought to bear. Informal and illegal settlements developed where the inhabitants felt confident that they could exert sufficient pressure on the authorities to let them stay—or at least to receive an alternative land site.[14] Decisions about which site to occupy and when to do so often reflected careful planning, good timing and well-informed trade-offs between the best locations and the best possibilities of being allowed to stay there and avoid eviction.[15] And when political circumstances permitted, intense pressure was brought to bear on the public authorities either for infrastructure and services or for legal tenure or both. In many cities, large sections of the middle-class were also active in such lobbying as they too had to develop their homes in illegal settlements, as inefficient land markets and cumbersome government regulations pushed land prices for legal plots beyond their means. However as Chapters 6 and 7 describe in more detail, these were generally in illegal subdivisions where the purchase of the land was legal but no approval for its use for housing or its subdivision had been obtained from the relevant public authorities. Although the form of this 'building cities from the bottom up' took many forms, each much influenced by a great range of local factors such as political and economic circumstances, landowning structures, income distribution and official rules and regulations governing land use and building, it was responsible for a high proportion of all the housing that exists in most cities in the South today.[16]

Since in most countries, national and local government agencies were either unable or unwilling to supply basic urban services to these burgeoning popular settlements—at least not at the pace and quality that the people were demanding—various patterns of community organization and self-help activities developed almost everywhere. There also developed a diverse range of NGOs who worked with them. The role and scope of community action and of NGO support for this was usually restricted and often repressed under non-democratic regimes. For instance, during the 1960s and 1970s, NGOs in Latin America occupied the narrow political space between local communities and formal institutions in the domain of social services and the promotion of local development. When many northern countries and foundations did not want to give assistance to authoritarian governments or government-dominated political parties, they were prepared to support local NGOs, which often worked with community groups. In some countries, NGOs helped to maintain political pluralism; in others, they helped keep authoritarianism at bay. But the political importance of community organization and of the NGO work associated with them increased considerably with democratic rule. As Albert Hirschman suggests, such developments may be part of a worldwide trend in which basic economic (and therefore political) rights are being demanded by all citizens.[17] For example, in Brazil, beginning in the late 1970s:

civil society breathed the air of the political 'opening', which heralded a return to democratic rule after 20 years of authoritarianism. Mobilization took root in the factories, but soon spread beyond the labour movement and political parties. In both poor neighbourhoods . . . and middle-class areas, the population organized to demand the right to basic services—water supply, sewerage, school facilities, health facilities, roads—and protested against ecological dangers, development plans which ignored residents' interests, housing evictions and a host of other causes.[18]

The emergence of urban social movements in Mexico and Peru, involving particularly the mobilization and organization of low-income communities predated the Brazilian awakening. But the 1985 earthquake in Mexico City, and a growing concern over urban environmental risk—especially as a result of high levels of air pollution in the capital—led to a diverse range of protests and popular activity in the area of human settlements. As most Latin American countries became predominantly urban, the link between protests and organizational activity to secure land and improved urban services, and demands for the reduction and control of air and water pollution in the cities became more pronounced. Both, in any case, were central to the democratization process in Latin America:

social movements were crucial to democratic recovery; they served as a means of developing social identity and of organizing political mobilization against dictatorships in Peru, Uruguay, Argentina and Chile.[19]

Eventually, with the return of democracy in much of South America in the 1980s, the activity of social movements was considerably reduced—but community organization linked to particular sites or more widespread citizen mobilization

against particular projects still remained. So too did the role of NGOs whose role often expanded, as governments or international agencies channelled funding through them.

In the countries in the North, the development of an environmental movement had important roots in local communities—very often as they mobilized against a new road, power plant, wastesite or some other development that they felt would threaten their environment. Well-publicized environmental disasters such as the accidental release of methyl iso-cyanate in Bhopal in 1985 or the fire and release of radioactive material from the Chernobyl nuclear power plant in 1986 or the release of oil by the Exxon Valdez in 1989 helped to create and maintain a high level of public apprehension over environmental risk. These concerns were nourished—both in Europe and North America—by the increasing prominence among the public at large of what may be called 'postmaterialist' values. In the affluent societies of the postwar period, in which basic human needs such as employment security, housing and material possessions were satisfied to a relatively high degree, a shift to nonmaterial needs such as self-expression, esteem and aesthetic satisfaction became much more prominent. Surveys in nine major European countries showed, for a large group of respondents, a strong clustering of five nonmaterialist goals: 'more say on the job', 'a less impersonal society', 'more say in government', 'ideas count', and 'freedom of speech'. In seven of the nine countries (showing most strongly in West Germany), the goal of 'more beautiful cities' was also strongly associated with the first five items. On the other hand, materialist goals such as 'strong defence forces', 'fighting rising prices', 'achieving a stable economy', 'fighting against crime', 'economic growth' and 'maintaining order' were strongly clustered for another group of respondents.[20]

Postmaterialist values have proved to be a strong support for environmentalism. Thus, in 1985, among 'materialists' in an opinion survey of the countries of the European community, 37 per cent 'strongly approved' of the ecology movement, while among 'postmaterialists' the approval level was 53 per cent. While 0.5 per cent of the 'materialists' claimed to be members of an environmental group, 3.3 per cent of the 'postmaterialists'—or almost seven times the proportion—did so.[21] In both Europe and North America, belief in environmental values are strongly correlated with education, and with youth. As one writer puts it in commenting on the situation in North America, '[e]volving environmental values were closely associated with rising standards of living and levels of education'.[22]

Support for the environmental movement has been strongest in the more affluent regions of Canada and the United States, and weakest in the less developed regions.[23] Overall, support for environmental groups increased considerably during the 1970s and 1980s. In Canada, for example, in 1973, the government listed 344 'citizens' environmental organizations'.[24] By the late 1980s, the number had risen to some 1,800, with a membership exceeding 1 million, or about 4 per cent of Canada's total population.[25] In the United States, a poll found that 7 per cent of the whole population considered themselves 'environmentally active', while another 55 per cent said they were sympathetic with the aims of the environmental movement.[26] In 1990, a Gallup poll found that 76 per cent of Americans 'called themselves environmentalists, and half contributed to environmental organizations'.[27] By 1991, it was estimated that the larger national environmental organizations had a membership of no less than 14 million individuals, or about one in every seven adults in the country![28]

Although membership and contribution figures in the large environmental organizations were falling by the mid 1990s (largely, observers suggested, because of the parlous state of the economy which reduced the marginal propensity for donations), the environmental movement had already had a major impact on local activism. This was particularly evident in the area of solid waste management—whether the concern was toxic industrial wastes, or the siting of a refuse dumpsite at the neighbourhood level. This grassroots activism which was often focused on the municipalities that were responsible for the land-use and effluent-control regulations affecting the communities in which people lived and raised their children, was much more heavily influenced by the participation of women than were the large national organizations. One of the most lasting legacies of the environmental movement—at least in the North—has been a greater involvement of a wide range of local groups in the local governance process.

5.2 Changes in Urban Governance in Latin America

Introduction

In Latin America, three shifts in patterns of governance can be identified during the post-war era, each with a different relationship between civil society and the state. In the immediate post-war era, many Latin American countries were ruled by populist political parties and the role of political organizations in civil society was pronounced. Extending roughly from the mid-1960s to the mid-1980s, many of these populist regimes were replaced by military dictatorships of varying political tendencies. In most cases, the role of civil society in running the nations' affairs was

significantly reduced. However, in response to mounting domestic and international pressure, and often to economic mismanagement, many of Latin America's military regimes were replaced by democratically elected governments. Once again, the role of civil society was on the rise.

The restoration of many democratically elected governments took place during the 'lost decade' of the 1980s when, as Chapter 3 described, wages usually declined, prices increased and the proportion of people with below poverty-line incomes grew considerably. There was often a severe contraction of productive activity, and a significant reduction in the public sector. As a result, while the inauguration of democratic regimes restored civil society to its former role, its interlocutor, the state, was considerably reduced in size and importance. It is primarily during the last decade—with the widespread return to democracy—that the issue of local governance and local government reform has become a critical element in the larger project to improve governance as a whole.[29] There are two manifestations of this. The first is that many central governments have embarked on decentralization programmes designed to devolve a wide variety of powers and responsibilities to subnational governments. The second, and an integral part of the decentralization programs, is a democratization of local government to enhance civic participation in local government, and to provide mechanisms for more efficient and effective service delivery at the local level. Each is discussed below.

Decentralization and central–local government relations

The wave of democratization has brought with it an equally broad programme of decentralization of government power and authority to subnational levels of government. In Latin America, decentralization programmes have been implemented in the vast majority of countries, affecting over 90 per cent of the population.[30] Each programme is country specific and is predicated both on the previous governing structure and fiscal regimes. Some central governments have devolved power to regional governments while others have concentrated upon strengthening municipal governments directly. One of the preconditions for improving urban governance is reflected in changes in the level of public sector expenditure at the municipal level. As Table 5.1 shows, although municipal expenditures are increasing, they still constitute a relatively small proportion of overall expenditure. Two countries which have recently launched major decentralization programmes to the municipal level are Brazil and Bolivia. The impact of Brazil's programmes launched in 1988 is still being worked out (see below for more details) while Bolivia only launched its reform in 1994. Under Bolivia's *Ley de Participacion Popular*, municipal governments will automatically receive 20 per cent of all central government revenues through fiscal transfers from the government.

TABLE 5.1 Municipal spending in selected countries

Country	Municipal Spending as a Percentage of Total Public Sector Expenditure by year (percentage)		
	1970–83	**1985**	**1992**
Colombia	10.5% (1980)	16.2%	15.7%
Argentina	5.4% (1983)		8.6%
Chile	4.7% (1970)		12.7%
Peru	2.2% (1980)	2.2%	9.2%

Source: Inter-American Development Bank, *Economic and Social Progress in Latin America 1994 Report; Special Report: Fiscal Decentralization*, Washington DC, 1994.

However, despite the adoption of decentralization programmes, attempts to assess the impact of decentralization upon urban governance are limited. Evaluations of various decentralization programmes tend to concentrate on legal and administrative analysis and relatively little work has been done to see whether the objectives of decentralization to enhance civic participation or improve service delivery in urban areas have been achieved.[31] Given this scenario, it is important to consider what exactly local governments are responsible for providing.

In Latin America, the heritage of the administrative structures of government, with the exception of Brazil, are based on the Spanish model which is a unitary structure. Brazil's political traditions emerge from the Portuguese tradition in which local governments have traditionally had much more autonomy than in Spain.[32] Brazil's 1988 Constitution transferred significant autonomy and power to municipal governments and as a result, urban governance in Brazil is widely seen to be amongst the leaders in the hemisphere. Brazilian municipalities are run by democratically elected mayors assisted by municipal councils. Municipalities are responsible for the provision of services—some exclusively, others in conjunction with state and central government. Municipalities are exclusively responsible for providing lighting, markets, local roads, urban public transport, fire protection, land-use control and armed night guards. The functions which they exercise concurrently with the state governments include education, public health, recreation, culture, social assistance, agriculture and public utilities. But the allocation of services is less straightforward than

the clear divisions would appear, in part because federal and state governments have continued to invade municipal spheres, and in part because of a '*de facto* renunciation of functions by the municipalities themselves'.[33]

Revenues for Brazilian municipalities are generated from own sources as well as direct transfers from central and state governments. In Brazil, municipalities account for over 16 per cent of all public sector expenditure, one of the highest levels in Latin America. Local government elections based on the 1988 constitution returned a large number of 'Left-leaning parties'[34] to power but the impact of the new electoral system on urban governance is still under debate. A preliminary evaluation of the impact of the first wave of popularly elected municipal governments is:

that the administrations experimenting with more democratic forms of municipal government have met with more success in altering the priorities in municipal budgeting, increasing the weight of social investment in low-income areas, than in constructing new effective channels for participation by urban movements. In particular, the territorially based forms of participation through popular councils to be set up in political administrative regions seem to have advanced little because of localism, fragmentation, corporatism, and the rejection of representation by the neighbourhood associations.[35]

In Ecuador, although the number of municipalities has increased dramatically during the last decade, municipalities have, since 1970, progressively lost functions and powers to the central government because much of the oil wealth has accrued to the central government and the funding formula for local governments has been haphazard.[36] This is despite the fact that the military period ended in 1978 and a new constitution established the basis for democratic government. Municipal governments are responsible for the provision of water and sewerage; solid and liquid waste disposal; public lighting; control of food products; land-use; markets; tourism promotion; and authorization for the functioning of industrial, commercial and professional services.[37] As in many countries in the region, the capacity to manage urban issues within municipalities is weak both in terms of human and financial resources, and it is characterized by ineffectual and obsolete administrative systems and weak social participation.[38]

The transition to democratic rule in Chile began with the gradual strengthening of municipal governments. One of the first steps in this direction was the passing of the Municipal Rents Law of 1979 which tripled the level of resources available to municipalities. This was followed in 1981 by the transfer to municipalities of the responsibility for the administration of education and health. The next step was the modification of the Constitution in 1992 to allow for the direct election of local councillors and mayors.[39] Municipalities are responsible for public transport and traffic; urban planning; refuse collection; parks; promoting communal development; local roads; sewers, public lighting; managing health-care centres; and primary and secondary education. They are not responsible for the provision and treatment of water nor for regional public corporations. They share with the central government and other public institutions responsibility for social assistance, environmental protection, public housing, drainage, and support to special social programmes.[40]

Since the advent of the democratic period in 1988, Chile has embarked on a decentralization programme which has the potential of significantly strengthening the ability of local governments to play a more decisive role in urban governance. This decentralization has included both administrative and political aspects with the intention of enabling a more direct involvement of civic organizations in daily political life. In September 1992, the first popularly chosen mayors since 1972 were elected in 335 municipalities. Through various fiscal measures, real resources for municipalities increased by 36.1 per cent between 1985 and 1991.[41] In terms of urban governance the potential for greater civic participation is certainly evident and likely to increase as the democratic administration of municipalities is further entrenched.

In summary, compared to the period from the 1960s until the early 1980s, local governments in Latin America have been taking on an increasing share of public sector activity, usually leading to increased participation in health care, education, infrastructure, and basic services. An aspect of decentralization which is often overlooked, however, is that central and intermediate levels of government often continue to have a critical role in urban governance either through policy and regulatory reform, or through direct intervention. Decentralization from central to state and even to local governments has tended to be the focus of much of the discussion. The on-going relationship of the state to civil society, to which we turn in the next section, has received far less attention.

Character and functions of urban civil society

The very important political role of social movements in Latin America highlights the extent to which the daily livelihood (or survival) strategies of the urban poor can provide the foundation for more organized and articulate protest. While social movements are generally targeted at specific issues, it is clear that a number of them have had a significant impact upon urban governance in Latin America. Perhaps the most important dimension of civil society which social movements studies have illuminated is the critical role which women have had in the struggles for political and social change. Accounts of women's political participation in Guadalajara, Mexico; of neighbourhood handicraft organizations in Santiago, Chile; and of struggles for health care in Sao Paulo, Brazil are just some of the most salient examples.[42] Each points out the extent to which political participation in urban governance is gendered and should be understood in such a context.

Studies of social movements based on their social structure and dynamics highlight the important, and growing role, that organizations in civil society are taking in shaping political agendas and in dealing with local governments, parastatals, and central government bodies. Such studies tend to emphasize the horizontal nature of urban politics and the way in which social and political protest are focused on achieving very concrete goals. Other studies, which seek to come to terms with the nature of social movements in Latin America from the perspective of the state, have taken a different approach. Given the current focus on transforming local governments from a supply-driven to a demand-driven role, community participation has a much greater role in service delivery.[43]

The nexus between civil society and the state for local governance in Latin America centres on the important role of community participation in service provision and delivery. There has been a growing recognition of its importance for decades in various facets of urban development—especially land development and housing. Until recently, the participation of civil society in urban governance has been treated with suspicion by many, largely because of scepticism of the motive of governments to promote genuine community participation. The main objective of community-action programmes was

less to improve conditions for the poor or to modify forms of decision making than to legitimate the state. The main object of community action is how to help maintain existing power relation in society. The aim is not to change conditions for the poor as much as to make sure they cause no problems.[44]

With democratization, some more recent assessments of community participation programmes are more generous. There is growing recognition of the important openings which local elections have generated. With more recent shifts in national governance and the increasingly large role taken by civil society both in decision-making and organizing service delivery, community participation in urban governance is coming to be accepted as the norm, not the exception. In spite of these advances, the challenge of developing effective channels of communication and participation remains.

Local governance in the 1990s and beyond

As local governance takes on more importance in Latin America, two key issues will emerge. The first issue involves political participation while the second addresses the reform of the state and the development of new models of intergovernmental relations. As democratization in Latin America proceeds, the role of local governments in addressing local political issues and enabling civic participation to develop will take on greater significance. This includes not only the holding of elections at the local level, but also the ability of municipal governments to provide effective solutions to urban problems. Box 5.1 presents an assessment of recent municipal elections in La Paz, the largest urban concentration in Bolivia.[45] The emergence of the new party there suggests a dissatisfaction among many urban citizens with the traditional political parties. A study in Lima-Callao in Peru which examined data from four municipal elections (1980, 1983, 1986, and 1989) and three national elections found a similar dissatisfaction—that can be seen in a substantial rise in wasted ballots and absenteeism.[46] The study suggests that despite the presence of *Sendero Luminoso* (the 'shining path' guerrilla movement) in Lima and its active campaign during this period for boycotting elections, a major variable explaining the declining proportion of citizens who voted was a general disaffection with traditional political parties and the political system itself. As disaffection grew with solutions presented by the traditional Peruvian political parties, the electorate participated less and less in each election. The study's overall analysis of the voting pattern suggests that the previously nonexistent *Cambio 90* party of Ing. Fujimori swept to power in the 1990 elections on the basis of declining participation in municipal elections and the increasing fragmentation of the votes between different political parties. There is also some evidence of new kinds of city politicians being elected in Latin America who are not closely aligned to existing political parties[47] or who are trying new, more participatory, more socially oriented programmes.[48]

The second issue, which is posed in the context of the reform of the state apparatuses in many countries, is to develop more effective relationships between different levels of government. This involves both coming to terms with metropolitan government, as well as seeking more equitable and efficient forms of relationship between

---

BOX 5.1
Municipal elections in Bolivia

A study of local politics in La Paz in Bolivia, including the adjacent El Alto, examined the emergence of one political party, *Conciencia de Patria* (CONDEPA) and its charismatic leader, Carlos Palenque and the important role the party has come to play in the Bolivian politics. The authors conclude that the strength of the movement lies in a complex mix of populism based upon charismatic, utopian, religious and indigenist factors. The effective use of the media, given these elements, led to the emergence of CONDEPA as a major political force in the department of La Paz and Bolivia itself.

CONDEPA was created as a political party by Carlos Palenque after the government censured, and then closed his radio station in June 1988 after almost twenty years of operation. On September 21, 1988, CONDEPA was formally launched as a political party in Tiwanancu, the ancient capital of the Aymara world. In May 1989, CONDEPA won the majority of the votes in the national elections in the department of La Paz, became the fourth largest political party in Bolivia, and acted as a major political broker in the Bolivian Congress. In December 1989, CONDEPA won a majority of the votes in the municipal elections in La Paz, but was denied the mayoralty because the election to that post was indirect. However, the party won a sweeping victory in El Alto and a CONDEPA representative became the city's mayor. By March 1995, CONDEPA controlled both the cities of La Paz and El Alto and their support continued to grow. One explanation of the success of CONDEPA was its appeal to recent urban migrants through populist, religico-utopian elements in the people's own language—Aymara.

Sources: Joaquin Saravia C. and Godofredo Sandoval Z. *Jach'a Uru: ¿La Esperanza de un Pueblo? Carlos Palenque, RTP y Los Sectores Populares Urbanos en La Paz*, CEP and ILDIS, La Paz, 1991.

---

the various levels of government. Two issues are important here: first, the pressure to deal with metropolitanization of large cities; and second, the continuing role of all levels of government in urban governance.

The critical importance of central–local relations is highlighted by two issues which will need to be addressed during the coming decade as urban governance in Latin America takes on greater urgency. First, as civil society becomes increasingly concerned with urban poverty, the urban environment, and the urban economy, the need to manage cities on a metropolitan basis will become politically more significant. Following from this, the second issue, and one which will continue in each country, is working out the respective roles of the various levels of government in improving urban government. While local, or municipal governments are responsible for certain critical services in urban settings, the role of regional and national governments is also critical, and will continue to be so. The metropolitan mobilization in Buenos Aires was directed against the central government because there was no effective interlocutor at the metropolitan level with which to consult. There is also the complication that the central area of the city (the Federal District) is under the jurisdiction of the Federal Government while all the surrounding municipalities which have more than two thirds of the urban agglomeration's population are in the Province of Buenos Aires, and under the jurisdiction of the Provincial Government. Improving urban governance will depend not only on strengthening municipal management and developing alternative service delivery mechanisms, but also on developing more effective inter-governmental relations between municipal, regional, and national governments.

Conclusions

This review of the changes in patterns of urban governance in Latin America shows that changes in governance as a whole have begun to shift toward local governance. With the recent advent of the democratization, the widespread efforts of many national governments to 'modernize' their public sectors has included the decentralization of many functions and responsibilities to the municipal level. While these shifts augur well for the future, the rapid pace of urbanization during the last two decades coupled with the continuing unmet demands for basic services in many of Latin America's cities will place an immediate strain on the 'democratic governance' of the urban centres. The pressure to meet the demands of low-income urban residents is increasing and it is not clear that civil society will continue to be patient for much longer. A recent example of the increasingly organized and active role played by organizations in civil society is provided by the case of Guadalajara, Mexico, in response to the tragic gas pipeline explosion in 1992. Protests against various levels of government illustrate a new form of politics, which

rely upon an ethic or moral economy that claims a legitimate right to customary arrangements evolved with urbanization such as renters' rights to continued occupancy, rights of the poor to urban services as part of a just social wage rather than a contingent political bargain, and increasingly a set of internationally defined human rights to health, safety, freedom from oppression and, at bottom, dignity. That is not to say that these rights have been won, nor that civil society has supplanted other interest-group bases of organization. It does mean that the terrain of political conflict in the third world city is shifting—and never so markedly as in the last decade of neo-liberal economic reform and its associated political reform. Patron-client models that worked in an economically expanding and often authoritarian third world from the 1950s to the 1980s are collapsing. The *damnificados* of Guadalajara and their confederates in other cities have given us a glimpse of what is coming.[49]

As this example shows, the patterns of urban governance which are emerging will put even

more stress on local governments that are currently ill-equipped to deal with existing, let alone new concerns. The challenge for many local governments in Latin America will be to negotiate and enter into more fruitful partnerships with civil society to resolve their pressing problems.

5.3 Changes in Urban Governance in Africa

Introduction

By the 1990s, as African cities continued to grow at a pace that considerably exceeded the average for most other parts of the world, two central challenges were posed. The first was the challenge of more effectively managing urban services, so that (*a*) a minimum of efficiency could be assured for the continued functioning of the urban economy; and (*b*) the increasing numbers of urban poor would have access to clean water, health centres, education, public transport and other elements of public infrastructure. The second challenge, which in many ways subsumed the first, was to develop governance systems which provided access to local decisions by important groups in the community, while at the same time maintaining an institutional framework that was both legitimate in national terms, and more appropriate to the nature of modern urban life. This section will focus on the question of governance structures, although the technical functions of actually managing African cities can never be far from view.

There are important differences in the form of decentralization between francophone and anglophone countries which partially relate to their different colonial legacies. One of the most important components of local governance in Africa has been the colonial legacy of institutional structure. Britain and France, as the major colonial powers on the continent from the late nineteenth century to the 1960s, provided the basic framework for two, largely parallel approaches to local government. These two approaches overlapped to some degree by the 1990s, but their essential elements could still be distinguished. The pattern most common in Francophone countries can be called the communal structure, while the pattern in Anglophone countries may be called the representative council structure. The differences between the two are largely explained by history and the accretion of many decades of legal and administrative precedent.

Decentralization in Francophone countries

Most of the Francophone countries in Africa (with the major exception of Zaire, Rwanda and

Burundi, which were Belgian colonies) are former French colonies. Since the early part of the twentieth century, urban government has been structured according to the French law dating back to 1884, which provides for communes with mayors, municipal councils, and specific revenue and expenditure powers and procedures. The level of responsibility over finances and local decisions typically depends on the size and wealth of a 'commune', although the local authority has generally been considered to be an organizational modality internal to the unitary state. By the end of the colonial period in the late 1950s, the evolution of municipal institutions was such that the municipal councils (the administrative organs of the communes) in the larger cities had become responsible for a relatively important range of local services, and were presided over by elected mayors. For example, Abidjan, the capital of Côte d'Ivoire, was declared a 'full exercise commune' (the highest legal category) in 1955, electing a full council by universal suffrage in 1956. Prefects were appointed for another six major communes, replacing elected mayors. While a relatively wide range of functions were discharged by the communes and the larger 'City of Abidjan' (consisting of the central area of Abidjan and some adjoining communes), decisions on their implementation were taken by central government officials. This structure remained in place until 1980.[50] There was a somewhat similar situation in Dakar, the capital of Senegal, with much deeper historical roots. Dakar was then the largest French-speaking city in West Africa. From 1887, when Dakar (which had earlier been designated, along with three other towns, as a 'full exercise commune' under French law) was given French-style institutions. The city had an elected council, an elected mayor, and considerable influence over finance, services, and the hiring of personnel. By the early 1980s, however, the administration of the commune of Dakar was 'exclusively carried out by centrally appointed officials, which has led, as a consequence, to the setting aside of any direct participation by elected elements'.[51]

By the 1980s, the balance between central and local government began to change. Not only was there more attention placed on the development of metropolitan government structures, but a more democratic and decentralized framework began to take shape. By the end of the decade, several countries (such as Senegal, Côte d'Ivoire and Bénin) were organizing regular, even multi-party elections both at the local and national level, and a number of other countries were clearly moving towards multi-party democracy. Thus, Senegal, which began multi-party elections in the late 1970s, established in 1983 the Urban Community of Dakar, which created a working arrangement to incorporate the three

newly-created communes of Dakar, Pikine and Rufisque-Bargny. While the individual communes were governed by municipal councils selected both by selection (as representing interest groups) and open elections, their mayors were selected by secret ballot of their council.

By the 1980s, the balance between central and local government began to change in Francophone Africa. Not only was there more attention placed on the development of metropolitan government structures, but a more democratic and decentralized framework began to take shape. By the end of the decade, many countries (such as Senegal, Côte d'Ivoire and Bénin) were organizing regular, even multi-party elections both at the local and national level, and a number of other countries were clearly moving towards multi-party democracy. Thus, Senegal, which began multi-party elections in the late 1970s, established in 1983 the Urban Community of Dakar, which created a working arrangement to incorporate the three newly-created communes of Dakar, Pikine and Rufisque-Bargny. While the individual communes were governed by municipal councils selected both by selection (as representing interest groups) and open elections, their mayors were selected by secret ballot of their council. The mayor of the CUD (Dakar Urban Community) was likewise elected by secret ballot of the delegates of the communes to the ten-person governing body of the CUD. From 1983 until the present, the Mayor of the CUD has been the same individual, a high-profile politician with previous central government ministerial experience. As a leading member of an opposition party, representing the indigenous Lébou community, and having been able to assemble around him an impressive group of dedicated young technocrats, the mayor of Dakar has become:

one of the main players in the politics of national integration [whose role] … explains the tightening of central control over the implementation of the mayor's functions as well as the fragility of his status as a representative of the local community. This situation is facilitated by the lack of interest and/or confidence which the people express for these local institutions. In spite of a particularly dense and heavy set of laws and regulations, which allow the state to harass those communes which the opposition might control, it is significant that opposition leaders pay little attention to this question in their confrontations with the state. The political culture of the opposition, made up of different segments of the urban petty bourgeoisie, is dominated by an attitude of parliamentarism, and not by a preoccupation with the destruction of local structures of domination. Nevertheless, the nomination to the commune of Dakar of leading political personalities who maintain close links with the national political and administrative leadership, shows that the commune can have a important political role within the state.[52]

Aside from the political dynamics within which it operates, the CUD is also important because of its important functions. These include construction and maintenance of roads within its jurisdiction, cleaning and sweeping of streets, removal and destruction of household wastes, management of the municipal hospital, management of municipal abattoirs, management of both Christian and Muslim cemeteries, and a number of other functions which include the overall direction of technical services at the local level.

Of all the decentralization exercises to have been initiated in Francophone Africa, the most thoroughgoing, and by many measures, effective has been that of the Côte d'Ivoire. The initiative began in late December 1977, when a law was passed in the National Assembly confirming the establishment of the two existing 'full exercise' communes (Abidjan and Bouaké). A series of laws defined the powers and institutions of the new communes, elaborating a specific regime under which they would be controlled by the central government. Ten communes were created within the former single commune of Abidjan, presided over by the City of Abidjan, whose structure and powers were specified. The Mayor of the City of Abidjan was to be elected from among their number by the elected mayors of the ten component communes of the greater Abidjan area. Finally, in 1985, ninety-eight new communes were added to the list of local authorities, for a total of 135, plus the City of Abidjan. According to most observers, the decentralization exercise in Côte d'Ivoire has on balance been a positive experience. On the one hand, more explicit transfers of powers need to be effected between the central and local authorities, and more resources need to be given to the communes in the form of personnel and taxation powers for them to manage their own affairs. But on the other hand, the role of the communes 'in people's daily lives' is becoming increasingly evident. Functions such as maintaining the civil registry, public security, building and maintaining schools, maintaining urban roads, building and maintaining markets, removing household waste, and regulating abattoirs and public water taps are all within their jurisdiction. In addition, their elected mayors have often become very proactive, using, 'as best they can, their networks of personal friends and supporters, as well as the bureaucracy and the party in power to mobilize support. They also attempt to obtain additional resources for their new responsibilities from foreign embassies and international NGOs'. Partly as a result,' '[t]oday, at the local level, the people speak first to the commune, thus pushing aside the role of the central administration to the non-communalized [i.e. rural] parts of the country'.[53]

Decentralization in Anglophone countries

In English-speaking African countries, the centralist legacy of the colonial period was more ambiguous. Historically, the United Kingdom has placed more emphasis than has France on democratically elected local councils for the administration and finance of a very wide range of local services. Towards the end of the colonial period, there was a strong thrust to introduce an 'efficient and democratic system of local government' all over English-speaking Africa. By the 1960s, local councils proved unable to cope with burgeoning demands for improved education, health, and other local services. These shortcomings were particularly acute in the large, rapidly growing cities. And their inability to raise financing, in conjunction with central government restrictions on transfers, meant that their performance fell far short of their responsibilities. Partly as a result of both political and financial factors, in most English-speaking countries the political autonomy and fiscal resource base of municipal governments was progressively restricted during the 1960s and 1970s. Important exceptions were Nigeria, where for complex political reasons, military governments were favourable to local governments; and Zimbabwe which (after independence in 1980) opted to support local government as a major element in its development strategy.

A number of significant decentralization schemes were introduced during the 1970s, beginning with the exercise undertaken by President Nyerere in Tanzania in 1972, followed by the Nigerian initiative begun by the military regime in 1975 and continued through the return to civilian rule in 1979, and finalized by the sweeping introduction in Sudan of regional governments in both the south (in 1972), and in the north (in 1980).[54] The Tanzanian initiative, as many commentators observed, was little more than the deconcentration of central government functionaries to the regional and district level, where democratically elected local councils were abolished, to be replaced by committees dominated by officials. As for the Sudanese initiative, there was little commitment from central officials to work at the regional level, and ultimately conflicts between the North and the South prevented a decentralized system from functioning. The Nigerian reforms resulted in the 1976 Local Government Act, which established a uniform pattern of local government in the whole of the country. Elections followed for local councillors at the end of 1976, and by the end of the military regime, there were some 299 local governments established all over Nigeria. What distinguished this reform was 'the formal and unequivocal recognition of local government as constituting a distinct level of government with defined boundaries, clearly stated functions and provisions for ensuring adequate human and financial resources'.[55] The Revenue Allocation Act of 1981 guaranteed that established local governments were to receive 10 per cent of the funds which the states received from the federal government, even though this requirement was honoured more in the breach than the observance. Nigerian local government has gone through many difficulties since the 1970s, but the reforms themselves are generally considered positive, 'even though the gains have been complicated by other factors'.[56]

If the decentralization reforms of the 1970s were initiated by highly centralized governments, with little involvement of local communities and other groups in civil society, the reforms of the 1980s and 1990s have involved more give and take between government and other forces in the wider society. That this relationship has involved a struggle is evident in the case of Nairobi, the capital of Kenya.[57] With a population of 1,346,000 in 1989, Nairobi is by far the largest, and most economically important centre in the country. Since the 1920s the city was governed by an elected municipal council and mayor. In March, 1983, the Minister for Local Government called a press conference to announce that the central government had suspended all meetings of the Nairobi City Council, and that it further had decided 'to exclude indefinitely with immediate effect the mayor, the deputy mayor and all councillors from council premises'. Several weeks later, citing 'gross mismanagement of council funds and poor services to the residents', the minister placed Nairobi's approximately 17,000 municipal employees and all buildings and services under the direct control of a commission, which he himself appointed. Although the original intention of the commission had been to 'clean up' the council and reestablish elected local government, the central government passed various motions through the National Assembly extending the life of the commission until both national and local elections were held in December 1992. There was little evidence that the Commission was any more effective in managing the city's services than was the City Council before it. By 1991 a lengthy article in *The Weekly Review* (not considered a 'sensationalist' publication) entitled 'Filthy, Ailing City in the Sun' concluded:

Since central government took over the running of the city through appointed officials in 1983, services in Nairobi have grown unspeakably bad, with desperate changes from one administration to the next only making the situation worse. The inevitable conclusion is that the underlying problems of the city have never

ever been tackled, while a bloated and insensitive bureaucracy with around 19,000 employees consuming more than KShs. 70 million a month in wages [about $2.9 million] sits comfortably in place. Drastic action is clearly required before the corruption, incompetence and irresponsibility that have slowly eaten up City Hall lead to the final disintegration of the city.[58]

Kenya's first multiparty elections, held in December 1992, ushered in a new chapter in the turbulent history of Nairobi—and of urban local governance in Kenya. One of the major new parties specifically called in its election manifesto for the granting of increased autonomy to local government. As has always been the case in Kenya, local and national elections were held at the same time. But whereas the governing party, KANU, had always captured both levels of seats in the urban wards and constituencies in the past, in this election the opposition parties won most of the parliamentary seats in the major urban areas, and took control of twenty-three of the twenty-six municipal councils, including Nairobi. The new mayor of Nairobi (elected by the sitting councillors) was himself not a member of the governing party of the country. Political differences between the central government and the newly elected municipal councils soon came to the surface, with the Minister of Local Government issuing a series of directives that curtailed the powers of the mayors. For the government, these councils were a political force to be reckoned with; but for the emerging middle class, the councils were a vehicle by which to achieve a greater measure of local autonomy.

Conclusions

By the 1990s, issues of urban governance in Africa were being seriously considered in the development agenda, both by many national governments, but increasingly by the multilateral and bilateral assistance agencies that supported development projects across the continent. Three major factors were at play in this process. In the first place, as African governments were obliged to accept structural adjustment 'packages' involving cuts in the public service and more limited regulatory powers for the central government, local services could only be assured through some kind of coalition between local communities and their local governments. The logic of decentralization was reinforced by the argument that the most likely source of future funding for infrastructure and services would have to come from local, rather than national government. A second factor was undoubtedly the great interest of the donors—particularly the French government, USAID, and the World Bank—in decentralization as a strategy of development. These agencies came to a new awareness of the economic importance of urban development, just as the problems of governing African cities demonstrated that the institutional aspects of development were the most recondite. Finally, a slow process of democratization and the emergence of self-conscious groups in civil society could also be discerned. The most spectacular example of this trend was South Africa, which gained a democratic government in 1994 following a major struggle in which 'civic' organizations in the black urban townships played a major role. But elsewhere in Africa, as the formerly 'statist'

and highly centralized governments grew weaker under the twin assaults of globalization and structural adjustment, local communities and interest groups in the cities began to assert themselves both in the democratic election process, and in the day to day management of their communities.

5.4 Financing Local Services within Countries[59]

Introduction: The importance of local government finance

Three basic financial problems face local governments around the world, but especially in the South and among transitional countries:

- Local governments do not have enough money to carry out the functions assigned to them.

- Some local governments have a lot more money than others.

- Matters are getting worse rather than better because local revenues are not adequately responsive to changing needs.

Local government finance is important for several reasons. First, in countries as diverse as the Republic of Korea and Denmark, local governments already mobilize significant resources; in both these countries, in the late 1980s, local government revenue represented 31 percent of total government revenue (see Table 5.2). Locally generated resources may also be becoming more important; in many more countries, both North and South, hard-pressed national governments are increasingly shifting functions to local governments in the expectation that additional local resources can be mobilized to pay for them. Local expenditures and local revenues are thus likely to constitute an increasingly important component of total public sector activity.

A second reason why local government finance is particularly important is that, regardless of how large local governments may be, in most countries they have an important role in the provision and utilization of local public infrastructure and public services. These include both those that are essential to good quality housing and living conditions and those that contribute much to economic development. How local services are financed may have significant implications for national development patterns as well as for the political accountability and administrative efficiency of local government institutions themselves. However, as Table 5.2 shows, many local services, in many countries, are still financed to a considerable extent by transfers from central (or state) governments. Others are provided directly by central or regional agencies or by various

TABLE 5.2 The importance of local finance

Country	Year	Expenditure Ratio	Revenue Ratio	Local Autonomy Ratio	Local Control Ratio
Korea, Republic of	1987	33	31	99	33
Zimbabwe	1986	22	17	58	12
Algeria*	1986	14	16	101	14
Bangladesh	1987	12	8	39	5
South Africa*	1988	10	10	79	8
Chile	1988	8	6	61	5
Brazil*	1989	7	1	33	2
Thailand	1990	7	4	75	5
Philippines	1988	6	7	119	6
Morocco	1987	6	8	108	6
Paraguay	1989	4	3	88	4
Kenya	1989	4	7	134	4
Pakistan*	1987	4	6	100	4
Costa Rica	1988	3	3	123	3
Ghana	1988	2	2	71	1
Cote d'Ivoire	1985	2	2	115	2
Countries in 'the South'		9	9	88	7
Poland	1988	27	23	78	21
Czechoslovakia	1990	26	19	61	16
Hungary	1990	19	11	53	10
Romania	1989	9	8	103	9
Transition Countries		20	15	74	14
Denmark	1988	45	31	58	26
Finland	1989	41	29	63	26
Sweden	1989	37	30	78	29
Norway	1990	31	21	59	18
U.K.	1989	26	16	55	14
Ireland	1989	23	10	33	8
Netherlands	1990	23	5	16	4
Iceland	1986	23	26	99	23
Switzerland*	1984	22	22	87	19
USA*	1989	21	16	65	14
France	1988	18	12	63	11
Germany*	1988	17	14	73	12
Austria*	1990	16	17	89	14
Canada*	1989	16	11	53	8
Luxembourg	1988	15	7	42	6
Spain*	1988	13	10	62	8
Belgium	1987	12	6	41	5
Australia*	1990	5	5	83	4
Western Europe, North America, Australia		22	16	62	14

Notes: *In addition, there is another significant level of subnational government.

The figures shown for countries in the South, transition countries, and Western Europe, North America and Australia are unweighted averages.

Expenditure ratio is local government expenditure as percentage of total government expenditure.
Revenue ratio is local government revenue as percentage of total government revenue.
Autonomy ratio is local government revenue as percentage of local government expenditure.
Control ratio is local government revenue as percentage of total government expenditure.

Source: Bird, Richard M., *Financing Local Services: Patterns, Problems and Possibilities*, Background Paper for the Global Report, 1995.

groupings of local governments. Still others are provided by a wide variety of non-governmental organizations at the community level or by private firms; Box 5.2 shows the diverse range of government, mixed private-public and private institutions that may provide local services. The optimal role and structure of local government finance for any country depends in part upon the actual and potential role of different actors or institutions in providing local public services.

Patterns of local government finance

The structure of local government finance in any country is invariably unique, reflecting the

---

BOX 5.2
Alternative Ways to Provide Local Public Services

Public Sector Provision:
1. Central Government:
   (a) Department
   (b) Decentralized Agency
   (c) Enterprise
2. Regional Government:
   (a) Department
   (b) Decentralized Agency
   (c) Enterprise
3. Local Government:
   (a) Department
   (b) Decentralized Agency
   (c) Enterprise
4. Central-Regional Arrangement
5. Central-Local Arrangement
6. Central-Regional-Local Arrangement
7. Regional-Local Arrangement
8. Association of Local Governments
9. Special-Purpose Local Authority:
   (a) Encompassing more than one local government
   (b) Coterminous with a local government
   (c) Covering less area than a local government

Mixed Public-Private Provision
10. BOT or BOO (Build-Operate-Transfer or Build-Own-Operate) Arrangements
11. Other forms of public-private 'partnerships'
12. Development charges, exactions, and similar schemes

Private Provision
13. Compulsory provision by developers
14. Compulsory provision by individuals:
   (a) Vouchers
   (b) Self-financed
15. Voluntary provision:
   (a) Formal Arrangements
   (b) Informal Arrangements
16. Provision by Non-governmental Organizations (churches, enterprises)

Even this extensive list is less than complete. Many of the arrangements listed have a number of possible variants, and of course there are various possible combinations of all these organizational structures. Moreover, different structures might apply for e.g. policy-making, regulation, financing, production (delivery of services) and so on.

---

complex of historical and political factors that define governmental institutions in that country. Many countries have more than one level of local government, and a few countries, especially some of the larger ones, also have an important intermediate (state or regional) level of government that has a larger role in public finance than the municipal and local level (see Box 5.3). Although the focus of this section is on local government, meaningful comparisons of purely 'local' governments across countries are difficult because of the different governmental structures in different countries, the different functions and finances of various jurisdictional levels, and the deficiencies of available data. The term 'subnational' will be used to refer to all levels of government below the national or central level, while the term 'local' excludes the intermediate or regional governments, particularly those in federal states.

Despite this diversity, among certain broad patterns that recur in many countries, three are particularly important. The first is that local governments almost invariably have inadequate 'own resources' to finance the expenditure functions with which they are charged; thus, they are dependent upon transfers from higher levels of government. This is sometimes called the problem of 'vertical imbalance'. The second is that not all local governments are equal. In even the smallest and most homogeneous countries, there are big cities and small cities, heavily urbanized municipalities and rural municipalities, rich areas and poor ones. The resulting unevenness in access to local public resources gives rise to what is known as 'horizontal imbalance'. The third is that few countries permit local governments to levy taxes that are both economically sensible and capable of yielding enough in revenue to meet expanding local needs.

The data needed to establish the importance of local finance within total public finance is surprisingly hard to find—and this perhaps accounts for the fact that different studies give rather different answers. In one study covering twenty-one countries in the South, local governments accounted for between 6 and 50 per cent of total government spending, with a median share of 23 per cent.[61] In eight transitional countries, the share of subnational governments similarly ranged from 11 to 53 per cent of total expenditure with an unweighted average share of 26 per cent.[62] In ten OECD countries, local expenditure ranged from 12 to 45 per cent of total expenditure, with an average share of 21 per cent.[63] Table 5.2 shows that the average share of local government expenditure (the expenditure ratio) is 22 per cent for a broader sample of eighteen wealthy countries, and 20 per cent for a smaller sample of four transitional countries. On the other hand, the average share for the sixteen countries from

BOX 5.3
The special case of federalism

Many countries have not one but two (or more) subnational levels of government. Sometimes the intermediate (state or provincial) level has a more important role in public finance than the municipal or local level, as in the case of Canada's provincial governments; sometimes it is less important, as with Colombia's departmental governments. Countries in which the intermediate level of government is more important are often countries that are at least nominally 'federal', such as Canada, Germany, India, Papua New Guinea, and Nigeria. In such countries, most transfers from the central government go at least in the first instance to the states, and the states often have a tutelary or supervisory role with respect to the municipalities. The latter feature means that the degree of autonomy of local governments—which may themselves have two or three tiers—may vary significantly from state to state in such countries.

As wide a range of institutional structures and relations is found within federal as within unitary countries. Indeed, the difference between a 'tight' federation such as Malaysia or Germany and most unitary countries is probably less than that between such federations and 'looser' federations such as India and Canada, in which state governments have more power to act independently with respect to expenditure and taxing patterns. The constitutional label matters less than the reality of how the intergovernmental relations that constitute the essence of the public sector in all countries work out in practice. If, as is usually the case, especially in the South, the central government basically confines the range of action of subnational governments to a very limited domain, those governments may for most purposes be considered to be more agents of the central government—or, in some federal countries, of state governments—than independent actors. On the other hand, where there are real geographic or ethnic differences within a country, a certain degree of local 'autonomy' often emerges in practice even if the constitutional structure is formally unitary. In particular, in most countries central governments must work with the local governments they have, in the sense that even if the central government is ultimately responsible for the size, structure, and functioning of local governments, these characteristics can ordinarily be altered only in an incremental fashion. Since the essence of the federal finance problem is how to adjust intergovernmental fiscal transfers to achieve tolerable results in the face of what is generally a clearly nonoptimal assignment of functions and finances, the intergovernmental problem in every country is in this sense 'federal' to some extent. It is only in the few 'true' federations that such a constraint is long-term in nature, however. In other countries, a closer approach to an efficient public sector may in principle be attained over time by judicious and feasible restructuring of the functions and finances assigned to each level of government. For simplicity, the case of federal states in which the intermediate level of government has a special degree of policy autonomy is not discussed further here.[60]

Africa, Asia and Latin America included in this Table is only 9 per cent, although it is much higher in a few countries (notably Republic of Korea and Zimbabwe).

In many more countries local governments are important for the wide variety of important services they deliver. For example, local public utilities are responsible for such essential services as water supply, sewerage, electric power, public transit, and sometimes also for telecommunications.[64] Local governments (and related agencies) also provide local streets and a variety of related services including refuse removal and disposal, street lighting, and street cleaning. In addition, local governments in most countries are responsible for providing police and fire protection, and in some countries they also have an important role in providing such social services as primary education, health care, and social assistance. In the transition countries, local governments are also largely responsible for housing and heating. Other local activities found in different countries include the provision of markets and slaughter houses, tourist services, and sports and cultural facilities, including parks.

In most countries in Africa, Asia and Latin America, the absolute level of resources available to local governments is seldom adequate to provide even the most minimal level of many of the services with which they are charged. In 1991, for example, local governments in the United States spent, on average, over $US2,000 per capita (see Table 5.3), and state and local governments combined spent about $3,000.[65] In contrast, in the early 1980s, although some Korean cities spent as much as $US200 per capita, other cities such as Dhaka in Bangladesh spent less than $US2 per capita.[66] A very similar picture is shown for the countries contained in Table 5.3. If anything, this estimate seems on the low side for such low-income countries as Malawi and Paraguay. What is also notable in Table 5.3 is the very low level of local capital expenditures per person for local governments in most countries.

Another source of information about the resources available to local governments comes from the Housing Indicators Programme. Figure

TABLE 5.3 Local government finance, selected countries and years (US$ per capita)

Country	Year	Population (millions)	GDP, 1991 ($US per cap)	Local Government Expenditures ($US per capita)	Local Capital Expenditures ($US per capita)
Brazil	1991	153.3	2,940	153	36
Chile	1988	12.8	2,160	47	13
Colombia	1986	29.2	1,260	14	3
Iran	1989	54.2	2,170	7	2
Israel	1990	4.7	11,950	78	16
Kenya	1990	24.9	340	5	1
Malawi	1984	6.8	230	3	1
Paraguay	1989	4.2	1,270	4	2
South Africa	1990*	35.3	2,560	120	38
Thailand	1992*	57.8	1,570	24	11
Zimbabwe	1986	8.4	650	64	8
U.S.A.	1991	252.7	22,240	2054	255

Notes: *Preliminary.

Sources: GDP per capita from World Bank, *World Development Report 1993*, 238–9; Oxford University Press, Oxford and New York, 1993. Other data from country tables in International Monetary Fund, *Government Finance Statistics Yearbook 1993*. Washington DC, 1993—population and exchange rate for year indicated from summary table, and local government data from Table L.

5.1 maps the expenditure per person by government agencies on water supply, sanitation, garbage collection and other forms of infrastructure and services for the cities for which there was data against the per capita income of the country. While in general, infrastructure expenditures per person in the cities are higher, the larger the per capita income of the country, the range of per capita expenditures for cities in countries with comparable levels of per capita income is very considerable. This can be seen in Figure 5.1 in the different levels of infrastructure expenditure in Caracas, Athens and Seoul, although each was the national capital and largest city in nations with comparable levels of per capita income in 1991. Major differences are also noticeable between the capitals of the more prosperous European countries.[67]

Inadequate 'own-source' revenues

However much local governments spend in different countries, the revenues under their direct control are invariably less. In the United States, for example, only 65 per cent of local expenditure was financed out of local revenue in 1989 (see Table 5.2). The comparable unweighted average figure for eighteen countries in West Europe, North America and Australia was 62 per cent, but the range was between a low of 16 per cent in the Netherlands and a high of 87 per cent in Switzerland.

In seven transitional countries, if shared taxes are counted as local revenues, the average (for subnational governments) was 63 per cent, ranging between a low of 15 per cent in the Czech Republic and a high of 95 per cent in Russia.[68] If shared taxes are instead considered to constitute revenues of the central government (see Box 5.4), the average increases to 74 per cent for the four transitional countries included in Table 5.2.

The variation found within countries in the South is similar. A study of eighteen such countries found that own-source revenue provided as little as 30 per cent of total local revenue in some countries but over 90 per cent in others.[73] A similar pattern is shown for the sixteen countries in Table 5.2. In some instances, local revenues even exceed local expenditures, while in others local

FIGURE 5.1
Infrastructure expenditure per person (1990) (selected cities)

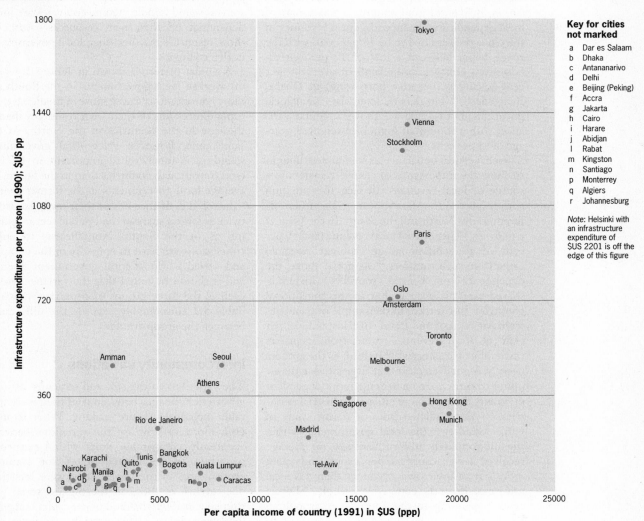

BOX 5.4
Local income taxes

Strictly speaking, a 'local' tax might be defined as one that is (1) assessed by local governments, (2) at rates determined by local governments, (3) collected by local governments, and (4) with its proceeds accruing to local governments. In many countries, few taxes have all these characteristics.

In Hungary, for example, part of the income tax accrues to local governments, but the rates of the tax are set by the central government, which also assesses and collects the tax.[69] The result is the same as if the central government simply allocated a grant to local governments in proportion to the amount of national income tax collected locally. In contrast, in Canada, where the central government similarly assesses and collects the income tax, the provinces can set different rates and therefore affect through their own actions the amount of revenue accruing to them. (On the other hand, Canadian local governments cannot levy income taxes of any description.) Unlike the Hungarian case, the Canadian provincial income tax is usually considered to be a provincial 'own-source' revenue. Somewhat similar systems exist in the five Nordic countries (Denmark, Finland, Iceland, Norway, and Sweden), where local governments can set their own tax rates on the same tax base as the national income tax and where the local taxes are collected by the national government and remitted to the taxing local authorities. Other Northern countries with significant subnational—state or local or both—income taxes of various sorts include Belgium, France, Japan, Germany, and Switzerland[70] (see Table 5.4). Although local income taxes have occasionally been levied in a few African cities,[71] they are not common in Africa, Asia or Latin America. In contrast, in many transitional economies, subnational governments have been assigned significant shares of income tax revenues. In Russia, for example, they receive all of personal income tax revenues, in Bulgaria, 50 per cent, in Poland, 30 per cent, and in Hungary (as noted above), 25 per cent.[72] Since in none of these countries, however, do local governments have any freedom in establishing the tax rate, the resulting distribution of revenues seems better considered as a combination of a national tax and a related intergovernmental fiscal transfer based on locally-collected national tax revenues rather than as a really 'local' source of revenue. If local governments are not politically responsible for the revenues they receive, it seems to stretch reality unduly to consider such revenues as local taxes. The principal reason local governments have seldom been given access to income taxes in the North is because of the reliance of central governments on this source of revenue. In the South, of course, even central governments have trouble collecting much from the income tax and tend to rely more heavily on taxes such as the value-added tax which are inherently less suitable for local government use.

revenues are inadequate to finance even the current spending of local governments. In their survey, Bahl and Linn found the median share of local expenditures financed by local revenues in the cities they studied to be 78 per cent, with the range being between a low of 30 per cent in Kingston, Jamaica, and a high of over 100 per cent (owing to negative borrowing) in Dhaka, Bangladesh.[74] The data for later years for all local governments in Table 5.2 shows a similar variance, with a somewhat higher unweighted average of 88 per cent.

Such 'vertical imbalance' is sometimes thought to show the importance of central transfers as a source of local revenues. In fact, the situation with respect to transfers appears to be rather different in the North and the South. In the OECD countries, 37 per cent of local revenue (and 39 per cent of all subnational government revenue) came from such transfers.[75] As noted above, the dependence on central transfers (including shared taxes) is even higher in the transitional countries. In contrast, in the sample of countries from Africa, Asia and Latin America, only 22 per cent of local revenues came from transfers (including shared taxes).[76] Indeed, as the authors note, 'it is not even clear that large cities in developing countries are on average more dependent on grants than are large cities in industrial countries.'[77] Along related lines, a recent study of Chile found that the local governments within the metropolitan area of Santiago on average received fewer transfers per capita and spent more out of their own resources than did local governments in the country as a whole.[78] Direct central spending in the Santiago metropolitan area was also much lower—less than half in per capita terms—than the national average. In appears that some local governments in at least some low and middle income countries are more dependent on their own resources—scarce as those resources may be—than local governments in rich countries.

A similar pattern is shown in Table 5.2, where on average local governments in the South are more 'autonomous' in the sense of financing their expenditures out of their own resources than is the case in the countries in the North. At the same time, however, since local government spending is much more important in OECD (and transitional) countries than in the South, on average local governments in the former groups 'control' (i.e. finance out of their own resources) twice as large a share of total public sector spending as in the South. Nonetheless, sweeping conclusions are hard to come by in the complex and varied world of local government finance, and it should be noted that the variance within each of the three groups of countries shown in Table 5.2 considerably exceeds the differences between the group averages.

Intercommunity variations

The variations in the size and structure of local government finance between countries at comparable income levels are striking. What is often even more striking are the variations between apparently comparable units within particular countries. In the United States, for example, expenditures in the lowest state were less than one-seventh of those in the highest state.[79] In Romania in 1992, the ratio of per capita budgeted local expenditures in the lowest district (judet) was a quarter that in the highest.[80] In Chile, in 1990, the ratio of per capita municipal revenues in the lowest 'zone' was 44 per cent of that in the highest[81] while in Indonesia in 1990/1, it was only 7 per cent.[82] In the case of Chile, the variations within the metropolitan area were equally marked, with the city of Santiago receiving less than six per cent of its revenues from Chile's local 'equalization' fund (designed to even out the resources available to local governments to some extent), and other municipalities receiving 60 per cent. Similar variations are likely to exist in other countries.

A striking feature in almost every country is the difference between big cities and other local governments. In Colombia in the late 1970s, for example, per capita tax revenues were ten times higher in the capital, Bogota, than in the many small rural municipalities.[83] In Canada in the same period, the ratio of per capita local revenues among provinces was almost the same, with the more urbanized areas having ten times the 'own-source' per capita revenues of the more rural areas.[84] Such variation reflects two different factors in most countries: big cities are richer, and their governments tend to carry out a wider range of functions.

Direct comparisons across countries among local governments are difficult to make, but inter-provincial variations similar to those in Canada have been observed in many other countries, both in the North and in the South. A recent example from India shows this but such variations may reflect not only differences in wealth but different policy choices.[85] Kerala and Tamil Nadu, for example, are two states in India at more or less the same income levels; but Kerala has chosen to levy higher taxes and to spend much more on education and health in both relative and absolute terms (see Box 5.5).

The structure of local revenues

As the example just mentioned illustrates, local choices can and do make a difference. On the whole, however, the patterns of local finance sketched above for the most part result from conscious choices made by the central governments in the various countries.

The size and pattern of local government taxation varies greatly from country to country; Table 5.4 shows this for OECD countries. Income taxes are the most important source of local tax revenue in all of the ten countries where local taxes account for more than 10 per cent of total taxes. However, only in one of these countries (Sweden) are income taxes the sole important local tax. In contrast, there are four countries in which property taxes are the only significant local tax. Consumption taxes (often local 'business' taxes of various sorts rather than conventional

---

BOX 5.5
Local choices make a difference

Even when the incentives facing local government are perverse, a number of examples around the world show that local policies can make a real difference. A recent comparison of the provision of education in China and India, for example, found China far ahead in most respects. But one state in India, Kerala, with universal literacy among adolescent males and females and near-universal literacy among the adult population came out better than any province in China. In the words of the study: 'This remarkable achievement reflects more than a hundred years of creative interaction between state commitment to, and public demand for, the widespread provision of public education.'[86] Another study of state finance and poverty alleviation in India similarly found that Kerala was much more successful in this field than either its income level or its state revenues would suggest.[87] Similar 'anomalies' exist in many countries. In Brazil, for example, a few cities are well run and efficiently provided with services; others, superficially similar in character and resources, are poorly run and equipped. In Colombia, some departments (regional governments) provide superior health services than others with similar resources. Almost everywhere, some local governments in at least some areas do much better than others. The reason may be because of historical circumstance: for one reason or another they started to do something well some time ago, and they continue to do so. Or it may be because of a caring and charismatic local leader or some other chance circumstance. Whatever the cause, such experiences emphasize two important points: (1) even in the perverse situations in which many local governments are placed by inappropriate central policies, there is usually some scope for local initiative; and (2) such local initiative can make a real difference in the lives of local people. The aim of effective decentralization is to make it easier for such 'good examples' to occur and to be emulated elsewhere.

---

sales taxes) account for more than 10 per cent of local tax revenue in nine countries, property taxes in thirteen countries, and income taxes in fifteen countries. Only a few countries have a 'balanced' local revenue structure in the sense of not being dominated by just one tax. Nine OECD countries may be categorized as income-tax countries and five (all predominantly English-speaking) as property-tax countries in the sense that over 75 per cent of their local tax revenue comes from the source indicated.

The structure of local revenues in the OECD countries suggests several tentative conclusions:

1. OECD countries may clearly exercise considerable discretion in deciding how large a role their local governments play, the extent to which local activities are financed from local revenues, and the types of taxes levied by local governments. There is no reason to think this is any less true in other countries.

2. Countries influenced by British traditions are those that rely most heavily on taxes on real

TABLE 5.4 The pattern of local taxation in the OECD, 1988

Country	Local taxes		As %age of local taxes		
	As % of total taxes	As % of local revenues	Income	Sales	Property
Australia	3.3	43.2*	0.0	0.0	99.6
Austria	10.8	52.7*	50.6	33.2	9.2
Belgium	5.0	37.4*	76.8	0.0	0.0
Canada	9.1	39.1	0.0	0.3	84.5
Denmark	30.0	49.6	92.1	0.1	7.8
Finland	25.6	45.0*	99.1	0.0	0.9
France	8.9	44.3	14.7	4.9	34.2
Germany	8.7	36.7	81.9	0.3	17.1
Greece	9.9	n.a.	0.0	33.2	0.0
Ireland	2.2	6.2*	0.0	0.0	100.0
Italy	1.8	3.6	41.7	22.3	0.0
Japan	25.9	n.a.	61.0	11.5	22.4
Luxembourg	11.9	55.4*	80.5	15.1	3.7
Netherlands	2.2	5.9	0.0	1.3	73.5
New Zealand	5.5	n.a.	0.0	1.4	92.4
Norway	20.9	n.a.	88.9	0.0	7.6
Portugal	5.4	n.a.	43.6	29.4	23.7
Spain	11.3	57.3*	31.7	29.6	27.1
Sweden	27.6	61.1*	99.6	0.4	0.0
Switzerland	15.8	n.a.	86.3	0.4	13.3
Turkey	10.1	n.a.	41.0	37.4	3.4
United Kingdom	10.5	32.6*	0.0	0.0	100.0
United States	12.2	40.0*	6.0	15.3	74.2

Notes: Percentage shares of Local Taxes will not add to 100% owing to other taxes. *1987 data.

Source: Calculated from OECD Revenue Statistics for OECD Countries, 1965–89, Organization for Economic Cooperation and Development, Paris, 1990.

property and least heavily on income taxes. This 'British' influence is also clear in countries formerly colonized by Britain in areas such as the Caribbean and Africa.[88]

3. Since no country seems able to raise much more than 10 per cent of total taxes from property taxes, local tax revenues are likely to exceed this proportion only when local governments have access to either sales or income taxes. As Table 5.4 suggests, property-tax countries tend to have either less important local governments (Ireland, Australia) or local governments that are more dependent on intergovernmental transfers (Canada, US, UK). In these five countries, local taxes on average constituted only 32 per cent of local revenues (including grants), compared to an average of 48 per cent for the six income-tax countries for which this information is available (see Table 5.4).

4. Although user charges have been becoming more important in some countries in recent years—for example, in Canada they accounted for 12 per cent of local revenue in 1990 compared to only 7 per cent in 1975[89]—in no country, North or South do they come close to dominating local finance. Nor, as a rule, are the charges imposed those that economic theory[90] would suggest. The potential for user charges as a means of financing local government remains more potential than reality.

Although the data are even less tractable for Africa, Asia and Latin America, similar variations are apparent within this heterogeneous group of countries. Although a large variety of local taxes are levied in different countries, the property tax is both the most common and often the most important source of local revenue. The median share of property-tax revenues in local tax revenues in the thirty-seven cities in twenty-one countries covered in the Bahl and Linn study was 42 per cent, with a marked decline in this share being apparent over the 15 years or so covered in this study.[91]

The only other major source of 'own' revenue in a number of countries is some form of business tax such as the octroi (tax on goods entering cities) in India and Pakistan and the industry and commerce tax or patente in a number of countries of Latin America and Africa. Such taxes have been much more successful than property taxes in providing revenues that expand with economic activity and expenditure needs. Unfortunately, most local business taxes are both economically distorting and to some extent conducive to political irresponsibility, owing to the ease with which they lend themselves to 'exporting' part of the tax burden to non-residents.[92]

Apart from taxes, which accounted for about half of local revenues, the only other significant source of local financing in most countries in Africa, Asia and Latin America are user charges levied by 'self-financing' public utilities, again with wide variations from country to country, depending upon the extent to which such utilities are under the control of local governments and upon the pricing policies that are adopted. In a few countries such as Colombia and the Republic of Korea—as also in some countries in the North such as the United States—significant use is also made of 'benefit-related' charges in financing urban infrastructure, as discussed later.

Trends and patterns in local government own revenues are important. As Bahl and Linn conclude with respect to their sample of cities in the South:

it would appear that changes in locally raised resources determine the ability of an urban government to expand its services. Where locally raised revenues fare badly, urban government expenditure suffers; where they do well, urban expenditure thrives.[93]

The generally low 'control' ratios for Southern countries shown in Table 5.2 suggest that, viewed from this perspective, local government expenditure is probably 'thriving' in very few countries.

If a central government wishes local governments to play an active and expanding role in the provision of public services, it must both provide them access to an adequate revenue source (such as the income tax or, less desirably owing to the possibility of tax export, some form of local sales or business tax) and permit and encourage them (e.g. through the design of intergovernmental fiscal transfers, as discussed below) to make efficient use of the resources thus provided. Essentially for this reason, some transitional countries that have devolved significant expenditure responsibilities to local governments have been urged to give more power to local governments to levy supplementary local surcharges on the national income tax (see Box 5.4). Taxes on real property, although a useful and appropriate source of local revenues, are unlikely to be able to provide sufficient revenue in the near future in such countries. Even countries that have devoted considerable effort and attention to improving property tax valuation and collections, such as Colombia[94] have seldom managed to do more than to maintain the relative importance of this tax (see Box 5.6).

The role of the central government

One reason for concern about the possible effects of decentralizing public sector activities is the poor quality of local government administration in many countries. To a considerable extent each country gets the local government that those in power want. Local government officials, like central government officials, respond to the incentives with which they are faced. If those incentives discourage initiative and reward inefficiency and even corruption, then it is not surprising to find corrupt and inefficient local governments. The answer to this problem is obviously to alter the incentive structure to make

it possible and attractive for honest, well-trained people to make a career in local government. Similarly, one answer to local governments that make 'wrong' decisions is to provide an incentive structure that leads them, in their own interests, to make the 'right' decisions, that is, decisions that are both economically efficient and politically acceptable.

It is, as always, easier to state such propositions in general than it is to demonstrate concretely how they may be implemented in particular circumstances. None the less, as a recent World Bank study notes, the institutional settings within which many local governments in Africa, Asia and Latin America must work may be categorized into three groups: (1) the over-controlled local public sector, (2) the under-controlled local public sector, and (3) the perversely regulated local public sector.[99] The first of these categories is perhaps the most commonly observed: central governments control all the details of local government—who they hire, what salaries they pay, even where the buses run . . . —and leave no freedom of action for local initiative. In such countries, local citizens tend to look to the national government to fix potholes on their street—and they are generally right to do so.

While less common, the opposite ill of 'under-control' is beginning to emerge in a number of countries as a result of inappropriate decentralization strategies. For example, a number of transitional countries in eastern and central Europe have given their local governments access to a substantial share of centrally raised revenues as well as responsibility for important public service

---

Local property taxes

Property tax is the most widespread form of local taxation. Unfortunately, experience suggests that such taxes are not easy to administer, particularly in countries where inflation is endemic (e.g. Brazil), and that they are never politically popular owing to their visibility and to certain inherent administrative difficulties. Even in the most sophisticated countries, local property taxes can seldom yield enough to finance local services. As noted elsewhere, no country in the North which depends significantly upon property taxes for local fiscal resources has a local government sector that accounts for more than 10 per cent of total public spending.[95] Similarly, property taxes seldom account for more than 20 per cent of local current revenues—or less than 1 per cent of total public spending—in countries in the South. Moreover, despite substantial efforts in some countries and considerable foreign assistance, these figures have not changed.[96]

The property tax, it appears, may be a useful, even a necessary, source of local revenue, but it is most unlikely to provide sufficient resources to finance a significant expansion of local public services in any country. Indeed, countries have often been hard-pressed even to maintain the present low relative importance of property tax revenues in the face of varying price levels and political difficulties. A recent study concludes that a number of conditions must be satisfied for local property taxes to play a more important role in financing local activities.[97] The political costs of reliance on the property tax are so high that no government with access to 'cheaper' sources of finance will willingly do so. Intergovernmental transfers which can be spent as local governments wish, like access to taxes on business which can largely be exported, must therefore be curtailed not simply to make property taxes more attractive but, more importantly, to confront local decision-makers with the true economic (and political) costs of their decisions. Even if this essential structural pre-condition is met, a

number of other policy reforms are needed to turn the property tax into a responsive instrument of local fiscal policy. First, and importantly, local governments must be allowed to set their own tax rates; very few central governments give their local governments freedom in this respect. Secondly, the tax base must be maintained adequately; in countries with high inflation, some form of index adjustment is advisable. In other countries, the assessing agency must be provided direct financial incentives to keep the tax base up to date. Finally, a series of procedural reforms is often needed to improve collection efficiency, valuation accuracy, and the coverage of the potential tax base.[98] None of these steps is easy, either politically or, in some instances, in terms of available technical resources. None the less, countries that want to have local governments that are both responsive and responsible must follow this difficult path; there are no short cuts to successful local property taxation.

functions. In most cases, these countries have not yet established an adequate institutional structure to ensure that the central funds are being properly spent in, say, maintaining minimum standards of service in education or health.[100]

Finally, whether over- or under-controlled, local governments in all too many countries receive perverse signals from national governments in a number of ways. In some countries, for example, the amount of national funding received depends upon the size of the local budget deficit—a rather perverse way of encouraging over-spending and poor budget management. In others, national funding is available for infrastructure investment at no cost but there are no funds for operation and maintenance. It pays localities to let existing facilities deteriorate (since they would have to pay maintenance out of their own funds) in order to strengthen the apparent need for new facilities (which the central government will pay for).

The lack of an appropriate central government structure to monitor and support local governments is a common problem in transitional economies and in the South. Among the tasks for which central governments should in principle be responsible is that of monitoring and assessing the finances of subnational governments, both in total and individually. Central authorities need to have a much better understanding of both the existing situation of their local governments and of the likely effects of any proposed changes in local finance than is usually the case.

Financing infrastructure

Local governments, particularly in the larger urban areas of the South in principle have a critical role in providing the basic infrastructure without which modern economic life would not be possible. But how can this infrastructure be financed? The meagre tax resources available to most local governments, especially in the South make it difficult for them to finance costly projects from their own current revenues, so three other approaches to infrastructure finance are often considered. The first possibility is to borrow the money. A second possibility is for users, actual or prospective, to finance the infrastructure. And a third is for the investment to be financed by the central government, with the local government being responsible only for financing the recurrent costs of operation. Each of these approaches has its own difficulties.

When the benefits from infrastructure projects are enjoyed over a period of time, in some instances it may be both fair and efficient to finance such projects in part or whole by borrowing. In any case, borrowing may often be the only practical way to finance large capital projects without large and undesirable fluctuations in local tax rates from year to year.

In most countries, however, local government access to capital markets is limited in practice both because capital markets themselves are poorly developed and because central governments are seldom keen to allow any but very restricted access by local governments. When local borrowing is permitted, it generally requires central approval and is heavily restricted (see Box 5.7). In many cases, local capital finance through borrowing takes place mainly from government-sponsored and financed agencies such as municipal development funds. Unfortunately, the record of such agencies in most countries is poor, with many loans not being repaid and local governments having few incentives to repay.[101]

BOX 5.7
Restrictions on local borrowing

Local government access to capital markets is often restricted. Since central governments generally implicitly guarantee local debt at least to some extent, they understandably wish to restrict and control local governments' access to the treasury and to obviate the possibility of local bankruptcy and hence demands on central funds. In Canada, for example, local government borrowing is severely restricted in a number of ways: the amount of debt, the type of debt instrument, the length of term, the rate of interest, and the use of debt funds, are all, as a rule, strictly controlled. Some provinces require provincial government approval before debt is issued; others require the specific approval of local electors. Sometimes the restrictions are different for different categories of municipalities or for short-term as opposed to long-term debt. But in no case are local governments allowed to borrow as they wish.[102] In Colombia, it was estimated a few years ago that a local government wishing to borrow required the approval of over 100 officials, and that it took, on average, at least a year to achieve the needed approvals.[103] In Hungary, on the other hand, local governments have, by law, unlimited borrowing authority, subject only to the approval of the local assembly: some analysts have expressed concern about the possibility of inexperienced local authorities getting into difficulty by injudicious borrowing and have urged that controls should be instituted to ensure that local access to capital markets does not cause unwanted difficulties.[104]

Some transitional countries in Eastern and Central Europe appear to have given their newly created local governments virtually unlimited authority to borrow from commercial banks or other sources. Unrestrained local access to credit in a situation in which financial markets are not well-regulated and local governments are desperate to expand local economic activity may result in disaster. A better alternative, despite the problems mentioned in the preceding paragraph, might be to develop more appropriate modalities for local government capital financing and borrowing, in the first instance through centrally-controlled sources. Such borrowing, however, should be on close to commercial terms: operating redistributive policy through loan finance is even less appropriate than through matching grants (see below).

An attractive and feasible way to finance local infrastructure in some instances may be through some variant of benefit taxation. In Latin America, for example, street improvements, water supply, and other local public services have been financed by a system of taxation known as 'valorization,' in which the cost of the public works is allocated to affected properties in proportion to the benefits estimated to be conferred by the work in question. Such systems have had varying success in different circumstances.

Studies in Colombia, where valorization has been most used, suggest that critical to its success are careful planning and execution of projects, participation of beneficiaries in both planning and managing projects, an effective collection system, and, in many instances, significant initial financing of the valorization fund from general government revenues (so that works can be begun in a timely fashion, without requiring prospective beneficiaries to put up all the funds in advance). Somewhat similar lessons have emerged from experience with an alternative approach called 'land readjustment' in Korea, in which large land parcels are consolidated and developed by the local government and then part of the property is returned to the original owners in proportion to their ownership, while the balance is sold by the government at market prices in order to recoup development costs. Again, careful planning and fairly sophisticated management are required for success.[105]

These experiences demonstrate that local governments can in some circumstances develop urban infrastructure, in effect by playing the role of a developer. Recently, another way in which beneficiaries may finance local infrastructure has been developed extensively in North America through the use of so-called 'exactions', 'lot levies', 'development charges', and similar systems, under which governments impose levies on would-be property developers in proportion to the estimated costs the development will impose on the urban infrastructure.[106] For example, if new residences are to be erected, and the average cost of adding them to the urban water and sewerage system is $100, the development charge—to be paid up front before the project is authorized—would be $100 (or possibly some discounted equivalent). While such schemes are far from perfect, they have been increasingly used in some countries by financially pressed urban governments to accommodate population expansion without deteriorating service levels, though not always successfully (see Box 5.8).

BOX 5.8
Public-private infrastructure finance

Some countries have turned in recent years to 'mixed' public-private financing of urban infrastructure such as roads and transit systems. Such schemes have potential and deserve careful consideration where they seem appropriate. However, care must be taken to ensure that certain conditions are satisfied if such 'mixed' financing is to produce beneficial results. As in the case of Colombia's valorization or Korea's land adjustment schemes, for example, mixed financing is most likely to prove successful when projects are carefully designed and implemented, and when the responsible public agencies are technically and financially able to meet their responsibilities. Weak governments cannot rely on private agents to overcome their weaknesses and expect to make the best possible bargains for the public they represent. In particular, governments must be careful that they do not end up assuming the 'downside' risk of projects, while allowing their private partners to reap any 'upside' gains. Similarly, care must be exerted to ensure that what occurs is not simply the replacement of public sector borrowing by (often more expensive) private sector borrowing, as some have said has occurred in Canada's 'development charge' financing of projects.[107] Both the economic and the budgetary gains of such arrangements may leave much to be desired. Even sophisticated local governments in wealthy countries have arguably made major errors along these lines in recent years. Inevitably, weaker local governments in countries in the South seem even more prone to such mistakes. As in other spheres, 'privatizing' the design, construction, and operation of urban infrastructure may have many merits: but it is neither a panacea, nor is it free.

Of course, all formal systems of 'user-pay' infrastructure development can operate successfully only in the formal sector. To the extent that housing and urban development takes place primarily outside this sector—for instance in illegal subdivisions or squatter settlements—less formal systems must be used if there is to be any beneficiary-related finance. Chapters 9 and 10 include several examples of less formal systems of infrastructure and service provision that have been successful within illegal or informal settlements, including those that are independent of external agencies and those that have been done in partnership with governments and international agencies.

Earmarking

A pervasive feature of local government finance in the South is the prevalence of earmarking. In Gujarat state in India, for example, a portion of the state entertainment tax is earmarked for urban local governments, and some of this portion is in turn earmarked for investment in capital projects that are co-financed by the municipalities.[108] In many Latin American countries, the earmarking of substantial parts of intergovernmental transfers to localities to local infrastructure investment has characterized much of the recent decentralization: this feature is found in Argentina (for housing) and in Brazil, Colombia, Chile, Ecuador, Guatemala, and Venezuela.[109] Although earmarking is seldom fully effective—there is usually some substitution of transfers for own-source revenues—the result of this practice may be to expand capital spending to some extent, while exacerbating the already difficult problem of funding operating and maintenance expenditures. Presumably motivated by the desire to prevent local governments from 'wasting' transfers on expanding local payrolls, such earmarking may have the paradoxical effect of exacerbating local fiscal problems.

In general, the earmarking that marks local finances in many countries has little to recommend it. It distorts local preferences, exacerbates perverse incentives already found in the local finance system, and sometimes (as in the Gujarat case) connects revenue sources with expenditures in totally illogical ways. Such earmarking has often deservedly received criticism. Yet there is also 'good' earmarking. When there is a strong benefit link between the payment of an earmarked tax (or fee) and the use of the tax to finance additional expenditures, not only is the source of financing eminently sensible in equity and political terms, but it may also serve the important efficiency purpose of signalling local preferences.[110]

Well-designed earmarked benefit taxes are, in effect, surrogate prices. Like prices, when set appropriately such taxes may provide useful guidance both to the more efficient utilization of existing infrastructure and to better investment decisions. In the conditions of many countries in Africa, Asia and Latin America, to establish such prices may seem a counsel of perfection. None the less, the interdependence of pricing and investment decisions, and the potentially important role of earmarking in linking revenues and expenditures, means that this practice deserves careful consideration when it comes to financing local infrastructure.

The recurrent cost problem

Most countries in the South are clearly short of capital. Even when capital projects get built, they are often inadequately maintained. In many countries, local governments, even when (as is usually the case) they have not been involved in the selection or execution of projects, are assumed to be willing and able to look after the subsequent costs required to keep the infrastructure operating and in good condition. This assumption is often mistaken: not only may local governments lack the financial resources or technical capacity to undertake this task, but the

incentives facing them seldom encourage them to do so. These incentives are often perverse in the sense that the less a local government does to maintain its infrastructure the more likely it is to be rescued from above.

Funding recurrent costs through user charges are often criticized for their distributional effects, but these have little validity when the under-financing of recurrent costs means that any redistributive objective sought through the free or subsidized supply of services cannot be achieved.[111] On the other hand, it is not particularly difficult to design pricing schemes that incorporate some relief for low-income users but are none the less economically efficient.[112] As Davey argues:

Services, such as water supply and sewerage, are improved for all if charges fully cover both operating and capital costs. . . . If water supply costs are not fully recovered, for example, low-income groups end up with a few hours of treated water a day, or none at all. If fares remain static (unchanged in Cairo for thirty years, for example), buses simply break down. The public does not really gain from subsidy, least of all the poor. [113]

Infrastructure finance is a serious problem when the resources available for local capital expenditure are as scarce as in many countries in the South (see Table 5.3 and Figure 5.1). Nevertheless, there are usually possibilities for improvement. In some instances, borrowing may offer one means of capital finance; in others, users can be called upon to pay a substantial fraction of the cost of infrastructure, either up front (as in Colombia's valorization system) or after the fact (through appropriately earmarked user charges). Chapter 8 documents how in many cities, the lower income groups who used water vendors were paying many times the price per litre of wealthier groups receiving piped supplies. There is no reason in principle why more cannot be done to harness this potential to provide (usually cheaper and often safer) public water.[114]

The special case of transitional economies

These and other problems of local government finance are now arising in many of the transitional countries of eastern and central Europe, although of course the circumstances of these countries are very different from those of, say, sub-Saharan Africa or India. Decentralization in the transitional countries represents both a reaction from below to the previously tight political control from the centre and an attempt from above to further the privatization of the economy and to relieve the strained fiscal situation of the central government. Although there are many variations in this process from country to country, some important common elements arise from the similar institutional starting point in all countries[115] and the common transitional problems most of them are facing.[116]

Under the previous socialist regime the fiscal system was essentially unitary. Local governments were little more than administrative units or 'departments' of the centre, with no independent fiscal or legislative responsibility. Policy-making was controlled and centralized, and local governments had virtually no independent tax or expenditure powers—part of a larger picture in which the budget itself was seen only as the means to implement the Plan.[117] Now, virtually every transitional country is to varying degrees decentralizing, deconcentrating, and delegating functions and responsibilities.

In most transitional countries, autonomy and control over (often poorly-defined) 'local matters' is increasingly being devolved to local governments (see Table 5.5). The general intent is to free local governments from central control and to let local democracy flourish. It is not clear that the local fiscal systems being established will achieve this goal—at least not without compromising the attainment of such broader reforms in the transitional economies as price-liberalization and privatization.

The traditional analysis of intergovernmental finance examines the fiscal functions of local and central governments in terms of their respective roles and responsibilities for stabilization, income distribution, expenditure provision, the appropriate assignment of tax functions, and the design of a transfer system that provides appropriate incentives. The 'benefit model' of service provision described in Box 5.9 suggests that local governments—whose role in this analysis is essentially that of service provider—should be financed to the extent possible by charging for the services they provide, with local taxes making up the remaining

gap, supplemented as appropriate by transfers and, perhaps, some limited borrowing.[118]

This perspective is also important in the transitional economies. The obvious need for flexibility in today's rapidly changing environment has led many central governments to attempt to preserve some degrees of freedom by continuing with the 'negotiated' tax sharing systems of the past under which local governments received a variable share of central revenues as determined virtually unilaterally by the central government.[120] Such an approach seems unlikely to be acceptable for long in countries in which demands for 'fair' treatment and equalization are strong, and local governments are seeking greater autonomy (see below). New intergovernmental fiscal arrangements are therefore under discussion in virtually every transitional country of Europe—and similar concerns are likely to surface in other countries (e.g. Vietnam) that had adopted similar 'planning' structures.

Discussion of this issue is rendered more difficult in transitional economies by several key features of local government roles, responsibilities and economic functions. First, the important roles of local government as producer and as owner, as well as the complicated and critical relationships between enterprises and local government in most transitional economies, must be taken into account. Local governments have a major role as potential impediments to, or supporters of, privatization. Moreover, the asset stock conferred on them in the decentralization process represents a potential source of revenue (or, in some instances, loss). The interaction of local government finance and privatization thus merits careful attention in the transitional economies.

Second, the traditional approach ignores the shrinking role of government in general as shown in Table 5.5. Under the former system, government, both local and central, had a major production role. It was also the major investor in the economy, and the expenditure side of the budget was full of expenditures—not only subsidies, but direct investment, inventory finance and wages—which in a more market-oriented economy are not the responsibility of government. In all the transitional countries government revenue is declining more rapidly than governments are able to divest themselves of these expenditure responsibilities, thus contributing to stabilization problems. One response in countries such as Russia has been to try to shift the deficit downwards by making local governments responsible for more expenditures, while simultaneously reducing central transfers to the subnational sector. This approach seems unlikely to be sustainable for very long.

A third important factor is related to the present role of local governments with respect

TABLE 5.5 Transitional economies: the changing size of local government

Country	Total Exp. as % of GDP	Subnational Exp. as % % of GDP	Subnational Exp. as % of Total Exp.	Total Exp. as % of GDP	Subnational Exp. as % of GDP	Subnational Exp. as % of Total Exp.
		Pre-1989			Post-1989	
Hungary	62.7	14.3	25.4	57.4	10.4	18.2
Poland	49.7	14.7	35.3	40.1	4.00	11.0
Romania	45.1	3.6	11.4	24.6	6.07	10.8
Bulgaria	55.2	N.A.	N.A.	43.0	25.0	23.0
CSFR	58.4	20.5	34.5	60.1	20.2	34.3
Russia	51.0	20.7	16.0	41.0	17.0	43.0

Sources and Notes: Bird, Richard M. and Christine Wallich, 'Fiscal Decentralization and Intergovernmental Relations in Transition Economies', Working Paper No. WPS 1122, World Bank, Washington, DC, 1993. The figures in this Table—other than for Russia—do not show the degree of real decentralization very clearly, partly because the government sector as a whole is shrinking rapidly and partly because, although local governments may have been large under the old system, they had no real freedom of action; they were more like departments of the central government than local governments.

BOX 5.9
Two models of local government finance

Two models of local government finance may be found in the literature. The first views local government, like any other government, primarily in an 'ability-to-pay' framework. The second, in contrast, views local governments, unlike general national governments, primarily as agencies providing identifiable services to identifiable local residents and thus applies what is called a 'benefit' framework of analysis. The 'benefit' model of local finance fits best into economic analysis. In this framework, local governments are essentially viewed as firms that provide services, for the last (marginal) units of which recipients are willing to pay a price or charge that is just equal to the benefit they receive. This approach to local finance is logically appealing (at least to economists), equitable in the sense that no one pays less (or more) than he or she would be willing to pay in a free market, and economically efficient. There are, however, two problems with the benefit model.

First, it is difficult to implement appropriate pricing policy for local public services; and second, it is not politically appealing. The first of these problems may be dealt with to some extent by structuring local government finances along the following lines:[119] (1) Price appropriately those services that flow to identifiable individuals; (2) Where such pricing is not possible, link local expenditures and revenues through such devices as earmarking and matching service benefit areas and the spatial dimension of the financing sources; (3) Ensure that taxes financing local services are raised primarily from local residents; and (4) Design intergovernmental transfers to ensure that, at the margin, the costs and benefits of local fiscal decisions are borne locally, while taking adequately into account such interjurisdictional spillovers as are deemed relevant. Imposing a 'hard budget constraint' on local decision-makers in this way will never be politically popular, either with local decision-makers or, in most instances, with their constituents. In contrast, the political attractiveness in many countries of the ability model is undeniable, although it is often as nebulous

how 'ability' is to be assessed in this framework as to how 'benefit' can be measured in the benefit framework. In countries in the South, where most tax bases are occupied by the central government, what an ability approach to local government usually means is that central transfers (or the analytical equivalent of a national tax 'shared' according to some formula) end up financing most local services. There is no assurance, of course, that the local recipients of central largesse are necessarily less 'able' to pay for what they get than those whose incomes are reduced as a result of the central taxes. If local governments themselves attempt to implement differentiated 'ability' taxes, their tax bases are likely to leave for more congenial climes, with the result that the package of local services provided may be lower than it would be if the benefit approach were followed. In particular, richer local governments are likely to attract tax base from poorer ones, thus accentuating disparities. Overall, pursuing active distributional policies through local finances seems unlikely to be a very sensible strategy.

---

to the so-called 'social safety net' that varies from country to country. Problems are likely to arise in the future because of the combined effect of weakening central government capacity to maintain social protection and a growing need for such assistance as a result of economic restructuring. Even if the need for the bottom (local) layer of the social safety net increases, it is unlikely that local governments, even if they may sometimes be the appropriate executing agencies, should or can be responsible for financing such assistance. At present, for example, state enterprises provide a wide range of social sector outlays: with privatization, many of these outlays will have to be taken over by local governments. Since the revenue sources assigned to local governments in most countries seem unlikely to be adequate to finance even 'ordinary' local activities, one result of thus shifting responsibility for distributional expenditures downward may be, paradoxically, an increased demand for intergovernmental transfers.

Current solutions

Central governments in most transitional countries appear to view fiscal decentralization as an opportunity to reduce central expenditures in two ways: by spinning off expenditure responsibilities to the subnational level and by reducing fiscal transfers—purportedly to make local governments more 'independent,' but with the welcome side effect of reducing central outlays. In particular, some countries are transferring increasing responsibility for social

expenditures and the social safety net to local government.

The most dramatic example is that of Russia, where the central government transferred social expenditures equivalent to some 6 per cent of GDP (1992) to the subnational level, with the objective of 'pushing the deficit down'.[121] Since Russia is a federal country, in the first instance the shift has been to the regional (oblast) level. Many oblasts seem, in turn, to have passed the pressure on to the local (rayon) level of government. The hope seems to have been that lower-level governments would perform the politically painful cutting required. More recently, responsibility for key national, interjurisdictional investments (e.g. in transport) has also been transferred to the subnational sector. In contrast, in Albania, although responsibility for social assistance has similarly been pushed 'downstairs,' the central government has retained primary responsibility for financing such assistance.

Fiscal difficulties at the national level have led some countries to reduce intergovernmental transfers. The principle of 'budgetary independence' has been interpreted to mean that subnational governments should be financially self-sufficient, which in turn implies that direct transfers should be reduced and even eliminated. However, in most of the transition economies, central transfers to local government sector remain very large (see Table 5.6), reflecting the rudimentary tax bases that have been made available to local governments as a result of the centre's reluctance to give local governments access to any major tax base.

TABLE 5.6 Transitional economies: structure of subnational government finance (recent year)

	Hungary	Poland	Romania	Czech R.	Slovak R.	Bulgaria	Russia
Own Resources	18%	50%	25%	9%	71%	4.4%	–
Shared Tax	13%	25%	0%	6%	4.7%	49.4%	95%
Total Local	31%	75%	25%	15%	76%	53.8%	95%
Transfers from Central Government	68.5%[1]	25%	75%	85%	24%	46.2%	5%

Source: Bird, Richard M. and Christine Wallich, 'Fiscal Decentralization and Intergovernmental Relations in Transition Economies', Working Paper No. WPS 1122, World Bank, Washington DC, 1993.

[1] 51.4% as grants and 17.1% as Social Security Funds transfers.

The amount and distribution of intergovernmental transfers in most countries continues to be determined annually on a discretionary basis in accordance with central fiscal exigencies. Such budgetary flexibility is clearly desirable from the central government's short-run view. None the less, it is a mistake to view intergovernmental transfers as an easily compressible portion of the national budget. Many of the services provided by subnational governments, particularly in view of the 'pass-down' phenomenon already discussed, constitute essential expenditures for political stability or for future economic development. The many small local governments that have been created in response to political pressures in most countries cannot finance the provision of these services at an adequate level out of their own resources (see Box 5.10).

In the current macro-economic environment, an underfunded local government sector seems all too likely to result in a situation in which the only way local governments can cope with budgetary pressure is by using economically undesirable sources of revenue such as profits derived from the exploitation of income-earning assets transferred to them and from direct public ownership of local businesses. At the same time, local governments' open-ended expenditure responsibility for social assistance in some countries may result in emergency recurrence to the central government for additional funds, or simply the unsustainable accrual of arrears through short-term borrowing, as has happened in Russia. One way or another, intergovernmental transfers seem likely to be an important component of the central budget for years to come in most transitional countries.

The level, design and effects of intergovernmental fiscal transfers obviously constitute key elements in the emerging intergovernmental and local finance systems of the transitional economies[125]—as they do in other countries. Critical decisions must be made in regard to the overall size of such transfers (the 'distributable pool') and to the distribution formulas to be

BOX 5.10
The need for larger local governments

In many countries, the average size of local governments is small. In six transitional economies in eastern Europe, for example, the average population of the newly created local governments is less than 10,000.[122] In Hungary, three-quarters of the new local governments have less than 2,000 inhabitants. Similar situations exist in many countries in Africa, Asia and Latin America. Many of these local governments are too small to provide efficiently all the public services demanded from them. Some countries in the North have developed 'two-tiered' local government structures in response to this problem. In Finland, for instance, where the average population of local governments is little more than 10,000, the 460 local governments (communes) are organized on a voluntary basis to provide particular services. There are 100 such federations in the health care field, for example.[123] Similar special purpose municipal federations exist in other Nordic countries to provide such services as health care and certain types of education. Other services are provided by so-called 'secondary communes', or counties, which are responsible for certain services provided to an area encompassing a number of communes. Still other services are provided by regional agencies of the central government such as highway construction and maintenance and, in some cases, the collection of local taxes. Canada too has developed a number of variant forms of 'two-tiered' local government.[124] In the province of Ontario, for example, regional governments are responsible for some social and health services, water supply, sewage treatment, and refuse disposal, while local governments are responsible for refuse collection, fire protection, parks, and recreation. Some functions, such as water distribution, police, and roads, are jointly controlled. Primary and secondary education is provided by special-purpose school districts.

employed. These must take into account both the severe fiscal pressures on the central government and the vital tasks to be performed by the local governments in the emerging new structure of the public sector (see Box 5.11).

As in many countries in the South, local governments in the transitional economies need substantial help and guidance in developing adequate local revenue systems. In most such countries, for example, the principal local tax is some form of property tax.[130] In some instances (e.g. Romania), however, national governments have greatly limited the revenue potential of this tax both by granting exemptions to newly privatized land, housing, and enterprises and by fixing a uniform national tax rate. In other instances (e.g. Hungary) local governments are supposed to receive some share of certain national taxes, often on a derivation basis (e.g. origin, or residence).[131] Such provisions often raise both technical and allocative problems, in addition to biasing national tax policy decisions in unfavourable ways.[132] Even when a local property tax is feasible

BOX 5.11
Redesigning government transfers

Three aspects of intergovernmental fiscal transfers need further attention in most countries: the size of the 'distributable pool,' the basis for distributing transfers, and conditionality. Some countries (e.g. Morocco) set aside a fraction of a particular central tax as the amount to be distributed to local governments but this can introduce an undesirable bias into national tax policy. Finance ministries will be reluctant to raise taxes for the benefit of other governments. A better solution is, as in Colombia, to establish a certain percentage of all central revenues as the 'pool' to be distributed to local governments. This approach both provides more certainty to local governments than a purely discretionary system and permits the central government to retain budgetary flexibility. Another approach would be to have a 'horizontal equalization' transfer, as in Germany and Denmark, under which, in effect, rich local governments directly transfer resources to poor localities without directly affecting central revenues. Chile appears to be the only country in the South to have such a system.[126] A good transfer system should distribute funds on the basis of a formula. Discretionary or negotiated transfers, such as are still common in many countries in East and Central Europe and the South are clearly undesirable. The essential ingredients of most formulas for general transfer programs (as opposed to 'matching grants' which are specifically intended to finance narrowly-defined projects and activities) are needs, capacity, and effort. Needs may be adequately proxied in many cases by some combination of population and the type or category of municipality.[127] Effort may be adequately taken into account by a proper specification of capacity.[128] The key ingredient is some measure of the 'capacity' of local governments to raise resources, given the revenue authority at their disposal. Once the total amount to be distributed has been decided, and the basic distribution formula determined, the remaining question is whether the transfer should be made conditional on the provision of certain services at specified levels. As a general rule, in the circumstances of most countries in Africa, Asia and Latin America, in which the 'benefit' model of local governments (see Box 5.9) seems applicable, such conditionality seems desirable,[129] though matters may be different for regional governments in some federal states (see Box 5.3).

and adequate in principle, realistically it will take some years before such a tax can be expected to produce sufficient revenues to meet perceived local needs, if it ever can (see Box 5.6).

Many local expenditures cannot be postponed until the revenue side is improved. Even if local expenditures are rationally assigned, and designed, the paucity of locally-controlled tax resources in most transitional countries, when combined with the universal reluctance of politicians to tax constituents too directly and openly, makes it almost inevitable that hard-pressed local governments will turn to other avenues for revenue. They will demand increased transfers, they will try to borrow, and they will try to exploit to the full the new assets they have acquired as part of the decentralization-privatization process. Each of these paths carries with it dangers for the transition process as a whole.

While many of the problems and critical areas in the transitional economies are similar to those in the South generally, a broader framework than usual is thus needed to analyse fiscal decentralization and local and intergovernmental fiscal issues in the transitional economies. This framework must incorporate such elements as the likelihood of continuing structural changes in the economy and continuing political shifts, the need to undertake intergovernmental reforms while coping simultaneously with stabilization pressures and the increased importance of the social safety net, the likelihood of continued (local) public ownership on a significant scale, the financial implications of such ownership and its possible conflicts with the overall privatization objective, and continued vestiges of price and wage controls and other rigidities. Each country is different, and each will need close examination to determine the precise structure of the relevant incentives, constraints, and opportunities in order to design as 'hard' a budget constraint as may prove acceptable.

Notes and References

1. Sections 5.1–5.3 are a slightly shortened and amended version of a background paper prepared for the Global Report entitled *The Governance of Human Settlements* by Richard Stren and Christie Gombay, Centre for Urban and Community Studies, University of Toronto.

2. World Bank, *Sub-Saharan Africa: From Crisis to Sustainable Growth*, The World Bank, Washington DC, 1989, 5.

3. Wunsch, James and Dele Olowu, 'The failure of the centralized African state' in James Wunsch and Dele Olowu (editors), *The Failure of the Centralized State;*

Institutions and Self-Governance in Africa, Westview, Boulder, 1990, 4–5.

4. Prud'homme, Remy, 'Main Issues in Decentralization', in World Bank, *Strengthening Local Governments in Sub-Saharan Africa; Proceedings of Two Workshops*, EDI Policy Seminar Report, no. 21, The World Bank, Washington DC, 1988, 71.

5. Dillinger, William, *Decentralization and its Implications for Urban Service Delivery*, Urban Management Programme Discussion Paper No. 16, The World Bank, Washington DC, 1993, 8.

6. See Smith, B. C., *Decentralization; The*

Territorial Dimension of the State, George Allen and Unwin, London, 1985, esp. ch. 1.

7. The best discussion of this typology is to be found in Shabbir Cheema and Dennis Rondinelli (eds.), *Decentralization and Development; Policy Implementation in Developing Countries*, Sage, Beverly Hills, 1983.

8. See, for example, Prud'homme 1988, *op. cit.*

9. Huntington, Samuel P., *The Third Wave; Democratization in the Late Twentieth Century*, University of Oklahoma Press, Norman, Oklahoma, 1991, 7.

10. Huntington 1991, *op. cit.* 113.

11. Huntington 1991, *op. cit.* 26. Only states with a population of over 1 million were included in this calculation.

12. These estimates, and definitions of the categories, can be found in the newsletter *Africa Demos*, issued by the Carter Center of Emory University, Atlanta, Georgia. The 1991 estimates are taken from vol. 1, no. 4 (May 1991); and the 1994 estimates are taken from vol. 3, no. 3 (Sept. 1994). The key definitions are those of a democratic and an authoritarian political system. Thus, a democratic system is 'a system enjoying wide competition between organized groups, numerous opportunities for popular participation in government, and elections that are regularly and fairly conducted. Constitutional guarantees of civil liberties and human rights are effectively enforced.' An authoritarian system is 'a system with highly restricted opportunities for political mobilization. Power is exercised by a leader or small group who are not formally accountable to an electorate. There are no effective constitutional limits to the exercise of political power'.

13. Examples of these are given in Chapters 9, 10 and 11.

14. See Peattie, Lisa, 'Participation: a case study of how invaders organize, negotiate and interact with government in Lima, Peru', *Environment and Urbanization*, vol. 2, no. 1, April 1990, 19–30 for one detailed description of this. Also Cuenya, Beatriz, Diego Armus, Maria Di Loreto and Susana Penalva, 'Land invasions and grassroots organization: the Quilmes settlement in Greater Buenos Aires, Argentina', *Environment and Urbanization*, vol. 2, no. 1, April 1990, 61–73.

15. *Ibid.*

16. Hardoy, Jorge E. and David Satterthwaite, *Squatter Citizen: Life in the Urban Third World*, Earthscan Publications, London, 1989.

17. Hirschman, Albert O., *Getting Ahead Collectively; Grassroots Experiences in Latin America*, Pergamon Press, New York, 1984, 100.

18. Valladares, Licia, and Magda Prates Coelho, 'Urban Research in Brazil and Venezuela: Towards an Agenda for the 1990s', in Richard Stren (ed.), *Urban Research in the Developing World; Volume 3: Latin America*, Centre for Urban and Community Studies, Toronto, 1995, ch. 3, 36.

19. Rodriguez, Alfredo, Vicente Espinoza and Hilda Herzer, 'Argentina, Bolivia, Chile, Ecuador, Peru, Uruguay: Urban Research in the 1990s—A Framework for an Analysis' in Richard Stren (ed.), *Urban Research in the Developing World; Volume 3: Latin America*, Centre for Urban and Community Studies, Toronto, 1995, ch. 5, 11.

20. Inglehart, Ronald, *Culture Shift in Advanced Industrial Society*, Princeton University Press, Princeton, 1990, 137–9.

21. *Ibid.* 267.

22. Hays, Samuel, *Beauty, Health and Permanence: Environmental Politics in the United States 1955–1985*, Cambridge University Press, Cambridge, 1987, 22.

23. On the Canadian pattern, see Doug Macdonald, *The Politics of Pollution*, McClelland and Stewart, Toronto, 1991, 90–1. Kirkpatrick Sale sums up the American pattern of support. 'Generally the strength [of the environmental movement] came from the more urbanized and often more liberal sections of the country—chiefly the conurbations known as Bos-Wash, Chi-Cin, Pitt-Phil, Sea-Port, and San-San, the last in California—and petered out in the Heartland and Plains, dwindling even more in such areas dependent on petrochemicals and extraction as the Rockies and the Gulf. Generally the shock troops as well as the directors and the staffs were younger, richer, and better educated than the American average, leading to criticism that it was an "elitist" movement concerned only with the luxuries of a good life for those who already had a good living. And generally both the organizations and their supporters were predominantly white, with little impact in black or brown populations where ecological matters at this point seemed trivial compared with economic ones and the connections between the two rarely made' (Kirkpatrick Sale, *The Green Revolution: The American Environmental Movement 1962–1992*, Hill and Wang, New York, 1993, 44–5).

24. Macdonald 1991, *op. cit.* 98–9.

25. Government of Canada, *Canada's Green Plan for a Healthy Environment*, Minister of Supply and Services, Ottawa, 1990, 135.

26. Sale 1993, *op.cit.* 44.

27. *Ibid.* 80.

28. *Ibid.* 79.

29. Herzer, Hilda, and Pedro Pirez, 'Municipal government and popular participation in Latin America', *Environment and Urbanization*, vol. 3, no. 1, April 1991, 79–95.

30. Campbell, Tim with G. Petersen and J. Brakarz, *Decentralization to Local Government in LAC: National Strategies and Local Response in Planning*, Spending and Management, Latin American and the Caribbean Technical Department, The World Bank, Washington DC, 1991.

31. Rodriguez, Alfredo, and Lucy Winchester, 'The City: Governance and Urban Poverty in Six Countries in Latin America', Unpublished paper, SUR, Santiago, 1994.

32. De Mello, Diogo Lordello, 'Brazil', in Samuel Humes IV, *Local Governance and National Power: A Worldwide Comparison of Tradition and Change in Local Government*, Harvester, London, 1991, 155.

33. *Ibid.* 162.

34. *Ibid.* 167.

35. Assies, Villem, 'Urban Social Movements in Brazil. A Debate and Its Dynamics', *Latin American Perspectives*, Issue 81, vol. 21, no. 2, Spring 1994, 93.

36. Carrion, Diego, 'The role and functions of municipal government in Ecuador', in *The Role and Functions of Municipal Government in Selected Countries*, Centre for Urban and Community Studies and Federation of Canadian Municipalities, Toronto, 1995, 116.

37. Carr, Michelle, 'A Case Study of Quito, Ecuador', in *Metropolitan Planning and Management in the Developing World: Abidjan and Quito*, UNCHS, Nairobi, 1992, 94.

38. Carrion 1995, *op. cit.* 119.

39. Rodriguez and Winchester 1994, *op. cit.*

40. Rosenfeld, Alex, 'The role and functions of municipal government in Chile', in *The Role and Functions of Municipal Government in Selected Countries*, Centre for Urban and Community Studies and Federation of Canadian Municipalities, Toronto, 1995, 89.

41. Rosenfeld 1995, *op. cit.* 95.

42. For these cases, see Nikki Craske, 'Women's Political Participation in Colonias Populares in Guadalajara, Mexico'; and Leda M. Vieira Machado, '"We learned to think politically": The influence of the Catholic Church and the feminist movement on the emergence of the health movement of the Jardim Nordeste area in Sao Paulo, Brazil', in Radcliffe and Westwood 1993, *op. cit.*; and Veronica Schild, 'Recasting "Popular" Movements: gender and political learning in neighborhood organizations in Chile' *Latin American Perspectives*, Issue 81, Volume 21, no. 2, 1994. In her conclusion, Schild makes a point common to many studies of women in local social movements: 'Inequalities based on gendered class relations (and limiting subjectivities) have traditionally rendered citizenship marginal for most poor and working-class women. However, during the period of enforced public silence [i.e. during the authoritarian period] many of these women found new resources with which to question limiting subjectivities, while some also engaged in crafting new political subjectivities. Thus women's neighborhood organizations have been important sites of struggles in which women have begun to acquire their own voices as part of the creation of new political identities. These new voices will no doubt help to make the so-called reconstitution of civil society currently taking place in Chile more a redefinition than a restitution' (p. 75).

43. World Bank, *Urban Policy and Economic Development. An Agenda for the 1990s*, The World Bank, Washington, 1991.

44. Gilbert, Alan, and Peter Ward, *Housing, the State and the Poor: Policy and Practice in Three Latin American Cities*, Cambridge University Press, Cambridge, 1985, 175.

45. Saravia, Joaquin C. and Godofredo

Sandoval Z. *Jach'a Uru: ¿La Esperanza de un Pueblo? Carlos Palenque, RTP y Los Sectores Populares Urbanos en La Paz*, CEP and ILDIS, La Paz, 1991.

46. Pflucker, Piedad Pareja and Aldo Gatti Murriel, *Elecciones Municipales en las Provincias de Lima y el Callao*, Fundacion Friedrich Ebert, Lima, 1993.

47. For instance, the recently elected mayor of Bogota.

48. Guerrero V., Rodrigo, 'Innovative programs for the urban poor in Cali, Colombia', in Bonnie Bradford and Margaret A. Gwynne (eds.), *Down to Earth: Community Perspectives on Health, Development and the Environment*, Kumarian Press, West Hartford, 1995, 17–22.

49. Shefner, Jon, and John Walton, 'The *damnificados* of Guadalajara: The politics of domination and social movement protest', *International Journal of Urban and Regional Research*, vol. 17, no. 4, December 1993, 621.

50. Attahi, Koffi, 'Planning and management in large cities: a case study of Abidjan, Côte d'Ivoire', in UNCHS (Habitat), *Metropolitan Planning and Management in the Developing World: Abidjan and Quito*, UNCHS, Nairobi, 1992, 31–82.

51. Lapeyre, Charles, 'La ville de Dakar: commune et région', in Centre d'études et de recherches en administration local, *L'Administration des grandes villes dans le monde*, PUF, Paris, 1986, 339.

52. Diop, Momar Coumba and Mamadou Diouf, 'Pouvoir central et pouvoir local. La crise de l'institution municipale au Sénégal', in Sylvy Jaglin and Alain Dubresson (eds.), *Pouvoirs et cités d'Afrique noire; Décentralisations en questions*, Karthala, Paris, 1993, 114–15 [Author's translation].

53. Attahi, Koffi, 'The Functions and Powers of Municipal Government in Côte d'Ivoire', in Centre for Urban and Community Studies, *The Role and Functions of Municipal Government in Selected Countries*, University of Toronto for Federation of Canadian Municipalities, Toronto, 1995, 72.

54. Kasfir, Nelson, 'Designs and dilemmas: an overview', in Philip Mawhood (ed.), *Local Government in the Third World. The Experience of Tropical Africa*, John Wiley and Sons, Chichester, 1983, 25–47.

55. Adamolekun, Lapido, 'The idea of local government as a third level of government', in L. Adamolekun and L. Rowland (eds.), *The New Local Government System in Nigeria; Problems and Prospects for Implementation*, Heinemann, Ibadan, 1979, 39.

56. Olowu, Dele, 'Centralization, self-governance, and development in Nigeria', in Wunsch and Olowu (eds.) 1990, *op. cit.*

57. The following section on Nairobi is based on a longer account in Richard Stren, Mohamed Halfani and Joyce Malombe, 'Coping with Urbanization and Urban Policy' in Joel Barkan (ed.), *Beyond Socialism and Capitalism in Kenya and Tanzania*, Lynne Rienner, Boulder, 1994, 175–200.

58. *The Weekly Review* (Nairobi) 12 July 1991, 18.

59. Section 5.4 is a shortened version of a background paper written by Richard M. Bird.

60. See Bird, Richard M., *Federal Finance in Comparative Perspective*, Canadian Tax Foundation, Toronto, 1986 for further discussion.

61. Surveyed by Bahl, Roy W. and Johannes Linn, *Urban Public Finance in Developing Countries*, Oxford University Press, New York, 1992, 14–15.

62. Bird, Richard M. and Christine Wallich, 'Fiscal Decentralization and Intergovernmental Relations in Transition Economies,' Working Paper no. WPS 1122, World Bank, Washington, DC, 1993, 22.

63. Developed countries surveyed in OECD, Fiscal Affairs Secretariat, 'The Role of Intermediate and Local Levels of Government: The Experience of Selected OECD Countries,' Background Document for Seminar on Fiscal Federalism in Economies in Transition, Paris, 1991.

64. The extent to which such activities are reflected in the data included in Table 5.2 varies from country to country. The full range of local government activities has been thoroughly analyzed in few countries outside the industrial world, and even when such data have been gathered in special studies, they have not been kept up to date.

65. Advisory Commission on Intergovernmental Relations, *Significant Features of Fiscal Federalism*, Washington DC, vol. 2, 1992, 58.

66. Bahl, Roy W. and Johannes Linn, *Urban Public Finance in Developing Countries*, Oxford University Press, New York, 1992, 14–15.

67. World Bank/UNCHS, *The Housing Indicators Program Volume III; Preliminary Findings*, a Joint Programme of the United Nations Centre for Human Settlements (Habitat) and the World Bank, Washington DC, April 1993.

68. Bird and Wallich 1993, *op. cit.*

69. Bird, Richard M. and Christine Wallich, 'Financing Local Government in Hungary,' Working Paper no. WPS 869, World Bank, Washington, DC, 1992.

70. See Bird, Richard M. and Enid Slack, 'Financing local governments in OECD countries: the role of local taxes and user charges', in Owens, Jeffrey and Giorgio Panella (eds.), *Local Government: An International Perspective*, North-Holland, Amsterdam, 1991.

71. Bahl and Linn 1992, *op. cit.* 36–7.

72. Bird and Wallich, 1993, *op. cit.* 44.

73. World Bank, *World Development Report 1988*, Oxford University Press, 1988.

74. Bahl and Linn 1992, *op. cit.*

75. OECD 1991, *op. cit.* 66.

76. Covered by Bahl and Linn 1992, *op. cit.* 34–5.

77. Bahl and Linn 1992, *op. cit.*, 40

78. World Bank, *Chile: Subnational Government Finance*, Washington DC, 1993, 57.

79. This variation partly reflects differences in the roles of state and local governments in different US states. Even if state and local expenditures are combined, however, the variation is still from 68 to 291 per cent of the national average. (See Advisory Commission on Intergovernmental Relations 1992, *op. cit.* vol. 2, 224–5 and 220–1.)

80. Bird, Richard M. and Heng-fu Zou, 'Financing Local Government in Romania', Draft; World Bank, Washington DC, 1992

81. World Bank, *Chile: Subnational Government Finance*, Washington DC, 1993.

82. World Bank, 'Indonesia: Fiscal Decentralization: Towards a New Partnership for Progress', Report no. 12407–IND, Oct. 1993.

83. Bird, Richard M., *Intergovernmental Fiscal Relations in Colombia*, Harvard Law School International Tax Program, Cambridge, Mass, 1984, 267.

84. Kitchen, Harry M., *Local Government Finance in Canada*, Canadian Tax Foundation, Toronto, 1984, 175.

85. Rao, M. Govinda and A. Das-Gupta, 'Intergovernmental Transfers as an Instrument to Alleviate Poverty', Economic Development Institute, World Bank, 1993.

86. Dreze, Jean and Mrinalini Saran, 'Primary Education and Economic Development in China and India: Overview and Two Case Studies', no. 47, Development Economics Research Programme, London School of Economics, Sept. 1993, 73.

87. Rao and Das-Gupta 1993, *op. cit.*

88. Keith, Simon H., *Property Tax in Anglophone Africa: A Practical Manual*, World Bank Technical Paper no. 209, Washington DC, 1993.

89. Kitchen, Harry, *Efficient Delivery of Local Government Services*, Discussion Paper 93–15, School of Policy Studies, Queen's University, Kingston, 1993, 30.

90. See for instance Bird, Richard M., *Charging for Public Services: A New Look at an Old Idea*, Canadian Tax Foundation, Toronto, 1976.

91. Bahl and Linn 1992, *op. cit.*

92. As Thirsk notes with respect to Canada, the same argument may be made with respect to that portion of the property tax—frequently half or more of the total—that applies to nonresidential property; see Thirsk, Wayne R., 'Political Sensitivity versus Economic Sensibility: A Tale of Two Property Taxes', in W. R. Thirsk and J. Whalley (eds.), *Tax Policy Options in the 1980s*, Canadian Tax Foundation, Toronto, 1982.

93. Bahl and Linn 1992, *op. cit.* 43.

94. World Bank, *Colombia: Decentralizing Revenues and the Provision of Services—a Review of Recent Experience*, Report no. 7870–CO, Oct. 1989.

95. Bird and Slack 1991, *op. cit.*

96. Dillinger, William , *Urban Property Tax Reform*, World Bank, Washington DC, 1991.

97. Dillinger, 1991, *op. cit.*

98. Kelly, Roy, 'Implementing property tax reform in transitional countries: the experience of Albania and Poland', *Environment and Planning C: Government and Policy*, vol. 12, 1994.

99. World Bank, '*Indonesia: Fiscal Decentralization: Towards a New Partnership for Progress*, Report no. 12407–IND, Oct. 1993.

100. Bird and Wallich 1993, *op. cit.*

101. Davey, Kenneth J. , 'Municipal Development Funds and Intermediaries', Working Paper no. 32, World Bank, Washington DC, 1990.

102. Bird, Richard M. and Enid Slack, *Urban Public Finance in Canada*, 2nd edn., John Wiley, Toronto, 1993.

103. Bird, Richard M., *Intergovernmental Fiscal Relations in Developing Countries*, World Bank Staff Working Paper no. 304, Oct. 1978.

104. Bird and Wallich 1992, *op. cit.*

105. World Bank 1988, *op. cit.*

106. Bird and Slack 1993, *op. cit.*

107. Slack, Enid and Richard M. Bird, 'Financing urban growth through development charges', *Canadian Tax Journal*, 39: 1288–304, 1991.

108. Rao, M. Govinda, 'State Government Transfers to Urban Local Bodies', National Institute of Public Finance and Policy, New Delhi, 1991.

109. Campbell, Peterson and Brakarz 1991, *op. cit.*

110. Thirsk, Wayne R. and Richard M. Bird, 'Earmarked Taxes in Ontario: Solution or Problem?', in Allan Maslove (ed.), *Taxing and Spending: Issues of Process*, University of Toronto Press, Toronto, 1994, 129–84.

111. Bird, Richard M. and Barbara Miller, 'Taxes, Prices and the Poor', in Richard M. Bird and Susan Horton (eds.), *Government Policy and the Poor in Developing Countries*, University of Toronto Press, Toronto, 1989.

112. Lee, Terence and Andre Jouravlev, 'Self-financing Water Supply and Sanitation Services', *Cepal Review*, no. 48, Dec. 1992.

113. Davey, Kenneth J., *Elements of Urban Management*, World Bank, Washington DC, 1993, 22.

114. See Cairncross, Sandy, 'Water supply and the urban poor', in Jorge E. Hardoy, Sandy Cairncross and David Satterthwaite (eds.), *The Poor Die Young: Housing and Health in Third World Cities*, Earthscan Publications, London, 1990, 109–26.

115. Kornai, Janos, *The Socialist System*, Princeton University Press, Princeton NJ, 1992.

116. Tanzi, Vito (ed.), *Fiscal Policies in Economies in Transition*, International Monetary Fund, Washington DC, 1992 and Tanzi, Vito (ed.), *Transition to Market: Studies in Fiscal Reform*, International Monetary Fund, Washington DC, 1993.

117. Kornai, 1992, *op. cit.*

118. Bird, Richard M., 'Threading the Fiscal labyrinth: some issues in fiscal decentralization', *National Tax Journal* vol. 46, 1993, 207–27.

119. Bird 1993, *op. cit.*

120. Bahl, Roy and Sally Wallace, 'Revenue Sharing in Russia', *Environment and Planning C: Government and Policy*, vol. 12, 1994.

121. Wallich, Christine, *Fiscal Decentralization: Intergovernmental Relations in Russia*, World Bank, Washington DC, 1992.

122. Bird and Wallich 1993, *op. cit.*

123. Soderstrom, Lars, 'Fiscal Federalism: The Nordic Countries' Style', in Remy Prud'homme (ed.), *Public Finance with Several Levels of Government*, Koenigsteing: Foundation Journal Public Finance, The Hague, 1991.

124. Bird and Slack, 1993, *op. cit.*

125. Bird and Wallich, 1992, *op. cit.*

126. World Bank, *World Development Report 1993*, Oxford University Press, 1993.

127. See, for example, Bird, Richard M., *Intergovernmental Fiscal Relations in Colombia*, Harvard Law School International Tax Program, Cambridge, Mass., 1984.

128. See Bird, Richard M. and Enid Slack, 'Redesigning intergovernmental transfers: A Colombian example,' *Environment and Planning C: Government and Policy*, vol. 1, 1983, 461–73.

129. Bird 1993, *op. cit.*

130. Kelly, Roy, 'Implementing Property Tax Reform in Transitional Countries: The Experience of Albania and Poland', *Environment and Planning C: Government and Policy*, vol. 12, 1994.

131. Bird and Wallich, 1992, *op. cit.*

132. Bahl and Wallace 1994, *op. cit.*

PART II

Inside Human Settlements

6 Housing

6.1 Assessing Housing Conditions

Introduction

The central importance of housing to everyone's quality of life and health is often forgotten. The importance of secure, safe and adequately serviced housing to health was described in some detail in Chapter 4. But housing should do more than simply minimize disease and injury. If it meets the needs and priorities of its residents, it also contributes much to physical, mental and social well-being. The quality and size of housing, and the quality of the neighbourhood in which it is located, is obviously important for privacy, security and an enjoyable domestic life. Its location is important in terms of the access it provides its residents to city services and employment opportunities. For a considerable proportion of the world's population, their house is their most valuable asset and, for many, it is also their most significant item of expenditure. Thus, whilst housing has considerable importance as a proportion of a nation's total fixed capital, this measure cannot accurately represent its value to house dwellers. Its importance in people's health, quality of life and enjoyment of life is so much more than this. But these are aspects that are difficult to capture in statistics.

One of the most important changes in the last 10–15 years has been the move away from assessing the quantitative dimensions of housing 'deficits' or 'backlogs' within nations to whether people can find accommodation that meets their needs and priorities—and what constrains those with low incomes from being able to do so. In many instances, the problem is not one of too few housing units but of the poor quality and lack of basic services in a high proportion of the total housing stock.

But before considering this, a review is made of global housing conditions under four main aspects:

- The quality of housing—including its size relative to the number of inhabitants, the quality of construction and the extent of provision for water supply, electricity, sanitation and drainage.

- Housing tenure—the proportion of households who, as legally recognized owners or renters, have protection against sudden or arbitrary eviction.

- The quantity of housing (relative to the number of households).

- Housing accessibility—the proportion of people able to buy, rent or in other ways obtain adequate quality housing. Of special interest in this is whether those with low incomes or those unable to earn an income (for instance the elderly) are able to find adequate shelter.[1]

It is difficult to substantiate statistically whether housing conditions under these four aspects improved or not, worldwide, over the last 10–15 years. For many countries, there are no reliable statistics on housing; for many others, detailed data on housing conditions from their most recent census (1989/1990/1991) are still not available.

There is also the fact that in many countries, the statistics on housing do not provide much information on housing conditions. For instance, one of the most widely collected official statistics is the number of conventional dwellings constructed annually per 1,000 persons. This can be compared to the growth in the population in any country to see whether there is a large gap between the two.[2] But this statistic only has some validity as an indicator of housing conditions in countries where most housing is constructed as conventional dwellings, within a legal and administrative system which ensures that virtually all new housing units are recorded. This statistic has very little relevance in countries where most housing construction is unrecorded. According to international statistical compendia, that draw their data from government figures, in nations in Africa, Asia and Latin America, the number of conventional dwellings constructed annually is usually between 2 and 4 per 1,000 inhabitants—when the actual growth in the housing stock (including all illegal and informal housing) is likely to be between 15 and 30 units per 1,000 inhabitants. Most people are housed in shelters that are never recorded.

If most new housing units are not counted in official statistics, then figures for a country's or city's 'housing deficit' can be misleading—especially by emphasizing that the main problem is one of the quantity of housing units (the deficit) when the main problem is often the quality of new units.[3] In addition, since housing deficits also include the number of housing units which are 'sub-standard' and thus have to be 'replaced', the use of invalid criteria as to what is 'substandard' often leads to half a city's housing stock and nine out of ten of all new housing units currently being produced being given zero value. This includes large numbers of houses built, repaired and extended by their inhabitants which represent not only these people's homes but also their most valuable asset. Calculations for housing deficits within a city or nation may also misrepresent the problem as there may be no deficit in numbers nationally or city-wide but serious problems of many housing units being too expensive or in the wrong location.

However, since the last *Global Report on Human Settlements* was published in 1987, a considerable body of new data has become available on housing conditions. The first, covering only urban housing, is the data from the Housing Indicators Programme whose findings form the central part of this section on assessing housing conditions. The second is data on the health burden that arises from poor housing conditions and/or from poverty in general—which was summarized in Chapter 4. The third is a considerable number of new studies of housing conditions for particular nations, regions, cities or neighbourhoods within cities. Although these exist for only a minority of the world's settlements, they provide greater detail about housing conditions and the processes that influence housing conditions. As Section 6.2 explains, these also demonstrate the complexity of housing markets in most cities and their dynamic nature—and how little they conform to the widely used stereotype of the poor housed in 'slums'. They also demonstrate the great differences in conditions and trends between cities. They make clear that the quality and quantity of housing in many cities in the South has improved considerably in recent years. In other instances there is some improvement in housing conditions but the growth in the number of households is still greater than the increase in the number of households in better quality housing.

The Housing Indicators Programme

There is a stronger basis for comparing housing conditions in cities worldwide than in the previous *Global Report*, because of a new international programme on housing indicators. This programme undertook a survey of housing in 52 cities covering around 10 per cent of the world's urban population in 1990. Table 6.1 lists the cities while Box 6.1 gives more details about this programme.

The 52 cities are drawn from countries covering the greatest possible range of per capita incomes. The level of detail on housing conditions in this survey is substantially greater than any other international survey. However, care must be taken in extrapolating the findings to the

---

BOX 6.1

The Housing Indicators Programme

In 1990, the United Nations Centre for Human Settlements and the World Bank set up an international programme to create a more solid analytical, empirical and institutional base for the conduct of housing policy in the South. Two of its most important objectives are

—to provide a comprehensive, policy-sensitive framework for monitoring the performance of the housing sector; and
—to illustrate the benefits of good housing policies by providing new empirical information on the relationship between housing policies, housing sector outcomes and broader social and economic outcomes.

The Programme is collecting data from four sources:

1. An extensive survey of housing indicators (whose results are reported here)
2. An intensive survey of housing indicators in selected countries
3. Urban household surveys conducted by the World Bank in selected countries in recent years
4. Other relevant housing data

The extensive survey of housing indicators requested consultants based in each of the 52 countries to calculate values for 25 key indicators, 10 alternate indicators and 20 regulatory audit indicators. These were chosen to provide an overview of the performance of the housing sector in each city, including information on housing affordability, quality, finance, production, subsidies and the workings of the regulatory and institutional environment. All were based on existing data and expert estimates; no new household surveys were undertaken.

Source: The Housing Indicators Program Volume III; Preliminary Findings, A Joint Programme of the United Nations Centre for Human Settlements (Habitat) and the World Bank, Washington DC, April 1993.

---

rest of the world's urban centres since the sample is not representative of urban centres, either geographically (in terms of the proportion of cities chosen from different regions to represent the proportion of the world's urban population located there) or in terms of city-size. A high proportion of the sample were large cities; 44 had a million or more inhabitants in 1990. Little more than 2 per cent of the population in the 52 sample cities lived in cities with less than a million inhabitants when worldwide, in 1990, more than 60 per cent of the world's urban population lives in urban centres with less than one million inhabitants. The sample includes a high proportion of national capitals (39 out of the 52) and housing conditions and government responses to such conditions may be unusual in capital cities.

Housing quality

In general, perhaps not surprisingly, the research of the Housing Indicators Programme found that the higher the per capita income of the country,

TABLE 6.1 The 52 cities included in the Extensive Survey of Housing Indicators for 1990

Urban centre	Country
Cities from low income countries	
Dar es Salaam	Tanzania
Lilongwe	Malawi
Dhaka	Bangladesh
Antananarivo	Madagascar
Ibadan	Nigeria
Delhi	India
Nairobi	Kenya
Beijing (Peking)	China
Karachi	Pakistan
Accra	Ghana
Cities from low-mid income countries	
Jakarta	Indonesia
Cairo	Egypt
Harare	Zimbabwe
Dakar	Senegal
Manila	Philippines
Abidjan	Côte D'Ivoire
Rabat	Morocco
Quito	Ecuador
Amman	Jordan
Bogota	Colombia
Cities from middle income countries	
Bangkok	Thailand
Tunis	Tunisia
Kingston	Jamaica
Istanbul	Turkey
Warsaw	Poland
Santiago	Chile
Monterrey	Mexico
Algiers	Algeria
Kuala Lumpur	Malaysia
Johannesburg	South Africa
Cities from mid-high income countries	
Caracas	Venezuela
Rio de Janeiro	Brazil
Budapest	Hungary
Bratislava	Slovakia
Seoul	Korea, Republic of
Athens	Greece
Tel-Aviv	Israel
Madrid	Spain
Singapore	Singapore
Hong Kong	Hong Kong
Cities from high income countries	
London	United Kingdom
Melbourne	Australia
Amsterdam	Netherlands
Vienna	Austria
Paris	France
Toronto	Canada
Washington DC	United States
Munich	Germany
Oslo	Norway
Stockholm	Sweden
Tokyo	Japan
Helsinki	Finland

TABLE 6.2 Regional breakdown of the 52 cities

	The number of			Percentage of sample's population (1990)
	cities	national capitals	million-cities	
East Asia	7	7	7	23.6
EMENA*	10	8	8	13.9
West Europe, North America, Australasia**	15	11	14	33.8
Latin America and the Caribbean	7	5	6	12.9
South Asia	3	2	3	10.4
Sub-Saharan Africa	10	6	6	5.5
TOTAL	52	39	44	100.0

* EMENA is North Africa, the Middle East and some eastern, central and southern European countries.
** This was designated 'industrialized countries' but such a category has very limited validity as many so called 'non-industrialized' nations have a higher proportion of their workforce working in industry and a higher proportion of their GDP generated by industrial production.

the larger and better quality the housing and the higher the proportion of dwelling units that have water piped to the plot and are made of permanent building materials.[4] However, there are large differences in housing quality between the most prosperous cities in countries with comparable levels of per capita income. An analysis based on the data of the Housing Indicators Programme suggests that effective government housing policies, especially efficient systems that ensure an unconstrained supply of land, materials, infrastructure for housing and finance, are among the main reasons for this difference.[5]

The floor area per person[6] is a more precise indicator than persons per room for highlighting overcrowding. Among the 52 cities, the floor area per person generally gets larger, the higher the per capita income of the country but the large variation in this indicator between cities in countries with comparable per capita incomes suggest that many other factors are also influential (see Figure 6.1). Among the cities in countries with per capita incomes of over $US10,000, only Hong Kong had less than 20 square metres per person. Among the cities in countries with less than $US5,000 per capita income, only Istanbul had more than 15 square metres per person and most cities had less than 10. However, there is considerable variation between cities in countries with comparable levels of per capita income and preliminary analyses suggest that most of the variation is linked to land costs and construction costs. Among the cities in the low-income countries, all but Accra had less than 10 square metres; in Dhaka, there is only 3.7 square metres of floor area per person and in Nairobi, Dar es Salaam and Antananarivo, around 5. Among the high-income countries, all but Tokyo (15.8 square metres per person) and Amsterdam (23.8) had more than 30 with Stockholm, Oslo and Toronto with more than 40, Melbourne with more than 50 and Washington DC with more than 60.

Figure 6.1 shows the cities with large and small floor areas per person relative to their country's per capita income. Hong Kong (with 7 square metres) has an especially low floor area per person in comparison to per capita income;

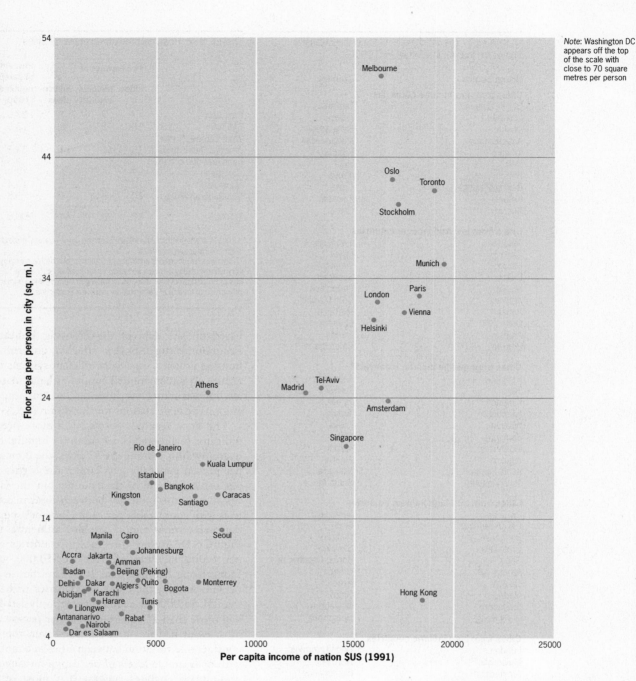

Note: Washington DC appears off the top of the scale with close to 70 square metres per person

**FIGURE 6.1
Housing Quality:
Floor area per
person**

Monterrey (with 8.6) and Seoul (with 13) also have low scores while Bangkok, Istanbul, Rio de Janeiro, Athens and Melbourne have relatively high scores. The score for Washington DC is particularly high—perhaps reflecting people's preference within Washington DC (and most cities in North America) for relatively large, detached housing within relatively low-density residential areas—although this is a preference that has been shaped by government policies and powerful economic interests.

City averages for floor area per person often obscure high levels of overcrowding for low-income groups in general—or for particular low-income groups or for those living in particular settlements. For instance, in Seoul in 1985,

the poorest 30 per cent of the population had an average of 2 square metres per person, many times less than the average.[7] In Karachi, the living space in many of the informal settlements (*katchi abadis*) where close to 40 per cent of the population live is between 2 and 3 square metres per person while those living in bungalows or the larger town houses or apartments had between 23 and 33 square metres per person.[8] In a study of Olaleye-Iponri, a centrally located informal settlement in Lagos, many tenant households lived in a single room with an average of around 1 square metre per person.[9]

The Housing Indicators Programme also collected data on persons per room[10] in the 52 cities and these indicate that overcrowding tends to

TABLE 6.3 Housing Quality

Income Grouping; cities in:	Floor area per person (m²)	Persons per room	%age of permanent structures	%age of dwelling units with water connection to their plot
Low-income countries	6.1	2.47	67	56
Low–mid-income countries	8.8	2.24	86	74
Middle-income countries	15.1	1.69	94	94
Mid–high-income countries	22.0	1.03	99	99
High-income countries	35.0	0.66	100	100

Source: *The Housing Indicators Program Volume III; Preliminary Findings*, A Joint Programme of the United Nations Centre for Human Settlements (Habitat) and the World Bank, Washington DC, April 1993.

decrease, the higher the country's per capita income. In all 12 of the high-income countries, there is less than one person per room; in Oslo and Toronto, there are two rooms to each person. Among the low-income countries, most have 2 or more persons per room with 3 or more in Dhaka, Antananarivo, Nairobi, Karachi and Accra. Among cities in low–mid-income countries, Manila and Amman are the most overcrowded with 3 or more persons per room; Jakarta is the least overcrowded with 1.3 persons per room. It is worth noting that Jakarta is thus relatively overcrowded in terms of floor area per person but much less overcrowded in terms of persons per room. Among cities in the middle-income countries, Warsaw was the least overcrowded (0.9 persons per room) with Algiers (2.6) the most overcrowded.

The proportion of dwellings in a city that are made of permanent materials also increases consistently with the country's per capita income, although there are very considerable variations in this indicator among cities in countries with comparable per capita incomes. One factor that helps explain this variation is the rate of growth of a city's population—the more rapidly growing cities tend to have a higher proportion of houses built on temporary materials. Cities with relatively low levels of infrastructure expenditure per person and lower percentages of dwellings with piped water also tend to have a smaller proportion of houses built of permanent materials. However, for many cities, the figures given for this indicator seem at odds with other research reports or official statistics. For instance, the data from the Housing Indicators Programme suggests that in Karachi, 97 per cent of the dwelling units are made of permanent materials—which does not accord with other sources.[11] Figures of 97 per cent for Accra, 80 per cent for Manila, 97 per cent for Amman and 99 per cent for Rio de Janeiro are also among figures that seem at variance with other research reports on housing conditions in these cities.

The proportion of dwellings in cities with water connections to the plot they occupy also increases as the country's per capita income increases—to the point where these are provided for nearly all households in the cities in the mid/high- and high-income countries—see Chapter 8 for more details. The expenditure per person by government agencies on water supply, sanitation, garbage collection and other forms of infrastructure and services also gives some indication of housing quality. The range of such expenditures in the 52 cities was enormous—from 1 or 2 $US per person per year in Antananarivo and Dar es Salaam to more than $US1,000 in Vienna, Stockholm, and Tokyo and $US2,201 in Helsinki. Table 6.4 shows the median values for cities grouped by their country's per capita income and by their geographic region. These expenditure figures per person cover operations, maintenance and capital for all government agencies for roads, sewerage, drainage, water supply, electricity and garbage collection. If this figure had been restricted only to capital investment, the contrasts would have been even more dramatic. As Chapter 5 described most city and municipal authorities in the South have an annual investment capacity of less than $US10 per person in their jurisdiction; many have less than $US1 per person. Cities with low per capita expenditures on infrastructure also tend to be cities with the largest gap between the price of undeveloped land and the prices of a land plot with infrastructure within a typical subdivision—as will be described in more detail in Chapter 7.

Housing tenure

It is well known that between 30 and 60 per cent of the housing units in most cities in the South are illegal in that either they contravene land ownership laws or they contravene building and planning laws or codes. Many contravene both sets of laws. Among the 52 cities, there is a dramatic fall in the percentage of the housing stock that is unauthorized, going from cities in the lowest to the highest income countries. Among the ten cities in the lowest income category, the mean is 64 per cent unauthorized and all but Beijing has 40 or more per cent (see Table 6.5). In Nairobi, Ibadan and Dhaka, three-quarters or more of the housing stock is unauthorized. In cities in the low/mid-income countries, the proportion of the housing stock that is unauthorized varies from 8 (Bogota) to 65 or more per cent (Jakarta, Cairo, Dakar and Manila)—although care must be taken in interpreting these figures. For instance, in the case of Bogota, a large proportion of housing that is now considered 'authorized' was built on illegal subdivisions.[12] In Jakarta, a considerable proportion of the housing stock considered

TABLE 6.4 Government expenditures per person on water supply, sanitation, drainage, garbage collection, roads and electricity

Income Grouping; cities in:	$US per person	Regional grouping; cities in:	$US per person
Low-income countries	15.0	Sub-Saharan Africa	16.6
Low–mid-income countries	31.4	South Asia	15.0
Middle-income countries	40.1	East Asia	72.5
Mid–high-income countries	304.6	Latin America and the Caribbean	48.4
High-income countries	813.5	Eastern Europe, Greece, North Africa and the Middle East	86.2
		West Europe, North America, Australasia	656.0

Source: The Housing Indicators Program Volume III; Preliminary Findings, A Joint Programme of the United Nations Centre for Human Settlements (Habitat) and the World Bank, Washington DC, April 1993.

'unauthorized' was in *kampungs* which are perhaps better considered as traditional rather than unauthorized residential areas.[13]

Among cities in other income groups, more than half the housing stock is unauthorized in Kingston, Istanbul and Caracas—although in Caracas, as in Bogota, a considerable proportion of those who live in 'unauthorized' housing stock have little or no possibility of eviction and have long been provided with public services.[14] Thus, care must be taken in interpreting these figures. In addition, in many cities, the proportion of people in 'unauthorized housing' is not the same as the proportion in 'squatter housing' in that they include dwellings built on illegal or informal subdivisions where the occupation of the land site is not illegal. Thus, the proportion of unauthorized housing in most of these cities is much higher than the proportion living in squatter settlements. The range of housing units within 'unauthorized housing' and the different aspects of their illegality in cities in the South is discussed in more detail in Sections 6.2 and 6.4; these sections also discuss in more detail the different forms of tenure under which people live in city dwellings.

TABLE 6.5 Housing tenure for the 52 cities

Income Grouping: cities in:	%age of dwelling units owned by the occupants	%age of dwelling units that are public housing	%age of total housing stock that is unauthorized
Low-income countries	33	13	64
Low–mid-income countries	52	11	36
Middle-income countries	59	14	20
Mid–high-income countries	55	53	3
High-income countries	51	13	0

Source: The Housing Indicators Program Volume III; Preliminary Findings, A Joint Programme of the United Nations Centre for Human Settlements (Habitat) and the World Bank, Washington DC, April 1993.

Housing availability and affordability

The Housing Indicators Programme investigated not only housing affordability—for instance through the ratio of house price to income—but also the factors that help keep down house prices relative to incomes and thus increase the proportion of people able to purchase or rent adequate quality housing. One of the most common measures for housing affordability is the house price–income ratio i.e. how many years' income is needed to purchase a house.

What is perhaps most notable about this indicator is the relatively small differences between the median price–income ratio for housing for low-, low/mid-, middle-, mid/high- and high-income countries but the very large variation among cities within each category. In many of the cities, the prospects for most people of being able to buy a house appear poor as the house price–income ratio is 5 or more. A ratio of between 2:1 and 3:1 would generally imply that a significant proportion of the population could afford to purchase housing (although highly unequal income distribution would push down this proportion). If the country has well-developed housing finance institutions, this can considerably increase the proportion since it increases the amount the household can afford, by permitting repayment of the total housing cost over a longer period—although it is rare for housing finance institutions to provide house purchase loans or mortgages in excess of three times a household's annual income. The findings from the Housing Indicators Programme suggest that housing is cheap relative to incomes in cities such as Lilongwe, Nairobi and Karachi, Abidjan and Quito, Johannesburg and Santiago, and Caracas and Rio de Janeiro. Among the high-income countries, there is no city with a ratio below 3.7, although these cities are also in countries with among the most highly developed housing finance systems. Some caution is needed in interpreting the city figures since the value for this indicator can change quite rapidly. For instance, the price–income ratio for housing in Greater London, fell by 27 per cent between 1988 and 1993.[15]

A comparison between house prices in Tokyo and Washington DC in 1990 illustrates the differences in housing affordability. Reported house prices for median dwelling units in this year were $US442,000 for Tokyo and $US196,000 for Washington DC; the average size of these dwellings was 41 square metres in Tokyo and 161 square metres in Washington DC.[16] In some cities, one factor in high price to income ratios is the proportion of housing in public ownership. Some of the cities where the ratios are particularly high are also cities where a high proportion of the housing stock is publicly owned—for instance Beijing and Hong Kong. However, some cities with a high proportion of housing in public ownership also have relatively low house-price-to-income ratios—for instance Helsinki, Paris, Stockholm and Amsterdam.

The price of rental housing

In most cities, the price of rental housing has great importance to lower-income groups. Rental housing is not only cheaper because no payment has to be made for the asset and for the security that owning provides—it is also because smaller units can be rented rather than purchased. It is possible to rent a room in a multi-room building and even a bed but these cannot be purchased. Renting tends to be particularly important for those who work in low-paid jobs in central city locations and for those who earn an income from casual work or other work sources that require them to move constantly. As will be discussed in more detail in section 6.4, the price and availability of cheap rental accommodation in cities in the North is one important influence on the level of homelessness.

The Housing Indicators Programme found that rent levels per square metre of dwelling space were about three times as variable among cities in the South, compared to cities in the North. In addition, it was in the cities in the low-income countries that rent levels per square metre appeared to be highest, relative to the country's per capita income.[17] The mean for the rent to income ratio for all cities was 0.16, i.e. on average, 16 per cent of the income of renters was being spent on rent. In certain cities, it was much lower than this. For instance, it was only 3 per cent in Dar es Salaam and Bratislava and between 5 and 10 for many cities. In some of these cities, where a high proportion of all renters are accommodated in public housing, this may reflect the fact that rents in public housing are subsidized—for instance in Beijing, Hong Kong and Bratislava; in others, it may reflect a high degree of rent control. The preliminary analysis of the Housing Indicators Programme suggested that this ratio of rent to income rises, as a country's per capita income increases, to reach a peak in middle-income countries and then falls.[18] It also suggested that cities with a rapid growth in the number of households have relatively high rent-to-income ratios—and that these ratios also appear to be associated with residential mobility and tenure choice. When rents are low, especially in countries with pervasive rent controls, people generally move less frequently. When rents are relatively high, owning a house becomes more attractive and the proportion of households owning their home rises. Section 6.2 will describe in more detail the scale of renting and home ownership in different cities and who rents.

Another source of information about the relative cost of rental housing between cities is a survey undertaken in 53 cities by the Union Bank of Switzerland in Zurich. This survey included rent levels for two kinds of accommodation: local rent levels; and rent levels for furnished apartments of 'international' standard. Perhaps the most dramatic difference between these two is the lack of correspondence between international rent levels and the per capita income of the country. Thus, in cities such as Jakarta, Bombay, Bangkok, Sao Paulo, Lagos, Rio de Janeiro and Kuala Lumpur, it was more expensive to rent an 'international level' four-room apartment than in most cities in Europe and North America. The most expensive city of all was Hong Kong—much more expensive than Tokyo, New York and all the major European cities. Of course, this is biased by the type of apartment considered—which in this instance had to be built after 1975, be furnished to satisfy the tastes of Europeans in middle management positions, located in a 'choice' residential area with a garage. The premium paid just for a garage is likely to be very considerable in the wealthiest and most densely populated cities.

In contrast, there is a much closer correspondence between local rent levels and the country's per capita income. According to this, cities such as Cairo, Jakarta, Seoul, Hong Kong and Tokyo have among the highest rents relative to their country's per capita income while cities like Lagos, Prague, Caracas, Montreal and Houston have among the lowest. It is also interesting to note the variation between the four cities in the United States. Local rent levels in Houston are half the rate in Los Angeles, Chicago and New York. Although Houston is substantially smaller than the other three cities, it has also had a booming economy and a much more rapid growth in population in recent decades. Houston's rapid population growth has taken place without constraints on its expansion or internal land use whereas in New York–New Jersey, there are many controls; the proportion of households who move each year in Houston has also been twice or more than that of New York–New Jersey since 1970.[19]

Costs of land, construction and finance for housing

The final cost of housing is obviously much influenced by the cost of land, construction and finance for housing construction (including land purchase). Variations in the cost of these inputs help explain the large differences in housing quality between cities in countries with comparable per capita incomes. For instance, in Athens, in 1990, median dwellings had 70 square metres while in Hong Kong, they had 26 square metres; in Athens, they were valued as $US54,000 compared to $US112,000 in Hong Kong. The differences in costs are attributable to differences in both land and construction costs.[20] Below are discussed the influence of housing finance and construction costs; Chapter 7 considers land costs.

An overview of institutional housing finance

Next to land and building materials, housing finance is perhaps the most important factor in housing production—and may even be considered the most important, given that adequate finance can help the purchase of the land and materials.[21] Indeed, the extent to which housing finance is available, the terms under which it is available and the proportion of the population that can obtain it is a major influence not only on housing but on cities.[22]

Analyses and inferences in the sections above notwithstanding, current, comparable and comprehensive data on housing demand, housing supply and housing finance around the world are extremely inadequate. International agencies have been unable to mobilize the funds and elicit the co-operation of member countries in collecting and supplying adequate information on the sector. This is indicative of the lack of organization in the sector and of the priority attached to housing by policy-makers and their administrative systems. An enormous amount of research into the issues of housing and housing finance remains to be done, but cannot be done until the basic task of adequate data collection and dissemination has been completed. This section seeks to provide an overview of institutional housing finance around the world by presenting such data and information as have been collected and developed.

Experience in housing finance development around the world demonstrates that broad, market-based systems are the most effective vehicle through which to provide financial resources for shelter development. A fundamental problem facing Governments, however, is that formal-sector financial institutions seldom lend downmarket to serve the needs and requirements of low-income households. Low-income families are denied credit altogether, because the mode of operation followed by formal financial institutions is not compatible with their economic characteristics and financing needs. For example, commercial lending institutions require that borrowers have a stable source of income out of which the principal and interest on loans can be paid according to the agreed terms, whereas the income of self-employed people is usually not stable regardless of its size. Lenders also look for collateral with a clear title that many low-income urban people do not have. In addition, financial institutions tend to think that low-income households are a bad risk, although there is no proven evidence for it.[23]

Governments often try to address the problem of lack of access to credit for low-income households by creating specialized lending institutions. In so doing, most governments also provide capital or low-cost funds to the special circuit housing finance institutions so that they could extend credit to the low-income clientele at subsidized interest rates.[24] Interest rate subsidies are usually justified on social policy grounds that the low-income borrowers cannot afford to service the loans offered on commercial terms.

Virtually all the countries in the North have identifiable financial institutions specializing, to one degree or another, in housing finance. Many countries in the South have also established housing finance institutions or systems. However, enabling legislation and even an initial grant of operating capital, is not enough to assure the success of a housing finance system. Many of the housing finance systems in the South are all but moribund; they are housing finance systems in name only. Many have also prospered for a time, only to fall prey to macroeconomic policies and external shocks that allowed the operating environment to deteriorate to the point at which they could no longer function (see Box 6.2). It is thus hardly surprising to find that most housing finance in the South comes from non-institutionalized sources such as family savings, assistance from friends and other relations or loans from employers or informal credit-groups or unions.[25] For instance, among the owner-occupiers of housing in informal settlements in Abidjan which house around a fifth of the city's population, housing finance either came from personal savings or from kinship networks or employers in the form of loans.[26]

Housing credit, as a proportion of the financial assets of a country's banking system, generally increases with the level of per capita income. Thus, among the low income country category for the Housing Indicators Programme, only 3 per cent of the outstanding credit is held in the form of housing loans, compared to 27 per cent in the high-income countries—with figures for the other country categories ordered by per capita income falling between these two extremes. However, there is considerable variation between countries in each of the five categories, reflecting, among other things, variations in the extent of development of housing markets, housing finance institutions and government policy towards housing finance. Contrasting this indicator in the centrally planned economies and Latin American countries in the 52-country sample illustrates this. Latin America, with a rich set of financial institutions dealing with housing finance has an unusually high share of the assets of its banking system allocated to housing loans; the median for the countries in the region was 21

BOX 6.2
Examples of financial distress

Argentina: The failure of a large private bank sparked the 1980–1982 banking crisis. By 1983, 71 of 740 financial institutions had been liquidated.

Bangladesh: Four banks that accounted for 70 per cent of total credit had an estimated 20 per cent of non-performing assets in 1987. Loans to two loss-making public enterprises amounted to fourteen times the banks' total capital.

Bolivia: In late 1987 the central bank liquidated two of twelve private commercial banks; seven more reported large losses. In mid-1988 reported arrears stood at 92 per cent of commercial banks' net worth.

Chile: In 1981 the government liquidated eight insolvent institutions that together held 35 per cent of total financial systems assets. In 1983 another eight institutions (45 per cent of system assets) were taken over; three were liquidated, five restructured and recapitalized. In September 1988, central bank holdings of bad commercial bank loans amounted to nearly 19 per cent of GNP.

Colombia: The 1995 losses of the banking system as a whole amounted to 140 per cent of capital plus reserves. Between 1982 and 1987 the central bank intervened in six banks (24 per cent of system assets), five of which in 1985 alone had losses equal to 202 per cent of their capital plus reserves.

Costa Rica: Public banks, which do 90 per cent of all lending, considered 32 per cent of loans 'uncollectible' in early 1987. This implied losses of at least twice capital plus reserves. Losses of private banks were an estimated 21 per cent plus reserves.

Ghana: By mid-1988 the net worth of the banking system was negative, having been completely eroded by large foreign exchange losses and a high proportion of

nonperforming loans. The estimated cost of restructuring is $300 million, or nearly 6 per cent of GNP.

Greece: Non-performing loans to ailing industrial companies amount to several times the capital of the largest commercial banks, which hold more than 80 per cent of total bank assets.

Guinea: The Government that assumed power in 1984 inherited a virtually defunct banking system; 99 per cent of loans proved unrecoverable. All six state-owned banks were liquidated, and three new commercial banks were established.

Kenya: Many of the non-bank financial institutions that have sprung up since 1978 are insolvent, and in 1986 several of the larger ones collapsed.

Kuwait: Because of the large losses sustained by speculators in stock and real estate markets, an estimated 40 per cent of bank loans were nonperforming by 1986.

Madagascar: In early 1988, 25 per cent of all loans were irrecoverable, and 21 per cent more were deemed 'difficult to collect'. Given the low level of reserves (less than 5 per cent of assets), the banking system as a whole was insolvent.

Norway: Commercial and savings banks suffered heavy losses in 1987 and 1988 owing to the collapse of the price of oil and imprudent lending.

Philippines: Between 1981 and 1987, 161 smaller institutions holding 3.5 per cent of total financial system assets were closed. In addition, the authorities intervened in two large public and five private banks. The public banks were liquidated in 1986 and their largest bad assets (equal to 30 per cent of the banking system's assets) were transferred to a separate agency.

Republic of Korea: Seventy-eight insolvent firms, whose combined debts exceeded

assets by $5.9 billion, were dissolved or merged during 1986 and 1987.

Spain: Between 1978 and 1983 fifty-one institutions holding nearly a fifth of all deposits were rescued; two were eventually liquidated, and the rest were sold to sound banks

Sri Lanka: Two state-owned banks comprising 70 per cent of the banking system have estimated non-performing assets of at least 35 per sent of their total portfolio

Thailand: The resolution of a 1983 crisis involving forty-four finance companies that held 12 per cent of financial system assets cost $190 million, or 0.5 per cent of GNP. Between 1984 and 1987, the Government intervened in five banks that held one quarter of bank assets.

UMOA Countries: More than 25 per cent of bank credits in the UMOA countries are non-performing. At least twenty primary banks are bankrupt; non-performing credits are almost six times the sum of their capital, reserves, and provisions.

United Republic of Tanzania: In early 1987 the main financial institutions had long-standing arrears amounting to half their portfolio, and implied losses were nearly 10 per cent of GNP.

United States: Between 1980 and 1988 nearly 1,100 savings and loan associates (S&Ls) were closed or merged. In early 1989, more than 600 (one-fifth of all S&Ls) were insolvent, and the cost of restructuring was estimated to be roughly $80 billion in terms of present value. By 1989, 10 per cent of commercial banks were on the regulator's 'watch list'.

Uruguay: After several banks failed in 1981/2, the central bank began to aid banks by purchasing their worst assets; by 1983 it had acquired $830 million in bad loans. The potential cost of recapitalizing the banks has been estimated at $350 million, or 7 per cent of GNP.

Source: UNCHS (Habitat), Integrated Housing Finance into the National Finance Systems of Developing Countries: Exploring the Potentials and Problems, Nairobi, 1991—drawing on a report prepared for UNCHS by James W. Christian III.

per cent. For the formerly centrally planned economies, which lack market-based lending for housing and market oriented housing finance institutions, housing finance makes up a much smaller proportion of total investment.

The findings from the Housing Indicators Programme also emphasize the extent to which formal financial institutions come to dominate total housing investment in the high income countries but still have a relatively small role in low-income countries. When viewed regionally, the 'credit-to value' ratio (the proportion of total housing investment provided by mortgage loans) is particularly low in sub-Saharan Africa and South Asia. This is unsurprising, given that the higher a country's per capita income, the higher

the proportion of income the average household spends on housing and the more important housing finance becomes within financial systems.[27] However, in most countries in the South, the unavailability of housing finance for a large proportion of low- and lower middle-income groups who have considerable capacity to save, invest in housing and repay loans is a major constraint on improving their housing quality—and housing quality in the city overall. It also slows down housing construction, especially where (as is common in many cities in the South) a high proportion of new housing units are constructed by self-help. One of the reasons why self-help construction takes so many years is that the households can only fund it out of their income as no long-term loan can be obtained—and this helps explain why many urban dwellers live in housing units that are only partially completed with construction undertaken incrementally over many years.[28] Many innovative housing finance initiatives—most of them undertaken by NGOs but also some by governments—have shown how individuals or households who cannot obtain loans for house purchase or improvement or land acquisition from conventional finance institutions have a considerable capacity to save and take on loans—and often achieve better repayment rates than more wealthy individuals using the formal institutions.[29] The credit-to-value ratio appears to have considerable importance in terms of housing quality as it was positively associated with every indicator of housing quality and space—and with residential mobility and owner occupancy.

Construction costs

The Housing Indicators Programme found that construction costs per square metre for a median-priced dwelling unit differed much less between cities relative to the per capita income of the nation than might have been expected, given the very large differences in levels of per capita income. However, there was great variation between cities within countries of comparable per capita incomes—sometimes by a factor of 10. Construction costs were considerably higher relative to incomes in the lowest income countries, which suggests that the efficiency of the residential construction industry generally increases, as a country's per capita income increases. Construction costs were particularly high in cities in sub-Saharan Africa, relative to per capita income, which could be partially explained by high building material prices (that also relate to monopoly elements in the building materials industries), the scarcity of skilled labour, high transport costs, inappropriate standards and (when the research was undertaken) over-valued exchange rates. For instance, in South Africa, at least until recent years, building material costs have been kept high because of the highly concentrated ownership within the building materials industry and restrictions on the import of building materials; for most building materials, only one or two firms control production and distribution.[30]

Many cities with high house price-to-income ratios also have high construction costs per square metre—although a strong correlation between high construction costs and high price-to-income ratios only appears common for cities in the middle, mid/high- and high-income countries. For instance, Hong Kong and Seoul with the highest price–income ratios in their group

also have among the highest construction costs while Caracas and Rio de Janeiro with the lowest house price–income ratio also have among the lowest construction costs. Tokyo with much the highest house price–income ratio also has much the highest construction cost per square metre.[31]

The effects of government regulation

One of the most debated aspects of government's role in housing provision over the last ten years is its role as regulator of land sales, land conversion and development, land-uses and construction standards and as the body responsible for defining housing and infrastructure standards. At one extreme, unrealistically high standards demanded for housing plot sizes, construction and building material standards, and standards for piped water, sewers, drains and roads relative to most of the population's income, ensures that legal housing is too expensive for most of the population. If it also proves to be a cumbersome process to obtain the necessary permissions and approvals, the costs will go up still further. And it is common for anyone building a house who wants to do so legally to have to obtain permission for different aspects of the work from different agencies—for instance the land purchase, the use to which it is to be put, the provision for infrastructure and services, the house design, the standard of the house construction, and so on. At the other extreme, no regulation and no standards will allow housing and land developers to avoid all the basic standards for infrastructure and service provision, structural safety and plot size that are so needed for health and safety. It can also lead to highly exploitative, large-scale landlordism as in the *thika* tenants of Calcutta, the beehive buildings in Seoul, and the cage people of Hong Kong.[32] For the cage people, several thousand people live in 'cages', rows of double or triple bunk beds in rooms with 30 or more beds; they are called the cage people since many of the beds are surrounded with a wire cage surrounding each bed and a lock for security.[33]

The Housing Indicators Programme looked at a variety of indicators that would influence the cost of all houses that were built with official permission—including minimum lot size, the speed with which a permit could be obtained for a residential land subdivision and the proportion of land in that subdivision that could be sold (i.e. the saleable land ratio). It also looked at the amount of time needed to get approvals, permits and titles for a new medium-size residential subdivision in an area on the urban fringe where residential development is permitted—and this varied from under 5 months for around a third of the cities to over 20 months for a quarter of cities. A 'restrictiveness index' was constructed as the unweighed sum of positive answers to a list of questions concerning the existence of legal restrictions on the development and exchange of land, on the production of housing and building materials and on the provision of housing finance. The value of the index generally declines as per capita incomes rise; the highest values were among the low income countries with the lowest values among the high-income countries. Higher values for this index are also associated with a high degree of land concentration (see Chapter 7), lower vacancy rates, higher ratios of house price to income and relatively lower amounts of housing finance.

A recent paper suggested a very strong correlation between the level of government regulation and public housing ownership on the one hand and the extent to which people move house.[34] It suggested that in countries with high levels of government regulation and ownership, 5 per cent or fewer households moved annually. In countries with few controls on landlords and investors such as Switzerland, Thailand and the USA, 16–19 per cent moved annually. In countries with an intermediate amount of intervention in building, rents and finance, around 9 per cent moved annually. A high proportion of households in public housing or in rented accommodation where rents are controlled is likely to keep down residential mobility. Households in subsidized housing are obviously more reluctant to move. Residential mobility is likely to be particularly low for public housing, if for most households it requires several years waiting to get the housing and as the administrative systems that allocate and manage public housing have difficulties managing continuous changes in tenants within each unit.

However, the variation between cities in the wealthiest nations in terms of the proportion of people who moved in one year is notable and not obviously linked to the proportion of housing in public ownership—see Figure 6.2.

Thus, Amsterdam with a high proportion of housing units in public ownership has among the highest level of mobility with London and Stockholm also having relatively high mobility and significant proportions of their housing stock in public ownership—while cities such as Munich, Oslo and Tokyo with low proportions in public ownership also have low levels of mobility. Some of the cities with low levels of residential mobility relate to particular circumstances—for instance in Hong Kong and Singapore, the very small size of these city-states would allow more people to move jobs without necessarily moving house. Among the cities in low to middle income countries, some of those with among the lowest levels of residential mobility also had among the highest proportions of public housing stock. Certain cities with a high proportion of their rented housing stock subject to

rent control in 1990 also had relatively low mobility rates—for instance Manila, Dar es Salaam, Budapest and Rio de Janeiro—but Toronto, Amsterdam and Beijing that also had a high proportion of their rental accommodation subject to rent control in 1990 also had relatively high mobility rates.

6.2 Housing Markets and Tenure

Introduction

This section reviews conditions and trends in housing markets and in housing tenure. Its main interest is in the extent to which those with relatively modest means can find adequate quality and secure accommodation. It draws on a considerable number of detailed descriptions and analyses of such housing markets published since the last *Global Report*.[35] These served as a reminder that a high proportion of low-income groups rent accommodation in most cities, if rental accommodation is available—a fact that had been documented in the 1960s and early 1970s but not given much attention in housing policies during the 1970s and 1980s. They also revealed how complex and varied housing markets often are—and how simplistic and often inaccurate it is to assume that most low-income groups lived in 'slums' or 'slums and squatter settlements'. They showed how many 'illegal settlements' are not 'squatter settlements' at all as the land had not been occupied illegally. Many 'illegal' settlements have also been shown to have had the tacit approval of government officials or politicians and in some, officials or politicians had a leading role in their development.

Recent research on housing and land markets in cities in the South has not replaced the old generalizations with new ones. But it has shown how these markets are too diverse to permit much valid generalization. A focus on a city-specific understanding of how housing markets work and the ways in which poorer individuals and households find some form of accommodation—even if it is only a temporary structure, erected on a pavement—produces a more precise understanding of the needs of low-income groups and how these are currently met (however inadequately) in each particular city. It also demonstrates how a detailed understanding of housing problems cannot be abstracted out of the particular city. Such problems are too rooted in the particulars of that city—especially the supply and price of land for housing (described in more detail in Chapter 7), the extent and spatial pattern of roads, water supply, provision for public transport and other forms of infrastructure and public services and the cost of constructing a house (including the costs of loans and building materi-

FIGURE 6.2
**Residential
mobility—the
percentage of
households who
moved their unit
in 1989**

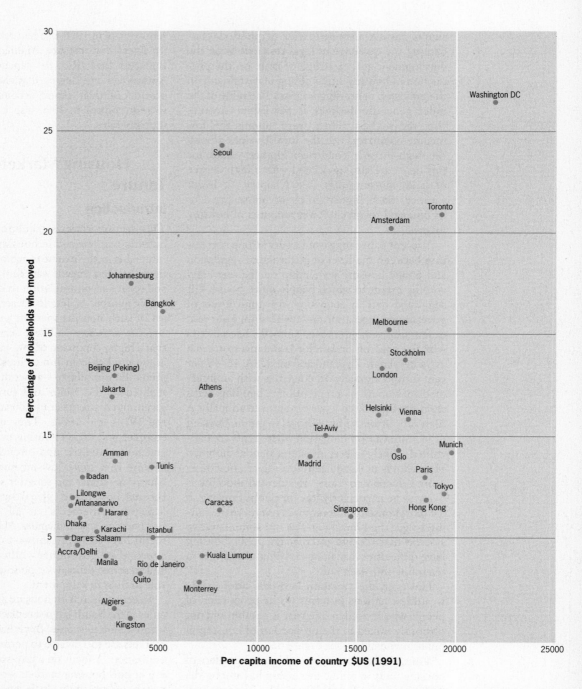

als). Government policies and the laws, codes and standards that underlie them have a great direct and indirect influence on all of these. So too does the nature of land ownership and the formal and informal mechanisms that influence its development for housing—legally or illegally. Governments' macro-economic and pricing policies can also have a major influence, especially where a significant proportion of the population have large outstanding loans to allow them to buy or build a house. What is evident in housing, as in land (see Chapter 7) and in environmental problems (Chapter 4) is the extent to which social and economic change in cities in the South have outpaced governments' willingness or capacity to change their institutional frameworks for managing urban change. This is a theme to which this chapter will return in its conclusions.

Housing demand from low-income groups

A recent World Bank policy paper on housing noted how one of the most striking findings about expenditures for housing is their regularity across countries:

Spending for housing, like that for most commodities, increases with household income in every urban society. Moreover, as economic development proceeds, the average fraction of income spent on housing in countries at different levels of economic development increased from about 5 per cent to about 30 per cent, before beginning to decrease again. This is, to a considerable degree, because households give increased priority to housing as incomes increase and as food becomes less of a problem. This shift of expenditures towards housing creates the possibility of rapid improvement in housing conditions, as economic development proceeds.[36]

In a study of Cairo, Manila, Bogotá and Seoul in the mid-1980s, patterns of spending were remarkably similar, despite the considerable differences in average monthly income between these cities.[37] In each of the cities, the proportion of income spent on housing declined systematically at relatively similar rates, as household income increased. Thus, lower-income households spent a higher proportion of their income on housing than more prosperous households.

However, this regularity across countries or cities does not imply any valid generalizations as to how much different low-income individuals or households want to spend on housing. Studies of urban housing markets or of particular sub-markets used by lower-income groups demonstrate a great diversity of 'demand'. This diversity stems from two factors. The first is how much income they have available to spend on housing; the lowest-income individuals or households may have nothing to spend on housing as all income is needed to purchase their immediate daily necessities.[38] The second is each individual's or household's choice as to how much they want to spend on housing; this decision will be influenced by what kinds of accommodation currently available within the city or its periphery best serve their needs in terms of cost relative to location (especially in relation to sources of employment), size and quality of dwelling and associated infrastructure and services and level of security. Their priorities in regard to location, size of dwelling, amount they want to pay and many other factors will be much influenced by their age, employment status, whether they are single or a couple and whether or not they have children—and how many children they have and their ages.

In most cities, there is a large section of the population who want to spend as little as possible on housing and certainly do not want to own a home—at least in their current circumstances. Many single people or parents working in cities with their families living elsewhere choose to spend as little as possible on housing to maximize their income or minimize costs. For instance, in Thika (Kenya) 'the poor do not squat' because most of the population prefer to rent accommodation; they are in Thika to earn money and do not intend to make their home there.[40]

A proportion of those who are considered

BOX 6.3

Constraints on investment in housing by low-income households

In addition to their very limited capacity to pay for housing, low-income households face other constraints if they seek better quality accommodation:

Inability to get credit: Many households with sufficient income to repay a long-term loan cannot obtain such a loan because they cannot meet official criteria for being creditworthy—for instance, working in the informal economy and lacking proof of employment or lacking the required collateral. Women headed households face particular problems, because of widespread gender biases in credit-vetting procedures.

Locational needs: Many low-income households could afford the cost of better quality housing on the city periphery but not the time and money needed to go to and from work. Improvements in public transport will tend to widen the range of choices open to low-income households.

Lack of 'free-time': The assumption that most 'low-income' households have 'free time' in which they can organize and build their own housing and work with neighbours in developing community-level infrastructure has often been shown to be wrong because of the long hours worked by the heads of household—or all adults or even, in extreme circumstances, all adults and many children. There has long been a confusion between 'low income' and 'unemployment' or 'underemployment'. Those with very low incomes, working in the informal economy, are assumed to be out of work because they are not working in a job that is registered but in fact they are working long hours. Single-parent households (most of them headed by women) face the greatest constraint on 'free time' as they have to combine income earning, child-rearing and household maintenance.[39]

'homeless' in the sense that they sleep in public buildings, parks or other open spaces may have sufficient income to rent a room or bed indoors but prefer to avoid these costs to maximize their savings or to permit them to send more funds to their family living elsewhere. It is also common for migrants newly arrived in a city to spend as little as possible on accommodation by relying on family members, relatives or friends to provide accommodation initially and help in finding employment that then permits them to pay for their own accommodation.[43] At the other extreme, relatively low-income households may be spending a high proportion of their income on a house—for instance a family that has acquired a plot of land with reasonably secure tenure who invest as much income and labour as possible in building, developing or improving their home as this not only improves their house but also represents an asset whose value is increasing. Box 6.4 presents the reasons why the inhabitants of precarious settlements in Abidjan were attracted to live there.

BOX 6.4
Choosing a neighbourhood among precarious settlements in Abidjan

For both owner-occupiers and tenants, housing opportunities, access to areas of economic activity and potential employment and the presence of relatives were the most important attractions for people moving to the precarious settlements. The table shows the main factor that attracted owners and tenants, based on interviews with 620 people.

Attraction	Owners	Tenants	All
Land available	196 (39.2)	–	196 (31.6)
Accommodation available	23 (4.6)	8 (6.7)	31 (5.0)
Presence of relatives	89 (17.8)	37 (30.8)	126 (20.3)
Easy access	78 (15.6)	–	78 (12.6)
Close to employment	107 (21.4)	29 (24.2)	136 (22.0)
Low cost of living	3 (0.6)	44 (36.7)	47 (7.6)
Community lifestyle	4 (0.8)	2 (1.7)	6 (1.0)
All	500 (100.0)	120 (100.0)	620 (100.0)

Proximity to one's job, the most important factor for 22 per cent of those interviewed, has about the same weight as the presence of relatives (20.3%). However, it is logical that owners should be more attracted by the availability of land (39.2%), whereas tenants are more likely to look for neighbourhoods with a low cost of living (36.7%) or where their relatives live or close to areas of economic activity.

Living close to their places of work may reduce but does not remove the high cost of transport. According to various studies, transport represents between 6 to 12 per cent of the expenses of heads of household in informal housing.[41]

Whether transport and proximity to places of work, or competitive rents and property opportunities, appear amongst criteria for choosing neighbourhoods, these elements show that low-income groups' residential strategy cannot be reduced to a simple equation. Choice is generally based on a combination of several inter-acting factors. There are many illustrations of this, in the life-histories of city dwellers that have been recorded in various neighbourhoods of Abidjan.[42]

Source: Yapi-Diahou, Alphonse, *The informal housing sector of the metropolis of Abidjan, Ivory Coast*, Background Paper for the United Nations Global Report on Human Settlements, 1994.

FIGURE 6.3
The factors that influence housing supply and housing demand
Source: The framework is drawn from Mayo, Stephen K. and Shlomo Angel, *Enabling Housing Markets to Work*, A World Bank Policy Paper, The World Bank, Washington DC. The factors that influence housing supply and demand have been added.

The factors that influence housing demand

- **Disposable income** available to households (which in turn is influenced by government fiscal policy) and its distribution within the population. Lower income groups having little or nothing to spend on housing
- **nature of employment** (secure, long term employment perhaps more associated with desire for home ownership? Also with possibility of obtaining mortgage or loan)
- **household priorities**; the extent to which individuals and households want to own their own shelter that is also influenced by whether owning a house, apartment or land site is considered a good investment or has tax advantages
- **availability of housing finance** for different income groups and types of household or other means to permit entry for all individuals and households (gender biases may restrict women's access)
- **age and household size and structure** (including number of individuals or households seeking housing)
- **occupation** (adult students and those wanting to remain mobile not wanting owner occupation or long-term tenancies).

The factors that influence housing supply

- **price and availability of land** for housing (that is influenced by ease with which it can be bought or sold and subdivision/minimum plot size regulations; also by demand for land from other sectors; also by the scale and nature of road construction and public transport provision)
- **price and availability of skilled and unskilled labour** for housing (also influenced by demand for labour from other sectors)
- **the efficiency of the official framework** supervising the construction and purchase/sale of housing including the time and cost involved in receiving official permission or sanction to buy or sell housing or land or build housing
- **official standards** on building, building materials, infrastructure and services and land use and development
- **extent to which illegal or informal housing and land developments are tolerated** (in many urban centres in the South, this is the most critical influence on the possibilities of lower income groups of ever owning or building their own house)
- **building material and component costs**
- **availability and price of infrastructure and services for housing**

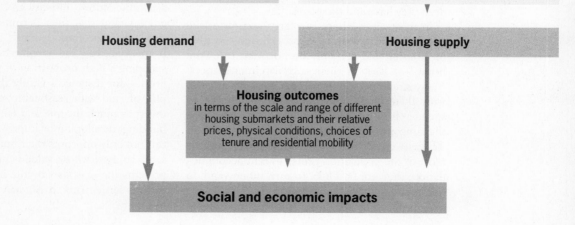

Housing demand

Housing supply

Housing outcomes
in terms of the scale and range of different housing submarkets and their relative prices, physical conditions, choices of tenure and residential mobility

Social and economic impacts

Housing supply for low-income groups

Figure 6.3 lists various factors that influence the supply of housing for low income groups. The factors that influence housing demand have already been discussed. On the supply side, one obvious factor is the price and availability of land for housing that in turn is influenced by the demand for land from other sectors and by the attitude of national, city and municipal authorities to different kinds of illegal developments (whose range and influence is discussed in Chapter 7). Another major influence is the scale and nature of road construction and public transport provision. A cheap and efficient public transport system can greatly expand the choices available to those seeking housing and keep prices down by greatly expanding the land area within reach of the main centres of employment. A large highway and freeway road system can have a similar effect, although generally with a much larger land area and with obvious biases towards middle- and upper-income groups since access to cheap land will depend on a household owning one or more automobile.

One of the most significant influences on the supply of housing for low-income groups in the South has been the extent to which illegal or informal housing and land developments are tolerated. In many cities in the South, this is the most critical influence on the possibilities of low- and often middle-income groups of owning or building their own house. The proportion of a city's population living in illegal and informal settlements is not necessarily a good measure of housing problems in that rudimentary houses or shacks in illegal or informal settlements often meet the cost, location and space needs of low-income households better than other available alternatives.

As Chapter 7 will describe in more detail, in nearly all instances, the state, much influenced by the main landowners, sets the limits within which illegal or informal land markets can operate. Here, as in most other aspects of housing supply, there are great variations in what is tolerated and the scale and nature of illegal developments are sensitive to this. In some cities, there is very little control of illegal or informal land markets, as long as these do not impinge on the more valuable sites. In some cities, the extent of these illegal or informal developments is much enhanced by the large amounts of well-located land that is too dangerous or expensive to develop commercially—for instance the *suburbios* built over the floodplain in Guayaquil[44] and dozens of other cities or the low income *barrios* built on the steep hillsides around Caracas[45] and in the *favelas* in Rio de Janeiro, or the *tugurios* built in ravines in San Salvador.[46] In others, they are enhanced by the fact that the state owns large amounts of land and has been tolerant of illegal land develop-

ments on it—as in Karachi,[47] Valencia,[48] or Lima.[49]

A further factor in housing supply (and price) is the availability of piped water, provision for sanitation and drainage and other forms of infrastructure and services needed by housing and residential neighbourhoods. Where municipal agencies or the companies responsible for the supply of these fail to keep up with demand, the price of land or land developments with infrastructure and services acquires a 'scarcity premium'.[50] The Housing Indicators Programme found that in cities such as Bangkok, these scarcity premiums were relatively small and the price of land with infrastructure was only slightly higher than the combined cost of raw land and the installation of infrastructure. In other cities such as Manila, Seoul, Kingston and Cairo, land sites with infrastructure and services were of the order of 10–15 times the price of raw land—which is far more than the cost of installing the infrastructure.[51]

Another major influence on housing supply is the efficiency of the official legal and regulatory framework within which those who supply housing operate.[52] This includes the framework that regulates and supervises the development and purchase of land and the construction and purchase/sale of housing including the time and cost involved in receiving official permission or sanction to buy, sell or build housing or land. It also includes official standards on building, building materials, infrastructure and services and land use and development. The impact on housing prices of the legal and regulatory frameworks for land are considered in Chapter 7.

Housing submarkets for low-income groups

A city's housing market is the final outcome of the interaction of all the factors that influence supply and demand. Within any city, it is usually possible to detect a range of housing submarkets that have developed as the best compromise between poorer groups' needs and their inability to pay much for housing. These can be divided into 'rental' and 'owner-occupier' with the relative balance between the two varying greatly, from city to city and, within any city, varying over time. For instance, inner-city tenements and houses developed on illegal subdivisions are two common housing sub-markets—the first with mostly tenants, the second generally with a predominance of 'owner occupiers', even if government has not recognized their status as such. Each sub-market for owners or tenants has its relative price—influenced by, among other things, location, size, physical conditions, and forms of tenure.

This is illustrated by Table 6.6 that gives examples of the types of housing available in Karachi and the typical income range of their occupants. The housing types range in value from the one room dwelling built of semi-permanent material in an illegal or informal settlement (*katchi abadi*) worth around 3,750 rupees to large apartments and bungalows worth 1–2 million rupees. For the lowest-income groups, the choices are to build their own dwelling in a *katchi abadi* (in which around 37 per cent of Karachi's population live) or to rent a room in an existing house there. If they build their own home, they can generally only afford to build a one room structure of semi-permanent materials—and in an area with no piped water or electricity. Those with a little more income have the possibility of building two or three rooms in a structure built of semi-permanent material in an illegal subdivision with a toilet and bathroom. As per capita income rises, so too does the choice of housing types.

Various studies have documented the scale and range of housing sub-markets within cities—or in particular those used by low-income groups. For instance, in Dhaka, there are six major sub-markets in which the poorest two-thirds of the population live: squatter settlements, refugee rehabilitation colonies and squatter resettlement camps, *bastis* (cheap rental accommodation in one or occasionally two-storey buildings), conventional inner-city tenement housing, and employee housing (including accommodation provided by government agencies for some of their staff and accommodation provided by middle- or upper-income households for servants)—with another 2.5 per cent living in housing that does not fall within these six categories (for instance boats or shared rooms with multiple occupancy that are widely used by single women working in garment factories).[53] In San Salvador, the majority of low-income groups find accommodation in one of four kinds of housing: tenements (*mesones*), illegal sub-divisions (*colonias ilegales*), what were once temporary camps (*campamentos*) and squatter settlements (*tugurios*).[54] In Tunis, the main sources of housing for low-income groups are within the traditional

TABLE 6.6 The range of housing types in Karachi

Type of housing	Plot size (square metres)	House or apartment size	Living space; m² per person	Dweller status	Persons per room	Income range of occupant	Property value
						Rupees	
A. Katchi abadis with homes built of semi-permanent materials							
1 room, sharing toilet, no water, bathroom or electricity	30–40	12–15	2.45	Illegal	5.0	501–1000	30,000
1 room, no water, bathroom or electricity	30–40	12–15	2.11	Illegal	5.0	501–1000	3,750
2 rooms, squatter settlement next to waterways	50–70	25–50	4.38	Renter	2.5	1001–1800	25,000
2–3 rooms, illegal subdivision with bathroom and toilet	70–90	50–70	5.31	Owner	2.5	1500–2000	60,000
B. Old house built with semi-permanent materials							
2–4 rooms, 1–2 levels in the old city centre	70–90	55–120	5.03	Illegal	4.0	2001–6500	200,000
C. Houses built with permanent materials							
2–3 rooms, new development, small plot size	70–100	30–60	5.38	Owner	2.5	2001–2500	46,900
2–4 rooms, 1–2 levels, small plot size	70–100	60–85	6.76	Owner	1.2	2501–5000	200,000
2–4 rooms, 1–2 levels in Metroville, medium plot	100–250	60–85	6.80	Owner	1.8	5001–8000	200,000
4–5 rooms, 1–2 levels, medium plot	120–250	70–95	9.01	Owner	1.5	10001 +	800,000
5–8 rooms, 2 levels, townhouse	120–180	90–120	23.49	Owner	1.0	20001 +	900,000
D. Bungalow							
5–10 rooms, large plot size	300+	150–400+	26.74	Owner	0.8	25,001 +	1.5 m
E. Apartment							
1–2 rooms in a building of 4–5 storeys	FAR:2.2	25–45	8.00	Owner	2.5	4001–6000	100,000
3–5 rooms in a building of 4–5 storeys	FAR:1.7	50–140	11.57	Owner	1.6	15000 +	500,000
3–5 rooms in a building of 4–18 storeys	FAR:1.3	70–180	33.00	Owner	1.0	25001 +	1 m

Source: Hasan, Arif, *Profiles of three Pakistani Cities; Karachi, Faisalabad and Thatta*, Background paper prepared for the Global Report on Human Settlements, 1994. FAR is floor-to-area ratio.

city centre (*medina*), a great variety of *gourbivilles* (illegal or informal settlements), illegal sub-divisions (mostly on the periphery) and social housing.[55] A study of Lagos also pointed to a great variety of different housing sub-markets used by low-income groups.[56] A study in La Paz (Bolivia) pointed to the range of housing sub-markets used by lower income groups, including one that was neither rental nor owner-occupation but where a dwelling or space in a dwelling is temporarily lent without charging rent.[57] These and other studies[58] are important not only for providing a more accurate basis on which to develop housing policy in these cities but also for showing the extent to which the social, economic and political structure of the city, its region and the nation and the particular topographical characteristics of a city shape the scale and nature of housing provision.

Rental housing and their tenants

There is great variety between cities in the proportion of households who are tenants—from cities where less than 10 per cent are tenants to cities where 90 per cent or more are tenants. This includes great variety not only internationally but between cities in the same country. For instance, in India in 1981, the proportion of urban households living in rented accommodation varied from 19 per cent in the state of Kerala to 79 per cent in Arunachal Pradesh while among India's largest cities, it varied from 30 per cent in Lucknow to 76 per cent in Calcutta.[59] In Brazil, more than 40 per cent of households in the Southeast were tenants in 1984, compared to less than 30 per cent in the North-East.[60] There are also large variations in the proportions of tenants in different districts or neighbourhoods within cities. In most cities, there are districts where most of the population is in rented accommodation, especially in areas with high concentrations of cheap boarding and rooming houses or tenements—and also districts (including many suburban areas) with most of the population as owner-occupiers.

There is also great variety in the form of housing that is rented—from, at one extreme, beds in shared rooms that are rented by the hour and land plots rented for short periods on which tenants have to build their own temporary shelter, through to high-quality houses or apartments. There is also great variety in the landlords who own the beds, rooms, houses, shacks, apartments or land plots that they rent. In some cities, rental markets are dominated by the public sector; in others they are almost entirely within the private sector. Then within the public sector, there is considerable variety as to whether the owner is central government, local government or a public enterprise. There are also many forms of social housing that are part private and part public or that are privately owned and managed but which receive public funding.

Within market or mixed economies, the proportion of a city's population who are tenants is generally smallest, the higher the proportion of people who can afford to purchase or build their own house—although this is not always the case, as can be seen by the high proportion of middle- and upper-income households who are tenants in many of Europe's most prosperous cities. For instance, many cities in Germany, Switzerland and the Netherlands have a high proportion of households who rent accommodation. In cities where illegal or informal land acquisition is tolerated, the proportion of the city population able to afford to become owner-occupiers obviously increases considerably, even if the 'owner-occupiers' are not recognized as such in law. In many cities in the Russian Federation and in certain countries of East and Central Europe, a considerable proportion of the population are tenants of public authorities, although in most instances, the proportion of owner-occupiers is increasing rapidly through the sale of publicly owned dwellings and the restitution of property that was confiscated.[61]

This great variety in the scale and form of renting is only partially explained by factors on the demand side—for instance, the preferences of those seeking accommodation. As one of the specialists who has helped stimulate a much greater interest in rental accommodation in recent years comments, 'The fact . . . that the poor in Lima invade land, those of Bogotá buy land and those of Lagos rent accommodation is only partly due to different household preferences. Much more important are the structural conditions that limit the choice.'[62]

Table 6.7 shows the diversity between cities in terms of the proportion of households who rent accommodation and how there are examples of cities in the wealthiest and the poorest countries where most households are tenants. The table also includes examples of cities where there has been a rapid decrease in the proportion of households who rent accommodation. There has been a clear trend towards a decrease in the proportion of tenant households in many Latin American and Asian cities.[63] This is less evident in several cities in sub-Saharan Africa for which there is data and the proportion of tenant households to total households remains very high in many cities. There are also instances where the proportion of tenant households remains very high in Asian cities—as in the case of Seoul. There is also little or no data on changes in the proportion of households who were tenants in the late 1980s and early 1990s and it may be that the proportion of urban households who were tenants increased in many countries during the 1980s and early 1990s.[64]

TABLE 6.7 The proportion of city populations who rent accommodation

City	Date	Percentage of households		Notes
		Renting	Owning	
Africa				
Benin City (Nigeria)	1986	65	20	13 per cent of households as 'other'.[65]
Cairo (Egypt)	1986	59		[66]
Kumasi (Ghana)	1986	62		7 per cent of households rented dwellings with 55 per cent renting one or two rooms, usually in compound houses.[67]
Port Harcourt (Nigeria)	1984	88	12	Relatively little change as the proportion of renters was 89.7 per cent in 1973.[68]
Port Louis (Mauritius)	1990	31	60	9 per cent in 'other'.
Rabat (Morocco)	1981	52	33	[69]
Thika (Kenya)	1985	91	8	74 per cent of all households were private tenants, 17 per cent were tenants in public or staff housing.[70]
Tunis (Tunisia)	1989	28	59	
Asia				
Greater Amman (Jordan)	1985	25	c.66	The rest have no legal title.[71]
Bombay (India)	1987/88	48	43	The proportion who were renters has fallen from 90 per cent in 1961.[72]
Calcutta (India)	1987/88	56	33	The proportion of households who are tenants has fallen considerably as 83 per cent of households were reported to be tenants in 1961.[73]
Delhi (India)	1987/88	37	53	The proportion of households who are tenants have fallen from 66.5 per cent in 1961.[74]
Jakarta (Indonesia)	1988	30	55	[75]
Lucknow (India)	1981	30		This is the proportion of households who were tenants—and this is down from 61.7 per cent in 1961.[76]
Seoul (Republic of Korea)	1987	59	41	The proportion in rented accommodation had grown in previous decades.[77]
Tokyo (Japan)	1990	53	42	7 per cent in 'other'.[78]
Urban centres in India	1988	37		The proportion of renters is down from 46.4 per cent in 1981 and 53.7 in 1961.[79]
Europe				
Bratislava (Slovak Republic)	1988	47		Most of the rest owned by co-operatives[80]
Budapest (Hungary)	1992	45		It was 60 per cent in the early 1980s but had fallen to 44.5 per cent by January 1992.[81]
Greater London (UK)	1993	40	57	Of the 40 per cent who were tenants, 22 per cent were in local authority public housing, 6 per cent in housing association accommodation and 14 per cent were private sector tenants.[82]
Hamburg	1987	77	16	
Helsinki (Finland)	1989	39	59	
Munich (Germany)	1987	79	17	
Oslo (Norway)	1990	24	76	
Prague (Czech Republic)	1988	61		Most of the rest owned by co-operatives[83]
Stockholm	1990	66	11	
Urban centres in Poland	1990	77		Around half this is co-operative housing and a proportion of the apartments within co-operative housing are privately owned.[84]
Zurich (Switzerland)	1980	90	7	

TABLE 6.7 continued

City	Date	Percentage of households		Notes
		Renting	Owning	
Latin America				
Bogotá (Colombia)	1985	40	57	The percentage of tenants has declined from 50 per cent in 1973.[85]
Cali (Colombia)	1985	27	68	The proportion of tenants has declined from 42 per cent in 1973.[86]
Caracas (Venezuela)	1981	31	63	6 per cent 'others'; the proportion of tenant households within the Federal District of Caracas was 47 per cent in 1950.[87]
La Paz (Bolivia)	1986	20	49	Although only 20 per cent of households were tenants, another 28 per cent were living in accommodation lent them by others, rent-free.[88]
Lima (Peru)	1985/6	30	61	
Sao Paulo (Brazil)	1982	35	56	Around 1900, more than 80 per cent of Sao Paulo's dwellings were rented.[89]

Notes: Care must be taken in comparing the figures between cities for at least two reasons. The first is the problem discussed in Chapter 1 with regard to city boundaries. Where the figures above are only for central cities, the proportion of tenants may be higher than if a wider boundary had been used. The second is differences in the way that households are classified—for instance whether those living in illegal or informal settlements are classified as 'owner-occupiers' or 'other' or whether members of housing co-operatives are classified as 'tenants' or 'owner-occupiers'.

Sources: Drawn mainly from UNCHS (Habitat), *Support Measures to Promote Rental Housing for Low Income Groups*, United Nations Centre for Human Settlements, HS/294/93E, Nairobi, 1993, and from data drawn from United Nations, *Human Settlements Statistics Questionnaire 1992*, reported in Table 9 of the Statistical Annex.

In most cities in the South, over the last 20–30 years, much the most important way by which most low-income and many middle-income households have become owner-occupiers is by developing their own shelter on land that was either illegally occupied or illegally subdivided. The importance of the informal land market for housing is described in more detail in Chapter 7. But as cities grow in size and wealth, and competition increases for the best quality and best located land sites, the possibilities for low-income households of acquiring a land plot for housing—by purchase or illegal occupation—are likely to diminish. As land becomes more valuable, illegal land occupations become more difficult and there is hardly any land for which ownership is not already claimed (whether legally or illegally).[90] Cheap land sites are almost always available in the least commercially attractive areas but in general, the larger the city, the greater the distance between these and the locations where most low-income households can earn an income. As demand for housing begins to concentrate in areas where there is no affordable land on which someone with a modest income can acquire their own home (legally or illegally), rental markets develop as those with land there can adjust or extend their structures to allow part or all to be rented.[91] Many renters become locked into rental accommodation with increasing rents and no possibility of owner-occupation.[92] However, this can change if the city structure changes—for instance if industry, commerce and services dis-

perse to less central sites (or even into suburbs or the urban periphery)—so that cheap land sites for housing are once again within reach of employment opportunities. It may also change through a much-improved public transport system or the installation of new urban–suburban links (for instance an efficient and cheap commuter railway service)—both of which increase the land area that is accessible to employment opportunities.

In all cities, there is a section of the population that prefers rental accommodation—and a section that needs to rent because their incomes or employment make owner occupation impossible. As a report on housing in the United Kingdom commented, 'what is accepted by all except the most ideologically committed to a "property owning democracy" is that this tenure is not suitable for everyone and that it should be complemented by other methods of providing housing'.[93] The proportion of a city's population who prefer to rent may be very high, especially if there is a competitive and diverse rental market and if there are few financial advantages in owner occupation compared to renting. As was noted earlier, in many European cities, a high proportion of the population rent their accommodation and most of these choose to do so. In many sub-Saharan African cities, one reason for the high proportion of households who are tenants is that they regard their stay in that city as temporary.[94]

There are also individuals or households whose only possibility of finding accommodation is renting because their income is too low to afford the cheapest 'owner-occupation', even if they wanted to. It is now much rarer to find low-income households able to find cheap or free land in the larger and more prosperous cities in the South. In the North, there is always a proportion of the city population that also lacks the means to own their own home. For instance, in the United States, more than a third of all households do not own their home[95] and it has always been difficult for low-income families to buy their own home. During the 1980s, access to owner-occupation became more difficult even for many families who had assumed that they would be able to purchase their own home.[96] During the 1980s, the rate of home ownership fell for nearly every demographic group.[97] Without a substantial shift in the distribution of wealth and income, large numbers of young families and many older and poorer families cannot afford their own home. In the United Kingdom too, during the late 1980s, the proportion of people able to purchase their own home decreased.[98]

In many cities in both North and South, women-headed households are more likely to be tenants or sharers than owners. This is linked to the discrimination they face in comparison to men in housing and employment markets. But it is also linked to the fact that it is usually the mother rather than the father that takes responsibility for the children, when parents separate (see Box 6.5).

Sharers

Among the people who do not own the house in which they live, there are also 'sharers' i.e. people who are permitted to share the dwelling with the owner or tenant without payment. They may represent a significant proportion of the city population—for instance in Abidjan, Benin City, Delhi, Khartoum, Kumasi, La Paz, Lima and Santiago de Chile, sharing houses is common.[105] In some cities, the sharing of housing plots is also important (see Chapter 7).

It is important to draw a distinction between the sharing of a house, apartment, room or land site that becomes common because many single adults or households lack the income to be able to find any alternative and sharing which is done by choice. Sharing driven by necessity often leads to high levels of overcrowding and a high number of persons relative to provision for water supply and sanitation. But sharing by choice is common in many societies as adult children remain in the home of their parents—for instance as they complete secondary and higher education. Among low-income groups in many cities, it is also common for young married couples to stay in the house of their parents. For young adults (whether single or married), remaining with parents may be

---

BOX 6.5

Gender dimensions to renting and gender-related constraints to owner-occupation

Female-headed households are more likely to be tenants or sharers than owners. Research in Guadalajara, Mexico City, Queretaro and Puebla found that there was a higher incidence of female-headed households among tenants.[99] This was also found in West Africa.[100] A study of informal settlements in Abidjan found that a higher proportion of women-headed households were tenants, compared to male-headed households.[101] A study in a low-income settlement in Khulna (Bangladesh) found that female-headed and supported households were concentrated in the poorest and potentially most vulnerable group of households.[102]

There are several reasons for this. First, women are often excluded from official housing programmes offering owner-occupation.[103] Secondly, female-headed households tend to be poorer and since poorer households frequently rent, women tend to be tenants. Female-headed households also frequently lack 'both skills and time to self-build but are often required to do so in the absence of funds for professional labour'.[104] Experience in Cordoba, Argentina, on a housing programme for squatters that were relocated found that women-headed households who formed around a third of all households had similar aspirations to other beneficiaries but had particular difficulties that were not recognized and which meant they were least able to develop their homes. For instance, no special provision was made for the fact that women-headed households lacked the free time to permit them to develop their own homes—and no provision was made for child-care that might have permitted them to work more on self-help construction. Among the different types of housing sites or core houses available, the ones allocated to women-headed households were generally those that least suited their needs and priorities both in the design and in the amount of self-construction they required.

Source: Drawn principally from UNCHS (Habitat), *Support Measures to Promote Rental Housing for Low Income Group*, United Nations Centre for Human Settlements, HS/294/93E, Nairobi, 1993. The case study in Argentina is from Falu, Ana and Mirina Curutchet, 'Rehousing the urban poor: looking at women first', *Environment and Urbanization*, vol. 3, no. 2, Oct. 1991, 23–38.

---

particularly important in giving them time to save, and thus allowing them to avoid the poorest quality rental accommodation when their earnings are low. Indeed, for young adults with low-income jobs, having parents in the city with whom they can stay is an important economic advantage.

Sharing is obviously important in many cities for those able to share, i.e. those who have parents or children in a city, or, in societies where there is an obligation to house kin, also other relatives. Housing conditions would be worse without sharing. An increase in sharing in any city may be one indicator of an increasing proportion of the population unable to afford accommodation. In some cities, it is clear that many families are forced to share because of a lack of alternatives. In Santiago de Chile, as many as one-fifth of households were sharing in the 1980s—and sharing had become important because few families could afford to pay the high rents and cheap land was unavailable.[106] The sharers and *allegados* in Santiago were typically much poorer than tenants and owners. A survey in Delhi found that households share accommodation because of the very high rent levels and the difficulties in building their own home.[107] Karachi is likely to be one among many cities where young couples are now tending to stay in their parents' home for longer periods.[108]

Sharers may also include 'disguised renters'. For instance, family members who are considered sharers may be making significant payments to the home-owners but not considering this as rent.[109] In addition, 'sharers' may pay no rent but still make important contributions to household expenditures and to domestic work or child-care and their contribution can be particularly important for households having to cope with declining real incomes or rising costs.[110]

Private landlords in cities in the South

Although it is clear that the lowest income groups tend to rent, various studies in particular cities or particular settlements in cities have found that the contrasts between tenants and their landlords are not very great. For instance, in Karachi's *katchi abadis*, the renters include a number of singularly poor people or those unable to earn much such as widows and aged people and large young families with one income-earner but they do not in general exhibit any striking characteristics distinguishing them from the owners.[111]

Detailed information on private-sector landlords is rare. Among the detailed studies of renting in illegal or informal settlements on which the sections above have drawn, there are few examples of large-scale landlordism. Several studies of Latin American cities and in Indonesia and Turkey found that the typical landlord is a former self-help builder.[112] Many reside in the same property as the tenants and few have more than a couple of properties. In the consolidated periphery of Santiago de Chile, seven out of ten landlords rent only to one tenant household, in Mexico City three-quarters and in Caracas two-thirds. Even in the central areas of these cities, most landlords operate only on a small scale. In Mexico City, subdivision of property through inheritance has gradually reduced the level of property concentration.

The few available studies in Asian cities also suggests a predominance of small-scale landlords. A similar pattern of small-scale ownership seems to hold for most African cities.[113] It has been suggested that 'the rental market has been dominated by the small landlord; rarely except perhaps in North Africa, have private investors built large blocks of tenements for the relatively poor'.[114] In a survey in Cairo, 91 per cent of landlords live in the building and 76 per cent of surveyed landlords had less than ten tenants.[115] In a survey in Benin City (Nigeria), 86 per cent of the 50 landlords interviewed own only one property and only one had more than three properties.[116] The typical landlord is self-employed and built the accommodation originally for their and their family's own use.

There is evidence of some relatively large-scale landlords renting to low-income individuals or households in certain cities—for instance in Kibera in Nairobi,[117] Bangkok[118] and urban areas in Nigeria but what is not known is their share in the city's overall rental market. Certain studies have also shown the complexity that has to be unravelled to establish the scale and nature of landlordism. For instance, in a study of an informal settlement within Lagos, three-quarters of the population were tenants and the landlords could be divided into three categories: seven large landowners who lived outside the settlement; small landowners who had freehold titles to their plots and most of whom live within the settlement; and landlords who lease their land from landowners.[119]

The characteristics of most landlords in cities in the South seem to be generally rather similar to those of other owners and sometimes even to those of their tenants. Clearly, landlords, owners and tenants living in the same consolidated settlements may be drawn from the same social class. The main characteristic that may distinguish landlords from the rest of the population is their age. Landlords tend to be older than other owners and much older than most tenants. In Cairo, almost half of the landlords interviewed had been renting for more than 30 years. Because of their age, landlords are much more likely to be retired, live in larger properties than other families and have lived longer in their current home.

There are also what might be termed 'reluctant' landlords—for instance those who let their premises out of sheer need—to finance a daughter's marriage, to rebuild or expand a house, to pay off debts—and do so only for a limited period.[120]

Rental sub-markets

Table 6.8 lists the different kinds of rental housing that are commonly used by low income groups. Some are only found in relatively few cities; others are almost universal. The Table shows the range of different rental sub-markets evident in cities—that include not only houses, apartments or rooms but also land sites on which a temporary shack may be built by the tenant. At the cheapest end of the range, the tenant rents a

TABLE 6.8 The different kinds of rental housing used by low-income groups in many cities

Types of rental accommodation	Common characteristics	Problems
Rented room in subdivided inner-city tenement building	Often the most common form of low-income housing in early stages of a city's growth. Buildings originally built legally as residences for middle/upper-income groups but subdivided and turned into tenements when they move to suburbs or elsewhere. Advantage of being centrally located so usually close to job or income earning opportunities. Sometimes rent levels are controlled by legislation. Many cities in the South never had sufficient quantities of middle/upper-income housing suited to conversion into tenements to make this type of accommodation common.	Usually very overcrowded and in poor state of repair. Whole families often in one room, sometimes with no window. Facilities for water supply, cooking, storage, laundry and excreta/garbage disposal very poor and have rarely been improved or increased to cope with much higher density of occupation caused by sub-division. If subject to rent control, landlord often demanding extra payment 'unofficially'. Certain inner-city areas with tenements may be subject to strong commercial pressures to redevelop them (or their sites) for more profitable uses. Building often very poorly maintained
Rented room in custom-built tenement	Government built or government approved buildings specially built as tenements for low income groups; sometimes publicly owned. Common in many Latin American cities and some Asian cities and usually built some decades ago. Some public housing estates fall into this category.	Similar problems to above in that the original building never had sufficient provision for the high density of inhabitants in regard to adequate provision for water supply, cooking, ventilation, food storage, laundry, excreta and garbage disposal. Building often very poorly maintained, especially fabric and public and semi-public areas
Rented room, bed or bed hours in boarding or rooming house, cheap hotel or pension	Often, these kinds of accommodation are most in evidence near railway station or bus-station though they may also be common in other areas, including illegal settlements. Perhaps common for newly arrived migrant family or single person working in the city to use these. Single person may hire bed for a set number of hours each day so more than one person shares cost of each bed. Usually relatively cheap and centrally located.	Similar problems to above in terms of overcrowding, poor maintenance and lack of facilities. A rapidly changing population in most such establishments inhibits united action on the part of users to obtain improvements or lower charges.
Rented room or bed in illegal settlement	In many cities, rented rooms in illegal settlements represent a larger stock of rental accommodation than in tenements which were originally legally built (see above). May take the form of room or bed rented in a house or shack with *de facto* owner-occupier; may be rented from small or large-scale landlord who lives elsewhere.	Problems in terms of poor quality of building and lack of infrastructure (paved roads, sidewalks, storm drainage . . .) plus site often ill-suited to housing as in squatter settlements and illegal subdivisions. Also, insecurity of tenure which is even greater than for *de facto* house/shack owners.
Rented land plot on which a shack is built	The renting of plots in illegal subdivisions or renting space in another person's lot, court-yard or garden is common in certain cities; in some cities, even the flat roofs on top of apartment blocks are rented out to people who build a shack there. Their extent and relative importance are not known.	Similar problems to those listed above in terms of insecure tenure and lack of basic services and infrastructure. Additional burden on household to build shack, despite no tenure and no incentive to improve, since the owner may require them to move at short notice.
Rented room in house or flat in lower- or middle-income area of the city	Declines in the purchasing power of many lower-middle income or formal sector worker households have encouraged many to rent out rooms in their own houses/apartments to supplement their incomes and to help them pay off loans or mortgages on their house or apartment.	Probably relatively good quality compared to above options. Tenant–landlord relationship not usually subject to contract. Such rooms are often in locations at considerable distances from the city areas where most jobs or income-earning possibilities are concentrated.
Employer-housing for low-paid workers	In many cities, a considerable proportion of the higher income groups provide accommodation for servants. Some large enterprises provide rented rooms for some of their workforce. This is common in plantations but is also evident in some city-based enterprises or for some public authority employees.	The quality of this housing is usually very poor with several people crowded into each room and very inadequate provision for basic services. Rules may prevent workers' families living there and these have to live elsewhere so two separate forms of accommodation have to be paid for and household members have to live apart for much of the time.

TABLE 6.8 continued

Types of rental accommodation	Common characteristics	Problems
Public-housing unit	In many cities, public housing units represent a considerable proportion of all rental accommodation although the extent to which low income groups obtain access to them varies greatly. In some cities, most public housing units are allocated to government employees or military personnel. Some may be sublet from their original tenants. In many cities, the proportion of public housing stock that is rented is declining, as governments promote their sale to tenants.	The size and quality of the buildings vary greatly—but many have suffered from inadequate or no maintenance. Many have also been very small, relative to the size of household using them.
Renting space to sleep at work	The extent is simply not known. A study in Lagos found that space to spread a sleeping mat can be rented in a warehouse or some other commercial establishment—often with caretakers organizing this, without the knowledge of the owner or manager. Some families find accommodation through agreeing to live as caretakers in uncompleted or empty buildings or workshops and they in turn may sublet spaces within these buildings. Many young people who are very low paid including apprentices are allowed to sleep in the commercial or industrial establishments in which they work.[121]	In most instances, a lack of facilities for washing and food preparation and a complete lack of security.
Renting a space to sleep	Where there are large numbers of people who sleep outside or in public places e.g. railway/bus stations, graveyards or temples, local officials or protection gangs may demand money.	The problems are obvious—not only the insecurity and lack of shelter and basic services but also the need to pay for this space and often to pay people who have no right to demand such payments.

Source: Based on a table in *Squatter Citizen: Life in the Urban Third World*—Jorge E. Hardoy and David Satterthwaite, Earthscan Publications, London, 1989.

bed in a room rather than a room—and may indeed only rent the bed by the hour. In Calcutta, the 'hotbed' system permits two or three persons to use the same bed over a 24-hour period and thus pay less than they would have done, if they rented the bed for their sole use.

In most cities, there is a considerable range of rental sub-markets. Central city areas or the areas immediately surrounding them often retain tenements or other forms of cheap rental accommodation (for instance cheap boarding and rooming houses) that may be declining in the proportion of the population living there but none the less remain important. A study of historical city centres in Latin America found that tens of thousands of individuals or households lived in tenements, lodging houses or cheap 'hotels' in Buenos Aires, Montevideo, Santiago de Chile, Lima, Mexico City, Bogota and many other large cities and metropolitan centres in Latin America.[122] Centrally located rental accommodation serve those low-income individuals or households whose source of income is in central cities or other prime locations where all forms of legal or illegal 'owner-occupation' are far beyond their means. Many work long hours in industrial or service occupations for low incomes—and the cost in time and fares on public transport travel-

ling to and from the nearest house, shack or land site they could own and afford is also far beyond their means.[123]

In many cities, the bulk of affordable rental housing is now provided in the homes of low-income homeowners—whether they have legal, semi-legal or no legal tenure of their land and house.[124] This is generally because the returns to landlords of organized renting are not sufficiently high to encourage large-scale formal-sector capital investment.[125] The proportion of housing that is rented out or has renters within it varies greatly from some areas given over almost entirely to renters to others with virtually all *de facto* owners. In some instances, the tenure of the owner-occupier is too insecure for any renting—for instance, in a study of an illegal settlement within Khartoum in 1986, no renting was found because the occupants were afraid that tenants might challenge their right to stay in that house, if and when the public authorities legalized their settlement.[126] A United Nations survey of nineteen different 'slums and squatter settlements' found that eight had more than a third of the buildings either rented out or with mixed tenure (i.e. partially rented out) while five had more than half; two had more than 80 per cent of the buildings rented out.[127] In a 1979 study of Kibera, a large, informal residential settlement in Nairobi, most of the houses or shacks were rented out and there was large-scale and highly profitable land-lordism there.[128] In Lusaka, in upgraded areas, over half the population were tenants in 1986.[129] In interviews with 122 households in one district of a large informal settlement in Khartoum, two-thirds of households had a tenant, 19 per cent with the owner and one tenant family, the rest with a mix of tenants and sub-tenants.[130]

The illegal or informal settlements that have a more central location and a greater degree of consolidation are likely to have the largest pro-portion of renters. In a survey of three low-income settlements in Santa Cruz (Bolivia) undertaken in 1985–6, the proportion of people who were tenants was much higher, the older and more consolidated the settlement. In the oldest settlement, located quite near the city centre and founded in the late 1950s, 65 per cent of house-holds were non-owners. A second settlement founded in the late 1970s near the city's current edge had 48 per cent of households as non-own-ers. The third, on the edge of the city and devel-oped from a land invasion in 1984 had virtually no non-owners.[131] In George, one of the largest squatter areas in Lusaka, what began as a settle-ment dominated by *de facto* owners in the late 1960s slowly developed a rental market so that by 1989, around a third of the population were tenants.[132]

In many cities, there are also what might be termed rental shantytowns—*ciudades perdidas* in Mexico, *favelas de quinta* in Brazil, *corralones* in El Salvador, rentyards in the Caribbean and *bustees* in Calcutta.[133] In many African cities, low-income compounds may have become almost entirely given over to rent—for instance tenements that house between twelve and twenty families each are common in the low-income compounds of Kumasi,[134] Lagos[135] and Nairobi.[136] The physical quality of the housing is very poor, services are almost non-existent and tenure is usually illegal. These areas represent the worst living conditions of any kind of low-income rental housing. Illegal or informal settlements with predominantly rental accommodation are likely to be common where there are supply constraints, a high level of demand for cheap rental accommodation and few or no controls on the quality of housing that can be rented and the rents charged.[137]

Many cities have rental sub-markets other than the renting of rooms. These include tenants rent-ing house-plots[138] or roof-space or space in another person's backyard on which a temporary structure is built. There may even be a rental market for people sleeping on pavements or in public spaces—with small payments made to offi-cials or to people demanding 'protection money' for the right to sleep there. Chapter 7 discusses in more detail 'land renting' while Section 6.4 on homelessness discusses in more detail the nature of 'homelessness'.

State-owned housing

In many urban centres in the North and in many cities in the South, public housing represents a significant proportion of all housing—and among the largest sources of rental accommodation. Some Latin American governments managed to build the equivalent of 15 per cent of the housing stock in major cities such as Bogota, Caracas, Mexico City and Santiago de Chile and even larger proportions in new cities such as Brasilia and Ciudad Guyana.[139] In the 52 cities in both the North and the South covered by the Housing Indicators Programme, most had over 10 per cent of their total housing stock in public ownership while nine from the South and five from the North (four of them in West Europe) had more than 25 per cent. 92 per cent of the housing stock in Beijing was reported as public housing stock.[140] In Hong Kong, by 1994, half the popu-lation live in public housing.[141] Some care must be taken in interpreting figures in some coun-tries, as apartments within public housing units have been sold and have thus become owner-occupied. For instance, Singapore presents this case of the country with the highest proportion of its housing stock built by the public sector—but also a high degree of owner-occupiers, as people who were formerly tenants of public housing were encouraged to become owners. In Hong Kong too, a considerable proportion of the apart-ments in public housing have been sold.

Public housing programmes became popular with many governments in the North and South during the 1950s—although for different reasons. In West Europe, they were seen as ways of rapidly expanding housing and rebuilding cities damaged during the Second World War as well as providing cheap, good-quality accommodation for low-income groups. In Eastern Europe and the former Soviet Union, they were seen both as this and as a way of creating an egalitarian society and avoiding exploitative landlordism.[142] In Latin America, where most countries had long had independence, public housing programmes were a response to rapidly growing city populations—although such programmes had been started in many countries in the region prior to World War II.[143] In Africa and Asia, they were favoured by many newly inde-pendent governments—although they were often rooted in colonial precedents that had previously housed colonial staff or provided cheap accom-modation for the workers in certain key institu-tions and industries.

It was during the 1960s and early 1970s that most governments in the South either launched large public-housing programmes or greatly enlarged existing ones.[144] In Latin America, from the early 1960s, aid was available for the first time, on a large scale to finance housing projects—from the Inter-American Development Bank but funded largely by the US government under the 'Alliance for Progress'.[145] Most such public housing programmes were initially to provide rental accommodation for low-income groups and/or government workers. Large public-housing programmes were initiated during the 1950s or 1960s in many countries—with efforts during the 1970s to expand them.[146] In many others, new public housing agencies were set up during the 1970s—although these often consolidated existing agencies.[147] Many governments also set up new housing finance institutions or overhauled existing ones. Certain public-housing programmes achieved a considerable scale. For instance, the National Housing Bank of Brazil set up in 1964 and closed down in 1986 had provided the core of a housing finance system that had produced around 4 million units.[148] In Egypt, some 456,000 public-housing units were produced between 1960 and 1986.[149] In Singapore, some 230,000 units were constructed between 1960 and 1975 and around as many again between 1975 and 1985.[150]

During the 1980s, the scale of support for public-housing programmes diminished in most countries with market or mixed economies—and in East and Central Europe and the Russian Federation, after their political realignments during the late 1980s or early 1990s.[151] The reaffirmation of the importance of market forces influenced this in many countries—particularly in the United Kingdom, the United States and the former communist bloc. In many countries in the South, recession and the cuts in public expenditures linked to debt crises and structural adjustment also had a role. Both in the North and the South, it also relates to difficulties in the public-housing programmes themselves. First, public housing was often unpopular with the tenants because it was too small or poorly designed or poorly maintained. In addition, bureaucratic allocation systems found it difficult if not impossible to cope with the diversity of priorities within low-income groups in terms of each individual's or household's preferred trade-off between type of dwelling, size and location. Individuals or families who have often waited many years to obtain a public-housing unit are reluctant to move, if the possibilities of finding comparable accommodation elsewhere are limited or non-existent.

In many countries in the South, problems of inadequate or no maintenance were added to the failure to build the planned number of units, despite large sums spend on public housing. In many public-housing programmes, less than a quarter of the initial target was met and in some, less than 10 per cent.[152] Many public-housing programmes suffered problems of very high unit costs. And even with subsidized rents, a substantial proportion of the 'low-income groups' could not afford them.[153] If governments reduced the scale of the subsidy given to each unit so more could be built, the units generally became too costly for low-income households. In many other countries, low-income groups simply did not get the public housing as they were allocated to civil servants or military personnel or to middle or higher income groups.[154] Even where efforts were made to ensure that low-income households received public-housing units, the eligibility criteria often excluded the poorest households—especially women-headed households.[155]

Few governments now have large public-housing programmes building rental accommodation and in most countries where there had been large public-housing programmes for rent, much of the public-housing stock has been sold—or at least the tenants of such stock encouraged to purchase it. In some countries, this change dates back to the late 1970s. For instance, as noted above, a considerable proportion of the public-housing in Singapore and Hong Kong has been sold and in Singapore, the sale of apartments in public-housing blocks began in the 1970s. In India, it was in the late 1970s that the Federal Government resolved to convert public-housing tenants into owner-occupiers and the property was offered for sale to the occupants—and the only rental housing provided by the Federal Government is to its own employees. State governments in India have generally followed the same policy.[156] In Nigeria and Egypt, public-housing units were increasingly sold during the 1980s. And in Egypt, the state has withdrawn from the production of subsidized housing.[157]

In the United Kingdom, there has been a rapid decline in the number of public-housing units built since 1980 and a major programme to promote the sale of public-housing to their tenants.[158] By the end of 1992, some 1.4 million tenants of public-housing had purchased their dwelling.[159] Government policy placed strong controls on the possibilities of local authorities continuing to build public-housing units and encouraged the sale of public-housing estates to private buyers or housing associations.[160]

The most dramatic declines in public-housing construction and in public-sector rental housing are evident in East and Central European countries. The privatization of the state housing stock may be the single most distinguishing feature of the transition in these countries. There is a clear pattern across this diverse group of countries in the form of decentralization of the ownership of state housing to local authorities and the cut in national funding for public-housing construction.[161] In every country where privatization has been undertaken, the tenants of public housing have been offered generous terms—at least at the outset—and by 1992, more than 20 per cent of public housing had been transferred in Slovenia, Hungary and Bulgaria.[162] There is also the change in property rights since 1989 and the restitution of property to its former owners that is affecting housing in these countries—see Box 6.6.

BOX 6.6
The change in property rights and restitution of property in East and Central European countries

The economic and political transition in East and Central European countries has also marked the beginning of a return to capitalist property relations through private ownership. This has raised the issue of restitution of property to its original owners.

Private property in Eastern Europe was treated, for most of the period since World War II as something inconsistent with the social and economic system. It was gradually eradicated through communist legal acts that secured mass collectivization of land and nationalization of factories, businesses, shops, hotels, restaurants—and houses—although the extent to which it was carried out varied considerably from country to country. All the post-1989 democratic governments have recognized that some amends have to be made for the expropriation of such property.

There is an important distinction between property returned in its original form (i.e. natural restitution) and provision of compensation (financial restitution). Natural restitution is considered fairer but financial restitution answered the economic imperative of speeding up privatization and thus economic development. Natural restitution is also complex—for instance, those who receive back housing may find tenant protection and rent control still in operation. For instance, in the Czech Republic, many former owners have received back their property but find that the repair and maintenance costs far exceed the rental income. The owners could not evict the tenants, unless they provided alternative accommodation to the same standard. In other instances, restitution is difficult since the property no longer exists and no documentation is available to set its value. There is also the difficulty of setting a fair price, as property's value has increased manyfold since World War II.

Source: Carter, F. W., 'East Europe: population distribution, urban change, housing and environmental problems', background paper for the Global Report, 1994.

Owner-occupied housing

There are large variations in the proportion of a nation's or a city's population that owns the house or apartment in which it lives—in both the North and the South. Table 6.9 shows the proportion of housing that is occupied by owners for a range of countries for which statistics were available. Not surprisingly, various countries that until the late

1980s were centrally planned economies with the state having the central role in housing provision are among the countries with the lowest proportion of housing that is owner-occupied—Russia, the Czech Republic and Poland. But what is perhaps more surprising is to find several countries from this same region with among the highest proportion of housing that is owner-occupied—for instance Bulgaria and Hungary. It is also evident that countries with the highest per capita incomes are not necessarily countries with the highest proportion of housing that is owner-occupied. It tends to be the countries in the North with among the lowest per capita incomes that have among the highest proportion of housing that is owner-occupied—Ireland, Greece and Spain—although this partially reflects the fact that these countries have a higher proportion of their national populations in rural areas—where owner-occupation predominates—than other countries in the North. But this is not the case for Finland, where in 1990, around 64 per cent of the urban housing stock was owner-occupied.[163] Most of Norway's urban housing stock is also owner-occupied. But there is no simple correlation between wealth and proportion of housing that is owner-occupied as countries that are among the wealthiest can have 60–80 per cent of housing that is owner-occupied (USA, Norway, Japan, Belgium, Luxembourg), only 40–50 per cent (Germany and the Netherlands) or in between these two extremes (France and Denmark).

In several countries, the proportion of the population who own their main house has increased considerably in recent years. For instance, in France, there has been a considerable increase in the proportion of households who own their main home; between 1963 and 1992 it rose from 42 to 54 per cent.[164] In the United Kingdom, it grew from around 41 per cent in 1961 to just over 50 per cent in 1971 to around two-thirds in 1992.[165] The proportion of home-owners in the Russian Federation has also increased rapidly in recent years, as large numbers of public units have been sold.

Owner-occupiers within cities

Table 6.7 included statistics on the proportion of households who are owner-occupiers in many cities. These proportions are generally lower than national averages, as a higher proportion of rural populations tend to be owner-occupiers. However, for many cities in the South it is difficult to produce accurate statistics on owner-occupation, since a considerable proportion of the population live in shelters for which they are *de facto* owner-occupiers but not *de jure* and the proportion of households that are 'owner-occupiers' will vary considerably,

TABLE 6.9 The proportion of housing that is owner-occupied

Country—in categories according to the proportion of housing that is owner-occupied	Date	Proportion of dwellings owner-occupied	Proportion of dwellings rented		Other
			Proportion in public rental units	Proportion Other in private rental units	
70 per cent or more					
Ireland	c.1986	74	12	10	
Greece	c.1986	70		27	
Spain	c.1986	88	1	11	
Bulgaria	1990	87	9	3	1
Hungary	1990	80	20		
Finland	1990	c.73	c.14	c.10	
Norway	1990	78			
New Zealand	1991	72	8	14	5
Tunisia	1989	80	11	8	1
60 to 70 per cent					
United Kingdom	1991	66	20		10
United States of America	1990				
Italy	c.1986	64	5	24	
Belgium	c.1986	62	6	30	
Luxembourg	1991				
Slovenia	1991				
Canada	1986	63			
Chile	1992	63		17	20
Brazil	1984	63			
Japan	1990	61	7	26	6
50–60 per cent					
France	1990	54	15	25	2
Denmark	c.1986	56	21	22	
Portugal	c.1986	56	4	36	20
Hong Kong	1994				
40–50 per cent					
Germany[a]	c.1986	40	17	43	
Netherlands	1990	c.44			
Poland	1990	41	31	4	25[b]
Under 40 per cent					
Russia	1990	26	67		7
Former Czechoslovakia	1988	26	45		26[c]

Notes:
[a] Statistics for the former West Germany.
[b] Co-operatives—11 per cent owners, 14 per cent renters.
[c] Co-operative—owners.

Sources: For Bulgaria, Hungary, Poland and Russia: Baross, Pal and Raymond Struyk, 'Housing transition in Eastern Europe', *Cities*, vol. 10, no. 3, Aug. 1993, 182. For countries with data c.1986: Ghékiere, L., *Marchés et Politiques du Logement dans la CEE*, La Documentation Française, 1991, quoted in Mary Daly, *European Homelessness—the Rising Tide*, The first report of the European Observatory on Homelessness, FEANTSA, 1992. For Finland: Andersson, Kari and Anneli Juntto, 'The effect of the recession on the Finnish housing market', *European Network for Housing Research Newsletter 1.93*, 1993, 3–6. For Hong Kong, Government Information Service 1994. For Chile: Rojas, Eduardo and Margarita Greene, 'Reaching the poor: Lessons from the Chilean housing experience', *Environment and Urbanization*, vol. 7, no. 2, Oct. 1995. For all others: United Nations, *Human Settlements Statistics Questionnaire 1992*, see Table 8 in the statistical annex.

depending on how these are classified. Many are illegally occupying the land on which the shelter is built. Others are closer to being *de jure* owner-occupiers as they purchased the land from the landowner and it is the shelter or the subdivision that is illegal, not the land occupation. Although the Housing Indicators Programme collected statistics on owner-occupancy in 52 cities, in cities with a high proportion of the population living in illegal or informal settlements, the proportion that were 'owner-occupiers' varied greatly, depending on the extent to which the *de facto* owner-occupiers

living in illegal or informal settlements were classified as 'owner-occupiers'.

Table 6.7 also shows how the proportion of households who were owner-occupiers had grown considerably in many cities of the South. This is linked to two factors: the first is the much-increased demand for owner-occupation (as an increasing proportion of households have higher incomes); the second is that illegal land subdivisions and illegal land occupation lowered the cost of housing and brought 'ownership' within reach of a larger proportion of the low-income households.[166] The extent of owner-occupation among low-income households is much influenced by the extent to which cheap land sites are available—whether in legal or illegal subdivisions or through illegal occupation—and the cost of developing a house is not too high.[167] A third factor, in many cities, was government support for owner-occupation.

In many Latin American cities, the proportion of city inhabitants who are owner-occupiers has increased—although the number of tenants has not.[168] Mexico City provides a dramatic example of the decline in renting. Between 1850 and 1950, most of the rapidly growing low-income population was housed in rental accommodation and in 1950, three-quarters of the housing stock was rental accommodation.[169] But by 1980, close to two-thirds of the population were owner-occupiers. Among the reasons for the decline in renting were: rapid economic growth and political stability that made investments in other sectors more profitable; government decrees that froze rents and reduced the return on housing investment; and implementation of building regulations that made the construction of rental-housing for low-income groups unviable.[170] The proportion of households who are owner-occupiers has also increased very considerably in many other cities over the last few decades, although the increase in owner-occupation and decline in renting may have slowed or even reversed in some cities with the economic stagnation of the 1980s.[171]

The possibilities for non-house owners to become owners obviously varies greatly from city to city and within each city over time. One of the key questions is—under what circumstances do low-income households who want to become owners (including those who currently rent or share) find it possible to become owners? The proportion of low-income tenants or sharers who want to become owners will obviously vary greatly from city to city. In certain cities, for certain periods, a considerable proportion of low-income households have found it possible to become owner-occupiers. Perhaps the most important condition is a plentiful supply of cheap or free land in or close to the city. In different cities, for different periods, this condition has been present, although in different forms. In Karachi, the land was available because the city is located on semi-desert land that is for the most part in public ownership and the government did not oppose its occupation by squatters and its development by illegal subdividers.[172] In Santa Cruz (Bolivia), land was also available to squatters when the political authorities tolerated land invasions—because the city is surrounded by flat, low-value agricultural land much of which is uncleared scrubland.[173] This issue of land availability is discussed in more detail in Chapter 7 since in general, the larger the land area that is accessible to the main centres of employment and the easier it is for low-income households to obtain land, the higher the proportion of households who are owners. The motivation for becoming owners in illegal settlements is obviously strongly linked to the likelihood of being able to avoid eviction—and eventually acquiring legal tenure and infrastructure and services.

In considering cities with a high or a low proportion of housing that is owner-occupied, there are certain other factors that are known in particular instances to have affected this balance. For instance, the high rate of owner-occupation in most cities in the United States and the United Kingdom is certainly related to the widespread availability of housing finance and a considerable financial advantage given to owner-occupiers by government policies. The particularly high rate of owner-occupation in Indonesian cities has been attributed to greater access to land with a reasonable degree of tenure security, development of a water supply and provision for sanitation that is simpler and less costly and no onerous land-use and building regulations (or if they exist they are not rigorously enforced).[174] Rising incomes for a considerable proportion of a city's population and the availability of land for housing through informal or illegal land markets has obviously been important for the many Latin American cities where the proportion of households who are owner-occupiers has increased.

Since there is a general tendency for well located land sites in cities (and thus the housing on them) to become more valuable if the city grows in size and prosperity, those who own property in such cities benefit from this rising value—while those who rent do not. In effect, those that own property in cities benefit from the increment in land values created by the combination of public and private investment concentrated there. Owner-occupiers also generally have more secure tenure. This would encourage owner-occupation rather than renting, at least for those able to afford this—although as previous sections noted, there is a sec-

tion of the population in most cities who prefer to rent, even when they can afford to purchase a dwelling. But this does not explain the great differences between cities in the proportion of people who choose to rent or become owner-occupiers, including prosperous cities where most middle- and upper-income groups prefer to rent. What has to be considered in each city at any point in time is the relative advantages and disadvantages of owner-occupation—whether of a completed house or apartment or of a legal, semi-legal or illegal plot on which a dwelling is built. And central to this is the direct and indirect influences of government policies. In many of the wealthiest market economies, owner-occupiers have long been given generous financial incentives—for instance in the United Kingdom, the United States and Australia.[175]

Many low-income households may particularly value the possibility of becoming property owners, if circumstances permit this.[176] First, they acquire a capital asset—and possibly their first significant capital asset. As noted in Chapter 3, it is often low-income groups' lack of assets that make them so vulnerable to economic changes and an asset can be used as a collateral against a loan or sold or part of it rented if a more pressing need presents itself. Building, improving or extending their own home can also take the form of a savings account, as their own labour input into this is translated into a more valuable asset. A house and the land on which it is developed have often proved among the safest capital assets during times of inflation. But, equally important for many low-income households, owning their own dwelling provides more security, unless in an illegal settlement threatened with eviction. And if a household can acquire or build a home without a loan, it removes the necessity of regular rent payments—something that people with irregular incomes find particularly useful.[177]

In many nations—or particular cities—there are also obvious constraints to households who want to become owner-occupiers from doing so. For instance, a major deterrent is where potential owners find it difficult to obtain property titles that guarantee their ownership—for instance where property markets are not well developed and where title to land and property is often not clear, as in many African cities.[178] A lack of availability of long-term finance for housing purchase is also a major constraint since a well-functioning housing finance system greatly increases the amount any individual or households can afford to pay—by spreading repayment over a long period.

Owner-occupier markets

Housing submarkets where the occupiers 'own' the house (even if this ownership is not recognized by law) are also diverse and vary from city to city in the form they take and their relative importance. Table 6.10 outlines various kinds of housing in which it is common for low-income households to be 'owner-occupiers' although in two of them, the occupation of the land or building is illegal and in all but one, some aspect of the building is illegal.

The costs and benefits of different forms of housing tenure

Table 6.11 is drawn from a study that compares housing production systems in Europe, with a special concentration on comparing housing produc-tion in Britain, Sweden and France. But this summary of the costs and benefits of different form of tenure has a wider relevance. The inclusion of 'self-provided owner-occupation' might be considered an unusual category for Europe and of much greater relevance to countries in the South where most housing is 'self-provided owner-occupation' even if most units are built illegally with many built on illegally occupied land. Yet during the 1980s, self-provided owner-occupation accounted for over half of all housing completions in France[180] and over a quarter of all housing completions in Sweden.

Self-provided housing covers all housing in which an individual household takes the responsibility for getting the house built for themselves and

TABLE 6.10 Different kinds of 'owner-occupation' housing used by low-income groups in many cities in the South

Types of owner-occupation	Common characteristics	Problems
Building a house or shack in a squatter settlement	As city grows and so too does the number of people unable to afford a legal house (or house site on which they can organize the construction of a house), illegal occupation of land site and the construction of a house there becomes more common. Advantage to users of (usually) being a free site—although as the settlement develops, a monetized market for sites often appears and land sites can be expensive in better quality, better located settlements. The extent to which households actually build most or all their house varies considerably; many people lack the time to contribute much and hire workers or small firms to do much or all the construction	Lack of secure tenure and settlement often subject to constant threat of destruction by government. Lack of legal tenure inhibits or prevents households offering site as collateral to bank for loan to help pay for construction. No government provision of water, drains, sewers (or other forms of sanitation), roads, electricity, schools, public transport—or even where government does so, this is usually years after the settlement has been built and is usually inadequate. Poor quality sites often squatted on (e.g. subject to flooding or landslides) because these have lowest commercial value and thus give inhabitants the best chance of not being evicted.
Building a house or shack in an illegal subdivision	With housing built in squatter settlements, this represents the main source of new housing in most large cities. The site is bought (or sometimes leased) from landowner or land agent who acts as the developer for the landowner. Or where customary law is still common, the site may be obtained through receiving permission to use it from the chief who acts for 'the community'. Governments often prepared to tolerate these while strongly suppressing squatter invasions since illegal subdivisions do not threaten land owning classes. Often relatively well-off households also organize their house construction on illegal subdivisions. As in squatter settlements, extent to which people build own houses varies considerably.	Comparable problems to those above except land tenure is more secure and landowner or developer sometimes provides some infrastructure (e.g. a road and some water faucets). The site is usually planned (although so too are some squatter settlements). The better located and better quality illegal subdivisions are also likely to be expensive. If the city's physical growth is largely defined by where squatter settlements or illegal subdivisions spring up, it produces a haphazard and chaotic pattern and density of development to which it will be very expensive to provide infrastructure and services. Very large cost-savings can be made if new settlements are planned and located close to existing roads, pipes and sewers.
Building a house or shack on a legal land subdivision on the city periphery	Often a popular solution, especially if there is good quality public transport to keep down the time and costs of getting to and from work.	Low-income households generally having to buy land at a considerable distance from the city centre and the main sources of employment as legal land plots that are better located are too expensive.
Invading empty houses or apartments or public buildings	Known to be common in a few cities; its overall importance in the South is not known.	Obviously insecure tenure since occupation is illegal. May be impossible to get electricity and water even if dwelling was originally connected to these.
Building a house or shack in government sites-and-services scheme or core housing scheme	An increasing number of governments have moved from a concentration on public-housing schemes (which rarely were on a scale to make much impact and often did not benefit poorer households) to serviced sites or core housing schemes. Very rarely are these on a scale to have much impact on reducing the housing problems faced by lower income groups. In addition, it is often middle or upper income groups which receive the serviced plots or core housing units.	Public agency responsible for projects often finds it impossible to acquire cheap, well-located sites. Sites far from low-income groups' sources of employment are chosen, since the public agency finds these cheaper and easier to acquire. Extra cost in time and bus fares for primary and secondary income earners can make household worse off than in squatter settlement. Eligibility criteria often bar women-headed households. Regulations on repayment and building schedule often make many ineligible. Rules often forbid workshops in house or renting out of rooms which limit household income.
Building or developing a house or shack in a 'temporary camp'	Many examples known of governments who develop 'temporary' camps for victims of disasters or for those evicted by redevelopment. Usually located on the city periphery. Many become permanent.[179]	Land and house tenure is often ambiguous; the provision of infrastructure and services at best inadequate, at worst non-existent. The location is often far from the inhabitants' sources of income.

Source: Developed from a table in Hardoy, Jorge E. and David Satterthwaite, *Squatter Citizen: Life in the Urban Third World*, Earthscan Publications, London, 1989

TABLE 6.11 A comparison of the costs and benefits of different forms of housing tenure

	Social renting	Private renting	Cooperative tenant-ownership	Purchased owner-occupation	Self-provided owner-occupation
Entry costs	lowest	low	medium	highest	high
Form of access	queue	market	queue/market	market	self-help
Choice of location and dwelling type	variable	variable	medium	medium	high
Current expenditure	lowest	variable	medium	highest	high
Security of tenure	highest	variable	high	medium	high
Dwelling control	variable	lowest	medium	high	high
Responsibility for repairs & maintenance	low	low	medium	high	high
Property ownership	none	none	mixed	mortgaged	mortgaged
Capital gains	none	none	low	medium	highest

Source: Barlow, James and Simon Duncan, *Success and Failure in Housing Provision: European Cities Compared*, Pergamon, 1994.

includes self-build (i.e. where the household also takes responsibility for building the house) and self-management with the building undertaken by a builder or by a specialist firm supplying the household's chosen prefabricated dwelling.[181] In the case of France, a fifth of the self-promoted housing completions during the 1980s were self-build with another fifth through one-off contracting and the rest through specialist mass-producing 'catalogue' builders.

Table 6.11 also highlights the way in which co-operative tenant-ownership is placed between renting and owner-occupation in terms of entry costs, current expenditure, level of dweller's control, responsibility for maintenance and capital gains. This intermediate category between full ownership rights and no ownership rights has proved very important in several European countries. In Sweden, housing co-operatives produce units for tenant-owners where the co-operative owns the unit but the tenant owns the 'occupancy rights' which are also bought and sold—and housing co-operatives produced a quarter of all the housing produced in Sweden during the 1980s.[182] In Norway, 14 per cent of all housing is managed by co-operative building and housing associations—with higher proportions in urban areas (for instance in Oslo, they manage two-thirds of all homes).[183] In other countries, there are possibilities for occupants of social housing to become part-owners. Forms of housing tenure such as these that are more secure than renting and in which the occupier has a stake in the house or apartment's capital value but which none the less are much cheaper than owner-occupation may have considerable relevance to other countries—although care should be taken in assuming that a model that worked in one country necessarily works in another. In Sweden, the importance of housing co-operatives is linked to long-established political developments; social housing co-operatives are long established and had strong links with the labour movement and with other people's movements.[184]

6.3 The Construction Sector for Housing and Infrastructure Delivery

Construction's importance to national development

The construction industry makes significant contributions to the socio-economic development process in most countries. The level of that contribution has been measured in several ways—notably in terms of its contribution to a nation's gross domestic product or to its capital assets or gross fixed capital formation. In countries in the South, major construction activities account for about 80 per cent of total capital assets. And investment in the construction sector yields continuous benefits over a long period. Investments in shelter are also significant to national development, even though a large part of such investments are often not accounted for, especially those undertaken in illegal or informal settlements. There are also the many indirect benefits from the construction sector—for instance the multiplier effects that the sector stimulates in other sectors and the significant contribution in terms of conserving and generating foreign exchange. However, there are many constraints on the construction sector delivering these direct and indirect benefits in most countries in the South—and this is the focus of this section.

Existing limitations in the construction sector

The underlying problems of the construction sector can be classified into two main groups. The first arises from the fact that the sector is not viewed and planned in a holistic manner, but, rather, operates with fragmented, unrelated and often conflicting components resulting in wastage, duplication, inefficiency and inability to plan for total development. The second set of problems is related to deficiencies in the specific inputs required for the supply of construction output and to unfavourable characteristics of the sector in terms of demand. For instance, key building materials are scarce and expensive; access to finance is limited; much needed equipment and machinery are not easily available; skilled workforce is underdeveloped; and other supporting mechanisms, such as regulatory systems and research efforts, have had little or no impact on the development trends of the industry. A further problem is that large amounts of capital are needed to pay for large scale infrastructure with the financial returns coming over a long period. Such projects are only profitable when considered over a time period that is longer than most commercial investments. Investors are reluctant to commit capital to long term projects when other investment opportunities give a more rapid pay-back and when there is uncertainty about the future demand for new infrastructure.

Primary resource inputs required by the construction sector

Building materials

Building materials generally constitute the single largest input into the construction of housing, accounting for as much as 80 per cent of the total value of a simple house. It is, therefore, important that building materials be made available in sufficient quantities and at affordable costs. The building materials available on the market, in most countries in Africa, Asia and Latin America are either prohibitively expensive and in scarce supply or of low quality. In some low-income settlements, the use of traditional building materials is in decline. This is probably due to the low quality of the traditional materials or to the higher level of maintenance their use requires or to the higher value and greater attractiveness of 'contemporary' building materials. Whatever the reason, this has had negative consequences on the low-income shelter-construction market.

In many countries in the South, the formal construction industry depends almost exclusively on contemporary building materials that have to be imported—and for which very high prices often have to be paid. Among the 52 cities considered in the Housing Indicators Programme, eighteen had imported materials representing more than 20 per cent of the value of residential construction materials with imported materials representing more than 40 per cent in Accra, Dakar and, not surprisingly, the small city-states of Singapore and Hong Kong.[185] There are numerous examples of well-intended government-sponsored low-cost housing programmes being entirely shelved or abandoned before completion, mainly because of the unavailability of the specified materials. Sometimes, low-cost housing projects undergo frequent upward budget revisions, while awaiting the requisite supplies of 'modern' materials, to the point where the project becomes unfeasible.

The above-mentioned constraints in the building materials sector have the same negative effect on the provision of basic infrastructure as they have on housing supply. For instance, in rural areas and in urban squatter settlements, the predominant practice is to use non-durable materials for the construction of pit latrines. In a few cases where public-sponsored programmes have provided water supply and sanitation systems, items such as sewers, septic tanks, latrine slabs and pavement tiles have mainly been procured from conventional production systems, so that they have been also affected by the usual limitations of high cost and inadequate supply.

A good indicator of the relative costs of building materials is represented by the price changes of these materials over time in relation to the average cost of living. Data from Africa show drastic rises in prices of building materials, outpacing the general inflationary trends in the economy. For example in the United Republic of Tanzania, between 1982 and 1989, three basic materials—sand, cement, and steel—increased in price more than fivefold, substantially more than the increase in the cost-of-living index.[186] Similarly, recent data from Nigeria show that three components of a small building—reinforced concrete work, steel roof-sheets and timber doors—have increased in price by more than twice the Nigerian consumer price index during the last decade.[187]

Energy is one of the most crucial inputs required for the production of building materials and the rise in the cost of energy contributes directly to price rises for basic building materials. For example cement, steel, bricks and lime are all energy-intensive materials and the direct fuel costs can contribute by more than 50 per cent to the cost of production of these materials.

Although there is a move towards alternative

fuels such as agricultural waste and low-grade oils, these fuels are also in demand elsewhere, and their prices are quickly catching up with those of conventional fuels. The limited supply and the high price of electricity also prohibits upgrading of traditional technologies using machinery. Even in India, where a range of fuels is available, energy prices to the consumer have increased over the last decade by 25 per cent in real terms.[188]

An important prerequisite for wide-scale production of low-cost/appropriate building materials is that the technologies involved are tested and widely known at the local level. Appropriate technologies for the low-cost building materials production have multiple advantages, including a reduction in the dependence on imported inputs, opportunities for developing substitute inputs from abundant indigenous resources, and potentials for generating new and improved skills among the local workforce. Appropriate technologies can also be useful for reducing the cost of construction output, which is particularly significant for the construction requirements of the poor.

Many governments have found it feasible to establish large-scale factories for the production of basic building materials, particularly cement, steel, roofing sheets, bricks, tiles and concrete products with mainly imported technologies. However, within a short period, many of these factories have been faced with numerous difficulties, arising primarily from the choice of technology. The absence of stable markets and production interruptions resulting from the lack of spare parts and irregular energy supply have often made production planning difficult, resulting in low capacity utilization. For example, the average capacity utilization of cement factories in some African countries in the 1980s was only 58 per cent, and, in some cases, as low as 30 per cent.[189]

The small-scale sector of the building-materials industry, however, has shown remarkable potential in meeting the local demand, despite the fact that they are often forced to operate in an environment that favours large-scale enterprises. For example, in Sri Lanka small-scale enterprises producing bricks, tiles, sand and lime supply more than 35 per cent by value of the total building materials used in the country.[190] However, the continued reliance of the small-scale industries on traditional and outdated production technologies, which are wasteful of raw materials and energy, has been the biggest stumbling block in improving productivity in this sector.

Transportation and distribution costs can claim a significant share of the total cost of a building material. In the South, especially in sub-Saharan Africa, distribution costs can be disproportionately high because of run-down infrastructural facilities and high trucking costs. Small-scale producers, on the other hand, can meet the needs of proximate markets with price advantage. Their strength, essentially, lies in keeping overheads and distribution costs low and meet the local demand. Nevertheless, they lack in managerial and marketing skills for progressive market penetration through forward planning and product diversification.

The lack of requisite knowledge or techniques in the appropriate use of low-cost building materials in construction is an important factor limiting marketing and the wide-scale adoption of such materials. An indigenous building material may be sold at a low cost on the market but, where skills are deficient, the overall objective of low-cost construction will be defeated, because of the excessive use of materials in construction or simply as a result of the prohibitive cost of labour in construction. Where skills are deficient good-quality products may be wrongly employed and thereby lead to unsafe and non-durable constructions and, consequently, render a particular set of building materials unpopular.

Even when low-cost building materials are attractive in terms of market price, there is still the problem of consumer biases against the products. For example, preference for Portland cement, as against lime or lime-pozzolana may not be based on considerations of cost but rather on the lack of information on the technical properties of lime and lack of awareness of the fact that cement can easily be replaced by lime in the construction of 1–2 storey simple houses. The failure to use low-cost materials in government-sponsored construction projects is another serious constraint which limits the wide-scale adoption of these materials. Governments in the South are often the single largest clients of the construction industry and their efforts can easily popularize the use of these materials by private low-income house builders.

Regulatory instruments

Building acts, regulations and codes are the means by which authorities control construction activities for the purpose of ensuring safety and health in the built environment. Similarly, standards and specifications for building materials production and use, ensure stipulated quality construction of products. To a large extent, these regulatory procedures can determine the types of building materials, skills and construction techniques to be used in a given construction process. In this way, an opportunity is created to promote the use of appropriate building materials, so that the capacity of the shelter delivery can be enhanced: conversely, regulatory instruments can be formulated in a manner so as to prohibit the use of certain materials which are normally accessible to the low-income population and, thereby, limit the delivery of low-income shelter. For example, the use of soil in construction probably offers the best opportunity for most low-income settlements: however, to build a safe and durable house in soil requires some basic technical guidelines which can be provided through standards and specifications and permitted by building regulations.

The inadequacies of existing regulatory instruments have negative effects on the provision of basic infrastructure to the low-income population in much the same way as on shelter supply. Typically, existing public health acts and regulations, covering water supply, sanitation and solid-waste disposal, ignore actual practices in low-income settlements and do not offer any corrective devices to the unhealthy state of affairs and faulty trends in the minimal available infrastructure in low-income settlements. Rather, the regulations stipulate infrastructure standards which are far too costly for the target group and which, even if they were provided, could not be maintained with local resources and know-how.

Finance

The construction industry is dependent on financing to purchase required inputs and to pay for labour costs. Shelter and infrastructure construction for the low-income population, even though termed 'low-cost', is still dependent on financing, especially if conventional approaches are adopted. Any constraint in cash flow, therefore, could jeopardize a construction programme and, worse still, lead to cost escalations. In most countries in the South, existing public financial institutions do not respond adequately to the demands for financial resources which are required for critical inputs in construction. The few available financing institutions have had little impact and the normal practice in private-sector low-income shelter construction is to depend on the builder's own finances which often are limited. Financial resources are more readily available in the private sector than in the public sector. Yet, in most countries, the financing of public construction projects, which usually require large investments, are borne by public sources of finance. However, private-sector investment can be attracted, with suitable conditions and interest rates. An example of this is the collection of tolls on highway projects as a means of paying back the investment.

Small contractors

Contractors are one of the key components of the construction sector, as they are directly responsible for the physical realisation of the designs prepared in response to the client's needs and objectives. Small contractors often make a very large contribution to the provision of housing (or its improvement or upgrading) and infrastructure. But they are often affected by several constraints which include: lack of technical and managerial expertise; lack of adequate finance; difficulty in obtaining essential resources— materials, equipment and skilled personnel; and inadequate supervisory capabilities. These constraints can be removed, if adequate policies are in place and necessary support can be provided to them by governments, local and international communities. The ultimate goal, which is to increase progressively the share of local construction activities and attain sustainable development and maintenance of built environment, calls for strengthening small-scale contractors' involvement in the sector, which should have an impact on improving quality of outputs and reducing costs.

Maintenance and upgrading

The expected life-span of a building or infrastructure element requires that some basic regular maintenance will be provided during the service period of the facility. In normal practice buildings and infrastructure also tend to be exposed to unexpected deterioration, thus requiring repair in addition to routine maintenance. Because of the low quality of construction in most low-income settlements, the concept of maintenance is even more relevant than in 'high-cost construction'. Maintenance is also crucial for low-income construction, because most low-income families cannot afford the replacement cost, should a building deteriorate to the point of failure. Finally, given the low rate at which new dwellings and infrastructure are provided for the low-income population, a logical option is to ensure that the little that is already available is sustained in use to the utmost point of its service life.

Sustainable construction industry[191]

The construction industry, while contributing, largely to overall socio-economic development in every country, is a major exploiter of natural non-renewable resources and a significant polluter of the environment. The need, therefore, to introduce more sustainable construction practices is taking new urgency in the overall development context of human settlements. The process of socio-economic development through increased construction activities and protection of the environment are not separate challenges. The sustainability of development cannot be ensured in a climate where growth plans consistently fail to safeguard the environment and arrest the degradation of the natural-resource base and the ecosystem as a whole. It is for this reason that

Agenda 21, adopted by the United Nations Conference on Environment and Development, underscores the importance of the sustainable construction industry activities as a major contributor to the sustainable human settlements development.

While increased awareness and knowledge of the implications of resource depletion and environmental degradation caused by the activities of the construction industry have resulted in some action being taken in the North, there has been little progress in countries of the South, especially in sub-Saharan Africa. Their position is even more desperate given that many of them are faced with fragile environments, involving aridity, desertification, flooding, etc.

Construction and the deterioration of physical environment

The highly dispersed character of construction activities in most countries makes it difficult to monitor the physical disruption caused by them. There is a growing concern, in many countries, about increasing land dereliction caused by the quarrying of sand and gravel, extraction of brick clay, etc. which ultimately reduces the land available for human settlements development. The degradation of the marine environment, caused by coral mining for the production of building lime, and the disruption of wildlife habitats and water tables, by excavations are now attracting the increasing attention of physical planners and coast-conservation authorities.

Appropriate land-use policies and planning, specially aimed at eco-sensitive zones, are very often lacking in the South. One of the main reasons for the lack of clear policies is that data on which to carry out environmental impact assessment and cost-benefit analysis are seriously lacking. The assignment of priorities to alternative environmental needs is not a very difficult task to undertake. However, ultimately, the allocation of land-use priorities would involve an economic decision between costs and returns and safeguarding the environment.

Construction activities similarly contribute to the loss of forests, wetlands and other natural areas by their conversion to other uses and by their unsustainable exploitation for building timber. Timber, because of its superior characteristics and almost zero-energy content, has been one of the basic building materials for centuries. It is estimated that in the Philippines, the demand for wood in building construction is likely to rise from 173,000 m³ in 1990 to 433,000 m³ by the year 2000. In Indonesia, the demand for wood in housing construction is likely to exceed nearly 4 million m³. Japan imports 18 million m³ of sawn wood for the 1.5 million homes annually built there. In Chile 60 per cent of the annual produc-

tion of sawn timber is used in houses and other building construction.[192] These figures mean that wood is going to be an essential building material both for modern structures as well as for traditional building construction in the years to come and their unsustainable exploitation will cause rapid deforestation in many countries.

Construction and depletion of non-renewable resources

The construction industry is responsible for the consumption of commercial energy in two principal ways: (1) in the production of buildings and other facilities, and (2) in the subsequent use of them. It has been found that the consumption of energy in the manufacture of building materials and components is about 75 per cent of the energy requirement for the production of a building, the remaining 25 per cent being primarily used during on-site construction activities.[193] However, in the context of lower-income countries, where construction activities are labour-intensive, the amount of energy required in construction is mainly used in the manufacture and transport of building materials. A high proportion of the energy used in the production of building materials is in a small number of key materials such as steel, aluminium, cement, bricks, glass and lime. Similarly different types of construction systems (sets of materials) can result in considerable differences in the total embodied energy requirements in complete house systems.

Energy is also used in buildings for cooking, space-heating and cooling, lighting and for productive activities. In areas where there is a substantial annual heating requirement, coal-burning stoves are often used in urban housing: insulation standards in such housing are frequently very poor by comparison with those of industrialized countries, and the combustion products add considerably to urban air pollution.

Construction and atmospheric pollution

Pollution caused by construction activities and the production of building materials includes water pollutants from quarrying activities and effluents from chemicals, particulates from fuel combustion and manufacturing processes, carbon oxides (CO and CO_2) from burning fuel, sulphur dioxide (SO_2) from high-temperature burning, and hydrocarbons from the manufacture of chemicals and allied products such as paints.

At local scale, construction and building materials industries create air pollution through emissions of dust, fibre, particles and toxic gases from site activities and building materials production processes. It contributes to regional pollution through emissions of nitrogen and sulphur oxides in building materials production and it contributes to pollution on a global scale in two important ways: (*a*) by the use and release of chlorofluorocarbons (CFCs) for refrigeration which contribute to the depletion of ozone layer; and (*b*) by the emission of carbon dioxide and other 'greenhouse gases'.

6.4 Homelessness

Introduction

Worldwide, the number of homeless people can be estimated at anywhere from 100 million to 1 billion or more, depending on how homelessness is defined. The estimate of 100 million would apply to those who have no shelter at all, including those who sleep outside (on pavements, in shop doorways, in parks or under bridges) or in public buildings (in railway, bus or metro stations) or in night shelters set up to provide homeless people with a bed. The estimate of 1 billion homeless people would also include those in accommodation that is very insecure or temporary, and often poor quality—for instance squatters who have found accommodation by illegally occupying someone else's home or land and are under constant threat of eviction, those living in refugee camps whose home has been destroyed and those living in temporary shelters (like the 250,000 pavement dwellers in Bombay). The estimate for the number of homeless people worldwide would exceed 1 billion people if it were to include all people who lack an adequate home with secure tenure (i.e. as owner-occupiers or tenants protected from sudden or arbitrary eviction) and the most basic facilities such as water of adequate quality piped into the home, provision for sanitation and drainage.

The European Observatory on Homelessness has developed a fourfold classification that can be used to define the condition of homelessness and evaluate its extent:

—rooflessness (i.e. sleeping rough);
—houselessness (i.e. living in institutions or short-term 'guest' accommodation);
—insecure accommodation; and
—inferior or substandard housing.[194]

The fact that widely differing estimates are given for the number of homeless people in any city or country reflect different definitions for homelessness and the difficulty of measuring how many homeless people there are. In Europe and North America, the number of 'homeless' people is generally equal to the number of people registered with some official body as 'homeless' or the number of people using night shelters. They rarely include many of those who sleep outside or in public places because they are not registered as homeless and do not use night shelters. The number using night shelters is often a poor indi-cation of the scale of homelessness—for instance where the quality of night shelters is very poor or authoritarian so homeless people avoid using them, or very inadequate in relation to the number of homeless people, or they fail to provide for those in need.

There is also what can be termed 'concealed homelessness' made up of all the individuals or households who are sharing accommodation or are in temporary accommodation when they need their own home. The previous section noted how in many cities a considerable proportion of adults who would like to have their own accommodation stay for long periods in the home of family members, because they cannot afford their own accommodation. Many young people also find temporary accommodation by illegally occupying a building or by staying with friends or family. There are also the many instances of women wishing to leave an unhappy marriage or relationship but are unable to do so, because they cannot afford separate accommodation.[195] A significant proportion of women in the North who become homeless do so because they are fleeing domestic violence[196]—but many are discouraged from doing so because of the limited possibilities of finding accommodation. This helps explain why in the UK, the average length of time that women tolerate domestic violence before leaving home is 7 years.[197] There may be many disabled people presently accommodated in institutions who have the desire and the capacity to live in their own home but are not able to do so because of costs or lack of suitable housing. These people whose need for housing remains unmet are rarely included in statistics on homelessness. Thus, any statistic given for the number of homeless people for a particular neighbourhood, city or country needs to be qualified with a definition as to what part of 'the homeless' population it is measuring.

The scale of homelessness

Homelessness is certainly not concentrated in low-income countries. The proportion of people who are homeless in the sense of sleeping rough or in a night shelter or temporary accommodation may be higher in some of the world's wealthiest cities than in some cities in the lowest-income countries, largely because they have a higher proportion of people who lack the income to find the cheapest accommodation.

Several million people are homeless in Europe and North America. Using a conservative definition of homelessness, around 2.5 million people were estimated to be homeless in the early 1990s within the twelve countries that made up the European Union (see Box 6.7).[198] This includes 1.8 million who in the course of a year depend on public or voluntary services for temporary shelter or squat or sleep rough, and another 0.9 million in cheap boarding houses and furnished rooms who pay for their own accommodation or are temporarily doubling up with friends and relatives.[199] If the definition was widened to include people in seriously substandard accommodation, the number would be much higher—at least another 15 million people are living in substandard housing and in overcrowded conditions (with more than two persons per room).[200] If the definition was widened further to include all single persons and households who want but are not able to obtain their own home, the number would rise still further; one estimate suggested that 10 per cent of the population of the European Union, some 35 million people would be homeless by this definition.[201] A survey in London in 1986/7 found 188,000 'sharers', people who were living as part of another household when they would prefer to live in their own separate accommodation.[202]

Given the scale of domestic violence and its health impact on women and children in many countries in the North, a more comprehensive service to find new accommodation for the women and children seeking this as a result of domestic violence and sexual abuse would probably reveal a large 'concealed homeless' problem. To give an idea of the scale of the problem, in the United States, battering is the leading cause of injury to women and accounts for nearly one third of all emergency room visits by women.[203]

In the United States, most figures on 'homelessness' refer to people who have no accommodation or who may use temporary night shelters. Official estimates for the mid-1980s suggest between 250,000 and 350,000; the National Coalition for the Homelessness puts the figure much higher—at over 3 million with between 60,000 and 80,000 in New York alone. In Canada, estimates for the number of homeless people based on the number using temporary night shelters and those living and sleeping outside suggest between 130,000 and 250,000.[204]

No comparable figures exist for most nations in Latin America, Asia or Africa. The number who are 'roofless' and have no home and sleep in public buildings or open space is likely to be tens of millions. In India, it is common to see individuals and families taking shelter under bridges and fly-overs, in culverts and even unused water pipes.[205] Those who are 'roofless' include many who move constantly in response to where work is available—for instance building construction workers who live with their families on construction sites.[206] Many street children sleep in open spaces—although the proportion of street children that do so is generally relatively small.[207] In many cities, a proportion of the people who sleep in the open or in public buildings are not home-

---

BOX 6.7

The extent of homelessness in the European Union in the early 1990s

In the early 1990s, around 18 million citizens within the European Union were homeless or extremely badly housed. This included 1.8 million people who in the course of a year depended on public or voluntary services for temporary shelter or who squat or sleep rough. Another 900,000 were estimated to be in cheap temporary accommodation for which they pay themselves—for instance boarding houses or furnished rooms—or were temporarily doubling up with friends and relatives. Another 15 million people were living in housing of very poor quality in overcrowded conditions (with more than two persons per room). A much higher number live in dwellings that do not meet their own national criteria for housing of good quality. Drawing data from ten of the twelve European Union countries, 71.3 million people lived in dwellings which did not meet their own national criteria for housing of good quality. Although most of West Europe's population live in housing with adequate provision for water and sanitation, none the less, in the second half of the 1980s, around 20 million people within the European Union lived in a dwelling without a water closet while around 30 million lived in a dwelling without a bathroom or shower.

Figures are available for most European Union countries on 'the number of homeless people' but these are generally based on the number of people who have been dependent on some public or voluntary sector service for homeless people. If these figures are used as 'the number of homeless people', it tends to be countries with relatively good provision for the homeless that appear to have the highest proportion of homeless people. For instance, by such statistics, Greece, Spain and Portugal appear to have a relatively small homeless population but there are large numbers of people in each of these countries sleeping rough or living in tents, caravans, shacks or other forms of temporary accommodation who are not considered as 'homeless' by official statistics.

Source: Avramov, Dragana, *Homelessness in the European Union: Social and Legal Context for Housing Exclusion in the 1990s*, FEANTSA (European Federation of National Organizations Working with the Homeless), Brussels, 1995.

---

less in that they have homes in rural areas or small towns but they move to cities for temporary work and sleep outside to maximize the amount of money that can be saved or sent home—for instance, many people who work in agriculture move temporarily to cities during periods of the year when there is less work needed on farms.

There are also the large numbers of people who live in tents or shelters made of temporary materials on land on which they have no hope of remaining—who should also be considered homeless. These include the 'pavement dwellers' that can be seen in the largest Indian cities; recent estimates suggest that there are around 250,000 pavement dwellers in Bombay and 130,000 in Delhi[208] (see Box 6.8 for more details of pavement dwellers in Bombay). In Karachi, they include those who live over and along storm drains, on road reserves or on land set aside for parks and playgrounds that had not been realized.[209] Similar kinds of what might be termed 'temporary squatting' can be seen on similar sites in many other cities throughout Africa, Asia and Latin America. These are really the last resort for poor households unable to find rental accommodation they can afford or more secure 'illegal' sites.[210] And the very precarious nature of their tenure ensures that they keep their shelters made of temporary and easily transportable materials. As one person living in an illegal settlement in Abidjan commented:

Wooden houses are more expensive than permanent houses, but the land does not belong to us; we have no papers from the Town Hall or Government, so as we cannot use permanent materials, we build in wood . . . If we are thrown out of here, I can take my wood and go and set up somewhere else, which I could not do with a brick house: you lose a lot, apart from the metal sheeting and wood which you can pick up to take elsewhere.[211]

The number of people in Africa, Asia and Latin America that live in accommodation that is both insecure and substandard is much higher, as described already—for instance the hundreds of millions who live in illegal settlements that are under threat of eviction and with their shelters lacking basic services such as piped water and provision for sanitation and drainage and services such as schools and health care centres. These could be defined as homeless using the broadest definition. Millions of rural households also live in insecure and substandard dwellings— for instance plantation workers, tenant-farming households or temporary or seasonal workers living in communal shacks in very poor conditions. The number living in substandard but relatively secure accommodation would run into the hundreds of millions in rural areas.

Trends

Data about homelessness in the South is too sparse to be able to comment on trends. However, the increasing commercialization of land markets in many cities described in Chapter 7 and the increasing difficulties that low-income groups are having in finding cheap rental accommodation and housing plots that was described earlier suggests that the proportion of people unable to find an adequate quality and secure home is on the rise. The large and possibly rising scale of forced evictions described in Chapter 7 would also support the idea that homelessness in the South is growing.

The evidence in the North suggests that homelessness rose during the 1980s—although here too, the lack of data does not allow precise estimates, especially for the broader categories of 'homelessness'. In the United States, during the 1980s, the number of shelter beds available for the homeless in cities of over 100,000 inhabitants

---

BOX 6.8
Pavement dwellers in Bombay

Pavement dwellers live in small shacks made of temporary materials on pavements and utilize the walls or fences that separate building compounds from the pavement and street outside. They can been seen in most large cities in India but are mostly concentrated in Bombay and Calcutta. They are not a new phenomenon; an English woman, who lived in Bombay in the 1920s, wrote of her shock and distress at the numbers of people for whom the pavements were the only home. The only real change since then has been in the magnitude of the problem and in the nature of official reaction to it.

Most households living in pavement dwellings have at least one household member employed—and hardly any make their livelihood through begging. Far from being a burden to the city's economy, they are supplying it with a vast pool of cheap labour for the unpleasant jobs which organized labour does not like to do. Most are employed in the informal economy as petty traders,

hawkers, cobblers, tailors, handcart pullers, domestic servants and waste-pickers. They can only work for such low wages because they are living on pavements that minimizes their housing costs and incur no overheads on either shelter or transport (most walk to and from work).

The inhabitants of pavement dwellings come to live there initially as a temporary measure, until they can locate and afford better housing. Unfortunately, most are never able to acquire better housing and live out their lives on the footpath. In a census of pavement dwellers undertaken by the Indian NGO SPARC in one ward of Bombay, almost all the families have been living on the pavement ever since their arrival in Bombay—which could be as much as 30 years previously. Fourteen per cent of household heads were not first-generation migrants but born in the city and 23 per cent had been living in the city for more than three decades. Most pavement dwellers moved to Bombay because of poverty, landlessness or lack of employment; most were agricultural labourers, before moving to Bombay.

In a sample of 375 pavement dwellers, half

lived in huts of less than 5 square metres. Given the size of the hut, the pavement in front of the shelter becomes an important part of the domestic space—and is where most children eat, sleep, study and wash. Most pavement dwellers had to obtain water from housing nearby (probably where the women work as domestic helps). For toilets, most used public toilets for which a nominal charge had to be paid while 30 per cent used the railway tracks. When mothers of children under 6 were asked about the main problems they face in staying in their current location, problems of water and sanitation were the ones most frequently mentioned.

Pavement dwellers also had many characteristics in common with most other low-income households in terms of their incorporation within the city. Around two-thirds had their names on electoral roles and just over half the children attend school. Three-quarters of the children had been born in municipal hospitals. Just over a third of all households said they had savings and 28 per cent had loans with banks.

Source: 'We the Invisible' a census of pavement dwellers, SPARC, 1985; Patel, Sheela, 'Street children, hotel boys and children of pavement dwellers and construction workers in Bombay: how they meet their daily needs', Environment and Urbanization, vol. 2, no. 2, Oct. 1990, 9–26.

BOX 6.9
Homeless people in Europe and North America

Most studies of homeless people draw their information from the people who use public services set up for the homeless. Although population censuses record the condition of homelessness and poor quality housing, they do not catch all homeless people, they are generally only undertaken once every ten years and they usually have limited information about the immediate and underlying causes of homelessness.[215] But studies on the extent of homelessness and on who is homeless and why that draw on those using public services are only representative of the homeless who use these public services. A survey of those using night shelters cannot be representative of homeless people if most homeless people do not use night shelters.

In recent years, studies of homeless people in the North that use the most restricted definition of homelessness—i.e. people who use public or voluntary services for the homeless—have undermined the idea that it

tends to be older, single men who account for most of the homeless.

Women: In both Europe and the United States, a significant and growing proportion of homeless people are women—many with children.[216] Around 40 per cent of the people receiving services for the homeless within the European Union are women.[217] A third of the young single homeless people arriving at an emergency shelter in Central London (Centrepoint) each year are female.[218] Single parent households, most of which are headed by women, are particularly vulnerable to homelessness because of the combination of higher costs than single people and very restricted income-earning possibilities for the single parent, especially if the children are too young to go to school.

Younger age groups: The average age of those who are homeless has also fallen. In the 12 countries that formed the European Union in 1994, over 70 per cent of the homeless were younger than 40 years of age. While the age profile varies from country to country, in general there is a fall in the average age of homeless people. In Denmark, both the 18–24 and the 25–34 age groups doubled as

a proportion of homeless people between 1976 and 1989. In Spain, the proportion of those assisted as homeless under the age of 30 grew from 19 to 32 per cent of the total between 1984 and 1991.[219] In the United Kingdom, more than 150,000 young people are homeless—and nearly half of them have been in care and nearly half are young women who left home because of sexual abuse.[220]

Level of education: Homeless people tend to have below average levels of education and it is generally their difficulties in finding work that makes them homeless. In Germany, 80 per cent of those in shelters had not progressed beyond primary schooling; in Spain, over 70 per cent of homeless people have only basic reading and writing skills and most of the rest have no more than middle-range education.[221] Although most homeless people in Europe and the United States rely mostly on subsistence incomes paid by government agencies, a proportion actually have work but the work pays them too little to allow them to find secure accommodation.

Sources: Most of the information in this box is based on the first, second and third report of the European Observatory on Homelessness by Mary Daly, the fourth research report by Dragana Avramov, FEANTSA, Brussels, and Burt, Martha R., *Over the Edge; the Growth of Homelessness in the 1980s*, The Urban Institute Press, Washington DC, 1992.

nearly tripled—from 41,000 to 117,000.[212] In the United Kingdom, where provision for homeless people is less oriented to single males and more oriented to parents with young children or pregnant women and other 'priority groups'[213], the number of households recognized as 'homeless' by public authorities rose from around 20,000 in 1970 to 117,900 in 1986 to 167,300 in 1992.[214] Box 6.9 outlines some characteristics of the homeless in the North.

The causes of homelessness

Much of the research on homelessness tends to describe characteristics of the homeless such as those outlined in Box 6.9 or immediate causes that precipitated a person or family being homeless—for instance the loss of a job or a fall in income that meant the rent could no longer be afforded or the break-up of a relationship leaving one parent and often the children homeless. The underlying causes are sometimes not mentioned at all—for instance a decline in the availability of cheap rental accommodation to allow these people to find accommodation without becoming homeless, the decreased emphasis given by most governments to social housing, and changes in the labour market that make it increasingly difficult for substantial sections of the adult population to find employment, or the possibility of earning an income or (in the North) the decline

in the value of the subsistence income available to the unemployed and the limits on its availability for unemployed people.

Most homelessness is the result of people unable to find adequately paid work and it is often exacerbated by housing markets where adequate accommodation is beyond the means of those with low incomes. The clear links between poverty and homelessness were noted in Chapter 3 when describing the scale and nature of poverty.

Although the general causes of homelessness will have common elements in most countries in the North and the South, its scale and the groups most affected by it will vary greatly. It is also likely that the causes of homelessness vary for different groups—for instance comparing men and women and considering the special circumstances that make young groups or older groups or those with physical or mental difficulties more at risk of homelessness. Minority groups and refugees are often more at risk of homelessness because of greater difficulties in finding jobs and because of discrimination against them by landlords and possibly by agencies selling or renting housing or selling mortgages. In many countries, women also face discrimination in job markets, housing markets and access to housing finance.

In regard to gender differences, the European Observatory on Homelessness noted that male and female homelessness tend to be precipitated by different conditions. For women, relationship problems are the most common stated cause of homelessness—often arising from marital difficulties, a considerable proportion of which include domestic violence. Men are more likely to be made homeless by either material problems (for instance loss of job, shortage of money) or personal difficulties of some kind. Men who are homeless are more likely to seek and receive accommodation from the available services (which are typically more suited to the needs of lone individuals) or are more visible on the streets and in public places. Women who are homeless or potentially homeless (for instance having left their home and are staying with a family member or a friend) often have responsibility for children.[222]

In regard to homelessness among young adults, the most critical factor is the extent of employment opportunities and their level of pay. For instance, perhaps the most fundamental underlying cause of increased homelessness among the young in Britain (and probably in most European countries) is their deteriorating economic position that has its roots in the rapid changes in the labour market.[223] In Britain, young people have experienced dramatic rises in unemployment, particularly long-term unemployment, a downward pressure on wages for young workers and reductions in entitlements to a minimum income if unemployed.[224]

A study of the growth of homelessness in the United States during the 1980s was unusual in that it investigated in considerable detail the variety of underlying causes.[225] One of the most important was the change in labour markets—like the disappearance of many casual-labour and manufacturing jobs that had paid relatively high incomes to people with relatively little formal education. This was part of the increase in inequality in the United States; during the 1980s, the average incomes of lower-income groups declined. These changes had the greatest effects on people with the highest risk of experiencing homelessness—minorities and low-skilled men and families headed by women. A second underlying cause was rising rents, especially in relation to the incomes of those who rented accommodation; in many cities, there were also increases in living costs. The third was changes in government 'safety net' programmes during the 1980s that generally withdrew or reduced resources for very poor households. The fourth was the increase in the number of households with only one income-earner; low-income households who rented accommodation in the 1980s were more likely than in the 1970s to be single-person households or households that included only one adult (usually these were households headed by women). Both household types are less able to weather a crisis than husband–wife households.

They are less able to support disabled or unemployed family members—and if some crisis pushes them into homelessness (e.g. losing a job or eligibility for welfare), their lack of assets are less likely to be able to get them back into their housing market. Their circumstances combined with increasing housing costs put them and their wider network of family and friends at higher risk of homelessness.

A fifth underlying cause was the decrease in government support for people with mental illnesses or problems of chemical or alcohol dependency. A significant proportion of the people using homeless services have problems with chemical dependency or mental illness—and the proportion increased rapidly during the 1980s. However, they were still a minority among those using homeless services[226] and a proportion of these people were able to avoid homelessness when cheap rental accommodation and casual work was available. Their numbers were also increased by reduced government provision for those with mental illnesses, including a greater tendency to release people too early, without support. The proportion of homeless people with problems of chemical dependency or mental problems would be much lower, if a broader definition was used for defining the homeless.

Studies of homelessness in Europe and North America stress the broad range of people who are homeless or at risk of becoming homeless. They also show how the relative importance of different underlying causes varies considerably from country to country and city to city—and often, in any country or city over time. The study of homelessness in the United States also found that a city's poverty rate rarely contributed to explaining differences in homeless rates between cities. The author suggests that

poverty should be viewed as a factor making one vulnerable to homelessness but homelessness depends less on the proportion of the city's population that are poor than on external conditions affecting poor people. Poverty reduces a household's ability to cope with heavy pressures but it is the structural pressures of poor quality jobs, high living costs, pressures from middle class and tight housing markets that tip poor people into homelessness.[227]

However, despite the great variety in the scale and nature of homelessness between countries and cities, certain common themes recur in research findings. The most common is the extent to which poverty, poor housing and homelessness are concentrated in households with only one income-earner—and especially so in single-parent households where the single parent (almost always a woman) has to combine responsibility for child-rearing and for all housekeeping tasks with earning an income. Another common theme is that the scale of homelessness in any country is much influenced by the extent and quality of government action in three areas:

- Providing a framework in both housing policy and macro-economic policy and tax structure that ensures housing costs are kept down and constraints on the supply of housing (including rental accommodation) and on inputs into housing (land, finance, materials) are kept to a minimum. Cheap rental accommodation is often of particular importance to individuals or households most at risk of becoming homeless;

- The provision for education and training and for health care that increases people's capacity to earn income and minimizes the time that potential income earners are sick or injured; and

- The extent and quality of safety nets or social

security schemes that ensure at least a minimum income and access to accommodation for those who are sick, disabled, fleeing domestic violence (usually women, often with children) or otherwise unable to find a source of income.

These reasons underlie homelessness and many other aspects of deprivation in both North and South. The safety net must include adequate provision for the people with mental illnesses and problems of alcohol or drug abuse but it should be recognized that these are only part of the people who are 'roofless' and a very small proportion of the homeless, using the broader definition for homelessness. And as a study on homeless within the European Union noted, since homelessness is largely the outcome of social and economic factors, it also means it can be much reduced by reducing the social and economic factors that cause or precipitate homelessness.[228]

Notes and References

1. Burt, Martha R., *Over the Edge; the Growth of Homelessness in the 1980s*, The Urban Institute Press, Washington DC, 1992, see p. 31.

2. This gives only a crude measure of housing adequacy since what might appear as a system in balance within a nation may hide significant regional imbalances.

3. This discussion of the validity of the concept of 'housing deficit' is drawn from Hardoy, Jorge E. and David Satterthwaite, *Squatter Citizen: Life in the Urban Third World*, Earthscan Publications, London, 1989.

4. Defined as the percentage of dwelling units likely to last 20 years or more given normal maintenance and repair, taking into account locational and environmental hazards (e.g. floods, typhoons, mudslides and earthquakes).

5. Mayo, Stephen K. and Shlomo Angel, *Housing: Enabling Markets to Work, A World Bank Policy Paper*, World Bank, Washington DC, 1993.

6. Defined as the median usable living space per person last year.

7. Asian Coalition for Housing Rights, 'Evictions in Seoul, South Korea', *Environment and Urbanization*, vol. 1, no. 1, April 1989, 89–94. This was quoting from statistics released by the Economic Planning Board and the Ministry of Construction in 1985.

8. Hasan, Arif, 'Profiles of three Pakistani Cities: Karachi, Faisalabad and Thatta', background paper prepared for the Global Report on Human Settlements, 1994.

9. Aina, Tade Akin, *Health, Habitat and Underdevelopment—with Special Reference to a Low-Income Settlement in Metropolitan Lagos*, IIED Technical Report, London, 1989.

10. Defined as the ratio between the median

number of persons in a dwelling unit and the median number of rooms in a dwelling unit.

11. See for instance Hasan 1994, *op. cit.*

12. Hamer, Andrew, *Bogota's Unregulated Subdivisions*, World Bank Staff Working Paper, The World Bank, Washington DC, 1981.

13. Silas, Johan, 'Surabaya', background paper prepared for the Global Report on Human Settlements, 1994.

14. See Perez Perdomo, Rogelio and Pedro Nicken (with the assistance of Elizabeth Fassano and Marcos Vilera), 'The law and home ownership in the barrios of Caracas', in Alan Gilbert, Jorge E. Hardoy and Ronaldo Ramirez (eds.), *Urbanization in Contemporary Latin America*, John Wiley and Sons, Chichester, 1982, 205–29; also Ramirez, Ronaldo, Jorge Fiori, Hans Harms and Kosta Mathey, 'The commodification of self-help housing and state intervention: household experiences in the Barrios of Caracas, in Kosta Mathey (ed.), *Beyond Self-Help Housing*, Mansell, London and New York, 1992, 95–144.

15. This draws on a different price–income ratio to the Housing Indicators Programme; the price-income ratio for Greater London was reported at 5.5 in 1988, falling to just over 4.0 in 1993; Council of Mortgage Lenders, UK, 1994.

16. Mayo and Angel 1993, *op. cit.*

17. *Ibid.*

18. UNCHS/World Bank, *The Housing Indicators Program Volume III; Preliminary Findings*, Washington DC, April 1993.

19. Strassmann, W. Paul, 'Oversimplification in housing analysis, with reference to land markets and mobility', *Cities* vol. 11, no. 6, Dec. 1994, 377–83.

20. Mayo and Angel 1993, *op. cit.*

21. Okpala, Don C. I., 'Financing housing in developing countries: a review of the pitfalls and potentials in the development of formal housing finance systems', *Urban Studies*, vol. 31, no. 9, 1994, 1571–86.

22. See Okpala 1994, *op. cit.*; also Renaud, Bertrand, 'Another look at housing finance in developing countries', *Cities*, vol. 4, no. 1, Feb. 1987, 28–34.

23. Kim, Kyung-Hwan: 'Access to credit, terms of housing finance and affordability of housing', Paper presented at the Asia Regional Conference on Housing Finance Strategies for Habitat II, Seoul, Korea, 20–22 March 1995. Chapter 11 includes examples of innovative housing finance schemes for low income groups where virtually all borrowers repaid the loans on time.

24. *Ibid.*

25. Okpala 1994, *op. cit.*

26. Yapi-Diahou, Alphonse, 'The informal housing sector of the metropolis of Abidjan, Ivory Coast', *Environment and Urbanization* vol. 7, no. 2, Oct. 1995, 11–30.

27. The proportion will tend to decrease again in countries with still higher per capita incomes—see Mayo and Angel 1993, *op. cit.*

28. *Ibid.*

29. Arrossi, Silvina, Felix Bombarolo, Jorge E. Hardoy, Diana Mitlin, Luis Perez Coscio and David Satterthwaite, *Funding Community Initiatives*, Earthscan Publications, London, 1994.

30. Mayo and Angel 1993, *op. cit.*

31. World Bank/UNCHS 1993, *op. cit.*

32. Society for Community Organization, *Photo Album of Cages*, Hong Kong, 1993; Asian Coalition for Housing Rights, 'Evictions in Seoul, South Korea', *Environment and Urbanization*, vol. 1,

no. 1, April 1989, 89–94; Hardoy and Satterthwaite 1989, *op. cit.*

33. Society for Community Organization 1993, *op. cit.*

34. Strassmann 1994, *op. cit.*

35. These include papers commissioned for this Global Report including Stambouli, Fredj, 'The urban profile of Tunis City today', Background Paper for the United Nations Global Report on Human Settlements, 1994 and Yapi-Diahou, Alphonse, 'The informal housing sector of the metropolis of Abidjan, Ivory Coast', Background Paper for the United Nations Global Report on Human Settlements, 1994, subsequently published in Yapi-Diahou 1995, *op. cit.*

36. Mayo and Angel 1993, *op. cit.*

37. This paragraph is drawn from Box S-1 of Mayo and Angel 1993, *op. cit.*

38. Peattie, Lisa, 'Shelter, development and the poor', in Lloyd Rodwin (ed.), *Shelter, Settlement and Development*, Allen and Unwin, Boston and London, 1987, 263–80.

39. See Moser, Caroline O. N. and Linda Peake (eds.), *Women, Housing and Human Settlements*, Tavistock Publications, London and New York, 1987, especially Moser, Caroline O. N., 'Mobilization is women's work: struggles for infrastructure in Guayaquil, Ecuador', 166–94.

40. Andreasen, Jorgen, 'The poor don't squat: the case of Thika, Kenya', *Environment and Urbanization*, vol. 1, no. 2, Oct. 1989, 16–26.

41. Yapi-Diahou 1995, *op. cit.*

42. *Ibid.*

43. For La Paz (Bolivia) and Bamako (Mali), see van Lindert, Paul and August van Western, 'Household shelter strategies in comparative perspective: evidence from low income groups in Bamako and La Paz, *World Development* vol. 19, No 8, 1991, 1007–28; for Abidjan, see Yapi-Diahou 1995, *op. cit.*

44. Moser, Caroline O. N., 'A home of one's own: squatter housing strategies in Guayaquil, Ecuador', in Alan Gilbert, Jorge E. Hardoy and Ronaldo Ramirez (eds.), *Urbanization in Contemporary Latin America*, John Wiley and Sons, Chichester, UK, 1982.

45. Perez Perdomo and Nicken 1982, *op. cit.*

46. Stein, Alfredo, 'The Tugurios of San Salvador: a place to live, work and struggle', *Environment and Urbanization*, vol. 1, no. 2, Oct. 1989, 6–15.

47. Hasan 1994, *op. cit.*

48. Gilbert, Alan, 'Pirates and invaders; land acquisition in urban Colombia and Venezuela', *World Development*, vol. 9, 1981, 657–78.

49. Riofrio, Gustavo, *Producir la Ciudad Popular de los. '90; Entre el Mercado y el Estado*, DESCO, Lima, 1991; also Peattie, Lisa, 'Participation: a case study of how invaders organize, negotiate and interact with government in Lima, Peru', *Environment and Urbanization*, vol. 2, no. 1, April 1990, 19–30.

50. Mayo and Angel 1993, *op. cit*

51. *Ibid.*

52. *Ibid.*

53. Islam, Nazrul, 'The poor's access to urban land for housing', in Islam, Nazrul and Amirul Islam Chowdhury (eds.), *Urban Land Management in Bangladesh*, Ministry of Land, Gov-ern-ment of Bangladesh, Dhaka, 1992.

54. Stein 1989, *op. cit.*

55. Stambouli 1994, *op. cit.*

56. Aina, Tade Akin, 'Metropolitan Lagos: population growth and spatial expansion; city study', Background paper for the Global Report on Human Settlements, 1995.

57. More than a quarter of all households in La Paz live rent-free in a room, apartment or house with the permission of the owner. This form of tenure is called *cedida*—see Beijaard, Frans, 'Rental and rent-free housing as coping mechanisms in La Paz, Bolivia', *Environment and Urbanization*, vol. 7, no. 2, Oct. 1995, 167–82.

58. Edwards, Michael, 'Cities of tenants: renting among the urban poor in Latin America', in Alan Gilbert, Jorge E. Hardoy and Ronaldo Ramirez (eds.), *Urbanization in Contemporary Latin America*, John Wiley and Sons, Chichester, 1982.

59. Census data quoted in Wadhva, Kiran, 'Rental housing in India: compulsion or choice?', in UNCHS, *Rental Housing: Proceedings of an Expert Group Meeting*, UNCHS (Habitat), Nairobi, 1990, 20–31.

60. Official statistics quoted in Pasternak Taschner, Suzana, 'Housing in Brazil: diagnosis and challenges', in Leslie Kilmartin and Harjinder Singh (eds.), *Housing in the Third World*, Concept Publishing Company, Delhi, 1992, 93–112.

61. Baross, Pal and Raymond Struyk, 'Housing transition in Eastern Europe: progress and problems', *Cities*, vol. 10, no. 3, Aug. 1993, 179–88; Carter, F. W., 'East Europe: population distribution, urban change, housing and environmental problems', background paper for the Global Report on Human Settlements, 1994.

62. Gilbert, Alan, 'The housing of the urban poor', in Alan Gilbert and Josef Gugler, *Cities, Poverty and Development; Urbanization in the Third World* (Second Edition), Oxford University Press, Oxford, 1992, 121.

63. UNCHS 1993, *op. cit.*

64. Table V.3 in United Nations, *Report of the World Social Situation 1993*, ST/ESA/235, New York, 1993, suggests that proportion of urban households who were 'renter households' increased in several Latin American countries when comparing the 1980s to the 1970s—and also in Malawi, Zambia and the Republic of Korea.

65. Ozo, A. O., 'The private rented housing sector and public policies in developing countries: the example of Nigeria',

Third World Planning Review, vol. 12, no. 3, 1990, 261–79.

66. Serageldin, H., *Support Measures to Promote Low-income Rental Housing: the Case of Egypt*, UNCHS (Habitat), mimeo, 1993.

67. Tipple, A. G. and K. G. Willis, 'Tenure choice in a West African city', *Third World Planning Review*, vol. 13, no. 1, 1991, 27–46.

68. Oruwari, Yomi, 'Conditions of low-income housing, with special reference to rental stock and rental housing strategies in Nigeria', in UNCHS, *Rental Housing: Proceedings of an Expert Group Meeting*, UNCHS (Habitat), Nairobi, 1990, 32–43.

69. UNCHS 1993, *op. cit.*

70. Andreasen 1989, *op. cit.*

71. Municipality of Amman, 'Greater Amman: urban development', *Cities*, vol. 10, no. 1, Feb. 1993, 37–49.

72. Data for 1987/8 from Wadhva, Kiran, 'Support measures to promote low-income rental housing: the case of India', UNCHS (Habitat), mimeo, 1993; earlier data from the 1961 census quoted in Wadhva 1990, *op. cit.*

73. Data for 1987/8 from Wadhva 1993, *op. cit.*; data from 1961 from census quoted in Wadhva 1990, *op. cit.*

74. Data for 1987/8 from Wadhva 1993, *op. cit.*; data from 1961 from census quoted in Wadhva 1990, *op. cit.*

75. Hoffman, M. L., C. Walker, R. J. Struyk and K. Nelson, 'Rental housing in urban Indonesia', *Habitat International*, vol. 15, 1990, 181–206.

76. Wadhva 1990, *op. cit.* drawing on census data.

77. Urban Poor Institute, *Information Packet on the Urban Poor of Korea*, Seoul, South Korea, 1988 quoted in Asian Coalition for Housing Rights, 'Evictions in Seoul, South Korea', *Environment and Urbanization*, vol. 1, no. 1, April 1989, 89–94.

78. United Nations, *Human Settlements Statistics Questionnaire 1992*; see Table 9 in the statistical annex.

79. Data for 1987/8 from Wadhva 1993, *op. cit.*; data from 1961 from census quoted in Wadhva 1990, *op. cit.*

80. Kingsley, G. Thomas, Peter Tajcman and Sarah W. Wines, 'Housing reform in Czechoslovakia: promise not yet ful-filled', *Cities*, vol. 10, no. 3, Aug. 1993, 224–36.

81. Hedegus, Jozsef, Katharine Mark, Raymond Struyk and Ivan Tosics, 'Local options for transforming the public rental sector: empirical results from two cities in Hungary', *Cities*, vol. 10, no. 3, Aug. 1993, 257–71.

82. Central Statistical Office, *Regional Trends 29*, HMSO, 1994.

83. Kingsley, Tajcman and Wines 1993, *op. cit.*

84. Herbst, Irena and Alina Muziol-Weclawowicz, 'Housing in Poland: problems and reforms', *Cities*, vol. 10, no. 3, August 1993, 246–56.

85. For 1985 data, Gilbert, Alan, 'Land and shelter in mega-cities: some critical issues', in Roland J. Fuchs, Ellen Brennan, Joseph Chamie, Fu-Chen Lo and Juha I. Uitto (eds.), *Mega-City Growth and the Future*, United Nations University Press, Tokyo, 1994, 307–31; for earlier data, see Edwards 1982, *op. cit.* which draws on and comments on official data.

86. UNCHS 1993, *op. cit.*; for 1973, official data quoted in Edwards 1982, *op. cit.*

87. Gilbert 1993, *op. cit.*

88. Beijaard 1995, *op. cit.*

89. The 1982 figures are from Sachs, Celine, *Sao Paulo—Politiques Publiques et Habitat Populaire*, Editions de la Maison des Sciences de l'Homme, Paris, 1990; the figures for 1900 are from Bonduki, Nabil, 'Habitaçao popular: contribuiçao para o estudo da evoluçao urbana de Sao Paulo', in Lícia do Prado Valladares (ed.), *Repensando a Habitaçao no Brasil*, Zahar, Rio de Janeiro, 1983, 135–68 quoted in Caldeira, Teresa, 'Building up walls: the new pattern of spatial segregation in Sao Paulo', *International Social Science Journal*, no. 147, March 1996.

90. Van der Linden, Jan, 'Rental housing of the urban poor in Pakistan: characteristics and some trends', in UNCHS, *Rental Housing: Proceedings of an Expert Group Meeting*, UNCHS (Habitat), Nairobi, 1990, 50–5.

91. Baross, Paul, 'The impact of urban development and management of the spatial location of rental-housing stock in Third World cities', in UNCHS, *Rental Housing: Proceedings of an Expert Group Meeting*, UNCHS (Habitat), Nairobi, 1990, 132–3.

92. Van der Linden 1990, *op. cit.*

93. Daunton, M. J., *A Property Owning Democracy? Housing in Britain*, Faber and Faber, London, 1987, quoted in UNCHS (Habitat), *Support Measures to Promote Rental Housing for Low Income Group*, United Nations Centre for Human Settlements, HS/294/93E, Nairobi, 1993.

94. See for instance Andreasen 1989, *op. cit.*

95. In 1992, the home ownership rate in the United States was 63 per cent—Chinloy, Peter and Isaac F. Megbolugbe, 'Real estate market institutions in the United Kingdom: implications for the United States', *Housing Policy Debate*, vol. 5, Issue 3, 1994, 381–99.

96. UNCHS 1993, *op. cit.*

97. Megbolugbe, I. F. and P. D. Linnerman, 'Home ownership', *Urban Studies*, vol. 30, 659–82.

98. Boléat, Mark, 'The 1985–1993 housing market in the United Kingdom; an overview', *Housing Policy Debate*, vol. 5, Issue 3, 1994, 253–74.

99. Chant, Sylvia and Peter Ward, 'Family structure and low-income housing policy', *Third World Planning Review*, vol. 9, 1987, 5–19, Gilbert 1993 *op. cit.*

100. Barnes, S. T., 'Public and private housing in urban West Africa: the social implications', in M. K. C. Morrison and P. C. W. Gutkind (eds.), *Housing the Urban Poor in Africa*, Maxwell School, Syracuse University, Syracuse, 1982, 5–29; and Peil, M. and P. O. Sada, *African Urban Society*, John Wiley and Sons, Chichester, 1984.

101. Yapi-Diahou 1995, *op. cit.*

102. Pryer, Jane, 'The impact of adult ill-health on household income and nutrition in Khulna, Bangladesh', *Environment and Urbanization*, vol. 5, no. 2, Oct. 1993, 35–49.

103. Klak, T. and J. K. Hey, 'Gender and state bias in Jamaican housing programs', *World Development*, vol. 20, 1992, 213–27; Moser, Caroline O. N. and Linda Peake (eds.), *Women, Human Settlements and Housing*, Tavistock Publications, New York and London, 1987.

104. See Moser, Caroline O. N., 'Women, human settlements and housing: a conceptual framework for analysis and policy-making', in Caroline O. N. Moser and Linda Peake (eds.), *Women, Housing and Human Settlements*, Tavistock Publications, London and New York, 1987, 12–32.

105. UNCHS (Habitat), *Support Measures to Promote Rental Housing for Low Income Group*, United Nations Centre for Human Settlements, HS/294/93E, Nairobi, 1993. For sharing in Khartoum, see Ahmad, Adil Mustafa, 'Housing submarkets for the urban poor—the case of Greater Khartoum, the Sudan', *Environment and Urbanization*, vol. 1, no. 2, Oct. 1989, 50–9. For sharing in Abidjan, see Yapi-Diahou 1995, *op. cit.*

106. Necochea, A., 'El allegamiento de los sin tierra, estrategia de supervivencia en vivienda', *EURE* Nos. 13–14, 1987, 85–100; Gilbert, Alan, *In Search of a Home*, UCL Press, London, 1993.

107. Wadhva 1993, *op. cit.*

108. Van der Linden 1990 and Ahmad 1989, *op. cit.*

109. For an example of this, see van der Linden 1990, *op. cit.*

110. See for instance Latapí, Augustín Escobar and Mercedes González de la Rocha, 'Crisis, restructuring and urban poverty in Mexico', *Environment and Urbanization* vol. 7, no. 1, April 1995, 57–75.

111. van der Linden 1990, *op. cit.*

112. UNCHS 1993, *op. cit.* lists the many studies that support this including Beijaard, Frans, *And I promise you . . . .; Politics, Economy and Housing Policy in Bolivia, 1952–87*, Free University, Amsterdam, 1992; Coulomb, R., 'La vivienda de alquiler en las areas de reciente urbanización', *Revista de Ciencias Sociales y Humanidades*, vol. VI, 1985, 43–70; Gilbert, A. G. and A. Varley, *Landlord and Tenant: Housing the Poor in Urban Mexico*, Routledge, London, 1991; and Edwards 1982, *op. cit.* See also Hoffman and others 1990, *op. cit.*

113. See for instance Ozo, A. O., *Support Measures to Promote Low-income Rental Housing: the Case of Nigeria*, UNCHS (Habitat), mimeo, 1993; Lloyd, Peter, 'Epilogue', In Philip Amis and Peter Lloyd (eds.), *Housing Africa's Urban Poor*, Manchester University Press, Manchester, 1990, 278–98; Rakodi, Carole, 'Upgrading in Chawama, Lusaka: displacement or differentiation', *Urban Studies* vol. 25, 1987, 297–318; Barnes, S., *Patrons and Power: Creating a Political Community in Metropolitan Lagos*, Manchester University Press, Manchester, 1987.

114. Lloyd 1990, *op. cit.* 294

115. Serageldin, H., *Support Measures to Promote Low-income Rental Housing: the Case of Egypt*, UNCHS (Habitat), mimeo, 1993.

116. Ozo, A. O., *Support Measures to Promote Low-income Rental Housing: the Case of Nigeria*, UNCHS (Habitat), mimeo, 1993.

117. Amis, Philip, 'Squatters or tenants: the commercialization of unauthorized housing in Nairobi', *World Development* vol. 12, no. 1, 1984, 87–96.

118. Pornchokchai, Sopon, *Bangkok Slums; Review and Recommendations*, School of Urban Community Research and Actions, Bangkok, 1992.

119. Aina, Tade Akin, 'Many routes enter the market place: housing sub-markets for the urban poor in Metropolitan Lagos, Nigeria', *Environment and Urbanization*, vol. 1, no. 2, Oct. 1989, 38–49.

120. Wahab, E. A., *The Tenant Market of Baldia Township*, Urban Research Working Papers No 3, Amsterdam Free University, Amsterdam, 1984, quoted in van der Linden, Jan, 'Rental housing of the urban poor in Pakistan: characteristics and some trends', in UNCHS, *Rental Housing: Proceedings of an Expert Group Meeting*, UNCHS (Habitat), Nairobi, 1990, 50–5.

121. Aina 1989, *op. cit.*

122. Hardoy, Jorge E., 'The inhabitants of historical centres; who is concerned about their plight', *Habitat International*, vol. 7, no. 5/6, 1983; Hardoy, Jorge E. and Mario dos Santos, *Impacto de la Urbanizacion en los Centros Historicos Latinamericanos*, PNUD/ UNESCO, Lima, 1983.

123. For more details about renters' needs and priorities, see UNCHS 1993, *op. cit.*; Gilbert, Alan, *In Search of a Home*, UCL Press, London, 1993; and van Lindert and van Western 1991, *op. cit.*

124. Edwards, Michael, 'Characteristics of the rental-housing market: the supply side', in UNCHS, *Rental Housing: Proceedings of an Expert Group Meeting*, UNCHS (Habitat), Nairobi, 1990, 67–75.

125. Edwards 1990, *op. cit.*

126. Ahmad, Adil Mustafa, 'Housing submarkets for the urban poor—the case of Greater Khartoum, the Sudan', *Environment and Urbanization*, vol. 1, no. 2, Oct. 1989, 50–9.

127. UNCHS (Habitat), *Survey of Slums and Squatter Settlements*, Tycooly International, Dublin, 1982.

128. Amis 1984, *op. cit.*

129. Edwards, Michael, 'Rental housing and the urban poor: Africa and Latin America compared', in Philip Amis and Peter Lloyd (eds.), *Housing Africa's Urban Poor*, Manchester University Press, Manchester, 1990, 253–72, quoting a 1985 survey of the Lusaka Urban District Council.

130. El Agraa and Shaddad 1988, *op. cit.*

131. Green, Gill, 'A case study of housing tenure and rental accommodation in Santa Cruz, Bolivia', in UNCHS, Rental Housing: Proceedings of an Expert Group Meeting, UNCHS (Habitat), Nairobi, 1990, 56–66.

132. Schlyter, Ann, *Twenty Years of Development in George, Zambia*, Swedish Council for Building Research, Stockholm, 1991.

133. Edwards 1990, *op. cit.*

134. Malpezzi, S., A. G. Tipple and K. G. Willis, 'Costs and benefits of rent control: a case study of Kumasi, Ghana', *World Bank Discussion Papers no. 74*, World Bank, Washington DC, 1990.

135. Aina 1989, *op. cit.*

136. Amis 1984, *op. cit.*

137. Edwards 1990, *op. cit.*

138. Kioe Sheng, Yap, 'Some low income housing delivery sub-systems in Bangkok, Thailand', *Environment and Urbanization*, vol. 1, no. 2, Oct. 1989, 27–37.

139. UNCHS 1993, *op. cit.*

140. Qi, Liu, 'Housing and reform: an introduction to Beijing's housing reform program', Paper presented at the Second Symposium on Housing for the Urban Poor, European Network for Housing Research, Birmingham, April 1994.

141. Government Information Services, *Hong Kong 1995; A Review of 1994*, Hong Kong, 1995.

142. Carter 1994, *op. cit.*

143. Hardoy and Satterthwaite 1989, *op. cit.*

144. Hardoy, Jorge E. and David Satterthwaite, *Shelter: Need and Response; Housing, Land and Settlement Policies in Seventeen Third World Nations*, John Wiley and Sons, Chichester, 1981.

145. Blitzer, Silvia, Jorge E. Hardoy and David Satterthwaite, 'The sectoral and spatial distribution of multilateral aid for human settlements', *Habitat International* vol. 7, no. 1/2, 1983, 103–27.

146. See many examples in Hardoy and Satterthwaite 1989, *op. cit.*

147. *Ibid.*

148. Batley, Richard, 'National housing banks in India and Brazil', *Third World Planning Review* vol. 10, no. 2, May 1988.

149. Soliman, Ahmed M., 'Housing consolidation and the urban poor: the case of Hagar El Nawateyah, Alexandria', *Environment and Urbanization*, vol. 4,

no. 2, Oct. 1992, 184–95.

150. Hardoy and Satterthwaite 1989, *op. cit.*

151. Baross and Struyk 1993, *op. cit.*

152. Hardoy and Satterthwaite 1989, *op. cit.*

153. Linn, J. F., *Policies for Efficient and Equitable Growth of Cities in Developing Countries*, World Bank Staff Working Paper, Washington DC, 1979.

154. Hardoy and Satterthwaite 1989, *op. cit*; Ekpenyong, Stephen, 'Housing, the state and the poor in Port Harcourt', *Cities*, vol. 6, no. 1, Feb. 1989; Chogill, C. L., *Problems in Providing Low-Income Urban Housing in Bangladesh*, Centre for Development Planning Studies, University of Sheffield DPS 2, June 1987; Wadhva 1993, *op. cit.*

155. Moser, Caroline O. N., 'Women, human settlements and housing: a conceptual framework for analysis and policy making', in Moser and Peake 1987, *op. cit.*

156. UNCHS 1993, *op. cit.*

157. El Kadi, G., 'Market mechanisms and spontaneous urbanization in Egypt: the Cairo case', *International Journal of Urban and Regional Research*, vol. 12, 1988, 22–37.

158. Morris, Jenny and Martin Winn, *Housing and Social Inequality*, Hilary Shipman, London, 1990.

159. Central Statistical Office, 'Housing', chapter 8 in *Social Trends 24*, HMSO, London, 1994, 109–18.

160. Morris and Winn 1990, *op. cit.*

161. Baross and Struyk 1993, *op. cit.*

162. *Ibid.*

163. Andersson, Kari and Anneli Juntto, 'The effect of the recession on the Finnish housing market', European Network for Housing Research Newsletter 1/93, 1993, 3–6.

164. Official figures quoted in Horenfeld, Gilles, 'Changes in the rental housing sector in France', *Villes en Développement*, no. 25, Sept. 1994.

165. Department of the Environment figures quoted in Central Statistical Office, 'Housing', *op. cit.* Figure for 1970 from Willman, John, 'A deafening silence on the politics of housing', *Financial Times*, Sept. 21/2, 1991, p. ix.

166. Edwards 1982, *op. cit.*

167. Gilbert 1983, *op. cit.*

168. Gilbert, Alan, *The Latin American City*, Latin American Bureau, London, 1994.

169. Connolly, Priscilla, 'Uncontrolled Settlements and Selfbuild: What kind of solution? The Mexico City Case', in Peter Ward (ed.), *Self Help Housing: a Critique*, Mansell Publishers, London, 1982, 141–74.

170. Connolly 1982, *op. cit.*

171. See for instance Coulomb, René, 'Inquilinos o proprietarios? La crisis del sistema de la vivienda popular en la ciudad de México', *Medio Ambiente y Urbanización*, vol. 7, no. 24, 1988, 25–33. Table V.3 in United Nations, *The World Social Situation 1993*, New York, 1993 suggests that the proportion of households in urban areas who were

renters went up rather than down when comparing figures for the 1980s with those of the 1970s in several Latin American countries.

172. Van der Linden 1990, *op. cit.*

173. Green 1990, *op. cit.*

174. Hoffman and others 1990, *op. cit.*

175. UNCHS 1993, *op. cit.*

176. See for instance UNCHS 1993 and Edwards 1982, *op. cit.*; also Green, Gill, 'The quest for tranquilidad: paths to home ownership in Santa Cruz, Bolivia', *Bulletin of Latin American Research*, vol. 7, no. 1, 1988, 1–15.

177. Van der Linden 1990, *op. cit.*

178. Lloyd 1990, *op. cit.*

179. See for instance the case of *campamentos* in San Salvador or what were originally refugee camps in many cities in India and Pakistan that formed soon after Partition.

180. Barlow, James and Simon Duncan, *Success and Failure in Housing Provision: European Cities Compared*, Pergamon, 1994.

181. *Ibid.*

182. *Ibid.*

183. NBBL, *Sustainable Development and Housing*, The Norwegian Federation of Co-operative Housing and Building Associations, Feb. 1995.

184. Barlow and Duncan 1994, *op. cit.*

185. World Bank/UNCHS 1993, *op. cit.*

186. Government of the United Republic of Tanzania, Ministry of Planning and Economic Affairs, *Review of the Economy, 1988* (March 1989).

187. Spence, R. J. S., Cambridge Architectural Research Limited, Cambridge (UK), 'Affordable building materials for housing', unpublished draft report prepared for the United Nations Centre for Human Settlements (Habitat), Aug. 1992.

188. Gupta, T. N., 'Technology delivery for the modernisation of the building materials industry in developing countries,' unpublished draft report prepared for the United Nations Centre for Human Settlements (Habitat), Aug. 1992.

189. United Nations Centre for Human Settlements (Habitat), 'The Small-scale Production of Building Materials', Report of the Executive Director to the Commission on Human Settlements at its ninth session, 5–16 May 1986 (HS/C/9/5 and HS/C/9/5 Add.1; and United Nations Centre for Human Settlements (Habitat), *The Economic and Technical Viability of Various Scales of Building Materials Production* (Nairobi, 1989) (HS/180/89/E).

190. United Nations Centre for Human Settlements (Habitat), *Development of National Technological Capacity for Production of Indigenous Building Materials* (HS/247/91E), Nairobi, 1991.

191. United Nations Centre for Human Settlements (Habitat), *Development of National Technology Capacity for Environmentally Sound Construction*

(HS/293/93E), Nairobi, 1993; and United Nations Centre for Human Settlements (Habitat), *Journal of the Network of African Countries on Local Building Materials and Technologies*, vol. 2, no. 3, Aug. 1993 (ISSN 1012–9812).

192. See previous two notes.

193. *Ibid.*

194. Daly, Mary, *The Right to a Home; the Right to a Future*, Third Report of the European Observatory on Homelessness, FEANTSA, Brussels, 1994.

195. See for instance Morris and Winn 1990, *op. cit.*

196. See Section 3.3.

197. Shelter, *The Impact on Women of National Housing Policy since 1979 and Prospects for the Future*, London, 1987.

198. The number of countries within the Union increased to fifteen in 1995. This statistic is from Avramov, Dragana, *Homelessness in the European Union: Social and Legal Context for Housing Exclusion in the 1990s*, FEANTSA (European Federation of National Organizations Working with the Homeless), Brussels, 1995.

199. *Ibid.*

200. *Ibid.*

201. Daly, Mary, *Abandoned: Profile of Europe's Homeless People*, the second report of the European Observatory on Homelessness, Brussels, 1993.

202. London Research Centre, *London Housing Survey 1986/7: Access to Housing in London*, April 1988 quoted in London Housing Foundation, *Funding Single Homelessness*, A report prepared by Raynsford and Morris Ltd., January 1991, with appendices.

203. Cohen, Larry and Susan Swift, 'A public health approach to the violence epidemic in the United States', *Environment and Urbanization*, vol. 5, no. 2, Oct. 1993, 50–66.

204. McLaughlin, Maryann, *Homelessness in Canada; the Report of the National Inquiry*, Canada Mortgage and Housing Corporation, no date.

205. Das, S. K. and Manju Gupta, 'Housing, living and environmental conditions in Indian cities', Background paper for the Global Report, 1994

206. See Patel, Sheela, 'Street children, hotels boys and children of pavement dwellers and construction workers in Bombay: how they meet their daily needs', *Environment and Urbanization*, vol. 2, no. 2, Oct. 1990, 9–26.

207. Within 'street children', it is useful to distinguish between children who work in the street but live in a stable home, usually with their parents, and children who live and work on the streets. UNICEF has suggested three categories of street children. The first is 'children on the street' which is much the largest category of 'street children'; these are children who work on the streets but have strong family connections, may attend school and, in most cases, return home at the end of the day. The second category is 'children of the street'; these see the street as their home and seek shelter, food and a sense of community among their companions there. But ties to their families exist, even if they are remote and they only visit their families infrequently. The third category is 'abandoned children'; these are difficult to distinguish from children of the street since they undertake similar activities and live in similar ways. These children have no ties with their families and are entirely on their own—and are most likely to sleep in the open. However, in most cities, the proportion of 'street children' who are abandoned is relatively small, although in the largest metropolitan areas it can still run into thousands.

208. Das and Gupta 1994, *op. cit.*

209. Van der Linden 1990, *op. cit.*

210. *Ibid.*

211. Yapi-Diahou 1995, *op. cit.*

212. Burt 1992, *op. cit.*

213. Local governments in the UK have a statutory duty to help homeless people in defined categories of 'priority need'— and these are essentially families with young children, women expecting babies and those vulnerable through old age, physical disability, mental handicap or illness (Central Statistical Office, *Social Trends 24*, 1994 Edition, HMSO, London, 1994). This means that services for homeless families are probably much better than in the United States—but a large number of homeless people or people wishing for their own home and unable to find one do not receive support (see for instance Morris and Winn 1990, *op. cit.*)

214. Department of the Environment, Welsh and Scottish Office, quoted in *Social Trends 1994*, *op. cit.*

215. Avramov 1995, *op. cit.*

216. Burt 1992 and Daly 1994, *op. cit.*

217. Daly 93, *op. cit.* In some instances, this might reflect the fact that such services are prioritized for families with children and the fact that many families become homeless through a breakdown in the relationships between the parents with the woman generally taking responsibility for the children.

218. Randall, Geoff, *No Way Home: Homeless Young People in Central London*, June 1988.

219. Daly 1993, *op. cit.*

220. National Children's Home, *The NCH Factfile*, NCH, London, 1993 quoted in Commission on Social Justice, *Social Justice: Strategies for National Renewal*, Vintage, London, 1994.

221. Daly, Mary, *European Homelessness—the Rising Tide*, The first report of the European Observatory on Homelessness, FEANTSA, 1992.

222. Daly 1993, *op. cit.*

223. Doogan, K., 'Falling off the treadmill: the causes of youth homelessness', in G. Bramley and others, *Homelessness and the London Housing Market*, School of Advanced Urban Studies, Bristol, 1988 quoted in Morris and Winn 1990, *op. cit.*

224. Morris and Winn 1990, *op. cit.*

225. Burt 1992, *op. cit.*

226. 57 per cent had never experienced institutionalization for chemical dependency or mental illness—see Burt 1992, *op. cit.*

227. *Ibid.*

228. Daly 1992, *op. cit.*

Land, Land Markets and Settlement Planning

7.1 Land Markets for Housing[1]

Introduction

The price and availability of land for housing remains an important influence on housing price (and on housing conditions) in most urban centres.[2] This is also true in rural areas where the value of the land is related to its locational advantage rather than its agricultural value. The price and availability of land for housing is especially influential on housing conditions and prices in urban centres in the South with rapidly growing populations and inadequate housing stocks in relation to the number of households—and where the other monetary costs of housing construction are kept down by self help construction and by widespread use of local (often semi-permanent or temporary) building materials.

The issue of how to ensure that urban land markets serve the economic and social needs of urban inhabitants and enterprises remains one of the most complex—perhaps the most complex— tasks for urban governments. The economic and social benefits from good land management are enormous; one of the main determinants of the economic success and quality of housing and living conditions in any city is the price and availability of land—for commercial and industrial use, for housing, infrastructure, public services and the various forms of public space—playgrounds, parks, public squares. The social costs of poor or no land management are also enormous, as earlier chapters have described, where a large proportion of the city's population (including most of its labour force) have to resort to illegal practices in occupying, renting or purchasing land to find a home. The economic costs of poor land management are often the failure to attract productive investment, especially as many enterprises now give a higher priority to good quality infrastructure and services both for the enterprise itself and for their workforce when choosing locations. Chapter 4 also documented the high environmental health costs and ecological costs of inadequate or inappropriate land policies.

The Recommendations for National Action endorsed at the first United Nations Conference on Human Settlements (Habitat) in 1976 recognized the central importance of land policies. Many of the recommendations were addressed to improved management of urban land. The recommendations also noted that

Land, because of its unique nature and the crucial role it plays in human settlements, cannot be treated as an ordinary asset, controlled by individuals and subject to the pressures and inefficiencies of the market. Private landownership is also a principal instrument of accumulation and concentration of wealth and therefore contributes to social injustice; if unchecked, it may become a major obstacle in the planning and implementation of development schemes. Social justice, urban renewal and development, the provision of decent dwellings and health conditions for the people can only be achieved if land is used in the interests of society as a whole.[3]

What was not fully recognized in these recommendations was how inappropriate government legislation, administration or intervention in urban land markets could contribute as much to economic, social and environmental costs as no management. This includes inappropriate legal frameworks and inefficient administrative procedures for defining land tenure and land transfer (including its purchase and sale) and for managing land use and land development. As in housing markets, too little attention had been given to what constrains land supply and as such, directly or indirectly increases its price. This section (7.1) focuses on urban land markets for housing, while section 7.2 reviews the overall urban land-use planning frameworks in which these processes take place.

Illegal or informal land markets for housing

Overview

The 'solution' to the rigidities and inefficiencies of public action and administration on land and the high proportion of city populations with very limited capacity to pay for 'housing' has been the development of illegal or informal land markets. These have provided the land sites for most additions to the housing stock in most cities in the South over the last 30 to 40 years.[4] They have also proved important in some cities in the North—for instance studies in Lisbon (Portugal) show that where the demand for residential land is much greater than the formal channels of supply, extensive informal markets have emerged.[5] A study of urban issues in Pakistan[6] suggested the reasons why—because informal or illegal land developments provide land for housing at a cost that is affordable by many low-income households and with the advantages of immediate possession and no paper work. Standards for plot sizes and infrastructure adjust to the capacity to pay. This system is exploitative in that a high proportion of housing plots have very inadequate or no provision for infrastructure and services; in many instances, the occupier pays substantial sums for the plot and may not even receive secure tenure. The illegal land system serves many powerful vested interests—including in many instances politicians and real estate companies. But housing conditions would be much worse without it. This is a conclusion that has validity in most cities in the South.

Three points about these illegal markets should be stressed:

- There is far less squatting in the sense of illegal occupation of the land than that suggested in most of the general literature on urban issues in the South. Only rarely do illegal land markets develop in the face of strong opposition from governments, landowners and real estate companies. In most instances, illegal land markets operate within limits that do not threaten the interests of governments and landowners, real estate companies and developers.

- In many cities, what might be considered as the key actors in legal land markets—real estate companies, politicians and the staff of government agencies—are also active within informal or illegal markets.

- There is great variety in the nature of the illegality between households and settlements. Although illegal land markets provide most new housing plots in most cities in the South, the precise nature of the illegality differs enormously both between countries and cities and, within cities, between different neighbourhoods.

Studies of particular cities have shown the great variety in the nature of the illegality for different settlements. Although it is common to label all people who live in 'illegal settlements' as squatters, most are not squatters since they occupy the land with the permission or implicit approval of the landowner. There is a great range in the nature of the illegality—in the occupation of the land, in the registration of ownership, in the way the land site is subdivided, in the use to which the land is put and in the nature of the building on it. At one extreme, there is illegal occupation (squatting) and at the other, fully legal occupation of the land but with one aspect of the house or the plot or the wider subdivision not meeting official standards or perhaps even meeting official standards but not having received official approval. There are also various forms of land acquisition that fall somewhere between these two extremes—for instance in countries where traditionally land is owned by the community, a person may develop their home on a site for which they received permission to do so from the chief or traditional authority that has had the right to bestow this—but not from the municipal planning office.

Then among squatter settlements, i.e. settlements built on land that has been illegally occupied, there is considerable differentiation in terms of whose land is occupied, the likelihood of those occupying the land being able to stay there (or being evicted with or without compensation), the terms under which they are permitted to stay and, if they do succeed in obtaining legal tenure, the time taken for this to happen and the delay in receiving public services. There are also settlements that are partly legal and partly illegal—for instance as a new legal settlement develops on the periphery of a city, sanctioned by government, illegal houses and settlements may develop around it.[7]

There are also large variations between cities and countries in such aspects as the nature of the legislation governing land ownership or use, the extent of concentration in land ownership, the extent to which international investors are active in a city's real estate market and the extent of public ownership of land. In all countries, people's access to land within illegal markets is influenced by traditional and/or legal attitudes to land ownership rights and by government attitudes.[8]

A review of how people obtain land in different cities[9] suggested that these be divided into three categories: administrative, non-commercial and commercial. Within the non-commercial category there are settlements on the following types of land: customary land (usually with permission from the traditional authorities); government land; abandoned land (for instance after foreign settlers moved away when a nation achieved independence); and marginal land that has little commercial value. Within the category of commercial land acquisition, there are 'mini-plots' within existing settlements, mostly from the subdivision of existing plots within illegal settlements; renting land; and finally illegal subdivisions.[10] Box 7.1 outlines how this range fits within broader commercial and non-commercial markets.

But in any illegal or informal settlement, there are usually a considerable variety of ways through which the people currently living in the settlement acquired the site. For instance, in a survey of households living in informal settlements in Abidjan, 61 per cent obtained their land through a 'gift', 15 per cent through purchase, 15 per cent through occupation of the site without payment, 7 per cent through leasing and 3 per cent through inheritance.[11] In one of the many informal settlements built on the municipal floodplain on which around three-fifths of Guayaquil's population

BOX 7.1

The range of ways through which people obtain land for housing in cities in the South

Formal

Commercial

- public or private residential development of serviced sites available through purchase or renting

- land purchase with approval obtained for its use for housing

Semi- or non-commercial

- government subsidized site and services schemes

- 'regularization' of tenure in what were illegal settlements
- inheritance or gift

Informal and/or illegal

- purchase of plot on illegally subdivided public land
- purchase of plot in illegal subdivision
- purchase of house site formed by subdivision of existing plot
- Renting of land site on which a shelter (often only a temporary shelter) can be built
- purchase or renting of permission to develop a house on a plot without tenure rights to the plot

- settlement on customary land with permission of traditional authority or farmer—although the size of 'gifts' given for this may reach a level where this is better considered as commercial
- squatting on government land
- squatting on marginal or dangerous land which has no clear ownership
- squatting on private land
- 'nomadic' squatters who use land site temporarily

Source: Based on Table 1 in Payne, Geoffrey, *Informal Housing and Land Subdivisions in Third World Cities: A Review of the Literature*, CENDEP, Oxford, 1989.

---

lives, a study found that there were eight distinct ways in which the inhabitants had obtained their housing plot—from opening up the land for themselves by cutting the mangrove (14 per cent of the inhabitants) to paying a 'professional squatter' to cut the mangrove and mark out the plot (19 per cent), to buying the plot without a house (30 per cent) or with a house already built (11 per cent). Most of the rest obtained the plot by individual invasion—9 per cent without paying, 6 per cent with paying. In all, two-thirds of the population had paid to acquire their plot.[12] Research in three unplanned areas of Dar es Salaam found that a quarter of those interviewed owned land; of these, a third had acquired it through the purchase of vacant land while 10 per cent had bought the land with a house (or in one instance the land with a foundation). Among the others, 21 per cent had inherited the land while 12 per cent were allocated it by a friend or a relative and 8 per cent occupied it without permission. Only 15 per cent of those who had land held the official Certificate of Title or a Letter of Offer.[13]

In many cities in the South, customary patterns of land tenure still apply to large tracts of urban land—or such patterns of tenure overlap with imported models of land legislation that were generally imposed by colonial rulers. For instance, in many urban centres in West Africa, land for a house can be obtained from its customary owner or the person who has the right to allocate land. One example of this is the case of land acquisition within informal settlements in Abidjan noted above where 60 per cent of households surveyed acquired their land through a gift.

However, this form of land acquisition has become more commercialized. To take again the case of Abidjan, the gifts that were given to traditional leaders or farmers when a land plot is allotted were once symbolic—'the price of a drink' and the 'price of pulling up' crops; now they involve much more substantial gifts and may occasionally reach a size that is comparable to the commercial value of the land.[14] In Bamako (Mali), unauthorized housing almost invariably complies with customary land rights, even if it is in violation of traditional norms and formal legislation, but here too the land market has become commercialized through the sale of rights by those who retain traditional land rights and a range of 'land-brokers'.[15]

Illegal or informal land markets for housing are markets in the sense that in most instances, the individual or household seeking a housing plot has to pay for it. In most instances, the person who sells them the plot is the landowner or a developer acting on the owner's behalf—or a developer who subdivides public land, with the tacit approval or acceptance of the government. Where customary tenure prevails, what might be sold is the temporary or permanent right to live on a plot—but not the tenure of the plot itself. A review of the literature on illegal or informal land markets noted how this usually took the form of developers who acquire land from the original landowners, often on the urban fringe

and subdivide it for sale to individual purchasers at whatever rate the local market will bear. In doing this, they generally circumvent or ignore official standards concerning plot size and levels of initial service provision in order to achieve a product which lower income groups can afford. Households are then left to build whatever type of dwelling they want or can afford without any imposed obligation to conform to official norms and procedures. It is their ability to cut corners—and costs—which has helped the commercial subdividers to expand their operations and to provide plots which are more appropriate, affordable and easily available than any other housing option.[16]

Illegal subdivisions are likely to emerge as an important supplier of land for housing wherever there is an effective demand for land sites for housing that official rules and procedures prevent from being fulfilled. For instance, a study in Hyderabad shows how illegal subdivisions evolved as a response to élitist standards, urban land demand and the ineffectiveness of local management agencies. The study also shows how the process was initiated by the landlord or colonizer and is sustained by political support for the provision of services and inaction in enforcing planning regulations.[17] Box 7.2 gives an example of how an illegal subdivision in Karachi developed. It illustrates how the development of illegal subdivisions is often a complex process—in this instance involving not only the official owner of the land (a government agency) but also a tribe which had established the right to use the site. It is a reminder of how any illegal subdivision often has a complex array of actors and how the whole process of illegal subdivision is rooted in the particulars of each country's and city's legal, administrative and political structure, including the structure of land-ownership.

Many studies of illegal land markets in Africa, Asia and Latin America have shown the central role of particular agents or brokers in the development of illegal subdivisions. The variety of agents involved in illegal land development was stressed in a study covering Bogota, Mexico City and Valencia—where the agent responsible for developing the land (that could be public, private or communal) could be a party politician, a real-estate developer, a community that invaded or purchased land or a popular leader or organization.[18] A case study in Karachi showed the involvement of political leaders, administrative leaders, administrative personnel, devel-

opers, developers' personnel and dwellers.[19] 'Professional subdividers' and subdivision companies have also had a central role in the illegal or informal land developments around Cairo.[20] Customary landowners in Papua New Guinea who control almost 97 per cent of the land have taken to providing low-income households with plots at low rents on which households build a temporary shelter; consolidation or improvement is strongly discouraged and the provision of services denied so as not to prejudice the long-term interests of the landowners.[21] A study of informal housing areas in Abidjan also described the complex range of intermediaries who were important in the acquisition of land for housing—including neighbourhood leaders, kinship networks and public and private agencies.[22]

For illegal subdivisions, a distinction should be drawn between where the land occupation is legal and where it is not. In most illegal subdivisions, the occupation of the land is legal and is done by landowners acting as developers or developers who have purchased land to develop the subdivisions. In some instances, it is through customary landholders 'renting' sites as in the above case of Papua New Guinea or selling sites—as is common in and around many cities in Mexico where *ejido* land that is owned by rural communities has been subdivided and sold—although in theory such land can be neither subdivided nor sold.[23] In other instances, where the government itself is a major landowner or perhaps where the city has grown in a site without a commercial land market in its surrounds, subdividers can operate even though they do not own the land. This was the case in Yakoobabad described in Box 7.2 and is common in other settlements of Karachi. In Tunis too, 'pirate subdividers' have become important and include individuals who without official sanction subdivide land that is not legally theirs—including land that belongs to the state.[24] This is an interesting variation in that these developers have the knowledge and contacts to permit them to develop land belonging to other people (usually a government agency) whereas individuals who tried to occupy the same land that these developers subdivide would probably not be permitted to stay there. Developers become important because of their ability to anticipate what was likely to be officially or politically acceptable[25] or because their political and economic power is such that their subdivisions are not challenged, even while squatter settlements are being cleared.[26]

Increasing commercialization of urban land markets

In many of the cities for which detailed research has been undertaken on informal land markets, the non-commercial informal land markets are in

BOX 7.2
The development of Yakoobabad illegal subdivision in Karachi, Pakistan

Yakoobabad is a settlement on the north-western fringes of Orangi township in Karachi. The land belongs to the Central Board of Revenue. The land to the north of Yakoobabad belongs to an elder of the Rind tribe and this tribe has lived next to Yakoobabad since 1839. The tribe has also had the right to use the site under an annual contract dating back to the 1880s. The tribe, through the elder, also retains certain rights over the site including the right of pre-emption in matters of contract or purchase, if it is put up for sale (this is known as *shifa*).

The land is rocky and uneven. Although it had been used for damming water to aid cultivation of crops, agriculture was poor and the land was virtually worthless before the development of Orangi township. By 1976–8, most of the plots in settlements adjacent to Yakoobabad had been occupied. The value of the remaining vacant plots increased beyond what poorer groups could afford. The West Karachi subdividers felt that the time had come to colonize new land. The plan to colonize the area was first conceived by a well-established developer whom we shall call Mr X. He was also involved with the development of adjacent sites and, some years previously, had begun work on a plan for the development of Yakoobabad.

People who had been settled in the neighbouring areas kept informing Mr X of their friends and relations who needed plots of land. Many social welfare organizations and public-spirited people also approached him, asking for help in settling refugees, widows and the destitute. At some point in 1977, Mr X drew up a list of 100 families and made informal representations on their behalf to government officials. They agreed to the development of Yakoobabad. The developers say that Karachi Municipal Corporation officials were to be paid Rs200 (about $US10)

for each plot sold and the police also collected this amount for each construction undertaken in the settlement. These negotiations took place in the evenings in the tea shops of Orangi.

Early in 1977, Mr X moved 100 destitute families onto the Yakoobabad site. With the families were transported the bamboo posts and mats needed for the initial construction. The Rind tribe followed them onto the land and threatened to kill those who remained. It was agreed that the destitute could stay but no houses would be erected until an agreement had been reached. The next day, the tribe's elder went to court and, through a lawyer, argued for his right of pre-emption. This case was admitted. The subdivider filed a report in the local police station accusing the tribe of causing 'bodily harm' to his clients and associates.

Further negotiations took place; one source said that these were arranged by mutual friends who received several plots as their 'fee' while others suggested the talks were set up by the local police. Agreement was reached whereby the Rind tribe received Rs 500 ($US25) for every plot developed (although the first 100 destitute families were exempt from this payment). The Rind tribe then withdrew their case against the development although they have continued to press their case against the government for permitting the colonization of the land.

The subdivider then laid out the settlement with about 2,000 plots on a grid iron plan. Roads were levelled by informally hiring (at a reduced rate) tractors and a bulldozer from the Karachi Municipal Corporation. Space was set aside for a mosque and school, and plots on the main road were left for communal purposes. It is reported that informal representations were made by government officials and local informants state that about 30 per cent of all plots were set aside for speculative purposes with the subdivider agreeing to sell these at an appropriate time on behalf of government officials. Additional speculative plots were held by the subdivider.

In total, ten years after development started, 32 per cent of plots are still vacant.

In 1979, there were local elections. Residents have told of how the subdivider gave small sums of money to elected councillors and also tried, successfully in some cases, to make them office-bearers of his welfare organization. (It is common for illegal subdividers to formally register a social welfare society formed by residents. This strengthens their ability to push for service provision to the area, thereby increasing the value of the land.)

The subdivider engaged people with donkey carts to first supply water to the residents. The water was acquired illegally from the water mains in Orangi. The subdivider paid for the first supply but after this the residents bought direct from the water-vendors. Initially, residents collected this water in containers but later built their own concrete storage tanks which served each small street (lane), with a committee of residents organizing the purchase and distribution of water.

Transportation links to and from the new settlement are poor. The nearest regular transport is a mile (1.6 kilometres) away. Buses now go to and from the settlement itself but these are privately owned. The permits for the route were given to the operator due to pressure from the subdivider's welfare organization.

Electricity is provided commercially to a few households from a privately operated generator. This is illegal but can function because of police protection. The subdivider is pressurizing people to apply for regular electricity connections. When a sufficient number of applications have been collected, pressure for electricity connections will be put on the Karachi Electricity Supply Corporation through the subdivider's welfare organization. The subsequent increase in the value of the property will benefit the subdivider and government officials holding speculative plots in the area.

Source: Hasan, Arif, *A Study of Metropolitan Fringe Development in Karachi (focusing on informal land subdivision)*, report prepared as part of the United Nations ESCAP study on metropolitan fringe areas in major cities in the region, April 1987.

---

decline and the informal commercial land markets are expanding rapidly.[27] Many researchers point to the increasing commercialization of informal land markets as city economies and populations grow.[28]

Two characteristics of this increasing commercialization of informal land markets were noted above—the emergence of land-brokers or agents operating on land that is not officially theirs and the increased amount of 'gift' that has to be given to farmers or traditional authorities to secure the right to use a plot. Another is the emergence of 'land rental' where it is the land site for a shelter that is rented rather than a shelter itself. For

instance, in Bangkok, short-term leases for land plots on which the tenant develops a shelter are often provided by landowners but the lease is only temporary (perhaps renewed on a yearly basis); the advantage for the landowner is a return on land that is undeveloped but the land remains available when the landowner chooses to develop more profitable uses.[29] The *bustees* in Calcutta are shelters that the occupants rent from middle-men (*thika* tenants) who in turn have leased the land from the landowners.[30] Land leasing became important for low-income groups on the periphery of Fez (Morocco) as central-city rental accommodation became saturated, although a paper in 1988 also reported that landowners were finding it more profitable to sell rather than lease land.[31] It was also reported in the informal settlements of Abidjan, although only for a small proportion of plots.[32] In Latin America, case studies have also given examples of small land plots rented out by the owners of lots that are large enough to permit this but their extent and relative importance is not known.[33]

Temporary squatting may also be another characteristic of the increasing commercialization of illegal land markets. In many cities in the South, there are thousands of people who live in rudimentary shacks built on sites that are illegally occupied on which they can have little hope of permanency or secure tenure. This may reflect the fact that there is no free or very cheap land available on which these people would have some chance of avoiding eviction and even obtaining tenure in the longer term—although 'temporary squatting' may provide temporary accommodation for seasonal workers or people who plan only a short stay in a city.

Highly commercialized land markets can also produce new variations in illegal land occupation and use. For instance, in most cities of the South, there is also the problem of private encroachment onto public space—for instance influential real estate interests being allowed to site new developments on public land, including parks and greenbelts. It is also common to find private developments encroaching onto public roads or sidewalks—or, as in a recent example in Karachi, onto a major stormwater drain.[34]

One final and obvious characteristic of increasingly commercialized land markets is the increasing concentration of the lower-income groups on a small proportion of the land area. One study in Dhaka revealed the level of inequality in the use of land; in 1987, the wealthiest 2 per cent of the city's population used almost as much of the city's residential land as the poorest 70 per cent and 2.8 million of the poorest people lived on just 7 square kilometres of land.[35] A study in Nairobi found that one-third of the population lived in illegal or informal settlements which covered less than 4 per cent of the land area.[36] This high concentration of low-income groups in very small proportions of the land area does not imply that overall densities are high. Indeed, in most of the largest cities in the South, there is sufficient vacant or underutilized land within the city or metropolitan boundaries to provide good-quality housing for all those currently living in overcrowded tenements or high density illegal or informal settlements.[37]

Squatting and evictions

Large-scale invasions of urban land are relatively rare. They are too much of a threat to the established structure of asset ownership. Where they happen, they constitute one of the few examples of a redistribution of assets towards lower-income households—although some case studies of squatter invasions have also revealed that not all those taking part in invasions are low-income.

There are certain characteristics that land invasions tend to have in common. First, they often occur under particular political circumstances. For instance, the large-scale land invasions in Buenos Aires in late 1981 took place because the (then) military government was in crisis. In Santa Cruz (Bolivia), large-scale land invasions coincided with particular political circumstances that permitted the invasions.[38] In Karachi, despite the fact that illegal land markets are the main means by which low-income groups obtain land for housing, relatively few low-income households have managed to get land free. Some land invasions have occurred and succeeded—typically they coincide with specific political events—for instance, the hanging of ex-Prime Minister Bhutto in Pakistan or the announcement of the five-point government plan for low-income housing by ex-Prime Minister Junejo. Almost all of those who took part in these invasions were renters or sharers. Most said that they could never afford to settle in an illegal subdivision both because of the costs and because they fear they cannot survive outside their socio-spatial network which gives them access to jobs and some help when needed.[39]

A second characteristic of land invasions is that they are generally carefully planned, with the sites selected for invasion chosen either for the good possibility of being able to stay there or for the strong negotiating position that occupying that site will provide.[40]

In one important sense, most evictions are the opposite of successful invasions in that they involve the transfer of high value land from the inhabitants of the settlements who are evicted to middle- or upper-income groups or to free land for the construction of houses, commercial developments, roads and other forms of infrastructure that primarily benefit wealthier groups. An analysis of who benefited from the *favela* eradication programme in Rio de Janeiro in the late 1950s and early 1960s showed that it was primarily middle- and upper-income groups and industry and construction firms:

The re-organization of space . . . freed land from occupation by the most deprived classes and placed it at the disposal of the wealthier groups. The program aimed to stimulate upper and middle class residential construction by clearing the most desirable areas of the city from the presence of the poor. 'Clearing' took the double meaning of physically opening new sites for construction and symbolically freeing the well-to-do from daily confrontation with the misery of the favelas.

Other sites were cleared to serve the needs of industry and construction firms were given an additional boost by receiving government contracts to build public housing projects. Needless to say, all of this was done in the name of the government's concern for the welfare of the 'less favoured' families.[41]

Developments in Rio de Janeiro in the mid-1990s parallel those thirty years earlier as the communities in Tijuca lagoon are evicted or threatened with eviction to clear land for middle- and upper-income groups and the construction companies which would build for them.[42] Perhaps the most notable change in these thirty years is the extent to which protecting 'the environment' is invoked as a justification for the eviction, although the existing communities are making major efforts to safeguard the mangrove swamps while the middle- and high-income housing developments being built there are not.

The increasingly comprehensive information base on evictions suggests that several million people are evicted by force from their homes in urban areas each year.[43] The annual total is almost certainly higher in rural areas as people are evicted from their homes or lands to make way for reservoirs and building works associated with dams or other 'infrastructure works' or as farmers, pastoralists and huntergatherers are evicted from lands they traditionally 'owned' and managed.[44]

It would be wrong to suggest that no redevelopment should take place within cities which displaces people. Inevitably, in any rapidly growing and developing city, there will be a need to redevelop certain areas and for public agencies to acquire land for infrastructure and services. The issue is not that such redevelopments should never take place but their scale, the way in which they are currently implemented with little or no dialogue with those who will be displaced, the lack of respect for the needs of those evicted and the lack of any attempt to develop solutions which minimize the scale of the evictions and the disruption caused to those who have to move. Table 7.1 lists some of the recent cases of evictions that have been identified and documented by the Habitat International Coalition. Six of these cases involved more than 100,000 people.

It is difficult to know if the scale of evictions in urban areas is increasing. There were certainly massive eviction programmes in many countries during the 1960s, 1970s and 1980s.[45] Probably the largest was in Seoul in South Korea where millions were evicted from their homes between 1966 and 1990. Between 1983 and 1988, 720,000 people lost their homes to demolitions and redevelopments and 90 per cent of those evicted did not obtain an apartment in the redeveloped site.[46]

One factor that has probably helped moderate the scale of evictions has been the move towards more democratic governments.[47] But another factor which works in the opposite direction by increasing the scale of evictions is action by governments to make up for the backlog in urban infrastructure with large road, drainage and other developments. In the more prosperous cities with rapidly growing private car ownership and where the 'solution' to traffic problems is still seen in terms of ever increasing provision for private automobile use, the potential scale of evictions is very high.

Although evictions share one common characteristic—the removal of one group of people currently occupying (and often owning) land at the behest of a more powerful group—there are a variety of underlying causes. Some evictions arise because wealthier groups do not want settlements of low-income groups near them.[48] Others arise through a systematic process of oppression or control imposed by one people or group in society on another,[49] while others arise because of public works programmes. An overview of many recent cases of evictions that took place between 1987 and 1993 considered the role of local authorities in evictions. In most evictions, local governments had a major role either in initiating the evictions—for instance for public works or city beautification programmes—or in sanctioning them.[50]

Governments usually justify evictions in one of three ways. The first (and perhaps the most common) is to 'improve' or 'beautify' the city. Major eviction programmes often take place just prior to some international event—for instance in Seoul prior to the 1988 Olympics,[51] in Manila prior to the Miss Universe contest and the visit of the Pope, and in Bangkok to beautify the city for the meeting there of the Board of the World Bank. Authoritarian governments are more likely to implement large 'city beautification' plans with large scale evictions; a lack of dialogue with citizens and their organizations, a lack of representation for citizen views within government and a style of government which represses popular protest greatly limits the possibility of successful opposition to such plans. The negotiation of a compromise between those undertaking the redevelopment (whether government or private company) and those to be evicted is more common in nations with representative forms of government, although many of the evictions described in the review of these 40 cases were implemented in countries with elected governments.

A second way in which government justifies evictions is to claim that 'slums' are centres of crime and havens for criminals. Thus, evictions not only make the city more 'beautiful' but rid it of 'centres of crime'. When a new eviction programme was launched in Manila in mid-1982, the then Mayor of Metro Manila talked of 'professional squatters' who were 'plain landgrabbers taking advantage of the compassionate society'.[52] In Tibet, the authorities in Lhasa tried to portray the people living in the

TABLE 7.1 Recent examples of evictions

Location	Date	Persons evicted	Motive for eviction	Agent responsible for eviction
Argentina (Buenos Aires)	1992	1,200	illegal occupation	Landowner
Bhutan	1990–1	500	military control	Royal Bhutan Army
Brazil (Sao Paulo)	1990–1	10,000	illegal occupation	Landowners & judiciary
Chile (Santiago)	1981–90	11,325	urban development	Municipality
Dominican Republic (Santo Domingo)	1987–92	180,000	500-year anniversary commemoration	Municipality & government
El Salvador	1991	450	illegal occupation	Government
France (Paris)	1990	240	real-estate speculation	Municipality
Guatemala	1987–90	11,825	illegal occupation	Municipality
India (Bhopal)	1991	3,000	urban renovation	Municipality
India (Bombay)	1988	200	illegal occupation	Municipal council
India (Calcutta)	1993	500	real-estate speculation	Municipality
India (Narmada Valley)	1985–?	610,000	dam construction	Federal & state govts.
Indonesia (Jakarta)	1991	29,247	urban renovation	Municipality
Kenya (Nairobi)	1990	2,000	real-estate speculation	Municipality
Korea (Seoul)	1983–90	720,000	Olympic Games	Government
Malaysia	1990	250	real-estate speculation	Government
Mexico (Alto Balsas)	1990–2	46,000	dam construction	Federal government
Nexico (Chiapas)	1991	230	ethnic discrimination	Political boss/ land owner
Mexico (Guadalupe)	1992	775	ecological reserve	Local authorities
Mexico (Pensil)	1992	700	real-estate speculation	Owner & local authorities
Myanmar (Rangoon)	1988–92	500,000	political control	Government
Nicaragua (Managua)	1992	25,000	illegal occupation	Municipality
Nigeria (Lagos)	1990	300,000	urban renovation	Government
Panama (Panama City)	1990	5,800	illegal occupation	Municipality
Papua New Guinea (Lae)	1991	600	illegal occupation	Government
Philippines (Quezon City)	1988	60,000	urban renovation	Municipality
Senegal (Dakar)	1991–2	1,035	real-estate speculation	Municipality
Sudan (Khartoum)	1987–90	500,000	ethnic discrimination	Federal government
Thailand (Bangkok)	1984–9	214,500	real-estate speculation	Municipality
Thailand (Bangkok)	1991	2,930	World Bank Meeting	Municipality
Uruguay (Montevideo)	1987–92	750	illegal occupation	Owner & municipality
USA (Atlanta)	1993–?	10,000	Olympic Games prep.	Municipality
Zambia (Lusaka)	1987–91	2,290	urban renovation	Local authorities
Zimbabwe (Harare)	1991	2,500	Visit Queen Elizabeth II	Municipality

Source: Habitat International Coalition

houses being demolished as beggars and unemployed people.[53] Many other instances have been documented where the authorities undertaking the evictions seek to portray those being evicted as criminals or racketeers.[54]

Governments have also used the health problems evident in inner-city tenements or squatter settlements as a justification for their clearance, although eviction and slum or squatter clearance will usually increase rather than decrease health problems. If no alternative accommodation is provided for those displaced, they have to find space in other cheap areas and increase overcrowding there. Or the health problems of those evicted increases because of the very poor quality and location of the land on which they are forcibly 'resettled'.

A third justification for evictions is 'redevelopment', to use the cleared land more intensively or to build public works or facilities. Here, underlying reasons and official justifications are more likely to coincide. Centrally located areas in a city and other strategically located sites (for instance close to airports or main roads) become increasingly valuable, as the city's economy develops. In many cities, cheap tenement districts developed in central areas but as the city grows, so too does the pressure to redevelop central locations for offices or other uses which yield higher returns. This helps to explain the rapid decline in the number of people living in the central areas of cities such as old Delhi, Bombay, Karachi, Bangkok, Santiago and Lima.[55] Similarly, squatter settlements which developed on what was once the city's periphery some decades (or years) ago are often on land that has become very valuable, as the city expands. Landowners or developers can make very large profits redeveloping such sites, especially if they can avoid the cost of rehousing those evicted from these sites. If settlements are judged to be 'illegal'—even if they have been there many decades—this is a convenient excuse to bulldoze them with no compensation paid to former inhabitants.

In 'redevelopments' of areas where the housing

that is to be replaced is legal, house-owners usually receive compensation although not necessarily enough to allow them to purchase another house of comparable quality and value to the one they lose. But it is very rare for tenants to receive any compensation. In many redevelopment schemes in Seoul, home-owners received some compensation although not enough to allow them to purchase another house or flat in the new development. But tenants—who often made up 60 per cent or more of all those displaced—usually received nothing but a notice to quit and at best a small token payment. When government officials were asked about this by the Asian Coalition for Housing Rights, it became obvious that they had never considered the idea of tenant rights and indeed had difficulty understanding the concept. The implication is that government views tenants as second-class citizens with fewer rights than those rich enough to afford the purchase of their own house or flat. The same is true in the large-scale evictions in Santo Domingo, initiated in 1988; here too, home-owners received very inadequate compensation but tenants (again the majority) received nothing.

More attention is also being given in recent case studies to the trauma of evictions where people are forced from homes and neighbourhoods in which they have lived for years or even decades. It is not only that they lose their homes—in which they have often invested a considerable proportion of their income over the years—or their possessions, as no warning is given before the bulldozers destroy their settlement. But they also lose their friends and neighbours as they scatter in the search for other accommodation.[56] They also lose the often complex reciprocal relationships which provided a safety net of protection against the costs of ill-health, income decline or the loss of a job, and which allowed many tasks to be shared. They often lose one or more sources of livelihood as they are forced to move away from the area where they had jobs or sources of income.[57] Where provision is made for resettlement, this is almost always at a distant site where the people are expected to build their homes once again, but on land with little or no provision for infrastructure and services. Those evicted rarely receive any financial support for rebuilding. The land site on which they are relocated is also very often of poor quality.[58] There are also the deaths and injuries caused by the violence in many evictions and the injuries or the murder of community leaders who oppose the evictions.[59]

The role of government in informal land markets

In most countries in the South, one characteristic of government involvement in urban land is a combination of official policies that restrict and constrain legal land markets and unofficial tolerance of illegal or informal land operations. This has been the case in a great range of countries with very diverse social, economic and political structures. What is also common to most is that this tolerance of informal land markets is only as long as such markets are kept within limits that neither threaten most landowners nor question the primacy of private or public land ownership, nor gravely endanger public safety and the environment in general.

In regard to the legal land market, most governments adopted policies that have contributed to land shortages, rather than land availability. Government policies have emphasized the control and regulation of land use rather than supporting and facilitating the supply and development of land to ensure demand is met as quickly and cheaply as possible. Government land-use policies have often been subsumed under some other heading—such as shelter needs or masterplanning. Governments have also failed to act on the fact that one of the most effective ways to support a city's economy and to improve housing conditions is to ensure that land with basic infrastructure is available for a great range of activities at the lowest possible price. Few governments have used their powers and investment capacities to stimulate increased supplies. Yet stimulating increased supplies can often meet economic, social and environmental goals more effectively than controlling use.

However, as already described, a range of informal and illegal land markets have provided the means by which the cost of housing—for renting, self building or purchase—could be brought down sufficiently to become affordable by a much larger proportion of each city's population. Governments have tolerated informal land markets to defuse what was potentially a huge political problem—the fact that a high and growing proportion of the population could not afford the cheapest legal house or site. But this toleration was virtually always within strict limits so most land for housing was not occupied illegally—and where it was occupied illegally, only rarely was it on valuable privately owned land. Most illegal land occupation took place on government land or land of very poor quality with limited commercial value. And over time, conventional land and housing markets developed in most illegal or informal settlements so what originally appeared to be a threat to the existing order ended up fully integrated into that order.[60]

There are also many documented examples of government involvement in illegal or informal land markets. In some instances, this takes the form of providing tenure to those living in illegal settlements; perhaps not surprisingly, announcements regarding the provision of secure tenure for the inhabitants of particular illegal settlements often take place just before elections.[61] There are also examples of government authorities targeting their programmes that provide land tenure and basic services to those illegal settlements that appear to be the most substantial political threat to the government in power and not doing so to other, long established illegal settlements that did not represent a centre of opposition.[62] Providing those living in illegal settlements with secure tenure can thus be used to counteract urban popular movements that threaten the established political order.[63]

The extent to which governments develop a major programme to provide secure tenure and basic infrastructure and services to those living in illegal settlements and the choice of settlements that get priority is likely to be influenced by the extent to which those living in illegal settlements are organized. There are many case studies of squatter movements or popular movements in Latin America negotiating successfully with the state. At the other extreme, there are few if any organizations based in low-income settlements that represent 'the settlement'; for instance, a study in Bamako pointed out that people are active in organizations along ethnic and religious lines or based on being from the same area of origin and not on the basis of where they now live.[64]

A study in Mexico City highlighted three different forms of government response to demands from low-income settlements:[65]

- no formal government structure for the government–community interaction, with community leaders serving as intermediaries between residents and the government in an informal network of patron–client relationships;

- an opening of the official government agencies to petitions and a greater readiness to respond to demands but with no formal structure to manage this; and finally

- a formal structure established to manage government–community interactions (although not necessarily succeeding in doing so).

These distinctions may be useful in considering how other governments currently respond to demands from low-income settlements. Certainly the case studies of the role of government officials and politicians in illegal or informal land markets suggest that most remain in the first of these.

The cost of developing land for housing

Converting raw land into land for housing is often a long, complex and expensive process, if undertaken legally. Table 7.2 outlines the different stages that are often involved in transforming raw (often agricultural) land into a housing plot.

The Housing Indicators Programme developed two indicators to measure how much the price of land increased as it became legally available for housing or developed for housing. The first was the *land development multiplier*—stage 5 in Table 7.2—that reflects the premium that had to be paid for a land plot developed for housing, in comparison to raw, undeveloped land. Data was collected on the price of 'raw' land and of land with services on the urban fringe. The land development multiplier was the average ratio between the median land price of a developed housing plot and the median price of raw undeveloped land in an area currently being developed. This not only reveals the size of the premium that has to be paid for land with infrastructure and services but in effect also the availability of infrastructure and services as well as of other constraints on the availability of land for housing—such as complex land development regulations and/or monopolistic land ownership patterns.

The second indicator was the *land conversion multiplier* (stages 2–4 in Table 7.2) that reflects the premium paid for a legal land plot for housing that meets zoning regulations and has planning permission in comparison to land in agricultural use. This measures the extent to which regulations governing changes of land use and its development for housing restrict the conversion of land from agriculture to urban housing.

There was considerable variation between cities for both these indicators and with the premium being paid for a legal housing plot and a housing plot with services often being much higher, in cities in relatively low income countries. For instance, for the land development multiplier, there was a tendency for cities in the wealthiest nations to have smaller land development multipliers—see Figure 7.1. Very large premiums had to be paid for land with infrastructure and services compared to undeveloped land in cities such as Lilongwe, Harare and Accra and, among the more prosperous nations, Madrid. Within the country groupings defined by per capita income, the cities in the high-income countries had the lowest land development multiplier; the median figure for price of the land plot with infrastructure was only 2.25 times that of the undeveloped land and no city had a land development multiplier of more than 5. The mid/high-income countries as a group had a land development multiplier of 5, the highest of any country group; in Madrid, it was 12 although Singapore, Hong Kong and Seoul had among the lowest land development multipliers of any country. The median figure for the other groups of countries based on income varied between these two extremes—but as Figure 7.1 shows, with great variation between them. Among

TABLE 7.2 The different stages in transforming raw (often agricultural) land into a housing plot

	The different costs that have to be met	Factors that influence price
	1. Raw land price.	Perhaps high because of high concentration of land ownership and very little incentive to develop it or penalty for not developing it—e.g. Manila.[66] Or poor road network so land close to roads having inflated prices. Tending to be lower in cities which grew up in areas with land largely unused or desert?
Land conversion costs	**2.** The cost of obtaining permission to convert it from agricultural or non-urban use to use for housing.	Supply restricted by large green belt—as in Seoul—or areas around the city zoned for uses other than housing or with new developments strictly controlled—common around most European cities—or long and cumbersome bureaucratic processes.
Land conversion costs	**3.** The cost of obtaining approval for the subdivision plan.	The cost may be high, especially because of long delays in getting official approval—and permission may be needed from several agencies with each checking one aspect of the subdivision e.g. provision for roads, community facilities, plot sizes etc.
Land conversion costs	**4.** The influence of subdivision regulations on the price of the plot—for instance the minimum plot size, the requirements for provision for roads, community facilities, the plot to building area ratio etc.	Dependent on official standards that may be unrealistic. For instance, very large minimum plot sizes push up plot prices and often exclude low-income groups.
	5. Land development costs—the costs involved in meeting official standards for infrastructure and services.	Where government agencies provide these, one of the main costs may be the delays in obtaining this. Plot costs are obviously much increased if the developer is responsible for paying for these or installing them.
	6. Cost of finance for subdivider.	
	7. Cost to person seeking to purchase the plot of doing so—including fees that have to be paid for legal services, registering the plot ownership, taxes and duties if any.	Influenced by ease with which the legal requirements for the purchase of a plot and registering its ownership can be met.
	8. Cost to land purchaser of obtaining funds to permit this transaction.	Influenced by availability of and terms for long-term loans.

the cities within low-income countries, the land development multiplier was very high in Accra and Lilongwe but very low in Ibadan and Dhaka. Among cities within low/mid-income countries, it was very high in Harare and Cairo and relatively low in Abidjan, Karachi and Jakarta. Among cities in middle-income countries, it was very low in Kingston and relatively low in Bangkok, Bogota and Santiago and relatively high in Istanbul and Rio de Janeiro. With the exception of Madrid, the variation in this indicator in cities in the wealthiest countries is much smaller than in the low-, low/mid- and middle-income countries.

Many of the cities in low- and middle-income countries that have low land development multipliers are also cities that have a relatively high proportion of housing plots with piped water, relative to their country's per capita income—notably Dhaka, Ibadan, Jakarta, Kingston and Seoul. Three cities in sub-Saharan Africa had particularly high values—Lilongwe, Harare and Accra—and in general, in this region, provision of basic infrastructure and services to residential areas lags far behind need. The good performance among the cities in the wealthiest nations is obviously helped by the slow population growth that most have—or indeed in some instances, population decline (although the number of households may be increasing).

For the land conversion multiplier, which reflects how expensive it is to get official permission to develop agricultural land for residential use, there are even larger variations between cities (see Figure 7.2). Here, it was generally cities in low-, low/mid- and middle-income countries that had the lowest land conversion multipliers—especially Ibadan, Bejing, Dar es Salaam, Bangkok, Santiago, Dhaka and Caracas—but some of the cities in the high-income countries also had relatively low figures—for instance Toronto, Munich and Stockholm. Three cities had unusually high land conversion multipliers—Oslo with 115 (which went off the scale for Figure 7.2), Amsterdam with 80, Rio de Janeiro with 40. For Amsterdam, this is likely to reflect the strong public controls on the conversion of land from agriculture to urban use to prevent urban sprawl.[67]

Care should be taken in assuming that these figures necessarily reflect the cost of land for housing or of housing itself. For instance, the land conversion multiplier in Dar es Salaam

FIGURE 7.1
**The land
development
multiplier: the
premium paid for
developed land**

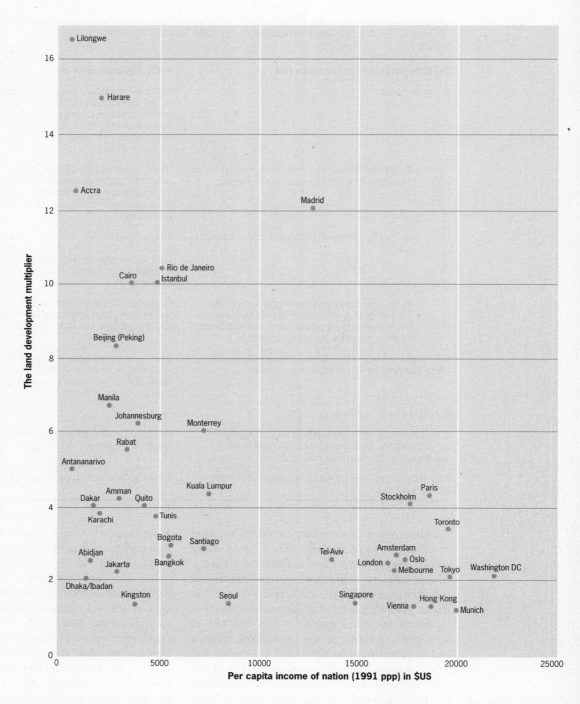

might be very low but the availability of legal plots for housing is very restricted; it is not price that is the constraint on obtaining a legal plot for housing but availability.[68] In several of the cities covered by the Housing Indicators Programme and many others in the South, it is common for much of the land that has been illegally developed for housing to be 'regularized' in the sense of the tenure of the people there being legalized. It might be considerably cheaper (and more common) for relatively low-income households wanting their own home to purchase a plot on agricultural land that has been illegally subdivided or (in some instances) to occupy illegally

agricultural land and then negotiate or lobby for their occupation to be legalized. In several of the cities covered by the Housing Indicators Programme and in many others in the South, there is relatively little risk of eviction or sanctions for most of those who live on or develop illegal subdivisions. Those who illegally occupy land also tend to avoid the more valuable land sites from which they are likely to be evicted. Households who follow this route may save large amounts of money and still end up with a legal house plot—although often with considerable delays and perhaps considerable insecurity while tenure is being negotiated or eviction fought.

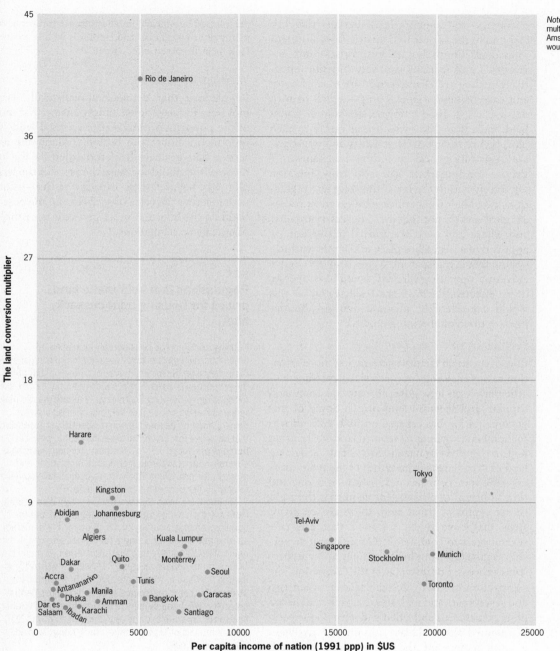

Note: Oslo with a land multiplier of 115 and Amsterdam with one of 80 would not fit onto this figure

FIGURE 7.2
The land conversion multiplier: the premium paid for a legal house plot when converted from agricultural use

The land conversion multiplier may also have less influence on housing prices in many of the large cities in the North that already have a large housing stock relative to their populations and a relatively small increase in demand for housing. In addition, the number of housing units may increase substantially without requiring more agricultural land—as in residential developments in unused sites for housing or the redevelopment of commercial or industrial sites or buildings with other uses for housing. Many of the cities in Europe and the older commercial and industrial cities in North America have substantial residential developments in central areas that were once predominantly commercial or industrial.

The land conversion multiplier will also have less influence on housing prices in cities in the South with large amounts of undeveloped land within the urban boundaries—as long as that land can be developed for housing.

Constraints on government as an enabler

The growing understanding of how government must act as an 'enabler' rather than a 'provider' of housing also has great relevance to urban land. As in housing, government's role is now increasingly understood as less on controlling the supply and more in setting the framework to encourage and support land markets that can respond to the variety of demands from different individuals, households, enterprises and investors. Land markets can only function effectively if they are characterized by ease of entry and ease of buying and selling—which in turn depend on a good information system about land, including who owns or has rights to each plot, secure tenure arrangements and appropriate registration and recording mechanisms.[69] Private land markets can also only function effectively within the law if the rules and regulations that landowners or developers must follow are clear and do not require unnecessary expense and where any need for formal permission or approval of a plan takes place efficiently, within a system that is transparent. Many land developers currently operating illegally could also operate more effectively within the legal system as this would considerably increase the possibilities open to them of obtaining credit.[70]

Inefficient government procedures[71]

One of the main factors encouraging more attention to this enabling approach is the growing documentation on how governments constrain land supplies and increase land prices. Some of this documentation has centred on how difficult it is for someone wishing to acquire land for housing to do so legally. For instance, in Ghana, acquiring land in urban areas from either of the main owners—the state or tribal authorities—is a long and time consuming process; for acquiring the right to use a plot of tribal land, there are 20 major steps that have to be followed that can take several years to complete.[72] Getting land ownership registered can also be a long and cumbersome process. For instance, in the Cameroon, the registration of land titles can take between two and seven years and with less than a fifth of urban plots demarcated and titled and with no properly maintained cadastral maps, it is difficult to obtain a clear picture of the land tenure situation. Although every country is a special case and procedural details vary greatly, the slow pace and complexity of land registration in Cameroon is not untypical of countries in the South.[73]

Getting approval for development plans, once the land has been acquired, can also be slow and costly. In Lima, subdivision approval takes an average of 28 months and must go through three stages, all of which must be overseen by the city council; it then takes another 12 months to have building permits approved. As one specialist in land legislation has commented:

The sole result of regulatory laws which price legal houses beyond the reach of the urban poor is that the poor are forced to live in accommodation of a quality poorer than they could in fact afford. For quite sensibly, the poor will not spend money on houses likely to be demolished by officialdom and they are forever at the mercy of venal officials and landlords willing to overlook their illegal status for a price.[74]

Inappropriate standards

Regulations that demand unrealistically large plot sizes for each house simply ensure that most of the population cannot afford a legal land site on which a house can be built. Many site and service schemes have been too expensive for low income households because the price of the large plot was beyond their capacity to pay—along with meeting the costs of services and the cost of building the house. Box 7.3 gives some examples of unrealistic regulations.

BOX 7.3

Regulations that help make land prices for housing unnecessarily high

Housing costs can be considerably increased by unrealistically high standards required for housing sites—for instance on the minimum size of a housing plot or for the proportion of a residential subdivision that can be used for housing. In Serpong (Indonesia), a recent master plan requires that 65 per cent of the total planned area for development be devoted to non-residential purposes and that densities for residential areas be kept to only 100 persons per hectare.[75] In Seoul, land for housing is also severely restricted through greenbelt regulations and master-plan provisions that limit residential developments to only 25 per cent of the total land area.[76]

Minimum lot sizes that are set very high also greatly increase the cost of the cheapest legal land site for housing. Among a survey of 48 cities for the minimum lot size permitted for a single family-housing unit within a new 50 to 200-unit residential subdivision, in many it was 300 or more square metres.[77] In Accra it was 445, in Ibadan 558 and in Washington DC 836. Minimum lot sizes of 300 or more square metres imply residential areas for which the density is too low to support public transport. By contrast, the minimum lot size was 30 square metres or less in Tokyo, Hong Kong, Madrid, Bogota and Delhi.

Few countries have made a concerted effort to revise their building regulations so as to allow more appropriate standards. In some countries and cities, the building regulations are more than 50 years old and are still, in theory, in operation. For instance, in Madras, the refusal to permit cheap and unconventional building materials and practices in site and service schemes ensured that most of the low-income population could not afford to take part.[78]

An insistence on inappropriate standards for, for instance, plot size and infrastructure standards have increased prices to the point where a high proportion of all land developments take place illegally. Many of these standards have their origins in standards imposed during colonial times that were originally intended only for the high quality residential areas of the colonial rulers in circumstances where demand for urban land was far lower as urban centres were much smaller and in most instances, urban populations kept down by strong restrictions on the rights of the native populations to live there. There are few examples of governments revising standards—although many have permitted particular projects, including government projects, to use more realistic standards.[79]

Other constraints

Governments have often imposed inappropriate legal regimes onto long established traditional land tenure practices that have inhibited the release of land with clear urban titles. In Africa, there are many examples of inappropriate government policies to deal with customary land tenure. In Lesotho, a World Bank inspired land-reform programme failed because of suspicions that it was designed to facilitate foreigners acquiring choice urban plots under a law that only they could understand.[80]

In theory, cities with a high proportion of all land under public ownership are the ones which should achieve a balance between the economic and social needs of all the different actors within the city. These cities should also have a comparative advantage in developing infrastructure and services since acquiring the land to do so should present them with no problems. They should be able to keep down land prices, by releasing land, as demand grows. In practice, in both North and South, the record of cities with a high proportion of land owned by the public authorities is often poor. For instance, in Tanzania and Zambia, a refusal to countenance a market in urban land and a failure to provide a responsive and efficient land-allocation system has simply led to large unofficial markets with all the problems these pose for urban authorities in terms of haphazard development, insecure tenure and lack of records for ownership or tenure. One example of this is provided by Dar es Salaam where the problem is more related to the fact that the demand for legal house sites outstrips the administrative capacity to allocate them—see Box 7.4.

Another example is provided by the Delhi Development Authority. 20,000 hectares of land has been marked for compulsory acquisition while the Authority has failed to substantially increase the supply of land for low-cost residential developments. A substantial part of the land it releases goes to high-income groups with less than 10 per cent going to lower-income groups. Urban development and capital authorities in Pakistan, Nigeria, Tanzania and Brazil also have a poor record in providing affordable land for the majority of urban dwellers.[81]

This adds up to a system that if not designed to facilitate the exploitation of the poor at least is adapted to do so. By being weighed so heavily to those who have the financial or political power—the latter often precedes the former but the two usually go together—the system facilitates the development of the exploitative relationship of landlords and tenants rather than those of owner occupiers. Shelter is a scarce good sold to the highest bidder. The more commercialized the markets, the more the poor are forced to use the least satisfactory land with the fewest rights.

International influences on cities' land markets

Inevitably, many cities worldwide are influenced by the new international division of labour that is organized and managed on a global scale. This new mode of global production is closely related to the growing importance within the world economy of the global corporation that can internalize many specific product markets, allocate capital globally to the most profitable locales and gather, process and communicate information on a global scale to carry out its functions.[82] The process has been accelerated recently with the development of regional trade blocs such as NAFTA and the European Union[83] (which expanded from the original six countries to nine, to twelve, and in 1995 to fifteen, with more hoping to join).

The municipal authorities responsible for managing urban development in these cities are no longer doing so in isolation from global forces. The housing and land markets and demands for infrastructure are influenced by the foreign (often multinational) firms and the firms that service their needs (and all their employees). This influence is evident in what have come to be called the 'world cities' that are the commanding nodes of the global system, with London, New York and Tokyo at the top and a range of other key cities that articulate large national or regional economies into the global system or have a particularly important multinational role.[84] This influence is also evident in cities or particular zones that are not so much centres of command and control but centres of production for multinational companies or firms contracted by them. In addition, a growing number of cities are also influenced by foreign investment in real estate. Despite the decline and even disintegration of some local and regional real-estate markets, real-estate markets in many cities were so thoroughly globalized during the 1980s boom that this will not be reversed.[85]

Although detailed and accurate information

BOX 7.4
The urban land delivery system in Tanzania

Between 1978/9 and 1991/2, the Dar es Salaam City Council received 261,668 applications for land plots, but was able to produce and allocate only 17,751 plots. In other words, only 7 per cent of the applicants got an allocation. The rest had to look elsewhere for their land needs. Over 70 per cent of Dar es Salaam's population live in unplanned areas, where, invariably, land is obtained through informal means. These findings suggest that the official system of land allocation has been outstripped by the acquisition of land through informal means.

Within the formal land-delivery system, land is allocated administratively. Application for a land plot is made to the district land officer, who submits all applications to an allocation committee which makes the final decision. In view of the numerous conflicts over land allocation powers, the Ministry of Lands issued a directive in 1988 whereby urban councils were empowered to allocate only high density residential plots (and even then, to the exclusion of 'projects' plots like the externally financed sites and services plots). Industrial, commercial, institutional and medium and low density residential land is allocated either by the Ministry of Lands, or by Regional Authorities.

If an applicant's quest for land is successful, they receive a letter of offer outlining the conditions (including land rent, various fees, building covenants, allowed uses, timescale for development, etc) under which land is being allocated. If these are accepted, the applicant meets the preliminary conditions (like paying land rent) and they become the legal possessor of the title to land. Long-term rights of occupancy are granted for periods of 33, 66 or 99 years; while short-term rights are for a duration of 5 or less years. A certificate of title may later on be issued. Typical costs to be met on land allocation include fees for the certificate of occupancy, registration fees, survey fees, fees for deed plans, stamp duty, and one year's land rent—

and these are very low and have no relation to the cost that the government incurs to prepare the land, nor are they related to the value of this land. The rationale behind such a cheap land policy has always been that land was national property to which anybody, particularly low income households, was entitled, and that putting too high a cost on this land, would edge the urban poor out of its acquisition.

In fact, this policy, inherited from the colonial era, has only served to allow the socially powerful members of society to get access to planned land cheaply. Moreover, since the supply of land has been restricted, the open land allocation system has been replaced by 'informal' allocations, usually depending on the economic power or the social influence of the would-be grantee— qualities which the urban poor do not possess. They therefore stand little chance of being allocated planned land.

Land can be obtained informally by way of occupation without permit, allocation by local leaders or landowners, inheritance, and purchase. While spectacular land invasions such as those seen in Latin America have not taken place in urban Tanzania, 'slow' land invasion does take place particularly on marginal land. No systematic study of this process has been made but typical methods of invasion include the use of land for cultivation for several seasons before finally deciding to build; the putting up of a makeshift structure before eventually deciding to go permanent; and the invitation of others by an early settler to create solidarity.

Land can be obtained from acknowledged owners. In some cases, particularly in the case of village-owned peripheral land, the local political (10-cell) leader or the local elders can allocate land to a newcomer, for a token fee. Inheritance is also a major way of getting land especially in the older areas, be they planned or unplanned. A study carried out recently over a sample of landowners in the inner city Kariakoo area in Dar es Salaam found that 55 per cent of those who owned land had got it by way of inheritance, while this

proportion dropped to nil in the new Mbezi area.

But it is more common for land to be purchased from recognized owners in unplanned areas. These subdivide and sell it either as building plots, or as agricultural land (Shamba). Most households with land in Dar es Salaam are likely to have obtained their land in this way. A study carried out in the Mabibo and Manzese unplanned areas of Dar es Salaam indicated that 75 and 79 per cent of the landowners in the respective areas obtained land through purchase. Typically, the land-sellers and the land-buyers are brought together through an intermediary and should a deal be struck, the parties will register the transaction with a 10-cell leader or a local branch of a political party, in front of witnesses, some of whom are usually neighbours or relatives.

Government (planned) land may also be allocated informally through private dealings which involve the exchange of money. Three ways can be identified:

- Land officials 'selling' unallocated or abandoned land, or land where earlier allocations may have been revoked; or new plots (locally known as 'creations') added to an already approved land use scheme.

- Plot allottees selling their undeveloped plots. This is illegal but such transfers are allowed if made 'for love and affection', and this loophole could be invoked to sell land to third parties.

- Plot allottees selling developments on their land. This is legal, but in most instances, the true transfer price is never officially disclosed to avoid it being known that the price far exceeded the value of developments; and also to avoid capital gains tax.

A survey over a sample of landowners in two planned areas of Dar es Salaam revealed that 12 per cent of the landowners in Kijitonyama and 45 per cent in Mbezi had bought empty plots from the 'owners'; and 15 and 2 per cent respectively had been sold government plots. In the case of Kijitonyama, a further 44 per cent had bought a house or a foundation.

Source: Kironde, J. M. Lusugga, 'The access to land by the poor in Urban Tanzania: some findings from Dar es Salaam', *Environment and Urbanization*, vol. 7, no. 1, April 1995.

about international investments in real-estate are difficult to obtain, it is clear that foreign investment in real-estate is a major influence on real-estate markets in many US and Canadian cities, in Australia (especially Sydney and Melbourne), in South-East Asia and Europe. European investors have long been involved in the property markets of other European nations but the globalization of European real-estate markets in the 1980s brought heightened attention to global property investment and particularly to investment in Europe from Asia.[86] In the United States,

Canadian investment in real-estate is the largest foreign source of investment followed by the Europeans and the Asians.[87] The Japanese were very active in real-estate investment in the 1980s but the decline of the Tokyo market in the 1990s dampened their enthusiasm for North American property.

The dominance of the service sector in advanced economies and the relative (and often absolute) decline in goods production is related to the new international division of labour. This is due in part to lower wages in other countries, in

Addressing the housing and land implications of globalization: the case of Vancouver

Vancouver on the west coast of Canada has a population of around 1.5 million in its metropolitan area. With a diverse population and a strategic location on the Pacific Rim, it has sought to attract global investment and tourism and, along with the province in which it is located (British Columbia), to reduce its reliance on natural resource exploitation and the US market. In the early 1980s, the provincial economy was largely directed to the United States and dominated by natural resource products such as lumber, pulp, non-ferrous metals and coal. Tourism has now moved ahead of mining as the province's second largest industry with Vancouver having a central role in this. The proportion of exports to Asia and Europe has also increased rapidly. The success in attracting new international business and investment to Vancouver also brought increasing pressure on the housing and land market and necessitated changes in government policy to help expand housing choice, increase densities and maintain supplies to moderate housing price pressures and maintain Vancouver's attractiveness to new investment.

Source: Goldberg, Michael A., *Some Thoughts on The Current and Potential Impacts of the Globalized Economy on Land and Housing Markets in World Cities,* background paper for the Global Report on Human Settlements, 1994.

part to growing environmental controls, and in part to rapid technological change reducing employment in goods-producing industries. Certain service activities seem to be much less dependent on wages so that locational choice for services will be increasingly driven by quality of life because employees and management of service firms want to locate in high-quality physical settings. This helps explain the increase in income inequality as managerial and professional jobs pay more and unskilled or semi-skilled jobs in the service sector pay less.

7.2 Approaches to Urban Land-Use Planning

Introduction

The main approaches to urban planning in both the North and the South essentially set out to document a finite long term plan which, once legally adopted, forms the basis for public sector infrastructure and services investment and a detailed system of land use regulation and control. A study of urban planning which surveyed and reviewed city planning and city plans in India (Madras and Calcutta), Nigeria (Kano, Abuja), Morocco (Rabat), Iraq (Baghdad), and Mexico, among others, concluded that many urban plans fail in practice because they are over-ambitious, considering the capabilities of the administrative system to enforce their implementation.[88] The reasons

for this include the lack of a proper legal and administrative framework, inadequate technical skills and financial resources, unrealistic assumptions emanating from the foreign base of the plans and lack of participation by the population. It has also been suggested that traditional land-use systems generally do not adequately control the quality, pace or distributional effects of land development and that, even when a plan exists, development activity is too often disorganized. This is mostly because the stated goals are unrealistic, and because there is lack of co-ordination between planning and financing agencies, or because there is a shortage of trained personnel.

In addition, the institutional capacity of many countries in Africa, Asia and Latin America to absorb change is usually disproportionately small compared with the level of their aspirations. The analogy of the master plan as a building 'blueprint' has often been stressed. Implementation of such plans assumes the involvement of formal organizations in the residential, commercial and industrial sectors through processes of institutional bargaining, where the rules of the game are known and development is meant to conform to set procedures, planning/building applications, development briefs, public hearings, etc.[89] In the past, this form of urban planning tended to mirror the development model that was widespread in the post-World War II period with considerable state economic planning which relied on central government finance and the technical capacity of public agencies to control most urban activity.[90] These procedures worked well in many OECD countries with urban conditions characterized by slow growth, high average household incomes and effective enforcement practices, as well as in some countries in Africa and Asia to which they were exported as part of a colonial inheritance, particularly in the 1940s and 1950s, when most urban areas were still relatively small.

Traditional approaches to urban land-use planning

There were two broad traditions of urban planning. One, supplied by French, British and other European practice, grew out of concerns for public health and other urban concerns and involved an often centralised tradition of public urban intervention through strong land-use regulations and public sector investments, often with a strong emphasis on civic design (e.g. Chandigarh in India and Brasilia in Brazil). The other, arising from practice in North America, emphasised land use zoning and land subdivision regulations, in keeping with a strong tradition of private property rights and values.

BOX 7.6
Master-planning in India

In India many states enacted Town and Country Planning laws during the 1960s under which master plans were prepared for a very large number of cities and towns across the country. The first Delhi Master Plan (1961–81) is indicative of the major themes of that era:

1. Demographic projection and decision on the level at which the population shall be contained;
2. Allocation of population to various zones depending on existing density levels, infrastructure capacity and acceptable future density levels;
3. Land-use zoning to achieve the desired allocation of population and activities in various zones as projected; and
4. Large-scale acquisition of land with a view to ensuring planned development.

Source: Dharmarajank, Kapoor R. M. and P. B. Anand, 'Urban Planning in Asia', 1994.

BOX 7.7
Dhaka's master plan

The current master plan for Dhaka, Bangladesh was produced in 1959 for an anticipated future population of 2 million, compared to a current figure of over 6 million that is growing by some 250,000 persons per year. The plan remains the only legal document for land-use regulation, even though it covers only about 40 per cent of the current built-up area and was produced 12 years before the country's independence and Dhaka's development as the national capital. The plan included recommendations that it should be updated from time to time and that local plans should be detailed to act as the basis for regulations, but neither recommendation was carried out.

However, since the 1960s, such traditional approaches have been found wanting in cities in both the North and the South, even if they continue to be used in many countries. In many cases the reasons are similar for both groups of countries—for instance the divorce of planning from resource assessment and the absence of community consensus in the plan-making process. Master plans often took too long to prepare and were extremely costly. Master-plan preparation was almost always measured in years, and where the plan had to be embodied in a statutory development order, sometimes in decades. Many master plans remain not only unimplemented but very out of date, as the example in Box 7.7 illustrates. At the same time there was a trend to produce national spatial plans based on 'top-down' allocations of urban functions, land uses and communications based on rank-size and other theories of optimal urban population distribution. Again such strategies were predominantly physical and did not reflect the real world requirements of economic development, political priorities and the weak role of the planner in enforcing these plans. Consequently, few such national plans had any real impact on national or inter-regional population distribution.

Particularly in countries in the South, traditional approaches are often completely inappropriate to meeting the needs of the many cities which since the 1960s have been characterised by rapid growth of a low-income population which has overwhelmed the financial, human and institutional resources of the government, particularly at the city level. As earlier chapters have described, the net effect of such inadequacies is that the majority of urban growth has long taken place outside the planning 'rules of the game'. 'Informal' residential and business premises and developments increasingly dominate new urban areas.

Even where half or more of a city's population and many of its economic activities are located in illegal or informal settlements, urban planners may still rely on traditional master-planning approaches with their role restricted to servicing the minority, influential high income clients and trying to bring some coordination of development and services to 'informal' areas, or ignoring such areas altogether. Although the official conception of urban development is of 'planning—servicing—building—occupation', this is often reversed as the sequence is occupation—building—servicing—planning.

Lack of co-ordination

In nearly all cities in the South and many in the North, there have been shortfalls of public-sector finance for the provision and maintenance of urban infrastructure and services and land for urban expansion. Very few traditional master plans addressed the financial implications of the programmes and projects they recommended—either the actual costs involved or how they would be financed. They also failed to consider which components of the plan could or should be scrapped or standards modified as a result of budget constraints.

Master plans also generally fail to reflect the priorities, resource constraints and programmes of the agencies responsible for infrastructure provision. Even where plans attempt to co-ordinate the proposals of a range of infrastructure and other line agencies, there have often been problems because of the way 'horizontal' planning systems relate poorly to 'vertical' systems of resource allocation. In many cases, spatial planning has no power to co-ordinate the sectoral spending agencies, which themselves may have little commitment to the spatial plan. Planners are thus at a disadvantage in having few or no financial resources to negotiate with and having to rely largely on persuasion to get co-operation and support for the spatial plan. Lack of co-ordination is compounded where, as frequently happens, the process of specifying development budgeted priorities has little to do with spatial objectives or policies.

In response to these deficiencies in master-planning approaches, from the 1970s, many countries adopted a project-by-project approach, i.e. individual spending agencies preparing projects which might or might not correspond with the master plan but which at least were financially feasible. This sectoral approach led to a lack of co-ordination in development activities and has contributed to the search for improved urban planning mechanisms.

Traditional master-planning has shown uncertainty about the relationship between economic and spatial planning initiatives in promoting urban development. Part of this uncertainty stems from the fact that the actual mechanisms of the urban economy are not well understood (for instance the scale and nature of the informal economy and the links between formal and informal employment). In addition, many decisions affecting the city economy are in fact dependent on regional or sub-regional objectives and policies. The relationship becomes even more complex with the advent of sustainable development objectives. The uncertainty also stems from the traditional role of the public *vis-à-vis* the private sector in which the planning system has tended to be reactive rather than proactive.

A two-dimensional approach to urban development

The prevailing assumption in traditional master planning has been that 'the plan' is an end in itself rather than just one component in the management of urban processes. This two-dimensional approach originates from the view that plan-making is a technocratic process alone rather than also a socio-economic and political process. This is one reason why it so often leads to the formulation of policies and programmes which are ignored or rejected by politicians and the community. To give only one example of this deficiency, urban planners often have little understanding about a key component of any master plan—the real world operations of land markets (i.e. land prices, impacts on demand, supply, 'actors' in the market, etc). Where most development is taking place outside the formal sector, such information gaps are even larger. Such gaps lead to plans which do not take account of the impact of infrastructure investment on land prices, and which may ignore potential environmental hazards such as settlement on land that is subject to flooding. Planners have also often ignored the impact of unclear property rights resulting from inadequate cadastral, registration and tenure records, and the existence of informal and formal land tenure

systems, on the formulation of urban expansion strategies.

Inappropriate land-use regulations

Traditional master-planning has often relied on rigid regulations using zoning, subdivision and building policies and standards which generate more costs than benefits to residents and businesses in the city. In parallel with such excessive regulations, there is often a lack of effective regulations designed to address environmentally-sensitive areas such as steep slopes, wetlands and earthquake-prone land. In both situations the traditional planning approach has rarely concerned itself with the critical issue of impacts on low-income households.

While regulatory measures such as minimum plot size, density limits, building set-backs, maximum land ownership, road widths, permissible building materials, floor-area ratios, and compulsory connections to water and sanitation systems may have been introduced to overcome undesirable environmental 'spillover' effects arising from land development, they may have the effect of forcing up land and property prices and reducing most household's access to shelter. As a result, households and businesses are forced to move into the informal, unregulated land market, often settling in environmentally sensitive locations. Poorly designed regulations impact on historic city neighbourhoods as well. Such areas are often subject to laws and regulations, such as restrictions on use and rent control, which have the effect of encouraging progressive deterioration, rather than providing economic incentives to encourage new land uses.

As earlier sections on inefficient government procedures and inappropriate standards noted, affordability and efficient access to land is also affected where there are complex development permission procedures built into the planning and land-development process. Box 7.8 gives examples of inappropriate land-use regulations or procedures.

Institutional shortcomings

Administrative frameworks

The preparation and enforcement of urban plans has often been based on obsolete planning ordinances which place all planning powers and responsibilities with the central government. This centralization has often helped to enlarge the gap between the planning process and the executive system at the local level.

Three further institutional shortcomings have often been exacerbated by centralization. First, in many cases the responsibility for spatial planning in central government has frequently shifted from ministry to ministry, having at one time or another

BOX 7.8
Examples of inappropriate land-use regulations or procedures

Malaysia: A 1989 study suggested that land-use regulations and standards increased housing costs by up to 50 per cent. The area per house provided for roads is up to four times greater in the typical Malaysian subdivision than in comparable North American or West European examples. According to accepted international practices, about 25 per cent of the land set aside is wasted through over-generous standards for street width, setbacks and community facilities. House prices rose at an annual rate of 18.9 per cent in the 1972–82 period, partly because of the above and partly because of overly complex and time-consuming housing-project approval procedures. It can take 5–8 years to obtain necessary permits from 15–20 government agencies for subdivision approval. In Thailand by contrast the figures are 5 months and 5 agencies.

India: In India, the 1976 Urban Land (Ceiling and Regulation) Act imposed a ceiling on vacant land ownership within urban agglomerations, ranging from 2,000 square metres in the smallest towns to only 500 square metres in the metropolitan centres of Delhi, Bombay, Calcutta and Madras. The state governments would then take over the surplus vacant land (at a low price). However, only 1.5 per cent of the land declared as surplus has actually been acquired under the Act since public authorities have been unable to continue acquiring surplus land under existing land-acquisition statutes. Thus not only has this limited the supply of land which can be offered by the public sector, but large amounts of privately owned 'surplus' land have been frozen in administrative procedures and litigation for most of the period since enactment of the Act, precluding the private sector from legally supplying land, except in a limited number of cases where exemptions have been granted. In addition, these problems have had the effect of accelerating land values in inner urban areas for plots exempted under the Act. It has been calculated that at least 300,000 hectares of land have been declared 'excess', and effectively frozen, as a result of the Act.

Sources: World Bank, *Malaysia: The Housing Sector—Getting the Incentives Right*, Infrastructure Division, Country Department II, Asia Regional Office, Washington DC, 1989; World Bank, *India Urban Land Management Study*, Washington DC, 1986.

been attached to the Ministry of Lands, Public Works, Housing, Economic Planning or Local Government. This usually leads to the bypassing of urban planning authorities by both infrastructure delivery agencies and private developers. Second, statutory legislation is often not enforceable over the entire country, but only in statutory planning areas. Such a non-comprehensive approach to traditional urban planning contributed to problems of co-ordination and enforcement and reinforced a process whereby planning tended to follow development. Third, the approval process for planning instruments is frequently over-centralized, lengthy and cumbersome, as already noted, and this represents another deterrent to efficient plan-making and plan implementation processes.

The role of public and private sectors

The increasing inability of the comprehensive planning approaches of the 1960s to meet the needs of rapid rates of urban growth in most countries in Africa, Asia and Latin America coupled with the unwillingness of central government to increase the powers and resources needed for cities to manage themselves, led to increasing public/private-sector antagonisms. Thus for example, developers and the community as a whole were increasingly unable to rely on the public sector to provide infrastructure and services and saw only a negative and irrelevant system of land-use regulation. As ever-increasing proportions of urban households relied on informal or illegal land markets, conflicts between planners and local communities grew over critical issues such as land uses.

In many instances, such antagonisms were made worse because community leaders and business interests were not meaningfully involved in the master planning process. Typically, master plans were prepared by professional planners and/or consultants working in agencies cut off from channels of community expression and only at the end of the plan-preparation process was a perfunctory discussion period allowed.

Time horizons and sustainability

While master plans have often looked strategically 20–30 years ahead, they have rarely set out to meet the goals of sustainable development. While the conservation of natural and other resources is a familiar theme for planners, at least in the North, the marrying of sustainable resource use and urban growth has only very recently gained importance. In part, this arises from the institutional fragmentation of the organizations who are responsible for components of sustainable urban development (water, agriculture, forestry, energy, transport, housing, industry). Some of these actors in the process may well have developed their thinking on long term sustainability well ahead of urban planners.

It is important to emphasize, also, that the vilification and criticisms of settlement planning, is largely in the context of countries where the rate of urban growth and development in many cities has been so high as to overwhelm attempts at orderly rational development planning, and where the requisite institutional framework is still relatively weak and in a constant state of flux. In most countries in the North, settlements planning and management has, to substantial degrees been effective. It has been easier to implement as the rate of growth of urban populations has slowed to very low levels, and as appropriate legal and institutional frameworks had been in place for some time and had gained substantial strength and maturity and could therefore more effectively handle the ensuing challenges of settlement planning, development and management. In Australian cities (including Sydney and Perth), for example, strategic urban plans are being prepared directed at the geographic, economic and social structure of the development of the cities over a long time scale, with the main aims to:[91]

- Set broad parameters for the direction of future urban growth, taking account of topographical constraints and environmental considerations such as the protection of water catchment areas, places of natural beauty or environmental sensitivity.

- Facilitate the co-ordination of a wide range of future commercial activities and public-services affecting economic development, employment, transport, housing, education and social welfare.

- Provide adequate level of certainty to participants in the land supply and development process.

- Provide for staged urban development within particular areas or growth corridors in order to maximize efficiency in the provision of key infrastructure items such as water, sewerage, electricity and roads.

Such plans establish the conceptual land-use framework for a city or region and identify new areas for future development over a period of 20 years or more. They may also provide guidelines on major urban planning issues such as urban consolidation and regional development.

The planning system in England, as another example, has been judged to have been 'highly successful' in the pursuit of the main planning policy objectives, namely: containment of the growth of major urban areas,[92] curbing the amount of agricultural land taken for urban development, maintaining greenbelts around major cities and urban agglomerations, allocating sites for new development and sustaining conservation policies.

In spite of the criticism of the perceived ineffectiveness of planning, however, the process is widely acknowledged by all governments as very relevant. Very few countries today, do not have urban settlements planning programme activities in their development agenda. The absence of urban planning in national or local settlement development activities and processes in inconceivable. Settlements planning, with its built-in land-development regulations as a set of rules governing activities that form part of social and economic life currently exists in all countries.

The lessons learnt

From a review of the experiences of urban settlements planning and management in both the North and the South, the following lessons are apparent:

- Traditional master planning has often been ineffective because too much emphasis is put on plan-making and too little on implementation, and the process has been slow and expensive. In addition, such master-planning has paid little or no attention to the necessary resource-allocation needs and financial feasibility of policies and programmes.

- Inappropriate regulations and standards have often reduced land availability for housing and businesses by imposing unnecessary costs and fuelling the growth of informal land markets. Planners have too often used a two-dimensional approach to land development, viewing it as a matter of zoning, networks and forecasts. A greater understanding of land markets, property rights, affordability and the multidimensional character of land will help planners to focus on the day-to-day needs of residents and thereby help to make the urban planning system more relevant to the needs and priorities of citizens and businesses. The planner needs to learn how to utilize the latent resources of the community to manage facilities. They also need to learn how informal employment is generated and sustained and how to reduce negative land-use controls to the minimum required for maintenance of public health and environmental safeguarding—and to ensure that the needs of all groups in the city are addressed.

- A shift in emphasis in the typical planning system is needed. Whatever the scale of plan being considered (metropolitan/sub-regional/city/local), a first question is: what tools are available to implement the plan over the next five years? In many cities, for example, the only effective methods of trying to direct city growth are by the location of new arterial or access roads and the location of public facilities. Other tools, such as land-use zoning or compulsory purchase, may exist on paper or in legislation but are not effective in practice. Plans that recognize the limitations of implementation tools, at least in the short term, are much more likely to be effective policy instruments.

- A shift in emphasis may also be needed in the traditionally hierarchical view of planning. In many instances, local plans are required to fit into the framework of plans and policies emanating from higher levels of government (a 'top-down' view of implementation). As will be seen in Chapter 9, a shift towards 'bottom-up' planning means a greater emphasis on designing plans around available implementation tools, and on 'action planning', co-ordinated at the city government level.

- The increasing complexities and inter-dependencies of urban areas (urban growth dynamics, inter-sectoral choice mechanisms, the role of the private sector and the increasing emphasis on sustainable development) require a re-evaluation of the traditional role of public-sector urban planning in the urban management process.

- Urban-sector interventions characterized by a 'project' approach based on public-sector capital expenditure as the prime means of achieving urban objectives cannot hope to meet the massive need for improved urban services and shelter in cities, let alone contribute significantly to economic growth. Instead, interventions need to address the management of processes. A much greater emphasis on an enabling approach is needed whereby the public sector's main efforts are to support the private sector's role in urban development, through policy measures and sympathetic land regulation systems, i.e. to capitalize on the energies and resources of individuals, households, community groups and commercial enterprises.

- As economic conditions have deteriorated in many countries in Africa, Asia and Latin America, putting more pressures on non-renewable natural resources and the absorp-

tive capacity of the city environment, more integrated approaches to urban development are required. This integration needs to be technical (co-ordination of urban planning with ecological management, energy, transport and other key sectors), equitable (explicit impact on all income groups in both the household and commercial sectors), and institutional (both vertical and horizontal co-ordination of urban planning, sectoral investment, financial resources, cost-recovery and administrative functions).

Thus, in conclusion, planning has to be the fundamental strategic tool of good management. Without planning, there can be no management to speak of, and without management, planning becomes nothing more than a depository of good intentions entirely separate from reality. The change that needs to take place is one from 'planning the city' to 'a city that plans' and from product (i.e. a graphic image of a desirable future produced by specialized technical departments) to process (i.e. consultations, initiatives and actions through which a city collectively maps its present situation, identifies problems and opportunities, develops an inherent vision of the future and translates it into social, economic and physical objectives supported by clear and realistic strategies).[93]

Notes and References

1. Section 7.1 draws heavily on McAuslan, Patrick, 'Land in the City', mimeo, 1994 and Payne, Geoffrey, *Informal Housing and Land Subdivisions in Third World Cities: A Review of the Literature*, CENDEP, Oxford, 1989.

2. Very little is known about land markets for housing in most small and inter-mediate-size urban centres in the South. It may be that in many small administrative centres and market towns which lack a buoyant economy, land prices for housing are not very high—but there are many small urban centres with rapid economic growth (for instance successful tourist centres or market towns for high-value crops) where low-income groups have increasing difficulty obtaining land for housing.

3. Preamble, Section D., United Nations, *Report of Habitat: United Nations Conference on Human Settlements*, A/CONF.70/15, United Nations, New York, 1976, 61.

4. See for instance Shlomo Angel, Raymon W. Archer, Sidhijai Tanphiphat and Emiel A. Wegelin (eds.), *Land for Housing the Poor*, Select Books, Singapore, 1983; Payne, 1989, *op. cit.*

5. See for instance Soares, B. and R. Stussi, 'Parallel land markets in the Lisbon region', in Pal Baross (ed.), *The New Suburbs*, Gower, 1989.

6. Hasan, Arif, *Community Development Groups in the Urban Field in Pakistan*, Arif Hasan and Associates, Prepared for the Swiss Development Corporation, 1989.

7. See for instance El Agraa, Omer M. A., Adil M. Ahmad, Ian Haywood and O. M. El Kheir, *Popular Settlements in Greater Khartoum*, Sudanese Group for Assessment of Human Settlements, Khartoum University Press, Khartoum, 1985.

8. Baross, Paul, 'The articulation of land supply for popular settlements in Third World cities', in Shlomo Angel, Raymon W. Archer, Sidhijai Tanphiphat and Emiel A. Wegelin (eds.), *Land for Housing the Poor*, Select Books, Singapore, 1983; Gilbert, Alan and Peter Ward, *Housing, the State and the Poor*, Cambridge University Press, 1985.

9. Baross 1983, *op. cit.*

10. Baross 1983, *op. cit.*

11. Yapi-Diahou, Alphonse, *The Informal Housing Sector in the Metropolis of Abidjan, Ivory Coast*, background Paper for the Global Report on Human Settlements, 1994, subsequently published in *Environment and Urbanization* vol. 7, no. 2, Oct. 1995.

12. Moser, Caroline O. N., 'A home of one's own: squatter housing strategies in Guayaquil, Ecuador', in Alan Gilbert,

Jorge E. Hardoy and Ronaldo Ramirez (eds.), *Urbanization in Contemporary Latin America*, John Wiley and Sons, Chichester, UK, 1982.

13. Kironde, J. M. Lusugga, 'Access to land by the urban poor in Tanzania: some findings from Dar es Salaam', *Environment and Urbanization*, vol. 7, no. 1, April 1995, 77–95.

14. Yapi-Diahou 1994, *op. cit.*

15. Van Lindert, Paul and August van Western, 'Household shelter strategies in comparative perspective: evidence from low income groups in Bamako and La Paz', *World Development*, vol. 19, no. 8, 1991, 1007–28.

16. Payne 1989, *op. cit.*, page 2.

17. Padmaja, Nayani, *Process of Illegal Subdivision of Land and Housing Consolidation*, School of Architecture, New Delhi, mimeo, 1987, quoted in Payne 1989, *op. cit.*

18. Gilbert, Alan and Peter Ward, *Housing, the State and the Poor*, Cambridge University Press, 1985.

19. Van der Linden, Jan, 'Rental housing of the urban poor in Pakistan: characteristics and some trends', in UNCHS, *Rental Housing: Proceedings of an Expert Group Meeting*, UNCHS (Habitat), Nairobi, 1990, 50–5.

20. El Kadi, Galila, 'Market mechanisms and spontaneous urbanization in Egypt:

the Cairo case', *International Journal for Urban and Regional Research*, vol. 12, no. 1, 1988, 22–37.

21. Payne, Geoffrey K., 'Housing Agents in the Towns of Papua New Guinea', *Built Environment*, vol. 8, no. 2, 1983, 125–37.

22. Yapi-Diahou 1994, *op. cit.*

23. Varley, Ann, 'Clientisism or technocracy? The political logic of urban land regularization', in N. Harvey (ed.), *Mexico: The Dilemma of Transition*, University of London and I. P. Tauris, 1994.

24. Chabbi, Morched, 'The pirate subdeveloper: a new form of land developer in Tunis', *International Journal for Urban and Regional Research*, vol. 12, no. 1, 1988, 8–21.

25. Payne 1989, *op. cit.*

26. Hasan 1989, *op. cit.*

27. Payne 1989, *op. cit.*

28. *Ibid.*; Doebele, William A., 'Land policy', in Lloyd Rodwin (ed.), *Shelter, Settlement and Development*, Allen and Unwin, Boston, 1987, 110–32.

29. Wegelin, E. A. and C. Chanond, 'Home improvement, housing finance and security of tenure in Bangkok slums', in Shlomo Angel, Raymon W. Archer, Sidhijai Tanphiphat and Emiel A. Wegelin (eds.), *Land for Housing the Poor*, Select Books, Singapore, 1983, 75–97.

30. Roy, Dilip, 'The supply of land for the slums in Calcutta', in Angel, 1983, *op. cit.* 98–109.

31. Ameur, Mohammed, 'Le logement des pauvres à Fes: processus de production et tendances de l'évolution', *Revue Tiers Monde*, vol. 29, no. 116, Oct.–Dec. 1988, 1171–81.

32. Yapi-Diahou 1994, *op. cit.*

33. See for instance the description of *favela de quintal* in Rio de Janeiro and *corralon* in Lima, in Leeds, Anthony, 'Housing-settlement types, arrangements for living, proletarianization and the social structure of the city', in F. M. Trueblood and W. A. Cornelius (eds.), *Latin American Urban Research*, Sage Publications, USA, 1974.

34. Urban Resource Centre, *Facts and Figures*, vol. 3, no. 3, Karachi, March 1995, 4.

35. Islam, Nazrul, 'Land ownership pattern in Dhaka City' in Islam, Nazrul and Amirul Islam Chowdhury (eds.), *Urban Land Management in Bangladesh*, Ministry of Land, Government of Bangladesh, Dhaka, 1992.

36. Alder, Graham, 'Tackling poverty in Nairobi's informal settlements: developing an institutional strategy', *Environment and Urbanization*, vol. 7, no. 2, Oct. 1995.

37. Hardoy, Jorge E. and David Satterthwaite, *Squatter Citizen: Life in the Urban Third World*, Earthscan Publications, London, 1989.

38. Green, Gill, 'A case study of housing tenure and rental accommodation in Santa Cruz, Bolivia', in UNCHS, *Rental Housing: Proceedings of an Expert Group Meeting*, UNCHS (Habitat), Nairobi, 1990, 56–66.

39. Van der Linden 1990, *op. cit.*

40. See for instance Peattie, Lisa, 'Participation: a case study of how invaders organize, negotiate and interact with government in Lima, Peru', *Environment and Urbanization*, vol. 2, no. 1, April 1990, 19–30.

41. Portes, Alejandro, 'Housing policy, urban poverty and the state: the favelas of Rio de Janeiro', *Latin American Research Review*, no. 14, Summer 1979, 3–24.

42. Kothari, Miloon, 'Rio de Janeiro', *Environment and Urbanization*, vol. 6, no. 1, April 1994, 63–73.

43. This has been developed by the Habitat International Coalition.

44. The Ecologist, *Whose Common Future: Reclaiming the Commons*, Earthscan Publications, London, 1992.

45. Hardoy and Satterthwaite 1989, *op. cit.*

46. Asian Coalition for Housing Rights, 'Evictions in Seoul, South Korea', *Environment and Urbanization*, vol. 1, no. 1, April 1989, 89–94; Urban Poor Institute, *Information Packet on the Urban Poor of Korea*, Seoul, South Korea, 1988.

47. Hardoy and Satterthwaite 1989, *op. cit.*

48. Hunsley Magebhula, Patrick, 'Evictions in the new South Africa: a narrative report from Durban', and Fernandes, Kenneth, 'Katchi abadis: living on the edge', *Environment and Urbanization*, vol. 6, no. 1, April 1994.

49. Leckie, Scott, *Destruction by Design: Housing Rights Violations in Tibet*, Centre on Housing Rights and Evictions (COHRE), Utrecht, 1994; Schechla, Joseph, 'Forced eviction as an increment of demographic manipulation', *Environment and Urbanization*, vol. 6, no. 1, April 1994, 89–105. See also the *Ecologist* 1992 and Portes 1979, *op. cit.*

50. Audefroy, Joël, 'Eviction trends worldwide—and the role of local authorities in implementing the right to housing', *Environment and Urbanization*, vol. 6, no. 1, April 1994, 8–24.

51. 'Asian Coalition for Housing Rights', NGO profile in *Environment and Urbanization*, vol. 5, no. 2, 1993, 153–65

52. Asian Coalition for Housing Rights 1993, *op. cit.*

53. Leckie 1994, *op. cit.*

54. Schechla 1994, The Ecologist 1994 and Portes 1979, *op. cit.*

55. Hardoy and Satterthwaite 1989, *op. cit.*

56. Khan, Shahed Anwer, 'Attributes of slums affecting their vulnerability to eviction: a study of Bangkok's informal settlements' and Murphy, Denis and Ted Anana, 'Evictions and fear of evictions in the Philippines', *Environment and Urbanization*, vol. 6, no. 1, April 1994.

57. See for instance Audefroy 1994, and Hunsley 1994, *op. cit.*

58. See for instance Audefroy 1994, Hunsley 1994 and Fernandes 1994, *op. cit.*

59. See for instance Kothari 1994 and Murphy and Anana 1994, *op. cit.*

60. See Ramirez, Ronaldo, Jorge Fiori, Hans Harms and Kosta Mathey, 'The commodification of self-help housing and state intervention: household experiences in the Barrios of Caracas', in Kosta Mathey (ed.), *Beyond Self-Help Housing*, Mansell, London and New York, 1992, 95–144.

61. Hardoy and Satterthwaite 1989, *op. cit.*

62. See Varley 1994, *op. cit.*

63. *Ibid.*

64. Van Lindert and van Western 1991, *op. cit.*

65. Varley 1994, *op. cit.*

66. Strassmann, W. Paul, 'Oversimplification in housing analysis, with reference to land markets and mobility', *Cities*, vol. 11, no. 6, Dec. 1994, 377–83.

67. Strassmann 1994, *op. cit.*

68. Kironde 1995, *op. cit.*

69. Farvacque, Catherine and Patrick McAuslan, *Reforming Urban Land Policies and Institutions in Developing Countries*, Urban Management Program Policy Paper No. 5, The World Bank, Washington DC, 1992.

70. Durand-Lasserve, Alain, 'Land and housing in Third World cities: are public and private strategies contradictory?', *Cities*, vol. 4, no. 4, Nov. 1987, 325–38.

71. Section drawn from Farvacque and McAuslan 1992, *op. cit.*

72. *Ibid.*

73. *Ibid.*

74. McAuslan, Patrick, 'Legislation, regulation and shelter', *Cities*, vol. 4, no. 1, 1987, 23–7.

75. Bertaud, Marie Agnes and Douglas Lucius, *Land Use, Building Codes, and Infrastructure Standards as Barriers to Affordable Housing in Developing Countries*, Working Paper, World Bank, Urban Development Department, Washington DC, 1989, quoted in Mayo, Stephen K. and Shlomo Angel, *Housing: Enabling Markets to Work*, A World Bank Policy Paper, World Bank, Washington DC, 1993.

76. Mayo and Angel 1993, *op. cit.*

77. UNCHS/World Bank, *The Housing Indicators Program Volume III; Preliminary Findings*, Washington DC, April 1993.

78. Land in the City—Patrick McAuslan, mimeo, 1994.

79. See for instance Schilderman, Theo, 'Building codes and planning regulations as enabling tools', Paper presented at the Second Symposium on Housing for the Urban Poor, European Network for Housing Research, Birmingham, April 1994.

80. McAuslan 1994, *op. cit.*

81. *Ibid.*

82. Taylor, Michael and Nigel Thrift (eds.), *The Geography of Multinationals*, Croom Helm, London, 1982; Thrift, Nigel, 'World Cities and the world city prop-

erty market: The case of Southeast Asian investment in Australia', Working Paper, Australia National University, Research School of Pacific Studies, Department of Human Geography, 1983, mimeo.

83. Kresl, Peter K., *The Urban Economy and Regional Trade Liberalization*, Praeger, Westport, 1992; Epstein, G., J. Graham, and J. Nembhard (eds.) *Creating a New World Economy: Forces of Change and Plans for Action*, Temple University, Philadelphia, 1993.

84. Friedmann, John, 'Where we stand: a decade of world city research', Paper prepared for the Conference of World Cities in a World System, Center for Innovative Technology, April 1993; Sassen, Saskia, *Cities in a World Economy*, Pine Forge Press, Thousand Oaks, London, New Delhi, 1994.

85. Goldberg, Michael A., *Some Thoughts on The Current and Potential Impacts of the Globalized Economy on Land and Housing Markets in World Cities*, background paper for the Global Report on Human Settlements, 1994.

86. Harper, Timothy, 'European retail lacks customer service,' and 'In recession Europe seeks leadership,' *Shopping Centers Today*, 100, 104, and 112, vol. 14, issue 5, May 1993; Young, Nicholas E. and Michael Evans, 'Japanese real estate investment in Europe accelerated in 1989 as investors sought higher yields and diversification', *Real Estate Newsline*, March/April 1990, 1; and *Urban Land*, 'First International Property Market Held in France,' vol. 49, no. 7, July 1990, 21–2 and 'Outlook for European Investment in US Real Estate,' vol. 49, no. 9, Sept. 1990, 28–9.

87. *Land Use Digest*, vol. 23, no. 9, Sept. 1990, 'Trends in Japanese Real Estate Investment', 2; and vol. 24, no. 7, July 1991, 'Report on World Property Performance, Costs,' 1, and 'Offshore Investors See US Markets as Exceptional', 2.

88. McAuslan, Patrick, *Urban Land and Shelter for the Poor*, Earthscan, London, 1985.

89. UNCHS (Habitat), *Integrated Action Planning; Urban Management Programme Analysis and Synthesis Report*, Nairobi, 1989.

90. World Bank, *Urban Policy and Economic Development—An Agenda for the 1990s*, Washington DC, 1991.

91. Commonwealth of Australia, *The National Housing Strategy: The Efficient Supply of Land and Housing—The Urban Challenge*, Issue Paper no. 4, 1991, 48.

92. Hall, Peter, *The Containment of Urban England*, Unwin Hyman, London, 1973.

93. UNCHS (Habitat), *The Management of Human Settlements: The Municipal Level*, Nairobi, 1993.

8 Infrastructure and Service

8.1 Introduction

Provision for water, sanitation, drainage and the safe disposal of wastes are obviously central to good housing and living conditions and to health. They and certain other forms of infrastructure are also central to prosperous economies—for instance roads, ports and railways, electric power and telecommunications. If consideration is given only to what might be termed 'economic infrastructure' that does not include education and health care, the services associated with it usually account for between 7 and 11 per cent of a country's GDP.[1] The share usually increases with income. Transport and communications generally represents the largest sector in low-, middle- and high-income countries and its share generally increases, the higher the per capita income.[2] Investment in infrastructure was found to represent around 20 per cent of total investment in a sample of low- and middle-income countries and to account for 40 to 60 per cent of public investment.[3]

The quality of infrastructure and service provision within any city or country has become increasingly important in attracting new investment. The capacity to attract industries or service enterprises that can operate successfully in international markets is particularly dependent on high quality infrastructure, especially in the rapid and cost-effective handling of freight and sophisticated telecommunications systems.[4] As the recent World Development Report on *Infrastructure for Development* noted, 'Surveys of prospective foreign investors over a wide range of countries show that the quality of infrastructure is an important factor in ranking potential sites for location of direct investment.'[5] All the countries or regions that have had the most success in attracting enterprises that have a role within the increasingly globalized world economy have also greatly improved the range and quality of their infrastructure.

In theory, demand for infrastructure accompanies economic growth so the two can support each other. What has proved difficult for most governments is developing the institutional means to ensure that the two go together. This includes the means to raise the funds for infrastructure investment, to ensure sufficient funding for operations and maintenance and to develop the capacity within municipalities, cities and regions to make the best choices over which forms of infrastructure receive priority in each

location and how best to charge those who benefit from such investment. It is also difficult to predict how demand will change for many forms of infrastructure, although large infrastructure investments require many years for their planning and construction. Overestimating future growth in demand can prove very expensive, as in, for instance, new power stations whose full capacity is not needed or industrial estates that remain empty. But there are also large costs from underestimating growth in demand—for instance where power and water shortages hold back the economic growth of a city or region.

There are also the more serious problems for cities and countries that have not enjoyed economic prosperity. As in most cities in the North, cities in the South experienced a deterioration in their infrastructure over the last 10–15 years as little or no new infrastructure was constructed and much of the existing infrastructure deteriorated through inadequate provision for maintenance. Yet these are also cities with the greatest need to improve the quality and coverage of infrastructure and services both to attract new investment and to improve living conditions for their population. But effective demand may be low, the resources available to city and municipal authorities very inadequate (see Chapter 5) and there is a lack of technical and institutional experience in funding, constructing, operating and maintaining infrastructure. In addition, most of the countries in the South that have undergone economic problems during the last 10–15 years also underwent structural adjustment that was often accompanied by a marked deterioration in infrastructure and a cut in provision for its maintenance.[6] Capital spending on investment is often among the first items to be cut with operations and maintenance not far behind. Despite the long-term economic costs of doing so and the substantial employment benefits from well-organized labour-based approaches, this is less costly politically than cutting incomes or public employment.[7]

This chapter begins by describing the inadequate scale and nature of investment in water supply, sanitation and solid-waste collection and management in Africa, Asia and Latin America. It is in these regions that the deficits in terms of people unserved or inadequately served are concentrated. It then discusses transport and communications in both the North and the South and describes how few wealthy or rapidly growing

...he growth in the num-... most cities in both ..., traffic congestion has become a major ... cost, while attempts to resolve it that are based on increasing provision for private automobiles bring a large range of social and environmental costs. The inadequate investments in infrastructure that characterize most countries in the South during the last few decades and the desire by many governments in the North to reduce public expenditure have led to many initiatives to encourage private-sector investment but these will be described in later chapters.

8.2 Water Supply[8]

Despite considerable progress in improving or extending water supplies in the South during the International Drinking Water Supply and Sanitation Decade that began in 1980, by the end of the decade, 245 million urban dwellers and over one billion rural dwellers still had no alternative but to use contaminated water or water whose quality is not assured. Although there has been a considerable increase in the number of people with access to safe drinking water during the early 1990s, the latest estimates (for 1994) suggest the number without suitable water services had increased to about 280 million for urban dwellers while the number of unserved rural dwellers had been reduced to 835 million.[9]

'Access to piped water supplies' does not necessarily mean adequate or safe supplies. For instance, in 1990, close to half the urban population in the South and more than 90 per cent of its rural population still lacked a water supply piped into their home. The quantity of water available to a household and the price that has to be paid can be as important to a family's health as its quality.[10] Thus, while those served by public standpipes, boreholes with handpumps and protected dug wells may have access to uncontaminated water, the difficulties in getting access to it and the distance that the water has to be carried often limit water use so the full health benefits are not enjoyed.

This means that much less was achieved during the 1980s than had been hoped. One of the most important achievements of Habitat I, the first UN Conference on Human Settlements in 1976 had been to highlight the importance of improving water supply and sanitation. This enthusiasm among government representatives and international agencies led finally to the United Nations General Assembly proclaiming the period 1981–90 the International Drinking Water Supply and Sanitation Decade. The primary goal was to ensure full access to water supply and sanitation to all inhabitants of the South by 1990.[11] But in 1990, at least 30 per cent lacked access to safe water and at least 40 per cent were without adequate sanitation.[12] In addition, unless governments and international agencies substantially change their approach and their commitment, the numbers lacking access to safe water and adequate sanitation will grow rapidly during the 1990s.[13]

For urban areas in the South, an assessment in 1991 suggested that around half the population had water piped into their homes while around a quarter were supplied through less convenient means—public standpipes, yard taps, protected dug wells and boreholes/handpumps.[14] The remaining 350 million or so urban dwellers did not have a safe, protected water supply. They usually relied on one of two sources: water from streams or other surface sources that in urban areas are often little more than open sewers; or water purchased from vendors whose quality is not guaranteed—often at prices per litre which are between 4 and 100 times the amount paid by richer households for publicly provided piped water.[15] For instance, pavement dwellers in central Bombay pay twenty times more for water per litre than the municipal rate charged to other residents of the city.[16] Water-vendors probably serve 20 or more per cent of the South's urban population;[17] Box 8.1 illustrates how much those so served often have to pay.

BOX 8.1

Differentials in the cost of water (ratio of price charged by water vendors to prices charged by the public utility)

City	Price ratio of water from private vendors:public utility
Abidjan	5:1
Dhaka	12:1 to 25:1
Istanbul	10:1
Kampala	4:1 to 9:1
Karachi	28:1 to 83:1
Lagos	4:1 to 10:1
Lima	17:1
Lomé	7:1 to 10:1
Nairobi	7:1 to 11:1
Port-au-Prince	17:1 to 100:1
Surabaya	20:1 to 60:1
Tegucigalpa	16:1 to 34:1

Source: World Bank, *World Development Report 1988*, Oxford University Press, Oxford, 1988, 146.

The 1991 assessment found that in rural areas, most households with 'safe' water supplies depended on boreholes and handpumps or protected dug wells; these were the water sources on which over a third of the rural population in the

South relied. Only 10 per cent had water piped into their homes with another 10 per cent served by yard taps or public standpipes. Around a billion people, nearly two-fifths of the total rural population, had no safe water source or at least a water source where some attempt was made to ensure that it was uncontaminated and of reasonable quality. Figure 8.1 shows the number of people with access to functioning, safe water supply in 1991 by region, and the form in which the water was provided.

In Africa, in this year, over half the population was not served with safe drinking water and of those who were served, only a small proportion had a house connection (see Figure 8.1). Most relied on one of three sources: public standpipes, boreholes/handpumps and protected dug wells. Of Africa's 440 million rural inhabitants in 1991, less than 15 million had water piped to their homes. Most of the house connections were in urban areas but only one in three urban dwellers in Africa had water piped to their home. Close to

half of the urban population served with safe drinking water did not have house connections; around 32 million relied on public standpipes while 15 million had taps in the yard with the rest relying on some other source.

For Asia and the Pacific, around a quarter of the population lacked safe water in 1991, although the size of the region's population still meant that around 800 million people lacked access to safe water (see Figure 8.1). Less than a quarter of this region's total population had water piped into the home; boreholes with handpumps, protected dug wells and public standpipes provide water for around half the population that had safe water supplies. The rural population especially relied on borehole/handpumps and protected dug wells, although rainwater collection and public standpipes each supplied around 100 million people. For the urban population with provision for safe water, around two-thirds had house connections with around a fifth relying on public standpipes.

Within Latin America and the Caribbean, a much higher proportion of the population had house connections for water. However, close to 30 per cent of the population still lacked safe water. In urban areas most of the people with safe water had house connections; it was the only region in the South where this was the case. In rural areas, most of the people with safe water were supplied by boreholes/handpumps or protected dug wells.

Table 8.1 shows the increase in the proportion of the population with access to water and sanitation between 1975 and 1990 for low-income and middle-income countries. The figures for 1990 still suggest that more than a third of the population in low-income countries and a quarter of the population in middle-income countries lacked access to water. When broken down by urban and rural areas, more than 80 per cent of the urban population and close to 60 per cent of the rural population was reported to have access to water supply in 1990. Although most of the population in high-income countries are covered, none the less, in the second half of the 1980s, around 20 million people within the European Union lived in a dwelling without a water closet, while around 30 million lived in a dwelling without a bathroom or shower.[18]

However, as the United Nations organizations who are responsible for collecting this data state,[19] the statistics given for the proportion of the world's population with safe drinking water are exaggerated. This is for two reasons. The first relates to the definitions used; what is officially considered by governments as an 'adequate' amount of safe drinking water and at a 'convenient distance' from the user's dwelling is often too little water at too great a distance to allow

FIGURE 8.1
The number of people with access to a functioning, safe water supply in 1991

Source: Water Supply and Sanitation Collaborative Council, *Water Supply and Sanitation Sector Monitoring Report 1993*, World Health Organization and UNICEF, 1993

Africa

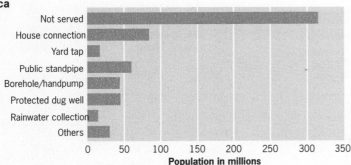

Asia

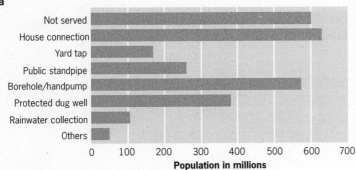

Latin America and the Caribbean

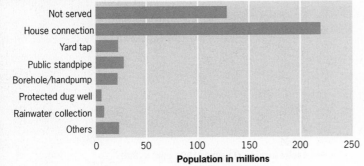

TABLE 8.1 The expansion in water supply and sanitation, 1975–1990 (percentage of population with access)

	Coverage in low-income countries		Coverage in middle-income countries		Coverage in high-income countries
	1975	**1990**	**1975**	**1990**	**1990**
Water	40	62	54	74	95+
Sanitation	23	42	44	68	95+

Source: World Bank, *World Development Report 1994; Infrastructure for Development*, Oxford University Press, Oxford and New York, 1994.

sufficient for washing, laundry, personal hygiene and house cleaning. The second is a tendency for governments to exaggerate the proportion of the population with safe drinking water.[20]

The Housing Indicators Programme collected statistics on the proportion of dwelling units with a water connection in the plot they occupy for 52 cities. This is a more reliable indicator of adequate and convenient water supply than water available at a 'convenient distance'. The proportion of dwellings with water piped to the plot varied from 30–50 per cent for the cities with the worst performance (and all cities with under 50 per cent were in sub-Saharan Africa and were among the poorest countries) to 95–100 per cent for cities in countries with per capita incomes that exceeded $10,000. Given that such a high proportion of these cities are national capitals and the largest and most prosperous cities within their countries, the proportion of their populations with water piped to the house plot are likely to be untypically high when compared to other urban centres within the same country. Figure 8.2 maps the proportion of these cities' population with a water connection to their plot with the per capita income of the country in 1991.

Figure 8.2 shows that in general, the higher the per capita income of the country, the higher the proportion of the city's population with water piped to their plot. It also shows that some cities have a much higher proportion of their population with water piped to their plot, relative to their country's per capita income while others have a much lower proportion. For instance, Caracas has a low proportion, relative to the per capita income of the country. Among cities in low-income coun-

FIGURE 8.2
The proportion of a city's population with water piped to the plot

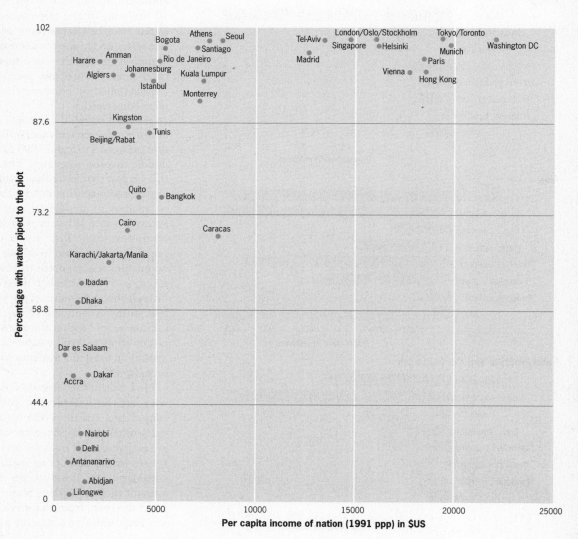

BOX 8.2
Examples of the inadequacies in provision for water supply in cities

Dar es Salaam (Tanzania): From a survey of 660 households drawn from all income levels in 1986/87, 47 per cent had no piped water supply either inside or immediately outside their houses while 32 per cent had a shared piped water supply. Of the households without piped water, 67 per cent buy water from neighbours while 26 per cent draw water from public water kiosks or standpipes. Only 7.1 per cent buy water from water-sellers. Average water consumption per person is only 23.6 litres a day.

Khartoum (the Sudan): The water supply system is working beyond its design capacity while demand continues to rise. The coverage is poor, with low-income groups in squatter settlements suffering the cost of all through paying the most for water, often bought from vendors. Breakdown and cuts in the supply system are common.

Kinshasa (Zaire): Around half the urban population (some 1.5 million people) are not served by a piped water network. High-income areas are often 100 per cent connected while many other areas have 20–30 per cent of houses connected—essentially those along the main roads. The sale of water flourishes in areas far from the network—in these areas water is usually obtained from wells, the river or deep wells.

Calcutta (India): With a total population of around 10 million, some 3 million people live in 'bustees' and refugee settlements which lack potable water, endure serious annual flooding and have no systematic means of disposing of refuse or human wastes. Some 2.5 million others live in similarly blighted and unserviced areas. Piped water is only available in the central city and parts of some other municipalities.

Faisalabad (Pakistan): Over half of the population have no piped water and most of those that do not have piped water have to rely on hand-pumps with water of poor quality.

Karachi (Pakistan): In 1988, 66.6 per cent of households had piped water; among the *katchi abadis*, only 50.3 per cent had piped water—perhaps not surprisingly, only 36 per cent of the housing in the *katchi abadis* inhabited by the lowest income quintile had piped water.

Jakarta (Indonesia): Less than a third of the population have direct connections to a piped water system; around 30 per cent depend solely on water vendors whose prices per litre of water are up to fifty times that paid by households served by the municipal water company. Over a third of the population rely on shallow wells (most of which are contaminated), deep wells or nearby river water. Over half of all dwellings have no indoor plumbing and much of the population have to use drainage canals for bathing, laundry and defecation.

Madras (India): Only 2 million of the 3.7 million residential consumers within service area of the local water supply and sewerage board are connected to the system. On average, they receive some 36 litres per capita day per day. The rest within the service area must use public taps which serve about 240 persons per tap. Another million consumers outside the service area must rely on wells—but supplies are inadequate too because of falling groundwater levels.

Sources: See note. [24]

tries, the proportion of dwellings with water piped to their plot varies from 86 per cent in Beijing to 31 (Lilongwe), 36 (Antananarivo), 38 (Delhi) and 40 (Nairobi). Among cities in the other income ranges, Harare, Bogotá and Amman have a high proportion of households with piped water to their plot, relative to their country's per capita income with Abidjan and Dakar having a low proportion. In regional terms, cities in sub-Saharan Africa are the worst served—although these are also the cities whose population growth rates have generally been much higher than in Asia or Latin America in recent decades.

Some caution is needed in reading too much into these statistics since a city's performance would also depend on the reliability and quality of the water. In addition, for each city, the proportion of the population with water piped to their plots will also depend on what boundaries were used to define the city. City boundaries that exclude a significant proportion of the peripheral settlements can often mean statistics that appear to show an impressive performance in infrastructure and service provision, as it is in the peripheral settlements that infrastructure and services are most lacking.

Box 8.2 gives some summaries of the inadequacy in water supply provision in cities for which there are recent reports. The extent of the inadequacies are perhaps surprising, given that most of these cities are either capitals or among the most prosperous cities in their countries. Where data is available for a range of urban centres within a country, the proportion of the population with piped supplies is generally much lower in smaller urban centres. For instance, in Argentina, the smaller the urban centre, the higher the proportion of households lacking piped water (and connection to sewers).[21] In Bolivia, a much higher proportion of the populations of the two largest and most prosperous cities—La Paz and Santa Cruz—have safe water than in Tarija and Sucre where close to half the population lacked provision for water supply.[22] However, this is not always so; for instance, in Ecuador in 1988, many of medium-sized cities in the *Sierra* had a higher percentage of houses with piped water (and sewerage) than Quito, the largest city in this region (and also the national capital) while in the coastal area, several medium-sized cities had a higher percent of houses with water than Guayaquil, Ecuador's largest city although all had a lower proportion of houses with sewerage.[23]

The fact that official statistics are often optimistic on the extent of progress in improving water supplies during the 1980s should not detract from the considerable achievements of many governments in improving water supplies. For instance, it is clear that major progress has been made in Brazil in improving the provision of water supply (and sanitation) during the late 1970s and the 1980s.[25] In Sao Paulo, for instance, although there is still a need to improve the quality and reliability of the water supply, especially for low-income groups, the public water supply network reaches some 95 per cent of all households.[26] Similarly, in Chile, the proportion of the urban population with piped water grew from 78 per cent in 1976 to 98 per cent in 1987 although here too, the coverage for the lowest income groups are also particularly low.[27]

8.3 Sanitation

Official statistics for 1991 suggest that at least a third of the South's urban population and more than half its rural population have no hygienic means of disposing of excreta[28] and an even greater number lack adequate means to dispose of waste waters.[29] Close to 2 billion people still lacked provision for sanitation in 1991 and for most of those with provision, the simple pit latrine was still the most common method of excreta disposal. Of those that had provision for sanitation, most (1 billion) had a simple latrine; only some 550 million had a house connected to a public sewer with around 220 million having a septic tank system. Estimates for 1994 suggest that the number of people lacking adequate sanitation in the South had increased considerably during the early 1990s, to 588 million in urban areas and 2.28 billion in rural areas, up from 452 million and 2.15 billion respectively in 1990.[30] Projections to the year 2000 show that if the present rates of provision for sanitation are maintained, the number of people without adequate sanitation will total 3.31 billion, that is more than half the world's population. This will include 846 million urban dwellers and 2.5 million rural dwellers; most will be in Asia.[31]

There are three obvious criteria by which to judge provision for sanitation. The first is convenience and hygiene for the user; people need a toilet that, if not in their home, is at least very close and available. The second is the extent to which human contact with the excreta can be avoided. The third is the extent to which the facility is easily maintained. Different kinds of provision can meet these criteria, depending on the size, nature and density of the settlement. Thus, a simple pit latrine in a small rural settlement may meet all three criteria—but it rarely does in cities.

Figure 8.3 shows the number of people with provision for sanitation in 1991 by region, and the form of the provision. In Africa, over half of the population had no provision for sanitation in this year. For Africa's rural population, most of those with provision for sanitation had a simple latrine. The simple latrine was also still among the most widely used forms of provision for those with sanitation in urban areas. In 1991, around 20 per cent of Africa's urban population used simple latrines, around 20 per cent had homes connected to public sewers and around 20 per cent were connected to septic tank systems.[32]

In Asia, in this same year, close to half the population, a total of 1.5 billion people, did not have provision for sanitation; of those that did, the majority relied on simple latrines (see Figure 8.3). The vast majority of the rural population with provision for sanitation had simple latrines; less than 100 million had the safer pour-flush latrines and less than 50 million had ventilated improved pit latrines. Ten per cent of the region's population was connected to public sewers; virtually all such connections were in urban areas although overall, only a third of the region's urban population was connected to public sewers. Most of the rest of the urban population with provision for sanitation had septic tanks or pour-flush latrines.

Within Latin America and the Caribbean, a much higher proportion of the population had provision for sanitation in 1991. Within urban areas, around three-fifths of the population had house connections to public sewer systems although small-bore sewers and septic tanks each served around 15 million people. In rural areas, most of the people with sanitation used simple latrines. However, around a quarter of the urban population and more than three-fifths of the rural population lacked provision for sanitation.

As with water supply, official figures suggest a considerable improvement in the proportion of the population with access to sanitation between 1975 and 1990—see Table 8.1—although the figures for 1990 still suggest nearly three-fifths of the population in low-income countries and close to a third in middle-income countries lacked access to sanitation. When broken down by urban and rural areas, more than 70 per cent of the urban population and about 40 per cent of the rural population were reported as having access to sanitation. However, as with official figures for water supply, official statistics on provision for sanitation in many nations are also known to overstate the proportion of people with provision that is convenient, accessible and adequate from a health perspective.[33]

The problems with sanitation are often most apparent in urban centres where the size and density of settlements make defecation outside difficult or impossible—or for women, often dangerous. There are also the obvious conflicts—as those living or working in and around areas where many defecate in the open object to them doing so.[34] High concentrations of people also make the cheaper and easier sanitation solutions such as simple latrines less appropriate. In high-density residential areas, it is generally only sewers or toilets connected to septic tanks that can ensure adequate provision for sanitation. Most cities in Africa and many in Asia have no sewers at all.[35] This is not only the smaller cities; many major cities with a million or more inhabitants have no sewers. Most of their inhabitants

Africa

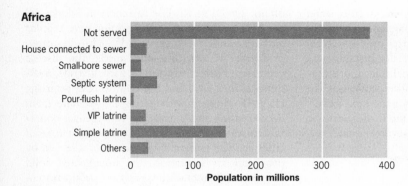

Asia

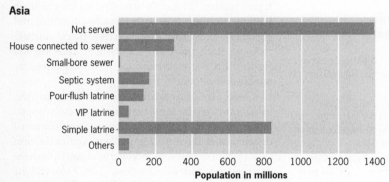

Latin America and the Caribbean

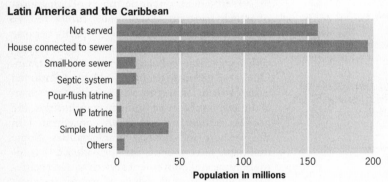

FIGURE 8.3

The number of people with provision for sanitation in 1991

Source: Water Supply and Sanitation Collaborative Council, *Water Supply and Sanitation Sector Monitoring Report, 1993,* World Health Organization and UNICEF, 1993, 57 pages.

also lack connection to septic tanks. Most human excrement and waste water ends up in rivers, streams, canals, gullies and ditches, untreated. Where there are sewers, rarely do they serve more than a small proportion of the population—typically they are located in the richer residential, government and commercial areas.

Box 8.3 gives some examples of the extent of provision for sanitation in selected cities. These are generally cities which are either capitals or if not capitals among the largest and most prosperous cities within their nations. The provision for sanitation in these is likely to be much better than in most smaller cities and market towns.

8.4 Solid-Waste Collection

Most city governments are facing mounting problems with the collection and disposal of solid wastes. In high-income countries, the problems usually centre on the difficulties (and high costs)

Examples of cities with inadequate provision for sanitation

Dar es Salaam (Tanzania): From a survey of 660 households drawn from all income levels in 1986/7, 89 per cent had simple pit latrines. Most households have to share sanitary facilities. Overflowing latrines are a serious problem, especially in the rainy season and provision to empty septic tanks or latrines is very inadequate.

Khartoum (the Sudan): The municipal sewage system serves only about 5 per cent of the Khartoum urban area. Even that system is susceptible to breakdowns when waste is discharged either directly into the river or onto open land. Most of the population rely on pit latrines while a significant proportion of the population has no toilet facility at all.

Calcutta (India): The sewage system is limited to only a third of the area in the urban core. Poor maintenance of open drains and periodic clogging of the system have made flooding an annual feature.

Faisalabad (Pakistan): Two-thirds of the population have no connection to sewers and only 3.2 per cent had connection to a septic tank. The sewer system was built for a population of 300,000 but the city now has more than 2 million inhabitants.

Karachi (Pakistan): 85 per cent of the houses in the planned areas are estimated to have sanitation but only 12 per cent in the *katchi abadis* where most of the population lives.

Jakarta (Indonesia): The city has no central waterborne sewage system. Septic tanks serve about 68 per cent of the population with 17 per cent relying on pit latrines or toilets which discharge directly into ditches or drains, 6 per cent using public toilets (generally with septic tanks) and about 9 per cent with no formal toilet facilities.

Madras (India): The sewage system serves 31 per cent of the metropolitan population.

Kingston (Jamaica): Only 18 per cent of the population are connected to sewers while 27 per cent have soak away pits, 47 per cent use pit latrines and 8 per cent report no sanitary facilities at all. A significant percentage of the population (especially those in low-income communities) defecate in open lots, abandoned buildings or into plastic bags that are then thrown into gullies. The sewage system in the central city area is old and in need of repair. There are also frequent blockages as solid waste is disposed of, down the manholes.

Sources: See note.[36]

of disposing of the large quantities of wastes generated by households and businesses. In lower-income countries, the problems are more to do with collection. In most cities in the South, between a third and half of the solid wastes generated within urban centres remains uncollected and such wastes generally accumulate on open spaces, wasteland and streets and bring with them serious health and environmental problems.[37] These wastes generally add greatly to water pollution, when it rains, as much of this waste is organic matter and ends up swept into water bodies. In many of the urban centres in the lowest-income countries, perhaps only 10–20 per cent of solid waste is collected. For instance, in a survey of 34 municipalities in India, more than three-fifths of the municipalities collected less than 40 per cent of the wastes generated daily.[38] Box 8.4 includes examples of the inadequacies in garbage collection services in several cities.

BOX 8.4

Examples of cities with inadequate provision for solid-waste collection and disposal

Dar es Salaam: Some two-thirds of all solid wastes from both residential areas and from commercial enterprises remains uncollected.

Kinshasa: The collection of household waste is only undertaken in a few residential areas. In the rest of the city, household waste is put out on the road, on illegal dumps or in storm-water drains or buried on open sites.

Jakarta: Around 40 per cent of the solid wastes generated within Jakarta are not collected; much of it ends up in canals and rivers and along the roadside where it clogs drainage channels and causes extensive flooding during the rainy season.

Karachi: Only two-fifths of the solid waste produced by households in the city is being collected and transported to dump sites.

Faisalabad: The estimated total daily production of solid waste in 1985 was 1,000 tonnes of which less than 50 per cent was collected by the Faisalabad H. C.

Sources: See note.[39]

Among many municipalities in the South, solid-waste collection and management often consumes as much as 20–40 per cent of municipal revenues and it often suffers more than other municipal services when budget allocations and cuts are made.[40] The agencies responsible for the collection and disposal of household wastes are often understaffed and underfunded—and since virtually all have to use collection trucks that are imported, there are often serious problems with collection trucks out of use because of a lack of spare parts. Too little attention to servicing and maintenance adds to this problem. One illustration of this is from Tanzania where

Virtually all urban authorities . . . have a totally inadequate number of refuse collection vehicles, as compared to the daily amount of refuse produced in urban areas. The refuse collection capacity is low partly because most of the vehicles are either in poor mechanical condition or are not working at all. As a result . . . urban authorities can only collect a small amount (24 per cent) of the estimated refuse produced each day.[41]

The poorest areas of any city are generally the worst served by garbage-collection service—

or not served at all. For instance, in Dhaka, 90 per cent of the 'slum' areas do not have regular garbage collection services.[42] The resulting problems are obvious—the smells, the disease vectors and pests attracted by garbage (rats, mosquitoes, flies etc.) and the overflowing drainage channels clogged with garbage. Leachate from decomposing and putrefying garbage can contaminate water sources.[43] Since the poorest areas of cities are also generally the ones worst served by provision for sanitation, the uncollected solid wastes usually include a significant proportion of faecal matter. The risks are obvious for children playing on open sites with faecally contaminated garbage—and also for waste-pickers sorting through such garbage.[44] Flies and cockroaches feeding on such garbage can also subsequently contaminate food.[45]

These problems are especially serious for the inhabitants of the larger and most densely populated informal or illegal settlements or tenement districts that have no regular garbage collection service since there is nowhere close-by where such wastes can be dumped. The informal or illegal settlements on the periphery of cities, most of which have no paved roads, rarely receive regular waste-collection services—partly because the roads are so poor that it is difficult or impossible for garbage-collection trucks to enter them. One also returns to the problem mentioned earlier that in large cities where service provision is the responsibility of municipal authorities, the poorest settlements are often concentrated in the weakest and poorest municipalities. Some municipal governments may provide a less comprehensive and convenient service to such settlements in an effort to reduce costs—for instance, communal pick-up points or communal garbage skips. But the further away these are from the household, the less frequently people use them and the more garbage is dropped on the way to them.[46] In addition, collections from such communal points are often irregular and overflowing skips or dumps become a serious health hazard in themselves and also discourage households from using them.

There are also the environmental problems caused by residents who try to reduce their own garbage problems—for instance by burning it. A study of household-level environmental problems in Jakarta in 1991 found that the occurrence of respiratory diseases in children and their mothers was correlated to a problem with uncollected garbage and this may be because households with no collection services burn their garbage.[47]

As countries become wealthier and local authorities become more competent, the proportion of solid wastes collected and the proportion of households served with a regular collection generally rises. Garbage-collection problems are less extreme in most of the middle-income countries in Asia and Latin America where a higher proportion of the urban populations have regular collections for their household wastes. For instance, in Sao Paulo City, 95 per cent of households have a regular garbage-collection service[48]—although the proportion of the population served in many of the outer municipalities of the wider metropolitan region is lower.[49] In Bangkok City, by 1990, 80 per cent of the solid wastes generated were being collected.[50] In the world's wealthiest countries, regular garbage-collection services—like piped water and connection to main sewers—are even extended to much of the rural population.

The volume of waste per person also tends to rise with per capita incomes, so the authorities in the larger and more prosperous cities are faced with very large waste volumes. This is especially so in cities with a rapid growth in prosperity since this generally coincides with a rapid growth in population and a growth in the volume of wastes generated per person—and there is usually a considerable backlog of people who are not served by garbage-collection services that the authorities have to address. Thus, the volume of wastes that the municipal authority should collect may be growing three to four times more rapidly than the growth in population. As the city area expands, so too does the distance that the wastes must be carried before disposal and this adds greatly to disposal costs. In Bangkok, the transport of refuse to one of the present dump sites is responsible for 70 per cent of the total waste-management opera-

tional budget; in Manila, with the closing of the 'Smoky Mountain' dump site, the budget of the Metro Manila Authority responsible for waste management had to be increased by around 30 per cent because of increased haulage costs.[51] The more heavily populated the city and its wider region, the more difficult it becomes to find sites for solid-waste disposal—not least because no one wants solid-waste disposal sites and the large traffic in heavy lorries they imply located close to their homes.

Table 8.2 shows how the quantity and composition of municipal wastes vary, depending on the per capita income of the country. In low-income countries, average municipal waste levels per person per year can be as low as 100 kg; in high-income countries they can be close to 1,000 kg although in most wealthy European countries, they average between 300 and 500.[52] In a recent study of five Asian cities (Karachi, Manila, Kanpur, Bangkok and Jakarta), the average for domestic solid waste was 216 kg per person per year.[53] Per capita figures tend to rise with income, although there is a considerable range of per capita figures among the wealthiest countries. For instance, the per capita figures for Sweden and France are only 40 per cent that of the United States and less than half those of Canada and Australia.[54] The limited data that is available on municipal refuse volumes per person from cities in the South also suggests considerable variation for cities with comparable levels of per capita income—although here too, this may reflect different production bases (for instance a heavily industrialized city against an important administrative and commercial city) or different methods for measuring municipal wastes which may or may not include industrial wastes or construction wastes. For instance, in Karachi, different sources give the waste generation per person per year as only 128 kg per person per year or as 365 kg per person per year—with the latter figure including construction wastes and street-sweeping.[55]

The figures in Table 8.2 are for municipal wastes and so include not only domestic wastes but also commercial and institutional refuse, street-sweepings and construction and demolition debris. They may also include industrial wastes. Residential wastes generally account for between 60 and 80 per cent of total solid wastes in cities in the South—but generally rather less in the North. For instance, in the Netherlands in 1986, household waste accounted for only a fifth of total solid wastes—with construction and demolition wastes accounting for 32 per cent, industrial wastes for 23 per cent and wastes from streets, markets, offices and shops accounting for most of the rest.[56] In the USA, industrial refuse is not considered as part of municipal refuse and its quantity is about 3 times that of municipal refuse.[57]

TABLE 8.2 Municipal wastes—quantities and characteristics for low-, middle- and high-income countries

	Low-income countries	Middle-income countries	High-income countries
Waste generation (kg per person per year)	100–220	180–330	300–1,000
Moisture content (% net weight at the point of generation)	40–80	40–60	20–40
Composition (% by wet weight)			
Paper	1 to 10	15 to 40	15 to 50
Glass, ceramics	1 to 10	1 to 10	4 to 12
Metals	1 to 5	1 to 5	3 to 13
Plastics	1 to 5	2 to 6	2 to 10
Leather, rubber	1 to 5	-	-
Wood, bones, straw	1 to 5	-	-
Textiles	1 to 5	2 to 10	2 to 10
Vegetables/putrescible	40 to 85	20 to 65	20 to 50
Miscellaneous inerts	1 to 40	1 to 30	1 to 20

Source: Drawn from Cointreau, Sandra, *Environmental Management of Urban Solid Waste in Developing Countries*, Urban Development Technical Paper No 5, The World Bank, Washington DC, 1982. The ranges of waste generation in low- and high-income countries have been extended, reflecting new data on municipal waste generation in different cities.

A table similar to Table 8.2 could also be constructed for any city to contrast the differences in the scale and composition of the wastes of high-, middle- and low-income households. Many high-income households in cities in Africa, Asia and Latin America may have waste levels per person similar to those in Europe and North America; it is only the fact that they represent a smaller proportion of the city population that keeps down city averages. For instance, in the municipality of Olinda in Brazil the inhabitants of an illegal settlement (*favela*) produce only 100 kilograms per person per year while the middle- and higher-income groups produce between 180 and 550.[58] Part of the reason is that low-income households are more inclined to separate out and reuse or sell paper, tins, glass containers and other wastes. Waste-pickers particularly value domestic waste from middle- or upper-income residential areas because it has far more material that can be recovered and sold. Another illustration of the diversity within nations is provided by figures for urban areas in Argentina—where the average level of solid-waste production per person per year is around 240 kg but in Buenos Aires it is 400 kg.[59] If figures were available for waste levels per person per year by income group in Buenos Aires, very considerable differences are likely.

However, this view of solid-waste collection systems that are inadequate or breaking down or facing serious cost problems misses the large and complex 'waste economy' that exists in most cities in the South. The reclamation and reuse of materials may be so intensive that only a small proportion of the solid wastes generated may need to be disposed of. For instance, in Bangalore, one of India's largest and most prosperous cities (with more than 4 million inhabitants within the municipality), the municipal corporation only has to dispose of around 335 tonnes of solid wastes a day because around 2,700 are recycled or reused—see Box 8.5. Thus, the annual average solid waste generation per person in Bangalore may be around 270 kilograms but the amount that is unused and has to be disposed of is around 30 kilograms.

The 'waste economy' also provides a livelihood for tens of thousands of people in many large cities. The scale and nature of this 'waste economy' is now much better understood.[60] Box 8.5 describes its dimensions in Bangalore in India where over 40,000 people earn their living from waste recovery and recycling. Many other Asian cities have 'extensive "waste economies", structured through itinerant waste buyers, waste pickers, small waste shops, second hand markets, dealers, transporters and a range of recycling industries.'[61] In Calcutta, around 40,000 people make a living from waste-picking and many

thousands more from farming or fishing that are based on the solid (composted) or liquid wastes from the city.[62] In Manila, some 30,000 people are involved in informal waste recycling.[63] This large and complex 'waste economy' is not restricted to Asia; in Bogotá (Colombia), between 30,000 and 50,000 people have the reclamation and recycling of waste as their principal income-earning activity[64] while in Cairo (Egypt), some 20,000 people rely on collecting and sorting waste for their livelihood.[65] Chapter 12 discusses the integration of those involved in the waste economy into official solid-waste management systems so cities can retain the immense ecological and economic advantages that their operations provide while also improving solid-waste collection, especially to the poorer and more peripheral settlements, and reducing health risks and improving incomes for the lower-income groups engaged in the waste economy.

8.5 Transport*

Introduction

The last 10–15 years brought a continuing rise in the number of motorized road vehicles worldwide and continued growth in air traffic. For instance, road traffic in the European Union grew by 70 per cent between 1970 and 1985 and is expected to increase by a further 50 per cent between 1985 and 2000.[66] The growth in automobile use and in air travel has been a major factor in growing levels of fossil fuel use and in greenhouse-gas emissions. In most nations in the North, by the early 1990s, transport accounts for around 30 per cent of total energy consumption—although with considerable variation between countries. For instance, in the United States, it accounted for 37 per cent while in Japan it was 27 per cent and in the Netherlands 22 per cent;[67] since all three are among the world's wealthiest nations, it is clear that the variation is not simply due to differences in per capita income. The average share in the South was estimated at 22 per cent in 1985,[68] although there are also large variations between countries—for instance, in Mexico in the early 1990s, transport represented 35 per cent of total energy consumption.[69] Virtually all motorized transport uses oil-based fuels and most of this consumption is for road vehicles.

Nearly all cities have been transformed by motorized road vehicles. This is obvious in cities

---

* This section draws on Newman, Peter, *Transport And Cities: Resolving The Dilemma Of Automobile Dependence*, Background Paper for the Global Report on Human Settlements, 1995.

BOX 8.5
The scale and nature of the waste economy in Bangalore, India

In Bangalore, India's sixth largest city (with 4.1 million inhabitants within the municipality), between 40,000 and 50,000 people make a living by waste recovery or recycling. This represents between 1.6 and 2.0 per cent of the workforce. The waste economy also means that Bangalore recovers and recycles most of the solid wastes that are generated.

The recovery and trading network consists of: c.25,000 waste-pickers (predominantly women and children); 3,000–4,000 itinerant waste-buyers of newspapers, plastics, glass, metals, clothes and other materials; c.800 small dealers, 50 medium-size dealers and 50 wholesalers in wastes; a great variety of enterprises using recycling materials including two glass- and four paper-recycling plants, eight aluminium recyclers, 350–500 plastic factories using waste materials and an uncounted number of small recycling enterprises; householders, household servants and around 7,600 municipal street-sweeping and garbage-collection workers, shop cleaners and office caretakers; piggery and poultry workers who collect food wastes from hotels and institutions; and farmers who collect compost from the garbage dumps or persuade garbage truck drivers to deliver wastes direct to their farms

Street pickers are estimated to retrieve about 15 per cent of wastes put out on the streets and from over 12,000 street bins—amounting to perhaps 300 tonnes of materials per day within the city. Municipal collectors and sweepers are estimated to take out 37 tonnes per day, in addition to the wastes removed by pickers. Itinerant buyers recover about 40 kg of material per day and this implies a recovery of between 400,000 and 500,000 tonnes of materials per year. Middle- and lower middle-income households are their main residential customers although they also buy wastes from offices and shops. High-income households with their own motor vehicles often store their own waste materials such as newspapers and plastics and take them directly to a dealer or even a wholesaler although they will sell old clothes to itinerant buyers.

The fact that so much material is recovered from wastes by residents and shopkeepers or by waste-pickers allows the remaining wastes that are largely composed of organic wastes to be taken directly to farms and for natural composting to take place on garbage dumps. At one dump in 1990 about 15 truck-loads (each with around five tonnes of fresh wastes) are delivered per day and about 12 farmers' truck-loads of compost are removed. There is also a semi-mechanical compost plant that processes 50–100 tones of market wastes per day, producing about 20 tonnes of compost. About 210 tonnes of cow dung is collected each day from the roads for use as fuel by low-income people. A considerable amount of kitchen wastes, leaves, and tree trimmings are eaten by stray dogs, cows and pigs from street bins, amounting to perhaps 5 per cent by weight of garbage put in bins. Recently, some citizen groups have been experimenting with decentralized composting and vermicomposting so a small amount of further household organic waste is being recycled.

No study has been done of industrial wastes (metals, wiring, batteries, plastics, rubber, leather scraps etc.) diverted by waste-exchange or trading, nor of bones sent to fertilizer factories and food wastes used by pig and poultry farms. None of the major industrial recyclables reach the dumps. Food wastes generated by restaurants and hotels are traded. Construction wastes are used for filling low-lying land.

Largely due to these varied activities of recovery and reuse, only about 335 tonnes of solid waste per day is handled by the corporation.

Although not all Indian cities have the capacity to recover and recycle as thoroughly as Bangalore, this study demonstrates that where convenient markets exist, traditions of separation and informal-waste trading thrive. It suggests that frugal habits are well established across a spectrum of household classes and that financial incentives reinforce these habits in lower-income groups, shops and factories, Such waste-reducing practices are found in other Third World countries, although the proportions of materials taken by itinerant waste-buyers and waste-pickers and the patterns of control in the trade may vary.

Sources: Furedy, Christine, 'Socio-environmental initiatives in solid waste management in Southern cities; developing international comparisons', in M. Huysman, B. Raman and A. Rosario (eds.), *Proceedings of the Workshop on Linkages in Urban Solid Waste Management*, Karnataka State Council for Science and Technology, Bangalore, 1994; and Huysman, Marijk, 'The position of women-waste pickers in Bangalore', in Ida Baud and Hans Schenk (eds.), *Solid Waste Management: Bangalore*, Manohar, Delhi, 1994.

with high levels of automobile ownership but there are also many cities which still have relatively few passenger cars relative to their population but where the use of cars, trucks, buses and other forms of motorized vehicle has greatly increased the size of the urban area. In addition, most major cities throughout the world developed before the widespread use of automobiles[70] and were thus 'pedestrian cities' with small streets, high densities and a great mix of commercial and residential activities. All such city centres have difficulty coping with automobile traffic. Moreover, many cities have faced 'explosive' growth in the number of road vehicles—for instance, in Bangkok, the number of road vehicles grew more than sevenfold between 1970 and 1990.[71] Many of the Asian cities within the more prosperous economies are likely to have had a tripling or quadrupling in the number of passenger cars over the last 10–15 years. For instance, the number in Seoul more than doubled in just five years between 1980 and 1985 while the number in Karachi and Jakarta also grew very rapidly in this period.[72] This section reviews first the growth in the number of road vehicles in countries and in cities. Then it considers the costs and benefits of the increasing dependence on automobiles.

The number of road vehicles

The growth in the number of cars worldwide in recent decades has been far more rapid than the growth in the urban population. For instance, in 1950, there were around 53 million cars on the world's roads, three-quarters of them in the United States; by 1990, there were more than 400 million and another 100 million trucks, buses and commercial vehicles. Around one-third of these were in Europe, another third were in North America and the final third divided between the rest of the world.[73]

Although in Africa, Asia and Latin America, the number of road vehicles per person remains far below the level in Europe and North America, certain countries in these regions have had the most rapid growth in the number of road vehicles—and a few of the wealthiest countries in these regions have levels of car ownership comparable to those of Europe. Table 8.3 shows the number of passenger cars per 1000 inhabitants for selected countries. It reveals the very large contrasts between some of the world's poorest countries with 1 or 2 passenger cars per 1,000 inhabitants in 1985 and some of the wealthiest countries with 400 or more. In the United States, by 1985, there were more than one passenger car for every two persons; by 1991, several other countries had reached or were close to reaching this ratio—including Italy, Switzerland, Canada, Australia and New Zealand.[74]

This Table also shows how the number of passenger cars per person still remains relatively low in some of the most prosperous Asian nations. In 1985, Hong Kong had a tenth of the ratio of passenger cars to people of the wealthiest countries while Singapore had a fifth of this ratio—although these are unusual instances as both are essentially city-states with high population densities and with governments prepared to take highly effective economic and regulatory actions to control car populations. But this table also indicates that it is difficult to generalize the relationship between per capita income and the number of private automobiles per person. Japan and Denmark were among the world's most wealthy nations in 1985 but had much fewer passenger cars per 1,000 inhabitants than other nations with comparable per capita incomes. As will be described in more detail below, the number of passenger cars per person in any society is often influenced by factors such as the extent and quality of provision for alternatives to private automobiles and by the density of urban areas.

In many countries, the number of passenger cars per 1,000 inhabitants doubled between 1975 and 1985—for instance in Botswana, Mexico, Colombia and Ecuador. In Malaysia, Greece and Thailand, the numbers per person tripled between 1975 and 1987. But Table 8.3 also shows many countries with no increase in the number of passenger cars per 1,000 inhabitants and some such as Zambia and Burkina Faso with an overall decline.

The number of automobiles and other forms of transport in cities

The convenience of private automobiles for those able to afford them and the extent to which many developments in retailing (drive-in stores, hypermarkets, out-of-town shopping malls), in the concentrations of job opportunities and in new residential developments encourage (or necessitate) their use suggests that it may be difficult to shift car-users to other transport modes. An increasing reliance on private automobile use has been built into much of the urban landscape and this is not easily changed. In many cities in the North, a significant proportion of the population now live in low-density suburbs within which no public transport can operate cost-effectively[75] and in which at least two private cars per household are almost a necessity.[76] Even in a small, compact country such as Denmark where gasoline consumption per person was found to be relatively low in relation to per capita income in its major city,[77] each person (including children and the elderly) travel an average of 40 kilometres a day with this average projected to rise to 55 kilometres a day by the year 2010.[78] As one paper commented:

In the postwar era falling energy prices and rising car ownership have transformed cities, allowing the increased physical separation of activities and the progressive spread of urban hinterland at lower densities. The dispersal of employment, retailing and service facilities creates an equivalently dispersed pattern of trips that is anathema to public transport operation. Lower average densities mean a decline in pedestrian accessibility, longer trip lengths and reduced catchment populations for public transport routes. The result is increased car dependence, profligate energy use and global pollution.[79]

However, the extent to which a city's population has become dependent on the use of private automobiles varies greatly, even for cities where the inhabitants have comparable levels of income. A detailed study of thirty-two major cities in North America, Europe, Australia and Asia that looked at the extent of automobile dependence and the factors that helped explain this found that the cities could be divided into five categories of automobile dependence.[80] Most US and Australian cities were within categories 1 and 2 which have a high or very high automobile dependence and at most a minor role for public transport, walking and cycling. Most European cities fell into categories 3 and 4 which had moderate or low automobile dependence and an important role for public transport. However, Munich and Paris, both among the most prosperous cities in Europe, along with three of the most prosperous Asian cities (Tokyo, Singapore, Hong Kong) had a very low automobile dependence with public transport, walking and cycling more important than cars.

Figure 8.4 plots fuel consumption per person in these 32 cities against urban density (persons per hectare). It shows not only the very large differences in fuel consumption per person between cities but emphasizes the fact that wealthy, prosperous and desirable cities can have relatively low levels of fuel consumption per person. For instance, cities such as Vienna, Copenhagen and Stockholm are among the most wealthy and

TABLE 8.3 The number of passenger cars per 1,000 inhabitants; selected countries

	1975	1980	1985 or latest year	Comment
Africa				
Botswana	5	7	13	Numbers per person up 3fold, 1975–85
Burkina Faso	2	2	1	Overall decline in number per person, 1975–85
Cameroun		24	39	
Congo	15	15	15	
Cote D'Ivoire	11	14	18	Numbers per person more than doubled, 1975–85
Ethiopia	1	1	1	
Gabon		15	16	
Malawi	2	2	2	
Nigeria	4	4	9 (1991)	
South Africa	84	74	93	
Tunisia	17	23	40 (1991)	Numbers more than doubling, 1975–91
Zambia	19	10	10	Substantial decrease in number, 1975–87
Zimbabwe		26	31	The figure for 1991 (18.5) implies a sharp fall
North America				
Canada	382	404	476 (1991)	
United States	491	495	588 (1991)	
Central America and the Caribbean				
Costa Rica	30	33		
Cuba	15	16	21	
Dominican Rep.	14	15	16	
Haiti	4	4		
Mexico	39	53	83 (1991)	Numbers per person more than doubled, 1975–91
Trinidad & Tobago	100	133	204	Numbers per person more than doubled, 1975–85
South America				
Argentina	89	99	126	Highest number of autos/person in region
Bolivia	6	5	5	
Brazil		45	83 (1991)	
Chile	25	37	52	Numbers per person up 144 percent, 1975–85
Colombia	16	18	28	Numbers per person more than doubled, 1975–85
Ecuador	7	7	15	Total number more than doubled, 1975–85
Peru	17	16	19	
Uruguay		73	102	
Venezuela	75	87	92	
Asia				
Bangladesh	less than 1.0 for all three dates			
Hong Kong	27	33	29	
India	1	1	1	
Indonesia	3	4	6	
Japan	155	196	303 (1991)	Number per person almost doubled, 1975–91
Kuwait	202	233	244	
Malaysia	39	56	90	Number per person increased 3fold, 1975–87
Pakistan	3	3	4	
Philippines	9	8	7	Decline in number per person, 1975–85
Singapore	66	64	92	
Thailand	6	8	14	Number per person nearly tripled, 1975–85
Europe				
Austria	229	300	337	
Denmark	257	273	295	
France	290	334	382	
Germany[a]	289	380	424	
Greece	48	87	127	Number per person more than tripled, 1975–87
Hungary	55	95	135	Number per person nearly tripled, 1975–87
Italy	272	310	394	
Netherlands	249	314	338	
Poland	32	64	99	Total number nearly quadrupled, 1975–87
Spain	135	196	240	Total number more than doubled, 1975–87
Switzerland	280	347	404	
United Kingdom	254	276	313	
Oceania				
Australia	357	368	434	
New Zealand	369	401	460	
Papua New Guinea	7	5	5	

[a] Statistic for former West Germany.

Source: Table 29 in United Nations, *Compendium of Social Statistics and Indicators 1988*, New York, 1991—with statistics for 1991 drawn from AAMA, *World Motor Vehicle Data: 1993 Edition*, Washington DC, 1993, quoted in WRI, *World Resources Report 1996–7*, World Resources Institute, Washington DC, 1996.

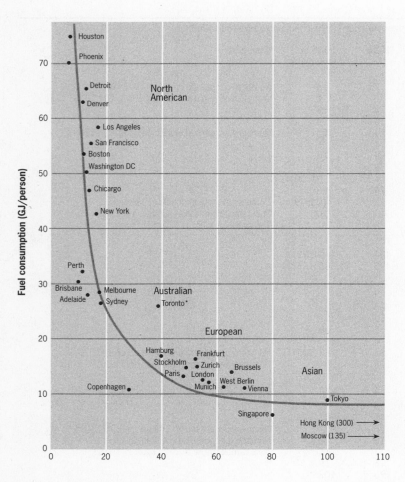

South also have a high proportion of trips made by walking. But it is not only cities in relatively low-income countries that have a high proportion of trips made by walking or bicycling. For instance, in cities in West Germany in 1989, 27 per cent of trips were made by walking with 10 per cent by bicycle.[84] In many cities in Denmark, France, Sweden, Germany and the Netherlands, a high proportion of all trips are made by bicycle; in Delft (the Netherlands) where special attention has been given to encouraging bicycle use, 43 per cent of trips are made by bicycle with 26 per cent made by walking.[85]

The differences in the average densities of inner and outer areas and in the overall metropolitan densities in Table 8.4 are particularly notable. Figure 8.5 shows the differences between the traditional 'walking' city that generally has between 100 and 200 persons per hectare to the 'transit city' with 70–100 persons per hectare to the 'automobile dependent city' with densities of 10–20 persons per hectare.

These same kind of relationships are found *within* cities as some areas—especially between outer suburbs and historic areas, central business districts and residential and commercial areas that developed before it was common for households to have their own automobiles. Figure 8.6 shows how gasoline use per person remains relatively low for those in central New York but is nearly twice as high for those in the inner city area and some five times higher for those in the outer areas.

Comparable contrasts were found in a study in Toronto in 1986 where those living in the dense city core travelled on average 9.4 kilometres a day by automobile compared to 13.4 by those in less dense inner suburbs and 21.7 for those in low density outer suburbs.[86] Many cities have a small *walking city* centre and a distinctive *transit city* with higher density and very different transport patterns, surrounded by an *automobile dependent city* with uniformly low density suburbs and high car use.[87] In most cities, there are also large variations in rates of car ownership and use between high-, middle- and low-income areas.

Although the general trend has been for increasing car dependence and decreasing density, as cities become more prosperous, there are many instances of wealthy cities in which densities have increased in recent years—for instance in many historic urban cores or in new urban villages in Europe—and in which public transport and walking or cycling have grown at the expense of car travel.[88] The section in Chapter 9 on responses to transport problems has several examples of cities in which high quality public transport and other measures to support inner city development have encouraged more people to live in central areas.

FIGURE 8.4
Population density against gasoline consumption per person for 32 cities (data for 1980)

Source: Newman, Peter W. G. and Jeffrey R. Kenworthy, *Cities and Automobile Dependence: an International Sourcebook*, Gower Technical, Aldershot, 1989. * Toronto falls within the 'Australian' rather than the 'North American' norm.

desirable cities in which to live yet they have a fifth to a tenth of the fuel consumption of US cities. Many European cities have per capita incomes higher than Australian cities and yet have two to three times less use of automobiles.

The relatively low levels of automobile dependence in the Asian and some of the European cities are associated with higher population densities, a more efficient public transport system and effective demand management measures. In the three Asian cities in Table 8.4, nearly two-thirds of all travelling in terms of passenger-km was undertaken on public transport. Many other large cities in Asia also have most passenger movements undertaken by public transport—for instance, in the mid-1980s, over two-thirds of all motorized trips in Seoul, Bombay, Shanghai, Manila[81] and Calcutta as well as Tokyo and Hong Kong were made by bus, rail or subway.[82]

Table 8.4 also shows large contrasts between the cities in terms of the proportion of workers walking or cycling. Cities in China such as Shanghai and Tianjin have among the highest rates of bicycle use in the world,[83] although in both, these rates may be declining rapidly, with the rapid growth in the number of automobiles and with transport plans oriented towards increasing automobile use. Most cities in the

FIGURE 8.5
Different city forms according to dominant mode of transport

Source: Newman, Peter, Jeff Kenworthy and Peter Vintila, *Housing, Transport and Urban Form*, Institute for Science and Technology Policy, Murdoch University, Australia, 1992.

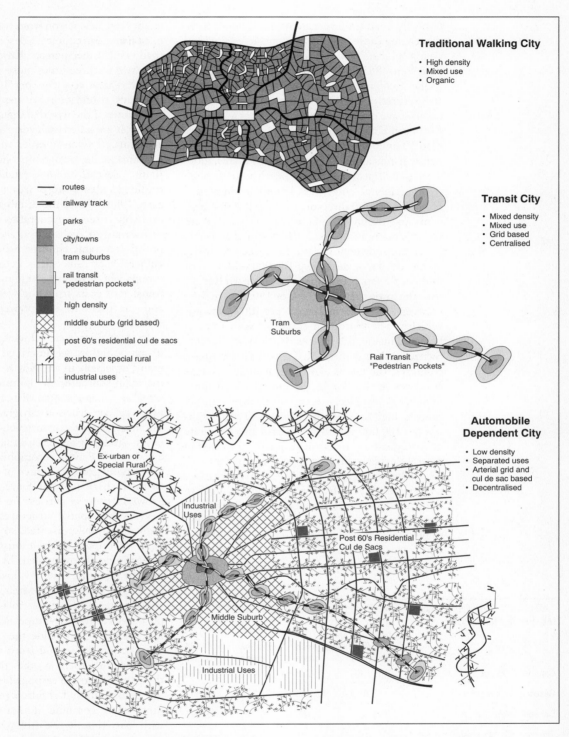

The costs and benefits of automobile dependence

Few cities have been successful in coping with the rapid growth in the number of road vehicles. The economic costs of congestion in many major cities are estimated in terms of billions of US dollars a year and any city with serious congestion is likely to lose new investments to other, less congested areas. Congested roads and a lack of an efficient public transit system also means high costs for low-income households. In large cities lacking effective public transport systems, it is common for low-income households to spend 20 or more per cent of their incomes on transport and for those living in peripheral areas to spend 3–4 hours a day travelling to and from work.[89]

Those who own and use road vehicles rarely pay for the full range of social and environmental costs they directly or indirectly generate.[90] For instance, there are the very considerable health costs associated with road vehicles, much of which are borne by those not using motor vehicles.

Globally, road traffic accidents are thought to be the leading cause of death among adolescents and young adults.[91] One recent estimate suggested that some 885,000 people die each year from traffic accidents[92] and many times this number are seriously injured.[93] More than a million people have died from traffic accidents within the European Union over the last 20 years, and more than 30 million have been injured and/or permanently handicapped.[94] In the United States, more than 40,000 people are killed each year through road accidents and over 3 million injured.[95] However, around three-quarters of all traffic accidents now occur in the South, even though there are still many more road vehicles in the North. There are enormous variations between countries in the rate of road deaths per 100,000 vehicles. For instance, in Japan and among countries in Europe with the lowest rates, in 1990 or 1991, there were between 18 and 22 road deaths per 100,000 motor vehicles. The European countries with rates of below 22 included Netherlands, Norway, Sweden, Switzerland and the UK.[96] In some European countries, the rate is 3–4 times as high. In many countries in the South, the rate is 15–30 times higher. For instance, in Kenya, the rate is some 30 times as high (in 1991 there were 580 road fatalities per 100,000 vehicles).[97] Kenya also has a rate of road deaths per person comparable to that in several European nations, despite having far fewer road vehicles per person. In India, there are more fatalities each year from road accidents than in the United States yet it has less than a twentieth of the road vehicles.[98] One estimate for Thailand suggested that around half of the 20,000 lives that are lost each year to accidents are from traffic accidents,[99] which would give Thailand a higher

fatality rate per person from traffic accidents than most European countries, despite having far fewer road vehicles per person. Kuwait and Venezuela have two to three times more people dying from motor vehicle accidents per 100,000 inhabitants than most countries in Europe.[100]

In some of the world's largest cities, thousands of people are killed each year through automobile accidents.[101] Even in cities with very low levels of automobile ownership, such as Delhi and Beijing, several hundred fatalities per year from traffic accidents were being reported in the early 1980s[102] and the number of fatalities have probably risen considerably since then. It is pedestrians or cyclists who are most often killed or injured—and children who are particularly vulnerable.[103] Since it is generally low-income groups who walk or bicycle most, there is also a transfer of costs from the wealthier car owners and car users to the poorer pedestrians and cyclists.

In most cities, road vehicles are a major source of air pollution, as described in Chapter 4; in many, especially in the North, they have become the main source of air pollution in cities. They are also a major source of noise while road and highway construction programmes are among the most disruptive construction projects within cities—and they are often a major cause of forced evictions.[104] Private automobiles are also a major and rapidly growing source of greenhouse gases, as their share in total fossil-fuel consumption grows in most countries. And as city transport systems and spatial structures become increasingly automobile oriented, so those who cannot drive or cannot afford motor vehicles become increasingly disadvantaged. This affects in particular the poor, the elderly who do not drive or can no longer drive and children and youth. There are often particular gender biases as public transport services decline—especially as they become more infrequent outside the 'rush hours' when most people go to and from work. This affects those who use them at other times—for instance the people who are responsible for looking after the household and children (usually women) or those who combine domestic responsibilities with part-time work (usually women) whose journeys to and from work are outside the conventional rush hours.

It has also become clear that building ever more highways and freeways is no solution. Even if traffic congestion is reduced (which is rarely the case), the level of resource use and greenhouse-gas emissions increases greatly. What is perhaps most dramatic about Table 8.3 is the scale of the differences in passenger vehicles per 1,000 inhabitants. Most of the most populous Asian and African countries have less than one-hundredth of the passenger cars per person of the world's

TABLE 8.4 Comparing cities in terms of use of cars and public transport (All statistics for 1980)

	Wealthy Asian cities	European cities	Australian cities	US cities
Cars per 1,000 people	88	328	453	533
Gasoline use per person	5,493	13,820	29,829	58,541
Car vehicle-kms per person	1,067	3,485	5,794	8,715
The share of public transit in total passenger-kms	64	25	8	4
Public transport vehicle-km of service per person	103	79	56	30
Proportion of workers walking or cycling	25	21	5	5
Metropolitan population density	160	54	14	14
Inner area population density	464	91	24	45
Outer area population density	115	43	13	11

Source: Sustainable Urban Transport Systems Project, ISTP. The Asian cities were Tokyo, Singapore and Hong Kong.

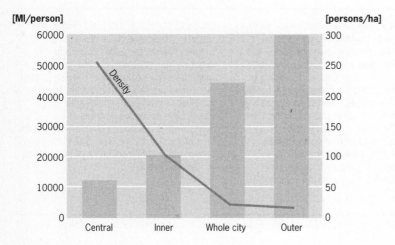

[MI/person] ... [persons/ha]

Central Inner Whole city Outer

FIGURE 8.6
Gasoline use and urban density in New York's centre and its inner and outer area

Source: Based on data drawn from Newman, Peter W. G and Jeffrey R. Kenworthy, *Cities and Automobile Dependence: an International Sourcebook*, Gower Technical, Aldershot, 1989.

wealthiest nations. Even with major advances in the fuel efficiency of automobiles and in resource conservation (for instance through high levels of recycling for automobile parts and through automobiles that lasted longer), the increase in fossil-fuel use and resource use if these countries sought to reach levels of private automobile use comparable to those that are now common in the wealthiest countries would place enormous strains on the world's finite resource base and finite capacity to absorb greenhouse gases without major climatic change.

Transport and cities in the South[105]

Most city and municipal authorities in the South face great difficulties in improving what are currently grossly inadequate public transport systems—to the point where they not only meet the needs of low-income groups but also encourage many middle- and upper-income groups to use them, instead of private automobiles. Many major cities in the South face comparable problems to Northern cities in regard to traffic congestion and air pollution arising from road vehicles.[106] Within the richer cities, rates of automobile ownership per capita can be as high as in cities in the North. Even where they are much lower, less provision for roads in cities, poor road maintenance and poorly functioning traffic management systems often ensure high levels of congestion. Congestion combined with less efficient and poorly maintained engines and higher levels of lead-based additives in gasoline can also mean comparable or higher levels of automobile-related air pollution, even when the number of road vehicles in use is substantially less.[107]

In many if not most cities in the South, the quality of public transport is poor and, in recent years, has been falling further and further behind demand. In most cities in Africa, Asia and Latin America, the growth in the supply of public transport by the formal sector is slower than popula-

tion growth—and the deficit in the supply of services is further widened because the larger the city grows, the larger the average length of travel. In several sub-Saharan African cities, there has even been a major decline in the supply of public transport, despite growing populations. In others, such as Nairobi and Abidjan, the main public transport operators increased the number of vehicle kilometres during the 1980s, but at a rate that was much slower than population growth. In India, the supply of public transport services stagnated in Bombay, did not match population growth in Bangalore and only in Madras did it increase faster than the population. There are usually too few vehicles relative to demand and a serious problem of maintenance as existing vehicles are over-used and too little attention is given to maintenance. For many nations, there is also the problem of the high import costs of oil and public transport vehicles (and of all spare parts); only a minority of nations produce automobiles, buses and trucks and most that do simply assemble imported components.

In many cities, a high proportion of all trips on public transport are provided by informal private-sector services. By the end of the 1980s, the informal sector had between 40 and 80 per cent share in public transport in most capital cities of sub-Saharan Africa—see Box 8.6. It also dominates public transport in many cities in South Asia, except the large ones where institutionalized transport usually has the lead. Where routes and timetables are not defined, informal transport is more expensive than regular transport, is often hardly affordable by the urban poor and it may be dangerous—see Box 8.6.

One other common problem is the fact that revenues for most publicly owned bus, railway and metro systems do not cover the costs so there are no revenues on which to draw to improve maintenance and the quality of the service and to invest in expanding the service. Politicians are reluctant to raise fares because of the political protests this would cause, not least because many low-income households would be seriously affected. But a failure to address this simply means a continuous deterioration in the quality of the service while unmet demands continue to grow.

There is also the problem of the spatial incoherence of the built-up area within and around the city. In most cities, there are many districts into which no buses can go. These include historic city centres where roads and lanes are too narrow for buses and all the illegal or informal settlements that have developed on sites which are often flooded or waterlogged or on steep slopes with no motorable roads or at a considerable distance from paved roads. In addition, most cities have developed and expanded with such a spatial incoherence that it

Public transport by private companies in Africa

As the large, generally publicly owned bus companies in Africa began to falter in the economically depressed 1980s and 1990s (see Chapter 2 for more details), private transport became increasingly important, especially for the low-income groups. Often the service was more direct, faster, and certainly more accessible, particularly to and from outlying areas where roads were bad and the large buses could not easily function. These smaller, privately owned vehicles had a variety of local names, derived according to a number of different principles, according to the location: for example, the Nairobi *matatus*, the Dar es Salaam *dala-dalas*, the Bamako *duru-duruni* and the Brazzaville *cent-cent* are based on the coins, or fares that were charged for the service when it was first initiated; and the speed of the vehicle is reflected in the *car rapide* of Dakar, the *kimalu-malu* of Kinshasa, or the *zemidjan* of Cotonou; the age and lack of comfort and security is indicated in the *alakabon* of Conakry, the *congelés* of Douala and Yaoundé, the *gbakas* of Abidjan, and the *mammy-wagons* of Lagos.[108] Typically, they were reconstituted pick-up trucks, small minibuses, or minivans, holding up to 36 passengers in various degrees of overcrowding depending on the route and the time of the day. By the late 1980s, they had carved out a significant share of the market, as Table 8.5 shows.

TABLE 8.5 Division of market between mass transit—companies and informal transporters (1989 estimates)

City	Company		Informal transport	
Conakry	SOGETRAG	40%	Ala Kabons	60%
Nairobi	KBS	40%	Matatus	57%
	NBSC	3%		
Dar es Salaam	UDA	10%	Dala-dalas	90%
Abidjan	SOTRA	75%	Gbakas	25%
Dakar	SOTRAC	32%	Cars rapides	68%
Kinshasa	SOTRAZ	30%	Fulas-fulas	44%
	All companies together	56%		
Lagos	LSTC	2%	Molue/Danfoe	98%
Bamako	SPGA/CTUB	2%	Durunis/Sotrama	98%
Douala & Yaoundé	SOTUC	20%	Taxis collectifs	80%
Brazzaville	STB/STUB	5%	Fulas fulas	95%
	RATB		Taxis collectifs	

Sources: For Table 8.5, Xavier Godard et Pierre Teurnier, *Les Transports urbains en Afrique a l'heure de l'ajustement*, Karthala, Paris, 1992, 51. For the text, Stren, Richard and Christie Gombay, *The Governance of Human Settlements*, Background paper for the Global Report, 1995.

is very difficult to organize cost-effective public transport. In the absence of land-use planning, and where illegal settlements become the only viable source of housing for most low-income groups, cities expand in a haphazard manner, with very densely populated settlements of different sizes interspersed with large areas with little or no development and often low density suburban developments for middle and upper-income groups.[109] This greatly increases the cost of providing public transport.

8.6 Communications

The growth in the communications industry

The world is in the midst of what is often termed an 'Information Revolution', in which advances in computers and telecommunications technology have transformed the way that many people work, shop, learn, and communicate, and, increasingly, where they live and work. These technological advances have also changed the way that many goods are made, many services provided and most companies or corporations are organized. They are affecting settlement patterns all round the world—and the scale of their influence is likely to increase. The scale and nature of the changes that they are bringing—or could bring—should be of concern to every policy-maker and every city authority.

The growth in the telecommunications industry has been dramatic. There are more than 500 million connections to telephone main lines,[110] and in 1994, more than 38 million new subscribers were connected.[111] Between 1975 and 1990, the number of telephone connections grew rapidly in most countries in the South. For instance, to take only examples from some of the more populous countries, the number of connections more than doubled in China, Mexico, Peru, Iran and the Philippines in this 15-year period while it more than tripled in India, Colombia, Brazil and Pakistan and more than quadrupled in Egypt, Thailand, Republic of Korea and Indonesia. In Turkey and Saudi Arabia, it increased more than ninefold. The rate of increase was less dramatic in the wealthiest nations, as they already had high ratios of connections to people in 1975. By 1990, there was more than one telephone line for every two persons in many of the world's wealthiest countries.[112] There is also the dramatic increase in the number of people with cellular phones; the cellular phone networks had some 50 million subscribers in 1994 and worldwide, one new telephone subscriber in six gets a mobile phone.[113] The twenty-five leading telecommunications companies had revenues of $400 billion in 1994 and in this same year, the ten largest of these made bigger profits than the twenty-five largest commercial banks.[114] With a world average of around one telephone connection for every ten persons compared to one connection to two persons in high-income countries, the potential for expansion is obvious.

The implications for settlements

What is perhaps more important for settlements is not the size of the industry but the implications of two factors. The first that a computer, a modem (for sending data from the computer down the telephone line) and a telephone connection in a remote, small village allows just as much connection to other users and information services that are 'on-line' as one in the centre of a large city. The cost of the computer and the modem has fallen rapidly; in many countries, the two together cost only a few hundred dollars.[115] The second is the growth in the scale and nature of data transmission that is possible through the telephone line, and the fall in costs. While telephone lines were once considered only as the means by which people can talk to each other, now they can do far more. Faxes can transmit 'facsimiles' of both text and graphics. Electronic mail connects computer users through telephone lines—and allows the transmission of any form of data (text, statistics, graphics). Cables made of fibre optics enormously increase the capacity of phone lines and lower the cost of data transmission—and allow, for instance, the transmission of television pictures between those with connections. Meanwhile, digital telephone exchanges and digital connections between telephones or computers plus computer-controlled communications systems make connections between users easier and cheaper. A review of telecommunications in *The Economist* in 1995 was

entitled 'the death of distance' as international telephone calls become as cheap for telephone companies as local telephone calls—even if their pricing structure does not reflect this.

The fall in the cost of communications and the dramatic increase in the scale and nature of communications that is possible through telecommunications systems introduces new uncertainties for all cities, as these undermine one of their main comparative advantages as centres which promote information-exchange. This link between telecommunications systems and computers certainly allows a new division of labour and new patterns of urban economic specialization within nations and internationally,[116] but it seems more likely to change the location of many of the world's most prosperous cities rather than to undermine the economic dominance of cities. The role of the city may not be so much as a centre of communications but a centre for the control of communications and access to information.[117] Telecommunications networks and most of the information services that they can tap are not public goods but privately owned and only available to those who pay for them. They certainly increase access to information for those who live outside the large cities and are able to pay for this access, but much of this information and equipment is produced in cities by companies or corporations that are based in cities. The combination of rapid advances in telecommunications and computers has reinforced the comparative advantage of transnational corporations in three aspects: (1) as the producers of the computers, telecommunications networks and telecommunications equipment; (2) as the owners of most of the information services and entertainment to which they provide access; and (3) as the enterprises who can utilize computer networks in planning and organizing production in different locations around the world. This boosted the economy of many cities (and other settlements) where the multinational corporations invested or subcontracted and fewer cities where they concentrated their own offices—while at the same time contributing to the decline of many cities that had enterprises that lost their market to the multinationals. As Chapter 1 described, a few of the largest and most long-established cities have had their role reinforced by their role within the world economy—especially the three main 'command and control' centres of the multinational corporations—London, New York and Tokyo.

Much-improved telecommunications systems and computers have been an important facet in several of the changes in the world economy noted in Chapter 1—for instance, the much increased importance of the service sector within the world economy, the rapid growth in financial services (and speculation in international currencies) and the increasing proportion of the world's economic activities controlled by multinational corporations. By much increasing the possibilities for communication and co-ordination between the different offices and production sites scattered around the world, they have also separated many of the activities that were formerly concentrated in one city. There can be a complete separation between production and control as a corporation based in London, San Francisco or Sydney commissions a design studio in Milan to design a new good, a bank in Tokyo to finance it, a factory in Shenzhen (China) to produce it, and an advertising firm in New York to promote it—with the corporate office (and the city where it is based) never having to handle the good whose production and sale it organized. So it is not clear where the actual production of goods will take place in the future, except that much less will take place in the largest and most prosperous cities.

There is also a comparable move of many service-sector enterprises out of major cities or the more expensive countries. At first, companies in the wealthiest nations moved much of their office staff to cheaper locations outside the major cities or to the city periphery—a move that was encouraged in some instances by high crime rates in central cities. Many government agencies or offices also moved, for similar reasons (and also, in some instances, to push jobs to poorer, high unemployment areas). Now, it is possible to move a large part of office work to cheaper countries as telecommunications systems allow companies with headquarters in Europe and North America to have much of the 'information processing' in their accounting, payroll, invoicing or sales done in nations in Asia and the Caribbean, where wage rates are much lower. Airline companies were among the first to move part of their office operations to cheaper countries in the South where there was the telecommunications infrastructure and the workforce to do this. Publishing companies have long had branches, subsidiaries or subcontractors in low-wage countries that undertook much of the typesetting and printing of books and advanced telecommunications systems simply make this transfer easier and more rapid. This subcontracting of work to lower-wage countries can include highly skilled tasks—as in software development or in animation; many of the children's cartoons on US television are largely drawn by animators in low-wage Asian countries. Information and entertainment services that are available through the telephone can also be located in lower-cost countries—for instance those provided by computer companies and computer software companies. It was even possible to 'export' part of a security firm's work as the pictures from television cameras monitor-ing buildings in Europe or North America go directly to televisions in low-wage countries—with the people monitoring them being able to alert the police or other security staff in the original country, if there is any suspicious activity.[118] Not only does this mean much lower wages for the staff supervising the cameras but because this monitoring is done on the other side of the world, much of the night-time surveillance in Europe can be done as a daytime job in Asia.

Although the most advanced computer networks which allow the largest and most rapid transmission of data and the possibility of permanent electronic connection between distant sites are privately owned, with access to them strictly controlled to those who pay for them, much improved telecommunications systems and computers have also increased the possibilities for smaller firms or for individuals. Small companies or individuals can also send business overseas—for instance commissioning typing or data inputting into records or translation to businesses in countries with lower wages—with electronic mail, faxes and telephone lines providing the links. Of particular importance is the Internet which provides electronic connections between subscribers at a low cost—and allows subscribers to send each other letters and data through their computer and modem with the cost of sending 'e-mail' letters being little more than the cost of the local telephone call needed to send the data to their local e-mail network. There are some 30 million users within the Internet on 50,000 different networks in 65 countries and around 1 million new users are joining the system each year.[119] The range of information services available to Internet subscribers has also increased considerably and an increasing number of international agencies, companies and voluntary organizations make information available to those who are connected to Internet.

There are also the many ways in which computer networks reduce the necessity to work in or visit cities. For instance, 'teleshopping' allows people to purchase goods from their homes, choosing either from the television or from catalogues, with no need to visit a shop and with the people who take their order and package and send the goods also not needing to be in a city. Such teleshopping depends on the use of credit cards or charge cards and the staff responsible for managing the purchase of goods by these cards also need not be located in cities. Home-shopping sales in the United States and the major European Union Countries grew rapidly in the late 1980s and early 1990s.[120] The possibilities for teleshopping are further increased where consumers can receive full details of companies' products through computer information systems and use these systems to order the goods or services they want. 'Telebanking' is also growing and this allows many transactions formerly done by visiting one's bank to be done over the telephone—and, of course, the bank staff who answer the telephone and organize the transaction also need not be in major cities. 'Telecommuting' or 'teleworking' is also made much easier, through a computer in the home connected through the telephone system to the computer system at work. One report suggested that about 25 per cent of all jobs in the Netherlands could be done in telework[121] while one estimate suggested that there could be as many as 33 million teleworkers in the USA and 10 million in the UK by the year 2010.[122] Advanced telecommunications systems also allow many activities to be done through a telephone line rather than through face-to-face contact—including 'teleteaching,' 'teleconferencing' and 'teleconsulting' and each can reduce the demand for service activities that are usually concentrated in cities (i.e. schools, universities, conference centres and consultants). Many information services accessed over the telephone such as telephone directory enquiries or computer hardware or software 'help-lines' have the staff who answer the calls located outside the larger and more expensive cities. 'Telemetry' can be used to monitor any building's consumption of water, electricity and gas and allow accurate billing without anyone needing to visit the building to read the water, electricity or gas meter.

In theory, this substitution of telecommunications for people's journeys should considerably reduce energy use in transport. The substitution of telecommunications links for visits to work, conferences, shops, banks, schools, and other places reduces the need for transport and implies a considerable reduction in energy use for transport. But these may also increase energy use by allowing a more dispersed pattern of settlements which implies longer journeys and often more reliance of the use of the private automobile.[123]

Thus, the possibilities for changing the location of economic activities and of where people live within countries and internationally are very large. Nations, regions and cities which have good-quality telecommunications infrastructure are clearly at a great advantage to those that do not. Countries with a well-educated workforce that are also able to use computers are also, obviously, at an advantage, although to attract business from the wealthier countries also implies that this workforce must speak the language of the wealthier countries. It is no coincidence that most of the examples of countries in the South which have attracted information-processing jobs from the North are countries in which English is the first language or a language widely spoken among middle- and upper-income groups. However, the actual form of the rearrangement of economic activities

within nations and internationally remains unclear. As one commentator notes, 'contrary to early, simplistic expectations that telecommunications would "eliminate space", rendering geography meaningless through the effortless conquest of distance, such systems in fact produce new rounds of unevenness, forming new geographies that are imposed upon the relics of the past'.[124] But the underlying trend will be that the cost of transport is unlikely to fall and will probably rise while the cost of communications is likely to continue falling—and this implies a tendency towards spatial diffusion.[125]

The implications for city authorities[126]

The two critical questions for city authorities are first, what these advances imply for the prosperity of their city and what steps they can take to promote this prosperity and secondly what they imply for the spatial distribution of people and economic activities within their jurisdiction. Far-sighted policies on telecommunications can considerably enhance a city's economy but unrealistic assumptions about the potential of a city to attract new enterprises that then underpin large public investments in 'wiring the city' and in improving the communications links between the city and outside can also prove expensive and ineffective.

The growing economic importance of what is often termed the 'information economy' has meant increased competition between cities for the jobs and investments associated with it. The information economy is very large, if taken to include all economic activities and employment primarily associated with the production, processing and distribution of information.[127] Using such a broad definition, by 1981, between 40 and 50 per cent of the labour force in OECD nations worked in the information economy, with the proportion being considerably higher in certain major metropolitan centres.[128] But this definition includes teachers and lecturers and the media (who are included within 'information distributors') and the administrative and managerial staff of private firms and the public sector ('information processors') as well as those who produce information (including researchers and consultant services) and those who build and run the information infrastructure (for instance the staff of postal and telecommunications services).[129] In this broad definition, the information economy has long been central to most city economies as for centuries, most large cities have concentrated government bureaucracies, legal services, the headquarters of merchant organizations and banks and schools and universities. What is new is the much increased economic value of the information and the extent to which many of those working within the information economy need not be in the largest, wealthiest cities.

The competition between cities can be seen in two aspects. The first is in the buildings and high technology estates where the buildings incorporate the latest information technology—or in a more widespread development to 'wire the city' so all businesses have access to an optic-fibre cable network. The second is in improving the quality and capacity of the city's telecommunications links with the outside—for instance through teleports. Teleports are to the transport of information what seaports and airports are to freight and passenger transport: a consolidated point of entry into (or out of) a region from which information is distributed to their final destinations or collected from their origins.[130]

The first teleport in the United States was the teleport of New York, a satellite communication centre and office park built on 142 hectares of Staten Island and opening in 1985.[131] The city of New York was an active financial and management partner in the venture (which also included Merrill Lynch and the Port Authority of New York and New Jersey), and its main motivation was to stem business movement out of New York. The telecommunications infrastructure in downtown Manhattan had become extremely congested—and this was solved by connecting the teleport to a fibre-optic network serving Manhattan. The teleport site itself also offered business location opportunities within the city.[132] Many other teleports have been built since then, not only in the United States but also in Europe, Japan and other locations.[133] Even where the teleport had been funded entirely by the private sector—as was the Harbor Bay Teleport near Oakland, California, across the Bay from San Francisco where real-estate development was linked with high-capacity telecommunications infrastructure—this had major implications for the local authority. And the urban planners who approved the project certainly hoped that it would produce substantial economic benefits for the city.

The examples of New York and Oakland illustrate two, somewhat distinct functions a teleport can serve: as a *regional* provider of telecommunications capacity and competitive service, and as a *local* magnet for business. The economic development potential of the first function seems to be more important than that of the second. Among the seventy or more teleports in the United States, most appear to be primarily 'antenna' or 'dish farms', serving a collector–distributor role for the telecommunications of the region, without generating much new business opportunities on site. Nearly all are privately owned—and few were initiated by local policy-makers.[134] Businesses need not locate at a teleport to enjoy its services, but the absence of the advanced communications capabilities offered by such a facility may put a region at a competitive disadvantage in terms of attracting or retaining firms with such advanced communication needs.

Many city authorities have become involved in improving telecommunications cabling within their city or within particular zones in the city. This is generally in the hope that this will attract new business or keep existing ones but there can also be other important objectives. For instance, other objectives might be to keep down the growth in private automobile use or to encourage new jobs in poorer or more run-down areas within the city. Advanced telecommunications systems also bring many other possibilities—for instance increasing access to information in schools or allowing local cable television channels through which the city authorities make their workings more open and accountable by televising meetings. City authorities can also maintain up-to-date computer bulletin boards about decisions and ensure that comprehensive information about the work of the city authorities and the services they provide is available 'on line'. There are also many possibilities for improving access to information for the people who have the most difficulty moving around the city—older people, children, those with physical handicaps and low-income groups in general.

Thus, telecommunications technologies present a number of challenges and opportunities for city authorities. Cities must avoid unrealistic investment and promotion policies on communications infrastructure but must continually monitor the changing technological landscape as they explore policy and planning alternatives. City authorities should also be aware of the social polarization that they can exacerbate, both in labour markets and in terms of who has access to valuable information and who has not. One specialist suggested the following:

A city should also be interested in promoting diversity in its telecommunications infrastructure and in the use of that infrastructure, rather than looking for a technological fix for whatever economic ills it may be undergoing. In the 1960s, many cities [in the US] thought cable television could solve the urban problems of poverty and political participation; in the 1980s, teleports and smart buildings have been regarded as high-technology solutions to economic development problems. City leaders must realize that telecommunications can no longer be taken for granted but should be considered an important strategic component of the community's infrastructure. While telecommunications is not, in and of itself, a sufficient condition for economic development, it appears to be a necessary one. Increasingly, cities that can effectively use telecommunications as a development and service delivery tool will enjoy a competitive advantage over cities that are oblivious to the opportunities at hand.[135]

Box 8.7 summaries some of the key issues in regard to telecommunications planning.

8.7 Concluding Comments

The first few sections of this chapter concentrated on describing the lack of infrastructure and services that underlie many of the most serious health problems evident in urban areas in Africa, Asia and Latin America. But a broader view is also needed in assessing how improved infrastructure and services makes a good living environment—for instance what makes particular inner-city areas, suburbs, neighbourhoods or villages and shelters more pleasant, safe and valued by their inhabitants—and thus more healthy.[136] Improvements in the quality of housing, water, sanitation, drainage, roads and paths not only reduces disease but also makes life more pleasant—perhaps most especially for those people within households (usually women) who are responsible for looking after the children and for managing the household. So too does a

---

BOX 8.7

Some of the main issues relating to cities' telecommunications planning

- Improving telecommunications infrastructure can encourage a loss of jobs from a city or region as well as bringing them in. Telecommunications facilitates the closure of small branch banks, insurance offices and other service enterprises. It facilitates the entry of large national chain stores at the expense of small and diverse local shops and other enterprises.

- High-quality telecommunications infrastructure may bring jobs to a depressed region (urban or rural), but it may also lock the economy of that region into low-wage, low-skill information-processing jobs such as back-office processing.

- Isolated attention to various demonstration projects may result in a region having certain communication 'hot spots' within which novel services may be available, but which are not linked to the rest of the region. Uneven access to the technology and its benefits may be the result.

- Cities should take care that attention to high-technology attractions do not divert them from the provision of conventional services. 'Investment at the expense of other, more traditional priorities in times of local financial stringency may not even produce the best economic results for the area. It could be argued that investment in more traditional infrastructure is more likely to produce more immediate economic development benefits. Indeed, telematics strategies may increase social polarization within cities unless specific steps are taken to counteract this.'

Source: Drawn mainly from Gibbs, David, 'Telematics and urban economic development policies: time for caution?', *Telecommunications Policy*, vol. 17, no. 4, 1993, 250–6

---

good public transport system, especially for low-income groups as it increases their access to family and friends and also to open space and social activities. Provision within each city neighbourhood for well-designed and managed open space and space and facilities for safe and stimulating play for children of different ages is also important, as is minimum noise and a lack of violence.[137] Telephones are not only invaluable for their role in rapidly calling on emergency services when needed but also for many aspects of urban life linked to work, domestic life and pleasure. The relative importance given to each of these will vary greatly from person to person—and it is difficult to be precise about how pleasant environments contribute to a greater sense of wellbeing and lessen stress. But it is clear that they do. The reverse is also true as many psychosocial disorders are associated with poor quality housing, infrastructure and services.[138] One of the themes that consistently emerges in discussions with people about what influences wellbeing is the importance of being able to command events that control their lives.[139] This includes being able to avoid all the injuries and diseases associated with a lack of provision for water, sanitation and drainage and to have a reliable and regular public transport system.

Increasing income generally brings improvements in infrastructure and service provision. This is both the case within cities, if the environmental quality of the homes of high and low income groups are compared, and between cities. Recent World Bank publications have stressed how the scale and relative importance of different environmental problems change, as a country's economy becomes more prosperous and as more investments can be made in infrastructure and services.[140] In general, the higher a country's per capita income:

- The higher the proportion of rural and urban population with safe water.

- The higher the proportion of urban population with adequate sanitation.

- The larger the municipal wastes but also the more comprehensive the service to regularly collect such wastes.

However, certain other environmental problems also increase with per capita income including:

- Fossil-fuel consumption (especially through rising electricity demand and use of motor vehicles) and thus carbon dioxide emissions per capita.

- Concentrations of particulate matter in the air in urban areas, until a certain per capita income is reached—and this concentration then declines.

- Concentrations of sulphur dioxide in the air in urban areas until a certain per capita income is reached and then a rapid decrease.[141]

This is an identifiable tendency, even if there are large variations in these indicators for cities in countries with comparable per capita incomes. One should recall the large variations between cities in the proportion of people with water piped to their plots in nations with comparable per capita incomes—or the very large differences in per capita gasoline use among the world's wealthiest cities.[142] But this tendency is largely a result of increased capacity to invest in and to manage infrastructure and services.

This tendency for improved environmental quality to be associated with higher income was demonstrated by a study of household-level environmental problems in three cities: Sao Paulo (the largest city in Brazil and one of the wealthiest cities in the South); Accra (the largest city in Ghana, a relatively low-income country); and Jakarta (the largest city in Indonesia, a middle-income country). With surveys covering 1,000 or more households in each city, the environmental problems associated with water, sanitation, solid waste, indoor air quality and pests were found to lessen with the per capita income of the country—see Table 8.6. But as importantly, most household level environmental problems also tended to lessen within each of these cities, the wealthier the household.[143]

The fact that the scale and relative importance of environmental problems change, the higher the per capita income of the city or nation, allows a classification of urban centres, according to which set of environmental problems is likely to be most pressing—see Table 8.7. In the cities in category 1, many households are still struggling with a lack of provision for water and sanitation; by category 4, the main environmental problems are no longer within the city but are the collective impact of the consumption and waste produced by city inhabitants and city businesses on regional and global resource bases and systems. Most urban centres will never fit neatly into one of these categories—but this table helps to stress the dynamic and changing nature of environmental problems in cities with growing economies.

The initial environmental problems for all urban centres are those caused by the absence of infrastructure—the environmental health problems that arise from a concentration of people and enterprises when there is a lack of provision for piped water supplies, sanitation and drainage, solid-waste collection and health care. Increased prosperity brings with it increased potential to invest in the needed infrastructure and services. For those with rising incomes, this also means rising capacity to pay for these and if provided efficiently, most or all costs of provision can be recouped from the users. As these initial 'environmental health' problems are addressed, and as the city's economic base grows, so chemical and physical hazards grow, many of them originating in enterprises.[144] If growing economic prosperity is based on rapid industrialization, this can mean serious air and water pollution and growing problems with hazardous wastes. In cities with rapid industrial growth, there are often strong pressures brought by industrial and commercial concerns to limit pollution control. Rapid industrial growth in the absence of pollution control can produce very unhealthy cities—of which Cubatao in Brazil is one of the best known examples, although environmental quality in this city has improved greatly since it was known as 'the Valley of Death'.[145]

As chemical and physical hazards are addressed, through much improved pollution control, waste management and attention to occupational health and safety, they usually give way to environmental problems linked to high-consumption lifestyles and an increasing number of private automobiles. Problems of industrial pollution are often lessened too, through the deindustrialization of cities or more effective pollution control. The mix of air pollutants also changes, reflecting the increased role of automobile emissions and the reduced role of industry and power stations. And the large cities also have an increasing impact on their wider regions.

This movement through the four different categories in Table 8.7 can also be interpreted as

TABLE 8.6 Incidence of household environmental problems in Accra, Jakarta and Sao Paulo

Environmental indicator	Incidence of problem (percentage of all households surveyed)		
	Accra	Jakarta	Sao Paulo
Water			
No water source at residence	46	13	5
No drinking-water source at residence	46	33	5
Sanitation			
Toilets shared with more than 10 households	48	14–20	<3
Solid waste			
No home garbage collection	89	37	5
Waste stored indoors in open container	40	27	14
Indoor air quality			
Wood or charcoal is main cooking fuel	76	2	0
Mosquito coils used	45	28	8
Pests			
Flies observed in the kitchen	82	38	17
Rats/mice often seen in the home	61	82	25

Source: McGranahan, Gordon and Jacob Songsore, 'Wealth, health and the urban household; weighing environmental burdens in Accra, Jakarta and Sao Paulo', Environment, vol. 36, no. 6, July/Aug. 1994, 9. Data drawn from surveys conducted by the Stockholm Environment Institute in collaboration with a local research team in each of these cities in late 1991 and early 1992. Sample sizes were 1,000 for Accra and Sao Paulo and 1,055 for Jakarta.

TABLE 8.7   Typical environmental problems for urban centres of different sizes and within nations with different levels of per capita income

Environmental problems and influences	Category 1: Most urban centres in most low-income nations and many middle-income nations	Category 2: More prosperous cities in low- and middle-income countries—including many that have developed as industrial centres	Category 3: Prosperous major cities/metropolitan areas in middle- and upper-income countries	Category 4: Cities in upper-income countries
Access to basic infrastructure and services —water supply and sanitation —drainage —solid-waste collection —primary health care	Many or most of the urban population lacking water piped into the home and adequate sanitation. Also many or most residential areas lacking drainage so such areas often having mud and stagnant pools. Many residential areas at risk from flooding. Many or most residential areas also lacking services for solid-waste collection and health care, especially the poorer and more peripheral areas.	Piped water supplies and sanitation systems reaching a considerable proportion of the population but a large proportion of low-income households not reached, especially those in illegal or informal settlements on the city periphery. Typically, solid-waste collection and health care reaching a higher proportion of the population than in category 1 but still with between one- and two-thirds of the population unserved.	Generally acceptable water supplies for most of the population. Provision for sanitation, solid-waste collection and primary health care also much improved, although 10–30 per cent of the population still lacking provision (or adequate provision). The proportion of people lacking adequate services generally smaller than in category 2 but in very large cities, this can still mean millions who lack basic services. In large metropolitan areas, service provision often least adequate in weakest, peripheral municipalities.	Provision of all four services for virtually all the population.
Pollution & waste —water pollution	The main water 'pollution' problems arise from a lack of provision for sanitation and garbage collection.	Most local rivers and other water bodies polluted from industrial and urban discharges and storm and surface run-off.	Severe problems from untreated or inadequately treated industrial and municipal liquid wastes that are usually dumped without treatment in local water bodies.	Much improved levels of treatment for liquid wastes from homes and productive activities. Concern with amenity values and toxic wastes.
—air pollution	Often serious indoor air pollution, where soft coal or biomass fuels used as domestic fuels—especially where indoor heating is needed.	Often severe problems from industrial and residential emissions. Indoor air pollution in households lessened as households with higher incomes switch to cleaner fuels.	Increasingly important contribution to air pollution from motor vehicles. Perhaps less from industry as city's economic base becomes less pollution intensive and as measures begin to be taken to control industrial emissions.	Motor vehicles becoming the major source of air pollution. Little or no heavy industry remains in the city and the control of air pollution becomes a greater priority for citizens.
—solid-waste disposal	Open dumping of the solid wastes that are collected.	Mostly uncontrolled landfills; mixed wastes.	A proportion of landfills controlled or semi-controlled.	Controlled sanitary landfills, incineration, some recovery.
—hazardous waste management	No capacity but also volumes generally small.	Severe problems; limited capacities to deal with it.	Growing capacity but often still a serious problem.	Moving from remediation to prevention.
Physical and chemical hazards in the home and workplace	The main physical hazards associated with poor-quality living and working environments—especially domestic and workplace accidents. There may be serious occupational hazards among certain small-scale and household enterprises.	A great increase in the problems with occupational health and safety at all levels and scales of industry. Government often not giving occupational health and safety adequate priority. A high proportion of low-income households living in illegal or informal settlements with high risks of accidental injuries—especially if they settle on dangerous sites.	Improved government supervision or worker organization to ensure improved occupational health and safety. Often, a decline in the proportion of the population working in hazardous jobs. A rise in the contribution of traffic accidents to premature death and injury. Improved provision of water, sanitation, drainage and health care lessening physical hazards in residential areas.	A high level of occupational health and safety and active programmes promoting injury reduction for homes and on the roads.

TABLE 8.7 continued

Environmental problems and influences	Category 1: Most urban centres in most low-income nations and many middle-income nations	Category 2: More prosperous cities in low- and middle-income countries—including many that have developed as industrial centres	Category 3: Prosperous major cities/metropolitan areas in middle- and upper-income countries	Category 4: Cities in upper-income countries
Land	Urban expansion taking place with few or no controls—or where controls exist, they are largely ignored.	Urban expansion continuing to take place with few or no controls; uncontrolled or ineffective land use controls; often rapid growth in illegal or informal settlements, including illegal land subdivisions for wealthier groups; loss of farmland to expanding urban areas and to demand for building materials and aggregate.	More controls imposed on urban expansion but these often prove ineffective as illegal residential developments continue, in the face of a considerable section of the population unable to afford to buy or rent the cheapest 'legal' land site or house. Different groups often in conflict over use of best located undeveloped land sites or of use of agricultural land for urban purposes.	Land use tightly regulated—perhaps to the point where house prices begin to rise as land supplies for new housing become constrained.
Other environmental hazards	No provision by the public authorities for disaster preparedness; disasters (floods, storms .....) often common with severe damage and loss of life. In cities with an industrial base, inadequate provision to guard against industrial disasters and to act to limit the damage and loss of life, when they occur.		No provision by the public authorities for disaster preparedness; disasters (floods, storms .....) often common with severe damage and loss of life. In cities with an	industrial base, inadequate provision to guard against industrial disasters and to act to limit the damage and loss of life, when they occur.

Source: Based on a table in Bartone, Carl, Janis Bernstein, Josef Leitmann and Jochen Eigen, *Towards Environmental Strategies for Cities; Policy Considerations for Urban Environmental Management in Developing Countries*, UNDP/UNCHS/World Bank Urban Management Program, 18, World Bank, Washington DC, 1994.

an increasing capacity for individuals and households to pass on the environmental costs and the responsibilities for environmental management to higher levels.[146] As a recent paper noted:

many environmental services such as piped water, sewerage connections, electricity and door to door garbage collection not only export pollution (from the household to the city) but also shift both the intellectual and practical burdens of environmental management from the household to the government or utility.[147]

Thus, connection to a sewer allows a household to get rid of excreta and waste waters with no hazard to the household itself and with great convenience—but the aggregation of all households' liquid wastes within a city when disposed of untreated can seriously damage regional water bodies. The same is true for solid wastes. If coal- or wood-fuelled stoves are replaced with electric cookers, the air pollution burden may be transferred from the home and the settlement to the power station.[148]

But cities do not have to successively undergo the four different phases summarized in Table 8.7. In most urban centres in relatively low-income countries, far more could be done to improve water supply, sanitation, drainage and health care using existing resources—to the point where it matches the performance of urban centres in category 2 or 3—through using existing resources allocated in different ways. This

also brings other important advantages—for instance the stimulus that infrastructure improvement in residential areas brings to household investment in improving or extending housing that also creates employment.[149]

Similarly, no city has to 'wait' until a certain per capita income is reached before action is taken. It is not necessary for cities to undergo a 'dirty industry' phase as part of their development—as most of the older North American and European cities have undergone and as many industrial centres in the South are also undergoing. The costs of pollution control are often less important in the total costs of an industry than industrialists like to claim, especially when new industries are set up and 'clean' industrial technology can be installed. In addition, a clean, well-managed city is in itself an important asset in attracting many kinds of new enterprise. Similarly, the problems of pollution and traffic congestion associated with many of the world's wealthiest cities today, most of which are 'post-industrial' cities as they have very little industry, are also problems that can be avoided or much reduced with foresight. It is the way that cities expand and new settlements develop on their periphery and the spatial form of these new developments that will strongly influence the extent of private automobile use and the scale of rural land loss to urbanization.

The extent to which urban centres in low-income nations can address the deficiencies in infrastructure and services and in so doing address also the most serious life-threatening and health-threatening environmental problems will be much influenced by local political and economic circumstances. The uniqueness of each city must be stressed again—not least in the form of its political economy. Each city has within it a great range of actors and institutions that contribute to the city's economy and built form and that are also seeking changes in policy and approach from all agencies in government. Most are in competition with each other for scarce public resources and political favours. Many are seeking official approval for land developments that can multiply one hundredfold or more the value of land. Evidence of this competition is evident in every city's local newspaper and often in national or regional newspapers as citizen groups demand action against polluters or castigate the performance of utility companies or as those illegally settled in the city's watershed try to avoid eviction. It is the outcome of this process that largely determines what investments are made in infrastructure, which environmental problems receive priority and who benefits (and who does

not). In political systems that inhibit organized action by low-income groups or that are undemocratic, most investments in infrastructure and services may end up serving middle- and upper-income groups.

One possible way to greatly improve the quality and range of infrastructure and services in relatively low-income countries is to draw on the knowledge and resources of low-income communities.[150] There are precedents that show how much can be achieved with modest resources.[151] But achieving this will require more resources and powers devolved to community level—and not just more responsibilities.[152] It should also be remembered that most low-income individuals and households have limited 'free time' to devote to community initiatives, as most adult members have to work long hours. In addition, no assumptions should be made by external agencies as to how much community participation the inhabitants of a particular settlement want; low-income households may prefer to spend a larger proportion of their income to obtain provision for water, sanitation, garbage collection and environmental management that does not involve community management.

Notes and References

1. World Bank, *World Development Report 1994; Infrastructure for Development*, Oxford University Press, Oxford and New York, 1994.

2. *Ibid.*

3. *Ibid.*

4. *Ibid.*

5. *Ibid.*

6. *Ibid.*

7. *Ibid.*

8. Most of the statistics on global and regional coverage for water supply and sanitation are drawn from Water Supply and Sanitation Collaborative Council, *Water Supply and Sanitation Sector Monitoring Report 1993*, World Health Organization and UNICEF, 1993.

9. Water Supply and Sanitation Collaborative Council, *Water Supply and Sanitation Sector Monitoring Report 1994*, World Health Organization and UNICEF, 1994.

10. Cairncross, Sandy, 'Water supply and the urban poor' in Jorge E. Hardoy and others (eds.), *The Poor Die Young: Housing and Health in Third World Cities*, Earthscan Publications, London, 1990.

11. Water Supply and Sanitation Collaborative Council, *Water Supply and Sanitation Sector Monitoring Report 1990 (Baseline Year)*, World Health Organization and UNICEF, 1992.

12. *Ibid.*

13. *Ibid.*

14. Water Supply and Sanitation Collaborative Council, *Water Supply and Sanitation Sector Monitoring Report 1993*,

World Health Organization and UNICEF, 1993.

15. Cairncross 1990, *op. cit.*

16. SPARC, 'Waiting for water: the experience of poor communities in Bombay', Bombay, 1994, cited in Swaminathan, Madhura, 'Aspects of urban poverty in Bombay', *Environment and Urbanization*, vol. 7, no. 1, April 1995.

17. Briscoe, John, 'Selected primary health care revisited', in Joseph S. Tulchin (ed.), *Health, Habitat and Development*, Lynne Reinner, Boulder, 1986.

18. Avramov, Dragana, *Homelessness in the European Union: Social and Legal Context for Housing Exclusion in the 1990s*, FEANTSA (European Federation of National Organizations Working with the Homeless), Brussels, 1995.

19. WHO, *Our Planet, Our Health*, Report of the Commission on Health and Environment, Geneva, 1992.

20. Cairncross, Sandy, Jorge E. Hardoy and David Satterthwaite, 'The urban context', in Jorge E. Hardoy and others, *The Poor Die Young: Housing and Health in Third World Cities*, Earthscan Publications, London, 1990, 1–24.

21. Hardoy, Jorge E., Diana Mitlin and David Satterthwaite, *Environmental Problems in Third World Cities*, Earthscan Publications, London, 1992.

22. Water Supply and Sanitation Collaborative Council 1993, *op. cit.*

23. Official sources quoted in Carr, Michelle, 'Metropolitan planning and management in the Third World: a case

study of Quito, Ecuador', in UNCHS (Habitat), *Metropolitan Planning and Management in the Developing World: Abidjan and Quito*, Nairobi, 1992, 83–137.

24. Sources for Box 8.1: This is an updated version of a box published in Hardoy, Jorge E., Diana Mitlin and David Satterthwaite, *Environmental Problems in Third World Cities*, Earthscan Publications, London, 1992. For Dar es Salaam, Kulaba, Saitiel, 'Local government and the management of urban services in Tanzania', in Stren, Richard E. and Rodney R. White (eds.), *African Cities in Crisis*, Westview Press, USA, 1989, 203–45. For Khartoum, El Sammani, Mohamed O., Mohamed El Hadi Abu Sin, M. Talha, B.M. El Hassan and Ian Haywood, 'Management problems of Greater Khartoum', in Stren, Richard E. and Rodney R. White (eds.), *African Cities in Crisis*, Westview Press, USA, 1989, 246–75. For Kinshasa, Mbuyi, Kankonde, 'Kinshasa: problems of land management, infrastructure and food supply', in Stren, Richard E. and Rodney R. White (eds.), *African Cities in Crisis*, Westview Press, USA, 1989, 148–75. For Calcutta, Madras and Jakarta, Sivaramakrishnan, K. C. and Leslie Green, *Metropolitan Management— The Asian Experience*, Oxford University Press (for the World Bank), 1986. For Faisalabad and Karachi, Hasan, Arif, *Profiles of three Pakistani Cities; Karachi, Faisalabad and Thatta*,

Background paper prepared for the Global Report on Human Settlements 1996, Karachi, 1994.

25. Oya-Sawyer, Diana, Rogelio Fernandez-Castilla and Roberto Luis de Melo Monte-Mor, 'The impact of urbanization and industrialization on mortality in Brazil', *World Health Statistics Quarterly*, vol. 40, 1987.

26. Jacobi, Pedro R., 'Household and environment in the city of Sao Paulo; problems, perceptions and solutions', *Environment and Urbanization*, vol. 6, no. 1, April 1994.

27. Castaneda, Tarsicio, *Para Combatir la Pobreza: Politica Social y Descentralizacion en Chile durante los '80*, Centro de Estudios Publicos, Santiago, 1990.

28. Water Supply and Sanitation Collaborative Council 1993, *op. cit.*

29. Sinnatamby, Gehan, 'Low cost sanitation' in Jorge E. Hardoy and others (eds.), *The Poor Die Young: Housing and Health in Third World Cities*, Earthscan, London, 1990.

30. Water Supply and Sanitation Collaborative Council 1994, *op. cit.*

31. *Ibid.*

32. Water Supply and Sanitation Collaborative Council 1993, *op. cit.*

33. See Cairncross, Hardoy and Satterthwaite 1990, *op. cit.*

34. See for instance the Indian fortnightly environment and science journal *Down to Earth* reports on these conflicts in Indian cities.

35. Hardoy, Jorge E. and David Satterthwaite, *Squatter Citizen: Life in the Urban Third World*, Earthscan Publications, London, 1989.

36. These draw on the same sources as the previous Box (see no. 24) except for Kingston, which comes from Robotham, Don, 'Redefining urban health policy: the Jamaica case', Paper presented at the Urban Health Conference, London School of Hygiene and Tropical Medicine, 6–8 Dec. 1994, and additional material drawn on Khartoum from Ahmad, Adil Mustafa and Ata El-Hassan El-Batthani, 'Poverty in Khartoum', *Environment and Urbanization*, vol. 7, no. 2, Oct. 1995.

37. Cointreau, Sandra, *Environmental Management of Urban Solid Waste in Developing Countries*, Urban Development Technical Paper No. 5, The World Bank, Washington DC, 1982.

38. Nath, K. J. and others, 'Urban solid waste: appropriate technology', Proceedings of the 9th Water and Waste Engineering for Developing Countries Conference, Loughborough University of Technology, England 1983, quoted in UNCHS, *Refuse Collection Vehicles for Developing Countries*, HS/138/88E, UNCHS (Habitat), Nairobi, Kenya, 1988.

39. Same sources as Boxes 8.2 and 8.3; also UNCHS (Habitat), *Report of the Regional Workshop on the Promotion of Waste Recycling and Reuse in Developing Countries*, Nairobi, 1993.

40. Cointreau 1982, *op. cit.*

41. Kulaba, Saitiel, 'Local government and the management of urban services in Tanzania', in Stren, Richard E. and Rodney R. White (eds.), *African Cities in Crisis*, Westview Press, USA, 1989, 203–45.

42. Momin, M. A., 'Housing in Bangladesh', *The Bangladesh Observer*, 12 Feb. 1992 quoted in ESCAP, *State of Urbanization in Asia and the Pacific 1993*, Economic and Social Commission for Asia and the Pacific, ST/ESCAP/1300, United Nations, New York, 1993.

43. UNCHS, *Refuse Collection Vehicles for Developing Countries*, HS/138/88E, UNCHS (Habitat), Nairobi, Kenya, 1988.

44. Cointreau 1982, *op. cit.*

45. *Ibid.*

46. White, Rodney R., *North, South and the Environmental Crisis*, University of Toronto Press, Toronto, 1993. See also Hoque, Bilquis A., M. M. Hoque, N. Ali and Sarah E. Coghlan, 'Sanitation in a slum in Bangladesh: a challenge for the 1990s', *Environment and Urbanization*, vol. 6, no. 2, Oct. 1994, 79–85.

47. Surjadi, Charles, 'Respiratory diseases of mothers and children and environmental factors among households in Jakarta', *Environment and Urbanization*, vol. 5, no. 2, Oct. 1993, 78–86.

48. Jacobi 1994, *op. cit.*

49. See Carrion, Diego, Mario Vasconez and Jorge Garcia, 'La problematica del acceso a los servicios urbanos para los sectores populares en America Latina: desafios e ideales en la busqueda de soliciones', Economic Development Institute, World Bank, 1989.

50. UNCHS (Habitat), *Report of the Regional Workshop on the Promotion of Waste Recycling and Reuse in Developing Countries*, Nairobi, 1993.

51. UNCHS 1993, *op. cit.*

52. Table 21.4 in World Resources Institute, *World Resources 1992–93: a Guide to the Global Environment: Toward Sustainable Development*, Oxford University Press, Oxford, 1992, 385 pages, drawing from OECD and Economic Commission for Europe sources; OECD, *The State of the Environment*, Organization for Economic Cooperation and Development, Paris, 1991; also OECD, *OECD Environmental Data Compendium 1991*, Organization for Economic Co-operation and Development, Paris, 1991.

53. UNCHS 1993, *op. cit.*

54. OECD 1991, *op. cit.*

55. UNCHS 1993, *op. cit.*

56. Jonker, J. F. and J. W. A. Verwaart, 'Comparison of solid waste management practices', in Peter A. Erkelens and George van der Meulen (eds.), *Urban Environment in Developing Countries*, Eindhoven University of Technology, Eindhoven, 1994, 137–45.

57. Cointreau 1982, *op. cit.*

58. De Coura Cuentro, Stenio and Dji Malla Gadji, 'The collection and management of household garbage' in Hardoy and others (eds.), 1990, *op. cit.* 169–88.

59. Fernandez Aller, Norberto, 'Nuevas tecnologias para la solucion del problema de los residuous solidos', Madrid, 1988 quoted in di Pace, Maria, Sergio Federovisky, Jorge E. Hardoy, Jorge E. Morello and Alfredo Stein, 'Latin America', ch. 8 in Richard Stren, Rodney White and Joseph Whitney (eds.), *Sustainable Cities: Urbanization and the Environment in International Perspective*, Westview Press, Boulder, 1992, 205–27.

60. See for instance Furedy, Christine, 'Social aspects of solid waste recovery in Asian cities', *Environmental Sanitation Reviews*, no. 30, Dec. ENSIC, Asian Institute of Technology, Bangkok, 1990, 2–52.

61. Furedy, Christine, 'Garbage: exploring non-conventional options in Asian cities', *Environment and Urbanization*, vol. 4, no. 2, Oct. 1992.

62. Furedy 1990, *op. cit.*

63. UNCHS 1993, *op. cit.*

64. Pacheco, Margarita, 'Recycling in Bogota; developing a culture for urban sustainability', *Environment and Urbanization*, vol. 4, no. 2, Oct. 1992.

65. UNCHS (Habitat), 'The role of human settlements in improving community health in Africa', International Conference on Community Health in Africa, Brazzaville, Congo, Sept. 1992.

66. Løvig Simonsen, Ole, 'Sustainable transport', speech presented at the Symposium on Sustainable Consumption, Oslo, 19/20 Jan. 1994.

67. IEA/OECD, *Energy Balances of OECD Countries, 1992–1993*, Paris, 1995, quoted in OECD, *OECD in Figures: Statistics on the Member Countries*, 1995 ed. Paris.

68. Parson, E.A., *The Transport Sector and Global Warming*, J.F. Kennedy School of Government, Cambridge, Mass., 1990.

69. OECD 1995, *op. cit.*

70. See Ch. 1 for more details.

71. Paboon C., J.R. Kenworthy, P. W. G. Newman and P. Barter, 'Bangkok: anatomy of a traffic disaster', Paper presented at the Asian Studies Association of Australia Biennial Conference 1994, Murdoch University, Perth, 1994.

72. Institut d'Estudis Metropolitans de Barcelona, *Cities of the World: Statistical, Administrative and Graphical Information on the Major Urban Areas of the World*, Institut d'Estudis Metropolitans de Barcelona, Barcelona, 1988, vol. 5.

73. MacKenzie, James J. and Michael P. Walsh, *Driving Forces: Motor Vehicle Trends and their Implications for Global Warming, Energy Strategies and Transportation Planning*, World Resources Institute, Washington DC, 1990.

74. AAMA, *World Motor Vehicle Data: 1993 Edition*, Washington DC, 1993, quoted

in World Resources Institute (WRI), *World Resources 1996–7*, Oxford University Press, Oxford and New York, 1996.

75. Density is closely linked to effective public transport as it enables sufficient people to be in reasonable proximity to any one transit stop. Many other factors can diminish the role of density through below 30 persons per hectate it becomes almost impossible to provide other than an irregular bus service. See Newman, Peter, Jeff Kenworthy and Peter Vintila, *Housing Transport and Urban Form*, National Housing Strategy Paper 15, Dept of Health, Housing and Community Services, Canberra, 1992.

76. Scimeni, G., 'Recent urban development trends in North America and Europe, and their impact upon the global environment', Paper presented to the Osaka International Forum on Global Environment and the City, July 1990.

77. Newman, Peter and Jeffrey Kenworthy, *Cities and Automobile Dependence: an International Sourcebook*, Gower, Aldershot, 1989.

78. Løvig Simonsen 1994, *op. cit.*

79. Barton, H., 'City transport: strategies for sustainability', in M. J. Breheny (ed.), *Sustainable Development and Urban Form*, European Research in Regional Science 2, Pion, London, 1992, 197–216.

80. Newman and Kenworthy 1989, *op. cit.*

81. Including jitneys and other forms of paratransit.

82. ESCAP, *State of Urbanization in Asia and the Pacific 1993*, Economic and Social Commission for Asia and the Pacific, ST/ESCAP/1300, United Nations, New York, 1993.

83. ESCAP 1993, *op. cit.*

84. WRI 1996, *op. cit.*

85. European Environment Agency, *Europe's Environment: the Dobris Assessment*, Copenhagen, 1995. See also the example of Almere in the Netherlands described in Ch. 9.

86. Gilbert, Richard, 'Cities and Global Warming', in James McCulloch (ed.), *Cities and Global Change*, Climate Institute, Washington DC, 1992.

87. Newman, Kenworthy and Vintila 1992, *op. cit.*

88. Newman, Peter and Jeff Kenworthy with Les Robinson, *Winning Back the Cities*, Australian Consumers' Association, Pluto Press, Australia, 1992.

89. UNCHS (Habitat), *Urban Public Transport in Developing Countries*, UNCHS (Habitat), Nairobi, 1994.

90. WRI 1996, *op. cit.*

91. Mohan, D. and C. J. Romer, 'Accident mortality and morbidity in developing countries', in M. Manciaux and C. J. Romer (eds.), *Accidents in Childhood and Adolescence; The Role of Research*, World Health Organization, Geneva, 1991, 31–8 quoted in Odero, W., 'Road traffic accidents in Kenya', Paper presented at

the Urban Health Conference, London School of Hygiene and Tropical Medicine, 6–8 Dec. 1994.

92. WHO, *The World Health Report 1995: Bridging the Gaps*. Geneva, 1995.

93. WHO 1992, *op. cit.*

94. European Environment Agency 1995, *op. cit.*

95. OECD 1995, *op. cit.*

96. Department of Transport, UK, quoted in Central Statistical Office, *Social Trends*, 1994 edn., HMSO, London, 1994.

97. Odero, W., 'Road traffic accidents in Kenya', Paper presented at the Urban Health Conference, London School of Hygiene and Tropical Medicine, 6–8 Dec. 1994.

98. India was reported to have 60,000 fatalities a year from road accidents—see WRI 1996, *op. cit.*

99. Centre for Health Economics, 'Economic costs of traffic accidents', *Health Economics Issues*, vol. 1, no. 1, Chulalongkom University, Bangkok, 1994, 2–5.

100. See tables 4a, 4b, 5a and 5b in Bourbeau, Robert, 'Analyse comparative de la mortalité violente dans les pays développés en dans quelques pays en développement durant la période 1985–89', *World Health Statistics Quarterly*, vol. 46, no. 1, 1993, 4–33.

101. For instance, in 1991, there were 8,863 deaths from traffic accidents in Sao Paulo and 1,365 in Seoul; in Buenos Aires, there were 3,750 in 1988. Figures from the Governor of Tokyo and Summit Conference of the Major Cities of the World, *Major Cities of the World*, Tokyo Metropolitan Government, Tokyo, 1991, quoted in Sassen, Saskia, *Cities in a World Economy*, Pine Forge Press, Thousand Oaks, London, New Delhi, 1994.

102. ESCAP 1993, *op. cit.*

103. See for instance European Environment Agency 1995, *op. cit.*

104. See the papers in *Environment and Urbanization* vol. 6, no. 1, April 1994 on evictions.

105. This section draws on UNCHS (Habitat), *Urban Public Transport in Developing Countries*, UNCHS (Habitat), Nairobi, 1994.

106. UNCHS 1994, *op. cit.*

107. Hardoy, Mitlin and Satterthwaite 1992, *op. cit.*

108. Godard, Xavier and Pierre Teurnier, *Les transports urbains en Afrique à l'heure de l'ajustement*, Karthala, Paris, 1992, 139.

109. Hardoy, Jorge E. and David Satterthwaite, *Squatter Citizen: Life in the Urban Third World*, Earthscan Publications, London, 1989.

110. World Bank 1994, *op. cit.*

111. Cairncross, Frances, 'The death of distance; a survey of telecommunications', *The Economist*, 30 Sept. 1995.

112. World Bank 1994, *op. cit.*

113. Cairncross 1995, *op. cit.*

114. *Ibid.*

115. Obviously, the price varies considerably from country to country—and depending on the power and speed of the computer and the speed with which the modem transfers data. But in many countries in the North, a computer plus modem can be purchased for this price, if starting with the cheapest available model.

116. Hepworth, Mark E., 'Planning for the Information city; the challenge and response', in Joanne Fox-Przeworski, John Goddard and Mark de Jong (eds.), *Urban Regeneration in a Changing Economy—an International Perspective*, Clarendon Press, Oxford, 1991, 24–52.

117. Gillespie, A., 'Communications technologies and the future of the city', in M. J. Breheny (ed.), *Sustainable Development and Urban Form*, European Research in Regional Science 2, Pion, London, 1992, 67–78.

118. Cairncross 1995, *op. cit.*

119. Baker, Timothy H., 'The consumer in the global market', *OECD Observer*, no. 192, Feb./March 1995, 13–15.

120. Baker 1995, *op. cit.*

121. Weijers, Thea, Rob Meijer and Erno Spoelman, 'Telework remains "made to measure"; the large-scale introduction of telework in the Netherlands', in *Information Technology and Society CD-ROM*, Block 5: IT Futures, The Open University, Milton Keynes, 1995.

122. Gray, M., N. Hodson and G. Gordon, *Teleworking Explained*, John Wiley and Sons, Chichester, 1993.

123. Gillespie 1992, *op. cit.*

124. Warf, Barney, 'Telecommunications and the changing geographies of knowledge transmission in the late 20th century', *Urban Studies*, vol. 32, no. 2, 1995, 375.

125. De Sola Pool, Ithiel, 'Communications technology and land use', *The Annals of the American Academy of Political and Social Science*, no. 451, Sept. 1980, 1–12.

126. This section draws heavily on Mokhtarian, Patricia L., 'Telecommunications in urban planning selected North American examples' prepared for Habitat II Global Workshop on Transport and Communication for Urban Development, Singapore, 1995.

127. Porat, M., *The Information Economy: Definition and Measurement*, Office of Telecommunications, Special Publication 77–12(1), US Department of Commerce, Washington DC, 1977, quoted in Hepworth, Mark E., 'Planning for the Information city; the challenge and response', in Joanne Fox-Przeworski, John Goddard and Mark de Jong (eds.), *Urban Regeneration in a Changing Economy—an International Perspective*, Clarendon Press, Oxford, 1991, 24–52.

128. Hepworth 1991, *op. cit.*

129. After Porat 1977, *op. cit.*

130. Mokhtarian 1995, *op. cit.*

131. For a case study of the teleport, see Jennings, Larkin and Harmeet S. Sawhney, 'New York', ch. 6 in

Schmandt, Jurgen, Frederick Williams and Robert H. Wilson (eds.), *Telecommunications Policy and Economic Development: the New State Role*, Praeger, New York, 1989.

132. Blazar, William A., Mary Ellen Spector and John Grathwol, 'The sky above, the teleport below', *Planning*, Dec. 1985, 22–6.

133. Gillespie 1992, *op. cit.*

134. Graham, Stephen D.N., 'The role of cities in telecommunications development', *Telecommunications Policy*, vol. 16, no. 3, 1992, 187–93.

135. Schmandt, Jurgen, Frederick Williams, Robert H. Wilson and Sharon Strover (eds.), *The New Urban Infrastructure: Cities and Telecommunications*, Praeger, New York, 1990.

136. Hardoy, Mitlin and Satterthwaite 1992, *op. cit.*

137. Ekblad, Solvig and others, *Stressors, Chinese City Dwellings and Quality of Life*, D12, Swedish Council for Building Research, Stockholm, 1991.

138. WHO 1992, *op. cit.*

139. Duhl, Leonard J., *The Social Entrepreneurship of Change*, Pace University Press, New York, 1990.

140. World Bank, *World Development Report 1992*, Oxford University Press, 1992; Bartone, Carl, Janis Bernstein, Josef Leitmann and Jochen Eigen, *Towards Environmental Strategies for Cities; Policy Considerations for Urban Environmental Management in Developing Countries*, UNDP/UNCHS/World Bank Urban Management Program, no. 18, World Bank, Washington DC, 1994.

141. World Bank 1992, *op. cit.*

142. Newman and Kenworthy 1989, *op. cit.*

143. Bartone and others 1994, *op. cit.*

144. Although in cities in locations where domestic heating is necessary for part or most of the year, dirty, smoky fuels used in the home can be a major contributor to ambient air pollution.

145. See Hardoy, Mitlin and Satterthwaite 1992, *op. cit.*

146. McGranahan, Gordon and Jacob Songsore, 'Wealth, health and the urban household; weighing environmental burdens in Accra, Jakarta and Sao Paulo', *Environment*, vol. 36, no. 6, July/Aug. 1994, 4–11 and 40–5.

147. McGranahan and Songsore 1994, *op. cit.*

148. Although this is only so if a thermal power station is used and it lacks emission controls.

149. Strassmann, W. Paul, 'Oversimplification in housing analysis, with reference to land markets and mobility', *Cities*, vol. 11, no. 6, Dec. 1994, 377–83.

150. Douglass, Mike, 'The political economy of urban poverty and environmental management in Asia: access, empowerment and community-based alternatives', *Environment and Urbanization*, vol. 4, no. 2, Oct. 1992.

151. Chapter 11 will give some examples.

152. Douglass 1992, and McGranahan and Songsore 1993, *op. cit.*

PART III

Responses to Conditions and Trends

9 Settlements Planning and Management

9.1 Introduction

Various new approaches to settlements planning and management have been developed over the last 10–15 years—or innovations dating from earlier years applied more widely. This can be seen in settlement planning, land use control, the management of infrastructure and transport planning and management. In each, there is a greater stress on public authorities working with the private sector and community organizations and in many aspects of their work, moving from control to enablement. Planning is seen less as 'development control' and more as encouraging and supporting the multiplicity of private initiatives from citizen groups, NGOs and local, national and international enterprises that make a settlement prosper. There is also a much greater stress placed on integrating social, economic and environmental goals. One other important change over the last ten to fifteen years is the extent to which many international agencies are also giving a higher priority to increasing the capacity of city and local authorities in settlements planning and management.

This chapter reviews seven areas. The first and second are new directions in settlement planning and land development and management where public authorities place a greater stress on enablement—including more actively supporting the initiatives of the private sector and of community-based organizations. The third is the management of environmental infrastructure where private-sector institutions have a greater role, including non-profit institutions and NGOs. The fourth is in transport where city and municipal authorities seek to ensure the efficient movement of people and goods within their boundaries but with less automobile-dependent models than in the past and with more attention to meeting the transport needs of those unable to use private automobiles. The fifth and sixth areas reviewed in this chapter are about means. The first describes new participatory tools and methods through which public authorities (and international agencies) can fully involve the citizens in each locality in development projects. The second describes new approaches to training and education. The final area reviewed is the increased international assistance given to settlements planning and management.

9.2 New Directions in Settlements Planning[1]

The role of planning

Settlement planning is central to ensuring that urban development and management meets sustainable development goals—and is still widely recognized and used by both national and local governments. But as Chapter 7 noted, there are serious shortcomings within many current approaches. In light of the increasingly pressing urban problems described in earlier chapters, the traditional approaches to planning and the use of planning instruments have been critically reviewed and revised with a view to making them more effective.

The need to reappraise the urban planning process was given added urgency by the social and environmental impacts of rapid urbanization in the South and the heightened concern for sustainable development promoted by the action plan of the Earth Summit, Agenda 21. The Human Settlements chapter of Agenda 21 (Chapter 7) urges, among other things:

- The promotion of understanding among policy-makers of the adverse consequences of unplanned settlements in environmentally vulnerable areas and of the appropriate national and local land use and settlements policies required for this purpose.

- The promotion of sustainable land-use planning and management, with the objective of providing for the land requirements of human settlements development through environmentally sound physical planning and land use.

- That all countries, as appropriate, and in accordance with their national plans, objectives and priorities . . . adopt innovative city planning strategies to address environmental and social issues.

- The creating as appropriate, of national legislation to guide the implementation of public policies for environmentally sound urban development, land utilization, housing and for the improved management of urban expansion.

- The development of fiscal incentives and land use control measures, including land use planning solutions for a more rational and environmentally sound use of limited land resources.

- The development and support of the implementation of improved land management practices which deal comprehensively with potentially competing land requirements for agriculture, industry, transport, urban development, open spaces, preserves and other vital needs.

The challenge of planning is not only how to contain urban growth but also how to marshall human, financial and technical resources to ensure that social, economic and environmental needs are addressed within urban growth. Within this, issues of sustainable urban development are now of increasing concern, signposted by *Our Common Future*, the 1987 Brundtland Commission Report[2] and the 1992 Earth Summit. The challenge of planning is to make the activity be seen as a process that ensures that social, environmental and economic goals are met, rather than as an 'end state' activity.

Improved planning and implementation processes and approaches

As a reaction to the shortcomings of traditional master planning, and more recently to address the needs of sustainable development, various countries have adopted new processes and approaches to urban plans, including Malaysia, Indonesia, Tanzania, China, Sri Lanka and the UK. These approaches can be grouped under Structure Planning, Action Planning and Strategic Planning. These are outlined below,

with examples given in boxes. Box 9.1 describes the use of structure planning in Malaysia.

Action planning

Action Planning is generally defined as an implementation-orientated process to solve problems at a local level. It has a short term perspective, resolving issues in the most direct manner with a minimum of data collection and traditional planning procedures. The problems to be remedied may be physical, social, or economic and local community participation in decision-making is a key to success. Action planning also draws on the local adaption of experiences that proved successful in other contexts—a 'learning by doing' approach. Box 9.2 outlines how in Sri Lanka, local upgrading initiatives are prepared through workshops that bring together representatives from the community, the local authority and the national agency responsible for this work—the National Housing Development Authority.

The action planning approach fits well with the view of planning as 'process' rather than 'product' and with the parallel emphasis on community involvement at an early stage in the planning process. However, overemphasis on an action planning approach may run the risk of producing a number of uncoordinated projects or programmes which do not deal with underlying problems. For this reason, it is generally agreed that action planning should be implemented within the framework of a city-wide strategic planning approach.

BOX 9.1
Structure Planning in Malaysia

Malaysia's Town and Country Planning Act 1976 introduced a system of structure planning modelled very closely on the equivalent British legislation of 1971, including much of the procedure for preparation and approval of structure plans. As in Britain, the aim was to introduce a framework of strategic planning and policies to guide the social, economic and physical development of urban areas. According to the Act, structure plans consist of written statements accompanied by diagrams and illustrations, and provide the basis for the preparation of detailed local plans. In Malaysia, structure planning replaced the previous system of map-based plans, prepared under the Town Board Enactment, which had come to be seen as rigid and

unable to cope with the rapid pace of urban development.

The first structure plan was for Kuala Lumpur and this was approved in 1984. In the decade following the Act, only two other structure plans were completed and approved, with a further eleven in preparation. The structure planning system in Malaysia has considerable advantages over the previous system; it is much more comprehensive in terms of its consideration of the various factors which influence development; it is much more flexible to allow for changing circumstances; it is much better able to respond to community needs and aspirations; and it distinguishes between the broad goals and strategies on the one hand and the detailed physical development involved in local plans on the other.

However, it has also revealed serious shortcomings. The process of plan preparation has taken too long, with the risk

that plans are out of date before they are approved. The delay in preparation has been due partly to a shortage of skilled planning staff, but also to a tendency to be too comprehensive, to collect too many data, and to involve too many committee stages. The legislation itself imposes heavy obligations in terms of survey, often in areas where information is not readily available, and of time-consuming procedures which if not carried out precisely as prescribed could render the plan null and void.

Whilst it is clear that there is a need in Malaysia for some form of development strategy planning for the urban areas, and that the present system of structure planning represents a considerable improvement over what was there before, there must be questions about the appropriateness to Malaysia's current situations of the model of structure planning imported virtually wholesale from Britain.

Source: Devas, Nick, 'Evolving approaches', in Nick Devas and Carole Rakodi (eds.), *Managing Fast Growing Cities; New Approaches to Urban Planning in the Developing World*, Longman, Harlow, 1993, 63–101; drawing on Lee, G. B. and T. T. Siew, 'Urban land policies: towards better management of Asian metropolises: the case of Penang, Malaysia', Paper presented at the First International Workshop on Urban Land Policies, Penang, Malaysia, February 1991 and Lee, G. B., *Urban Planning in Malaysia: History, Assumptions and Issues*, Tempo Publishing, Petaling Jaya, 1991.

BOX 9.2
Action Planning in Sri Lanka

In Sri Lanka, the preparation of the Community Upgrading Plan is one of the main events of the Community Action Planning Cycle. When a settlement is identified for upgrading, a 2-day workshop is conducted by a representative group from the community, the National Housing Development Authority and Local Authority officials. The objective of this exercise is for the community to prepare a development programme for the settlement in partnership with the technical and health officials. The workshop has six main stages:

1. Identification: What are the Problems?
2. Strategies: What are the Approaches?
3. Options and Tradeoffs: What are the Actions?
4. Planning for Implementation: Who does What When and How?
5. Monitoring: What is the Performance and What Have we Learned?
6. Presentation of Community Action Plan to the community.

Source: National Housing Development Authority, Sri Lanka, 1988. See also Box 9.23 for more details of Community Action Planning.

Strategic planning

The key characteristics of strategic planning are:

- cross-sectoral coordination and integration
- financial feasibility
- agreement on comparative advantage of public and private sectors in urban development and management
- enabling role of public sector in support of private sector
- inter- and intra-sectoral choice mechanisms
- linkages to and from national policy issues
- concern with rural-urban relationships
- resolution of conflicts among participants
- regular monitoring and evaluation

Strategic planning is increasingly seen as a participatory approach to integrated urban development to achieve growth management and remedial actions at both the city-wide and local scales. The output of the process is not just a physical development plan for the city but a set of inter-related strategies for city development (including land, infrastructure, finance and institutions). These strategies aim at enabling all public and private initiatives to promote economic growth, provide basic urban services and enhance the quality of the environment. At the city-wide scale the process involves multi-sectoral co-ordination of spatial planning, sectoral investment plans, financial resources and institutional frameworks to meet inter-sectoral city development objectives over a longer time period of say 10–15 years—strategic

planning. At the local scale, the process involves co-ordinated processes of intensive change for a limited area over a short time period (2–5 years)—action planning. At both scales, techniques of multi-sectoral investment planning can be used to prioritize and define a capital plan. The particular form of integrated urban development will vary according to the country and city context. The critical variables will include the degree of decentralization of decision-making and financial autonomy, the relative roles of the public and private sector and the health of the macro-level and local economies. Box 9.3 outlines the strategic planning approach used in the Jakarta city region and how this sought to move beyond a previous over-concentration on physical objectives to an integration of economic, financial and institutional aspects and increased attention to ensuring co-ordination between different sectoral programmes.

Improved standards and regulations

The most common techniques for land use regulations and control are: building regulations, infrastructure regulations (on- and off-site) and zoning. Underlying all three is the question of standards. The correct application of standards will make a crucial impact on the effectiveness of land use regulations as a whole. Where existing standards are unsatisfactory the choices are to do nothing, reduce standards to a level affordable by low income groups or reduce standards for selective areas where low-income groups are or will be encouraged to locate. By modifying existing standards to a level which is affordable by low-income groups, existing settlements can become 'legal' and standards can be enforced. Low-income households can also use new rights to land as security for obtaining loans and they will have more incentives to improve their living conditions. The disadvantages may include the need strictly to enforce environmental controls to avoid standards dropping too low in poor districts, social and political resistance in general and a resistance by city officials to implementing the reduced standards. Box 9.4 describes recent proposals to upgrade planning and building regulations in Dhaka, the capital of Bangladesh.

In some countries it may be appropriate to use a performance standard approach. Performance standards allow a number of ways and means of satisfying objectives for land use rather than the traditional 'prescriptive' approach. In theory, the approach allows objectives for land uses to be met within community priorities and capabilities over time. However, they do present certain difficulties of operation which limit their application. Prescriptive regulations, which may be highly

BOX 9.3
Strategic Planning in Indonesia

A strategic planning approach was used in the Jakarta city region (Jabotabek) in the early 1980s. The new approach followed a period in the 1960s and early 1970s in which planning for the city and region was dominated by physical objectives and the concept of a 'closed city'. During the 1970s there had been a move to sectoral project approaches in water supply, sewerage, railways, toll routes etc. with no coordination. The new strategic approach aimed to ensure linkages between the different issues involved, i.e. economic objectives, urban growth dynamics, inter- and intra-sectoral choices, financial resources, the role of the community and implementation capabilities.

The critical elements of the Jabotabek strategic planning approach were:

- Agreement on key inter-sectoral objectives (e.g. upgrade defined inner-city areas using infrastructure, socio-economic and land-readjustment mechanisms) between departments and agencies at local, regional and, where relevant, national levels.
- Development of a city-wide structure plan with inputs by sectoral, financial, and institutional 'actors' in the public and private sectors. This plan emphasized the formulation of policies, plans and sectoral investment programmes according to income groups, i.e. giving the opportunity for a more rigorous assessment of poverty impact. Thus, where city objectives stress the distributional impact of policies and programmes, compromises between sectors may be made by delaying implementation in some areas and giving priority to those likely to achieve the greatest equity. Compromises within sectors may be made by designing for lower standards initially, to be improved incrementally as individual or city resources permit. Given that planning controls were very weak, the structure plan emphasised, for example, infrastructure development and limited land reservations rather than detailed land-use zoning allocations.
- Agreement on the main roles of the public and private sectors in implementing the plan.
- Development of improved techniques for forecasting city revenues, co-ordinating central government allocations to local government, and prioritizing sectoral investments in relation to financial feasibility.
- Development of a capital investment programme incorporating, a 3–5 year 'rolling programme' within a 10 year forecast of financial resources.
- The co-ordination and synchronisation of structure plan policies and the capital investment programme in a form which could be used as an agreed point of reference by central and local government departments and by external support agencies who wished to coordinate their work in the city and sub-region.
- The capacity to monitor both the progress of planned activity and changes in the external environment. In the former, monitoring was necessary to ensure that action was taken on time or that, pending this, corrective action was put in hand. In relation to the external environment, monitoring had to check constantly that the structure plan/capital investment programme remained relevant to its environment.

To implement a strategic planning approach, a modified institutional structure was established in the city government. The department previously concerned only with city finances, expanded its role to co-ordinate both the formulation and implementation of the spatial planning/capital investment programme. To improve efficiency, seven inter-sectoral groups were established which brought the sectoral and spatial planning teams together for the first time, with direct access to the Governor of Jakarta.

---

inhibitive in terms of development, are never the less exact and easily understood. Consequently, such regulations can be applied by staff with low skill levels. Performance standards which relate to the effect of development, rather than to the form or content, pose questions of measurements and of interpretation which require much higher levels of skill.

In mixed-use zoning, for example, a commercial or industrial use may be permissible in proximity to residential uses, as long as it does not cause a nuisance by the emission of dust, smoke or fumes, by strong lights, heavy traffic or other environmental impairment. However, the measurement of these environmental impacts must be made in respect of degree, duration and occasion and therefore depend for their effectiveness on systems of monitoring.

Improved zoning techniques

Zoning of urban land use by ordinances and codes is the most common form of land regulation. Traditionally, zoning has often been applied rigidly, involving single or limited use of land parcels for housing, commercial, industrial, community and other activities and geared to the development of one parcel at a time.

Recent improvements in zoning techniques used mostly in OECD countries include: *mixed use zoning*, a technique for incorporating integrated project components within a coherent plan that stipulates the type and scale of uses, permitted densities and related items; *floating zoning*, in which a district is described in the zoning ordinances but not located on the zoning map until the need arises (i.e. the city in effect sets a development performance standard for a district); and *conditional or contract zoning*, under which the city bargains with a developer for certain social benefits such as park land to be provided in return for permission to develop commercial land uses (i.e. 'planning gain'). *Phased zoning* is another technique whereby a permit is required before development can occur. Such permission may be granted when adequate infrastructure to service the site is agreed to and installed by the city government.

A related issue in many countries is that of plot and sub-division standards which assume individual house construction. Some countries have provided for more efficient layouts in the form of semi-detached or terrace housing layouts. Box 9.5 describes a modification of land sub-division regulations that encouraged the development of housing on vacant plots around Amman that had been serviced and the advantages that this brought.

BOX 9.4
Improved standards and regulations in Bangladesh

In Dhaka, Bangladesh, planning and building rules have been based on the Building Construction Rules 1984 and the Town Improvement Act 1953. However planning provisions are contained in building codes and vice versa—a confusing situation. Recently proposals have been made for a comprehensive updating in parallel with the introduction of a new strategic/structure planning process for the city. Proposals address the following:

• a clear distinction between planning, infrastructure and building standards and regulations.

• a range of standards for infrastructure and building appropriate to different income levels and capable of incremental upgrading.

• reduced minimum plot sizes.

• more appropriate standards for floor-area ratio and density limits.

• interim measures for areas not yet covered by local plans.

• a simpler and more effective system of development control.

Dhaka now has the tools to implement appropriate land use regulations which respect local socio-economic conditions, household income levels, and the limited resources of the city to implement and enforce regulations.

Source: Asian Development Bank and Government of Bangladesh, *Dhaka Land Development Project*, 1993.

Choices in development control systems

Country choices in development control systems to implement land use regulations and standards can be grouped under a 'policing' model or an 'enabling' model.

The policing model presupposes that all or nearly all land development projects from the individual plot level to large development projects require the developer to meet a detailed schedule of planning, environmental and building standards, obtain numerous permissions and often pay numerous fees, with the end objective of obtaining a building permit for construction. The model assumes the availability of skilled and plentiful staff to enforce the system. The policing model puts a responsibility not only on the development control department but on other government departments such as the city engineers, public health, water, drainage, sanitation, utilities and others, to carry out detailed analysis and the processing of the application.

The alternative 'enabling' model of development control assumes that (*a*) the physical planning department, or whichever department is responsible for land regulations, needs a positive, innovative, relationship with the private sector

BOX 9.5
Improved subdivision of land in Jordan

Large areas on the fringe of Amman, Jordan have been subdivided and serviced but remain vacant since (*a*) the plots are mostly laid out at too high a standard for prevailing demand and (*b*) there is no disincentive for holding land in an undeveloped state. The 1987 Jordan National Housing Strategy recommended that vacant plot owners should be allowed to apply for the redivision of their plot, resulting in clear ownership titles for each sub-plot. Buildings on the sub-plots would have to be entirely within the envelope as defined by the zoning regulations applying to the original plot, and sub-plot titles would have to specify access rights to back-plots should the plot configuration require it. Minimum sub-plot areas would be specified and each new plot would have to have access to the street to conform with the existing planning law. The resulting semi-detached built form would not vary appreciably from what is allowed under present building regulations. Since existing building regulations would be respected, maximum densities would not be increased, nor would the quality of air, light and open space be affected.

There were numerous advantages of this modification to the original subdivision. The landowner could probably gain more by selling subdivided plots than by selling the original plot, and the developer could provide a greater variety of infill and semi-detached row house opportunities to the much larger lower income housing market. Owners of buildings on plots adjacent to vacant plots may perceive that this will 'lower the quality of the neighbourhood' but since building standards would not be lowered in the area, such objections should not be a major constraint. Lastly, there would be a financial gain to the local government. Since it is currently obliged to issue building permits and provide infrastructure connections to any development taking place on planned and subdivided land, this in effect means it provides a significant subsidy in sparsely settled subdivisions. The costs of providing these connections will be less per unit with a more intensive development of the subdivision and the returns from taxes and user charges will be higher.

and wishes to play a full role in promoting land development policies to support city development objectives; (*b*) staff shortages and other resource constraints will continue to afflict city governments in most countries in Africa, Asia and Latin America; and (*c*) controls on development can only be introduced incrementally as resources and, more importantly, political and social consensus, permit.

Certain key components of this enabling model can be identified:

• The objective of the development control system using planning and/or building permission procedures is that the system should be permissive in character, i.e. the initial assumption by the planning authority is that the individual or business developer should be allowed to proceed with the particular residential, commercial, mixed use, industrial, social or other project subject to the minimum of restrictions.

- In view of continuing staff shortages the development control system is concentrated in critical areas, only at a later stage being extended city-wide.

- Whenever possible, development control decisions are taken at the lower level in the city hierarchy where staffing allows, with referral upwards to the city level only for large and/or disputed cases.

- Whenever possible the functions of planning/zoning/subdivision and building control should be located in a single local government department.

- The system of planning controls is concerned with matters such as land use, densities, planning and design standards. Building controls are concerned with the structure and safety of buildings.

- There is a choice of development control systems where there are severe staff shortages. Either there can be exemptions in the types of development for which planning permission is needed or a system of automatic grants of permission. The exemption system relies on developers being knowledgeable about which classes of development require permission and they may knowingly or otherwise claim that they did not realize permission was needed. A system of automatic grants of permission would avoid that situation by requiring most or all development to be notified to the planning authority, but using junior staff to give routine planning approval for certain classes of development. Even with this simplified system it is likely that not all development categories could be controlled. Thus, for example, small additions to existing buildings, simple changes of land use and temporary structures could be omitted from the system.

Permitted use development can (*a*) specify the kind of development not needing planning permission (mainly small-scale development) and (*b*) allow change of use within specified land use categories, requiring permission only for changing from one category to another. Box 9.6 describes the use of Enterprise Zones in the United Kingdom to encourage the development of particular land sizes with the incentives including a greatly simplified planning regime that allowed developers to begin developments more quickly.

Improved tools

There are a number of technical 'tools of the trade' which are now becoming widely used as part of more effective urban planning approaches. Space does not allow a full review of such innovative tools but two should be highlighted; Geographic Information Systems and Land Market Surveys.

BOX 9.6
Enterprise Zones in the United Kingdom

The UK Government set up a number of Enterprise Zones (EZs) in the UK in the early 1980s. The individual sites vary widely from 50 to 500 acres, but all contain land ripe for development. The benefits are available for a 10-year period from the date on which each zone is designated and include:

- Exemption from rates on industrial and commercial property.
- Exemption from Development Land Tax.
- 100 per cent allowances for corporation and income tax purposes for capital expenditure on industrial and commercial buildings.
- A greatly simplified planning regime; developments that conform to the published scheme for each zone will not require individual planning permission.
- Applications from firms in EZs for certain customs facilities will be processed as a matter of priority and certain criteria relaxed.

Overall, however, it seems most new development would have occurred anyway, though not necessarily in the designated areas. Simplified planning controls have not proved a major incentive and the need for negotiation with developers and local authorities remains. In many cases, planning controls are retained along boundaries, special industrial uses are still subject to control and on occasion environmental regulations are written into the declaration. The positive advantage of EZs is that they can help the developer to get on site more quickly. EZs have conditions that are set out and known from the beginning. EZs offer substantial financial benefits which are much more important than any change in 'planning'.

Geographical Information Systems

Geographical information systems (GIS) are gaining increasing importance as a tool for decision-making in planning. Such systems enable speedy and easy access to large volumes of data and allow the data to be manipulated in order to select, update, combine, model 'what if' questions and display the information on maps and diagrams or as lists of addresses. The essence of any GIS is the ability to link together different data sets and present them clearly and concisely in a variety of ways. In any planning office there is a great reservoir of such information which is costly to collect, even more so if this process is repeated unnecessarily. GIS offers the tool to manage and present this information.

Start-up costs can be expensive but as a tool to the planner GIS is a very useful addition especially when requirements as to its end use have been thought through and are 'programmed in' at an early stage. Its application and development to full potential must include changing the culture in which people and planners work. GIS systems can also aid short-staffed local governments in better managing rapid urban growth.

GIS systems are now common in planning departments in OECD countries and are starting to be used in other countries. For instance in Dhaka, Bangladesh, a GIS system has been installed in the city planning office as part of the reorganization of the department and an introduction of a new typology of plans (with assistance by UNCHS). It is anticipated that the system will not only benefit the day to day work of the planning department (e.g. development control, local and action planning etc.) but will also benefit the city council as a whole by providing the hardware and software for updating property valuation, land transactions and other land-related responsibilities of the government.

In Sri Lanka, the Urban Development Authority is currently installing GIS to help in its planning, development control and other responsibilities for the Greater Colombo area and other urban centres throughout the country. It is hoped to link this system with a new GIS being installed by the Government Survey Department. Again, a major benefit of GIS should be to eliminate the large backlog of land subdivision applications and address improved land registry functions in both urban and rural areas.

In a few countries, remote sensing using high resolution satellite data can be used with GIS. Such integrated systems are particularly useful for evaluating urban growth scenarios, planning new transport routes and sites for infrastructure facilities, environmental zoning analysis and mitigation of natural hazards.[3]

Land Market Assessments

Many urban planning departments are trying to plan for future development without a realistic data base on the prime commodity that they deal in—land. Land market assessments are implemented to fill this information gap and to provide accurate and up to date information on land prices, the supply of serviced land, present and future land projects, housing typologies, and other aspects of the housing and land market.[4] Land market assessments can be used to support four broad activities: government planning and decision-making; the evaluation of government policies and actions (including urban planning): private-sector investment and development decisions and structuring of land-based taxation systems. The availability of high capacity statistical and spreadsheet computer packages at low cost means that comprehensive data banks can be established for even large cities with only modest staff and technical resources. In some instances, land market assessments can be incorporated in Geographical Information Systems.

Institutional implications

The implications of the move from traditional master planning are significant for the role of the urban planner and the planning system within the general goal of improved urban management.

Delegation of planning powers

The powers of local government to prepare plans, regulate land use and co-ordinate the actions of the public and private sector in land development are often very restricted by central government. Such a situation may have been acceptable when the urban sector was rather small, but the increasing demands of rapid urban growth make such a centralized approach less and less relevant. Such cities may need city-specific regulatory powers and delegated authority to make land use decisions which avoid the costs and delay of referring cases to higher levels of government. The extent to which delegated or decentralized powers are needed will vary according to national and local political realities and to the particular motivations for plan-making and land regulation already discussed in earlier chapters. For example, if there is to be an emphasis on promoting social equality through intervening in the land market by using financial tools to facilitate low income housing, there may be a need for strong centralized legislation applied across urban areas. If on the other hand the emphasis is to be more limited, e.g. to promote 'good neighbour' planning, then a stronger emphasis on locally-administered legislation may be sufficient, (e.g. building regulations).

Role of the public and private sector

In considering the degree of local responsibility for tasks in plan formulation and land use regulation, the role of the private sector, i.e. enterprises, community groups and their organizations and NGOs, should be considered. Community participation may be a natural part of the city life in some countries, whether in local plan making, surveys, giving priorities to projects, etc, but in many cases there will be in-built resistance by government to such involvement and the direct role of the private sector may be very restricted for some years. It may often be the case that government is happier to enlist direct private-sector support in 'downstream' activities such as the contracting-out of certain municipal services. In parallel to this direct involvement by the private sector, it is now increasingly recognized that government needs to be more explicit about which activities in urban development can best be carried out by the private sector (such as the provision of shelter, job creation) and which can best be carried out by the public sector, such as investments in advance infrastructure measures, policies to make land transactions cheaper and developing realistic standards which will benefit all income groups. In some instances this policy is being applied to the planning profession itself, e.g. consultants are employed to take over the city's traditional role in plan-making.

Increased co-ordination

It might be thought that the agenda for reforming urban planning policies and the techniques outlined above are more than sufficient for governments to absorb, quite apart from the new demands of meeting sustainable development objectives. However, urban planners are explicitly or implicitly involved in important components of ecological sustainability, for instance in land development and the conservation of resources, and there should be opportunities to extend this involvement.

In summary the move towards strategic planning will require stronger co-ordination of urban planning functions with those sectoral and financial agencies at the local level in order to deliver the integrated development approach. This 'horizontal' co-ordination also extends to public/private sector linkages, i.e. day to day links between the planners and the private sector, both formal bodies such as land development companies, major manufacturing and service businesses, as well as community-based organizations and individuals. Mechanisms for such co-ordination are generally poor at present—although there are examples of cities where such co-ordination has been much improved. For instance, the city of Curitiba is well known for its co-ordinated planning and management, in particular the close co-ordination of transport and land use policies which have encouraged higher densities along public transport routes, reduced dependency on private automobile use and encouraged travel by bicycle and on foot. This example is described in more detail in Section 9.5. Box 9.7 describes a programme in Indonesia that improved co-ordination in infrastructure development.

9.3   Innovations in Land Development and Management

Supporting innovative land development

The achievement of sustainable development goals within urban development requires that land development initiatives take account of impacts of development on the environment and other land based resources. There are now many examples of innovative land development mechanisms that promote the combining of social, economic and environmental goals, using appropriate standards, working with rather than against land markets and using new forms of public/private partnerships. Some of these mechanisms include:

BOX 9.7
Integrated urban infrastructure development in Indonesia

The Integrated Urban Infrastructure Development Programme (IUIDP) is an excellent example of improved infrastructure planning co-ordination. In its idealized form, the process entails the following steps: (1) meetings are held with provincial governments to prioritise cities for attention; (2) project teams in the selected cities (local staff with technical assistance provided from the centre) review and update local master plans or develop a new 'structure plan' where none is available; (3) teams then use those plans as a guide in developing a proposed local multi-year investment programme (PJM) integrated across several sectors; (4) the teams are also required to prepare a complete financing plan (RIAP) that covers the enhancement of local revenues and borrowing, as well as support from the central budget and/or external donors; (5) plans (LIDAP) are also prepared for building the capacity of local government to assume ever increasing responsibility for infrastructure development, operation, and maintenance; (6) on the basis of the multi-year PJMs, individual cities prepare annual budget requests; (7) the programme and budget requests so defined are reviewed at the provincial and central levels and decisions are made about the allocation of central loan and grant funds.

Despite over-ambitious targets in the early years, IUIDP has generally been regarded as a major accomplishment. Its basic characteristics (integrated planning across sectors based on city-specific conditions, the linkage to financial discipline through the RIAPs and to capacity building through the LIDAPs) in and of themselves have been a dramatic improvement over the approach of the past. Also, efforts continue to be made to rectify problems as they are identified by revising IUIDP guidelines.

Source: Urban Management Programme, *Multi Sectoral Investment Planning,* UNCHS/UNDP/World Bank, 1994.

- Increasing the supply of new urban land by direct and indirect interventions in private land markets, i.e. by public land acquisitions and land readjustment as has been demonstrated in Bangladesh (see Box 9.8) and several other countries.

- Implementing guided land development programmes as a joint public/private-sector initiative. This has been implemented in Indonesia (see Box 9.8), among other countries.

- Increasing access of low income groups to existing and new urban land through cross-subsidies, sites and services projects, land-sharing, the use of appropriate land development standards and the more intensive use of low-density built-up areas.

- Recognizing the legitimacy of informal settlements and incorporating informal settlements into formal systems of land management, identifying those areas capable of improvement and those where resettlement is imperative. This has been successfully demonstrated in many countries including Jordan (see Box 9.8).

BOX 9.8
Examples of innovations in land development and management

Land readjustment in Bangladesh: On the fringe of Dhaka, a group of landowners have designed a land readjustment project covering some 30 hectares, now in process of implementation with only minimal government involvement. The objectives are to bring access roads, school sites and other social services into the neighbourhood by a process of plot readjustment. The technique also permits the replotting of landholdings into more rational and hence more viable holdings for sale or development. The benefits of such schemes to the landowners are clear. They get replotted land with higher value and better access to services. The costs and benefits of the land readjustment process are shared among the owners equitably and they are free to develop their land according to individual needs. The benefits to the city are also clear—the opportunity to structure urban fringe development in a timely manner and to provide appropriate infrastructure and land for public uses at little or no cost to government.

Guided land development in Indonesia: The

Guided land development approach, first considered in Jakarta, Indonesia, in the early 1980s, incorporated elements of public/private co-ordination in land development with an emphasis on encouraging the legal participation of low-income groups in urban development. The programme included the construction of roads to induce growth into preferred urban expansion areas, the incremental introduction of essential urban services, into these areas starting with land drainage and at a later stage water supply mains, and the creation of an administrative, planning and financial structure to ensure an effective joint public/private management and implementation of such growth. The physical aims of the programme were to provide a large supply of ordered and planned land so that the private market could help meet the city's projected housing needs for some 250,000 new residents annually, while using the positive relation between levels of access to an area and the resulting price of land to benefit the majority demand by low-income groups. Various administrative measures were proposed to simplify and reduce the cost to poor households of obtaining legal rights to land, and a more equitable tax structure involving betterment taxes was proposed to

allow recovery of all public development costs other than the purchase of land for key community services.

Legalization of unregistered subdivisions in Jordan: In the fringe areas of Amman, many unregistered subdivisions are made on land which was granted decades ago to various tribal groups. Although the government does not legally recognize such claims, and still officially considers the land to be in public ownership, individuals representing the tribes have been able to subdivide the land and sell-off individual plots, using 'hejah' or customary contracts. The boundaries of the parcel are inspected and physically marked; it is in the buyer's interest to immediately construct a wall, or at least boundary corners, if there is likely to be any confusion. The buyer can hold their land vacant for as long as they wish, but most begin at least some symbolic construction. Once the building is roofed it is considered inhabited and demolition cannot take place. The government began a process of legalizing individual holdings in the early 1970s and is now establishing rights-of-way for roads, etc., as a recognition that these areas will form a permanent component of the expanding city.

Facilitating land titling and land transactions

Another vital instrument of land development often given low priority in government funding and staffing is the functions of land survey, cadastral mapping, registration and tenure records. Typically, existing systems are based on long established practices which have failed to keep up with the growth in land transactions and subdivisions. In addition, the process of land transfer is often costly, including staff time, transfer taxes and stamp duties, and further complicated in cities where both modern and customary land tenure rules apply. The resulting impacts on residents include poor access to credit for land development, insecurity of tenure, and long and costly disputes over land ownership.

Various countries are now introducing quicker and cheaper systems of titling, registration and tenure—see for instance the use of Occupancy Licences in Zambia (Box 9.9). Although systems are usually provided by government, there is increasing use of the private sector (i.e. private licensed surveyors) to speed up the process of land titling and development.

BOX 9.9
Occupancy licences in Zambia

In Lusaka, Zambia, under the Housing (Statutory and Improvement Areas) Act, 1974, an Occupancy Licence was introduced to provide tenure to squatters without the necessary costs and complications of issuing legal titles. The licence gives the right to occupy a building for 30 years; the occupant does not own the land, but, subject to their paying municipal charges for services, they are legally protected from eviction. They can improve the house, sell it, or mortgage it, without restriction. Once the land has been gazetted as an Improvement Area, all existing house locations are numbered using an air photograph of the area. This demarcation forms the basis for identifying the property and is properly entered in a register of titles. Land disputes in the upgraded squatter areas are resolved by community leaders, subject to customary law. While the licence does not address the issue of the original ownership of land nor the issue of its legal transfer, which thereby brings about disputes involving claims and counter claims by various owners and tenants of individual houses, it does have the major benefit of simplicity in providing tenure security without complicated surveys, legal proceedings and bureaucratic forms. It may be gradually upgraded into a legal title scheme as property boundaries become consolidated and eventually recognized in the years to come.

Public/private-sector partnerships in land development projects

In many countries, both North and South, there are examples of new forms of public/private sector partnerships in urban land development projects. In general, the public sector's comparative advantage is in land assembly, fast track plan approval and coordination of infrastructure investment for the project, while the private sector enjoys the advantages of finance raising, marketing of floor-space and efficient relationships with building contractors. Teaming up creates mutual benefits. The possible benefits to the public sector include: urban redevelopment of decayed neighbourhoods considered too 'risky' by developers to tackle on their own; increased economic activity and taxes as under-used and surplus urban land becomes developed; and financial gains from grouped ground leases and participation in cash flows from joint development projects. In addition, developers may sign agreements to provide public amenities such as recreation spaces and/or cash contributions to public-sector projects in exchange for planning approvals.

Box 9.10 gives three examples of public/private-sector partnerships or agreements. The first is the reassessment of the role of the Sri Lankan government's Urban Development Authority. The second is the application of the principle of 'planning gain' within the United Kingdom through which developers are required to help meet the cost of needed infrastructure or services. The third is 'Least Cost Planning' in the United States of America whose application can require developers to take actions outside their own development—for instance to reduce demand for water elsewhere to the point where it equals the increased water demand the development will require.

Infrastructure-led development

It is common for urban planners not to co-ordinate their work sufficiently with the public agencies and private enterprises whose developments have a large impact on the form of urban development. For instance, plans for a city may be developed without co-ordination with the infrastructure and utilities sectors of water

---

BOX 9.10

Public/private-sector agreements in development projects

Public/Private-Sector Partnerships in Sri Lanka: In Sri Lanka, the Urban Development Authority (UDA) has been involved in large and small commercial industrial and residential development projects for many years, usually in partnership with private sector interests. Recently, a reassessment of the comparative advantages of public- and private-sector roles in such projects has been undertaken. In summary, UDA's future role was assessed as follows:

- UDA should take the lead role as a catalyst in promoting commercial and industrial projects which are analysed to give satisfactory social, economic, financial and environmental returns. It has the legal authority to undertake land assembly and acquisition.

- UDA should have an intensive but limited involvement (say 5 years) in the planning, design, funding arrangements and implementation of projects, but should not be involved financially in the long term. However, it may have a long-term stake in the funding of and revenues from particular components of the project (such as commercial/shopping floorspace).

- UDA should coordinate the roles of the many infrastructure, service and other sectoral agencies having an interest in the project.

Planning Gain or Contract Zoning in the UK: In the UK the principles of 'planning gain' are closely associated with betterment which was abandoned in the early 1980s. The term 'planning gain' has two meanings. It can denote facilities which are an integral part of a development; but it can also mean 'benefits' which have little or no relationship to the development, and which the local authority require as 'the price of planning permission'. The experience of this technique is mixed. Essentially, the issue is the extent to which local authorities can legitimately require developers to take on the wider costs of development associated with the urban environment; i.e. much needed infrastructure, schools, and other essential local services. Under UK law there are three key tests, i.e. that the gain:

- is needed to enable the development to go ahead, for example the provision of adequate access or car parking; or

- in the case of financial payment, will contribute to meeting the cost of providing such facilities in the near future; or

- is otherwise so directly related to the proposed development and to the use of the land after its completion, that the development ought not to be permitted without it, e.g. the provision, whether by the applicant or by the authority at the applicant's expense, of car parking in or near the development, of reasonable amounts of open space related to the development, or of social, educational, recreational, sporting or other community

provision the need for which arises from the development.

Least-cost planning (LCP) in USA: A demand management technique applied especially in the USA, LCP aims to optimize the performance of networks (usually infrastructure) by equal considerations of supply and demand side measures, and their social, environmental and economic implications in an integrated policy framework.

Increasingly LCP is being used to force developers and utilities to implement demand management policies over infrastructure provision in new developments. In California, LCP applications are playing a major part in developments receiving permissions. For example if a development is going to receive permission, the developer has to formulate a strategy of water conservation measures in adjacent development to reduce demand in the existing area by the same level that the new development will increase demand; thus at the very least maintaining equilibrium and ensuring the new development is highly water-efficient.

The benefit of a LCP approach to the planning process is that is focuses attention on demand management options rather than increasing levels of supply. Thus it shifts planning away from focusing solely on the direct environmental problems associated with specific development to one which needs to take a view of problems in relation to the whole city or urban fabric, making linkages with a much wider range of actors than would usually be involved in the formulation of planning policies.

resources and supply, solid and liquid waste management, drainage and sewerage, electricity and telecommunications, road and rail transport. However, many countries and cities are now making efforts to achieve better co-ordination as part of the new emphasis on the enabling approach and also as a result of the failure of zoning and other 'negative' land use control systems to influence urban growth.

One key part of this is termed 'infrastructure-led development' where full use is made of public investment to guide urban development but in ways that also support the private sector's role in such development. For example, road construction can be used to guide the direction of urban expansion into desirable development zones and away from hazardous land areas or areas of particular ecological value. One example of this is Guided Land Development in Jakarta through which industrial estates can be located downstream of residential areas and where provision is made for the treatment of all the factories' wastes, which is more efficient (and cheaper) than treatment within each factory, scattered across the urban area. Landfill activities can also be planned and phased to prepare areas for future urban growth more efficiently than through the landfill actions of different developers. Since such strategic public investment can also bring about significant increases in land and property values, especially the extension or improvement of roads or public transport systems and of water and sanitation systems, adoption of infrastructure-led development techniques will also need effective means to recover the costs of such investments—for instance through user charges, betterment taxes, planning gain agreements, and land readjustment schemes.

This use of infrastructure to guide urban growth and redevelopment requires the planner to be involved in new forms of infrastructure provision. Box 5.1 in Chapter 5 noted the great range of ways through which infrastructure can be developed ranging from the various alternatives for public sector provision through mixed private/public provision to private provision. Section 9.4 develops this further, describing various ways in which public authorities can involve the private and voluntary sector in the management of environmental infrastructure.

A central issue here is the provision of 'off-site' infrastructure. Typically, the public sector will provide off-site roads, power supply, water mains, treatment works, etc, but faced with resource shortages is looking for innovative methods of cost recovery. For example, in Dhaka, Bangladesh, land reservations along a major new central road were sold to developers as a means of partial cost recovery; the next stage in thinking is how to attract 'Build-Operate-Transfer' private sector enterprises to provide such roads by granting land alongside a road on which the enterprise can develop saleable properties.

Urban economic development

Innovative land development in the context and framework of appropriate urban planning approaches can contribute to economic development in several ways, namely:

- through strengthening the management of urban infrastructure with particular emphasis on maintenance
- through improving the city-wide regulatory framework to increase market efficiency and private sector participation
- through improving the financial and technical capacity of municipal institutions; and
- through strengthening financial services for urban development.

Many of these innovative mechanisms contribute to capacity building in a much wider sense. The impact of such contributions would be greatly enhanced and better targeted if there were much better co-ordination of policy and programme-making between urban planners and the wide range of local business interests in both formal and informal sectors. To take one obvious example, the introduction of mixed-use zoning (residential/commercial) would be of immediate benefit to small household-based businesses, which form an important core of the informal sector and which are not provided for under traditional master plans with their emphasis on separate land use zoning.

There is an increasing tendency for cities, especially in OECD countries, to establish economic development units that report directly to the Chief Executive and that have a very focused mandate for such aspects as employment creation, industrial renewal, environmental upgrading, and advisory services for small businesses. Given that these agencies are by definition in close touch with local business they provide a two-way channel of guidance and information between urban planning and economic development.

Improved investment decision-making

Strategic planning requires, among other things, close linkages between spatial planning, financial resources and sectoral strategies. The Urban Management Programme (UNCHS/World Bank/UNDP) has analysed techniques used in different countries for investment prioritization and has developed the technique of Multi-Sectoral Investment Planning.[5] This has its roots in both spatial planning and annual operating and capital budgeting traditions. Its product is a multi-year capital plan, showing what investments take place across sectors, how this investment will be financed and the repercussions of investments on the operating and maintenance budgets of public agencies. Multi-Sectoral Investment Planning is built around four themes:

- investment planning should be demand driven,
- all public agencies with a significant role in investment decisions should be part of the process,
- when the process is inaugurated, every step should be simplified as much as possible,
- comprehensiveness is critical, i.e. there should be a strategy for allocating scarce investment measures across all sectors and all projects. However, Multi-Sectoral Investment Planning should not rely on a central planning group alone; decision-making can be decentralized to markets, line agencies and community-level groups.

The steps in implementing it are:

1. Establish an inter-agency steering group and coordinating agency to be responsible for investment prioritizing.

2. Decide on the mechanisms to be used for measuring user demand and incorporating this information within the priority-setting process.

3. Identify the capital improvement priorities of the community.

4. Obtain information on investment activities in progress or about to start.

5. Prepare lists of prioritized projects by agency or individual sector.

6. Decide on cross-sectoral project priorities.

7. Plan for the revenue side of the budget.

An advantage of Multi-Sectoral Investment Planning is that the process can be tailored to staff resources available and can be expanded incrementally from certain core activities/sectors. A further advantage is that many community-level projects can be integrated and prioritized at the local level and do not have to go through city-wide planning (in many cases this delegation of decision-making can be coordinated with the Action Planning approach discussed earlier).

Box 9.11 gives two examples of initiatives to improve investment decision making. The first is from Tianjin (China) and this seeks to improve inter-sectoral coordination and to involve the finance bureau in guiding investment project choices which draw in finance specialists. The second is the Capital Investment Folio process used in Metro Manila, Philippines, a well known example of Multi-Sectoral Investment Planning in practice.

Technically, the priority setting system of the Capital Investment Folio Process in Manila described above attracted a good deal of favourable attention in the Philippines and elsewhere. It led to practical recommendations regarding types of projects that should be advanced in the capital-improvements queue and others that should be postponed. However, its fate illustrates the potential problems associated

---

BOX 9.11
Innovations in investment decision making

Inter-agency steering froup for Tianjin, China: Tianjin traditionally has had an Urban and Rural Construction Commission (URCC) which co-ordinates policies, programmes, and budgets across the different bureaux responsible for infrastructure planning and construction, such as the Municipal Engineering Bureau or Public Utilities Bureau. This has reflected a technical and supply-driven approach to infrastructure provision that emphasizes units built. In the new urban management approach being developed in collaboration with the World Bank, a steering group, called the Planning and Management Improvement Leading Group, has been created to guide investment project choices. It is chaired by the Chief Engineer of URCC but also includes the Chief Economist of the Finance Bureau, the Director

of the Infrastructure Division of the Planning Commission, as well as the Deputy Director of URCC and others. Task forces will be set up to prioritize projects in each functional area, chaired by a member of the Leading Group and comprised of staff from affected Bureaux. One of the goals is to introduce financing constraints, planning principles, and up-to-date information on user demand into a rolling five-year capital plan.

Priority-setting under the Capital Investment Folio Process in Metro Manila, the Philippines: The Capital Investment Folio process first screened out projects that, though they appeared on agencies' project lists, were insufficiently elaborated or had no possible funding source. Small projects were grouped together by type of activity for evaluation. All projects or classes or projects were then scored on a scale of 1–10 according to different evaluation criteria, including:

- socio-political acceptability
- capital-financing requirements and availability of dedicated funds
- debt-servicing requirements
- economic rate of return
- targeting on poor communities and poor households.

Rankings were made under alternative assumptions about future economic growth. Based on this analysis, projects were grouped into first, second, and third priorities. First priority investments included, among others, slum upgrading, garbage collection and disposal sites, and sites and services projects. Low priority programmes included a primary roads programme, sewer rehabilitation, and the construction of completed housing units. For highly ranked projects, a further investigation of agency implementing capacity was carried out, before the projects were placed in the recommended Core Investment Program.

Sources: For Tianjin, World Bank, *Tianjin Urban Development and Environment Project*, Washington DC, 1992; for Manila, Clark, Giles, *Reappraising the Urban Planning Process as an Instrument for Sustainable Urban Development and Management*, UNCHS (Habitat), Nairobi, 1994.

with technical solutions that do not involve public or local government participation. The Capital Investment Folio Process was primarily an exercise for coordinating the major parastatal providers under the aegis of a politically powerful inter-agency forum, with local governments in a subordinate role. When Imelda Marcos was removed as Governor of Metro Manila, the entire concept of a formally recognized metropolitan planning jurisdiction with capital-allocating power disappeared with her.

This highlights an issue that has been raised in almost all efforts to apply Multi-Sectoral Investment Planning in practice: should analytical priority-setting methods replace, merge with, or serve as background information for political selection of investment projects? Different answers to this question have evolved over time in different locations. However, when first established, Multi-Sectoral Investment Planning probably should not attempt to supplant political decision making. Rather, it is best used as a tool to help rationalise or constrain political choices.[6]

9.4 Management of Environmental Infrastructure

Major changes are now taking place in the ways in which urban water resources and environmental infrastructure are managed. These are in response to the continuing failure in most countries in the South to meet environmental infrastructure needs despite the efforts of national governments with the assistance of external support agencies (both bilateral and multilateral). This has led to water sector professionals, urban planners, and some government ministers and city authorities concluding in several meetings and conferences that new ways must be sought.[7] These meetings have also helped to consolidate new actions and strategies for building capacity in water resource and environmental management and in the management of environmental infrastructure.

The experiences of the International Drinking Water Supply and Sanitation Decade from 1981 to 1990 have also shown the need for new approaches. To improve low-income groups' access to safe water and sanitation, drainage, and solid waste management on a sustainable basis will require more effective utilization of limited investment resources, an active search for better approaches to enhance services, expansion of both technological and service delivery options to tailor choices to people's demands, a re-think of the roles of government and the private sector, more investments in human resources and capacity-building initiatives, and the strengthening of country level institutions which can ensure that the improved infrastructure is maintained.

Box 9.12 outlines some of the initiatives underway by various international agencies.

Integrated management of services

In most countries in the South, environmental infrastructure has not been managed in an integrated manner, even where the different forms of infrastructure provision were under the same

---

government agency, local authority, or parastatal. However, integrated management is needed as inadequate water supply leads to poor sanitation while inadequate provision for sanitation can mean a contamination of surface and ground-water resources. Similarly, the absence of a well managed solid waste collection and disposal system often leads to refuse blocking drains, causing flooding in low lying areas, and water pollution. An integrated approach is also needed to promote the conservation of water resources both in terms of quality and quantity, and the efficient and equitable allocation of scarce water resources among competing uses.

In response to this and to other needs, UNCHS (Habitat) launched its Settlement Infrastructure and Environment Programme. This includes a global demonstration project with the objective of formulating policy options and strategies to improve the integrated management of urban water resources at the municipal level. The programme also seeks to develop practical planning and implementation tools for local government and communities through research, city and national workshops for all stakeholders (government, local authorities, all categories of consumers, communities, private sector, and NGOs). The programme is also documenting best practice in promoting community participation in the implementation of water and sanitation programmes focused on the urban poor—see Box 9.13.

Financing investments

In the past and to a large extent in many countries today, investments in environmental infrastructure has been financed largely from tax revenues and government borrowing. Thus, government bore all the associated risks. However public funds fall far short of the required level of investment to cover the rapidly growing demand in many urban areas, especially in the South, and the economic problems faced by most countries in Africa, Asia and Latin America have further reduced the availability of these funds. An estimated $80 to $120 billion a year needs to be invested by countries in the South to cater for the population growth between 1990 and 2000, but only about 5 to 10 per cent of the yearly requirement (about $2.5 billion per year) has been provided by external support agencies in the form of aid and non-concessionary loans. The need to quickly identify other means of financing investments is obvious.

While there are arguments for government financing of infrastructure, since government is the most credit-worthy entity in some cases, and is also able to borrow at lower interest rates, there are many reasons why other options should

be sought. These include the inefficiencies in government, the difficulties of maintaining accountability, implementation delays and serious cost and time overruns, and the general failure or unwillingness to recover full costs of investments along with operation and maintenance costs. These often greatly increase the unit cost of service provision, and make continued government financing unsustainable.

Financing investments with bilateral aid also has its own problems. The requirement that the funds be spent on goods and services from specified countries often leads to higher costs, and to the import of technology that is, in some cases, unfamiliar and inappropriate. More importantly, there is insufficient bilateral aid available to cover the funding gap, and the overall amount available is decreasing, in real terms.

Mobilizing private capital is another way to fill the funding gap. However private capital is not unlimited and environmental infrastructure has to compete with sectors which yield a higher return on investment. To date, only limited amounts of private capital have been used to finance investment in the sector. A survey published in October 1993 by *Public Works Financing* showed that of 148 private infrastructure projects funded worldwide since the early 1980s at a total cost of over $60 billion, only 16 per cent of the projects were for environmental infrastructure, and none of the projects were in low income countries. As better strategies are devised to ensure more private sector financing of infrastructure projects, more environmental infrastructure projects will qualify for such financing. An estimated 250 infrastructure projects in the South are being considered for future private sector financing, 72 of which are in low income countries.

Another source of funds for sectoral investments is generation from the services through user charges. If tariffs are set high enough to recover operation and maintenance costs as well as the investment costs, this can generate adequate funding for future investments. While agencies like the World Bank, the African Development Bank, the Asian Development Bank, and other external support agencies are actively promoting this idea, and in some cases making it a condition for the loans or grants they provide for infrastructure, recipient governments have been slow to embrace the idea, mainly for political reasons. However, there is evidence of slowly increasing support with reasonable results, particularly in countries like Côte d'Ivoire, Guinea, and the Gambia, where services have been leased to the private sector or privatized.

Households, communities, and the informal sector are also sources of limited amounts of capital as well as non-financial inputs for the construction of infrastructure. However the lack of

BOX 9.13
Settlement Infrastructure Environment Programme (SIEP)

The Settlement Infrastructure and Environment Programme (SIEP) was launched by UNCHS (Habitat) in July 1992 to help countries achieve the infrastructure related goals of Agenda 21. The programme seeks to improve the living environment of human settlements by assisting governments and communities to develop practical policy options, planning and implementation aids and local capacity in critical areas of infrastructure delivery and management. Funded mainly by the Governments of Denmark, the Netherlands and Germany, the programme is currently active in ten countries in Africa, Asia and Latin America.

The strategic focus
Sharply focused on Agenda 21 priorities, the programme addresses capacity-building needs in the following areas:

- Promoting the integrated provision of environmental infrastructure: water, sanitation, drainage and solid-waste management (*Programme area D of Chapter 7 of Agenda 21*).
- Water resources management for sustainable urban development (*Programme area E of Chapter 18 of Agenda 21*).
- Environmentally sound management of solid wastes and sewage (*all programmes areas of Chapter 21 of Agenda 21*).
- Promoting sustainable energy and transport systems in human settlements (*Programme area E of Chapter 7 of Agenda 21*).
- Supporting co-operation and capacity-building for the use of environmentally sound technologies for sustainable development of human settlements (*Chapter 34 of Agenda 21*).
- Reducing health risks from environmental infrastructure deficiencies (*Programme area E of Chapter 6 of Agenda 21*).

Programme implementation
In programme execution, primary emphasis is given to strengthening the means of implementation identified in Agenda 21, particularly *the scientific and technological means*, which are critical for addressing successfully the above-mentioned priorities.

The programme is, therefore, implemented through a series of carefully designed projects, focusing on:

- *Bridging the knowledge gap in critical areas* through research and studies; developing policy and technical options, management tools and aids; field testing research results and targeted dissemination of proven research outputs.
- *Documenting and disseminating 'best practice applications'* in the provision and management of environmental infrastructure services.
- *Implementing demonstration projects* for the dissemination of appropriate technologies and effective models of delivery mechanisms.
- *Building 'capacity for capacity'*, in other words, strengthening the capacity of key local institutions which can, in turn, help enhance the capacity of other local actors.
- *Information exchange*, through regional networks linking private and public research institutions and NGOs, and through computerised databases and expert systems.

---

appropriate mechanisms for the systematic organization and mobilization of communities has limited the regular and large-scale mobilization of this type of capital at a level sufficient to have significant impact on current demands.

Institutional arrangements

Many public-sector institutions involved in environmental infrastructure management have been found to be monopolistic, lacking transparency and accountable only to the government machinery and not to the stakeholders and consumers. They also generally lack the capability to respond to consumer demands. Among the challenges of the future are the needs to introduce competition, transparency and accountability, and financial soundness into such institutions.

One of the factors limiting the availability of private capital for environmental infrastructure is the lack of a reliable track record by the operators. There is thus a move promoted by agencies such as the World Bank to privatization or leasing the management of services to private companies with proven track records. Another option is to enter into joint management contracts with such companies with a view to improving service delivery and management, operating on sound commercial principles, and using the private company's proven track record to attract financing. Such private/public partnerships have often proved useful to municipal authorities who lack the funding to provide or manage infrastructure but can do so through forming partnerships with private sector enterprises or with NGOs or on occasion, community based organizations. Such partnerships are also particularly useful, as demands for infrastructure become too large and varied for the government authorities to supply efficiently. They can vary in scale from the contracting out or privatization of city-wide infrastructure (for instance for water supply or sanitation) to support provided to an NGO or community based organization to install infrastructure in one particular low-income settlement. Box 9.14 gives the example of the private firm in Côte d'Ivoire which operates and maintains the water supply system in Abidjan and in most other urban centres, with the government remaining responsible for investment and construction.

The Republics of Guinea and the Gambia entered into management leasing arrangements with private companies for the operation and maintenance of services including billing and revenue collection with the respective governments retaining responsibility for capital investments. While the Guinean contract is still in place, contractual problems in the Gambia resulted in premature termination barely 2 years into a 10-year contract. The lessons of the Gambian case have been used to develop what is believed to be a better management leasing contract for the water utility in Senegal. Once the initial problems are

BOX 9.14
The private operation of water services; the case of SODECI in Côte d'Ivoire

SOCECI (Societé des Eaux du Côte d'Ivoire) is an Ivorian company that provides water supply in Abidjan and for all urban centres in the country and also manages Abidjan's sewerage system. Originally founded as a French firm, its capital is now 52 per cent owned by local interests with 46 per cent held by Saur, the French water distributor, and 2 per cent by a government investment fund. It began operations with the Abidjan water supply system 30 years ago and now manages more than 300 piped water supply systems across the country. This includes 300,000 individual connections that serve some 70 per cent of Côte D'Ivoire's 4.5 million urban residents with the number of connections growing by between 5 and 6 per cent a year.

Since the early 1970s, full cost recovery has been the rule and revenues from water sales have fully covered capital, operation and maintenance costs. During the past ten years, unaccounted-for water has never exceeded 15 per cent and collection from private consumers has never fallen below 98 per cent—although collection from government agencies has proved more problematic. The staff to connection ratio is four persons per 1,000 connections which reflects best-practice standards.

The company retains part of the rates collected to cover its operating costs, depreciate its assets, extend and rehabilitate distribution networks and pay dividends to shareholders. It also pays government a rental fee to service the debt attached to earlier projects financed by the government.

SODECI provides service standards close to the standards of countries in the North but the cost to consumers is no higher than in neighbouring countries in similar economic conditions or in other Francophone African countries where water tariffs rarely cover capital, operation and maintenance costs. SODECI's bonds are one of the main items traded in Abidjan's financial market, and it has distributed dividends to its shareholders. The company has also paid taxes since its inception.

Source: World Bank, *World Development Report 1994; Infrastructure for Development*, Oxford University Press, Oxford, 1994.

BOX 9.15
Garbage collection and resource recovery by the informal sector; the zabbaleen in Cairo

In Cairo, an informal-sector group of garbage collectors, known as *zabbaleen,* and local contractors, known as *wahis* were transformed into the private Environmental Protection Company (EPC). EPC has the contract for waste collection in several parts of the city. Although the responsibilities for solid-waste management have long been shared by the municipal sanitation service and the zabbaleen, the formation of the EPC established wahis and zabbaleen as key participants in the local governor's programme to upgrade solid-waste management in Cairo. The wahis administer the system, market the company's services, collect household charges, and supervise service deliveries. The zabbaleen collect and transport the waste, supplying their labour in exchange for rights to recycle the waste. After establishing the EPC, the wahis increased their earnings and the zabbaleen earned additional income and were able to reduce collection time by 30–50 per cent. The Cairo Governorate is seeking to extend the EPC service to other areas of the city.

Source: Environmental Quality International, quoted in UNCHS (Habitat), *Sustainable Human Settlements Development: Implementing Agenda 21,* Report for the Commission on Sustainable Development, Nairobi, March 1994.

resolved, there are likely to be more such contracts for the management of environmental infrastructure services.

One of the most common forms of private/public partnership in both the North and the South is for urban authorities to contract out solid-waste collection and disposal. Many (although not all) case studies find that private-sector solid-waste collection has lowered costs. There are also an increasing number of instances where informal-sector groups of garbage collectors have been contracted to collect and dispose of solid wastes. Box 9.15 gives one of the best known examples—the *zabbaleen* in Cairo. Chapter 12 will return to this issue, since there is considerable potential for improved recycling and reclamation within solid-waste collection and management through contracts with local groups, including community-based groups, and this also has considerable potential for employment creation at local level.

There is considerable variety in what aspects of infrastructure can become the responsibility of private enterprise, NGO, or community-based organizations. Such groups may be contracted to undertake one or more areas of—feasibility-study, design, construction, supervision or management; or to provide some service like the collection of solid waste; or to administer infrastructure such as the management of water distribution and sewerage networks, which includes operation and maintenance, rehabilitation, and the systems' expansion. Box 9.16 describes the example of AGETIP, a private, non-profit agency in Senegal that executes urban infrastructure and service projects for central and municipal authorities. Similar agencies operate in Benin, Burkina Faso, Mali, Mauritania, and Niger, and others are being formed in Chad, the Gambia, Madagascar, and Togo.

There is also considerable diversity in the form that a public/private partnership in infrastructure provision or maintenance takes and in the extent of ownership or control retained by the public sector. At one extreme, the private sector owns and manages what had previously been the responsibility of the government. This may be through privatization as what had previously been a government company is sold to the private sector (as in many water supply companies). Or it may be through what is often termed BOO

Private-sector infrastructure provision; the example of AGETIP in Senegal

The Agence d'Exécution des Travaux d'Interêt Public (AGETIP) is a private, non-profit legal enterprise that contracts with Senegal's Government to execute urban infrastructure works and urban service projects. The arrangement is stipulated in several documents including a manual defining the duties and responsibilities of the two parties. Municipal and central governments sign specific delegated contract management agreements with AGETIP each time they submit a sub-project for execution. AGETIP hires consultants to prepare designs and bidding documents and to supervise works, issues calls for bids, evaluates and adjudicates the bids, and signs the contracts, and evaluates progress, pays the contractors, and represents the owner at the final hand-over of the works. As of January 1993, Senegal's AGETIP had implemented 330 projects with a total value of $55 million. These projects are located in 78 municipalities and have created 50,600 temporary jobs and 1,500 permanent jobs. Over half of the projects executed have dealt with the environment (drainage, garbage collection, canal clearing, sidewalk improvements and road maintenance). The AGETIP model creates jobs for low-income groups through its labour-intensive methods. The 'contracting-out' approach created demand for the services of local contracting and consulting industries, thus stimulating their development and increasing spending in local effective management information systems, and a sense of a accountability that allows for timely decision making. These also inspired other agencies to improve their own performance.

Source: World Bank, *World Development Report 1994: Infrastructure for Development,* Oxford University Press, Oxford & New York, 1994.

(build, own and operate) schemes, where the private company builds, owns, and operates the infrastructure. In these instances where there is no public sector ownership, the public sector continues, in theory, to monitor prices and quality. Another common variant of this is through residents' organizations, including those formed in illegal or informal settlements, improving their own infrastructure (for instance paving roads or installing drains) with some support from local authorities. There is also the 'Build, Operate and Transfer' model where the private company builds and operates some form of infrastructure, a treatment plant for example, with the infrastructure being transferred to the public sector after an agreed period of time.

For the public sector to successfully involve the private sector in providing or managing environmental infrastructure, the government authorities should have the capacity to manage the process—for instance to ensure that people's needs are met with services of appropriate quality and price. The legal framework must both support the government authorities in managing the process while at the same time not hindering decision-making by a private partner.

Although the examples of SODECI in Côte d'Ivoire, the Environmental Protection Company in Cairo given in the boxes above, and the Orangi Pilot Project in Karachi given in Box 9.18 below, suggest new ways and means by which governments can work with the private and voluntary sector in infrastructure provision or management, care must be taken in assuming that these provide solutions in all instances. The experience of private-sector performance in the management of infrastructure development in countries in the South is still too limited to draw general conclusions, although there is agreement that the private sector has great potential of taking a more active role in this area.

Capacity building

Building up national and local capacities is a complex process, involving policies, institutions, and people. At the policy level it involves improving the rules governing the sector along with the regulations and practices to provide an enabling environment for its development. Experience in the past has shown that unless an enabling environment is created with the right policies and regulations, investments and other development efforts will not be sustainable.

The UNCHS (Habitat) and other programmes listed in Box 9.12 help build up the capacity of local authorities, communities, private sector and local NGOs to provide and manage the services. Multilateral development assistance agencies now include capacity building programmes in their lending packages, while bilateral agencies provide technical assistance to build up capacity of institutions and individuals and to provide enabling environments for sustainable service provision and delivery.

Community participation

It has for long been assumed that communities do not know their infrastructure needs—especially low-income communities. Thus, decisions about provision were made from above and passed down. It is increasingly being recognised that this top-down approach has been the reason for the failure of many initiatives, and that the communities know their needs, and should to be consulted and involved in the decision making process. Community participation is gradually becoming a component of all environmental infrastructure planning and decision making.

One example of the need to involve communities in the decision making process has been demonstrated in the rapidly growing body of research into their willingness to pay for services. While it had long been assumed that low-income communities were unable and unwilling to pay for infrastructure services, research quickly established that such communities living in unplanned and unserviced settlements were often paying 10 to 100 times more for water supply (per litre) than their counterparts in planned areas. UNCHS is currently conducting research to develop a manual for a community self-survey to determine effective demand for services under the SIEP programme described in Box 9.13. There are some 20 other studies on the subject of willingness to pay covering cities in West and East Africa focusing on vending, as well as bidding games in Asia and Latin America, sponsored mainly by the World Bank and the US Agency for International Development (see Box 9.17).

Community participation in the decision making process not only ensures that communi-

---

BOX 9.17
Willingness to pay: assessing community water demand

Two main methods exist for evaluating willingness to pay. The first is a direct method, using rapid appraisal surveys assessing what consumers already pay for water. This has been widely used for surveys of water-vending practices, and the contingent valuation studies which employ bidding games asking people what they would be prepared to pay for improved services in future. The second is an indirect method which aims at establishing what people living in similar circumstances to the target population are already paying for water. These approaches have one common drawback in that they both depend on external resources to generate information, and are therefore subjected to biases.

To address this problem, UNCHS (Habitat) within its Community-based Environmental Management Information System (CEMIS), is undertaking research to develop and test a manual for assessing effective demand by communities for environmental infrastructure services, in association with Atma Jaya University in Indonesia. The approach is to train communities to assess their own demand for services through community self-surveys and community workshops. It uses community leaders and volunteers, and reduces the need for external resources and also the biases, and leads to community empowerment and self-determination. It can also mobilize locally available information and resources.

To do this, after community mobilization, a community meeting is called by the community leader to discuss and prioritize environmental problems. It is common for environmental infrastructure issues to top the agenda. In the case of water supply, for example, the community would decide to determine effective demand for water. First a workshop is held for community volunteers to familiarize them with the methodology and develop a plan for the self-survey. Then the survey is conducted by the volunteers and the data collated and analysed, and the results presented at a community meeting during which a consensus is reached on commitments of individual households to contribute to the provision, operation and maintenance of a service, in this case, water supply.

---

ties are provided with what they want as opposed to what the experts think they want, but it also provides a sense of belonging and ownership and better care for the investments, and it reduces costs. Box 9.18 gives the example of the Orangi Pilot Project in Karachi which has become one of the best known examples of NGO community collaboration in developing infrastructure. It has demonstrated that low-income households can afford to pay the full cost of installing basic drainage and sewage, if all households within a street or 'lane' worked collectively, generally collecting small contributions from each household and sub-contracting out the work.[8] The NGO, the Orangi Pilot Project, provided technical and organizational support. This showed how a partnership between NGOs and citizens organized in small neighbourhood groups can not only prove effective but can also be so on a very large scale. The estimated cost per household is one seventh of what the local authority wanted to charge to complete such investment. Once the households in a 'lane' became involved in installing the drains, they automatically assumed responsibility for regular maintenance and repair. As Box 9.18 notes, the municipal authority is now helping to fund this approach and Orangi Pilot Project is now working with local NGOs and community organizations in other settlements in Karachi and in other urban centres in Pakistan.

The UNCHS/Danida Community Participation Training Programme was launched in 1984 out of the recognition that an enabling approach to improve living conditions in low income settlements requires a partnership between government agencies, project staff and participating communities. It also recognized that the building of trust and cooperation for this partnership requires the use of skills and sensitivities that are new to all parties. The Training Programme aims to institutionalize community participation in all low-income housing projects and programmes.

As a result of governments' inability to meet existing demands, communities, households and NGOs are also becoming more involved in mobilizing funds to build their water and sanitation schemes or to operate and maintain existing ones. Women, in particular, play an important role in organizing their communities and mobilizing local resources. However these activities often do not evolve into sustainable forms of settlement development and resource management since they are carried out in a non-formal manner, reacting to immediate needs, with varying degrees of success. A number of the above programmes as well as NGO programmes are focused on raising awareness and building up capacity for participation in the execution of activities on water and sustainable urban development to help communities achieve better results.

BOX 9.18
The Orangi pilot project in Karachi, Pakistan

Orangi is an unauthorised settlement with around 1 million inhabitants extending over 8,000 hectares. Most inhabitants built their own houses and none received official help in doing so. There was no public provision for sanitation; most people used bucket latrines which were emptied every few days, usually onto the unpaved lanes running between houses. More affluent households constructed soakpits but these filled up after a few years. Some households living near creeks constructed sewage pipes which emptied into the creeks. The cost of persuading local government agencies to lay sewage pipes in Orangi was too much for local residents—who also felt that these should be provided free.

A local organization called the Orangi Pilot Project (OPP) was sure that if local residents were fully involved, a cheaper, more appropriate sanitation system could be installed. Research undertaken by OPP staff showed that the inhabitants were aware of the consequences of poor sanitation on their health and their property but they could neither afford conventional systems nor had they the technical or organizational skills to use alternative options. OPP organized meetings for those living in 10–15 adjacent houses each side of a lane and explained the benefits of improved sanitation and offered technical assistance. Where agreement was reached among the households of a lane, they elected their own leader who formally applied for technical help. Their site was surveyed with plans drawn up and cost estimates prepared. Local leaders kept their group informed and collected money to pay for the work. Sewers were then installed with maintenance organized by local groups. The scope of the sewer construction programme grew as more local groups approached OPP for help and the local authorities began to provide some financial support. Over the last eight years, households in Orangi have constructed close to 69,000 sanitary pour-flush latrines in their homes plus 4,459 sewerage lines and 345 secondary drains—using their own funds and under their own management. One indication of the viability of this work is shown by the fact that some lanes have organized and undertaken lane sewerage investments independently of OPP; another is the households' willingness to make the investments needed in maintenance.

Women were very active in local groups; many were elected group leaders and it was often women who found the funds to pay for the sewers out of household budgets. But women had difficulty visiting health centres since custom dictates that they should stay at home. OPP developed a health programme, working through women's groups, also at the level of the lane, with advice provided on hygiene, nutrition, disease prevention, family planning and kitchen gardens.

Sources: Arif Hasan, 'A low cost sewer system by low-income Pakistanis', in Bertha Turner (ed.), *Building Community: a Third World Case Book,* Habitat International Coalition, 1989; Hasan, Arif, 'Community organizations and non-government organizations in the urban field in Pakistan' *Environment and Urbanization,* vol. 2, no. 1, April 1990, 74–86; and Khan, Akhter Hameed, *Orangi Pilot Project Programmes,* Orangi Pilot Project, Karachi, 1991.

For optimum results, there needs to be more coordination linking the activities of NGOs with activities being executed by the public sector and other external support agencies. There is also a need to provide the appropriate legal and institutional environment to facilitate NGO operations. The UNDP inter-regional Local Initiative Facility for Urban Environment (LIFE) launched at UNCED to promote 'local-local' dialogue among municipal governments, NGOs and CBOs to improve the urban environment, is an important initiative in this area (see Chapter 11 for more details).

Sustaining the resource base

Chapter 4 noted how excessive exploitation of water resources to supply urban areas has often led to the depletion or irreversible degradation of freshwater resources, while unrestricted urban groundwater abstractions in many coastal cities has led to saline intrusions into freshwater aquifers. Increasing urban populations and growing industrial production requires large increases in the freshwater supplies. Cities often have to compete with agriculture for local freshwater and this often makes it necessary for cities to tap new, more distant sources.

Chapter 4 also noted how the discharge of urban domestic and industrial wastewater into freshwater bodies reduces their productivity, and affects fisheries, agriculture, and their downstream use by communities. The discharge of untreated sewage into seas can damage fragile marine and coastal ecosystems. Uncontrolled dumping of urban solid wastes causes contamination of surface and groundwater resources, blockage of drainage channels and flooding of low lying areas.

In the past the focus was on the design of more efficient, environmentally sound waste treatment and disposal facilities. But financial restrictions and increasing waste production have brought about a change of focus to promoting waste minimization and a reduction of pollutant load at source, waste recycling, the use of water saving devices, metering of services, and new tariff structures. The UNCHS project on the Integrated Management of Water Resources and Environmental Infrastructure is developing strategies and action plans for improved water resources management focusing on control of depletion and degradation of water resources and their equitable allocation. The Centre has also developed an efficient low cost solid waste management system for Pune Municipality, in India (Box 9.19).

Raising awareness

The examples given above of new approaches to environmental infrastructure management are now well documented and known to sector experts working in the North and in development assistance agencies. However, it is becoming increasingly apparent that the stakeholders in the field involved with delivery and management of environmental infrastructure services in Africa, Asia and Latin America are

BOX 9.19
Low cost and rapid delivery technical assistance for solid-waste management; Pune Municipality, India

UNCHS (Habitat) was requested to review the waste disposal problems of Pune and to make recommendations as to possible improvements in the existing local solid waste management practices. As a first priority, the existing refuse collection fleet was examined. It appeared that most vehicles were generally not entirely suited to local conditions in refuse collection and, in view of local waste densities, they were often not operating at full capacity. In particular, the ergonomics of the trucks' design appeared to be unsuitable. It was also found that labour efficiency could be improved, as could the organizational aspects of waste collection, notably shift durations and undesirable delays at landfill sites. The landfill sites were essentially open dumps and one of the four landfill sites was an obvious environmental threat to a nearby water course.

To address these problems, the advisory team from SIEP took the following actions:

- Under UNCHS (Habitat)'s direction, one of the more recently purchased garbage collection vehicles was modified by a local engineering firm so as to increase the vehicles body volume, allowing for the collection of more waste during one trip. The addition of a simple loading platform to reduce the loading height and comfortable seating arrangements during the collection runs considerably improved the tasks of the waste collectors.

- Changes in the workers' daily schedule and an incentive scheme based on productivity was suggested. These would allow for substantially reduced labour requirements and it was further recommended that the surplus labour so created be used to increase the level of service coverage, particularly in low-income areas where primary waste collection was considered a necessity.

- A new design of waste collection hand-cart was proposed to replace the grossly inefficient existing hand-carts and implements. The new hand-cart proposed could be easily and cheaply constructed, using wheels with tyres made of the inner beading of discarded truck tyres.

The advisory study was completed with a workshop to disseminate its findings and to share the experience with other municipalities. All of these activities were carried out in a space of eight months and for a total cost of $US20,000.

not always aware of the innovative approaches. For all the above developments to be meaningful, information about them needs to be more widely available. Only through dramatic change in attitudes employing the above ideas and concepts will there be any chance of achieving the goal of ensuring affordable access to adequate levels of environmental infrastructure services to all people and in the earliest possible time.

9.5 Transport[9]

Introduction

National and city governments in both the North and the South are questioning the future of cities and urban systems in which private automobiles have the central role in the transport of people. This stems from a greater recognition of the economic, social and environmental costs of 'automobile dependent' cities that were described in Chapter 8. More attention is also being given to the social and environmental costs of freight transport by road. To this is added an interest in the extent to which advanced telecommunications and computer networks can reduce the need for people to travel.

Automobiles and trucks can be 'civilized' through technological advances that greatly reduce fuel use and polluting emissions and increase safety both for the vehicle users and for other road users.[10] Sophisticated traffic management systems can increase the efficiency of the use of road spaces and the number of vehicles using road systems without congestion. But increasingly, even if the incorporation of these advances was accelerated, it is seen as insufficient as the sheer volume of cars, trucks and other motorized road vehicles overwhelms cities. This is especially so in high density cities that have a low proportion of their total area devoted to roads, as is the case in many cities in Europe and in the South. Seeking to expand road systems to cope with projections of increased automobile use in high density cities also produces such disruption to the urban fabric and displaces large numbers of people. It was the scale of this disruption in cities in the North that helped generate a re-evaluation of the priority that was being given to private automobile users. For many of the major cities in the South, the number of automobiles is growing much more rapidly than the number of people and building the roads and highways to cope with projections for increased automobile use will mean the displacement of tens of thousands (or more) people in each such city. There is also the more recent recognition that people who do not have access to a car are significantly disadvantaged as automobile dependence within a city or region increases since this also leads to a deterioration in public transport and a city in which access to workplaces, schools, shops and services is increasingly difficult without a car.

Despite the doubts as to whether the use of private cars can be controlled, not least because of the power of the economic interests behind the automobile-dependent model, there is a growing awareness of the need to plan to reduce automobile dependence within cities.[11] Many cities have pedestrianized their central districts; for most, this was easily done as these were historic city centres that originally developed as 'walking cities' before the advent of motorized transport. But there are also many examples of cities which have reduced automobile dependence through innovations in public transport and controls on automobile use in both the North and the South. They include Hong Kong, Singapore and Surabaya in Asia, Curitiba in Latin America, Zurich, Copenhagen and Freiburg in Europe, Toronto and Portland in North America and Perth in Australia and the means by which they achieved this are outlined in this section. The fact that this list includes some of the wealthiest cities in both the North and South shows that reducing automobile dependence is possible even in societies with high levels of automobile ownership.

There is also much discussion about the need for development oriented towards public transport as the basis for any sustainable city.[12] The link with sustainable development comes from the fact that there is a rapid growth in the number of automobile-dependent cities and in most of these cities, automobile dependence is still increasing. Chapter 8 noted the very rapid growth in the number of automobiles worldwide and their growing role in greenhouse gas emissions. The world's consumption of fossil fuels and total emissions of greenhouse gases would increase dramatically, if the whole world's population came to be as automobile dependent as North America, West Europe or Australia. The OECD and the World Bank have begun to recognise this and are stressing how transport funding needs to be more critically evaluated.[13] But in a globally connected world, the reduction of automobile dependence (and its associated energy, resource use, air pollution and greenhouse gas emissions) should be directed both to cities where automobile dependence is highest and to cities in the South where short-term and long-term measures can reduce their automobile-dependence while also enhancing their prosperity and quality of life.

Some of the world's wealthiest and most successful cities have been reducing the dependence of their citizens on private automobiles. This can be seen in a comparison between Los Angeles, Zurich and Singapore in how their car use and transit use changed between 1980 to 1990. In Los Angeles, car use continued to grow rapidly, with a decline in the use of public transport whereas in Zurich and Singapore, there was far less growth in car use and a considerable increase in the use of public transport. Thus the substantial increases in income which have occurred in the past 10 years in Zurich and Singapore have gone mostly into public transport use and not into private car use and this reflects their cities' overall plans and priorities to achieve this. Los Angeles on the other hand has not attempted to control automobile dependence; here, it is accepted that there is a culture which has little belief in planning other than the facilitation of individual household values. The use of private automobiles has almost inevitably grown as a result.

Key policy conclusions

Four key conclusions of relevance to public policy can be drawn from the data on cities around the world:

- *Public Transport Infrastructure.* Investment in transit infrastructure can help shape the city as well as ease traffic problems—for instance, encouraging 'walking cities' to develop around the stations of light railways or rapid busways. There is a considerable range of technological options too, varying in price, capacity and speed and these include options such as express busways that do not require heavy investments. It is also possible to 'upgrade' as demand rises and as cities grow in size and wealth—for instance as light railways or trams replace express busways. It is also possible to draw on private-sector resources—for instance through city authorities providing the framework within which private bus companies bid for particular routes or areas. But this can only be achieved if public transport is part of a broader policy that discourages low density developments and unnecessary automobile use. If public transport is left as a supplementary process in streets designed for the automobile, there will be no resolution of the transport dilemma.

- *Pedestrian/Cycle Orientation.* If the goal is to provide for the most efficient, equitable and human form of transport, this means a city with provision for cycling, good walking space on streets and in public squares and traffic-free shopping streets. Any city that neglects this dimension will find social and economic problems as well as the obvious environmental ones.

- *Density.* The need to maintain land use efficiency is linked closely to transport. Dispersing land uses at low density creates automobile dependence. Dense urban villages linked by public transport creates the opportunity for Walking and Transit City characteristics to be introduced into the automobile-dependent city—see Figure 9.1 which should be compared to Figure 8.5 in Chapter 8. Similarly, introducing new and efficient public transport lines into rapidly growing cities can encourage the development of such dense urban settlements and limit low density sprawl, especially if land use planning helps encourage such developments.

- *Planning and Control.* All three of the above policies have strong market pressures behind them. But they also require planning to facilitate them. This planning is not heavy-handed bureaucracy but an expression of any city's cultural values—and also of the needs and priorities of pedestrians and cyclists and of children, youth and all other citizens who cannot or do not use cars. It highlights the priority on urbanization and access to city services for all people. All cities have some commitment to this social value. If automobile dependence is not resisted through conscious planning, it will erode or help to destroy most attempts to maintain community life in an urban setting. For all cities but particularly those in the South, strong neighbourhoods need to be protected from the dispersing and disruptive aspects of the automobile, while in many cities in the wealthiest market economies of the world, the policy of reducing automobile dependence is part of a process to reclaim residential neighbourhoods.

FIGURE 9.1
The remodelling of the automobile dependent city

Source: Newman, Peter, Jeff Kenworthy and Peter Vintila *Housing, Transport and Urban Form*, Institute for Science and Technology Policy, Murdoch University, Australia, 1992.

Case studies in resolving or limiting private automobile dependence

Apart from general principle, it is important to learn from individual cities how they have been able to overcome automobile dependence. It is also important to learn of the challenges that need to be faced by cities that are seeking to address problems of increasing traffic congestion and rising levels of private automobile ownership and/or use. Below are short sketches of the measures taken to reduce automobile dependence in a range of cities. Examples of governments who are developing 'enabling' frameworks that encourage city and municipal authorities to reduce automobile dependence and to improve public transport are given in Chapter 12.

Singapore and Hong Kong

Both Singapore and Hong Kong have remarkably successful transit systems and very low car usage. They have not always been so well balanced but faced the dilemma of the automobile and constantly opted to provide more for public transport than for the car. In order to achieve this, Singapore and Hong Kong have made city-wide planning a very high priority.[14] The transit system in both cities is both fixed, rapid and comfortable (electric rail) and is also flexible and local (minibus). This is supplemented by non-motorized means such as walking and cycling. Central to the success of this model is high density urban development that is closely integrated around the transit system. Such densities seem

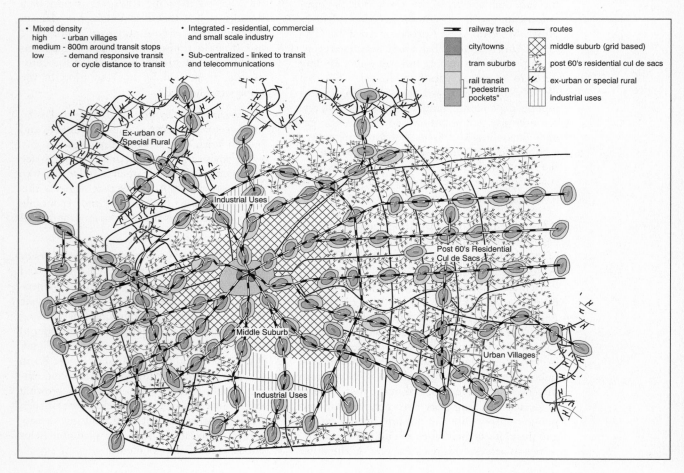

excessive to Anglo-Saxon perceptions but are not so culturally unacceptable particularly when they are associated with good planning that results in high levels of health and other quality-of-life indicators.[15] In Singapore, high-quality provision of public transport is also supplemented by heavy taxes on car ownership and an 'area licensing scheme' that charges cars that enter the central city—although car pools of four or more riders are allowed to enter free.[16] Many other measures are being taken to encourage walking and cycling—for instance separated bikeways along roads and in the new towns to facilitate access to the mass rapid transit stations and extensive pedestrian precincts and malls.[17]

Many of the larger cities in Africa, Asia and Latin America already have high levels of automobile ownership—and many have a much more rapid growth in car ownership than in population. Most are seeking to address this with transport priorities dominated by new roads and highways and increased provision for car parking. Many such cities already have huge traffic problems as well as associated environmental and social problems. For them there is the obvious solution—to implement public transport systems similar to those of Hong Kong, Singapore or Curitiba (see Box 9.20 for more details on Curitiba). The density of development in most cities in these regions is more than adequate to enable good transit sys-

tems to be built. And for rapidly growing cities, decisions made now about good public transport can ensure that the city's physical growth in the future avoids the problems of automobile-dependent, low-density sprawl. Many proposals and plans for transit systems (usually with a mixture of finance from private and public sources) exist in cities like Bangkok which are becoming overwhelmed by automobiles.

Curitiba

The problem for most cities whether in the North or the South is how to minimize the cost of public transport whilst putting in sufficient investment to make it a viable alternative to increasing private automobile use. Curitiba in Brazil is a city which has shown how to do this by channelling investment of scarce urban resources into a coherent, city-wide transit service that is closely integrated with land use policy and other social policies in the city. Box 9.20 describes its public transport system.

Three other aspects of Curitiba's transport policy are also worth noting:[18]

1. It has one of the lowest accident rates per vehicle in Brazil.
2. There are considerable savings for inhabitants in expenditure on transport (on average, residents spend only about 10 per cent of their

---

BOX 9.20

Public transport and other environmental initiatives in Curitiba, Brazil

The public transport system which has been developed over the last 20 years began with the use of express buses on exclusive busways on axes radiating out of the city centre. These proved much cheaper and less disruptive than conventional metro or light railway systems. Over the years, these axes have been further developed and new urban developments have been encouraged to concentrate along them. There are five main axes, each with a 'trinary' road system. The central road has two exclusive bus lanes in the centre for express buses and is flanked by two local roads. Each side of this central road, one block away, are high capacity, free-flowing, one way roads—one for traffic flowing into the city, the other for traffic flowing out of the city. In the areas adjacent to each axis, land use legislation has encouraged high density residential developments, along with services and commerce. The express buses running along these axes are served by inter-district buses

and conventional feeder buses with connections between different buses organized in a series of bus terminals.

With a more deconcentrated pattern of employment, the central city areas could be pedestrianized and the historic buildings protected from redevelopment. Several main thoroughfares have been closed to traffic and converted into tree-lined walkways. One important complementary action was the municipal government's acquisition of land along or close to the new transport axes, prior to their construction. This allowed the government to organize high density housing programmes close to the transport axes; in all, some 17,000 lower-income families were located close to these.

At present there are 53 km of express lines, 294 km of feeder lines and 167 km of inter-district lines. Buses are colour coded: the express buses are red, inter-district buses are green and the conventional (feeder) buses are yellow. There is full integration between express buses, inter-district buses and conventional (feeder) buses. Large bus terminals at the end of each of the five express busways allow people to transfer to inter-district or feeder buses and one single fare is valid for all buses. Along each express

route, smaller bus terminals are located approximately every 1,400 metres, equipped with newspaper stands, public telephones and post office facilities. Here passengers arrive on feeder buses and transfer to the express buses. The latest innovation is the introduction of the 'direct' express buses with fewer stops and where passengers pay before boarding the buses in special raised tubular stations. These new stations (with platforms at the same height as bus floors) cut boarding and deboarding times. This rapid bus system with 'boarding tubes' can take twice as many passengers per hour as the other express buses and three times as many passengers per hour when compared to a conventional bus operating in a normal street. The boarding tubes also eliminate the need for a crew on the bus to collect fares, which frees up space for more passengers.

Curitiba's public transportation system is used by more than 1.3 million passengers each day. Twenty eight per cent of express bus users previously travelled in their cars. This has meant savings of up to 25 per cent of fuel consumption city-wide. Curitiba's public transportation system is a major reason for the city having one of the lowest levels of ambient air pollution in Brazil.

Source: Jonas Rabinovitch, 'Curitiba: towards sustainable urban development', *Environment and Urbanization* vol. 4, no. 2., Oct. 1992.

income on transport which is relatively low for Brazil).

3. Social policies have been integrated with the system through the insistence on low cost fares across the city, the access to the system for those with disabilities (wheelchairs can enter the bus directly once in the bus-boarding tube, and old buses are used to provide special services for the heavily disabled).

The next phase of Curitiba's growth is to develop higher capacity rail services along the main axes which can now be done as the city develops based on its original low cost buses.

Surabaya

Cities without the funding potential for major transit systems must try other ways of managing the automobile or it will quickly destroy their cities. In the South, what is termed the 'non-motorized transport sector' which includes bicycles and walking is largely neglected and is seen as an expression of older, less fashionable values—ironically, at a time when it is seen once again as fashionable and modern in Europe. In both the North and the South, it has huge potential if it is properly facilitated.[19]

Surabaya provides an excellent example of support for non-motorized transport. Surabaya is a dense, walking-oriented city with little motorized transport. The goal of Surabaya was to build on this strength whilst providing improved quality of life for its residents. The city developed an extensive programme to improve housing, infrastructure and services in the traditional Kampungs. But the upgrading also retained narrow alleys and these were made attractive with planting and a strong emphasis on pedestrians.[20] This is a demonstration of how planning can work in cities in less urbanized and industrialized economies. It also shows how an emphasis on participation and grassroots involvement can work in such a city environment.

Zurich, Copenhagen and Freiburg

Each of these are examples of cities that have made concerted efforts to contain the automobile whilst improving the quality of life of their citizens. In Zurich, there has been a spectacular increase in the use of public transport and a containment in the growth in car use. This has occurred despite substantial growth in per capita incomes in Zurich. How has Zurich managed to channel its wealth into such positive city-building processes rather than the city-destroying processes of dispersal, pollution and community disturbance associated with automobile dependence? In the 1970s, Zurich had to make decisions about its trams. Instead of bowing to the car lobby and scrapping the tram system (as most European cities had done before them), it expanded its old tram system and upgraded the services so tram-users never had to wait more than 6 minutes and had total right of way at traffic lights.

As trams became fashionable, public attention was directed to other amenities—pedestrian malls and outdoor cafés, that were allowed to take up road space and parking lots. The strategy, was 'to point out other better possibilities of use'. People began to respond to the attractions of the public realm and made private sacrifices to be part of that. This is the key to resolving the dilemma of the automobile: a city should provide something more appealing to its citizens than automobile-based decisions can provide.

Copenhagen is an example of a city that has sought to resolve the dilemma of the automobile using innovative social planning. The city has a transit-oriented urban form but it was not enough in itself as the use of private automobiles was growing and there was a need to resist this.

By the 1960s, American values had begun to catch on—separate isolated homes and everyone driving. The city was suffering so how could we reverse these patterns? We decided to make the public realm so attractive it would drag people back into the streets, whilst making it simultaneously difficult to go there by car.[21]

Each year, the amount of space for car parking was reduced by three per cent and more streets were pedestrianized. Each year, city housing was built or refurbished, and streets were made more attractive to pedestrians and to street life in general through landscaping, sculptures, and seating (including 3,000 seats in sidewalk cafés). And each year they introduced more street musicians, markets and other street life and street festivals that became increasingly popular. 'The city became like a good party'.[22] The result has been not only a reduction in the traffic but growth in the vitality of the city area. Social and recreational activity has tripled in Copenhagen's major streets. And this was despite the conventional wisdom that:

—'Denmark has never had a strong urban culture'
—'Danes will never get out of their cars' and
—'Danes do not promenade like Italians'.

This turnaround from what had appeared to be a strong trend towards increasing automobile dependence took only twenty years. The newly invigorated public realm of the city is so attractive that there is a declining market for single detached homes on the urban fringe; they are apparently 'too far away' and 'too private'.

Freiburg in Germany is another city that has shown how it is possible to virtually stop the growth of car use, even when car ownership is growing. Freiburg's car ownership rose from 113 per 1,000 people in 1960 to 422 per 1,000 in 1990, only a little under the average for the Zurich agglomeration, and only 12 per cent less than the national average for West Germany (481 per 1,000).[23] Table 9.1 shows how, despite this growth in the availability of cars, car use has virtually remained constant since 1976. Public transport passengers have increased 53 per cent and bicycle trips have risen 96 per cent between 1976 and 1991.

The growth in car trips in Freiburg over 15 years was only 1.3 per cent, yet total trips increased 30 per cent. The growth in mobility was supplied principally by increased public transport and bicycling. In fact the share of trips by car *reduced* over the 15 years from 60 per cent to 47 per cent. The growth in car ownership has also begun to slow down;[24] Freiburg had previously had higher than average car ownership within what was West Germany as a whole, whereas now it has below average car ownership.

The success in Freiburg in 'taming the automobile' was the result of a combination of transportation and physical planning strategies:

First, it has sharply restricted auto use in the city. Second it has provided affordable, convenient, and safe alternatives to auto use. Finally, it has strictly regulated development to ensure a compact land use pattern that is conducive to public transport, bicycling and walking.[25]

Restricted automobile use has been achieved through mechanisms such as pedestrianization of the city centre, area-wide traffic calming schemes (including a city-wide speed limit of 30 km per hour in residential areas) and more difficult, expensive parking. Freiburg's improvements to public transport have focused on extending and upgrading its light rail system as opposed to buses. Buses are used as feeders to the light rail system. Land use regulations are similar to many other parts of Europe and have involved limiting the overall amount of land available to development and strictly zoning land for agriculture, forests, wildlife reserves or undeveloped open space.

The important savings in automobile use arising from the more compact urban patterns that have resulted from these latter policies should also be noted.[26]

Toronto and Portland

North America has been the area most associated with high levels of automobile ownership and use. Toronto and Portland are now however, among the cities that have overcome the dominant paradigm of automobile-based planning. Central to both stories is how community organizations forced planners to think again about freeway proposals.

Toronto has made a deliberate policy of transit-oriented development for a number of decades. Whilst not always consistently applied, it has been more successful than any other North American city.

Toronto is far less dominated by cars and indeed is the best North American example of transit-oriented development. From 1960 to 1980, the use of Toronto's public transport grew by 48 per cent. The central city of Toronto grew and the overall density increased by 8 per cent (particularly along its transit lines). The Mayor of Toronto from that period tells the story of how it happened. The authorities in Toronto were very influenced by the book *The Death and Life of Great American Cities*[27] which stressed the need for people to go back to a more urban character and to rediscover public spaces. The author, Jane Jacobs, went to live in Toronto and was very influential in a movement there that was designed to stop the building of a major freeway called the Spadina Expressway. This began a whole public community-based move for a different kind of city.

Once the halting of the freeway had defined the city's direction, the decision was made to emphasize transit-oriented development. Toronto changed in 20 years from a city that was very car-based to one that is substantially based around public transport. As a result it has been able to revitalise the downtown area and develop a series of transit-centred sub-cities.

The overall process was something that the Mayor said they were never confident about; they were not sure that they would be able to achieve a city that was moving away from the automobile. But they were surprised by how well it worked. It is now a very vibrant city. It is a city that planned its development around public transport. It has even built 30,000 houses in the past 10 years in the city centre and this has reduced the morning peak by 100 cars for every 120 units built.[28] There are families living in the city centre in the European tradition, which contributes much to the vitality and safety of the public spaces.

Portland in the United States has shown that an increasingly automobile-dominated city is not inevitable. During the 1970s, there were plans to build the Mt Hood Expressway through the city. When it was decided by the community not to

TABLE 9.1 Transport trends in Freiburg, Germany, 1976–1991

Transport factor	1976	1991	% Increase 1976–1991
Total daily trips	385,000	502,000	+ 30.4%
Total daily auto trips	231,000	234,000	+ 1.2%
Auto's share of non-pedestrian trips	60%	47%	n.a.
Bicycle's share of non-pedestrian trips	18%	27%	n.a.
Public transport share of non-pedestrian trips	22%	26%	n.a.

Source: Pucher, S and Clorer, J., 'Taming the automobile in Germany', *Transportation Quarterly*, vol. 46, no. 3, 1992, 383–95.

build it but instead to go for a light rail system (MAX), the majority of transport experts laughed—and the new system planned was even dubbed the 'streetcar named expire' as the experts claimed that in a modern city you cannot get people out of their cars.

The new system proved to be a transport success story with a doubling of the patronage over the bus system it replaced and a large off peak usage by families going into the city. The only political problem with the decision to go for light rail instead of a freeway is that many other corridors want the MAX system extended along them—so plans are being developed to extend it. There have also been several other important side effects. One is that the city centre has come alive after the business community recognised the opportunity provided by MAX and took the initiative to help re-pave the city streets and installed lots of seats, flower planters and other elements of good urban design at the street level. The city centre is among the most attractive in the USA. The downtown area went from 5 per cent to 30 per cent of the city's total retailing because of the light rail and added housing rather than parking. There was even a central city car park that was replaced with a public meeting place and a downtown freeway that was replaced with a riverfront park.[29] Another development has occurred in the suburbs where citizens, encouraged by their victory over the freeway have started to push for traffic calming. In response to this, the City Government began a 'Reclaim Your Street' project where residents and the government architect plan together how to slow down traffic and make it easier for pedestrians and cyclists (see Box 9.21 for an example of the benefits of traffic calming). Finally the city has now recognised that MAX provides the opportunity to develop an integrated approach to land development. They have now developed a plan to curtail outer area growth and redirect it to urban redevelopment around transit stops so 85 per cent of all new growth must be within 5 minutes walk of a designated transit stop.[30]

Perth

For over 50 years new suburbs have been built in Australia on the assumption that the majority of people will not need a public transport service. Suburbs were built at uniformly low densities of 10–12 dwellings per hectare and without access to rail services. This left suburbs with a subsidized bus service that rarely came more than hourly at off-peak times. It is not surprising that the Australian suburban lifestyle rapidly became highly automobile-dependent.

One such corridor in Perth was that of the city's northern suburbs which grew rapidly in the 1960s and 1970s on the low-density, car-

BOX 9.21
Traffic calming: the European experience

There are many examples of traffic-calming schemes in Europe that have greatly reduced accidents. One example is the German Federal Government which has sponsored area-wide traffic calming schemes in cities of different sizes from Berlin down to a village of 2,300 inhabitants. In the Netherlands, the Federal government has also sponsored a wide range of traffic-calming initiatives since 1977, including area-wide traffic-calming demonstration projects in Eindhoven and Rijswijk. Both the number and severity of accidents is usually significantly reduced, as reducing speed greatly reduces the risk of serious injury and the danger to pedestrians and cyclists. Berlin's area wide scheme resulted in the following reductions in accidents:

Type of traffic	Measure	% reduction in accidents
All traffic	Fatal accidents	57
	Serious accidents	45
	Slight accidents	40
	Accident costs	16
Non-motorized	Pedestrians	43
	Cyclists	16
	Children	66

Most other schemes report similar results—for instance in Heidelberg, accidents fell by an average of 31 per cent with casualties falling by 44 per cent, after a residential speed limit of 30 km per hour and other traffic-calming measures were introduced.[31] Area-wide schemes in the Netherlands have reduced accidents in residential areas by 20 per cent overall and accidents involving injury by 50 per cent (measured per million vehicle km) and there was no increase in accidents in surrounding areas.[32]

Source: Newman, Peter and Jeff Kenworthy with Les Robinson, *Winning Back the Cities*, Australian Consumers' Association, Pluto Press, Australia, 1992. The Table on Berlin is drawn from Pharoah, T. and J. Russell, *Traffic calming: Policy evaluation in three European countries*, Occasional Paper 2/89, Department of Planning, Housing and Development, Southbank Polytechnic, London, 1989.

dependent form. Two original rail services were removed in the 1960s as planners saw no future for transit other than back-up bus services. However by the 1980s, the freeway serving the corridor was highly congested at peak hours and the community was dissatisfied with the bus service. A strong political push for a rail service resulted in the Northern Suburbs Rapid Transit System.[33] The 33-kilometre electric rail service has only 7 stations which allows a very rapid service. It also features trains that are linked by bus services interchanging passengers directly onto the stations. This allows cross-suburban bus services to be provided once the station nodes become the focus for bus routes rather than the Central Business District.

The new service has been successful but it reveals the problem of transport planners who do not believe that good public transport can succeed in modern cities. Three predictions were made about the rapid transit system which proved to be wrong:

Prediction 1: Rail will lose patronage over buses as people don't like transferring.
Result: 40 per cent *increase* with Rail-Bus over Bus-only in the corridor.
Conclusion: People will transfer if they can move to a superior form of service.

Prediction 2: You will never get people out of their cars as the freeway is so good and parking so easy in Perth.
Result: 25 per cent of the patrons on the northern line gave up using their cars.
Conclusion: Even in an automobile-dependent city, people can give up their cars.

Prediction 3: It will be a financial disaster.
Result: It was completed on-budget and on-time, winning many awards for engineering and architecture. It is almost breaking-even in running costs.
Conclusion: If people are given a good option then rail infrastructure can be viable in modern cities.

Perth still has a long way to go before it overcomes its automobile dependence. One of the positive trends has been the growth in transit-oriented urban villages around the new electric rail service stations. These urban villages provide not only a good, close, rail option for residents and employees in the villages but much of the need for a car is replaced by a short walk to local services. This process can continue as more people discover the value of a less automobile-dependent lifestyle.

Alternative planning models in new cities

Two new cities, Milton Keynes in the United Kingdom and Almere in the Netherlands, illustrate the difference between a new city developed on the assumption that most people would travel by private automobile and a new city developed at a density similar to traditional settlements—i.e. to a settlement pattern that predated the automobile. The Garden City concept developed by Ebenezer Howard was first proposed 100 years ago in response to the smoky, overcrowded industrial cities of Britain. The concept has been the inspiration for many New Towns since. However not all have kept to the key concepts as developed by Howard. In particular, the density of residential areas has been lowered in their New Towns considerably on the basis of 'Nothing gained by overcrowding' the slogan of the Town and Country Planning Association through most of this century. This dislike of high density seems to be an Anglo-Saxon characteristic that has been exported to most English-speaking cities.[34]

What is lost by lowering densities below 35 to 40 dwellings per hectare is the walking scale of cities and their viability for public transport. What is left is an automobile dependence that creates so many of the problems outlined in earlier chapters. This can be seen most clearly in the difference between Milton Keynes, a UK New Town and Almere a similarly sized Dutch New Town. Both were inspired by Garden City concepts but Milton Keynes reduced its densities to 20 dwellings per hectare and also separated its housing from employment and shopping zones by large distances. Almere was denser and more mixed as in traditional Dutch settlements.

Perhaps the most marked difference is in the degree of automobile dependence which is expressed by the proportion of people who see a car as 'essential', and the related difference in confidence in allowing children to be unsupervised on streets. This difference is about confidence in the public realm. It is obviously related to many social factors but its link to the structure and form of the city cannot be underestimated. A walking environment is not created by scattering land uses at densities which demand the use of an automobile.

Conclusions

The private automobile poses a dilemma in all cities. It raises significant questions about the economic, social and environmental impact of technology, whether as part of the planning

TABLE 9.2 A comparison of travel and land use in two new towns: Milton Keynes (UK) and Almere (Netherlands)

	Milton Keynes	Almere
Modal Split		
Car	59%	35%
Public Transport	17%	17%
Bicycle	6%	28%
Walk	18%	20%
Land Use		
Average Travel Distance	7.2 km	6.9 km (much less for non-work)
% of Trips more than 3 km	45%	85%
Density (dwellings per hectare)	20	35–40
Form	scattered, separated use	organic, mixed use
Automobile Dependence		
Proportion who see a car as 'essential'	70%	50%
% Households with children under 12 years who are always supervised outside home	52%	16%
% who are never supervised outside home	8%	48%

Source: Roberts, J., *Changed Travel—Better World? A Study of Travel Patterns in Milton Keynes and Almere*, TEST, London, 1992.

process in cities in the North or South, or as part of development assistance. Many development assistance agencies explicitly or implicitly favour the automobile-dependent city in the transport and infrastructure projects they support. The inappropriateness of such a model can be seen in the scale of the problems with traffic congestion and pollution related to internal combustion engines in cities in the South and the very high rates of accidental deaths and injuries, even though most cities have much lower levels of private automobile ownership per person than cities in the North. Much of the advice on solving the problem is still within the automobile-dependent model in the form of plans that spread cities outwards in reduced densities and in the building of freeways that usually bring an enormous displacement of people. These just create further automobile dependence.

Examples given in this section suggest that the problem can be resolved, as most cities have not developed to the scale and low density that makes public transport options unfeasible. But the difficulties in doing so should not be underestimated. First, very rarely is there an agency in a city or metropolitan area that has the authority to promote comprehensive solutions—and different agencies or ministries have their own objectives, priorities and resources.[35] Second, ministries or agencies concerned with roads are often more powerful than agencies concerned with public transport—and are also backed by powerful lobbies that represent automobile owners, automobile manufacturers and construction companies.

However, the case studies in this section do show that these constraints can be overcome. Ironically, it may be the increasing realization that all major cities must remain competitive in a world market to attract productive investment that will, once again, legitimize substantial government intervention in limiting automobile dependence and the economic, social and environmental costs it implies. The case studies also show how automobile dependence in cities in the North can be slowed and even reversed through planning that puts greater emphasis on public transport and non-motorized travel. The case studies offer some hope although few cities have integrated, coherent plans to overcome automobile dependence and most are relying too much on technological advances to resolve more fundamental problems in the planning of their cities. Solutions in cities in the South are also being found either through an emphasis on public transport or non-motorized travel. Both require a commitment to planning that is in essence the recognition that social aspects of development are essential for sustainable and civilized cities.

9.6 Participation and the Tools and Methods to Support it

Introduction

The 1980s brought many important developments in the ways and means of more fully involving low-income groups and their community organizations in development projects. Although most of these developments were pioneered in rural or agricultural projects, more recently, these have been modified for use in urban areas or new initiatives developed within urban contexts. This section reports on recent developments in participatory tools and methods, illustrating them with three case studies: 'Planning for real' in the UK, Community Action Planning in Sri Lanka, and the India–South Africa community-to-community exchange.

The importance of involving the inhabitants of any settlement in decisions about the development of their settlement or in larger developments that will affect them is receiving increasing recognition.[36] New methods have been developed to collect and process information about, with, and by local people and their own conditions and livelihoods. When first developed during the late 1970s and early 1980s, these procedures were primarily concerned with gathering accurate and detailed information efficiently. At that time, the emphasis was on the word 'rapid' within 'rapid appraisals', and most of the analyses and actions were controlled by outside agencies or researchers. As experiences and insights grew, it became evident that local people, who had previously been viewed as passive 'subjects', 'clients' or 'beneficiaries', had much to contribute to the research and development process. As these approaches were adapted and modified further, the depth and validity of local people's experiences and knowledge became clear. By the late 1980s, much of the emphasis had shifted from 'rapid' to 'participatory' planning and research. Participatory approaches and the tools and methods that help their implementation are now being applied in a wide range of social and ecological contexts and are shaping and influencing development programmes and projects worldwide.[37]

Participatory approaches

Participatory methodologies are sets of tools and techniques that have been developed in order to better realize high levels of community members' involvement in development projects or to allow the inhabitants of a particular settlement to design, implement and/or evaluate their own initiatives. Participation is now commonly accepted to be an important component of successful development programmes although the term is used in many different senses. Table 9.3 illus-

TABLE 9.3 Different levels of participation within any project

Self-Mobilization	Project initiated by the population themselves who develop contacts with external institutions for resources and technical advice they need, but retain control over how resources are used. Can 'go to scale' if governments and NGOs can provide the 'enabling' framework to support a wide range of such initiatives. Also, within any low-income settlements, this is less of a project and more part of a process by which people organize to get things done and negotiate with external agencies for support in doing so.
Interactive Participation	Project initiated by external agency working with local population (and often in response to local people's demand). Participation seen as a citizen's right, not just as a means to achieve project goals. People participate in joint analysis, development of action plans and formation or strengthening of institutions for implementation and management. As such, they have considerable influence in determining how available resources are to be used.
Functional Participation	Participation seen by external agency as a means to achieve project goals, especially reduced costs (through people providing free labour and management). For instance, people participate by forming groups to meet predetermined objectives but after major decisions have been made by the external agency. At its worst, the population is simply coopted to serve external agency's goals which accord little with their goals. However, this limited form of participation has brought real benefits to 'beneficiaries' in many instances.
Participation for Material Incentives	People participate but only in implementation in response to material incentives (e.g. contributing labour to a project in return for cash, food or other material incentives; building a house within a 'self-help' project as a condition for obtaining the land and services).
Consultation and Information-Giving	People's views sought through a consultation process whose aim is to elicit their needs and priorities but this process is undertaken by external agents who define the information gathering process and control the analysis through which the problem is defined and the solutions designed. No decision-making powers given to the population and no obligation on the part of the project designers to respond to their priorities. Great variety in extent to which people's views are accurately elicited and incorporated into project design and implementation.
Passive Participation	People are told what is going to happen but without their views sought and with no power to change what will happen.
Manipulation and Decoration	Pretence of participation—e.g. with 'peoples' representatives on official boards but who are not elected and have no power.

Sources: Drawn from Hart, Roger A., *Children's Participation; from Tokenism to Citizenship*, Innocenti Essays, no. 4, March, UNICEF International Child Development Centre, Florence, 1992, and Pretty, Jules, 'Participatory inquiry for sustainable agriculture', IIED, London, mimeo (draft), 1993. These in turn drew on Arnstein, S. R., 'Eight rungs on the ladder of citizen participation', *Journal of the American Institute of Planners*, 1979.

trates how at one extreme, 'participation' is simply 'passive participation' where people are simply told what is going to happen to them, to 'self-mobilization' at the other extreme in which the inhabitants of a settlement work together to develop and implement their own initiative, independent of external agents.

Participatory approaches are meant to facilitate higher levels of participation in which the inhabitants of a settlement have some control over the development process. They have, in general, been initiated by development practitioners and agencies concerned that much of the decision-making process is designed by and limited to professionals. Participatory approaches are intended to facilitate the integration of residents into such debates and to bring out the needs and priorities of all those living in the settlement. In some cases, they are also intended to enhance collective control of the development process.

Participatory approaches include a range of different activities designed to:

- increase available information about the settlement and residents

- increase available information about the locality
- identify development options
- identify resources for such options
- enable residents (individually and collectively) to prioritize their needs
- develop residents' self-confidence and collective capacity
- develop mechanisms to bring out the priorities and needs of all residents, especially those that may face particular social or cultural barriers to their full involvement—for instance the many societies in which the needs and priorities of women, children and youth receive too little attention.

The development of participatory approaches

Participatory approaches have largely been developed within two sectors, rural development and public health.[38] While they have separate traditions, there is some acknowledgement of their related origins. Within rural development, these approaches are associated with the term 'Rapid Rural Appraisal' (RRA) and within the public health sector 'Rapid Assessment Procedures' (RAP). Other names for similar methodologies include Participatory Learning Methods, Participatory Action Research, Rapid Rural Systems Analysis and *Méthode Accélérée de Recherche Participative*. RRA methodologies have drawn on other methodological traditions and have further developed into Participatory Rural Appraisal (PRA). Robert Chambers who has done much to develop these approaches and promote their use argues that these influences include participatory research and participatory action research approaches developed from the work of Paulo Freire, agro-ecosystems analysis, applied anthropology and field research on farming systems.[39]

Participatory rural appraisal uses similar methods to rapid rural appraisal but, in addition to obtaining the information, it is also concerned with enhancing local people's active participation in the research and development process. The concepts, principles and methods employed are those that encourage low-income households (or groups within households) to take control of the project or programme for which the research and/or development activity is being undertaken. The process of Participatory Rural Appraisal demonstrates to, and reinforces within these local groups, the breadth, depth and validity of their own understanding of their needs and priorities. It builds on people's innate visual literacy by employing a variety of diagramming and visualization methods that enable both literate and non-literate persons to participate actively. Within the health sector, rapid assessment procedures have been used since the early 1980s when anthropological investigation methods were adapted into tools and procedures that could be used to rapidly obtain information on household and community health and nutrition-related behaviour.[40]

Participatory approaches in an urban context

There has been far less development of participatory tools and methods for use in urban contexts. Although there are an increasing number of case studies of urban community development, in general, little emphasis has been placed on methodology. One of the best known examples is the approach taken by the Million Houses Programme in Sri Lanka described in Box 10.13 in which the specific methodology for residents' involvement has always had a clear role. More recently there has been an increased interest in drawing on methodologies developed within a rural context for urban work. This interest includes a broad spectrum of agencies and areas of work that are trying out rapid assessment procedures for urban poverty and programme assessments and the incorporation of PALM tools within the UK Overseas Development Administration's Indian Slum Improvement Programme.[41]

As with the use of such approaches in a rural development context, there is an important distinction between participatory tools and methods being used to simply obtain information and such tools being used to initiate a local development process. Where the intention is to initiate a development process, information gathering is very much a first step, designed to demonstrate to all the residents the depth of their knowledge and their capacity to analyse such information. It is this second use that is illustrated in the boxes included in this section. In its first use, i.e. using these techniques simply to gather information, the exercises are completed once that information is obtained and there is no further discussion of problems facing the community, and how such problems might be overcome. In this form, it is essentially rapid appraisal rather than participatory appraisal.

While some participatory approaches have clearly drawn on traditions developed in other sectors, particularly participatory rural appraisal and rapid assessment procedures, it is also evident that there has been a widespread experimentation with different participatory tools and methods by groups working in urban areas.[42] In many different contexts, similar tools and techniques have been developed based around the use of diagrams, maps and pictures to replace written descriptions. Box 9.22 describes some of the tools and techniques used in urban areas.

One of the most comprehensively documented examples of the use of participatory methods in urban development is community action planning in Sri Lanka. The community action planning approach of Sri Lanka's National Housing Development Authority was developed to implement the urban component of the Million Houses Programme (1984–1989). Community action planning sees people as the main resource for development rather than as an object of the development efforts or as mere recipients of benefits. The objective is to motivate and mobilize the population of an urban low-income settlement to take the lead in planning and implementing an improvement programme. The role of the National Housing Development Authority and the urban local authorities, is to support this process where necessary, but the intention is for the inhabitants of low-income settlement to take the initiative themselves. Box 9.23 describes community action planning, while more details of the Million Houses Programme are given in Chapters 10 and 11.

BOX 9.22
Examples of participatory tools and techniques

- Participative Mapping of the settlement by the inhabitants, including the plotting of important landmarks such as rivers, roads, churches, and public services plus indications of features such as topography. Such maps may be drawn in any open space within the settlement and are put together by drawing on a number of different participants.
- Community members undertaking surveys of the settlement to collect socio-economic data such as numbers of children or information about particular resources such as skills of household members.
- Collective modelling of new housing designs that will better meet the needs of residents. House models can be made from any easily available material such as cardboard. Models can then be discussed and revised with different groups in the community in order to identify the preferred model and discuss trade-offs between size and materials on the one hand and cost on the other.
- Collective planning of new settlement design that will better meet the needs of residents. Once a plan of the existing settlement has been made, residents can discuss how to change buildings to improve access roads and allow space for infrastructure, reblock plots and/or improve services.
- Collective identification of resources including access, management and control and including sources of income, health and links to other settlements.
- Transect walks—for example, to identify the different informal sector activities taking place in the settlement or to identify housing conditions within the settlement.
- Seasonal calendars to identify seasonally occurring events such as illness, availability of employment, food prices and food intake.
- Wealth ranking of all households in the settlement either through households being ranked from first to last or using different colours to indicate different levels of wealth. (A similar exercise can be done for 'well-being' once the community has identified appropriate characteristics.)
- An understanding of the processes by which a particular settlement developed can be obtained either through trend analysis or life histories. In trend analysis, discussions with older people or those who have been in the settlement many years are used to plot the provision of basic services in the settlement, or to consider how factors such as population and social customs have changed over time. Through small group discussions with accounts of individual life histories, critical events in people's lives and in the life of the settlement can be identified.
- Perceived relations with other groups and organizations can be identified through Venn diagramming techniques. Different sized circles are given to small groups of participants who then use the circles to illustrate the importance of other groups (e.g. local government officials) to the community. The size indicates their importance; the distance on the ground indicates their closeness, or not, to the community. Different symbols (squares, triangles etc. may be used to indicate different kinds of groups or individuals).
- Identification of priorities through collective ranking of different development options.
- Acting of 'life stories' based on individuals in the community in order to provoke discussion about opportunities and constraints facing residents.
- Establishment of formal and informal groupings that can provide a focus for and maintain the momentum of community driven development.

BOX 9.23
Community Action Planning

'the real authors of the methodology are the community and the officials who worked alongside each other.' [43]

Community action planning is initiated by workshops at which the inhabitants of a low-income settlement work with staff from the National Housing Development Authority (NHDA), the local (municipal) authority and the non-governmental organisations. They discuss the problems within the settlement, identify solutions and formulate plans of action. Local residents take responsibility for implementing these action plans in collaboration with the NHDA and other organizations, and also for maintaining and managing the built environment after the completion of the project.

Settlement regularization: Community action planning has been used to implement the regularization of illegal or informal settlements. A workshop determines the broad principles within which the regularization process should take place, such as the width of roads and footpaths. The workshop participants are divided into three groups: a women's team, an officials' team and a team of community members and builders. The groups meet separately to identify the needs for land in the settlement for residential plots, roads and footpaths, amenities, a community centre, a playground, a clinic and any other needs. Each group presents its findings in a plenary session and the presentations are discussed until consensus is reached. Next, the three groups meet again separately to find locations for the land uses and to allocate land. Once this has been agreed, participants consider the logistics for the on-site blocking-out exercise.

The decisions of the workshop on the principles and guidelines for re-blocking are distributed to all households in the settlement. Community leaders inform clusters of households of the day the blocking-out exercise will be conducted in their cluster and request the households to be at home on that day. The action planning team visits the cluster to discuss the plot boundaries with each of the households. The team meets with the families in each block to discuss the size of the area and whether or not it can accommodate all the households and, if not, how the problem will be dealt with. As soon as there is an agreement, plot markers are placed to allow all involved to see the implications of the decisions. This often leads to objections and further negotiations by the affected families. The process of negotiation between the families is the most important part of the exercise. The role of the officials is to ensure that no household can grab more land than has been agreed by the workshop (which establishes a maximum size for plots in the settlement). In the process, all land disputes are settled on the spot and finally consensus is reached about the re-blocking of the land in the settlement.

Sources: UNCHS (Habitat), *The Urban Poor as Agents of Development: Community Action Planning in Sri Lanka*, United Nations Centre for Human Settlements (Habitat), Nairobi, 1993; UNCHS (Habitat), *The Community Construction Contract System in Sri Lanka*, Nairobi, 1994.

Despite relatively few publications about the use of such methodologies within an urban context, they are being used in many countries by groups working in settlements in urban areas to consider a wide range of issues including neighbourhood and community development. A recent review drew attention to a considerable diversity of approaches between North and South; between their use by the state and the voluntary sector; and whether they were developed specifically within an urban context or were techniques or approaches originally developed in rural contexts and modified for use in urban areas.[44] However, it also noted the similarities in approaches, despite great differences in context.

Similarities in participatory methodologies between North and South have developed in response to a common need. Professionals throughout the world share similar training standards and very few had any training in the use of participatory tools or methods or indeed in participation itself. As urban development has officially become the work of architects, engineers and planners, so small scale household building processes (whether self-build or by contractor) were excluded from professional consideration except as 'eyesores' to be declared illegal and to be later replaced.[45] Examples from throughout Africa, Asia and Latin America suggest that there is a rich tradition of community-based urban development efforts.[46] Many of these have developed appropriate methodologies to improve work with local residents. Examples of this include:

- In Fortaleza, Brazilian NGOs have worked with community groups to collectively redesign houses and settlements.

- In Manila, the Philippines, women have been exploring critical events in the development of settlement through sharing life histories.

- In India, participatory methods have been used to assist in identifying appropriate responses to the earthquake in Maharashtra.

- In Chile, houses have been designed by non-specialists using house modelling exercises.

- In Pakistan, the Orangi Pilot Project makes rapid and low-cost surveys of areas that are to be provided with secondary drains by drawing on the community's expertise.

- In Zambia, Participatory Rural Appraisal methodologies have been used to identify appropriate donor support for income-generation projects in Lusaka.

- In Birmingham, England, participatory tools have helped to initiate discussions and development programmes with Bangladeshi immigrants.

In an initiative between South Africa and India, exchanges between residents from different settlements have been combined with participatory methodologies in order to 'root' the learning process more solidly within communities and rapidly to accelerate the capacity of community leaders and members to adopt new roles within the development process.[47] This partnership is between the People's Dialogue in South Africa together with the South African Homeless People's Federation and a group of three organisations in India: SPARC, the National Slum Dwellers Federation and *Mahila Milan*, a federation of women's collectives.[48] Exchange visits have been organized between representatives from squatters or pavement dwellers in India and in South Africa.

These community-to-community exchanges have meant that members of the People's Dialogue in South Africa have been able to benefit from community-based shelter training programmes in India where the National Slum Dwellers Federation and *Mahila Milan* have been engaged in such programmes for over eight years. They have since experimented with and developed the training process within communities in South Africa. In this process, they have demonstrated the potential of South-South exchanges to transform the capacity of local residents to address their own development needs. The tools and methods that are used for developing detailed maps of informal settlements, models of houses that meet the needs and resources of the inhabitants and the development of savings groups are described in Box 9.24. This description has been drawn from their application in South Africa. These tools and methods are disseminated by local residents (and facilitated by federations of community based organizations) who, once trained in their settlement, visit other settlements and train new 'experts'.

The examples given here demonstrate that, although often associated with NGOs and community based organizations, they have also been initiated and supported by government agencies willing to support greater community involvement in development processes. The India–South Africa exchange programme described above is unusual because community leaders themselves have been responsible for demonstrating the different tools and methods and therefore for spreading this approach to members within their organizations. A more common strategy has been the use of trained professionals to initiate activities within the settlement.

Some conclusions

The development and use of participatory tools and methods have helped to transform the capacity of the inhabitants of informal or illegal settlements—or other settlements or neighbour-

BOX 9.24
The India-South Africa community exchange and the methods used

The experience-based learning of the training process has two separate but interrelated purposes. First, it enables low-income people to develop their own understanding of their social and economic context, not just on a micro-level but via exchange in regional and global arenas. Second, it equips the participants (low-income residents of informal settlements) with the ability to carry out and drive their own experimental learning programmes.

Shack-Counting in informal settlements: Once the community leadership is ready to undertake the training, a start date is arranged with the training team. Normally the training begins with the physical counting and mapping of all houses and other structures in the settlement and this shack-counting exercise always starts with a huge celebration which might be a concert, drama, or a welcome for visiting dignitaries or representatives from other low-income communities. The training team prepares for the activities of the next day by completing a few practical tasks. A rough map of the settlement, drawn a few days before, and a series of photographs of the settlement are displayed. Everybody should be ready at the start of the day to begin the counting. One member of the training team is assigned to each section. They become the leaders of groups of people who will assist in counting all the structures in the sections. While counting the shacks with training-team members these people receive a thorough experience-based training.

The informal exchanges that take place during this process are the core of the process. This simple process of dialogue and exchange only occurs when the people from communities do the counting. The informal discussions that accompany community driven enumerations are both an outstanding method of mobilization and an exceptionally accurate way of identifying issues that people in the community regard as relevant. Community-driven enumerations, where they are backed up by a strong but loosely structured federation of informal settlements, achieve what professional enumerators are unable to do. The process helps identify and release the real feelings, frustrations and expectations of the inhabitants. The way a squatter responds to the inquiries of a fellow squatter is very different from, and more relevant than, the way that same squatter responds to the social scientist or researcher. In tandem with the shack-count and numbering, the training groups draw rough maps of the settlement.

Mapping: As the groups progress through the settlement numbering and counting shacks, shops, crèches, churches and so on, they draw a simple one dimensional drawing of the streets and structures. Key landmarks are included, such as drains, sewers, electric lights, rivers and other major features. Once the shack-counting and mapping have been completed, the sections are combined into one by a community member who draws well. The result is that the community members have produced their own physical map of the settlement in which they live: a concrete example as to how the attainment of knowledge through practice generates energy and power.

Source: Bolnick, Joel and Sheela Patel, *Regaining Knowledge: An Appeal to Abandon Illusions*, People's Dialogue and SPARC, Cape Town and Bombay, 1994.

hoods—to work together to achieve agreed goals. By strengthening the process of collective decision making, they have resulted in:

- residents being aware of their skills and gaining self-respect
- community groups being able to negotiate as equals with government and other agencies
- community groups being able to strategize to improve their situation
- community members being made more able to resolve differences within the settlement.

From experiences to date, three particular questions have emerged about the use of participatory methodologies. The first is what is the time scale of implementation, particularly given their development from 'rapid' methodologies? Second, how participatory are such methodologies? And thirdly, how can such local development programmes link with higher level planning structures?

Although having emerged from methods whose essential feature was their rapid execution in contrast to more traditional forms of information gathering, participatory methodologies are generally not so quick. As rapid assessment has moved towards and merged with participatory development, speed is considered of less importance. While some of the methods may result in the relatively quick gathering of information, the establishment of programmes to support such activity is likely to take some years. For instance, in the use of participatory approaches in the development of artisanal fisheries in port areas of Dakar, their introduction has not been rapid due primarily to the need to train government officials.[49] The tools and methods might still be used for rapid assessment,[50] but development participation in programmes takes more time.

Community participation is a complex process and reservations have been expressed about the nature of participation within programmes using participatory tools and methods. Drawing on the experience of participatory approaches in rural areas, it is likely that the application of such tools and methods will not be quick if the community is to understand and accept the purpose of the external agents coming into the settlement.[51] The need to establish some form of representative community development council has been recognised in many of these projects such as the Million Houses Programme. However, even within these formal structures many issues remain. Particular groups including women, children and those on the lowest incomes may not participate equally in the activities that take place. Many settlements are divided by political or other affiliations and these differences need to be recognised and, where possible, addressed before other collective activities can take place. Community participation may favour stronger groups in the community who can reinterpret their private interests as public concerns.[52]

How to link local planning within the community to higher level planning structures? As community capacity to plan local settlements increases, there is a need to ensure that municipal and city officials permit and encourage such developments. Such autonomous and community-driven development may rest uneasily within city plans. At a city level, participation is likely to be a more formal process and there is a need to address how cities can plan in order to be flexible and responsive to local initiatives.

Despite these concerns, there is evidence of growing interest in the use of participatory methodologies for neighbourhood improvement programmes in both urban and rural areas.[53] The experiences described here demonstrate a new direction for planning methodologies that is being used by governments, communities and professional training institutions. Both the scale of present interest and their widespread acceptance in rural development suggest that their application will continue to grow

9.7 Training for Settlement Management and Development[54]

Introduction

Governments and international agencies are responding to the great lack of adequately trained and qualified personnel for settlement management and development, and many new approaches have been developed to make training more relevant to addressing the wide range of settlement problems outlined in earlier chapters. However, the scale of support for training from governments and international agencies remains far below that needed. In addition, much of the training remains inappropriate to the tasks that the personnel will face when they work in institutions for settlement management. This section considers the scale and nature of need for qualified personnel and the qualitative and quantitative deficiencies in the 'supply' side. It also outlines how training is changing to more relevant approaches and the role of governments and international agencies in this.

The scarcity of qualified human resources

A scarcity of adequately trained, qualified personnel—for policy, management and technical aspects—has long been one of the main obstacles to the improvement of human settlements. This is especially the case at local (for instance district or municipal) level. The need to address this scarcity has become even more pressing since mid-1980s as a result of various global developments:

- The new roles and responsibilities placed on local governments as a result of decentralization and the new importance given to public/private partnership.
- The need for far more effective local responses to environmental degradation and to poverty (and, in many countries, to the social impacts of structural adjustment).
- In the 'transition' countries, the basic restructuring of economic and political systems and of the nature of land and property ownership is completely changing the management of local development, and presenting authorities with entirely new problems and opportunities.
- In the wealthiest market economies, where settlement problems were thought to be diminishing, there are many problems that remain poorly addressed including urban violence, poverty and homelessness, and the social and economic strategies needed in urban centres or particular city districts that lose their economic dynamism.
- The importance of integrating sustainable development issues into public policy and public/private partnerships.
- The new awareness of gender discrimination and the need for new responses to address this in housing, transport, settlement and environmental policies.
- The demands placed on governments at all levels by non-governmental organizations, community-based institutions, women's groups, and the private sector for much broader participation in development decisions and actions.

Neither the staff nor the elected officials of the organizations responsible for the management of cities, municipalities and districts are, by and large, prepared to meet this challenge. But even where they are, they often lack the knowledge of how to do so. Addressing these issues requires new content and methods of training, as well as the obvious need to greatly increase the number of qualified personnel. There are also the great difficulties that local governments and other agencies working in settlements management face in attracting, motivating and retaining qualified staff and officials, as they often do not have adequate salary scales, career-development opportunities and other incentives.

The supply side

The programmes of the academic institutions, and of other pre-service educational organizations, that train people for settlements management, have been slow to respond to the increased magnitude and new nature of needs and demands. National institutions that should provide training courses in rural and urban development or should help develop the capacity of settlements institutions (including on-the-job training) are rarely in a position to do so.

In addition, the training and capacity-building they provide is often inappropriate to the tasks facing those responsible for settlements management and development. The conceptual framework on which education and training in general is based is in a process of change, or as some call it 'paradigm shift'. As a result of scientific discoveries and of awareness of changes in the world, 'the fragmentation of knowledge into jealous and secretive "disciplines" and of activities into bureaucratic and competitive "sectors" is now widely decried'.[55] As Fritjof Capra states, 'In the old paradigm it was believed that in any complex system the dynamics of the whole could be understood from the properties of the parts. One tried to construct explanatory pictures from building blocks, starting with jig-saw puzzle pieces instead of disaggregating a whole'.[56] As Capra goes on to say, 'in the new paradigm, the relationship between the parts and the whole is reversed. The properties of the parts can be understood only from the dynamics of the whole. Ultimately, there are no parts at all. What we call a part is merely a pattern in an inseparable web of relationships'.[57]

This new paradigm is central to improving practice in the complex multi-dimensional process of settlements management and development. At the same time, translating such general principles into training and capacity-building practice requires major rethinking and restructuring of current strategies, methods and institutions.

The concept of 'enablement' that is integral to the 'Global Strategy for Shelter to the Year 2000' and the new partnerships between government and other sectors that it implies also require major changes in training and capacity building. For instance, it implies entirely new relationships between settlements development institutions and population at large, especially with the lowest income groups. This requires radical change in the roles of officials and professionals which in turn necessitates major changes in the content and form of their education and training.

National responses

Most countries in the South lack national human resource development policies and strategies for settlement management and development. Much of the training for settlements management comes through academic education, primarily in architecture related to planning schools, but also in geography, public administration, socio-logy, economics, and law (among others). Many countries also have specialized, pre-service, professional education in local government management—for instance special programmes for town clerks or treasurers. In Latin America many countries have technical-level education for human settlements, especially for work with low-income settlements (what is sometimes termed the 'barefoot architects' concept).

One characteristic of training for planning and for other specialist disciplines during the late 1970s and early 1980s was their increasing fragmentation into more specialized departments, programmes, and careers. In the 1990s, there are signs that this fragmentation is being reversed. This applies to post-graduate education and to in-service training. Several institutions, or training programmes that were previously narrowly focused (for example on housing) have widened their scope to settlements management in general, and reflect the paradigm shift mentioned above. Examples can be found in training institutions in Europe that concentrate on settlements-related training for the South (for instance the Institute of Housing and Urban Studies in the Netherlands and the Development Planning Unit and CARDO in the UK) and in training institutions in the South (the Centre for Housing Studies, Ardhi Institute, Tanzania and the Human Settlements Management Institute in India).

In terms of subject focus, in pre-service education and even more in-service training, there is a new emphasis on management, in addition to the planning and preparation of new capital projects. This also includes greater emphasis on the operation and maintenance of existing assets. The range of subjects covered by education and training for settlements management has also widened to include a broad range of social, economic, political and environmental concerns, including organizational development and settlements management within a sustainable development framework.

There are many new initiatives and approaches within in-service training. These include:

- A move from supply-based standard courses to demand responsive, client-centred capacity-building services to local government and other settlements management organizations;

- The combining of training (residential and on-the-job) with problem-solving consultancies, research, and the production of training materials;

- A move from knowledge content only, to practical skills and to the development and strengthening of attitudes. This remains contentious as some experts believe that training should concentrate only on technical issues while others insist that changes in behaviour and attitude are central to making effective settlement managers. Among these important changes in attitude are how to work in teams, an understanding of gender issues and how to act on gender-discrimination, 'can do' attitude, and a readiness to listen to and work with low-income groups in participatory ways.

- A shift from classroom teaching to on-the-job, experiential learning.

Such innovations are still limited only to some institutions but they represent a significant, and very positive, new trend.

In parallel with these developments in the content of training and in the methods taught, there are also important changes in the nature and status of the settlements management training institutions, and in the greater number and diversity of training and settlements management advisory services. These include:

- Government training institutions that have become more autonomous with often a parastatal status with the elimination of budget financing and the reduction of subsidies and other supports. In most cases, the objective is complete financial self-reliance, based on services paid for by clients and, in some instances, by third-party donors.

- Universities and other academic institutions, in the North and South opening in-service training programmes in settlements management and development.

- An increase in the number of training and local development-support institutions with an NGO base, linked with national associations of municipalities, or associated with political parties.

- The creation of a large number of private commercial training and consultancy enterprises.

National networks of settlement management capacity-building institutions already function in some countries (for instance Peru, Nicaragua, Poland and Zambia) and are in a process of development in others (for instance Lithuania and Mozambique).

International responses

The support for training in settlements management and development by international bilateral and multilateral agencies falls into three broad categories:

—The direct training or internships, in the donor country
—Direct individual training in the 'recipient' countries and regions
—The strengthening of national and local capacity-building institutions: building 'capacity to build capacity'.

Although there is a variety of programmes and activities in all 3 categories, there is a clear trend away from the donor-country based training, to training in the regions and countries concerned, and ultimately towards the strengthening of national capacity to respond to that country's need for personnel trained in settlements management. Direct training in donor countries will probably remain an important factor within aid programmes as it allows foreign assistance funds to remain largely in the donor country and it supports the donor country's own academic institutions. However, the programmes themselves are increasingly focusing on mid-career training of university professors and trainers, and on the short-term high-level 'executive training'. Internships in donor countries for professionals and officers from recipient countries should also be included in this category. This has been widely used, especially since the beginning of 1990, for Transition Countries of Central and Eastern Europe, although it has received some criticism in terms of its low impact and low multiplier effect.

The support for direct training in 'recipient' countries and regions sponsored and organized by the external agencies is not declining, although it is receiving a lower proportion of total international assistance. Furthermore, some new training of this kind is a relocation, to the South, of the former donor-country based training.

There are many examples of the rapidly growing category of strengthening national 'capacity to build capacity'. These fall into various types of activities and programmes such as:

- Regional workshops, seminars and policy consultations on the development of policies and strategies for training in settlements management and development.

- Assistance in creating regional, collaborative networks of national and local capacity-building institutions for exchange of experiences, mutual assistance and joint programmes and activities.

- Assistance in training needs assessments, and assessments (including self-assessment) of capabilities and support requirements of training institutions.

- Assistance in strategic planning and business planning by capacity-building institutions.

- Regional, or inter-regional, workshops and seminars on innovative approaches to current key policy issues.

- Development and testing, jointly with the national and local capacity-building institutions of innovative generic training materials, handbooks, instruments and management tools in key areas of settlements management and development.

- Specific assistance in gender-aware approaches

in settlement planning, management and development.

- Programmes focusing on capacity-building for local development NGOs—see Box 9.26 for one example of this.

- Training of trainers and advisors in subjects of particularly high need—for instance in the use of participatory tools and methods that are described in a later section—often in conjunction with development of training manuals and management tools.

- 'On-the-job' assistance in curricula development, application of new training methods, and use of new learning tools and instruments.

- Assistance with capital investments, equipment, and library support.

- Assistance through evaluation of activities, programmes and their impact, as input into strategic planning of the national and local capacity-building institutions. This is still a relatively new direction, although support for it is growing. Strengthening its effectiveness, coverage and resulting impact is a major challenge.

Box 9.25 gives an example of an international capacity-building project for municipal development.

BOX 9.25
Support for municipal development: the SACDEL Project

The regional Support System for Training for Local Municipal Development in Latin America (SACDEL) is a capacity-building project executed by the CELCADEL training centre in Quito, Ecuador. Its main objective is to bolster the decentralization processes taking place in Latin America through training activities and assistance to public and private national training institutions charged with the development of local government. Most of its work is policy seminars, the training of trainers in key areas of municipal administration, technical assistance to national training institutes, support for municipal associations and development and dissemination of innovative training materials, manuals and on-the-job handbooks. The pilot phase of the project, completed in 1993, concentrated on Colombia, Costa Rica, Ecuador and Peru. The current stage initiated in 1994 is gradually increasing its coverage with three sub-regional programme groups: Central America, Andean Region and Southern Cone. An important characteristic of this project is a high level of inputs, substantive and financial coming from the countries themselves. It also receives support from the Economic Development Institute of the World Bank, UNCHS (Habitat), the Canadian Federation of Municipalities, the Canadian International Development Agency and the International Union of Local Authorities (IULA), Swedish International Development Co-operation Agency and other donors.

Lessons from the new approaches

To address the scale and complex nature of housing and settlement problems described in earlier chapters, national and local capacity-building institutions will need to be strengthened in most countries. The needed capacity-building must also respond to national and local context and culture and to changing problems and opportunities. Among the greatest challenges is to ensure that training for settlement management is in the national languages and that it trains people to be gender sensitive and understand how to involve all the key actors, (governmental, NGO, community and private enterprise). This can be done only by national and local capacity-building institutions.

These institutions must also go beyond traditional concepts of class-room training to include all aspects of human resource development and institutional capacity-building. They should also support the development of national policy and help build societal awareness. But these institutions' effectiveness will also depend on supportive policies from national governments and on the extent to which the legal, institutional and regulatory environment supports the actions of the professionals they train.

This 'building capacity to build capacity' is still new, with its coverage still limited—and the ways and means of achieving it still not fully known. The experience to date should be used to improve practice and to expand coverage to all regions. It should also emphasize the enabling approaches and close partnerships between operational settlements management institutions and capacity-building organizations, and between those organizations themselves at national and regional levels.

There is also a need to scale up new approaches. For instance, the process of training trainers and advisors, and the development and dissemination of manuals and handbooks in national languages (the only way to reach all critical actors) needs to be greatly expanded. So too does the scale of training activities, especially for elected local government officials—the elected municipal or city councillors. This is especially relevant, given the introduction or return to elected local councils in so many countries and the fact that their responsibilities for settlements management have often been increased.

Another area meriting increased attention in the future is management training for staff from NGOs, community based organizations and other voluntary organizations involved in urban development. The FICONG Programme in Latin America, is a useful model—see Box 9.26. Such training should not only help these organizations to improve their own effectiveness but should also cover policy consultations, problem-solving workshops and other activities aimed at improving their collaboration with local and central governments, including the creation of a legal and regulatory framework that is supportive of their activities.

BOX 9.26
Training NGOs: the FICONG Programme

In Latin America, there is a long tradition of specialist NGOs working with the inhabitants of low-income settlements (often illegal or informal settlements) in programmes to improve housing conditions or provide basic services. The role of NGOs has also been much increased in many countries as economic reform during the 1980s has often been accompanied by a withdrawal of the state from direct provision of services. Many of the programmes of international agencies also support NGOs or channel funding to low-income groups through NGOs—for instance through Social Funds as outlined in Chapter 11. However, greater participation for NGOs in projects to help improve the living conditions and incomes of the poor and to improve environmental health has to be matched by a greater effectiveness among NGOs and a growth in the scale of their programmes. With these goals in mind, in September 1991, IIED-America Latina in Buenos Aires launched a new programme for the institutional strengthening and training of non-governmental organizations (FICONG). The programme is implemented through a large network of NGOs and other settlements institutions and it aims to enhance the capacity of NGOs and public agencies in responding to the needs of poorer groups and to increase their effectiveness and the scale of their activities. FICONG also encourages NGOs and State organizations to develop more effective partnerships with residents' associations in low-income communities. Training courses, seminars and workshops are undertaken throughout Latin America in conjunction with a large network of affiliated institutions and organizations. Among the main supporters of the FICONG Programme are the Economic Development Institute of the World Bank and the bilateral aid programmes of Sweden, the Netherlands and Japan.

Source: IIED-América Latina, 'About FICONG', *Pobreza Urbana y Desarrollo*, Special issue on 'The role of NGOs in policies and projects for development and against poverty in Latin America and the Caribbean', Oct. 1994.

One final area that needs development which remains very weak methodologically, is the area of impact evaluations of training and of other capacity-building activities. Techniques for evaluating training programmes themselves are better developed and more frequently and systematically practised. A lack of adequate and reliable impact evaluation limits the quality of capacity-building in general, not only in settlements management and development. The development and testing of this strategic tool for managing of human resource development investments is an important and urgent task.

9.8 International Assistance to Urban Management

Interest among development assistance agencies in urban management has been growing in recent years. There was considerable interest in the late 1950s and early 1960s in the strengthening of local government but at this time, there were many fewer development assistance agencies and this was not an interest that was sustained through the 1960s and 1970s. In most African and many Asian nations, newly independent governments were too intent on consolidating the position of national institutions. In virtually all nations, national economic planning to maximize economic growth also implied neglect of local governments' development role.[58] The development functions of local government (including urban government) was not seen as a priority.

The 1970s brought a new interest among some governments and many aid agencies in agriculture and rural development and many development-assistance agencies avoided urban investments. Although virtually all nations in the South urbanized rapidly during the last four decades, in most, very little attention was given either by governments or by development assistance agencies to ensuring that urban governments had the power, skills and resources to manage this rapid growth and to provide rapidly expanding populations and economic activities with the infrastructure and services they needed. The exception was the Inter-American Development Bank that made many investments in urban shelter, water and sanitation in Latin America during the 1960s although at this time, little attention was given to urban management. One result of this lack of interest among governments and international agencies was that the institutions that were meant to manage urban development remained (in the words of a survey in the early 1980s) 'fragmented, confused about their functions and all too often either invisible or largely ceremonial'.[59]

It also became clear that the funds available for urban development from donor agencies prepared to support urban development were small in scale, in relation to need. For instance, despite the fact that the World Bank's loan commitments to urban shelter, infrastructure and service projects in Latin America represent much the largest commitments from any agency to the region, it was estimated that total capital investments by sub-national governments in the region were more than 45 times the volume of Bank loans[60]—and despite this, urban investments in the region still failed to keep up with urban growth. The fact that international funding was limited in relation to needs encouraged some of the largest agencies to move away from support for urban projects to support for developing governments' institutional capacity to invest in and to manage urban development. One example of this will be described in more detail in Chapter 12—the move by the World Bank and the US AID Housing Guaranty Program from support to shelter projects to support to national housing finance institutions. Instead of supporting a single shelter project, the aim is to develop financial institutions within the nation which can support a large multiplication of projects or individual house loans. Similarly, there was also a move within the World Bank away from funding integrated urban development projects to funding national institutions concerned with funding municipal projects.

This move away from projects to building institutional capacity can also be seen in the greater emphasis given by some agencies to urban management—i.e. on building the institutional capacity of city authorities to address their own needs with regard to urban development and to enhancing urban government's capacity to install and maintain infrastructure and services. One reason for this move may stem from a recognition of the unsustainability of many of their previous project interventions; many projects in the 1980s were to rehabilitate urban infrastructure or services built only a few years previously in development-assistance funded projects, or had components within larger projects to do so.[61] Another reason is that this will increase the capacity of recipient governments to manage and invest in infrastructure and services. This new interest in urban management has been most evident in the project commitments of the World Bank Group (although many agencies have recognized the importance of this subject) and, in technical assistance, in the joint UNDP-World Bank-UNCHS (Habitat) program to strengthen urban management (see Box 9.27).

The first sign of an increasing interest in urban management was for it to become common for 'institution building' or 'strengthening institutional capacity' to be included as a component in many projects so that the implementation of a water supply project or an upgrading project often includes funds and technical assistance to strengthen the national or local agencies involved. Many 'integrated urban development' projects included components for training or strengthening institutional capacity. However, this developed into projects that were specifically about building institutional capacity, rather than having this as one component.

The World Bank was the first to provide significant amounts of funding to this with various funding commitments to improve urban management in the first half of the 1980s. Over 40 project

BOX 9.27
The Urban Management Programme

The Urban Management Programme (UMP) is a global technical co-operation programme in which agencies of the United Nations and other external support agencies work together to strengthen the capacity of cities and towns to manage economic growth, social development, and the alleviation of poverty. Initiated in 1986 by the United Nations Development Programme (UNDP), the United Nations Centre for Human Settlements (Habitat) and the World Bank, this Programme assists cities in implementing innovative programmes in five areas: urban land management; infrastructure management; municipal finance and administration; urban environmental management; and urban poverty alleviation.

Through its regional offices in Africa, the Arab States, Asia and the Pacific, and Latin America and the Caribbean, the Urban Management Programme seeks to strengthen urban management by harnessing the skills and strategies of regional networks of experts, communities, and organizations in the private sector. The goal of the Programme is to strengthen this local and regional expertise.

Regional co-ordinators and their networks address the five programme areas in two ways:

- *City and Country Consultations*, which brings together national and local authorities, the private sector, community representatives, and other actors to discuss specific problems and propose reasoned solutions. Consultations are held at the request of a country or city, and often provide a forum for discussion on a cross-section of issues. These consultations generally result in a concrete action plan for policy and programme change. By 1995, 61 such consultations had been held.

- *Technical Co-operation*, in which the Programme uses its regional networks of expertise to follow-up on the country and city consultations by providing technical advice and co-operation to implement action plans and to mobilize the resources needed for their implementation.

Nucleus teams at UNCHS (Habitat) in Nairobi and at the World Bank in Washington DC support the regional programmes and networks by synthesizing lessons learned, conducting state-of-the-art research, and supporting dissemination of programme materials. The Urban Management Programme has many publications covering the description and analysis of urban problems and their causes and reviewing new approaches and tools that can be used in resolving them.

Source: Urban Management Programme, *Annual Report 1994*, a partnership of the United Nations Development Programme, the United Nations Centre for Human Settlements (Habitat) and the World Bank, 1995; and internal Urban Management Programme documents.

commitments were made between 1980 and 1993 with a total value of $US2 billion to build the institutional and financial capacity of urban governments or to fund institutions which support urban development. Well over half this commitment was made in the years 1989–93.[62]

Most of the World Bank loans are to strengthen

institutional capacity for urban investments, urban development planning and urban management. These include loans for strengthening specific city governments (for instance Amman in Jordan, Pusan in South Korea and Santo Domingo in the Dominican Republic) and loans which provide assistance to national-level institutions to support local governments (as in loans to Mexico, Sri Lanka and Guinea). Several loans are specifically to strengthen the capacity of municipal governments (as in loans to Nepal and Brazil). Many of these loans include a training component. Several loans are for national institutions responsible for providing funding to local governments—as in loans to support the work of the Cities and Villages Development Bank in Jordan, the Autonomous Municipal Bank in Honduras and the Fonds d'Equipement Communal in Morocco and in a loan to the Philippines to help establish a revolving municipal development fund. Other loans to Zimbabwe and Brazil have provided credit direct to certain urban authorities. Box 9.28 below gives some examples of these kinds of projects, including those receiving support from other agencies although to date, the World Bank is the only institution which has a major programme in this area.

The Inter-American Development Bank has also given several loans totalling $244 million between 1990 and 1993 to improve urban management; most combine providing a pool of funding that municipal governments can draw on to make investments in infrastructure and services with support for institutional reforms. In recent years, the US AID's Housing Guaranty Program has also authorized loans to strengthen the institutional capacity within nations to invest in urban infrastructure and services—for instance the municipal finance programme authorized in 1988 for Indonesia described in Box 9.28 and the loan to Jamaica authorized in 1988 to support their national shelter strategy by providing capital and technical assistance to public and private utilities which provide water and electricity.

One final example of an international initiative designed to improve planning and management within urban areas is the 'Healthy Cities programme'. This aims to get all the key actors within a city (government, business, community organizations, professional groups, NGOs) to agree on what they can do jointly to improve the health and quality of the living environment in their city.[63] Although these groups have different and often contradictory priorities, there is often a common, agreed agenda in regard to improving the quality of the city environment and working together to address social and environmental problems. Municipal Health Plans are also being prepared to promote collaboration between sectors, generate awareness of health and environmental problems

---

BOX 9.28
Examples of development assistance to build the capacity of municipal governments

Indonesia: $100 million five year municipal finance programme initiated in 1988 by the US AID Housing Guaranty Program. This will help strengthen the local government finance system and help develop links between this system and private sector capital markets. Thus, it will also increase the participation of the private sector in providing and funding urban infrastructure and services and improve the role of central government through a system of loans and grants which encourage the mobilization of local resources.

Brazil: $100 million non-concessional loan commitment from the World Bank in 1989 to provide technical assistance, training and equipment to municipalities and to urban sector state institutions in Parana state to strengthen their financial management and overall administrative capacities. In addition, the loan will help fund municipal government investments in urban infrastructure throughout the state and a pilot project for low-income self-help housing construction.

Sources: US AID Office of Housing and Urban Programs, *Annual Report; Fiscal Year 1988*, Washington DC, 29; World Bank, *Annual Report 1989*, Washington DC, 156.

---

and mobilize resources to deal with the problems.

Initially, most of the 'healthy city' initiatives took place in Europe, North America, Australasia and Japan. The movement started in Europe to create action oriented approaches to Health in Cities; this has been supported by the Healthy Cities Project of the World Health Organization's European Office since 1986. In recent years, all WHO regional offices have been helping comparable developments within their region.

- In the Eastern Mediterranean region, many countries are developing national networks of Healthy Cities. For instance, in Iran, a Healthy Cities office has been set up in Teheran and projects have begun to upgrade a number of low-income areas in the city. In Pakistan, a national network of Healthy Cities has been established and projects are planned in 12 cities. Comparable plans are underway in Saudi Arabia, Egypt, Yemen, Tunisia and Morocco.

- In Africa, Accra was one of the first to develop a Healthy Cities project that reviewed health problems in the city and developed plans to address them. A network of healthy cities has also been established in Francophone Africa that includes Garoua (Cameroon), N'Djamena (Chad), Abidjan and Toumodi (Côte d'Ivoire), Libreville (Gabon), Niamey and Dosso (Niger) and Dakar, Rufisque and St Louis (Senegal). Projects are also underway in Ibadan (Nigeria) and Dar es Salaam (Tanzania).

- In Asia, a network of cities committed to the

Healthy Cities Programme has developed—including Bangkok (Thailand), Kuching and Johor Bahru (Malaysia), Bangalore (India), Chittagong and Cox's Bazaar (Bangladesh) and Surabaya (Indonesia). In Latin America, Healthy City initiatives are underway in Rio de Janeiro and Sao Paulo and in various cities in Bolivia and Colombia.

Notes and References

1. Sections 9.1 and 9.2 draw on Clark, Giles, *Reappraising the Urban Planning Process as an Instrument for Sustainable Urban Development and Management*, UNCHS (Habitat), Nairobi, 1994.

2. WCED (World Commission on Environment and Development), *Our Common Future*, Oxford University Press, 1987.

3. Paulsson, Bengt, *Urban Applications of Satellite Remote Sensing and GIS Analysis*, Urban Management Programme, UNCHS/UNDP/World Bank, Washington DC, 1992.

4. Dowall, David E., *The Land Market Assessment: a New Tool for Urban Management*, Urban Management Programme, UNCHS/UNDP/World Bank, Washington DC, 1991.

5. Peterson, George E., G. Thomas Kingsley and Jeffrey P. Telgarsky, *Multisectoral Investment Planning*, UNCHS (Habitat), Nairobi, 1990.

6. *Ibid.*

7. Notable among these meetings and conferences are the 1990 Global Consultation on Safe Water and Sanitation in New Delhi; the 1991 UNDP Capacity Building Symposium in Delft; the 1991 Water Supply and Sanitation Collaborative Council (WSSCC) Global Forum in Oslo; the 1992 International Conference on Water and Environment in Dublin; the 1992 UN Conference on Environment and Development in Rio de Janeiro; the 1993 WSSCC Global Forum in Rabat; and the 1994 Ministerial conference on Drinking Water and Environmental Sanitation in Noordwijk.

8. Arif Hasan, 'A low cost sewer system by low-income Pakistanis', in Bertha Turner (eds.), *Building Community: a Third World Case Book*, Habitat International Coalition, 1989; Hasan, Arif 'Community organizations and non-government organizations in the urban field in Pakistan', *Environment and Urbanization*, vol. 2, no. 1, April 1990, 74–86; and Khan, Akhter Hameed, *Orangi Pilot Project Programmes*, Orangi Pilot Project, Karachi, 1991.

9. This is an edited version of the first section of Newman, Peter, *Transport and Cities: Resolving the dilemma of Automobile Dependence*, background paper for the Global Report on Human Settlements, 1995.

10. Lovins, Amory B. and L. Hunter Lovins, 'Least-cost climatic stabilization', *Annual Review of Energy and Environment*, vol. 16, 1991, 433–531.

11. Newman, Peter, Jeff Kenworthy and Peter Vintila, 'Can we overcome automobile dependence? Physical planning in an age of urban cynicism', *Cities*, vol. 12, no. 1, Feb. 1995, 53–65; Laquian, A. A., *Planning and Development of Metropolitan Regions*, Proceedings of Conference, Bangkok, June/July, Asian Urban Research Network, Centre for Human Settlements, School of Community & Regional Planning, UBC, Canada, 1993; Mitlin, Diana and David Satterthwaite, *Cities and Sustainable Development*, Background paper for Global Forum '94, Manchester City Council, Manchester, 1994.

12. Hope, C. and S. Owens, *Moving Forward: Overcoming the Obstacles to a Sustainable Transport Policy*, Cambridge University, White Horse Press, Cambridge, 1994; Calthorpe P., *The Next American Metropolis: Ecology and Urban Form*, Princeton, 1993.

13. Kreimer A., T. Lobo, B. Menezes, M. Munasinghe and R. Parker, *Towards a Sustainable Urban Environment: The Rio de Janeiro Study*, World Bank Discussion Papers 195, Washington DC, 1993; Serageldin, I. and R. Barrett, *Environmentally Sustainable Urban Transport: Defining a Global Policy*, World Bank, Washington DC, 1993.

14. Wang, L. H. and A. G. O. Yeh (eds.), *Keep a City Moving: Urban Transportation Management in Hong Kong*, Asian Productivity Organization, Tokyo, 1993.

15. Newman, Peter, 'Cities and development—an emerging Asian model', *Development Bulletin*, vol. 27, 1993, 20–2.

16. Kenworthy, Jeff, Paul Barter, Peter Newman and Chamlong Poboon, 'Resisting automobile dependence in booming economies; a case study of Singapore, Tokyo and Hong Kong within a global sample of cities', Paper presented at the Asian Studies Association of Australia Biennial Conference 1994, Murdoch University, Perth, 1994.

17. Urban Redevelopment Authority, *Living the Next Lap: Towards a Tropical City of Excellence*, Singapore, 1991, quoted in Kenworthy and others 1994, *op. cit.*

18. Rabinovitch, Jonas, 'Curitiba: towards sustainable urban development', *Environment and Urbanization*, vol. 4, no. 2, Oct. 1992.

19. Replogle, M., *Non-Motorised Vehicles in Asian Cities*, World Bank Technical Paper no. 162, World Bank, Washington DC, 1992; and Replogle, M., *Bicycles and Cycle Rickshaws in Asian Cities: Issues and Strategies*, in *Transp. Res. Rec.* no. 1372 on non-motorized transportation.

20. Silas, Johan, *Surabaya—the Fast Growing City of Indonesia—the Housing Experience*, Municipal Government of Surabaya, 1989.

21. Gehl J., 'The challenge of making a human quality in the city', in *Perth Beyond 2000: A Challenge for a City*, Proceedings of the City Challenge Conference, Perth, Sept. 1992.

22. Gehl 1992, *op. cit.*

23. Pucher, S. and J. Clorer, 'Taming the automobile in Germany', *Transportation Quarterly*, vol. 46, no. 3, 1992, 383–95.

24. Pucher and Clorer 1992, *op. cit.*

25. *Ibid.*

26. *Ibid.*

27. Jacobs, Jane, *The Death and Life of Great American Cities*, Pelican, London, 1965.

28. Nowlan, D. M. and G. Stewart, 'The effect of downtown population growth on commuting trips: some recent Toronto experience', *Journal of the American Planning Association*, vol. 57, no. 2, 1992, 165–82.

29. Arrington, M. 'Portland: transportation and land use—a shared vision', *Passenger Transport*, vol. 2, no. 3, 1993, 4–14.

30. Arrington 1993, *op. cit.*

31. Hass-Klau, C., *An Illustrated Guide to Traffic Calming: the Future Way of Managing Traffic*, Friends of the Earth, London, 1990.

32. Hass-Klau, C. (ed.), New Ways of Managing Traffic, Special issue of *Built Environment*, vol. 12, no. 1/2, 1986.

33. Newman, Peter 1993, *op. cit.*

34. Newman, P. W. G. and T. L. F. Hogan, 'A review of urban density models: towards a resolution of the conflict between populace and planner', *Human Ecology*, vol. 9, no. 3, 1981, 269–303.

35. UNCHS (Habitat), *Urban Public Transport in Developing Countries*, Nairobi, 1994.

36. Chambers, Robert, Arnold Pacey and Lori Ann Thrupp (eds.), *Farmer First: Farmer Innovation and Agricultural Research*, Intermediate Technology Publications, London, 1989; Turner, Bertha (ed.), *Building Community*, Building Community Books/Habitat International Coalition, London, 1988.

37. Cornwall, Andrea, Irene Guilt and Alice Welbourne, 'Acknowledging process: challenges for agricultural research and extension methodology', Sustainable Agricultural Programme Research Series, vol. 1, no. 1, IIED, 1993, 21–47.

38. Scrimshaw, Nevin S. and Gary R. Gleason (eds.), *RAP: Rapid Assessment*

Procedures, Qualitative Methodologies for Planning and Evaluation of Health Related Programmes, International Nutrition Foundation for Development Countries, 1992.

39. Chambers, Robert, 'The origins and practice of Participatory Rural Appraisal', in *World Development*, vol. 22, no. 7, 1994, 53–969; Chambers, Robert, 'Participatory Rural Appraisal (PRA): analysis of experience' in *World Development*, vol. 22, no. 9, 1994, 1253–68; Chambers, Robert, 'Participatory Rural Appraisal (PRA): challenges, potentials and paradigm', in *World Development*, vol. 22, no. 10, 1994, 1437–54.

40. Scrimshaw, Susan C. M., 'Adaptation of anthropological methodologies to rapid assessment of nutrition and primary health care', and other papers in Scrimshaw and Gleason 1992, *op. cit.*

41. See: Francis, Sheelu, 'PALM in Slum Improvement Projects: a training experience from India'; Norton, Andy, 'Observations on urban applications of PRA methods from Ghana and Zambia: participatory poverty assessments'; and Leach, Martin, 'Targeting aid to the poorest in urban Ethiopia—is it possible? Rapid urban appraisal', in *RRA Notes* 21, *Special Issue on Participatory Tools and Techniques for Urban Areas*, International Institute for Environment and Development, London, 1994.

42. *RRA Notes* 21, 1994, *op. cit. Participatory Rural Appraisal: Abstracts of Sources—An Annotated Bibliography*, Institute of Development Studies, University of Sussex, 1994.

43. Lankatilleke, L., *Integrating Urban Livelihoods with Environmental Concerns in the Million Houses Programme Settlements: the Case of Colombo*, Sri Lanka, 1989.

44. Mitlin, Diana and John Thompson, 'Addressing the gaps or dispelling the myths? Participatory approaches in low-income urban communities', in *RRA Notes* 21, 1994, *op. cit.*

45. Lankatilleke, Lalith, 'Build Together: National Housing Programme of

Namibia', paper presented at a workshop on Participatory Tools and Methods in Urban Areas, IIED, London, 1995.

46. Arrossi, Silvina, Felix Bombarolo, Luis Coscio, Jorge E. Hardoy, Diana Mitlin and David Satterthwaite, *Funding Community Initiatives*, Earthscan Publications, London, 1994; Turner, Bertha (ed.), *Building Community*, Building Community Books, London, 1988; and 'Funding Community Level Initiatives: the role of NGOs and other intermediate institutions in funding and supporting low-income households to improve shelter, infrastructure and services', *Environment and Urbanization*, vol. 5, no. 1, 1993.

47. Bolnick, Joel and Sheela Patel, *Regaining Knowledge: An Appeal to Abandon Illusions*, People's Dialogue and SPARC, Cape Town and Bomba, 1994.

48. Bolnick, Joel, 'The People's Dialogue on Land and Shelter: community-driven networking in South Africa's informal settlements', *Environment and Urbanization*, vol. 5, no. 1, 1993; SPARC, NGO profile, *Environment and Urbanization*, vol. 2, no. 1; and D'Cruz, Celine and Sheela Patel, 'The *Mahila Milan* crisis credit scheme: from a seed to a tree', *Environment and Urbanization*, vol. 5, no. 1, 1993.

49. Rensen, Rene and Jan Johnson, 'Linking government agents and local users: PUA for artisanal fishing ports', in *RRA Notes* 21, 1994, *op. cit.*

50. Norton, Andy, 'Observations on urban applications of PRA methods from Ghana and Zambia: participatory poverty assessments' in *RRA Notes* 21, 1994, *op. cit.*

51. Mosse, D, 'Authority, gender and knowledge: theoretical reflections on the practice of Participatory Rural Appraisal', *Development and Change*, vol. 25, no. 3, 1994, 497–526 (earlier draft as ODA Agricultural Administration (Research and Extension) Network Paper no. 44).

52. Mosse 1994, *op. cit.*

53. In addition to *RRA Notes* 21, 1994 (*op.*

cit.) and other reviews mentioned in earlier footnotes, the World Bank, Rooftops Canada and the Asian Coalition for Housing Rights have all been considering the use of such approaches.

54. This section draws on a paper prepared by Thomasz Sudra.

55. Turner, John F. C., *Global Change, Development Concepts and Implications for Housing: a Discussion Paper with reference to learning in a time of paradigm change*, Paper prepared for UNCHS (Habitat), 1994.

56. Capra, Fritjof and David Stendl-Rast with Thomas Matus, *Belonging to the Universe: New Thinking about God and Nature*, Penguin Books, Harmondsworth, 1992.

57. *Ibid.*

58. McAuslan, Patrick, *Land in the City: The Role of Law in Facilitating Access to Land by the Urban Poor*, Mimeo, 1994.

59. Cochrane, Glynn, *Policies for Strengthening Local Government in Developing Countries*, World Bank Staff Working Paper no. 582, Washington DC, 1983, 5.

60. Guarda, Gian Carlo, 'A new direction in World Bank urban lending to Latin American countries', *Review of Urban and Regional Development Studies*, vol. 2, no. 2, July 1990, 116–24.

61. The basis for this analysis was the Aid Project Database of the International Institute for Environment and Development which has details of human settlements projects going back to 1970. This allowed a comparison of urban infrastructure and services projects by country between projects that received support during the 1970s and the first half of the 1980s and projects that received support during the second half of the 1980s and the early 1990s.

62. *Ibid.*

63. WHO, *Our Planet, Our Health*, Report of the Commission on Health and Environment, Geneva, 1992 with updated information from Greg Goldstein from WHO.

10.1 From Housing Supply to Enablement

A review of what governments have done to improve housing conditions since Habitat I, the first United Nations Conference on Human Settlements in 1976 came to three main conclusions.[1] The first is that there is no evidence that housing conditions for the lower income groups in cities in the South have improved since Habitat I in terms of affordability, tenure, standards and access to services. The absolute number of urban residents living in inadequate shelter has certainly grown, although the information about housing conditions is too limited to know whether the overall proportion has also grown. The second is that housing conditions are not deteriorating in all nations—and in many they have improved considerably. Trends vary greatly from city to city and nation to nation—and within nations and cities, according to income group, location and other characteristics. The third is that in many cities in both the North and the South, inequality in incomes and in housing conditions has increased, and with it the attendant dangers of social and political conflict.

The last 10–15 years brought major changes to the ways that most governments sought to tackle housing problems. These were influenced by many factors but among the most important are changes in economic conditions (and in government responses to them), changes in the concept of what governments should do (and should not do) to improve housing conditions, and, in many countries in the South, democratic pressures. There were also contradictions that arose that have yet to be resolved—for instance, a diminution in the role of the state in housing but also growing pressure for government action from those with inadequate housing. And as will be described in more detail later in this chapter, there is the growing use of national and international pressures by citizen groups and NGOs to demand that governments recognize people's right to adequate housing. There is also a growing movement to end discrimination against women in access to housing and basic services.

In the South, the economic stagnation and debt crisis that faced many nations during the 1980s that had previously achieved economic growth brought cuts in public expenditure, including that on housing programmes. In addition, the falling incomes experienced by many people also meant less capacity to pay for housing. For the many nations undergoing structural adjustment, further cuts in public expenditures were also required which often meant cuts in investments on housing-related infrastructure and services. Macro-economic policy can have powerful effects on the performance of the housing sector, through such instruments as directed credit, trade policy, interest rates, fiscal and monetary policy, state intervention in housing (including ownership and control of production) and laws governing property rights.[2] Over the past 10–15 years, the housing sector has been particularly vulnerable in countries undergoing structural adjustment as policies designed to address broad economic problems have been formulated with little regard for their impacts on housing investments.[3]

At the same time, there were changes in the concept of what governments should do to improve housing conditions. There are three distinct concepts of the role of government in housing programmes: state provision; the 'enabling' approach; and 'leave provision to the market'. Although no government's position falls entirely within one of these approaches—and within either state provision or the enabling approach, there is a great variety in what government does and how it does it—the scale and nature of any government intervention in housing will reflect which of these concepts its official position is nearest to.

The enabling approach helped to develop what might be termed a new agenda for shelter as it relied on market forces for many aspects of shelter provision, but within a framework that addressed those areas where private, unregulated markets do not work well. Thus, it used the advantages of private markets for land, building materials, finance and finished housing in terms of cost reductions, rapid response to changing demands and a diverse range of housing available for sale or rent. But it is not only private-sector firms but also third-sector institutions such as NGOs, voluntary agencies and community organizations that are seen as more cost effective producers and providers of housing, housing finance, land development and many forms of housing-related infrastructure and services than government bureaucracies. In addition, governments retain a key role in ensuring that land

and housing finance are available and in ensuring that the provision of water, sanitation, drainage and other infrastructure and services expands to match the expansion of the housing stock—although here too, private firms or voluntary organizations may have central roles in actual provision.

This new approach accepts that the privatization of some services can bring major benefits but that privatization is no longer the standard response for all services. The results achieved in some of the highly privatized social service systems in the North are not encouraging, not least for low-income groups. Within the many very unequal societies of the South, such problems are likely to be exacerbated.[4] The tendency in market economics on short-term optimization at the expense of longer-term investment and planning is of concern as is the lack of attention paid to the influential role of interest groups and other non-economic factors in manipulating the way markets work to the advantage of some and the detriment of others.[5] These and other observations encouraged a re-emphasis on the limits of market mechanisms and reasserted the importance of strong government and social action.

The 'enabling' approach is also associated with political reforms, especially democratization. Popular participation and decentralization now receive more official support than they used to.[6] Civil society is also given a much greater role through NGOs, community based organizations and citizens movements. There is a more explicit and informed attempt to ensure that housing provision better matches the needs and priorities of lower-income groups. This includes removing discrimination against women in housing and basic service provision and ensuring that the different needs of men and women in housing provision and production are understood and addressed.

Housing policies that have moved from 'supply to enablement' during the 1980s have antecedents in many programmes such as the Kampung Improvement Programme in Indonesia that had been initiated in Jakarta and Surabaya in the late 1960s and the Urban Basic Services Programme in India. These broke away from specific projects to focus on developing a more appropriate framework within which people living in informal or illegal housing could create or develop housing more effectively.[7] The new approach gained strength throughout the 1980s, supported by two related, international initiatives. The first, promoted by UNCHS (Habitat), centred on the concept of the 'enabling approach' that was elaborated in the Global Strategy for Shelter. Here, the role of government was redefined to focus on managing the legal, regulatory and economic framework so

that people, NGOs and private-sector actors were more able to produce housing and related services, more effectively. Scarce government resources could then be directed to areas such as capital-intensive infrastructure which the poor could not fund, and which commercial interests would not finance themselves. Given added impetus by the United Nations 'International Year of Shelter for the Homeless' in 1987, and formalized by UNCHS (Habitat) in the 'Global Shelter Strategy to the Year 2000' in 1988, the principles set out in the enabling approach marked a considerable break with the past.

The second international support for a new approach to shelter policy in the 1980s and early 1990s came from the World Bank. Although the World Bank's approach shared and supported many of the characteristics of the 'enabling approach', during the second half of the 1980s, its shelter policy developed more of a focus on economic issues, especially the role of markets, and paid less attention to social and political matters. As the title of the most recent World Bank policy statement makes clear, the focus is on 'enabling housing markets to work' rather than on enabling poor people to gain access to housing and land markets.[8] This is a subtle but important distinction. The World Bank's interest in the enabling approach was already clear in earlier evaluation reports[9] and policy statements,[10] with a move away from investment in housing projects in the mid-1980s, to housing finance in the latter part of the decade, and on to urban management around 1985 (see Chapter 11 for more details). The World Bank also responded to the negative impacts of structural adjustment on many low income groups and on many previously middle- or lower-middle-income households who became impoverished. As these negative impacts became clear by the mid-1980s, the World Bank added social funds or other forms of 'social safety-net' to its portfolio of urban interventions which sought to mitigate economic stress via a range of welfare and compensatory measures.[11] Growing attention was also paid by the World Bank throughout the 1980s to the links between economic development and shelter. As two of its staff commented, 'it is less government's spending in the housing sector than its role in defining regulatory frameworks, pricing policies, and policies affecting the financial sector that comprise the major instruments for influencing the performance of the sector, and, in turn, the way its performance affects the macro-economy.'[12] This approach was formalized in the World Bank's 1991 paper, *Urban Policy and Economic Development: an Agenda for the 1990s*, which had an explicit focus on the need to remove constraints to urban productivity arising from the legal, fiscal and other frameworks, and on the role of the private sector in addressing these concerns.[13] It was further developed in the 1993 Policy Paper *Housing: Enabling Markets to Work*, which advocated the reform of government policies, interventions and regulations to 'enable housing markets to work more efficiently', while simultaneously managing housing and urban development as part of a broader economic strategy.[14] The most important elements in this new agenda included secure property rights, developing private mortgage finance, rationalizing subsidies, promoting cost-recovery in infrastructure development, reducing shelter standards and regulatory complexity, and promoting private-sector activity in all areas.

Thus, different interpretations of 'enablement' mean different kinds and levels of government intervention. 'Housing enablement' can imply very extensive or very limited government intervention. For instance, Sweden's housing policy during the 1980s could certainly be termed enablement as state intervention ensured that cheap land and housing finance were widely available and that most of the housing was actually constructed by private firms or individuals. However, most private-sector construction was as clients of housing co-operatives, communes or 'restricted profit' schemes and virtually all housing construction during the 1980s received government funding and had to meet the conditions laid down by such funding.[15] This is an example of an enabling policy that does not imply no state intervention—but a change as to where the state intervenes and a reliance on market forces where appropriate to bring down costs and ensure a good match between supply and diverse demand.

It is also important to recall the complex political economy of each nation that conditions any new housing initiative and that cautions against international comparisons. Both Sweden's and Sri Lanka's housing policies during the 1980s can be described in terms of housing enablement but the contrasts in the economic and political conditions of the two countries are so extreme that it is difficult to compare them. There are also historic factors that help explain why a new initiative was or was not taken during the 1980s. Many governments in the North and the South may have given a lower priority to public housing, but many public housing programmes or programmes of subsidized housing finance remained in place, because they had long benefited government employees or some other group with sufficient influence within government to ensure that their access to subsidized housing provision or to subsidized housing finance was not halted.

Obviously, the ideological base of governments will strongly influence the nature of state intervention in housing but a government may be strongly market-oriented in most aspects of economic policy, yet still interventionist in regard to housing. This remains the case in many European countries, although the form of government intervention in housing has tended to change and often to diminish. In the South, Singapore is the most obvious example of heavy state intervention within housing within an economic policy that is strongly market-oriented. With one of the world's most successful economic performances over the last few decades because of its expanding role within international production, trade and services, it also has much the largest public housing programme in terms of the proportion of the population living in such units. Over 90 per cent of all housing units built over the last forty years were built by the public sector—although most have been sold to their occupiers so in terms of housing tenure, it does not appear as state housing provision. Singapore has also long had a degree of control over land use with the government also a major landowner that is much closer to social democratic countries in Europe than might be implied by its overall economic policy.

One important influence on the housing policies of many governments over the last 10–15 years has been the introduction of or return to democractic rule. This has brought more readiness on the part of governments to provide legal tenure for many of those living in illegal or informal settlements and less readiness to support large-scale 'slum' and squatter eviction programmes. Most of the large-scale eviction programmes from cities during the 1970s and 1980s and most of the repression of community organization took place in countries that had non-democratic regimes.[16] The wider acceptance by governments of upgrading programmes (described in more detail below) may also be linked to increasing democratic pressures. It is difficult for a democratic government to justify an entirely market-oriented approach to housing, since the rapid expansion in the scale and nature of housing problems often coincides with the decades when priority was given to economic growth and economic growth was seen as the means by which housing problems would solve themselves. And if 'enablement' is taken to mean that those with low incomes, few (if any) monetary assets and little political voice are to be 'enabled' to obtain better quality housing, it implies a transfer of power and resources to them.[17] Such transfers are unlikely, if political structures are unresponsive to citizen and social pressures.

10.2 How Government Policies have Changed since Vancouver

Housing enablement in the North

Not surprisingly, the changes in the political orientation of many governments towards neo-liberalism during the 1980s also brought changes in the way that governments viewed their role within housing (and within social policy in general). This can be seen in Europe with the erosion of the post-war consensus on the role of the welfare state[18] that also brought major changes in housing policies in many countries. The changes were particularly abrupt in the United Kingdom which up to 1980 had one of the highest proportions of its national population in public (municipal) housing. The powers of local governments to build social housing and the resources they could use to do so were much reduced; the production of social (rental) housing fell from 140,000 in 1977 to 31,000 in 1992.[19] Meanwhile, the proportion of the population living in municipal housing was much reduced as large financial incentives were offered to those who lived in such housing to purchase it. Owner-occupiers in general also received large tax incentives and were not taxed for the capital gains they made when housing was sold; in 1990/1, these tax advantages for owner-occupiers cost the government twice as much as the cost of providing housing benefits to low-income renters.[20] However, there was no agreement within the European market and mixed economies as to the best role for governments in housing policy. Indeed, a comparative study of housing policies in eighteen countries concluded that there was increasing divergence during the 1970s and 1980s.[21] Two factors underpinned this divergence: the nature of the building industry and how housing was promoted; and the broad ideological base of the society.[22]

The thrust of housing policies in countries in Europe and North America can be partly explained by their ideological base. Housing policies and the range of housing types and forms of tenure they influence are very different in Europe's social-democratic welfare states such as Sweden and Norway compared to liberal welfare states such as the United States and, increasingly, Britain. In social democratic welfare states, there is extensive state intervention in many areas to promote equality which includes extensive state intervention in housing while using market forces to keep down prices and promote diversity in types of housing and forms of housing tenure. Countries which are characterized as social democracies tend to have governments with a much greater role in land supply and a greater emphasis on social housing and restricted profit private promotion. For instance, in Sweden, during the 1980s, more than half of all housing completions were non-profit social housing (housing co-operatives and municipal housing companies largely run by local communes) with 19 per cent of completions by the restricted private profit sector producing for sale and rent; virtually all housing production was funded by the state housing loan system. In liberal welfare states, the market is favoured over other forms of housing provision with very limited government involvement, generally only in the form of housing provision to a residual population who lack the means to enter 'the market', or some form of welfare payment to help pay for housing. Here, as in other aspects of welfare provision in liberal welfare states (and unlike social democracies) there is a stigma attached to living in public housing.

Most countries in the North fall between these two extremes both in their ideological base and in the form of government intervention in housing. And even in the countries with the most market-driven approaches, there are still innovative public programmes to improve housing conditions for lower-income households.[23] There is also an important third category that can be termed the corporatist welfare state where the state is prepared to displace the market as a provider of welfare but not to the extent of promoting equality (as in social-democratic welfare states), and in principle the state only intervenes when the capacity of the family to address problems is no longer adequate.[24] In these and in many social-democratic welfare states, a considerable proportion of new housing units are produced by households who organize their construction themselves—including a proportion who are also self-builders. For instance, in France, over half of all housing output during the 1980s was undertaken by households promoting their own unit. Most (with 30 per cent of all completions) were built by specialist mass production 'catalogue' builders although 10 per cent of all completions were self-built with roughly 10 per cent through one-off contracting.

Liberal welfare countries tend to have the highest proportion of housing built where land supply is through conventional market means and most units produced by the private sector. Nearly 75 per cent of all units completed in the United Kingdom during the 1980s were in this category. Box 10.1 contrasts housing provision in 'high growth' zones in Sweden, Britain and France as a way of considering the relative performance of housing markets in the three distinct forms of welfare state.

BOX 10.1

Housing quality, cost and diversity: a comparison between prosperous regions in Britain, France and Sweden

One study which compared the quality, diversity and cost of housing produced during the 1980s in a prosperous region in Britain and Sweden and two such regions in France found that the most regulated housing system performed best and the least regulated performed worst. The region in Sweden (where housing production was most regulated) performed best when considering output levels, building costs, land prices and final output prices; the British region (within the least regulated production system) performed the worst. The most regulated (in Sweden) produced the most diversity with those seeking a house or apartment having the option of purchased owner-occupation, self-promoted owner-occupation, co-operative tenant ownership and social renting; the most market driven area—in Britain—had the least diversity. In terms of consumer cost, the region in Britain had the highest costs, especially for poor households. The Swedish region had lower costs and less-marked social differentiation. The regions in France came between these two extremes.

The study was undertaken in high-growth regions in France, Britain and Sweden, each of which experienced above average growth in population. In Sweden, the study concentrated on three communes north of Stockholm[25] and the contiguous Kista parish in Stockholm; the number of jobs in this area

grew by 139 per cent between 1980 and 1987 with a relative emphasis on high-growth sectors and high-status jobs. In Britain, the study area was the county of Berkshire where employment only grew by 6 per cent over the period but it began from a larger base and should be seen within the context of Britain's poor economic performance. In France, two regions were chosen: the urban agglomeration of Toulouse (which is relatively free-standing) and an area on the southern fringe of Paris (which like the British and Swedish examples are close to and strongly influenced by the country's largest city).

In terms of housing output per person, the Swedish region had the highest figure followed by Toulouse, then Berkshire, then the southern Paris region. Output in Berkshire showed the most volatility. The comparison of costs looked at the costs of building, the cost of land and final output costs. In regard to land costs, in Toulouse and the Swedish region, land costs were both relatively low and quite stable, although there was a rise in the Swedish region by 43 per cent in the economic boom of 1987–9. In Berkshire, the UK region, land prices were comparable at the beginning of the decade but they rose by 436 per cent between 1980 and 1988. By 1988, the land-cost element of housing costs had risen to 60 per cent by 1988. In Toulouse, the land-cost element was estimated to have declined from about 40 per cent to just over 30 per cent during the decade while in south Paris, it remained at roughly 40 per cent of final house costs. In the Swedish region, it is unlikely that the land cost element exceeded 10 per cent of a single dwelling costs and 5

per cent of an apartment.

Overall, taking into account output levels, building costs, land prices and final output prices, the Swedish region performs best: output was high, building costs and land prices relatively low and stable and total output costs comparatively low. In Berkshire, the costs were generally highest and certainly most volatile. There was also a much greater diversity in the forms of housing tenure available in the Swedish region, compared to the British region, with the two French regions falling between these two extremes. For a household in Berkshire, there was increasingly only one choice—buying a house from a speculative development or from existing owner-occupied stock. An examination of housing costs for various class groups and household types also found that in general, those in the Swedish region paid a smaller proportion of their incomes on housing—and there was also less inequality between groups in the proportion of income spent on housing. In the Swedish region, there was also no association between household income and housing quality or age; income differentials only became apparent for housing size.

The structure of housing promotion and production in Britain favoured the establishment of short-term goals based around business strategies that focused on speculation in the land and housing markets. In the Swedish region, they concentrated on improving labour productivity and product quality and diversity. However, in Sweden these are problems of emerging power of large oligopolistic firms that tended to subvert the existing system of regulation.

Source: Barlow, James and Simon Duncan, *Success and Failure in Housing Provision: European Cities Compared*, Pergamon, 1994.

Towards housing enablement in the South

In the South, there was a clear retreat from government as major providers of housing during the 1980s. In some countries, this was a trend that had begun prior to the 1980s and was associated with the shift from provision to enablement. Many governments had already made significant changes in their housing policies during the 1970s—for instance in the shift away from public housing programmes and a greater priority given to upgrading programmes.[26] During the 1980s, there was a coincidence of several influences:

- a greater market orientation encouraged by many powerful governments in the North and by many multilateral and bilateral donors that was often enforced through structural adjustment;

- for most nations, economic stagnation or decline that in turn limited the capacity of gov-

ernments to embark on high cost housing interventions;

- democratic pressures from the bottom up and some international donor pressure from the top down that demanded a stronger support for community organizations, NGOs and participation and that explicitly or implicitly supported the expansion of the human rights movement to include consideration of the 'right to housing';

- the growing strength and influence of the movement to reduce the discrimination against women and 'gender-blindness' in housing and basic service provision;

- Increasingly less international funding available for housing projects from the international agencies that had been much the largest supporters of such projects—especially the World Bank and US AID's Housing Guaranty Program (see Chapter 11 for more details); and

- the development of 'the enabling approach' within the Global Shelter Strategy.

Of course, the relative strength of these different influences varied enormously from country to country—and often with considerable change over time. There were also many countries that retained or returned to non-democratic regimes and where few if any of these influences were evident. There are also nations where economic decline and/or civil strife meant little or no attention to housing. In seeking to highlight the most important innovations in housing policy in the South over the last 10–15 years, perhaps five deserve attention. The first is the development of national shelter strategies by many governments that broadly follow the guidelines of the Global Strategy for Shelter. The second is the higher priority given to upgrading programmes and the development of new approaches to upgrading. The third is the increasing attention given to identifying and reducing discrimination against women and 'gender-blindness' in housing and service provision. The fourth is the increasing influence of human rights movements or campaigns within housing. The fifth is the recognition by governments of the importance of rental housing, with some initiatives to support its development. Each of these is described below. There were also many innovative programmes of housing finance developed during the 1980s by governments and by NGOs, but these are described in Chapter 11. Some of these are also mentioned briefly in this chapter because they combine housing finance with support for upgrading and other elements of housing construction or improvement. One example of this is the urban component of the 'Million Houses Programme' in Sri Lanka which is mentioned both in this Chapter and in Chapter 11. A final section draws some conclusions.

National shelter strategies and the global shelter strategy

Relatively few governments had developed national shelter strategies before the elaboration of the Global Shelter Strategy in 1988. The United Nations International Year of Shelter for the Homeless in 1987 had stimulated a good deal of action in preparing draft national strategies: out of 145 countries that had participated in this International Year, 55 established new shelter policies or strategies, 11 started preparations for new strategies, and the rest 'had made at least one significant policy change or new programme'.[27]

The Global Shelter Strategy laid down four requirements for national strategies:[28]

- the definition of clear and measurable objectives;

- gradual reorganization of the shelter sector (including the legal and regulatory framework and shelter production);

- mobilization and distribution of increased financial resources (including housing finance, rationalization of subsidies and cost-recovery); and

- production of shelter and management of land, infrastructure and the construction industry.

Agenda 21 from the Earth Summit (the United Nations Conference on Environment and Development in 1992) added one further requirement to this list, namely that national shelter strategies should include measures to promote 'sustainable energy development and transport systems'.[29]

Over the last few years, a number of studies have reviewed progress in developing national shelter strategies.[30] A good deal of information is therefore available on strategy formulation, especially from Colombia, Nigeria, Thailand, India, Kenya, Zimbabwe, Uganda, Indonesia, the Philippines, Costa Rica, Nicaragua, Jamaica, Mexico and Sri Lanka. In general, a start has been made in developing national shelter strategies in most countries. The output of the strategy-formulation process also varies widely from one country to another; some have concentrated on modifying existing plans from earlier years, while others have focused on particular sectors of shelter development.[31] In most cases, some elements of strategy were already in place prior to 1988 as a result of earlier attempts at policy-formulation.[32] For example, Costa Rica and Zimbabwe have concentrated on changes at central government level; Nicaragua and Uganda have emphasized the development of district and municipal strategies; and Indonesia and the Philippines have focused on the development of links between central and local-level planning and action.[33] Some countries (such as Uganda and Zimbabwe) have kept to their original schedules, with strategies and mechanisms for implementation agreed and adopted by 1992 but most have fallen behind schedule for one reason or another. In Indonesia, the government recognized the need to adopt an 'enabling approach' to shelter in its Five-Year Plan for 1989–94, though it still has no single, explicit strategy document.[34] Kenya signalled its move away from state-dominated shelter policies to the enabling approach with a 'Sessional Paper on Housing' in 1986, followed a year later by a National Shelter Strategy and in 1990 by a new Housing Policy Paper. However, one observer reports that the impact of these changes has been 'disappointing', in part because housing policies have been fragmented and uncoordinated, and because of institutional difficulties in implementing them.[35] Similar problems have been noted in Tanzania.[36]

India's new National Housing Policy (1992) evolved from an earlier policy adopted in 1988, and embodies a clear commitment to the principles enshrined in the Global Shelter Strategy: 'the Government will devise and implement strategies which will enable the various agencies to complement the efforts of one another and to ensure the most efficient utilization of resources'.[37] However, Indian NGOs have yet to be persuaded that the new policy will be implemented effectively; 'although India has continued to describe its policy for housing as an enabling one, it has done little to create mechanisms which assure in concrete terms the enabling principle.'[38] A similar judgement comes from Bolivia, where one observer reports that, though 'bold in its outlook and wide in its application', the National Plan for Housing (1989–93) has not been implemented.[39] Mechanisms for implementation have also been the weakest area of strategy development in the four countries reviewed by UNCHS in 1990 (Barbados, Zimbabwe, Jamaica and Kenya). A common failing is that the functions of, and linkages between implementing agencies are not spelled out in any detail.[40] All four country strategies define an increased role for the private sector in shelter production and qualitative changes in the roles of government agencies, but again this means different things in each case. For example, government maintains a more significant role in Zimbabwe than in the other three countries reviewed. This study, in common with other similar studies, found wide variations in the details of scheduling, the groups and institutions involved in drawing up the strategies, the degree of technical assistance involved, and the precise steps that were taken.

Key factors in differentiating successful strategies from those that remain 'on paper' are high-level and continuous political support, careful research on housing market conditions prior to strategy formulation, and local control. Attempts by international donors to initiate the process should be avoided.[41] There is also evidence that broad-based consultation among public, private and third-sector institutions produces a stronger outcome, whether this is achieved through a committee structure (as in Kenya) or via a series of hearings (as in Indonesia). In Nicaragua, an innovative process of workshops and data-collection at municipal level produced a number of 'diagnoses' of shelter issues that were then discussed at meetings of all the relevant actors, resulting in the production of local action plans during 1990 and 1991.[42] A similar process was undertaken in the Philippines, which focused on developing strategies at the regional level. Uganda was also successful in involving a wider range of staff at both local and district levels in the development of a new National Shelter Strategy

in the early 1990s, the focus being on building from the district level upwards rather than the central level downwards. A similar 'bottom-up' process in Zimbabwe did not work so well, since the state system is more highly centralized than in Uganda.[43]

Taking the four requirements for national shelter strategies laid out in the Global Shelter Strategy to the Year 2000, the following conclusions can be drawn:

(a) clear objectives: national shelter strategies have made good progress in reframing traditional policies in terms of the general objectives of the enabling approach, but progress towards implementing these objectives has been weak. The aims of Colombia's new shelter strategy are to create a national social-housing system that maximizes the use of available resources under efficiency and equity criteria, and that optimizes the construction process. These aims are representative of most shelter strategies in the South in the sense that they follow the broad framework of the Global Shelter Strategy while allowing for local adaptation. However, more detailed, measurable and time-bound goals are comparatively rare. The new strategies are beginning to take effect in some countries—for example in the Philippines, evictions have fallen from an annual level of around 100,000 people between 1986 and 1992, to less than 25,000 in 1993.[44] There is also some evidence of a lack of integration between objectives, as in Indonesia where urban renewal policies may run counter to measures to increase the supply of land.[45] Indicators are beginning to be identified to enable policy-makers to measure progress towards the objectives laid out in national shelter strategies. The UNCHS/World Bank Housing Indicators Programme and the sub-regional seminars held in 1990/1 to develop monitoring guidelines for shelter strategies have developed a wide variety of indicators, though even when aggregated there are probably still too many for easy monitoring.[46]

(b) reorganization of the shelter sector: most national shelter strategies make explicit reference to the roles and responsibilities of public, private and third sectors in the shelter process, and to the role of government in creating and maintaining an 'enabling environment' within which people and private enterprise can build their own housing. 'Mexico has managed to do more with less' by increasing the efficiency and effectiveness of municipal management.[47] The new National Shelter Strategy for the Philippines signifies a clear move to a less interventionist role for government which is already producing some interesting results, such as the 'Joint Venture Programme' and the Community Mortgage

Programme[48] that is described in Chapter 11 on housing finance.

Public–private partnerships of this kind are explicitly recognized in most strategies as a central mechanism to enable different institutions to concentrate on areas of comparative advantage in the shelter process.[49] 'The fundamental policy role for governments is to identify, within acceptable political parameters, where the management of human settlements will be enhanced by decentralizing, devolving or subcontracting any particular component of their current responsibility to any particular level.'[50]

(c) mobilization and distribution of financial resources: reforms in housing finance, infrastructural investment and cost-recovery, property taxation and other fiscal measures receive high priority in all national shelter strategies, though again implementation is often disappointing. Mexico's success in 'doing more with less' cited above can be attributed in part to the increased revenues captured by government from the regularization of land around major cities, reforms in housing finance (with mortgage repayments indexed to adjustments in wages), the creation of specialist intermediaries to promote access to affordable finance among lower-income groups, and the more efficient targeting of subsidies.[51] The expansion of the 'Kampung Improvement Programme' in Indonesia was made possible by increased financing from public and private sources, supplemented by increased local (property and other) taxes.[52] The strategy process in Costa Rica was stimulated in part by the difficulties experienced in the 1980s by municipal authorities, who found they lacked the means to finance housing and infrastructure works originating from central government.[53] Zimbabwe's new National Shelter Strategy is based on the goal of home ownership for all via incentives to building societies and increasing access to loans among the urban poor.[54]

(d) production of shelter and management of land, infrastructure and the construction industry: National shelter strategies formulated after 1988 mark a major break with the past in scaling-down government's role in shelter production and in focusing instead on promoting incentives to private- and third-sector production, within a framework intended to guard against speculation and ensure access among the poor. Most strategies identify a central role for government in infrastructure investment (less so in the provision of services), re-defining housing and building standards, promoting small-scale construction efforts and investment in local building materials, and removing 'imperfections' in the land market. In Zimbabwe, for example, the new strategy makes explicit reference to the need to lower building and planning standards, a significant move since the Zimbabwe Government had previously maintained standards inherited from the colonial era as a reaction in part to the lower standards endured by Africans under colonial rule.[55]

In summary, substantial progress was made during the 1980s and early 1990s in many countries in redefining aims and objectives to coincide with the principles of the enabling approach. In many cases there was also wide consultation with private-sector groups and NGOs and community organizations, although (necessarily) the details of who was involved at what stage vary widely. However, most 'strategies' lack a detailed plan of action, a timescale, provision for ensuring resources are available to implement the actions proposed, and indicators for monitoring and evaluation. They are closer to 'policies' than 'strategies'. This is one reason why implementation has so far been disappointing. The lessons learned from this phase of strategy development confirm the results of an earlier evaluation of the enabling approach, that identified four preconditions for success:

- governments must take unambiguous decisions that provide for autonomy at local level;

- measures to foster local initiative must be accompanied by others to address barriers that stand in the way of these initiatives;

- governments must accept the demands of poor communities as legitimate, and respond to them; and

- professionals involved in human settlements development must be prepared to redefine their roles.[56]

It is also evident that if 'enabling policies and strategies' are to enable low-income groups to buy, rent or build better quality housing, this involves changes that are far beyond the capacity and competence of housing ministries or agencies and such changes are unlikely to happen without more democratic and accountable governments.[57]

Upgrading

Upgrading programmes for inner-city tenement districts and illegal or informal settlements have become so widespread that it is difficult to recall how recently these became a significant part of most government's housing policies. Some have achieved a significant scale (though often with considerable disguised subsidies). Indonesia's 'Kampung Improvement Programme' has been implemented in over 500 urban areas since 1968 and is responsible in part for the fact that dwelling size and residential densities in Indonesian cities are actually improving over time, despite the continued poor performance of the formal construction sector.[58] In India, the Urban Basic Services Programme for the Poor is intended to cover 500 urban centres between 1992 and 1997—and after two years of operation, there is progress in 280 urban centres with community structures evolving and in place and with nearly 30,000 volunteers and over 4,000 neighbourhood groups of women.[59] The upgrading of 'slums and shanties' became a central part of the urban component of Sri Lanka's 'Million Houses Programme' in the mid-1980s.[60] In Pakistan, although the *Katchi Abadis (squatter settlement) Improvement and Regularization Programme* has not managed to meet its targets and faces other problems—as will be described below—it still represents a central part of Pakistan's housing policy. Other successful upgrading programmes (such as Aguablanca in Cali, Colombia, and Ruamjai Samakki in Bangkok, Thailand) demonstrate that the failings of earlier projects are being tackled—costs and subsidies have been reduced significantly, access to the very poor (though still not the poorest) has been promoted, and security of tenure granted.[61]

One of the underpinnings of upgrading programmes has been the greater tolerance by governments for illegal and informal settlements. This, in turn, has often been helped by a return to democratic rule. Those living in illegal settlements have shown themselves to be politically adept at negotiating for legal tenure or basic services in return for votes.[62] Their numbers have also increased so much that they can represent a sizeable portion of a city's voters—and they often include a sizeable part of the city's lower-middle and middle-income groups, although these tend to be in settlements developed on illegal subdivisions rather than on illegally occupied land. A greater official tolerance for illegal or informal settlements is also helped by the number of individuals and businesses who make money out of their development. Chapter 7 noted how an increasing proportion of illegal or informal settlements develop on land that the occupiers have to purchase from landowners, land developers acting on their behalf or land developers who simply subdivide government land. In other instances, landowners are less worried about the illegal occupation of their land, as government authorities prove ready to provide them with compensation. Certain landowners have also profited from land invasions; there are even cases of landowners organizing or encouraging squatters to invade their land because they could receive more money in compensation from the government than the land itself was actually worth, before it was invaded. [63]

Governments could therefore afford to be tolerant, as long as low-income groups did not try to invade prime real estate—either that which was privately owned (so the invasion was in direct conflict with private landowners) or that which was publicly owned and was to be used for some public investment. Low-income groups usually avoid using land sites which were easily visible from the centre of the city or a major road since these might be subject to the threat of eviction because of a government plan to 'beautify' the city.

Perhaps the two most serious difficulties with upgrading programmes are how to sustain the initial impetus and how to expand them to the point where they reach most or all of those in need. The 'upgrading' aims to make up for a lack of past public investment in basic infrastructure and services by a single intervention—for instance, paved roads, drains, water supply and electricity. These should have been installed in the first place and maintained and improved on a continuous basis by the local government or utility company. Upgrading programmes may improve conditions considerably at first but very rarely do they increase the capacity of the local government to maintain the new infrastructure and services and to continue with the upgrading process.[64] Upgrading momentarily makes up for a deficiency in local government's investment and implementation capacity but the basic institutional deficiency is not removed. Even in successful 'slum' upgrading schemes such as Hyderabad and Visakhapatnam in India, it has proved difficult to sustain community interest in maintaining services after the initial period of investment in housing and infrastructure is completed, particularly in 'softer' areas such as health, education and social development.[65] As two Indonesian specialists suggest, reviewing the experience in Indonesia with the Kampung Improvement Programme,[66] fully involving the residents in the upgrading programme can provide a substitute, so that local residents and community organizations take on the responsibility for maintenance. But this is rare in upgrading schemes. It might also be considered somewhat inequitable for poorer communities to have to take on responsibility for maintenance when richer areas not only receive higher quality public services but also have these maintained by local government or other public agencies.[67]

The *Katchi Abadis (squatter settlement) Improvement and Regularization Programme* in Pakistan illustrates the second difficulty—expanding the programme to the point where it reaches most or all of those in need.[68] This programme has been in operation in its present form since 1978. It seeks to regularize 2,320 *katchi abadis* with a population of over 5.5 million and also to provide water, sanitation, electricity, paved roads and social facilities. The beneficiaries are meant to pay for this improvement through land and development charges known collectively as 'lease charges'. However, between 1978 and 1989, only 13.9 percent of *abadis* were in the process of being developed.[69] Among the reasons given for the slow pace of work are lack of funds (although the agencies responsible are able to spend only 50 per cent of what is allocated to them annually), heavy government subsidy in development along with lack of recovery of development charges and lack of community involvement. Under the present programme, 30,000 houses are upgraded annually although to keep up with the increasing backlog, this would have to increase to 100,000 a year. In addition, the planning standards are unnecessarily high and their implementation means the uprooting of up to 35 per cent of the population of a *katchi abadi*. Their resettlement also poses major political, social and financial problems.[70]

The Indonesian *Kampung* Improvement Programme can be taken as an example of a programme that expanded to the point where it reached a high proportion of all low-income households. This was also one of the first large upgrading programmes and remains one of the largest ever implemented. It was started in the late 1960s in Jakarta and Surabaya and later expanded to include a large range of urban centres. It is generally judged to have been a success because at a relatively low cost, millions of households were reached. Infrastructure and services were improved for a high proportion of lower-income households. However, there are signs that in some cities or some districts within cities, upgrading also led to rising land prices, and a marked decrease in cheap rental accommodation.[71] Furthermore, where no provision was made to work with the inhabitants of the *kampungs* in designing and implementing the upgrading (and thus no provision made to ensure maintenance and repair for the new infrastructure and services), considerable problems with maintenance soon arose.[72] Box 10.2 gives an example of how improvements stimulated by an upgrading programme in Surabaya were sustained and how 'a programme' became a continuous process involving government authorities and the inhabitants of the *kampungs*. Although now widely considered as one of the most

---

BOX 10.2
Sustaining improvements in housing and living conditions: the Kampung Improvement Programme in Surabaya, Indonesia

The Kampung Improvement Programme in Surabaya, Indonesia's second largest city, is regarded as one of the most successful government initiatives to improve housing and living conditions in Asia. Unlike many upgrading programmes, the improvements made in water supply, drainage and other aspects have been sustained with households and community organizations making major contributions both to maintenance and to further investments. It was conceived not as a public works programme but as a partnership with community organizations with the kampung inhabitants involved in determining priorities and preferences. The Kampung Improvement Programme sought to avoid taking over what individuals, households or community organizations can do for themselves. The scale of the improvement programme in terms of the number of people reached has helped to avoid the process by which housing and land prices rise in improved kampungs with poorer groups moving out.

In the early 1960s, housing and living conditions in cities were put under further strain as city populations grew rapidly and public and open space were invaded. In the late 1960s, local governments in Surabaya and Jakarta began to evict the people who had settled on land not designated for housing but also to improve conditions in existing kampungs. The first post-war Kampung Improvement Programme in Surabaya, known as the W. R. Supratman KIP, was introduced in 1968. With limited public funding available, the city government of Surabaya only provided basic construction elements for infrastructure in the kampungs, mainly pre-cast concrete slabs and gutters. The inhabitants of the kampungs had to request these and take responsibility for installing them and constructing paths and drains.

From 1976, funding from the World Bank became available to support the upgrading programme in Surabaya. The main objective of the assistance was to increase the scale, scope and coverage of the programme. The financial support was a soft loan of around 65 per cent of the project cost with repayment over a 20-year period. National and provincial government also provided a counterpart fund that represented around one-fifth of the total cost. The kampungs had to provide the land and space needed for the project which meant the removal of front fences and use of house frontage and, on occasion, the removal of houses, with provisions made to rehouse those who lost their house. After the project was completed, many people improved their own front yard and houses and community infrastructure and services also improved—

for instance playgrounds and community halls (that were often used for kindergartens), street lighting, guard houses (to improve security).

In the second stage, after 1974, a fixed sum was made available in the annual city development budget to respond to improvement requests from kampungs. The requests were prepared by kampung development committees with technical assistance from PWD staff and these had to conform to municipal standards and provide a detailed plan and cost estimate. After approval, the inhabitants also had to provide matching funds; these varied from more than half the total costs in kampungs with a high proportion of high income groups to a third for settlements where most of the inhabitants had low incomes.

Interest in the programme has been sustained and it is still widely used for local infrastructure. Each year, not all applications for funding can be met and there is some variation in the total funding allocated by the city government to this programme. For instance, more funding was available between 1984 and 1986 as part of a programme to prevent flooding. Other international agencies have also provided support for different aspects—for instance, UNICEF helped support improved standards of water provision and garbage collection and support for children's facilities.

Sources: Silas, Johan, *Impact Assessment on Kip Urban III*, and *Community Based Urban Environment Management: Case study of KIP in Surabaya*, background papers prepared for the Global Report on Human Settlements, 1994.

successful large scale upgrading programmes, initially the upgrading programme in Surabaya was regarded as 'too slow', largely because of the time needed to develop agreements between public authorities and the *kampung* inhabitants.[73]

Perhaps of greater significance worldwide than the large, well-known and well-documented upgrading programmes are the large number of small, largely *ad hoc* 'upgrading' schemes in which the inhabitants of a low income settlement negotiate with a local government or some other public agency for tenure of the plots on which they live and for some basic infrastructure and services. The significance of these schemes lies in their numbers and in the fact that they demonstrate a much wider acceptance of this approach by city and municipal authorities. Where these small 'upgrading' schemes have been documented, they often show this process to be slow and inefficient—for instance, with support for paved roads negotiated at one point, then later drains or improved water supplies when there would be major cost savings if provision for water supply, sanitation, drainage and paved roads were combined. But their importance lies in the fact that they represent a fundamental change in the attitude of local authorities to illegal or informal settlements. If municipal authorities can acquire increased power, resources and capacities within the many decentralization programmes around the world, so too can their capacities expand to respond more effectively to these kinds of demands. One-off, *ad hoc* upgrading projects can then develop into continuous programmes where infrastructure and service provision is improved and partnerships developed between public agencies and resident organizations to keep down costs and ensure provision for maintenance and for further improvements. Box 10.3 gives an example of one such small scale upgrading programme that arose not from some government programme but from demands made by the inhabitants to the local municipality—but also a settlement where the inhabitants had already worked with external (non-government) agencies in a variety of initiatives to improve conditions.

One measure of a government's commitment to 'enabling policies' would be the extent to which it has moved from 'upgrading projects' to institutionalizing upgrading within city and municipal authorities who develop the capacity and knowledge to continuously work with the inhabitants of low-income settlements in upgrading the quality and extent of infrastructure and service provision and in regularizing land tenure. In this, there are few examples of the needed institutional restructuring. Certainly, progress has been made in this direction in Indonesia, although the impetus from upgrading was rarely sustained as it has been in Surabaya.[74] Progress was also made in Sri Lanka during the Million Houses Programme, as local (urban) authorities and community development councils took on much of the upgrading work.[75] Progress has also been made in India, as the programme becomes one implemented in hundreds of urban centres although there are worries that the much expanded programme will run into difficulties because of a lack of properly trained staff and the difficulty of ensuring that it does not become a top-down government directed programme with little or no community participation.[76]

Towards gender-aware housing policies and programmes

One of the most significant developments in housing during the 1980s and early 1990s was the increasing understanding of the discrimination faced by women in most if not all aspects of housing and basic services. This can be seen in discriminatory practices (more often incipient) that prevent or inhibit women owning or purchasing land for housing or obtaining a credit to purchase or build a house or getting access to a public programme or to private rental accommodation. Although this discrimination affects single women, it usually affects women-headed households more in their search for an adequate shelter and basic services for their household. For instance, women-headed households often cannot successfully apply for housing credit or for a place in a public housing or serviced-site programme, even though up to a third of all households (and up to half of the households in many low-income areas) are headed by women. In some instances, only men could apply on behalf of a household. In others, proof of formal, stable employment was required but women-headed households are rarely able to find a formal job—given both the discrimination against women in the job market and the fact that a formal job is very difficult to combine with rearing and caring for infants and children.[77] Discrimination against women outside of housing often disadvantages them in getting access to housing—for instance discrimination against women in access to employment and in wage levels also means they have less income and thus less choice within housing markets.

There is increased awareness of possible 'gender blindness' in housing and basic service programmes. Such programmes are gender blind because they do not recognize and make provision for the particular needs and priorities of women for income-earning, child-rearing and household management, and community-level action and management. Low-cost housing or serviced-site programmes rarely consider the needs and priorities of women in terms of site

BOX 10.3

Barrio San Jorge, Argentina: an example of change in the attitude of local authorities to informal settlements

Barrio San Jorge is one of the many informal or illegal settlements located in a municipality on the periphery of Buenos Aires metropolitan area. Around a third of the 450 families living there have incomes too low to meet their basic nutritional needs. There are also serious environmental problems, partly because the settlement is located on a site prone to flooding. One of its boundaries is set by a river which is seriously polluted by untreated industrial effluents. Most roads are unpaved and provision for water supply, site drainage and sanitation is very inadequate.

Since 1987, various community projects have been implemented to improve conditions, with funding raised from a variety of local, national and international sources. They include the construction and development of a mother-and-child crèche/day-care/health centre and a conversion of an existing house into a community centre (the house of the *barrio*), the provision of a piped water and sanitation system, a health-education programme, a

sewing and clothing workshop; and the surfacing of some internal roads. A community-managed building materials store has also been opened to lower prices and to make it easier to obtain materials. But what has also proved important is the changing relationship with the local authority.

Until recent years, Argentina's political history has been one of military coups and military dictatorships alternating with weak civilian governments. Local and provincial governments have mistrusted community organizations and NGOs became a major source of technical and financial support. Many low-income communities came to doubt the capacity and competence of government, after decades of promises by politicians that were rarely if ever fulfilled. Prior to 1987, the inhabitants of Barrio San Jorge had only intermittent contact with the municipal government, although most of the site on which they were living is public land. Although buses used the one paved road in the settlement, the unpaved and often muddy streets in the settlement were used as the excuse by the municipal government not to provide emergency services to the Barrio and for trucks not to empty the latrines and cesspits which are used by 89 per cent of the residents.

Until 1987 (3 years after Argentina returned

to civilian rule), the local (municipal) government had no programme for those living in illegal settlements. In recent years, the municipality has been showing increased interest. A new integrated development programme for Barrio San Jorge has been developed with the support of the settlement's population and an NGOs' technical support team, the Provincial Government of Buenos Aires and the local municipal government. It aims to improve living conditions in the settlement by promoting the inhabitants' participation and organization in coordinated actions in such areas as employment, education, recreation, health and housing and by co-ordinating the efforts of various actors: the special interests of different age groups, state organizations, private institutions and different funding sources. This integrated development programme is seeking secure tenure of the land for the inhabitants. It is also introducing some restructuring within the neighbourhood to reduce densities by developing new sites for housing on land adjacent to Barrio San Jorge to permit the relocation of some households. To this end, the municipal government has provided Barrio San Jorge with seven hectares of land free of charge on an adjoining site.

Sources: Barrio San Jorge, Annual Reports 1989/90 and 1990/1; Hardoy, Ana, Jorge Hardoy and Richard Schusterrman, 'Building community organization: the history of a squatter settlement and its own organization', *Environment and Urbanization*, vol. 3, no. 2, 1991; Ana Hardoy, personal communication.

---

design, house design and nature of infrastructure and service provision that meet their needs. Few housing and basic service programmes make special provision for single-parent households, most of whom are headed by women, even though it is common for a high proportion of all households to be headed by women. And as Chapter 3 described, the proportion of women-headed households is generally even higher among low-income groups.

There have also been many initiatives in recent years to reduce this discrimination against women. Significant progress, however, tends to be limited as discrimination is often deeply embedded in societal attitudes and perceptions, and in laws and institutional structures. It is also embedded in patterns of property ownership; at the outset of the United Nations Decade for Women in 1975, it was noted that women constitute half the world's population but own only one percent of its property.[78] These initiatives began in the early 1970s as a move to ensure that women's roles and contributions within development (and later natural resource management) became better understood. They then developed into a focus on 'gender and development' which recognized the need to consider not just women's needs and priorities in isolation but to understand

these within the broader context of the social relationship between men and women and how this relationship underpinned discrimination against women.[79] It was also spurred by evaluations of the social impact of structural adjustment programmes that found that their social impact was often particularly severe on women.[80] Box 10.4 outlines the changes that are needed in any move towards a 'gender aware city'.

During the 1980s and early 1990s, there was a rapid growth in the number of professionals, NGOs, coalitions and associations that are committed to ensuring a greater voice and influence for women's needs and priorities in housing and more generally in human settlements.[81] These are part of a much larger and broader group of women's organizations including grassroots organizations.[82] There was a tendency to give more attention to women's needs for income-generation rather than their housing and human settlements needs[83] and there have also been some notable successes in credit schemes for women in different countries—for instance the credit programme of the Working Women's Forum in Madras and that of the Grameen Bank in Bangladesh that lends to both men and women but most of those taking on loans are women.[84] There are examples of innovative emergency

BOX 10.4
Moving towards a gender-aware city

Women and men have different roles and responsibilities—within households, communities and the labour market. In these different roles, women and men have different access to and control over resources. This is reflected at a number of different levels. For example, in the household in some parts of the world, girl children may have less access to education than boy children. In many parts of the world, women have unequal access to decision-making positions. Women also face discrimination in job and housing markets. Moreover, women are generally far more severely affected by poor and overcrowded housing conditions, inadequate provision of water, sanitation, health care, schools and nurseries because they take most responsibility for looking after infants and children, caring for sick family members and managing the household.

Urban policies, planning and management must contribute to a reduction in such gender-based inequities and ensure that women and men get equal access to credit (for housing or small-scale enterprises), vocational training and government housing schemes. But they must also respond to the fact that women and men have different needs and priorities. Programmes or projects that target 'the household', 'the community', 'the neighbourhood' or 'low-income groups' must recognize that the needs and priorities of women within each household, community or neighbourhood or within low-income groups will differ from those of men.

Integrating gender issues into urban policy, planning and management will make urban development more effective. First, it helps ensure that limited resources are used more effectively, as both women's and men's needs and priorities are addressed. Second, it facilitates the active involvement of both women and men in all stages of development which will reduce project failures and wasteful expenditure. Integrating gender issues is not something 'extra' for practitioners to consider but a regular part of good practice.

Source: Drawn from Jo Beall and Caren Levy, *Moving Towards the Gendered City*, Overview paper prepared for the Preparatory Committee for Habitat II, Geneva, 11–22 April 1994.

credit schemes for low-income women, like the crisis credit scheme developed by Mahila Milan, a federation of women's collectives in Bombay.[85] But it is now more common to find discussions of women's livelihood and housing needs together, when previously there was a tendency to concentrate only on livelihoods.[86] Some of the credit programmes that developed for income generation and emergency credit have also developed credit programmes for housing purchase, construction or improvement. The Grameen Bank which began as a bank to provide low-income groups with small loans for productive activities has provided more than 300,000 housing loans[87] while the crisis credit scheme developed by Mahila Milan has developed a savings and credit programme for housing (see Chapter 11 for more details).

There has been a rapid growth in the docu-

mentation of the ways and means in which discrimination against women takes place,[88] including evaluation of the extent to which particular projects or programmes meet the needs and priorities of women.[89] Some initiatives have developed housing specifically to meet women's practical or strategic needs—some arising out of facilities set up to help women and children who were victims of domestic violence who after 'emergency' support also needed help in finding their own accommodation. There are also more professionals and institutions who provide 'gender awareness' training for staff of government and development assistance agencies and many international agencies who have taken measures in recent years to eliminate gender blindness in their work.[90] Several initiatives are underway to disaggregate economic and social statistics to reveal the differentials between men and women. For instance, indicators to measure women's participation in shelter strategies at community level have been developed and are now being applied in eight countries.[91]

The role of women at grassroots or community level is also becoming better appreciated by external agencies. There are examples of how and in what way women have organized at grassroots level to make demands for housing-related infrastructure or services[92] or address their own housing needs[93] or organize service provision themselves. In regard to services, one of the best known examples is the communal kitchens and 'glass of milk' committees organized by women in Peru in response to their survival needs during the economic crisis—with many of these initiatives later expanding their area of operation to health and leadership training.[94] Women's organizations are getting involved in demanding tenure for low income households or women having a central role in resisting evictions.[95] Several case studies that suggest community organizations in which women have a major role are more effective than those controlled by men. For example, in the Integrated Slum Improvement Programme in Visakhapatnam (India), it is 'in the few examples of settlements that are led by women that the rhetoric of urban community development has most closely been translated into reality'.[96]

Women's housing projects

In a number of countries, there are examples of women's housing projects or of housing projects that address the particular needs of women or of women headed households. Box 10.5 gives some examples of women's housing projects in Canada during the 1980s. Another example is Cefemina, a non-profit organization in San Jose, Costa Rica, that has promoted women's participation in the design and planning of new communities.[97]

The Global Strategy for Shelter to the Year

BOX 10.5
Women's housing projects in Canada

In Canada, women's groups have helped develop non-profit housing to fill gaps in both shelter and service provision. Direct service-providers, housing-advocacy groups and women's community groups have become developers of permanent affordable housing for women. In the process they have pioneered new models to go beyond shelter to include child care, life skills training and participatory housing management.

There is considerable diversity in women's housing projects. For instance, single parents, groups of women over the age of 40 and lesbians have developed non-profit housing projects to meet their own particular needs. Several have also been designed for teenage mothers and their children. Immigrant, visible minority and aboriginal women have also developed housing that responds to their own particular cultural needs.

A survey of 56 housing projects that included more than 1,500 housing units developed and controlled by women found that they fell into three broad categories:

1. Second-stage transitional housing or next-step housing with a limited stay of a few months to a year for abused women and their children. These often included services such as counselling, child care and opportunities for job upgrading. Second-stage housing has generally been developed by women's shelters that are set up as refuges for women who have been subjected to domestic violence.

2. Non-profit women's housing projects developed by existing community and women's service organizations such as the Young Women's Christian Association or local groups such as the Young Mothers' Support Group for teenage mothers in Toronto. In these cases, the non-profit community organization owns and manages the housing and residents are tenants.

3. Non-profit housing co-operatives that have been developed by groups of women and are controlled and managed by the residents that live there.

One example of this third category is the Women's Community Co-operative in Hamilton, Ontario completed in 1988. It is a six-storey-building with 47 units located in a suburban neighbourhood adjacent to a regional shopping mall. Its objective was to provide housing for women aged 40–59 at the time of application who were not well served by either the private market or the social housing that was available. Committees of residents are responsible for maintenance, interviewing applicants and social events.

Source: Wekerle, Gerda R., 'Responding to diversity: housing developed by and for women', in Hemalata C. Dandekar (ed.), *Shelter, Women and Development: First and Third World Perspectives*, George Wahr, Ann Arbor, 1993, 178–86.

2000 was also amended to incorporate gender concerns. In 1991, the following text was introduced:

In addition to actors already involved in the shelter-production process, an important place must be found for the integration of the potentially powerful but hitherto largely excluded contribution of women.

Women are subject to special constraints in obtaining adequate housing and in participating in human settle-ments development efforts at all levels. While some of these constraints are the result of *de jure* and/or *de facto* gender discrimination, others are the result of their severe poverty, their lack of education and training, and their double and triple burden as household workers and workers in the formal and informal sectors of agriculture, industry and commerce. Removing these constraints is important not only because equity in distribution of development benefits is a fundamental principle but also because increasing numbers of households are either solely or largely supported by women. Depriving women of access to shelter and infrastructure deprives large numbers of families as well. There are concrete and identifiable implications for women in all human settlements and shelter-related policies, programmes and projects, whether they deal with land, finance, building materials, construction technologies, housing or community design. It is necessary, therefore, to enhance women's participation in shelter and infrastructure management as contributors and beneficiaries, and to put particular emphasis on the integration of women's activities with all mainstream development activities, on an equal basis with those of men. There is also need to assess women's demands for shelter, good and services and to encourage the design and implementation of innovative programmes that will increase women's participation in shelter management.[98]

Certain countries have introduced special programmes for women-headed households. Box 10.6 gives an example of the programme that developed in Colombia. Also in Colombia, the national federation of popular housing groups *Construyamos* encourages the development of 'women's committees' and their participation in decision-making at neighbourhood level and at higher levels in the system.[99]

It is important not to overstate the extent to which this pressure to reduce discrimination against women and to promote 'gender-aware' housing and basic service policies has been successful. The fact that this discrimination is deeply embedded in laws and institutions and in societal attitudes was noted earlier. Generally speaking, gender-aware training and research continues to have little influence on mainstream researchers and policy-makers.[100]

From housing needs to housing rights

One significant change during the 1980s and early 1990s was the increasing influence on government actions of international and national law on people's right to housing. This was largely the result of a much greater use of international and national law by citizen groups and NGOs—which in turn helped stimulate important developments in international and national law concerning people's right to housing. Citizen groups and NGOs used the law as a defence for those facing the threat of forced eviction, as a justification for demanding adequate compensation for those already evicted—and, more generally, as

Colombia's programme for the development of families headed by women

In Colombia in 1990, a local Non-Government Organization and the Women's World Bank began a credit programme targeted at female heads of household in Cali, the third largest city. Following on from the new constitution passed in 1990 and after the 1991 elections, the Presidential Programme for Women, Youth and the Elderly decided to take up this programme and make it national and permanent, in part to address one of the articles of the new constitution that prescribed special support for women-headed households.

In 1992, the programme was launched in five cities and in 1993 in a further ten, covering 2,570 households. It was supported by many institutions, both governmental and non-governmental. The programme was seen as an effective way of institutionalizing gender-aware policy and, in the context of decentralization, of involving local-level institutions.

The objective of the programme was to improve the quality of life of families headed by women at the lowest socio-economic level in urban areas through the improvement of income generation, household wellbeing, the condition of children and the promotion of human development of women and their families. The target group is urban women heads of households working in the informal economy in their own small enterprises. The programme includes credit schemes, management training, promotion and support for person development—including training in self-esteem, health care, legal education and family life.

Source: Beall, Jo, *The Gender Dimensions of Urbanisation and Urban Poverty,* Paper prepared for the seminar on Women in Urban Areas, Division for the Advancement of Women, United Nations Office at Vienna, 8–12 Nov., Vienna, 1993.

Examples of national constitutions with the right to housing

Nicaragua: The Nicaraguan constitution of 1987 states that 'Nicaraguans have the right to a decent, comfortable and safe housing that guarantees familial privacy. The state shall promote the fulfilment of this right.'

Spain: The Spanish constitution states that 'All Spaniards have the right to enjoy decent and adequate housing.'

Netherlands: Article 22(2) of the Dutch constitution states that 'It shall be the concern of the authorities to provide sufficient living accommodation.'

Philippines: 'the state shall by law, and for the common good, undertake in cooperation with the private sector a continuing programme of urban land reform and housing which will make available at affordable cost decent housing and basic services to underprivileged and homeless citizens in urban centres and resettlement areas' (Article 13/9).

Source: Leckie, Scott, *From Housing Needs to Housing Rights: an Analysis of the Right to Adequate Housing Under International Human Rights Law,* Human Settlements Programme, IIED, London, 1992.

a way of backing the demand that governments act to ensure people's housing needs are met.

Although few governments or international agencies actively support people's right to housing, almost none will deny that the right to housing is part of human rights. Most countries with new constitutions in the last 10–12 years have included the right to housing within them or at least a formal acceptance that the state has a responsibility for ensuring people find housing. Fifty-three national constitutions have some provision within them for housing rights. Box 10.7 gives some examples. International conventions on housing rights has also changed dramatically in the last few years. International human rights law includes a series of clear governmental legal obligations and a broad series of individual and group entitlements to these. Many changes at local and national level will be influenced by these. What is also new is the extent to which the actions of government in housing are now subject to regular scrutiny by various human rights bodies.

This greater use of national and international

law within housing was not so much because of major innovations in international law but more because of the extent to which citizens groups and NGOs organized their demands around the issue of 'rights' rather than the issue of 'need'. Housing rights have long been within international covenants or conventions. For instance, the Universal Declaration on Human Rights of 1948 states that:

Everyone has the right to a standard of living adequate for the health and wellbeing of himself and his family, including food, clothing, housing and medical care and necessary social services . . .

When adopted, this was not seen as a legally binding agreement but a common standard of achievement that should form the basis of national and international human rights policies.[101] Various other pieces of international covenants have included within them 'the right to housing' including the Vancouver Declaration on Human Settlements at Habitat I in 1976. But the most important from a legal perspective is the International Covenant on Economic, Social and Cultural Rights which has been ratified by over 90 states.[102] The states that have ratified this Covenant are bound to prove that they comply with this Covenant and individuals can formally complain to human rights bodies if they feel the state has violated this convention.

The International Year of Shelter for the Homeless in 1987 helped to give impetus to the development and use of national and international covenant on housing rights. In 1987, at its 42nd session, the United Nations General Assembly adopted the following resolution:

The General Assembly,

1. Expresses its deep concern that millions of people do not enjoy the right to adequate housing;

2. Reiterates the need to take, at the national and international levels, measures to promote the right of all persons to an adequate standard of living for themselves and their families, including adequate housing;

3. Calls upon all states and international organizations concerned to pay special attention to the realization of the right to adequate housing in carrying out measures to develop national shelter strategies and settlement improvement programmes within the framework of the global strategy for shelter to the year 2000;

4. requests the Economic and Social Council (ECOSOC) and its appropriate functional commissions to keep the question of the right to adequate housing under periodic review;

5. Decides to consider the question again following its consideration by the Economic and Social Council (ECOSOC).[103]

The United Nations Committee on Economic, Social and Cultural Rights is charged with helping the Economic and Social Council in monitoring member governments' compliance with their obligations under the International Covenant on Economic, Social and Cultural Rights. Between 1992 and 1994, this Committee scrutinized the housing rights situation in sixteen countries and issued recommendations to several governments concerning complicity in forced evictions. This Committee has become the main international legal mechanism in the struggle against forced evictions.[104]

The United Nations Commission on Human Rights which is the principal United Nations body responsible for the promotion of human rights appointed a Special Rapporteur responsible for reporting to the United Nations on all aspects of the right to adequate housing under international law—and this rapporteur's reports[105] have contributed not only to the development of housing rights but also of economic, social and cultural rights in general.[106]

Although international law may have implicitly recognized that the practice of forced eviction violated human rights, only since 1991 has the United Nations explicitly recognized this. In August 1991, the UN Sub-Commission on Prevention of Discrimination and Protection of Minorities unanimously adopted resolution 1991/12 which condemned forced evictions as a major infringement of human rights law. This has subsequently been reaffirmed by additional resolutions, including resolution 1993/77 adopted in March 1993 which reaffirmed that forced evictions are a gross violation of human rights. It also demanded that governments confer security of tenure to all dwellers currently without such legal protection and that sufficient compensation be paid to all persons and communities which have already been forcibly removed from their homes and land. It also stressed that governments should desist from tolerating or sponsoring evictions in the future.[107]

Government and rental housing

Chapters 6 and 7 noted the importance of renting in terms of the proportion of people who rely on renting in urban areas and the fact that a large proportion of those who rent are among the lowest income groups. There are examples of successful government intervention in rental housing but far less of effective policies. In Bombay, the Maharashtra state government has supported a programme to repair the inner-city tenement housing. Between 1969 and 1989, some 13,000 buildings were repaired and those that were beyond repair were purchased by the government for redevelopment. The cost of the programme was shared between landlords, tenants and state and federal government funds. Although the management of the scheme has been criticized, the principle appears sound[108] and attempts are now being made to involve the tenants and landlords more directly. Box 10.8 gives more details of the scheme in the centre of Mexico City that combined a rapid reconstruction of housing destroyed by the earthquake with improved provision of housing for the tenants who had lost their housing.

The general record of official support to the rental market has been disappointing.[109] Despite the obvious (and in many cities growing) importance of renting and sharing, housing policies have been slow to respond. National shelter strategies usually identify the promotion of rental housing as an objective, but have done little to promote it. There are some exceptions to this rule—for example, in Colombia and Indonesia, where credit is being provided specifically for investment by landlords in small-scale rental housing.[111] The Mexican government offered a series of incentives to the private sector to build housing for rent during the 1980s, but the Ministry of Urban Development admitted disappointment with this, as too few companies showed a real interest.[112] Government figures suggest that some 60,000 units were completed but most were in the main tourist resorts.[113] In the Republic of Korea, the government has attracted private investment in the provision of rental housing through the offer of subsidized loans and exemption from capital gains tax and discounting the sale of serviced land; between 1982 and 1986, land to accommodate 34,000

BOX 10.8
Renovación Habitacional
Popular: **The post-earthquake**
reconstruction programme in
Mexico City

The earthquakes of September 1985 hit
Mexico City's densely populated central area
hardest. An estimated 100,000 dwellings
were affected, including high-rise
public-sector housing, 4–5 storey flats and
condominiums and, especially, the run-down
tenements, known in Mexico as 'vecindades'.
The Renovación Habitacional Popular
programme was geared to the rebuilding of
dwellings within this last category. In all,
44,000 units were built or rehabilitated, most
of them on the original plots and to the benefit
of the original tenants, in the space of just
over two years. This amount represents an
additional 15 per cent over and above the
number of houses financed by the public
sector in Mexico during those same years.
The programme was handled by a specially
created body—Renovación Habitacional
Popular—and was financed by FONHAPO and
the World Bank. Below are listed the most
outstanding innovative features of the
programme.

- The programme was drawn up as a direct
  response to concrete demands from

potential beneficiaries. It was those who
had lost their homes and were living on the
street who demanded the expropriation of
the affected lots and the basic operational
principles that developed. During the first
stage, the demands were presented and
obtained by means of intense political
mobilization of those affected. For the
second stage, after the expropriation,
people's participation was channelled into
the 'Democratic Agreement for
Reconstruction', a negotiated document
that laid out the programme's operational
rules. The way in which the beneficiaries
actively participated in the setting up of this
programme contrasts strongly with most
public housing institutions which were
generally created without regard to the
concrete demands of prospective
beneficiaries.

- The political measure that was of greatest
  importance to the programme was the
  expropriation of 4,332 properties,
  containing 3,311 vecindades which were
  occupied by 44,788 families. The
  expropriation solved one the main problems
  facing low-cost housing programmes,
  namely access to land, and met the
  earthquake victims' main demand, the right
  to remain in their respective
  neighbourhoods. This included residents
  and also people whose shops and

workshops had been affected. The legal
terms of the expropriation determined who
were to be the programme's beneficiaries:
those families who had been occupying the
expropriated lots, at that time, or
immediately prior to the earthquake. This
eliminated (or substantially reduced) the
traditional (often corrupt) mechanisms for
allocating housing credits. It became
practically impossible for anybody to gain
political (or economic) capital out of the
programme using clientelistic tactics.

- Because of the legal obligation, derived
  from the expropriation, to rehouse all the
  affected population
  in situ, the programme's financial terms had
  to be accessible to all. This meant a fairly
  high level of subsidy, although not
  necessarily higher than those applied in
  conventional public housing programmes.
  The subsidies were concentrated in the part
  of the programme financed by the Mexican
  government: land and indirect cost.

- In addition to World Bank funding, the
  programme introduced other financial
  innovations, allowing the participation of
  non-governmental resources. These were
  allowed either in the cases of those families
  or individuals who were unable to pay under
  the programme's standard credit terms, or
  to 130 expropriated lots, whose occupants
  opted out of the Renovación project.

Source: Connolly, Priscilla, 'The go between; CENVI, a Habitat NGO in Mexico City', *Environment and Urbanization*, vol. 5, no. 1, 1993, 68–90.[110]

units was made available.[114]

Most governments have also been slow to
encourage an expansion of rental accommodation, in upgrading and serviced-site programmes.
Various studies have suggested that upgrading
programmes in settlements where there are
tenants as well as 'owner-occupiers' (even if
their land occupation is illegal) can lead to rent
rises.[115] In other instances, there is less evidence
of this—or even evidence of net benefits for
renters, as owner-occupiers were encouraged by
the upgrading to extend their housing to include
rooms for rent.[116] Whether or not an upgrading
programme encourages the displacement of tenants is likely to vary according to the scale of the
upgrading programme (a very large upgrading
programme would tend to keep down rises in
value for the upgraded housing stock) and to its
location—where the legalization and upgrading
of a settlement in a valuable location will generally lead to price rises and demand for houses
there by higher-income groups.[117] Legalization
of a settlement will generally push up the value of
housing there and rents for any tenants. But it
may also promote an expansion of rental accommodation, where prior to legalization, those seeking tenure to the land were reluctant to rent since

the tenants might compete with them in claiming
rights to tenure.[118]

Where provision for maintenance of rental
housing by landlords is inadequate, the transfer of
tenure from landlords to tenants and the provision of credit to permit tenants to purchase their
units from landlords have been suggested.
Tenants could jointly manage a tenement building through co-operative ownership—although
those who only plan a short stay in a tenement
will be reluctant to take on extra responsibilities
and costs. In addition, tenants are unlikely to
commit funding and self-help to a cooperatively
managed building if they cannot sell their
'tenure' when they leave—and this implies provision for such a sale and recognition by housing
credit-agencies of the validity of such tenant-
ownership.

Thus, in general, instead of promoting the
widest possible range of housing alternatives so
that people can choose from a range of options
shelter strategies still tend to promote home
ownership. This is despite the fact that in most
urban centres in the South, landlordism among
the urban poor is usually a small-scale and non-
exploitative affair;[119] that many low-income
individuals and households actually prefer rent-

ing to ownership; and that a variety of policy measures are already in hand to stimulate rental housing production.[120] These include rent decontrol, relaxing planning standards (to promote the building of extra rooms), and fiscal incentives to landlords.[121]

Other developments during the 1980s

Although there is no comprehensive survey of the scale and nature of government support for housing, it appears that support for serviced-site projects decreased, as the difficulties in implementing them became more obvious and as international support for them decreased. Government-sponsored site and service projects were an attempt to come to terms with the lack of cheap, legal housing plots but however successful they were at project level, they fail to tackle the real problem—a legal urban land market which excludes poorer groups who want to develop their own housing.[122] When governments tried to scale up 'site and service projects' into a continuous programme, they ran into problems in implementing and financing this because they could not acquire the land they needed. The difficulty in acquiring land through expropriation (and the long delays in doing so) often led to serviced sites being developed in locations where land was easily obtained—but these are usually in locations which least suit lower income groups. If governments purchasing land for serviced-site programmes pay 'market rates', the main beneficiaries of an expanded serviced-site programme will be the landowners, not the poor.[123] And the costs of the land will probably be so high that the scale of the programme remains very limited. Perhaps not surprisingly, a review of serviced-site projects commented that most governments have adopted this kind of project on a trial basis and not as a central part of housing policy.[124] The review also found that it was pressure on public agencies to reduce unit costs that was the main reason for their implementation—rather than a genuine attempt to develop more appropriate solutions for low-income groups. In pursuit of such cost reductions, government tends to use cheap land sites in locations too distant from employment sources to suit poorer households. Many low-income recipients either default on payments or sell out to middle-income groups.[125] The limitations of site and service projects are also becoming more evident. Serviced sites are only cheaper than public housing units because the public authorities make the recipients responsible for house construction (and additional cost savings may be achieved by having lower standards for plot sizes, infrastructure and services). Many serviced-site schemes

have suffered from problems similar to those experienced in public housing projects, i.e. being too expensive for poorer groups, in the wrong location and with plot sizes and site lay-outs which ill-match the needs and priorities of the intended beneficiaries.[126] In other cases, official procedures ensured that poorer households did not receive the serviced sites. In a site and service project in Thika (Kenya) started in 1971, elected town councillors prepared lists of people to receive the serviced sites; those they proposed were not low income households and some councillors received substantial payments from the persons they placed on the list for receiving serviced sites.[127] There are examples of a new generation of serviced-site schemes, often implemented by city or municipal authorities,[128] which seek to address these disadvantages but it is not known whether these are isolated examples or representative of approaches being more widely implemented.

Experience shows that employment-generating activities must be integrated into shelter programmes at the design stage to take maximum advantage of the links between them as the programme unfolds. Data from illegal subdivisions in Medellin (Colombia) demonstrate that the use of dwellings for income-generation increased consistently between 1964 and 1984.[129] The use of housing as a combined space for living and working (and organizing!) is characteristic of the urban poor, especially for women who need to be able to balance the demands of employment, income-generation, domestic work and childcare and therefore have special requirements for the design and use of their housing that permits income-earning activities.[130] The mixed use of buildings needs to be promoted and planning standards adjusted to encourage this. Location-specific jobs (such as portering, rickshaw-pullers and some forms of informal-sector petty commerce) have obvious implications for the siting of low-income settlements. A key factor behind the success of the Kampung Improvement Programme in Indonesia was the early recognition of, and support for, the economic potential and productivity of the upgrading process, both via construction itself and via a variety of indirect contributions to the urban economy.[131] The UNICEF-assisted Urban Basic Services programme also recognizes the importance of establishing the necessary linkages between physical upgrading, social mobilization, and economic development.[132] The long-term economic potential of upgrading for the poor does, however, tend to be limited by the process of commercialization and filtering which occurs unless preventive measures are adopted.

10.3 The Construction Sector— Challenges and Opportunities

Introduction

The current trends and limitations of the construction sector for delivery of low-cost housing and infrastructure, as discussed in Chapter 6 point to a very demanding set of criteria if the capacity of the sector has to be strengthened. Despite the gloomy picture of constraints facing the sector, however, progress has been made in some countries. In several instances, these efforts have lacked comprehensiveness, by focusing only on one issue and with geographically restrictive impacts. Yet, these minimal developmental efforts are noteworthy since they represent moves in the right direction and could be moulded into a desirable comprehensive strategy for the ultimate solution of the low-income shelter crisis. The following is a summary of challenges and efforts which have been made in some countries, to tackle specific issues for low-income shelter and infrastructure construction.

New technologies and materials

Over the past 10–20 years, mainly through a wide range of research activities carried out in a number of countries in both the North and the South, several new technologies and materials have been identified which are based entirely on local resources. Even though these research efforts, in many cases, have not been adopted on a wide scale, mainly because of weak information flow and technology transfer mechanisms, experience has shown that if these limitations are removed, considerable improvements could be achieved in the construction sector for low-cost housing and infrastructure delivery. Among the more promising developments in this area are the following.

Small-scale production of cement, lime and alternative binding materials

Cement is one of the most important and commonly used construction materials throughout the world, and the per capita production and consumption rate of cement is often used as an indicator of development, especially in the South. The total cement production in the world was 1,147 million tons in 1991, most of which was from large cement plants with capacities varying from 2,000 to 20,000 tons per day.[133]

In view of a number of constraints facing the large-scale cement plants in the South, particularly the under-utilization of installed capacities and resource wastages, a new generation of production plants is now in operation, mainly in China and India. These produce cement of a quality identical to those produced in conventional large-scale factories, but at scales as low as 20 tons per day. The plants use small, local raw-material deposits, can be brought into production rapidly, and involve a level of investment which can be afforded by local entrepreneurs. In 1990, more than 50 per cent of China's and about 10 per cent of India's cement production was from mini-cement plants and the production rate is increasing every year.[134] By meeting the demands of local captive markets mini-cement plants also provide for participation of local small entrepreneurs and, thus, help in building up local economies.

The inherent flexibility of small-scale operations to cope with volatile and shifting demands, and their ability to take best advantage of available factors of production in the South are the main sources of their strength. Yet, the total installed capacity of mini-cement plants outside China and India has remained very limited, mainly because of the lack of wide-scale dissemination of the required information relating to this technology among prospective entrepreneurs.[135]

Similarly, in lime production, small-scale vertical-shaft lime-kiln technology has shown the possibility of producing high-quality building lime, which can replace cement in many low-cost housing construction processes. Lime, even though it has less strength than Portland cement and a slower setting rate, is perfectly adequate for most low-strength applications. Moreover, lime, because of its good workability, ability to accept movement without cracking, and retentivity resistance to water penetration, is very often, more suitable for masonry, plastering etc. than Portland cement.[136]

Even though cement is widely used in construction, because of its high cost and chronic shortages, efforts are made in some countries to replace it with cheaper materials. In this connection, the production and use of alternative binders for low-cost construction purposes is attracting greater attention in recent years in many countries. Natural and artificial pozzolanas such as volcanic ashes, pumice, rice and groundnut-husk-ashes and fly-ash are offering excellent potentials as substitutes for cement or lime, thus, reducing considerably the use of cement in low-cost construction.[137]

Innovations in soil-construction

In recent years, new and innovative techniques have been developed for the production of high-quality, low-cost walling blocks made from earth using a stabilizer, such as a small amount of cement or lime, to make it strong, durable and impervious to water. The UNCHS (Habitat) in collaboration with appropriate technology development organizations worldwide and a number of building research institutions in the South have actively promoted the wide-scale production and use of stabilized-soil blocks as a cost-effective alternative to burnt-clay bricks and concrete blocks. The process of making stabilized-soil blocks is not complicated and can be done on a small-scale with simple hand-operated block-presses using a wide range of soil types. A variety of block-presses are now available worldwide and many countries have started manufacturing them locally (see Box 10.9).[138]

BOX 10.9
Stabilized soil-block press-manufacturing in Kenya

Among the East African countries, Kenya is one of the pioneering countries which has achieved great success in manufacturing stabilized soil-block (SSB) presses. Based on a number of imported presses, a non-governmental organization in charge of developing low-cost building materials and technologies and training local artisans, succeeded in developing a new and improved design for SSB presses in the late 1980s, which was proved to have more efficiency, durability and strength than the imported ones. The idea of designing a new SSB-press in Kenya, which is named Action-Pack Block-Press (APBP), was conceived only after a close examination of all other imported presses were completed and found that not only are they exorbitant in price, they are technically also not fully suitable to local conditions.

Reported figures indicate that a total of 800 APBPs have been manufactured, mainly by two private metal working enterprises (including the Undugu Society) in the past 5–6 years, and at least 300 of them have been exported to neighbouring countries: Uganda and the United Republic of Tanzania. The technology is now in the hands of the private sector, with entrepreneurs investing in the technology as a business. Currently an average of 10 presses are manufactured and sold every month and the prospects show that the demand will grow in the years to come. For example, the upgrading of the Mathare Valley slum in Nairobi (a project supported by the Government of Germany) is designed to use SSBs for the walls of houses. This is just an indication of how the technology has widely spread and been readily accepted.[139]

Source: Action Aid-Kenya, stabilized soil-block technology adaptation and progress, and Appropriate Technologies for Enterprise Creation (APPROTEC), Nairobi, Kenya.

Fibre-concrete roofing

Roofing accounts for between 30 and 50 per cent of the total cost of a simple house. Therefore, any savings in this component are an essential first step towards improving housing affordability in the South.

In recent years, considerable research has been carried out on fibre-concrete roofing (FCR) technology (sheets and tiles) most of which has been published and disseminated, and the technology is gaining considerable popularity in many countries in the South. Production techniques and equipment are widely available for the small-scale manufacture of tiles, using simple locally made equipment (manual/electrical vibrators and moulds) requiring little energy and largely unskilled labour. Fibres from a wide range of locally available plants (such as sisal and coconut) can be used. The feasibility of fibre-concrete roofing has been demonstrated successfully in more than 70 countries covering more than 2.5 million square metres of roofing area.[140]

Use of industrial and agricultural wastes in building materials

One of the greatest challenges of the construction industry is its potential to utilize wastes from agriculture and industry, as raw materials and as fuel substitutes. Among many other opportunities, phospho-gypsum can be produced as a by-product of fertilizer manufacture; sulphur removed from chimney stacks can be used for producing sulphur blocks; and 'red mud' can be used both in block production and cement. The utilization of these industrial wastes can also help control environmental pollution. In China and India, for example, millions of tons of fly ash is used annually for block production. Similarly, in most rice-growing countries, the residues of rice processing (rice husk) after some processing (to convert it into rice-husk ash)—is used as a partial substitute to cement.

Timber wastes and agricultural wastes can be processed to form building boards. The residues from rice processing, palm-nut processing, and coconut and groundnut residues are all materials which can be used as fuels in brick-burning and lime-burning. In short, almost all non-hazardous industrial and agricultural wastes can be used in construction.[141]

Environmentally sound construction: energy-efficient and low-polluting technologies

The construction industry, as a major consumer of the world's natural resources and a potential polluter of the environment, is being closely scrutinized by the international community and many governments. Owing to the expansion of the construction sector in many countries, tropical hardwood, metallic and non-metallic minerals and non-renewable energy resources are used extensively.

To reduce the material content of buildings however, solid masonry walls could be replaced by cavity walls, solid concrete slabs by hollow-block joist slabs, timber beams by lightweight trusses and forest timber by secondary species of wood. Similarly, in the production of certain energy-intensive materials, such as lime and brick, considerable energy savings can be achieved by using continuous kilns instead of intermittent ones. Gasifiers can also improve energy-efficiency of traditional fuels. Appropriate architectural design (particularly in regions with extreme hot or cold climates) such as proper insulation of external walls or providing natural cooling ducts in rooms are important measures which result in reducing the energy consumption in buildings in use.[142]

In addition to adverse environmental aspects of construction activities, health hazards associated with certain building materials is also attracting great attention in recent years. Materials such as asbestos, certain solvents, insecticides and fungicides, toxic metals and radon exhaled from materials containing radium have been proved to be hazardous to health in a variety of ways, including respiratory diseases such as asthma, heart diseases, cancer, brain damage and poisoning. In the absence of adequate information and public awareness, the construction industry and the decision-makers have unfortunately not been able, so far, to respond effectively to the challenges of controlling the health hazards associated with building materials. There is, therefore, an urgent need to design and implement programmes so as to raise the understanding of the health implications of building materials on a continuing basis.[143]

Information flow and transfer of technology through networking

One of the crucial prerequisites for the development of the construction sector in the South is the existence of relevant information on technological aspects of the industry. Systematic information flow is a vital component to technology transfer and adaptation and its absence would lead to a trend of wasting scarce resources and a general lack of progress in the construction sector for low-cost housing.

The process of information collection and dissemination through specialized information services and data centres in the South is undergoing gradual development. However, because of a number of reasons, such as inadequate managerial skills and lack of financial resources these centres have not been able to fully satisfy the information needs of researchers and professionals in the construction sector. In recent years, some important regional networking initiatives have been taken by the United Nations to promote the flow of information and regional cooperation with a view to transferring appropriate technologies from country to country and strengthening capacity in the building materials and construction sector (see Box 2). Another innovative measure for the diffusion of appropriate technologies to small-scale building materials producers is through establishment of countrywide building centres. The 'Building Centres Movement' in India which was initiated in the recent past, is an excellent example of this trend which can be replicated in many other countries (see Box 10.10).

BOX 10.10
Network of African countries on local building materials and technologies

The UNCHS (Habitat) as part of its efforts to support the initiatives of countries in the African region for developing local building materials industries, established (in 1985), in collaboration with the Commonwealth Science Council (CSC) a Network of African Countries on Local Building Materials and Technologies. During the first 4 to 5 years, the Network in addition to facilitating flow and exchange of technological information, organized a number of national workshops in Ghana, Malawi and Kenya aimed at supporting these countries in formulating standards and specification for locally produced building materials. These efforts have made it possible to convince policy- and decision-makers in a number of African countries to take effective measures for formulate and put in place new standards and specifications, for the utilization of locally produced materials such as fibre-concrete roofing, stabilized-soil-block technology, lime and other types of binding materials.

The Network, in pursuit of its overall objective of 'strengthening local technological capacity through information flow, regional cooperation and transfer of appropriate technologies in the low-cost building materials sector', has been publishing a biannual Journal since 1989, disseminating a wide range of information on research activities, production technologies and case studies on issues relevant to the objective of the Network.

While seeking to expand its current activities, the Network is also seeking to strengthen its role in field operations with a view to facilitating more regional cooperation and transfer of technology. It also plans to launch a regional programme on 'Domestic capacity-building in the local building-materials sector in sub-Saharan African countries'. The Network currently has 15 member-countries comprising: Cameroon, Ethiopia, Ghana, Kenya, Lesotho, Malawi, Malta, Mauritius, Namibia, Nigeria, Sierra Leone, Uganda, United Republic of Tanzania, Zambia and Zimbabwe.

Similarly, the appropriate technology development organizations (ATDOs) such as the Intermediate Technology Development Group (ITDG), in the United Kingdom, the German Appropriate Technology Exchange (GATE) of the Deutsche Gesellschaft Fuer Technische Zusammenarbeit (GTZ) and the Small Industries Development Organizations (SIDOs) such as the one in the United Republic of Tanzania have had significant roles in diffusion of appropriate technologies in many countries and regions.

The role of communities

Experience over the past several years has shown that involvement of communities, the informal

BOX 10.11
The building centres movement in India

The first building centre was launched in 1986 in Quilon, Kerala. Its aim was to disseminate innovative building-materials production techniques through the training of artisans and unemployed youth, for use of meeting the state's massive housing needs swelled by the impact of recent natural disasters.

Under the guidance of a dynamic district administrator, the Nirmithi Kendra (Building Centre)—a community-based, non-governmental organization (NGO)—created a movement for the rapid production of building components such as ferro-cement rafters, funicular shells, filler-slab roofing, plate-floors, rubble filler blocks and soil-stabilized pressed blocks, among others, to replace cement and its dwindling supplies of timber. The Kendra also undertook construction and upgrading of housing, flood shelters, water tanks and wells—all at much lower costs. The Movement demonstrated the cost-effectiveness and aesthetic qualities of local materials and techniques, some of which were nearly lost to local artisans. In a few years, thousands of artisans—both men and women—have been trained in 14 district centres, set up on a similar model, and many now operate independently. The young artisans trained in these centres have become agents for change. The Kerala State Government has supported this initiative by awarding contracts for numerous high-visibility government projects to the Centre.

By 1992, under the guidance and support of the Ministry of Urban Development and of the Housing and Urban Development Corporation, 280 centres had been identified all over the country, 105 of which were already functional. They follow different models—some are led by government initiative, others by NGOs—and they promote different technologies in response to local resources. Some emphasize production, some entrepreneur-training, some artisan-training. The Rajasthan model emphasizes entrepreneur-training, providing a market for what is produced by buying the components for use in the housing projects of the Rajasthan Housing Board. A highly dedicated professional group in Auroville Building Centre is promoting vaulted earth-based construction and a range of ferro-cement products. In Andhra Pradesh, trainee artisans not only produce materials, but also assist villagers in the construction of houses. Building centres with similar aims have also been set up by NGOs, a construction workers' cooperative and a school of architecture. The Building Centre in Delhi trains young architects on new and innovative building products and systems and deploys them to set up building centres in places like Manipur, Sikkim, and the Andaman and Nicobar Islands.

Source: Suresh, V., 'Techno-financing issues in the building materials sector for housing delivery in the Asian region', unpublished draft report prepared for the UNCHS (Habitat), August 1992.

sector and women in construction activities can considerably help in improving the conditions of human settlements. Positive experiences in encouraging local initiatives by community-based groups and the informal sector in the local production of building materials have taken place in several countries, e.g. in Brazil, Jamaica, the Philippines and Zambia.[144] They have demonstrated the many advantages and social opportunities such an approach can provide to marginalized groups by mobilizing the skills and financial resources of the community, generating income and employment opportunities, and giving the community an experience of participating in wider decision-making.

There are many successful examples of women's co-operatives in the manufacture of building materials. For example, block-making operations in Ghana involve large numbers of women, and in Zimbabwe the rural brick-making industry is dominated by women. Awareness-raising programmes and training projects set up to increase the number of women entering the construction industry have been found to be successful in a number of countries. Women are in many cases successful entrepreneurs in building-materials production (see Box 10.12).

BOX 10.12
Kabiro and Dandora women's self-help groups, Kenya

The Kabiro Women's Group located in the western suburbs of Nairobi is registered with the Ministry of Culture and Social Services as a local self-help group. The group of 70 women has divided itself into seven subgroups of 10 and produces building blocks on a rotating basis, i.e. every subgroup works only once a week in block-making.

The Dandora group is located in a densely populated low-income housing area of Nairobi. Consisting of 38 women, the group carries out block-making operations on a plot of about one acre. The group purchased a second-hand block-making machine through contributions of Kshs.100 from each member. Since its formation in 1985, the group has managed to obtain a grant of land, built a small storage shed and a temporary cover for concrete-block curing, and acquired various sundry items to support production. The group works on an almost full-time basis, with subgroups of seven women each operating daily shifts on a rotational basis.

The Kabiro and Dandora groups have a number of similar features: (*a*) both groups are in formal existence; (*b*) when a woman is absent for personal reasons her family may substitute for her in production activities; (*c*) identical machines are used in making blocks; (*d*) both groups are grappling with the demands of an industrial activity on a part-time basis, whilst being mothers and housewives at the same time.

The production of building materials seems to be a good opportunity for women to move into non-traditional industrial operations. Whilst women in Africa have often practised group or communal activities, industrial production demands regular attendance at fixed times and some commitment to abandon other tasks in favour of the production unit. There are signs that women are rapidly adapting to new lifestyles demanded by these non-traditional activities.

10.4 New Partnerships

One characteristic of many of the innovative policies and programmes described in earlier sections of this Chapter is the partnerships that allowed a combining of resources from national government agencies, municipal authorities, private sector, NGOs, international funding agencies, voluntary or community sector resources, and individuals/households. The Kampung Improvement Programme in Surabaya (Box 10.2) relied on the active support of community organizations and on the integration of other government programmes within its framework.[145] The example of Barrio San Jorge in Argentina (Box 10.3) that was given as one among many possible examples of upgrading projects depends for its long term success on agreements reached between community organizations, support NGOs and the municipal authorities. The example of Renovación Habitacional Popular that rebuilt inner city housing in Mexico City for the benefit of low-income former tenants (see Box 10.8) also involved a partnership between community organizations, NGOs, government agencies and an international funding agency. There is also a considerable range of public--private partnerships in housing construction, improvement, maintenance or management in other countries, including many in West Europe, Japan, Australia and North America.[146]

This section on new partnerships will present four very different examples of new partnerships—with one from Africa and Asia and two from Latin America. None are intended as a 'model' and each have their limitations. But three represent an attempt by a government to work in partnership with households and residents' or community organizations and, in the examples in Latin America and Asia, with national government agencies working with city and municipal agencies. The Million Houses Programme in Sri Lanka (Box 10.13) represented a reduction in the scale of national government investment in housing and an active policy to stimulate and support the investments of individual households, community organizations and municipal authorities. The development in Guatemala of a Committee for Attention to Precarious Areas in Guatemala City (Box 10.14) brought together representatives from national government agencies, different city authorities, NGOs, community organizations and aid agencies to work together to improve housing, infrastructure and services in the informal or illegal settlements in which close to half the city's population lives.[147] The initiative of the government of Burkina Faso was to mobilize individual and community labour to improve infrastructure and service provision in its largest city and was underpinned by a programme to

provide legal rights of occupancy to more than 60,000 households[148] (see Box 10.16). The fourth example is one of partnerships between low-income groups and their community organizations and a local non-profit institution. The Carvajal Foundation and its work in Aguablanca in Cali, Colombia represents the example of a private Foundation set up by a successful printing company that began in Cali. Its programme worked extensively not only with low income groups and their organizations but also with the city authorities and with national agencies (see Box 10.15). There are enormous contrasts between these examples in the economic and social context in which they worked, but each represents an example of the kind of support that low-income groups need from government or other actors to allow them to improve housing and living conditions.

One of the most innovative aspects of the urban sub-programme of the Million Houses Programme was the system of community construction contracts that were awarded to community organizations who then undertook the construction of infrastructure that had previously been done by a contractor. This process lowered costs, often improved the quality of the product, made maintenance more likely and generated employment within the community.[149] The fact that urban infrastructure (such as roads, markets and drainage networks) can be developed using local labour, as demonstrated by the community contracts in Sri Lanka has also been tried in similar 'community contracts' in Zambia and Bolivia. Results from the UNDP/ILO 'Employment Generation in Urban Works Programme' show that labour-intensive public works can compete with capital-intensive methods in terms of cost and quality, though not in terms of time.[151] It is also a reminder of the strong links that can exist between improving infrastructure and service provision in urban and rural areas and creating employment. In countries or regions where only a modest income is needed to fully meet the cost of food, housing, fuel and other necessities, improving infrastructure and services, including helping to staff and maintain schools, health centres and day care centres, remains relatively low cost.[152] It can provide incomes for large numbers of people who previously had inadequate incomes—and particular jobs can be established that meet the needs of poorer or more vulnerable groups. And almost all the income will be spent in the locality.

The Million Houses Programme and the range of initiatives in Guatemala City described below reflect what is essentially a new model of urban development, although in the Million Houses Programme, its incremental development from earlier initiatives hides the extent to which it differs from conventional approaches. But even in low-income countries in the South,

BOX 10.13
The Million Houses Programme in Sri Lanka

The Million Houses Programme in Sri Lanka launched in 1984 represented a shift in the role of government within housing from 'provider' with a high level of government expenditure in housing to enabler and supporter of individual or household efforts (and in urban areas community efforts) with a much lower level of government expenditure.

In the early 1980s, Sri Lanka's economic performance began to deteriorate, after several years of very rapid economic growth. There was also an escalation in costs of the direct construction programme and of building materials in general; the direct construction programme of the '100,000 houses programme' had reached only around a third of its target before being suspended in 1983. The government had to reduce the allocation of public funds to housing and urban development. A Task Force set up to examine the results of the 100,000 Houses Programme and to develop a new five-year programme for housing identified various weaknesses including the high cost and unrealistically high standards implicit in a conventional public housing construction programme, the failure to recognize the constraints on the key components of housing (e.g. finance, labour, building materials) and the failure to recognize the fact that most housing was constructed by households without government support and such housing was generally cheaper and more suited to

their needs than government produced units. The recommendations of this Task Force contributed to the change in approach when a new housing programme, the 'Million Houses Programme' was announced in 1983.

The Million Houses Programme was based on 'minimal intervention but maximum support by the state; maximum involvement of the builder families'. The core of the programme was small housing loans to low income rural and urban households to enable them to build or improve their houses. The Million Houses Programme was made up of six sub-programmes. Two were the responsibility of the National Housing Development Authority: the Urban and the Rural Housing Sub-Programmes. The other four were the Plantation Housing, the Mahaweli Housing, the Private Sector Housing and the Major Settlement Scheme Housing Sub-Programmes.

In both the rural and the urban sub-programmes, a considerable range of 'housing options and loans packages' were available for upgrading or repairing an existing house, for developing a new house where land is already available, for the provision of utilities (for instance water, sanitation, electricity) and registration of deeds, or where land, shelter and services were needed. The rural sub-programme was essentially loans to individual households; the urban sub-programme was far more organized around particular projects, because a loan programme for individual house-builders was not sufficient to improve conditions. Most low-income urban households live in settlements without formal land tenure, so

land tenure has to be regularized to create sufficient security of tenure to make the investment in housing worthwhile. Most urban settlements lacked roads, drains, piped water, and a system to dispose of human wastes and these could not be left to individual initiatives. Housing in urban areas is also subject to complicated planning and building regulations that need to be waived for low income housing projects. Thus, the project-based approach was indispensable.[150]

There was also a decentralization of decision-making, planning and implementation to local authorities and low-income communities themselves, largely through elected community development councils within each project area.

The rural sub-programme reached 258,762 families between 1984 and 1992; the urban sub-programme reached 38,125. By 1991, the Urban Housing Division had started the implementation of over 300 low-income housing projects, more than 100 of which were in Colombo and these included 75 slum and shanty settlement regularization and upgrading projects and 21 sites and services scheme. The urban sub-programme also pioneered Community Action Planning and Management—a methodology for poor communities to mobilize themselves and agree on what is to be done.

The Million Housing Programme was then superseded by the 1.5 million houses programme that seeks to reach 1.5 million households between 1990 and 1995 with one of 11 sub-programmes.

Sources: Sirivardana, Susil, 'Sri Lanka's experience with mobilization strategy with special reference to housing and poverty alleviation', Paper presented at the South Asian Regional Housing Conference, Colombo, June 1994; UNCHS (Habitat), *The Community Construction Contract System in Sri Lanka*, UNCHS (Habitat), Nairobi, 1994; UNCHS (Habitat), *The Urban Poor as Agents of Development: Community Action Planning in Sri Lanka*, UNCHS (Habitat), Nairobi, 1993; Pigott, Marni, *The Origin and Implications of the Million Houses Programme*, Sectoral Activities Programme Working Papers, International Labour Office, Geneva, 1986; Gamage, Nandasiri, 'Praja Sahayaka Sewaya (Community Assistance Service)', *Environment and Urbanization*, vol. 5, no. 2, Oct. 1994, 166–72.

the conventional wisdom remains that government agencies (usually at city or municipal level) have the responsibility for the provision and maintenance of infrastructure and services. Such responsibilities are set by law and embodied in specified norms and standards, irrespective of the institutional capacity to meet these responsibilities. The alternative model starts from the fact that it is people and the organizations they form that are responsible for developing housing and residential areas and that the role of government is to support their efforts. In terms of what they want to achieve, the two models do not differ much but they do differ in the relative roles (and powers) of the different actors and in the implementation.

Within the alternative model, community participation is integral because the basis of the government intervention is to identify what

individuals, households and community or neighbourhood organizations are doing (or would like to do if they had the resources) and seek to support this for the achievement of better results. Community participation in the traditional model may have been introduced but usually this was more to help in the rapid implementation of government-designed and implemented interventions and to help with maintenance—i.e. as a means to achieve ends, rather than as integral to the whole intervention. By contrast, in the example given in Box 10.14 of community initiatives in Guatemala City, external support responded to community priorities and community organizations often chose to take responsibility for organizing and managing the initiative. This helps explain the diversity of initiatives—for instance conventional 'upgrading' programmes usually offer a standard package which may not include aspects regarded as a priority. Where low-income communities have a say in what is provided and where women express their priorities, aspects such as health care and day-care often receive a high priority yet most upgrading programmes make little or no provision for either.

The work of the Orangi Pilot Project in supporting low-income groups to build and manage their own sewers was described in Chapter 9. Orangi is also an example of partnerships in the development of schools and health centres. While the government has provided 72 schools, private entrepreneurs and the inhabitants have developed over 600.[153] Orangi Pilot Project has a programme to help upgrade the physical and academic conditions of private schools.[154] The Carvajal Foundation in Cali (see below) set up a programme to improve the quality of schools run by low-income communities themselves.[155] There may be considerable potential for government support for schools developed by local residents or community organizations that prove much cheaper for government. This can also improve standards, coverage and equipment for the schools concerned. In the illegal or informal settlements in many urban centres, there are various voluntary organizations, charities and international private voluntary organizations running or contributing funding to schools, health care centres and other community services. This is usually without much coordination and with little or no support from government. The quality and coverage of such services would probably be much improved if the national agencies or ministries, the local authorities, the different third sector institutions and community organizations coordinated their work and sought to support each other's initiatives.

Box 10.15 describes the Carvajal Foundation's support for self-build housing and for paving streets in Aguablanca, a large, informal settlement of around 350,000 people in Cali, Colombia. This is only one of various support programmes by this Foundation. There is also a long-established programme of support for micro-enterprises and also programmes for food-shop owners and for education. The Foundation also works with the city authorities and other institutions in one of the most effective primary health-care systems in Latin America.[156] The work of the Foundation in Cali is much enhanced not only by its partnership with low income households and community organizations but also by its collaboration with the city authorities, government agencies and other institutions. The recycling programme described in Box 10.15 was to support a programme of road and pavement improvement and sewerage provided by the City Mayor's Office while the support for self-build housing also complements a major pro-gramme of serviced sites launched by the city government.[157]

Box 10.16 describes a programme that has similarities to the Million Houses Programme and the initiatives in Guatemala City in that it sought to mobilize individual and community resources that were combined with support from national and provincial government and it bene-fited a significant proportion of the population of Ouagadougou. It secured legal land tenure for more than 60,000 households and improved a range of services for a considerable portion of the lower income households. However, it differs in how it was implemented and in the extent and nature of 'participation'. It also failed to change the nature of the urban administration. It was a single initiative that did not lead to a change in what was a highly centralized administrative structure and to improved urban management. It proved incapable of supporting large scale tasks in which management was needed—for instance, efforts to improve sanitation, drainage and garbage collection. It also did not redistribute resources since most major investments during these years continued to go to the central area of Ouagadougou.

Citizen mobilization cannot promote the democratiza-tion of the decision-making process as well as providing a means of combating urban inequalities unless it is accompanied by a vigorous public policy taking respon-sibility for long-term financial and management options on the one hand and mechanisms for arbitra-tion and evening out socio-spatial inequalities on the other.[158]

Conclusions

Questions have been raised about 'who really benefits' from 'enabling approaches'. As noted by John Turner whose work did much to develop and promote the enabling approach, 'in high-income industrialized countries, as well as those still undergoing rapid urbanization, supra-local, corporate interests appear to be gaining more from enabling policies than those they are meant to support.'[159] The danger here is that the bal-ance between public responsibilities and private freedoms in the shelter process is in danger of shifting too far towards the latter, with the result that those with less 'market power' in the city (the urban poor) are denied access to adequate shelter and services. These dangers are inherent when more reliance is placed on market mechanisms in highly-unequal societies with imperfect markets and a weak state apparatus. Substandard housing, exploitative rents, hazardous jobs and very inade-quate provision for water, sanitation, drainage and other forms of infrastructure and services are just as likely as the thriving land, housing and employment markets which theory predicts.

BOX 10.14
Building local-national-international partnerships to address city problems in Guatemala City

In 1986, a newly elected government established a Committee for Attention to the Population of Precarious Areas in Guatemala City (COINAP). This became the official government counterpart to an urban basic services programme that UNICEF had initiated some years earlier. Committee members included representatives from several ministries, the different city authorities, local universities, NGOs and aid agencies, and representatives from community organizations where projects were underway. A considerable range of initiatives developed, including community health-promoters and pharmacies, improved water supplies managed by community organizations, house improvement and construction, community day care centres, improved sanitation, reafforestation and education. Some of these are described below.

The network of health-promoters: By 1993, 600 community health-promoters were active in 60 illegal or informal settlements and were serving over 150,000 inhabitants. Each was elected by their neighbourhood and gave eight hours a week of voluntary service. These health-promoters undertook a physical survey of the settlement, noting on a map all relevant social and geographic information. This provided project organizers with a precise idea of the resources available in a given area—for instance a health clinic, church, public water tap or shop—as well as health hazards such as garbage dumps or polluted streams. The health-promoters then worked with a technical team from COINAP to help identify the main causes of ill health and possible solutions that they could realistically address, drawing mainly on local resources. Each undertook house-to-house surveys to discover the specific health or social problems within their micro-zone. This formed the basis for developing a workplan and with training and technical support to help their efforts, the health promoters helped the inhabitants prevent diarrhoeal diseases—and to rapidly treat it when it occurred. They maintained health records for all the families in their micro-zone and helped ensure that all children received vaccinations. They also helped encourage the inhabitants to use local health services and developed health

education materials and 'community' pharmacies; some community-based laboratories have also been set up to carry out simple tests on blood, urine and faeces.

Water supply and sanitation: As health services improved, with a strong emphasis on education, community members sought ways to address other problems, especially water supply. Two different models for an improved water supply developed: the single-source tank and the well. Both combined the active involvement of a community group, reliance on technical assistance, and institutional co-operation from COINAP members. In the first, residents requested that Empagua, Guatemala's municipal water enterprise, install a single, large water tank in the neighbourhood. From this single source, the community created a supply network to reach individual residences, with UNICEF providing the funds for the pipes and other materials. Each family carried out the work necessary for their own home connection. The local community association receives one large bill from the water company and then collects fees from residents according to usage measured by individual meters. A resident, chosen by the community, was trained to manage billing and the collection of fees. Most of the fees are to cover actual costs but a portion is set aside for maintenance and the surplus will go towards other local infrastructure needs such as drains and sewers. For the community-managed well, a deep well is dug and water pumped from this is then distributed to households. The community has formed a small, private enterprise managed by local residents to operate the new water project.

Housing and urban improvement: A new programme was initiated in one of the settlements, El Mezquital, to improve housing conditions and water supply and provide paved roads and a park. This was to be funded through loans provided to the residents at a monthly cost that the relatively low-income households can afford. Entitled PROUME (Programme for the Urbanization of El Mezquital), this receives support from the World Bank, the government of Guatemala, the community and UNICEF. With regard to housing, 1,000 new homes will be built and 500 improved. Each family can choose one of five designs for its home, depending on its needs and the size of the lot. The designs allow for the construction of a second storey in later years. Loans are available for families wishing to upgrade their homes—or for

constructing a new unit with the loan covering construction materials and labour. The plan also includes street-paving, the installation of drains and sewers and the construction of a park and community centre. Each household will have to contribute labour towards these improvements and help to pay for materials.

New models for community-based day care: A young trainee-teacher developed a new model for day care in one precarious settlement through inviting children between the ages of four and six into her home during the afternoon, at a time when these children would normally be playing or wandering around the settlement. With no pre-school support, they were ill-prepared when they entered school at the age of seven and often had to repeat grades. Many were on the way to becoming street children as parents, discouraged by their lack of progress at school, allowed them to drop out and put them to work—but again in work for which the youngsters were usually ill-prepared. The improved performance of the young children when they entered school was so impressive that both parents and educators developed a pre-school centre. All aspects of the day care are agreed during meetings between the staff (that include two community health promoters) and the mothers. The local technical team helped design and build furniture for the Centre. The health promoters also monitor the growth and development of the children and within a year of the Centre's opening, more than three-quarters of the children met or surpassed standards in all areas. Fees are charged on a sliding scale, according to family income.

A different kind of day-care model was developed in another settlement where there was no space to construct a centre. A 'home day-care network' was set up with support from UNICEF and COINAP. With the help of a local health-promoter, five community women received one month's training in early childhood development. Each home day-care mother receives a small salary and her home is remodelled to provide water, toilets and appropriate outdoor space for ten children. Home day-care mothers from one community then helped to train others using printed materials and their own experience. The same model soon began operating in other crowded settlements, so that by 1993 about 250 children were receiving care in 25 homes that are part of the 'network'.

Source: Lair Espinosa and Oscar A. López Rivera, 'UNICEF's urban basic services programme in illegal settlements in Guatemala City', *Environment and Urbanization* vol. 6, no. 2, Oct. 1994.

BOX 10.15
The housing, recycling and education programme of the Carvajal Foundation in Cali, Colombia

Aguablanca is a large informal settlement with some 350,000 inhabitants in the city of Cali, Colombia. It contains three of the 20 communes that make up Cali. When the Carvajal Foundation began working in Aguablanca, there was no sanitary infrastructure, no electricity, no medical care and no public transport services. Horse-drawn carts sold water by the gallon (4.4 litres) at a very high price, and dangerously overloaded small jeeps carried people on very poor quality roads to the nearest bus stop. However, in spite of such adverse conditions, many people continued trying to turn their shacks into brick houses.

Among the most serious constraints on self-construction were the very high prices that people had to pay for construction materials because a large number of intermediaries were involved between the producer and the final retailer. Other problems were that the people did not know how to draw plans or structures, they had no access to credit for financing their homes, and even when they had designed their structures and raised finance, they could not get building construction licences from the city government.

Self-Build Housing: The Foundation's first project to support self-build housing was to build a construction materials warehouse. The warehouse is located in the middle of the squatter area and provides an outlet for producers of construction materials who can rent space from which to sell their products at wholesale prices. Some of those selling construction materials through the warehouse are micro-entrepreneurs, assisted through the Foundation's micro-enterprise programme.

Securing a retail outlet within the materials warehouse is, in effect, a guarantee of sales and therefore allows the entrepreneurs to rationalize production and produce at a lower cost than would otherwise have been possible. The Foundation charges each enterprise a small percentage of the sales value to cover the administrative costs of the project, including the cost of the warehouse, insurance and security. To meet the need for better technical assistance, the Foundation signed agreements with the two schools of architecture, to involve their students in helping people draw plans and structures, and build their homes.

The city government also established a small office in the warehouse from which people could obtain building licences. A second office was opened by the government owned Central Mortgage Bank to encourage people to open savings accounts and obtain loans to finance their housing construction. The Foundation has deliberately sought to promote the involvement of state agencies in providing housing loans and in developing improved guidelines for sub-dividing and construction work.

The self-build housing programme includes a series of practical workshops where people learn a range of skills including how to read plans, how to build foundations, walls and roofs and how to do the plumbing and wiring. The design of the process is such that 60 days after the first workshop, the family has a basic unit to move into. When a household begins to develop its own house and stops paying rent, it can afford to invest more of its budget in its home and, in two to three years, it can have a well-finished house. The programme also includes training in construction management for families who cannot do the building work themselves. On this course, they learn how to budget for the house and how to control the cash flow.

This method of guided self-construction has been particularly effective in reaching those with very low incomes. The programme has

directly built 11,160 homes and has contributed to the construction of a further 27,000. The city government of Cali has launched a large housing project for minimum wage families by selling lots and services to 22,500 families who will build their own homes, and the Foundation has offered assistance to 10 other Colombian cities and four countries to set up similar programmes.

Recycling and street paving: Since the district of Aguablanca had no sewage system, the government was unable to pave the streets. With no paved roads for the garbage collection trucks, the garbage collection service was unreliable, and people threw their rubbish onto the roadside or onto piles scattered throughout the settlement. A joint programme for road development was negotiated in which the base layer (foundation), sewerage system and pavements would be provided by the City Mayor's Office. The community's contribution was to pave the streets with cement blocks (which can be removed to construct the sewer and then laid back), and to collect materials for recycling to pay for the blocks. The community organized itself into committees, each committee being formed by the families living in one block, on both sides of the same street.

The Foundation opened a recycling centre. Each committee holds an account at the centre and receives a credit for the value of the materials that they bring in and weigh. As soon as each committee accumulates enough money to pay for the cement blocks, the municipality prepares the street for paving and the neighbours organize a 'block-laying day'. A whole neighbourhood has paved its streets in this way. During the process, members have learned more about the value of garbage. The centre has extended its services and individual households have opened accounts to earn funds for construction materials, utility bills, mortgage payments and medical or dental visits.

Source: Cruz, Luis Fernando, 'NGO Profile: Fundación Carvajal; the Carvajal Foundation', *Environment and Urbanization*, vol. 6, no. 2, Oct. 1994.

The distinction between 'enabling' policies and 'market-driven' policies becomes very significant. As noted already, the enabling policies recommended within the Global Shelter Strategy do not necessarily imply less government intervention—but a different kind of government intervention. Governments intervene to help those whose housing needs and priorities are not met by the 'market' (for instance those who lack the income or assets to enter the housing market) or have particular needs that the market does not cater for, like vulnerable groups or the elderly. Its interventions usually centre on ensuring that the resources needed for housing purchase, construction or improvement

are available at the lowest possible price— especially land, building materials and finance. It also structures its intervention in ways that support the resources and skills that low-income individuals, households and neighbourhood and community organizations can bring to housing construction or improvement. In many instances, its interventions are best realized through non-profit intermediaries as in NGOs providing technical and legal advice to the residents of low-income settlements in need of improvement. Or social banks such as the Grameen Bank or government institutions that directly support community initiatives such as FONHAPO or the

BOX 10.16
Why mobilize town dwellers? Joint management in Ouagadougou (1983–1990)

Between 1983 and 1990, the government of Burkina Faso sought a new way of providing infrastructure and service provision in the settlements that had formed around the central areas of Ouagadougou. This centred on mobilizing individual and community labour and resources organized by 'revolutionary committees' in 30 different urban neighbourhoods with national and provincial government agencies providing technical assistance and some counterpart funding.

In this period, more than 60,000 plots of land were provided with legal rights of occupancy. Having obtained security of tenure, the residents were invited to organize themselves under the aegis of their revolutionary committees to supply the necessary labour and cash resources to provide facilities in their areas, in exchange for which government agencies undertook to provide technical supervision and a limited amount of 'counterpart funds'. This achieved very substantial improvements in local public facilities and helped the poorer peripheral areas 'catch up' with the central city.

Elected by the population of the thirty urban sectors, the revolutionary committees allocated the plots and were mainly responsible for the construction of schools, dispensaries, crèches, sports grounds, and markets. These committees also managed certain services such as the distribution of drinking water from public hydrants. In managing these hydrants, the committees purchased the water from the national water and sanitation agency and sold the water to users. Although prices to users rose, this also meant a service that reached a higher proportion of the population and that operated more effectively than previously as water was more often available, maintenance was properly done and closure as a result of non-payment relatively rare.

Initially, local resources came mostly from taxes illegally imposed on the newly defined plots but later, as this revenue source ran out, more commonly from user-fees (including those for water) and fees raised for other tasks (for instance school construction).

This mobilization worked well for projects that could be completed quickly and rapidly gave citizens a return on their efforts. It was responsible for constructing many schools with a successful partnership between local residents (who raised funds and contributed some labour), the revolutionary committees who organized the process and the various state agencies which provided particular components (for instance the roofing sheets, metal doors, windows and furniture and also the teachers to run them). 117 new classrooms were built in the periurban areas of Ouagadougou between 1984 and 1989. Health facilities, drug stores, sports grounds, crèches, public latrines and offices for the revolutionary committees were also built in similar ways.

This system of joint management has both positive and negative aspects. It proved possible to tap into new human and cash resources in ways that brought substantial benefits to populations who had previously been largely excluded from the benefit of urban development. Whilst regularizing the land title situation in the outlying areas was the decisive trigger for this mobilization of town dwellers, it was deployed within an extremely centralized institutional framework which was not tempered by any subsequent administrative reform.

However, the system proved incapable of undertaking large-scale tasks in which management was needed. For instance, efforts to improve sanitation, drainage and garbage collection, all much needed, failed because they required a sustained investment and involvement. It did not trigger autonomy but encouraged each urban sector to lobby for more resources from the government and to compete with each other in doing so. It also did not redistribute resources since most major investments during these years continued to go to the central area of Ouagadougou.

Source: Jaglin, Sylvy, 'Why mobilize town dwellers; joint management in Ouagadougou, 1983–1990', *Environment and Urbanization*, vol. 6, no. 2, Oct. 1994, 111–32.

Urban Community Development Office in Thailand—whose work is described in more detail in Chapter 11. Or it finds that the scale and scope of its work is much enhanced by working with NGOs such as the Orangi Pilot Project or private foundations such as the Carvajal Foundation. Government may also have to intervene to ensure that market forces keep a downward pressure on prices, in ensuring that a competitive market exists for housing finance, building materials and land. Where there is no competitive market to do so, prices need to be kept at reasonable levels and the quality of products or services needs to be monitored (for instance where private businesses provide piped water services). It is difficult to generalize from the examples of government programmes as social, economic and political circumstances vary from city to city and country to country. Democratic pressures are important to ensure that market failures are addressed and that the needs of those who cannot enter 'the market' are catered for. In most societies, the capacities of individuals, households and resident or community organizations to invest in and help build and manage infrastructure and services remains underappreciated.

The potential conflict in enabling shelter strategies between the need for liberalization ('freedom to build', private-sector incentives) and the need for regulation (to correct market imperfections and curb speculation) is a particular illustration of the wider dilemma facing all economies that aim to be more equitable but also to remain competitive within regional and international markets. The successful implementation of an enabling approach depends on the ability of governments and citizens to find the right balance between these two sets of principles.[160] The two should also not always be seen as opposites in that many programmes that improve infrastructure and housing conditions and that increase the incomes and assets of lower-income groups also contribute considerably to economic growth.

As the study on European housing policies whose findings were summarized earlier in this chapter notes, the key issue is 'what sort of market–state mix' will produce what sort of outcome.[161] This study notes that governments must act to ensure sufficient supplies of inexpensive land and capital for housing. It also suggests that governments should intervene to promote a diversity of forms of housing type and tenure—

especially forms of housing tenure that are less costly than owner-occupation but where the occupier has secure tenure. It stresses the need for more autonomous local authorities who can respond to the particular needs and priorities of their inhabitants and localities. But the ambitions of more autonomous local authorities must also be checked by democratic structures. These are issues that are as relevant to the South as to the North and more pressing, given much worse housing conditions, more inequality in the distribution of incomes and assets and, in most instances, a more rapid expansion in both need and demand.

Notes and References

1. UNCHS (Habitat), *Review of National Action to Provide Housing for All Since Habitat I: The United Nations Conference on Human Settlements*, HS/C/15/5, 1994; and Edwards, Michael A., *Review of National Action to Provide Housing for All Since Habitat I*, a report for UNCHS (Habitat), Nairobi, 1994. Sections 10.1 and 10.2 of this chapter draw heavily on these documents.

2. Mayo, Stephen K. and Shlomo Angel, *Housing: Enabling Markets to Work*, A World Bank Policy Paper, World Bank, Washington DC, 1993.

3. *Ibid.*

4. Colclough, C. and J. Manor, *States or Markets? Neo-Liberalism and the Development Policy Debate*, Clarendon Press, Oxford, 1991.

5. UNCHS (Habitat), *Public/Private Partnerships in Enabling Shelter Strategies*, Nairobi, 1993.

6. There is some contradiction in some donor agencies and governments between participation as a political process (i.e. as an end) and as a means to achieve cost recovery and greater efficiency in economic development.

7. UNCHS (Habitat), *Evaluation of Experience with Initiating Enabling Housing Strategies*, Nairobi, 1991, 4.

8. Mayo and Angel 1993, *op. cit.*

9. World Bank, *Learning by Doing: World Bank Lending for Urban Development 1972–82*, Washington DC, 1983.

10. World Bank, *Shelter: Poverty and Basic Needs*, Washington DC, 1980; World Bank, *Urban Policy and Economic Development: an Agenda for the 1990s*, Washington DC, 1991.

11. Moser, Caroline O. N., Alicia J. Herbert and Roza E. Makonnen, *Urban Poverty in the Context of Structural Adjustment; Recent Evidence and Policy Responses*, TWU Discussion Paper DP #4, the Urban Development Division, World Bank, Washington DC, 1993.

12. Buckley, Robert and Steve Mayo, 'Housing Policy in Developing Economies: evaluating the macroeconomic impacts', *Review of Urban and Regional Development Studies*, vol. 2, 1989, 27.

13. Cohen, Michael A., 'Macroeconomic adjustment and the city', *Cities*, vol. 7, no. 1, Feb. 1990, 49–59.

14. Mayo and Angel 1993, *op. cit.*, 2.

15. Barlow, James and Simon Duncan, *Success and Failure in Housing Provision: European Cities Compared*, Pergamon, 1994.

16. Hardoy, Jorge E. and David Satterthwaite, *Squatter Citizen: Life in the Urban Third World*, Earthscan Publications, London, 1989.

17. Berghäll, Outi, 'The enabling concept: an unachievable ideal or a practical guide to action', Paper prepared for the UNU/WIDER Conference on 'Human Settlements in the Changing Global Political and Economic Processes', Helsinki, 1995.

18. Cahill, Michael, *The New Social Policy*, Blackwell, Oxford and Cambridge, Mass., 1994.

19. Barlow and Duncan 1994, *op. cit.*

20. *Ibid.*

21. Schmidt, S., 'Convergence theory, labour movements and corporatism: the case of housing', *Scandinavian Housing and Planning Research*, vol. 6, no. 2, 1989, 82–102 quoted in Barlow and Duncan 1994, *op. cit.*

22. *Ibid.*

23. See for instance the work of Housing Trust Funds created by local and state governments in the United States. See also van Vliet, William (ed.), *Affordable Housing and Urban Development in the US; Learning from Failure and Success*, Sage Publications, Newbury Park, California, 1996.

24. Esping-Anderson, G., *The Three Worlds of Welfare Capitalism*, Polity, Cambridge, 1990.

25. Sigtuna, Sollentuna, Upplands-Vasby.

26. Hardoy, Jorge E. and David Satterthwaite, *Shelter: Need and Response; Housing, Land and Settlement Policies in Seventeen Third World Nations*, John Wiley and Sons, Chichester, 1981.

27. UNCHS (Habitat), *Shelter: From Projects to National Strategies*, Nairobi, 1990, 35.

28. UNCHS (Habitat), *The Global Shelter Strategy to the Year 2000*, Nairobi, 1990, 14–15.

29. Para 7.52, UNCED, *Agenda 21: Promoting Sustainable Human Settlements Development*, 1992.

30. Struyk, R., 'Early experience with enabling national housing strategies', *Cities*, vol. 7, no. 4, Nov. 1990, 315–22; Wakely, Patrick, Ronaldo Ramirez, and Babar Mumtaz, *The Formulation of National Shelter Strategies: Six Case Studies*, Working Paper 59, Development Planning Unit, University College London, 1992; UNCHS (Habitat) 1991, *op. cit.*; UNCHS (Habitat), *Global Shelter Strategy to the Year 2000: GSS in Action*, Nairobi, 1992; UNCHS (Habitat), *Developing a National Shelter Strategy: lessons from four countries*, Nairobi, 1990.

31. UNCHS (Habitat), *Global Shelter Strategy to the Year 2000: GSS in Action*, Nairobi, 1992, 91–100.

32. UNCHS (Habitat), *Evaluation of Experience with Initiating Enabling Housing Strategies*, Nairobi, 1991.

33. Wakely, Patrick, Ronaldo Ramirez, and Babar Mumtaz, *The Formulation of National Shelter Strategies: Six Case Studies*, Working Paper 59, Development Planning Unit, University College London, 1992, 2.

34. Hoffman, M. L., C. Walker, R. J. Struyk and K. Nelson, 'Rental housing in urban Indonesia', *Habitat International*, vol. 15, 1990, 181–206; van der Hoff, Robert and Florian Steinberg, *The Integrated Urban Infrastructure Development Programme and Urban Management Innovations in Indonesia*, IHS Working Papers no. 7, Rotterdam, 1993.

35. Mitullah, W., 'Formulation and implementation of shelter strategies for the urban poor in Kenya: the missing link', Paper presented to the 2nd Symposium on *Housing for the Urban Poor*, Birmingham.

36. Stren, Richard, 'Urban Housing in Africa: the changing role of government policy', in P. Amis and P. Lloyd (eds.), *Housing Africa's Urban Poor*, Manchester University Press/International African Institute, Manchester, 1990.

37. UNCHS (Habitat), *Strategies and practical modalities for increased co-operation in human settlements between government institutions, NGOs and CBOs at the local, state/provincial and national levels*, Nairobi, 1992, 21.

38. Patel, Sheela and S. Burra, 'Forging a link: an institutional strategy to access housing finance for the urban poor', Paper presented to the 2nd Symposium on Housing for the Urban Poor, Birmingham, 1994, 1.

39. Richmond, P., 'Policy and practice in the provision of housing for the low-income sectors of Bolivia', Paper presented to the 2nd Symposium on Housing for the Urban Poor, Birmingham, 1994.

40. UNCHS (Habitat), *Developing a National Shelter Strategy: lessons from four countries*, Nairobi, 1990, 15.

41. Struyk 1990, *op. cit.*

42. Wakely and others 1992, *op. cit.*

43. *Ibid.*

44. Murphy, D., *The Urban Poor: Land and Housing*, Asian Coalition for Housing Rights/Habitat International Coalition, 1993.

45. Marcussen, L., *Third-World Housing in Social and Spatial Development*, Avebury-Gower, Aldershot, 1990.

46. UNCHS (Habitat), *Global Shelter Strategy to the Year 2000: Sub-regional Seminars to Support National Action*, Nairobi, 1991.

47. Jones, G. and P. Ward (eds.), *Methodology for Land and Housing Market Analysis*, UCL Press, London, 1994.

48. Wakely and others, 1992, *op. cit.*

49. UNCHS (Habitat), *Public/Private Partnerships in Enabling Shelter Strategies*, Nairobi, 1993.

50. *Ibid.* 14.

51. Zearly, T., 'Housing Reforms in Mexico', *Finance and Development*, March 1994.

52. Van der Hoff and Steinberg 1993, *op. cit.*

53. Wakely and others, 1992, *op. cit.*

54. *Ibid.*

55. *Ibid.*

56. UNCHS (Habitat), *Global Report on Human Settlements 1986*, Oxford University Press, Oxford, 1987.

57. Berghall 1995, *op. cit.*

58. Silas, Johan, 'Surabaya; background paper', background paper prepared for the Global Report, 1994.

59. Mehta, Dinesh, 'Community based programmes of urban poverty alleviation in India', Paper presented at the RWCBP-UPA, Kuala Lumpur, 1994.

60. UNCHS (Habitat), *The Urban Poor as Agents of Development: Community Action Planning in Sri Lanka*, Nairobi, 1993.

61. UNCHS (Habitat), *Evaluation of Experience with Initiating Enabling Housing Strategies*, Nairobi, 1991.

62. See for instance Peattie, Lisa, 'Participation: a case study of how invaders organize, negotiate and interact with government in Lima, Peru', *Environment and Urbanization*, vol. 2, no. 1, April 1990, 19–30; Sobreira de Moura, Alexandrina, 'Brasilia Teimosa—the organization of a low income settlement in Recife, Brazil', *Development Dialogue*, 1987, 152–69; Moser, Caroline O. N., 'Mobilization is women's work: struggles for infrastructure in Guayaquil, Ecuador', in Caroline O. N. Moser and Linda Peake (eds.), *Women, Housing and Human Settlements*, Tavistock Publications, London and New York, 1987, 166–94; van der Linden, Jan, 'Squatting by organized invasion—a new reply to a failing housing policy?', *Third World Planning Review*, vol. 4, no. 4, Nov. 1982, 400–12.

63. Perez Perdomo, Rogelio and Pedro Nicken (with the assistance of Elizabeth Fassano and Marcos Vilera), 'The law and home ownership in the barrios of Caracas', in Alan Gilbert, Jorge E.

Hardoy and Ronaldo Ramirez (Editors), *Urbanization in Contemporary Latin America*, John Wiley and Sons, Chichester, 1982, 205–29.

64. Hardoy and Satterthwaite 1989, *op. cit.*

65. Asthana, S., 'Integrated slum improvement in Visakhapatnam, India', *Habitat International*, vol. 18, no.1, 1994, 57–70.

66. Silas, Johan and Eddy Indrayana, 'Kampung Banyu Urip', in Bertha Turner (Editor), *Building Community, a Third World Case Book*, Habitat International Coalition, London, 1988.

67. Hardoy and Satterthwaite 1989, *op. cit.*

68. This paragraph draws its information from Hasan, Arif, *Housing Policies and Approaches in a Changing Urban Context*, Paper prepared for UNCHS (Habitat) and the PGCHS, Katholieke Universiteit, Leuven, Draft, 1994.

69. Asian Development Bank, *Pakistan Low Cost Housing Project*, 1989, quoted in Hasan, Arif, *Housing Policies and Approaches in a Changing Urban Context*, Paper prepared for UNCHS (Habitat) and the PGCHS, Katholieke Universiteit, Leuven, Draft, 1994.

70. Hasan 1992, *op. cit.*

71. For one example, see Silas, Johan, 'Spatial structure, housing delivery, land tenure and the urban poor in Surabaya, Indonesia', in Shlomo Angel, Raymon W. Archer, Sidhijai Tanphiphat and Emiel A. Wegelin (eds.), *Land for Housing the Poor*, Select Books, Singapore, 1983.

72. Silas and Indrayana 1988, *op. cit.*

73. Silas 1994, *op. cit.*

74. *Ibid.*

75. UNCHS (Habitat) 1993, *op. cit.*

76. Mehta, Dinesh, 'Community based programmes of urban poverty alleviation in India', Paper presented at the RWCBP-UPA, Kuala Lumpur, 1994.

77. Moser, Caroline O. N., 'Women, human settlements and housing: a conceptual framework for analysis and policy-making', in Caroline O. N. Moser and Linda Peake (eds.), *Women, Housing and Human Settlements*, Tavistock Publications, London and New York, 1987, 12–32.

78. UNCHS (Habitat), *Women in Human Settlements Development: Getting the Issues Right*, UNCHS (Habitat), Nairobi, 1995.

79. Moser, Caroline O. N., *Gender Planning and Development; Theory, Practice and Training*, Routledge, London and New York, 1993.

80. Elson, D. 'Male bias in macro-economics: the case of structural adjustment' in D. Elson (editor), *Male Bias in the Development Process*, Manchester University Press, Manchester, 1991; Moser 1993, *op. cit.*

81. See for instance different issues of *Women and Shelter*, the newsletter published by the Women and Shelter Network of the Habitat International Coalition. See also Bell, Judith Kjellberg, 'Guide to the literature: Women, environment and

urbanization', *Environment and Urbanization*, vol. 3, no. 1, Oct. 1991.

82. Moser 1993, *op. cit*; Sen, Gita and Caren Grown, *Development, Crises and Alternative Visions: Third World Women's Perspectives*, Development Alternatives with Women for a New Era (DAWN), Earthscan Publications, London, 1987.

83. See Moser, Caroline O. N., 'Introduction' in Moser, Caroline O. N. and Linda Peake (eds.), *Women, Housing and Human Settlements*, Tavistock Publications, London and New York, 1987, 1–11.

84. UNCHS (Habitat), *Women in Human Settlements Development: Getting the Issues Right*, Nairobi, 1995.

85. Patel, Sheela and Celine D'Cruz, 'The Mahila Milan crisis credit scheme; from a seed to a tree', *Environment and Urbanization*, vol. 5, no. 1, 1993, 9–17.

86. See Lee-Smith, Diana and Hinchey Trujillo, Catalina 'The struggle to legitimize subsistence: Women and sustainable development', *Environment and Urbanization*, vol. 4, no. 1, April, 1992, 77–84.

87. Global Forum '94, Report of the speech by Mohamed Yunus, executive director of the Grameen Bank.

88. These include Moser, Caroline O. N. and Linda Peake (eds.), *Women, Housing and Human Settlements*, Tavistock Publications, London and New York, 1987, incl. conceptual chapters and case studies in Guayaquil, Managua, Querétaro, Brazil, Nairobi, Colombo and Sri Lanka; Dandekar, Hemalata C. (ed.), *Shelter, Women and Development; First and Third World Perspectives*, George Wahr, Ann Arbor (USA), 1993, incl. 50 papers from an international conference held in May 1992; and a series of case studies published by the National Swedish Institute for Building Research including: Schlyter, Ann, *Women Householders and Housing Strategies: the case of George, Lusaka*, Social and Behavioural Sciences Series No. 14; Larsson, Anita, *Women Householders and Housing Strategies: the case of Gabarone, Botswana*, 1989; Schlyter, Ann, *Women Householders and Housing Strategies: the case of Harare, Zimbabwe*, Stockholm, 1990; and Larsson, Anita and Ann Schlyter, *Gender Contracts and Housing Conflicts in Southern Africa*, 1994.

- Among other recent published material on women and human settlements are:
- Banaynal-Fernandez, Tessie, 'Fighting violence against women: the Cebu Experience', *Environment and Urbanization*, vol. 6, no. 2, Oct. 1994.
- Beall, Jo, 'The Gender Dimensions of Urbanisation and Urban Poverty', Paper prepared for the seminar on Women in Urban Areas, Division for the Advancement of Women, United Nations Office at Vienna, Vienna, 1993.
- Beall, Jo and Caren Levy, 'Moving towards the gendered city', Overview paper prepared for the Preparatory

Committee for Habitat II, Geneva, 1994.

- Beall, Jo, 'Integrating the gender variable into urban development', Background paper to the DAC Meeting on Aid for Urban Development, Paris, Nov. 1992.
- Falu, Ana and Mirina Curutchet, 'Rehousing the urban poor: looking at women first', *Environment and Urbanization*, vol. 3, no. 2, Oct. 1991, 23–38.
- Feijoo, Maria del Carmen and Hilda Herzer (eds.), *Las Mujeres y la Vida de las Ciudades (Women and Urban Life)*, GEL/IIED-America Latina, Buenos Aires, 1991.
- Huysman, Marijk, 'Waste picking as a survival strategy in Bangalore; a case study of women waste pickers', *Environment and Urbanization*, vol. 6, no. 2, Oct. 1994.
- Kanji, Nazneen, 'Gender, poverty and structural adjustment in Harare, Zimbabwe', *Environment and Urbanization*, vol. 7, no. 2, April 1995.
- Klak, T. and J. K. Hey, 'Gender and state bias in Jamaican housing programs', *World Development*, vol. 20, 1992, 213–27.
- Lee-Smith, Diana and Ann Schlyter, 'Women, environment and urbanization', *Environment and Urbanization*, vol. 3, no. 1, Oct. 1991.
- Levy, Caren, 'Gender and the environment: the challenge of cross-cutting issues in development policy and planning', *Environment and Urbanization*, vol. 4, no. 1, April 1992, 120–35.
- Mazingira Institute, *Women's Participation in Shelter Strategies at Community Level in Urban Informal Settlements*, Prepared for UNCHS (Habitat), Nairobi, 1993.
- McLeod, Ruth, *Daughters of Sysiphus; a Study of Gender-Related Behaviour Differences in the Search for Shelter among Low-Income Heads of Household in Kingston, Jamaica*, UNCHS (UNCHS) Habitat, Nairobi, 1990.
- Mitullah, Winnie, 'Hawking as a survival strategy for the urban poor in Nairobi: the case of women', *Environment and Urbanization*, vol. 3, no. 2, Oct. 1991, 13–22.
- Moser, Caroline O. N., 'Housing policy and women: towards a gender aware approach', DPU Gender and Planning Working Paper no. 7, University College London, 1985.
- Moser, C. O. N. and S. Chant, *The Role of Women in the Execution of Low-Income Housing Projects Training Module*, DPU Gender and Planning Working Paper no. 6, University College London, 1985.
- Moser, Caroline O. N., *Gender Planning and Development; Theory, Practice and Training*, Routledge, London and New York, 1993.
- Oruwari, Yomi, 'The changing role of women in families and their housing needs: a case study of Port Harcourt, Nigeria', *Environment and Urbanization*, vol. 3, no. 2, Oct. 1991, 6–12.

- Sylvia Chant (ed.), *Gender and Migration in Developing Countries*, Belhaven Press, London, 1992, 197–206.
- UNCHS (Habitat), *Building-Related Income Generation for Women: Lessons from Experience*, HS/197/90E, Nairobi, 1990.
- UNCHS (Habitat), *Women in Human Settlements Development: Getting the Issues Right*, Nairobi, 1995.
- UNCHS (Habitat), *Focus on Women*, Nairobi, 1991.

89. See for instance Falu, Ana and Mirina Curutchet, 'Rehousing the urban poor: looking at women first', *Environment and Urbanization*, vol. 3, no. 2, Oct. 1991, 23–38 and Machado, Leda M. V., 'The problems for woman-headed households in a low-income housing programme in Brazil', and Nimpuno-Parente, Paula, 'The struggle for shelter: women in a site and service project in Nairobi, Kenya', in Moser and Peake (eds.), 1987, *op. cit.*

90. See Moser 1993, *op. cit.*

91. UNCHS (Habitat), *Women in Human Settlements Development: Getting the Issues Right*, Nairobi, 1995.

92. Moser, Caroline O. N., 'Mobilization is women's work: struggles for infrastructure in Guayaquil, Ecuador', in Moser and Peake (eds.), 1987, *op. cit.* 166–94.

93. See for instance Vance, Irene, 'More than bricks and mortar: women's participation in self-help housing in Managua, Nicaragua', in Moser and Peake (eds.), 1987, *op. cit.* 139–65.

94. Barrig, Maruja, 'Women and development in Peru: old models, new actors', *Environment and Urbanization*, vol. 3, no. 2, Oct. 1991, 66–70.

95. See the example of Canteras in Bogota in NGO Profile—Fedevivienda, the National Federation of Self-Help Community Housing Organizations in Colombia, *Environment and Urbanization*, vol. 3, no. 2, Oct. 1991, 87–91 and the story of Regina Ntongana in Crossroads in NGO Profile—Habitat International Coalition Women and Shelter Network, *Environment and Urbanization*, vol. 3, no. 2, Oct. 1991, 82–6.

96. Asthana, Sheena, 'Integrated slum improvement in Visakhapatnam, India: problems and prospects', *Habitat International*, vol. 18, no. 1, 1994, 66.

97. HIC Women and Shelter Network, *Women and Shelter*, no. 6, April 1993, 8.

98. UNCHS (Habitat), *Global Strategy for Shelter to the Year 2000*, HS/266/91E, Nairobi, 1991, 28–9.

99. UNCHS (Habitat), *Evaluation of Experience with Initiating Enabling Housing Strategies*, Nairobi, 1991.

100. Moser 1993, *op. cit.*

101. Leckie, Scott, 'Housing as a human right', *Environment and Urbanization*, vol. 1, no. 2, Oct. 1989, 90–108.

102. This covenant has a long history in that the Commission on Human Rights drafted this Covenant between 1947 and

1954 and originally it was part of a single covenant that included civil and political rights as well. This covenant was adopted by the United Nations General Assembly in 1966 and came into force in 1976.

103. UNGA Resolution 42/146, 7 Dec. 1987.

104. NGO Profile: The Centre on Housing Rights and Evictions (COHRE), *Environment and Urbanization*, vol. 6, no. 1, April 1994, 147–57.

105. See for instance UN documents E/CN.4/Sub.2/1992/15 and E/CN.4/Sub.2/1993/15.

106. COHRE 1994, *op. cit.*

107. *Ibid.*

108. Dua, A., *Management of Bombay Housing Renewal Programme—a Critique*, 27th Research Report, IHSP Human Settlement Management Institute, New Delhi, 1991; Wadhva, Kiran, 'Support measures to promote low-income rental housing: the case of India', UNCHS (Habitat), mimeo, 1993.

109. UNCHS (Habitat), *Support Measures to Promote Rental Housing for Low Income Groups*, HS/294/93E, Nairobi, 1993.

110. See also *Estudio Demográficos y Urbanos*, vol. 2, no. 1, 1987, El Colegio de México (special issue on the post-earthquake reconstruction); Ziccardi, A. (1986), 'Política de vivienda para un espacio destruido', *Revista Mexicana de Sociología*, vol. 48, no. 2; Connolly, P., R. Coulomb y E. Duhau, *Cambiar de Casa pero no de Barrio*, México DF, CENVI/Universidad Autónoma Metropolitana, Azcapotzalco, 1991.

111. Hoffman and others 1990, *op. cit.*.

112. Gilbert, Alan and Ann Varley, *Landlord and Tenant: Housing the Poor in Urban Mexico*, Routledge, London, 1991.

113. *Ibid.*

114. UNCHS (Habitat), *Support Measures to Promote Rental Housing for Low Income Groups*, HS/294/93E, Nairobi, 1993.

115. Payne, Geoffrey, *Informal Housing and Land Subdivisions in Third World Cities: A Review of the Literature*, CENDEP, Oxford, 1989; Nientied, P., P. Robben and J. van der Linden, 'Low-income housing improvement and displacement: some comparative evidence', in B. C. Aldrich and R. S. Sanhu (eds.), *Housing in Asia: Problems and Perspectives*, Rawat Publishers, Jaipur, 1990, 25–42.

116. Baken, Riovert-Jan, Peter Nientied, Monique Peltenburg and Mirjam Zaaier, *Neighbourhood Consolidation and Economic Development of Informal Settlements*, IHS Working Papers 3, Institute for Housing and Urban Development Studies, Rotterdam, 1991; Strassmen 1982, Salmen 1989; Taylor, J. L., 'Evaluation of the Jakarta Kampung Improvement Programme', in R. J. Skinner, J. L. Taylor and E. A. Wegelin (eds.), *Shelter Upgrading for the Urban Poor: Evaluation of Third World Experience*, Island Publishing Housing, Manila, 1987.

117. See for instance Baken and others 1991, *op. cit.*

118. UNCHS (Habitat), *Support Measures to Promote Rental Housing for Low Income Groups*, HS/294/93E, Nairobi, 1993.

119. Edwards, M. 'Rental housing and the urban poor: Africa and Latin America compared', in Amis and Lloyd 1990, *op. cit.*; Gilbert and Varley 1991, *op. cit.*

120. UNCHS (Habitat), *Rental Housing: Proceedings of an Expert Group Meeting*, Nairobi, Kenya, 1990.

121. Malpezzi, S. 'Rental housing in developing countries: issues and constraints', in *Rental Housing: Proceedings of an Expert Group Meeting*, UNCHS (Habitat), Nairobi, 1990.

122. Hardoy and Satterthwaite 1989, *op. cit.*

123. *Ibid.*

124. Payne, G. K., 'Introduction', G. K. Payne (ed.), *Low Income Housing in the Developing World—the Role of Sites and Services and Settlement Upgrading*, John Wiley and Sons, Chichester, 1984.

125. *Ibid.*

126. *Ibid.*; and Rodell, M. J., 'Sites and services and low-income housing', in R. J. Skinner and M. J. Rodell (eds.), *People, Poverty and Shelter*, Methuen, London and New York, 1984.

127. Andreasen, Jorgen, 'The poor don't squat: the case of Thika, Kenya', *Environment and Urbanization*, vol. 1, no. 2, Oct. 1989, 16–26.

128. See for instance the large scale serviced site programme implemented in Cali, Colombia which is one among many initiatives to reach lower income groups with improved incomes and housing conditions—Guerrero V., Rodrigo, 'Innovative programs for the urban poor in Cali, Colombia', in Bonnie Bradford and Margaret A. Gwynne (eds.), *Down to Earth: Community Perspectives on Health, Development and the Environment*, Kumarian Press, West Hartford, 1995, 17–22.

129. Raj, M. and P. Nientied (eds.), *Housing and Finance in Third-World Urban Development*, Oxford and IBH, New Delhi, 1990.

130. UNCHS (Habitat), *Improving Income and Housing: Employment-generation in Low-income Settlements*, Nairobi, 1989.

131. Silas 1994, *op. cit.*

132. Iskander, M. *UNICEF Co-operation with Municipal Governments*, UNICEF, New York, 1992.

133. United Nations, *Industrial Statistics Yearbook 1991* vol. II, *Commodity Production Statistics 1982–1991*, New York, 1993.

134. UNCHS (Habitat), *Journal of the Network of African countries on Local Building Materials and Technologies*, vol. 2, no. 2, May 1993.

135. For a detailed treatment of the subject see UNCHS (Habitat), *Small-scale Production of Portland Cement*, HS/281/93E, 1993.

136. For detailed treatment of the subject see: UNCHS (Habitat), *Vertical-Shaft Limekiln Technology*, HS/303/93E, 1993; Neville Hill, Stafford Holmes and David Mather, *Lime and Other Alternative Cements*, Intermediate Technology Publications, London, 1992; and UNCHS (Habitat), *Endogenous Capacity-building for the Production of Binding Materials in the Construction Industry—Selected case studies*, HS/292/93E, 1993.

137. For a detailed treatment of the subject see Hill, Holmes and Mather 1992, *op. cit.*; UNCHS (Habitat), *Endogenous Capacity-building for the Production of Binding Materials in the Construction Industry—Selected Case Studies*, HS/292/93E; BASIN-NEWS, Building Advisory Service and Information Network, GATE, SKAT, IT, CRATerre (all issues), Switzerland; UNCHS (Habitat), *A Compendium of Information on Selected Low-cost Building Materials*, HS/137/88E, 1988; UNCHS (Habitat), *Journal of the Network of African Countries on Local Building Materials and Technologies*, vol. 1, no. 1, April 1989.

138. UNCHS (Habitat), *Earth Construction Technology*, HS/265/92E, 1992; UNCHS (Habitat), *Journal of the Network of African Countries on local Building Materials and Technologies*, vol. 1, no. 4, Sept. 1991; UNCHS (Habitat), *Bibliography on Soil Construction*, HS/169/90E, 1990; BASIN-NEWS, Building Advisory Service and Information Network, GATE, SKAT, IT, CRATerre (all issues), Switzerland; UNCHS (Habitat), 'Data Sheets on Soil Construction', no date; UNCHS (Habitat), *A Compendium of Information on Selected Low-cost Building Materials*, HS/137/88E, 1988.

139. For detailed treatment of the subject see UNCHS (Habitat), *Journal of the Network of African countries on Local Building Materials and Technologies*, vol. 2, no. 2, May 1993.

140. For detailed treatment of the subject please see BASIN-NEWS, Building Advisory Service and Information Network, GATE, SKAT, IT, CRATerre (all issues), Switzerland; UNCHS (Habitat), *A Compendium of Information on Selected Low-cost Building Materials*, HS/137/88E, Nairobi, 1988; UNCHS (Habitat), *Journal of the Network of African Countries on Local Building Materials and Technologies*, vol. 1, no. 3 Aug. 1991 and vol. 2, no. 3 Aug. 1993; German Appropriate Technology Exchange (GATE), *Fibre Concrete (FCR) Roofing Equipment*, Product Information, 1991; Swiss Centre for Appropriate Technology (SKAT), *Fibre Concrete Roofing*, A comprehensive report on the potential of FCR, the limits of application, the state of the art, 1987; and Parry, J. P. M., *Fibre Cement Roofing*, Intermediate Technology Workshop, UK, 1985.

141. For a detailed treatment of the subject see UNCHS (Habitat), *Endogenous Capacity-building for the Production of Binding Materials in the Construction Industry—Selected case studies*, HS/292/93E, Nairobi, 1993; UNCHS (Habitat), *A Compendium of Information on Selected Low-cost Building Materials*, HS/137/88E, Nairobi, 1988; Feliciano, Lauricio M., *Technology Manual on Rice-hust Ash Cement*, UNDP/UNIDO Regional Network in Asia for Low-cost Building Materials Technologies and Construction Systems, Manila, Philippines, 1987; ESCAP, *Building Materials and Construction Technologies for Low-cost Housing in Developing ESCAP Countries*, Bangkok, Thailand; and UNCHS (Habitat), *Journal of the Network of African Countries on Local Building Materials and Technologies*, vol. 1, no. 1, April 1989.

142. UNCHS (Habitat), *Development of National Technological Capacity for Environmentally Sound Construction*, HS/293/93E, 1993.

143. UNCHS (Habitat), *Information Document on Building Materials and Health*, Nairobi, 1995.

144. UNCHS (Habitat), *Co-operative Housing, Experiences of Mutual Self-help*, HS/179/89/E, Nairobi, 1989.

145. Silas 1994, *op. cit.*

146. See UNCHS (Habitat), *Public/Private Partnerships in Enabling Shelter Strategies*, Nairobi, Kenya, 1993.

147. Lair Espinoza and Oscar A. López Rivera, 'UNICEF's urban basic services programme in illegal settlements in Guatemala City', *Environment and Urbanization* vol. 6, no. 2, Oct. 1994.

148. Jaglin, Sylvy, 'Why mobilize town dwellers; joint management in Ouagadougou, 1983–1990', *Environment and Urbanization*, vol. 6, no. 2, Oct. 1994, 111–32.

149. UNCHS (Habitat), *The Urban Poor as Agents of Development: Community Action Planning in Sri Lanka*, Nairobi, 1993.

150. UNCHS (Habitat), *Shelter for Low-income Communities: Sri Lanka Demonstration Project Case Study—Part I*, Nairobi, 1985.

151. UNCHS (Habitat), 'Housing for the urban poor: housing, poverty and developing countries', Paper presented to the 2nd Symposium on Housing for the Urban Poor, Birmingham, 1994.

152. Sen, Amartya, *Mortality as an Indicator of Economic Success and Failure*, Innocenti Lecture given at the UNICEF-IUSSP Conference on Demography and Poverty, Florence, 1995.

153. Khan, Akhtar Hameed, OPP Programmes, OPP-RTI, 1992 quoted in Hasan 1994, *op. cit.*

154. Hasan, Arif, *Manual for Rehabilitation Programmes for Informal Settlements based on the Orangi Pilot Project*, OPP-RTI, May 1992.

155. Cruz, Luis Fernando, 'NGO Profile: Fundación Carvajal; the Carvajal Foundation', *Environment and Urbanization*, vol. 6, no. 2, Oct. 1994.

156. Cruz 1994, *op. cit.*

157. *Ibid.*

158. Jaglin 1994, *op. cit.*

159. Turner, John F. C., *Managing the*

Recovery of Local Initiative, Paper
presented to the Seminar on Low-Cost
Housing in the Arab Region, Sana'a,

1992, 17.
160. UNCHS (Habitat), *Evaluation of
Experience with Initiating Enabling*

Housing Strategies, Nairobi, 1991.
161. Barlow and Duncan 1994, *op. cit.*

11 Finance for Housing, Infrastructure and Services

11.1 Introduction

The first half of this chapter concentrates on highlighting the lessons learnt from recent housing finance programmes that sought to reach lower-income groups in the South; the second half reviews the scale and nature of finance from donor agencies to housing, infrastructure and services. This concentration in the first half of the chapter on such a narrow focus is for two reasons. The first is the fact that the last 10–15 years have brought considerable innovation in this field from many governments and non-government organizations in the South. The second is that limitations of space prevent a more wide-ranging review of recent trends and innovations in housing finance in both the North and the South. This means that many interesting and important innovations are not covered here.

Most of the housing finance programmes described in this chapter include finance for some infrastructure and services so it is difficult to separate the discussion of housing finance from that of infrastructure and services. In most countries in the South, relatively few low-income households can afford to purchase a house with piped water and connection to sewers. Loans provided to individual households to build a new unit often have to cover the cost of installing a water supply and provision for sanitation with no connection available to municipal or city water supply and sewage systems—or connections only available at a relatively high unit cost. The same is true for many loans provided to low-income households to improve existing housing units. The primary focus in this chapter is on housing and there is no discussion of government loan programmes only for infrastructure and services.

In government housing finance programmes, there is a recognition that a large portion of the population cannot afford to purchase conventional housing but can afford to develop their own housing, if credit, technical assistance and services are available that match their needs and capacities to pay. There is also a recognition that new kinds of housing finance institutions are needed and that conventional housing finance or mortgage institutions which many governments set up or strengthened in the 1970s and early 1980s were not serving low-income groups. At the same time, it has been recognized that informal finance is being used for housing improvement or construction. Although differing in detail, many relatively new housing finance institutions have sought to provide subsidized credit to help finance (generally incremental) housing development for low-income communities. This section describes the experiences of some of these programmes: Mutirao (the National Programme of Mutual Aid Housing) in Brazil, the Community Mortgage Programme from the Philippines, the Urban Community Development Office from Thailand, FONHAPO in Mexico and Build-Together National Housing Programme in Namibia. It also includes details of some other programmes such as the Million Houses Programme in Sri Lanka and recent experiences in Colombia. It describes how these programmes enabled households and communities to obtain access to land, building materials and finance for housing, and support for housing production processes.

The government programmes for housing finance drew on earlier NGO experience in credit programmes that had successfully provided low-income groups with small sums of credit for income earning activities. Such government and NGO programmes seek to address the fact that most low-income households cannot obtain credit for housing construction or improvement from conventional banks or housing credit institutions. Without credit, households have far fewer housing options. They generally cannot afford to purchase a secure land site legally and are generally forced to build incrementally, in ways which increase overall costs.

One Indian NGO calculated that the total expenditure incurred by a pavement dweller in Bombay in maintaining their shelter would be equivalent to the mortgage repayments on a small permanent dwelling.[1] But, without being able to obtain a loan, 20 years' expenditure is wasted and they are left with neither a secure home nor an asset. Such experiences showed the need for housing credit.

The lack of formal sector credit for low-income households arises for many reasons:

- Low-income household's lack of verifiable or regular flow of income and of collateral that is acceptable to housing finance agencies.

- The high transaction costs for the housing finance agency, in relation to the size of the loan (processing and monitoring a small loan is often as time-consuming as that of a large loan).

- A belief that the poor will not repay.

- A lack of offices by the conventional banks and housing finance agencies in low-income areas.
- The complexity of the application and the level of bureaucracy associated with the provision of loans including the need to be literate to complete forms.[2]

Many of these are similar to the problems faced by small entrepreneurs in obtaining credit for business investment. But in the case of housing, there are three further factors that reduce available credit: the longer loan periods; the larger loans needed; and the lack of increased income arising directly from the investment. Nevertheless, as the discussion in this chapter shows, these programmes for low-income housing finance are similar in some aspects to informal and innovative credit programmes for micro-enterprises.

11.2 Government Programmes For Housing Finance[3]

New models of housing finance

In both their form and historical development, the new government housing finance initiatives described here show the influence of NGO experiences. In many countries, NGOs have succeeded in identifying the successful 'ingredients' of credit programmes for housing and neighbourhood development, but they lack the capital to provide opportunities for low-income communities on a large scale. Although development from NGO initiatives to a government programme has often taken a long time a national fund does offer advantages to both government and NGOs. For NGOs, it offers a way to take their programmes to scale; for governments, they draw on models that have succeeded in implementing effective housing credit and neighbourhood improvement programmes that also make maximum use of the communities' own capacity to invest, build and organize.

Governments seeking to adopt such strategies have to develop systems to make available sufficient land and financial resources. They also have to identify ways in which they can support the present housing production process of low-income households. Each of these elements is discussed below. One particular innovative aspect of such government policies is that they seek to involve many groups other than government and the new roles and responsibilities of the different actors involved in such programmes are also considered below.

Land

Housing loan programmes generally have to provide ways by which low-income households can obtain land or obtain tenure of the land they already occupied. Significant housing investment does not make sense unless tenure is secure and assistance in securing land is generally a first step in a process of housing consolidation.

Most low-income households have a very limited capacity to purchase land at market prices if they are also to cover the costs of building materials and construction. The loan programmes of both the Community Mortgage Programme in the Philippines and the Urban Community Development Office in Thailand have observed that households who take a first loan for land can rarely afford to take a second to help meet the costs of housing construction. In such circumstances, governments can make a significant contribution to a community development process either by making public land available for housing or by requiring municipalities to provide land as their contribution to the improvement programme (as encouraged by the *Mutirão* programme in Brazil).

When FONHAPO was established it benefited from being able to use a land bank that had been established by a previous government programme in the late 1970s. This supply of land was of considerable help to FONHAPO in helping communities to acquire the land they needed for housing. Once a suitable plot had been identified, communities could borrow from the fund to finance their land purchases. In the Philippines, the Community Mortgage Programme was set up to help low-income urban households to acquire title to the land that they occupied (illegally) and then to improve infrastructure and services (see Box 11.2). In Colombia, the shortage of land that can be afforded by low-income households is being addressed through a new government housing programme that offers municipalities an incentive to provide low-income communities with land. Groups living within municipalities that have made land available have an increased chance of receiving a housing subsidy from national government.

When supplying infrastructure and services, experience suggests that the development process works to the advantage of low-income communities if the provision of infrastructure and services follows rather than precedes housing development. Once investments in infrastructure and services are made, the price of the land usually rises steeply, especially since the demand for land for housing with infrastructure and services considerably exceeds supply in many countries and it rapidly becomes too expensive for low-income households. Undeveloped land is considerably cheaper and acquiring land without infrastructure and services enables the increase in value arising from development to be 'captured' by the low-income residents. By developing and

BOX 11.1
FONHAPO

FONHAPO is a national fund for low-income housing established by the Mexican government in late 1981. The Fund sought to:

- double the low-income housing stock between 1980–2000;
- finance housing construction by people with modest incomes who organized the development of their own housing;
- finance incremental housing development, not just new houses;
- redistribute national government funds in favour of people with low incomes to reinforce principles of equity and social justice;
- support the development of democratic processes from the community upwards;
- ensure that government support was used efficiently;
- be decentralized; and
- institutionalize the fund within government.

FONHAPO was designed by professionals with long experience of working with low-income communities and realistic assumptions were made about how much the people could afford and where credit was needed. It authorized credit principally to public sector organizations (such as housing or state-level real-estate institutions and municipalities) and to organised community groups seeking housing (such as housing co-operatives, civil associations, unions, and peasant organizations). All groups receiving credit had to be legally constituted and the credit was authorized to lend to the group as a whole, not to its individual members. When the Fund was fully operative, there were 800 accounts and 250,000 households receiving loans.

Title to the land on which the housing units were developed or improved could not be individualized until the loan had been completely repaid. In some cases, communities maintained a collective land-holding. Occasionally, a single loan was turned into two loans if there were divisions in the community. The most common reason for this was that one group wished to repay the loan faster than other groups.

Credit could be used to fund any part of the housing process, with great flexibility for people to choose how the funding was used. Five main programmes developed: site and services, incremental housing development, improvement and/or extension of existing housing, new finished houses and the production and distribution of building materials. The credit lines correspond to different phases of the housing process: site acquisition, technical assistance to develop projects, provision of basic services (water, drainage, electricity and roads); and either mutual aid construction processes or construction by third parties. The combination of possibilities gave the fund great flexibility to respond to the different needs, potentials and preferences of the participating groups. The programme had very few technical standards but many standards for social processes. For example, there were no limits to the size of rooms but communities had to have regular meetings and fixed numbers had to participate when making critical collective decisions.

The financial system was designed according to the ability of the people to repay. The maximum size of loan was 2,000 times the daily minimum wage of the region although the actual amount of credit was set according to the repayment possibilities of the soliciting group. A deposit of 10–15 per cent of the value of the loan was required before the loan was provided and the value of loan repayments could not exceed 25 per cent of the monthly income of the head of the household. Loans were given for 7–8 years. Communities that successfully repaid their first loan could apply for a second loan. Land was used as collateral for the loan.

A subsidy was included in the programme and half the total value of this subsidy was earmarked for those with an income of less than 1.5 times the minimum monthly wage. Up to 40 per cent of the total cost of a project could be subsidized; 25 per cent was given immediately and the remaining 15 per cent if the repayment schedule was maintained.

Repayment did not follow a conventional form with the repayment of capital and interest. At the time the loan was taken out, the equivalent value of a monthly repayment (at nought per cent interest rate) was converted into a percentage of the minimum monthly wage. As the monthly minimum wage changed, so did the value of the repayment. This system of calculating repayments was supported by the communities who recognized the need to maintain the capital value of the Fund and felt that their repayments were fair. An additional charge equivalent to an interest rate of 2 per cent was later added and passed to the communities to cover administration costs.

In 1983, when the programme began operations, 25 per cent of all loans were given to communities and 75 per cent to other institutions such as local and state government departments. Within a few years, the structure of the programme had succeeded in shifting a much greater share of resources to community development. Between 1985 and 1987, 66 per cent of the total number of loans were to community organizations. Administrative costs fell from 10 per cent of the total value of loans at the beginning of the programme to 4 per cent after five years.

The 4 per cent government allocation to housing which was given to FONHAPO was soon producing 22 per cent of all government funded housing investment. In the first year, 5,000 units were completed and 15,000 started; by 1987, 63,000 units had been completed and a further 53,000 started. ('Units' does not mean a new house but a completed programme of incremental improvement.)

Source: Asian Coalition for Housing Rights/Habitat International Coalition, 'Finance and resource mobilization for low income housing and neighbourhood development: a workshop report', Pagtambayayong Foundation, Philippines, 1994.

supporting strong community organization, the housing finance programme can assist communities to negotiate and lobby to ensure that infrastructure and services are provided, once the land is acquired; such strategies and mechanisms are discussed in more detail below.

There is a need for governments to adopt integrated urban development strategies in the provision of land. The value of land is related to the availability and quality of services in the area. Good-quality public transport services, in particular, can partially compensate for having to use land in remote locations. Governments add to the value of land allocated to or obtained by low-income communities through not only ensuring basic infrastructure and services but also ensuring good-quality public transport and encouraging investments in suitable productive activities on nearby sites. Such public investment can clearly add considerably to the value of land. Governments entering into major new transport developments should consider reserving a proportion of land for housing developments for low-income households. In Curitiba, for example, the planning authorities recognized the importance of ensuring low-income households obtained land with good access to employment by reserving areas for low-income housing

BOX 11.2
The Community Mortgage Programme, the Philippines

The Philippines government launched a Community Mortgage Programme in 1988 to help poor urban households acquire title to the land they occupy and develop the site and their housing in 'blighted and depressed' areas. The Programme was placed within the National Home Finance Corporation. It focused on the bottom 30 per cent of households to obtain access to housing especially those living illegally on land. The Programme provides loans to allow community associations to acquire land on behalf of their members, improve the site, develop individual titling of the land and provide individual housing loans for home improvement or house construction. It is innovative in that it emphasized the importance of non-government groups in developing a solution to housing in the Philippines and in its focus on achieving land security.

To acquire the loan, the residents have to organize themselves into a community association which becomes responsible for collecting repayments and for ensuring that the loan continues to be serviced. If the development is to take place within an existing residential settlement, 90 per cent or more of residents have to agree to be a party to the loan and improvement programme. The land is purchased on behalf of the members and initially remains under the common ownership of the association. It is the association which is responsible for collecting monthly rentals and amortization from member beneficiaries until the community loan has been individualized. Both community based organizations and NGOs (and municipal governments) can take out loans and provide assistance in organizing member-beneficiaries and informing them about loan availability.

Loans are available for up to 90 per cent of appraised value of property. Where residents were already on the site by February 25th 1986, this valuation is no longer required if an agreement has been reached between the land owner and the community association as to the value of the land—although this must not exceed ten million pesos. Loans are provided for 25 years at 6 per cent interest.

As of April 1994, the Programme had already assisted 330 communities (39,992 households) with a total loan value of more than 835 million pesos. The average loan for each household is P21,000. Another 40,000 households have begun the process of obtaining a loan. Repayments rates are about 65 per cent.

An essential part of the programme is that either a government agency or an NGO acts as an intermediary, helping the residents form an association and supporting them while they negotiate for official title to the land, apply and secure the land, and begin site development and the financial operation of the loan. Just over half of the intermediary institutions which have acted as originators for loans are NGOs although some have been undertaken by local government units, national government agencies and financial institutions. Originators receive a small payment of 500 pesos per household from the government for this service.

Source: Asian Coalition for Housing Rights/Habitat International Coalition, 'Finance and resource mobilization for low income housing and neighbourhood development: a workshop report', Pagtambayayong Foundation, Philippines, 1994.

---

alongside the express bus routes into the city centre.[4]

Finance, subsidies and repayments

The housing finance programmes considered here all involve the combined funds of governments and households. This section explores two critical issues: first, the reasons why governments have been willing to finance (and subsidize) these programmes, and second, the strategies that are used to secure a high level of repayment.

The governments' financial contribution to such programmes is primarily the loan capital which is usually available to households or community organizations at subsidized rates. The NGO experience in housing finance has been subsidized housing finance, which reflects their primary focus on assisting the poor and their local knowledge of the communities they are supporting. On the other hand, the experience of government programmes offering subsidized finance is that such programmes are attractive to higher income groups who are often successful in 'capturing' the subsidy. The issue of finance and subsidies are therefore critical to the design of government programmes.

Those arguing for loan provision on economic grounds emphasize that credit markets in many countries in Africa, Asia and Latin America are inefficient and that profitable investment opportunities are foregone because credit is not available to low-income communities at interest rates approaching those of competitive market rates.[5] While much of this debate has centred on credit for micro-enterprise investment, the same arguments have been applied to housing. Thus, it is argued, there is a role for government to ensure low-income households can obtain housing credit. And it has been suggested that this strategy may be more efficient than the more common public policy response of the 1970s and early 1980s which was to provide public housing, core housing or serviced sites for 'low-income' households.[6] Credit programmes to enable low-income households to build or purchase their own housing are therefore a solution emerging from conventional economic analysis of the housing needs of low-income communities. In such programmes, the emphasis is overwhelmingly on the provision of investment capital for housing and the focus of the programme is primarily financial. Subsidies may be considered unnecessary and even detrimental to the effectiveness of such programmes. They are unnecessary because the major problem is lack of credit, not the cost of credit; and they are detrimental because the subsidy is attractive to higher income groups who try to obtain funds through the programme.

The second rationale for credit provision for housing concentrates on its effectiveness in ensuring the basic needs of low-income households are met. Market-based development is considered to be inadequate without a redistribution of income or assets towards low-income groups although this redistribution will bring wider economic benefits such as increased demand for goods and services. Housing credit programmes, it is argued, have proved to be an effective and efficient way of delivering subsidies because they avoid or reduce problems such as the selection of recipients and dependency. Households contribute directly to the development process as they are required to provide 'counterpart' funding through savings and loan repayments. Households and communities are therefore, in part, self-selected. Subsidy funds are allocated more efficiently than might otherwise be the case because the households and/or communities are also spending their own funds and become involved in the allocation decisions with some sense of ownership in the project. The subsidy finance goes further because it automatically draws in additional resources. Within such a perspective, low-income housing loan programmes are seen as one component within a poverty-reduction strategy. Subsidies are seen as an integral component of such strategies. And as was noted in Chapter 6, it is not unusual for wealthier groups to receive tax relief or some other subsidy on their housing loans. In Mexico, the level of subsidy available to low-income households through FONHAPO was less than that received by many more wealthy households.[7]

In all the programmes described here, subsidies have been provided both through subsidized loan finance and through capital subsidies. For example, households were only expected to repay some 40 per cent of the loans obtained from FONHAPO. A major advantage of interest rate subsidies for the government agency is that they spread the cost over the full period of the loan. In some cases, the communities argue strongly for such an approach. In Thailand, the Community Development Office charges an average rate of 7 per cent with differential interest being charged on community revolving funds, housing and micro-enterprise credit. In the case of the Community Mortgage Programme, interest rates subsidies have led to a very specific problem because, managed by a conventional government financing institution, there is an incentive to redirect financing away from the Programme towards investments with higher interest rates. From the perspective of the community, there is some evidence to suggest that communities benefit from having as much choice as possible in regard to the balance between interest rate and capital subsidies. One NGO programme in Mexico offered households within one credit programme three repayment options in which the total subsidy was equal but it was differently divided. All three options were used by the households.[8]

In Latin America, a common practice is to link repayments to the minimum monthly wage as is the case with FONHAPO. At a time of rising inflation (varying between 40 and 165 per cent a year in Mexico during the 1980s) this maintained the real value of repayments more effectively than conventional interest repayments. Moreover, it reduced uncertainty for the households having to maintain repayments and was seen as 'fair' by those repaying loans, despite the falling value of real wages.

A common and important feature of these funds is that the loan is taken out by the community. Major government programmes such as FONHAPO, Mutirâo, the Community Mortgage Programme and the Urban Community Development Office have been innovative in offering loans through communities or providing 'collective credits'. Such a structure has a number of advantages for the different parties involved. For the programme's managers, administrative costs are lower because the community organization manages the individual loan allocations and repayments. Collective housing developments also allow for greater efficiency and cost-effectiveness in the production process. For the government, the insistence of community organization is one strategy for reducing the risk of the fund being taken over by middle-class residents. However, more fundamental to the development process is the strengthening of the community by encouraging the formation of a formal organization; encouraging the collective process within the community can assist low-income households in combating the adverse effects of poverty.

High repayment rates have, in general, been secured by the programmes described here. For example, Build-Together in Namibia has a repayment rate of 92 per cent.[9] FONHAPO's repayment rate at the end of 1988 was 93 per cent. Repayment has been encouraged through a number of measures, all of which are common to effective NGO programmes. Perhaps the most universal is the requirement that a community has operated a savings programme before becoming eligible for loan financing. For example, the Urban Community Development Office requires a compulsory three-month saving period for any community wishing to obtain a loan. Other measures include requiring the community organization to take responsibility for obtaining the loan repayments.

Housing production

The way in which such credit programmes interact with the housing production process is also an important element of the programme structure in the innovative schemes considered here. The programmes have been designed to promote a local development process within communities receiving loans in order to reduce poverty and vulnerability to crises. In order to reach this objective, the programmes seek to encourage three specific elements:

- To maximize household receipt of funds.
- To maximize non-financial support for households.
- To maximize local economic multipliers.

Maximizing household receipt of funds

Housing production is the process by which building materials, labour and land are combined to become housing. In general, subsidized government housing programmes that focus only on contractor-built units or even serviced sites for low income groups result in much of the value of the subsidy being captured by the construction company. Low-income households do not benefit as much as they might have done and the final product is too expensive for the government to be able to afford production on a scale appropriate to need.[10]

Alternative strategies have been used to ensure that as much as possible of the subsidy reaches those in most need. Loans specifically directed at low-income households are one such strategy. By providing the subsidy through the loan, which is managed at the level of the household or community, the subsidy can be used in the way that is most effective to the community. For example, they can either self-build, or negotiate with local contractors for building services. A further advantage of this strategy is better value for money. In Karachi, low-income communities can install sewers at one-seventh of the cost of the government.[11] In Namibia, homes built by low-income communities have a market value over five times that of the cost of materials invested in the house.[12] An evaluation at the end of the FONHAPO programme demonstrated that the houses constructed had cost about half of what they would have cost if the government had built a house of equivalent size. By delivering the subsidy direct to the people who are responsible for managing the housing construction or improvement process, the full value of the subsidy reaches those for whom it was intended. These experiences suggest that government housing subsidies must be allocated directly to low-income communities if limited funds are to be used most effectively.

Maximizing non-financial support for low-income households

Credit programmes provide an opportunity to reduce poverty or vulnerability not only through improved housing conditions and through providing households with an asset but also through strengthening community organization. A strong community organization is considered an essential element of the government programmes considered here and each programme has been designed to encourage and support this element. The experience of low-income housing finance suggests that there are many advantages attached to 'collective credits' or community loans. One of the most important is that such loans can be designed to support the formation and strengthening of community organizations that then have a central role in the development process within low-income settlements. A strong community organization also offers a number of specific advantages to the realization of a development programme through loan finance:

Community design: if the development is to work, it must draw on the knowledge of local residents about their needs. Individual voices are not generally heard against those of the professionals who dictate the development of the house and/or neighbourhood. Even if the individual voices are heard, such individuals cannot be representative. Some forum is required for all the experiences and perceptions of individuals to come together and assess what makes sense for the community.

Community management: through community based design and management, the housing process is democratised and the people have the opportunity to determine their housing and its standard. As argued by the Urban Community Development Office in Thailand, the richest resource available to low-income communities is their capacity to work and to organize and the process must be one that realises and enhances this resource (see Box 11.5)

Maximizes availability of funds: by working through community organizations, these programmes draw on the use of savings and other resources from community members. Although small, these resources made a real difference to the success of the project.

Efficient use of funds: the households who receive credit in these programmes have very limited monetary assets and incomes so it is important that costs are minimized in all stages of the production process. Experience suggests that the community will be able to build at lower costs than either private or public contractors. Incorporating part of the households' savings into the programme increases the responsibility with which the community manages funds. In general, people look after their own money better than they look after the money of others.

Community insurance: lack of income and assets means that households are particularly vulnerable to changes in circumstances. Collective management of funds reduces the risk of loan default by individual households. For example, if the main income earner in a household is sick or injured, the household's repayments may be temporarily paid by the community. In some cases, community insurance schemes have been made more formal with a special fund or special provision. For instance, in Guadalajara in Mexico, a community with 82 households purchased a plot of land with 110 plots, with the extra plots sold to cover the costs these households had incurred in developing this initiative. The community agreed to keep three plots both to provide some insurance for community members and as a resource that could be rented out, providing small amounts of income for the community. If government funds are given community organizations, residents can plan to increase group security.

Collective strength: the loan may be the start of the development process but it is not considered to be sufficient by itself. Low-income settlements require the continuing provision of investment and maintenance in infrastructure and services. In order to secure these, they need to be able to negotiate and put pressure on municipal government and other state institutions. Some form of community organization is essential to this process.

It is also important to note that the argument is not one way. Although the form of credit programmes has been designed to strengthen communities, so the success of such programmes may also require that a given level of capacity for, and experience in, community organization has been reached. What was important in the establishment of the Urban Community Development Office in Thailand in 1992 was that there had been a qualitative change in the knowledge and experience of community organizations in the country and a qualitative increase in their capacity over the last 10 years. These changes brought new possibilities including the prospect of large-scale impact for the programme of the Development Office. Without a given level of community organization, it would not have been possible to implement this programme.

Maximizing the economic multiplier effects

Another strategy often used by innovative housing finance programmes is to ensure that funds circulate as many times as possible in the local economy through using housing production to stimulate local economic growth. In several of the innovative housing finance programmes discussed in Section 11.3, there has been a move away from housing to more comprehensive neighbourhood development. The need for this expansion of housing programmes into neighbourhood development was stimulated by the ineffectiveness of some interventions orientated towards housing alone. In particular, the new programmes are intended to assist in increasing household incomes and therefore the capacity of these households to take on and repay loans. Certain government programmes have also developed this integration of income-generation and housing finance.

BOX 11.3
Lessons learnt about community management

Many government housing loan programmes have both depended on and attempted to strengthen, the ability of communities to manage their own development. Although the context and situation of communities varies considerably, a number of factors are likely to be necessary for communities to be successful in such management.

- The importance of understandable and up-to-date information about all aspects of the programme. It also proved a considerable help for communities beginning the process to be able to draw on a broad range of other community experiences. Local experiences must be complemented by an information programme at the level of the municipality or district with details of available land plots, city resources and other government programmes. Information should be appropriate for the different groups for whom it is intended, state institutions, municipal governments, NGOs, private contractors and communities.

- The need for transparent and easily understood loan processes at all levels. There also needs to be a clear logical framework with a legal role for community leaders and community members. Without such a framework, it is difficult for community leaders to act with legitimacy.

- The need for training for most or all the actors involved in the process (community leaders, trainers, members, technical advisers) including those who will be trainers within the programme. Lack of adequately prepared trainers has been a constraint on the development of several government programmes, including those discussed here. Training needs to be targeted to the different groups involved and should deliberately aim to ensure that all the groups necessary to the success of the programme are drawn into the process. While the form of the training programme will vary according to the local context, training needs are likely to include training in community organization, financial management, housing construction techniques and negotiation skills. Training in financial management has been particularly important.

- The financial needs of community organizations. These need to be addressed in some way if their participation is to be maximized. The management of community development inevitably involves the community and its leaders in some level of expenditure and a mechanism needs to be developed to ensure that the community has access to the funds that it needs. The mechanism most commonly used to date is that a proportion of the loan repayments is returned to the community organization for collective management.

- The need to minimize bureaucracy and complexity. A major problem with government credit programmes for low-income communities is the amount of bureaucracy that is involved. Despite attempts to simplify procedures as much as possible, experience suggests that problems with bureaucracy remain.

There are a variety of different income opportunities that are related to improved housing. For example, housing finance programmes can help finance the building of rooms for rent and may include space for micro-enterprise development. Further income-earning opportunities are provided through housing construction and the production of building materials, fixtures or fittings. In general, such developments have been restricted in government programmes (although FONHAPO permitted loans for building materials production by co-operatives) because of traditional problems in working across different ministries. However, the new fund in Thailand, despite being located under the National Housing Authority, has 50 per cent of the loan capital allocated to micro-enterprise development.

Improved income-earning opportunities increase household capacity to repay loans and enables them to invest more in housing. At the community level, successful new or expanded micro-enterprises ensure the circulation of money within the local economy. A development of the *Mutirâo* programme initiated by one community in Fortaleza has been the construction of small workshops and enterprise units within the community (see Box 11.4). These serve the dual purpose of encouraging individual entrepreneurs and offering them a local base, and providing rental income from the units for the community organization.

A further advantage of developing a more comprehensive programme of activity is that the focus on housing may not always be helpful in maintaining organizational enthusiasm within the community. In the experience of the *Mutirâo* programme in Brazil, the emphasis on housing has not helped the process of community organization. While the communities have been motivated to organize and achieve housing, once the homes have been constructed, the focus of community organization has been removed and energies fade rapidly.

One further long-term economic benefit of housing finance is that, by allowing a low-income household to acquire a house or land site, it provides them with the possibility of incremental investment that both improves their home and adds to the value of their asset. The scale of housing investment that takes place after land tenure is secure has been frequently observed.[13] In the Community Mortgage Programme, most of the loans are for land because it is land that the communities find it hardest to acquire. But five years after acquiring land, the estimated total value of the investment in the residential area is about three times the size of the loan for land purchase.

The contributions of local government, NGOs and other actors

Government credit programmes for low-income housing usually involve a range of institutions including national governments, local or municipal governments, NGOs and community organizations. Some conclusions as to different roles and responsibilities of these groups have emerged from the experiences described here.

Non-governmental organizations

Many of the innovative government housing credit programmes have emerged from the experience of NGO staff who were brought into government to improve low-income housing strategies and programmes. In such programmes, NGOs have been given an important role in providing technical advice and assistance to communities participating in the programme. Such support usually involves a broad range of activities including the development of community organization and self-help processes, and training and direct assistance in financial management and housing production. In addition to supporting community loan management, NGOs may have further responsibilities in assisting communities to secure additional government services and infrastructure, once their housing improvement programme has begun.

The experience of government programmes for low-income housing to date is that such programmes may have been too dependent on NGOs and their capacity to support the process. A number of weaknesses associated with both the NGO sector and some individual organizations have emerged. First, there are often not enough NGOs to support the scale of community initiatives that need to take place. Even in the many Asian and Latin American countries which have long had extensive NGO involvement in housing, there are rarely sufficient experienced NGOs to be able to support a large scale programme. Second, government programmes demand new skills from NGOs and few NGOs have extensive experience in financial management and project implementation. NGOs are often sectorally specialized and those that have a housing focus may not have the necessary experience in community enterprises. Third, the NGOs need to find additional income to that which they receive through participation in the programme because the amount they receive for supporting the government programme has not been sufficient to meet all their costs.

In the experience of FONHAPO in Mexico, very few of the 800 communities receiving credit within the programme had a high level of input from NGOs, even though Mexican NGOs have long been among the most innovative in working on housing issues with low-income groups.[14]

BOX 11.4
The national programme of mutual aid housing—*Mutirâo*

In 1986, the Federal government of Brazil launched a programme aiming to build 400,000 dwellings by 1990. The programme was financed by a tax on the proceeds of the national football lottery. At the time, the National Housing Bank that had been the main source through which the government had made credit available for housing was bankrupt and therefore funds passed directly to the Ministry for Housing and Community Action. In this move, housing was placed clearly within the social policy agenda. Federal resources were distributed to state and municipal agencies and the new programme was called the Mutirao, a Brazilian term meaning mutual aid which has been popularized through housing programmes.

In 1990, federal support for the Mutirao programme ended although the original target had not been achieved. The programme continued in only two cities, Fortaleza and Sao Paulo, with funds from the state and municipal authorities. In 1990, Fortaleza Metropolitan Region had a population of 2.4 million (1.8 million of which lived in Fortaleza) with an official housing deficit of 130,000. The state had previously received funds from the federal government for the Mutirao programme. The state government had passed this funding to Compania de Habitacao (Cohab) for implementation of the programme. Within the municipality of Fortaleza, funding was passed to the Social Services Department. Both Cohab and the Social Services Department collaborated in establishing Communal Societies for People's Housing—perhaps the

most original aspect of the entire programme. Communal societies have now been established throughout Fortaleza with representation from non-organized communities and already established organizations including federations of CBOs, unions and neighbourhood councils. Each communal society is a mixed government/voluntary organization with three elements:

—a general assembly of beneficiaries;
—a bank account or fund (to which households pay back the credit); and
—a council made up of three community representatives and two government representatives, one from the federal government and the other from the local authority or state.

Through these institutions, the Mutirao programme provides funding for the purchase of building materials. The communities construct their new houses either individually or with collective self-help. Generally, the families build everything together (although there are a few exceptional projects in which households build individually) and, once the settlement is complete, the houses are allocated to members.

Since 1987, 100 communal societies have been formed in Fortaleza and about 11,000 houses have been constructed in the city (with an additional 3,000 in the remainder of the state). Most communities consist of between 50 and 100 households. The Mutirao programme pays the cost of materials but this money is given as a loan to participants who are expected to pay a part of this cost back to the community of which they are a member. A monthly charge, equivalent to 10 per cent of the minimum monthly wage, is made for a

fixed period, generally five years. From the beginning, the social organizations and the neighbourhood associations involved in the programme argued that this level of monthly repayment was too high and it has now been reduced to 2–5 per cent of the monthly wage (for the same period of five years).

The repayments are given to the community to form a fund which is managed by community members. Up to half the community fund may be used by the people to invest in their homes and the remainder is to be used for projects which benefit all members of the community; for example, to repair a sewerage system, to pay the transport costs of those fighting for water, to provide electricity to a meeting room. In practice, all funds have been used for community projects and nothing has been allocated to improving individual houses.

The costs involved in a Mutirao project are about $US1,200 for a house of 30 square metres with the land being provided free. About one-third of this is labour costs which are provided by the households participating in the programme. The remaining $US800 is provided as a subsidy by the government. If 10 per cent of the minimum salary is repaid to the community organization over a five-year period, the households repay about 50 per cent of the value of this subsidy into the community fund. The scale of the subsidy, even in the most expensive example, is very small compared to many subsidized housing projects in Brazil. Taking account of the land and service charges doubles the cost of the project, but the total cost remains relatively low.

Source: Asian Coalition for Housing Rights/Habitat International Coalition, 'Finance and resource mobilization for low income housing and neighbourhood development: a workshop report', Pagtambayayong Foundation, Philippines, 1994.

Many communities applied for support from FONHAPO with only minimal technical support such as groups of students. In one project, the community was divided into several groups; the one using an NGO successfully completed the programme, the community being assisted by students never finished their new homes. There were few alternative institutions to NGOs offering assistance.

In the Philippines, the lack of support for NGOs did not prove an immediate problem for the Community Mortgage Programme especially as there was significant international support from which the NGOs could obtain additional resources. The NGOs were offered a fee of P500 per household to cover the costs of their support for the communities within the Community Mortgage Programme. As the initial estimate of costs was P250, it was hoped that this amount would be sufficient but a number of

problems emerged. The bureaucracy of the Programme was complex and time consuming. The amount proved to be insufficient to cover all NGO costs and international donors were reducing funding into the Philippines. NGOs have been forced to think about new strategies for fund-raising in order to maintain their involvement in the programme.

Local Government and Municipalities

Local government is usually responsible for zoning and for applying land use and building regulations and, in most cases, the provision of services. Their involvement is crucial for large scale programmes to improve housing conditions for low-income groups. Many local authorities also own land and virtually all will have the main role in providing legal tenure to those living in illegal settlements. Local government also has an important potential role in supporting credit and technical assistance programmes for low-income households but as Chapter 5 described, in most countries in the South, local authorities lack resources, revenue-raising capacities and technical staff.

Local government could offer an alternative source of support and training to NGOs. In practice, however, they are often under-resourced and have little experience in dealing with local development projects in partnership with low-income communities. Local government structures may be very bureaucratic and place additional obstacles before low-income communities, for example delay in obtaining building permits or in undertaking the paperwork needed for legalizing their tenure.

National/state government

Governments have a particular responsibility in setting the broad framework within which the other actors take part. This includes making it simple for individuals or households to develop their own housing. For governments intent on changing their role from the delivery of housing to support for households and communities developing their own, this requires considerable institutional change. One dilemma is whether to set up new offices for innovative housing programmes or to work through existing government institutions. Although clearly based on a limited number of examples, those programmes that have been set up within new government institutions appear to have had fewer problems than those located within existing state institutions with a more traditional approach to finance and housing provision. In both Mexico and the Philippines, establishing innovative financing processes within existing government departments resulted in the resistance of some government staff and a delay in the implementation of the programme. One experience emerging from the *Mutirâo* programme in Brazil is that governments should not divide their strategies for meeting land, infrastructure and housing needs.

Governments that seek to support households and communities developing their own housing will usually also have to modify housing standards. The Mexican experience had shown that minimum standards soon became maximum standards for the poor. Within FONHAPO, the concept of minimum standards (for both improvement and newly built housing) was replaced by that of incremental housing improvement. Standards may be introduced for good reasons—for example those concerned with health and safety—but their enforcement usually compounds problems for low-income self-build households. Governments need to find innovative alternatives. For example, within the Sri

Lankan government's Million Houses Programme, urban communities were allowed to propose new standards for development within their residential areas which were then accepted by the government authorities.[15]

The experience of government loan programmes for low-income housing demonstrates that the importance of the external context within which such programmes are implemented should not be underestimated. The importance of government policy on land has already been discussed. Housing loan programmes have also been influenced both directly and indirectly by structural adjustment programmes. Direct impacts include the reduced magnitude of the capital fund available to the programme and reduced expenditure on advisory and technical services. Indirect impacts have been felt as economic recession has made it increasingly difficult for communities to manage credit successfully and afford different housing options. For instance, FONHAPO's achievements described in Box 11.1 were achieved during one of the most severe economic crises in recent Mexican history. Successive cuts in government expenditure reduced the extent of technical assistance offered by FONHAPO. A high level of technical assistance later proved to be a critical element of successful loan programmes.

However, where economic conditions improve, this can also be used to the advantage of low-income groups. In Thailand, one justification used to support a new loan fund for low-income communities was that those who were not landowners had not benefited from rapid economic growth to the extent of landowners and houseowners. Between 1975/6 and 1992, the share of total income received by the highest 10 per cent of income earners increased from 33 per cent to 43 per cent. As a consequence of putting forward arguments such as these, there was increased support for the setting up of an Urban Community Development Office—see Box 11.5.

Private Sector

Large private companies have generally had a limited role in innovative government programmes providing credit to low-income communities. In general, private contractors have remained outside such programmes. One of the most innovative aspects of FONHAPO was the attempt to make the private sector produce solutions that were acceptable to a social system of production. They achieved this through competitions in which commercial firms bid for tenders to build a certain quality of house at the lowest price. This is also a method used in several countries in the North where government agencies (national or municipal) or social housing institutions put to tender the 'low-price' housing

BOX 11.5
The Urban Community Development Office (UCDO) in Thailand

In March 1992, the Thai government approved a budget of the equivalent of $US50 million to initiate an Urban Poor Development Programme within the Seventh National Economic and Social Development Plan. The approval of this budget led to the establishment of a new organization, the 'Urban Community Development Office' with responsibility for implementing the Programme nationwide. By the end of June 1995, loans totalling some 340 million baht (around $13.6 million) had been approved, benefiting some 140 communities with around 11,500 families. Loans had been made both in Bangkok and in the regional cities. By the end of 1996 the Office aims to have more than 850 'saving and credit organizations' in urban communities and more than 120,000 households belonging to them. It is also intended that at least 80 per cent of the urban poor who are members of 'savings and credit organizations' will have secure jobs and reasonably secure incomes. A considerable range of regional NGOs, federations of community organizations, municipalities and professionals are also involved in these initiatives.

The overall objective of the Programme is to strengthen the capacity of the urban poor and those living in illegal settlements to obtain increased and secure incomes, appropriate housing with secure rights, an improved environment and better living conditions. The people are considered to be the main actors in the community development process. The Office considers that local authorities, NGOs and other agencies external to the community, both governmental and non-governmental, also have an essential role but as supporters of the people's development process. Based on this understanding, there are six main working objectives:

1. To assist in the setting up of community savings groups and support for the operation of community saving and credit activities.
2. To support and enhance the managerial and organizational capacity of the saving groups.
3. To support the formation and development of community savings and credit federations and other forms of community networking.
4. To provide integrated development credit for communities (including credit for housing construction or improvement and micro-enterprises).
5. To support community groups in planning for an integrated community development process.
6. To support those already working in development activities to work together and enhance their working capacity.

The Urban Community Development Office is a special organization within the National Housing Authority, but its Board has the power to make decisions autonomously. The concept of partnership is fundamental to the composition of the Board, which has nine members. Three are drawn from government organizations (the Bank of Thailand, the Finance Ministry and the National Economic and Social Development Board), three are community leaders, two come from NGOs, and the final member is from the private sector. The Governor of the National Housing Authority is the Chair of the Board and the Managing Director of the Development Office acts as Secretary to the Board.

A major aim of the Urban Community Development Office is to strengthen communities' managerial capacity. It seeks to encourage and enable, in all possible ways, different forms of community organisations and federations to be set up and be involved in the Programme. 'Credit' is used as a mechanism to strengthen the capability of communities to collectively deal with their own development issues.

To be eligible for a loan, each community must operate a savings programme, with a clearly defined management structure, for at least three months. Loans can be granted for up to a maximum of ten times the amount saved. All loans are conditional on there being a community management structure and operating mechanism as well as clearly defined beneficiaries and a project development management process. All committee members are required to sign their names as guarantors of the loan. The Development Office considers that the resources it provides should be supplementary to the financial resources of the communities themselves.

Through the careful use of credit, the role of the community as initiator, organizer, planner and manager is enhanced. At every stage, the role of the community as the main actor in the implementation process as well as the main actor in development is reinforced. The credit system and associated management activities seek to gradually change the quality of the community organization to enable it to become a strong development unit able to more effectively deal with forces external to the community as well as becoming a nucleus for an internal integrated development process.

The Programme provides an 'integrated credit system' for community development with different loans available, including those for income generation, small revolving funds and housing. This approach responds to the multiple and related needs of the communities. The Office charges an average rate of 7 per cent interest a year with differential interest being charged on community revolving funds (10 per cent), housing (3 per cent) and micro-enterprise credit (8 per cent). A further 2–5 per cent may be added by communities to provide their organizations with a small fund for collective projects. This enables the savings and credit organization to increase and strengthen its capacity. By mid-1995, around two-thirds of the credits had gone to 15 new housing projects developed by slum community organizations that registered themselves into housing co-operatives and around 20 housing improvement projects. One-fourth had gone to income-generation but since income-generation credits were on average much smaller than credits for housing, there were many more income-generation projects.

Source: Asian Coalition for Housing Rights/Habitat International Coalition, 'Finance and resource mobilization for low income housing and neighbourhood development: a workshop report', Pagtambayayong Foundation, Philippines, 1994; and Somsook Boonyabancha, personal communication, 1995.

they want and rely on competition between building firms to produce the best-value final product. Smaller informal construction companies have benefited from such programmes because they increase local demand for building materials and building skills.

Non-profit Construction Companies
There are relatively few 'social producers' of housing, i.e. non-profit-making organizations able to work with low-income households and communities in establishing their own housing. FONHAPO consciously tried to develop the capacity of certain communities to provide this service but without success. In its experience, it is very difficult to encourage a community which came together for the purpose of building housing, and which successfully completes its own programme, to then become a social developer in other locations. The level and type of organiza-

tion required to support the process of neighbourhood development elsewhere is different, and experience shows that most groups stop once they have developed their own housing; there was only one exception to this in 800 communities receiving loans.

Box 11.6 gives the example of the 'Build-Together' national housing programme in Namibia which is also centred on housing loans and working with and supporting community organizations.

Looking ahead

This section has concentrated on the recent experience of seven housing finance initiatives in the South. These are only a sample of the innovations and initiatives that have been tried. There are also many initiatives that have sought to increase the efficiency of housing finance institutions so they can reach households that are further down the income scale with non-subsidized housing finance. For instance, Zimbabwe's new National Shelter Strategy pays considerable attention to improving the efficiency and reach of mortgage finance. With high-level backing from central government, it has proved possible to persuade building societies to reduce the cost of housing loans in return for greater access to capital—in this case, tax-exempt bonds with 25 per cent of each issue earmarked for on-lending to 'lower-income groups.'[16]

Considering the programmes discussed here, current trends include three separate but related

---

BOX 11.6
'Build-Together' national housing programme of Namibia

At Independence in March 1991, Namibia inherited a very skewed pattern of settlement development. The homelands policy had restricted the majority of people to small settlement areas within communal lands. The apartheid laws had prevented people from moving freely about the country including to urban areas. In urban areas, much low-income housing was also of poor quality. There were also particular problems with 'single quarters' accommodation that had been constructed for male migrant workers who had been refused permission to bring their families. With the lifting of movement restrictions, many households became established in a space intended to accommodate a single individual. In 1994, it was estimated that the housing need in urban areas was about 37,000 units. Estimates of need in rural areas, where three-quarters of the population live, are difficult to assess accurately.

The Namibian National Housing Policy made a strong commitment to develop an enabling housing process that would provide all households with a serviced site and facilitate access to housing. The government of Namibia has made housing one of its four development priorities following independence and, as such, it is committed to spending 5 per cent of its capital budget on housing. In order to assist low-income households improve their housing, the government launched the Build-Together Programme for those with an income of less than $Nam1,250 a month ($US357). Within urban areas, just under two-thirds of households have incomes below this level.

The government supports households through technical assistance, subsidized credit and encouragement for the communities to follow a structured framework. Within three years, the programme had reached about 3,500 households at a total cost of $US12 million. The programme has also been successful in reaching women-headed households. Two-fifths of Namibian households are headed by women and to date, about 45 per cent of households receiving loans have been headed by women. Land is free in Namibia but people have to pay for the development costs of the land. In the capital city this is very high and many low-income earners cannot afford to get serviced land.

When a community starts a project, they hold a workshop and go through the following five stages:

—identify problems
—agree on problems
—work out solutions to the problems
—select practical options from solutions
—plan for implementation

Housing loans are available in the form of options for different housing needs. Loans range from $Nam1,050–17,500 ($US300–5,000). Families, particularly those of informal workers, are encouraged to take out very small loans. However, people want to take out the biggest loan possible for their income. Loans are given for 20 years at an interest rate of 9 per cent for loans up to $Nam14,000. An additional 1 per cent is charged for every additional $Nam1,000 loaned over $Nam14,000. The current annual market rate of interest is between 14–16 per cent and the inflation rate is 12–13 per cent.

A Community Housing Development Group (CHDG) is established in each community interested in participating in the programme. This group is the decision-making body at the community level. To date, Groups have been established in twenty-two towns and villages. The Groups assess the major problems faced by the community and how best to solve them. The Group submits an implementation programme to the Ministry of Regional and Local Government and Housing. The Group receives the individual loan application forms from community members and has to decide whether or not to recommend them for approval. The final decision rests with the Ministry. A new act is being drafted to give more authority to the Groups and to devolve the programme.

To receive the loan each beneficiary opens an individual account in any private bank. Once the loan is agreed, the work programme begins and the central government transfers the progress payment directly to the individual's account. All monies pass through a private bank. Some villages participating in the programme are served by a mobile bank. Technical assistance is provided on request to households from the Directorate of Housing and is available for such tasks as the reblocking of settlements or community installation of infrastructure.

Groups are responsible for checking on the progress of the work and for monitoring repayments. The current repayment rate is 92 per cent. Many of these households have built one-room houses with a toilet for $Nam5,000. If the government builds such a house it would cost $Nam27,000.

Within each settlement, households receiving loans are encouraged to organize themselves into a community-based organization in order to strengthen solidarity within communities and to be able to negotiate with external agencies including the local authorities and Development Groups. This organization may take on responsibility for managing communal services.

Source: Asian Coalition for Housing Rights/Habitat International Coalition, 'Finance and resource mobilization for low income housing and neighbourhood development: a workshop report', Pagtambayayong Foundation, Philippines, 1994; and Ministry of Regional and Local Government and Housing, 'Build-Together, National Housing Programme: Implementation Guidelines', UNDP/UNCHS Project NAM/90/018, 1994.

aspects. The first is a tendency to individualize housing finance with loans being held by the individual household and not the community. In the Philippines, there is now much-increased pressure to individualize community mortgages into individual titles within two years of the start of the credit. In FONHAPO this tendency is also evident. This trend means that none of the benefits to community organization for development can be realized. The second trend is an emphasis on private-sector production, rather than production through local community enterprises. In this, it is sometimes forgotten that community enterprises or non-profit enterprises can themselves use market forces to keep down costs. The third trend is towards reducing the cost of subsidies. In order to achieve this, governments are trying to target subsidies more accurately on the poorest groups. As a consequence, there is a reduction in the scope of such programmes.

In addition to these general trends in housing for low-income communities, innovative government programmes for housing credit have found it difficult to maintain their momentum and continue their development. Experience to date suggests that working within government to establish processes that are favourable to low-income communities and their housing needs is a slow and difficult process. Certainly working within existing government institutions proved difficult for both FONHAPO and the Community Mortgage Programme. Reflecting on FONHAPO and why the programme failed to maintain the successes of the first five years, three reasons may be put forward. First, insufficient attention was given to demonstrating the success of the programme. Although the community organizations were strongly behind it, their support was not mobilized effectively and the potential support of the other groups was not identified, developed and maintained. Second, the process was not sufficiently institutionalized within the organization. Setting up a programme within government inevitably meant working with staff who were not familiar with the processes required to work effectively with low-income communities. And innovative and successful programmes always face the risk of being closed or replaced, when governments change, as they are too strongly associated with the previous regime. Third, the success of a programme can also make it particularly attractive to politicians seeking to strengthen their own power base and this too can bring disadvantages.

11.3 NGO Programmes for Financing Housing and Basic Services

Formal and informal institutions for housing finance

Because of the lack of credit available to low-income households in either the private sector or the government, NGOs began to experiment with housing finance programmes. This section describes some of the characteristics of such programmes including their relationship with formal financial sector institutions, subsidies, risk and repayment and additional support mechanisms.

NGOs who identified the need to intervene in financial markets to provide credit for housing investment have used different strategies in their relationship with formal finance institutions. Some have remained sceptical about the ability of the formal financial sector to address the needs of low-income households and have sought to establish alternative financial institutions. Others have established new financial institutions offering bridging or small-scale finance while encouraging links between the informal and formal financial sectors. Yet others have assisted the integration of low-income housing loans within the formal financial sector. Each of these strategies is described below.

In many cases, NGO experiences start with very small independent revolving loan funds in which households repay funds to a capital fund which then makes the funds available to another household. The revolving loan fund of Catholic Social Services in Karachi, Pakistan is typical of such programmes.[17] The fund has a capital base of $US150,000 and between 1981–92, it supported 830 households with about one-third of the loans being outstanding at the end of this period. As NGOs have sought to increase the scale of such programmes, some have found that formal sector institutions are unable to respond adequately to low-income groups. The first strategy is concerned with establishing alternative financial institutions. NGOs have therefore obtained donor and/or government support to establish alternative institutions that seek to combine the best of formal and informal sector finance. The founder of the Grameen Bank only set up the Bank, after failing to persuade conventional banks that people with low incomes (especially women) were credit-worthy and would repay loans.[18] Although best known for its credit programme to low-income households (primarily women) for income-generation, the Grameen Bank has also developed a large housing loan programme that is described in Box 11.7.

The second strategy is to develop a credit scheme that provides an alternative lending insti-

BOX 11.7
Grameen Bank housing loans

Although the Grameen Bank's main focus has been on providing credit for income-earning activities to poor rural households, it has also developed a housing loan programme which has been in operation since 1984. Members of the Grameen Bank who are borrowing to finance income-generating activities and who have met loan conditions and are up to date with repayments are also eligible for housing loans. The average loan made in May 1990 was $US298. The annual interest rate is 5 per cent and the period of the loan is about 10 years although borrowers are advised to try to repay more quickly. Up to May 1990, just under 80,000 loans had been disbursed, over 80 per cent to women. This programme is integrated into the Bank's other credit programmes, in which those seeking loans must form themselves into groups of five and several groups then come together to form a Centre. All group members and an elected 'Centre Chief' must approve a loan made to any of their members. The housing loan package includes four reinforced concrete pillars, two bundles of galvanized iron sheets, one sanitary latrine and additional material for the walls and roof. Some of this material is produced by manufacturing units supported by the Bank.

Source: Anzorena, Jorge (1989–91), reports in *SELAVIP* papers. Some additional information about the Grameen Bank comes from UNCHS (Habitat), *IYSH Bulletin* Tenth Issue, July 1987.

tution in the short term but has as its long-term objective the integration into formal-sector housing finance of low-income groups who take part. FUPROVI is a Costa Rican NGO that was established as part of the official development assistance programme of Sweden and its housing loan programme is described in the last section of this chapter. FUPROVI offers preliminary loan finance to households which then transfer their loans to the National Financing System for Housing; this allows FUPROVI to recover their capital and to extend credit to other households.[19]

The third strategy is to facilitate the immediate integration of low-income groups into the formal sector. For instance, NGOs establish loan-guarantee schemes to provide the collateral that low-income households need to obtain credit from formal-sector credit institutions. In such schemes, the NGO takes on the risk of loan default and relies on the formal-sector institution to provide the loan. One example is the Housing and Local Management Unit (EVGL) in Chile that has operated such a guarantee successfully, persuading a commercial bank to commit its own money.[20] Another, working at international level, is Homeless International which is developing a loan guarantee to support housing programmes in the South.[21] Another method of facilitating the integration of low-income groups into the formal sector is shown by the Fundación Carvajal in Colombia which offers training in self-build

techniques and a materials bank with the loans being provided by a formal bank.[22] The case of the Villa El Salvador Self-managed Urban Community (CUAVES) illustrates a different kind of support. In this case, credit was received from the formal sector but conditions imposed by this institution became too onerous for the community after an economic crisis in Peru. CUAVES helped negotiate a more acceptable solution.[23]

The relationship between any innovative credit scheme and the formal sector clearly depends on the particular strategy chosen. There are no obvious lessons emerging in regard to whether one strategy is more successful than another. Some schemes have successfully managed to integrate low-income groups into the formal sector, others have been less successful. Some attempts to set up alternative institutions have worked, others have not. The necessary conditions for success are dependent on the particular context within which the scheme is operating.

Subsidies and loan finance

While there appears to be broad agreement among many NGOs and international agencies that subsidized credit should be avoided for micro-enterprise loans, there is less agreement in regard to housing finance.[24] Most NGO housing finance programmes use fixed interest rates. In some cases, these are intentionally subsidized at below market rates. In others, the loan becomes subsidized as inflation levels increase and the real interest rate is not maintained. Within some large NGO credit programmes, housing is treated as a special case with subsidized loans being available for housing investment but not for income-generation activities.

Additional measures and support

Many innovative credit schemes include a package of additional measures to supplement and enhance the provision of credit. Some are multi-faceted community development programmes within which credit provision has a small part; others are primarily for the provision of credit with some small-scale extra support services being offered.

In the case of programmes where the main focus is on credit provision, the kinds of additional services frequently offered include assistance in obtaining legal tenure, and training in the activities for which credit is being extended or in financial/business management. For example, communities may require assistance in financial management so that they can handle large amounts of money without creating dissension within the community. Households that are using the finance for housing improvement are likely to benefit from technical advice in materials and methods to use.[25] For example, EVGL in Chile offered technical assistance to improve the quality of housing development.[26] They also set up a materials bank to ensure that households received maximum benefit from the funds by being able to obtain discounted prices by bulk purchase of materials and saving on transport costs.

Some of the more ambitious credit schemes use group development techniques to establish a structure through which borrowing can take place. In many cases, the group also provides a guarantee of repayment. In such cases, it may be several years before credit can be provided. In Bombay, three agencies, SPARC, the National Slum Dwellers' Federation and *Mahila Milan* (a collective of grassroots women's organizations) work together in low-income communities to establish two complementary loan programmes, the first for emergency credit and income-generation loans, and the second for housing investment.[27] The agencies estimate that it takes between three and six months working with a new community to establish the savings programme and associated financial management skills prior to emergency and income-generation loans being operational. Housing loans take significantly longer as a new site needs to be identified and additional sources of finance obtained.

A number of integrated urban community-development programmes have included housing loan components.[28] Such programmes commonly provide infrastructure improvements such as water and sanitation, health services, improved employment opportunities and support for housing improvements such as technical assistance, material banks and/or housing credit. Such programmes can be structured to maximize the benefits to each individual component. For example, housing investment can assist in achieving income generation objectives in several ways:

- training courses can enhance the construction skills of building labourers within the community;
- credit for income-generation can assist such informal sector workers to obtain the tools they need; and
- providing finance directly to households ensures that it will be spent within the immediate community thereby supporting the local economy.

Box 11.8 describes the Toilet Block Project of three agencies working collectively in India, SPARC, the National Slum Dwellers' Federation and *Mahila Milan*. This project is just one component within the comprehensive strategy of these agencies to provide infrastructure, services, improved employment opportunities and housing to low-income communities. Within the component, multiple objectives have been achieved; in particular, the strengthening of community organization, the provision of sanitation and enhancement of incomes. The promotion of communal toilet blocks was also something that was initially opposed by various international agencies, despite the difficulties identified with individual toilets (see below).

Risk and repayment

In housing projects (which may include the provision or improvement of infrastructure for individual housing units), there are a number of special characteristics that affect risk and repayment. The large capital cost and slow depreciation of the capital asset mean that repayments are often spread over an extended period. In some housing projects, loan periods are often significantly longer than in loans for income-generating activities. For example, those participating with FUPROVI and Koperasi Kredit Borromeus repay their housing loans over 15 years.[29] In many other cases, much shorter loan periods are used; for example, Catholic Social Services requires their borrowers to repay the loan in three years.[30] For the household, the shorter the period of repayment the higher the monthly repayments and the smaller the loan which can be afforded. But longer loan periods raise the amount of capital needed by the NGO to reach a given number of people.

A second characteristic is that housing construction or improvement does not usually add directly to household income, although such investments may improve the magnitude and stability of such income. In general, the investment does not generate additional funds to help meet the costs of repayment. For this reason, the requirement that participants save at a rate equivalent to their future repayments for a period before obtaining a loan may be particularly important to ensure that households who cannot afford the repayments do not participate. In many NGO housing loan programmes, loans are only available to households that have successfully completed a savings programme.

A third characteristic is that the money may be invested in a property for which the residents lack legal tenure. In most urban centres, projects which only offer loans to those households with legal tenure of the house site will not reach a high proportion of low-income households. It is common for between 30 and 60 per cent of a city's population (and a much higher proportion of the low income population) to live in illegal settlements.[31] For this reason, the NGO may also need to assist participants in obtaining legal tenure. In several case studies—for instance that of Barrio San Jorge in Argentina described in Chapter 10—the NGO

BOX 11.8
The construction of toilet blocks in Bombay

The development of a model communal toilet block began in 1987, when SPARC, the National Slum Dwellers' Federation and Mahila Milan were working with women pavement dwellers to consider how best to provide infrastructure and services within new housing developments. It immediately became apparent that there were a number of problems with the individual household toilets that were included in conventional development plans for low-income communities. The major problems include (1) the size of the houses, which are often too small for toilets to be easily accommodated; (2) sporadic water supply and low pressure compound the problems of ensuring that the toilets are kept clean; (3) The individual toilets are expensive and add 15–20 per cent to the cost of the basic dwelling unit, and houses with individual toilets are more desirable to richer groups, with the result that low-income households are under greater pressure to sell and find alternative accommodation.

The women pavement dwellers argued in favour of communal toilets. Although these had not been successful in previous projects, the women believed that this was because they had been appropriated by powerful individuals within the settlement who charged a fee for use. The women believed that communal toilets would help to develop a sense of community awareness and solidarity. Such solidarity is an invaluable asset in

reducing the vulnerability of low-income households both individually and collectively. As women, they also valued a common washing area within the settlement. In order that the facilities were not over-used, it was estimated that there should be one toilet block for every 20 households and one toilet for every four households. Separate facilities should be provided for men, women and children. Where needed, water stand-pipes and refuse collection points were also provided.

In Bombay, the Municipal Corporation has been much criticized both for a failure to provide and maintain toilet blocks. When SPARC started working in Dharavi, one of the largest informal settlements, there was one toilet for every 800 people. Unable to obtain state funds, SPARC looked elsewhere and obtained assistance from a Northern NGO. The funds were used to construct five blocks and the Corporation agreed to refund the costs once the toilets were completed.

Mahila Milan with SPARC and the National Slum Dwellers' Federation suggested to the Corporation that the communities are best placed to ensure that the toilets were kept clean and functioning. However, in order to ensure a sense of ownership, communities need to be involved in developing and constructing the toilet blocks. SPARC have targeted women construction workers living in the settlements to be involved in working on the model toilet blocks. Experience on the first sites has shown that women can learn the techniques fully after participating in the construction process of three blocks. The skills they learn enable them to obtain a 200

per cent increase in their wages.

Some four to five blocks have been built in Bombay. In each of the locations there is a community organization with membership of the Federation to provide local management for the project. Although progress has been slow because of bureaucracy within the local government offices responsible for approving plans and connections, these model toilet blocks together with those constructed in other cities in India have demonstrated that communities can both build the blocks and can collect contributions (of between 2–5 Rps a month) from members for cleaning and small maintenance costs. There are significant cost savings compared to the private sector. Construction costs in the pilot toilet blocks are only 40 per cent of the cost charged by a private contractor and costs are likely to fall further as production systems become more efficient. More income is also generated by toilet blocks that are on main roads or thoroughfares, from their use by passers-by.

The long-term intended model is that the government will contribute the land and the costs of the construction, and the community will build the structure themselves. In this way they will be involved in the process and will therefore feel a commitment to maintaining it. In January 1995, the Bombay Municipal Corporation agreed to support the scaling-up of this programme to provide a total of 2,000 toilet blocks throughout the city. Similar programmes for these communal toilet blocks are also being developed in Kanpur and Bangalore, among other cities.

Source: UNDP, 'People's Participation in Improving Sanitation—A case of Kanpur Slums, Caselet 3, UNDP/World Bank Water and Sanitation Program, New Delhi, 1994; and Patel, Sheela and Michael Hoffmann, 'Homeless International, SPARC IS13 Toilet Block Construction, Interim Report', Homeless International, 1993.

---

is working with the inhabitants to secure the transfer of tenure to the inhabitants.[32] The experience of FUPROVI in Costa Rica is interesting in this respect because the organization offers possibilities to those who cannot achieve legal status. In other cases, the land may be legally owned but the housing design may infringe building regulations. The NGO may have to support the community in negotiations with the city or municipal authorities.

A fourth characteristic occurs in much infrastructure and basic services provision where the investment is, by necessity, provided to the community as a whole. The provision of credit for investment in infrastructure or services which benefit a group of households or community clearly has different characteristics to the provision of credit for individuals. Certain services may be funded through charges made to residents as they use the service—for instance, building-materials stores set up within low-income settlements which obtain wholesale or discount prices through bulk purchase; the materials can be pur-

chased by the inhabitants, as they require them. Other services for which there is a constant demand might also be financed in this way—for example, child-care centres and the collection of garbage. Loans for larger, more capital intensive schemes that depend on regular repayments from most or all inhabitants in a settlement may be more problematic, although there are case studies of settlement-wide piped water supply schemes which have had good records of cost recovery. Certain forms of infrastructure such as roads and site drains can present particular problems in terms of recovering costs from all beneficiaries since their use cannot be denied to those who do not pay. There may be little incentive for individual households to repay once the investment has been made. One possibility, evident in some upgrading schemes, is a regular payment levied on all households to recover costs for an integrated package of infrastructure and service improvements. Although costs per household can be kept down, especially where all inhabitants are prepared to contribute to the improvements, such integrated schemes for whole settlements or neighbourhoods will still demand relatively large amounts of capital up-front, with repayment having to take place over a number of years. If cost recovery is sought from such integrated schemes—or from the more capital intensive aspects such as piped water systems and sewers—the inhabitants must be fully involved in discussions about what should be done and the cost implications of different options. Consensus reached within low-income settlements as to what should be done and its cost implications for each household are obviously more likely to produce good cost recovery.

Conclusion

The NGO experience in the last twenty years provided a basis for many of the innovative government programmes described earlier. The weight of experience has been in housing rather than infrastructure provision and it is this aspect that many government programmes have sought to replicate. Such experiences have demonstrated that lack of loan finance for housing is an important factor in increasing household expenditures and delaying house consolidation. As well as demonstrating the need for appropriate housing finance, they have also demonstrated that low-income households are willing and able to repay—and indeed often achieve repayment rates that are much higher than wealthier groups repaying to many commercial banks or housing finance institutions. The household's involvement in loan repayments achieves important development objectives at both a micro- and macro-level. At the micro-level, it enables households and communities to participate directly in the development process and reinforce a sense of self-reliance and independence. Through community-based loan repayment structures, communities are brought together in a forum that enables households to identify and explore the benefits of collective action. At the macro-level, loan programmes enable governments to recover some funds for use by other communities. Few development programmes offer support to more than a small number of households and, if programmes are to be able to respond to the scale of needs, resources need to be allocated efficiently and recycled wherever possible.

11.4 International Finance for Housing, Infrastructure and Services[33]

Introduction

Funding for human settlements projects from development assistance agencies comes from three principal sources. The first (and much the largest) is from multilateral agencies, especially development banks with the World Bank Group being much the largest single source. The second is from the bilateral agencies of donor governments—for instance the bilateral agencies of the US, German, Japanese, French and British governments. The third is from the enormous number and range of international private voluntary organizations such as MISEREOR (Germany), CEBEMO (Netherlands), CARE (the United States), Christian Aid (UK)—and the different Save the Children and OXFAM organizations that exist in different OECD countries. Although total funding-flows from these are much smaller than those from the first two sources, the priority they give to basic services makes them significant in total funding for such services. Arab-funded bilateral and multilateral agencies are also important in total development assistance but less so in funding for human settlements projects.

Before describing the scale and nature of these funding-flows, two points should be noted: first, how in most international agencies, funding for human settlements lacks any coherent framework and second how low a priority funding for human settlements receives.[34] In most agencies, there is no department that provides a coherent framework for funding for human settlements projects, although in some agencies, initiatives are underway to develop these. Few agencies have a special section for 'human settlements' or for 'urban'. For official projects (that need the approval of the recipient government), funding for human settlements is simply the aggregate of a great range of projects initiated by different ministries or agencies in the recipient government and different sectors or country offices in the donor agencies. However, most fall within two broad categories:

- Funding for the basic infrastructure and services that is central to adequate housing and living conditions and health—water supply, sanitation, drainage, health care and, where needed, solid-waste collection. These are justified in terms of improving housing and living conditions and reducing ill health and premature death.

- Funding for large urban infrastructure projects such as ports, airports, underground or light-rail city transit systems, highways and city electrification, or urban services such as hospitals and centres of higher education in recognition of the importance of urban infrastructure for economic growth.

This overview of funding-flows to housing, infrastructure and services to both rural and urban areas from multilateral banks, bilateral agencies and international Private Voluntary Agencies is organized in four sections. The first looks at funding to shelter projects and how the scale and nature of this funding has changed since 1980. The second considers funding-flows to the infrastructure and services associated with residential areas; short subsections also consider funding-flows to social funds and to 'women in development' projects. The third is funding-flows to urban infrastructure and services. The final section considers what constrains a greater flow of funding to projects that reach lower-income groups with improved housing and basic services.

Shelter

In recent years, shelter projects and housing finance combined have attracted less than 3 per cent of the commitments of most development assistance agencies. Table 11.1 gives figures for selected multilateral and bilateral agencies. The largest sources of donor-funding for shelter have come from the World Bank Group, the Inter-American Development Bank and US AID's Housing Guaranty Programme. Some bilateral agencies fund projects that seek to reach

low-income groups with improved housing conditions but in general, these receive a very low priority. An OECD estimate suggested that the total commitment to urban housing projects of all the bilateral aid programmes of OECD countries averaged less than $90 million a year between 1986 and 1990;[35] this represents less than one-eighth of the annual average commitments of the World Bank to housing projects and housing finance during these same years. Overall, the proportion of funds allocated to shelter from multilateral and bilateral agencies is declining.

During the period 1980–1993 a few donor agencies provided considerable sums to low-income housing projects in urban areas, most of them in large cities. Perhaps more importantly, most went to projects that differed considerably from conventional public housing. For instance, support was provided for 'slum' and 'squatter' upgrading schemes that sought to improve conditions within existing low-income settlements by providing or improving water supply, provision for sanitation and drainage and often community facilities. Many such projects also provided

TABLE 11.1 The proportion of aid and non-concessional loan commitments to shelter projects and housing finance, 1980–93

Agency	Total funding (US$ billion)	Proportion of commitments to SHELTER PROJECTS	Proportion of commitments to HOUSING FINANCE	Proportion of total commitments to shelter projects & housing finance 1980–93	1990–91	1992–93
Aid (concessional loans or grants)						
International Development Association						
** Africa	27.9	1.2	0.0	1.2	1.4	1.1
** Asia	38.6	1.3	0.0	1.3	0.1	0.0
** Latin America & Caribbean	1.9	1.4	0.0	1.4	0.0	0.0
African Development Bank	10.2	0.4	0.0	0.4	0.0	0.0
Asian Development Fund	14.3	0.9	0.1	1.0	0.7	0.0
Inter-American Development Bank	6.5	3.4	0.0	3.4	0.0	4.4
Caribbean Development Bank	0.7	0.0	1.2	1.2	1.8	0.6
Arab Fund for Economic & Social Develt (1980–91)	4.7	1.2	0.0	1.2*	0.0	
Overseas Economic Cooperation Fund, Japan (1987–91)	36.5	0.8	0.1		0.1	
Non-concessional loans						
International Bank for Reconstruction and Development (IBRD)						
** Africa	29.6	2.1	1.2	3.3	0.3	11.4
** Asia	90.6	1.3	0.9	2.3	1.5	0.0
** Latin America & Caribbean	68.7	1.7	2.1	3.8	3.3	4.5
African Development Bank	17.6	0.1	0.0	0.1	0.0	0.0
Asian Development Bank	30.9	1.2	0.0	1.2	0.0	0.0
Inter-American Development Bank	41.7	2.1	0.0	2.1	0.4	0.9
Caribbean Development Bank	0.5	0.0	1.0	1.0	0.0	0.5

* 1980–91

Notes and Sources: Satterthwaite, David, 'The scale and nature of international donor assistance to housing, basic services and other human-settlements related projects', Paper presented at the UNU/WIDER Conference on 'Human Settlements in the changing global political and economic processes', August 1995. Shelter projects include slum- and squatter-upgrading, serviced-site schemes, core-housing schemes and community-development projects which include housing improvement. These funding-flows only apply to commitments to countries in the South—for instance, they do not include World Bank commitments to East and Southern European nations. The figures are based on analyses drawn from two computer databases. The first contains each agency's total annual commitments to each nation, with total commitments converted into $US at their 1990 value. The second database is an aid project database with details of all human settlement projects or projects with human settlements components.

secure tenure to the inhabitants whose house or occupation of the land (or both) had previously been considered 'illegal'. Although upgrading projects did improve conditions for several million urban households at a relatively low cost, there were often problems with maintaining the upgraded infrastructure and services. These programmes made up for a lack of investment in the past that should have been made on a continuous basis by local authorities and while they improved conditions considerably, rarely did they also increase the capacity of local authorities and citizen groups to maintain them.[36]

Site and service projects provided cheaper units than public housing units by providing only a house site within a residential subdivision with roads, often electricity and some provision for water supply (and sometimes provision for sanitation). The construction of the shelter was left to the households who received the plot. The hope was that unit costs would come down to the point where these could be provided to relatively low-income households who could pay their full costs. Core housing schemes included a one room 'core' as well.

Donor agencies faced many difficulties with serviced-site schemes. Under pressure to reduce unit costs, recipient governments often developed them on cheap land sites that were in locations too distant from employment sources to suit poorer households. And governments rarely took these up as a form of housing intervention that was implemented on a large enough scale to have much impact.[37] While the particular projects could reduce unit costs by being exempt from zoning and land use regulations, few efforts were made to change these regulations as they affected all other sites.[38] In addition, the fact that many serviced-site projects obtained government land at below market prices also meant they were not easily replicable.[39] The priority given to such projects by the few agencies that had funded them declined—for instance, most of the World Bank and US AID commitments to serviced site projects were made between 1975 and 1985. Both upgrading projects and serviced site projects also 'projectized' city problems when more fundamental reforms were needed—for instance in changing building codes, improving the availability of housing finance and reforming city and municipal government to address all the weaknesses noted in Chapter 5.[40]

One of the first responses by the agencies involved in supporting shelter was to channel funding to support housing finance—in recognition of how many countries lacked an efficient housing finance system. For instance, between 1980 and 1993, the World Bank Group made commitments totalling $6.5 billion to shelter: two-fifths went to support housing finance

with around 30 per cent to slum- and squatter-upgrading, serviced sites and core-housing projects; most of the rest went to what can be termed 'integrated community development' projects that contained too many components to be classified as 'shelter' or 'water and sanitation.'[41] This contrasts with the period 1972–84 when housing finance received very little support and most funding for shelter was for projects, i.e. for upgrading slums or squatter settlements, serviced sites or low-cost housing. The average size of loans also increased considerably, and an increasing proportion of loans went to middle income groups.[42]

However, in the longer term, within the World Bank Group there was a third shift to 'housing policy development' that sought to address some of the city-wide structural constraints that had limited the impact of 'projects'. In this third shift, the aim of loans is to improve the performance of the housing sector as a whole—see Box 11.9. It appears that the Bank, in general, is giving less priority to shelter in recent years; total commitments in 1991 and 1993 were among the lowest since 1980 and no commitment to housing finance was made in 1993. A recent sector report stated that upgrading projects will remain a critical component of Bank lending in the future.[43]

This new emphasis locates support for shelter within the broader macro-economic framework and includes within it explicit goals for improving macro-economic performance as well as improving housing conditions.[44] It couches support for housing within a broader framework of 'enabling markets to work'.[45] This evolution in the World Bank's housing policies is consistent with broader changes of thinking about development within and outside the Bank.[46]

Changes within US AID also reflect broader changes in thinking. US AID's Housing Guaranty Programme made much fewer loan commitments to shelter in the years 1989–93 compared to the period 1980–88. Loan commitments to shelter projects made between 1980 and 1993 totalled close to $1.8 billion. However, this Programme has, in recent years, given increasing importance to finance for environmental infrastructure and improved municipal management as will be described below.

The Inter-American Development Bank was the first multilateral agency to have a major programme to fund shelter projects. This dates back to the 1960s and the Alliance for Progress during which a considerable number of housing projects were funded in both rural and urban areas. During the 1980s and early 1990s, the emphasis changed away from 'shelter' projects to projects to improve shelter-related infrastructure and services. During the period 1980–93, loans to shelter projects totalled some $1.1 billion, three-fifths of them for

BOX 11.9
Changes in the World Bank's housing policy: 1970s to 1990s

Objectives

1970s: Implement projects to achieve affordable land and housing for the poor; achieve cost recovery, create conditions for large-scale replicability of projects

1980s: Create self-supporting financial intermediaries capable of making long-term mortgage loans to low- and moderate-income households; reduce and restructure housing subsidies

1990s: Create a well-functioning housing sector that serves the needs of consumers, producers, financiers and local and central governments; and that enhances economic development, alleviates poverty and supports a sustainable environment

Role of Government

1970s: Emphasis on direct provision by government of land, housing and finance to facilitate progressive development of housing conditions by project beneficiaries

1980s: Emphasis on provision of housing finance, mainly by public institutions, and rationalization of housing subsidies (reduction, improved targeting and shift from financial to fiscal)

1990s: Adoption by government agencies with policy-making co-ordination and regulatory responsibilities of an enabling role, to facilitate the provision of land and housing by the private sector; and improved co-ordination of sector and macro-economic policy

Policy and Lending Instruments

1970s: Sites and services demonstration projects emphasizing affordable housing and infrastructure standards, tenure security and internal cross-subsidies

1980s: Housing finance projects emphasizing interest-rate reform (to enhance resource mobilization and improve mortgage-instrument design); subsidy design and improved institutional financial performance of public agencies involved in direct provision of land, infrastructure and housing

1990s: Integrated array of policy and lending instruments to stimulate demand (property-rights development, housing finance, and targeted subsidies); facilitate supply (infrastructure provision, regulatory reform; and building industry organization); and manage the housing sector as a whole (institutional reform and co-ordination with macro-economic policy).

Source: Mayo, Stephen K. and Shlomo Angel, *Enabling Housing Markets to Work,* A World Bank Policy Paper, The World Bank, Washington DC, 1993.

---

integrated community-development projects and most of the rest for serviced sites or upgrading. Nearly two-thirds of this was committed in the years 1986, 1987 and 1989 and annual commitments since then have fallen off.

The low priority given by other multilateral agencies to shelter-related projects is evident in Table 11.1. The Asian Development Bank has given a very low priority to shelter and made no commitments to shelter projects during 1992 and 1993.

Among other bilateral programmes, many examples can be cited of shelter projects that received bilateral support, especially where official bilateral aid was channelled through international private voluntary organizations such as SELAVIP, MISEREOR and Homeless International. However, shelter has never been a priority of any bilateral agency except the US AID Housing Guaranty Programme. This is borne out by an analysis of who co-financed projects with the World Bank and the regional development banks which found less interest among bilateral agencies on co-financing shelter projects than co-financing urban infrastructure and services.[47] The shelter programme of the Swedish International Development Cooperation Agency (SIDA) in Latin America, and the United Kingdom Overseas Development Administration's expanded support to India for slum- and squatter-improvement programmes are two examples of shelter projects that received direct bilateral support. Among other bilateral agencies, the German technical co-operation agency GTZ has a long established and varied programme of support for shelter projects, targeted at poorer groups. Swiss Development Cooperation has also supported some urban shelter projects including squatter-upgrading in Douala and social housing in Bujumbura. FINNIDA has provided support for the preparation of national shelter strategies in six countries, in co-operation with UNCHS.

Many international Private Voluntary Organizations allocate a higher priority to shelter projects or community-based housing finance schemes than official agencies. Although their contribution within total aid flows is not very large—an estimate for 1991 suggested a total aid flow of $US5.2 billion compared to official development assistance of $55.8 billion[48]—they have financed many innovative projects and have also developed new ways of reaching low-income groups and working in partnership with local community organizations and NGOs.

Infrastructure and services for shelter

When analysing international donor flows to infrastructure and services for shelter, the decision was made to include not only funding to water supply, sanitation and drainage but also to two other kinds of projects that are not normally associated with housing: primary health-care centres including dispensaries, health centres and initiatives to control infectious or parasitic diseases; and primary schools and other educational programmes aimed at literacy or primary education. Although health care and education investments are not under the control of housing or public works ministries or agencies—and in many countries, these are the direct responsibility of ministries of health and education—these are among the most important interventions to improve living conditions and among the most important in reducing disease, disablement and premature death within shelters and the residential areas in which they are located. Primary health-care centres and literacy are central to improving health and controlling disease within villages and urban residential areas.

The infrastructure and services associated with housing and residential areas receive a higher priority from both multilateral and bilateral agencies than housing itself or housing finance. In some agencies, these do receive a high priority (see Table 11.2). This table also shows the noticeable increase in the priority given to such infrastructure and services in the early 1990s.

The World Bank is much the largest donor for this group of projects both in terms of aid (through its concessional loans) and in terms of non-concessional loans. Around $22 billion was committed to the infrastructure and services associated with shelter between 1980 and 1993, most of it to urban areas. Close to half went to water supply, sanitation and drainage with around a quarter to primary health care and just over a

fifth to basic education and literacy. Virtually all the rest went to social funds or social employment schemes that are described in a later section. For the non-concessional loans, three-fifths of commitments during these fourteen years were for water and sanitation with close to a fifth for primary health care and for primary or basic education. Thus, while the scale of the World Bank's commitments specifically to shelter have declined, the scale of the commitments to interventions that are central to improving housing and living conditions and providing services that every village or urban settlement needs (primary health care and schools) has increased considerably.

Among the other multilateral agencies, the Inter-American Development Bank with loan commitments of $4.4 billion in these fourteen years is the largest donor; Table 11.2 also shows the high priority that this Bank gave to shelter-related infrastructure and services in recent years. The Asian Development Bank generally gives a low priority to these kinds of projects although as Table 11.2 shows, these received an unusually high proportion of total commitments for soft loans for 1992 and 1993. Just over half were for water supply and sanitation. The African

TABLE 11.2 The proportion of aid and non-concessional loan commitments to shelter-related infrastructure and basic services, 1980–93.

Agency	Total funding (US$ billion)	Proportion of total project commitments				Percent of total commitments		
		WATER AND SANITATION	PRIMARY HEALTH CARE	BASIC EDUCN	POVERTY REDN & JOBS	1980–93	1990–91	1992–93
Aid (concessional loans or grants)								
International Development Association								
** Africa	27.9	3.6	2.7	4.3	1.9	12.7	20.0	15.3
** Asia	38.6	5.5	5.3	2.7	1.4	15.0	22.1	36.2
** Latin America & Caribbean	1.9	3.8	3.5	1.8	7.6	16.8	41.1	11.8
African Development Bank	10.2	7.3	2.7	4.3	1.3	15.7	15.8	15.3
Asian Development Fund	14.3	4.4	1.6	1.7	0.3	7.9	7.7	22.6
Inter-American Development Bank	6.5	18.0	1.4	3.1	1.3	29.6	28.0	37.8
Caribbean Development Bank	0.7	4.1	—	—	0.5	4.9	3.1	2.2
UNICEF	6.6	13.7	33.5	7.9	—	55.1	57.4	47.9
Overseas Economic Cooperation Fund, Japan (1987–91)	36.5	3.8	—	0.4	—	4.5	3.7	
Non-concessional loans								
International Bank for Reconstruction and Development (IBRD)								
** Africa	29.6	8.0	1.2	0.9	0.1	10.4	12.3	12.9
** Asia	90.6	3.3	0.9	0.9	0.04	5.1	7.9	6.6
** Latin America & Caribbean	68.7	5.1	1.6	2.1	0.0	8.9	12.2	11.1
African Development Bank	17.6	9.0	0.4	1.6	0.4	11.5	13.5	14.5
Asian Development Bank	30.9	4.5	1.0	—	—	5.6	1.3	0.7
Inter-American Development Bank	41.7	6.3	0.3	0.3	0.6	7.5	13.0	17.3
Caribbean Development Bank	0.5	6.7	0.0	0.0	0.0	6.7	8.5	0.0

Notes and Sources: Satterthwaite, David, 'The scale and nature of international donor assistance to housing, basic services and other human-settlements related projects', Paper presented at the UNU/WIDER Conference on 'Human Settlements in the changing global political and economic processes', Helsinki, 1995. Water and sanitation are part of Primary Health Care so the column headed Primary Health Care includes all its components other than water and sanitation. Basic education is taken to include primary education, literacy programmes and basic education programmes. UNICEF figures are for disbursements, not commitments so they are not directly comparable; they are included here to give an idea of the scale and relative importance of UNICEF funding in this project category. The disbursements for basic health care include support for child health and nutrition and for child and family basic health services. The funding totals noted above including funding for both rural and urban projects. For the totals reported here for water supply, sanitation and drainage, these only included projects whose main focus was delivering or improving these for residential areas. City-wide investments in improved drainage and investments in water supplies whose main focus was not improving supplies to residential areas are included in Table 11.4. These funding-flows do not include commitments to East and Southern European nations.

Development Bank Group has, historically, given a relatively high priority to water supply and sanitation and it continues to do so. This bank allocated close to $4 billion to shelter-related infrastructure and services with most going to water and sanitation. However, in recent years, primary health care, primary or basic education and social funds have received more support and the proportion to water and sanitation has declined. The priority given to basic education has also increased in recent years.

UNICEF disbursements to shelter-related infrastructure and services totalled over $4.5 billion during these fourteen years, three-fifths of the support going to primary/basic health care services (including support for child health and nutrition and for community or family basic health services). This makes it the second largest multilateral aid programme to projects in this category, despite the fact that UNICEF's total annual funding commitments appear small relative to most multilateral and bilateral agencies.

Among all the largest multilateral banks (the World Bank, the African, Asian and Inter-American Development Bank), non-concessional loans represent a larger source of funding for shelter related infrastructure and services and most of these loan commitments are with countries with relatively high per capita incomes and most such support goes to urban projects.

When viewing trends in the support given to these kinds of projects by the different agencies listed in Table 11.2, in general, they received a higher priority when comparing the years 1990–1 and 1992–3 to the average for 1980–93. This is the case for the World Bank for all three regions (Africa, Asia, Latin America and the Caribbean) and for the Inter-American and African Development Banks.

There were also some notable changes in priority among the different kinds of project within this category. Within the World Bank, the most noticeable change is the higher priority given to primary health care and to primary or basic education. The World Bank had become the single most important source of funding for primary health care worldwide. The increased funding to primary health care was particularly noticeable in Asia. The change in priority to primary and basic education is comparable with total commitments being especially high for the years 1988–93; for each year from 1991 to 1993, annual commitments exceeded $650 million. The increased priority to primary and basic education was particularly noticeable in Latin America.

It is much more difficult to provide a comprehensive overview of the commitment of bilateral agencies to human settlements projects. Unlike the multilateral agencies, few publish details of all the projects they fund with enough detail to allow an analysis comparable to that provided above for the agencies listed in Table 11.2.[49] The most up-to-date figures available for the bilateral agencies' priorities in this area are shown in Table 11.3. They are reported under a category termed 'social and administrative infrastructure' under which health and population, education, planning and public administration and water supply and 'other' fall. This is the category used by the OECD Development Assistance Committee to report on funding flows from the bilateral aid programmes of OECD countries and no more detailed statistics are available that allow comparisons between these bilateral agencies. These statistics show a low priority to water and sanitation, and to health and population. Water supply did not receive much more; the average for water supply and 'other' was 4.9 per cent with ten of the nineteen bilateral programmes giving less than 5 per cent. Education receives a higher priority but in most bilateral programmes, this does not reflect a priority to basic education since most bilateral assistance to education goes to support scholarships for students from the South to study in the higher education institutions in the donor country. As such, most of the donor assistance to education remains in the donor country.

In recent years, several bilateral and multilateral agencies have shown a greater interest in urban poverty, even if this had not yet become apparent in the latest statistics showing their sectoral priorities. For instance, the Dutch Government's bilateral aid programme has a new programme on urban poverty while the United Nations Development Program launched a new funding initiative in 1992 to support local initiatives to improve the urban environment—see Box 11.10.

Overall, the scale of funding that has gone into water, sanitation and health care has been well below what is needed to achieve the ambitious goals set by the International Drinking Water Supply and Sanitation Decade and the World Health Organization's 'Health for All'. For the Decade, the primary goal was to ensure full access to water supply and sanitation to all inhabitants of the South by 1990;[50] Chapter 8 described how large the shortfall remains in the early 1990s. There were also important lessons learned during the 1980s about how difficult it is to improve water supply and sanitation provision where local authorities remain weak and where the institutional structure to maintain new investments is simply not there. One review of the Decade's performance suggested too much attention to the 'hardware', i.e. the capital equipment and too little to the 'software'—the institutional structure

TABLE 11.3 The priority given by bilateral aid programmes to different project categories within 'social and administrative infrastructure' in 1991

Countries	The % of official development assistance to				
	Educ-ation	Health & Popn.	Planning & public Admin.	Water Supply & other	Total for social and administrative infrastructure
Australia	30.1	1.1	4.8	7.9	43.9
Austria	22.3	0.6	0.2	5.4	28.5
Belgium	14.9	12.6	3.8	1.6	32.9
Canada	7.1	1.8	0.5	4.9	14.3
Denmark	9.4	11.9	0.4	17.9	39.6
Finland	4.9	1.2	2.7	11.1	19.9
France	22.5	3.2	2.4	3.8	31.9
Germany	12.9	1.6	2.4	7.8	24.7
Ireland	21.3	6.2	5.1	3.7	36.3
Italy	6.6	4.4	0.7	8.4	20.1
Japan	6.3	1.6	0.4	3.9	12.2
Netherlands	12.3	2.0	2.8	8.3	25.4
New Zealand	41.3	2.5	5.3	2.3	51.4
Norway	5.0	2.2	1.1	3.3	11.6
Spain	5.0	1.5	1.1	4.4	12.0
Sweden	9.1	8.8	2.8	5.4	26.1
Switzerland	6.4	3.6	0.2	4.5	14.7
United Kingdom	12.6	2.7	3.3	5.4	24.0
USA	2.8	4.4	4.4	3.6	15.2
Total DAC	8.7	3.2	2.4	4.9	19.2

Source: OECD Development Assistance Committee, *Development Cooperation 1993 Efforts and Policies of the Members of the Development Assistance Committee*, Paris, 1994, table 26, pp. 190–1.

that must operate to ensure efficient operation and maintenance—whether by a public authority, a private company or a community organization.[51] But here, perhaps the most important reason is the low priority given by governments in the South to water supply and sanitation. An analysis of who funded capital investments in water supply and sanitation based on a sample of countries found that the total contributions from international funding agencies were comparable to those of governments both for new systems and for rehabilitating existing ones and both in water supply and sanitation.[52] Here, donor agencies' priorities to water supply and sanitation is likely to have increased, if recipient governments had given these a higher priority in their negotiations for development assistance.

Most international private voluntary organizations give a higher priority to water supply, sanitation, health care and basic education than official development assistance agencies. Most have been oriented to rural settlements although in recent years, an increasing number of these organizations have increased the scale and scope of their work in low-income urban settlements, especially illegal and informal settlements.

Social funds

A new kind of project or programme became increasingly important in the last ten years at the World Bank and in certain other multilateral

New initiatives to address urban problems

The Urban Poverty Programme (Netherlands): In 1990, a special unit, the Spearhead Programme to Combat Urban Poverty, was set up in the Netherlands Ministry of Foreign Affairs and Development Co-operation, along with three other special programmes—on women in development, on research and on environment. This will promote greater attention to employment and income-generation programmes for poorer groups in urban areas, empowerment strategies for community-based organizations and programmes directing support to poorer sections of the urban population, including those to help improve housing and living conditions. As from 1992, all projects are being screened to check their likely impact on poverty, environment and women.

Local Initiative Facility for Urban Environment (LIFE): This is a programme set up by the United Nations Development Programme in 1992 to promote and fund local initiatives to improve the quality of the urban environment. Most of the support goes to funding community based actions to address such problems as inadequate provision of water supply and sanitation or of services to collect and manage solid and liquid wastes, poor environmental health or lack of environmental education. The programme was initiated in eight countries. In each, a participatory consultation was held, bringing together NGOs, community-based organizations, local authorities and the private sector to establish priorities and guidelines for the selection of local projects to receive support. Selection committees have been formed to review and consider applications for funding. The programme is now to extend its activities to more countries. A particular focus is now being given to 'local-local dialogue', the bringing together of all stakeholders to identify and consider further the policy implications.

Sources: Milbert, Isabelle, *Cooperation and Urban Development; Urban Policies of Bilateral and Multilateral Cooperation Agencies* Second edition (draft), IUED/SDC, Geneva, 1992; and UNDP, 'Brief on the Local Initiative Facility for Urban Environment (LIFE)' New York, 1992.

and bilateral agencies: social-action programmes targeted at poorer groups, most of them aimed at protecting poorer groups who would otherwise be adversely affected by structural adjustment programmes. These include donor support for Social Funds (sometimes called Social and Economic Funds) and employment programmes targeted at poorer groups. These usually seek to combine support for a wide range of social projects (for instance health care centres, schools) with employment generation. The World Bank is the single largest contributor to these funds; these only began to receive support in the second half of the 1980s but by 1990 they had become a regular and significant part of commitments; total commitments exceeded $200 million in 1991 and 1992 and exceeding $570 million in 1993.[53] Most commitments have been to African countries although in 1993, three Latin American countries also received loan commitments for this (Guatemala, Nicaragua and Bolivia). Commitments from the Inter-American Development Bank to social funds totalled over $300 million; most were non-concessional loans and also made in recent years.

Women in development

Another important innovation in many bilateral and some multilateral programmes is a greater attention to the needs and priorities of women in development. A greater understanding of women's needs may be one reason for the increased priority given by several agencies to primary health care since in societies where most or the responsibility for child-rearing and caring for the sick falls to women, effective, easily accessible health care is one of women's most immediate practical needs.

Certain agencies also seek to better meet women's strategic needs, i.e. to lessen the discrimination against women in terms of access to employment, credit and land ownership.[54] One example is employment and credit programmes targeted at women to increase their income-earning opportunities. In some social fund and emergency employment programmes, special attempts are made to ensure that women's practical and strategic needs are met. However, the strength of donor agencies' commitment to women in development cannot be measured by the proportion of funding allocated to women's programmes. A more fundamental realignment is to ensure that all projects consider whether they make sufficient provision for women's needs—as is now done in the Netherlands' aid programme. The Swedish International Development Cooperation Agency (SIDA) has sought to ensure that women's practical and strategic needs are met in all its aid projects, with both its staff and the staff of agencies who work with them undergoing training in gender awareness and with gender-programme officers now working in SIDA's development co-operation offices.[55]

NORAD and the UK Overseas Development Administration are also among the bilateral agencies which seek to give due attention to women's practical and strategic needs in their aid programmes and both have supported training in gender awareness for their staff. In 1991, an estimated 12 per cent of Norway's total bilateral development assistance went to measures 'where women were defined as a target group and where women participated actively in the planning of projects'.[56] However, a recent paper which discussed how to integrate the gender variable into urban development noted the need not only for more gender awareness from professionals but also for more consultation with women at all levels in the formulation and implementation of development interventions and for

more attention within capacity building to ensuring that women and men have equal representation on the staff of institutions and equal access to the services, resources and technical assistance that they provide.[57]

Urban infrastructure and services

Many of the agencies listed in Table 11.4 have increased the priority they give to urban infrastructure and services other than that directly related to shelter. Table 11.4 also includes commitments made to urban management and to integrated urban development projects that combine investments in different kinds of urban infrastructure and services, often in more than one city, and often include components to train local government staff and strengthen local institutions. Many integrated urban development projects are in cities that have been badly hit by a natural disaster and the project is to help rebuild or repair the damage.

Among the multilateral agencies listed, the World Bank remains much the largest source of development assistance to urban infrastructure and services with commitments totalling close to $27 billion between 1980 and 1993. Urban services such as secondary and higher education and hospitals received around two-fifths of the funding with a third to urban infrastructure, 18 per cent to integrated urban development and 7.5 per cent to improving urban management. The trend over these fourteen years has been a shift away from large infrastructure projects to support for secondary and higher education, strengthening the capacity and competence of city or municipal authorities in urban management and integrated urban development.

The World Bank has also been giving a greater priority to pollution control in urban areas in recent years. Although loan commitments were made before 1990—indeed, a loan commitment to Sao Paulo to help control river pollution is recorded in the Bank's 1971 Annual Report—it is only since 1990 that one or two projects received funding each year. In 1993, three projects received support with commitments totalling more than $700 million.

The Inter-American Development Bank made commitments totalling $4.2 billion during these fourteen years. Commitments were almost evenly divided between urban infrastructure (especially urban electrification and city water supply schemes[58]), urban services (especially secondary and higher education and hospitals) and integrated urban development projects. The priority given to health and to secondary and tertiary education has grown in recent years, while that given to integrated urban development has diminished.

TABLE 11.4 The proportion of aid and non-concessional loan commitments to urban infrastructure, urban services and urban management, 1980–93

Agency	Total funding (US$ bill.	Proportion of total project commitments					Per cent of total commitments		
		URBAN INFRA-STRUCTURE	COLLEGES AND HOSPITALS	PUBLIC TRANS-PORT	URBAN MANAGEMENT INTEGD. URBAN	DEVELT.	1980–93	1990–91	1992–93
Aid (concessional loans or grants)									
International Development Association									
** Africa	27.9	1.8	4.4	0.0		2.6	8.8	10.0	11.3
** Asia	38.6	1.1	5.3	0.3		3.6	10.3	16.1	12.4
** Latin America & Caribbean	1.9	4.0	0.0	0.0		2.7	6.5	0.0	0.0
African Development Bank	10.2	3.5	9.1	0.0		0.5	13.1	14.7	14.7
Asian Development Fund	14.3	2.7	6.2	0.0		2.8	11.8	12.9	17.7
Inter-American Development Bank	6.5	2.9	8.0	0.0		6.0	16.9	8.3	7.1
Caribbean Development Bank	0.7	4.4	2.6	0.0		6.3	14.3	8.2	15.4
Arab Fund for Economic & Social Develt	4.7	9.1	2.3	0.0		0.5	11.8	7.6	
Overseas Economic Cooperation Fund, Japan (1987–91)	36.5	6.6	1.4	2.4		2.2	n.a.	20.1	
Non-concessional loans									
International Bank for Reconstruction and Development (IBRD)									
** Africa	29.6	4.0	3.8	0.1		3.4	11.3	15.4	15.3
** Asia	90.6	3.9	3.2	0.2		3.0	10.3	16.6	14.9
** Latin America & Caribbean	68.7	4.0	1.4	1.5		3.9	10.8	5.8	16.8
African Development Bank	17.6	4.4	3.6	0.1		0.1	8.2	3.4	9.1
Asian Development Bank	30.9	6.9	4.4	0.0		3.4	14.8	18.4	16.1
Inter-American Development Bank	41.7	2.5	1.7	0.0		3.1	7.4	4.2	3.3
Caribbean Development Bank	0.5	13.0	0.2	0.0		5.0	18.6	20.4	3.8

Notes and Sources: Satterthwaite, David, 'The scale and nature of international donor assistance to housing, basic services and other human-settlements related projects', Paper presented at the UNU/WIDER Conference on 'Human Settlements in the changing global political and economic processes', Helsinki, 1995: Urban infrastructure includes ports, airports, urban electricity and water supply projects that were not included in Table 11.2. Urban electricity includes all projects with major electrification components in urban areas and/or electricity generating facilities directly linked to improving the service in a city or group of cities; it does not include general investments in power or in national or regional grids. Funding for colleges and hospitals do not include support for primary education, literacy programmes and primary health care which were included in Table 11.2. Public transport includes buses, intra-city and commuter-line railways and subways. Funding for urban management includes projects or programmes whose main focus was urban cadastral surveys, institution building, training or research at city/municipal level, urban government finance, urban planning and urban traffic management. Integrated urban development: when a multi-sectoral or multipurpose project has components which come under four or more of the other categories listed in this table or table 11.2, it is categorized as an 'integrated urban development' project. The category on urban management and integrated urban development also includes funding for urban markets and industrial estates, city-wide investments in solid-waste collection and management and in pollution control and in urban gas supplies. Aid and non-concessional loan commitments to each of these can be disaggregated separately, but space does not permit this in this report. The database on which this table is based also records commitments to intra-urban roads and bridges and to building material industries although these too are not reported here.

The Asian Development Bank made commitments totalling $6.4 billion between 1980 and 1993. Just over two-fifths went to urban infrastructure (mainly ports and urban electrification) with just under two-fifths to urban services (mainly secondary and higher education) and 20 per cent to integrated urban development. The Bank also made its first loan for a comprehensive urban environmental improvement project in 1992—to Qingdao in China. The African Development Bank Group committed about $2.9 billion during these fourteen years. Most went to secondary and higher education, hospitals and city electrification.

US AID's Office of Housing and Urban Programs made large commitments to urban infrastructure, especially water and sanitation, during the period 1990–3. For instance, during 1992–3, over $400 million was authorized for various initiatives to support private sector or municipal investments in water, sanitation and other forms of urban environmental infrastructure. In 1994, this Office became a unit within a new Environment Centre that US AID has set up to provide technical and programmatic leadership and support to itself (including its field missions) and its 'domestic and international development partners on global and sustainable development environmental problems'.[59] The Office of Housing and Urban Programs has been renamed as the 'Office of Environment and Urban Programs'.[60]

The data available on other bilateral agencies was too incomplete to permit a detailed analysis of funding to urban infrastructure and services. One source of information about bilateral aid to urban development comes from the Development Assistance Committee of the OECD which drew from their own database to come up with figures on the scale of support from bilateral agencies to urban development. Their calculations are based on a more aggregated set of project categories over a more limited time period and their findings are presented in Table 11.5. These figures suggest that multilateral donors are far more significant sources of funding for urban infrastructure and services than bilateral donors.

BOX 11.11
Examples of project loans made in 1993 by the World Bank for the control of pollution

China: $250 million committed to the Southern Jiangsu Environmental Protection Project that will focus on cost-effective water-pollution control investments in urban and industrial projects. It will also strengthen the institutional, regulatory and environmental management capabilities of local agencies. Southern Jiangsu region is one of China's most industrialized areas.

Mexico: $220 million committed to the Transport Air Quality Management Project for Mexico City Metropolitan Area. This is the government's programme to reduce pollution in Mexico City that is being supported by technical and financial assistance in developing low-emission vehicles and in the conversion or replacement of old high-use vehicles. It will also help finance the installation of vapour-recovery systems at gas stations.

Brazil: $245 million committed to the Sao Paulo Water-Quality and Pollution-Control Project. This seeks to implement a cost-effective approach to controlling water pollution in two of the most congested and polluted metropolitan areas of the country. This will be achieved through the creation of two urban water-basin authorities—for the Guarapiranga river near Sao Paulo and for the upper Iguacu river in Curitiba—and the financing of water pollution-control investments.

Sources: The World Bank, *Annual Report 1993*, Washington DC, 1993; Monthly Operational Summary of Bank and IDA Proposed Projects, IBRD, 4 January, 1993

TABLE 11.5 Bilateral agencies' official development finance commitments for urban development by purpose, 1986–1990 ($US million constant—1990 value)

	86	87	88	89	90	ALL
Urban development	93.9	33.3	66.6	31.7	26.0	251.5
Housing	52.7	74.4	73.0	168.6	62.0	430.7
Water and waste management	617.2	741.5	1,195.4	998.5	917.0	4,469.5
Transport	72.1	138.8	120.3	457.9	540.0	1,329.0
Gas distribution	38.9	0.0	576.7	68.5	1.0	685.1
Electricity distribution	175.2	570.5	522.0	984.2	397.0	2,648.9
Pollution control	0.0	0.0	0.0	0.0	5.0	5.0
Harbours/docks/ airports	478.6	652.7	629.4	716.4	334.0	2,811.1
Health	95.0	108.8	165.4	191.1	100.0	660.3
Cultural activities	35.5	93.2	68.7	35.8	21.0	254.2
TOTAL	1,659.1	2,413.1	3,417.5	3,652.6	2,403.0	13,545.3

Note: The figures in this table differ from the original for two reasons. First, all totals have been converted to $US at their 1990 value. Second, support for telecommunications has been excluded.[61]

Source: OECD Development Co-operation Directorate, *Urban Development—Donor Roles and Responsibilities Issues Paper*, note by the secretariat, Paris, 1992.

Constraints on increased development assistance to human settlements

Various factors constrain a greater priority to human settlements from donor agencies. One reason is simply that recipient governments and/or development assistance agencies do not view human settlements projects as a priority or they equate 'human settlements' with 'urban' and choose to give a low priority to urban investments. There was certainly an 'anti-urban' bias among many development assistance agencies during the late 1970s and for much of the 1980s. Some changes can be detected in the attitude of agencies towards human settlements projects. One reason may be a better understanding of the economic role of cities (and urban systems) and the difficulty for any nation in achieving a successful economic performance without a well-functioning urban system which includes adequate provision for the infrastructure that enterprises need. Another may be an acknowledgement within agencies that 'human settlements' is not a sector but the physical context within which virtually all their development investments take place and a critical determinant both of economic growth and of people's quality of life.

A more intractable constraint is the operational difficulties experienced by development assistance agencies in expanding their commitments to human settlements projects. One study that included interviews with a range of staff from different development assistance agencies found a variety of institutional constraints in increasing the priority to many human settlements projects—especially for shelter, water supply and sanitation, primary schools and primary health care and community development.[62] One reason is that human settlements specialists within the agencies find it difficult to convince others in the agency that a higher priority should be given to human settlements projects. A second reason is that many agencies' institutional structures do not allow them to expand their funding to a multiplicity of small scale projects; this is especially the case in development banks where one important measure of their 'efficiency' is the scale of their lending relative to their staff costs.

A third reason is the inability or reluctance of donor agencies to fund recurrent costs, often part of an institutional legacy as they were set up to fund capital projects. Yet the capital cost of building a school, community centre or health clinic within a low income area is relatively modest but the recurrent costs are often much more difficult to fund.

Box 11.12 summarizes some characteristics of successful shelter and basic services projects that reached poorer households and contrasts them with project characteristics that the institutional structure of development assistance agencies tends to favour. For instance, slum- or squatter-upgrading projects which seek to be participatory, working with community organizations formed by poorer groups in the settlement, take many years to implement and require a high

---

BOX 11.12

Most important aid project characteristics from two different viewpoints

Characteristics of Many Successful Basic Needs Projects	**Project Characteristics which Make Implementation Easy for Outside Funding Agency**
Small-scale and multi-sectoral—addressing multiple needs of poorer groups	Large-scale and single-sector
Implementation over many years—less of a project and more of a longer term continuous process to improve housing and living conditions	Rapid implementation (internal evaluations of staff performance in funding agencies often based on volume of funding supervised)
Substantial involvement of local people (and usually their own community organizations) in project design and implementation	Project designed by agency staff (usually in offices in Europe or North America) or by consultants from funding agency's own nation
Project implemented collaboratively with beneficiaries, their local government and certain national agencies	Project implemented by one construction company or government agency
High ratio of staff costs to total project cost	Low ratio of staff costs to total project cost
Difficult to evaluate using conventional cost-benefit analysis	Easy to evaluate
Little or no direct import of goods or services from abroad	High degree of import of goods or services from funding agency's own nation

Source: Jorge E. Hardoy and David Satterthwaite, 'Aid and Human Settlements', report prepared for the Institute for Research on Public Policy, Canada, 1988.

---

input of staff time relative to the project cost. Yet there are great pressures on virtually all development assistance agencies to minimize the amount of staff time per unit of expenditure. Such pressures will mean that agencies tend to favour large, easily supervised projects. In addition, the fact that most development assistance agencies have a relatively small proportion of their staff based in recipient nations and that these staff have relatively small decision-making powers make it difficult to design projects which mesh with the local context and local processes.

Development assistance agencies would find it easier to increase the scale of their human settlements commitments if there were effective counterpart institutions within recipient nations who could take on most of the responsibility for project formulation, implementation and evaluation and could do so working closely with the project-households and their community organizations. This is one reason why a greater priority has been given to building the capacity and competence of local authorities most of which are weak and ineffective as was described in Chapter 5. The development of stronger, more competent and more representative local governments within recipient nations would remove a major constraint on increasing development assistance flows to human settlements and would certainly increase the quality of donor-assisted urban projects. However, many donor agencies find it difficult to strengthen 'institutional capacity' since again their main expertise and experience is in project-funding.

Another constraint is the poor match between the 'project orientation' of most development assistance agencies and the funding needs of local institutions. Inadequate provision for infrastructure and services within most urban centres in the South can be attributed largely to a lack of resources and trained personnel at the level of the city and municipal authorities. An aid project can remedy such deficiencies within a project site—but in effect, it makes up for a failure of local bodies to make such investments in previous years. The project may improve conditions considerably at first but rarely does it increase the capacity of local bodies to maintain the new infrastructure and services and to make similar investments in other areas of the city. Urban authorities need a continuous capacity to invest in and maintain infrastructure and services—or to oversee other bodies (private enterprises, community organizations, cooperatives etc) which provide some services. Funds available on an irregular basis for specific projects are not an effective substitute. This suggests not only a need for increased priority among development assistance agencies for shelter (including the basic infrastructure and services which are part of shelter) but also that such development assistance should be provided within a long-term strategy to develop the capacity of national and local governments to plan, invest in and manage infrastructure and service provision and to involve other key local actors in this process (including private sector institutions, NGOs and community organizations).[63]

Notes and References

1. Sheela Patel, SPARC, personal communication.

2. Remenyi, Joe, *Where Credit is Due: Income-generating Programmes for the Poor in Developing Countries*, Intermediate Technology, London, 1991; Mehta, Dinesh, *Community Based Programmes of Urban Poverty Alleviation in India*, Paper presented at the RWCBP-UPA, Kuala Lumpur, 1994; and ESCAP, *Guidelines on Community Based Housing Finance and Innovative Credit Systems for Low-income Households*, United Nations, ST/ESCAP/1003, 1991.

3. This section draws on the discussions that took place at two workshops. The first was in the Philippines in October 1993 and the workshop report has been published: Asian Coalition for Housing Rights and Habitat International Coalition (ACHR/HIC), *Finance and Resource Mobilization for Low Income Housing and Neighbourhood Development: A Workshop Report*, Pagtambayayong Foundation Inc., Philippines, 1994. The second workshop was organized to develop this chapter for the Global Report; participants were Yves Cabannes, Francisco Fernandez, Alejandro Florian, Diana Mitlin, Enrique Ortiz and Randy Sachs. Further comments on issues raised during this workshop were made by Somsook Boonyabancha.

4. Rabinovitch, Jonas, 'Curitiba: towards sustainable urban development', *Environment and Urbanization*, vol. 4, no. 2, 1992, 62–73.

5. Remenyi 1991 and ESCAP 1991, *op. cit.*

6. Arrossi, Silvina, Felix Bombarolo, Jorge E. Hardoy, Diana Mitlin, Luis Perez Coscio and David Satterthwaite, *Funding Community Initiatives*, Earthscan Publications, London, 1994.

7. Asian Coalition for Housing Rights and Habitat International Coalition, 'Finance and resource mobilization for low income housing and neighbourhood development: a workshop report', Pagtambayayong Foundation, Philippines, 1994.

8. *Ibid.*

9. Lankatilleke, Lalith, 'Build Together: National Housing Programme of Namibia', Paper presented at a workshop on Participatory Tools and Methods in Urban Areas, IIED, London, 1995.

10. Arrossi and others 1994, *op. cit.*

11. Khan, Akhter Hameed, *Orangi Pilot Project Programs*, OPP, Karachi, 1991.

12. Ministry of Regional and Local Government and Housing, 'Build-Together, National Housing Programme: Implementation Guidelines', UNDP/UNCHS Project NAM/90/018, 1994.

13. Hardoy, Jorge E. and David Satterthwaite, *Squatter Citizen: Life in the Urban Third World*, Earthscan Publications, London, 1989.

14. See for instance details of COPEVI, CENVI and Ciudad Alternativa in Connolly, Priscilla, 'The go between; CENVI, a Habitat NGO in Mexico City', *Environment and Urbanization*, vol. 5, no. 1, 1993, 68–90; Turner, Bertha (ed.), *Building Community—A Third World Case Book from Habitat International Coalition*, Habitat International Coalition, London, 1988; and ACHR/HIC 1994, *op. cit.*

15. UNCHS (Habitat), *The Urban Poor as Agents of Development: Community Action Planning in Sri Lanka*, Nairobi, 1993.

16. UNCHS (Habitat), *Developing a National Shelter Strategy: lessons from four countries*, Nairobi, 1990.

17. Ghouri, Naeem Shahid and Hector Nihal, 'The housing loan programme of the Catholic Social Services', *Environment and Urbanization*, vol. 5, no. 1, 1993, 9–17.

18. The speech at Global Forum '94 by Mohamed Yunus, Executive Director of the Grameen Bank, Bangladesh.

19. Arrossi and others 1994, *op. cit.*; and Sevilla, Manuel, 'New approaches for aid agencies: FUPROVI's community based shelter programme', *Environment and Urbanization*, vol. 5, no. 1, 1993, 111–21.

20. Arrossi and others 1994 *op. cit.*

21. See the NGO profile of Homeless International, *Environment and Urbanization*, vol. 4, no. 2, 1992, 168–175.

22. Cruz, Luis Fernando, 'Fundacion Carvajal: the Carvajal Foundation', *Environment and Urbanization*, vol. 6, no. 2, 1994, 175–82.

23. Arrossi and others 1994, *op. cit.*

24. *Ibid.*; also the papers included in the special issue, 'Funding Community Level Initiatives: the role of NGOs and other intermediate institutions in funding and supporting low-income households to improve shelter, infrastructure and services', *Environment and Urbanization*, vol. 5, no. 1, 1993.

25. *Ibid.*

26. *Ibid.*

27. Patel, Sheela and Celine D'Cruz, 'The Mahila Milan crisis credit scheme: from a seed to a tree', *Environment and Urbanization*,1993, 9–17.

28. See Arrossi and others 1994, *op. cit.*; and Anzorena, Jorge, *Housing the Poor: the Asian Experience*, Asian Coalition for Housing Rights, 1994.

29. Arrossi and others 1994, *op. cit.*

30. Ghouri and Nihal 1993, *op. cit.*

31. Hardoy and Satterthwaite 1989, *op. cit.*

32. Hardoy, Ana, Jorge E. Hardoy and Ricardo Schusterman, 'Building community organization: the history of a squatter settlement and its own organizations in Buenos Aires', *Environment and Urbanization*, vol. 3, no. 2, Oct. 1991, 104–20.

33. This section is based on Satterthwaite, David, 'The scale and nature of international donor assistance to housing, basic services and other human-settlements related projects,' Paper presented to the UNU/WIDER Conference on 'Human Settlements in the changing global political and economic processes', Helsinki, Aug. 1995.

34. See the last few 'Financial and other assistance provided to and among developing countries on human settlements and on the human settlements activities of the United Nations system' prepared by UNCHS; also Satterthwaite, David, 'La Ayuda Internacional'—chapter in *Construccion y Administracion de la Ciudad Latinoamericano*—Nora Clichevsky and others GEL, Buenos Aires, 1990, and Arrossi and others 1994, *op. cit.*

35. OECD Development Cooperation Directorate, *Urban Development—Donor Roles and Responsibilities Issues Paper*, note by the secretariat, Paris, 1992.

36. There are exceptions, including the upgrading programme in Surabaja described in Chapter 10.

37. Payne, G. K., 'Introduction', G. K. Payne (ed.), *Low Income Housing in the Developing World—the Role of Sites and Services and Settlement Upgrading*, John Wiley and Sons, Chichester, 1984.

38. Mayo, Stephen K. and Shlomo Angel, *Enabling Housing Markets to Work*, A World Bank Policy Paper, The World Bank, Washington DC, 1993.

39. Mayo and Angel 1993, *op. cit.*

40. Cohen, Michael A., 'Macroeconomic adjustment and the city', *Cities*, vol. 7, no. 1, Feb. 1990, 49–59.

41. For instance a project in a squatter settlement may have project components for water, sanitation, garbage disposal, primary health care, housing-tenure regularization and building-material production.

42. Mayo and Angel 1993, *op. cit.*

43. *Ibid.* 55

44. Pugh, Cedric, 'Housing policy development in developing countries; the World Bank and internationalization, 1972–93', *Cities*, vol. 11, no. 3, June 1994, 159–80.

45. The title of the most recent World Bank policy paper on Housing was *Housing: Enabling Markets to Work*.

46. Pugh 1994, *op. cit.*

47. The analysis in this section is based on a database that contains details of all human settlements projects that received support from the agencies listed in Tables 11.1, 11.2 and 11.4 between 1980 and 1993. This database also includes details of co-funders and thus allowed an analysis of the involvement of other agencies in co-financing.

48. OECD Development Co-operation Directorate, *Urban Development—Donor Roles and Responsibilities Issues Paper*, note by the secretariat, Paris, 1992.

49. The difficulties of producing accurate, detailed statistics on the sectoral priorities of different development assistance agencies have long been recognized. There are two problems that have to be overcome. The first is that most agencies developed their own classification systems for sectoral priorities; with no common base used in the definition of sectors or sub-sectors, figures for sectoral priorities cannot be compared between agencies. The second is that the sectoral classification systems that do exist—that can form the common base for all agencies—do not have a classification system that is appropriate for monitoring development assistance to human settlements. It is still possible to compare the priorities in human settlements assistance between agencies, where each agency publishes details of each project or programme commitment that it makes since each of these can be classified according to a common human settlements classification system; this is how the statistics in Tables 11.1, 11.2 and 11.4 were developed. However, most bilateral agencies do not publish a complete listing of all the projects or programmes they support with sufficient detail given about each to permit its classification within such a common system.

50. Water Supply and Sanitation Collaborative Council, *Water Supply and Sanitation Sector Monitoring Report 1990 (Baseline Year)*, World Health Organization and UNICEF, 1992.

51. Warner, D. B. and L. Laugeri, 'Health for all: the legacy of the water decade', *Water International*, vol. 16, 1991, 135–41.

52. Water Supply and Sanitation Collaborative Council, *Water Supply and Sanitation Sector Monitoring Report 1993*, World Most Health Organization and UNICEF, 1993. This also reports on how many countries reported on the relative balance of investments into water supply and sanitation coming from governments, international agencies and communities for rehabilitation and new systems

53. Although this was largely the result of a single commitment of $US500 million for a social safety-net programme in India.

54. Women's practical gender needs are 'those needs which arise from the concrete conditions of women's positioning, by virtue of their gender, within the sexual division of labour. Within these positions, needs are formulated by women themselves, in response to the living conditions which they face daily. Therefore in many contexts need such as adequate housing, clean water supply or community creche facilities are identified as the practical gender needs of low income women, both by planners as well as by women themselves . . . Strategic gender needs are those needs identified from the analysis of women's subordination, and, deriving out of this, the formulation of an alternative more satisfactory organization of society to those which exist at present, in terms of the structure and nature of relationships between men and women.' Moser, Caroline O. N., 'Women, human settlements and housing: a conceptual framework for analysis and policy-making', in Caroline O. N. Moser and Linda Peake (eds.) *Women, Housing and Human Settlements*, Tavistock Publications, London and New York, 1987.

55. SIDA, *Striking a Balance: Gender Awareness in Swedish Development Cooperation*, Swedish International Development Authority, Stockholm, 1990.

56. NORAD, *Annual Report NORAD 1991*, Norwegian Agency for Development Cooperation, Oslo, 1992.

57. Beall, Jo, 'Integrated the gender variable into urban development', background paper to the DAC Meeting on Aid for Urban Development, Paris, Nov. 1992 and originally drafted at the request of the Expert Group on Women in Development.

58. These did not include city water supply schemes whose main goal was increasing or improving water supplies for households since these were included in Table 11.2.

59. US Agency for International Development, *Proposed Strategic Objectives and Program Outcomes for the Strategic Plan of the Centre for Environment*, Bureau for Global Programs, Field Support and Research, Centre for Environment, Nov. 1994.

60. US Agency for International Development, *Annual Report, 1993*, Office of Housing and Urban Programs, Bureau for Global Programs, Field Support and Research, Washington DC, 1994.

61. Certain kinds of projects—especially projects for electricity supply, electrification and telecommunications—present special difficulties for classifying whether or not there are 'urban' projects. The OECD DAC statistics chose to classify telecommunications projects as urban. The database on which Tables 11.1, 11.2 and 11.4 are drawn only includes telecommunication projects which are directly linked to urban services—for instance to installing or improving telephone equipment in a specific city. Similarly, when Table 11.4 reports on 'urban electricity', this only includes electrification projects which had a major urban component and electricity generating or other equipment which was specifically to improve coverage or quality of service within urban areas.

62. The initial findings of this study are reported in Satterthwaite, David, 'The scale and nature of international donor assistance to housing, basic services and other human-settlements related projects', Paper presented to the UNU/WIDER Conference on 'Human Settlements in the changing global political and economic processes', Helsinki, Aug. 1995.

63. For a discussion of the role and relevance of these new actors in urban management, see Lee-Smith, Diana and Richard E. Stren, 'New perspectives on African urban management', *Environment and Urbanization*, vol. 3, no. 1, April 1991. See also UNCHS (Habitat), *Shelter for the Homeless: the Role of Non Governmental Organizations*, UNCHS (Habitat), Nairobi, 1987.

12 Environmental Protection and Resource Management

12.1 Limitations to Current Approaches

There is no shortage of innovative examples of buildings or settlements in which the level of resource use and waste generation has been greatly reduced. There are also many examples of companies and city governments that have greatly reduced resource use and wastes. There are the many traditional buildings and settlements that have always used resources efficiently and kept wastes to a minimum. What is less evident is governments prepared to develop national frameworks to promote resource conservation and waste minimization in all sectors and at all levels. This chapter includes many examples of innovations—for instance the great improvements in energy efficiency in most aspects of housing and housing appliances, the trend towards recognizing waste streams as resource streams and innovations in urban agriculture and urban forestry that reduce cities' 'ecological footprints'. But these tend to be the exceptions rather than the rule.

There is a growing recognition of the need to make all investment decisions by governments and the private sector respond to environmental issues. This is both in the depletion of the different kinds of environmental assets listed in Box 12.1 and in the environmental hazards that arise within human settlements. Chapter 4 described the direct health costs that environmental hazards impose on the population and how such costs are most evident in cities in the South where the level of environmental risk experienced by citizens is strongly associated with their income. Middle- and upper-income households can afford to live in the least polluted areas of the city and to avoid the jobs with the highest levels of environmental risk. The areas in which they live generally enjoy the best provision for basic infrastructure and services—while low-income households often live in the most polluted areas, work in the most dangerous jobs and live in the most dangerous sites (for instance floodplains, steep slopes or sites contaminated with industrial wastes) with little or no infrastructure and services. There are also examples of lower-income groups being more exposed to environmental hazards in the North—for instance in the systematic siting of the more dangerous waste dumps in or close to low-income areas.[1]

There remain many unresolved questions in improving environmental protection and resource management such as how to value the different kinds of environmental assets widely used in production and consumption[2] and how to ensure that this revaluation contributes to greater inter-generational and intra-generational equity. If one considers the four different kinds of environmental assets listed in Box 12.1, most progress in reducing their depletion has been on two of them. The first is limiting the right of industries to use local sinks for wastes—for instance disposing of untreated wastes in rivers, lakes or other local water bodies or in high levels of air pollution. Environmental legislation has restricted this right in virtually all countries, although the extent to which the environmental legislation is enforced varies widely and in some countries, there is little enforcement.[3] The second is a less wasteful use of renewable resources; in many countries where fertile soil and fresh water are in short supply, and forests are being rapidly depleted, measures have been taken to protect them or, in the case of fresh water, to promote less wasteful patterns of use. But Chapter 4 also noted how consumers and businesses in the wealthier nations or cities can 'appropriate' the soils and water resources of distant ecosystems by importing the land- and water-intensive goods from these regions. Thus, the depletion of soil and the over-exploitation of fresh water to meet the demands of city consumers and producers may simply be switched from the city's own region to distant regions. On the third and fourth kinds of environmental assets, the use of non-renewable resources and sinks for non-biodegradable wastes, there has been much less progress. This includes the use of the 'global sink' for greenhouse gases and Chapter 4 outlined the direct and indirect economic, social and environmental costs this brings or may bring. The need is to halt or modify investment decisions which imply serious social and environmental costs either in the immediate locality or in distant ecosystems or for future generations. To achieve this implies major changes in ownership rights for land and natural resources.[4] Achieving this is made all the more difficult by incomplete knowledge about the scale and nature of the environmental costs that current production and consumption patterns are passing on to current and future generations.[5]

12.2 Resource Conservation and Waste Management

The opportunities for resource conservation

There is a great range of opportunities for resource conservation and waste reduction in the wealthier nations of both the North and the South. For many actions taken to improve environmental performance, the economic and environmental benefits greatly outweigh the economic and environmental costs.[6] Capital costs are rapidly repaid by lower running costs—as in lower fuel bills for better-insulated buildings or through replacement of inefficient cooling or heating systems—so there is little diminution of economic activity. For others, there are economic and employment costs which will have to be borne in the present or immediate future, but as part of a reduction in the costs passed on to future generations. One example of this is the economic costs of a major programme to cut greenhouse gas emissions—for instance through some dampening in total economic activity as carbon taxes raise the cost of using motor vehicles, of heating and cooling buildings and of most energy-intensive goods. But on the positive side, not only does this diminish the cost passed on to future generations but in addition, technological innovation can certainly diminish these costs and many new jobs will be created.

One of the main resource issues in the North is the transition to a much less fossil fuel intensive society. The policies that can promote such a transition are well known and well documented.[7] They include:

- Strong encouragement for improving the energy efficiency of residential, commercial, industrial and public-sector buildings—working on the basis of installing new equipment and insulation whose cost will be repaid within a few years (or less) from lower fuel bills. This can achieve very substantial reductions in fuel use with no loss in comfort.

- A range of incentives and the provision of technical advice to industries on how to improve energy efficiency; many industries have multiplied several-fold the energy productivity of their processes in recent decades.[8]

- A rethink of pricing and regulation for road vehicles, of pricing for fossil fuels in general, and of provision for public transport and support for increasing bicycling and walking as described in Chapter 9.

Box 12.2 gives examples of energy savings that are possible in different aspects of buildings and domestic appliances, most of which are already being implemented. There are also many examples of much improved performance in terms of resource use for buildings in general. For instance, in the Netherlands, new homes built in recent years require only a third to a quarter of the energy for heating compared to homes built 20 years ago.[9]

Ensuring the widespread adoption of such energy saving technologies or techniques implies changes to building norms and codes to encourage conservation and energy efficient equipment and to public information services to promote this. It also implies the labelling of vehicles and appliances so their energy efficiency (and fuel cost implications) are known to consumers, and the implementation of settlement-planning and traffic-management techniques that have positive social and environmental impacts. Finally, it includes a reappraisal of the energy-producing sector.

One important concept first developed by some utility companies in the United States is to treat potential savings in fuel or electricity as an alternative energy source. This has become a common response by electricity companies that are having difficulty meeting peak demand or that are planning to increase capacity. The costs of increasing electricity generation capacity are very high—especially if stringent environmental standards are met. It often proves much cheaper for the company to encourage its main users to invest in insulation and more resource-efficient equipment than to invest in new generating capacity. Although there are obvious problems in implementing such an approach, especially where a company is privately owned and the conservation option proves less profitable than the option of increasing supply, the advantages to society and to the environment are obvious. For instance, the very rapid expansion in the production and use of refrigerators in China in recent years has also required a large increase in electricity capacity to power them—and the high cost of expanding

BOX 12.2

Energy savings in different aspects of buildings and domestic appliances and in their construction

Walls: Improved insulation can be introduced into the walls of many buildings in Europe and North America, with reductions in fuel demand for heating or cooling by up to 25 per cent.

Windows: New window technology is greatly reducing heat loss both through the glass and as a result of gaps. Between 1984 and 1994, advanced windows with two or three panes of glass have claimed 38 per cent of the residential market in the United States—and this has saved the residents some $US5 billion in energy bills each year.[10]

Roof: Installing or upgrading insulation in the roof of many existing buildings in the North can reduce fuel demand for heating by up to 25 per cent with costs often repaid through lower fuel bills in less than a year.

Reducing Space-Heating and Cooling Requirements: In addition to improved insulation of walls, windows and the roof noted above, various other measures can reduce space heating and cooling requirements. For instance, light-coloured roofing and cladding

materials that reflect sunlight can cut peak cooling needs by as much as 40 per cent in hot climates—while planting trees around existing buildings can cut cooling needs by up to 30 per cent.

Lighting: New compact fluorescent lamps that can replace conventional light bulbs require less than a quarter of the electricity of the bulbs they replace—and since their introduction in 1982, they have captured a significant portion of the market in Europe and North America; in Japan, where electricity is particularly expensive, these are now used in 80 per cent of home fixtures.[11]

Appliances: Energy use in domestic fridges has fallen significantly, due mainly to better insulation and more efficient electric motors. Electricity use by fridges in the USA fell by around half between 1972 and 1992 while some 1994 models use 30–50 per cent less than the current average. Further improvements are possible so that overall, refrigerators and home freezers can now consume 80–90 per cent less electricity than conventional models. Major savings in electricity use by televisions, computers and photocopying machines can also be achieved through the use of the most energy-efficient models.[12]

Air-Conditioners: The need for air-conditioning buildings in hot climates can be considerably reduced by the measures noted above which reduce heat gain from the sun and also greatly reduce the amount of waste heat produced by lighting and appliances within the building. Air-conditioners themselves vary greatly in their efficiency; the most efficient use around a third of the electricity of the least efficient ones.

Space-Heating: Major advances have been made in the fuel efficiency of space-heaters in the last two decades. They are not only highly cost effective for new buildings through the fuel costs they save, but in many instances new models can be used to replace inefficient space-heaters in existing buildings.

Building Materials: There have been considerable improvements in the energy efficiency in building materials production—for instance the improved energy efficiency of cement production. Energy inputs into buildings have also been reduced through many innovations in the structural elements of large buildings that reduce the need for energy intensive materials and through measures to recycle building materials.

---

power supply could have been much moderated, if a more efficient refrigerator design had been chosen.[13] Similarly, the promotion of energy-efficient lightbulbs in many cities in the South would often considerably reduce the size of the evening peak demand.[14]

In the last few years, several states in the USA have adopted reforms that allow electricity companies to profit from increasing efficiency; in one instance, that of Pacific Gas and Electric in California, three-quarters of its new energy needs during the 1990s should be met through increased energy-efficiency programmes with the rest coming from renewable energy sources.[15]

Managing the transition to resource efficient cities

In the North and in the wealthier cities in the South, the potential for employment creation in greatly reducing resource use and wastes and in recycling or reusing the wastes that are generated are very considerable. The main reason is that levels of resource use, waste generation and pollution are so high that there are many possibilities for substituting labour and knowledge for resource use and waste. There is great potential for combining employment generation with the transition to a more resource-efficient, minimum waste production and consumption pattern in:

- Improving insulation levels in residential, commercial and industrial buildings and in

adopting other innovations which limit electricity or fossil-fuel consumption.

- The manufacture, installation and maintenance of machinery and equipment that are more resource efficient and less polluting.

- The industrial and service enterprises associated with waste minimization, recycling, reuse and resource reclamation.

Extending the life of capital goods to reduce levels of resource use also generally means more employment in maintenance and repair, although for many old capital goods and polluting equipment, the focus should be on replacement (including inefficient, high pollution level motor vehicles, poorly insulated CFC-coolant fridges, and inefficient space- and water-heaters and electric lights).

One of the factors constraining action by governments towards resource conservation and waste reduction is the worry about the employment costs. There are employment losses arising from the greater cost of certain goods or services, especially those whose production or use requires major changes to reduce unacceptable levels of resource use or waste generation. But there are many examples of industrial processes where resource use and pollution levels have been cut with no overall increase in costs and, in some cases, with significant cost savings. In addition, even if costs do rise, they only do so to compensate for environmental costs that previously had been ignored.

A shift to patterns of production that are far more resource conserving with wastes also minimized implies shifts in employment, including:

- Declining employment in the manufacture of automobiles and the material inputs into this process with expanding employment in public transport equipment and systems, traffic management, air pollution control equipment for motor vehicles and reclamation and recycling of materials used in road vehicles. A study in Germany suggested that investment in public transport equipment and infrastructure creates more jobs than those lost in car manufacture.[16]

- Declining employment in the coal, oil, natural gas and electricity industries and increasing employment in energy conservation in all sectors and in the manufacture and installation of energy-efficient appliances; also in the means to tap renewable energy sources. It is quite feasible in the North for living standards and the number of households to continue growing but with a steady decline in the level of fossil-fuel use.[17] Investments in energy conservation are generally far more labour intensive than investments in increasing the energy supply—especially when comparing the cost of increasing the electricity supply with the cost of reducing demand through conservation or the use of more efficient appliances, so that supplies no longer need to increase.

- Declining employment in mining and primary metals industries and paper and glass industries (and other industries associated with packaging production) and expanding employment in urban management systems that maximize recycling, reuse and reclamation, and promote waste minimization.

- Declining employment in producing and selling the fertilizers and biocides now widely used in industrial agriculture and horticulture but with increased employment in lower-input farming, ecologically based farming and land management, and resource-efficient, high-intensity crop production systems such as those based on hydroponics and permaculture.

In many areas, there are likely to be substantial increases in employment opportunities—for instance in the water supply and sewage treatment industries as higher standards are met and water conservation programmes implemented, and in the managerial and technical staff within municipalities and companies or corporations whose task is environmental management.

There are also the employment benefits that arise from cost-savings in conservation as highlighted by the Rocky Mountain Institute in the United States. For instance, the output from a $7.5 million compact fluorescent lamp factory saves as much electricity as a $1 billion power plant makes, as its products are installed to replace conventional light bulbs. While consuming 140 times less capital, the factory also avoids the power plant's fuel cost and pollution. A $10 million 'superglass' factory making windows that block heat but allow light to pass can produce more comfort than the air-conditioners run by $2 billion-worth of generating stations. Over 30 years, a single glass factory's output would save $12.25 billion in power investments.[18]

Although overall there are employment benefits in moving towards more ecologically sustainable patterns of production and consumption, the employment losses fall heavily on certain employees and on urban centres or regions that have the traditional logging, 'smokestack' and mining industries. Most of the job losses in these industries in Europe and North America over the last two decades have little to do with environmental regulation and much more to do with the gradual shift in production to cheaper areas or to new technologies that greatly reduce the need for labour. But it is little comfort to the miners and steelworkers and their families, when jobs disappear and there are few prospects for new employment in towns where unemployment rates are often 30 per cent or more, to know that policies promoting resource conservation and waste minimization are creating more employment elsewhere. Thus, one important role for government is addressing the needs of the workforce of the resource- and waste-intensive industries that lose their employment.

Certain cities in the North have managed the transition from centres of 'smokestack' industries towards the development of alternative economic bases, as industries close down, move elsewhere or reduce their workforce. There are also examples of city or regional governments which have begun such a process—for instance Hamilton-Wentworth in Canada whose programme is described in the later section on local Agenda 21s[19] or Leicester in the UK,[20] or the state of Nord-Rhine-Westphalia in the Emscher region in the Ruhr valley in Germany[21] or certain 'eco-municipalities' in Sweden.[22] Many urban regeneration programmes in Europe have also included ecological goals—from ensuring high levels of energy efficiency and reduced water use in the rebuilt or renovated buildings to the development of new parks or green areas.[23]

There is also an important international dimension to this as resource conservation and waste minimization in the North implies less purchase of goods from the South. For instance, strong support in the North for waste minimization and recycling may substantially reduce demand for paper and pulp from the South while any general tax applied globally on petroleum fuels would penalize exporters of high-volume low-value goods, most of whom are also in the South. Measures must be sought to reconcile the 'green trade' aspects of more sustainable patterns of production and consumption with support for more prosperous economies in the poorer Southern nations.

For practices such as those noted above that are currently the exceptions to become the norm requires a strong commitment and coherent support for local, city and regional action from national government. Such a commitment is also required to address the needs of the inhabitants of cities with the least comparative advantage in the transition to resource conservation and minimum waste. There are likely to be major long-term advantages for cities and nations which are among the first to promote such moves, as enterprises and municipalities there develop the kinds of products, services and knowledge that will be in high demand worldwide. A high-quality living and working environment has also become an increasingly important factor in attracting many kinds of new or expanding enterprises in the North and in some city-regions in the South.

Resource conservation in the South

In most cities in the South, the potential for new employment in resource conservation (including recycling) is rather less, given that levels of resource use are so much lower and levels of recycling, reclamation and reuse often much higher.[24] Ironically, many cities in the South, where housing and living conditions are very poor, are at the same time models of 'ecological sustainability' in that levels of resource use and waste generation are low and so much waste is reused or recycled.[25] Very low levels of resource and waste generation reflect very inadequate incomes for a high proportion of the population. Very low averages for water use per person are usually the result of half or more of the city's population having no piped water supply to their shelter or plot. Having to fetch and carry water from public standpipes greatly reduces consumption levels, often to below that needed for good health. High levels of reclamation and recycling are the result of tens of thousands of people eking out a precarious living from reclaiming or recycling metals, glass, paper, rags and other items from city wastes—and often with very serious health problems for those so engaged and with the work unpleasant and laborious. For instance, as Christine Furedy points out, 'Asian cities have extensive "waste economies", structured through itinerant waste buyers, waste pickers, small waste shops, second-hand markets, dealers, transporters, and a range of recycling industries.'[26] Chapter 9 gave several examples of cities where tens of thousands of people make a living from the reclamation, recycling or reuse of waste.

Most city authorities in the South seem set on copying Northern models for solid-waste collection and management—although usually only providing garbage collection services to the middle and upper-income areas and the main commercial and industrial areas. This indicates very little commitment to recycling or waste reduction and no consideration for the current or potential role of those who make their living picking saleable items from waste. Indeed, waste-pickers may lose their source of income as technical changes in waste collection inhibit informal recovery—for instance through requiring that all households put out their garbage in plastic bags making it difficult for pickers to sort through the garbage. The conventional Northern model also collects and compresses all wastes, with waste-pickers only able to obtain access to such waste at municipal dumps; waste-picking is more profitable and less hazardous if waste-pickers can sort through the waste at neighbourhood level 'transfer stations' before wastes become too compressed and mixed-up.[27]

However, over the last ten years, an increasing number of city authorities have moved from what can be characterized as 'waste management' to 'resource recognition'—see Box 12.3. Some city authorities are seeking to introduce social and environmental goals into their solid waste collection and management. In some cities, there is a recognition that the people previously regarded as 'scavengers' and 'pickers' are in fact recyclers and reclaimers who can be incorporated into city-wide waste management schemes in ways which benefit them and the city environment. For instance, in Bogotá, waste-pickers have formed co-operatives that have successfully bid for some municipal waste collection contracts.[28] In Cairo, as described in Chapter 9, the Environmental Protection Company that developed out of a group of informal garbage collectors (the *zabbaleen*) and local contractors have been awarded the contract for waste collection in several parts of the city and the Cairo Governorate is seeking to extend the company's services to other parts of the city.[29] There may be possibilities for further developing the contribution of waste-pickers towards a clean and resource-efficient city while also improving the returns that they receive from this work and addressing the health problems which accompany this work. An increasing number of initiatives, most started by Southern NGOs, are seeking to improve solid-waste collection and recycling and improve conditions for low-income groups which make a living as waste-pickers.[30] There are obvious linkages to be developed between social goals such as increased employment, better working conditions and higher wages for waste-pickers, and environmental goals such as better quality collection services, greater coverage for solid-waste collection (especially in the illegal or informal settlements where regular collection services are needed) and improved levels of recycling.

BOX 12.3

Resource recognition, not waste management

A new philosophy of resource management is beginning to transform solid-waste management worldwide, grounded in what can be called 'resource recognition'. Most waste material can be regarded as unused resources, so environmentally sound waste management entails the reduction of waste in production and distribution processes and the enhancement of reuse and recycling. In Northern cities these principles are being translated into practice through government regulation, stakeholder co-operation and citizens' initiatives. In Southern cities, solid-waste management is still focused on improving the conventional engineering systems (essentially, the collection, transport and disposal of solid wastes). Established environmental movements are not yet much interested in this subject, while city cleansing departments tend to look to higher technology and privatization for solutions to the environmental problems of uncollected and unsafely dumped wastes.

However, there are many small-scale non-conventional approaches to solid-waste management in cities of the South which not only change the conventional collect-transport-dispose organization of waste services but also have some general social and ecological goals linking 'resource recognition' to social betterment and attitudinal change at the local level. These include: assisting poor people whose livelihoods depend on wastes to do safer, more acceptable work; promoting the separation of wastes to facilitate more thorough or more efficient recycling (including decentralized compost-making); developing community/private sector/municipal partnerships; furthering environmental education; and pragmatic accommodation of informal activities in waste recovery and recycling.

Source: Furedy, Christine, 'Garbage: exploring non-conventional options in Asian Cities', *Environment and Urbanization*, vol. 4, no. 2, Oct. 1992, 42–61.

Some caution is needed in setting up recycling schemes as can be seen by the number of schemes that have failed. There are also conflicts or potential conflicts between different goals. For instance, promoting the separation by each household of recyclables and organic wastes from the rest of their wastes ensures much higher levels of recycling—and safer working conditions for those who collect the recyclables, compared to waste-picking. It probably means an overall increase in employment. But it also reduces the returns for waste-pickers—or may even remove their livelihood as most material with any value is removed from the garbage before they can pick through it. The crews of conventional garbage trucks may oppose a separate collection of recyclables from households since they also make

money separating out the more valuable recyclables or items that can be resold as they collect garbage. Some schemes to promote household separation have sought to employ former waste-pickers in household collection of recyclable materials,[31] whilst others have concentrated on making the tasks of waste-pickers at city dumps less hazardous.[32]

Perhaps the most important way to promote the successful integration of social and environmental goals into conventional solid-waste collection and management is the careful evaluation of initiatives to date and a greater sharing of experiences.[33] The experiences documented to date suggest that all new initiatives should be based on a detailed city-specific understanding of how wastes are currently generated and managed in each city—formally and informally from household level through to city level. They must recognize that there are often a great range of actors involved in some form of waste separation and reuse or recycling including:

- Households themselves who often keep separate some recyclables for direct sale.
- Waste-pickers who may 'pick' from household garbage cans or garbage on the street or at transfer stations or at the city dump.
- The staff of garbage collection trucks who look for the more valuable recyclable materials or items that can be resold as they collect garbage.
- Waste-buyers who range in the scale of their operation from itinerant buyers who go from house to house or from business to business to small waste-purchasing shops or enterprises, to larger buying operations, to factories or businesses who use the waste.
- Those involved in collecting, repairing and selling goods or items working in second-hand markets.

New initiatives need to be assessed in terms of how far they help poorer groups meet their needs and earn sufficient income and how far they reduce exploitation and discrimination against waste-pickers and other people making a living from wastes—as well as how much they increase the efficient use of wastes as resources.[34] The ideal would be for no one to need to make a living picking recyclable or reusable waste from a city dump both because this is a dangerous and unpleasant job and because separation of recyclables at source is a far more efficient way to reduce overall resource use.

Minimizing wastes[35]

While the initial interest in waste management centred on better ways to collect and dispose of it, there has also been a growing interest in what is termed 'waste minimization'. This seeks to reduce wastes at all points from the extraction of raw materials, their use in production, in packaging and distribution and in use and disposal. As a review of business perspectives on environment and development prepared for the Earth Summit noted:

Under the pressure of tightening regulations, increasingly 'green' consumer expectations and new management attitudes towards extended corporate responsibility, companies are recognizing that environmental management now requires the minimization of risks and impacts throughout a product's life cycle, from 'cradle to grave'. This is in turn leading to the industrial ideal of an economic system based on 'reconsumption'—that is the ability to use and reuse goods in whole or in part over several generations.[36]

Waste minimization can bring many advantages. For instance, there are many examples of industries that reduced costs or increased profits at the same time as reducing solid and liquid wastes.[37] One of the best known examples is that of the 3M Company in the US whose 'Pollution Prevention Pays' programme has been applied to more than 3000 projects and which has brought major reductions in air pollution, waste water and solid wastes—with the company managing to save $537 million.[38] New plant designs often allow process chemicals that were formerly dumped as wastes to be recovered and used again. In other instances, what was originally a production-waste from one factory has become a feedstock for another industry—for example the organic residues from many industries serve as feedstock for the manufacture of animal feed, packaging material, chemicals and pharmaceuticals, fertilizers, fuel, food and construction materials.[39]

For a municipality, encouraging waste minimization among households and commercial enterprises can considerably reduce the costs of collecting and disposing of solid wastes. Such encouragement could include providing recycling credits which the local authority pays to a household or business for paper, glass, metal or other materials they separate and make available for collection or lower charges for households or enterprises who generate very little waste for collection. This can be paid for through the amount the authority saves from not having to collect and/or dispose of the waste and through the revenue from selling the materials for recycling. But national governments are often reluctant to encourage waste minimization by, for instance, taxing packaging, as they fear that the increased taxation will dampen economic activity—even though this also means a cleaner environment and less pressure on the authorities responsible for solid-waste collection and management.

Various governments have taken measures to encourage waste minimization within industries. One is the use of 'take-back' agreements through which industry has to take back the waste that it generates. Take-back initiatives have also been developed in voluntary agreements between governments and industry—or between companies themselves, as in the example in Box 12.4. Charging companies the full cost of waste disposal, including paying for the short- and long-term environmental costs, can also promote waste minimization. As the review of business perspectives noted above stresses, one powerful stimulus to waste minimization and to recycling process chemicals within OECD countries is the growing cost of waste disposal; waste processing can cost companies an average of $380 a ton rising to $3,000–10,000 per ton for toxic and hazardous wastes.

BOX 12.4

An example of waste minimization

The Upper Canada Brewing Company in Toronto has managed to reduce the amount of waste it generates by 99 per cent, resulting in savings of over $US200,000 a year from fees associated with landfill and collection costs. Initiatives to reduce wastes were primarily targeted at the company's suppliers through requests to eliminate excess packaging. For suppliers that were uncooperative, the company sent back excess packaging at the suppliers' expense. The company also arranged for supplies to be shipped using packing material consisting of compostable materials such as popcorn or newspaper. Recycling initiatives focused on fine paper, beverage containers, newsprint, corrugated cardboard, plastics and organic materials. Spent grains generated from the brewing process were used as feed grain. The costs of starting up this initiative was around $15,000.

Source: McRae, L. S., '3 RS regulations in Ontario; compliance and cost savings', proceedings of R'95 International Congress, Geneva, 1995.

Incorporating environmental protection and resource conservation into decisions

During the last 10–15 years, a greater use has been made of environmental impact assessments and of new accounting techniques developed by environmental economics to more fully incorporate environmental issues into decision-making. Recent developments in both are considered briefly below and an example is given as to how environmental economics can feed into urban planning.

Environmental impact assessments (EIAs) are increasingly the means by which governments and development assistance agencies identify and predict the scope of the environmental consequences of a particular development project or activity.[40] Many also seek to ascertain the social impacts of projects. The objective is to anticipate the consequences and avoid or mitigate them through amending the design or implementation of the project or activity. There are several stages to such an assessment. The first is to accurately identify all possible environmental impacts related to the proposed project, and consider both the natural ecosytems and the different communities affected by the impacts. The second is to measure the severity of the impacts for a range of possible plans each of which realizes the objectives of the development project or activity. Finally the assessment should propose different options through which to minimize harmful environmental impacts. For projects in which the small scale of investment or the minimal predicted environmental impacts do not justify a full environmental impact assessment, estimates of the expected major impacts may be used to make a rapid and/or preliminary investigation. Most Northern countries have some form of EIA guidelines in law or through government regulations. The international bilateral and multilateral development agencies also have regulations which cover the use of EIA for development projects and the Development Assistance Committee of the OECD is currently working to standardize procedures. The form of such guidelines is not often contentious; the more controversial area is when and where such guidelines should be used.

Environmental impact-assessment techniques were developed during the 1960s in North America and began to spread significantly to other regions in the following decade. Although EIAs for projects in urban areas are common in the North, most experience with such assessments in the South to date is for rural development projects and activities. The focus on the rural environment reflects the fact that only recently has there been a growing awareness of the scale and severity of environmental problems in urban areas.[41] It is now accepted that large urban development projects have major impacts on natural resources within the urban area. These include increased use and reduction of the area of groundwater recharge zones depleting the water table, over-extending the capacity of the local environment to absorb waste (due to pollution), and significant reductions in the quality of the local environment for residents during construction and perhaps afterwards.[42] For example, the Environmental Guidelines for Hong Kong identifies over 70 different land use activities and scores each into one of three groups, depending on the severity of the environmental impact.[43] A particular problem occurs when urban developments have significant impacts on rural areas—or rural developments on

urban areas—and the planning authorities cannot easily take account of such impacts.[44] More recently, UNCHS (Habitat) has helped Sri Lanka to develop guidelines for environmental impact appraisal of industries and infrastructure projects for use in urban development control. The Urban Management Programme of the World Bank, UNCHS (Habitat) and UNDP has also been developing a framework for environmental planning and management in the South, identifying the particular environmental problems and their causes and major impacts on the livelihoods (both income and well-being) of local populations.[45]

Within environmental economics, there is considerable debate about how to assign appropriate values to natural resources and to ecosystems within economic decision-making. Many environmental goods are rarely bought and sold on the market but they have a very real value. They provide a flow of goods or services for productive activities (for example, water used in industry), they contribute to health and well-being (for example, clean air and access to parks) or they may be such that people value their continued existence without necessarily being able to measure the benefit (for example, access to historic buildings). In cities located in particularly beautiful natural surroundings, there is often a failure to recognize the value of the surroundings and to ensure their protection.[46]

There is a considerable body of literature on project-appraisal techniques and cost-benefit analyses which incorporate estimated valuations of environmental goods[47] although very little of this literature deals specifically with urban environments in the South. Box 12.5 illustrates the possibilities, drawing on a study of Mexico City which was one component of an assessment of the cost of aggregate environmental damage in Mexico.

A number of different techniques can be used to measure environmental values.[48] For example, the health-related costs of water and air pollution can be estimated through days of work lost, medical expenses and lives lost. The value of clean water can be assessed by the price people are willing to pay for bottled water. And the value of clean air can also be considered through examining house price differentials. In some cases, pollution levels are so high that the government is forced to incur direct additional expenses through shutting schools; or the shortage of water means incurring large infrastructure investment.[49] Although most research in this area has taken place in the North, there is increasing interest in considering such issues in the South.

There are obvious limitations in using such cost-benefit analysis techniques to evaluate projects which include an environmental component. Valuation of environmental benefits is difficult and

The costs of environmental damage in Mexico City

Research in Mexico City has sought to measure the costs of environmental damage using three steps. The first is a measure of the level of environmental quality or degradation. The second is to relate such levels to damage to health, productivity and materials. The third is to assign costs to the predicted damage. The discussion below considers air and water pollution.

Data on air quality is recorded for the city by the Departamento del Distrito Federal and by the air pollution unit of Mexico's environmental agency, SEDUE. One particular problem in assessing the damage is that little is known as to the health effects of different pollutants at high altitudes. In the case of the Mexico City Metropolitan Area the major health impacts of air pollution originate from three major pollutants: suspended particulate matter, ozone (a secondary pollutant) and lead. In regard to particulate matter, the major health effects are restricted activity and increase in overall mortality rates. Restricted activity can be assessed through restricted activity days (i.e. days for which normal activity was not possible), work-days lost, visits to emergency rooms, minor respiratory disease and chronic children's cough. Using data collected from Mexico City and elsewhere, it was estimated

that some 11.2 million work-days would be saved each year by reducing pollution emissions to those specified in legislated standards. Using the average industrial wage in Mexico City ,the current annual cost associated with this pollution, ignoring suffering and medication expenses, is $US358 million.

Drawing on other studies that have estimated the number of premature deaths associated with particulate matter, 6,400 people a year are dying prematurely with an average of 12.5 years of life being lost because of pollution emissions which exceed legislated standards. The valuation of life is very controversial. The author uses an estimate based on the hourly wage, resulting in an annual aggregate value of $US480 million.

In regard to ozone pollution, respiratory-related restricted-activity days are also the source of a major health cost. There are a number of other serious health problems including asthma attacks, eye irritation, mild cough, sore throat, headache and chest discomfort but little comprehensive data exists on the impacts. Estimated costs arising from pollution levels in excess of legislated standards are $US102 million.

Lead is a particularly dangerous air pollutant. Health studies on children living in Mexico City suggest that the main determinant of blood lead level is the place of residence. Little recent US data is helpful on

predicting health responses because in many cities, gasoline is now lead-free. Nearly 95 per cent of gasoline in the Mexico City Metropolitan Area still contains lead. Using what research is available results in an estimated cost of $US60 million based on screening of all children with a blood lead level above 25 µg/dl and 1 per cent of all children requiring chelation therapy. An additional $US21.5 million is required in compensatory education for children, due to a reduction in IQ as a result of lead poisoning. In adults, high levels of lead result in a number of health problems including high blood pressure and, as a result, myocardial infarctions. Annual costs from these two health problems equal $US47.9 million.

The water supply is another major environmental problem in Mexico City Metropolitan Area. Since the middle of the last century, underground water has been used. At present, only 15 per cent of consumption comes from surface water with the remainder being drawn from underneath the city. The average pumping height is now 80 metres. Significant subsidence damage has been caused in the city itself with the ground level falling by eight metres or more in the historical part of the city. Prices charged by the municipality for water are below the average cost, resulting in a total annual subsidy to those receiving municipal water of $US1 billion in direct costs alone.

Source: Margulis, Sergio, *Back-of-the-Envelope Estimates of Environmental Damage Costs in Mexico*, Policy Research Working Paper, WPS 824, World Bank, Washington DC, 1992.

therefore the process allows practitioners to distort the results to favour the outcome they prefer.[50] Some of the more fundamental criticisms to cost-benefit analysis are particularly pertinent when considering environmental goods: can environmental systems be treated as divisible; can we assume environmental systems achieve an equilibrium position; and are changes to ecological systems likely to be reversible?[51] The combined effects of two pollutants may also be very different from the simple sum of each individual component.

12.3 Developing local Agenda 21s

Hundreds of local authorities around the world are developing 'local Agenda 21s' as the means to introduce or strengthen environmental concerns into their plans and operations.[52] Chapter 28 of the Earth Summit's Agenda 21, entitled 'Local Authorities Initiatives in Support of Agenda 21' states succinctly why local governments have such an important role in implementing Agenda 21.

Because so many of the problems and solutions being addressed by Agenda 21 have their roots in local activities, the participation and cooperation of local authorities will be a determining factor in fulfilling its objectives. Local authorities construct, operate and maintain economic, social and environmental infrastructure, oversee planning processes, establish local environmental policies and regulations and assist in implementing national and sub-national environmental policies. As the level of governance closest to the people, they play a vital role in educating, mobilizing and responding to the public to promote sustainable development (28.1).[53]

This same chapter listed four objectives, the most important of which is that by 1996, most local authorities in each country should have undertaken a consultative process with their populations and achieved a consensus on a local Agenda 21. Another important objective was the need for all local authorities to implement and monitor programmes which aim to ensure that women and youth are represented in decision-making, planning and implementation processes.

At the meeting of the European Towns and Development Consortium several months after the Earth Summit, this idea received further support.[54] The idea of local strategies for sustainable

BOX 12.6
Hamilton-Wentworth's plan for sustainable development

Hamilton-Wentworth is a regional municipality in Canada, located in the centre of Canada's manufacturing heartland. Covering an area of 1,140 square kilometres, it has around 452,000 inhabitants. Since 1989, it has been developing its own sustainable development plan with strong social, economic and ecological objectives. These include helping to re-orient its economic base away from steel production towards knowledge based industries and enterprises involved in environmental improvement while also protecting its natural resource base, limiting urban expansion, reducing resource use and greatly improving the quality of the environment.

During the 1950s and 1960s, Hamilton-Wentworth's prosperity depended heavily on the steel mills located there and it was the key steel-maker for Toronto, Canada's largest metropolitan centre, 60 km away. Since then, especially during the 1980s, a new economic base became increasingly necessary with the decline in steel production and with technological changes in steel mills which greatly reduced the number of jobs. Some local industries also closed or moved away after the 1990 Canada–US Free Trade Agreement. There was the legacy of a large steel town with a heavily polluted bay and contaminated land around the steel mills. In recent years, there has been a major clean up with salmon and trout returning to the Hamilton harbour which had become almost devoid of fish. The soil around the harbour was also decontaminated and air pollution considerably reduced. The environmental clean-up also helped develop local enterprises based on waste management or environmental improvement.

In 1989, the regional government's management team found that they lacked a framework with which to evaluate proposals put forward for budget approval. They requested the formation of a Taskforce on Sustainable Development which was set up in 1990 to explore the concept of sustainable development and its application to Hamilton-Wentworth. Over a three-year period, this Task Force sought the opinion of a wide range of local citizens and specialists through town-hall meetings, focus-group discussions, community fora and specialized working teams. They produced a report entitled Vision 2020—A Sustainable Region with two additional reports, the first on directions needed to

achieve this, the second on strategies and actions. These covered topics such as air and water quality, the protection of natural areas, waste reduction, energy consumption, transport, land use planning, agriculture and other economic activities and personal health. They also identified the decisions and actions which the regional government and other levels of government, community groups, business and individual citizens need to make to achieve sustainable development goals. The Task Force's outreach programme also increased people's awareness and knowledge about sustainable development. These documents helped the regional government develop a draft plan Towards a Sustainable Region which is currently being discussed and amended, before implementation begins.

One notable aspect of the draft Plan (and the Task Force documents) is the integration of resource conservation, land-use planning, transport and energy conservation. For instance, energy conservation will be promoted through promoting a compact urban form. The plan seeks to accommodate 96 percent of future growth up to the year 2020 within existing urban areas—with the promotion of compact mixed land use in the regional centre and municipal centres and along corridors. As the draft plan states, mixed forms of development within an urban area are preferable to widespread low density residential development and scattered rural development because:

- growth can be accommodated by building on vacant or redeveloped land, without taking up agricultural lands or natural areas;
- higher density development can reduce per capita servicing costs and makes more efficient use of existing services;
- efficient and affordable public transit systems can be established;
- effective community design can ensure people are close to recreation, natural areas, shopping and their workplace; and a compact community makes walking and bicycling viable options for movement. (p. C-13).

The Plan has a strong commitment to protecting good-quality farmland from urban encroachment, and also of ensuring that farmers can obtain an adequate livelihood through sustainable farming practices. For instance, it supports the establishment of value-added or food-processing facilities on or close to farms and encourages local authorities to support farmer markets.

The linkages between land use, transport, energy and resource conservation are also

explicit in the draft Plan's sub-section on transport which states that 'because there is a direct link between land use planning (densities, mix and proximity of uses) and transportation, emphasis will be placed on accessibility and reducing reliance on the automobile by promoting alternative modes of transportation, such as public transit, walking and cycling to all urbanized areas of the Region' (p. C-28). A regional bicycle commuting network plan has been developed to guide improved provision of bicycle lanes and other facilities to support increased bicycle use.

Energy conservation is also encouraged through incorporating energy conservation practices in the design, construction and operation of the regional government's capital works and equipment (and requests that other local government agencies also do so). Public and private agencies, industrial and commercial operations and individuals are also encouraged to take part in energy conservation programmes and the regional authorities aim to promote innovations in housing design to encourage the construction of energy efficient housing and the utilization of solar energy for space heating, where feasible.

Many other initiatives are also planned to continue improving air and water quality. Vision 2020 outlined a plan to develop a system of interconnected protected natural areas threading through both rural and urban areas in the region including natural core areas such as wetlands, forests and other ecologically significant habitats used by local wildlife which will be linked by stream corridors, farm hedgerows and newly created linear links with vegetative buffers. These will allow wildlife to move from one geographic area to another and also link natural areas to municipal parks, rights-of-way, bike paths and hiking trails—making open space and natural areas more easily accessible to a higher proportion of the population. Vision 2020 also emphasises that a new ethic must be adopted on waste reduction, minimizing consumption and substantially reducing the amount of waste.

Apart from the guidance set by Vision 2020 for the different government sectoral plans and reviews, there is also a Staff Working Group on Sustainable Development which is mandated by the Regional government to help integrate the principles of sustainable development into the capital budget and departmental work programmes. There is also a programme to involve the population in evaluating what has been achieved and helping set priorities.

Source: Wilkins, Charles, 'Steeltown charts a new course', *Canadian Geographic*, vol. 113, no. 4, July/Aug. 1993, 42–55; Regional Municipality of Hamilton-Wentworth, *Implementing Vision 2020; Directions for Creating a Sustainable Region*, The Regional Chairman's Taskforce on Sustainable Development, 1993; and Regional Municipality of Hamilton-Wentworth, *Towards a Sustainable Region: Hamilton-Wentworth Region, Official Plan (Draft)*, Sept. 1993, Regional Planning and Development Department, September, Hamilton-Wentworth, 1993; Staff Working Group on Sustainable Development, *Hamilton-Wentworth's Sustainable Community Decision-Making Guide*, Regional Municipality of Hamilton-Wentworth, Aug. 1993.

development was not new to local government representatives. In 1990, the World Congress of Local Governments for a Sustainable Future founded the International Council for Local Environmental Initiatives (ICLEI), and this has been working for some years to support local authorities seeking to resolve environmental problems.[55] Box 12.6 gives an example of how a municipality can develop a sustainable development plan. It describes the plan developed by a Canadian municipality, Hamilton-Wentworth, and serves as an illustration of a local government seeking to address a wide range of sustainable development goals within a coherent planning framework.

Local Agenda 21 processes will differ from city to city since they reflect the different local contexts in which they are working and the existing institutional structures. In some countries, they can build on a considerable experience at local authority level in environmental planning and management; in others, there is no such base on which to develop them and as Chapter 5 described, many municipal governments have few powers and resources. There is also considerable variation as to how many local authorities in any country are developing local Agenda 21s and as to whether these are becoming integrated into other aspects of urban planning and management.

Some countries have national programmes of support for such initiatives including Australia, the Netherlands, Denmark, Sweden, the UK and Finland.[56] In the UK, such initiatives have several purposes:

- To promote local consultative processes on sustainable development.

- To disseminate guidance for UK local authorities on how to move towards sustainability at a local level and on how to develop models of community consultation, participation and local consensus.

- To involve and fully participate with other sectors and major groups in the local Agenda 21 process at a national level.[57]

In Sweden, all local authorities have environmental strategies that include provision for waste minimization and recycling and most municipalities have started or decided to start work on Local Agenda 21s.[58] Several European countries are exploring the possibilities of linking work on Local Agenda 21 to formal land-use planning systems. For instance, the city of Stockholm is currently preparing a new structure plan which takes a more strategic and longer term view than previous plans and will explicitly promote the integration of environmental, social and economic goals—and the new plan will become

part of the Local Agenda 21 for the city.[59] In Denmark, existing planning instruments are being adapted to Agenda 21 requirements so that municipal plans become overall action plans for the environment.[60]

Certain local authorities in the South have also developed local Agenda 21s. For instance, each of the municipalities which make up the Bogotá metropolitan area in Colombia are developing their own local environmental agendas, sponsored by the metropolitan authority, NGOs and academics[61]—see Box 12.7. Other urban centres in Colombia such as Manizales also have a well-established local Agenda 21 process.[62] Among other cities in the South that are developing Local Agenda 21s are Cajamarca in Peru, Durban in South Africa, and Santos in Brazil.[63]

To date, there has been no comprehensive assessment of local Agenda 21 processes. ICLEI has recently initiated a research programme to look more closely at this work in 21 cities throughout the world. An obvious constraint on local Agenda 21s is their national context. Chapter 5 noted the lack of resources and technical capacity within most local authorities in the South and the fact that local governments are often restricted by central government both in respect of raising finance and in other activities.[64]

12.4 Reducing cities' Ecological Footprint

Introduction

Chapter 4 described how the 'ecological footprint' of wealthy cities draws on the ecological productivity of an area many times that of the city itself. There are obvious measures which permit a reduction in any city's ecological footprint. Most are linked to one of the following:

- Increasing biomass production within the city or its immediate surrounds (e.g. crops, fish, trees).

- Reduced waste or increased use of 'waste' as an input into production (e.g. organic waste used for compost; waste water used for urban agriculture; improved performance on reclamation and recycling of materials).

- Increased efficiency in the use of resources imported into the city (e.g. fresh water, fossil fuels and other mineral resources).

Some of these issues have been considered already. For instance, earlier sections discussed how to reduce the use of resources which then implies less resource extraction is needed—and also innovations in waste minimization that reduce the volume of wastes generated within cities that then has to be disposed of in the wider

BOX 12.7
Developing Local Environmental Agendas in Santa Fé de Bogotá, Colombia

In Colombia, in recent years, there has been a considerable strengthening of environmental action—at all levels—and also institutional changes to give a higher priority to local action and to participation. The Colombian legal framework in the 1991 Constitution helped increase the decentralization process from national to regional and local agencies. The approval by Congress for setting up a new Ministry of Environment in December 1993 also implies increased political support for urban environmental policies.

This increased priority to environmental action at local level can be seen in Santa Fé de Bogotá, the capital and much the largest urban area (with 6.4 million inhabitants, according to the 1993 census). Environmental Agendas are being developed by each of the 20 municipalities that make up Bogotá metropolitan area with support from Bogotá's Department of the Environment (DAMA), NGOs and academics. Each district has Local Administrative Councils made up of directly elected councillors on three year terms of office. They are supported by local development funds which strengthen their decision making powers. Local environmental agendas are seen as ways in which local environmental problems can be identified and acted on, but which also feed into city planning or which allow districts with comparable problems to work together in addressing them.

The first step in developing a Local Agenda within a municipality is to develop a local environmental profile. This identifies environmental resources and problems and locates them within the municipality's physical and socio-economic structure. These are then discussed in workshops and the areas in need of immediate attention are identified. This leads to a priority list for environmental action. The second step is defining the Local Agendas (including the programmes and projects to receive priority, the financial responsibilities of the organizations involved, and a timetable for an investment plan) and developing the partnerships between the Local Administrative Councils and community based organizations, NGOs and other groups within the locality.

One funding source for the Local Agendas is the Ecofondo Corporation which was set up to provide financial and technical support for citizen's environmental initiatives. In 1994, it had 408 environmental organizations on its register, many of which work in Bogotá. It is providing funds to some of the Local Agenda projects in Bogotá—for instance the Entrenubes park project contained in the Usme and San Cristobal Agendas and the programme to protect the *humedales* of Tibabuyes and Juan Amarillo from unauthorized settlements and the dumping of wastes.

This decentralization of resources and responsibilities and the need for greater co-ordination between local, regional and national bodies has not been without difficulties. For instance, many government departments resisted the emergence of an environmental co-ordinating body for Bogotá and the municipal governments have long had inadequate resources and trained staff for the environment actions they are required by law to undertake. In addition, planning in Bogotá has traditionally been centralized with little participation.

The greater attention given to environmental issues has also been supported by a greater priority given to environmental education at all levels of the education system.

Source: Pacheco Montes, Margarita, *Development of Environmental Agendas in Districts of Santa Fé de Bogotá, Colombia*, Background Paper prepared for Global Report, Urban Environmental Studies programme, Instituto de Estudios Ambientales (IDEA), Universidad Nacional de Colombia

city region. Two aspects which have not been covered and which deserve attention are urban agriculture (see below) and urban forestry (see Box 12.9).

Urban agriculture

In many urban centres in the South, a high proportion of the population grows a significant proportion of their own food or derives an income from selling crops or livestock. In many cities in both the North and the South, a considerable proportion of the fruits and vegetables and certain other crops consumed in the city are produced within metropolitan boundaries or just outside them.

The importance of urban agriculture has rarely been fully grasped by city authorities or by researchers. As a recent overview of urban agriculture notes,

cities can be transformed from being only consumers of food and other agricultural products into important resource-conserving, health-improving, sustainable generators of these products. In particular, agriculture in towns, cities and metropolitan areas can convert urban wastes into resources, put vacant and under-utilised areas into productive use, and conserve natural resources outside cities while improving the environment for urban living.[65]

This overview also noted the tremendous diversity in urban agriculture since it includes:

- Aquaculture in tanks, ponds, rivers and coastal bays.
- Livestock (particularly micro-livestock) raised in backyards, along roadsides, within utility rights-of-way, in poultry sheds and piggeries.
- Orchards, including vineyards, street trees, and backyard trees.
- Vegetables and other crops grown on roof tops, in backyards, in vacant lots of industrial estates, along canals, on the grounds of institutions, on roadsides and in many suburban small farms.[66]

Urban agriculture can combine environmental goals such as reducing the ecological footprint of cities and utilizing city wastes with broader economic and social goals. It can generate or support many jobs and contribute significantly to the food or fuel needed by poorer groups; the review noted above pointed to the many studies which show the extent to which poorer households gain food or income from urban agriculture, even within cities where such agriculture is not encouraged. For instance, a study by Mazingira Institute in Kenya found that almost two-thirds of the 1,500 urban households questioned in six Kenyan towns grew some of their own food or fuel while about half kept some livestock.[67] In Lusaka, Zambia's capital and largest city, more than half of all households in some low-income areas grew a proportion of their own food either on plots next to their shelters or on plots elsewhere cultivated during the rainy season; for many families in Lusaka, the food they grow themselves provides a vital or useful food supplement although insufficient information is available to gauge its importance.[68]

However, it is not only in the South where urban or peri-urban agriculture is important; in the USA and in many European countries, a significant proportion of the total value of agricultural production is produced within metropolitan boundaries. This is especially so if the value of home-grown produce from gardens, balconies and backyards which is consumed by the household is also taken into account. There are also some innovative examples where urban agriculture has been combined with other services. For instance, the examples given in Box 12.8 include a 4-hectare farm that is right in the middle of a completely urbanized residential area and a series of small gardens developed by a group of neighbours in one of the poorer districts of South Philadelphia. In New York, one estimate suggested that 1,200 vacant lots had been reclaimed for community gardens.[69]

Urban agriculture can also bring other environmental benefits. It can make use of the city's organic wastes (through composting it) and in so doing, reduce considerably the volume of waste

which has to be disposed of. It can reduce water pollution when crop production is integrated with waste water disposal; this also has the advantage of limiting urban agriculture's demand for fresh water in cities where freshwater resources are scarce. Nutrient-rich sewage water is commonly used to irrigate crops or trees or support fishponds—and one in ten of the human population currently consumes food produced by the direct use of waste water.[70] The hazards to human health from pathogens or vectors within sewage water can easily be managed, either through relatively low-cost treatment measures or through the cultivation of non-food crops or crops which can safely be irrigated with sewage water.[71]

Urban agriculture can also make use of land not easily used for any other purpose—for instance land directly under electricity transmission lines as in the case of the successful commercial production of salad vegetables by Produce Gardens in Los Angeles[72] or land with sufficient risk of flooding to discourage permanent structures but where food production can be encouraged. It can also make use of vacant land-sites, until these are to be developed. In many cities, people make use of balconies, rooftops and small internal spaces for vegetables and fruit trees but also for more unusual products such as medicinal herbs (as in Santiago de Chile), silkworms (on balconies in Delhi), orchids in Bangkok and rabbits in Mexico City's informal or illegal settlements.[73] Urban agriculture can also reduce energy inputs into food production and distribution by minimizing the distance between production and consumption.[74]

Acting on rural–urban interactions

Earlier sections outlined the serious economic and ecological costs to the regions in which cities are located which can arise from urban demand for rural resources, urban pollution and unplanned and uncontrolled city expansion. Many are best addressed by action within the city—for instance the damage to forests, soils and water resources arising from city-generated pollution is generally best addressed through pollution control and waste reduction within the city. Most of the other problems—the loss of agricultural land, the destruction of natural landscapes and public open spaces and the ecological costs inherent in any unplanned low density urban sprawl—need a public control over land-use changes. These have to balance economic, social and ecological goals and resolve potential conflicts between them. For instance, housing prices in any city are much influenced by the availability and cost of land for housing—so too high a priority to halting development with an 'ecological belt' around a city where

---

BOX 12.8

Examples of urban agriculture in the United States

Fairview Gardens Farm: This 4-hectare farm is within one of California's more fertile valleys that has been surrounded by high-density, urban residential developments on three sides with a highway on the fourth. It is completely surrounded by urban development. The site was undeveloped in 1974, when purchased by a couple who were committed to growing food without chemicals, although the soil had been removed. The land has since been developed into a highly productive farm producing some 75 different varieties of fruit and vegetables. The food produced here feeds some 500 families. In a good year, over 30,000 lbs of peaches, plums and citrus fruits are harvested along with 25,000 lbs of avocadoes and tons of fresh vegetables. The farm also serves as a centre of education for schools in the vicinity.

The Garden of Eatin': In one of the poorer areas of Philadelphia, a group of neighbours developed highly productive food gardens on lots on a site that had been left undeveloped. Now, the different plots grow kale, cotton, black-eyed beans, okra, corn, lima beans, sweet potatoes, Jerusalem artichokes and blackberries as well as roses and calla lilies.

Source: Ableman, Michael, *From the Good Earth; a Celebration of Growing Food around the World*, Harry N. Abrams, New York, 1993.

demand for housing is growing will drive up housing prices. They must also be flexible enough to respond to different kinds of settlements and differing local needs and priorities. They must also reconcile the different aims and objectives of different local government units and of the populations they represent.

BOX 12.9
Urban forestry

Trees are an important part of urban environments. London has almost six million trees and hedges, and more than 65,000 woodlands and stands of trees. About 64 per cent of these trees are in residential areas—often in gardens. The increased awareness of the importance of urban trees has led to tree-planting programmes to increase the tree population in many towns and cities. In Quito, Ecuador the mayor declared a goal of planting 200,000 trees during his administration. In Guatemala City, a campaign to 're-green the city' was initiated in 1986 and over 1.5 million trees were planted. In the UK, tree-planting has been an important part of urban regeneration programmes.

The reasons for the considerable number of trees being planted or already existing in urban environments are the benefits they bring to improving the quality of urban life. First there are the material benefits. Trees in the South provide a variety of products that are used by urban dwellers to meet both subsistence and income generation needs. In areas in which the primary source of energy is wood fuel, either as wood or charcoal, the most vital benefit of trees in the South is the production of fuelwood. In both North and South, trees are a valuable source of food—particularly fruits, but also leaves, shoots and flowers. In many countries in the South, they are also used as fodder for livestock grazing in the urban areas. Trees are also important in the construction of urban settlements. Large amounts of timber are consumed for the construction of buildings and furniture. Other benefits include landscape enhancement, educational value, recreation and wildlife habitats. They can act as visual or acoustic screens and help to complement the buildings, and to keep the city in touch with nature. Trees can also provide pollution sinks for contaminants in land and air. Tree-planting has a significant effect in cleansing the air of pollutants and trees have a role in energy conservation by providing shade in summer and reducing the cooling effects of wind in winter. An additional benefit is the control of serious soil erosion and coastal erosion.

With the rapid growth of many towns and cities, there have been accompanying environmental problems, but some attempts have been made to improve the urban environments. Tree-planting has a role in this improvement and several schemes have been undertaken to increase the number of trees in these urban areas. In other instances, tree-planting has been used as part of urban regeneration. For instance, Knowsley Borough Council in the UK plants trees on vacant industrial land with the forestry type and treatment closely linked to the length of time the land is likely to remain idle and this initiative has been incorporated into the Mersey Forest, one of several community forests being created around urban areas in Britain.

Sources: Countryside Commission, *Action For London's Trees*, London, 1993; Carter, J. 'The Potential Of Urban Forestry In Developing Countries: A Concept Paper', Food and Agriculture Organization of the United Nations, 1993; Department of the Environment, *Trees in Towns*, London, 1993; European Union Expert Group on the Urban Environment, *European Sustainable Cities*, First report, Oct. 1994, XI/822/94–EN.

Here, as in other areas of environmental concern, the needed measures are more easily conceived than implemented. For instance, the loss of agricultural land from urban expansion can usually be avoided or minimized if local government guides the physical expansion and ensures that vacant or under-utilized land within the urbanized area is fully used. In most cities in the South, there is sufficient vacant land left undeveloped or only partially developed within the urbanized area to accommodate a very considerable increase in residential and commercial development with no expansion in the urbanized area.[75] Here, as in low-density suburbs in cities in the North, it is possible to promote higher densities and mix homes, workplaces, and retail and leisure activities around public transport nodes.[76] Even in cities with rapidly expanding populations, city expansion can combine adequate provision of land for housing and urban enterprises on the urban periphery with the protection of natural landscapes and the areas needed as public open space. Provision for urban agriculture and for parks, playgrounds and other forms of open space can be integrated with the protection of watersheds and agricultural land. The new urban developments on the city periphery can promote high energy efficiency in all buildings and energy supplies. Fossil-fuel use in transport can be kept down by ensuring that these relatively dense new developments on the urban periphery are centred around public transport nodes where mixed developments are encouraged and the use of private automobiles discouraged.[77]

The main difficulties in achieving such measures is in implementation. A recent paper on 'planning the sustainable city region'[78] noted that environmental planning must recognize three crucial characteristics of environmental processes:

- their trans-media nature through air, land and sea
- their trans-sectoral nature which cuts across traditional policy boundaries
- their trans-boundary nature cutting across political frontiers.

Solutions imply co-ordinated action between city authorities and the public authorities who have jurisdiction over the areas around a city unless there is a metropolitan authority which has jurisdiction over both. The local governments in the provinces, districts or municipalities which surround the urbanized area often have different aims and objectives to those within the urbanized area. Solutions imply integrated action by a wide range of government agencies and private companies who have long pursued their own sectoral goals largely in isolation. Many potential conflicts are not easily resolved. For instance, most cities have examples of the opposition of wealthier groups living in suburbs or 'exburbs' to new developments there—including improved provision of public transport (since this would put at risk the exclusive nature of the area), support for increased supplies of modest-priced housing and encouragement of new commercial or industrial enterprises. There is also the difficulty of developing an appropriate institutional structure to manage this process, especially in most cities in the South where urban authorities at all levels (metropolitan, city and municipal) are weak and ineffective. Making this institutional structure protect the public interest and do so in ways which are transparent and accountable is particularly difficult, given the scale of windfall profits which can accrue to landowners and developers from public decisions about land-use changes, the location of new roads or railways or where they are to be improved, and the kind and density of development permitted. Such decisions—or the failure of public authorities to control the conversion of agricultural land to residential, commercial or industrial use—can mean that land values increase by 100-fold or even 1,000-fold. The scale of possible profits from land transactions and the power of the landowners or developers who are the main beneficiaries help explain the inadequacies of public action on this issue.

12.5 International Innovations

Various international innovations have been described in earlier sections of this chapter—for instance the work of the Urban Management Programme in developing a framework for environmental planning and management and the work of the OECD Development Assistance Committee in developing environmental impact-assessment procedures. Chapter 11 also reported on the increasing attention given by various international donor agencies to environmental issues in their funding programmes.

Two other examples are the Sustainable Cities Programme and the Metropolitan Environmental Improvement Programme. The Sustainable Cities programme is a joint initiative of UNCHS (Habitat) and UNEP to provide municipal authorities and their partners in the public, private and community sectors with an improved capacity for environmental planning and management.[79] It has initiated in many cities demonstration projects that seek to involve all the public- and private-sector actors in the city to develop a broadly based environmental strategy and high priority capital investment projects. Each city project also aims to

stimulate comparable initiatives within the same country—and to promote the sharing of know-how between cities in different regions of the world. Sustainable City projects are underway in Dar es Salaam, Accra, Ibadan, Ismailia, Concepcion, Katowice, Jakarta and Madras; examples drawn from Dar es Salaam and Ismailia are given in Box 12.10.

BOX 12.10

Sustainable Cities Programmes in Dar es Salaam and Ismailia

Dar Es Salaam (Tanzania): Dar es Salaam has begun to develop and apply new approaches to urban planning and management with an explicit emphasis on sustainable development. Its main areas of work are in solid-waste management, providing services for urban land, improved air and surface water quality, the management of coastal area resources and of recreational and tourism resources and the development of urban agriculture. New urban management techniques have been introduced, working with local authorities. The programme has also brought private sector and community interests into the planning and management process and in so doing, has also helped to mobilize private sector and community resources. The new sustainable development planning process is also developing strategic plans, action plans and packages of investment projects that reinforce each other. This initiative has also stimulated the Government of Tanzania to initiate a national programme for sustainable urban management to replicate the lessons learnt in Dar es Salaam in eight other cities.

Ismailia (Egypt): Ismailia is an important administrative capital within the Suez Canal region with a population of 750,000. The Sustainable Cities Project has developed an environmental profile and a city environmental management information system. It also held a city-wide consultation that brought academics, the private sector, NGOs and community-based organizations into discussion with public institutions and politicians. This led to the formation of working groups that included representatives from these diverse groups. A City Environmental Strategy Review Workshop is co-ordinating environmental management and planning strategies based on the recommendations of working groups on

- managing land for agricultural development
- the management of Lake Timsah
- industrial development and
- urban strategic planning of the city, with human resource development as a cross cutting issue with particular attention given to generating job opportunities for youth and to the needs and priorities of women.

This process is leading to preparation of detailed investment projects, including feasibility studies and the identification of national and transnational sources of funding. A national consultation on Urban Environmental Strategies in Egypt is planned to allow the development of initiatives similar to those in Ismailia in other Egyptian cities.

Sources: UNCHS (Habitat), *Sustainable Human Settlements Development: Implementing Agenda 21*, Paper prepared for the Commission on Sustainable Development, United Nations Centre for Human Settlements (Habitat), Nairobi, 1994, with internal UNCHS documents.

The Metropolitan Environmental Improvement Programme is a UNDP-funded programme executed by the World Bank and this initiated work in five Asian cities in 1990 (Beijing, Bombay, Colombo, Jakarta and Manila).[80] It aims to develop and implement an environmental management strategy in each of these cities. This includes support for strengthening the capacity of pollution control and environmental protection agencies, especially in working with powerful economic planning and sectoral agencies at the local and national levels.

There are also numerous international agencies or networks that promote environmental planning and management or broader sustainable development goals. Box 12.11 gives some examples of the many that do so and of the various international conferences that have helped to generate a greater interest in cities' environmental problems in recent years.

BOX 12.11

Networks promoting environmental and sustainable development in urban areas

Formal and informal networking between cities has become increasingly important for the sharing of ideas and experiences in the development, management and implementation of policies and projects. Although both formal and informal city networks and city-twinning arrangements have existed for many years or even decades, as governments and international agencies have given more attention to urban problems, so have urban authorities become more involved in international, regional and national networks.

The international networks include CITYNET in Asia and EUROCITIES in Europe and the Cities for Climate Protection Campaign, whose work is supported by ICLEI. In March 1993, 83 European cities launched the European Cities for Climate Protection campaign. They also include networks that focus on particular issues—for instance the Urban Management Programme run by UNCHS (Habitat), the World Bank and UNDP that within its broader brief has a particular interest in environmental issues and the Healthy Cities network supported by the World

Health Organization that forms a network of cities committed to action on environment and health. The European Union supports a Sustainable Cities project through its Expert Group on the Urban Environment which encourages good practice and the exchange of information and is developing policy recommendations for the Union and member states.

There are many specialized networks operating within particular regions—for instance in Europe: Environet in the field of economic development; ECOS, POLIS, Public Transport Inter-change and the Car-Free Cities Club in Transport; and ROBIS that deals with the recycling of land for residential and commercial development in land use planning. In Asia, the Asia-Pacific 2000 programme is also promoting innovation and inter-city exchanges between groups working in urban areas.[81] The Africa Research Network for Urban Management (ARNUM) links over 300 researchers and urban practitioners in Africa in both national workshops and research projects. Certain agencies are particularly active within countries to promote action on Agenda 21 and an exchange of experiences—for instance the UK Local Government Management Board that is supporting a national programme to help local authorities in the UK to develop Local Agenda 21 plans.

Certain international events have been

important in stimulating this networking. These include

- The meeting in Toronto (Canada) in 1991 that led to 130 cities signing the *Toronto Declaration on World Cities and the Environment.*
- The *Berlin Declaration*, arising from an expert meeting in Berlin in 1992, that stressed the importance of each city building and updating a local environmental action plan for sustainable urban development.
- The meeting of the World Urban Forum in 1992 where representatives from 45 cities signed the *Curitiba Commitment* for sustainable urban development.
- *The Earth Summit* in Rio de Janeiro in 1992 where governments committed themselves, within Agenda 21, to supporting the development of Local Agenda 21s.
- *Global Forum '94* in Manchester (UK) where delegations from 50 cities met to discuss how citizen groups, NGOs, the private sector, trade unions and city authorities can work together to achieve sustainable development goals.
- *The First European Conference on Sustainable Cities and Towns* in Aalborg, Denmark in 1994.

Sources: European Union Expert Group on the Urban Environment, *European Sustainable Cities*, First report, Oct. 1994, XI/822/94–EN; Parenteau, René 'Local action plans for sustainable communities', *Environment and Urbanization*, vol. 6, no. 2, Oct. 1994; and UNCHS (Habitat), *Sustainable Human Settlements Development: Implementing Agenda 21*, Paper prepared for the Commission on Sustainable Development, United Nations Centre for Human Settlements (Habitat), Nairobi, 1994.

Notes and References

1. Bullard, Robert D., 'Anatomy of environmental racism', in Richard Hofrichter (ed.), *Toxic Struggles: The Theory and Practice of Environmental Justice*, New Society Publishers, Philadelphia, 1992, 25–35.

2. Serageldin, Ismail, 'Making development sustainable', *Finance and Development*, vol. 30, no. 4, Dec. 1993, 6–10; Winpenny, J.T., *Values for the Environment: A Guide to Economic Appraisal*, HMSO, London, 1991.

3. Hardoy, Jorge E., Diana Mitlin and David Satterthwaite, *Environmental Problems in Third World Cities*, Earthscan Publications, London, 1992.

4. Von Amsberg, Joachim, *Project Evaluation and the Depletion of Natural Capital: an Application of the Sustainability Principle*, Environment Working Paper no. 56, Environment Department, World Bank, Washington DC, 1993.

5. Serageldin 1993, *op. cit.*

6. Lovins, Amory B. and L. Hunter Lovins, 'Least-cost climatic stabilization', *Annual Review of Energy and Environment*, vol. 16, 1991, 433–531.

7. See for instance Lovins and Lovins 1991, *op. cit.*

8. Schmidheiny, Stephan, with the Business Council for Sustainable Development, *Changing Course: A Global Business Perspective on Development and the Environment*, The MIT Press, Cambridge, 1992.

9. 'Living under a grass roof', *Environmental News from the Netherlands*, no. 4, Ministry of Housing, Spatial Planning and the Environment, The Hague, 1994, 5–6.

10. Roodman, David Malin and Nicholas Lenssen, 'Our buildings, ourselves', *World Watch*, Dec. 1994, 21–9.

11. Roodman and Lenssen 1994, *op. cit.*

12. Fickett, Arnold P., Clark W. Gellings and Amory B. Lovins, 'Efficient use of electricity', *Scientific American*, Sept. 1990, 65–74.

13. Lovins, Amory B., 'Energy, people and industrialization', paper presented at the Hoover Institution conference on 'Human Demography and Natural Resources', Stanford University, 1–3 Feb. 1989.

14. *Ibid.*

15. Webb, Jeremy, 'Rebel with a cause; a profile of Amory Lovins', *New Scientist*, vol. 145, no. 1964, 1995, 32–5.

16. Hesse and Lucas, *Die Beschäftigungspolitische Bedeutung der Verkehrswirtschaft in Nordrhein-Westfalen*, Institut für Ökologische Wirtschaftsforschung, Wuppertal, 1990 quoted in Wikima Consulting, *The Employment Implications of Environmental Action*, Report prepared for the Commission of the European Communities, Directorate-General on Employment, Industrial Relations and Social Affairs, London, 1993.

17. Several studies in the late 1970s and early 1980s demonstrated this—for instance see Leach, Gerald and others, *A Low Energy Strategy for the United Kingdom*, London, Science Reviews Ltd., 1979 for details of how increasing prosperity need not imply increased fossil-fuel use in the UK.

18. Lovins and Lovins 1991, *op. cit.*

19. See Box 12.6.

20. Environ, *Environmental Achievements in Leicester—Britain's First Environment City*, Leicester, September 1993.

21. European Union Expert group on the Urban Environment, *European Sustainable Cities*, First report, October 1994, XI/822/94–EN.

22. Mansson, Tommy, 'The new urban dream', *Down to Earth*, 31 May 1993, 26–31.

23. European Union Expert group on the Urban Environment 1994, *op. cit.*

24. This and the following paragraphs on solid waste management draw heavily on the work of Dr Christine Furedy from York University, Toronto, Canada.

25. Hardoy, Jorge E., Diana Mitlin and David Satterthwaite, 'The future city', in Johan Holmberg (ed.), *Policies for a Small Planet*, Earthscan publications, London, 1992, 124–56.

26. Furedy, Christine, 'Garbage: exploring non-conventional options in Asian cities', *Environment and Urbanization*, vol. 4, no. 2, Oct. 1992, 42–61.

27. Furedy, Christine, 'Socio-environmental initiatives in solid waste management in Southern cities: developing international comparisons', Paper presented at a workshop on 'Linkages in Urban Solid Waste Management', Karnataka State Council for Science and Technology, University of Amsterdam and Bangalore Mahanagara Palike, Bangalore, 18–20 April 1994.

28. Pacheco, Margarita, 'Recycling in Bogota; developing a culture for urban sustainability', *Environment and Urbanization*, vol. 4, no. 2, Oct. 1992, 74–9.

29. UNCHS (Habitat), *Sustainable Human Settlements Development: Implementing Agenda 21*, Paper prepared for the Commission on Sustainable Development, United Nations Centre for Human Settlements (Habitat), Nairobi, 1994.

30. Furedy, Christine, 'Social aspects of solid waste recovery in Asian cities', *Environmental Sanitation Reviews*, no. 30, Dec., ENSIC, Asian Institute of Technology, Bangkok, 1990, 2–52. Also Furedy 1992, *op. cit.*, Huysman, Marijk, 'Waste picking as a survival strategy for women in Indian cities', *Environment and Urbanization*, vol. 6, no. 2, Oct. 1994, 155–74.

31. See for instance the experience of the 'garbage recycling project' in Metro Manila described in Furedy 1992 (*op. cit.*) and Furedy 1994 (*op. cit.*) and that of Waste Wise and Civic Exnora in India (Furedy 1992, *op. cit.*).

32. See for instance the GTZ funded project in Kathmandu described in Furedy 1992, *op. cit.*

33. Furedy 1994, *op. cit.*

34. Furedy 1990, *op. cit.*

35. This draws on a background paper by Graham Alabaster on *Waste Minimization Strategies for Developing Countries*, UNCHS, Nairobi, 1995.

36. Schmidheiny, Stephan, with the Business Council for Sustainable Development, *Changing Course: a Global Business Perspective on Development and the Environment*, The MIT Press, Cambridge, 1992, 98–9.

37. *Ibid.*

38. *Ibid.*

39. Vimal, O. P., 'Recycling of organic residues—status and trends in India, *Industry and Environment*, UNEP Europe, Paris, April-June 1982, 7–10.

40. ODA, *Manual of Environmental Apprasial*, Overseas Development Administration, London, 1992,

41. Hardoy, Jorge E., Diana Mitlin and David Satterthwaite, *Environmental Problems in Third World Cities*, Earthscan Publications, London, 1992.

42. *Ibid.*

43. Hong Kong Government, *Environmental Guidelines for Planning in Hong Kong*, an extract from the Hong Kong Planning Standards and Guidelines, Hong Kong. 1990.

44. See Ch. 4

45. Leitmann, Josef, Carl Bartone and Janis Bernstein, 'Environmental management and urban development: issues and options for Third World cities', *Environment and Urbanization*, vol. 4, no. 2, Oct. 1992.

46. See for instance Camargo, Jose Marcio, 'Rio de Janeiro: natural beauty as a public good' and Kreimer, Alcira, Thereza Lobo, Braz Menezes, Mohan Munasinghe, Ronald Parker and Martha Preece, 'Rio de Janeiro—in search of sustainability', in Alcira Kreimer, Thereza Lobo, Braz Menezes, Mohan Munasinghe and Ronald Parker (eds.),

Towards a Sustainable Urban Environment: The Rio de Janeiro Study, World Bank Discussion Papers No. 195, World Bank, 1993.

47. Winpenny 1991, *op. cit.*

48. See Winpenny 1991 for a description of the specific use of such techniques in urban areas.

49. White, Rodney R., 'The international transfer of urban technology: does the North have anything to offer for the global environmental crisis?', *Environment and Urbanization*, vol. 4, no. 2, Oct. 1992, 109–20.

50. Bowers, John, *Economics of the Environment—The Conservationists Response to the Pearce Report*, British Association for Nature Conservationists, 1990.

51. Norgaard, Richard B., 'Environmental economics: an evolutional critique and a plea for pluralism', *Journal of Environmental Economics and Management*, vol. 12, 1985, 382–94.

52. See for instance European Union Expert group on the Urban Environment 1994, *op. cit.*, and World Resources Institute, *World Resources Report 1996–97*, Washington DC, 1996. The second of these two reports quoted an estimate from the International Council of Local Environmental Initiatives that some 1,200 local authorities in 33 countries have established local agenda 21 campaigns.

53. Robinson, Nicholas A. (ed.), *Agenda 21: Earth's Action Plan*, Oceania, New York–London–Rome, 1993.

54. Smith, Vernon, 'Environmental imperialism?', *Edge*, 1 June 1993.

55. Morris, Jane, 'Local Agenda 21', *Edge*, 1 June, 1993.

56. International Environmental Agency for Local Governments, 'The local Agenda 21 Initiative', January, Ontario, 1993; and European Union Expert group on the Urban Environment 1994, *op. cit.*

57. Local Government Management Board, *The UK's Report to the UN Commission on Sustainable Development: An Initial Statement by UK Local Government*, Local Government Management Board, Luton, 1993.

58. European Union Expert group on the Urban Environment 1994, *op. cit.*

59. *Ibid.*

60. *Ibid.*

61. UNCHS (Habitat), *Sustainable Human Settlements Development: Implementing Agenda 21*, Paper prepared for the Commission on Sustainable Development, United Nations Centre for Human Settlements (Habitat), Nairobi, 1994, drawing from Pacheco Montes, Margarita, 'Building the local agenda process in Bogotá', Instituto de Estudios Ambientales (IDEA), Universidad Nacional de Colombia, 1993.

62. Pacheco Montes, Margarita, *Building the Local Agenda Process in Bogotá*, first draft of a Background Paper prepared for

Global Report, 1995, Instituto de Estudios Ambientales (IDEA), Universidad Nacional de Colombia.

63. ICLEI, UNCHS (Habitat) and UN Commission on Sustainable Development, *The Role of Local Authorities in Sustainable Development; 14 case studies on the Local Agenda 21 Process*, Prepared for the Day of Local Authorities Programme, Commission on Sustainable Development, Third Session, April 1995.

64. Local Government Management Board, *The UK's Report to the UN Commission on Sustainable Development: An Initial Statement by UK Local Government*, Local Government Management Board, Luton, 1993.

65. Smit, Jac and Joe Nasr, 'Urban agriculture for sustainable cities: using wastes and idle land and water bodies as resources', *Environment and Urbanization*, vol. 4, no. 2, Oct. 1992, 141.

66. Smit and Nasr 1992, *op. cit.*

67. Lee-Smith, Diana, Mutsembi Manundu, Davinder Lamba and P. Kuria Gathuru, *Urban Food Production and the Cooking Fuel Situation in Urban Kenya—National report: Results of a 1985 National Survey*, Mazingira Institute, Nairobi, Kenya, 1987.

68. Rakodi, Carole, 'Self reliance or survival: food production in African cities with particular reference to Zambia', Paper presented at a Workshop on Urban Food Supplies and Peri-Urban Agriculture, Centre for African Studies, University of London, 1988.

69. Ableman, Michael, *From the Good Earth; a Celebration of Growing Food around the World*, Harry N. Abrams, New York, 1993.

70. Smit and Nasr 1992, *op. cit.*

71. *Ibid.*

72. Tillman Lyle, John, *Regenerative Design for Sustainable Development*, John Wiley and Sons, New York and Chichester, 1994.

73. Smit and Nasr 1992, *op. cit.*

74. *Ibid.*

75. Sarin, Madhu, 'The Rich, the Poor and the Land Question', in Shlomo Angel, Raymon W. Archer, Sidhijai Tanphiphat and Emiel A. Wegelin (eds.), *Land for Housing the Poor*, Select Books, Singapore, 1983, pp. 237–253; Hardoy, Jorge E. and David Satterthwaite, *Squatter Citizen: Life in the Urban Third World*, Earthscan Publications, London, 1989.

76. Breheny, Michael and Ralph Rookwood, 'Planning the sustainable city region', in Andrew Blowers (ed.), *Planning for a Sustainable Environment*, Earthscan Publications, London, 1993, 150–89.

77. See Breheny and Rookwood 1993, *op. cit.*

78. *Ibid.*

79. UNCHS (Habitat), *Sustainable Human Settlements Development: Implementing Agenda 21*, Paper prepared for the Commission on Sustainable Development, United Nations Centre for Human Settlements (Habitat), Nairobi, 1994.

80. *Ibid.*

81. See for instance Fazal, Anwar and Sri Husnaini Sofjan, *Networks for Urban Action; a Guide to Who's What and Where on Urban Management in Asia and the Pacific*, Urban Management Programme, UNDP, Kuala Lumpur, 1995.

13 New Directions for Human Settlements: Addressing Sustainable Development Goals

Over the last two and a half decades, the focus of human settlements policies in most countries in the South has shifted several times. In the 1970s, the focus was on housing the urban poor. This was to be achieved largely through national government programmes for upgrading in illegal or informal settlements and for sites and services and core housing programmes that were meant to be affordable by low-income households. By the mid-1980s, the limitations of this approach had become evident; these are now generally well known and they were reviewed in the last Global Report on Human Settlements.[1] Their main shortcoming was the inability of governments to reach sufficient people through such approaches, largely because these did little to address the more fundamental constraints regarding the supply of land, housing finance and building materials and the provision for infrastructure and services. In addition, improvements arising from upgrading projects were often not maintained either by the communities upgraded or by their local authority while serviced site projects often proved inappropriate to the needs of lower income groups. The adoption of the Global Strategy for Shelter to the Year 2000 in 1988 promoted a shift in focus and propelled the 'Enabling Approach' and the related idea of 'Partnerships' to the forefront of human settlements policy. The latest shift in policy focus has been towards the concept of 'Sustainable Development.' This was the central theme and message of Agenda 21, which was adopted in Rio de Janeiro in May 1992 at the United Nations Conference on Environment and Development (UNCED). However, as this chapter will describe, the enabling approach also has great relevance to promoting sustainable development.

Earlier chapters described how these shifts in policy focus have been against the background of an increasingly urbanized world where within the next ten years or so, more than half the world's population will live in urban areas. An increasing proportion live in large cities, including some of unprecedented size. Given this background, and the recent policy changes mentioned above, the main challenge in the next two decades is how to manage the development of human settlements in a rapidly urbanizing world in such a way as to satisfy the social, economic and environmental goals of sustainable development, overcome the limitations of past human settlements policies, and satisfy the growing demand for democratic governance at all levels of society.

13.1 A Rapidly Urbanizing World: Cities as Solutions

Moving away from a negative view of cities

Cities have long been blamed for many human failings. Capital cities are often blamed for the failures or inadequacies of the government institutions located there. The wealthiest cities are often blamed for the inequalities in income that the contrasts between their richest and poorest districts make visible. Cities in general and industrial cities in particular are blamed for environmental degradation. Images such as 'exploding cities' and 'mushrooming cities' are often used to convey a process of population growth and urbanization that is 'out of control'. Cities are often blamed for corroding the social fabric. Within the current concern for 'sustainable development', cities are often cited as the main 'problem'.

Yet this Report, in surveying the evidence, found little substance to these criticisms. These criticisms forget the central role that cities and urban systems have in stronger and more stable economies, which in turn have underpinned great improvements in living standards for a considerable portion of the world's population over the last few decades. As Chapter 3 described, average life expectancy, worldwide, grew by more than 12 years between 1960 and 1992 while in many countries, it grew by 18 or more years. Chapter 1 showed the close association between urbanization and economic growth and the fact that urbanization is not 'out of control'; it also showed the high concentration of the world's largest cities in the world's largest economies. The tendency to consider 'rapid urbanization' as a problem forgets that the world's wealthiest nations also underwent periods of rapid urbanization and that the rate of increase in the level of urbanization in countries in the South is rarely larger than that experienced in earlier decades by countries in the North.[2] While it is true that many cities have grown very rapidly, this is largely a reflection of the rate at which their economies grew.[3]

The attempts to imply a link between 'exploding cities' and 'rapid population growth' in the South ignore the fact that those who live in or move to cities generally have smaller families than those living elsewhere and that the countries with the largest increase in their level of urbanization over the last 20–30 years are also generally those with the largest falls in population growth rates.[4] Chapter 1 also noted that cities are not 'mushrooming'; indeed most of the world's largest cities have long histories and a high proportion of the major cities that do not are in North America and Australia. This hardly suggests that the appearance of major new cities is associated with poverty.

Many cities certainly have a high concentration of poverty and Chapter 3 described how the scale of urban poverty and its depth in terms of the deprivation, ill health and premature death it causes have been greatly under-estimated. But worldwide, the scale and depth of poverty in rural areas remains higher, if sometimes less visible. In general, the higher the level of urbanization in a country, the lower the level of absolute poverty.

Anti-city polemic also obscures the real causes of social or ecological ills. It fails to point to those responsible for resource over-use and environmental degradation, and fails to perceive the great advantages (or potential advantages) that cities offer for greatly reducing resource use and wastes. It is not cities that are responsible for most resource use, waste, pollution and greenhouse-gas emissions—but particular industries and commercial and industrial enterprises (or corporations) and middle- and upper-income groups with high-consumption lifestyles. Most such enterprises and consumers may be concentrated in cities but a considerable (and probably growing) proportion are not. In the North and in the wealthier cities or regions of the South, it is the middle- or upper-income household, with two or three cars living in rural areas or small towns or low-density outer suburbs of cities, that has the highest consumption of resources—generally much more so than those with similar incomes living within cities.

The positive role and advantages of cities

Cities have the potential to combine safe and healthy living conditions and culturally rich and enjoyable lifestyles with remarkably low levels of energy consumption, resource use and wastes.[5] The fact that cities concentrate production and population gives them some obvious advantages over rural settlements or dispersed populations.

The first advantage is that high densities mean much lower costs per household and per enterprise for the provision of piped, treated water supplies, the collection and disposal of household and human wastes, advanced telecommunications and most forms of health care and education. It also makes much cheaper the provision of emergency services—for instance fire-fighting and the emergency response to acute illness or injury that can greatly reduce the health burden

for the people affected. The concentration of people and production may present problems for waste collection and disposal, but these are not problems that are insuperable, especially where a priority is given to minimizing wastes. Chapter 8 also noted the long-established traditions in many cities in the South which ensure high levels of recycling or reuse of wastes on which governments' solid-waste management can build. Within the largest cities, the concentration of population can make the treatment and disposal of sewage problematic given the volume of excreta and waste water that needs to be disposed of. But this is rarely a major problem in smaller cities and towns—where most of the world's urban population live. There are many examples of the successful and safe utilization of sewage for intensive crop production.[6] There are also an increasing number of examples of effective sanitation systems that do not require high volumes of water, including some that require no water at all[7] (although water is always needed for hand washing and personal hygiene in general). The techniques for enormously reducing the use of fresh water in city homes and enterprises, including recycling or directly reusing waste waters, are well known, where freshwater resources are scarce[8]—although it is agriculture, not cities, that dominate the use of fresh water in most nations.[9]

The second advantage that cities provide is the concentration of production and consumption, which means a greater range and possibility for efficient use of resources—through the reclamation of materials from waste streams and its reuse or recycling—and for the specialist enterprises that ensure this can happen safely. Cities make possible material or waste exchanges between industries. The collection of recyclable or reusable wastes from homes and businesses is generally cheaper, per person served. Cities have cheaper unit costs for many measures to promote the use of reusable containers (and cut down on disposable containers) or to collect chlorofluorocarbons from fridges and other forms of cooling equipment.

The third advantage is that a much higher population concentration in cities means a reduced demand for land relative to population. In most countries, urban areas take up less than 1 per cent of the national territory. The entire world's urban population would fit into an area of 200,000 square kilometres—roughly the size of Senegal or Oman—at densities similar to those of high-class, much-valued inner-city residential areas in European cities (for instance Chelsea in London).[10] In most cities around the world, there are examples of high-quality, high-density residential areas and Chapter 9 noted the increased popularity of housing in the central districts of certain cities, as governments controlled private automobiles, improved public transport and encouraged a rich and diverse street life. Although unchecked urban (or more often suburban) sprawl is often taking place over valuable agricultural land, this can often be avoided. And as Chapter 12 noted, in many cities in the South the scale of urban agriculture is such that a significant proportion of the food consumed by the city is also produced within its boundaries.[11] This chapter also pointed to the many advantages of urban forestry.

The fourth advantage of cities in climates where homes and businesses need to be heated for parts of the year is that the concentration of production and residential areas means a considerable potential for reducing fossil-fuel use—for instance through the use of waste process heat from industry or thermal power stations to provide space-heating for homes and commercial buildings. Certain forms of high-density housing such as terraces and apartment blocks also considerably reduce heat loss from each housing unit, when compared to detached housing. Chapter 12 also noted the many measures that can be taken to reduce heat gain in buildings to eliminate or greatly reduce the demand for electricity for air-conditioning.

The fifth advantage of cities is that they represent a much greater potential for limiting the use of motor vehicles—including greatly reducing the fossil fuels they need and the air pollution and high levels of resource consumption that their use implies. This might sound contradictory, since earlier chapters described how most of the world's largest cities have serious problems with congestion and motor-vehicle generated air pollution. But cities ensure that many more trips can be made through walking or bicycling. They also make possible a much greater use of public transport and make economically feasible a high-quality service. Thus, although cities tend to be associated with a high level of private automobile use, cities and urban systems also represent the greatest potential for allowing their inhabitants quick and cheap access to a great range of locations, without the need to use private automobiles.

Cities are also among societies' most precious cultural artifacts. This can be seen in the visual and decorative arts, music and dance, theatre and literature that develop there and in the variety and diversity of street life evident in most cities. In most cities, there are buildings, streets, layouts and neighbourhoods that form a central part of the history and culture of that society. Some of the most lively expressions of popular culture are evident in many of the poorer areas in cities—both in art[12] and in music.[13] Many cities or particular city districts demonstrate how cities can provide healthy, stimulating and valued housing and living environments for their inhabitants without imposing unsustainable demands on natural resources and ecosystems.

Cities are also places in which the 'social economy' has developed most—and where it must prosper, not only for the benefits it brings to each street or neighbourhood but also for the economic and social costs it saves the wider society.[14] The social economy is a term given to a great variety of initiatives and actions that are organized and controlled locally and that are not profit-oriented. It includes many activities that are unwaged and unmonetized—including the work of citizen groups, residents' associations, street or *barrio* clubs, youth clubs, parent associations that support local schools and the voluntary workers who help ensure that a preventive-focused health-care system reaches out to all those in need within its locality. It includes many voluntary groups that provide services for the elderly, the physically disabled or other individuals in need of special support. It often includes many initiatives that make cities safer and more fun—helping provide supervised play space, sport and recreational opportunities for children and youth. It may provide formal or informal supervision or maintenance of parks, squares and other public spaces. But it includes enterprises and initiatives that employ paid workers and sell goods and services—for instance local enterprises which combine social as well as commercial aims, owned by people within a defined locality or who share other forms of common interest. It also includes initiatives to support such enterprises—for instance the many community enterprise development trusts set up in recent years and the local exchange trading systems that are now in evidence in more than 20 countries—see Box 13.1.

The social economy within each locality creates a dense fabric of relationships that allow local citizens to work together in identifying and acting on local problems or in taking local initiatives.[15] Its value to city life is often enormous, but this is often forgotten by governments and international agencies, as it is almost impossible to calculate its value in monetary terms. A considerable proportion of the economic growth in the wealthier countries in recent decades has come from shifting functions from the social economy where their value was not counted in economic terms (and not recorded in GNP statistics) to the market economy. Energies once invested in developing and maintaining family and community relationships and in building or supporting local initiatives and institutions had to be redirected to earn sufficient income to pay the taxes that then funded government responses to the problems the social economy had helped address or keep in check—for instance structural

BOX 13.1
Local exchange trading systems (LETS)

Many cities have various forms of community exchanges operating within particular localities. During the 1980s and early 1990s, Local Exchange Trading Systems became increasingly popular as formal systems by which people in any locality or neighbourhood could exchange goods and services without money. These serve, in effect, to increase the purchasing power of those involved and the range of goods and services they can afford, while also retaining value within the locality.

LETS schemes function by publishing a list of goods and services offered for sale by their members, priced in particular units of account set up by their particular scheme. This allows members to exchange goods and services with no money changing hands. As a member provides goods or services to another member, so they run up credit that is recorded by the scheme. A member that 'purchases' these goods or services has a debit that is then paid off by providing goods or services to another member. All members receive regular statements to keep them informed of their position.

There are LETS groups in many countries—including more than 200 LETS groups in the UK and close to 200 in Australia. Some have grown to a considerable size—for instance one in the Blue Mountains in Australia has 1,000 accounts involving more than 2,000 people. A survey in the UK found that the average membership is 70 and that groups tend to double in size in a year until they reach a membership of around 250, when their growth rate slows down. In this same survey, 25 per cent of members were unemployed, and 12 per cent worked part time. Over a third of the LETS have businesses as members—rather than individuals.

Sources: Graham Boyd, 'The urban social economy', *Urban Examples*, UNICEF, New York, 1995; and Long, Peter, *Lets Work; Rebuilding the Local Economy*, Grover Books, Bristol, 1994.

unemployment, insecurity, vandalism, crime and a sense, among many low-income households and youth, of being excluded from social and political processes.

The role of governance

Perhaps the single most important—and difficult—aspect of urban development is developing the institutional structure to manage it in ways that ensure that the advantages noted above are utilized—and also done in ways that are accountable to urban populations. Most of the problems described in this Report in terms of very poor housing, lack of piped water and provision for sanitation and drainage, the lack of basic services such as health care, the serious and often rising problem of urban violence, the problems of traffic congestion and air and water pollution arise largely from a failure of government institutions to manage rapid change and to tap the knowledge, resources and capacities among the population within each city. Indeed, governments have

often helped destroy or stifle the 'social economy' in cities that is so central to their prosperity and to the capacity of the inhabitants in each locality to identify and act on their own priorities.

Making full use of the potential that cities have to offer requires 'good governance'. The evidence of the 1980s and early 1990s is that 'good governance' can bring major economic and social gains, and much less environmental degradation. This can be seen in the extent to which such critical social indicators as infant mortality and life expectancy vary between countries with comparable levels of per capita income or between cities of comparable size and prosperity. As Chapter 3 described, for nations with relatively low incomes per person, 'good governance' at the level of a city or nation can deliver a 10–15 year increase in levels of life expectancy above the average. There is also no contradiction between high social achievement and good economic performance; indeed, the link may be that high social achievement is associated with better than average economic performance.

'Good governance' can also be assessed in the extent to which city, regional and national governments ensure that people within their boundaries have safe, sufficient water supplies, provision for sanitation, education and health care. Although, in general, the proportion of the population with access to these rises, the wealthier the city and the higher the country's per capita income, there is great variation in performance between nations and cities with comparable levels of per capita income. In most nations, there has also been a failure to consider the economic costs—as well as the immense social costs—of not ensuring basic service provision to their populations.

A successful city is one where the many different goals of its inhabitants and enterprises are met, without passing on costs to other people (including future generations) or to their regions. It is also one where the social economy is allowed to thrive. But in the absence of 'good governance', as Chapter 4 described, cities tend to be centres of pollution and waste. Even when pollution levels are much reduced in the city—as they have been in most cities in the North—this is often because environmental costs are being passed on to other regions—for instance through acid rain and water pollution and dumping wastes generated within the city outside its boundaries. City enterprises and households can also pass on costs to future generations through over-use of scarce resources and through their contributions to greenhouse-gas emissions. Worldwide, city-based enterprises and consumers account for a high proportion of all resource use. They also produce a high proportion of all wastes, including toxic and hazardous wastes and air and water pollution.

In the absence of 'good governance', cities can be unhealthy and dangerous places in which to live and work. Each household and enterprise can reduce its costs by passing its environmental problems of solid and liquid wastes and air pollution on to others. At least 600 million urban dwellers in the South live in very poor conditions—many of them in illegal settlements—with very inadequate provision for water, sanitation, drainage, garbage collection and other basic services. Meanwhile, in the absence of a planning framework, city expansion takes place haphazardly and often with urban sprawl over the best quality farmland. Hundreds of millions of low income households live in illegal or informal settlements that developed on land ill-suited to housing—for instance on floodplains or steep slopes with a high risk of landslides or mudslides. They live here because these are the only land sites which they can afford or where their illegal occupation will not be challenged, because the land site is too dangerous for any commercial use. Hundreds of millions of city inhabitants have been forced to find or build homes in illegal settlements, where the threat of forced eviction is always present.

13.2 Sustainability in Human Settlements Development

From environmental concerns to sustainable development

Sustainable development brings together two strands of thought about managing human activity. The first concentrates on development, including a concern for equity, while the second looks to ensuring that development does not damage the planet's life support systems or in other ways jeopardize the interests of future generations.

Within the context of human settlements, a commitment to sustainable development means adding additional goals to those that are the traditional concerns of local authorities. Meeting human needs has long been a central responsibility of city and municipal authorities. Their objectives generally include a desire for greater prosperity, better social conditions (and fewer social problems) and (more recently) better environmental standards within their jurisdiction. These have long been important concerns for urban citizens.

A concern for 'sustainable development' retains these conventional concerns but with two more added. The first is a concern for the impact of city-based production and consumption on the needs of all people, not just those within their jurisdiction. The second is an understanding of the finite nature of many resources (or eco-

systems from which they are drawn) and of the capacities of ecosystems in the wider regional, national and international context to absorb or break-down wastes.

Historically, these have not been considered within the remit of city authorities. Indeed, as Chapter 4 described, while many cities in the North have made considerable progress in achieving sustainable development goals within their own boundaries (i.e. reducing poverty, ensuring high-quality living environments, protecting local ecosystems and developing more representative and accountable government), they still have a large 'ecological footprint' as they draw heavily on the environmental capital of other regions or nations and on the waste absorption capacity of 'the global commons'.[16] But in the long term, no city can remain prosperous if the aggregate impact of all cities' production and their inhabitants' consumption draws on global resources at unsustainable rates and deposits wastes in global sinks at levels that undermine health and disrupt the functioning of ecosystems.

Adding a concern for 'ecological sustainability' to existing development concerns means setting limits on the rights of city enterprises or consumers to use scarce resources and to generate non-biodegradable wastes. This has many implications for citizens, businesses and city authorities. Perhaps the most important for cities in the North and the wealthier countries in the South is how to uncouple high standards of living/quality of life from high levels of resource use and waste generation.

Sustainable development and cities

Figure 13.1 illustrates the multiple goals of sustainable development within cities. It is based on the central goal of sustainable development in *Our Common Future*, the Report of the World Commission on Environment and Development (also known as the Brundtland Commission), published in 1987. This states that we must meet 'the needs of the present generation without compromising the ability of future generations to meet their own needs'.[17] Figure 13.1 elaborates on the different social, economic, political and ecological goals that fall under this. The development goals that aim at 'meeting the needs of the present' are not new. They include economic, social, cultural, health and political needs. Many city authorities have these broad goals. These are also the goals contained in the United Nations Universal Declaration of Human Rights—i.e. meeting each person's right to a standard of living adequate for health and well-being including food, clothing, housing and medical care and necessary social services.[18] This Declaration, subsequent United Nations documents and *Our*

Common Future all stress that development goals should include the right to vote within representative government structures.

While the economic dimensions of 'sustainable development' are increasingly well understood and strongly woven into the current literature on sustainability, the social dimension is less well formed, although just as crucial. Social equity, social justice, social integration and social stability are of fundamental importance to a well-functioning urban society. Their absence leads not only to social tension and unrest, but also to civil wars, violent ethnic conflicts and other human-made disasters. Chapter 1 described the very rapid growth in the number of refugees worldwide and the number of people displaced by wars or civil strife within their own national boundaries. Beirut, Jerusalem, Belfast, Sarajevo and Mogadishu and many other cities have hit world headlines as places where opposing communities have engaged in internecine strife. Unless society is at peace, development can be stifled at source or destroyed. Without peace, all development gains are under threat. Strategies for achieving social equity, social integration and social stability are essential underpinnings of sustainable development. In the human settlements context, this implies two things. The first is reducing deprivation and avoiding social exclusion through the creation of adequate income-earning opportunities and improvement of living and working conditions for all social strata. The second is improving governance through the decentralization of decision-making and development implementation to democratic local authorities who remain accountable to their citizens and more transparent in their modes of working.

The 'sustainable' component, i.e. ensuring that present needs are met 'without compromising the ability of future generations to meet their own needs', requires action to prevent depletion or degradation of environmental assets so that the resource base and ecological base for human activities may be sustained indefinitely. Chapter 12 described the different kinds of environmental assets—the renewable and non-renewable resources and sinks—and the kinds of actions that can ensure ecological sustainability. These are also summarized in Figure 13.1. This implies the need for city and municipal authorities to consider how their policies and actions affect these different kinds of environmental assets and how, in the long term, to avoid depleting them. Some progress has been made in this, as can be seen in the examples given earlier of Local Agenda 21s developed in certain countries, cities and regions. Box 13.2 summarizes some of the specific actions needed at the local, national and international levels in implementing the concept of sustainable human settlements.

In the final analysis, and taking into account both the development and environment components of sustainable development, the main criteria for judging sustainable development in human settlements should be:

- the quality of life of the inhabitants, including existing levels of poverty, social exclusion and integration and socio-political stability;
- the scale of non-renewable resource use, including the extent to which waste recycling or re-use reduces it;
- the scale and nature of renewable resource use, including provisions to ensure sustainable levels of demand for, for instance, freshwater resources and consideration of the settlement's wider ecological footprint; and
- the scale and nature of non-reusable wastes generated by production and consumption

FIGURE 13.1
The multiple goals of sustainable development as applied to cities

Source: Mitlin, Diana and David Satterthwaite, *Cities and Sustainable Development*, the background paper to Global Forum '94, Manchester City Council, June 1994.

Meeting the needs of the present . . .

- Economic needs: includes access to an adequate livelihood or productive assets; also economic security when unemployed, ill, disabled or otherwise unable to secure a livelihood.

- Social, cultural and health needs: includes a shelter which is healthy, safe, affordable and secure, within a neighbourhood with provision for piped water, sanitation, drainage, transport, healthcare, education and child development. Also a home, workplace and living environment protected from environmental hazards, including chemical pollution. Also important are needs related to people's choice and control — including homes and neighbourhoods which they value and where their social and cultural priorities are met. Shelters and services must meet the specific needs of children and of adults responsible for most child-rearing (usually women). Achieving this implies a more equitable distribution of income between nations and, in most, within nations.

- Political needs: includes freedom to participate in national and local politics and in decisions regarding management and development of one's home and neighbourhood — within a broader framework which ensures respect for civil and political rights and the implementation of environmental legislation.

. . . without compromising the ability of future generations to meet their own needs

- Minimizing use or wase of non renewable resources: includes minimizing the consumption of fossil fuels in housing, commerce, industry and transport plus substituting renewable sources where feasible. Also, minimizing waste of scarce mineral resources (reduce use, re-use, recycle, reclaim). There are also cultural, historical and natural assets within cities that are irreplaceable and thus non-renewable — for instance, historic districts and parks and natural landscapes which provide space for play, recreation and access to nature.

- Sustainable use of renewable resources: cities drawing on freshwater resources at levels which can be sustained; keeping to a sustainable ecological footprint in terms of land area on which producers and consumers in any city draw for agricultural crops, wood products and biomass fuels.

- Wastes from cities keeping within absorptive capacity of local and global sinks: including renewable sinks (e.g. capacity of river to break down biodegradable wastes) and non-renewable sinks (for persistent chemicals; includes greenhouse gases, stratospheric ozone-depleting chemicals and many pesticides).

BOX 13.2
Implementing the concept of sustainable human settlements in an urbanizing world

Resolution 15/11, adopted by the United Nations Commission on Human Settlements at its fifteenth session (Nairobi, 25 April to 1 May, 1995), identifies the key measures necessary for the successful implementation of the concept of sustainable development within the context of human settlements, including specific measures relating to urban land and mitigation of natural disasters. The preamble to the resolution outlines the main concerns and premises on which the resolution is based, namely:

(a) The call for sustainable development in Agenda 21 is not simply for environmental protection, but also for a new concept of economic growth which provides for fairness and opportunity for all people in the world without destroying the world's natural resources and without further compromising the carrying capacity of the globe.

(b) Sustainable development rests on three pillars, namely, environmental sustainability, economic sustainability, and social sustainability.

(c) Because of their concentrated nature, human settlements are significant consumers of natural resources and the development and management of human settlements may represent a substantial component in unsustainable production and consumption patterns.

(d) As urban development occurs, it may have severe impacts on land and water resources and on the atmosphere, unless vigorous action is taken to prevent such adverse effects.

(e) In many countries, especially developing ones, the pressure of population growth and urbanization is having adverse implications for the supply of adequate shelter, environmental infrastructure and services.

(f) Cities play a very important role in national economic growth, contribute disproportionately to national productivity and have a valuable role in facilitating cultural advancement and social development.

(g) As part of the rapid increase in urban populations, rural settlements on urban fringes are being absorbed into the urban domain and agricultural areas and forest resources are being converted to urban use, often in wasteful and environmentally damaging ways.

(h) The poor are often unable to afford urban land and that which they can afford is often unsuited to settlement, they often lack security of land tenure, and reside in areas with grossly inadequate infrastructure.

(i) Natural disasters are an outcome of the interaction between natural hazards and vulnerable conditions which cause severe losses to people and their environments and they usually require outside intervention and assistance at national and international levels in addition to individual and communal responses.

(j) The challenge of comprehensive disaster mitigation programmes in urban areas is to continue general economic development and provide jobs, shelter and basic amenities while addressing the environmental and equity problems which are the real causes of vulnerability to natural hazards.

In the first part of the operative section, the resolution recommends that governments adopt and ensure the implementation (at national and local levels) of the following general measures for the sustainable development of human settlements:

(i) Decentralization of decision-making and creation of an enabling environment to support the initiatives of local authorities and community organizations.

(ii) Formulation and implementation of local Agenda 21 plans and improvement of inter-sectoral co-ordination at the local, regional and national levels.

(iii) Establishment of regulatory and incentive structures to encourage sustainable use of resources.

(iv) Promotion of the use of non-polluting appropriate technologies in human settlements activities, particularly in the areas of energy and transport, so as to minimize and to eliminate, if possible, negative impacts on the environment.

(v) Increasing financial resources at the level of the local authority for promoting national sustainable urban development objectives;

In the second part of the operative section, the resolution also calls upon Governments to adopt and facilitate the implementation of the following specific measures for sustainable urban land development and management:

(i) Promotion of access to land and security of tenure for all urban residents, particularly the poor, through improved land market transparency and innovative mechanisms to utilize public and private land, including fiscal incentives to bring unutilized land into use, improved land delivery and tenure systems and, where appropriate, direct government land ownership.

(ii) Decentralization and simplification of land registration and, where appropriate, privatization of land survey departments, as well as improvement of urban land-use planning and management methods.

(iii) Promotion of land-use planning, taking into account the density factor in a way which allows adequate social services and sustainable infrastructure to be provided, including measures to promote utilization of under-utilized plots.

(iv) Strengthening of conservation measures at all levels, both preventive and remedial, aimed at minimizing physical degradation of land and eliminating pollution, in particular from industrial waste.

(v) Strengthening of the role of land as the cornerstone of urban municipal finance, including measures for more effective taxation of the value added on privately owned land resulting from public infrastructure investments, as well as adoption of land and property taxes designed to encourage more economical use of land and discourage speculative withholding of land suitable for development.

(vi) Compilation of national inventories of land and other ecological resources and formulation of long-term spatial strategies to guide land resources development.

In the third part of the operative section, the resolution further urges governments to promote and facilitate implementation of the following measures specifically for the mitigation of natural disasters.

(i) Setting up of institutional structures and decision-making processes which ensure that mitigation of natural disasters becomes an integral part of sustainable human settlements development.

(ii) Building up of national collective memories of disasters, their effects, methods used to combat them and means to reduce their impacts.

(iii) Improvement and regulation of access to land for housing the poor in order to limit encroachment of residential settlements on to hazardous sites.

(iv) Encouragement of and assistance to local authorities to direct human settlements development on to vacant public land in relatively safe locations through the provision of infrastructure.

(v) Identification of hazardous sites and their conversion into alternative productive uses, thereby protecting them from illegal occupation for residential purposes.

(vi) Reduction of the threats of already identified hazardous sites.

(vii) Development and use of housing designs, building materials and construction methods which can mitigate the effects of natural disasters.

(viii) Enhancement of technical assistance to regional and local institutions and provision of training in management of natural disasters to technicians, professionals and administrators.

Finally, the resolution urges UNCHS (Habitat) and, by implication, other international organizations, to: increase efforts to assist

---

---

activities and the means by which these are disposed of, including the extent to which the wastes impact on human health, natural systems and amenity.

13.3 The Enabling Approach and Partnerships

The enabling framework

The 'enabling framework' gives government a central role in setting the framework for urban development but a lesser role in providing the investment. This framework encourages and supports the multiplicity of large and small initiatives, investments and expenditures by individuals, households, communities, businesses and voluntary organizations. By supporting the processes that are building and developing the city and the social economy, what appeared as insurmountable problems begin to appear more manageable.

The 'enabling framework' developed in response to housing problems and the failure of conventional public-sector responses.[19] It has a wider relevance to broader issues of city management. The origins of the idea that government actions in regard to housing should concentrate on 'enabling' and supporting the efforts of citizens and their community organizations to develop their own housing goes back at least to the 1950s and perhaps earlier. The concept of enablement has also spread to many other sectors—for instance, in the supply and maintenance of water systems and in the promotion of 'healthy cities and communities' where individuals' capacity to be able to take effective action and to influence their own environment is seen as central to their well-being.[20]

The concept of enablement is based on the understanding that most human investments, activities and choices, all of which influence the achievement of development goals and the extent of environmental impacts, take place outside 'government'. Most are beyond the control of governments, even where governments seek some regulation. In Southern cities, the point is particularly valid since most homes, neighbourhoods, jobs and incomes are created outside of government and often in contravention of official rules and regulations.[21] The emphasis on 'enabling policies' has received considerable support from the growing

recognition that democratic and participatory government structures are not only important goals of development but also important means for achieving such development. Participation and enablement are inseparable since popular priorities and demands will be a major influence on the development of effective and flexible enabling policies.

The 1980s brought a growing realization that inappropriate government controls and regulations discourage and distort the scale and vitality of individual, family and community investments and activities, all of which are essential for healthy and prosperous cities. But there is also recognition that, without controls and regulations that are scrupulously enforced, individuals, communities and enterprises can impose their externalities on others. Preventing this is one of the main tasks of governance.

One of the key issues is then—what kind of 'enabling' institution is needed that best compliments the efforts of individuals, households, communities and voluntary organizations and ensures more coherence between them all so they all contribute towards city-wide improvements. How can funding and technical advice be made available in ways that match the diverse needs and priorities of different settlements—with accountability and transparency built in to their disbursement of funding. Some important precedents have been described already—for instance the large-scale kampung improvement programme in Surabaja that did involve citizens and community organizations in determining priorities, the Million Houses Programme in Sri Lanka and the support for community-level organization and action in its urban sub-programme, and the work of FONHAPO in Mexico, COINAP in Guatemala, the Urban Community Development Office in Thailand, each of which has funded and supported a great diversity of community-level initiatives in housing improvement and site development. Chapter 9 also included a review of the participatory tools and methods now increasingly used in development projects.

Cities built from the bottom up

All cities are the result of an enormous range of investments of capital, expertise and time by individuals, households, communities, voluntary organizations, NGOs, private enterprises, investors and government agencies. In most cities in the South, the total value of the investments made by people in their own homes and neighbourhoods usually exceeds many times the total capital investment made by city and municipal authorities. Yet in most cities in Africa, Asia and Latin America, the individual, household and community efforts that have such a central role in building cities and developing services have long been ignored by governments, banks and aid agencies.[22]

Deficits in housing and basic services seem unmanageable when aggregated at the level of the city or nation. Yet housing gets built, new residential areas appear and basic (if inadequate) services are provided in the absence of government action. In most cities in the South, most new housing is being developed by those for whom there is no official support, and no credit or technical assistance available. Any attempt by a government organization to increase the housing stock of a major city by many thousand units a year is unthinkable and yet the housing stock in most of the larger cities in the South is increasing by tens of thousands of new units built outside the law and most with no government help. What can be achieved by supporting the efforts of several hundred community organizations in a single city (and where possible doing so in partnership with municipal agencies) vastly outweighs what any single government agency can do itself. As a prominent Argentine urban specialist has noted,

Much could be achieved in terms of direct improvements to living conditions in urban areas if governments no longer chained and repressed but supported a vast range of activities at present invisible to them—individuals, households and communities building or extending their own homes and creating a living for themselves.[23]

The challenge for city governance is to ensure that this great multiplicity of investments and initiatives, in aggregate, improves living conditions, attracts private sector investment and encourages new enterprises.

The capacity to manage rapid change is one of the key attributes of good governance. The capacity to manage urban change is often confused with the investment capacity of city or municipal authorities. The two are not necessarily the same since such authorities can do much to encourage and support private investment not only in enterprises but also in a city's built environment and in infrastructure and services. As earlier chapters noted, governments in the South that have worked with and supported the investments of individuals, households and community or neighbourhood organizations in their own homes and neighbourhoods have helped improve housing and living conditions and expand the provision of infrastructure and services, despite limited government funds. City authorities can greatly improve the quality of public transport by providing the framework for private firms; it is often forgotten that the public transport system of Curitiba in Brazil that is much admired for its quality and comprehensiveness is provided by private-sector bus companies but within a framework set up by the city authorities.[24] City authorities should also have the main role in enforcing legislation on air and water pollution and occupational health and safety. This does not require large investments by public authorities, but it can do much to improve health and the quality of life in a city.

Good governance also means coping with conflicting goals and the competing claims of different interests. All cities face a variety of contradictions that are not easily managed and for which sophisticated yet accountable regulations and institutions are needed. For instance, the most powerful economic interests on whose prosperity the city depends will want infrastructure and services provided to meet their needs but will also seek to keep down costs and pay as little as possible, both for these and for the infrastructure and services needed by city inhabitants. They will also seek to keep down wages for their workforces yet this in turn diminishes the amount that their workforce can pay for housing and basic services. Enterprises and their workforce will often disagree about the level of provision for occupational health and safety. In competing with other cities for productive investment, each city authority has to keep down costs for residents and enterprises and offer attractive sites for enterprises yet also ensure sufficient funding is available so that infrastructure and services are available and citizen needs are also met. In addition, as the power and resources available to city authorities grow, so too does the potential for their misallocation. The larger and more prosperous the city, the greater the potential for corrupt practices, as government contracts for public services or for infrastructure projects grow ever larger, and as government decisions (about the location of roads or about potential uses of particular land sites) can multiply tenfold, a hundredfold or even a thousandfold the value of particular land sites. But within these areas of disagreement and conflict, there is often a large degree of common ground between enterprises, trade unions (or other forms of workers' organizations) and residents. This is especially as private enterprises are increasingly looking for cities that are well managed with high-quality living environments and good-quality infrastructure and services.

City authorities must also look to encourage local innovation. For example, a local initiative to improve garbage collection and recycling levels may have immediate beneficial effects for the environment of a local community. Health may improve as rubbish dumps are cleared and breeding sites for disease vectors and pests reduced. The project itself may provide local employment. But if it is to spread beyond one locality, it requires a supportive local authority to encourage similar initiatives in other parts of the city. It also requires regulations to minimise risk from large-scale waste dumps and may require further incentives to encourage local business to use recycled products. National and international controls on waste may also be needed; few local authorities will promote recycling and waste reduction if it remains cheaper to dump untreated wastes or export them to another region or nation. There is also little point in a community reducing locally generated waste if their health is endangered by toxic or otherwise hazardous wastes from other sources.

Achieving the balance between addressing the needs of citizens as consumers and employees and addressing the demands of private enterprises needs a representative political and administrative system through which the views and priorities of citizens and businesses can influence policies and actions. Democratic structures remain among the best checks on the mis-allocation of resources by city and municipal governments. Actively involving a wide range of local groups in developing 'city governance' helps ensure that the different priorities of a wide range of groups are addressed. Decentralizing governance from capital cities to regions, cities and municipalities can be one of the best means of promoting participation as government projects become more relevant and more effective, as the communities concerned have a real say in their planning and implementation.[25]

The principle of subsidiarity remains important as responsibilities, tasks and control over resources are decentralized to the lowest level where their implementation will be effective. Agencies that are supra-city, whether state/provincial or national agencies or ministries or international agencies, often misunderstand the nature of local developments, resources and constraints. They also cannot identify the full range of options from which to choose the most appropriate policies, programmes and plans. External agencies can bring knowledge, expertise, capital and advice. But, without effective local government acting to represent local views, external agencies are unlikely to implement the kinds of projects or programmes that respond directly to the needs and priorities of individuals, households, voluntary groups and the private sector within each locality.

The basis for 'good governance' at city and municipal level exists in most of the world's wealthier and more urbanized nations. But it has taken many decades to develop the institutional framework for this, especially in setting up democratic, transparent and accountable decision-making structures, and in moderating the influence of those interests which have the power and resources to form influential lobbies. In most nations in the South, as Chapter 5 described, the basis for 'good governance' is much weaker. City and municipal authorities lack the capacity to raise revenue and have tasks and responsibilities assigned to them that are far beyond their technical and financial capabilities. It is common for local government budgets to have little or no funds for capital investments and a great shortage of technical skills. It is rare for a city or municipal government to have any significant capacity for expanding or extending infrastructure and services. At best, significant new investments are occasional and *ad hoc*, funded by central government or some development assistance agency. Meanwhile, city and municipal authorities fail to control industrial pollution and to ensure good practice in occupational health, to promote environmental health, to ensure that city dwellers have the basic infrastructure and services essential for livelihoods and a decent living environment, to plan in advance to ensure sufficient land is available for housing for low-income groups and for economic development, and to implement preventive measures to reduce environmental problems or their impacts. It is this lack of investment capacity that necessitates a new approach that builds on and supports the 'bottom up' processes that are building the cities.

Partnerships

Governance extends beyond governments. It includes the strengthening of institutions for collective decision-making and the resolution of conflicts. It implies new alliances and partnerships. Good governance develops a framework that succeeds in encouraging and supporting innovation and partnerships at household, community, city and regional levels. The achievement of sustainable development goals within a city will need an enormous range of household or community projects whose individual impact may be small but whose collective impact is significant. City and municipal authorities must develop sustainable development frameworks that encourage and support a sufficient number of such initiatives for their cumulative impact to be significant for particular districts and for whole cities and city-regions. Institutions and partnerships between the different actors (NGOs, community organizations, business and commercial enterprises, professional organizations or associations, national and local government) are needed to achieve sustainable development across all sectors and geographic scales and promote beneficial inter-project linkages.

The activities of certain groups are particularly influential to urban development: citizen groups and community-based organizations; non governmental organizations (NGOs); city government; commercial and industrial enterprises; and international aid/development assistance agencies.

Citizen groups

These come under many names and are also known as grassroots groups, community-based organizations, self-help groups and base-level organizations. All represent some form of primary organization by residents or workers in a city (often formed by relatively poor households) to better their opportunities or fight against some hazard. Such groups are usually formed around a residential community or workplace.

The range and relative influence of such groups varies greatly from city to city. In many Southern cities, associations of residents formed within illegal or informal settlements or tenements are much the most important 'local authority' for their neighbourhood because of the lack of services provided by local government. In some, associations or federations of these residents' organizations have become powerful political forces,[26] although in most instances governments seek to limit their power and in many seek actively to suppress it. But their importance in many cities has grown in recent years, when long-established citizen movements have been given more scope to organize in countries that have recently instituted or returned to democratic rule, or as new movements have grown in importance—for instance around environmental issues or women's rights or alternative lifestyles.[27] Most such movements challenge the legitimacy of conventional forms of city governments. And despite their volatility, these civic movements may be decisive in ensuring that cities meet the diverse social and collective needs of their inhabitants.[28]

The capacity of citizen groups to identify local problems and their causes, to organize and manage community-based initiatives and to monitor the effectiveness of external agencies working in their locality represents one of the most valuable resources available to city and municipal authorities. This is especially so where municipal authorities remain too weak to ensure the provision of basic services to entire city populations. However, there is also the danger that, where city authorities are weak and ineffective, it is the more prosperous middle- and upper-income areas that are most effective at ensuring they benefit from limited government investment capacity and at avoiding any financial contribution towards the costs of managing a city effectively.

Each city neighbourhood has its own unique range of environmental problems and development priorities—and effective action demands local capabilities to identify problems and their causes and decide on the best use of limited resources. In many societies, this will require far more support channelled direct to citizen and community action. Various examples given in this Report showed how this can deliver immediate benefits to poorer groups more cheaply and effectively than more conventional state actions. It can also contribute to strengthening civil society by reinforcing democracy and participation and by developing partnerships between community-based organizations, NGOs and municipal governments.

Citizen pressure can and often has encouraged city and municipal governments to pursue more sustainable patterns of resource use and waste minimization, where the ecological impacts are local or regional or (on occasion) national. Chapter 9 also noted the role that citizen-groups had in opposing large highway projects and in promoting more attention to public transport—roles that were seen, at the time, as regressive but with the benefit of hindsight have proved very important for the economy and the quality of life of the cities. The influence of citizen pressure can also be seen in the environmental movements and in the role taken by environmental issues in election campaigns in the North. But many have been largely driven by citizen concern for their own health and quality of life. There needs to be sustained citizen pressure on city and municipal governments to press for changes in production and consumption patterns that have their most serious ecological impacts overseas or on global cycles. The achievement of sustainable development depends on cities responding to the ecological damage to which their enterprises and consumers contribute far beyond their boundaries and that affect citizens in other countries.

Non-governmental organizations

Non-governmental organizations (NGOs) exist in so many forms with such differences in the scale and type of their work that any summary risks being incomplete and inaccurate. In most countries, there are dozens of NGOs involved in urban projects; in many, there are hundreds. NGOs vary in scale from large, well-organized institutions working in many locations to small ones operating in one neighbourhood with a tiny budget and perhaps one (part-time) paid staff member. Some are based only on voluntary, unpaid work. They vary in orientation from those working in participatory ways with low-income groups and their community organizations developing innovative approaches to development problems to those with very traditional, top-down 'welfarist' approaches.

NGOs carry out many different kinds of activities which include emergency relief; technical or financial support to improve income-generating/ expenditure-saving capacity; support for self-help and grassroots democracy; and lobbying and advocacy for political changes to improve the macro-level conditions that have resulted in local and national poverty (for example, debt) and environmental degradation. The scope of their goals varies from those seeking to influence change within one particular urban neighbourhood to those seeking to change the policies of governments and international agencies. Many NGOs follow more than one strategy, with different projects realizing different kinds of needs.[29]

In regard to cities, three roles have been identified for NGOs:

- *Enablers* (i.e. community developers, organizers or consultants) alongside community-based organizations;
- *Mediators* between the people and the authorities which control access to resources, goods and services.
- *Advisers* to state institutions on policy changes to increase local access to resources and greater freedom to use them in locally determined ways.[30]

NGOs have emerged as critical intermediary institutions supporting citizen's organizations to obtain access to resources and to negotiate with local government and other state institutions. In some cases, they may also negotiate on behalf of the citizens with the private sector, for example, when a low-income community has settled on illegally occupied private land and is trying to negotiate legal tenure from the landowner or when the residents in an illegal subdivision seek to negotiate improved provision of infrastructure from the landowners or developers. The role that many NGOs have as intermediaries between citizens and external agencies is sometimes encouraged by the local authority, although it is also viewed with some suspicion by other authorities.

NGOs may help form community organizations within the areas in which they are active or they may respond to the needs of existing citizen groups. NGOs that work with citizen groups may also be involved in building coalitions to address common goals. For instance, coalition building has been used to combat violence in the Prevention Programme at the Contra Costa County Health Services Department (California) which brings together different groups who are either already concentrating on a particular form of violence (e.g. Battered Women's Alternatives) or serving a population that is particularly at risk. Instead of creating new, stand-alone programmes, existing community-based organizations join with the Programme to form a single coalition that co-ordinates comprehensive, prevention services. These coalitions may also include representatives of governmental agencies, non-profit groups, funding sources, or businesses.[31]

Many NGOs have developed innovative ways to support disadvantaged groups (for instance, pavement dwellers, street children and people with physical disabilities or chronic diseases). NGOs' capacity to work with low-income groups in participatory ways to improve shelter and provide or improve services, to negotiate with governments and donors for funds and to develop the alliances and networks which promote political change (very often with federations or coalitions of community-based organizations) gives them an important role within new models of urban development. As Chapter 9 described, NGOs and citizen groups have also pioneered the development of participatory tools and methods that permit a much more active involvement of citizens and their associations in identifying their needs and priorities and in determining how best to ensure these are met.

Some of the most important research on urban problems and potential solutions in the South have been undertaken by NGOs. This is perhaps most evident in Latin America, as research or action-research NGOs formed and developed during the 1960s and 1970s, largely staffed by researchers who had been expelled from universities or other state institutions under the influence of right-wing non-democratic (and often military) governments. More recently, new NGO models have developed—as in the research, publications and campaigns of the Centre for Science and Environment in India that covers both rural and urban dimensions of sustainable development.[32]

The work of NGOs is sometimes controversial. It often centres on demands for social change, perhaps inevitably if a major part of NGOs' work involves demanding a fairer deal for low-income or disadvantaged groups. Many Southern NGOs working in urban issues have been active in opposing forced evictions of low-income groups—for instance the Urban Poor Associates in Manila, the Urban Resource Centre in Karachi, SPARC in Bombay and the Brazilian Movement for the Defence of Life in Rio de Janeiro.[33] In recent years, NGOs have come to be considered as an important part of a movement of 'civil society'; a broad coalition of interests determined to ensure that public interest issues are not monopolized by the state.

Many NGOs whose main work is implementing projects have been criticized for their lack of accountability to the communities with whom they work. The communities may find that a development project has been defined either by the NGO or their funders, and their own role in determining the direction of the project is marginal. There is also the problem in many countries of limited NGO capacity. This is especially so in many countries where there is no established tradition of NGO involvement in human settlement projects and where official bilateral aid programmes have greatly increased the scale of funding they channel through national or local NGOs.

At an international level, NGOs campaign and lobby to influence governments and international organizations. In this, they have long been active in both environment and development issues, although prior to the Earth Summit in 1992, relatively few sought to combine environment and development and thus work for the simultaneous achievement of the development and ecological sustainability goals that make up sustainable development. In recent years, there has been a much greater awareness of the coalition of interest between development NGOs and environment NGOs.

The strength of international NGO networks has greatly increased in the last decade and networks between NGOs in urban areas are no exception. The Habitat International Coalition is an international network of NGOs working in shelter and settlement-related issues that has been operating for over 20 years;[34] it has over 200 NGO members and a major urban agenda.[35] Ten years ago, a regional network for Africa, Settlement Information Network Africa, was set up.[36] More recently in 1987, an Asian network has been established, the Asian Coalition for Housing Rights.[37] Such networks support local city-based NGOs and community organizations and put pressure on governments and international agencies to address the needs of poorer groups.

City government

Given the diversity of cities both in terms of their size and population growth rates and in their economic, social, political, cultural and ecological underpinnings, it is difficult to consider 'sustainable development' and cities in general terms. Much of the action to achieve sustainable development has to be formulated and implemented locally. The unique nature of each city and its culture and position within local and regional ecosystems means a need for local resources, knowledge and skills to achieve development goals within a detailed knowledge of the local and regional ecological carrying capacity. This demands a considerable degree of local self-determination, since centralized decision-making structures have great difficulty in developing and implementing plans that respond appropriately to such diversity.[38] However, there are common principles such as the need for good practice in each public agency's planning, project appraisal, budgeting, purchasing and tendering with full consideration given to environmental aspects, including waste minimization and the use of goods made of recycled materials.[39] Another common principle is the need to ensure the integration of environmental goals into all aspects of planning and management.

The achievement of sustainable development goals for any city depends on the capacity of city and district/borough/commune/municipal governments to develop the sustainable development framework outlined earlier in this chapter and to plan and manage the area under their jurisdiction. Both the institutional framework and the planning has to be guided by the needs and priorities of its residents. At local level, the priority is for each society to develop its own response to local environmental problems and resource limitations, using the tools most appropriate to its own unique situation.

As Chapter 9 described, physical plans and land-use management should provide a framework within which local households, enterprises and entrepreneurs can make choices and governments can make long-term plans for infrastructure and service development. Insufficient or poor quality planning implies enormous societal and environmental costs such as those arising from difficulties in installing infrastructure due to the chaotic expansion of cities; the development of illegal settlements in and around cities on flood plains, wetlands and other unsuitable sites due to a lack of affordable alternative sites; and the lack of provision for city dwellers (especially in poorer areas) of open space for recreation. Poor and insufficient physical planning and land use management also implies the development of cities that compound the problems of the urban poor. Only richer groups can afford to live in legal, well-serviced residential areas while most of the poor have to survive on marginal, dangerous and often peripheral sites whose monetary value is too low to prompt their eviction.

It is the city government which has to:

- Promote more sustainable patterns of resource use and waste minimization among consumers and producers.

- Ensure a good match between demand and supply for land for all the different land uses that are part of any city while using its planning and regulatory system to promote resource conserving buildings and settlement patterns.

- Invest in needed infrastructure and services (or

plan and co-ordinate their provision by other agencies/enterprises) again within a resource conserving framework.

- Work with local businesses to enhance the locality's attraction for new productive investment.
- Encourage and develop local partnerships to help achieve the above and other sustainable development goals within the city.

Just as all the actions and policies of city or municipal authorities can seek to improve environmental performance and reduce waste, so too can they all seek ways to contribute to poverty reduction—see Box 13.3.

The quality of governance determines the extent to which a city takes advantage of the potential environmental advantages of its concentration of production and population and avoids the potential disadvantages. City government also has to represent the needs and priorities of its citizens in the broader context—for instance in negotiations with provincial and national governments. It must work with international agencies and businesses considering investing in the city region. And it has to work with regional authorities to identify and minimize negative impacts and maximize positive ones.

Commercial and industrial enterprises

Governments at both a national and local level must develop the conditions to support and sustain economic prosperity but in most instances they are dependent on the private sector to respond to these opportunities. With the collapse of communist governments in Eastern Europe and the former Soviet Union and the privatization of many government agencies and responsibilities in most countries, investment opportunities are increasingly in the domain of the private sector. The private sector has a clear interest in the economic aspects of sustainable development and in the provision of infrastructure and services, but a more ambiguous position in regard to equity—both within contemporary society and inter-generationally.

Most commercial and industrial enterprises have some direct long-term interest in ecological sustainability as a depleted and degraded environment is likely to raise production costs and increase risks. For some medium and large companies, environmental degradation may also result in increasing costs in the short-term. But the main area of action on the environment among the private sector is in reducing adverse health and environmental impacts within their own facilities and in their immediate surrounds. Here, there is an immediate incentive to intro-

---

BOX 13.3
Options for municipal interventions in urban areas

Municipal governments can have a major role in alleviating or reducing poverty in urban areas, even when they have limited investment capacity at their disposal. A large part of this role is in encouraging and supporting the efforts of community-based organizations, NGOs and private-sector institutions in supplying or improving urban services such as water supply, sanitation, solid-waste management, public transport, health care and education. There is also considerable potential for poverty alleviation through changes in the regulatory framework for land management, urban agriculture and housing. For instance, low-income households often find it difficult to obtain land for housing legally as finding and obtaining (or registering) a legal house plot and obtaining permission to develop it for housing involves time consuming and costly procedures; here regulatory reform could increase the supply and reduce the cost of land for housing. Similarly, regulatory reform on building and planning regulations can reduce the cost of housing. Municipalities can also support urban agriculture and in so doing, improve food supplies and incomes for many low-income households. This can be done by developing and disseminating information on land tenure, land capacity, markets, and water, by providing technical assistance where needed, and by ensuring that provision is made for urban agriculture in urban planning.

Municipal programmes can also make major contributions to employment creation—especially through support for small-scale and informal enterprises. A new and much-neglected aspect of poverty alleviation is also improved access to justice and protection from crime. The urban poor rarely receive protection from the law and often turn to informal systems, as the formal judicial system is seen as slow, unpredictable and often biased against them. There are interesting precedents for municipal action to address the problems of crime and public safety which include community-mobilization and support. For instance, in Cali (Colombia), the municipal programme acknowledged the importance of operating at community level in its three action areas: law enforcement (public safety councils), education for peace (conciliation centres and school programmes), and social development (micro-enterprise development and sites for low-income housing).

Source: Drawn largely from Wegelin, Emiel A. and Karin M. Borgman, 'Options for municipal interventions in urban poverty alleviation', *Environment and Urbanization*, vol. 7, no. 2, Oct. 1995. The information about Cali is drawn from Guerrero, R., 'Cali's innovative approach to urban violence', *The Urban Age* (Urban Violence Issue), vol. 1, no. 4, 1993, 12.

---

duce environmentally clean technology in their own factories or to pressure government to strengthen controls on other companies. Some of the larger companies have been encouraged to introduce environmental improvements in their production processes due to consumer campaigns and changes in the goods which consumers prefer to purchase. What is termed 'green consumerism' in the North has helped to drive a number of new items onto corporate agendas including environmental audits of company's performance (and that of their suppliers) and eco-labelling (so consumers can identify goods whose production and use minimize harmful environmental impacts).[40] Trade unions have also been active in promoting 'eco-audits' at the workplace—see Box 13.4.

In addition, despite recession in much of the North, there is a new vigour to the debate about business and the environment and many business leaders no longer dismiss environmental movements and are even happy to discuss such concepts as full cost accounting (where the environmental and social costs of a company's production process and products must be taken into account) and inter-generational equity.[41] There are also examples of companies in both North and South that have made a major commitment to pursuing sustainable development goals.

BOX 13.4

Mobilizing action and eco-audits at the workplace

The International Confederation of Free Trade Unions (ICFTU) has stressed that the discussions of sustainable development have given too little attention to the workplace and to the role of workers and their trade unions in acting on sustainable development issues. These issues obviously include meeting workers' needs for health and safety but they also include an important role in acting on issues such as resource use (including energy consumption), pollution control and waste management.

ICFTU has stressed the importance of eco-audits of the workplace as a way of setting and promoting action on such issues. Eco-auditing can identify the areas where any enterprise can improve its performance in accordance with the goals of Agenda 21 and can also provide a means for involving employers and local trade unions or workers' groups in partnerships towards commonly agreed goals. Community groups and local government authorities can also be involved—for instance, through being invited to review and evaluate the process.

Source: International Confederation of Free Trade Unions, 'Eco-auditing: sustainable development and the workplace', Discussion paper submitted to the Second Session of the Commission on Sustainable Development, May 1994; and Lambe, Tony, 'Trade Unions and the CSD', Eco, NGO Newsletter at the Second Session of the Commission on Sustainable Development, 20 May 1994, 1.

While many enterprises will benefit from the shift in employment that is part of achieving sustainable development (and there is already a very large pollution control and waste management industry in Europe and North America)[42] for many, it will result in increasing costs. Companies may be reluctant to adopt environmentally clean production processes if they are not confident that their competitors will face the same increase in costs. A long-term programme of support and regulation can ensure a gradual but continuous improvement—for instance, through the gradual replacement of polluting industrial processes and

plants with new industrial plant designs which eliminate or reduce polluting wastes and recover and reuse process chemicals.

Within an appropriate government framework of incentive and regulation, it is possible to conceive of commercial and industrial sectors greatly decreasing the scale of polluting emissions and toxic and hazardous wastes and minimizing environmental hazards in the workplace. Many private enterprises have chosen to make great progress on this even without government regulation. This has often been encouraged by shareholder pressure or by banks or investment funds that require much improved environmental performance as a precondition for investment. In some instances, it has also been encouraged by the possible scale of liability faced by a company or corporation whose production processes cause or contribute to major health impairments for its workforce or for a section of the population. What is more difficult to foresee is the means to reduce the private sector's depletion of other environmental assets, especially the use of the global sink for greenhouse gases and the use of resources whose ecologically damaging impacts are outside the city or nation in which the enterprise is located. Private enterprises in any city or country cannot afford to accept stringent controls on their use of non-renewable resources or greatly reduce the scale of greenhouse-gas emissions if their competitors in other cities or nations can avoid these.

Different companies display contrasting attitudes towards environmental quality. For instance enterprises (and entrepreneurs) committed to particular cities are likely to have a greater commitment to environmental quality than enterprises that are 'footloose', whose commitment to any city is only as long as that city retains cost advantages over alternative locations. Enterprises committed to a city have an incentive to invest in maintaining and improving the quality of that locality.

At the smallest level, small-scale enterprises are critical to the economy of many cities in the North and the South, especially to low-income areas. Many remain small and earn little money for their owner/workers. Programmes of support to help such enterprises typically offer training in new technology and business skills plus credit (generally at market interest rates). Some of these enterprises have an important role in the improvement of conditions in low-income settlements. Small-scale enterprise production processes may result in local pollution[43] but in some instances, improvements are possible for relatively low unit costs, especially where a group of small enterprises share waste management or processing facilities. Sensitive and careful local planning with residents is required. This should fully recognize and support the important role of small-scale enterprises and, at the same time, minimize conflicts over land use. Certain urban authorities have set up special programmes to help small enterprises improve their environmental performance.[44]

The role of national governments

It is difficult for any city or municipal authority to act in isolation. There are serious dilemmas facing any city authority that tries harder to meet its global responsibilities for ecological sustainability. Any programme by a single city to improve its overall performance in terms of greenhouse-gas emissions, use of scarce resources and disposal of wastes may impose financial penalties on its residents and businesses that threaten the city's economic prosperity. While this Report has described the many ways in which consumers and businesses in most cities can improve their 'sustainable development' performance without such drastic consequences, without clear agreement and enforcement at the national and international level to ensure that all cities contribute more to meeting their global responsibilities, those that do contribute may lose business to those that do not.

National governments have the key role in linking local and global ecological sustainability. Internationally, they have the responsibility for reaching agreements to limit each nation's call on the world's environmental capital. Nationally, they are responsible for providing the framework to ensure local actions can meet development goals without compromising local and global sustainability. It is also the task of national government to consider the social and environmental impacts of their macro-economic and sectoral policies which may contribute to the very problems their sustainable development policies are seeking to avoid.

Despite the increased attention given to sustainable development, no national government has set up the regulatory and incentive structure to ensure that the aggregate impact of their economic activities and citizens' consumption is in accordance with global sustainability—although a few in Europe have taken many important steps towards some aspects. For instance, the Netherlands has a long-term environmental policy both to address environmental problems and to address more ambitious sustainable development goals in the long term with the environmental goals integrated into other sectoral policies—such as transport, water management and physical planning.[45] In most nations in the South, national governments still deny city and municipal governments the power and resources they need to promote development.

The achievement of urban development goals that also seek to promote ecological sustainability (or at least minimize the contribution of city-based activities to unsustainability) requires both incentives and regulations. Incentives are needed to encourage the private sector and individual, household and community initiatives to contribute to sustainable development. For instance, promoting a greater commitment among companies to recycling and waste minimization generally needs national action. Regulations are needed so that the workings of the market are not such that the weak and vulnerable are exploited (so development goals are not met) and air and water quality damaged, natural capital depleted and global systems degraded. Without such a framework, enterprises with good environmental practice will be always at a disadvantage to those which can reduce costs by exploiting the environment. The consumer will always bear a large part of the costs—but the issues are: what is the size of the costs, when do they occur and how are the costs distributed among different consumers?

There are also the policy options that help change the nature of demand for goods and services to those that are more compatible with sustainable development. These include ensuring that consumers are more knowledgeable about the environmental impacts of the goods they purchase or of the process which produced them. This can be achieved through information campaigns including 'eco-labelling' schemes. They also include shifting the raising of public finance from employment (as in taxes on employer's wage rolls or employees' wages) to general consumption and resource use or pollution (e.g. carbon taxes).

The broad regulatory and incentive structure needed to support the achievement of development goals, within a framework which promotes local and global ecological sustainability, is relatively easy to conceive as an abstract exercise. But translating this into reality within nations and globally is far more problematic. Powerful vested interests oppose most, if not all, the needed policies and priorities. The likely levels of reduction needed in the use of non-renewable resources (especially fossil fuels) will impinge most on richer groups' lifestyles. Richer groups are unlikely willingly to forsake the comfort and mobility that they currently enjoy, although the innovative public transport schemes described in Chapter 9 show that automobile-dependent cities are not inevitable. As noted earlier, technological change can help reduce resource use and waste without limiting mobility. But if combating atmospheric warming does demand a rapid reduction in greenhouse-gas emissions and if needs are to be met in the South (implying considerably increased fossil-fuel use overall), this will require changes in consumption patterns among the wealthier high-consumption house-holds worldwide. This will include limitations on their right to use private automobiles at the levels now common since this cannot be sustained even with new technologies and alternative fuels drawn from renewable resources—at least without a significant increase in costs.

The role of the international community

National governments in both North and South are unlikely to set the incentives and regulations needed to promote sustainable development outside their national boundaries without international agreements. One of the key international issues for the next few decades will be how to resolve the pursuit of increased wealth by national societies (most of whose members have strong preferences for minimal constraints on their consumption levels) within a global recognition of the material limits of the biosphere. There is little doubt that the world's natural resource endowments and natural systems can sustain the world's population both now and in the near future with absolute poverty eliminated, human needs met and all nations having life expectancies comparable to those in the richer nations. In the richest nations, it is also possible to envisage much more resource-conserving societies without a fall in living standards. What is far more in question is whether the political processes within nations and internationally can put in place both the agreements and the regulatory and incentive structures to ensure that this is achieved. The power and profitability of many major corporations and the authority of national

governments will be reduced by such a move. Many jobs may also be threatened although, as described in Chapter 12, a shift of patterns of production and consumption towards those which greatly reduce the use of non-renewable resources, protect soils, forests and watersheds and promote waste-minimization and recycling also create many new jobs. Some necessary measures are likely to prove politically unpopular. Even when international agreement is reached, the world has little experience of the institutions needed to ensure compliance.

There are also international factors far beyond the competence and capacity of national and municipal governments that influence the quality of city environments. The very poor environmental conditions evident in most Southern cities are an expression of the very difficult circumstances in which most Southern countries find themselves. Stagnant economies and heavy debt burdens do not provide a suitable economic base from which to develop good governance. Governments from the North and international agencies may promote environmental policies but there is little progress on changing the international economic system to permit more economic stability and prosperity among the poorest nations. Many Southern economies have no alternative but to increase the exploitation of their natural resources to earn the foreign exchange to meet debt repayments. In the discussions about new 'enabling frameworks' that the City Summit promotes, what must not be forgotten is the 'enabling framework' needed at international level that is far more supportive of economic stability and greater prosperity for the lower-income nations.

Notes and References

1. UNCHS (Habitat), *The Global Report on Human Settlements 1986*, Oxford University Press, Oxford, 1987.

2. See for instance Preston, Samuel H., 'Urban growth in developing countries: a demographic reappraisal', *Population and Development Review*, vol. 5, no. 2, 1979 and Satterthwaite, David, 'The scale and nature of urban change in the South', presentation to the 21st Century Trust Meeting on *Population Growth, Health and Development: Problems and Prospects for the 21st Century*, Oxford, 1995.

3. There are some exceptions, as described in Chapters 1 and 2, but most rapidly growing cities are also cities whose economy is growing.

4. The countries with the largest increases in levels of urbanization during the 1980s are also generally those with the largest increase in their economies—as described in Chapters 1 and 2. These

chapters also described how population growth rates are generally lowest in the countries with the highest per capita incomes and the highest levels of urbanization. Over the last 15–20 years, population growth rates have also generally declined most in the countries with the most rapid economic growth, although there are important exceptions—see Cleland, John, 'Population growth in the 21st century; cause for crisis or celebration', Paper presented to the 21st Century Trust meeting on *Population Growth, Health and Development: Problems and Prospects for the 21st Century*, Oxford, 1995.

5. This section draws from Satterthwaite, David, 'Sustainable Cities', *Resurgence*, Issue 67, Nov./Dec. 1994, 20–3.

6. Smit, Jac and Joe Nasr, 'Urban agriculture for sustainable cities: using wastes and idle land and water bodies as resources', *Environment and Urbanization*, vol. 4, no. 2, Oct. 1992;

Mara, Duncan and Sandy Cairncross, *Guidelines for the Safe Use of Wastewater and Excreta in Agriculture and Aquaculture*, World Health Organization, Geneva, 1990.

7. Winblad, Uno and Wen Kilama, *Sanitation without Water*, Macmillan, Basingstoke, 1985; Pickford, John, *Low-cost Sanitation: a Survey of Practical Experience*, Intermediate Technology Publications, London, 1995.

8. See for instance The Water Program, *Water Efficiency: A Resource for Utility Managers, Community Planners and other Decision Makers*, Rocky Mountain Institute, Snowmass, 1991.

9. See Table 22.1, pp. 330–1 in World Resources Institute, *World Resources 1990–91: A Guide to the Global Environment*, Oxford University Press, Oxford, 1990.

10. The example of Chelsea was chosen because it combines very high quality

housing, very little of which is in high rises (and most of which is pre-20th century) with a diverse economic base, large amounts of open space and among the best educational and cultural facilities in London. With a population density of around 120 persons per hectare, it is an example of how relatively high density need not imply overcrowding or poor quality living environments. The world's urban population of around 2.6 billion in 1995 would fit into an area of land similar to that of Senegal (197,000 square kilometres) or Oman (212,000 square kilometres) at a density comparable to that of Chelsea.

11. The scale of agricultural production in any city is obviously dependent on where the boundaries are drawn. Many cities and most metropolitan areas have boundaries that are considerably larger than the central highly built up core and include large areas which are intensively farmed.

12. See as one example the street art developed by young people in Dakar, Senegal that is shown in ENDA, *Set setal: des murs qui parlent—nouvelle culture urbaine a Dakar*, no. 143 in series Études et Recherches, ENDA, Dakar, 1991.

13. Examples would include the schools of samba within the *favelas* of Rio de Janeiro and the strength and diversity of so much modern African music that originates from poorer areas of African cities, a small proportion of which has found a wider international audience in recent years.

14. This material on the social economy is drawn largely from Korten, David C., *Civic Engagement to Create Just and Sustainable Societies for the 21st Century*, a Conference Issues Paper prepared for Habitat II, 1995; and Boyd, Graham, 'The urban social economy', *Urban Examples*, UNICEF, New York, 1995.

15. Korten 1995, *op. cit.*

16. Rees, William E., 'Ecological footprints and appropriated carrying capacity', *Environment and Urbanization*, vol. 4, no. 2, Oct. 1992, 121–30.

17. World Commission on Environment and Development, *Our Common Future*, Oxford University Press, 1987, 8.

18. See the Universal Declaration of Human Rights, Article 25 (1), United Nations.

19. See for instance Turner, John F. C., *Housing By People—Towards Autonomy in Building Environments*, Ideas in Progress, Marion Boyars, London, 1976; also Turner, John F. C. and Robert Fichter (eds.), *Freedom to Build*,

Macmillan, New York and London, 1971.

20. Duhl, Leonard J., *The Social Entrepreneurship of Change*, Pace University Press, New York, 1990.

21. Hardoy, Jorge E. and David Satterthwaite, *Squatter Citizen: Life in the Urban Third World*, Earthscan Publications, London. 1989.

22. Hardoy and Satterthwaite 1989, *op. cit.*

23. Jorge Hardoy in Epilogue, Hardoy and Satterthwaite 1989, *op. cit.*

24. Rabinovitch, Jonas, 'Curitiba: towards sustainable urban development', *Environment and Urbanization*, vol. 4, no. 2, Oct. 1992, 62–77.

25. UNDP, *Human Development Report 1993*, Oxford University Press, Oxford, 1993.

26. See for instance Davila, Julio D., 'Mexico's urban popular movements: a conversation with Pedro Moctezuma', *Environment and Urbanization*, vol. 2, no. 1, April 1990, 35–50.

27. Gómez Buendía, Hernando, 'Collective goods in human settlements: the urban transition in Latin America', Paper prepared for the UNU/WIDER Conference on 'Human Settlements in the Changing Global Political and Economic Processes', Helsinki, 1995.

28. Gómez Buendía 1995, *op. cit.*

29. Korten, David C., *Getting into the 21st Century: Voluntary Action and the Global Agenda*, Kumarian Press, West Hartford, 1990.

30. Turner, John F. C., 'Issues and Conclusions', in Bertha Turner (Editor), *Building Community, a Third World Case Book*, Habitat International Coalition, London, 1988.

31. Cohen, Larry and Susan Swift, 'A public health approach to the violence epidemic in the United States', *Environment and Urbanization* vol. 5, no. 2, Oct. 1993, 50–66.

32. See for instance the three volumes that the Centre for Science and Environment has published on 'The State of India's Environment' and the fortnightly journal *Down to Earth*. Their work was described in CSE, 'NGO Profile: The Centre for Science and Environment', *Environment and Urbanization* vol. 1, no. 1, April 1989, 84–8.

33. SPARC, 'SPARC—Developing new NGO lines', *Environment and Urbanization* vol. 2, no. 1, April 1990, 91–104. For more details on the work of the other three, see: Murphy, Denis and

Ted Anana, 'Evictions and fear of evictions in the Philippines', Fernandes, Kenneth, 'Katchi abadis: living on the edge', and Kothari, Miloon, 'Rio de Janeiro' in *Environment and Urbanization* vol. 6, no. 1, April 1994.

34. Habitat International Coalition was formerly Habitat International Council.

35. HIC, 'NGO Profile—Habitat International Coalition', *Environment and Urbanization* vol. 2, no. 1, April 1990, 105–12.

36. Pinsky, Barry, 'NGO Profile: Settlements Information Network Africa, *Environment and Urbanization* vol. 5, no. 1, Oct. 1993, 155–61.

37. ACHR, 'NGO Profile: the Asian Coalition for Housing Rights', *Environment and Urbanization* vol. 5, no. 2, Oct. 1993, 153–65.

38. Richard E. Stren, 'Administration of Urban services' in Richard E. Stren and Rodney R. White (eds.), *African Cities in Crisis*, Westview, Boulder, 1989.

39. European Union Expert group on the Urban Environment, *European Sustainable Cities*, First report, Oct. 1994, XI/822/94–EN.

40. Elkington, John, 'Business as unusual', in the *Guardian* special supplement on 'Changes: a report onto the environmental forces shaping our future', London, Thursday 2 June 1994, 10–11.

41. Elkington 1994, *op. cit.*

42. Elkington, John and Jonathan Shopley, *Cleaning Up: U.S. Waste Management Technology and Third World Development*, WRI Papers, World Resources Institute, Washington DC, 1989.

43. Benavides, Livia, 'Hazardous waste management for small-scale and cottage industries in developing countries', Paper presented at the International Workshop on Planning for Sustainable Urban Development., Dept. of City and Regional Planning, University of Wales, 13 July 1992.

44. European Union Expert Group on the Urban Environment 1994 (*op. cit.*) outlines different initiatives in cities such as Cork, Berlin and the London borough of Islington to help local businesses to improve their environmental performance.

45. European Union Expert group on the Urban Environment 1994, *op. cit.* and Jonkhof, Jos F., *Environment and Sustainable Developments in Dutch Municipalities*, Background paper for the Global Report, Oct. 1994.

PART IV

Statistical Annex

List of Tables

Introductory Notes

The Statistical Annex consists of 21 tables covering a wide range of topics, related to human settlements, including population data, land statistics, economic indicators, characteristics of housing and related facilities, infrastructure and services, environmental data, and social indicators. The tables in this Annex do not merely provide updated versions of the tables contained in the *1986 Global Report on Human Settlements*. It contains recent data on country and city levels, collected from different published and unpublished secondary sources and through the United Nations Human Settlements Statistics Questionnaire. An innovative feature is the inclusion of household projections data derived from an exercise undertaken by UNCHS (Habitat) in 1994. Another resourceful feature is the presentation of city data in addition to country data. This is in response to the need for city level data required to address human settlements problems in an urbanizing world.

Sources of data

The tables of the Statistical Annex to the *Global Report on Human Settlements* have been compiled by the United Nations Centre for Human Settlements (Habitat) from several statistical publications. Notable among these are:
United Nations. *World Population Prospects: The 1994 Revision. World Urbanization Prospects: The 1994 Revision. 1983 Energy Statistical Yearbook*, ST/ESA/STAT/SER.J/27 (New York, 1985, sales No. E/F.85.XVII.9). *1992 Energy Statistical Yearbook*, ST/ESA/STAT/SER.J/36 (New York 1994, sales No. E/F.94.XVII.9). *Statistical Yearbook thirty-ninth issue*, ST/ESA/STAT/SER.S/15 (New York, 1994, E/F.94.XVII.1). *African Statistical Yearbook 1990/91 Vol. 1 Part 1* (sales No. E/F.93.II.K.3). *African Statistical Yearbook 1990/91 Vol. 1 Part 2* (sales No. E/F.93.II.K.4). *African Statistical Yearbook 1990/91 Vol. 2 Part 1* (sales No. E/F.93.II.K.8). *African Statistical Yearbook 1990/91 Vol. 2 Part 2* (sales No. E/F.93.II.K.7). *Statistical Yearbook for Latin America and the Caribbean 1993*, LC/G.1786-P (sales No.

E/S.94.II.G.1). *Statistical Abstract of the Region of the Economic and Social Commission for Western Asia 1981–90*, E/ESCWA/STAT/1992/18 (Amman, 1992, sales No. A/E.93.II.L.1). *The Environment in Europe and North-America: Annotated Statistics 1992* (New York, 1992, sales No. I.92.II.E.14). *Statistical Yearbook for Asia and The Pacific 1992*, ST/ESCAP/1228 (sales No. E/F.93.II.F.1). United Nations Centre for Human Settlements. *Human Settlements Database: Version 4.0*. United Nations Children's Fund. *The State of The World's Children 1994* (Oxford University Press). *The State of The World's Children 1995* (Oxford University Press). United Nations Development Programme. *Human Development Report 1994* (Oxford University Press, 1994). United Nations Educational, Scientific and Cultural Organization. *Statistical Yearbook 1994*. United Nations Environment Programme. *Environmental Data Report 1991–92. Environmental Data Report 1993–94*. The World Bank. *Social Indicator of Development 1994* (Baltimore and London, The World Bank and The Johns Hopkins University Press, 1994); *World Tables 1994; Data on Diskette*. Food and Agriculture Organization of the United Nations. *FAO Production Yearbook Vol. 45 1991* (Rome, 1992). *FAO Production Yearbook Vol. 47 1993* (Rome, 1994). World Health Organization. *The International Drinking Water Supply and Sanitation Decade – Review of National Baseline Data (as at 31 December 1980)* (Geneva, 1984). *The International Drinking Water Supply and Sanitation Decade – Review of Mid-Decade Progress (as at December 1985)*, (Geneva, 1987). *The International Drinking Water Supply and Sanitation Decade – Review of Decade Progress (as at December 1988)* (Geneva,1980). *The International Drinking Water Supply and Sanitation Decade End of Decade – Review (as at December 1990)* (Geneva, 1992). *World Health Statistics Annual 1985* (Geneva, 1985). *World Health Statistics Annual 1991* (Geneva, 1992). World Health Organization and United Nations Children's Fund. *Water Supply and Sanitation Sector Monitoring Report 1993: Sector Status as of 31 December 1991*. World Resources Institute in collaboration with the United Nations Environment Programme and the United Nations Development Programme, *World Resources 1992–93* (New York, Oxford University Press, 1992); World Resources Institute in collaboration with the United Nations Environment Programme and the United Nations Development Programme, *World Resources 1994–95* (New York, Oxford University Press, 1994); World Resources Institute, *World Resources 1994–95: Data Base* [Diskette] (DSC Data Services Inc., 1994); Organization for Economic Co-operation and Development. *OECD Environmental Data Compendium 1993* (Paris, 1993). International Road Federation. *World Road Statistics 1984–88 Edition 1989*.

The Human Settlements Statistics Questionnaire (*HSSQ*) 1992 becomes one of the major sources of data for the Statistical Annex. HSSQ was developed and finalized by the United Nations Statistical Division (UNSD) in co-operation with UNCHS (Habitat). This questionnaire was sent to 230 national Statistical Offices in 1992. Responses were received from 112 countries, out of which 9 countries gave various reasons for not being able to provide any data. The HSSQ 1992 consists of 18 tables. The first six tables request data on country/area, urban and rural levels, covering topics such as population, households, living quarters, number of rooms, tenureship, duration of residence, housing facilities, housing constructions, and crime statistics. The rest of HSSQ tables cater for four largest cities data.

The respective sources of data are shown at the end of each table.

Nomenclature and order of presentation

Owing to space limitations, the countries or areas listed in the tables are generally listed by the commonly employed short titles in use in the United Nations; for example, the United Kingdom of Great Britain and Northern Ireland is referred to as 'United Kingdom', the United States of America as 'United States', the former Union of Soviet Socialist Republics as 'USSR (former)'. Countries or areas are listed in English alphabetical order within the following macro regions: Africa, Asia, Europe, Latin America, Northern Europe and Oceania. Tables 5, 17, 18, 20 and 21 contain data referring to 'USSR (former)', shown as a macro region.

Tables 4, 9, 10, 12, 14, 16 and 19 contain data on a city/urban agglomeration level. The arrangement of these data is done by country, listed in English alphabetical order within the shown above macro regions. 'Cities' are defined according to the legal boundaries established by the countries concerned. The definition of 'Urban agglomerations' is given in Table 4.

Where the table indicates 'selected' countries or cities, the selection was not based on any other consideration except on the availability of the appropriate data for the country or city under reference. The arrangement of data by region, country or area and city, is done irrespective of political status, and the geographical designations employed were adopted solely for statistical convenience.

Explanation of symbols

In presenting data, the meaning of symbols used in each table of the Annex is given under the footnotes of that table. The following symbols carry general meaning throughout the Annex.

Category not applicable   ..
Data not available   ...
Magnitude zero   -

(*) *More Developed Regions* comprise all countries and areas of Europe and Northern America; and Australia, Japan, and New Zealand.

(+) *Less Developed Regions* comprise all countries and areas of Africa, Latin America, Asia (excluding Japan), and Oceania (excluding Australia and New Zealand).

Note: This classification of More Developed and Less Developed Regions is intended for statistical convenience and does not necessarily express a judgement about the state reached by a particular country or area in the development process.

TABLE 1

Size and Growth of Total Population, 1975–2050

	Estimates and Projections (thousands)						Annual Growth Rate (%)					Population by Sex (%) 1995	
	1975	1990	2000	2010	2025	2050	1975-1990	1990-2000	2000-2010	2010-2025	2025-2050	Male	Female
WORLD TOTAL	4076985	5284832	6158051	7032294	8294341	9833208	1.73	1.53	1.33	1.10	0.68	50.4	49.6
More Developed Regions (*)	1044186	1143358	1185536	1212865	1238406	1207504	0.60	0.36	0.23	0.14	-0.10	48.6	51.4
Less Developed Regions (+)	3032799	4141474	4972515	5819430	7055935	8625703	2.08	1.83	1.57	1.28	0.80	50.8	49.2
AFRICA	413988	632669	831596	1069378	1495772	2140844	2.83	2.73	2.51	2.24	1.43	49.9	50.1
Algeria	16018	24935	31158	37489	45475	55674	2.95	2.23	1.85	1.29	0.81	50.6	49.4
Angola	6110	9194	13074	17660	26619	41182	2.72	3.52	3.01	2.74	1.75	49.4	50.6
Benin	3033	4633	6266	8300	12252	18649	2.82	3.02	2.81	2.60	1.68	49.4	50.6
Botswana	759	1276	1718	2226	2980	3996	3.46	2.97	2.59	1.94	1.17	49.0	51.0
Burkina Faso	6202	8987	11708	14974	21654	33365	2.47	2.64	2.46	2.46	1.73	49.5	50.5
Burundi	3680	5503	7339	9488	13490	19065	2.68	2.88	2.57	2.35	1.38	49.0	51.0
Cameroon	7526	11526	15245	20163	29173	43100	2.84	2.80	2.80	2.46	1.56	49.6	50.4
Cape Verde	278	341	448	565	735	959	1.36	2.73	2.32	1.75	1.06	46.9	53.1
Central African Republic	2057	2927	3731	4666	6360	8907	2.35	2.43	2.24	2.06	1.35	48.4	51.6
Chad	4030	5553	7307	9319	12907	18450	2.14	2.74	2.43	2.17	1.43	49.4	50.6
Comoros	316	543	778	1079	1646	2484	3.61	3.60	3.27	2.82	1.65	50.7	49.3
Congo	1447	2232	2970	3853	5677	8774	2.89	2.86	2.60	2.58	1.74	48.9	51.1
Côte d'Ivoire	6755	11974	16761	23058	36817	61441	3.82	3.36	3.19	3.12	2.05	50.7	49.3
Djibouti	205	517	645	801	1055	1403	6.17	2.21	2.17	1.84	1.14	49.4	50.6
Egypt	38841	56312	69146	81490	97301	117398	2.48	2.05	1.64	1.18	0.75	50.9	49.1
Equatorial Guinea	225	352	452	574	798	1144	2.98	2.50	2.39	2.20	1.44	49.2	50.8
Eritrea	2089	3082	4025	5153	7043	9613	2.59	2.67	2.47	2.08	1.24	49.6	50.4
Ethiopia	32221	47423	63785	85078	126886	194203	2.58	2.96	2.88	2.66	1.70	50.3	49.7
Gabon	637	1146	1517	1924	2697	3975	3.92	2.80	2.38	2.25	1.55	49.3	50.7
Gambia	548	923	1291	1611	2102	2762	3.48	3.36	2.21	1.77	1.09	49.4	50.6
Ghana	9831	15020	20172	26594	37988	54868	2.83	2.95	2.76	2.38	1.47	49.7	50.3
Guinea	4149	5755	7759	10301	15088	22607	2.18	2.99	2.83	2.54	1.62	50.2	49.8
Guinea-Bissau	627	964	1192	1473	1978	2766	2.87	2.12	2.12	1.97	1.34	49.2	50.8
Kenya	13741	23613	32577	43552	63360	92194	3.61	3.22	2.90	2.50	1.50	50.1	49.9
Lesotho	1187	1792	2338	3012	4172	5856	2.75	2.66	2.53	2.17	1.36	49.1	50.9
Liberia	1609	2575	3565	4829	7240	10997	3.13	3.25	3.03	2.70	1.67	50.5	49.5
Libyan Arab Jamahirya	2446	4545	6387	8724	12885	19109	4.13	3.40	3.12	2.60	1.58	52.1	47.9
Madagascar	7787	12571	17259	23326	34419	50926	3.19	3.17	3.01	2.59	1.57	49.6	50.4
Malawi	5244	9367	12144	15299	22348	33658	3.87	2.60	2.31	2.53	1.64	49.3	50.7
Mali	6169	9212	12559	16733	24575	36817	2.67	3.10	2.87	2.56	1.62	49.2	50.8
Mauritania	1371	2003	2580	3283	4443	6077	2.53	2.53	2.41	2.02	1.25	49.5	50.5
Mauritius	892	1057	1179	1306	1481	1654	1.13	1.09	1.02	0.84	0.44	49.9	50.1
Morocco	17305	24334	29637	34196	40650	47858	2.27	1.97	1.43	1.15	0.65	50.0	50.0
Mozambique	10498	14187	18991	24704	35139	52145	2.01	2.92	2.63	2.35	1.58	49.4	50.6
Namibia	900	1349	1752	2239	3049	4163	2.70	2.61	2.45	2.06	1.25	49.7	50.3
Niger	4771	7731	10805	14751	22385	34576	3.22	3.35	3.11	2.78	1.74	49.4	50.6
Nigeria	62770	96154	128786	168370	238397	338510	2.84	2.92	2.68	2.32	1.40	49.6	50.4
Reunion	483	604	697	783	901	1029	1.49	1.43	1.16	0.94	0.53	49.0	51.0
Rwanda	4384	6986	9048	11545	15797	21755	3.11	2.59	2.44	2.09	1.28	49.4	50.6
Sao Tome & Principe	81	119	146	174	215	294	2.56	2.04	1.75	1.41	1.25	...	...
Senegal	4806	7327	9495	12241	16896	23442	2.81	2.59	2.54	2.15	1.31	50.0	50.0
Seychelles	59	70	77	85	95	106	1.14	0.95	0.99	0.74	0.44	...	...
Sierra Leone	2931	3999	5069	6366	8690	12090	2.07	2.37	2.28	2.07	1.32	49.1	50.9
Somalia	5471	8677	10787	14470	21276	32062	3.07	2.18	2.94	2.57	1.64	49.5	50.5
South Africa	25669	37066	46215	56398	70951	90129	2.45	2.21	1.99	1.53	0.96	49.7	50.3
St. Helena	5	6	6	7	8	11	1.22	-	1.54	0.89	1.27	...	...
Sudan	16012	24585	32079	41534	58388	84829	2.86	2.66	2.58	2.27	1.49	50.2	49.8
Swaziland	482	744	980	1253	1647	2176	2.89	2.76	2.46	1.82	1.11	47.9	52.1
Togo	2285	3531	4818	6427	9377	13704	2.90	3.11	2.88	2.52	1.52	49.5	50.5
Tunisia	5611	8080	9694	11209	13290	15607	2.43	1.82	1.45	1.14	0.64	50.5	49.5
Uganda	11182	17949	24618	32308	48056	72131	3.15	3.16	2.72	2.65	1.62	49.5	50.5
United Republic of Tanzania	15900	25600	34074	44154	62894	91132	3.18	2.86	2.59	2.36	1.48	49.6	50.4
Western Sahara	117	230	342	467	627	796	4.51	3.97	3.12	1.96	0.95	...	...
Zaire	23251	37436	51136	68876	104639	164433	3.18	3.12	2.98	2.79	1.81	49.4	50.6
Zambia	4841	8150	10754	13657	19130	27173	3.47	2.77	2.39	2.25	1.40	49.4	50.6
Zimbabwe	6143	9903	12514	15260	19631	26622	3.18	2.34	1.98	1.68	1.22	49.6	50.4
ASIA	2405987	3186446	3735846	4263948	4959987	5741004	1.87	1.59	1.32	1.01	0.58	51.1	48.9
Afghanistan	15378	15045	26674	33992	45262	59960	-0.15	5.73	2.42	1.91	1.12	51.3	48.7
Armenia	2826	3352	3813	4201	4724	5240	1.14	1.29	0.97	0.78	0.41	49.2	50.8
Azerbaijan	5689	7117	7969	8815	10106	11299	1.49	1.13	1.01	0.91	0.45	49.0	51.0
Bahrain	272	490	633	758	922	1046	3.92	2.56	1.80	1.31	0.51	57.3	42.7
Bangladesh	76582	108118	134417	162501	196128	238512	2.30	2.18	1.90	1.25	0.78	51.6	48.4
Bhutan	1119	1544	1842	2309	3136	4329	2.15	1.76	2.26	2.04	1.29	50.2	49.8
Brunei Darussalam	161	257	312	359	425	492	3.12	1.94	1.40	1.13	0.59	52.3	47.7
Cambodia	7098	8841	11637	14601	19686	26272	1.46	2.75	2.27	1.99	1.15	48.2	51.8
China	927808	1155305	1284597	1388474	1526106	1605991	1.46	1.06	0.78	0.63	0.20	51.5	48.5
Cyprus	609	702	777	839	927	1006	0.95	1.02	0.77	0.66	0.33	49.9	50.1
Dem. People's Rep. of Korea	16562	21774	25979	29112	33386	37198	1.82	1.77	1.14	0.91	0.43	49.3	50.7

TABLE 1 *(continued)*

Size and Growth of Total Population, 1975–2050

	Estimates and Projections (thousands)						Annual Growth Rate (%)					Population by Sex (%) 1995	
	1975	1990	2000	2010	2025	2050	1975-1990	1990-2000	2000-2010	2010-2025	2025-2050	Male	Female
ASIA (continued)													
East Timor	672	740	884	1018	1200	1415	0.64	1.78	1.41	1.10	0.66	51.5	48.5
Gaza Strip (Palestine)	390	624	874	1087	1405	1909	3.13	3.37	2.18	1.71	1.23	...	...
Georgia	4908	5418	5527	5770	6122	6513	0.66	0.20	0.43	0.39	0.25	47.7	52.3
Hong Kong	4396	5705	5968	6039	5936	4944	1.74	0.45	0.12	-0.11	-0.73	51.1	48.9
India	620701	850638	1022021	1189082	1392086	1639863	2.10	1.84	1.51	1.05	0.66	51.7	48.3
Indonesia	135666	182812	212731	239601	275598	318802	1.99	1.52	1.19	0.93	0.58	49.9	50.1
Iran (Islamic Republic of)	33344	58946	74644	95215	123549	163108	3.80	2.36	2.43	1.74	1.11	50.8	49.2
Iraq	11020	18078	23753	31097	42656	57691	3.30	2.73	2.69	2.11	1.21	50.9	49.1
Israel	3455	4660	6062	6833	7808	8927	1.99	2.63	1.20	0.89	0.54	49.6	50.4
Japan	111524	123537	126472	127152	121594	110015	0.68	0.23	-0.05	-0.30	-0.40	49.1	50.9
Jordan	2600	4259	6407	8561	12039	16874	3.29	4.08	2.90	2.27	1.35	51.2	48.8
Kazakhstan	14136	16670	17694	19327	21748	24278	1.10	0.60	0.88	0.79	0.44	48.7	51.3
Kuwait	1007	2143	1818	2282	2805	3384	5.03	-1.64	2.27	1.38	0.75	50.2	49.8
Kyrgyzstan	3299	4362	5143	5970	7128	8637	1.86	1.65	1.49	1.18	0.77	49.1	50.9
Lao People's Dem. Republic	3024	4202	5602	7188	9688	13001	2.19	2.88	2.49	1.99	1.18	49.3	50.7
Lebanon	2767	2555	3289	3742	4424	5189	-0.53	2.53	1.29	1.12	0.64	48.8	51.2
Macau	234	342	459	497	546	575	2.53	2.94	0.80	0.63	0.21	...	...
Malaysia	12258	17891	22299	26239	31577	38089	2.52	2.20	1.63	1.23	0.75	50.5	49.5
Maldives	137	216	297	398	559	777	3.04	3.18	2.93	2.26	1.32	51.3	48.7
Mongolia	1447	2177	2661	3183	3827	4649	2.72	2.01	1.79	1.23	0.78	50.4	49.6
Myanmar	30441	41813	51539	61596	75564	94569	2.12	2.09	1.78	1.36	0.90	49.8	50.2
Nepal	13006	19253	24842	31236	40693	53272	2.62	2.55	2.29	1.76	1.08	51.0	49.0
Oman	847	1751	2626	3783	6094	10005	4.84	4.05	3.65	3.18	1.98	52.5	47.5
Pakistan	74734	121933	161827	210104	284827	381488	3.26	2.83	2.61	2.03	1.17	51.7	48.3
Philippines	43010	60779	74575	88157	104522	129532	2.31	2.05	1.67	1.14	0.86	50.3	49.7
Qatar	171	485	605	703	799	889	6.95	2.21	1.50	0.85	0.43	66.3	33.7
Republic of Korea	35281	42869	47149	50764	54418	56456	1.30	0.95	0.74	0.46	0.15	50.2	49.8
Saudi Arabia	7251	16048	21257	28880	42651	60897	5.30	2.81	3.06	2.60	1.42	55.7	44.3
Singapore	2263	2705	2967	3144	3355	3304	1.19	0.92	0.58	0.43	-0.06	50.6	49.4
Sri Lanka	13603	17225	19504	21796	25031	28350	1.57	1.24	1.11	0.92	0.50	49.8	50.2
Syrian Arab Republic	7438	12348	17329	23591	33505	47212	3.38	3.39	3.08	2.34	1.37	50.4	49.6
Tajikistan	3442	5287	6973	8881	11792	15534	2.86	2.77	2.42	1.89	1.10	49.8	50.2
Thailand	41359	55583	61909	67130	73584	81913	1.97	1.08	0.81	0.61	0.43	50.1	49.9
Turkey	40025	56098	67748	77883	90937	106284	2.25	1.89	1.39	1.03	0.62	51.2	48.8
Turkmenistan	2520	3657	4551	5463	6650	8180	2.48	2.19	1.83	1.31	0.83	49.4	50.6
United Arab Emirates	505	1671	2107	2500	2958	3423	7.98	2.32	1.71	1.12	0.58	63.8	36.2
Uzbekistan	13981	20420	25383	30703	37678	46810	2.53	2.18	1.90	1.36	0.87	49.6	50.4
Viet Nam	48030	66689	82648	98448	118151	143620	2.19	2.15	1.75	1.22	0.78	49.2	50.8
Yemen	6991	11311	17051	22946	33676	49280	3.21	4.10	2.97	2.56	1.52	50.2	49.8
EUROPE	**676389**	**721734**	**729803**	**728741**	**718203**	**677765**	**0.43**	**0.11**	**-0.01**	**-0.10**	**-0.23**	**48.3**	**51.7**
Albania	2424	3289	3624	4060	4668	5265	2.03	0.97	1.14	0.93	0.48	51.2	48.8
Andorra	25	52	81	110	153	194	4.88	4.43	3.06	2.20	0.95	...	...
Austria	7579	7705	8148	8251	8262	7811	0.11	0.56	0.13	0.01	-0.22	48.8	51.2
Belarus	9367	10212	10069	9996	9903	9717	0.58	-0.14	-0.07	-0.06	-0.08	47.0	53.0
Belgium	9796	9951	10248	10334	10407	10068	0.10	0.29	0.08	0.05	-0.13	49.0	51.0
Bosnia & Herzegovina	3747	4308	4330	4420	4474	4223	0.93	0.05	0.21	0.08	-0.23	49.5	50.5
Bulgaria	8722	8991	8576	8242	7768	7091	0.20	-0.47	-0.40	-0.39	-0.36	49.0	51.0
Channel Islands	127	142	153	162	173	182	0.74	0.75	0.57	0.44	0.20	...	...
Croatia	4263	4517	4433	4373	4234	4038	0.39	-0.19	-0.14	-0.22	-0.19	48.4	51.6
Czech Republic	9997	10306	10346	10444	10622	10875	0.20	0.04	0.09	0.11	0.09	48.8	51.2
Denmark	5060	5140	5207	5173	5081	4819	0.10	0.13	-0.07	-0.12	-0.21	49.4	50.6
Estonia	1432	1575	1495	1461	1422	1368	0.63	-0.52	-0.23	-0.18	-0.15	47.1	52.9
Faeroe Islands	41	47	48	49	50	51	0.91	0.21	0.21	0.13	0.08	...	...
Finland	4711	4986	5201	5314	5407	5373	0.38	0.42	0.21	0.12	-0.03	48.7	51.3
France	52699	56718	59024	60130	61247	60475	0.49	0.40	0.19	0.12	-0.05	48.8	51.2
Germany	78679	79365	81700	80466	76442	64244	0.06	0.29	-0.15	-0.34	-0.70	48.8	51.2
Gibraltar	28	28	28	28	28	28	-	-	-	-	-	...	...
Greece	9047	10238	10573	10458	9868	8591	0.82	0.32	-0.11	-0.39	-0.55	49.2	50.8
Holy See	1	1	1	1	1	1	-	-	-	-	-	...	...
Hungary	10532	10365	9940	9678	9397	9223	-0.11	-0.42	-0.27	-0.20	-0.07	47.9	52.1
Iceland	218	255	282	307	337	365	1.05	1.01	0.85	0.62	0.32	50.2	49.8
Ireland	3177	3503	3616	3777	3882	4103	0.65	0.32	0.44	0.18	0.22	49.9	50.1
Isle of Man	60	69	79	89	101	110	0.93	1.35	1.19	0.84	0.34	...	...
Italy	55441	57023	57254	55985	52324	43630	0.19	0.04	-0.22	-0.45	-0.73	48.6	51.4
Latvia	2474	2671	2471	2398	2335	2272	0.51	-0.78	-0.30	-0.18	-0.11	46.1	53.9
Liechtenstein	23	29	33	37	42	44	1.55	1.29	1.14	0.85	0.19	...	...
Lithuania	3308	3711	3692	3736	3816	3912	0.77	-0.05	0.12	0.14	0.10	47.3	52.7
Luxembourg	362	381	425	439	439	420	0.34	1.09	0.32	-	-0.17	49.3	50.7
Malta	304	354	377	399	422	439	1.02	0.63	0.57	0.37	0.16	49.5	50.5
Monaco	25	30	34	37	43	49	1.22	1.25	0.85	1.00	0.52	...	...
Netherlands	13653	14952	15934	16239	16276	15275	0.61	0.64	0.19	0.02	-0.25	49.5	50.5
Norway	4007	4241	4427	4556	4719	4791	0.38	0.43	0.29	0.23	0.06	49.5	50.5

TABLE 1 (continued)

Size and Growth of Total Population, 1975–2050

	Estimates and Projections (thousands)						Annual Growth Rate (%)					Population by Sex (%) 1995	
	1975	1990	2000	2010	2025	2050	1975-1990	1990-2000	2000-2010	2010-2025	2025-2050	Male	Female
EUROPE (continued)													
Poland	34022	38119	38786	39938	41542	43154	0.76	0.17	0.29	0.26	0.15	48.7	51.3
Portugal	9093	9868	9807	9791	9685	9140	0.55	-0.06	-0.02	-0.07	-0.23	48.3	51.7
Republic of Moldova	3839	4362	4510	4764	5130	5579	0.85	0.33	0.55	0.49	0.34	47.8	52.2
Romania	21245	23207	22607	22316	21735	20389	0.59	-0.26	-0.13	-0.18	-0.26	49.3	50.7
Russian Federation	134233	147913	145552	143134	138548	129831	0.65	-0.16	-0.17	-0.22	-0.26	46.9	53.1
San Marino	19	23	27	30	34	38	1.27	1.60	1.05	0.83	0.44	...	...
Slovakia	4736	5256	5468	5707	6014	6342	0.69	0.40	0.43	0.35	0.21	48.7	51.3
Slovenia	1742	1918	1945	1918	1825	1640	0.64	0.14	-0.14	-0.33	-0.43	48.4	51.6
Spain	35596	39272	39848	39514	37571	31765	0.66	0.15	-0.08	-0.34	-0.67	49.1	50.9
Sweden	8193	8559	8972	9266	9751	9991	0.29	0.47	0.32	0.34	0.10	49.5	50.5
Switzerland	6339	6834	7494	7717	7786	7422	0.50	0.92	0.29	0.06	-0.19	49.6	50.4
TFYR Macedonia	1676	2046	2247	2405	2571	2685	1.33	0.94	0.68	0.44	0.17	50.3	49.7
Ukraine	49016	51637	50974	50085	48715	47250	0.35	-0.13	-0.18	-0.18	-0.12	46.5	53.5
United Kingdom	56226	57411	59022	59919	61476	61635	0.14	0.28	0.15	0.17	0.01	48.9	51.1
Yugoslavia	9085	10156	10696	11085	11478	11855	0.74	0.52	0.36	0.23	0.13	49.7	50.3
LATIN AMERICA	**319893**	**439716**	**523875**	**603843**	**709785**	**838527**	**2.12**	**1.75**	**1.42**	**1.08**	**0.67**	**49.8**	**50.2**
Anguilla	6	7	8	9	10	13	1.03	1.34	1.18	0.70	1.05	...	...
Antigua & Barbuda	59	64	68	73	84	102	0.54	0.61	0.71	0.94	0.78	...	...
Argentina	26049	32547	36648	40755	46133	53121	1.48	1.19	1.06	0.83	0.56	49.1	50.9
Aruba	62	67	73	80	89	97	0.52	0.86	0.92	0.71	0.34	...	...
Bahamas	190	256	295	332	378	419	1.99	1.42	1.18	0.87	0.42	49.0	51.0
Barbados	246	257	268	283	309	325	0.29	0.42	0.54	0.59	0.21	48.2	51.8
Belize	134	189	245	304	386	499	2.29	2.60	2.16	1.59	1.02	50.5	49.5
Bolivia	4759	6573	8329	10229	13131	16967	2.15	2.37	2.05	1.66	1.03	49.6	50.4
Brazil	108032	148477	174825	199327	230250	264349	2.12	1.63	1.31	0.96	0.55	49.9	50.1
British Virgin Islands	11	16	21	26	32	40	2.50	2.72	2.14	1.38	0.89	...	...
Cayman Islands	14	26	36	46	57	72	4.13	3.25	2.45	1.43	0.93	...	...
Chile	10334	13154	15311	17220	19775	22450	1.61	1.52	1.17	0.92	0.51	49.4	50.6
Colombia	23776	32300	37822	42959	49359	56402	2.04	1.58	1.27	0.93	0.53	49.6	50.4
Costa Rica	1968	3035	3798	4534	5608	6902	2.89	2.24	1.77	1.42	0.83	50.6	49.4
Cuba	9306	10598	11385	11911	12658	12907	0.87	0.72	0.45	0.41	0.08	50.2	49.8
Dominica	72	71	71	73	82	105	-0.09		0.28	0.78	0.99	...	...
Dominican Republic	5049	7110	8495	9708	11164	13167	2.28	1.78	1.33	0.93	0.66	50.8	49.2
Ecuador	6907	10264	12646	14899	17792	21189	2.64	2.09	1.64	1.18	0.70	50.2	49.8
El Salvador	4085	5172	6425	7772	9735	12485	1.57	2.17	1.90	1.50	1.00	48.9	51.1
Falkland Islands (Malvinas)	2	2	2	2	3	4	-	-	-	2.70	1.15	...	...
French Guiana	57	117	179	242	305	387	4.79	4.25	3.02	1.54	0.95	...	...
Grenada	92	91	94	100	113	143	-0.07	0.32	0.62	0.81	0.94	...	...
Guadeloupe	329	391	462	515	579	641	1.15	1.67	1.09	0.78	0.41	48.9	51.1
Guatemala	6023	9197	12222	15827	21668	29353	2.82	2.84	2.58	2.09	1.21	50.5	49.5
Guyana	734	796	883	987	1141	1279	0.54	1.04	1.11	0.97	0.46	49.5	50.5
Haiti	4920	6486	7959	9770	13128	18564	1.84	2.05	2.05	1.97	1.39	49.1	50.9
Honduras	3017	4879	6485	8203	10656	13921	3.20	2.85	2.35	1.74	1.07	50.4	49.6
Jamaica	2013	2366	2543	2840	3301	3755	1.08	0.72	1.10	1.00	0.52	50.1	49.9
Martinique	329	360	397	428	470	504	0.60	0.98	0.75	0.62	0.28	48.4	51.6
Mexico	58871	84511	102410	117651	136594	161450	2.41	1.92	1.39	1.00	0.67	49.9	50.1
Montserrat	12	11	11	11	12	15	-0.58	-		0.58	0.89	...	...
Netherlands Antilles	166	190	207	225	248	266	0.90	0.86	0.83	0.65	0.27	48.8	51.2
Nicaragua	2426	3676	5169	6728	9079	12211	2.77	3.41	2.64	2.00	1.19	48.8	51.2
Panama	1723	2398	2856	3266	3767	4290	2.20	1.75	1.34	0.95	0.52	50.6	49.4
Paraguay	2682	4317	5613	6970	9017	11666	3.17	2.63	2.17	1.72	1.03	50.7	49.3
Peru	15161	21588	26082	30685	36692	43820	2.36	1.89	1.63	1.19	0.71	50.3	49.7
Puerto Rico	2993	3531	3825	4148	4553	4985	1.10	0.80	0.81	0.62	0.36	48.4	51.6
Saint Kitts & Nevis	45	42	41	42	47	60	-0.46	-0.24	0.24	0.75	0.98	...	...
Saint Lucia	108	133	152	171	199	253	1.39	1.34	1.18	1.01	0.96	...	...
St. Vincent & Grenadines	93	107	117	128	147	187	0.93	0.89	0.90	0.92	0.96	...	...
Suriname	364	400	447	502	599	706	0.63	1.11	1.16	1.18	0.66	49.6	50.4
Trinidad & Tobago	1012	1236	1380	1552	1808	2085	1.33	1.10	1.17	1.02	0.57	49.5	50.5
Turks & Caicos Islands	6	12	17	22	27	34	4.62	3.48	2.58	1.37	0.92	...	...
Uruguay	2829	3094	3274	3453	3691	4013	0.60	0.57	0.53	0.44	0.33	48.7	51.3
US Virgin Islands	95	102	108	117	133	169	0.47	0.57	0.80	0.85	0.96	...	...
Venezuela	12734	19502	24170	28716	34775	42152	2.84	2.15	1.72	1.28	0.77	50.4	49.6
NORTHERN AMERICA	**239289**	**277838**	**306280**	**331571**	**369566**	**388997**	**1.00**	**0.97**	**0.79**	**0.72**	**0.20**	**48.9**	**51.1**
Bermuda	53	61	65	69	73	80	0.94	0.64	0.60	0.38	0.37	...	...
Canada	23209	27791	31029	33946	38266	39870	1.20	1.10	0.90	0.80	0.16	49.5	50.5
Greenland	50	56	60	63	67	73	0.76	0.69	0.49	0.41	0.34	...	...
St. Pierre & Miquelon	6	6	7	7	8	8	-	1.54	-	0.89		...	...
United States	215972	249924	275119	297486	331152	348966	0.97	0.96	0.78	0.71	0.21	48.8	51.2

TABLE 1 (continued)

Size and Growth of Total Population, 1975–2050

	Estimates and Projections (thousands)						Annual Growth Rate (%)					Population by Sex (%) 1995	
	1975	1990	2000	2010	2025	2050	1975-1990	1990-2000	2000-2010	2010-2025	2025-2050	Male	Female
OCEANIA	21438	26428	30651	34814	41027	46070	1.40	1.48	1.27	1.09	0.46	50.2	49.8
American Samoa	30	47	63	82	104	126	2.99	2.93	2.64	1.58	0.77	...	...
Australia	13900	16888	19222	21367	24667	26060	1.30	1.29	1.06	0.96	0.22	49.9	50.1
Cook Islands	19	18	20	24	28	34	-0.36	1.05	1.82	1.03	0.78	...	...
Fiji	576	726	845	983	1161	1377	1.54	1.52	1.51	1.11	0.68	50.8	49.2
French Polynesia	130	197	242	285	340	408	2.77	2.06	1.64	1.18	0.73	51.7	48.3
Guam	95	134	164	188	219	252	2.29	2.02	1.37	1.02	0.55	52.9	47.1
Kiribati	55	72	87	108	144	196	1.80	1.89	2.16	1.92	1.23	...	...
Marshall Islands	30	46	63	86	127	190	2.85	3.14	3.11	2.60	1.61	...	...
Micronesia, Fed. States of	71	108	144	195	284	419	2.80	2.88	3.03	2.51	1.56	...	...
Nauru	6	10	12	17	24	34	3.41	1.82	3.48	2.30	1.39	...	...
New Caledonia	133	168	195	220	255	295	1.56	1.49	1.21	0.98	0.58	50.9	49.1
New Zealand	3083	3360	3759	4034	4376	4667	0.57	1.12	0.71	0.54	0.26	49.4	50.6
Niue	4	2	2	2	2	3	-4.62	-	-	-	1.62	...	...
Northern Mariana Islands	15	43	51	60	71	86	7.02	1.71	1.63	1.12	0.77	...	...
Pacific Islands (Palau)	11	15	19	25	35	49	2.07	2.36	2.74	2.24	1.35	...	...
Papua New Guinea	2729	3839	4809	5918	7532	9614	2.28	2.25	2.08	1.61	0.98	51.6	48.4
Pitcairn	-	-	-	-	-	-	..	..	..	..	..	...	...
Samoa	153	162	187	236	307	404	0.38	1.44	2.33	1.75	1.10	51.8	48.2
Solomon Islands	190	320	444	596	844	1191	3.48	3.28	2.94	2.32	1.38	51.5	48.5
Tokelau	2	2	2	2	2	2	-	-	-	-	-	...	...
Tonga	88	96	102	114	134	164	0.58	0.61	1.11	1.08	0.81	...	...
Tuvalu	6	9	10	12	15	18	2.70	1.05	1.82	1.49	0.73	...	...
Vanuatu	102	149	192	245	334	455	2.53	2.54	2.44	2.07	1.24	50.3	49.7
Wallis & Futuna Islands	9	14	15	18	22	26	2.95	0.69	1.82	1.34	0.67	...	...

Sources: United Nations, World Population Prospects: The 1994 Revision. World Urbanization Prospects: The 1994 Revision.

Total Population data refer to the mid year population of the world, region, country or area and present estimates and the medium variant of projections undertaken by the Population Division of the Department of Economic and Social Information and Policy Analysis in 1994. The United Nations updates, every two years, population estimates and projections by incorporating new data, new estimates and new analysis of data on population, fertility, mortality and international migration. Data from new population censuses and/or demographic surveys are used to verify and update old estimates of population or demographic indicators or to make new ones and to check the validity of the assumptions made in the projections. **Annual Growth Rate**, calculated by UNCHS (Habitat), refers to the average annual percentage change of population during the indicated period.

TABLE 2

Demographic Indicators: Age Structure and Life Expectancy, 1975–2025

| | Percentage of Population in Specific Age Groups | | | | | | | | | Life Expectancy at Birth (years) | | | | | |
| | 1975 | | | 2000 | | | 2025 | | | 1970-1975 | | 1995-2000 | | 2020-2025 | |
	0-14	15-24	>60	0-14	15-24	>60	0-14	15-24	>60	Male	Female	Male	Female	Male	Female
WORLD TOTAL	36.9	18.6	8.5	30.6	17.3	9.8	24.8	15.8	14.2	56.4	59.4	63.7	67.8	70.2	74.9
More Developed Regions (*)	24.2	16.9	15.4	18.7	13.5	19.2	17.1	11.6	26.4	67.6	74.7	71.2	78.6	75.4	81.7
Less Developed Regions (+)	41.3	19.2	6.1	33.4	18.2	7.6	26.1	16.5	12.1	53.9	55.4	62.4	65.3	69.4	73.3
AFRICA	44.8	19.1	4.9	43.2	19.6	5.0	35.7	19.5	6.5	44.5	47.6	52.7	55.7	63.7	67.2
Algeria	47.6	18.5	6.1	35.5	21.5	5.8	23.6	16.9	10.7	53.5	55.5	67.5	70.3	72.9	76.7
Angola	44.2	18.1	5.0	47.3	18.7	4.5	40.8	20.4	4.8	36.5	39.6	47.4	50.6	59.9	63.1
Benin	44.8	18.1	5.4	47.1	18.9	4.5	40.4	20.2	4.8	38.5	41.6	47.2	50.6	58.3	61.9
Botswana	50.1	19.6	3.3	41.5	20.5	4.4	30.1	19.3	8.2	51.5	55.0	65.3	69.2	73.2	77.7
Burkina Faso	44.0	18.2	4.7	44.9	18.8	5.0	39.7	20.0	5.0	39.7	42.8	45.3	48.1	58.1	61.7
Burundi	45.5	20.8	5.5	45.7	19.0	4.2	37.1	19.7	5.9	42.4	45.6	49.4	52.9	61.6	65.3
Cameroon	43.4	17.7	5.7	43.4	19.8	5.5	36.6	19.9	6.3	44.3	47.3	57.0	60.0	69.5	72.5
Cape Verde	46.8	19.8	8.1	40.6	20.7	6.2	28.6	18.8	7.6	56.0	59.0	65.5	67.5	71.4	74.0
Central African Republic	40.6	18.5	6.4	42.5	19.2	6.0	35.7	19.7	6.4	40.4	45.6	47.8	52.5	59.9	64.8
Chad	41.7	18.5	5.8	42.9	19.0	5.6	36.8	19.8	6.2	37.5	40.6	47.9	51.1	57.9	61.1
Comoros	47.2	18.3	4.3	48.3	19.4	3.8	39.4	20.6	4.5	47.0	48.0	57.5	58.5	66.9	68.3
Congo	44.4	18.1	5.5	45.7	19.4	4.9	39.3	20.1	4.9	44.1	49.3	47.8	52.0	63.1	68.2
Côte d'Ivoire	45.8	18.0	4.1	49.3	19.2	4.3	43.6	20.7	3.8	43.9	47.1	48.6	50.5	63.9	67.1
Djibouti	43.7	17.9	4.2	40.4	20.0	5.4	33.7	19.4	7.0	39.4	42.6	48.7	52.0	58.7	62.0
Egypt	40.0	21.1	6.5	35.2	20.0	6.7	23.8	16.6	11.9	50.8	53.4	64.7	67.3	71.8	75.5
Equatorial Guinea	40.1	18.7	6.8	43.2	18.5	6.0	37.0	19.6	6.3	39.0	42.1	48.4	51.6	58.4	61.6
Eritrea	44.6	18.7	4.2	43.5	19.1	5.0	34.4	19.8	6.6	42.8	45.9	51.4	54.6	63.9	67.1
Ethiopia	45.8	19.0	4.4	46.4	18.9	4.6	40.1	20.0	5.2	39.4	42.6	48.4	51.6	60.9	64.1
Gabon	32.4	17.5	9.1	40.7	16.4	8.7	37.4	19.4	7.7	43.4	46.6	53.9	57.2	63.9	67.2
Gambia	42.1	17.3	4.8	41.3	17.9	5.0	34.0	19.4	7.2	35.5	38.6	45.4	48.7	55.2	58.8
Ghana	45.4	19.3	4.4	44.1	19.5	4.7	36.3	19.8	6.4	48.3	51.7	56.2	59.9	66.2	69.8
Guinea	45.3	19.2	4.4	46.9	19.1	4.2	40.3	20.3	4.8	36.8	37.8	46.0	47.0	56.0	57.0
Guinea-Bissau	38.0	17.8	6.5	41.5	18.6	6.4	36.6	19.5	6.5	35.0	38.1	43.9	47.1	53.7	57.3
Kenya	49.1	18.6	5.5	46.7	21.1	4.1	36.6	20.9	4.9	49.0	53.0	53.0	55.4	69.0	73.4
Lesotho	41.7	18.3	5.7	41.1	19.7	6.2	33.9	19.2	7.7	48.0	53.0	60.5	65.5	69.5	74.5
Liberia	44.0	17.6	5.5	46.0	18.8	5.4	39.4	20.0	5.8	46.0	49.0	56.0	59.0	66.0	69.0
Libyan Arab Jamahiriya	46.0	18.6	3.7	44.7	19.4	4.7	36.7	20.1	6.1	51.4	54.5	63.9	67.5	71.1	75.7
Madagascar	44.7	19.0	4.8	45.2	19.6	4.5	37.2	20.1	5.6	45.0	48.0	57.5	60.5	67.9	71.7
Malawi	47.2	18.5	3.7	46.3	19.5	4.4	39.3	19.9	5.0	40.3	41.7	44.3	45.4	59.6	60.9
Mali	46.0	19.1	4.2	47.2	19.0	4.1	40.0	20.2	4.9	37.0	40.1	46.4	49.7	56.2	59.9
Mauritania	43.3	18.6	5.0	41.5	20.6	5.0	34.2	19.6	6.8	41.9	45.6	51.9	55.1	61.9	65.1
Mauritius	39.7	20.8	4.5	26.6	18.0	8.8	21.5	14.2	17.5	60.7	65.3	68.3	75.0	73.5	79.7
Morocco	47.2	19.2	5.2	33.6	20.5	6.5	23.3	15.0	12.0	51.4	54.5	63.9	67.5	71.1	75.7
Mozambique	43.8	18.0	5.2	44.5	19.3	5.1	38.5	19.9	5.4	40.9	44.1	45.4	48.3	58.5	62.2
Namibia	42.9	18.5	5.5	40.9	19.6	5.9	33.1	19.2	7.7	47.5	50.0	60.0	62.5	68.8	72.6
Niger	46.4	19.0	4.1	48.6	18.9	3.9	41.6	20.5	4.5	37.5	40.6	46.9	50.2	56.7	60.4
Nigeria	44.9	19.4	4.2	45.0	19.2	4.6	37.2	20.0	6.0	41.9	45.1	50.8	54.0	60.8	64.0
Reunion	41.8	19.8	6.1	27.4	17.6	9.9	21.7	14.0	17.3	60.4	68.1	70.9	78.7	76.1	83.1
Rwanda	48.2	17.8	4.0	44.6	21.3	4.1	35.4	20.7	4.9	43.0	46.2	45.2	48.0	60.1	63.7
Senegal	44.8	19.0	4.7	43.6	20.0	4.7	35.8	20.0	6.1	39.3	41.3	50.3	52.3	60.3	62.3
Sierra Leone	42.5	18.3	5.3	44.2	18.8	4.9	38.2	19.8	5.5	33.5	36.5	39.4	42.6	49.3	52.7
Somalia	45.4	18.9	5.0	47.3	19.1	4.2	39.8	20.5	4.9	39.4	42.6	47.4	50.6	57.4	60.6
South Africa	40.9	19.4	6.0	36.1	19.3	6.8	27.8	18.1	10.2	51.0	57.0	62.3	68.3	70.5	75.7
Sudan	44.4	19.1	4.5	42.8	20.1	4.8	36.5	19.7	6.2	42.3	45.1	53.6	56.4	63.6	66.4
Swaziland	45.7	18.7	4.7	41.4	21.0	4.5	30.1	19.6	7.2	45.1	49.6	57.7	62.3	67.5	73.1
Togo	44.2	18.5	5.1	45.4	19.1	4.9	37.7	20.1	5.8	43.9	47.1	55.2	58.8	65.2	68.8
Tunisia	43.8	19.9	5.8	31.9	20.3	7.4	22.9	15.1	13.0	55.1	56.1	68.4	70.7	73.6	77.1
Uganda	47.4	19.0	4.1	49.1	19.5	3.5	40.6	20.8	3.7	44.9	48.1	42.2	44.3	59.4	62.4
United Republic of Tanzania	47.9	18.2	3.8	45.0	20.0	4.2	36.8	20.1	5.3	44.9	48.1	50.2	52.9	64.7	67.8
Zaire	45.3	18.4	4.6	47.6	19.4	4.5	40.7	20.4	4.5	44.4	47.6	50.4	53.4	63.8	67.3
Zambia	46.5	18.7	4.3	46.2	20.8	3.7	36.1	20.6	4.4	45.7	49.0	45.4	46.8	64.9	66.8
Zimbabwe	49.0	19.4	4.2	43.0	20.5	4.3	29.7	20.0	6.3	49.8	53.3	49.8	51.8	68.2	72.2
ASIA	39.9	19.0	6.6	30.8	17.6	8.6	23.3	15.5	14.0	55.8	56.8	64.9	67.7	71.3	75.2
Afghanistan	43.8	17.3	4.2	40.4	17.3	4.6	34.3	20.4	6.6	38.0	38.0	45.0	46.0	55.0	56.0
Armenia	34.3	21.6	8.3	27.3	17.0	12.9	21.7	13.9	18.6	69.3	75.3	70.3	76.3	73.4	79.4
Azerbaijan	40.0	20.2	7.9	29.2	17.9	10.8	22.0	13.6	16.4	63.4	71.0	68.0	75.5	72.4	78.9
Bahrain	43.0	23.8	3.6	31.4	15.5	4.8	21.7	14.4	18.3	61.7	65.4	71.1	75.3	75.5	79.9
Bangladesh	45.9	18.4	5.7	37.1	21.1	5.1	24.1	18.1	9.3	45.6	44.1	58.1	58.2	68.4	70.1
Bhutan	39.9	18.8	5.3	40.9	18.8	5.7	34.5	19.3	6.9	40.0	41.5	51.6	54.9	63.9	67.4
Brunei Darussalam	40.1	19.5	5.6	30.8	19.3	6.4	22.5	14.0	16.5	66.9	69.9	73.3	77.3	76.7	81.2
Cambodia	41.6	19.7	4.7	43.6	17.8	4.2	33.1	18.8	6.8	39.0	41.7	52.6	55.4	64.9	67.9
China	39.5	19.1	6.9	25.3	15.4	9.9	20.4	12.8	18.0	62.5	63.9	68.2	71.7	72.6	76.7
Cyprus	25.9	20.4	13.9	24.8	15.0	14.5	20.6	12.9	22.4	70.0	72.9	75.6	80.0	78.0	82.6
Dem. People's Rep. of Korea	45.1	19.5	5.0	29.6	14.7	7.6	21.6	13.6	15.6	59.2	64.0	68.7	75.2	72.6	79.4
East Timor	42.0	19.1	4.5	38.9	18.8	4.4	26.8	17.3	9.1	39.2	40.7	46.6	48.4	59.1	60.9
Georgia	28.4	17.7	12.4	22.5	15.1	18.3	20.3	13.5	21.7	65.0	72.9	69.5	77.6	73.1	80.0
Hong Kong	30.4	21.9	8.8	16.5	14.2	15.8	12.4	8.7	34.0	68.5	75.6	76.2	82.3	78.3	84.5

TABLE 2 (continued)

Demographic Indicators: Age Structure and Life Expectancy, 1975–2025

	Percentage of Population in Specific Age Groups									Life Expectancy at Birth (years)					
	1975			2000			2025			1970-1975		1995-2000		2020-2025	
	0-14	15-24	>60	0-14	15-24	>60	0-14	15-24	>60	Male	Female	Male	Female	Male	Female
ASIA (continued)															
India	39.8	18.8	6.2	33.5	18.8	7.6	23.0	16.5	12.4	51.2	49.3	62.6	62.9	70.5	73.3
Indonesia	42.0	19.1	5.3	30.8	19.8	7.4	23.0	15.0	12.7	48.0	50.5	63.3	67.0	70.7	75.2
Iran (Islamic Republic of)	45.4	20.0	5.1	41.7	20.8	6.0	27.9	19.1	8.5	56.2	55.5	69.0	70.3	74.9	78.2
Iraq	46.6	19.2	4.1	42.5	19.6	4.8	32.1	19.5	7.4	56.1	57.9	66.5	69.5	72.4	76.1
Israel	32.8	19.0	11.8	27.8	17.1	12.7	21.5	14.5	18.0	70.1	73.3	75.4	79.2	77.9	82.1
Japan	24.3	15.4	11.7	15.3	12.7	22.4	13.9	10.6	31.8	70.6	76.2	76.8	82.9	78.8	84.9
Jordan	47.2	18.0	4.3	43.3	19.6	4.6	33.0	19.8	6.6	54.9	58.3	67.7	71.8	73.1	77.7
Kazakhstan	34.6	20.5	8.5	27.6	17.8	11.6	21.9	14.3	17.3	59.1	69.4	66.5	75.0	71.6	78.4
Kuwait	44.4	17.6	2.6	34.1	21.0	3.5	23.6	15.7	14.8	65.3	69.3	74.1	78.2	77.2	81.6
Kyrgyzstan	39.9	19.6	8.5	35.3	18.8	9.0	23.9	16.3	12.5	58.8	67.3	66.5	73.8	71.6	78.0
Lao People's Dem. Republic	42.1	19.5	4.6	44.5	18.7	4.8	33.2	20.2	6.3	39.1	41.8	52.0	55.0	64.3	67.3
Lebanon	41.2	20.0	7.5	32.9	18.3	8.2	23.3	14.6	12.2	63.1	67.0	68.1	71.7	72.5	76.7
Malaysia	42.1	20.4	5.6	35.3	18.8	6.5	23.7	15.8	12.5	61.4	64.7	69.9	74.3	74.7	79.3
Maldives	41.8	20.0	6.9	45.1	20.0	5.1	33.3	20.5	6.3	52.7	50.1	65.7	63.3	73.1	74.1
Mongolia	43.7	19.1	4.7	34.9	20.9	6.0	24.0	17.2	10.8	52.5	55.0	64.4	67.3	71.0	75.0
Myanmar	40.7	19.3	6.2	36.8	18.7	6.7	26.4	17.9	9.8	48.3	51.4	58.5	61.8	69.3	73.6
Nepal	42.3	18.9	4.9	41.2	20.1	5.6	30.6	19.8	7.1	44.0	42.5	56.5	56.5	67.3	69.0
Oman	44.7	18.7	4.6	47.2	18.9	4.2	41.2	20.3	5.6	47.8	50.2	68.9	73.3	73.9	78.5
Pakistan	45.5	20.2	4.8	43.0	19.0	4.8	31.3	19.4	7.8	50.6	50.5	62.9	65.1	70.8	74.4
Philippines	43.6	21.3	4.3	36.3	20.0	5.8	24.8	17.5	11.0	56.4	59.4	66.6	70.2	72.4	76.6
Qatar	33.4	20.0	3.1	26.8	13.4	4.7	23.1	15.4	23.6	60.7	64.4	70.0	75.4	74.6	80.0
Republic of Korea	37.7	21.3	5.8	22.1	16.4	10.4	19.0	12.9	20.9	59.3	66.1	68.8	76.1	73.9	80.4
Saudi Arabia	44.3	18.8	4.8	41.0	19.2	4.6	35.6	19.2	8.5	52.4	55.5	69.9	73.4	75.6	79.6
Singapore	32.8	23.9	6.7	21.6	13.5	11.2	17.5	10.8	27.8	67.4	71.8	73.5	78.6	78.0	83.0
Sri Lanka	39.4	20.0	6.1	27.6	19.3	9.3	21.9	14.0	16.7	64.0	66.0	70.9	75.4	75.3	60.0
Syrian Arab Republic	48.5	19.2	5.3	45.8	20.5	4.2	33.4	20.6	5.9	55.4	58.7	66.7	71.2	72.3	77.1
Tajikistan	45.4	18.7	6.7	41.7	18.9	6.7	29.6	18.7	8.9	60.8	65.9	68.8	74.0	73.2	77.9
Thailand	44.9	20.2	4.7	26.5	18.5	8.5	21.2	14.4	16.3	57.7	61.6	65.1	71.6	72.4	78.1
Turkey	40.1	20.2	6.9	32.6	17.8	8.4	22.7	15.4	13.8	55.9	60.0	66.5	70.7	72.4	77.0
Turkmenistan	43.5	19.8	6.8	37.5	19.4	6.5	24.5	17.3	10.7	57.1	64.1	63.5	70.0	70.3	75.4
United Arab Emirates	28.2	20.4	3.4	29.7	15.0	5.0	23.6	15.5	21.6	60.6	67.4	67.5	73.2	71.9	77.6
Uzbekistan	43.3	19.8	7.8	37.7	19.5	7.0	24.8	17.4	10.9	60.7	64.4	73.9	76.5	78.0	81.4
Viet Nam	43.7	19.2	6.4	35.7	19.8	7.1	23.6	17.2	11.1	47.7	53.1	64.9	69.6	71.8	76.5
Yemen	50.9	15.4	4.4	46.9	19.5	3.7	38.4	20.4	4.5	41.9	42.4	51.9	52.4	61.9	62.4
EUROPE	**23.7**	**16.4**	**16.4**	**18.0**	**13.8**	**20.0**	**16.3**	**11.3**	**26.7**	**67.1**	**74.2**	**69.3**	**77.3**	**74.2**	**80.8**
Albania	39.9	19.9	6.9	29.9	17.6	9.1	21.7	14.5	16.1	66.0	69.5	70.0	75.8	73.8	78.9
Austria	23.2	14.5	20.4	17.5	12.0	20.2	15.9	10.5	29.5	67.0	74.3	73.9	80.1	77.9	83.6
Belarus	25.6	17.5	14.2	19.5	15.1	19.4	17.9	12.2	23.6	66.6	75.5	64.5	75.1	69.5	79.1
Belgium	22.2	15.6	19.1	17.7	12.0	21.4	16.9	11.0	29.6	68.2	74.7	74.1	80.6	78.0	83.7
Bosnia & Herzegovina	30.9	21.2	8.1	19.9	14.9	14.7	16.6	11.2	25.1	65.2	69.5	70.5	75.9	73.9	79.0
Bulgaria	22.0	15.1	16.1	17.0	14.4	21.2	15.3	11.2	25.4	68.7	73.9	67.8	74.9	72.2	78.8
Croatia	21.5	16.6	15.5	17.5	14.1	20.5	16.9	11.7	25.7	66.2	72.9	68.1	76.5	72.6	79.6
Czech Republic	22.3	15.3	18.3	19.5	15.1	16.4	19.1	12.7	21.5	66.6	73.5	67.8	74.9	72.4	79.0
Denmark	22.6	14.7	18.7	18.0	11.4	19.9	16.7	10.9	27.9	70.9	76.4	73.0	78.7	75.5	81.2
Estonia	21.8	15.4	17.1	18.6	14.7	19.4	17.2	12.0	24.1	65.7	74.6	63.8	74.8	70.3	78.8
Finland	22.0	17.4	15.5	18.6	12.7	19.5	18.4	12.0	28.1	66.6	75.0	72.7	80.2	76.1	82.6
France	23.9	16.1	18.3	18.9	13.1	20.3	17.4	11.3	27.7	68.6	76.3	73.8	81.3	76.9	83.6
Germany	21.5	14.5	20.4	15.3	11.3	22.8	13.1	9.2	31.6	67.9	73.8	73.5	79.8	76.6	82.5
Greece	23.9	14.8	17.4	15.0	13.6	24.0	13.3	9.9	31.1	70.6	74.2	75.5	80.6	77.9	83.1
Hungary	20.3	16.3	18.3	18.0	14.6	19.3	17.9	12.5	22.6	66.5	72.4	64.5	73.8	69.5	78.1
Iceland	30.1	19.3	12.7	23.9	14.9	14.8	19.9	13.3	22.8	71.4	77.4	76.3	81.3	78.6	83.6
Ireland	31.2	16.9	15.5	22.2	17.8	15.1	19.5	13.8	22.0	68.9	73.8	73.4	78.9	76.5	81.9
Italy	24.2	14.2	17.4	14.5	11.8	23.5	12.0	9.2	33.4	69.2	75.2	75.1	81.4	78.5	84.3
Latvia	21.1	15.0	17.8	18.8	14.0	20.2	17.9	12.1	23.9	65.3	74.5	63.3	74.9	69.8	78.0
Lithuania	25.5	15.8	15.1	20.6	14.4	18.4	19.9	13.0	22.4	67.0	75.4	64.9	76.0	69.8	79.1
Luxembourg	21.6	14.6	18.6	16.9	12.1	19.7	16.4	11.4	28.8	67.2	74.4	72.8	80.2	76.1	83.7
Malta	24.7	17.8	13.1	20.8	14.9	16.4	19.3	12.7	25.0	68.5	72.8	74.6	79.1	77.4	81.9
Netherlands	25.3	16.8	15.1	18.4	11.6	18.2	15.7	10.4	30.0	71.1	77.0	75.1	80.9	77.6	83.2
Norway	23.8	15.2	19.1	20.3	11.9	19.1	18.7	12.4	25.5	71.4	77.6	74.1	80.6	75.9	82.0
Poland	24.0	20.1	13.8	20.5	16.9	16.1	19.7	13.4	21.7	67.0	67.0	66.7	75.7	71.7	79.1
Portugal	27.9	16.8	14.3	17.7	14.4	20.2	15.7	11.1	26.7	64.9	71.3	72.1	78.9	75.5	82.0
Republic of Moldova	28.9	19.6	10.8	24.2	17.1	14.0	21.5	14.5	18.3	61.6	68.5	63.5	71.6	69.5	76.4
Romania	25.2	16.8	14.3	18.7	15.7	18.6	16.0	11.6	22.3	66.8	71.3	66.6	73.3	71.6	77.6
Russian Federation	23.3	18.7	13.6	18.5	15.3	18.9	16.6	11.7	24.8	63.1	73.5	61.5	73.6	69.5	77.7
Slovakia	26.2	18.9	13.8	21.5	16.6	14.9	20.0	13.6	20.3	66.8	73.5	66.5	75.4	71.1	79.4
Slovenia	23.7	16.2	15.4	16.4	14.9	19.5	14.7	10.9	26.8	66.0	73.5	68.7	78.1	73.1	80.6
Spain	27.6	15.7	14.4	15.0	14.2	21.3	12.2	9.7	30.6	70.2	75.7	75.3	81.0	77.8	83.3
Sweden	20.7	13.4	21.0	20.0	11.3	21.5	18.5	11.9	27.3	72.1	77.5	76.1	81.9	79.2	84.6
Switzerland	22.4	14.6	17.5	18.0	11.2	19.3	16.3	10.7	30.5	70.8	77.0	75.4	81.7	77.8	83.8
TFYR Macedonia	30.7	19.6	9.2	22.1	16.3	13.9	19.6	13.1	21.5	66.1	68.9	69.8	75.8	73.8	78.9

TABLE 2 (continued)

Demographic Indicators: Age Structure and Life Expectancy, 1975–2025

	Percentage of Population in Specific Age Groups									Life Expectancy at Birth (years)					
	1975			2000			2025			1970-1975		1995-2000		2020-2025	
	0-14	15-24	>60	0-14	15-24	>60	0-14	15-24	>60	Male	Female	Male	Female	Male	Female
EUROPE (continued)															
Ukraine	23.0	16.2	15.8	18.5	14.5	21.0	17.4	12.1	24.0	65.3	74.0	64.2	74.2	70.7	78.4
United Kingdom	23.3	14.3	19.6	19.5	12.4	20.1	18.2	11.5	26.1	69.0	75.2	74.5	79.4	77.2	82.2
Yugoslavia	24.6	17.2	12.9	20.7	15.0	18.4	19.6	13.3	22.0	66.8	70.6	70.3	75.3	73.7	78.7
LATIN AMERICA	**41.1**	**19.7**	**6.4**	**31.9**	**19.0**	**8.1**	**23.6**	**15.6**	**14.2**	**58.8**	**63.5**	**67.1**	**72.4**	**72.4**	**77.7**
Argentina	29.2	17.2	11.4	27.4	18.0	13.5	22.1	15.1	16.9	64.1	70.8	69.6	76.8	74.0	81.1
Bahamas	41.2	18.9	5.9	26.7	18.0	8.4	21.0	13.8	18.4	63.2	69.9	69.9	78.7	74.7	81.8
Barbados	31.5	21.0	13.6	22.5	15.3	14.1	19.3	12.3	22.4	66.9	72.0	73.6	78.7	76.7	81.7
Belize	47.1	21.3	6.8	40.5	21.2	5.9	25.3	17.8	9.1	66.9	68.3	73.4	76.1	76.8	80.5
Bolivia	43.0	19.1	5.5	39.6	19.5	6.2	29.2	18.6	8.9	44.6	49.0	59.8	63.2	69.5	73.5
Brazil	40.1	20.5	5.8	30.1	19.0	8.4	22.3	15.2	15.6	57.6	62.2	65.5	70.1	71.8	76.4
Chile	37.0	19.9	7.8	28.5	16.3	10.2	22.3	14.4	17.8	60.5	66.8	71.1	78.1	74.2	81.2
Colombia	43.1	21.1	5.5	30.4	19.6	7.0	22.7	15.2	14.7	59.9	63.4	67.4	73.3	72.0	77.2
Costa Rica	42.2	21.6	5.2	33.1	18.6	7.5	25.3	15.9	14.3	66.1	70.2	74.5	79.2	77.0	81.9
Cuba	37.3	16.4	9.9	22.6	13.1	13.5	18.6	11.6	23.4	69.4	72.7	74.2	78.0	76.8	81.2
Dominican Republic	45.3	20.1	4.7	33.0	19.0	6.8	23.3	15.3	14.2	58.1	61.8	68.9	73.1	74.1	79.1
Ecuador	43.8	19.7	6.1	33.8	20.3	6.9	23.7	16.1	12.6	57.4	60.5	67.3	72.5	71.6	77.1
El Salvador	45.9	19.9	4.6	38.9	21.5	6.5	27.7	18.1	8.8	56.6	61.1	65.8	70.8	71.2	76.7
Guadeloupe	42.0	18.4	8.7	25.8	15.7	11.4	20.6	13.7	19.0	64.7	70.9	72.1	78.9	75.8	81.8
Guatemala	45.7	19.6	4.4	42.9	20.3	5.5	32.6	19.5	7.4	52.6	55.5	64.7	69.8	69.6	75.1
Guyana	44.1	21.2	5.5	30.2	18.0	6.3	22.3	14.1	14.2	58.0	62.1	64.4	69.5	70.5	75.1
Haiti	41.1	19.0	7.0	39.9	19.3	5.9	35.6	19.0	7.0	47.1	50.0	56.7	60.2	63.8	68.4
Honduras	48.0	19.4	4.2	41.6	20.6	5.2	28.5	18.5	8.6	52.1	56.2	67.5	72.3	72.5	77.5
Jamaica	45.2	18.7	8.5	28.4	18.5	9.0	21.5	14.1	15.5	66.6	70.8	72.4	76.8	75.9	80.6
Martinique	40.3	19.4	9.3	23.5	14.6	14.4	19.9	12.8	21.6	66.3	72.0	73.8	80.1	76.7	82.6
Mexico	46.3	19.1	5.6	33.6	19.6	6.7	23.0	15.1	13.3	60.6	65.3	68.9	75.0	73.3	79.4
Netherlands Antilles	32.9	22.7	8.6	24.7	15.4	11.3	20.6	13.3	20.5	63.3	69.1	71.4	76.4	74.6	79.4
Nicaragua	48.0	20.2	4.0	43.6	21.1	4.8	30.6	19.2	7.6	53.7	56.8	66.6	70.3	71.9	76.1
Panama	42.9	19.3	6.5	31.3	18.4	8.1	22.1	14.7	15.4	65.0	68.0	71.8	76.4	74.9	79.9
Paraguay	44.3	22.0	5.3	38.5	18.9	5.7	28.1	17.5	10.9	63.7	67.6	69.4	73.1	74.4	78.3
Peru	43.2	19.4	5.6	32.8	20.3	7.0	23.9	16.3	12.7	53.9	57.3	65.5	69.4	71.8	75.8
Puerto Rico	33.6	21.1	9.2	24.1	16.8	14.2	20.6	13.8	20.1	69.0	76.2	72.1	79.8	74.9	81.5
Suriname	47.6	18.9	5.8	32.4	18.8	7.9	23.4	14.2	12.7	61.7	66.5	69.0	74.0	73.9	78.8
Trindad & Tobago	38.0	21.4	7.6	28.7	19.6	8.4	22.5	14.4	15.8	63.4	68.1	70.5	75.2	75.0	79.8
Uruguay	27.7	15.6	14.1	23.9	16.1	17.0	21.2	14.3	18.4	65.6	72.2	69.6	76.1	71.3	77.9
Venezuela	43.3	20.1	4.9	34.0	19.5	6.6	24.2	16.2	13.2	63.5	68.9	70.0	75.7	74.2	80.0
NORTHERN AMERICA	**25.3**	**19.0**	**14.6**	**21.7**	**13.3**	**16.3**	**19.6**	**12.6**	**24.4**	**67.7**	**75.4**	**73.5**	**80.2**	**76.9**	**82.7**
Canada	26.1	19.7	12.3	20.6	13.0	16.2	19.3	12.3	25.7	69.7	76.8	75.0	81.2	77.8	83.5
United States	25.2	18.9	14.9	21.8	13.4	16.3	19.7	12.6	24.2	67.5	75.3	73.4	80.1	76.8	82.6
OCEANIA	**31.0**	**18.0**	**11.1**	**25.5**	**15.2**	**13.1**	**22.2**	**14.2**	**18.9**	**64.0**	**69.4**	**71.3**	**76.4**	**75.6**	**80.7**
Australia	27.6	17.4	12.8	21.0	13.6	15.7	19.4	12.2	23.4	68.4	75.2	75.4	81.2	77.9	83.6
Fiji	39.9	22.5	4.5	31.0	21.4	7.2	22.8	15.7	13.9	63.6	66.7	70.6	74.9	75.0	79.4
French Polynesia	42.0	20.3	4.9	33.7	17.7	6.6	23.9	16.2	12.9	59.3	63.0	68.6	74.1	73.8	79.1
Guam	37.3	21.2	3.8	31.1	15.2	8.2	22.1	14.3	17.7	68.8	73.3	73.7	79.1	76.9	82.1
New Caledonia	38.7	20.1	6.6	29.5	18.0	8.6	22.3	14.4	15.5	61.5	66.5	70.9	75.9	75.2	80.2
New Zealand	30.0	18.0	12.7	23.4	13.9	15.1	19.9	12.9	22.6	68.7	74.8	73.4	79.4	76.7	82.3
Papua New Guinea	42.0	18.8	5.2	38.7	19.7	5.0	29.5	19.2	7.3	47.7	47.6	57.2	58.7	66.7	68.7
Samoa	50.1	21.5	4.2	44.1	24.5	3.4	25.8	19.0	5.1	57.0	60.0	67.5	71.1	73.1	77.3
Solomon Islands	47.7	17.5	4.9	42.9	20.5	4.7	33.4	19.8	6.9	60.2	63.9	69.6	73.9	74.3	78.8
Vanuatu	46.0	19.7	3.8	41.4	20.0	4.9	31.8	18.8	8.1	52.4	55.7	65.5	69.5	71.9	76.4

Source: United Nations, World Population Prospects: The 1994 Revision.

The Percentage of Population in Specific Age Groups (0–14, 15–24 and over 60 years) have been computed from the 1994 revision of *The Sex and Age Distribution of the World Populations*. **Life expectancy at birth**—the average number of years that a newborn infant is expected to live if prevailing pattern of mortality for all people at the time of his or her birth were to stay the same throughout his or her life time.

TABLE 3

Urbanization Trends, Size and Growth of Urban and Rural Population, 1975–2025

	Level of Urbanization (% of total population in urban settlements)			Urban Population (thousands)			Annual Growth Rate (%)		Rural Population (thousands)			Annual Growth Rate (%)	
	1975	2000	2025	1975	2000	2025	1975-2000	2000-2025	1975	2000	2025	1975-2000	2000-2025
WORLD TOTAL	37.73	47.52	61.07	1538346	2926444	5065334	2.57	2.19	2538638	3231608	3229007	0.97	-
More Developed Regions (*)	69.84	76.28	83.98	729285	904288	1040049	0.86	0.56	314901	281249	198357	-0.45	-1.40
Less Developed Regions (+)	26.68	40.67	57.05	809062	2022156	4025286	3.66	2.75	2223737	2950359	3030649	1.13	0.11
AFRICA	25.15	37.30	53.77	104123	310158	804239	4.37	3.81	309865	521438	691534	2.08	1.13
Algeria	40.33	59.65	74.05	6460	18586	33675	4.23	2.38	9558	12573	11800	1.10	-0.25
Angola	17.79	36.17	55.59	1087	4729	14799	5.88	4.56	5023	8345	11820	2.03	1.39
Benin	20.45	33.88	51.78	620	2123	6344	4.92	4.38	2413	4143	5908	2.16	1.42
Botswana	11.95	33.31	55.42	91	572	1651	7.35	4.24	668	1146	1328	2.16	0.59
Burkina Faso	6.35	37.46	66.39	394	4386	14376	9.64	4.75	5808	7322	7279	0.93	-0.02
Burundi	3.22	9.01	21.15	118	661	2853	6.89	5.85	3562	6678	10637	2.51	1.86
Cameroon	26.87	49.33	66.86	2022	7521	19504	5.25	3.81	5503	7724	9669	1.36	0.90
Cape Verde	21.42	62.59	78.94	60	280	581	6.16	2.92	218	168	155	-1.04	-0.32
Central African Republic	33.67	41.60	58.88	693	1552	3745	3.23	3.52	1364	2179	2615	1.87	0.73
Chad	15.57	22.84	38.51	627	1669	4970	3.92	4.36	3403	5638	7937	2.02	1.37
Comoros	21.24	34.08	53.43	67	265	879	5.50	4.80	249	513	767	2.89	1.61
Congo	34.85	63.27	76.58	504	1879	4347	5.26	3.35	943	1091	1329	0.58	0.79
Côte d'Ivoire	32.09	46.95	64.13	2168	7869	23611	5.16	4.40	4587	8892	13206	2.65	1.58
Djibouti	68.49	84.25	89.75	140	543	947	5.42	2.22	65	102	108	1.80	0.23
Egypt	43.45	46.36	62.20	16877	32054	60519	2.57	2.54	21964	37092	36782	2.10	-0.03
Equatorial Guinea	27.06	48.35	68.51	61	218	547	5.09	3.68	164	233	251	1.40	0.30
Eritrea	12.24	19.02	35.66	256	766	2511	4.38	4.75	1833	3259	4532	2.30	1.32
Ethiopia	9.50	14.92	29.89	3061	9516	37929	4.54	5.53	29159	54270	88957	2.48	1.98
Gabon	30.61	53.77	69.58	195	815	1877	5.72	3.34	442	701	820	1.84	0.63
Gambia	16.58	28.92	48.63	91	373	1022	5.64	4.03	457	918	1080	2.79	0.65
Ghana	30.06	39.17	57.74	2955	7901	21934	3.93	4.08	6876	12271	16053	2.32	1.07
Guinea	16.30	33.56	53.28	676	2604	8039	5.39	4.51	3473	5155	7049	1.58	1.25
Guinea-Bissau	15.95	25.16	44.59	100	300	882	4.39	4.31	527	892	1096	2.11	0.82
Kenya	12.92	31.76	51.48	1775	10347	32616	7.05	4.59	11966	22230	30744	2.48	1.30
Lesotho	10.80	27.05	47.28	128	633	1973	6.39	4.55	1059	1706	2199	1.91	1.02
Liberia	30.35	48.05	64.55	488	1713	4674	5.02	4.02	1121	1852	2567	2.01	1.31
Libyan Arab Jamahirya	60.95	88.35	92.75	1491	5643	11951	5.32	3.00	955	744	934	-1.00	0.91
Madagascar	16.09	30.76	50.49	1253	5308	17378	5.77	4.74	6534	11951	17041	2.42	1.42
Malawi	7.66	15.60	31.69	402	1894	7083	6.20	5.28	4842	10250	15265	3.00	1.59
Mali	16.21	30.42	49.96	1000	3821	12277	5.36	4.67	5169	8739	12298	2.10	1.37
Mauritania	20.30	58.98	73.25	278	1522	3255	6.80	3.04	1093	1058	1189	-0.13	0.47
Mauritius	43.44	41.67	57.82	388	491	856	0.94	2.22	505	687	625	1.23	-0.38
Morocco	37.68	50.94	66.22	6520	15096	26917	3.36	2.31	10785	14541	13733	1.20	-0.23
Mozambique	8.62	41.07	61.09	905	7800	21468	8.62	4.05	9593	11191	13671	0.62	0.80
Namibia	20.61	42.93	63.59	186	752	1939	5.59	3.79	715	1000	1110	1.34	0.42
Niger	10.63	19.24	36.45	507	2078	8160	5.64	5.47	4263	8727	14225	2.87	1.95
Nigeria	23.38	43.29	61.64	14676	55751	146948	5.34	3.88	48094	73034	91449	1.67	0.90
Reunion	49.13	71.18	81.91	237	496	738	2.95	1.59	246	201	163	-0.81	-0.84
Rwanda	4.00	6.74	14.98	175	610	2367	4.99	5.42	4209	8438	13430	2.78	1.86
Sao Tome & Principe	27.94	50.55	67.24	23	74	145	4.67	2.69	58	72	71	0.86	-0.06
Senegal	34.18	45.07	62.17	1643	4280	10505	3.83	3.59	3163	5215	6391	2.00	0.81
Seychelles	33.26	58.88	73.85	20	46	70	3.33	1.68	40	32	25	-0.89	-0.99
Sierra Leone	21.14	40.21	59.10	620	2038	5136	4.76	3.70	2311	3031	3554	1.08	0.64
Somalia	21.27	27.85	45.87	1164	3004	9760	3.79	4.71	4308	7783	11516	2.37	1.57
South Africa	47.97	53.12	68.60	12314	24550	48673	2.76	2.74	13355	21665	22278	1.94	0.11
St. Helena	19.98	30.65	50.39	1	2	4	2.77	2.77	4	4	4	-	-
Sudan	18.94	27.25	46.37	3033	8742	27075	4.23	4.52	12979	23337	31313	2.35	1.18
Swaziland	14.01	36.12	56.61	67	354	933	6.66	3.88	414	626	715	1.65	0.53
Togo	16.32	33.66	52.32	373	1622	4906	5.88	4.43	1912	3196	4471	2.06	1.34
Tunisia	49.85	59.89	73.62	2797	5806	9784	2.92	2.09	2814	3888	3506	1.29	-0.41
Uganda	8.34	14.23	28.76	933	3504	13810	5.29	5.49	10250	21114	34237	2.89	1.93
United Republic of Tanzania	10.08	28.20	48.25	1602	9608	30344	7.17	4.60	14298	24467	32550	2.15	1.14
Western Sahara	45.79	63.14	76.07	54	216	477	5.55	3.17	64	126	150	2.71	0.70
Zaire	29.50	31.03	49.82	6860	15865	52129	3.35	4.76	16391	35271	52509	3.07	1.59
Zambia	34.84	44.70	59.94	1686	4807	11467	4.19	3.48	3155	5947	7664	2.54	1.01
Zimbabwe	19.56	35.97	55.39	1202	4502	10874	5.28	3.53	4942	8012	8758	1.93	0.36
ASIA	24.62	37.68	54.81	592282	1407806	2718435	3.46	2.63	1813705	2328040	2241553	1.00	-0.15
Afghanistan	13.27	22.19	39.90	2040	5920	18059	4.26	4.46	13338	20753	27204	1.77	1.08
Armenia	62.97	70.27	80.09	1780	2680	3783	1.64	1.38	1046	1134	941	0.32	-0.75
Azerbaijan	51.50	57.65	71.18	2930	4594	7194	1.80	1.79	2759	3375	2912	0.81	-0.59
Bahrain	79.23	92.22	95.85	215	584	884	4.00	1.66	56	49	38	-0.53	-1.02
Bangladesh	9.28	21.28	39.99	7108	28603	78430	5.57	4.03	69474	105814	117699	1.68	0.43
Bhutan	3.45	7.80	19.03	39	144	597	5.23	5.69	1080	1699	2539	1.81	1.61
Brunei Darussalam	61.99	58.98	72.47	100	184	308	2.44	2.06	61	128	117	2.96	-0.36
Cambodia	10.30	24.14	43.52	731	2809	8567	5.38	4.46	6367	8828	11119	1.31	0.92
China	17.25	34.49	54.51	160047	443057	831880	4.07	2.52	767761	841539	694225	0.37	-0.77
Cyprus	43.38	56.91	71.15	264	442	660	2.06	1.60	345	335	267	-0.12	-0.91
Dem. People's Rep. of Korea	56.49	63.10	75.16	9356	16392	25094	2.24	1.70	7205	9587	8292	1.14	-0.58

TABLE 3 (*continued*)

Urbanization Trends, Size and Growth of Urban and Rural Population, 1975–2025

	Level of Urbanization (% of total population in urban settlements)			Urban Population (thousands)			Annual Growth Rate (%)		Rural Population (thousands)			Annual Growth Rate (%)	
	1975	2000	2025	1975	2000	2025	1975-2000	2000-2025	1975	2000	2025	1975-2000	2000-2025
ASIA (continued)													
East Timor	8.91	7.52	14.43	60	66	173	0.38	3.85	612	818	1027	1.16	0.91
Gaza Strip (Palestine)	87.00	94.90	96.61	339	830	1357	3.58	1.97	51	45	48	-0.50	0.26
Georgia	49.54	61.07	74.22	2432	3375	4544	1.31	1.19	2476	2152	1578	-0.56	-1.24
Hong Kong	89.70	95.71	97.33	3943	5712	5778	1.48	0.05	453	256	158	-2.28	-1.93
India	21.31	28.56	45.24	132272	291901	629757	3.17	3.08	488429	730121	762329	1.61	0.17
Indonesia	19.36	40.34	60.74	26259	85819	167393	4.74	2.67	109408	126911	108205	0.59	-0.64
Iran (Islamic Republic of)	45.82	61.86	74.86	15278	46171	92491	4.42	2.78	18066	28472	31059	1.82	0.35
Iraq	61.39	77.08	85.42	6765	18308	36435	3.98	2.75	4254	5445	6221	0.99	0.53
Israel	86.64	90.92	93.60	2994	5512	7308	2.44	1.13	461	550	499	0.71	-0.39
Japan	75.69	78.39	84.86	84409	99145	103190	0.64	0.16	27115	27327	18404	0.03	-1.58
Jordan	55.31	74.48	83.95	1438	4772	10107	4.80	3.00	1162	1635	1932	1.37	0.67
Kazakhstan	52.16	62.05	74.75	7374	10980	16257	1.59	1.57	6762	6714	5491	-0.03	-0.80
Kuwait	83.81	97.65	98.56	844	1776	2765	2.98	1.77	163	43	40	-5.33	-0.29
Kyrgyzstan	37.91	40.49	57.23	1250	2083	4079	2.04	2.69	2049	3060	3048	1.60	-0.02
Lao People's Dem. Republic	11.38	25.12	44.55	344	1407	4316	5.63	4.48	2680	4195	5372	1.79	0.99
Lebanon	66.83	89.50	93.88	1849	2943	4154	1.86	1.38	918	345	271	-3.91	-0.97
Macau	97.70	98.92	99.28	229	454	542	2.74	0.71	5	5	4	-	-0.89
Malaysia	37.65	57.49	72.65	4616	12820	22942	4.09	2.33	7642	9478	8635	0.86	-0.37
Maldives	18.05	28.38	45.84	25	84	256	4.85	4.46	113	213	303	2.54	1.41
Mongolia	48.66	63.87	76.46	704	1699	2926	3.52	2.17	743	961	901	1.03	-0.26
Myanmar	23.92	28.41	47.32	7282	14640	35759	2.79	3.57	23159	36899	39805	1.86	0.30
Nepal	4.99	16.70	34.30	649	4148	13959	7.42	4.85	12357	20693	26733	2.06	1.02
Oman	6.28	15.67	32.54	53	412	1983	8.20	6.29	794	2215	4111	4.10	2.47
Pakistan	26.40	37.85	56.73	19733	61257	161579	4.53	3.88	55002	100570	123248	2.41	0.81
Philippines	35.56	59.01	74.26	15294	44005	77622	4.23	2.27	27715	30571	26900	0.39	-0.51
Qatar	82.94	92.56	95.38	142	560	762	5.49	1.23	29	45	37	1.76	-0.78
Republic of Korea	48.04	86.22	93.70	16947	40651	50987	3.50	0.91	18334	6498	3431	-4.15	-2.55
Saudi Arabia	58.70	81.80	88.20	4257	17388	37618	5.63	3.09	2995	3869	5033	1.02	1.05
Singapore	100.00	100.00	100.00	2263	2967	3355	1.08	0.49	-	-	-	..	..
Sri Lanka	22.04	24.21	42.59	2998	4722	10660	1.82	3.26	10605	14781	14371	1.33	-0.11
Syrian Arab Republic	45.06	54.87	69.57	3352	9508	23311	4.17	3.59	4086	7821	10194	2.60	1.06
Tajikistan	35.54	33.12	49.87	1223	2309	5881	2.54	3.74	2219	4663	5911	2.97	0.95
Thailand	15.10	21.90	39.08	6244	13555	28756	3.10	3.01	35115	48354	44827	1.28	-0.30
Turkey	41.60	74.84	86.99	16651	50701	79102	4.45	1.78	23375	17047	11835	-1.26	-1.46
Turkmenistan	47.56	45.78	61.15	1198	2084	4067	2.21	2.67	1322	2468	2584	2.50	0.18
United Arab Emirates	65.40	86.23	91.29	330	1817	2700	6.82	1.58	175	290	258	2.02	-0.47
Uzbekistan	39.09	42.80	59.19	5465	10865	22300	2.75	2.88	8516	14518	15378	2.13	0.23
Viet Nam	18.78	22.26	39.05	9021	18399	46135	2.85	3.68	39009	64249	72016	2.00	0.46
Yemen	16.40	38.42	58.42	1147	6550	19674	6.97	4.40	5844	10501	14002	2.34	1.15
EUROPE	**67.07**	**75.14**	**83.22**	**453668**	**548409**	**597660**	**0.76**	**0.34**	**222721**	**181395**	**120543**	**-0.82**	**-1.63**
Albania	32.77	39.54	56.99	794	1433	2661	2.36	2.48	1630	2191	2008	1.18	-0.35
Andorra	69.43	62.51	73.25	17	51	112	4.39	3.15	8	30	41	5.29	1.25
Austria	53.23	56.35	68.40	4034	4591	5651	0.52	0.83	3545	3557	2611	0.01	-1.24
Belarus	50.33	74.71	84.43	4714	7522	8361	1.87	0.42	4653	2547	1542	-2.41	-2.01
Belgium	94.92	97.36	98.36	9298	9977	10236	0.28	0.10	498	271	170	-2.43	-1.87
Bosnia & Herzegovina	31.29	53.18	69.34	1172	2303	3102	2.70	1.19	2575	2027	1372	-0.96	-1.56
Bulgaria	57.53	73.42	83.03	5017	6297	6450	0.91	0.10	3705	2279	1318	-1.94	-2.19
Channel Islands	33.51	30.17	46.74	43	46	81	0.27	2.26	85	107	92	0.92	-0.60
Croatia	45.13	68.52	80.97	1924	3037	3428	1.83	0.48	2339	1395	806	-2.07	-2.19
Czech Republic	57.82	66.37	76.22	5780	6867	8096	0.69	0.66	4217	3479	2525	-0.77	-1.28
Denmark	81.82	85.80	90.10	4140	4468	4577	0.30	0.10	920	739	503	-0.88	-1.54
Estonia	67.59	74.58	83.07	968	1115	1181	0.57	0.23	464	380	241	-0.80	-1.82
Faeroe Islands	27.94	36.05	55.48	11	17	28	1.74	2.00	30	31	22	0.13	-1.37
Finland	58.26	65.12	76.37	2745	3387	4129	0.84	0.79	1966	1814	1278	-0.32	-1.40
France	73.02	73.45	81.73	38481	43355	50055	0.48	0.57	14218	15669	11191	0.39	-1.35
Germany	81.17	87.69	91.98	63866	71644	70310	0.46	-0.08	14814	10056	6132	-1.55	-1.98
Gibraltar	100.00	100.00	100.00	28	28	28	-	-	-	-	-	..	..
Greece	55.31	67.82	79.10	5003	7171	7806	1.44	0.34	4043	3402	2062	-0.69	-2.00
Holy See	100.00	100.00	100.00	1	1	1	-	-	-	-	-	..	..
Hungary	52.79	67.28	78.67	5560	6688	7393	0.74	0.40	4972	3252	2004	-1.70	-1.94
Iceland	86.64	92.41	95.09	189	261	321	1.29	0.83	29	21	17	-1.29	-0.85
Ireland	53.63	58.66	70.59	1704	2121	2740	0.88	1.02	1473	1495	1142	0.06	-1.08
Isle of Man	52.40	76.83	84.67	31	61	85	2.71	1.33	28	18	15	-1.77	-0.73
Italy	65.64	67.11	76.25	36394	38422	39895	0.22	0.15	19047	18833	12428	-0.05	-1.66
Latvia	65.42	74.58	83.23	1618	1843	1943	0.52	0.21	855	628	392	-1.23	-1.89
Liechtenstein	19.98	23.30	41.61	5	8	17	1.88	3.02	18	25	24	1.31	-0.16
Lithuania	55.67	74.95	84.20	1842	2767	3213	1.63	0.60	1466	925	603	-1.84	-1.71
Luxembourg	73.71	91.09	95.13	267	387	418	1.48	0.31	95	38	21	-3.67	-2.37
Malta	80.42	90.64	94.14	245	342	397	1.33	0.60	60	35	25	-2.16	-1.35
Monaco	100.00	100.00	100.00	25	34	43	1.23	0.94	-	-	-	..	..
Netherlands	88.40	89.48	92.80	12070	14258	15105	0.67	0.23	1584	1676	1172	0.23	-1.43
Norway	68.19	74.27	82.21	2732	3288	3880	0.74	0.66	1275	1139	839	-0.45	-1.22

TABLE 3 *(continued)*

Urbanization Trends, Size and Growth of Urban and Rural Population, 1975–2025

	Level of Urbanization (% of total population in urban settlements)			Urban Population (thousands)			Annual Growth Rate (%)		Rural Population (thousands)			Annual Growth Rate (%)	
	1975	2000	2025	1975	2000	2025	1975-2000	2000-2025	1975	2000	2025	1975-2000	2000-2025
EUROPE (continued)													
Poland	55.40	67.11	78.39	18850	26029	32565	1.29	0.90	15172	12757	8977	-0.69	-1.41
Portugal	27.66	38.13	55.49	2515	3740	5374	1.59	1.45	6578	6067	4311	-0.32	-1.37
Republic of Moldova	35.85	55.58	71.09	1376	2507	3647	2.40	1.50	2463	2003	1483	-0.83	-1.20
Romania	46.17	57.78	71.31	9809	13063	15499	1.15	0.68	11436	9545	6236	-0.72	-1.70
Russian Federation	66.43	77.93	85.68	89168	113433	118705	0.96	0.18	45064	32119	19843	-1.35	-1.93
San Marino	71.70	95.78	97.77	14	26	34	2.48	1.07	5	1	1	-6.44	-
Slovakia	46.26	61.24	74.01	2191	3348	4451	1.70	1.14	2545	2119	1563	-0.73	-1.22
Slovenia	42.38	67.39	79.21	738	1311	1445	2.30	0.39	1004	634	379	-1.84	-2.06
Spain	69.57	77.71	84.87	24765	30964	31886	0.89	0.12	10831	8884	5685	-0.79	-1.79
Sweden	82.73	83.39	88.02	6778	7482	8583	0.40	0.55	1415	1490	1168	0.21	-0.97
Switzerland	55.75	62.44	74.01	3534	4679	5762	1.12	0.83	2805	2815	2024	0.01	-1.32
TFYR Macedonia	50.57	62.13	74.47	847	1396	1914	2.00	1.26	828	851	656	0.11	-1.04
Ukraine	58.27	72.81	82.51	28564	37115	40195	1.05	0.32	20452	13859	8519	-1.56	-1.95
United Kingdom	88.74	90.00	93.33	49896	53121	57375	0.25	0.31	6330	5901	4102	-0.28	-1.45
Yugoslavia	42.98	59.90	73.88	3905	6407	8479	1.98	1.12	5181	4289	2999	-0.76	-1.43
LATIN AMERICA	**61.32**	**76.61**	**84.67**	**196172**	**401361**	**600952**	**2.86**	**1.61**	**123720**	**122514**	**108833**	**-0.04**	**-0.47**
Antigua & Barbuda	34.22	36.95	52.35	20	25	44	0.89	2.26	39	43	40	0.39	-0.29
Argentina	80.73	89.40	93.39	21029	32762	43083	1.77	1.10	5021	3886	3050	-1.02	-0.97
Bahamas	73.44	88.67	93.21	139	262	353	2.54	1.19	50	33	26	-1.66	-0.95
Barbados	38.60	50.39	66.50	95	135	206	1.41	1.69	151	133	104	-0.51	-0.98
Belize	50.17	46.87	59.75	67	115	231	2.16	2.79	67	130	155	2.65	0.70
Bolivia	41.51	65.23	78.97	1975	5432	10370	4.05	2.59	2783	2896	2761	0.16	-0.19
Brazil	61.15	81.21	88.94	66065	141979	204791	3.06	1.47	41966	32846	25459	-0.98	-1.02
Cayman Islands	100.00	100.00	100.00	14	36	57	3.78	1.84	-	-	-	..	..
Chile	78.39	84.65	89.43	8101	12962	17684	1.88	1.24	2234	2350	2091	0.20	-0.47
Colombia	60.71	75.21	84.14	14434	28447	41532	2.71	1.51	9342	9375	7827	0.01	-0.72
Costa Rica	41.34	52.69	68.53	814	2001	3843	3.60	2.61	1154	1797	1765	1.77	-0.07
Cuba	64.23	78.14	85.97	5977	8896	10882	1.59	0.81	3329	2489	1776	-1.16	-1.35
Dominican Republic	45.34	68.14	79.63	2289	5789	8890	3.71	1.72	2760	2706	2274	-0.08	-0.70
Ecuador	42.36	61.94	75.63	2926	7833	13456	3.94	2.16	3981	4813	4336	0.76	-0.42
El Salvador	40.41	46.78	61.79	1651	3006	6015	2.40	2.77	2435	3420	3719	1.36	0.34
Falkland Islands (Malvinas)	56.35	89.68	96.13	1	2	3	2.77	1.62	1	-	-	..	..
French Guiana	69.12	78.38	85.94	40	140	262	5.01	2.51	18	39	43	3.09	0.39
Guadeloupe	82.94	99.73	99.91	272	461	578	2.11	0.90	56	1	1	-16.10	-
Guatemala	36.71	44.14	61.79	2211	5394	13389	3.57	3.64	3812	6827	8279	2.33	0.77
Guyana	29.97	39.53	58.52	220	349	668	1.85	2.60	514	534	473	0.15	-0.49
Haiti	21.73	34.87	53.90	1069	2775	7076	3.82	3.74	3851	5184	6052	1.19	0.62
Honduras	32.11	47.33	64.47	969	3070	6870	4.61	3.22	2048	3416	3786	2.05	0.41
Jamaica	44.13	56.23	70.26	888	1430	2319	1.91	1.93	1125	1113	982	-0.04	-0.50
Martinique	71.20	94.96	97.28	234	377	457	1.91	0.77	95	20	13	-6.23	-1.72
Mexico	62.76	77.71	85.82	36948	79580	117222	3.07	1.55	21923	22830	19372	0.16	-0.66
Montserrat	11.10	15.78	32.61	1	2	4	2.77	2.77	10	9	8	-0.42	-0.47
Netherlands Antilles	67.90	71.04	80.95	113	147	201	1.05	1.25	53	60	47	0.50	-0.98
Nicaragua	50.30	65.87	77.89	1220	3405	7072	4.11	2.92	1205	1765	2007	1.53	0.51
Panama	48.68	55.30	69.55	839	1579	2620	2.53	2.03	884	1276	1147	1.47	-0.43
Paraguay	38.98	56.44	71.82	1045	3168	6476	4.44	2.86	1636	2445	2541	1.61	0.15
Peru	61.46	74.52	83.54	9319	19437	30653	2.94	1.82	5843	6646	6039	0.52	-0.38
Puerto Rico	62.77	75.50	84.07	1879	2888	3828	1.72	1.13	1114	937	725	-0.69	-1.03
Saint Kitts & Nevis	35.03	45.73	63.57	16	19	30	0.69	1.83	29	22	17	-1.11	-1.03
Saint Lucia	41.03	50.54	65.71	44	77	131	2.24	2.13	64	75	68	0.63	-0.39
St.Vincent & Grenadines	20.57	51.88	68.22	19	61	100	4.67	1.98	74	56	47	-1.11	-1.70
Suriname	44.79	54.10	69.82	163	242	418	1.58	2.19	201	205	181	0.08	-0.50
Trindad & Tobago	63.00	74.36	83.57	637	1026	1511	1.91	1.55	374	354	297	-0.22	-0.70
Turks & Caicos Islands	42.81	47.39	64.86	3	8	17	3.92	3.02	4	9	9	3.24	-
Uruguay	83.05	91.43	94.58	2349	2994	3491	0.97	0.61	479	281	200	-2.13	-1.36
US Virgin Islands	44.50	46.84	62.56	42	51	84	0.78	2.00	52	58	50	0.44	-0.59
Venezuela	77.83	94.45	97.17	9911	22828	33791	3.34	1.57	2824	1342	984	-2.98	-1.24
NORTHERN AMERICA	**73.85**	**77.44**	**84.78**	**176712**	**237178**	**313336**	**1.18**	**1.11**	**62577**	**69102**	**56230**	**0.40**	**-0.82**
Bermuda	100.00	100.00	100.00	53	65	73	0.82	0.46	-	-	-	..	..
Canada	75.61	77.16	83.67	17548	23942	32018	1.24	1.16	5661	7087	6248	0.90	-0.50
Greenland	74.39	81.35	87.89	37	49	59	1.12	0.74	13	11	8	-0.67	-1.27
St. Pierre & Miquelon	88.56	92.12	94.77	5	6	7	0.73	0.62	1	1	-	..	..
United States	73.65	77.46	84.91	159069	213116	281179	1.17	1.11	56903	62003	49973	0.34	-0.86
OCEANIA	**71.78**	**70.25**	**74.86**	**15389**	**21532**	**30712**	**1.34**	**1.42**	**6050**	**9119**	**10315**	**1.64**	**0.49**
American Samoa	42.93	52.12	66.84	13	33	69	3.73	2.95	17	30	34	2.27	0.50
Australia	85.92	84.69	88.59	11943	16279	21852	1.24	1.18	1957	2943	2814	1.63	-0.18
Cook Islands	54.04	63.13	75.70	10	13	21	1.05	1.92	9	8	7	-0.47	-0.53
Fiji	36.72	42.75	59.60	212	361	692	2.13	2.60	364	484	469	1.14	-0.13
French Polynesia	56.01	57.20	70.08	73	138	238	2.55	2.18	57	104	102	2.41	-0.08
Guam	32.45	39.29	55.80	31	64	122	2.90	2.58	64	100	97	1.79	-0.12

TABLE 3 *(continued)*

Urbanization Trends, Size and Growth of Urban and Rural Population, 1975–2025

	Level of Urbanization (% of total population in urban settlements)			Urban Population (thousands)			Annual Growth Rate (%)		Rural Population (thousands)			Annual Growth Rate (%)	
	1975	2000	2025	1975	2000	2025	1975-2000	2000-2025	1975	2000	2025	1975-2000	2000-2025
OCEANIA (continued)													
Kiribati	30.14	37.42	53.62	17	33	77	2.65	3.39	39	55	67	1.38	0.79
Marshall Islands	60.66	72.16	82.36	18	45	105	3.67	3.39	12	17	22	1.39	1.03
Micronesia, Fed. States of	24.63	30.44	49.48	18	44	140	3.58	4.63	54	100	143	2.46	1.43
Nauru	100.00	100.00	100.00	6	12	24	2.77	2.77	-	-	-	..	..
New Caledonia	52.87	64.50	76.55	70	126	195	2.35	1.75	63	69	60	0.36	-0.56
New Zealand	82.78	87.20	91.64	2552	3278	4011	1.00	0.81	531	481	366	-0.40	-1.09
Niue	23.31	29.42	42.53	1	1	1	-	-	3	1	1	-4.39	-
Northern Mariana Islands	53.00	55.17	68.99	8	28	49	5.01	2.24	7	23	22	4.76	-0.18
Pacific Islands (Palau)	61.46	72.39	81.71	7	14	28	2.77	2.77	4	5	6	0.89	0.73
Papua New Guinea	11.93	17.50	32.27	326	842	2431	3.80	4.24	2403	3968	5101	2.01	1.00
Samoa	20.97	21.64	35.63	32	41	109	0.99	3.91	121	147	198	0.78	1.19
Solomon Islands	9.08	19.96	38.28	17	89	323	6.62	5.16	173	355	521	2.88	1.53
Tokelau	-	-	-	-	-	-	..	..	2	2	2	-	-
Tonga	20.30	46.80	65.90	18	48	89	3.92	2.47	70	54	46	-1.04	-0.64
Tuvalu	25.22	51.60	70.08	2	5	10	3.67	2.77	5	5	4	-	-0.89
Vanuatu	15.72	20.73	37.15	16	40	124	3.67	4.53	86	152	210	2.28	1.29
Wallis & Futuna Islands	-	-	-	-	-	-	..	..	9	15	22	2.04	1.53

Source: United Nations, World Urbanization Prospects: The 1994 Revision.

Level of Urbanization refers to the percentage of population residing in places classified as urban. Urban and rural settlements are defined in the national context and vary among countries (the definitions of urban are generally national definitions incorporated in the latest census). **Urban** and **Rural Population** data refer to the mid year population of the world, region, country or area. **Annual Growth Rate**, calculated by UNCHS (Habitat), refers to the average annual percentage change of population during the indicated period.

TABLE 4

Urban Agglomerations: Population Size and Growth Rate, 1975–2015

		Estimates and Projections (thousands)									Annual Growth Rate (%)			
		1975	1980	1985	1990	1995	2000	2005	2010	2015	1975-1985	1985-1995	1995-2005	2005-2015
AFRICA														
Algeria	Algiers	1627	2003	2464	3033	3702	4434	5157	5792	6276	4.15	4.07	3.31	1.96
Angola	Luanda	669	925	1240	1642	2207	2871	3636	4527	5548	6.17	5.77	4.99	4.23
Cameroon	Douala	380	522	723	1001	1322	1687	2105	2557	3026	6.43	6.03	4.65	3.63
Cameroon	Yaounde	276	396	571	823	1121	1460	1837	2238	2651	7.27	6.75	4.94	3.67
Congo	Brazzaville	338	458	609	793	1009	1242	1492	1764	2081	5.89	5.05	3.91	3.33
Côte d'Ivoire	Abidjan	960	1260	1653	2168	2797	3544	4412	5425	6611	5.43	5.26	4.56	4.04
Egypt	Alexandria	2241	2522	2835	3188	3577	3998	4470	5001	5546	2.35	2.32	2.23	2.16
Egypt	Cairo	6079	6852	7691	8633	9656	10731	11901	13193	14494	2.35	2.28	2.09	1.97
Egypt	Shubra El-Khema	353	490	661	892	1162	1426	1665	1893	2120	6.27	5.64	3.60	2.42
Ethiopia	Addis Ababa	929	1182	1488	1808	2209	2737	3465	4477	5850	4.71	3.95	4.50	5.24
Ghana	Accra	851	1004	1184	1405	1687	2053	2519	3092	3726	3.30	3.54	4.01	3.91
Guinea	Conakry	373	555	825	1127	1508	1978	2529	3156	3873	7.94	6.03	5.17	4.26
Kenya	Nairobi	677	863	1128	1519	2079	2730	3484	4363	5361	5.11	6.11	5.16	4.31
Libyan Arab Jamahiriya	Benghazi	329	491	733	888	1059	1268	1498	1733	1980	8.01	3.68	3.47	2.79
Libyan Arab Jamahiriya	Tripoli	675	1144	1938	2595	3272	3979	4674	5348	6044	10.55	5.24	3.57	2.57
Morocco	Casablanca	1765	2062	2409	2815	3289	3745	4205	4664	5114	3.11	3.11	2.46	1.96
Morocco	Rabat	639	801	1004	1258	1578	1904	2219	2508	2773	4.52	4.52	3.41	2.23
Mozambique	Maputo	532	762	1091	1561	2227	3138	4088	4877	5760	7.18	7.14	6.07	3.43
Nigeria	Ibadan	847	975	1121	1290	1484	1736	2073	2496	2982	2.80	2.81	3.34	3.64
Nigeria	Lagos	3300	4385	5827	7742	10287	13455	17037	20751	24437	5.69	5.68	5.05	3.61
Senegal	Dakar	768	984	1260	1613	1986	2419	2912	3469	4080	4.95	4.55	3.83	3.37
Somalia	Mogadishu	271	385	548	779	982	1233	1550	1954	2463	7.04	5.83	4.56	4.63
South Africa	Cape Town	1339	1609	1934	2294	2671	3073	3520	4017	4508	3.68	3.23	2.76	2.47
South Africa	Durban	894	939	985	1049	1149	1296	1489	1714	1939	0.97	1.54	2.59	2.64
South Africa	East Rand	943	991	1041	1111	1217	1372	1576	1813	2050	0.99	1.56	2.59	2.63
South Africa	Johannesburg	1498	1554	1613	1702	1849	2074	2371	2716	3059	0.74	1.37	2.49	2.55
South Africa	Pretoria	643	730	830	942	1073	1229	1417	1632	1847	2.55	2.57	2.78	2.65
South Africa	West Rand	489	565	653	753	865	996	1152	1329	1507	2.89	2.81	2.87	2.69
Sudan	Khartoum	887	1166	1533	1944	2429	3021	3769	4713	5782	5.47	4.60	4.39	4.28
Tunisia	Tunis	868	1114	1430	1741	2037	2321	2589	2849	3092	4.99	3.54	2.40	1.78
Uganda	Kampala	399	472	597	754	954	1213	1553	2006	2610	4.03	4.69	4.87	5.19
United Republic of Tanzania	Dar es Salaam	638	837	1096	1436	1734	2082	2577	3224	3965	5.41	4.59	3.96	4.31
Zaire	Kinshasa	1735	2197	2782	3455	4214	5121	6314	7946	9855	4.72	4.15	4.04	4.45
Zambia	Lusaka	385	533	723	979	1327	1726	2144	2570	3031	6.30	6.07	4.80	3.46
Zimbabwe	Harare	529	615	715	854	1044	1281	1557	1859	2186	3.01	3.79	4.00	3.39
ASIA														
Afghanistan	Kabul	674	977	1237	1565	2034	2756	3548	4410	5384	6.07	4.97	5.56	4.17
Armenia	Erevan	911	1042	1123	1210	1305	1403	1498	1591	1685	2.09	1.50	1.38	1.18
Azerbaijan	Baku	1429	1574	1660	1751	1853	1970	2105	2273	2461	1.50	1.10	1.28	1.56
Bangladesh	Chittagong	1017	1340	1642	1989	2410	2914	3559	4352	5212	4.79	3.84	3.90	3.81
Bangladesh	Dacca	1925	3210	4410	5877	7832	10193	12952	15970	18964	8.29	5.74	5.03	3.81
Bangladesh	Khulna	472	627	741	860	998	1167	1403	1714	2067	4.51	2.98	3.41	3.87
China	Anshan	1082	1175	1281	1432	1648	1926	2222	2509	2788	1.69	2.52	2.99	2.27
China	Baotou	918	1024	1108	1231	1414	1651	1907	2157	2400	1.88	2.44	2.99	2.30
China	Beijing	8545	9029	9797	10872	12362	14206	16086	17818	19423	1.37	2.33	2.63	1.89
China	Benxi	713	769	831	925	1063	1244	1441	1634	1823	1.53	2.46	3.04	2.35
China	Changchun	1558	1698	1900	2169	2523	2954	3398	3821	4228	1.98	2.84	2.98	2.19
China	Changsha	942	1036	1164	1334	1559	1833	2119	2393	2660	2.12	2.92	3.07	2.27
China	Chengdu	2076	2348	2601	2942	3401	3963	4545	5097	5623	2.25	2.68	2.90	2.13
China	Chongqing	2439	2577	2784	3086	3525	4087	4681	5247	5788	1.32	2.36	2.84	2.12
China	Dalian	1396	1455	1916	2491	3132	3777	4363	4894	5402	3.17	4.91	3.31	2.14
China	Daqing	627	722	831	972	1151	1363	1581	1791	1997	2.82	3.26	3.17	2.34
China	Datong	877	941	1009	1114	1275	1488	1720	1947	2168	1.40	2.34	2.99	2.31
China	Fushun	1082	1160	1253	1391	1595	1860	2146	2424	2694	1.47	2.41	2.97	2.27
China	Fuxin	572	623	680	762	880	1034	1200	1363	1523	1.73	2.58	3.10	2.38
China	Fuzhou	1012	1095	1193	1333	1535	1794	2072	2341	2602	1.65	2.52	3.00	2.28
China	Guangzhou	3102	3135	3307	3595	4056	4676	5344	5983	6591	0.64	2.04	2.76	2.10

TABLE 4 *(continued)*

Urban Agglomerations: Population Size and Growth Rate, 1975–2015

		Estimates and Projections (thousands)								Annual Growth Rate (%)			
		1975	1980	1985	1990	1995	2000	2005	2010	2015	1975-1985	1985-1995	1995-2005	2005-2015
ASIA (continued)														
China	Guiyang	1140	1265	1385	1554	1792	2095	2415	2725	3025	1.95	2.58	2.98	2.25
China	Handan	765	879	987	1131	1323	1557	1802	2039	2270	2.55	2.93	3.09	2.31
China	Hangzhou	1097	1164	1251	1383	1581	1843	2126	2402	2670	1.31	2.34	2.96	2.28
China	Harbin	2288	2467	2640	2905	3303	3825	4382	4915	5425	1.43	2.24	2.83	2.14
China	Hefei	716	790	872	985	1143	1343	1556	1763	1965	1.97	2.71	3.08	2.33
China	Hohhot	617	704	793	911	1067	1259	1461	1656	1847	2.51	2.97	3.14	2.34
China	Jilin	952	1041	1150	1299	1506	1766	2040	2305	2563	1.89	2.70	3.03	2.28
China	Jinan	1236	1308	1776	2365	3019	3663	4237	4755	5250	3.62	5.31	3.39	2.14
China	Jinzhou	530	562	705	883	1090	1313	1529	1732	1932	2.85	4.36	3.38	2.34
China	Jixi	656	733	800	896	1034	1213	1406	1595	1779	1.98	2.57	3.07	2.35
China	Kaohsiung	978	1157	1296	1480	1726	2027	2340	2641	2932	2.82	2.87	3.04	2.26
China	Kunming	1223	1365	1497	1683	1942	2269	2615	2948	3270	2.02	2.60	2.98	2.24
China	Lanzhou	1175	1307	1395	1534	1747	2032	2342	2643	2935	1.72	2.25	2.93	2.26
China	Liuzhou	464	548	640	758	905	1077	1253	1422	1589	3.22	3.46	3.25	2.38
China	Luoyang	797	921	1043	1202	1411	1662	1923	2175	2420	2.69	3.02	3.10	2.30
China	Nanchang	896	1011	1176	1386	1646	1948	2253	2543	2825	2.72	3.36	3.14	2.26
China	Nanjing	1938	2076	2285	2571	2965	3454	3966	4453	4919	1.65	2.61	2.91	2.15
China	Nanning	672	821	1004	1231	1498	1791	2077	2347	2609	4.01	4.00	3.27	2.28
China	Qingdao	1106	1154	1246	1383	1585	1850	2134	2411	2679	1.19	2.41	2.97	2.27
China	Qiqihar	1090	1184	1284	1430	1642	1916	2211	2496	2774	1.64	2.46	2.98	2.27
China	Shanghai	11443	11739	12396	13452	15082	17213	19435	21489	23382	0.80	1.96	2.54	1.85
China	Shantou	642	699	760	850	981	1150	1333	1513	1689	1.69	2.55	3.07	2.37
China	Shenyang	3697	3913	4219	4664	5310	6134	6999	7816	8588	1.32	2.30	2.76	2.05
China	Shijiazhuang	940	1030	1156	1324	1547	1818	2102	2374	2639	2.07	2.91	3.07	2.28
China	Suzhou	619	657	710	790	908	1065	1235	1402	1567	1.37	2.46	3.08	2.38
China	Taipei	1835	2156	2484	2900	3417	4012	4608	5166	5700	3.03	3.19	2.99	2.13
China	Taiyuan	1519	1698	1893	2154	2502	2926	3366	3786	4189	2.20	2.79	2.97	2.19
China	Tangshan	1198	1344	1424	1557	1767	2053	2364	2668	2962	1.73	2.16	2.91	2.26
China	Tianjin	6160	7268	8133	9253	10687	12369	14040	15573	16998	2.78	2.73	2.73	1.91
China	Urumqi	717	884	1090	1345	1643	1966	2279	2572	2857	4.19	4.10	3.27	2.26
China	Wuhan	2926	3155	3440	3840	4399	5101	5833	6525	7182	1.62	2.46	2.82	2.08
China	Wuxi	730	788	851	946	1086	1271	1471	1668	1861	1.53	2.44	3.03	2.35
China	Xian	1939	2120	2418	2800	3283	3849	4420	4958	5472	2.21	3.06	2.97	2.14
China	Xuzhou	667	745	824	933	1084	1274	1477	1674	1867	2.11	2.74	3.09	2.34
China	Yichun	664	761	823	914	1051	1230	1425	1616	1803	2.15	2.45	3.04	2.35
China	Zhengzhou	1227	1368	1518	1722	1999	2340	2697	3040	3371	2.13	2.75	2.99	2.23
Dem. Republic of Korea	Pyongyang	1328	1796	2011	2230	2470	2725	2966	3182	3390	4.15	2.06	1.83	1.34
Georgia	Tbilisi	993	1091	1180	1277	1353	1424	1496	1575	1651	1.73	1.37	1.00	0.99
Hong Kong	Hong Kong	3943	4609	5070	5369	5574	5712	5789	5833	5849	2.51	0.95	0.38	0.10
India	Agra	681	739	831	940	1063	1196	1360	1564	1803	1.99	2.46	2.46	2.82
India	Ahmedabad	2050	2484	2849	3242	3688	4158	4713	5372	6124	3.29	2.58	2.45	2.62
India	Allahabad	568	640	733	843	968	1103	1265	1459	1685	2.55	2.78	2.68	2.87
India	Bangalore	2111	2812	3384	4009	4749	5527	6379	7311	8324	4.72	3.39	2.95	2.66
India	Bhopal	488	646	819	1032	1299	1591	1903	2228	2571	5.18	4.61	3.82	3.01
India	Bombay	6856	8067	9898	12223	15093	18121	21208	24273	27373	3.67	4.22	3.40	2.55
India	Calcutta	7888	9030	9882	10741	11673	12660	13960	15639	17621	2.25	1.67	1.79	2.33
India	Coimbatore	810	907	1008	1120	1244	1379	1553	1778	2046	2.19	2.10	2.22	2.76
India	Delhi	4426	5559	6756	8171	9882	11678	13561	15513	17553	4.23	3.80	3.16	2.58
India	Dhanbad	526	658	735	807	887	974	1094	1252	1445	3.35	1.88	2.10	2.78
India	Hyderabad	2086	2487	3186	4126	5343	6678	8037	9354	10663	4.24	5.17	4.08	2.83
India	Indore	663	808	939	1083	1250	1428	1639	1888	2175	3.48	2.86	2.71	2.83
India	Jabalpur	621	740	811	878	950	1032	1150	1313	1514	2.67	1.58	1.91	2.75
India	Jaipur	778	984	1207	1475	1801	2153	2533	2941	3382	4.39	4.00	3.41	2.89
India	Jamshedpur	538	653	737	822	918	1022	1157	1328	1533	3.15	2.20	2.31	2.81
India	Kanpur	1420	1612	1829	2076	2356	2654	3011	3443	3941	2.53	2.53	2.45	2.69
India	Kochi (Cochin)	532	666	855	1102	1420	1773	2143	2518	2905	4.74	5.07	4.12	3.04
India	Kozhikode	412	528	645	781	946	1124	1321	1540	1780	4.48	3.83	3.34	2.98
India	Lucknow	892	993	1245	1590	2029	2512	3017	3529	4057	3.33	4.88	3.97	2.96
India	Ludhiana	479	590	758	978	1263	1579	1912	2249	2598	4.59	5.11	4.15	3.07
India	Madras	3609	4203	4725	5283	5906	6561	7357	8329	9451	2.69	2.23	2.20	2.50
India	Madurai	790	893	984	1080	1186	1302	1459	1667	1919	2.20	1.87	2.07	2.74
India	Meerut	432	523	654	822	1032	1263	1511	1771	2048	4.15	4.56	3.81	3.04
India	Nagpur	1075	1273	1447	1635	1847	2073	2350	2689	3085	2.97	2.44	2.41	2.72
India	Patna	643	881	993	1086	1187	1299	1453	1659	1910	4.35	1.78	2.02	2.73
India	Pune (Poona)	1345	1642	1995	2422	2940	3493	4089	4725	5407	3.94	3.88	3.30	2.79
India	Srinagar	494	592	709	850	1018	1200	1403	1631	1884	3.61	3.62	3.21	2.95
India	Surat	642	877	1138	1467	1890	2357	2845	3335	3837	5.72	5.07	4.09	2.99
India	Thiruvananthapur	454	512	636	801	1009	1237	1482	1739	2011	3.37	4.62	3.84	3.05
India	Ulhasnagar	490	628	805	1031	1322	1643	1982	2328	2687	4.96	4.96	4.05	3.04
India	Vadodara	571	722	887	1086	1329	1591	1877	2185	2519	4.40	4.04	3.45	2.94
India	Varanasi	682	783	890	1009	1145	1292	1471	1691	1949	2.66	2.52	2.51	2.81
India	Vijayawada	419	527	658	821	1024	1246	1486	1740	2012	4.51	4.42	3.72	3.03
India	Visakhapatnam	452	583	768	1014	1338	1703	2083	2459	2840	5.30	5.55	4.43	3.10

TABLE 4 (continued)

Urban Agglomerations: Population Size and Growth Rate, 1975–2015

		Estimates and Projections (thousands)									Annual Growth Rate (%)			
		1975	1980	1985	1990	1995	2000	2005	2010	2015	1975-1985	1985-1995	1995-2005	2005-2015
ASIA (continued)														
Indonesia	Bandung	1493	1774	2108	2505	2977	3527	4130	4739	5292	3.45	3.45	3.27	2.48
Indonesia	Bogor	406	535	704	927	1221	1573	1944	2288	2583	5.50	5.51	4.65	2.84
Indonesia	Jakarta	4814	5985	7440	9250	11500	14091	16748	19172	21170	4.35	4.35	3.76	2.34
Indonesia	Medan	1031	1249	1513	1834	2222	2675	3167	3654	4094	3.84	3.84	3.54	2.57
Indonesia	Palembang	597	746	933	1167	1459	1803	2171	2529	2846	4.46	4.47	3.97	2.71
Indonesia	Semarang	660	809	992	1215	1489	1811	2160	2506	2818	4.07	4.06	3.72	2.66
Indonesia	Surabaja	1471	1719	2009	2347	2742	3205	3725	4263	4762	3.12	3.11	3.06	2.46
Indonesia	Tanjung Karang	228	348	530	808	1232	1785	2365	2860	3240	8.44	8.44	6.52	3.15
Indonesia	Ujung Pandang	502	629	789	988	1239	1534	1851	2159	2434	4.52	4.51	4.01	2.74
Iran (Islamic Republic of)	Esfahan	767	897	978	1317	1915	2628	3373	4047	4618	2.43	6.72	5.66	3.14
Iran (Islamic Republic of)	Mashhad	685	952	1339	1676	2011	2367	2773	3210	3644	6.70	4.07	3.21	2.73
Iran (Islamic Republic of)	Shiraz	418	576	814	945	1022	1109	1240	1416	1614	6.66	2.28	1.93	2.64
Iran (Islamic Republic of)	Tabriz	662	861	1111	1294	1450	1617	1837	2106	2393	5.18	2.66	2.37	2.64
Iran (Islamic Republic of)	Teheran	4274	5067	5807	6351	6830	7347	8116	9122	10211	3.07	1.62	1.73	2.30
Iraq	Baghdad	2747	3355	3683	4044	4478	5068	5794	6574	7324	2.93	1.95	2.58	2.34
Israel	Tel-Aviv	1206	1416	1621	1790	1921	2057	2189	2299	2385	2.96	1.70	1.31	0.86
Japan	Hiroshima	505	731	797	840	886	908	923	931	933	4.56	1.06	0.41	0.11
Japan	Kitakyushu	1853	2030	2217	2448	2704	2873	2973	3014	3022	1.79	1.99	0.95	0.16
Japan	Kyoto	1622	1701	1714	1709	1703	1703	1703	1703	1703	0.55	-0.06	-	-
Japan	Nagoya	2293	2590	2708	2939	3196	3353	3444	3480	3488	1.66	1.66	0.75	0.13
Japan	Osaka	9844	9990	10351	10482	10601	10601	10601	10601	10601	0.50	0.24	-	-
Japan	Sapporo	978	1174	1379	1533	1699	1811	1880	1908	1913	3.44	2.09	1.01	0.17
Japan	Sendai	635	701	722	759	799	818	832	839	841	1.28	1.01	0.40	0.11
Japan	Tokyo	19771	21854	23322	25013	26836	27856	28424	28654	28701	1.65	1.40	0.57	0.10
Jordan	Amman	500	640	782	955	1187	1458	1752	2047	2327	4.47	4.17	3.89	2.84
Kazakhstan	Alma-Ata	834	938	1043	1158	1262	1360	1458	1567	1680	2.24	1.91	1.44	1.42
Kuwait	Kuwait City	682	831	942	1090	1090	1198	1336	1465	1572	3.23	1.46	2.04	1.63
Malaysia	Kuala Lumpur	645	921	1016	1122	1238	1383	1552	1735	1912	4.54	1.98	2.26	2.09
Myanmar	Yangon	1760	2215	2788	3302	3851	4506	5325	6342	7407	4.60	3.23	3.24	3.30
Pakistan	Faisalabad	907	1079	1284	1545	1875	2300	2826	3442	4106	3.48	3.79	4.10	3.74
Pakistan	Gujranwala	439	628	898	1253	1663	2115	2620	3193	3812	7.16	6.16	4.55	3.75
Pakistan	Hyderabad	667	741	824	940	1107	1346	1657	2029	2433	2.11	2.95	4.03	3.84
Pakistan	Karachi	3983	5023	6336	7965	9863	12079	14644	17554	20616	4.64	4.43	3.95	3.42
Pakistan	Lahore	2399	2882	3462	4190	5085	6201	7551	9109	10767	3.67	3.84	3.95	3.55
Pakistan	Multan	599	715	854	1032	1257	1548	1909	2334	2796	3.55	3.87	4.18	3.82
Pakistan	Peshawar	347	535	823	1219	1676	2163	2686	3273	3907	8.64	7.11	4.72	3.75
Pakistan	Rawalpindi	670	779	906	1072	1290	1580	1946	2379	2849	3.02	3.53	4.11	3.81
Philippines	Davao	488	614	723	851	1010	1199	1400	1586	1738	3.93	3.34	3.27	2.16
Philippines	Metro Manila	5000	5955	6888	7968	9280	10801	12354	13707	14711	3.20	2.98	2.86	1.75
Republic of Korea	Inchon	788	1067	1365	1785	2340	2843	3224	3457	3549	5.49	5.39	3.20	0.96
Republic of Korea	Kwangchu	600	721	893	1127	1424	1682	1879	2009	2069	3.98	4.67	2.77	0.96
Republic of Korea	Pusan	2415	3120	3490	3778	4082	4244	4377	4511	4584	3.68	1.57	0.70	0.46
Republic of Korea	Seoul	6799	8283	9549	10558	11641	12278	12719	13048	13139	3.40	1.98	0.89	0.32
Republic of Korea	Taegu	1296	1589	1999	2215	2432	2564	2672	2773	2832	4.33	1.96	0.94	0.58
Republic of Korea	Taejon	501	644	850	1048	1285	1481	1632	1737	1790	5.29	4.13	2.39	0.92
Saudi Arabia	Jeddah	584	745	952	1216	1468	1757	2076	2417	2771	4.89	4.33	3.47	2.89
Saudi Arabia	Riyadh	705	993	1401	1975	2576	3225	3865	4491	5117	6.87	6.09	4.06	2.81
Singapore	Singapore	2263	2414	2558	2705	2848	2967	3061	3144	3221	1.23	1.07	0.72	0.51
Syrian Arab Republic	Aleppo	879	1071	1288	1543	1855	2241	2710	3249	3824	3.82	3.65	3.79	3.44
Syrian Arab Republic	Damascus	1122	1376	1585	1790	2052	2408	2877	3440	4047	3.45	2.58	3.38	3.41
Thailand	Bangkok	3842	4723	5276	5894	6566	7320	8210	9282	10557	3.17	2.19	2.23	2.51
Turkey	Adana	471	568	751	901	1074	1278	1474	1639	1759	4.67	3.58	3.17	1.77
Turkey	Ankara	1709	1891	2261	2533	2826	3180	3537	3857	4095	2.80	2.23	2.24	1.46
Turkey	Bursa	345	478	645	816	1030	1281	1519	1707	1835	6.26	4.68	3.88	1.89
Turkey	Istanbul	3601	4397	5408	6507	7817	9316	10682	11713	12345	4.07	3.68	3.12	1.45
Turkey	Izmir	1046	1216	1472	1731	2031	2381	2718	2999	3198	3.42	3.22	2.91	1.63
Uzbekistan	Tashkent	1612	1818	1958	2109	2288	2523	2839	3244	3705	1.94	1.56	2.16	2.66
Viet Nam	Hanoi	816	911	1009	1117	1247	1419	1657	1973	2363	2.12	2.12	2.84	3.55
Viet Nam	Ho Chi Minh	2353	2735	2975	3237	3555	3992	4608	5430	6439	2.35	1.78	2.59	3.35
EUROPE														
Austria	Vienna	2001	2038	2049	2055	2060	2073	2096	2129	2181	0.24	0.05	0.17	0.40
Belarus	Minsk	1120	1318	1474	1648	1766	1841	1885	1909	1912	2.75	1.81	0.65	0.14

TABLE 4 *(continued)*

Urban Agglomerations: Population Size and Growth Rate, 1975–2015

		Estimates and Projections (thousands)									Annual Growth Rate (%)			
		1975	1980	1985	1990	1995	2000	2005	2010	2015	1975-1985	1985-1995	1995-2005	2005-2015
EUROPE (continued)														
Belgium	Brussels	1128	1190	1175	1148	1122	1123	1123	1123	1123	0.41	-0.46	0.01	-
Bulgaria	Sofia	960	1065	1182	1313	1384	1414	1423	1425	1425	2.08	1.58	0.28	0.01
Czech Republic	Prague	1125	1179	1196	1210	1225	1238	1253	1272	1297	0.61	0.24	0.23	0.35
Denmark	Copenhagen	1381	1382	1364	1345	1326	1326	1326	1326	1326	-0.12	-0.28	-	-
Finland	Helsinki	568	640	722	872	1059	1167	1230	1277	1316	2.40	3.83	1.50	0.68
France	Lille	943	937	945	960	970	982	996	1013	1035	0.02	0.26	0.26	0.38
France	Lyon	1185	1174	1207	1266	1311	1345	1370	1391	1416	0.18	0.83	0.44	0.33
France	Marseille	1194	1237	1243	1230	1230	1237	1250	1268	1293	0.40	-0.11	0.16	0.34
France	Paris	8885	8938	9105	9334	9469	9551	9584	9591	9591	0.24	0.39	0.12	0.01
Germany	Aachen	951	956	960	1001	1041	1060	1067	1067	1067	0.09	0.81	0.25	-
Germany	Berlin	3227	3247	3268	3288	3317	3317	3317	3317	3317	0.13	0.15	-	-
Germany	Bielefeld	1127	1132	1137	1201	1263	1293	1304	1305	1305	0.09	1.05	0.32	0.01
Germany	Bremen	823	819	815	840	867	880	884	884	884	-0.10	0.62	0.19	-
Germany	Cologne	2633	2674	2714	2855	2984	3046	3068	3069	3069	0.30	0.95	0.28	-
Germany	Dusseldorf	2590	2466	2349	2700	3031	3228	3308	3320	3320	-0.98	2.55	0.87	0.04
Germany	Essen	6448	6331	6217	6353	6481	6518	6526	6526	6526	-0.36	0.42	0.07	-
Germany	Frankfurt	3215	3254	3293	3456	3606	3676	3700	3702	3702	0.24	0.91	0.26	0.01
Germany	Hamburg	2479	2465	2451	2540	2625	2660	2672	2672	2672	-0.11	0.69	0.18	-
Germany	Hanover	1210	1202	1194	1230	1267	1283	1287	1287	1287	-0.13	0.59	0.16	-
Germany	Karlsruhe	861	865	869	912	955	977	985	985	985	0.09	0.94	0.31	-
Germany	Mannheim	1422	1427	1432	1503	1571	1603	1615	1615	1615	0.07	0.93	0.28	-
Germany	Munich	1957	1990	2023	2134	2238	2288	2306	2308	2308	0.33	1.01	0.30	0.01
Germany	Nuremberg	1034	1041	1048	1106	1161	1189	1199	1200	1200	0.13	1.02	0.32	0.01
Germany	Saarland	908	889	872	878	888	891	891	891	891	-0.40	0.18	0.03	-
Germany	Stuttgart	2300	2326	2351	2485	2608	2669	2691	2692	2692	0.22	1.04	0.31	-
Greece	Athens	2738	2987	3260	3492	3693	3838	3908	3908	3908	1.74	1.25	0.57	-
Greece	Thessaloniki	617	694	780	859	928	981	1013	1025	1027	2.34	1.74	0.88	0.14
Hungary	Budapest	2005	2057	2037	2017	2017	2020	2027	2036	2039	0.16	-0.10	0.05	0.06
Ireland	Dublin	833	903	920	916	911	916	933	967	1011	0.99	-0.10	0.24	0.80
Italy	Florence	916	903	865	820	778	778	778	778	778	-0.57	-1.06	-	-
Italy	Genoa	1086	1053	1000	943	890	890	890	890	890	-0.83	-1.17	-	-
Italy	Milan	5529	5334	4984	4603	4251	4251	4251	4251	4251	-1.04	-1.59	-	-
Italy	Naples	3624	3594	3421	3210	3012	3012	3012	3012	3012	-0.58	-1.27	-	-
Italy	Rome	2998	3019	2999	2965	2931	2931	2931	2931	2931	-	-0.23	-	-
Italy	Turin	1641	1598	1502	1394	1294	1294	1294	1294	1294	-0.89	-1.49	-	-
Latvia	Riga	789	845	882	921	924	924	924	929	934	1.11	0.47	-	0.11
Netherlands	Amsterdam	989	957	995	1053	1109	1153	1177	1182	1182	0.06	1.08	0.60	0.04
Netherlands	Rotterdam	1032	1026	1035	1047	1064	1082	1096	1098	1098	0.03	0.28	0.30	0.02
Poland	Gdansk	766	826	855	884	914	947	982	1021	1058	1.10	0.67	0.72	0.75
Poland	Katowice	3019	3238	3342	3449	3552	3648	3742	3840	3930	1.02	0.61	0.52	0.49
Poland	Krakow	698	760	792	825	859	893	928	965	1001	1.26	0.81	0.77	0.76
Poland	Lodz	971	1009	1026	1042	1063	1090	1125	1167	1208	0.55	0.35	0.57	0.71
Poland	Warsaw	1907	2070	2151	2235	2316	2392	2465	2541	2610	1.20	0.74	0.62	0.57
Portugal	Lisbon	1168	1313	1475	1658	1863	1979	2098	2225	2357	2.33	2.34	1.19	1.16
Romania	Bucharest	1869	1963	2004	2047	2090	2121	2154	2196	2237	0.70	0.42	0.30	0.38
Russian Federation	Chelyabinsk	966	1046	1098	1153	1175	1181	1184	1185	1185	1.28	0.68	0.08	0.01
Russian Federation	Ekaterinburg	1135	1231	1303	1379	1413	1425	1429	1430	1430	1.38	0.81	0.11	0.01
Russian Federation	Kazan	942	1007	1056	1108	1128	1133	1136	1138	1138	1.14	0.66	0.07	0.02
Russian Federation	Krasnoyarsk	734	812	868	928	959	973	981	984	984	1.68	1.00	0.23	0.03
Russian Federation	Moscow	7623	8136	8580	9048	9233	9282	9302	9306	9306	1.18	0.73	0.07	-
Russian Federation	Nizhni Novgorod	1273	1357	1401	1447	1454	1454	1454	1454	1454	0.96	0.37	-	-
Russian Federation	Novosibirsk	1250	1329	1387	1449	1469	1471	1471	1472	1472	1.04	0.57	0.01	0.01
Russian Federation	Omsk	933	1032	1097	1166	1199	1212	1217	1219	1219	1.62	0.89	0.15	0.02
Russian Federation	Perm	937	1011	1054	1098	1112	1114	1116	1117	1117	1.18	0.54	0.04	0.01
Russian Federation	Rostov-On-Don	874	946	986	1029	1043	1046	1048	1050	1050	1.21	0.56	0.05	0.02
Russian Federation	Saint Petersburg	4326	4645	4844	5053	5111	5111	5111	5111	5111	1.13	0.54	-	-
Russian Federation	Samara	1146	1221	1241	1260	1260	1260	1260	1260	1260	0.80	0.15	-	-
Russian Federation	Saratov	816	863	887	911	913	913	915	917	918	0.83	0.29	0.02	0.03
Russian Federation	Ufa	887	985	1041	1100	1126	1135	1140	1142	1142	1.60	0.78	0.12	0.02
Russian Federation	Volgograd	884	939	973	1008	1017	1017	1018	1020	1020	0.96	0.44	0.01	0.02
Russian Federation	Voronezh	732	797	847	900	926	937	944	947	947	1.46	0.89	0.19	0.03
Spain	Barcelona	2873	3070	3010	2913	2819	2820	2820	2820	2820	0.47	-0.66	-	-
Spain	Madrid	3823	4296	4273	4172	4072	4072	4072	4072	4072	1.11	-0.48	-	-
Sweden	Stockholm	1224	1380	1436	1490	1545	1591	1624	1646	1667	1.60	0.73	0.50	0.26
Switzerland	Zurich	713	707	761	826	897	969	1031	1075	1108	0.65	1.64	1.39	0.72

TABLE 4 (continued)

Urban Agglomerations: Population Size and Growth Rate, 1975–2015

		Estimates and Projections (thousands)									Annual Growth Rate (%)			
		1975	1980	1985	1990	1995	2000	2005	2010	2015	1975-1985	1985-1995	1995-2005	2005-2015
EUROPE (continued)														
Ukraine	Dnepropetrovsk	981	1081	1136	1192	1230	1255	1272	1282	1285	1.47	0.80	0.34	0.10
Ukraine	Donetsk	963	1033	1076	1121	1149	1169	1184	1193	1196	1.11	0.66	0.30	0.10
Ukraine	Kharkov	1353	1466	1544	1626	1680	1714	1734	1742	1742	1.32	0.84	0.32	0.05
Ukraine	Kiev	1926	2201	2410	2638	2809	2912	2957	2966	2966	2.24	1.53	0.51	0.03
Ukraine	Lvov	620	683	741	804	852	885	905	916	921	1.78	1.40	0.60	0.18
Ukraine	Odessa	982	1054	1081	1109	1122	1133	1144	1153	1157	0.96	0.37	0.19	0.11
Ukraine	Zaporozhye	730	795	844	896	933	958	976	986	991	1.45	1.00	0.45	0.15
United Kingdom	Birmingham	2430	2365	2302	2302	2302	2302	2302	2302	2302	-0.54	-	-	-
United Kingdom	Leeds	1508	1482	1457	1457	1460	1465	1467	1467	1468	-0.34	0.02	0.05	0.01
United Kingdom	London	8169	7741	7335	7335	7335	7335	7335	7335	7335	-1.08	-	-	-
United Kingdom	Manchester	2425	2350	2277	2277	2277	2277	2277	2277	2277	-0.63	-	-	-
Yugoslavia	Belgrade	975	1073	1180	1278	1405	1453	1531	1605	1669	1.91	1.75	0.86	0.86
LATIN AMERICA														
Argentina	Buenos Aires	9134	9899	10269	10623	10990	11378	11772	12121	12376	1.17	0.68	0.69	0.50
Argentina	Cordoba	878	977	1073	1179	1294	1411	1518	1607	1676	2.01	1.87	1.60	0.99
Argentina	Mendoza	534	601	675	758	851	946	1031	1099	1151	2.34	2.32	1.92	1.10
Argentina	Rosario	878	952	1017	1084	1155	1231	1307	1377	1436	1.47	1.27	1.24	0.94
Bolivia	La Paz	610	727	870	1041	1246	1461	1688	1925	2159	3.55	3.59	3.04	2.46
Brazil	Belem	736	828	1023	1269	1574	1879	2146	2354	2498	3.29	4.31	3.10	1.52
Brazil	Belo Horizonte	1974	2443	2859	3339	3899	4429	4894	5272	5540	3.70	3.10	2.27	1.24
Brazil	Brasilia	785	1162	1346	1547	1778	1997	2199	2376	2514	5.39	2.78	2.13	1.34
Brazil	Campinas	671	925	1116	1339	1607	1869	2102	2291	2429	5.09	3.65	2.69	1.45
Brazil	Curitiba	1035	1315	1579	1894	2270	2637	2959	3216	3399	4.22	3.63	2.65	1.39
Brazil	Fortaleza	1241	1492	1809	2193	2660	3116	3513	3821	4034	3.77	3.86	2.78	1.38
Brazil	Goiania	517	710	808	913	1033	1146	1256	1358	1444	4.47	2.46	1.95	1.39
Brazil	Manaus	439	626	778	962	1189	1417	1619	1779	1893	5.72	4.24	3.09	1.56
Brazil	Porto Alegre	1837	2218	2548	2921	3349	3750	4111	4419	4648	3.27	2.73	2.05	1.23
Brazil	Recife	1949	2125	2425	2772	3168	3538	3874	4163	4381	2.19	2.67	2.01	1.23
Brazil	Rio de Janeiro	7875	8789	9156	9515	9888	10213	10626	11121	11554	1.51	0.77	0.72	0.84
Brazil	Salvador	1387	1685	2002	2375	2819	3246	3620	3920	4134	3.67	3.42	2.50	1.33
Brazil	Santos	771	901	985	1075	1173	1265	1362	1463	1551	2.45	1.75	1.49	1.30
Brazil	Sao Paulo	9890	12101	13427	14847	16417	17803	19030	20067	20783	3.06	2.01	1.48	0.88
Chile	Santiago	3247	3717	4157	4588	5065	5439	5758	6029	6255	2.47	1.98	1.28	0.83
Colombia	Barranquilla	730	816	912	1019	1138	1262	1383	1491	1582	2.23	2.21	1.95	1.34
Colombia	Bogota	3012	3531	4139	4851	5614	6323	6904	7345	7677	3.18	3.05	2.07	1.06
Colombia	Cali	1038	1187	1359	1555	1769	1981	2173	2334	2467	2.69	2.64	2.06	1.27
Colombia	Medellin	1201	1317	1445	1585	1743	1912	2081	2233	2361	1.85	1.87	1.77	1.26
Costa Rica	San Jose	522	590	665	760	879	1021	1178	1344	1512	2.42	2.79	2.93	2.50
Cuba	Havana	1827	1909	2011	2124	2241	2346	2431	2494	2546	0.96	1.08	0.81	0.46
Dominican Republic	Santiago de los	346	474	649	830	1007	1170	1308	1419	1521	6.29	4.39	2.62	1.51
Dominican Republic	Santo Domingo	1082	1398	1807	2199	2580	2944	3254	3500	3720	5.13	3.56	2.32	1.34
Ecuador	Guayaquil	867	1082	1296	1492	1717	1976	2257	2532	2776	4.02	2.81	2.73	2.07
Ecuador	Quito	630	796	954	1089	1244	1423	1622	1822	2003	4.15	2.65	2.65	2.11
Guatemala	Guatemala City	715	749	785	842	946	1113	1342	1620	1917	0.93	1.87	3.50	3.57
Haiti	Port-au-Prince	575	701	854	1041	1266	1536	1855	2225	2641	3.96	3.94	3.82	3.53
Mexico	Ciudad Juarez	490	546	664	807	952	1087	1210	1310	1390	3.04	3.60	2.40	1.39
Mexico	Guadalajara	1857	2275	2554	2867	3165	3456	3753	4009	4209	3.19	2.14	1.70	1.15
Mexico	Leon de los Alda	471	595	725	883	1043	1192	1326	1435	1521	4.31	3.64	2.40	1.37
Mexico	Mexico City	11236	13888	14474	15085	15643	16354	17293	18161	18786	2.53	0.78	1.00	0.83
Mexico	Monterrey	1574	2012	2260	2539	2806	3068	3335	3567	3749	3.62	2.16	1.73	1.17
Mexico	Naucalpan	528	727	1001	1378	1793	2166	2456	2655	2798	6.40	5.83	3.15	1.30
Mexico	Puebla de Zarago	566	775	908	1065	1220	1367	1508	1627	1723	4.73	2.95	2.12	1.33
Mexico	Tijuana	382	431	571	755	954	1134	1282	1393	1477	4.02	5.13	2.96	1.42
Nicaragua	Managua	493	634	793	964	1195	1449	1710	1978	2245	4.75	4.10	3.58	2.72
Panama	Panama City	486	546	671	826	948	1071	1196	1323	1451	3.23	3.46	2.32	1.93
Peru	Lima	3660	4431	5357	6475	7452	8381	9228	9946	10526	3.81	3.30	2.14	1.32
Puerto Rico	San Juan	879	1087	1089	1092	1101	1129	1178	1238	1292	2.14	0.11	0.68	0.92
Uruguay	Montevideo	1178	1213	1249	1287	1326	1364	1398	1427	1448	0.59	0.60	0.53	0.35
Venezuela	Caracas	2282	2435	2598	2773	2959	3174	3407	3646	3858	1.30	1.30	1.41	1.24
Venezuela	Maracaibo	825	964	1139	1350	1600	1869	2116	2320	2475	3.23	3.40	2.80	1.57
Venezuela	Maracay	614	669	730	796	868	949	1036	1124	1203	1.73	1.73	1.77	1.49
Venezuela	Valencia	507	658	824	1019	1260	1523	1761	1949	2087	4.86	4.25	3.35	1.70

TABLE 4 (*continued*)

Urban Agglomerations: Population Size and Growth Rate, 1975–2015

		Estimates and Projections (thousands)									Annual Growth Rate (%)			
		1975	1980	1985	1990	1995	2000	2005	2010	2015	1975-1985	1985-1995	1995-2005	2005-2015
NORTHERN AMERICA														
Canada	Edmonton	543	623	677	809	991	1119	1223	1302	1369	2.21	3.81	2.10	1.13
Canada	Montreal	2792	2824	2892	3085	3320	3372	3445	3548	3676	0.35	1.38	0.37	0.65
Canada	Ottawa	676	729	770	893	1057	1162	1249	1321	1386	1.30	3.17	1.67	1.04
Canada	Toronto	2770	3008	3233	3770	4483	4930	5273	5518	5716	1.55	3.27	1.62	0.81
Canada	Vancouver	1150	1247	1349	1556	1823	1984	2117	2225	2323	1.60	3.01	1.50	0.93
United States	Atlanta	1387	1625	1879	2174	2464	2700	2864	2983	3095	3.04	2.71	1.50	0.78
United States	Baltimore	1670	1759	1825	1893	1969	2050	2133	2219	2309	0.89	0.76	0.80	0.79
United States	Boston	2666	2681	2729	2778	2842	2927	3026	3136	3251	0.23	0.41	0.63	0.72
United States	Buffalo	1041	1001	977	953	964	989	1028	1075	1126	-0.63	-0.13	0.64	0.91
United States	Chicago	6749	6780	6786	6792	6846	6962	7126	7320	7528	0.05	0.09	0.40	0.55
United States	Cincinnati	1117	1126	1169	1215	1266	1322	1381	1442	1507	0.46	0.80	0.87	0.87
United States	Cleveland	1848	1751	1713	1676	1692	1732	1792	1865	1943	-0.76	-0.12	0.57	0.81
United States	Columbus	813	836	890	948	1008	1066	1121	1174	1229	0.90	1.25	1.06	0.92
United States	Dallas	2234	2468	2819	3220	3612	3926	4142	4298	4443	2.33	2.48	1.37	0.70
United States	Denver	1198	1356	1437	1522	1611	1696	1774	1851	1929	1.82	1.14	0.96	0.84
United States	Detroit	3885	3806	3750	3695	3725	3798	3906	4035	4173	-0.35	-0.07	0.47	0.66
United States	Fort Lauderdale	797	1014	1123	1245	1365	1470	1553	1624	1695	3.43	1.95	1.29	0.87
United States	Houston	2030	2424	2658	2915	3166	3378	3539	3672	3802	2.70	1.75	1.11	0.72
United States	Indianapolis	829	838	877	917	961	1008	1056	1106	1159	0.56	0.91	0.94	0.93
United States	Kansas City	1100	1102	1188	1280	1373	1459	1534	1603	1673	0.77	1.45	1.11	0.87
United States	Los Angeles	8926	9523	10445	11456	12410	13148	13631	13967	14274	1.57	1.72	0.94	0.46
United States	Louisville	751	761	758	755	763	785	817	856	899	0.09	0.07	0.68	0.96
United States	Memphis	720	776	801	827	857	894	936	981	1028	1.07	0.68	0.88	0.94
United States	Miami	1410	1615	1762	1923	2082	2220	2332	2428	2524	2.23	1.67	1.13	0.79
United States	Milwaukee	1228	1207	1217	1227	1247	1284	1334	1392	1455	-0.09	0.24	0.67	0.87
United States	Minneapolis	1748	1794	1935	2088	2239	2373	2486	2586	2686	1.02	1.46	1.05	0.77
United States	New Orleans	1021	1077	1058	1039	1050	1078	1119	1170	1225	0.36	-0.08	0.64	0.91
United States	New York	15880	15601	15827	16056	16329	16640	16962	17291	17636	-0.03	0.31	0.38	0.39
United States	Norfolk	720	781	1024	1341	1682	1961	2135	2241	2332	3.52	4.96	2.38	0.88
United States	Oklahoma City	628	677	730	787	846	901	951	998	1047	1.51	1.47	1.17	0.96
United States	Orlando	427	583	723	897	1077	1225	1325	1394	1457	5.27	3.99	2.07	0.95
United States	Philadelphia	4069	4116	4170	4225	4304	4413	4544	4689	4844	0.25	0.32	0.54	0.64
United States	Phoenix	1117	1422	1696	2024	2353	2618	2794	2915	3025	4.18	3.27	1.72	0.79
United States	Pittsburgh	1827	1807	1740	1676	1692	1732	1792	1865	1943	-0.49	-0.28	0.57	0.81
United States	Portland	925	1030	1100	1176	1253	1327	1393	1457	1522	1.73	1.30	1.06	0.89
United States	Providence/War	796	797	822	848	878	915	957	1003	1052	0.32	0.66	0.86	0.95
United States	Riverside-San Bernardino	645	714	920	1185	1467	1697	1844	1937	2018	3.55	4.67	2.29	0.90
United States	Sacramento	714	803	942	1106	1270	1407	1504	1577	1646	2.77	2.99	1.69	0.90
United States	Saint Louis	1865	1851	1899	1949	2009	2080	2160	2246	2336	0.18	0.56	0.72	0.78
United States	Salt Lake City	573	677	732	793	854	911	962	1010	1058	2.45	1.54	1.19	0.95
United States	San Antonio	859	949	1038	1134	1231	1317	1390	1454	1519	1.89	1.71	1.21	0.89
United States	San Diego	1442	1718	2017	2367	2716	2996	3184	3315	3436	3.36	2.98	1.59	0.76
United States	San Francisco	3093	3201	3414	3641	3866	4065	4230	4377	4524	0.99	1.24	0.90	0.67
United States	San Jose	1135	1248	1341	1440	1540	1633	1714	1789	1865	1.67	1.38	1.07	0.84
United States	Seattle	1316	1399	1567	1754	1939	2094	2211	2306	2398	1.75	2.13	1.31	0.81
United States	Tampa	1094	1362	1530	1719	1905	2061	2178	2272	2363	3.35	2.19	1.34	0.82
United States	Washington, D.C.	2626	2782	3189	3655	4111	4474	4717	4890	5049	1.94	2.54	1.38	0.68
United States	West Palm Beach	379	493	630	805	990	1143	1244	1311	1371	5.08	4.52	2.28	0.97
OCEANIA														
Australia	Adelaide	882	940	993	1019	1039	1065	1102	1148	1203	1.19	0.45	0.59	0.88
Australia	Brisbane	928	1047	1170	1303	1450	1594	1716	1813	1898	2.32	2.15	1.68	1.01
Australia	Melbourne	2561	2731	2897	3003	3094	3193	3300	3417	3545	1.23	0.66	0.64	0.72
Australia	Perth	770	896	1023	1123	1220	1316	1402	1476	1547	2.84	1.76	1.39	0.98
Australia	Sydney	2960	3195	3425	3524	3590	3671	3771	3891	4031	1.46	0.47	0.49	0.67
New Zealand	Auckland	729	776	816	877	945	1014	1075	1120	1154	1.13	1.47	1.29	0.71

Source: United Nations, World Urbanization Prospect: The 1994 Revision.

This table contains revised estimates and projections for all urban agglomerations that had at least 750,000 inhabitants in 1990. These estimates and projections are in continuous process of revision, and the figures here may differ from some published in the other United Nations publications.

Urban Agglomeration refers to the contours of contiguous territory without regards to administrative boundaries. It comprises the city or town proper and also suburban fringe lying outside of, but adjacent to, the city boundaries. **Annual Growth Rate**, calculated by UNCHS (Habitat), refers to the average annual percentage change of population during the indicated period.

TABLE 5

Area, Population Density and Land Ratio, 1975–1992

	Area (000 ha)		Density (population per 1000 ha)		Land Ratio by Type of Use (ha per capita)							
					Arable Land and Land under Permanent Crops		Permanent Meadows and Pastures		Forests and Woodland		Other Land	
	Total Area	Land Area										
	1992	1992	1975	1992	1975	1992	1975	1992	1975	1992	1975	1992
WORLD TOTAL	13422362	...	311	421	0.34	0.27	0.81	0.67	1.02	0.71	1.03	0.81
More Developed Regions (*)	5146150	...	220	245	0.60	0.54	1.08	0.93	1.71	1.45	1.54	1.54
Less Developed Regions (+)	8276212	...	366	529	0.25	0.19	0.71	0.59	0.77	0.50	0.85	0.60
AFRICA	3029291	2963666	140	226	0.41	0.27	2.16	1.34	1.75	1.01	2.84	1.80
Algeria	238174	238174	67	110	0.47	0.30	2.26	1.18	0.26	0.15	11.88	7.49
Angola	124670	124670	49	79	0.56	0.35	4.75	2.93	8.87	5.25	6.23	4.07
Benin	11262	11062	274	446	0.58	0.38	0.15	0.09	1.39	0.69	1.53	1.08
Botswana	58173	56673	13	24	1.75	0.86	43.48	24.28	14.57	8.01	14.87	8.55
Burkina Faso	27400	27360	227	347	0.41	0.37	1.61	1.05	1.21	0.68	1.18	0.77
Burundi	2783	2568	1433	2277	0.34	0.23	0.23	0.16	0.02	0.01	0.11	0.04
Cameroon	47544	46540	162	262	0.85	0.58	1.10	0.68	3.48	2.00	0.75	0.56
Cape Verde	403	403	689	893	0.14	0.13	0.09	0.07	-	-	1.21	0.92
Central African Republic	62298	62298	33	49	0.92	0.66	1.46	0.97	17.47	11.63	10.44	6.99
Chad	128400	125920	32	46	0.74	0.56	11.17	7.70	3.45	2.15	15.89	11.14
Comoros	223	223	1416	2623	0.28	0.17	0.05	0.03	0.11	0.06	0.26	0.12
Congo	34200	34150	42	69	0.10	0.07	6.91	4.22	14.84	8.91	1.75	1.21
Côte d'Ivoire	32246	31800	212	404	0.43	0.29	1.92	1.01	1.65	0.55	0.70	0.62
Djibouti	2320	2318	88	236	-	-	0.98	0.37	0.03	0.01	10.30	3.87
Egypt	100145	99545	390	593	0.07	0.04	-	-	-	-	2.49	1.64
Equatorial Guinea	2805	2805	80	132	1.02	0.62	0.46	0.28	5.75	3.51	5.23	3.19
Ethiopia (former)	122190	110100	312	487	0.40	0.26	1.33	0.84	0.83	0.50	0.64	0.46
Gabon	26767	25767	25	47	0.58	0.38	7.53	3.87	31.38	16.36	0.94	0.62
Gambia	1130	1000	548	1002	0.28	0.18	0.16	0.09	0.45	0.14	0.94	0.58
Ghana	23854	22754	432	701	0.30	0.17	0.51	0.31	0.93	0.50	0.61	0.44
Guinea	24586	24572	169	249	0.17	0.12	1.48	0.90	3.73	2.36	0.55	0.63
Guinea-Bissau	3612	2812	223	358	0.45	0.34	1.72	1.07	1.71	1.06	0.60	0.32
Kenya	58037	56969	241	446	0.16	0.10	2.77	1.50	0.19	0.09	1.02	0.56
Lesotho	3035	3035	391	623	0.31	0.17	1.68	1.06	-	-	0.56	0.38
Liberia	9775	9675	166	284	0.23	0.14	3.54	2.07	1.33	0.62	0.91	0.69
Libyan Arab Jamahiriya	175954	175954	14	28	0.84	0.45	4.91	2.73	0.23	0.14	65.96	32.78
Madagascar	58704	58154	134	231	0.35	0.23	4.37	2.53	2.28	1.15	0.46	0.42
Malawi	11848	9408	557	1080	0.43	0.17	0.35	0.18	0.92	0.34	0.09	0.24
Mali	124019	122019	51	80	0.30	0.22	4.86	3.06	1.20	0.70	13.42	8.45
Mauritania	102552	102522	13	21	0.14	0.10	28.62	18.63	3.34	2.09	42.66	27.84
Mauritius [1]	204	203	4394	5315	0.12	0.10	0.01	0.01	0.07	0.05	0.02	0.03
Morocco	44655	44630	388	569	0.45	0.39	1.11	0.82	0.45	0.31	0.58	0.24
Mozambique	80159	78409	134	188	0.29	0.22	4.19	2.99	1.53	0.95	1.46	1.17
Namibia	82429	82329	11	17	0.73	0.47	42.20	26.70	20.62	12.65	27.88	18.04
Niger	126700	126670	38	65	0.45	0.44	2.23	1.06	0.61	0.23	23.27	13.60
Nigeria	92377	91077	689	1121	0.48	0.32	0.64	0.39	0.26	0.11	0.07	0.07
Reunion	251	250	1932	2496	0.10	0.08	0.02	0.02	0.20	0.14	0.20	0.16
Rwanda	2634	2467	1777	2985	0.21	0.16	0.14	0.06	0.14	0.07	0.08	0.04
Sao Tome & Principe	96	96	843	1292	0.44	0.30	0.01	0.01	-	-	0.73	0.47
Senegal	19672	19253	250	400	0.49	0.30	0.65	0.40	2.34	1.36	0.53	0.43
Seychelles	45	45	1311	1578	0.08	0.10	-	-	0.08	0.07	0.29	0.46
Sierra Leone	7174	7162	409	586	0.19	0.13	0.75	0.53	0.73	0.49	0.77	0.57
Somalia	63766	62734	87	141	0.18	0.12	7.86	4.85	1.68	1.02	1.75	1.09
South Africa	122104	122104	210	318	0.52	0.34	3.18	2.10	0.16	0.12	0.89	0.59
St. Helena [2]	31	31	165	194	0.39	0.33	0.39	0.33	0.20	0.33	5.10	4.17
Sudan	250581	237600	67	109	0.76	0.50	6.12	4.24	3.08	1.71	4.88	2.71
Swaziland	1736	1720	280	458	0.35	0.24	2.37	1.36	0.22	0.15	0.63	0.43
Togo	5679	5439	420	692	0.27	0.18	0.78	0.48	0.77	0.39	0.56	0.41
Tunisia	16361	15536	361	541	0.87	0.58	0.59	0.48	0.09	0.08	1.22	0.71
Uganda	23588	19965	560	965	0.48	0.35	0.16	0.09	0.56	0.29	0.58	0.31
United Republic of Tanzania	94509	88359	180	308	0.21	0.13	2.20	1.29	2.69	1.50	0.48	0.34
Zaire	234486	226705	103	176	0.32	0.20	0.65	0.38	7.71	4.35	1.08	0.75
Zambia	75261	74339	65	117	1.03	0.61	6.20	3.46	6.18	3.31	1.95	1.20
Zimbabwe	39076	38685	159	271	0.41	0.27	0.79	0.46	3.31	1.81	1.78	1.14
ASIA	2757465	2678433	778	1066	0.19	0.15	0.29	0.32	0.24	0.17	0.42	0.29
Afghanistan	65209	65209	236	255	0.52	0.48	1.95	1.80	0.12	0.11	1.64	1.52
Armenia	2980	...	961	1170	..	0.16	..	0.19	..	0.08	..	0.44
Azerbaijan	8660	...	661	847	..	0.26	..	0.30	..	0.13	..	0.49
Bahrain	68	68	3999	7647	0.01	-	0.01	0.01	-	-	0.23	0.12
Bangladesh	14400	13017	5883	8659	0.12	0.08	0.01	0.01	0.03	0.02	0.01	0.01
Bhutan	4700	4700	238	337	0.10	0.08	0.23	0.17	2.23	1.62	1.63	1.10
Brunei Darussalam	577	527	305	510	0.07	0.03	0.04	0.02	2.41	0.76	0.76	1.15
Cambodia	18104	17652	402	532	0.43	0.26	0.08	0.21	1.88	1.23	0.09	0.18
China	959696	932641	995	1269	0.11	0.08	0.32	0.34	0.15	0.11	0.42	0.26
Cyprus	925	924	659	777	0.26	0.21	0.01	0.01	0.20	0.17	1.05	0.89
Dem. People's Rep. of Korea	12054	12041	1375	1878	0.11	0.09	-	-	0.54	0.40	0.07	0.04
East Timor	1487	1487	452	518	0.12	0.10	0.22	0.19	1.64	1.43	0.23	0.20

TABLE 5 (continued)

Area, Population Density and Land Ratio, 1975–1992

	Area (000 ha)		Density (population per 1000 ha)		Land Ratio by Type of Use (ha per capita)							
	Total Area	Land Area			Arable Land and Land under Permanent Crops		Permanent Meadows and Pastures		Forests and Woodland		Other Land	
	1992	1992	1975	1992	1975	1992	1975	1992	1975	1992	1975	1992
ASIA (continued)												
Gaza Strip (Palestine)	38	38	10263	18211	0.05	0.03	-	-	0.01	0.01	0.03	0.01
Georgia	6970	...	711	789	..	0.19	..	0.37	..	0.50	..	0.23
Hong Kong	104	99	44402	58354	-	-	-	-	-	-	0.02	0.01
India [3]	328759	297319	2088	2975	0.27	0.19	0.02	0.01	0.11	0.08	0.08	0.05
Indonesia	190457	181157	749	1042	0.15	0.12	0.09	0.06	0.90	0.58	0.20	0.20
Iran (Islamic Republic of)	164800	163600	204	382	0.49	0.29	1.32	0.70	0.54	0.29	2.55	1.33
Iraq	43832	43737	252	435	0.48	0.29	0.36	0.21	0.18	0.10	2.95	1.71
Israel	2106	2062	1676	2442	0.12	0.09	0.03	0.03	0.03	0.03	0.40	0.27
Japan	37780	37652	2962	3300	0.05	0.04	-	0.01	0.22	0.20	0.06	0.06
Jordan	8921	8893	292	526	0.13	0.09	0.30	0.17	0.02	0.01	2.97	1.63
Kazakhstan	271730	...	53	63	..	2.11	..	11.04	..	0.57	..	2.39
Kuwait	1782	1782	565	1088	-	-	0.13	0.07	-	-	1.63	0.85
Kyrgyzstan	19850	...	167	228	..	0.29	..	1.99	..	0.16	..	1.96
Lao People's Dem. Republic	23680	23080	131	194	0.28	0.18	0.26	0.18	4.70	2.80	2.39	2.01
Lebanon	1040	1023	2705	2637	0.12	0.11	-	-	0.03	0.03	0.21	0,23
Macau	2	2	117000	185000	-	-	-	-	-	-	0.01	0.01
Malaysia	32975	32855	373	572	0.38	0.26	-	-	1.83	1.03	0.46	0.46
Maldives	30	30	4577	7700	0.02	0.01	0.01	-	0.01	-	0.18	0.11
Mongolia	156650	156650	9	15	0.57	0.62	96.63	54.91	10.51	6.12	0.52	7.27
Myanmar	67658	65755	463	664	0.33	0.23	0.01	0.01	1.06	0.74	0.76	0.53
Nepal	14080	13680	951	1482	0.18	0.12	0.14	0.10	0.19	0.26	0.54	0.20
Oman	21246	21246	40	90	0.04	0.03	1.18	0.52	-	-	23.87	10.57
Pakistan [3]	79610	77088	969	1677	0.27	0.16	0.07	0.04	0.04	0.03	0.66	0.36
Philippines	30000	29817	1442	2127	0.17	0.14	0.02	0.02	0.31	0.16	0.19	0.15
Qatar	1100	1100	156	470	0.01	0.01	0.29	0.10	-	-	6.12	2.02
Republic of Korea	9902	9873	3573	4427	0.06	0.05	-	-	0.19	0.15	0.03	0.03
Saudi Arabia	214969	214969	34	78	0.23	0.22	11.72	7.13	0.22	0.11	17.47	5.32
Singapore	62	61	37092	45311	-	-	-	-	-	-	0.02	0.02
Sri Lanka	6561	6463	2105	2734	0.14	0.11	0.03	0.02	0.13	0.12	0.17	0.11
Syrian Arab Republic	18518	18378	405	720	0.74	0.45	1.16	0.61	0.06	0.05	0.52	0.28
Tajikistan	14310	14060	245	399	..	0.18	..	0.62	..	0.07	..	1.64
Thailand	51312	51089	810	1115	0.40	0.35	0.01	0.01	0.45	0.24	0.37	0.29
Turkey	77945	76963	520	759	0.69	0.47	0.26	0.21	0.50	0.35	0.47	0.29
Turkmenistan	48810	...	52	79	..	0.38	..	10.12	..	1.04	..	1.19
United Arab Emirates	8360	8360	60	212	0.03	0.02	0.40	0.11	-	-	16.13	4.59
Uzbekistan	44740	...	314	480	..	0.23	..	1.07	..	0.06	..	0.73
Viet Nam	33169	32549	1476	2143	0.13	0.10	0.01	-	0.28	0.14	0.26	0.23
Yemen	52797	52797	132	237	0.21	0.12	2.30	1.28	0.58	0.16	4.46	2.66
EUROPE	**487659**	**...**	**302**	**324**	**0.30**	**0.27**	**0.19**	**0.16**	**0.33**	**0.31**	**0.19**	**0.19**
Albania	2875	2740	885	1228	0.27	0.21	0.17	0.12	0.42	0.31	0.27	0.18
Andorra	45	45	556	1289	0.04	0.02	1.00	0.43	0.40	0.17	0.36	0.16
Austria	8385	8273	916	944	0.21	0.19	0.29	0.25	0.43	0.41	0.16	0.20
Belarus	20760	...	460	501	..	0.61	..	0.31	..	0.68	..	0.43
Belgium	[4] 3050	[4] 3023	3240	3312	...	0.08	...	0.06	...	0.06	...	0.10
Bosnia & Herzegovina	5113	5100	735	773	..	0.24	..	0.25	..	0.53	..	0.27
Bulgaria	11091	11055	789	807	0.50	0.49	0.18	0.20	0.44	0.43	0.15	0.12
Croatia	5654	5592	762	808	..	0.26	..	0.24	..	0.46	..	0.28
Czechoslovakia (former)	12787	12536	1175	1244	0.36	0.32	0.12	0.11	0.31	0.30	0.07	0.08
Denmark	4309	4243	1193	1215	0.53	0.49	0.05	0.04	0.09	0.09	0.16	0.20
Estonia	4510	...	324	354	..	0.67	..	0.21	..	1.24	..	0.76
Faeroe Islands	140	140	293	336	0.07	0.06	-	-	-	-	3.34	2.91
Finland	33813	30461	155	165	0.56	0.50	0.03	0.02	4.92	4.61	0.96	0.92
France	55150	55010	958	1041	0.36	0.34	0.25	0.19	0.28	0.26	0.15	0.17
Germany	35691	34927	2253	2301	0.16	0.15	0.08	0.07	0.13	0.13	0.08	0.09
Gibraltar	1	1	28000	28000	-	-	-	-	-	-	0.04	0.04
Greece	13199	12890	702	802	0.43	0.38	0.58	0.51	0.29	0.25	0.13	0.11
Hungary	9303	9234	1141	1111	0.52	0.48	0.12	0.11	0.15	0.17	0.09	0.14
Iceland	10300	10025	22	26	0.04	0.02	10.45	8.75	0.55	0.46	34.94	29.33
Ireland	7028	6889	461	510	0.39	0.26	1.41	1.34	0.09	0.09	0.28	0.27
Italy	30127	29406	1885	1942	0.22	0.21	0.09	0.09	0.11	0.12	0.10	0.10
Latvia	6450	6205	399	425	..	0.65	..	0.31	..	1.07	..	0.33
Liechtenstein	16	16	1438	1813	0.17	0.14	0.22	0.21	0.13	0.10	0.17	0.10
Lithuania	6520	...	518	582	..	0.82	..	0.12	..	0.53	..	0.28
Luxembourg	[4] 260	[4] 257	1410	1518	...	0.15	...	0.18	...	0.22	...	0.12
Malta	32	32	9507	11219	0.04	0.04	-	-	-	-	0.06	0.05
Netherlands	3733	3392	4025	4473	0.06	0.06	0.09	0.07	0.02	0.02	0.07	0.07
Norway	32390	30683	131	139	0.20	0.21	0.03	0.03	2.08	1.95	5.35	4.99
Poland	31268	30442	1118	1257	0.44	0.38	0.12	0.11	0.25	0.23	0.08	0.08
Portugal	9239	9195	989	1071	0.34	0.32	0.09	0.09	0.33	0.34	0.25	0.19
Republic of Moldova	3370	3297	1164	1333	..	0.50	..	0.08	..	0.10	..	0.07
Romania	23750	23034	922	1004	0.49	0.43	0.21	0.21	0.30	0.29	0.08	0.07

TABLE 5 (continued)

Area, Population Density and Land Ratio, 1975–1992

	Area (000 ha)		Density (population per 1000 ha)		Land Ratio by Type of Use (ha per capita)							
	Total Area	Land Area			Arable Land and Land under Permanent Crops		Permanent Meadows and Pastures		Forests and Woodland		Other Land	
	1992	1992	1975	1992	1975	1992	1975	1992	1975	1992	1975	1992
EUROPE (continued)												
Russian Federation	1707540	...	81	89	..	0.89	..	0.53	..	5.26	..	4.85
San Marino	6	6	3167	4000	0.05	0.04	-	-	-	-	0.26	0.21
Slovenia	2025	2012	866	960	..	0.16	..	0.29	..	0.53		0.07
Spain	50478	49944	713	790	0.59	0.51	0.31	0.26	0.42	0.40	0.09	0.10
Sweden	44996	41162	199	210	0.37	0.32	0.09	0.06	3.40	3.24	1.17	1.14
Switzerland	4129	3955	1603	1765	0.06	0.07	0.26	0.16	0.17	0.18	0.14	0.16
TFYR Macedonia	2571	2543	659	824	..	0.29	..	0.33	..	0.48		0.11
Ukraine	60370	57935	846	891	..	0.67	..	0.14	..	0.20		0.11
United Kingdom	24488	24160	2327	2391	0.12	0.11	0.21	0.19	0.04	0.04	0.06	0.07
Yugoslavia	10217	10200	891	1025	..	0.37	..	0.19	..	0.26		0.16
Yugoslavia (former)	..	..	151	..	0.39	..	0.31	..	0.44	..	0.10	..
LATIN AMERICA	**2053315**	**2017495**	**159**	**226**	**0.40**	**0.33**	**1.73**	**1.30**	**3.04**	**1.93**	**1.14**	**0.86**
Antigua & Barbuda	44	44	1341	1477	0.14	0.12	0.05	0.06	0.10	0.08	0.46	0.42
Argentina	276689	273669	95	122	1.03	0.81	5.52	4.25	2.32	1.77	1.64	1.36
Aruba	19	19	3263	3579	0.03	0.03	-	-	-	-	0.27	0.25
Bahamas	1388	1001	189	264	0.05	0.04	0.01	0.01	1.71	1.23	3.52	2.52
Barbados	43	43	5711	6023	0.13	0.06	0.02	0.01	-	-	0.02	0.10
Belize	2296	2280	59	87	0.36	0.29	0.28	0.24	7.57	5.09	8.85	5.84
Bolivia	109858	108438	44	64	0.40	0.35	5.72	3.84	11.94	8.05	4.74	3.49
Brazil	851197	845651	128	182	0.37	0.38	1.53	1.21	4.91	3.17	1.02	0.73
British Virgin Islands	15	15	733	1133	0.27	0.24	0.45	0.29	0.09	0.06	0.55	0.29
Cayman Islands	26	26	538	1077	-	-	0.14	0.07	0.43	0.21	1.29	0.64
Chile	75695	74880	138	182	0.40	0.31	1.18	1.00	0.84	0.65	4.83	3.55
Colombia	113891	103870	229	322	0.22	0.16	1.55	1.21	2.30	1.46	0.30	0.27
Costa Rica	5110	5106	385	625	0.25	0.17	0.83	0.73	1.12	0.51	0.40	0.19
Cuba	11086	10982	847	982	0.33	0.31	0.28	0.28	0.26	0.21	0.30	0.22
Dominica	75	75	960	947	0.24	0.24	0.03	0.03	0.43	0.44	0.35	0.35
Dominican Republic	4873	4838	1044	1530	0.25	0.20	0.41	0.28	0.13	0.08	0.17	0.09
Ecuador	28356	27684	250	388	0.37	0.28	0.41	0.46	2.21	0.96	1.02	0.88
El Salvador	2104	2072	1972	2604	0.16	0.14	0.15	0.11	0.04	0.02	0.16	0.12
Falkland Islands (Malvinas)	1217	1217	2	2	-	-	600.00	604.50	-	-	8.50	4.00
French Guiana	9000	8815	6	15	0.05	0.09	0.09	0.07	128.07	56.59	26.44	11.5`
Grenada	34	34	2706	2676	0.17	0.12	0.01	0.01	0.04	0.03	0.14	0.21
Guadeloupe	171	169	1944	2402	0.12	0.07	0.06	0.06	0.21	0.16	0.12	0.12
Guatemala	10889	10843	555	899	0.27	0.19	0.21	0.15	0.82	0.37	0.50	0.41
Guyana	21497	19685	37	41	0.52	0.61	1.36	1.52	24.79	20.26	0.16	1.97
Haiti	2775	2756	1785	2451	0.17	0.13	0.11	0.07	0.01	0.01	0.26	0.19
Honduras	11209	11189	270	463	0.54	0.36	0.76	0.50	1.48	0.60	0.92	0.71
Jamaica	1099	1083	1859	2211	0.13	0.09	0.11	0.11	0.10	0.08	0.20	0.18
Martinique	110	106	3099	3472	0.07	0.05	0.04	0.05	0.12	0.13	0.09	0.06
Mexico	195820	190869	308	462	0.40	0.28	1.27	0.84	0.87	0.46	0.70	0.57
Montserrat	10	10	1200	1100	0.08	0.18	0.08	0.09	0.33	0.36	0.33	0.27
Netherlands Antilles	80	80	2078	2413	0.05	0.04	-	-	-	-	0.43	0.37
Nicaragua	13000	11875	204	333	0.51	0.32	1.90	1.39	2.08	0.81	0.41	0.48
Panama	7552	7443	232	335	0.32	0.26	0.73	0.60	2.51	1.28	0.85	0.84
Paraguay	40675	39730	67	115	0.43	0.50	5.63	4.75	7.78	2.81	0.98	0.64
Peru	128522	128000	118	175	0.21	0.17	1.79	1.21	4.76	3.03	1.68	1.30
Puerto Rico	890	886	3378	4051	0.05	0.03	0.11	0.09	0.06	0.05	0.07	0.07
Saint Kitts & Nevis [5]	36	36	1416	1361	0.27	0.28	0.02	0.02	0.11	0.12	0.29	0.31
Saint Lucia	62	61	1770	2246	0.16	0.13	0.03	0.02	0.07	0.06	0.31	0.23
St. Vincent & Grenadines	39	39	2385	2795	0.10	0.10	0.01	0.02	0.15	0.13	0.16	0.11
Suriname	16327	15600	23	26	0.12	0.17	0.04	0.05	40.92	36.19	1.72	1.74
Trinidad & Tobago	513	513	1973	2466	0.11	0.10	0.01	0.01	0.23	0.17	0.15	0.13
Turks & Caicos Islands	43	43	140	302	0.17	0.08	-	-	-	-	7.00	3.23
Uruguay	17741	17481	162	179	0.51	0.42	4.82	4.32	0.22	0.21	0.64	0.64
US Virgin Islands	34	34	2794	3029	0.06	0.07	0.09	0.09	0.02	0.02	0.18	0.16
Venezuela	91205	88205	144	232	0.28	0.19	1.32	0.87	2.71	1.45	2.62	1.80
NORTHERN AMERICA	**2012756**	**1913606**	**125**	**148**	**0.97**	**0.82**	**1.11**	**0.94**	**2.63**	**2.28**	**3.10**	**2.70**
Bermuda	5	5	10600	12400	-	-	-	-	0.02	0.02	0.08	0.06
Canada	997614	922097	25	31	1.90	1.60	1.01	0.98	14.23	12.67	22.60	17.12
Greenland	[6] 34170	[6] 34170	1	2	-	-	4.70	4.12	0.20	0.18	678.50	595.18
St. Pierre & Miquelon	24	23	261	261	0.50	0.50	-	-	0.17	0.17	3.17	3.17
United States	980943	957311	226	267	0.87	0.74	1.12	0.94	1.39	1.12	0.85	0.96
OCEANIA	**853698**	**845349**	**25**	**32**	**2.05**	**1.93**	**21.39**	**15.74**	**8.81**	**5.77**	**7.18**	**7.56**
American Samoa	20	20	1500	2500	0.13	0.06	-	-	0.47	0.28	0.07	0.06
Australia	771336	764444	18	23	3.05	2.93	31.97	23.88	9.91	6.10	10.06	11.08
Cook Islands	23	23	826	826	0.32	0.26	-	-	-	-	0.89	0.95
Fiji	1827	1827	315	408	0.40	0.35	0.11	0.23	2.06	1.59	0.60	0.28
French Polynesia	400	366	355	563	0.21	0.13	0.15	0.10	0.89	0.56	1.57	0.99

TABLE 5 (continued)

Area, Population Density and Land Ratio, 1975–1992

	Area (000 ha)		Density (population per 1000 ha)		Land Ratio by Type of Use (ha per capita)							
					Arable Land and Land under Permanent Crops		Permanent Meadows and Pastures		Forests and Woodland		Other Land	
	Total Area	Land Area										
	1992	1992	1975	1992	1975	1992	1975	1992	1975	1992	1975	1992
OCEANIA (continued)												
Guam	55	55	1734	2545	0.13	0.09	0.08	0.06	0.10	0.07	0.26	0.18
Kiribati	73	73	753	1027	0.65	0.49	-	-	0.04	0.03	0.60	0.45
Nauru	2	2	3000	5000	-	-	-	-	-	-	0.33	0.20
New Caledonia	1858	1828	73	95	0.11	0.08	1.88	1.25	5.32	4.09	6.43	5.15
New Zealand	27099	26799	115	128	0.13	0.12	4.39	3.97	2.29	2.15	1.88	1.56
Niue	26	26	154	77	1.75	3.50	0.25	0.50	1.25	2.50	3.25	6.50
Pacific Islands (Palau) [7]	178	178	314	584	1.05	0.57	0.43	0.23	0.71	0.38	0.98	0.53
Papua New Guinea	46284	45286	60	89	0.13	0.10	0.04	0.02	14.11	9.51	2.32	1.64
Samoa	284	283	541	583	0.77	0.74	0.01	0.01	0.90	0.81	0.17	0.16
Solomon Islands	2890	2799	68	123	0.26	0.17	0.20	0.11	13.45	7.46	0.79	0.42
Tokelau	1	1	2000	2000	-	-	-	-	-	-	0.50	0.50
Tonga	75	72	1222	1347	0.52	0.49	0.05	0.04	0.09	0.08	0.16	0.12
Tuvalu	3	3	2000	3000	-	-	-	-	-	-	0.50	0.33
Vanuatu	1219	1219	84	129	0.99	0.92	0.24	0.16	8.96	5.82	1.75	0.87
Wallis & Futuna Islands	20	20	450	700	0.56	0.36	-	-	-	-	1.67	1.07
U.S.S.R. (FORMER)	..	..	114	...	0.91	..	1.46	..	3.63	..	2.75	..

Sources: Food and Agriculture Organization of the United Nations, FAO Production Yearbooks Vol. 45, Vol. 47. Organization for Economic Co-operation and Development, OECD Environmental Data Compendium 1993. United Nations, World Population Prospects: The 1994 Revision.

Total area refers to the total area of the country or region, including area under inland water bodies. **Land area** refers to total land area, excluding area under inland water bodies. The definition of inland water bodies generally includes major rivers and lakes.

Population Density (population per 1,000 hectares of land area) and **Land Ratio** (hectares of land per capita) have been calculated, by UNCHS (Habitat), by using the population figures and land data from the above sources.

Arable land refers to land under temporary crops (double-cropped areas are counted only once), temporary meadows for mowing or pasture, land under market and kitchen garden, and temporary fallow (less than five years). The abandoned land resulting from shifting cultivation is not included in this category. **Land under permanent crops** refers to land cultivated with crops that occupy the land for long periods and need not be planted after each harvest, such as cocoa, coffee, and rubber; it includes land under shrubs, fruit trees, nut trees and vines, but excludes land under trees grown for wood or timber. **Permanent Meadows and Pastures** refers to land used permanently (five years or more) for herbaceous forage crops, either cultivated or grown wild (wild prairie or grazed land). The dividing line between this category and the category 'Forests and woodland' is rather indefinite, especially in the case of shrubs, savannas, etc., which may have been reported either under one or the other of these two categories. **Forests and Woodland** refers to land under natural or planted stands of trees, whether productive or not, and includes land from which forests have been cleared but that will be reforested in the foreseeable future. **Other Land** includes uncultivated land, grassland not used for pasture, built-on areas, wetlands, wastelands, and roads.

Notes:
1. Excluding dependencies.
2. Including Ascension and Tristan da Cunha.
3. Data relating to Kashmir-Jammu are included in figures for India and excluded from those of Pakistan. Data for Sikkim are included with those of India.
4. Data refer to 1990.
5. Including Anguilla.
6. Data refer to area free from ice.
7. Including the Republic of the Marshall Islands, the Commonwealth of the Northern Mariana Islands, the Federated States of Micronesia and the Republic of Palau.

TABLE 6

Labour Force and Economic Development Indicators

	Labour Force				GNP per Capita (US$)			GDP Distribution 1991			Gross Domestic Investment (% of GDP)		
	Total (000) 1975	Women (%) 1975	Total (000) 1990	Women (%) 1990	1975	1990	1993	Agriculture	Industry	Services	1975	1990	1993
AFRICA													
Algeria	3455	7.1	5819	9.6	950	2380	1650	14.0	50.0	36.0	45.2	28.1	27.6
Angola	2957	41.0	4081	38.6	...	...	...	...	...	...	...	...	...
Benin	1592	48.4	2195	47.4	220	360	420	36.1	13.2	50.7	19.3	14.2	15.2
Botswana	278	40.7	446	34.9	390	2260	2590	5.5	58.5	36.0	46.0	34.1	38.3
Burkina Faso	3111	48.1	4167	46.2	120	270	300	44.0	20.0	37.0	26.0	19.1	22.1
Burundi	2137	49.5	2820	47.3	110	220	180	55.0	16.0	29.0	7.6	16.9	2.3
Cameroon	3345	36.5	4365	33.3	340	910	770	23.0	29.4	47.6	20.0	14.6	10.8
Cape Verde	97	25.6	141	29.1	240	690	870	...	...	...	21.3	31.0	0.0
Central African Republic	1123	48.6	1384	45.7	180	410	390	41.0	16.0	42.0	13.9	10.2	8.6
Chad	1496	22.7	1971	21.1	160	180	200	43.0	18.0	39.0	23.0	9.4	9.4
Comoros	155	42.6	231	40.4	190	480	520	...	...	...	...	20.2	15.4
Congo	582	40.0	781	38.8	550	1010	920	13.2	38.2	48.7	39.1	16.4	14.2
Côte d'Ivoire	3153	36.6	4599	34.2	580	740	630	38.0	22.0	40.0	22.4	9.3	9.3
Djibouti	...	...	...	...	...	...	780	...	...	...	...	...	...
Egypt	10037	7.8	14574	10.1	340	620	660	18.0	30.0	52.0	33.4	21.9	19.6
Equatorial Guinea	149	41.6	182	39.9	...	300	360	...	...	...	15.0	26.6	25.1
Eritrea	...	...	...	...	...	...	...	...	...	...	...	...	...
Ethiopia	15912	39.7	21225	37.4	80	120	100	...	...	...	10.4	12.3	16.0
Gabon	481	39.7	536	37.3	2890	3800	4050	9.0	49.1	41.9	62.7	24.4	21.6
Gambia	263	42.6	329	40.3	230	330	360	28.5	13.8	57.6	12.2	19.7	...
Ghana	3813	41.9	5686	39.7	300	400	430	51.1	16.9	32.0	12.7	14.4	14.8
Guinea	2393	41.8	3097	39.8	...	480	520	32.0	32.6	35.4	...	17.6	16.4
Guinea-Bissau	323	42.6	458	40.8	200	190	220	46.3	15.8	37.9	15.4	24.5	24.0
Kenya	5890	42.1	10011	39.9	250	380	270	27.0	22.0	51.0	18.1	24.3	16.1
Lesotho	597	46.9	808	43.4	250	600	660	14.0	38.0	48.0	18.7	73.7	75.7
Liberia	636	32.0	912	30.2	450	...	...	...	...	...	...	...	...
Libyan Arab Jamahirya	628	6.7	1076	9.1	5130	...	...	...	...	...	...	...	...
Madagascar	3668	41.5	5004	39.3	300	240	240	33.0	14.0	53.0	8.1	17.0	11.7
Malawi	2382	44.7	3495	41.2	130	200	220	35.0	20.0	45.0	33.7	19.1	12.9
Mali	2089	17.5	2959	16.2	130	200	300	42.1	14.2	43.7	16.5	22.4	21.9
Mauritania	472	20.8	679	22.2	330	500	510	22.0	31.0	47.0	34.5	20.0	24.8
Mauritius	280	21.8	440	26.5	780	2310	2980	11.0	33.0	56.0	26.3	30.4	29.4
Morocco	4656	16.5	7824	20.7	550	990	1030	16.8	32.8	50.4	25.2	25.1	24.6
Mozambique	5531	50.0	8437	47.4	...	80	80	64.0	15.0	21.0	...	38.1	41.5
Namibia	389	24.2	537	23.8	...	1500	1660	10.0	28.0	62.0	...	20.7	...
Niger	2590	48.6	3619	46.7	230	320	270	34.8	15.9	49.3	14.3	8.1	5.7
Nigeria	27385	36.9	41857	34.8	530	350	310	37.0	38.0	26.0	25.2	14.6	...
Reunion	152	26.7	238	34.0	...	...	...	...	...	...	...	...	...
Rwanda	2274	49.7	3520	47.7	100	330	200	40.2	18.7	41.2	13.7	13.6	...
Sao Tome & Principe	...	...	...	...	470	420	350	...	...	...	...	...	...
Senegal	2245	41.3	3192	39.3	380	710	730	20.3	18.6	61.1	17.8	12.9	14.1
Seychelles	...	...	...	...	870	5170	6370	...	...	...	...	24.3	23.0
Sierra Leone	1216	35.2	1438	32.7	240	240	140	...	...	...	15.7	14.0	9.2
Somalia	1516	40.9	2143	38.7	140	120	...	...	...	...	22.5	15.5	...
South Africa	8854	33.6	12434	35.6	1590	2450	2900	5.0	44.0	51.0	32.0	19.1	15.1
Sudan	5328	20.0	8078	21.9	270	400	...	...	...	...	17.5	13.6	...
Swaziland	219	41.7	306	38.8	640	1060	1050	...	...	...	17.8	20.1	20.2
Togo	998	38.8	1396	36.4	280	420	330	33.0	22.2	44.8	27.7	25.4	11.7
Tunisia	1608	16.0	2594	24.4	770	1450	1780	18.0	32.0	50.0	28.0	25.5	25.1
Uganda	5331	43.0	8129	41.1	...	180	190	51.0	12.0	37.0	...	14.1	14.5
United Republic of Tanzania	8226	50.2	12597	47.9	170	100	...	61.0	5.0	34.0	21.1	46.6	...
Zaire	9503	40.0	13084	35.5	450	...	...	...	...	...	17.8	...	...
Zambia	1665	27.5	2644	29.0	600	470	370	18.2	45.3	36.5	40.9	17.3	10.7
Zimbabwe	2575	37.2	3921	34.6	600	700	540	20.0	32.0	49.0	26.3	20.4	22.5
ASIA													
Afghanistan	4569	6.9	6229	8.6	...	...	...	...	...	...	...	...	...
Armenia	...	...	...	...	...	2160	660	...	...	...	...	33.5	14.4
Azerbaijan	...	...	3977	...	...	1360	730	33.0	35.0	31.0	...	27.8	...
Bahrain	81	9.2	220	10.4	...	6930	...	...	...	...	...	...	...
Bangladesh	22548	5.8	33398	7.3	150	210	220	36.8	15.8	47.4	6.1	12.8	13.3
Bhutan	525	34.3	696	32.1	...	200	...	43.0	27.0	29.0	...	33.0	...
Cambodia	3205	41.5	3758	38.3	...	...	...	48.9	12.4	38.6	...	...	...
China	481759	42.4	679900	43.2	...	420	490	28.4	38.8	32.8	...	...	...
Cyprus	275	34.1	326	35.6	...	8410	...	...	...	...	...	...	...
Dem. People's Rep. of Korea	6812	45.5	10470	45.8	...	...	...	...	...	...	...	...	...
Georgia	...	...	...	...	...	2450	560	...	...	...	...	22.1	...
Hong Kong	2034	...	3115	...	2400	12100	...	...	...	...	...	...	...
India	243481	28.5	322944	25.2	180	360	290	31.0	27.0	41.0	20.8	26.5	24.5
Indonesia	50526	30.8	71314	31.2	230	570	730	21.4	39.3	39.2	23.7	36.1	30.6
Iran (Islamic Republic of)	9493	14.3	15253	18.0	...	2510	...	21.0	21.0	58.0	24.5	28.6	...
Iraq	2890	12.6	5119	21.6	1270	2170	...	...	...	...	...	...	...
Israel	1279	31.8	1806	33.7	4230	11500	13760	...	...	...	...	...	...
Japan	55678	38.3	62202	37.9	4930	26090	31450	2.5	42.0	55.5	32.8	32.8	...

TABLE 6 *(continued)*

Labour Force and Economic Development Indicators

	Labour Force				GNP per Capita (US$)			GDP Distribution 1991			Gross Domestic Investment (% of GDP)		
	Total (000) 1975	Women (%) 1975	Total (000) 1990	Women (%) 1990	1975	1990	1993	Agriculture	Industry	Services	1975	1990	1993
ASIA (continued)													
Jordan	634	7.1	992	10.3	...	1250	1190	7.0	26.0	67.0	...	28.8	30.1
Kazakhstan	...	...	9262	...	...	2370	1540	...	...	...	...	42.6	...
Kuwait	318	12.2	835	14.6	10140	...	...	0.6	51.0	48.4	...	...	...
Kyrgyzstan	...	...	...	...	...	1330	830	33.7	38.3	28.0	...	29.7	...
Lao People's Dem. Republic	1760	46.3	2239	44.3	...	200	290	...	...	...	...	12.3	...
Lebanon	771	20.5	914	27.8	...	...	...	...	...	...	...	...	...
Malaysia	4451	33.0	7071	35.1	890	2390	3160	...	...	...	25.3	31.5	33.2
Maldives	...	...	...	...	...	720	820	...	...	...	...	...	...
Mongolia	668	45.2	1029	45.5	...	...	400	16.6	33.5	49.9	...	42.3	18.8
Myanmar	13559	39.3	18324	36.9	...	...	...	...	...	...	10.0	13.4	...
Nepal	5588	34.9	7725	33.6	120	180	160	59.0	14.0	27.0	14.5	19.4	19.8
Oman	206	7.1	405	8.5	1450	5780	5600	3.3	57.7	39.0	35.6	13.1	...
Pakistan	21950	9.8	33698	12.5	150	490	440	26.0	26.0	49.0	16.2	18.9	20.4
Philippines	15814	32.8	22474	31.2	370	740	830	22.1	34.9	43.0	30.9	24.0	24.3
Qatar	83	3.8	186	7.1	8590	14370	...	...	...	...	...	...	...
Republic of Korea	13054	33.3	18664	33.8	630	5750	7670	9.0	44.7	46.3	27.1	36.9	34.3
Saudi Arabia	2042	5.9	4081	7.3	3690	6750	...	6.7	52.4	40.9	13.2	17.2	...
Singapore	909	30.7	1298	32.1	3080	12550	...	0.3	37.4	62.3	...	...	...
Sri Lanka	4773	25.6	6367	26.7	310	470	600	27.0	25.0	48.0	15.6	21.9	25.3
Syrian Arab Republic	1850	13.2	3101	17.3	940	990	...	29.8	23.4	46.8	25.0	15.4	...
Tajikistan	...	...	2468	...	...	...	880	...	...	...	...	23.4	...
Thailand	20491	47.1	29534	44.6	390	1510	2040	12.7	39.7	47.6	26.7	41.1	39.3
Turkey	17640	36.5	23696	33.7	910	1660	2130	18.0	34.0	49.0	23.2	23.1	...
Turkmenistan	...	...	1847	...	...	1600	...	...	...	...	...	40.0	...
United Arab Emirates	267	4.0	784	6.4	14850	22720	22470	...	...	...	...	...	...
Uzbekistan	...	...	...	...	...	1070	960	33.3	31.1	34.4	...	35.0	...
Viet Nam	22316	47.8	32916	46.7	...	...	170	38.6	23.7	37.7	...	...	...
Yemen	1764	10.0	2602	13.3	...	...	...	...	...	...	...	17.8	20.0
EUROPE													
Albania	1043	40.3	1591	41.2	...	...	340	...	...	...	...	...	...
Austria	3198	39.6	3570	40.1	5170	19290	23120	3.2	36.1	60.7	...	...	...
Belarus	...	...	...	...	...	3580	2840	...	...	...	...	29.9	...
Belgium	3767	32.2	4151	33.7	6480	17790	...	1.8	30.1	68.1	...	...	...
Bosnia & Herzegovina	...	...	...	...	...	...	...	...	...	...	...	...	...
Bulgaria	4496	45.6	4475	46.4	...	2270	1160	17.7	51.3	31.0	...	25.6	20.1
Croatia	...	...	...	...	...	...	...	...	...	...	...	...	...
Czech Republic	...	...	...	...	...	3470	2730	...	...	...	...	28.6	...
Denmark	2534	40.0	2852	44.6	7540	22610	26510	5.0	28.0	67.0	...	...	...
Estonia	...	...	796	53.1	...	4760	3040	15.6	46.8	37.6	...	30.2	32.9
Finland	2313	45.0	2552	47.0	5870	24470	18970	6.0	34.0	60.0	...	...	...
France	22617	37.7	25404	39.9	6540	19750	22360	3.4	29.0	67.6	...	...	...
Germany	44912	40.6	48651	40.5	6650	22350	23630	1.5	38.7	59.8	...	...	...
Greece	3460	25.9	3852	26.7	2590	6020	7390	17.0	27.0	56.0	27.0	19.9	...
Hungary	5445	42.0	5276	44.9	...	2870	3400	12.6	32.4	55.0	37.8	25.4	19.7
Iceland	103	38.1	136	42.7	6910	23110	23620	12.0	29.0	59.0	...	...	...
Ireland	1192	27.5	1481	29.4	3020	10970	12580	11.0	9.0	80.0	...	...	...
Italy	21332	30.1	23339	31.9	4020	17170	19620	3.2	33.3	63.5	...	...	...
Latvia	...	...	1409	...	...	4500	2030	18.1	47.4	34.5	...	40.1	10.5
Lithuania	...	...	1853	...	...	3440	1310	27.7	43.3	29.0	...	34.3	17.0
Luxembourg	144	29.1	155	31.9	8130	29880	...	...	...	...	...	...	...
Malta	120	21.5	146	23.2	1670	6790	...	...	...	...	23.5	33.4	0.0
Netherlands	5111	28.6	6153	30.9	6670	18110	20710	4.0	29.3	66.7	...	...	...
Norway	1780	35.0	2128	41.1	7210	23130	26340	3.1	35.6	61.3	...	...	...
Poland	18120	45.3	19704	45.6	...	1700	2270	8.4	54.2	37.4	...	27.5	19.1
Portugal	3875	30.9	4740	36.7	1680	5360	7890	8.7	37.1	54.2	24.3	29.1	...
Republic of Moldova	...	...	2429	...	...	2300	1180	30.7	39.4	29.8	...	25.2	6.5
Romania	11107	44.8	11825	46.5	...	1710	1090	18.0	53.9	28.1	...	30.2	27.4
Russian Federation	...	...	...	...	...	4100	2350	17.0	49.0	34.0	...	30.1	25.8
Slovakia	...	...	2478	44.5	...	3060	1900	...	...	...	...	33.5	25.1
Slovenia	...	...	...	...	...	...	6310	...	...	...	...	16.9	...
Spain	12369	21.7	14456	24.4	3010	11180	13650	5.3	35.0	59.7	...	...	...
Sweden	3923	39.8	4319	44.6	9110	24360	24830	3.0	34.0	63.0	...	...	...
Switzerland	3026	35.3	3212	36.6	8690	32760	36410	3.6	35.5	60.9	...	...	...
TFYR Macedonia	...	...	...	...	...	...	780	...	...	...	...	...	...
Ukraine	...	...	...	...	...	2750	1910	...	...	...	...	26.3	...
United Kingdom	25991	37.1	27766	38.6	4260	16220	17970	1.7	36.3	62.0	...	...	...
Yugoslavia	9629	37.1	10858	38.9	...	...	...	...	...	...	...	...	...
LATIN AMERICA													
Antigua & Barbuda	...	...	...	...	...	5510	6390	...	...	...	...	...	...
Argentina	9891	26.0	11548	28.1	2680	3310	7290	8.1	36.0	55.9	29.4	14.0	18.4
Bahamas	...	...	...	...	2970	11980	11500	...	...	...	...	...	...

TABLE 6 *(continued)*

Labour Force and Economic Development Indicators

	Labour Force				GNP per Capita			GDP Distribution 1991			Gross Domestic Investment (% of GDP)		
	Total (000) 1975	Women (%) 1975	Total (000) 1990	Women (%) 1990	1975	(US$) 1990	1993	Agriculture	Industry	Services	1975	1990	1993
LATIN AMERICA (continued)													
Barbados	107	43.3	137	47.3	1660	6550	6240	...	...	...	19.2	18.3	...
Belize	...	...	...	...	870	2160	2440	21.9	24.8	53.3	...	28.5	31.8
Bolivia	1565	22.0	2283	25.8	360	630	710	...	...	...	36.9	12.7	15.0
Brazil	37492	24.4	55026	27.4	1170	2770	3010	10.0	39.0	51.0	26.8	21.5	18.2
Chile	3322	24.8	4753	28.5	1030	2170	3070	...	...	...	17.0	24.7	26.2
Colombia	7060	21.9	10394	21.9	600	1000	1400	16.1	36.5	47.4	17.0	18.5	21.2
Costa Rica	638	19.7	1023	21.8	1030	1790	2160	15.8	25.7	58.5	21.6	27.2	30.4
Cuba	3047	24.6	4461	31.7	...	...	...	...	...	...	...	...	...
Dominica	...	...	...	...	410	2260	2680	...	...	...	...	...	...
Dominican Republic	1340	11.7	2187	15.0	720	830	1080	17.5	26.2	56.3	24.5	22.0	...
Ecuador	2136	17.7	3287	19.3	600	960	1170	13.4	37.9	48.7	26.7	17.5	21.1
El Salvador	1367	22.6	2155	25.1	470	1030	1320	11.2	23.3	65.5	22.1	11.8	16.3
Grenada	...	...	...	...	...	2120	2410	...	...	...	...	...	...
Guadeloupe	113	40.3	158	43.8	...	...	...	...	...	...	...	...	...
Guatemala	1775	13.5	2628	16.4	620	920	1110	25.7	19.7	54.6	16.1	13.6	18.7
Guyana	239	22.8	383	25.0	690	240	280	...	...	...	33.1	41.6	53.7
Haiti	2441	45.4	3131	41.6	160	380	...	...	...	...	14.7	10.9	...
Honduras	909	14.9	1576	18.8	390	670	580	20.0	23.5	45.6	19.0	23.0	26.7
Jamaica	803	44.6	1246	45.7	1380	1600	1390	5.0	43.9	51.1	25.8	20.5	...
Martinique	111	39.4	156	43.6	...	...	...	...	...	...	...	...	...
Mexico	17928	22.6	30487	27.1	1590	2670	3750	8.0	30.7	61.3	22.3	21.9	21.7
Nicaragua	722	20.6	1204	25.2	680	370	360	31.1	20.0	48.9	21.7	19.3	17.4
Panama	580	25.8	873	27.2	1120	2030	2580	9.9	10.0	80.1	30.8	17.1	22.0
Paraguay	882	21.0	1410	20.7	600	1150	1500	27.8	23.1	49.1	24.1	22.9	22.5
Peru	4548	22.3	7138	24.1	1000	1080	1490	...	...	...	24.7	16.8	18.6
Puerto Rico	928	...	1245	...	2690	6160	7020	...	...	...	...	...	...
Saint Kitts & Nevis	...	...	...	...	...	3620	4470	...	...	...	...	...	...
Saint Lucia	...	...	...	...	...	2520	3040	...	...	...	...	25.7	24.6
St. Vincent & Grenadines	...	...	...	...	380	1750	2130	...	...	...	...	...	...
Suriname	96	26.0	135	29.6	1470	1730	1210	11.1	26.8	62.1	39.5	20.4	...
Trinidad and Tobago	364	27.8	501	30.0	1910	3660	3730	2.5	38.6	58.9	27.3	12.6	13.6
Uruguay	1106	27.9	1216	31.1	1410	2640	3910	11.3	32.1	56.6	18.9	11.0	15.6
Venezuela	3909	23.3	6860	27.6	2600	2680	2840	5.4	50.2	44.4	32.8	10.2	18.0
NORTHERN AMERICA													
Bermuda	...	...	...	...	7400	...	...	...	...	...	...	...	...
Canada	10161	36.4	13360	39.8	7890	20600	20670	3.0	33.8	63.2	...	...	...
United States	97852	39.1	122005	41.4	8030	22340	24750	2.0	29.3	68.6	17.3	17.2	...
OCEANIA													
Australia	5993	34.4	7963	38.1	7770	16960	17510	3.3	30.9	65.8	...	...	...
Fiji	181	14.7	254	20.2	1130	1880	2140	...	...	...	20.6	17.5	...
Guam	...	...	...	...	...	...	...	...	...	...	...	...	...
Kiribati	...	...	...	...	...	700	710	...	...	...	...	...	...
Micronesia, Fed. States of	...	...	...	...	...	...	...	...	...	...	...	...	...
New Caledonia	...	...	...	...	...	...	...	...	...	...	...	...	...
New Zealand	1245	...	1570	...	5010	12900	12900	8.4	26.9	64.8	...	...	...
Papua New Guinea	1245	31.6	1570	34.9	570	880	1120	29.0	30.4	40.6	20.0	24.4	19.8
Samoa	...	...	...	...	...	930	980	...	...	...	...	34.4	...
Solomon Islands	...	...	...	...	310	740	750	...	...	...	...	29.0	...
Tonga	...	...	...	...	...	1210	1610	...	...	...	...	...	...
Vanuatu	...	...	...	...	...	1160	1230	...	...	...	...	43.6	...

Sources: The World Bank, World Tables 1994. The World Bank, Stars 3. World Resources Institute, World Resources 1994-95.

Labour Force: includes both civilian labour force and those serving in the armed forces. It includes employed, which comprises all persons, including unpaid family workers, and also unemployed, consisting of all persons who, during the reference period, were not working but who were seeking work or available for work.

GNP (Gross National Product) per capita at current purchaser values (market prices), in US dollars, are calculated by the World Bank according to *World Bank Atlas* methodology. **Gross Domestic Product** refers to the sum of the value added of resident producers plus import duties.

Gross Domestic Investment: the sum of gross domestic fixed investment and the change in stocks.

TABLE 7

Households: Number and Growth Rate, 1990–2050

	Number of Households: Estimates and Projections (thousands)						Annual Rate of Growth (%)			5-Year Increment (thousands)				
	1990	1995	2000	2010	2025	2050	1990-2000	2000-2010	2010-2025	1995-2000	2000-2005	2005-2010	2010-2015	2015-2020
WORLD TOTAL	1264620	1403330	1555428	1892782	2415016	3220037	2.07	1.96	1.62	152098	168224	169129	174588	173451
More Developed Regions (*)	414286	439316	464121	509227	568469	627350	1.14	0.93	0.73	24805	24019	21086	20637	19466
Less Developed Regions (+)	850334	964014	1091307	1383556	1846547	2592687	2.50	2.37	1.92	127293	144205	148043	153950	153985
AFRICA	108743	123531	141079	186076	279559	507969	2.60	2.77	2.71	17549	20724	24273	27504	31140
Algeria	3585	4162	4787	5944	7511	9624	2.89	2.17	1.56	625	603	554	564	538
Angola	1092	1285	1489	2028	3310	6916	3.10	3.09	3.26	204	234	306	367	425
Benin	705	764	841	1055	1512	2930	1.77	2.26	2.40	77	95	118	133	151
Botswana	206	224	241	271	300	445	1.55	1.18	0.69	17	15	15	13	10
Burkina Faso	1355	1442	1546	1845	2554	4936	1.32	1.77	2.17	104	132	167	194	234
Burundi	1145	1295	1487	2022	3110	5448	2.61	3.08	2.87	192	241	295	325	360
Cameroon	1812	2057	2359	3144	4913	9353	2.64	2.88	2.98	301	359	427	507	591
Cape Verde	64	74	86	114	168	248	2.99	2.86	2.57	12	13	16	17	18
Central African Republic	500	554	614	778	1140	2040	2.05	2.37	2.55	60	73	91	105	121
Chad	708	790	900	1156	1713	3146	2.41	2.50	2.62	110	115	141	164	186
Comoros	104	124	150	226	400	835	3.72	4.08	3.81	26	33	42	50	58
Congo	337	380	428	563	889	1820	2.39	2.74	3.05	48	59	76	90	108
Côte d'Ivoire	1876	2064	2289	2936	4560	10029	1.99	2.49	2.94	225	282	365	438	537
Djibouti	109	125	144	189	281	480	2.81	2.75	2.64	19	22	23	27	31
Egypt	11064	13219	15765	21560	30945	45313	3.54	3.13	2.41	2546	2876	2920	3058	3172
Equatorial Guinea	46	50	55	72	106	195	1.96	2.55	2.59	6	7	9	10	11
Eritrea	552	629	724	989	1522	2840	2.71	3.12	2.87	95	120	145	160	177
Ethiopia	8492	9802	11473	16320	27427	57379	3.01	3.52	3.46	1671	2148	2699	3140	3668
Gabon	163	176	194	242	355	674	1.73	2.19	2.56	18	22	26	33	37
Gambia	100	115	126	147	187	293	2.32	1.61	1.59	11	11	11	13	13
Ghana	2767	3029	3383	4246	5921	10442	2.01	2.27	2.22	354	411	452	500	557
Guinea	731	795	874	1095	1558	2960	1.78	2.25	2.35	79	99	122	136	153
Guinea-Bissau	154	159	167	192	245	414	0.86	1.38	1.63	8	11	14	16	18
Kenya	4530	5635	6683	9545	16239	29496	3.89	3.56	3.54	1048	1295	1567	1899	2247
Lesotho	318	351	392	490	681	1182	2.08	2.24	2.20	40	46	52	58	64
Liberia	380	416	462	590	858	1644	1.95	2.44	2.50	46	57	71	79	89
Libyan Arab Jamahirya	727	859	1013	1407	2229	4228	3.32	3.28	3.07	155	182	212	244	275
Madagascar	2615	3098	3711	5395	9122	18050	3.50	3.74	3.50	613	778	907	1060	1238
Malawi	1830	2195	2439	3282	5445	11240	2.87	2.97	3.38	244	335	508	603	717
Mali	1274	1305	1345	1462	1603	2962	0.54	0.84	0.61	40	53	65	56	47
Mauritania	281	307	338	403	534	870	1.84	1.76	1.88	32	30	35	40	44
Mauritius	236	263	289	352	462	627	2.03	1.97	1.80	27	27	36	37	37
Morocco	3926	4300	4628	5230	5730	7053	1.64	1.22	0.61	329	308	293	240	163
Mozambique	3137	3533	4254	5865	9368	18691	3.04	3.21	3.12	720	769	842	983	1162
Namibia	240	265	295	367	504	848	2.04	2.19	2.13	29	34	38	42	46
Niger	1134	1246	1386	1783	2659	5314	2.00	2.52	2.66	140	173	224	261	290
Nigeria	14167	15420	16980	21148	29295	51396	1.81	2.20	2.17	1559	1891	2277	2466	2699
Reunion	158	182	208	269	368	533	2.77	2.56	2.08	27	29	32	31	33
Rwanda	1470	1676	1911	2405	3439	5555	2.62	2.30	2.39	235	229	265	308	350
Sao Tome & Principe	35	41	48	64	92	183	3.16	2.88	2.42	7	7	9	8	10
Senegal	1077	1169	1284	1566	2121	3580	1.75	1.98	2.02	116	134	148	167	186
Seychelles	15	17	18	20	22	43	1.82	1.05	0.64	1	1	1	1	-
Sierra Leone	608	639	679	800	1050	1805	1.10	1.64	1.81	40	53	68	75	83
Somalia	1695	1799	2124	3047	5146	10606	2.25	3.61	3.49	325	409	514	600	697
South Africa	7108	7706	8390	9929	12654	18549	1.66	1.68	1.62	684	724	815	878	919
St. Helena	1	2	2	3	4	7	6.93	4.05	1.92	-	-	-	-	-
Sudan	3850	4415	5060	6606	9755	17798	2.73	2.67	2.60	645	727	820	930	1053
Swaziland	127	145	163	206	285	443	2.53	2.31	2.16	19	20	23	25	27
Togo	428	469	519	658	939	1709	1.92	2.36	2.38	50	62	76	84	93
Tunisia	1448	1605	1768	2040	2308	2819	2.00	1.43	0.82	163	149	124	107	89
Uganda	3314	3937	4567	6462	11184	23534	3.21	3.47	3.66	630	814	1081	1304	1563
United Republic of Tanzania	4558	5360	6306	8776	14376	27740	3.25	3.31	3.29	946	1131	1340	1587	1865
Western Sahara	29	34	39	49	68	101	2.96	2.28	2.18	5	5	5	6	6
Zaire	6675	7551	8705	11970	19653	41653	2.65	3.19	3.31	1154	1449	1816	2129	2542
Zambia	1652	1947	2289	3162	5198	9733	3.26	3.23	3.31	341	400	474	566	678
Zimbabwe	2031	2331	2664	3590	5540	9218	2.71	2.98	2.89	333	424	501	572	652
ASIA	683941	771117	867282	1083009	1401130	1834734	2.37	2.22	1.72	96165	108346	107382	109545	105661
Afghanistan	1980	2741	3588	4320	6237	9764	5.94	1.85	2.45	847	293	438	636	675
Armenia	736	786	850	970	1104	1274	1.44	1.32	0.86	63	65	55	45	42
Azerbaijan	1497	1588	1709	1978	2257	2571	1.32	1.46	0.88	122	144	125	101	83
Bahrain	64	67	71	80	89	104	1.08	1.22	0.68	4	4	5	4	3
Bangladesh	17770	19878	22298	26893	33823	43482	2.27	1.87	1.53	2420	2172	2423	2503	2383
Bhutan	252	261	289	364	507	818	1.38	2.30	2.21	28	34	41	44	48
Brunei Darussalam	43	48	53	62	69	83	2.08	1.54	0.74	5	5	4	3	2
Cambodia	1567	1761	2073	2947	4491	7590	2.80	3.52	2.81	312	406	468	479	505
China	292888	332532	375785	477435	621584	821841	2.49	2.39	1.76	43253	52546	49105	49938	47051
Cyprus	152	157	166	185	205	241	0.92	1.05	0.70	9	9	9	8	7
Dem. People's Rep. of Korea	5743	6627	7571	10154	14151	20140	2.76	2.94	2.21	944	1193	1390	1437	1318

TABLE 7 (*continued*)

Households: Number and Growth Rate, 1990–2050

	Number of Households: Estimates and Projections (thousands)						Annual Rate of Growth (%)			5-Year Increment (thousands)				
	1990	1995	2000	2010	2025	2050	1990-2000	2000-2010	2010-2025	1995-2000	2000-2005	2005-2010	2010-2015	2015-2020
ASIA (continued)														
East Timor	134	147	171	226	299	418	2.44	2.80	1.88	24	30	25	24	24
Gaza Strip (Palestine)	107	122	139	175	233	360	2.62	2.30	1.91	17	17	19	19	19
Georgia	1407	1411	1428	1468	1510	1516	0.15	0.28	0.18	18	22	18	14	12
Hong Kong	1576	1767	1970	2326	2719	2819	2.23	1.66	1.04	203	189	167	149	128
India	148617	166370	186914	231393	296823	368123	2.29	2.13	1.66	20544	21729	22749	22777	22052
Indonesia	40126	45037	49895	59068	70825	84993	2.18	1.69	1.21	4858	4713	4459	4442	4038
Iran (Islamic Republic of)	10518	11930	13240	17353	23357	33554	2.30	2.71	1.98	1310	2116	1997	1979	1996
Iraq	2336	2640	3091	4241	6431	10519	2.80	3.16	2.78	451	542	608	678	733
Israel	1258	1592	1772	2141	2681	3414	3.43	1.89	1.50	180	189	181	184	182
Japan	41243	43993	46173	48862	51244	51086	1.13	0.57	0.32	2180	1554	1136	1028	836
Jordan	494	635	741	1025	1612	2746	4.04	3.25	3.02	106	128	157	182	198
Kazakhstan	4424	4665	4992	5769	6806	8176	1.21	1.45	1.10	327	416	362	353	340
Kuwait	265	168	199	233	240	303	-2.87	1.58	0.21	31	24	10	4	2
Kyrgyzstan	775	788	817	893	937	863	0.53	0.89	0.32	29	40	37	25	14
Lao People's Dem. Republic	731	841	981	1388	2208	3743	2.94	3.47	3.10	141	180	227	249	273
Lebanon	428	503	555	675	836	1087	2.60	1.97	1.42	52	58	63	62	54
Macau	61	78	95	128	157	204	4.43	2.98	1.36	17	17	16	12	10
Malaysia	3485	3985	4660	6168	8263	11073	2.91	2.80	1.95	675	745	763	740	697
Maldives	30	34	40	54	80	127	2.94	3.02	2.59	6	7	7	8	9
Mongolia	475	584	717	1023	1571	2486	4.11	3.55	2.86	133	155	151	169	185
Myanmar	7799	8835	9999	13021	18461	27291	2.48	2.64	2.33	1163	1414	1608	1755	1831
Nepal	3154	3589	4114	5371	7761	11302	2.66	2.67	2.45	525	574	684	749	804
Oman	237	288	349	509	882	1928	3.85	3.79	3.67	60	72	88	104	124
Pakistan	16762	18920	21925	29726	43169	65300	2.68	3.04	2.49	3004	3716	4085	4309	4474
Philippines	11405	13294	15522	20670	29406	44060	3.08	2.86	2.35	2228	2449	2699	2860	2937
Qatar	63	70	77	91	105	127	2.08	1.59	0.99	7	7	6	5	5
Republic of Korea	11654	13781	16075	20677	28150	38601	3.22	2.52	2.06	2294	2189	2412	2527	2530
Saudi Arabia	2403	2638	3153	4314	6771	12316	2.72	3.13	3.01	515	541	619	715	822
Singapore	651	732	826	1049	1355	1719	2.39	2.38	1.70	94	109	114	109	100
Sri Lanka	3401	3734	4132	4807	5645	6598	1.95	1.51	1.07	398	343	333	303	269
Syrian Arab Republic	1880	2212	2627	3663	5658	9160	3.35	3.32	2.90	415	489	548	614	671
Tajikistan	872	968	1091	1407	1876	2391	2.24	2.55	1.92	123	157	160	158	155
Thailand	11409	12803	13989	16133	19631	25252	2.04	1.43	1.31	1186	1158	985	1103	1190
Turkey	11607	13281	15171	19657	26447	36424	2.68	2.59	1.98	1890	2195	2291	2344	2282
Turkmenistan	581	621	668	777	878	875	1.41	1.50	0.82	48	58	50	42	33
United Arab Emirates	298	333	373	456	558	711	2.24	2.01	1.34	40	45	38	34	34
Uzbekistan	3703	4106	4615	5804	7352	8698	2.20	2.29	1.58	509	611	579	549	514
Viet Nam	13295	15061	17033	21289	27703	35235	2.48	2.23	1.76	1971	1995	2261	2258	2178
Yemen	1589	2116	2501	3593	5975	11225	4.53	3.62	3.39	384	482	610	710	793
EUROPE	**262539**	**275444**	**287894**	**307194**	**328223**	**344692**	**0.92**	**0.65**	**0.44**	**12451**	**11473**	**7826**	**7534**	**6763**
Albania	911	997	1099	1374	1789	2333	1.88	2.23	1.76	102	129	146	146	139
Andorra	14	15	16	18	21	21	1.34	1.18	1.03	1	1	1	1	1
Austria	2991	3129	3265	3480	3702	3792	0.88	0.64	0.41	136	114	101	93	72
Belarus	3588	3691	3836	4043	4285	4648	0.67	0.52	0.39	145	148	59	61	74
Belgium	3883	4061	4232	4532	4920	5295	0.86	0.69	0.55	170	158	142	138	132
Bosnia & Herzegovina	1293	1082	1404	1509	1638	1715	0.82	0.72	0.55	326	63	41	46	40
Bulgaria	3143	3224	3282	3336	3368	3292	0.44	0.16	0.06	58	47	6	11	12
Channel Islands	52	56	60	68	82	95	1.43	1.25	1.25	4	4	4	5	4
Croatia	1356	1401	1438	1493	1550	1640	0.59	0.38	0.25	36	37	18	16	16
Czech Republic	4155	4491	4764	5252	6074	7351	1.37	0.98	0.97	273	246	242	278	281
Denmark	2239	2302	2343	2473	2615	2750	0.45	0.54	0.37	41	57	73	67	48
Estonia	608	608	614	622	621	616	0.11	0.12	-0.01	6	11	-3	-2	-1
Faeroe Islands	13	13	14	15	16	19	0.74	0.69	0.43	1	-	1	-	1
Finland	2013	2147	2281	2518	2838	3269	1.25	0.99	0.80	134	118	119	114	106
France	21922	23340	24772	27373	30738	34942	1.22	1.00	0.77	1432	1362	1240	1190	1103
Germany	33766	35408	36542	38506	39036	35882	0.79	0.52	0.09	1134	1181	783	462	75
Gibraltar	7	7	7	8	8	8	-	1.34	-	-	-	-	-	-
Greece	3372	3586	3753	3847	3813	3463	1.07	0.25	-0.06	167	78	16	-1	-14
Hungary	3961	4113	4191	4347	4665	5212	0.57	0.37	0.47	78	74	82	107	111
Iceland	95	104	113	134	166	208	1.81	1.67	1.43	10	10	11	11	11
Ireland	1022	1112	1200	1328	1526	1820	1.60	1.02	0.92	88	69	60	64	68
Isle of Man	26	27	28	30	33	38	0.74	0.69	0.64	1	1	1	1	1
Italy	21570	23002	24163	25924	27601	26744	1.14	0.70	0.42	1161	939	822	751	552
Latvia	993	969	965	966	957	956	-0.30	0.02	-0.06	-4	8	-7	-6	-5
Liechtenstein	11	12	13	15	18	18	1.67	1.43	1.22	1	1	1	1	1
Lithuania	1295	1312	1341	1398	1467	1599	0.35	0.42	0.32	29	37	20	17	22
Luxembourg	143	158	170	186	204	218	1.72	0.86	0.62	13	9	6	7	6
Malta	111	120	129	145	166	195	1.47	1.16	0.92	9	8	8	7	7
Monaco	14	15	16	18	20	21	1.34	1.18	0.70	1	1	1	1	-
Netherlands	6003	6399	6773	7497	8248	8670	1.21	1.02	0.64	374	369	354	322	249
Norway	1743	1828	1908	2106	2408	2787	0.91	0.99	0.89	80	92	106	112	104
Poland	12243	12970	13800	14853	16618	19260	1.20	0.74	0.75	830	632	421	492	601

TABLE 7 (continued)

Households: Number and Growth Rate, 1990–2050

	Number of Households: Estimates and Projections (thousands)						Annual Rate of Growth (%)			5-Year Increment (thousands)				
	1990	1995	2000	2010	2025	2050	1990-2000	2000-2010	2010-2025	1995-2000	2000-2005	2005-2010	2010-2015	2015-2020
EUROPE (continued)														
Portugal	3261	3413	3543	3758	4051	4228	0.83	0.59	0.50	130	98	117	110	96
Republic of Moldova	1422	1498	1594	1777	2053	2486	1.14	1.09	0.96	96	107	76	80	92
Romania	7131	7558	7904	8490	9129	9613	1.03	0.71	0.48	347	392	194	208	207
Russian Federation	50546	52135	54032	55895	56882	56923	0.67	0.34	0.12	1897	1812	51	113	250
San Marino	8	9	10	11	13	13	2.23	0.95	1.11	1	1	-	1	-
Slovakia	2118	2335	2518	2870	3438	4274	1.73	1.31	1.20	183	173	179	198	193
Slovenia	576	606	631	655	668	666	0.91	0.37	0.13	24	17	6	4	17
Spain	12390	13286	13912	14570	15158	14145	1.16	0.46	0.26	625	407	251	238	207
Sweden	3863	4031	4192	4648	5326	6189	0.82	1.03	0.91	161	204	251	251	230
Switzerland	3060	3364	3663	4197	4813	5361	1.80	1.36	0.91	299	280	254	241	209
TFYR Macedonia	614	674	729	821	941	1090	1.72	1.19	0.91	54	50	42	41	38
Ukraine	17481	17805	18150	18322	18296	18361	0.38	0.09	-0.01	346	274	-102	-57	-48
United Kingdom	22465	23651	25016	27984	32041	37651	1.08	1.12	0.90	1364	1472	1495	1462	1327
Yugoslavia	3048	3381	3469	3784	4203	4814	1.29	0.87	0.70	88	180	135	131	131
LATIN AMERICA	**97602**	**111879**	**127425**	**161115**	**213917**	**296246**	**2.67**	**2.35**	**1.89**	**15546**	**16441**	**17249**	**17629**	**17692**
Anguilla	2	2	2	3	3	4	-	4.05	-	-	1	-	-	-
Antigua & Barbuda	17	17	17	17	18	24	-	-	0.38	-	-	-	1	-
Argentina	8347	9187	9997	11617	14097	17511	1.80	1.50	1.29	810	819	802	819	839
Aruba	15	15	15	16	18	24	-	0.65	0.79	-	-	1	-	1
Bahamas	54	56	58	60	58	66	0.78	0.25	-0.19	2	2	-	-	-1
Barbados	73	75	78	85	96	107	0.63	0.88	0.81	3	3	4	4	4
Belize	36	42	49	65	91	126	3.08	2.96	2.22	7	8	9	9	9
Bolivia	1138	1199	1268	1427	1654	2359	1.08	1.18	0.98	69	75	84	86	77
Brazil	38690	46011	54194	72098	101757	148769	3.37	2.85	2.30	8183	8679	9225	9655	9950
British Virgin Islands	4	5	6	7	9	12	4.05	1.54	1.68	1	-	1	1	1
Cayman Islands	8	10	13	18	25	33	4.86	3.25	2.19	3	3	2	3	2
Chile	3091	3515	3986	5104	6845	9595	2.54	2.47	1.96	471	544	575	582	578
Colombia	5919	6680	7487	8989	10966	13119	2.35	1.83	1.33	807	757	745	710	665
Costa Rica	610	722	849	1149	1677	2625	3.30	3.03	2.52	127	144	156	166	176
Cuba	2833	2960	3080	3415	3792	4171	0.83	1.03	0.70	120	161	174	148	117
Dominica	19	19	20	21	23	31	0.51	0.49	0.61	1	-	1	1	-
Dominican Republic	1383	1568	1759	2177	2735	3655	2.40	2.13	1.52	191	210	208	199	186
Ecuador	2031	2368	2733	3500	4658	6383	2.97	2.47	1.90	365	377	391	394	388
El Salvador	1127	1354	1591	2152	3174	4846	3.45	3.02	2.59	238	261	300	331	345
Falkland Islands (Malvinas)	-	-	-	-	1	1	..	..	..	-	-	-	-	-
French Guiana	29	35	41	53	67	94	3.46	2.57	1.56	6	5	7	5	5
Grenada	21	20	21	22	25	33	-	0.47	0.85	1	-	1	-	1
Guadeloupe	112	128	143	173	217	272	2.40	1.88	1.53	15	14	16	16	15
Guatemala	1382	1557	1758	2225	2997	4654	2.41	2.36	1.98	201	224	243	256	261
Guyana	172	182	198	238	292	362	1.40	1.83	1.37	16	18	21	20	17
Haiti	1263	1397	1560	1984	2848	5108	2.12	2.40	2.41	164	196	228	258	287
Honduras	839	1007	1210	1707	2547	3810	3.66	3.44	2.67	203	234	263	276	282
Jamaica	568	584	602	652	697	818	0.59	0.80	0.44	19	23	27	19	15
Martinique	107	118	130	154	190	234	1.96	1.75	1.38	12	12	12	13	12
Mexico	15604	17352	19161	22950	27708	33855	2.05	1.80	1.26	1809	1887	1902	1777	1585
Montserrat	4	4	5	5	6	8	2.23	-	1.22	1	-	-	1	-
Netherlands Antilles	43	44	46	51	59	70	0.69	1.12	0.96	2	3	3	3	3
Nicaragua	621	780	953	1378	2162	3537	4.28	3.68	3.00	174	198	226	248	263
Panama	526	616	714	933	1262	1737	3.05	2.67	2.02	98	107	111	112	110
Paraguay	758	880	1031	1404	2033	3153	3.07	3.09	2.46	151	180	193	201	209
Peru	4193	4662	5136	5979	7073	8898	2.03	1.52	1.12	474	427	416	401	371
Puerto Rico	1081	1189	1290	1496	1809	2221	1.77	1.48	1.26	101	98	108	107	106
Saint Kitts & Nevis	13	13	14	16	19	25	0.74	1.34	1.15	1	1	1	1	-
Saint Lucia	28	30	31	34	36	48	1.02	0.92	0.38	1	1	2	1	-
St. Vincent & Grenadines	19	18	17	16	13	17	-1.11	-0.61	-1.38	-1	-1	-	-1	-1
Suriname	86	91	100	125	160	216	1.54	2.24	1.62	9	12	13	12	11
Trinidad & Tobago	265	287	320	385	483	631	1.88	1.86	1.51	33	33	32	32	32
Turks & Caicos Islands	3	3	3	4	6	8	-	2.88	2.70	-	1	-	1	-
Uruguay	905	954	993	1072	1195	1367	0.93	0.76	0.72	39	39	40	41	42
US Virgin Islands	35	39	43	50	61	81	2.06	1.51	1.33	4	4	3	4	4
Venezuela	3527	4084	4700	6084	8256	11527	2.87	2.58	2.04	617	681	703	716	727
NORTHERN AMERICA	**103547**	**112192**	**121606**	**143074**	**176303**	**216003**	**1.61**	**1.63**	**1.39**	**9414**	**10193**	**11275**	**11202**	**11002**
Bermuda	22	24	26	31	39	42	1.67	1.76	1.53	2	2	3	2	3
Canada	9916	10969	12114	14650	18687	23383	2.00	1.90	1.62	1145	1197	1339	1346	1347
Greenland	17	19	21	26	34	42	2.11	2.14	1.79	2	2	3	2	3
St. Pierre & Miquelon	2	2	2	2	2	2	-	-	-	-	-	-	-	-
United States	93590	101178	109443	128365	157541	192533	1.56	1.59	1.37	8265	8993	9930	9852	9649

TABLE 7 *(continued)*

Households: Number and Growth Rate, 1990–2050

	Number of Households: Estimates and Projections (thousands)						Annual Rate of Growth (%)			5-Year Increment (thousands)				
	1990	1995	2000	2010	2025	2050	1990-2000	2000-2010	2010-2025	1995-2000	2000-2005	2005-2010	2010-2015	2015-2020
OCEANIA	**8248**	**9169**	**10142**	**12314**	**15883**	**20393**	**2.07**	**1.94**	**1.70**	**974**	**1047**	**1125**	**1174**	**1193**
American Samoa	6	7	7	8	9	12	1.54	1.34	0.79	-	1	-	-	1
Australia	5839	6489	7177	8662	11045	13637	2.06	1.88	1.62	688	719	766	794	792
Cook Islands	4	4	4	4	5	7	-	-	1.49	-	-	-	-	1
Fiji	131	152	176	222	294	391	2.95	2.36	1.86	24	23	24	24	24
French Polynesia	41	47	53	69	93	129	2.56	2.57	2.00	6	8	8	8	8
Guam	34	38	41	52	65	83	2.02	2.22	1.53	4	4	6	5	5
Kiribati	11	12	13	16	18	23	1.67	2.08	0.79	1	1	2	1	-
Marshall Islands	5	6	7	10	13	17	3.36	3.57	1.75	1	2	1	1	1
Micronesia, Fed. States of	18	21	25	32	44	56	3.29	2.47	2.12	4	3	4	4	4
Nauru	2	2	2	3	3	4	-	4.05	-	-	-	1	-	-
New Caledonia	42	47	51	62	77	95	2.05	1.88	1.42	5	5	5	5	5
New Zealand	1118	1198	1271	1434	1654	1932	1.28	1.21	0.95	73	79	84	79	74
Niue	1	1	1	1	1	1	-	-	-	-	-	-	-	-
Northern Mariana Islands	4	5	5	7	10	13	2.23	3.36	2.38	-	1	1	1	1
Pacific Islands (Palau)	3	4	4	6	8	10	2.88	4.05	1.92	-	1	1	-	1
Papua New Guinea	845	968	1106	1445	2095	3199	2.69	2.68	2.48	138	161	179	201	219
Samoa	28	30	34	48	74	106	1.99	3.41	2.84	4	6	8	9	9
Solomon Islands	66	84	105	160	283	541	4.64	4.22	3.79	21	25	30	36	41
Tonga	16	16	16	17	18	26	-	0.61	0.38	-	1	-	-	1
Tuvalu	2	2	2	3	3	4	-	4.05	-	-	1	-	-	-
Vanuatu	28	30	34	43	57	87	2.14	2.31	1.80	4	4	5	4	4
Wake Islands	1	2	2	2	3	4	6.93	-	2.70	-	-	-	-	1
Wallis & Futuna Islands	3	4	5	7	12	17	5.11	3.36	3.59	1	1	1	2	2

Source: United Nations Centre for Human Settlements (Habitat), 1994.

Household: A unit reflecting the arrangements made by persons for living together and sharing housekeeping, budget and other essentials. A household may be either a one-person household or a multi-person household.

Data on number and size of households and their changes over time are important for the quantification of housing needs. Thus, the objective of the study, on which this table is based, was to project the number and size of households up to the year 2050. The methods applied are general in the sense that they allow for the inclusion of an unlimited number of historical data points and are applied to all countries for which data are available. Data starting from the 1970 census rounds up to the 1990 census rounds are included in the projections. For three regions sufficient household data have not been available to project future trends. These regions are Middle Africa, with only two countries having one year of household data; Southern Africa with only Botswana having two years of census data on households and no data available for the rest of the countries; and Micronesia with one census year for households in Guam and no data for the rest of the countries. Future growth of households in Middle and Southern Africa has been estimated from growth trends in Eastern and Western Africa, while the growth of households in Micronesia has been estimated from the regional trends of Melanesia and Polynesia.

Data bases for projections: (a) UNCHS (Habitat), *Human Settlements Statistical Database*; (b) United Nations, *Human Settlements Statistics Questionnaire 1992*; (c) United Nations, *World Population Prospects: The 1994 Revision* (the medium variant).

TABLE 8

Households' Housing Statistics, Selected Countries

			Number of Households in:				Number of Households by Tenure:					All Households	
			Housing Units			Collec-tive Living Quarters	Owner Occu-pants	Tenants			Other		
			Total	Conven-tional	Uncon-ven-tional			Total	Govern. Housing Units	Private Housing Units		Number	Size
AFRICA													
Burkina Faso	Total	1985	...	...	...	...	...	...	...	...	...	1274546	6.2
Burkina Faso	Urban	1985	...	...	...	...	...	...	...	...	...	161389	5.8
Burkina Faso	Rural	1985	...	...	...	...	...	...	...	...	...	1113157	6.3
Gambia	Total	1983	202199	...	...	...	[1] 52182	[1] 17933	[1] 3117	[1] 70112	[1] 8490	202199	3.4
Gambia	Urban	1983	...	...	...	...	[1] 6422	[1] 12920	[1] 1841	[1] 18916	[1] 3878	...	...
Gambia	Rural	1983	...	...	...	...	[1] 45760	[1] 5013	[1] 1276	[1] 51196	[1] 4612	...	...
Ghana	Total	1984	2480368	2480368	...	...	...	...	...	...	...	2480368	5.0
Ghana	Urban	1984	894138	894138	...	...	...	...	...	...	...	894138	4.4
Ghana	Rural	1984	1586230	1586230	...	...	...	...	...	...	...	1586230	5.3
Kenya	Total	1989	...	...	...	...	...	...	...	...	...	4352751	4.9
Madagascar	Total	1993	...	...	...	...	...	...	...	...	...	2688951	4.5
Malawi	Total	1987	...	...	...	...	...	...	...	...	...	1859572	4.3
Malawi	Urban	1987	...	...	...	...	...	...	...	...	...	198939	4.3
Malawi	Rural	1987	...	...	...	...	...	...	...	...	...	1660633	4.3
Mali	Total	1987	...	...	...	...	1148418	115520	...	...	77237	1364079	5.6
Mali	Urban	1987	...	...	...	...	...	...	...	...	...	282966	6.0
Mali	Rural	1987	...	...	...	...	...	...	...	...	...	1081133	5.6
Mauritius	Total	1990	236635	236347	288	176	179657	36026	...	...	20897	236811	4.5
Mauritius	Urban	1990	97441	97383	58	50	64101	25507	...	...	7812	97491	4.3
Mauritius	Rural	1990	139194	138964	230	126	115556	10519	...	...	13085	139320	4.6
Reunion	Total	1990	...	...	...	...	88844	56396	-	56396	[2] 12613	157853	3.8
Reunion	Urban	1990	...	...	...	...	86791	55967	-	55967	[2] 12371	155129	3.8
Reunion	Rural	1990	...	...	...	...	2053	429	-	429	[2] 242	2724	4.0
St. Helena	Total	1987	...	1392	...	...	...	...	...	...	...	1445	3.9
Tunisia	Total	1989	...	...	...	...	1168688	276897	160191	116706	12535	1458100	5.4
Tunisia	Urban	1989	...	...	...	...	649782	230066	155258	74808	7732	897600	5.2
Tunisia	Rural	1989	...	...	...	...	518906	46831	4933	41898	4803	560500	5.8
ASIA													
Brunei Darussalam	Total	1991	...	...	...	...	...	...	...	...	...	44769	5.8
Cyprus	Total	1982	144657	142613	2044	362	86959	23942	...	...	34129	145030	3.5
Cyprus	Urban	1982	90506	89411	1095	237	47597	21798	...	...	21355	90750	3.6
Cyprus	Rural	1982	54151	53202	949	125	39362	2144	...	...	12774	54280	3.4
Hong Kong	Total	1991	[3] 1547336	1481679	[4] 65657	[5] 32736	[6] 673067	[6] 837351	[6] 599432	[6] 237919	[6] 69654	1580072	3.5
India [7]	Total	1981	119772545	119772545	...	...	99069570	19545242	...	...	...	[3] 120402474	5.5
India [7]	Urban	1981	28905949	28905949	...	...	15272083	13269794	...	...	...	[3] 29115469	5.4
India [7]	Rural	1981	90866596	90866596	...	...	83797487	6275448	...	...	...	[3] 91287005	5.6
Indonesia	Total	1990	39695375	39695375	...	...	...	...	...	...	...	39695375	4.5
Indonesia	Urban	1990	...	11639073	...	...	...	...	...	...	...	...	...
Iraq	Total	1987	...	2111573	...	...	1379469	383116	90571	292545	246350	...	...
Iraq	Urban	1987	...	1532982	...	...	932260	362815	78152	284663	168340	...	...
Iraq	Rural	1987	...	578591	...	...	447209	20301	12419	7882	78010	...	...
Israel	Total	1983	...	...	...	...	...	...	...	...	...	[8] 1103232	3.7
Israel	Urban	1983	...	...	...	...	...	...	...	...	...	[8] 1037541	3.5
Israel	Rural	1983	...	...	...	...	...	...	...	...	...	[8] 65691	6.4
Japan [9]	Total	1988	37595200	...	...	217000	24059950	13091459	2875015	10216444	2167237	[3] 37595200	...
Japan [9]	Urban	1988	30087700	...	...	162400	17686969	11943981	2485615	9458366	1885833	[3] 30087700	...
Japan [9]	Rural	1988	7507500	...	...	54600	6372981	1147478	389400	758078	281404	[3] 7507500	...
Jordan	Total	1979	...	305429	...	1927	...	...	...	...	...	317810	6.7
Jordan	Urban	1979	...	210922	...	1444	...	...	...	...	...	190084	6.7
Jordan	Rural	1979	...	94507	...	483	...	...	...	...	...	127726	6.8
Kuwait	Total	1985	232731	227201	5530	9772	...	...	...	...	...	236729	7.2
Macau	Total	1991	98070	92978	5092	321	63985	26949	-	-	6170	98961	3.6
Maldives	Total	1990	...	...	...	...	...	...	...	...	...	29823	7.1
Maldives	Urban	1990	...	...	...	...	...	...	...	...	...	5613	9.8
Maldives	Rural	1990	...	...	...	...	...	...	...	...	...	24210	6.5
Myanmar	Total	1983	6495621	...	...	...	...	...	...	...	...	6495621	5.3
Myanmar	Urban	1983	1599343	...	...	...	...	...	...	...	...	1599343	5.3
Myanmar	Rural	1983	4896278	...	...	...	...	...	...	...	...	4896278	5.2

TABLE 8 (continued)

Households' Housing Statistics, Selected Countries

			Number of Households in:				Number of Households by Tenure:						All Households	
			Housing Units			Collec-tive Living Quarters	Owner Occu-pants	Tenants				Other		Number	Size
			Total	Conven-tional	Uncon-ven-tional			Total	Govern. Housing Units	Private Housing Units				
ASIA (continued)															
Pakistan	Total	1981	...	...	...	...	...	...	...	...		...	12587648	6.5
Pakistan	Urban	1981	...	...	...	...	...	...	...	...		...	3554173	6.7
Pakistan	Rural	1981	...	...	...	...	...	...	...	...		...	9033475	6.4
Qatar	Total	1986	...	...	...	...	10923	28774	8588	20186		10086	49783	7.4
Republic of Korea [10]	Total	1990	...	11357160	...	19239	5743728	5130434	...	...		[11] ...	[11] 11382955	3.8
Republic of Korea [10]	Urban	1990	...	8465826	...	14205	3518399	4642972	...	...		[11] ...	[11] 8486082	3.8
Republic of Korea [10]	Rural	1990	...	2891334	...	5034	2225329	487462	...	...		[11] ...	[11] 2896873	3.8
Singapore [12]	Total	1990	...	649100	...	...	585500	...	...	...		63600	...	...
Sri Lanka	Total	1981	[3] 2974608	2776646	197962	[13] 73897	1956349	...	[14] 287956	[2] 324399		[15] 245137	[16] 3048505	4.9
Sri Lanka	Urban	1981	[3] 559641	515509	44132	[13] 26794	296756	...	[14] 148796	[2] 37599		[15] 28659	[16] 586435	5.4
Sri Lanka	Rural	1981	[3] 2414967	2261137	153830	[13] 47103	1659593	...	[14] 139160	[2] 286800		[15] 216478	[16] 2462070	4.8
Syrian Arab Republic	Total	1981	1433800	1422348	11452	1228	...	...	...	...		...	1435028	6.3
Syrian Arab Republic	Urban	1981	706736	704619	2117	859	...	...	...	...		...	707595	6.0
Syrian Arab Republic	Rural	1981	727064	717729	9335	369	...	...	...	...		...	727433	6.6
Thailand	Total	1990	12224400	12160700	63700	...	...	...	...	...		[17] ...	[17] 12224400	4.5
Thailand	Urban	1990	2327800	2292500	35300	...	...	...	...	...		...	2342000	4.4
Thailand	Rural	1990	9897600	9869200	28400	...	...	...	...	...		...	9937000	4.5
Turkey	Total	1985	...	...	...	...	7533733	2196285	...	...		...	9730018	5.2
Turkey	Urban	1985	...	...	...	...	3491523	2007748	...	...		...	5499271	4.9
Turkey	Rural	1985	...	...	...	...	4042210	188537	...	...		...	4230747	5.6
Viet Nam	Total	1989	12927297	...	...	...	...	...	...	...		...	[3] 12927297	5.0
Viet Nam	Urban	1989	2464741	...	...	...	...	...	...	...		...	[3] 2464741	5.0
Viet Nam	Rural	1989	10462556	...	...	...	...	...	...	...		...	[3] 10462556	4.9
EUROPE														
Austria	Total	1981	...	2745028	...	21741	1326045	1163736	168654	995082		274089	2766770	2.7
Austria	Urban	1981	...	1728703	...	...	569971	992248	156149	836099		167647	1740930	2.4
Austria	Rural	1981	...	1016325	...	...	756074	171488	12505	158983		106442	1025839	3.3
Bulgaria [18]	Total	1985	2975819	2955457	20362	24950	2177276	491921	438347	2283496		[19] 33988	3014060	3.0
Bulgaria [18]	Urban	1985	1960599	1941602	18997	18871	1225995	457224	408000	1320291		[19] 29585	1984756	2.9
Bulgaria [18]	Rural	1985	1015220	1013855	1365	6079	951281	34697	30347	963205		[19] 4383	1029304	3.0
Channel Islands	Total	1991	[3] 53678	53678	...	...	30604	22277	6618	15659		977	54110	2.6
Finland	Total	1989	2008531	2008531	...	...	1436548	504527	...	...		37008	2008531	2.4
Finland	Urban	1989	1312822	1312822	...	...	896392	381981	...	...		17943	1312822	2.3
Finland	Rural	1989	695709	695709	...	...	540156	122546	...	...		19065	695709	2.7
France	Total	1990	...	...	...	...	11716580	8526440	3138640	5387800		[2] 1277680	21520700	2.6
France	Urban	1990	...	...	...	...	7791620	7588980	3006540	4582440		[2] 893640	16274240	2.5
France	Rural	1990	...	...	...	...	3924960	937460	132100	805360		[2] 384040	5246460	2.8
Germany	Total	1987	26506523	26468846	37677	...	9961871	15532980	...	...		1011672	26744081	2.3
Germany	Urban	1987	10658873	10646449	12424	...	2138673	8088742	...	...		431458	10834212	2.0
Germany	Rural	1987	15847650	15822397	25253	...	7823198	7444238	...	...		580214	15909869	2.6
Gibraltar	Total	1981	...	6945	...	...	361	6566	4503	2063		18	...	...
Hungary	Total	1990	...	3887590	...	...	2862880	[20] 912773	...	...		[21] 111937	3889532	2.7
Hungary	Urban	1990	...	2459607	...	...	...	...	...	...		...	2460475	2.6
Hungary	Rural	1990	...	1427983	...	...	...	...	...	...		...	1429057	2.8
Ireland	Total	1986	...	964882	[22] 11422	3380	667005	202054	111739	90315		26995	979684	3.6
Ireland	Urban	1986	550714	...	[22] 2129	...	328261	161465	87478	73987		10411	550714	3.5
Ireland	Rural	1986	414168	...	[22] 9293	...	338744	40589	24261	16328		16584	414168	3.6
Isle of Man	Total	1991	...	27316	...	...	18171	8882	5222	3660		263	...	...
Italy	Total	1991	...	19509362	...	...	...	...	...	...		...	19765679	2.9
Latvia	Total	1991	929019	929019	...	96335	...	...	725799	...		...	1114873	2.4
Latvia	Urban	1991	644598	644598	...	74201	...	...	557275	...		...	791082	2.4
Latvia	Rural	1991	284421	284421	...	22134	...	...	168524	...		...	323791	2.4
Netherlands	Total	1989	[3] 5937989	5912680	25309	...	[1] 2585281	[1] 3276538	[1] 284277	[1] 2992261		...	...	...
Netherlands	Urban	1989	[3] 4131847	4114974	16873	...	[1] 1507062	[1] 2559898	[1] 224018	[1] 2335880		...	...	...
Netherlands	Rural	1989	[3] 1806412	1797706	8436	...	[1] 1078219	[1] 716640	[1] 60259	[1] 656381		...	...	...
Norway	Total	1990	[23] 1751343	1751343	...	...	1368976	382367	...	...		...	[23] 1751343	2.4
Norway	Urban	1990	1288839	1288839	...	...	1008383	280456	...	...		...	1288839	2.3
Norway	Rural	1990	446938	446938	...	...	349670	97268	...	...		...	446938	2.7
Poland	Total	1988	11970440	11967021	3419	...	4218740	[24] 6488326	3574287	2914039		1259955	11970440	3.2
Poland	Urban	1988	7864162	7862725	1437	...	1377101	[24] 5752546	2941929	2810617		733078	7864162	2.9
Poland	Rural	1988	4106278	4104296	1982	...	2841639	[24] 735780	632358	103422		526877	4106278	3.6

TABLE 8 (*continued*)

Households' Housing Statistics, Selected Countries

| | | | Number of Households in: | | | | Number of Households by Tenure: | | | | Other | All Households | |
| | | | Housing Units | | | Collective Living Quarters | Owner Occupants | Tenants | | | | | |
			Total	Conventional	Unconventional			Total	Govern. Housing Units	Private Housing Units		Number	Size
EUROPE (continued)													
Romania	Total	1992	7288676	7281441	7235	...	5497870	1740539	...	...	43032	7288676	3.1
Romania	Urban	1992	3970435	3967201	3234	...	2419004	1526923	...	...	21274	3970435	3.1
Romania	Rural	1992	3318241	3314240	4001	...	3078866	213616	...	...	21758	3318241	3.1
Russian Federation	Total	1989	40531433	40531433	...	...	14097235	34832714	34376124	456590	1441974	[3] 50371923	2.8
Russian Federation	Urban	1989	28512934	28512934	...	...	6870387	29010637	28679197	331440	1122973	[3] 37003997	2.8
Russian Federation	Rural	1989	12018499	12018499	...	...	7226848	5822077	5696927	125150	319001	[3] 13367926	2.8
San Marino	Total	1991	...	...	...	...	...	...	...	...	...	8518	2.8
San Marino	Urban	1991	...	...	...	...	...	...	...	...	...	7780	2.7
San Marino	Rural	1991	...	...	...	...	...	...	...	...	...	738	3.2
Spain	Total	1991	...	...	...	...	9166124	1757469	...	...	[25] 901256		
Sweden	Total	1990	3830037	3830037	-	-	1556407	1569867	39075	1530792	703763	3830037	2.2
Sweden	Urban	1990	3260297	3260297	-	-	1108098	1495323	32169	1463154	656876	3260297	2.2
Sweden	Rural	1990	569740	569740	-	-	448309	74544	6906	67638	46887	569740	2.5
Switzerland	Total	1980	2449784	2447379	2405	9503	722247	1631154	...	...	[26] 93978	2459287	2.6
Switzerland	Urban	1980	1627249	1625670	1579	5119	...	...	...	...	...	1632368	2.4
Switzerland	Rural	1980	822535	821709	826	4384	...	...	...	...	...	826919	3.0
Yugoslavia (former)	Total	1981	...	6080988	...	...	4180435	[27] 1339019	[28] 1232144	[28] 99951	[29] 561534	...	...
LATIN AMERICA													
Aruba	Total	1991	19224	18538	673	20	12432	5945	1129	4816	[30] 845	19276	3.4
Bolivia	Total	1988	1117800	...	...	...	911800	197300	...	...	8800	[3] 1117800	5.6
Bolivia	Urban	1988	530100	...	...	...	353300	171400	...	...	5400	[3] 530100	6.2
Bolivia	Rural	1988	587700	...	...	...	558400	25900	...	...	3400	[3] 587700	5.0
Cayman Islands	Total	1989	8115	...	...	...	4308	3299	72	3227	508	8115	3.1
Chile	Total	1982	...	...	...	11639	1551579	459470	[31] 212163	[2] 204424	29506	2478292	4.6
Chile	Urban	1982	...	...	...	8999	1321648	437742	[31] 113209	[2] 159869	26078	2075145	4.5
Chile	Rural	1982	...	...	...	...	229931	21728	[31] 98954	[2] 44555	3428	403147	5.0
Cuba	Total	1981	2354915	...	...	...	...	...	...	...	...	2354915	4.1
Cuba	Urban	1981	1667915	...	...	...	...	...	...	...	...	1667915	4.0
Cuba	Rural	1981	687000	...	...	...	...	...	...	...	...	687000	4.4
Falkland Islands (Malvinas)	Total	1991	802	747	55	...	424	378	...	...	...	802	2.6
French Guiana	Total	1990	...	...	...	...	13742	15604	...	15604	[2] 3939	33285	3.4
French Guiana	Urban	1990	...	...	...	...	9714	14939	...	14939	[2] 3182	27835	3.3
French Guiana	Rural	1990	...	...	...	...	4028	665	...	665	[2] 757	5450	3.8
Guadeloupe	Total	1990	...	...	...	...	70369	36190	...	36190	[2] 5919	112478	3.4
Guadeloupe	Urban	1990	...	...	...	...	68994	35994	...	35994	[2] 5802	110790	3.4
Guadeloupe	Rural	1990	...	...	...	...	1375	196	...	196	[2] 117	1688	3.6
Guatemala	Total	1981	1151872	1096193	55679	3442	693073	130053	...	130053	328746	1155314	5.2
Guatemala	Urban	1981	393723	369005	24718	...	...	...	...	...	...	[3] 393723	5.0
Guatemala	Rural	1981	758149	727188	30961	...	...	...	...	...	...	[3] 758149	5.4
Haiti [32]	Total	1986	...	1164136	...	...	851938	228614	...	...	...	...	...
Haiti [32]	Urban	1986	...	285927	...	...	102679	163786	...	...	...	...	...
Haiti [32]	Rural	1986	...	878209	...	...	749259	64828	...	...	...	...	...
Honduras	Total	1988	...	[33] 780148	...	...	[1] 612507	[1] 92196	...	...	[1] 57414	...	...
Honduras	Urban	1988	...	[33] 329333	...	...	[1] 218933	[1] 79127	...	...	[1] 20010	...	...
Honduras	Rural	1988	...	[33] 450815	...	...	[1] 393574	[1] 13069	...	...	[1] 37404	...	...
Martinique	Total	1990	...	...	...	...	64861	34629	...	34629	[2] 7046	106536	3.3
Martinique	Urban	1990	...	...	...	...	58076	32122	...	32122	[2] 6073	96271	3.3
Martinique	Rural	1990	...	...	...	...	6785	2507	...	2507	[2] 973	10265	3.4
Mexico	Total	1990	16202846	...	...	...	12486898	2347459	...	...	1098682	[3] 16202846	5.0
Mexico	Urban	1990	11862627	...	...	...	...	...	...	...	...	[3] 11862627	4.9
Mexico	Rural	1990	4340219	...	...	...	...	...	...	...	...	[3] 4340219	5.4
Panama	Total	1990	526456	...	...	...	[1] 396046	[1] 82325	...	...	[1] 45913	[3] 526456	4.4
Panama	Urban	1990	296877	...	...	...	[1] 194349	[1] 74536	...	...	[1] 26220	[3] 296877	4.2
Panama	Rural	1990	229579	...	...	...	[1] 201697	[1] 7789	...	...	[1] 19693	[3] 229579	4.7
Paraguay	Total	1982	...	...	...	...	[1] 467980	[1] 59653	...	...	[1] 51081	...	...
Paraguay	Urban	1982	...	...	...	...	[1] 191093	[1] 50226	...	...	[1] 24103	...	...
Paraguay	Rural	1982	...	...	...	...	[1] 276887	[1] 9427	...	...	[1] 26978	...	...
Peru	Total	1990	4177189	4137519	39670	2895	2907005	710800	...	...	324336	4180084	5.2
Peru	Urban	1990	2849749	2820515	29234	2895	1751653	690016	...	...	224866	2852644	5.3
Peru	Rural	1990	1327440	1317004	10436	-	1155352	20784	...	...	99470	1327440	4.8

TABLE 8 (continued)

Households' Housing Statistics, Selected Countries

			Number of Households in:				Number of Households by Tenure:					All Households	
			Housing Units			Collective Living Quarters	Owner Occupants	Tenants			Other		
			Total	Conventional	Unconventional			Total	Govern. Housing Units	Private Housing Units		Number	Size
LATIN AMERICA (continued)													
Turks & Caicos Islands [34]	Total	1990	2022	2022	...	...	1330	504	...	...	[2] 188	2022	3.9
US Virgin Islands	Total	1990	32020	32020	...	...	14272	17748	...	...	...	32020	3.2
Venezuela	Total	1990	3750940	...	...	...	...	...	...	...	...	[3] 3750940	4.8
NORTHERN AMERICA													
Bermuda	Total	1991	22061	22061	...	369	9542	11520	...	...	[35] 999	22430	2.6
Canada	Total	1991	10018265	10002260	16005	21020	6273030	3718525	...	...	26715	10039545	2.6
United States	Total	1990	...	...	...	...	59024811	32922599	...	...	...	...	...
United States	Urban	1990	...	...	...	...	41375627	28669540	...	...	...	...	...
United States	Rural	1990	...	...	...	...	17649184	4253059	...	...	...	...	...
OCEANIA													
American Samoa	Total	1990	6959	6607	...	...	5161	1446	...	...	...	[3] 6959	6.7
American Samoa	Urban	1990	2378	2256	...	...	1608	648	...	...	...	[3] 2378	6.6
American Samoa	Rural	1990	4581	4351	...	...	3553	798	...	...	...	[3] 4581	6.8
Australia	Total	1986	5264516	5049170	139505	...	...	...	...	...	...	5264516	3.0
Australia	Urban	1986	4565271	4414139	88713	...	...	...	...	...	...	4565271	2.9
Australia	Rural	1986	699204	635010	50785	...	...	...	...	...	...	699204	3.1
Fiji	Total	1986	...	124098	...	225	92390	21343	...	...	6066	124323	5.8
Fiji	Urban	1986	...	49579	...	147	28114	15539	...	...	2514	49726	5.6
Fiji	Rural	1986	...	74519	...	78	64276	5804	...	...	3552	74597	5.9
French Polynesia	Total	1988	39513	39513	...	105	27072	8363	...	...	[36] 4078	39618	4.8
New Caledonia	Total	1989	40051	38975	1076	215	22717	12708	...	...	4841	40266	4.1
New Caledonia	Urban	1989	22258	21985	273	169	9189	10890	...	...	2348	22427	3.6
New Caledonia	Rural	1989	17793	16990	803	46	13528	1818	...	...	2493	17839	4.7
New Zealand	Total	1991	1175673	1161933	13740	7242	846342	[37] 262233	91560	160092	[38] 55839	1185396	2.9
New Zealand	Urban	1991	1011225	1001892	9333	5415	734913	[37] 235458	85824	140400	[38] 33354	1018476	2.9
New Zealand	Rural	1991	164445	160041	4407	1824	111429	[37] 26775	5736	19692	[38] 22485	166920	3.1
Tonga	Total	1986	...	...	...	...	...	...	...	...	...	15091	6.3
Tonga	Urban	1986	...	...	...	...	...	...	...	...	...	3233	6.6
Tonga	Rural	1986	...	...	...	...	...	...	...	...	...	11858	6.2
Wallis & Futuna Islands	Total	1990	2657	2640	17	...	2146	128	...	...	74	2667	5.1

Source: United Nations, Human Settlements Statistics Questionnaire 1992.

Housing Units: A housing unit is a separate and independent place of abode intended for habitation by one household.

Conventional dwelling refers to a room or a suite of rooms and its accessories in a permanent building or structurally separate part thereof, which by the way it has been built, rebuilt or converted, is intended for habitation by one household and is not, at the time of the census or other inquiry, used wholly for other purposes.

Unconventional dwellings refer to units that are occupied by households but that are considered inappropriate for human habitation. This unfitness for human habitation is expressed as a lack of elements that are needed for one structure to be a conventional dwelling. All those units which are not separate and independent places of abode, or built of waste materials, or in parts of permanent buildings that are not intended for human habitation are defined as unconventional dwellings. This category includes squatter settlements, slums and other improvised and marginal housing units.

Collective Living Quarters: This category includes structurally separate and independent places of abode intended for habitation by large groups of individuals or several households and occupied at the time of the census.

Tenure status indicates whether the household occupies the housing unit as owner, tenant, sub-tenant, free of charge or some other arrangement.

For additional information and definition of the term **'Household'** refer to technical notes of table 7.

TABLE 8 (continued)

Households' Housing Statistics, Selected Countries

Notes:

1. Data refer to housing units.
2. Data refer to households occupying a housing unit free of charge.
3. Data computed by UN.
4. Data refer to temporary housing.
5. Data refer to institutions and quarters.
6. Data refer to domestic households only.
7. Figures exclude Assam and some areas where 1981 Census could not be conducted.
8. Not including households in qibbuzim.
9. Data on Households by Tenure refer to 1990.
10. Data on Households by Tenure refer to 1992.
11. Data are preliminary.
12. Figures on population and households refer to Singapore Residents only (citizens and permanent residents). Figures on housing and households are preliminary data grossed up from the 10% sample data. Singapore is a city state.
13. Data refer to living quarters other than housing units.
14. Data refer to rented housing units.
15. Data include households whose tenure is unknown.
16. Including estates.
17. Data are displayed as received by the UN. However, the sum of the urban and rural differs from the total.
18. Data as reported.
19. The category 'Other' covers two categories, as follows:

	Total	Urban	Rural
Households that are owners and renters at the same time	30842	27893	2949
Other	3146	1692	1434

20. Households living under the title of tenant, co-tenant.
21. Households living under the title of sub-tenant, bed-tenant and without title.
22. The category 'Unconventional dwellings' here refers to Temporary Private Household, that is a private household occupying a caravan mobile home or other temporary dwelling and includes travelling people and homeless persons living rough on Census night.
23. Including 15,566 private households/living quarters with no information on densely/sparsely populated areas (33,400 persons).
24. Including households in conventional dwellings co-operatives.
25. Included are 538,752 principal residences occupied free of charge.
26. Data refer to households occupying units free of charge and sub-tenant households.
27. Tenants refer to holders of tenancy rights.
28. Data refer to dwellings occupied by a household whose member is a holder of tenancy rights.
29. Other refers to tenants and subtenants and unknown.
30. 'Other' includes 'not reported'.
31. Data refer to households paying their housing in service.
32. Data are estimated on the basis of 2.5 % sample.
33. Data include occupied housing units whether or not people were present or absent.
34. Data refer to Belongers (citizens of the Turks and Caicos Islands) only.
35. Data include 929 households occupying housing units free of rent and 70 households with status not stated.
36. 'Other' refer to dwellings occupied free of rent and dwellings offered by employer.
37. Tenanted dwellings include those for which no landlord is specified.
38. Data refer to dwellings occupied rent free and those of unspecified tenure.

TABLE 9

Households' Housing Statistics, Selected Cities

| | | | Number of Households in: | | | | Number of Households by Tenure: | | | | | All Households | |
| | | | Housing Units | | | Collective Living Quarters | Owner Occupants | Tenants | | | Other | | | |
			Total	Conventional	Unconventional			Total	Govern. Housing Units	Private Housing Units			Number	Size
AFRICA														
Angola	Cabinda	1983	...	...	...	...	...	...	...	...	...	21221	5.5
Angola	Luanda	1983	...	...	...	...	...	...	...	...	...	161120	5.7
Angola	Lubango	1983	...	...	...	...	...	...	...	...	...	16071	6.0
Ethiopia	Addis Ababa	1984	...	...	...	...	85765	...	157637	...	[1] 16153	...	...
Ethiopia	Asmara	1984	...	...	...	...	20859	...	33076	...	[1] 1567	...	...
Ethiopia	Dire Dawa	1984	...	...	...	...	8889	...	11621	...	[1] 1155	...	...
Ethiopia	Nazret	1984	...	...	...	...	6798	...	7483	...	[1] 287	...	...
Gambia	Banjul	1983	...	...	...	...	...	...	...	...	...	8026	5.3
Kenya	Kisumu	1989	...	...	...	...	...	...	...	...	...	47690	4.0
Kenya	Mombasa	1989	...	...	...	...	...	...	...	...	...	124468	3.7
Kenya	Nairobi	1989	...	...	...	...	...	...	...	...	...	382863	3.5
Kenya	Nakuru	1989	...	...	...	...	...	...	...	...	...	46800	3.5
Madagascar	Atananarivo	1993	...	...	...	...	...	...	...	...	...	149166	4.5
Madagascar	Fianarantsoa	1993	...	...	...	...	...	...	...	...	...	20857	4.7
Madagascar	Mahajanga	1993	...	...	...	...	...	...	...	...	...	25299	4.0
Madagascar	Toamasina	1993	...	...	...	...	...	...	...	...	...	29923	4.3
Malawi	Blantyre-Limbe	1987	...	...	...	...	...	...	...	...	...	83545	4.0
Malawi	Lilongwe	1987	...	...	...	...	...	...	...	...	...	50730	4.4
Malawi	Mzuzu	1987	...	...	...	...	...	...	...	...	...	9564	4.6
Malawi	Zomba	1987	...	...	...	...	...	...	...	...	...	9818	4.4
Mali	Bamako	1987	...	...	...	...	47963	44989	...	...	10489	105394	6.2
Mali	Mopti	1987	...	...	...	...	...	...	...	...	...	13442	5.6
Mali	Segou	1987	...	...	...	...	...	...	...	...	...	14745	6.0
Mali	Sikasso	1987	...	...	...	...	...	...	...	...	...	11543	6.4
Mauritius	Beau Bassin-Rose Hill	1990	22052	22045	7	8	14619	6068	...	...	1359	22060	4.2
Mauritius	Curepipe	1990	15954	15939	15	13	10658	3799	...	...	1492	15967	4.1
Mauritius	Port-Louis	1990	30636	30619	17	20	18258	9485	...	...	2890	30656	4.3
Mauritius	Quatre-Bornes	1990	16099	16090	9	6	11560	3598	...	...	936	16105	4.3
Reunion	Le Tampon	1990	...	...	...	...	8280	3800	...	3800	[2] 1230	13310	3.6
Reunion	Saint-Denis	1990	...	...	...	...	11097	21285	...	21285	[2] 2292	34674	3.5
Reunion	St. Paul	1990	...	...	...	...	12721	4168	...	4168	[2] 962	17851	4.0
Reunion	St. Pierre	1990	...	...	...	...	9265	5322	...	5322	[2] 1451	16038	3.6
South Africa	Cape Town	1985	483121	418000	65121	...	...	...	...	...	...	...	...
South Africa	Pretoria	1991	...	127680	...	...	...	...	...	...	...	...	...
Tunisia	Tunis	1989	...	...	...	...	98740	46842	...	...	15580	168464	4.8
ASIA														
Cyprus	Larnaca	1982	13166	13007	159	17	5616	2055	...	...	5513	13184	3.7
Cyprus	Limassol	1982	29845	29505	340	33	16240	7699	...	...	5941	29880	3.6
Cyprus	Nicosia	1982	41621	41122	499	182	21985	10967	...	...	8855	41807	3.6
Cyprus	Paphos	1982	5874	5777	97	5	3756	1077	...	...	1046	5879	3.5
India	Bombay	1981	...	...	...	...	608755	974340	...	...	...	...	...
India	Delhi	1991	...	...	...	...	1130710	508009	...	...	58109	...	...
Iraq	Baghdad	1987	...	511942	...	...	313527	121750	12127	109623	52950	...	...
Iraq	Basra	1987	...	112269	...	...	60038	27488	11829	15659	18026	...	...
Iraq	Kirkuk	1987	...	84824	...	...	50142	22633	8110	14523	8191	...	...
Iraq	Mosul	1987	...	206206	...	...	137740	29522	7284	22238	29036	...	...
Japan [3]	Osaka	1988	967250	...	...	5130	390289	563183	134130	429053	35680	[4] 967250	...
Japan [3]	Sapporo	1988	575950	...	...	2540	273890	308398	34053	274345	43991	[4] 575950	...
Japan [3]	Tokyo	1988	3137010	...	...	15530	1311884	1665945	268403	1397542	230361	[4] 3137010	...
Japan [3]	Yokohama	1988	1009020	...	...	4610	570644	418367	79432	338935	87180	[4] 1009020	...
Maldives	Male'	1990	...	...	...	...	...	...	...	...	...	5613	9.8
Myanmar	Mandalay	1983	102889	...	...	...	...	...	...	...	...	102889	5.2
Myanmar	Moulmein	1983	39869	...	...	...	...	...	...	...	...	39869	5.5
Myanmar	Pathein	1983	30270	...	...	...	...	...	...	...	...	30270	4.8
Myanmar	Yangon	1983	473997	...	...	...	...	...	...	...	...	473997	5.3
Pakistan	Faisalabad	1981	...	...	...	...	...	...	...	...	...	209768	5.3
Pakistan	Islamabad	1981	...	...	...	...	...	...	...	...	...	59019	3.5
Pakistan	Karachi	1981	...	...	...	...	...	...	...	...	...	811850	6.4
Pakistan	Lahore	1981	...	...	...	...	...	...	...	...	...	447509	6.7
Qatar	Doha	1986	30676	...	...	3595	...	...	...	...	...	[4] 30676	...
Qatar	Rayyan	1986	9995	...	...	715	...	...	...	...	...	[4] 9995	...
Qatar	Umm Said	1986	1039	...	...	55	...	...	...	...	...	[4] 1039	...
Qatar	Wakra	1986	1936	...	...	80	...	...	...	...	...	[4] 1936	...

TABLE 9 *(continued)*

Households' Housing Statistics, Selected Cities

			Number of Households in:				Number of Households by Tenure:					All Households	
			Housing Units			Collec- tive Living Quarters	Owner Occu- pants	Tenants			Other		
			Total	Conven- tional	Uncon- ven- tional			Total	Govern. Housing Units	Private Housing Units		Number	Size
ASIA (continued)													
Republic of Korea	Incheon	1990	486470	...	...	595	252408	224470	...	...	9592	[4] 486470	3.7
Republic of Korea	Pusan	1990	993206	...	...	1032	398155	571309	...	...	22016	[4] 993206	3.8
Republic of Korea	Seoul	1990	2817251	...	...	3060	1127178	1610535	...	...	68089	[4] 2817251	3.7
Republic of Korea	Taegu	1990	596701	...	...	1574	221256	359308	...	...	16157	[4] 596701	3.7
Syrian Arab Republic	Aleppo	1981	164423	164215	208	170	...	...	...	...	...	164593	6.0
Syrian Arab Republic	Damascus	1981	199024	198402	622	291	...	...	...	...	...	199315	5.6
Syrian Arab Republic	Homs	1981	56305	56204	101	44	...	...	...	...	...	56349	6.2
Syrian Arab Republic	Lattakia	1981	33799	33735	64	74	...	...	...	...	...	33873	5.8
Thailand [5]	Bangkok	1990	...	...	...	...	278871	166257	12701	97577	51686	1319000	4.5
Thailand [5]	Chon Buri	1990	...	...	...	...	67416	9465	238	7280	9083	202000	4.2
Thailand [5]	Nakhon Si Thammarat	1990	...	...	...	...	165989	4695	939	2383	13554	293000	4.8
Thailand [5]	Songkhla	1990	...	...	...	...	114389	4309	855	2619	7760	244000	4.5
Turkey	Adana	1985	...	...	...	...	232831	71971	...	...	...	304802	5.7
Turkey	Ankara	1985	...	...	...	...	450316	233521	...	...	...	683837	4.8
Turkey	Istanbul	1985	...	...	...	...	786987	506520	...	...	...	1293507	4.5
Turkey	Izmir	1985	...	...	...	...	389827	155621	...	...	...	545448	4.2
Viet Nam	Da Nang	1989	76565	...	...	...	...	...	...	...	...	[4] 76565	4.8
Viet Nam	Haiphong	1989	80165	...	...	...	...	...	...	...	...	[4] 80165	4.4
Viet Nam	Hanoi	1989	232573	...	...	...	...	...	...	...	...	[4] 232573	3.9
Viet Nam	Ho Chi Minh	1989	517606	...	...	...	...	...	...	...	...	[4] 517606	5.4
EUROPE													
Austria	Graz	1981	...	103353	...	[6] 672	40788	45546	7197	38349	17400	104025	2.3
Austria	Linz	1981	...	82785	...	[6] 5104	17965	54713	25985	28728	10891	87889	2.3
Austria	Salzburg	1981	...	59028	...	[6] 1253	24392	29110	5925	23186	5642	60281	2.3
Austria	Vienna	1981	...	723461	...	[6] 2482	121728	550237	57737	492501	53645	725943	2.1
Bosnia & Herzegovina	Sarajevo	1981	111416	111416	...	...	...	...	...	...	...	[4] 111416	3.3
Bulgaria	Bourgas	1985	...	70600	...	...	...	...	...	...	...	...	...
Bulgaria	Plovdiv	1985	...	118611	...	...	...	...	...	...	...	...	...
Bulgaria	Sofia	1985	...	445940	...	...	...	...	...	...	...	...	...
Bulgaria	Varna	1985	...	109400	...	...	...	...	...	...	...	...	...
Channel Islands	Guernsey	1991	...	21215	...	432	14516	6699	2208	4491	-	21647	2.7
Channel Islands	Jersey	1991	32463	32463	...	...	16088	15578	4410	11168	977	[4] 32463	2.6
Croatia	Zagreb	1981	234483	234483	...	...	...	...	...	...	...	[4] 234483	2.8
Finland	Espoo	1989	66493	66493	...	...	46766	17267	...	...	758	66493	2.6
Finland	Helsinki	1989	237589	237589	...	...	139149	92846	...	...	3800	237589	2.1
Finland	Tampere	1989	78253	78253	...	...	54400	21872	...	...	845	78253	2.2
Finland	Turku	1989	75033	75033	...	...	53172	20373	...	...	855	75033	2.1
France	Lyon	1990	189700	...	...	...	58980	121880	31460	90420	[2] 8840	[4] 189700	2.1
France	Marseille	1990	344500	...	...	...	148180	177840	58700	119140	[2] 18480	[4] 344500	2.4
France	Paris	1990	1090480	...	...	...	310860	683620	127600	556020	[2] 96000	[4] 1090480	1.9
France	Toulouse	1990	162600	...	...	...	54060	99120	25200	73920	[2] 9420	[4] 162600	2.1
Germany	Berlin (west)	1987	1094017	1092688	1329	...	114602	924309	...	...	55106	1111010	1.8
Germany	Bonn	1987	142396	142341	55	...	31863	102210	...	...	8323	147429	1.9
Germany	Hamburg	1987	828796	827198	1598	...	134285	642132	...	...	52379	841173	1.9
Germany	Munich	1987	650783	649116	1667	...	109197	511113	...	...	30473	666741	1.8
Hungary	Budapest	1990	850069	849798	271	...	356825	[7] 448296	...	...	[8] 44677	[4] 850069	...
Hungary	Debrecen	1990	78885	78854	31	...	51267	[7] 23960	...	...	[8] 3627	[4] 78885	...
Hungary	Miskolc	1990	73500	73487	13	...	41680	[7] 29631	...	...	[8] 2176	[4] 73500	...
Hungary	Szeged	1990	68893	68877	16	...	42113	[7] 23114	...	...	[8] 3650	[4] 68893	...
Ireland	Cork	1986	[4] 37014	36944	[9] 70	155	20485	14679	7747	6932	565	37169	3.6
Ireland	Dublin	1986	[4] 154168	153859	[9] 309	586	86550	60935	28243	32692	3079	154754	3.2
Ireland	Galway	1986	[4] 12458	12382	[9] 76	96	...	...	...	...	...	12554	3.8
Ireland	Limerick	1986	[4] 15455	15406	[9] 49	87	8381	6555	4392	2163	245	15542	3.6
Isle of Man	Douglas	1991	...	8447	...	...	4887	3483	2010	1473	77	...	...
Italy	Milan	1991	...	583104	...	...	...	...	...	...	...	591131	2.3
Italy	Naples	1991	...	...	...	...	...	...	...	...	...	309860	3.4
Italy	Rome	1991	...	988543	...	...	...	...	...	...	...	1003182	2.7
Italy	Turin	1991	...	...	...	...	...	...	...	...	...	405818	2.4
Latvia	Daugavpils	1991	40534	40534	...	5205	...	...	32315	...	...	51400	2.4
Latvia	Liepaja	1991	40128	40128	...	4747	...	...	37639	...	...	49092	2.3
Latvia	Riga	1991	308922	308922	...	38032	...	...	279352	...	...	383927	2.4
Netherlands	Amsterdam	1989	[4] 374106	372309	1797	...	[10] 36068	[10] 338038	[10] 18159	[10] 319879	...	...	...
Netherlands	Hague, The	1989	[4] 209515	208880	635	...	[10] 62149	[10] 147286	[10] 26633	[10] 120653	...	...	...
Netherlands	Rotterdam	1989	[4] 272933	271964	969	...	[10] 42813	[10] 230120	[10] 25268	[10] 204852	...	...	...
Netherlands	Utrecht	1989	[4] 111010	110200	810	...	[10] 29400	[10] 81610	[10] 15968	[10] 65642	...	...	...

TABLE 9 (continued)

Households' Housing Statistics, Selected Cities

			Number of Households in:				Number of Households by Tenure:					All Households	
			Housing Units			Collective Living Quarters	Owner Occupants	Tenants			Other		
			Total	Conventional	Unconventional			Total	Govern. Housing Units	Private Housing Units		Number	Size
EUROPE (continued)													
Norway	Bergen	1990	93949	93949	...	...	71701	22248	...	...	...	93949	2.3
Norway	Oslo	1990	244434	244434	...	...	185763	58671	...	...	...	244434	1.9
Norway	Stavanger	1990	42680	42680	...	...	33152	9528	...	...	...	42680	2.3
Norway	Trondheim	1990	60407	60407	...	...	46570	13837	...	...	...	60407	2.3
Poland	Krakow	1988	254521	254446	75	...	31549	[11] 201892	97362	104530	21005	254521	2.9
Poland	Lodz	1988	342235	342191	44	...	27242	[11] 290776	152882	137894	24173	342235	2.5
Poland	Warsaw	1988	640090	640032	58	...	68872	[11] 520268	242723	277545	50892	640090	2.6
Poland	Wroclaw	1988	222708	222645	63	...	27635	[11] 175474	98984	76490	19536	222708	2.9
Romania	Brasov	1992	105976	105851	125	...	62047	43406	...	...	398	[4] 105976	2.9
Romania	Bucarest	1992	742066	741937	129	...	437563	300987	...	...	3387	[4] 742066	2.7
Romania	Constanta	1992	111456	111393	63	...	77814	32796	...	...	783	[4] 111456	3.1
Romania	Timisoara	1992	115597	115421	176	...	78480	36325	...	...	616	[4] 115597	2.7
Russian Federation	Moscow	1989	2429095	2429095	...	...	288716	2800236	2797214	3022	59481	[4] 2429095	2.8
Russian Federation	Nizhny Novgorod	1989	376676	376676	...	...	66038	428318	426075	2243	7034	[4] 376676	2.9
Russian Federation	Novosibirsk	1989	363072	363072	...	...	77819	376999	373851	3148	7175	[4] 363072	3.1
Russian Federation	St. Petersburg	1989	974575	974575	...	...	221654	1332041	1329532	2509	65639	[4] 974575	2.9
Spain	Barcelona	1991	...	...	...	...	...	...	...	...	...	596186	...
Spain	Madrid	1991	...	...	...	...	...	...	...	...	...	1004786	...
Spain	Sevilla	1991	...	...	...	...	...	...	...	...	...	205263	...
Spain	Valencia	1991	...	...	...	...	...	...	...	...	...	261218	...
Sweden	Goteborg	1990	209779	209779	-	-	39601	123704	721	122983	46474	209779	2.1
Sweden	Malmo	1990	120464	120464	-	-	18558	60907	295	60612	40999	120464	1.8
Sweden	Stockholm	1990	351314	351314	-	-	37742	233271	1185	232086	80301	351314	1.8
Sweden	Uppsala	1990	72504	72504	-	-	20410	23823	1082	22741	28271	72504	2.2
Switzerland	Basel	1980	89364	89245	119	222	8562	78464	...	...	[12] 2219	89586	2.0
Switzerland	Berne	1980	69625	69507	118	211	6225	60636	...	...	[12] 2646	69836	2.1
Switzerland	Geneva	1980	81166	81085	81	233	2585	75370	...	...	[12] 3130	81399	1.9
Switzerland	Zurich	1980	182031	181837	194	431	11951	162949	...	...	[12] 6937	182462	2.0
TFYR Macedonia	Skoplje	1981	121658	121658	...	...	...	...	...	...	...	[4] 121658	4.1
Yugoslavia	Belgrade	1981	393678	393678	...	...	...	...	...	...	...	[4] 393678	3.0
LATIN AMERICA													
Bolivia	Cochabamba	1988	...	81714	...	...	48400	22800	...	...	14100	...	...
Bolivia	La Paz	1988	...	156601	...	...	75300	46400	...	...	33500	...	...
Bolivia	Oruro	1988	...	40306	...	...	18300	12600	...	...	7400	...	...
Bolivia	Santa Cruz	1988	...	105858	...	...	59100	26000	...	...	26300	...	...
Cayman Islands	Georgetown	1989	4445	...	...	...	1831	...	51	2298	265	4445	2.9
Cuba	Camaguey	1981	...	...	...	...	...	...	...	...	...	65235	3.8
Cuba	Havana	1981	...	...	...	...	...	...	...	...	...	519924	3.7
Cuba	Holguin	1981	...	...	...	...	...	...	...	...	...	45718	4.1
Cuba	Santiago de Cuba	1981	...	...	...	...	...	...	...	...	...	79701	4.4
Falkland Islands (Malvinas)	Stanley	1991	610	565	45	...	327	283	...	...	...	610	2.6
French Guiana	Cayenne	1990	...	...	...	...	3894	8436	...	8436	[2] 826	13156	3.1
French Guiana	Kourou	1990	...	...	...	...	982	2510	...	2510	[2] 548	4040	3.2
French Guiana	Remire - Montjoly	1990	...	...	...	...	1462	1628	...	1628	[2] 386	3476	3.4
French Guiana	Saint-Laurent-du-Moroni	1990	...	...	...	...	1466	1056	...	1056	[2] 865	3387	4.0
Guadeloupe	Abymes	1990	...	...	...	...	10025	8071	...	8071	[2] 676	18772	3.3
Guadeloupe	Basse-Terre	1990	...	...	...	...	1926	2208	...	2208	[2] 317	5175	2.7
Guadeloupe	Point-a-Pitre	1990	...	...	...	...	2056	6378	...	6378	[2] 261	8695	2.9
Guadeloupe	St. Martin	1990	...	...	...	...	2168	5872	-	5872	[2] 329	8369	3.4
Guatemala	Guatemala City	1981	...	...	...	...	75275	58328	...	58328	18920	152523	4.9
Guatemala	Mazatenango	1981	...	...	...	...	3506	2411	...	2411	1570	7487	5.1
Guatemala	Puerto Barrios	1981	...	...	...	...	6013	2156	...	2156	1700	9868	4.8
Guatemala	Quezaltenango	1981	...	...	...	...	8978	8144	...	8144	1396	13518	5.4
Haiti	Jacmel	1982	...	3006	...	...	...	...	...	...	...	...	...
Haiti	Jeremie	1982	...	3831	...	...	...	...	...	...	...	...	...
Haiti	Les Cayes	1982	...	6101	...	...	...	...	...	...	...	...	...
Haiti	Port-au-Prince	1982	...	150609	...	...	[13] 40725	[13] 108248	...	...	...	...	...
Honduras	Choluteca	1988	...	10022	138	...	[10] 6622	[10] 2458	...	...	[10] 743	...	...
Honduras	El Progreso	1988	...	10902	275	...	[10] 7719	[10] 2251	...	...	[10] 702	...	...
Honduras	San Pedro Sula	1988	...	55926	1384	...	[10] 32345	[10] 18248	...	...	[10] 3942	...	...
Honduras	Tegucigalpa	1988	...	108208	1203	...	[10] 69871	[10] 26277	...	...	[10] 6425	...	...
Martinique	Fort-de-France	1990	...	...	...	...	14397	16153	...	16153	[2] 1791	32340	3.0
Martinique	Lamentin	1990	...	...	...	...	5379	2613	...	2613	[2] 552	8544	3.5
Martinique	Sainte Marie	1990	...	...	...	...	3924	876	...	876	[2] 256	5056	3.9
Martinique	Schoelcher	1990	...	...	...	...	3115	2908	...	2908	[2] 296	6319	3.1
Mexico	Mexico City	1990	3172706	...	...	...	2169173	684506	...	...	247480	[4] 3172706	4.7

TABLE 9 (continued)

Households' Housing Statistics, Selected Cities

			Number of Households in:				Number of Households by Tenure:					All Households	
			Housing Units			Collective Living Quarters	Owner Occupants	Tenants			Other		
			Total	Conventional	Unconventional			Total	Govern. Housing Units	Private Housing Units		Number	Size
LATIN AMERICA (continued)													
Panama	Colon	1990	15520	...	...	...	10 1729	10 7837	...	...	10 5905	4 15520	3.5
Panama	Panama	1990	106887	...	...	...	10 56330	10 39367	...	...	10 9712	4 106887	3.9
Panama	San Miguelito	1990	51667	...	...	...	10 44796	10 4601	...	...	10 2248	4 51667	4.7
Paraguay	Asuncion	1982	...	...	...	...	10 56864	10 24246	...	...	10 10416	...	...
Peru	Arequipa	1991	122268	122268	...	3742	84272	24507	...	...	7092	126010	5.1
Peru	Callao	1991	90870	90870	...	22546	37112	34459	...	...	5834	113416	5.4
Peru	Lima	1991	899302	899302	...	223133	473544	304946	...	...	47707	1122435	5.4
Peru	Trujillo	1991	109304	108930	374	189	70697	19108	...	...	14345	109493	5.3
US Virgin Islands	Charlotte Amalie	1990	18433	18433	...	...	6397	9248	...	...	...	15645	3.1
Venezuela	Barquisimeto	1990	...	...	...	...	78735	15980	...	...	32897	...	...
Venezuela	Caracas	1990	...	...	...	...	204255	113955	...	...	97915	...	...
Venezuela	Valencia	1990	...	171920	...	...	100934	28246	...	...	65105	194391	...
NORTHERN AMERICA													
Canada	Montreal	1992	1235720	1234520	1205	1765	...	...	...	...	...	4 1237485	2.5
Canada	Ottawa	1992	349260	348205	1050	545	...	...	...	...	...	4 349805	2.6
Canada	Toronto	1992	1366700	1365330	1370	1645	...	...	...	...	...	4 1368345	2.8
Canada	Vancouver	1992	609430	609285	150	875	...	...	...	...	...	4 610305	2.6
United States	Chicago 14	1990	...	...	...	...	1795833	1112230	...	...	...	...	...
United States	Los Angeles 14	1990	...	...	...	...	2644998	2255722	...	...	...	...	...
United States	New York 14	1990	...	...	...	...	3373702	3247537	...	...	...	...	...
United States	Washington D.C. 14	1990	...	...	...	...	883612	575746	...	...	...	...	...
OCEANIA													
Australia	Brisbane	1986	387872	377046	7145	...	273810	93916	18525	75391	14847	387872	3.0
Australia	Canberra	1986	79309	77979	479	...	52204	24222	10261	13961	2520	79309	3.1
Australia	Melbourne	1986	960556	934057	10224	...	699283	207961	34454	173507	49981	960556	2.9
Australia	Sydney	1986	1145396	1110100	15761	...	767316	317493	70604	246889	55439	1145396	2.9
Fiji	Labasa	1986	4 3191	3191	...	2	...	...	...	...	...	3193	5.2
Fiji	Lami	1986	4 2551	2551	...	13	...	...	...	...	...	2564	6.5
Fiji	Lautoka	1986	4 7319	7319	...	21	...	...	...	...	...	7340	5.3
Fiji	Suva	1986	4 25040	24951	...	89	...	...	...	...	...	25040	5.6
New Caledonia	Noumea	1989	18593	18500	93	163	6556	10215	...	...	1985	18756	3.5
New Zealand	Auckland	1991	111993	110673	1320	744	67773	15 38775	12711	24537	16 4224	112833	2.8
New Zealand	Christchurch	1991	107214	106632	582	474	79116	15 24120	8484	14616	16 3411	107703	2.7
New Zealand	Manukau	1991	67152	66468	681	192	49503	15 14754	7506	6759	16 2211	67341	3.4
New Zealand	Wellington	1991	55473	55110	363	240	36150	15 16863	4200	11988	16 2112	55725	2.7
Tonga	Nuku'alofa	1986	...	...	...	...	...	...	...	...	...	3233	6.4
Wallis & Futuna Islands	Mata-Utu	1990	4 239	233	6	4 5	162	21	...	...	32	244	5.0

Source: United Nations, Human Settlements Statistics Questionnaire 1992

For additional information and definitions of the relevant terms refer to technical notes of tables 7 and 8.

Notes:

1. Data refer to households occupying a housing unit free of charge and 'not stated' tenure.
2. Data refer to households occupying a housing unit free of charge.
3. Data on Households by Tenure refer to 1990.
4. Data computed by UN.
5. Data on Households by Tenure refer to 1980.
6. Estimates.
7. Households living under the title of tenant, co-tenant.
8. Households living under the title of sub-tenant, bed-tenant and without title.
9. The category 'Unconventional dwellings' here refers to Temporary Private Household, that is a private household occupying a caravan mobile home or other temporary dwelling and includes travelling people and homeless persons living rough on Census night.
10. Data refer to housing units.
11. Including households in conventional dwellings co-operatives.
12. Data refer to units occupied free of charge and sub-tenant households.
13. Data are estimated on the basis of 2.5 % sample.
14. Data refer to the City Metropolitan Statistical Area (MSA).
15. Tenanted dwellings include those for which no landlord is specified.
16. Data refer to dwellings occupied rent free and those of unspecified tenure.

TABLE 10

Housing Construction, Number and Rate per Thousand Population, Selected Cities, 1987–1991

		Conventional Dwellings Constructed Annually									
		1987		1988		1989		1990		1991	
		Number	Rate	Number	Rate	Number	Rate	Number	Rate	Number	Rate
AFRICA											
Kenya	Kisumu	...	...	...	...	147	0.9	151	...	...	...
Kenya	Mombasa	...	...	...	...	239	0.5	363	...	...	...
Kenya	Nairobi	...	...	...	...	762	0.6	432	...	...	...
Kenya	Nakuru	...	...	...	...	154	0.8	49	...	...	...
Morocco	Casablanca [1]	5498	2.0	3436	1.2	3005	1.0	3752	1.3	...	...
Morocco	Fez [1]	480	0.5	483	0.5	510	0.5	416	0.4	...	...
Morocco	Marrakech [1]	1468	1.0	1264	0.9	1570	1.1	1205	0.8	...	...
Morocco	Rabat-Sale [1]	869	0.8	1385	1.2	1266	1.0	831	0.7	...	...
South Africa	Pretoria	1444	2.8	1769	3.4	1111	2.1	957	...	...	...
ASIA											
Cyprus	Larnaca [2]	807	15.3	779	...	836	13.7	1306	...	...	...
Cyprus	Limassol [2]	1628	13.8	1606	...	1616	12.2	1558	...	...	...
Cyprus	Nicosia [2]	1468	8.9	1950	...	1918	11.4	1714	...	...	...
Cyprus	Paphos [2]	326	14.4	450	...	697	25.1	657	...	...	...
Iraq	Baghdad	3714	1.0	5429	1.4	5770	1.4	4487	1.1	2200	0.5
Iraq	Basra	267	0.3	1092	1.2	7506	8.1	3867	4.1	735	0.8
Iraq	Kirkuk	4204	7.0	2997	5.0	3486	5.7	3573	5.8	1414	2.3
Iraq	Mosul	2139	1.4	2459	1.6	3809	2.4	3427	2.1	1694	1.0
Israel	Haifa [3]	690	3.1	605	2.7	865	3.9	910	3.7	755	...
Israel	Jerusalem [3]	2105	4.4	1090	2.2	2075	4.1	1650	3.1	1615	...
Israel	Tel Aviv-Yafo [3]	675	1.4	410	1.3	870	2.7	920	2.7	720	...
Turkey	Adana	3320	1.9	5700	3.1	10185	5.4	3960	2.1	...	...
Turkey	Ankara	18167	5.5	20646	6.3	28778	8.8	26480	8.2	...	...
Turkey	Istanbul	19924	3.2	21265	3.2	23648	3.4	23593	3.3	...	...
Turkey	Izmir	21162	8.7	21945	8.7	30151	11.6	27664	10.4	...	...
EUROPE											
Austria	Graz	722	3.0	1341	5.6	473	2.0	950	4.0	...	...
Austria	Linz	1469	7.6	889	4.6	1158	6.0	398	2.0	...	...
Austria	Salzburg	521	3.8	589	4.3	699	5.0	648	4.6	...	...
Austria	Vienna	6183	4.2	6537	4.4	6403	4.3	4142	2.8	...	...
Bosnia & Herzegovina	Sarajevo	2902	...	1983	...	2018	...	2126	...	...	...
Bulgaria	Bourgas	1548	...	1761	...	1074	...	496	...	878	...
Bulgaria	Plovdiv	3399	...	2991	...	1119	...	1107	...	1265	...
Bulgaria	Sofia	15762	...	14988	...	10766	...	6214	...	3976	...
Bulgaria	Varna	2889	...	2648	...	1771	...	1224	...	741	...
Croatia	Zagreb	4140	...	4420	...	2831	...	3739	...	...	...
Finland	Espoo	2217	13.7	2143	12.9	2814	16.7	2902	17.0	[4] 2070	11.9
Finland	Helsinki	4065	8.3	3820	7.8	4981	10.2	4421	9.0	[4] 4908	9.9
Finland	Tampere	1314	7.7	1883	11.0	2206	12.9	2029	11.8	[4] 1904	11.0
Finland	Turku	747	4.6	857	5.4	1297	8.1	1581	9.9	[4] 1405	8.8
Germany	Berlin (west)	4932	2.4	4568	...	4883	...	4107	...	...	...
Germany	Bonn	589	2.1	681	...	959	...	1414	...	...	...
Germany	Hamburg	3112	1.9	2624	...	3131	...	2597	...	...	...
Germany	Munich	7171	5.9	6924	...	5700	...	5935	...	...	...
Ireland	Cork	474	3.6	422	3.2	801	6.3	895	7.1	1057	8.3
Ireland	Dublin	1510	11.4	1579	3.2	2275	4.7	2125	4.6	2214	4.6
Ireland	Galway	287	6.0	409	8.5	546	11.4	765	15.9	786	15.4
Ireland	Limerick	183	3.3	323	6.1	456	9.1	478	1.0	469	9.0
Italy	Milan [5]	1692	...	2342	...	1621	...	2200	...	...	...
Italy	Naples [5]	2474	...	...	...	10	...	5	...	...	...
Italy	Rome [5]	4643	...	5766	...	5565	...	5746	...	...	...
Italy	Turin [5]	801	...	1230	...	908	...	1330	...	...	...
Latvia	Daugavpils	1480	12.0	1383	11.2	1428	11.3	1061	8.4	[6] 888	7.0
Latvia	Liepaja	975	8.6	937	8.2	484	4.2	732	6.4	[6] 186	1.6
Latvia	Riga	6514	7.3	5027	5.5	5575	6.1	4004	4.4	[6] 2078	2.3
Netherlands	Amsterdam	5727	8.3	5196	7.5	4346	6.3	4220	6.0	...	...
Netherlands	Hague, The	1763	4.0	3426	7.7	1466	3.3	1544	3.5	...	...
Netherlands	Rotterdam	4221	7.4	4882	8.5	3679	6.4	4209	7.2	...	...
Netherlands	Utrecht	1261	5.5	1134	4.9	752	3.3	748	3.2	...	...
Norway	Bergen	1182	5.7	1982	9.4	1360	6.4	1512	7.1	1190	5.5
Norway	Oslo	3078	6.8	3344	7.3	2853	6.2	3581	7.8	2258	4.9
Norway	Stavanger	906	9.4	821	8.5	1066	11.0	650	6.6	628	6.3
Norway	Trondheim	1174	8.7	1078	7.9	798	5.8	839	6.1	680	4.9
Poland	Krakow	2678	3.6	2800	3.7	1424	1.9	2313	3.1	...	...
Poland	Lodz	2944	3.5	2496	2.9	2046	2.4	2309	2.7	...	...
Poland	Warsaw	5430	3.3	5477	3.3	4227	2.6	3136	1.9	...	...
Poland	Wroclaw	2796	4.4	3000	4.7	2017	3.2	1961	3.0	...	...

TABLE 10 *(continued)*

Housing Construction, Number and Rate per Thousand Population, Selected Cities, 1987–1991

| | | Conventional Dwellings Constructed Annually | | | | | | | | | |
| | | 1987 | | 1988 | | 1989 | | 1990 | | 1991 | |
		Number	Rate	Number	Rate	Number	Rate	Number	Rate	Number	Rate
EUROPE (continued)											
Russian Federation	Moscow	57700	6.7	54900	6.3	47500	5.5	38900	4.5	...	...
Russian Federation	Nizhny Novgorod	11600	8.1	14000	9.8	10700	7.4	...		...	...
Russian Federation	Novosibirsk	11900	8.4	12400	8.7	10000	6.9	9600	6.6	...	...
Russian Federation	St. Petersburg	33300	7.6	29700	6.7	31500	7.1	18600	4.2	...	...
San Marino	Borgo Maggiore	22	5.0	32	7.1	39	8.5	43	9.1	...	...
San Marino	Domagnano	12	6.7	28	14.7	24	12.6	20	10.0	...	...
San Marino	San Marino	7	1.7	15	3.7	21	5.1	17	4.1	...	...
San Marino	Serravalle	39	5.6	39	5.6	47	6.5	26	3.6	...	...
Spain	Barcelona	4819	...	2824	...	2964	...	3415	...	...	...
Spain	Madrid	13314	...	13126	...	9593	...	10395	...	...	...
Spain	Sevilla	3289	...	3200	...	2746	...	2761	...	...	...
Spain	Valencia	13995	...	13851	...	12169	...	13511	...	...	...
Sweden	Goteborg	764	1.8	1507	3.5	1771	4.1	1503	3.5	1615	...
Sweden	Malmo	492	2.1	475	2.0	1101	4.7	807	3.4	1090	...
Sweden	Stockholm	1837	2.8	2063	3.1	2118	3.2	2370	3.5	2481	...
Sweden	Uppsala	495	3.1	1099	6.8	1431	8.7	1289	7.7	1697	...
Switzerland	Basel	1558	...	1290	...	1165	...	1053	...	...	...
Switzerland	Berne	969	...	1510	...	806	...	503	...	...	...
Switzerland	Geneva	1898	...	2335	...	1876	...	2331	...	...	...
Switzerland	Zurich	3986	...	3341	...	3332	...	2919	...	...	...
TFYR Macedonia	Skoplje	2785	...	733	...	2132	...	1352	...	...	...
Ukraine	Donetsk	7400	...	7600	...	7600	...	5100	...	...	...
Ukraine	Kharkov	14000	...	12600	...	10400	...	10100	...	...	...
Ukraine	Kiev	23400	...	23900	...	24600	...	19400	...	...	...
Ukraine	Odessa	7300	...	7800	...	7500	...	6300	...	...	...
United Kingdom	Birmingham	1684	...	2288	...	1335	...	2331	...	...	...
United Kingdom	Glasgow	1743	...	1912	...	2116	...	2239	...	...	...
United Kingdom	Leeds	2136	...	1716	...	1784	...	1677	...	...	...
United Kingdom	London	13189	...	14644	...	15324	...	16437	...	...	...
Yugoslavia	Belgrade	4917	...	6587	...	7722	...	6293	...	...	...
LATIN AMERICA											
Honduras	Choluteca	...	...	...	...	579	10.2	607	10.2	637	10.3
Honduras	El Progreso	...	...	...	...	618	9.8	648	9.9	680	9.9
Honduras	San Pedro Sula	...	...	...	...	2704	8.8	3014	9.4	3150	9.5
Honduras	Tegucigalpa	...	...	...	...	7757	12.9	8215	13.1	8700	13.3
NORTHERN AMERICA											
Canada	Montreal	36634	...	35591	...	24040	...	23756	...	17329	...
Canada	Ottawa	7275	...	7774	...	7015	...	5511	...	4179	...
Canada	Toronto	36525	...	34242	...	39397	...	27936	...	26007	...
Canada	Vancouver	14110	...	16773	...	18044	...	19925	...	14630	...
United States	Chicago [7]	41200	...	41000	...	41100	...	31800	3.9	28600	...
United States	Los Angeles [7]	138700	...	134000	...	118200	...	102400	7.0	58700	...
United States	New York [7]	70400	...	59200	...	48100	...	35000	1.9	27800	...
United States	Washington D.C. [7]	37700	...	36400	...	36800	...	25800	6.6	25000	...
OCEANIA											
Australia	Brisbane	6495	5.3	10352	8.3	14436	11.3	10947	8.4	...	...
Australia	Canberra	2550	9.6	2620	9.6	2650	9.6	2400	8.5	...	...
Australia	Melbourne	20551	6.9	20989	7.0	25618	8.4	18560	6.0	...	...
Australia	Sydney	17481	5.0	22722	6.3	23796	6.5	18207	5.0	...	...
New Zealand	Auckland	1104	...	887	...	772	...	861	...	628	2.0
New Zealand	Christchurch	513	...	523	...	754	...	807	...	876	3.0
New Zealand	Manukau	1686	...	1685	...	1871	...	1600	...	1058	4.7
New Zealand	Wellington	534	...	551	...	538	...	465	...	366	2.4

Source: United Nations, Human Settlements Statistics Questionnaire 1992.

For additional information and definition of the term '**Conventional dwelling**' refer to technical notes of table 8.

Notes:
1. Data refer to issued construction licenses.
2. Data refer to the Government controlled area only.
3. 'Conventional dwellings constructed' include also residential buildings with unknown number of dwellings.
4. Preliminary data.
5. Data refer to authorized dwellings constructed.
6. Data refer to individual buildings.
7. Data refer to the City Metropolitan Statistical Area (MSA).

TABLE 11

Living Quarters by Type, Selected Countries

			Number of Living Quarters	Total Housing Units	Conventional Housing Units			Unconventional Housing Units	Collective Living Quarters			Type not Stated
					Total	Occupied	Vacant		Total	Hotels/ Rooming	Others	
AFRICA												
Gambia	Total	1983	81719	...	...	...	...	...	...	...	...	...
Ghana	Total	1984	1216677	1204395	1204395	1204395	...	...	7831	177	7654	4451
Ghana	Urban	1984	290900	282997	282997	282997	...	...	4727	165	4562	3176
Ghana	Rural	1984	925777	921398	921398	921398	...	...	3104	12	3092	1275
Malawi	Total	1987	[1] 2474602	...	...	...	...	...	...	...	...	...
Malawi	Urban	1987	[1] 224831	...	...	...	...	...	...	...	...	...
Malawi	Rural	1987	[1] 2249771	...	...	...	...	...	...	...	...	...
Mali	Total	1987	787783	...	...	...	...	...	...	...	...	...
Mali	Urban	1987	166686	...	...	...	...	...	...	...	...	...
Mali	Rural	1987	621097	...	...	...	...	...	...	...	...	...
Mauritius	Total	1990	224124	223821	223526	215384	8142	295	303	189	114	...
Mauritius	Urban	1990	92892	92772	92711	90427	2284	61	120	53	67	...
Mauritius	Rural	1990	131232	131049	130815	124957	5858	234	183	136	47	...
Reunion	Total	1990	176581	...	...	...	...	...	...	...	...	...
Reunion	Urban	1990	173410	...	...	...	...	...	...	...	...	...
Reunion	Rural	1990	3171	...	...	...	...	...	...	...	...	...
Tunisia	Total	1989	1512300	1512300	1438900	1290800	148100	73400	...	...	...	...
Tunisia	Urban	1989	...	[2] 827100	...	807300	...	19800	...	...	...	...
Tunisia	Rural	1989	...	[2] 537100	...	483500	...	53600	...	...	...	...
ASIA												
Brunei Darussalam	Total	1991	40351	...	...	...	...	...	...	...	...	...
Cyprus	Total	1982	170987	170621	168588	141910	26678	2033	355	77	278	11
Cyprus	Urban	1982	103367	103129	102040	88849	13191	1089	231	48	183	7
Cyprus	Rural	1982	67620	67492	66548	53061	13487	944	124	29	95	4
Hong Kong	Total	1991	1507997	1463775	1399914	...	...	[3] 63861	[4] 44222	...	...	...
India	Total	1981	...	121752109	...	113735542	8046567	...	...	...	...	...
India	Urban	1981	...	27604947	...	27604947	2292544	...	...	...	...	...
India	Rural	1981	...	86130595	...	86130595	5754023	...	...	...	...	...
Iraq	Total	1987	...	...	...	1759176	...	...	...	...	...	...
Iraq	Urban	1987	...	...	...	1269005	...	...	...	...	...	...
Iraq	Rural	1987	...	...	...	490171	...	...	...	...	...	...
Japan	Total	1988	...	42007300	...	...	...	...	183600	...	...	...
Japan	Urban	1988	...	33722400	...	...	...	...	135400	...	...	...
Japan	Rural	1988	...	8284900	...	...	...	...	48200	...	...	...
Jordan	Total	1979	...	376822	353865	313193	40672	22957	1927	...	...	...
Jordan	Urban	1979	...	217889	210922	187560	23362	6967	1444	...	...	...
Jordan	Rural	1979	...	158933	142943	125633	17310	15990	483	...	...	...
Kuwait	Total	1985	269091	248826	243372	213591	29781	5454	9772	...	...	...
Macau	Total	1991	105700	103943	[5] 99405	82863	14056	4538	1222	292	930	[66] 535
Myanmar	Total	1983	6750884	...	...	...	...	...	...	...	...	...
Myanmar	Urban	1983	1581582	...	...	...	...	...	...	...	...	...
Myanmar	Rural	1983	5169302	...	...	...	...	...	...	...	...	...
Republic of Korea	Total	1990	...	7570922	...	...	...	...	...	...	...	...
Republic of Korea	Urban	1990	...	4840422	...	...	...	...	...	...	...	...
Republic of Korea	Rural	1990	...	2730500	...	...	...	...	...	...	...	...
Singapore [7]	Total	1990	...	...	...	677600	...	...	...	...	...	...
Sri Lanka	Total	1981	3029132	2924418	2665319	2631945	33374	280690	[8] 83111	...	...	...
Sri Lanka	Urban	1981	547306	518496	474325	471830	2495	46264	[8] 26717	...	...	...
Sri Lanka	Rural	1981	[9] 2481826	2405922	2190994	2160115	30879	234432	[8] 56400	...	...	...
Syrian Arab Republic	Total	1981	1623715	1622444	1610946	1305550	305396	11498	1271	559	712	...
Syrian Arab Republic	Urban	1981	810891	810021	807941	622056	185885	2080	870	509	361	...
Syrian Arab Republic	Rural	1981	812824	812423	803005	683494	119511	9418	401	50	351	...
EUROPE												
Austria	Total	1981	...	...	3052036	2692883	359153	...	...	...	...	...
Austria	Urban	1981	...	...	1887624	1693775	193849	...	...	...	...	...
Austria	Rural	1981	...	...	1164412	999108	165304	...	...	...	...	...
Bulgaria	Total	1985	2903080	2705560	2687689	...	...	17871	24950	8684	...	...
Bulgaria	Urban	1985	1848300	1706334	...	...	...	16734	18871	3159	...	...
Bulgaria	Rural	1985	1054780	982492	981355	...	...	1137	6079	5525	...	...
Finland	Total	1989	2152938	2152938	2152938	2001129	151809	...	...	...	...	...
Finland	Urban	1989	1411659	1411659	1411659	1309180	102479	...	...	...	...	...
Finland	Rural	1989	741279	741279	741279	691949	49330	...	...	...	...	...

TABLE 11 *(continued)*

Living Quarters by Type, Selected Countries

			Number of Living Quarters	Total Housing Units	Conventional Housing Units			Unconventional Housing Units	Collective Living Quarters			Type not Stated
					Total	Occupied	Vacant		Total	Hotels/ Rooming	Others	
EUROPE (continued)												
France	Total	1990	26205040	...	...	...	...	...	...	...	...	...
France	Urban	1990	18940060	...	...	...	...	...	...	...	...	...
France	Rural	1990	7264980	...	...	...	...	...	...	...	...	...
Germany	Total	1987	26595449	26360005	26312848	25840424	472424	47157	...	...	235444	...
Germany	Urban	1987	10637906	10465723	10454386	10279404	174982	11337	...	...	172183	...
Germany	Rural	1987	15957543	15894282	15858462	15561020	297442	35820	...	...	63261	...
Gibraltar	Total	1981	...	...	6945	6945	...	...	...	8	...	...
Hungary	Total	1990	...	3855192	3853288	3687996	165292	1904	...	...	...	...
Hungary	Urban	1990	...	2400000	2399152	2316108	83044	848	...	...	...	...
Hungary	Rural	1990	...	1455192	1454136	1371888	82248	1056	...	...	...	...
Italy	Total	1991	24802884	...	...	...	...	...	...	...	...	...
Latvia	Total	1991	1024188	952507	952507	938741	13766	...	71681	5310	66371	...
Latvia	Urban	1991	700258	642275	642275	640292	1983	...	57983	5146	52837	...
Latvia	Rural	1991	323930	310232	310232	298449	11783	...	13698	164	13534	...
Netherlands	Total	1989	...	...	...	5836512	...	25309	...	14633	2098	...
Netherlands	Urban	1989	...	...	...	4050087	...	16873	...	12778	2098	...
Netherlands	Rural	1989	...	...	...	1786425	...	8436	...	1855		...
Norway	Total	1990	[10] 1751343	[10] 1751343	[10] 1751343	[10] 1751343	...	...	...	...	...	...
Norway	Urban	1990	1288839	1288839	1288839	1288839	...	...	...	...	...	...
Norway	Rural	1990	446938	446938	446938	446938	...	...	...	...	...	...
Poland	Total	1988	10887113	10878092	10875031	10716758	158273	3061	9021	...	...	...
Poland	Urban	1988	7143671	7136540	7135219	7039802	95417	1321	7131	...	...	...
Poland	Rural	1988	3743442	3741552	3739812	3676956	62856	1740	1890	...	...	...
Romania	Total	1992	7675149	7666181	7659003	7186748	472255	7178	8968	3200	5768	...
Romania	Urban	1992	4085286	4079552	4076335	3923118	153217	3217	5734	2071	3663	...
Romania	Rural	1992	3589863	3586629	3582668	3263630	319038	3961	3234	1129	2105	...
Russian Federation	Total	1989	...	46049197	...	...	...	...	...	5068	29132	1360171
Russian Federation	Urban	1989	...	31548550	...	...	...	...	...	3611	20029	1301266
Russian Federation	Rural	1989	...	14500647	...	...	...	...	...	1457	9103	58905
Spain	Total	1991	[11] 17172680	16705038	16667427	14440864	2226563	12009	24807	...	...	480446
Sweden	Total	1990	4043378	3861803	3861803	3830037	31766	-	-	-	...	181575
Sweden	Urban	1990	3467274	3289853	3289853	3260297	29556	-	-	-	...	177421
Sweden	Rural	1990	576104	571950	571950	569740	2210	-	-	-	...	4154
Switzerland	Total	1980	2731017	2724350	[12] 2722432	2413185	69801	1918	6667	...	...	...
Switzerland	Urban	1980	1702478	1699201	[12] 1698150	1600580	33188	1051	3277	...	...	...
Switzerland	Rural	1980	1028539	1025149	[12] 1024282	812605	36613	867	3390	...	...	...
Ukraine	Total	1992	...	17827000	...	...	...	...	[13] 121000	[14] 58100	...	...
Ukraine	Urban	1992	...	11302800	...	...	...	...	[13] 120400	[14] 57700	...	...
Ukraine	Rural	1992	...	6524200	...	...	...	...	[13] 600	[14] 400	...	...
LATIN AMERICA												
Aruba	Total	1991	...	19224	...	18538	...	673	20	...	19	14
Bolivia	Total	1988	1318800	1315900	1247400	...	...	68500	2900	...	...	...
Bolivia	Urban	1988	662800	...	...	...	...	116000	...	...	...	...
Bolivia	Rural	1988	656000	...	...	...	...	...	...	...	...	...
Cayman Islands	Total	1989	10489	10459	...	...	2023	...	30	21	9	...
Chile	Total	1982	2534763	2522369	2522369	2361997	160372	...	12392	1261	11131	...
Chile	Urban	1982	2102792	2093340	2093340	1966317	127023	...	9452	1042	8410	...
Chile	Rural	1982	431969	429029	429029	395680	33349	...	2940	219	2721	...
Cuba	Total	1981	2368453	2367025	2366124	[15] 2309350	56774	[16] 901	1428	...	...	...
Cuba	Urban	1981	1660671	1659591	1659067	[15] 1620091	38976	[16] 524	1080	...	...	...
Cuba	Rural	1981	707782	707434	707054	[15] 689259	17798	[16] 377	348	...	...	...
Ecuador	Total	1990	2339281	2335551	2335551	2111121	224430	...	3730	...	...	...
Ecuador	Urban	1990	1264470	1262424	1262424	1195378	67046	...	2046	...	...	...
Ecuador	Rural	1990	1074811	1073127	1073127	915743	157384	...	1684	...	...	...
Falkland Islands (Malvinas)	Total	1991	802	802	747	747	...	55	...	...	...	...
French Guiana	Total	1990	38324	...	...	...	...	...	...	...	85	...
French Guiana	Urban	1990	31409	...	...	...	...	...	...	...	75	...
French Guiana	Rural	1990	6915	...	...	...	...	...	...	...	10	...
Guadeloupe	Total	1990	134816	...	...	...	...	...	...	...	409	...
Guadeloupe	Urban	1990	132598	...	...	...	...	...	...	...	404	...
Guadeloupe	Rural	1990	2218	...	...	...	...	...	...	...	5	...

TABLE 11 (continued)

Living Quarters by Type, Selected Countries

			Number of Living Quarters	Total Housing Units	Conventional Housing Units			Unconventional Housing Units	Collective Living Quarters			Type not Stated
					Total	Occupied	Vacant		Total	Hotels/ Rooming	Others	
LATIN AMERICA (continued)												
Guatemala	Total	1981	...	1256156	1197317	...	...	58839	3442	822	2620	...
Guatemala	Urban	1981	...	410857	385220	...	...	25637	...	...	...	...
Guatemala	Rural	1981	...	...	812097	...	...	...	...	...	...	...
Haiti	Total	1986	...	...	...	1164136	...	...	...	...	...	...
Haiti	Urban	1986	...	...	...	285927	...	...	...	...	...	...
Haiti	Rural	1986	...	...	...	878209	...	...	...	...	...	...
Honduras	Total	1988	891391	...	766385	[17] 762117	107665	13763	...	2954	624	...
Honduras	Urban	1988	366810	...	323722	[17] 318070	35679	5611	...	1232	566	...
Honduras	Rural	1988	524581	...	442663	[17] 444047	71986	8152	...	1722	58	...
Martinique	Total	1990	123317	...	...	...	...	...	...	...	287	...
Martinique	Urban	1990	109663	...	...	...	...	...	...	...	188	...
Martinique	Rural	1990	13654	...	...	...	...	...	...	...	99	...
Mexico	Total	1990	16197802	16183310	[18] 15773298	...	...	11736	14492	...	...	398276
Mexico	Urban	1990	11870435	11859156	11559264	...	...	7958	11279	...	...	291934
Mexico	Rural	1990	4327367	4324154	4214034	...	...	3778	3213	...	...	106342
Panama	Total	1990	601524	600799	587960	514587	73373	12839	725	208	517	...
Panama	Urban	1990	325642	325221	320013	291176	28837	5208	421	163	258	...
Panama	Rural	1990	275882	275578	267947	223411	44536	7631	304	45	259	...
Paraguay	Total	1982	579954	578714	[19] 571557	571557	...	7157	1240	...	...	...
Paraguay	Urban	1982	266205	265422	[19] 259626	259626	...	5796	783	...	...	...
Paraguay	Rural	1982	313749	313292	[19] 311931	311931	...	1361	457	...	...	...
Peru	Total	1990	4488236	4479073	4441000	3971000	470000	38073	9163	2963	6200	...
Peru	Urban	1990	2965220	2956057	2928000	2707000	221000	28057	9163	2963	6200	...
Peru	Rural	1990	1523016	1523016	1513000	1264000	249000	10016	...	...	...	...
Turks & Caicos Islands [20]	Total	1990	2022	2022	2022	...	...	...	...	...	...	...
Venezuela	Total	1990	...	4110019	3547416	3074026	...	557087	5516	...	...	...
Venezuela	Urban	1990	...	3400336	3077093	2708434	...	317981	5262	...	...	...
Venezuela	Rural	1990	...	709683	470323	365592	...	239106	254	...	...	...
NORTHERN AMERICA												
Bermuda	Total	1991	24552	24183	24183	22061	2122	...	369	369	...	...
Canada	Total	1991	10039545	10018265	10002260	...	...	16005	21020	7250	13510	[21] 260
United States	Total	1990	...	102263678	102263678	...	...	...	...	...	...	...
United States	Urban	1990	...	76212052	76212052	...	...	...	...	...	...	...
United States	Rural	1990	...	26051526	26051526	...	...	...	...	...	...	...
OCEANIA												
Australia	Total	1986	5829109	5808055	5592709	5049170	543539	139505	21054	9291	9747	75841
Australia	Urban	1986	4986055	4970784	4819652	4414139	405513	88713	15271	...	...	62419
Australia	Rural	1986	837230	832413	773036	635010	138026	50785	4817	...	...	13409
French Polynesia	Total	1988	47046	47046	45458	40793	4665	1588	...	...	...	...
New Caledonia	Total	1989	44176	43850	42774	38993	3781	1076	326	215	111	...
New Caledonia	Urban	1989	24240	24027	23754	22003	1751	273	213	169	44	...
New Caledonia	Rural	1989	19936	19823	19020	16990	2030	803	113	46	67	...
New Zealand	Total	1991	1185396	1175673	[22] 1161933	...	122711	[23] 13740	7242	3483	3756	2481
New Zealand	Urban	1991	1018473	1011225	[22] 1001892	...	79396	[23] 9333	5415	2796	2619	1833
New Zealand	Rural	1991	166923	164448	[22] 160041	...	43315	[23] 4407	1824	690	1137	651

Source: United Nations, Human Settlements Statistics Questionnaire 1992

Living Quarters: Living quarters are structurally separate and independent places of abode. Living quarters are either housing units or collective living quarters. For additional information and definitions of the terms 'Housing unit', 'Conventional dwelling', 'Unconventional dwelling' and 'Collective living quarters' refer to technical notes of table 8.

Occupied Housing Units: This category is defined as conventional dwellings or other housing units which are occupied by a household at the time of the census or other inquiry. Conventional dwelling may be either occupied, i.e. in use by a household, or vacant, i.e. in 'for sale' or 'for rent' status.

TABLE 11 *(continued)*

Living Quarters by Type, Selected Countries

Notes:
1. Data refer to dwelling units.
2. Data refer to occupied housing units only. Data on vacant units are included in the figure for Total at country level.
3. Data refer to temporary housing.
4. Data refer to institutions and quarters.
5. Included are secondary housing units, supplementary housing units and other units.
6. Data refer to 535 households living in fishing boats.
7. Figures on population and households refer to Singapore Residents only (citizens and permanent residents). Figures on housing and households are preliminary data grossed up from the 10% sample data. Singapore is a city state. Therefore separate data on urban and rural areas are not available.
8. Living quarters other than housing units.
9. Including estates.
10. Including 15,566 private households/living quarters with no information on densely/sparsely populated areas (33,400 persons).
11. Data are displayed as received by the UN. However, the sum of individual categories differs from the total.
12. The difference between the total number of conventional dwellings and the sum of occupied and vacant conventional dwellings refers to temporary occupied housing units.

13. Data refer to apartments shared by two or more tenants/households.
14. Data refer to the number of hotel suites.
15. Included are non-residential units.
16. Included are caves and other natural shelters.
17. Data include occupied housing units whether or not people were present or absent.
18. Data refer to a detached house, apartment in an apartment building, rooms in buildings for renting rooms and whose occupants share the facilities, servant's quarters usually built on the roof of a house and mobile units.
19. Data refer to one-family houses, apartments in apartment buildings and rented rooms whose occupants share one or more facilities.
20. Data refer to Belongers (citizens of the Turks and Caicos Islands) only.
21. Data refer to Hutterite Colonies.
22. Households (dwellings) and living quarters are synonymous by definition in the New Zealand Census of Population and Dwellings. Conventional dwelling is a permanent dwelling occupied by a private household.
23. Unconventional dwelling is a private dwelling that is temporary or mobile (such as a tent, caravan, campervan or boat) and occupied on census night

TABLE 12

Living Quarters by Type, Selected Cities

			Number of Living Quarters	Total Housing Units	Conventional Housing Units			Unconventional Housing Units	Collective Living Quarters			Type not Stated
					Total	Occupied	Vacant		Total	Hotels/ Rooming	Others	
AFRICA												
Mali	Bamako	1987	57386	...	...	...	...	...	...	...	...	...
Mali	Mopti	1987	6683	...	...	...	...	...	...	...	...	...
Mali	Segou	1987	8516	...	...	...	...	...	...	...	...	...
Mali	Sikasso	1987	5435	...	...	...	...	...	...	...	...	...
Mauritius	Beau Bassin-Rose Hill	1990	20963	20939	20932	20466	466	7	24	8	16	...
Mauritius	Curepipe	1990	15351	15331	15316	14850	466	15	20	13	7	...
Mauritius	Port-Louis	1990	29354	29313	29295	28604	691	18	41	22	19	...
Mauritius	Quatre-Bornes	1990	15243	15222	15212	14802	410	10	21	8	13	...
Reunion	Le Tampon	1990	15050	...	...	...	...	...	...	...	...	...
Reunion	Saint-Denis	1990	38048	...	...	...	...	...	...	...	...	...
Reunion	St. Paul	1990	20563	...	...	...	...	...	...	...	...	...
Reunion	St. Pierre	1990	18029	...	...	...	...	...	...	...	...	...
Tunisia	Tunis	1989	150422	...	1496701	143377	6293	...	...	...	...	752
ASIA												
Cyprus	Larnaca	1982	15241	15223	15064	12919	2145	159	17	7	10	1
Cyprus	Limassol	1982	34634	34600	34263	29345	4918	337	32	10	22	2
Cyprus	Nicosia	1982	46063	45882	45384	40863	4521	498	177	26	151	4
Cyprus	Paphos	1982	7429	7424	7329	5722	1607	95	5	5	...	...
Iraq	Baghdad	1987	...	...	...	419876	...	...	...	...	...	...
Iraq	Basra	1987	...	...	...	92005	...	...	...	...	...	...
Iraq	Kirkuk	1987	...	...	...	69273	...	...	...	...	...	...
Iraq	Mosul	1987	...	...	...	165963	...	...	...	...	...	...
Japan	Osaka	1988	...	1161020	...	...	...	...	4210	...	...	...
Japan	Sapporo	1988	...	653640	...	...	...	...	1960	...	...	...
Japan	Tokyo	1988	...	3502650	...	...	...	...	12340	...	...	...
Japan	Yokohama	1988	...	1096660	...	...	...	...	3680	...	...	...
Republic of Korea	Incheon	1990	...	327706	...	...	...	...	...	...	...	...
Republic of Korea	Pusan	1990	...	522720	...	...	...	...	...	...	...	...
Republic of Korea	Seoul	1990	...	1489784	...	...	...	...	...	...	...	...
Republic of Korea	Taegu	1990	...	300295	...	...	...	...	...	...	...	...
Syrian Arab Republic	Aleppo	1981	193326	193158	192962	149878	[1] 43084	196	168	107	61	...
Syrian Arab Republic	Damascus	1981	209132	208846	208270	163575	[1] 44695	576	286	209	77	...
Syrian Arab Republic	Homs	1981	66614	66560	66458	50548	[1] 15910	102	54	24	30	...
Syrian Arab Republic	Lattakia	1981	46557	46474	46410	32909	[1] 13501	64	83	55	28	...
EUROPE												
Austria	Graz	1981	...	...	109984	101941	8043	...	...	...	...	...
Austria	Linz	1981	...	...	84702	78791	5911	...	...	...	...	...
Austria	Salzburg	1981	...	...	63741	57221	6520	...	...	...	...	...
Austria	Vienna	1981	...	...	821174	717608	103566	...	...	...	...	...
Bulgaria	Bourgas	1985	...	...	64761	61779	2982	...	...	...	...	...
Bulgaria	Plovdiv	1985	...	...	108970	102041	6929	...	...	...	...	...
Bulgaria	Sofia	1985	...	...	403900	383905	19995	...	...	...	...	...
Bulgaria	Varna	1985	...	...	98122	92616	5506	...	...	...	...	...
Channel Islands	Jersey	1991	...	28725	28275	27611	1114	...	...	...	...	...
Finland	Espoo	1989	70229	70229	70229	66259	3970	...	...	...	...	...
Finland	Helsinki	1989	254470	254470	254470	236785	17685	...	...	...	...	...
Finland	Tampere	1989	85794	85794	85794	78001	7793	...	...	...	...	...
Finland	Turku	1989	82669	82669	82669	74857	7812	...	...	...	...	...
France	Lyon	1990	...	217220	...	...	...	...	...	...	...	...
France	Marseille	1990	...	389760	...	...	...	...	...	...	...	...
France	Paris	1990	...	1296820	...	...	...	...	...	...	...	...
France	Toulouse	1990	...	186900	...	...	...	...	...	...	...	...
Germany	Berlin (west)	1987	1088641	1070955	1069618	1042433	27185	1337	...	...	17686	...
Germany	Bonn	1987	143766	138646	138593	135437	3156	53	...	...	5120	...
Germany	Hamburg	1987	801095	788966	787415	778095	9320	1551	...	...	12129	...
Germany	Munich	1987	652314	638087	636692	625100	11592	1395	...	...	14227	...
Hungary	Budapest	1990	...	794022	793764	775523	18241	258	529	...	529	...
Hungary	Debrecen	1990	...	76700	76670	73850	2820	30	68	...	68	...
Hungary	Miskolc	1990	...	71602	71587	69463	2124	15	52	...	52	...
Hungary	Szeged	1990	...	67968	67954	64734	3220	14	56	...	56	...
Italy	Milan	1991	622425	...	...	...	...	...	...	...	...	...
Italy	Rome	1991	1175135	...	...	...	...	...	...	...	...	...
Latvia	Daugavpils	1991	46751	42823	42823	42823	...	...	3928	220	3708	...
Latvia	Liepaja	1991	40273	36765	36765	36402	363	...	3508	284	3224	...
Latvia	Riga	1991	327407	300179	300179	299451	728	...	27228	1929	25299	...

TABLE 12 (continued)

Living Quarters by Type, Selected Cities

			Number of Living Quarters	Total Housing Units	Conventional Housing Units			Unconventional Housing Units	Collective Living Quarters			Type not Stated
					Total	Occupied	Vacant		Total	Hotels/ Rooming	Others	
EUROPE (continued)												
Netherlands	Amsterdam	1989	...	...	...	361943	...	1797	...	928	...	...
Netherlands	Hague, The	1989	...	...	...	200292	...	635	...	1279	182	...
Netherlands	Rotterdam	1989	...	...	...	269004	...	969	...	588	453	...
Netherlands	Utrecht	1989	...	...	...	105344	...	810	...	935	...	...
Norway	Bergen	1990	93949	93949	93949	93949	...	...	...	...	...	...
Norway	Oslo	1990	244434	244434	244434	244434	...	...	...	...	...	...
Norway	Stavanger	1990	42680	42680	42680	42680	...	...	...	...	...	...
Norway	Trondheim	1990	60407	60407	60407	60407	...	...	...	...	...	...
Poland	Krakow	1988	231858	231527	231459	228245	3214	68	331	...	...	...
Poland	Lodz	1988	316396	316270	316231	313764	2467	39	126	...	...	...
Poland	Warsaw	1988	586059	585703	585646	581454	4192	57	356	...	...	...
Poland	Wroclaw	1988	197575	197354	197325	194403	2922	29	221	...	...	...
Romania	Brasov	1992	...	107745	107620	104836	2784	125	158	46	112	...
Romania	Bucarest	1992	...	761285	761156	733219	27937	129	110	50	60	...
Romania	Constanta	1992	...	110903	110842	108728	2114	61	110	33	77	...
Romania	Timisoara	1992	...	121436	121260	114873	6387	176	171	33	138	...
Russian Federation	Moscow	1989	...	2410137	...	...	...	...	...	173	...	234593
Russian Federation	Nizhny Novgorod	1989	...	412768	...	...	...	...	...	30	...	16208
Russian Federation	Novosibirsk	1989	...	368362	...	...	...	...	...	22	...	20364
Russian Federation	St. Petersburg	1989	...	991682	...	...	...	...	...	76	...	233025
Spain	Barcelona	1991	689281	685728	685713	615215	70498	15	925	...	...	2628
Spain	Madrid	1991	1169497	1143213	1141521	1028407	113114	1692	2019	...	...	24265
Spain	Sevilla	1991	245500	236670	236482	207865	28617	188	340	...	...	8490
Spain	Valencia	1991	329712	325130	325096	275428	49668	34	285	...	...	4297
Sweden	Goteborg	1990	226938	212372	212372	209779	2593	-	-	-	...	14566
Sweden	Malmo	1990	130412	121140	121140	120464	676	-	-	-	...	9272
Sweden	Stockholm	1990	386638	354069	354069	351314	2755	-	-	-	...	32569
Sweden	Uppsala	1990	77440	72637	72637	72504	133	-	-	-	...	4803
Switzerland	Basel	1980	91671	91514	[2] 91413	87819	1019	101	157	...	...	...
Switzerland	Berne	1980	70319	70204	[2] 70149	67719	395	55	115	...	...	...
Switzerland	Geneva	1980	88359	88247	[2] 88207	79628	1507	40	112	...	...	...
Switzerland	Zurich	1980	182648	182331	[2] 182235	176806	1912	96	317	...	...	...
Ukraine	Donetsk	1992	...	342100	...	...	...	...	[3] 3900	[4] 1600	...	...
Ukraine	Kharkov	1992	...	512700	...	...	...	...	[3] 23300	[4] 2000	...	...
Ukraine	Kiev	1992	...	833000	...	...	...	...	[3] 18000	[4] 7900	...	...
Ukraine	Odessa	1992	...	325800	...	...	...	...	[3] 17600	[4] 800	...	...
LATIN AMERICA												
Cayman Islands	Georgetown	1989	[5] 5625	5611	...	...	931	...	14	11	3	...
Cuba	Camaguey	1981	63731	63594	63552	[6] 62740	812	42	43	...	...	...
Cuba	Havana	1981	527348	526005	525830	[7] 504117	21713	175	371	...	...	...
Cuba	Holguin	1981	44691	44645	44629	[8] 44117	512	16	20	...	...	...
Cuba	Santiago de Cuba	1981	75275	75233	75216	[9] 72994	2222	17	42	...	...	...
Ecuador	Cuenca	1990	46992	46885	46885	44621	2264	...	107	...	...	...
Ecuador	Guayaquil	1990	343356	343084	343084	327889	15195	...	272	...	...	...
Ecuador	Machala	1990	34836	34806	34806	32530	2276	...	30	...	...	...
Ecuador	Quito	1990	283820	283426	283426	273885	9541	...	394	...	...	...
Falkland Islands (Malvinas)	Stanley	1991	610	610	565	565	...	45	...	...	...	...
French Guiana	Cayenne	1990	14680	...	...	...	...	...	...	...	25	...
French Guiana	Kourou	1990	4550	...	...	...	...	...	...	...	17	...
French Guiana	Remire - Montjoly	1990	3711	...	...	...	...	...	...	...	5	...
French Guiana	Saint-Laurent-du-Moroni	1990	3886	...	...	...	...	...	...	...	13	...
Guadeloupe	Abymes	1990	22387	...	...	...	...	...	...	...	85	...
Guadeloupe	Basse-Terre	1990	5175	...	...	...	...	...	...	...	7	...
Guadeloupe	Point-a-Pitre	1990	10210	...	...	...	...	...	...	...	72	...
Guadeloupe	St. Martin	1990	9680	...	...	...	...	...	...	...	165	...
Guatemala	Guatemala City	1981	...	154717	139338	...	...	15379	875	...	...	...
Guatemala	Mazatenango	1981	...	8092	7835	...	...	257	...	...	...	...
Guatemala	Puerto Barrios	1981	...	10594	10269	...	...	325	...	...	...	...
Guatemala	Quezaltenango	1981	...	12901	12826	...	...	75	119	...	...	...
Honduras	Choluteca	1988	11650	...	9884	[10] 9823	1555	138	...	46	27	...
Honduras	El Progreso	1988	12411	...	10627	[10] 10672	1444	275	...	62	3	...
Honduras	San Pedro Sula	1988	60434	...	54542	[10] 54535	...	1384	...	145	95	...
Honduras	Tegucigalpa	1988	116766	...	107005	[10] 102575	8049	1203	...	379	130	...
Martinique	Fort-de-France	1990	36330	...	...	...	...	...	...	...	103	...
Martinique	Lamentin	1990	9478	...	...	...	...	...	...	...	7	...
Martinique	Sainte Marie	1990	5779	...	...	...	...	...	...	...	3	...
Martinique	Schoelcher	1990	7024	...	...	...	...	...	...	...	8	...

TABLE 12 *(continued)*

Living Quarters by Type, Selected Cities

			Number of Living Quarters	Total Housing Units	Conventional Housing Units			Uncon-ventional Housing Units	Collective Living Quarters			Type not Stated
					Total	Occupied	Vacant		Total	Hotels/ Rooming	Others	
LATIN AMERICA (continued)												
Mexico	Mexico City	1990	3135669	[11] 3133634	[12] 3089110	...	...	2217	2035	...	...	42307
Panama	Colon	1990	16535	16520	16046	15069	977	474	15	9	6	...
Panama	Panama	1990	116941	116763	115878	104875	11003	885	178	76	102	...
Panama	San Miguelito	1990	54395	54385	53508	50957	2551	877	10	3	7	...
Paraguay	Asuncion	1982	91792	91526	86613	86613	...	4913	266	...	...	...
Paraguay	Ciudad del Este	1982	...	12602	...	...	...	...	...	...	...	...
Paraguay	Encarnacion	1982	...	9774	...	...	...	...	...	...	...	...
Paraguay	Pedro Juan Caballero	1982	...	9767	...	...	...	...	...	...	...	...
Peru	Arequipa	1991	124975	122254	122254	122254	...	...	2721	2721	...	...
Peru	Callao	1991	111073	88896	88896	88896	...	...	22177	15443	6734	...
Peru	Lima	1991	1099242	879760	879760	879760	...	...	219482	152830	66652	...
Peru	Trujillo	1991	105988	105805	105443	105443	...	362	183	116	67	...
Venezuela	Valencia	1990	...	...	...	159545	...	...	72	...	...	...
NORTHERN AMERICA												
Canada	Montreal	1992	1237485	1235720	1234520	...	...	1205	1765	490	1275	-
Canada	Ottawa	1992	349805	349260	348205	...	...	1050	545	180	370	-
Canada	Toronto	1992	1368345	1366700	1365330	...	...	1370	1645	755	975	-
Canada	Vancouver	1992	610305	609430	609285	...	...	150	875	210	670	-
United States	Chicago	1990	...	3105919	3105919	2908063	...	...	...	...	...	...
United States	Los Angeles	1990	...	5293072	5293072	4900720	...	...	...	...	...	...
United States	New York	1990	...	7096741	7096741	6621239	...	...	...	...	...	...
United States	Washington D.C.	1990	...	1556749	1556749	1459358	...	...	...	...	...	...
OCEANIA												
Australia	Brisbane	1986	415264	414374	403548	377046	26502	7145	890	...	...	3681
Australia	Canberra	1986	85027	84865	83535	77979	5556	479	162	...	851	...
Australia	Melbourne	1986	1044801	1042682	1016183	934057	82126	10224	2119	...	...	16275
Australia	Sydney	1986	1233277	1230405	1195109	1110100	85009	15761	2872	...	...	19535
French Polynesia	Papeete	1988	...	6567	6353	5468	885	214	...	...	...	...
New Caledonia	Noumea	1989	20373	20170	20077	18518	1559	93	203	163	40	...
New Zealand	Auckland	1991	...	111993	[13] 110673	...	9864	[14] 1320	744	357	387	99
New Zealand	Christchurch	1991	...	107214	[13] 106632	...	5721	[14] 582	474	228	246	15
New Zealand	Manukau	1991	...	67152	[13] 66468	...	3711	[14] 681	192	69	120	...
New Zealand	Wellington	1991	...	55473	[13] 55110	...	4071	[14] 363	240	153	87	12
Wallis & Futuna Islands	Mata-Utu	1990	680	662	656	656	...	6	18	18	...	...

Source: United Nations, Human Settlements Statistics Questionnaire 1992

For additional information and the definitions of relevant terms refer to technical notes for table 8 and 11.

TABLE 12   (continued)

Living Quarters by Type, Selected Cities

Notes:

1. Including dwellings under construction.
2. The difference between the total number of conventional dwellings and the sum of occupied and vacant conventional dwellings refers to temporary occupied housing units.
3. Data refer to apartments shared by two or more tenants/households.
4. Data refer to the number of hotel suites.
5. Including 235 living quarters occupied by 'visitors' on Census Day.
6. Including 26 commercial units and 56 residents.
7. Including 972 commercial units and 1954 residents.
8. Including 94 commercial units and 214 residents.
9. Including 105 commercial units and 283 residents.
10. Data refer to housing units whether or not people were present or absent.
11. Data include type not stated.
12. Data refer to a detached house, apartment in an apartment building, rooms in buildings for renting rooms and whose occupants share the facilities, servant's quarters usually built on the roof of a house and mobile units.
13. Households (dwellings) and living quarters are synonymous by definition in the New Zealand Census of Population and Dwellings. Conventional dwelling is a permanent dwelling occupied by a private household.
14. Unconventional dwelling is a private dwelling that is temporary or mobile (such as a tent, caravan, campervan or boat) and occupied on census night.

TABLE 13

Occupied Housing Units by Number of Rooms, Number and Percentage, Selected Countries

			Occupied Housing Units, Total and by Number of Rooms							Total Number of Rooms for all Units	Average Size (Rooms per Unit)
			Total	1-Room	2-Room	3-Room	4-Room	5+ Room	Unknown		
AFRICA											
Ethiopia	Total	1984	7377435	5325631	1399522	316895	83976	168470	82941	...	...
			100	72.2	19.0	4.3	1.1	2.3	1.1		
Ethiopia	Urban	1984	976180	359588	305034	121346	51399	114554	24259	...	...
			100	36.8	31.2	12.4	5.3	11.7	2.5		
Ethiopia	Rural	1984	6401255	4966043	1094488	195549	32577	53916	58682	...	...
			100	77.6	17.1	3.1	0.5	0.8	0.9		
Gambia	Total	1983	81719	...	...	...	...	...	...	336177	4.1
			100								
Gambia	Urban	1983	24575	...	...	...	...	...	...	67298	2.7
			100								
Gambia	Rural	1983	57144	...	...	...	...	...	...	268879	4.7
			100	...	...	...	...	...	...		
Malawi	Total [1]	1986	58705	14274	22454	10737	6199	5041	-	134193	2.3
			100	24.3	38.2	18.3	10.6	8.6	-		
Malawi	Urban [1]	1986	45106	9657	17487	8214	5207	4541	-	104377	2.3
			100	21.4	38.8	18.2	11.5	10.1	-		
Malawi	Rural [1]	1986	13599	4617	4967	2523	992	500	-	29816	2.2
			100	34.0	36.5	18.6	7.3	3.7	-		
Mali	Total [2]	1987	1364079	81382	854132	194055	188923	45587	-	...	...
			100	6.0	62.6	14.2	13.8	3.3	-		
Mauritius	Total [3]	1990	215384	13162	38562	37708	53954	71963	35	861826	4.0
			100	6.1	17.9	17.5	25.1	33.4	-		
Mauritius	Urban [3]	1990	90427	5347	14294	15986	21800	32986	14	370584	4.1
			100	5.9	15.8	17.7	24.1	36.5	-		
Mauritius	Rural [3]	1990	124957	7815	24268	21722	32154	38977	21	491242	3.9
			100	6.3	19.4	17.4	25.7	31.2	-		
Morocco	Total [4]	1985	...	...	...	...	...	...	-	...	...
			100	19.5	34.2	25.7	12.1	8.5	-		
Morocco	Urban [4]	1985	...	...	...	...	...	...	-	...	...
			100	20.9	33.6	26.4	11.4	7.7	-		
Morocco	Rural [4]	1985	...	...	...	...	...	...	-	...	...
			100	18.2	34.8	25.1	12.7	9.2	-		
Reunion	Total	1990	157853	6353	18462	35816	49466	47756	-	613828	3.9
			100	4.0	11.7	22.7	31.3	30.3	-		
Reunion	Urban	1990	155129	6271	18202	35431	48611	46614	-	602167	3.9
			100	4.0	11.7	22.8	31.3	30.0	-		
Reunion	Rural	1990	2724	82	260	385	855	1142	-	11661	4.3
			100	3.0	9.5	14.1	31.4	41.9	-		
Tunisia	Total	1989	1290778	185513	432891	374061	204376	87511	6426	...	...
			100	14.4	33.5	29.0	15.8	6.8	0.5		
Tunisia	Urban	1989	807282	61947	243843	274907	155310	67115	4160	...	...
			100	7.7	30.2	34.1	19.2	8.3	0.5		
Tunisia	Rural	1989	483496	123566	189048	99154	49066	20396	2266	...	...
			100	25.6	39.1	20.5	10.1	4.2	0.5		
ASIA											
Cyprus	Total [5]	1982	144310	4055	10309	17528	33920	78269	229	652743	4.5
			100	2.8	7.1	12.1	23.5	54.2	0.2		
Cyprus	Urban [5]	1982	90176	1478	4371	9290	20883	53984	170	426330	4.7
			100	1.6	4.8	10.3	23.2	59.9	0.2		
Cyprus	Rural [5]	1982	54133	2577	5937	8238	13037	24285	59	226413	4.2
			100	4.8	11.0	15.2	24.1	44.9	0.1		
India	Total [6,2]	1981	118614803	53046175	33948809	14496724	7482461	6852624	[7] 2788010	242795971	2.0
			100	44.7	28.6	12.2	6.3	5.8	2.4		
India	Urban [6,2]	1981	28541877	13072617	7947026	3484741	1804721	1626979	[7] 605793	60924094	2.1
			100	45.8	27.8	12.2	6.3	5.7	2.1		
India	Rural [6,2]	1981	90072926	39973558	26001783	11011983	5677740	5225645	[7] 2182217	181871877	2.0
			100	44.4	28.9	12.2	6.3	5.8	2.4		
Iraq	Total	1987	1759176	15284	111526	274402	316204	1041667	93	10383157	5.9
			100	0.9	6.3	15.6	18.0	59.2	-		
Iraq	Urban	1987	1269005	14315	106812	263597	303412	580868	1	5889555	4.6
			100	1.1	8.4	20.8	23.9	45.8	-		
Iraq	Rural	1987	490171	969	4714	10805	12792	460799	92	4493602	9.2
			100	0.2	1.0	2.2	2.6	94.0	-		
Israel	Total	1983	1104270	50010	220555	503775	253265	76665	-	3312810	3.0
			100	4.5	20.0	45.6	22.9	6.9	-		
Japan	Total	1990	39318646	2609019	4054479	6182025	7484949	18988174	-	...	...
			100	6.6	10.3	15.7	19.0	48.3	-		
Japan	Urban	1990	31516783	2487187	3684162	5399686	6364697	13581051	-	...	...
			100	7.9	11.7	17.1	20.2	43.1	-		
Japan	Rural	1990	7801863	121832	370317	782339	1120252	5407123	-	...	...
			100	1.6	4.7	10.0	14.4	69.3	-		

TABLE 13 *(continued)*

Occupied Housing Units by Number of Rooms, Number and Percentage, Selected Countries

			Occupied Housing Units, Total and by Number of Rooms							Total Number of Rooms for all Units	Average Size (Rooms per Unit)
			Total	1-Room	2-Room	3-Room	4-Room	5+ Room	Unknown		
ASIA (continued)											
Jordan	Total	1979	313193	...	...	...	...	...	...	...	...
			100	...	...	...	...	...	...		
Jordan	Urban	1979	187560	...	...	...	...	...	...	...	...
			100	...	...	...	...	...	...		
Jordan	Rural	1979	125633	...	...	...	...	...	...	...	...
			100	...	...	...	...	...	...		
Kuwait	Total	1985	[8] 228814	...	...	...	...	...	...	[8] 973032	4.3
			100	...	...	...	...	...	...		
Macau	Total	1991	87401	3583	12963	50949	15905	4002	-	...	...
			100	4.1	14.8	58.3	18.2	4.6			
Maldives	Total [2]	1990	29823	1108	2784	4898	5303	13381	2349	...	...
			100	3.7	9.3	16.4	17.8	44.9	7.9		
Maldives	Urban [2]	1990	5613	492	479	632	836	2446	728	...	...
			100	8.8	8.5	11.3	14.9	43.6	13.0		
Maldives	Rural [2]	1990	24210	616	2305	4266	4467	10935	1621	...	...
			100	2.5	9.5	17.6	18.5	45.2	6.7		
Pakistan	Total	1981	12587648	6487461	3721239	1356690	565251	457007	-	23916531	1.9
			100	51.5	29.6	10.8	4.5	3.6			
Pakistan	Urban	1981	3554173	1513465	1120401	486326	231236	202745	-	7819181	2.2
			100	42.6	31.5	13.7	6.5	5.7			
Pakistan	Rural	1981	9033475	4973996	2600838	870364	334015	254262	-	16097351	1.8
			100	55.1	28.8	9.6	3.7	2.8			
Qatar	Total [2]	1986	49783	5483	6136	8585	10056	19513	10	...	...
			100	11.0	12.3	17.2	20.2	39.2	-		
Republic of Korea	Total	1992	7374022	149975	1206629	2269273	1677760	2070385	-	29679211	4.0
			100	2.0	16.4	30.8	22.8	28.1			
Republic of Korea	Urban	1992	4749173	78904	472115	1195933	1216665	1785556	-	21396910	4.5
			100	1.7	9.9	25.2	25.6	37.6			
Republic of Korea	Rural	1992	2624849	71071	734514	1073340	461095	284829	-	8282301	3.2
			100	2.7	28.0	40.9	17.6	10.9			
Singapore	Total	1990	677600	...	...	...	...	...	...	...	...
			100	...	...	...	...	...	...		
Sri Lanka	Total	1981	2813844	862556	907815	504901	280120	258452	-	6967169	2.5
			100	30.7	32.3	17.9	10.0	9.2			
Sri Lanka	Urban	1981	511810	154282	148279	97494	54543	57212	-	1346381	2.6
			100	30.1	29.0	19.0	10.7	11.2			
Sri Lanka	Rural	1981	[9] 2302034	708274	759536	407407	225577	201240	-	5620788	2.4
			100	30.8	33.0	17.7	9.8	8.7			
Syrian Arab Republic	Total	1981	1305550	147382	398289	355438	223027	177152	4262	...	...
			100	11.3	30.5	27.2	17.1	13.6	0.3		
Syrian Arab Republic	Urban	1981	622056	48503	147009	169657	136294	118522	2071	...	...
			100	7.8	23.6	27.3	21.9	19.1	0.3		
Syrian Arab Republic	Rural	1981	683494	98879	251280	185781	86733	58630	2191	...	...
			100	14.5	36.8	27.2	12.7	8.6	0.3		
Turkey	Total	1985	[10] 9730018	310859	1787326	4052297	2574702	926831	32619	...	...
			100	3.2	18.4	41.6	26.5	9.5	0.3		
Turkey	Urban	1985	[10] 5499271	126034	866333	2491451	1626647	354162	16695	...	...
			100	2.3	15.8	45.3	29.6	6.4	0.3		
Turkey	Rural	1985	[10] 4230747	184825	920993	1560846	948055	572669	15924	...	...
			100	4.4	21.8	36.9	22.4	13.5	0.4		
EUROPE											
Albania	Total [11]	1989	674633	293025	241949	79614	[12] 27218	..	[13] 32827	...	...
			100	43.4	35.9	11.8	4.0	..	4.9		
Albania	Urban [11]	1989	288412	168041	85782	11161	[12] 2478	..	[13] 20950	...	...
			100	58.3	29.7	3.9	0.9	..	7.3		
Albania	Rural [11]	1989	386221	124984	156167	68453	[12] 24740	..	[13] 11877	...	...
			100	32.4	40.4	17.7	6.4	..	3.1		
Austria	Total	1981	2692883	426181	750788	722489	410683	361285	21457	7801247	2.9
			100	15.8	27.9	26.8	15.3	13.4	0.8		
Austria	Urban	1981	1693775	328920	533213	469683	207067	136297	18595	4402038	2.6
			100	19.4	31.5	27.7	12.2	8.0	1.1		
Austria	Rural	1981	999108	97261	217575	252806	203616	224988	2862	3399209	3.4
			100	9.7	21.8	25.3	20.4	22.5	0.3		
Bulgaria	Total	1985	2700039	353725	840952	832827	411423	261111	-	...	...
			100	13.1	31.1	30.8	15.2	9.7			
Bulgaria	Urban	1985	1711112	273478	632061	509298	197402	98873	-	...	...
			100	16.0	36.9	29.8	11.5	5.8			
Bulgaria	Rural	1985	988927	80247	208892	323529	214021	162238	-	...	...
			100	8.1	21.1	32.7	21.6	16.4			
Channel Islands	Total	1991	48826	1251	2662	4356	7503	33054	-	...	...
			100	2.6	5.5	8.9	15.4	67.7			

TABLE 13 (continued)

Occupied Housing Units by Number of Rooms, Number and Percentage, Selected Countries

			Occupied Housing Units, Total and by Number of Rooms							Total Number of Rooms for all Units	Average Size (Rooms per Unit)
			Total	1-Room	2-Room	3-Room	4-Room	5+ Room	Unknown		
EUROPE (continued)											
Finland	Total	1989	2001129	205855	262469	481960	452910	580540	17395	7193104	3.6
			100	10.3	13.1	24.1	22.6	29.0	0.9		
Finland	Urban	1989	1309180	160602	190362	327814	302092	320286	8024	4486229	3.4
			100	12.3	14.5	25.0	23.1	24.5	0.6		
Finland	Rural	1989	691949	45253	72107	154146	150818	260254	9371	2706875	3.9
			100	6.5	10.4	22.3	21.8	37.6	1.4		
France	Total	1990	21520700	1293340	2785400	5051160	6028900	6361900	-	81741920	3.8
			100	6.0	12.9	23.5	28.0	29.6	-		
France	Urban	1990	16274240	1197060	2401380	4087980	4486260	4101560	-	58973580	3.6
			100	7.4	14.8	25.1	27.6	25.2	-		
France	Rural	1990	5246460	96280	384020	963180	1542640	2260340	-	22768340	4.3
			100	1.8	7.3	18.4	29.4	43.1	-		
Germany	Total [14]	1987	25886220	733786	1565774	5440554	7560035	10586071	-	114226578	4.4
			100	2.8	6.0	21.0	29.2	40.9	-		
Germany	Urban [14]	1987	10290413	514607	950734	2929421	3361092	2534559	-	39836519	3.9
			100	5.0	9.2	28.5	32.7	24.6	-		
Germany	Rural [14]	1987	15595807	219179	615040	2511133	4198943	8051512	-	74390059	4.8
			100	1.4	3.9	16.1	26.9	51.6	-		
Gibraltar	Total	1981	6945	572	1321	2610	1708	733	1	21541	3.1
			100	8.2	19.0	37.6	24.6	10.6	-		
Hungary	Total	1990	3687996	[15] 71242	[15] 609939	[15] 1514017	1089348	403450	-	12325326	3.3
			100	1.9	16.5	41.1	29.5	10.9	-		
Hungary	Urban	1990	2316108	[15] 47612	[15] 405618	[15] 979074	644269	239535	-	7607176	3.3
			100	2.1	17.5	42.3	27.8	10.3	-		
Hungary	Rural	1990	1371888	[15] 23630	[15] 204321	[15] 534943	445079	163915	-	4718150	3.4
			100	1.7	14.9	39.0	32.4	11.9	-		
Ireland	Total [16]	1986	964882	17705	41798	97706	179602	627956	115	...	...
			100	1.8	4.3	10.1	18.6	65.1	-		
Isle of Man	Total [2]	1991	27316	173	964	2106	4707	19366	-	...	...
			100	0.6	3.5	7.7	17.2	70.9	-		
Latvia	Total	1991	938700	205500	351900	[17] 266900	..	..	114400	...	...
			100	21.9	37.5	28.4	..	..	12.2		
Latvia	Urban	1991	640300	163000	267000	[17] 210300	..	..		...	...
			100	25.5	41.7	32.8	..	..			
Latvia	Rural	1991	298400	42500	84900	[17] 56600	..	..	114400	...	...
			100	14.2	28.5	19.0	..	..	38.3		
Netherlands	Total	1989	5861820	43851	168010	547526	985006	4090020	27407	29435535	5.0
			100	0.7	2.9	9.3	16.8	69.8	0.5		
Netherlands	Urban	1989	4066960	39441	142318	454274	794130	2617826	18971	19841486	4.9
			100	1.0	3.5	11.2	19.5	64.4	0.5		
Netherlands	Rural	1989	1794860	4410	25692	93252	190876	1472194	8436	9594049	5.3
			100	0.2	1.4	5.2	10.6	82.0	0.5		
Norway	Total	1990	[18] 1751343	100108	255703	367954	430080	597498	-	7069333	4.0
			100	5.7	14.6	21.0	24.6	34.1	-		
Norway	Urban	1990	1288839	81587	211326	294287	313364	388275	-	...	...
			100	6.3	16.4	22.8	24.3	30.1	-		
Norway	Rural	1990	446938	17191	41464	70226	113199	204858	-	...	...
			100	3.8	9.3	15.7	25.3	45.8	-		
Poland	Total [19]	1988	10716758	[20] 457631	2073219	3731569	2901851	1552488	..	36286582	3.4
			100	4.3	19.3	34.8	27.1	14.5	..		
Poland	Urban [19]	1988	7039802	[20] 358909	1353934	2586302	1905986	834671	..	23142379	3.3
			100	5.1	19.2	36.7	27.1	11.9	..		
Poland	Rural [19]	1988	3676956	[20] 98722	719285	1145267	995865	717817	..	13144203	3.6
			100	2.7	19.6	31.1	27.1	19.5	..		
Romania	Total [21, 22]	1992	7186748	895750	3146677	2208184	724137	212000	-	17860712	2.5
			100	12.5	43.8	30.7	10.1	2.9	-		
Romania	Urban [21, 22]	1992	3923118	520053	1826879	1200181	316935	59070	-	9367266	2.4
			100	13.3	46.6	30.6	8.1	1.5	-		
Romania	Rural [21, 22]	1992	3263630	375697	1319798	1008003	407202	152930	-	8493446	2.6
			100	11.5	40.4	30.9	12.5	4.7	-		
Russian Federation	Total	1989	47409368	8972162	17064689	[17] 12582972	..	..	8789545	...	...
			100	18.9	36.0	26.5	..	..	18.5		
Russian Federation	Urban	1989	32849816	8005800	14799859	[17] 10044157	..	..	-	...	...
			100	24.4	45.1	30.6	..	..	-		
Russian Federation	Rural	1989	14559552	966362	2264830	[17] 2538815	..	..	8789545	...	...
			100	6.6	15.6	17.4	..	..	60.4		
San Marino	Total	1991	7241	27	241	1267	2624	1924	1158	32237	4.5
			100	0.4	3.3	17.5	36.2	26.6	16.0		
San Marino	Urban	1991	6613	22	205	1173	2389	1767	1057	29445	4.5
			100	0.3	3.1	17.7	36.1	26.7	16.0		
San Marino	Rural	1991	628	5	36	94	235	157	101	2792	4.4
			100	0.8	5.7	15.0	37.4	25.0	16.1		

TABLE 13 (continued)

Occupied Housing Units by Number of Rooms, Number and Percentage, Selected Countries

			Occupied Housing Units, Total and by Number of Rooms							Total Number of Rooms for all Units	Average Size (Rooms per Unit)
			Total	1-Room	2-Room	3-Room	4-Room	5+ Room	Unknown		
EUROPE (continued)											
Spain	Total[23, 24]	1991	11824849	55269	282624	1333021	3070596	7015981	67358	...	...
			100	0.5	2.4	11.3	26.0	59.3	0.6		
Sweden	Total	1990	3830037	85581	299116	855498	952564	1608610	28668	16471438	4.3
			100	2.2	7.8	22.3	24.9	42.0	0.7		
Sweden	Urban	1990	3260297	82127	280107	784990	820350	1270156	22567	13671885	4.2
			100	2.5	8.6	24.1	25.2	39.0	0.7		
Sweden	Rural	1990	569740	3454	19009	70508	132214	338454	6101	2799553	4.9
			100	0.6	3.3	12.4	23.2	59.4	1.1		
Switzerland	Total	1980	2413185	[25] 188342	[25] 326651	[25] 698079	[25] 620259	[25] 579854	-	[25] 9762967	4.0
			100	7.8	13.5	28.9	25.7	24.0	-		
Switzerland	Urban	1980	1600580	[25] 163364	[25] 259237	[25] 510542	[25] 384494	[25] 282943	-	[25] 5672499	3.5
			100	10.2	16.2	31.9	24.0	17.7	-		
Switzerland	Rural	1980	812605	[25] 24978	[25] 67414	[25] 187537	[25] 235765	[25] 296911	-	[25] 4090468	5.0
			100	3.1	8.3	23.1	29.0	36.5	-		
Ukraine	Total	1992	17827000	2762300	4611400	[17] 4555500	..	..	...	...	...
			100	15.5	25.9	25.6	..	..	-		
Ukraine	Urban	1992	11302800	2650200	4398300	[17] 4254300	..	..	-	...	...
			100	23.4	38.9	37.6	..	..	-		
Ukraine	Rural	1992	6524200	112100	213100	[17] 301200	..	..	...	...	...
			100	1.7	3.3	4.6	..	..	-		
Yugoslavia (former)	Total [26]	1981	5924217	1332221	2362228	1438303	521106	260665	9694	14041838	2.4
			100	22.5	39.9	24.3	8.8	4.4	0.2		
Yugoslavia (former)	Urban [26]	1981	2952643	...	...	...	...	...	...		
			100	...	...	...	...	...	...		
Yugoslavia (former)	Rural [26]	1981	2971574	...	...	...	...	...	...		
			100	...	...	...	...	...	...		
LATIN AMERICA											
Aruba	Total	1991	19224	778	1114	1459	2892	12862	121	[27] 98356	5.1
			100	4.0	5.8	7.6	15.0	66.9	0.6		
Bolivia	Total	1988	1318800	342000	413200	270000	154000	135800	3800	...	...
			100	25.9	31.3	20.5	11.7	10.3	0.3		
Bolivia	Urban	1988	662800	212500	162200	110500	79000	96700	2000	...	...
			100	32.1	24.5	16.7	11.9	14.6	0.3		
Bolivia	Rural	1988	656000	129500	251000	159400	75000	39100	1900	...	...
			100	19.7	38.3	24.3	11.4	6.0	0.3		
Cayman Islands	Total	1989	8115	632	783	1110	1561	4029	-	38140	4.7
			100	7.8	9.6	13.7	19.2	49.6	-		
Chile	Total [2]	1982	2457142	212329	413618	596532	634724	599939	-	...	...
			100	8.6	16.8	24.3	25.8	24.4	-		
Chile	Urban [2]	1982	2058546	160083	323558	503543	553330	518032	-	...	...
			100	7.8	15.7	24.5	26.9	25.2	-		
Chile	Rural [2]	1982	398596	52246	90060	92989	81394	81907	-	...	...
			100	13.1	22.6	23.3	20.4	20.5	-		
Cuba	Total [28]	1981	2290176	111727	262293	422117	608583	885456	-	...	...
			100	4.9	11.5	18.4	26.6	38.7	-		
Cuba	Urban [28]	1981	1609699	96176	200958	302581	428658	581326	-	...	...
			100	6.0	12.5	18.8	26.6	36.1	-		
Cuba	Rural [28]	1981	680477	15551	61335	119536	179925	304130	-	...	...
			100	2.3	9.0	17.6	26.4	44.7	-		
Ecuador	Total	1990	2008655	493090	561369	400656	273422	280118	-	...	...
			100	24.5	27.9	19.9	13.6	13.9	-		
Ecuador	Urban	1990	1148342	253107	282086	234397	175126	203626	-	...	...
			100	22.0	24.6	20.4	15.3	17.7	-		
Ecuador	Rural	1990	860313	239983	279283	166259	98296	76492	-	...	...
			100	27.9	32.5	19.3	11.4	8.9	-		
Falkland Islands (Malvinas)	Total	1991	802	110	177	280	122	59	54	...	...
			100	13.7	22.1	34.9	15.2	7.4	6.7		
French Guiana	Total	1990	33285	5652	7772	7026	7811	5024	-	101064	3.0
			100	17.0	23.3	21.1	23.5	15.1	-		
French Guiana	Urban	1990	27835	4317	5745	6145	6995	4633	-	87609	3.1
			100	15.5	20.6	22.1	25.1	16.6	-		
French Guiana	Rural	1990	5450	1335	2027	881	816	391	-	13455	2.5
			100	24.5	37.2	16.2	15.0	7.2	-		
Guadeloupe	Total [2]	1990	112478	7555	16623	24679	34901	28720	-	416081	3.7
			100	6.7	14.8	21.9	31.0	25.5	-		
Guadeloupe	Urban [2]	1990	110790	7464	16449	24354	34352	28171	-	409391	3.7
			100	6.7	14.8	22.0	31.0	25.4	-		
Guadeloupe	Rural [2]	1990	1688	91	174	325	549	549	-	6690	4.0
			100	5.4	10.3	19.3	32.5	32.5	-		

TABLE 13 *(continued)*

Occupied Housing Units by Number of Rooms, Number and Percentage, Selected Countries

			Occupied Housing Units, Total and by Number of Rooms							Total Number of Rooms for all Units	Average Size (Rooms per Unit)
			Total	1-Room	2-Room	3-Room	4-Room	5+ Room	Unknown		
LATIN AMERICA (continued)											
Guatemala	Total	1981	1102281 100	643375 58.4	235065 21.3	99879 9.1	57472 5.2	66490 6.0	-	...	...
Guatemala	Urban	1981	365453 100	...	...	...	...	...	...	...	...
Guatemala	Rural	1981	736828 100	...	...	...	...	...	...	...	...
Haiti	Total [29]	1986	1164136 100	252106 21.7	589528 50.6	172497 14.8	106289 9.1	43716 3.8	-	...	...
Haiti	Urban [29]	1986	285927 100	130913 45.8	68246 23.9	39234 13.7	26141 9.1	21393 7.5	-	...	...
Haiti	Rural [29]	1986	878209 100	121193 13.8	521282 59.4	133263 15.2	80148 9.1	22323 2.5	-	...	...
Honduras	Total [30]	1988	762117 100	194887 25.6	257233 33.8	146623 19.2	75415 9.9	87959 11.5	-	1890677	2.5
Honduras	Urban [30]	1988	318070 100	71827 22.6	75386 23.7	57075 17.9	44523 14.0	69259 21.8	-	918211	2.9
Honduras	Rural [30]	1988	444047 100	123060 27.7	181847 41.0	89548 20.2	30892 7.0	18700 4.2	-	972466	2.2
Martinique	Total [2]	1990	106536 100	3752 3.5	13124 12.3	29243 27.4	37646 35.3	22771 21.4	-	393251	3.7
Martinique	Urban [2]	1990	96271 100	3324 3.5	11766 12.2	26586 27.6	34211 35.5	20384 21.2	-	355027	3.7
Martinique	Rural [2]	1990	10265 100	428 4.2	1358 13.2	2657 25.9	3435 33.5	2387 23.3	-	38224	3.7
Mexico	Total	1990	[31] 16035233 100	1682020 10.5	3772533 23.5	3719354 23.2	2994636 18.7	3790480 23.6	76210 0.5	[32] 54769921	3.4
Panama	Total	1990	524284 100	123632 23.6	116867 22.3	124000 23.7	96037 18.3	63748 12.2	-	1474557	2.8
Panama	Urban	1990	295105 100	59667 20.2	55805 18.9	68469 23.2	64790 22.0	46374 15.7	-	900888	3.1
Panama	Rural	1990	229179 100	63965 27.9	61062 26.6	55531 24.2	31247 13.6	17374 7.6	-	573669	2.5
Paraguay	Total	1982	578714 100	278155 48.1	191257 33.0	72825 12.6	22533 3.9	9164 1.6	4780 0.8	...	...
Paraguay	Urban	1982	265422 100	94956 35.8	95133 35.8	47171 17.8	16504 6.2	7284 2.7	4374 1.6	...	...
Paraguay	Rural	1982	313292 100	183199 58.5	96124 30.7	25654 8.2	6029 1.9	1880 0.6	406 0.1	...	...
Peru	Total	1990	3971000 100	924665 23.3	1117083 28.1	739894 18.6	552146 13.9	637212 16.0	-	10773157	2.7
Peru	Urban	1990	2707000 100	485943 18.0	668104 24.7	537883 19.9	446791 16.5	568279 21.0	-	8064359	3.0
Peru	Rural	1990	1264000 100	438722 34.7	448979 35.5	202011 16.0	105355 8.3	68933 5.5	-	2708798	2.1
Turks & Caicos Islands	Total [33]	1990	2022 100	126 6.2	273 13.5	298 14.7	375 18.5	950 47.0	-	8901	4.4
US Virgin Islands	Total	1990	39290 100	20532 52.3	...	8817 22.4	...	8110 20.6	1831 4.7	...	...
Venezuela	Total	1990	3519384 100	217688 6.2	375763 10.7	657675 18.7	929780 26.4	1277344 36.3	61134 1.7	...	...
Venezuela	Urban	1990	2974529 100	170366 5.7	280972 9.4	531842 17.9	787648 26.5	1152186 38.7	51515 1.7	...	...
Venezuela	Rural	1990	544855 100	47322 8.7	94791 17.4	125833 23.1	142132 26.1	125158 23.0	9619 1.8	...	...
NORTHERN AMERICA											
Bermuda	Total	1991	22061 100	791 3.6	2103 9.5	3350 15.2	4840 21.9	10956 49.7	21 0.1	...	...
Canada	Total	1991	10018265 100	...	...	...	...	...	...	...	...
United States	Total	1990	91947410 100	1588833 1.7	3603703 3.9	9068028 9.9	16270533 17.7	61416313 66.8	-	498889544	5.4
United States	Urban	1990	70045167 100	1475281 2.1	3245345 4.6	7966221 11.4	12564435 17.9	44793885 64.0	-	...	...
United States	Rural	1990	21902243 100	113552 0.5	358358 1.6	1101807 5.0	3706098 16.9	16622428 75.9	-	...	...

TABLE 13 (continued)

Occupied Housing Units by Number of Rooms, Number and Percentage, Selected Countries

			Occupied Housing Units, Total and by Number of Rooms							Total Number of Rooms for all Units	Average Size (Rooms per Unit)
			Total	1-Room	2-Room	3-Room	4-Room	5+ Room	Unknown		
OCEANIA											
American Samoa	Total	1990	6959	779	1676	1868	797	662	1177	...	...
			100	11.2	24.1	26.8	11.5	9.5	16.9		
American Samoa	Urban	1990	2378	256	556	636	307	259	364	...	...
			100	10.8	23.4	26.7	12.9	10.9	15.3		
American Samoa	Rural	1990	4581	523	1120	1232	490	403	813	...	...
			100	11.4	24.4	26.9	10.7	8.8	17.7		
Australia	Total [34]	1986	5187422	296192	1349616	2638256	[35] 778256	[36] 1278	123824	...	...
			100	5.7	26.0	50.9	15.0	-	2.4		
Australia	Urban [34]	1986	4513692	266282	1224834	2298905	[35] 621655	[36] 873	101143	...	...
			100	5.9	27.1	50.9	13.8	-	2.2		
Australia	Rural [34]	1986	673689	29905	124774	339343	[35] 156596	[36] 404	22667	...	...
			100	4.4	18.5	50.4	23.2	0.1	3.4		
Fiji	Total	1986	124098	22991	24629	20466	21733	31502	2777	...	...
			100	18.5	19.8	16.5	17.5	25.4	2.2		
Fiji	Urban	1986	49579	5740	6489	8013	11290	17065	982	...	...
			100	11.6	13.1	16.2	22.8	34.4	2.0		
Fiji	Rural	1986	74519	17251	18140	12453	10443	14437	1795	...	...
			100	23.1	24.3	16.7	14.0	19.4	2.4		
French Polynesia	Total	1988	39513	1824	4302	11145	12227	10015	-	...	...
			100	4.6	10.9	28.2	30.9	25.3	-		
New Caledonia	Total [2]	1989	40266	4495	6530	10411	12196	6634	-	134115	3.3
			100	11.2	16.2	25.9	30.3	16.5	-		
New Caledonia	Urban [2]	1989	22427	2817	3133	5977	7287	3213	-	73515	3.3
			100	12.6	14.0	26.7	32.5	14.3	-		
New Caledonia	Rural [2]	1989	17839	1678	3397	4434	4909	3421	-	60600	3.4
			100	9.4	19.0	24.9	27.5	19.2	-		
New Zealand	Total [37]	1991	1164417	..	[38] 11532	34026	91560	944193	83106	7394130	6.4
			100	..	1.0	2.9	7.9	81.1	7.1		
New Zealand	Urban [37,39]	1991	1003725	..	[38] 10023	30822	83937	805425	73518	6288027	6.3
			100	..	1.0	3.1	8.4	80.2	7.3		
New Zealand	Rural [37,39]	1991	160689	..	[38] 1509	3201	7626	138765	9588	1106103	6.9
			100	..	0.9	2.0	4.7	86.4	6.0		
Wallis & Futuna Islands	Total	1990	2348	830	495	374	396	253	-	...	...
			100	35.3	21.1	15.9	16.9	10.8	-		

Source: United Nations, Human Settlements Statistics Questionnaire 1992

For additional information and definitions of the relevant terms refer to the source.

TABLE 13 *(continued)*

Occupied Housing Units by Number of Rooms, Number and Percentage, Selected Countries

Notes:

1. Data refer only to units covered by the sample for the National Household Survey 1986.
2. Data refer to households in housing units.
3. Excludes housing units occupied by institutional households.
4. Data are presented in percentages.
5. Data refer to the Government controlled area only.
6. Figures exclude Assam and some areas where 1981 Census could not be conducted. Also, not included are institutional households for which the number of living rooms in occupation of household was not canvassed.
7. Data include a total of 769,596 households with no exclusive room, of which 149,001 in urban and 620,505 in rural areas.
8. This category includes occupied conventional, occupied unconventional dwellings and occupied collective living quarters.
9. Including estates.
10. Difference between the sum of categories and total refers to tents, huts, caves, etc.
11. Data refer to apartments.
12. Data refer to four and more room units.
13. Data refer to units without any room.
14. Data refer to the territory prior to 3 October 1990, i.e., they relate only to the former Federal Republic of Germany.
    Note: In Germany the distinction between urban and rural areas is not of great importance. Therefore, 'Urban' refers to 'Kreisfreie Stadte'—that is a town not attached to administrative districts (Landkreise). Rural refers to 'Landkreise', that is an administrative district.
15. Estimated data.
16. Data refer to permanent households in permanent housing units.
17. Data refer to housing units with three or more rooms.
18. Including 15,566 housing units (dwellings) with no information on densely/sparsely populated areas.
19. Data refer to conventional dwellings only.
20. Including conventional dwellings with unknown number of rooms.
21. Data refer to occupied conventional dwellings only.
22. The definition of a 'room' does not cover kitchen even if it suits the definition of a room.

23. Data refer to principal residences only. According to census definitions principal residences refer to the housing unit occupied by one or more persons for most of the year. Secondary residence is a housing unit occupied seasonally and is not considered to be a usual residence.
24. Room is defined as bedroom, living room, dining room, reception, study room, play room, servant's quarters and kitchen.
25. Data do not include kitchens.
26. Data refer to the former Socialist Federative Republic of Yugoslavia.
27. Total number or rooms for all units excludes 121 cases where the number of rooms were not reported.
28. Data refer to occupied housing units with permanent residents. Excluded are huts and natural shelters.
29. Data are estimated on the basis of 2.5 % sample.
30. Data refer to the number of occupied housing units with people present.
31. Data don't include 11,763 'refugee' housing units which do not meet characteristics of a housing unit, also 136,341 housing units which were not occupied were excluded.
32. Data don't include 76,210 housing units with unknown number of rooms.
33. Data refer to Belongers (citizens of the Turks and Caicos Islands) only.
34. Data refer to units with number of bedrooms.
35. Data refer to units with 4 and more bedrooms.
36. Data refer to units without bedroom.
37. 'Occupied housing units' refer to conventional dwellings only (excluding unconventional dwellings) and 'Households in housing units' equates to 'Occupied housing units'.
38. Data refer to both one-room and two-room units.
39. Urban area refers to non-administrative centres which are regarded urban in character and have a population of 1,000 or greater. Rural refers to the area that is not specifically designated as 'urban'—includes rural centres (population 300-999), administrative county or district territory not included in an urban area and inland waters, coastal inlets, oceanic waters and islands, which are outside urban areas.

TABLE 14

Occupied Housing Units by Number of Rooms, Number and Percentage, Selected Cities

			Occupied Housing Units, Total and by Number of Rooms							Total Number of Rooms for all Units	Average Size (rooms per unit)
			Total	1-Room	2-Room	3-Room	4-Room	5+ Room	Unknown		
AFRICA											
Ethiopia	Addis Ababa	1984	259555	68413	78883	37853	20968	49041	4397	...	...
			100	26.4	30.4	14.6	8.1	18.9	1.7		
Ethiopia	Asmara	1984	55502	29760	8904	4772	2766	8310	990	...	...
			100	53.6	16.0	8.6	5.0	15.0	1.8		
Ethiopia	Dire Dawa	1984	21665	13132	4518	1304	553	1727	431	...	...
			100	60.6	20.9	6.0	2.6	8.0	2.0		
Ethiopia	Nazret	1984	14568	3357	5301	2582	1247	1783	298	...	...
			100	23.0	36.4	17.7	8.6	12.2	2.0		
Malawi	Blantyre-Limbe [1]	1986	20541	3953	8705	3700	2389	1794	-	53949	2.6
			100	19.2	42.4	18.0	11.6	8.7	-		
Malawi	Lilongwe [1]	1986	8201	1864	3183	1197	701	1256	-	23503	2.9
			100	22.7	38.8	14.6	8.5	15.3	-		
Malawi	Mzuzu [1]	1986	5197	664	1601	1392	910	630	-	15648	3.0
			100	12.8	30.8	26.8	17.5	12.1	-		
Malawi	Zomba [1]	1986	4550	1211	1685	784	562	308	-	11277	2.5
			100	26.6	37.0	17.2	12.4	6.8	-		
Mauritius	Beau Bassin-Rose Hill	1990	20466	1187	2830	3562	4855	8026	6	85623	4.2
			100	5.8	13.8	17.4	23.7	39.2	-		
Mauritius	Curepipe	1990	14850	510	1722	2485	3475	6655	3	66252	4.5
			100	3.4	11.6	16.7	23.4	44.8	-		
Mauritius	Port-Louis	1990	28604	2652	6421	5974	6978	6578	1	101350	3.5
			100	9.3	22.4	20.9	24.4	23.0	-		
Mauritius	Quatre-Bornes	1990	14802	574	1854	2061	3625	6685	3	65673	4.4
			100	3.9	12.5	13.9	24.5	45.2	-		
Reunion	Le Tampon	1990	13310	333	1040	2619	4381	4937	-	55009	4.1
			100	2.5	7.8	19.7	32.9	37.1	-		
Reunion	Saint-Denis	1990	34674	2615	4423	9845	9498	8293	-	124897	3.6
			100	7.5	12.8	28.4	27.4	23.9	-		
Reunion	St. Paul	1990	17851	427	2309	3809	5888	5418	-	70070	3.9
			100	2.4	12.9	21.3	33.0	30.4	-		
Reunion	St. Pierre	1990	16038	776	2284	3710	5087	4181	-	60028	3.7
			100	4.8	14.2	23.1	31.7	26.1	-		
Tunisia	Tunis	1989	167364	27042	51500	47583	27801	12417	1021	...	...
			100	16.2	30.8	28.4	16.6	7.4	0.6		
ASIA											
Cyprus	Larnaca [2]	1982	13096	131	608	1141	3580	7621	15	61847	4.7
			100	1.0	4.6	8.7	27.3	58.2	0.1		
Cyprus	Limassol [2]	1982	29716	507	1572	3982	6497	17112	46	136879	4.6
			100	1.7	5.3	13.4	21.9	57.6	0.2		
Cyprus	Nicosia [2]	1982	41542	702	1825	3502	9696	25730	87	200069	4.8
			100	1.7	4.4	8.4	23.3	61.9	0.2		
Cyprus	Paphos [2]	1982	5822	138	366	665	1110	3521	22	27535	4.7
			100	2.4	6.3	11.4	19.1	60.5	0.4		
India	Bombay	1991	[3] 1553845	1088460	267395	98185	30710	16770	52325	2234755	1.4
			100	70.0	17.2	6.3	2.0	1.1	3.4		
India	Calcutta [4]	1981	1712875	965255	413990	158000	70985	50800	53845	2992665	1.7
			100	56.4	24.2	9.2	4.1	3.0	3.1		
India	Delhi [4]	1991	1648553	758169	458350	263876	123870	41473	2815	...	...
			100	46.0	27.8	16.0	7.5	2.5	0.2		
India	Madras	1981	794322	...	...	...	...	...	...	...	...
			100								
Iraq	Baghdad	1987	419876	2589	23487	64914	96272	232614	-	2114728	5.0
			100	0.6	5.6	15.5	22.9	55.4	-		
Iraq	Basra	1987	92005	627	5204	14350	18599	53221	4	529178	5.8
			100	0.7	5.7	15.6	20.2	57.8	-		
Iraq	Kirkuk	1987	69273	446	4873	14121	14499	35333	1	375218	5.4
			100	0.6	7.0	20.4	20.9	51.0	-		
Iraq	Mosul	1987	165963	1251	9378	22394	23523	109402	15	1067708	6.4
			100	0.8	5.7	13.5	14.2	65.9	-		
Israel	Haifa	1983	80270	3560	18680	35785	17565	4680	-	...	...
			100	4.4	23.3	44.6	21.9	5.8	-		
Israel	Jerusalem	1983	108625	8775	23185	45855	23475	7335	-	...	...
			100	8.1	21.3	42.2	21.6	6.8	-		
Israel	Tel Aviv-Yafo	1983	128245	7690	37040	58085	19070	6360	-	...	...
			100	6.0	28.9	45.3	14.9	5.0	-		
Japan	Osaka	1990	989152	116137	176880	209493	248501	238141	-	...	...
			100	11.7	17.9	21.2	25.1	24.1	-		
Japan	Sapporo	1990	626279	57257	89169	141181	121357	217315	-	...	...
			100	9.1	14.2	22.5	19.4	34.7	-		
Japan	Tokyo	1990	3208190	617900	625238	687544	608614	668894	-	...	...
			100	19.3	19.5	21.4	19.0	20.8	-		
Japan	Yokohama	1990	1076191	96846	159962	205583	268909	344891	-	...	...
			100	9.0	14.9	19.1	25.0	32.0	-		

TABLE 14 (continued)

Occupied Housing Units by Number of Rooms, Number and Percentage, Selected Cities

			Occupied Housing Units, Total and by Number of Rooms							Total Number of Rooms for all Units	Average Size (rooms per unit)
			Total	1-Room	2-Room	3-Room	4-Room	5+ Room	Unknown		
ASIA (continued)											
Maldives	Male' [5]	1990	5613	492	479	632	836	2446	728	...	...
			100	8.8	8.5	11.3	14.9	43.6	13.0		
Pakistan	Faisalabad	1981	209768	95846	65356	25816	12959	9791	-	440513	2.1
			100	45.7	31.2	12.3	6.2	4.7	-		
Pakistan	Islamabad	1981	36973	8320	13452	6721	3514	4966	-	99827	2.7
			100	22.5	36.4	18.2	9.5	13.4	-		
Pakistan	Karachi	1981	811850	348146	258060	118435	49326	37883	-	1786070	2.2
			100	42.9	31.8	14.6	6.1	4.7	-		
Pakistan	Lahore	1981	447509	204639	129572	55679	30163	27456	-	984520	2.2
			100	45.7	29.0	12.4	6.7	6.1	-		
Republic of Korea	Incheon	1990	319363	5751	30089	107281	99717	76525	-	1281573	4.0
			100	1.8	9.4	33.6	31.2	24.0	-		
Republic of Korea	Pusan	1990	516413	11114	63524	106322	116403	219050	-	2404890	4.7
			100	2.2	12.3	20.6	22.5	42.4	-		
Republic of Korea	Seoul	1990	1463081	21934	119383	332658	366517	622589	-	6893805	4.7
			100	1.5	8.2	22.7	25.1	42.6	-		
Republic of Korea	Taegu	1990	296189	4188	22471	51683	75364	142483	-	1486060	5.0
			100	1.4	7.6	17.4	25.4	48.1	-		
Syrian Arab Republic	Aleppo	1981	149878	11076	33881	44630	34555	25736	416	...	...
			100	7.4	22.6	29.8	23.1	17.2	0.3		
Syrian Arab Republic	Damascus	1981	163575	9239	28957	39086	40156	45465	672	...	...
			100	5.6	17.7	23.9	24.5	27.8	0.4		
Syrian Arab Republic	Homs	1981	53282	5474	17210	15488	8453	6542	115	...	...
			100	10.3	32.3	29.1	15.9	12.3	0.2		
Syrian Arab Republic	Lattakia	1981	32909	3814	6553	8789	8027	5631	95	...	...
			100	11.6	19.9	26.7	24.4	17.1	0.3		
Thailand	Bangkok [6]	1980	902871	275609	282080	181472	[7] 89775	[8] 21316	52640	...	...
			100	30.5	31.2	20.1	9.9	2.4	5.8		
Thailand	Chon Buri [6]	1980	129899	63043	41346	12298	[7] 4310	[8] 2895	6017	...	...
			100	48.5	31.8	9.5	3.3	2.2	4.6		
Thailand	Nakhon Si Thammarat [6]	1980	214981	112258	71185	14967	[7] 3830	[8] 5479	7261	...	...
			100	52.2	33.1	7.0	1.8	2.5	3.4		
Thailand	Songkhla [6]	1980	158989	75874	57136	13271	[7] 4271	[8] 2062	6373	...	...
			100	47.7	35.9	8.3	2.7	1.3	4.0		
Turkey	Adana	1985	[9] 304802	15777	69990	125207	63702	19449	3494	...	...
			100	5.2	23.0	41.1	20.9	6.4	1.1		
Turkey	Ankara	1985	[9] 683837	8121	94393	300731	238873	37046	4115	...	...
			100	1.2	13.8	44.0	34.9	5.4	0.6		
Turkey	Istanbul	1985	[9] 1293507	33065	222707	640745	343339	51948	542	...	...
			100	2.6	17.2	49.5	26.5	4.0	-		
Turkey	Izmir	1985	[9] 545448	18596	105480	256626	139087	23073	397	...	...
			100	3.4	19.3	47.0	25.5	4.2	0.1		
EUROPE											
Albania	Durres [10]	1989	54888	25938	17752	5763	[11] 2075	..	[12] 3360	...	...
			100	47.3	32.3	10.5	3.8	..	6.1		
Albania	Elbasan [10]	1989	48548	21243	17336	6193	[11] 2026	..	[12] 1750	...	...
			100	43.8	35.7	12.8	4.2	..	3.6		
Albania	Shkoder [10]	1989	51926	25752	15997	5859	[11] 1935	..	[12] 2383	...	...
			100	49.6	30.8	11.3	3.7	..	4.6		
Albania	Tirana [10]	1989	95464	52954	28731	6511	[11] 1793	..	[12] 5475	...	...
			100	55.5	30.1	6.8	1.9	..	5.7		
Austria	Graz	1981	101941	20993	30312	24506	10784	7142	8204	247142	2.4
			100	20.6	29.7	24.0	10.6	7.0	8.0		
Austria	Linz	1981	78791	12333	27090	24677	9294	4325	1072	203114	2.6
			100	15.7	34.4	31.3	11.8	5.5	1.4		
Austria	Salzburg	1981	57221	11523	16320	17093	7415	4653	217	151810	2.7
			100	20.1	28.5	29.9	13.0	8.1	0.4		
Austria	Vienna	1981	717608	180416	260203	187062	59782	24864	5281	1645704	2.3
			100	25.1	36.3	26.1	8.3	3.5	0.7		
Bosnia & Herzegovina	Sarajevo [22]	1981	103144	33687	46156	19170	4423	1232	8	...	...
			100	32.7	44.7	18.6	4.3	1.2	-		
Bulgaria	Bourgas	1985	64761	9916	30236	16546	5859	2204	-	155804	2.4
			100	15.3	46.7	25.5	9.0	3.4	-		
Bulgaria	Plovdiv [13]	1985	234784	32934	68926	73071	36268	23585	-	664740	2.8
			100	14.0	29.4	31.1	15.4	10.0	-		
Bulgaria	Sofia	1985	403900	85866	165088	120907	23369	8670	-	919914	2.3
			100	21.3	40.9	29.9	5.8	2.1	-		
Bulgaria	Varna	1985	98122	20012	37150	28772	9580	2608	-	233348	2.4
			100	20.4	37.9	29.3	9.8	2.7	-		
Channel Islands	Guernsey	1991	21215	524	906	1755	2977	15053	-	...	...
			100	2.5	4.3	8.3	14.0	71.0	-		
Channel Islands	Jersey	1991	27611	727	1756	2601	4526	18001	-	...	...
			100	2.6	6.4	9.4	16.4	65.2	-		
Croatia	Zagreb [22]	1981	216364	63652	92015	45433	12963	4886	618	...	...
			100	29.4	42.5	21.0	6.0	2.3	0.3		

TABLE 14 (continued)

Occupied Housing Units by Number of Rooms, Number and Percentage, Selected Cities

			Occupied Housing Units, Total and by Number of Rooms							Total Number of Rooms for all Units	Average Size (rooms per unit)
			Total	1-Room	2-Room	3-Room	4-Room	5+ Room	Unknown		
EUROPE (continued)											
Finland	Espoo	1989	66259	6003	7326	13678	17291	21496	465	250061	3.8
			100	9.1	11.1	20.6	26.1	32.4	0.7		
Finland	Helsinki	1989	236785	45656	51687	52384	47615	38854	589	709481	3.0
			100	19.3	21.8	22.1	20.1	16.4	0.2		
Finland	Tampere	1989	78001	9666	12964	22138	17802	15074	357	254638	3.3
			100	12.4	16.6	28.4	22.8	19.3	0.5		
Finland	Turku	1989	74857	10469	11304	21214	17948	12916	1006	238343	3.2
			100	14.0	15.1	28.3	24.0	17.3	1.3		
France	Lyon [5]	1990	189700	24780	46860	53800	40540	23720	-	571480	3.0
			100	13.1	24.7	28.4	21.4	12.5	-		
France	Marseille [5]	1990	344500	28980	65520	126540	87020	36440	-	1083220	3.1
			100	8.4	19.0	36.7	25.3	10.6	-		
France	Paris [5]	1990	1090480	267760	366580	251420	123260	81460	-	2695800	2.5
			100	24.6	33.6	23.1	11.3	7.5	-		
France	Toulouse [5]	1990	162600	24760	33640	41420	38880	23900	-	503980	3.1
			100	15.2	20.7	25.5	23.9	14.7	-		
Germany	Berlin (west)	1987	1043719	24163	155726	389600	295492	178738	-	3681761	3.5
			100	2.3	14.9	37.3	28.3	17.1	-		
Germany	Bonn	1987	135489	10610	13507	31774	37897	41701	-	529118	3.9
			100	7.8	10.0	23.5	28.0	30.8	-		
Germany	Hamburg	1987	779605	20537	60190	239997	274143	184738	-	2995182	3.8
			100	2.6	7.7	30.8	35.2	23.7	-		
Germany	Munich	1987	626425	61008	77875	179105	181972	126465	-	2193450	3.5
			100	9.7	12.4	28.6	29.0	20.2	-		
Hungary	Budapest	1990	775523	35809	190335	277855	199602	71922	-	[14] 2424617	3.1
			100	4.6	24.5	35.8	25.7	9.3	-		
Hungary	Debrecen	1990	73850	2268	13286	29336	21441	7519	-	[14] 241129	3.3
			100	3.1	18.0	39.7	29.0	10.2	-		
Hungary	Miskolc	1990	69463	2560	12617	29900	19674	4712	-	[14] 221659	3.2
			100	3.7	18.2	43.0	28.3	6.8	-		
Hungary	Szeged	1990	64734	1328	8684	29198	18361	7163	-	[14] 217466	3.4
			100	2.1	13.4	45.1	28.4	11.1	-		
Ireland	Cork [15]	1986	36944	1073	1547	2484	5367	26466	7	...	...
			100	2.9	4.2	6.7	14.5	71.6	-		
Ireland	Dublin [15]	1986	153859	11441	10310	17751	30247	84081	29	...	...
			100	7.4	6.7	11.5	19.7	54.6	-		
Ireland	Galway [15]	1986	12382	237	581	973	1898	8691	2	...	...
			100	1.9	4.7	7.9	15.3	70.2	-		
Ireland	Limerick [15]	1986	15406	358	834	1108	3489	9617	-	...	...
			100	2.3	5.4	7.2	22.6	62.4	-		
Isle of Man	Douglas [5]	1991	8447	84	449	934	1295	5685	-	...	...
			100	1.0	5.3	11.1	15.3	67.3	-		
Italy	Milan	1991	583104	...	...	...	...	...	...	...	...
			100	...	...	...	...	...	...		
Italy	Naples	1991	306869	...	...	...	...	...	...		
			100	...	...	...	...	...	...		
Italy	Rome	1991	988543	...	...	...	...	...	...		
			100	...	...	...	...	...	...		
Italy	Turin	1991	392547	...	...	...	...	...	...		
			100	...	...	...	...	...	...		
Latvia	Daugavpils	1991	42800	8500	20700	[16] 13600	..	..	-	...	...
			100	19.9	48.4	31.8	..	..	-		
Latvia	Liepaja	1991	36400	10800	15800	[16] 9800	..	..	-	...	...
			100	29.7	43.4	26.9	..	..	-		
Latvia	Riga	1991	299500	79100	120200	[16] 100200	..	..	-	...	...
			100	26.4	40.1	33.5	..	..	-		
Lithuania	Kaunas	1991	126076	22331	53696	[16] 50049	..	..	-	...	...
			100	17.7	42.6	39.7	..	..	-		
Lithuania	Klaipeda	1991	59207	11798	27138	[16] 20271	..	..	-	...	...
			100	19.9	45.8	34.2	..	..	-		
Lithuania	Siauliai	1991	44164	7515	21466	[16] 15183	..	..	-	...	...
			100	17.0	48.6	34.4	..	..	-		
Lithuania	Vilnius	1991	162817	34137	66558	[16] 62122	..	..	-	...	...
			100	21.0	40.9	38.2	..	..	-		
Netherlands	Amsterdam	1989	363740	9017	30520	94978	112960	115396	869	1439447	4.0
			100	2.5	8.4	26.1	31.1	31.7	0.2		
Netherlands	Hague, The	1989	200927	2104	6283	31899	62585	97950	106	924879	4.6
			100	1.0	3.1	15.9	31.1	48.7	0.1		
Netherlands	Rotterdam	1989	269973	2467	14638	50568	90629	111290	381	1157512	4.3
			100	0.9	5.4	18.7	33.6	41.2	0.1		
Netherlands	Utrecht	1989	106154	2196	5684	14067	24610	59538	59	506812	4.8
			100	2.1	5.4	13.3	23.2	56.1	0.1		

TABLE 14 (continued)

Occupied Housing Units by Number of Rooms, Number and Percentage, Selected Cities

			Total	1-Room	2-Room	3-Room	4-Room	5+ Room	Unknown	Total Number of Rooms for all Units	Average Size (rooms per unit)
EUROPE (continued)											
Norway	Bergen	1990	93949	5376	17606	25788	23161	22019	-	341097	3.6
			100	5.7	18.7	27.4	24.7	23.4	-		
Norway	Oslo	1990	244434	30206	61022	73162	42047	37994	-	766900	3.1
			100	12.4	25.0	29.9	17.2	15.5	-		
Norway	Stavanger	1990	42680	2293	7914	9491	10315	12668	-	164000	3.8
			100	5.4	18.5	22.2	24.2	29.7	-		
Norway	Trondheim	1990	60407	4043	11765	14952	14899	14747	-	219527	3.6
			100	6.7	19.5	24.8	24.7	24.4	-		
Poland	Krakow [17]	1988	228245	[18] 19082	54246	78121	60231	16565	..	692376	3.0
			100	8.4	23.8	34.2	26.4	7.3	..		
Poland	Lodz [17]	1988	313764	[18] 34345	73215	128849	65224	12131	..	894125	2.8
			100	10.9	23.3	41.1	20.8	3.9	..		
Poland	Warsaw [17]	1988	581454	[18] 59944	142243	193485	149449	36333	..	1715722	3.0
			100	10.3	24.5	33.3	25.7	6.2	..		
Poland	Wroclaw [17]	1988	194403	[18] 12177	35682	69496	53438	23610	..	639103	3.3
			100	6.3	18.4	35.7	27.5	12.1	..		
Romania	Brasov [19, 20]	1992	104836	20394	50184	27030	6500	728	-	237083	2.3
			100	19.5	47.9	25.8	6.2	0.7	-		
Romania	Bucarest [19, 20]	1992	733219	108769	307200	243715	65216	8319	-	1819472	2.5
			100	14.8	41.9	33.2	8.9	1.1	-		
Romania	Constanta [19, 20]	1992	108728	7599	50761	36706	11474	2188	-	282047	2.6
			100	7.0	46.7	33.8	10.6	2.0	-		
Romania	Timisoara [19, 20]	1992	114873	20122	50977	34286	8116	1372	-	265659	2.3
			100	17.5	44.4	29.8	7.1	1.2	-		
Russian Federation	Moscow	1989	2644730	614276	1328447	[16] 689902	..	..	12105	...	...
			100	23.2	50.2	26.1	..	..	0.5		
Russian Federation	Nizhny Novgorod	1989	429476	89103	182448	[16] 124997	..	..	32928	...	...
			100	20.7	42.5	29.1	..	..	7.7		
Russian Federation	Novosibirsk	1989	388726	78902	151929	[16] 99205	..	..	58690	...	...
			100	20.3	39.1	25.5	..	..	15.1		
Russian Federation	St. Petersburg	1989	1224707	274672	602476	[16] 321239	..	..	26320	...	...
			100	22.4	49.2	26.2	..	..	2.1		
Spain	Barcelona	1991	590655	6837	29722	133990	183138	232148	4819	...	...
			100	1.2	5.0	22.7	31.0	39.3	0.8		
Spain	Madrid	1991	993286	6865	44663	151545	284877	498596	6739	...	...
			100	0.7	4.5	15.3	28.7	50.2	0.7		
Spain	Sevilla	1991	199375	954	5962	33670	52387	105404	998	...	...
			100	0.5	3.0	16.9	26.3	52.9	0.5		
Spain	Valencia	1991	253429	345	3977	28097	75400	144641	967	...	...
			100	0.1	1.6	11.1	29.8	57.1	0.4		
Sweden	Goteborg	1990	209779	5341	21346	65214	56914	58120	2844	804933	3.8
			100	2.5	10.2	31.1	27.1	27.7	1.4		
Sweden	Malmo	1990	120464	3252	10064	37373	36308	32023	1444	461990	3.8
			100	2.7	8.4	31.0	30.1	26.6	1.2		
Sweden	Stockholm	1990	351314	22888	59424	102761	88099	75358	2784	1229953	3.5
			100	6.5	16.9	29.3	25.1	21.5	0.8		
Sweden	Uppsala	1990	72504	1704	5778	17165	18755	28443	659	307055	4.2
			100	2.4	8.0	23.7	25.9	39.2	0.9		
Switzerland	Basel [21]	1980	87819	12732	22074	31856	12398	8759	-	264434	3.0
			100	14.5	25.1	36.3	14.1	10.0	-		
Switzerland	Berne [21]	1980	67719	9049	13899	24144	13311	7316	-	210893	3.1
			100	13.4	20.5	35.7	19.7	10.8	-		
Switzerland	Geneva [21]	1980	79628	21653	24513	19238	8356	5868	-	214896	2.7
			100	27.2	30.8	24.2	10.5	7.4	-		
Switzerland	Zurich [21]	1980	176809	30992	34603	64400	33193	13621	-	518501	2.9
			100	17.5	19.6	36.4	18.8	7.7	-		
TFYR Macedonia	Skoplje [22]	1981	116352	17586	45038	36003	13992	6881	189	...	...
			100	15.1	38.7	30.9	12.0	5.9	0.2		
Ukraine	Donetsk	1992	342067	83362	135921	[16] 122784	..	..	-	...	...
			100	24.4	39.7	35.9	..	..	-		
Ukraine	Kharkov	1992	512667	135045	192824	[16] 184798	..	..	-	...	...
			100	26.3	37.6	36.0	..	..	-		
Ukraine	Kiev	1992	832993	224141	345634	[16] 263218	..	..	-	...	...
			100	26.9	41.5	31.6	..	..	-		
Ukraine	Odessa	1992	325824	104903	114454	[16] 106467	..	..	-	...	...
			100	32.2	35.1	32.7	..	..	-		
Yugoslavia	Belgrade [22]	1981	354747	111048	140231	77709	18953	8107	1477	...	...
			100	31.3	39.5	21.9	5.3	2.3	0.4		

TABLE 14 (continued)

Occupied Housing Units by Number of Rooms, Number and Percentage, Selected Cities

			Occupied Housing Units, Total and by Number of Rooms							Total Number of Rooms for all Units	Average Size (rooms per unit)
			Total	1-Room	2-Room	3-Room	4-Room	5+ Room	Unknown		
LATIN AMERICA											
Bolivia	Cochabamba	1988	86100	17200	17900	15000	14100	21500	400	261900	3.0
			100	20.0	20.8	17.4	16.4	25.0	0.5		
Bolivia	La Paz [6]	1988	156500	49600	34300	26100	18600	26400	300	402900	2.6
			100	31.7	21.9	16.7	11.9	16.9	0.2		
Bolivia	Oruro [6]	1988	38400	12600	10500	5900	4600	4600	...	92700	2.4
			100	32.8	27.3	15.4	12.0	12.0	...		
Bolivia	Santa Cruz [6]	1988	112300	49300	24900	16200	10000	11700	100	246200	2.2
			100	43.9	22.2	14.4	8.9	10.4	0.1		
Cayman Islands	Georgetown	1989	4445	528	584	669	869	1795	-	18984	4.3
			100	11.9	13.1	15.1	19.6	40.4	-		
Cuba	Camaguey	1981	62624	3873	6863	12714	18616	20558	-	...	...
			100	6.2	11.0	20.3	29.7	32.8	-		
Cuba	Havana	1981	500198	48316	106125	111611	109932	124214	-	...	...
			100	9.7	21.2	22.3	22.0	24.8	-		
Cuba	Holguin	1981	43956	1875	4291	9088	12817	15885	-	...	...
			100	4.3	9.8	20.7	29.2	36.1	-		
Cuba	Santiago de Cuba	1981	72760	4328	9137	14716	18523	26056	-	...	...
			100	5.9	12.6	20.2	25.5	35.8	-		
Ecuador	Cuenca	1990	42417	6566	6534	6191	5799	17327	-	...	...
			100	15.5	15.4	14.6	13.7	40.8	-		
Ecuador	Guayaquil	1990	319900	78016	90040	69762	44823	37259	-	...	...
			100	24.4	28.1	21.8	14.0	11.6	-		
Ecuador	Machala	1990	30903	8366	8075	6820	4638	3004	-	...	...
			100	27.1	26.1	22.1	15.0	9.7	-		
Ecuador	Quito	1990	262709	54447	52905	47875	44299	63183	-	...	...
			100	20.7	20.1	18.2	16.9	24.1	-		
French Guiana	Cayenne	1990	13156	2178	2902	3172	3073	1831	-	39970	3.0
			100	16.6	22.1	24.1	23.4	13.9	-		
French Guiana	Kourou	1990	4040	465	809	1038	1170	558	-	12881	3.2
			100	11.5	20.0	25.7	29.0	13.8	-		
French Guiana	Remire - Montjoly	1990	3476	371	488	530	1058	1029	-	12756	3.7
			100	10.7	14.0	15.2	30.4	29.6	-		
French Guiana	Saint-Laurent-du-Moroni	1990	3387	908	1002	624	480	373	-	8711	2.6
			100	26.8	29.6	18.4	14.2	11.0	-		
Guadeloupe	Abymes	1990	18772	819	2654	4804	6393	4102	-	68599	3.7
			100	4.4	14.1	25.6	34.1	21.9	-		
Guadeloupe	Basse-Terre	1990	4451	309	607	1267	1385	883	-	15853	3.6
			100	6.9	13.6	28.5	31.1	19.8	-		
Guadeloupe	Point-a-Pitre	1990	8695	469	1600	2923	2710	993	-	28597	3.3
			100	5.4	18.4	33.6	31.2	11.4	-		
Guadeloupe	St. Martin	1990	8369	2512	2294	1576	1066	921	-	21290	2.5
			100	30.0	27.4	18.8	12.7	11.0	-		
Haiti	Port-au-Prince [23]	1986	158917	88493	27896	19337	10224	12967	-	...	...
			100	55.7	17.6	12.2	6.4	8.2	-		
Honduras	Choluteca [24]	1988	9823	2630	3112	1517	1065	1499	-	26507	2.7
			100	26.8	31.7	15.4	10.8	15.3	-		
Honduras	El Progreso [24]	1988	10672	2249	2573	2043	1884	1923	-	31855	3.0
			100	21.1	24.1	19.1	17.7	18.0	-		
Honduras	San Pedro Sula [24]	1988	54535	16340	10554	8040	7031	12570	-	164033	3.0
			100	30.0	19.4	14.7	12.9	23.0	-		
Honduras	Tegucigalpa [24]	1988	102573	24823	20235	15041	14034	28440	-	338036	3.3
			100	24.2	19.7	14.7	13.7	27.7	-		
Martinique	Fort-de-France [5]	1990	32340	1626	4959	10090	10340	5325	-	112173	3.5
			100	5.0	15.3	31.2	32.0	16.5	-		
Martinique	Lamentin [5]	1990	8544	234	961	2432	3130	1787	-	31735	3.7
			100	2.7	11.2	28.5	36.6	20.9	-		
Martinique	Sainte Marie [5]	1990	5056	109	499	1272	1922	1254	-	19506	3.9
			100	2.2	9.9	25.2	38.0	24.8	-		
Martinique	Schoelcher [5]	1990	6319	239	675	1514	2379	1512	-	23822	3.8
			100	3.8	10.7	24.0	37.6	23.9	-		
Mexico	Mexico City	1990	3120673	232645	561256	656345	627677	1031385	11365	[25] 12057475	3.9
			100	7.5	18.0	21.0	20.1	33.1	0.4		
Panama	Colon	1990	15471	8632	3947	1869	587	436	-	27015	1.7
			100	55.8	25.5	12.1	3.8	2.8	-		
Panama	Panama	1990	105409	22545	21302	22132	21450	17980	-	322818	3.1
			100	21.4	20.2	21.0	20.3	17.1	-		
Panama	San Miguelito	1990	51645	10347	8135	12495	13802	6866	-	156854	3.0
			100	20.0	15.8	24.2	26.7	13.3	-		
Paraguay	Asuncion	1982	91526	23872	29521	20460	9064	4401	4208	...	...
			100	26.1	32.3	22.4	9.9	4.8	4.6		

TABLE 14 (continued)

Occupied Housing Units by Number of Rooms, Number and Percentage, Selected Cities

			Occupied Housing Units, Total and by Number of Rooms							Total Number of Rooms for all Units	Average Size (rooms per unit)
			Total	1-Room	2-Room	3-Room	4-Room	5+ Room	Unknown		
LATIN AMERICA (continued)											
Peru	Arequipa	1991	124975	22369	18071	21458	18736	44341	-	419534	3.4
			100	17.9	14.5	17.2	15.0	35.5	-		
Peru	Callao	1991	111073	13062	17002	20914	27094	33001	-	383189	3.4
			100	11.8	15.3	18.8	24.4	29.7	-		
Peru	Lima	1991	1099242	129278	168258	206977	268135	326594	-	3792235	3.4
			100	11.8	15.3	18.8	24.4	29.7	-		
Peru	Trujillo	1991	105988	18971	15325	18198	15890	37604	-	355795	3.4
			100	17.9	14.5	17.2	15.0	35.5	-		
US Virgin Islands	Charlotte Amalie [26]	1990	18433	7859	...	[27] 5939	...	3815	820	[26] 75575	4.1
			100	42.6		32.2		20.7	4.4		
Venezuela	Barquisimeto	1990	127612	28157	38076	35135	14232	12012	-	...	...
			100	22.1	29.8	27.5	11.2	9.4	-		
Venezuela	Caracas	1990	416125	92936	138188	118032	33494	33475	-	...	...
			100	22.3	33.2	28.4	8.0	8.0	-		
Venezuela	Valencia	1990	194285	39391	58424	57354	19953	19163	-	...	...
			100	20.3	30.1	29.5	10.3	9.9	-		
NORTHERN AMERICA											
Bermuda	Hamilton	1991	388	22	52	82	104	127	1	...	...
			100	5.7	13.4	21.1	26.8	32.7	0.3		
United States	Chicago [29]	1990	2908063	58071	100811	271116	499366	1978699	-	15889714	5.5
			100	2.0	3.5	9.3	17.2	68.0	-		
United States	Los Angeles [29]	1990	4900720	248912	439187	726209	897222	2589190	-	23235386	4.7
			100	5.1	9.0	14.8	18.3	52.8	-		
United States	New York [29]	1990	6621239	251453	393763	1145821	1207119	3623083	-	33875975	5.1
			100	3.8	5.9	17.3	18.2	54.7	-		
United States	Washington D.C. [29]	1990	1459358	38704	69055	154127	190554	1006918	-	8759710	6.0
			100	2.7	4.7	10.6	13.1	69.0	-		
OCEANIA											
Australia	Brisbane [30]	1986	382573	18039	80663	215559	[31] 61995	...	[32] 6317	...	...
			100	4.7	21.1	56.3	16.2		1.7		
Australia	Canberra [30]	1986	78946	3207	9801	43921	[31] 20391	...	[32] 1626	...	...
			100	4.1	12.4	55.6	25.8		2.1		
Australia	Melbourne [30]	1986	957225	58297	255178	487388	[31] 130730	...	[32] 25631	...	...
			100	6.1	26.7	50.9	13.7		2.7		
Australia	Sydney [30]	1986	1140248	82827	362640	495075	[31] 166009	...	[32] 33697	...	...
			100	7.3	31.8	43.4	14.6				
New Caledonia	Noumea [5]	1989	18756	2678	2834	5208	5486	2550	-	64920	3.5
			100	14.3	15.1	27.8	29.2	13.6	-		
New Zealand	Auckland [33]	1991	110772	..	[34] 2136	5370	12870	77817	12576	629190	5.7
			100	..	1.9	4.8	11.6	70.2	11.4		
New Zealand	Christchurch [33]	1991	106647	..	[34] 1110	3576	10908	86040	5016	664383	6.2
			100	..	1.0	3.4	10.2	80.7	4.7		
New Zealand	Manukau [33]	1991	66471	..	[34] 432	1299	4257	52173	8310	407283	6.1
			100	..	0.6	2.0	6.4	78.5	12.5		
New Zealand	Wellington [33]	1991	55122	..	[34] 966	2478	4716	42636	4323	346065	6.3
			100	..	1.8	4.5	8.6	77.3	7.8		
Wallis & Futuna Islands	Mata-Utu	1990	215	58	46	42	34	35	-	...	...
			100	27.0	21.4	19.5	15.8	16.3	-		

Source: United Nations, Human Settlements Statistics Questionnaire 1992

For additional information and definitions of the relevant terms refer to the source.

TABLE 14 (*continued*)

Occupied Housing Units by Number of Rooms, Number and Percentage, Selected Cities

Notes:

1. Malawi National Housing Survey 1986 (unweighted sample)
2. Data refer to the Government controlled area only.
3. There were 51,135 households having no exclusive room and/or homeless.
4. Excluding institutional and homeless households.
5. Data refer to households in housing units.
6. Data as received by the UN. However the sum of the individual categories differs from the total.
7. Data refer to housing units with four or more bedrooms.
8. Data refer to housing units without any bedroom.
9. The sum of categories differs from the total because of tents, huts, caves, etc. Data refer to households in housing units and not to occupied housing units.
10. Data refer to apartments.
11. Data refer to four and more room units.
12. Data refer to units without any room.
13. Data refer to commune of Plovdiv.
14. Estimated data.
15. Data refer to permanent households in permanent housing units
16. Data refer to housing units with three or more rooms.
17. Data refer to conventional dwellings only.
18. Including conventional dwellings with unknown number of rooms.
19. Data refer to occupied conventional dwellings only.
20. The definition of a 'room' does not cover kitchen even if it suits the definition of a room.
21. Data do not include kitchens.
22. Data refer to occupied and vacant dwellings.
23. Data are estimated on the basis of 2.5% sample.
24. Data refer to the number of occupied housing units with people present at the time of census.
25. Data don't include 11,365 housing units with unknown number of rooms.
26. Figures are for the entire island of St. Thomas.
27. Figure represents the total number of two-, three- and four-room units, NOT only three-room units.
28. UN estimate.
29. Data refer to the City Metropolitan Statistical Area (MSA).
30. Data refer to units with number of bedrooms.
31. Data refer to units with 4 and more bedrooms.
32. Data include units without bedroom; being 28 units for Canberra, 153 units for Melbourne, 292 units for Sydney and 46 units for Brisbane.
33. 'Occupied housing units' refer to conventional dwellings only (excluding unconventional dwellings) and 'Households in housing units' equates to 'Occupied housing units'.
34. Data refer to both one-room and two-room units.

TABLE 15

Occupied Housing Units by Water and Toilet Facilities, Number and Percentage, Selected Countries

			Total Occupied Housing Units	Water Supply System			Without Piped Water	Unknown	Toilet Installation			Without Toilet of any Type	Unknown
				With Piped Water					With Toilet of any Type				
				Total	Inside	Outside			Total	Flush Toilet	Other Toilet		
AFRICA													
Ethiopia	Total	1984	7377435	...	...	...	...	...	...	...	...	...	...
			100	...	...	...	...	...	...	...	...	...	...
Ethiopia	Urban	1984	976180	501755	19314	482441	447874	26551	476874	75916	400958	485618	13688
			100	51.4	2.0	49.4	45.9	2.7	48.9	7.8	41.1	49.7	1.4
Ethiopia	Rural	1984	6401255	...	...	...	...	...	...	...	...	...	...
			100	...	...	...	...	...	...	...	...	...	...
Gambia	Total	1983	81719	17925	8062	9863	58228	5566	...	...	...	...	...
			100	21.9	9.9	12.1	71.3	6.8	...	...	...	...	...
Gambia	Urban	1983	24575	14488	6986	7502	7706	2381	...	...	...	...	...
			100	59.0	28.4	30.5	31.4	9.7	...	...	...	...	...
Gambia	Rural	1983	57144	3437	1076	2361	50522	3185	...	...	...	...	...
			100	6.0	1.9	4.1	88.4	5.6	...	...	...	...	...
Malawi	Total [1]	1987	2474602	548417	34321	514096	1926185	...	1199620	59765	1139855	659952	...
			100	22.2	1.4	20.8	77.8	...	48.5	2.4	46.1	26.7	...
Malawi	Urban [1]	1987	224831	169281	26104	143177	55550	...	187204	38425	148779	11735	...
			100	75.3	11.6	63.7	24.7	...	83.3	17.1	66.2	5.2	...
Malawi	Rural [1]	1987	2249771	379136	8217	370919	1870635	...	1012416	21340	991076	648217	...
			100	16.9	0.4	16.5	83.1	...	45.0	0.9	44.1	28.8	...
Mali	Total [2]	1987	1364079	82664	51104	31560	1265417	15998	724879	17591	707288	612595	26605
			100	6.1	3.7	2.3	92.8	1.2	53.1	1.3	51.9	44.9	2.0
Mali	Urban [2]	1987	282966	70716	47871	22845	207294	4935	...	...	...	...	...
			100	25.0	16.9	8.1	73.3	1.7	...	...	...	...	...
Mali	Rural [2]	1987	1081133	11948	3233	8715	1058123	11063	...	...	...	...	...
			100	1.1	0.3	0.8	97.9	1.0	...	...	...	...	...
Mauritius	Total	1990	215384	192079	120793	71286	23284	21	213661	135717	77944	1719	4
			100	89.2	56.1	33.1	10.8	-	99.2	63.0	36.2	0.8	-
Mauritius	Urban	1990	90427	88557	65553	23004	1860	10	90164	75720	14444	261	2
			100	97.9	72.5	25.4	2.1	-	99.7	83.7	16.0	0.3	-
Mauritius	Rural	1990	124957	103522	55240	48282	21424	11	123497	59997	63500	1458	2
			100	82.8	44.2	38.6	17.1	-	98.8	48.0	50.8	1.2	-
Morocco	Total [3]	1985	...	...	...	...	...	...	...	...	...	...	-
			100	32.1	...	...	55.7	12.0	52.5	...	...	47.5	-
Morocco	Urban [3]	1985	...	...	...	...	...	...	...	...	...	...	-
			100	62.7	...	...	27.8	5.5	90.1	...	...	9.9	-
Morocco	Rural [3]	1985	...	...	...	...	...	...	...	...	...	...	-
			100	1.6	...	...	80.6	17.8	18.8	...	...	81.2	-
St. Helena	Total	1987	1392	1279	1149	130	111	2	1389	1025	364	2	1
			100	91.9	82.5	9.3	8.0	0.1	99.8	73.6	26.1	0.1	0.1
Tunisia	Total [2]	1989	1458120	...	[4] 1020129	431448	...	6543	1099271	324454	774817	348808	10041
			100	...	70.0	29.6	...	0.4	75.4	22.3	53.1	23.9	0.7
Tunisia	Urban [2]	1989	887580	...	[4] 822035	61850	...	3695	842420	316381	526039	39580	5581
			100	...	92.6	7.0	...	0.4	94.9	35.6	59.3	4.5	0.6
Tunisia	Rural [2]	1989	570540	...	[4] 198094	369598	...	2848	256852	8074	248778	309229	4459
			100	...	34.7	64.8	...	0.5	45.0	1.4	43.6	54.2	0.8
ASIA													
Cyprus	Total [5]	1982	144309	143128	135278	7850	838	343	144094	122448	21646	...	215
			100	99.2	93.7	5.4	0.6	0.2	99.9	84.9	15.0	...	0.1
Cyprus	Urban [5]	1982	90176	89764	88742	1022	270	142	90027	85675	4352	...	149
			100	99.5	98.4	1.1	0.3	0.2	99.8	95.0	4.8	...	0.2
Cyprus	Rural [5]	1982	54133	53364	46536	6828	568	201	54067	36773	17294	...	66
			100	98.6	86.0	12.6	1.0	0.4	99.9	67.9	31.9	...	0.1
India	Total [6]	1981	118614803	27317532	12851006	[7] 14466526	...	...	...	...	...	...	...
			100	23.0	10.8	12.2	...	...	...	...	...	...	...
India	Urban [6]	1981	28541877	18049114	10302247	[7] 7746867	...	...	16596103	...	...	11945774	-
			100	63.2	36.1	27.1	...	...	58.1	...	...	41.9	-
India	Rural [6]	1981	90072926	9268418	2548759	[7] 6719659	...	...	...	...	...	...	...
			100	10.3	2.8	7.5	...	...	...	...	...	...	...
Indonesia	Total	1990	39695375	5152294	...	...	...	...	[8] 6829540	...	...	[9] 9836556	...
			100	13.0	...	...	...	...	17.2	...	...	24.8	...
Indonesia	Urban	1990	11693073	3857696	...	...	...	...	...	...	...	...	...
			100	33.0	...	...	...	...	...	...	...	...	...
Indonesia	Rural	1990	28002302	1294598	...	...	...	...	...	...	...	...	...
			100	4.6	...	...	...	...	...	...	...	...	...
Iraq	Total	1987	1759176	...	...	...	...	...	1588340	...	...	153128	17708
			100	...	...	...	...	...	90.3	...	...	8.7	1.0
Iraq	Urban	1987	1269005	...	...	...	...	...	1246527	...	...	19328	3150
			100	...	...	...	...	...	98.2	...	...	1.5	0.2
Iraq	Rural	1987	490171	...	...	...	...	...	341813	...	...	133800	14558
			100	...	...	...	...	...	69.7	...	...	27.3	3.0

TABLE 15 (continued)

Occupied Housing Units by Water and Toilet Facilities, Number and Percentage, Selected Countries

			Total Occupied Housing Units	Water Supply System — With Piped Water — Total	Inside	Outside	Without Piped Water	Unknown	Toilet Installation — With Toilet of any Type — Total	Flush Toilet	Other Toilet	Without Toilet of any Type	Unknown
ASIA (continued)													
Israel	Total	1983	1104270	...	...	...	...	...	[3] 99.9	[3] 99.9	...	...	...
			100	...	...	...	...	...			...	...	...
Israel	Urban	1983	1038565	...	...	...	...	...	[3] 99.9	[3] 99.9	...	...	...
			100	...	...	...	...	...			...	...	...
Israel	Rural	1983	65705	...	...	...	...	...	[3] 99.9	[3] 99.9	...	...	...
			100										
Japan	Total	1988	37413400	...	...	...	...	...	36962800	24843900	12118900	...	...
			100						98.8	66.4	32.4	...	...
Japan	Urban	1988	29922600	...	...	...	...	...	29485300	22210800	7274500	...	...
			100						98.5	74.2	24.3	...	...
Japan	Rural	1988	7490800	...	...	...	...	...	7477500	2633100	4844400	...	...
			100						99.8	35.2	64.7	...	...
Jordan	Total	1979	313193	240050	218023	22027	...	...	306227	294800	11427	6966	-
			100	76.6	69.6	7.0			97.8	94.1	3.6	2.2	
Jordan	Urban	1979	187560	171462	167192	4270	...	...	186642	183308	3334	918	-
			100	91.4	89.1	2.3			99.5	97.7	1.8	0.5	
Jordan	Rural	1979	125633	68588	50831	17757	...	...	119585	111492	8093	6048	-
			100	54.6	40.5	14.1			95.2	88.7	6.4	4.8	
Macau	Total	1991	87401	85680	...	...	...	[10] 1721	86763	81156	5607	638	-
			100	98.0	...	...		2.0	99.3	92.9	6.4	0.7	
Maldives	Total	1990	29823	...	...	...	...	...	...	...	...	...	...
			100	...	...	...	...	...	...	...	...	...	...
Maldives	Urban	1990	5613	...	...	...	...	...	...	...	...	...	...
			100	...	...	...	...	...	...	...	...	...	...
Maldives	Rural	1990	24210	...	...	...	...	...	...	...	...	...	...
			100	...	...	...	...	...	...	...	...	...	...
Pakistan	Total	1981	12587648	2560538	1588606	971932	10027110	-	...	...	...	...	...
			100	20.3	12.6	7.7	79.7						
Pakistan	Urban	1981	3554173	2071876	1359710	712166	1482297	-	2590818	890383	1700435	963355	-
			100	58.3	38.3	20.0	41.7		72.9	25.1	47.8	27.1	
Pakistan	Rural	1981	9033475	488662	228896	259766	8544813	-	...	...	...	...	...
			100	5.4	2.5	2.9	94.6						
Sri Lanka	Total	1981	2813844	496808	231386	265422	2245712	71324	1871827	135396	1736431	851239	90778
			100	17.7	8.2	9.4	79.8	2.5	66.5	4.8	61.7	30.3	3.2
Sri Lanka	Urban	1981	511810	248243	131319	116924	249936	13631	411136	81687	329449	84138	16536
			100	48.5	25.7	22.8	48.8	2.7	80.3	16.0	64.4	16.4	3.2
Sri Lanka	Rural	1981	2302034	248565	100067	148498	1995776	57693	1460691	53709	1406982	767101	74242
			100	10.8	4.3	6.5	86.7	2.5	63.5	2.3	61.1	33.3	3.2
Syrian Arab Rep.	Total	1981	1305550	842892	778401	64491	462388	270	864019	639671	224348	440675	856
			100	64.6	59.6	4.9	35.4		66.2	49.0	17.2	33.8	0.1
Syrian Arab Rep.	Urban	1981	622056	556379	542141	14238	65593	84	596154	498557	97597	25705	197
			100	89.4	87.2	2.3	10.5		95.8	80.1	15.7	4.1	
Syrian Arab Rep.	Rural	1981	683494	286513	236260	50253	396795	186	267865	141114	126751	414970	659
			100	41.9	34.6	7.4	58.1		39.2	20.6	18.5	60.7	0.1
Thailand	Total	1990	12224400	3627700	3151600	476100	8559200	37500	10714500	753200	9961300	1459100	50800
			100	29.7	25.8	3.9	70.0	0.3	87.6	6.2	81.5	11.9	0.4
Thailand	Urban	1990	2327800	1968100	1812800	155300	354300	5400	2307300	345600	1961700	14400	6100
			100	84.5	77.9	6.7	15.2	0.2	99.1	14.8	84.3	0.6	0.3
Thailand	Rural	1990	9896600	1659600	1338800	320800	8204900	32100	8407200	407600	7999600	1444700	44700
			100	16.8	13.5	3.2	82.9	0.3	85.0	4.1	80.8	14.6	0.5
EUROPE													
Albania	Total [11]	1989	385769	214618	...	...	168200	2951	383575	88223	295352	-	2194
			100	55.6	...	...	43.6	0.8	99.4	22.9	76.6	-	0.6
Albania	Urban [11]	1989	76103	71762	...	...	3343	998	75187	54407	20780	-	916
			100	94.3	...	...	4.4	1.3	98.8	71.5	27.3	-	1.2
Albania	Rural [11]	1989	309666	142856	...	...	164857	1953	308388	33816	274572	-	1278
			100	46.1	...	...	53.2	0.6	99.6	10.9	88.7	-	0.4
Austria	Total	1981	2692883	2553171	...	...	139712	-	2312348	...	...	380535	-
			100	94.8	...	...	5.2	-	85.9	...	...	14.1	-
Austria	Urban	1981	1693775	1603636	...	...	90139	-	1451757	...	...	242018	-
			100	94.7	...	...	5.3	-	85.7	...	...	14.3	-
Austria	Rural	1981	999108	949535	...	...	49573	-	860591	...	...	138517	-
			100	95.0	...	...	5.0	-	86.1	...	...	13.9	-
Bulgaria	Total	1985	2700039	2326634	2272859	53775	13051	360354	[12] 1392760	[12] 1331108	[12] 61652	[12] 1332229	...
			100	86.2	84.2	2.0	0.5	13.3	51.6	49.3	2.3	49.3	...
Bulgaria	Urban	1985	1711112	1620063	1614780	5283	9614	81435	[12] 1314231	[12] 1261149	[12] 53082	[12] 415752	...
			100	94.7	94.4	0.3	0.6	4.8	76.8	73.7	3.1	24.3	...
Bulgaria	Rural	1985	988927	706571	658079	48492	3437	278919	[12] 78523	[12] 69953	[12] 8570	[12] 916477	...
			100	71.4	66.5	4.9	0.3	28.2	7.9	7.1	0.9	92.7	...
Channel Islands	Total	1991	48826	...	...	...	...	...	48785	48785	-	41	-
			100	...	...	...	...	...	99.9	99.9	-	0.1	-

TABLE 15 (continued)

Occupied Housing Units by Water and Toilet Facilities, Number and Percentage, Selected Countries

			Total Occupied Housing Units	Water Supply System					Toilet Installation				
				With Piped Water			Without Piped Water	Unknown	With Toilet of any Type			Without Toilet of any Type	Unknown
				Total	Inside	Outside			Total	Flush Toilet	Other Toilet		
EUROPE (continued)													
Finland	Total	1989	2001129	1916362	1916362	...	...	84767	...	1872005	...	...	[13] 129124
			100	95.8	95.8	...	...	4.2	...	93.5	...	...	6.5
Finland	Urban	1989	1309180	1281551	1281551	...	...	27629	...	1266171	...	...	[13] 43009
			100	97.9	97.9	...	...	2.1	...	96.7	...	...	3.3
Finland	Rural	1989	691949	634811	634811	...	...	57138	...	605834	...	...	[13] 86115
			100	91.7	91.7	...	...	8.3	...	87.6	...	...	12.4
Germany [14]	Total	1987	25886220	...	...	...	...	...	25886220	25455064	431156	-	-
			100	...	...	...	...	...	100.0	98.3	1.7	-	-
Germany [14]	Urban	1987	10290413	...	...	...	...	...	10290413	10143703	146710	-	-
			100	...	...	...	...	...	100.0	98.6	1.4	-	-
Germany [14]	Rural	1987	15595807	...	...	...	...	...	15595807	15311361	284446	-	-
			100	...	...	...	...	...	100.0	98.2	1.8	-	-
Gibraltar	Total	1981	6945	6772	6713	59	173	-	6864	6864	-	81	-
			100	97.5	96.7	0.8	2.5	-	98.8	98.8	-	1.2	-
Hungary	Total	1990	3687996	3466916	3118217	348699	221080	-	...	2854519	...	...	...
			100	94.0	84.6	9.5	6.0	-	...	77.4	...	...	...
Hungary	Urban	1990	2316108	2149214	2149214	...	...	...	...	1982217	...	...	...
			100	92.8	92.8	...	...	...	...	85.6	...	...	...
Hungary	Rural	1990	1371888	969003	969003	...	...	...	...	795108	...	...	...
			100	70.6	70.6	...	...	...	...	58.0	...	...	...
Ireland	Total	1981	896054	850070	828061	22009	45048	936	834556	806452	28104	59980	1518
			100	94.9	92.4	2.5	5.0	0.1	93.1	90.0	3.1	6.7	0.2
Isle of Man	Total	1991	27316	...	...	...	...	...	27272	27272	-	44	-
			100	...	...	...	...	...	99.8	99.8	-	0.2	-
Latvia	Total	1991	938700	695000	695000	...	...	...	...	675900	...	...	...
			100	74.0	74.0	...	...	...	...	72.0	...	...	...
Latvia	Urban	1991	640300	544900	544900	...	...	...	...	539800	...	...	...
			100	85.1	85.1	...	...	...	...	84.3	...	...	...
Latvia	Rural	1991	298400	150100	150100	...	...	...	...	136100	...	...	...
			100	50.3	50.3	...	...	...	...	45.6	...	...	...
Lithuania	Total	1991	1165700	...	[15] 737600	...	...	...	...	...	...	...	...
			100	...	63.3	...	...	...	...	...	...	...	...
Lithuania	Urban	1991	755800	...	651000	...	...	...	...	...	...	...	...
			100	...	86.1	...	...	...	...	...	...	...	...
Lithuania	Rural	1991	409900	...	[15] 86600	...	...	...	...	...	...	...	...
			100	...	21.1	...	...	...	...	...	...	...	...
Netherlands	Total	1989	5861820	...	...	...	...	...	5711642	...	...	146482	3696
			100	...	...	...	...	...	97.4	...	...	2.5	0.1
Netherlands	Urban	1989	4066960	...	...	...	...	...	3941312	...	...	122264	3384
			100	...	...	...	...	...	96.9	...	...	3.0	0.1
Netherlands	Rural	1989	1794861	...	...	...	...	...	1770332	...	...	24217	312
			100	...	...	...	...	...	98.6	...	...	1.3	-
Norway	Total	1990	[16] 1751343	...	...	...	...	...	1751343	1682548	68795	-	-
			100	...	...	...	...	...	100.0	96.1	3.9	-	-
Norway	Urban	1990	1288839	...	...	...	...	...	1288839	1252228	36612	-	-
			100	...	...	...	...	...	100.0	97.2	2.8	-	-
Norway	Rural	1990	446938	...	...	...	...	...	446938	415639	31300	-	-
			100	...	...	...	...	...	100.0	93.0	7.0	-	-
Poland	Total [17]	1988	10716758	9266996	9024942	242054	[18] 1449762	-	7663429	7663429	-	[18] 3053329	
			100	86.5	84.2	2.3	13.5	-	71.5	71.5	-	28.5	
Poland	Urban [17]	1988	7039802	6791641	6678949	112692	[18] 248161	-	5976421	5976421	-	[18] 1063381	
			100	96.5	94.9	1.6	3.5	-	84.9	84.9	-	15.1	
Poland	Rural [17]	1988	3676956	2475355	2345993	129362	[18] 1201601	-	1687008	1687008	-	[18] 1989948	
			100	67.3	63.8	3.5	32.7	-	45.9	45.9	-	54.1	
Romania	Total [19]	1992	7659003	4106315	3950731	155584	...	...	...	3610371	...	...	...
			100	53.6	51.6	2.0	...	...	...	47.1	...	...	...
Romania	Urban [19]	1992	4076335	3593293	3542749	50544	...	...	...	3401157	...	...	...
			100	88.2	86.9	1.2	...	...	...	83.4	...	...	...
Romania	Rural [19]	1992	3582668	513022	407982	105040	...	...	...	209214	...	...	...
			100	14.3	11.4	2.9	...	...	...	5.8	...	...	...
Russian Federation	Total	1989	47409368	...	29460555	...	...	...	...	27821641	...	...	...
			100	...	62.1	...	...	...	...	58.7	...	...	...
Russian Federation	Urban	1989	32849816	...	26694065	...	...	...	...	25719446	...	...	...
			100	...	81.3	...	...	...	...	78.3	...	...	...
Russian Federation	Rural	1989	14559552	...	2766490	...	...	...	...	2102195	...	...	...
			100	...	19.0	...	...	...	...	14.4	...	...	...
San Marino	Total	1991	7241	...	...	...	...	...	7241	7241	-	-	-
			100	...	...	...	...	...	100.0	100.0	-	-	-
San Marino	Urban	1991	6613	...	...	...	...	...	6613	6613	-	-	-
			100	...	...	...	...	...	100.0	100.0	-	-	-
San Marino	Rural	1991	628	...	...	...	...	...	628	628	-	-	-
			100	...	...	...	...	...	100.0	100.0	-	-	-

TABLE 15 (continued)

Occupied Housing Units by Water and Toilet Facilities, Number and Percentage, Selected Countries

			Total Occupied Housing Units	With Piped Water Total	With Piped Water Inside	With Piped Water Outside	Without Piped Water	Unknown	With Toilet of any Type Total	Flush Toilet	Other Toilet	Without Toilet of any Type	Unknown
EUROPE (continued)													
Spain	Total [20]	1991	11824849	[3] ...	...	...	...	...	[3] ...	...	...	...	...
			100	98.7	...	...	...	...	97.1	...	...	...	...
Switzerland	Total	1980	2413185	...	...	...	...	...	...	...	...	...	...
			100	...	...	...	...	...	...	...	...	...	...
Switzerland	Urban	1980	1600580	...	...	...	...	...	...	...	...	...	...
			100	...	...	...	...	...	...	...	...	...	...
Switzerland	Rural	1980	812605	...	...	...	...	...	...	...	...	...	...
			100	...	...	...	...	...	...	...	...	...	...
Ukraine	Total [21]	1992	17827000	7988800	...	...	...	...	7727600	...	...	...	...
			100	44.8	...	...	...	...	43.3	...	...	...	...
Ukraine	Urban	1992	11302800	7705100	...	...	...	...	7507100	...	...	...	...
			100	68.2	...	...	...	...	66.4	...	...	...	...
Ukraine	Rural [21]	1992	6524200	283700	...	...	...	...	220500	...	...	...	...
			100	4.3	...	...	...	...	3.4	...	...	...	...
Yugoslavia (former)	Total	1981	5924217	4068670	[22] 3405344	[23] 663326	...	...	3193341	2938035	255306	...	...
			100	68.7	57.5	11.2	...	...	53.9	49.6	4.3	...	...
Yugoslavia (former)	Urban	1981	2952643	2711784	...	...	...	...	...	...	...	...	...
			100	91.8	...	...	...	...	...	...	...	...	...
Yugoslavia (former)	Rural	1981	2971574	1449169	...	...	...	...	...	...	...	...	...
			100	48.8	...	...	...	...	...	...	...	...	...
LATIN AMERICA													
Aruba	Total	1991	19225	...	...	...	...	...	18758	...	...	405	62
			100	...	...	...	...	...	97.6	...	...	2.1	0.3
Bolivia	Total	1988	1318800	791700	258500	533200	525000	2100	545800	299800	246000	773000	-
			100	60.0	19.6	40.4	39.8	0.2	41.4	22.7	18.7	58.6	-
Bolivia	Urban	1988	662800	591800	210800	381000	70200	800	461200	280700	180500	201600	-
			100	89.3	31.8	57.5	10.6	0.1	69.6	42.4	27.2	30.4	-
Bolivia	Rural	1988	656000	199900	47700	152200	454800	1300	[12] 85000	[12] 19100	[12] 65500	[12] 571300	...
			100	30.5	7.3	23.2	69.3	0.2	13.0	2.9	10.0	87.1	...
Cayman Islands	Total	1989	8115	8115	...	...	-	-	...	7789	...	...	326
			100	100.0	...	...	-	-	...	96.0	...	...	4.0
Cuba	Total [24]	1981	2290176	1697904	1209177	[25] 488727	592272	-	2084953	1137811	947142	205223	-
			100	74.1	52.8	21.3	25.9	-	91.0	49.7	41.4	9.0	-
Cuba	Urban [24]	1981	1609699	1453190	1120450	[25] 332740	156509	-	1542499	1086838	455661	67200	-
			100	90.3	69.6	20.7	9.7	-	95.8	67.5	28.3	4.2	-
Cuba	Rural [24]	1981	680477	244714	88727	[25] 155987	435763	-	542454	50973	491481	138023	-
			100	36.0	13.0	22.9	64.0	-	79.7	7.5	72.2	20.3	-
Ecuador	Total	1990	2008655	1137330	815284	322046	871325	-	1489995	1203492	286503	518660	-
			100	56.6	40.6	16.0	43.4	-	74.2	59.9	14.3	25.8	-
Ecuador	Urban	1990	1148342	864025	684697	179328	284317	-	1084985	984706	100279	63357	-
			100	75.2	59.6	15.6	24.8	-	94.5	85.8	8.7	5.5	-
Ecuador	Rural	1990	860313	273305	130587	142718	587008	-	405010	218786	186224	455303	-
			100	31.8	15.2	16.6	68.2	-	47.1	25.4	21.6	52.9	-
Falkland Islands (Malvinas)	Total	1986	788	...	...	...	...	...	...	...	...	...	...
			100	...	...	...	...	...	...	...	...	...	...
Guatemala	Total	1981	1102281	411420	...	...	690861	-	[2] 654282	[2] 214428	[2] 439854	[2] 497590	...
			100	37.3	...	...	62.7	-	59.4	19.5	39.9	45.1	...
Guatemala	Urban	1981	365453	254217	...	...	111236	-	[2] 347923	[2] 175193	[2] 172730	[2] 45800	...
			100	69.6	...	...	30.4	-	95.2	47.9	47.3	12.5	...
Guatemala	Rural	1981	736828	157203	...	...	579625	-	[2] 306359	[2] 39235	[2] 267124	[2] 451790	...
			100	21.3	...	...	78.7	-	41.6	5.3	36.3	61.3	...
Haiti	Total [26]	1986	1164136	68030	12276	55754	1008114	87992	665162	18594	646568	498974	-
			100	5.8	1.1	4.8	86.6	7.6	57.1	1.6	55.5	42.9	-
Haiti	Urban [26]	1986	285927	61965	12276	49689	200403	23559	248784	15489	233295	37143	-
			100	21.7	4.3	17.4	70.1	8.2	87.0	5.4	81.6	13.0	-
Haiti	Rural [26]	1986	878209	6065	-	6065	807711	64433	416378	3105	413273	461831	-
			100	0.7	-	0.7	92.0	7.3	47.4	0.4	47.1	52.6	-
Honduras	Total	1988	762117	502825	480576	22249	259292	-	448207	234648	213559	313910	-
			100	66.0	63.1	2.9	34.0	-	58.8	30.8	28.0	41.2	-
Honduras	Urban	1988	318070	277491	269766	7725	40579	-	279281	180064	99217	38789	-
			100	87.2	84.8	2.4	12.8	-	87.8	56.6	31.2	12.2	-
Honduras	Rural	1988	444047	225334	210810	14524	218713	-	168926	54584	114342	275121	-
			100	50.7	47.5	3.3	49.3	-	38.0	12.3	25.8	62.0	-
Mexico	Total [27]	1990	16035233	12258825	8072518	4186307	3644510	131898	[28] 11998430	7706353	4217752	3944043	92760
			100	76.4	50.3	26.1	22.7	0.8	74.8	48.1	26.3	24.6	0.6
Panama	Total	1990	524284	423168	271853	151315	101116	-	461794	231639	230155	62490	-
			100	80.7	51.9	28.9	19.3	-	88.1	44.2	43.9	11.9	-
Panama	Urban	1990	295105	287494	212617	74877	7611	-	290463	204417	86046	4642	-
			100	97.4	72.0	25.4	2.6	-	98.4	69.3	29.2	1.6	-
Panama	Rural	1990	229179	135674	59236	76438	93505	-	171331	27222	144109	57848	-
			100	59.2	25.8	33.4	40.8	-	74.8	11.9	62.9	25.2	-

TABLE 15 (continued)

Occupied Housing Units by Water and Toilet Facilities, Number and Percentage, Selected Countries

			Total Occupied Housing Units	Water Supply System With Piped Water Total	Inside	Outside	Without Piped Water	Unknown	Toilet Installation With Toilet of any Type Total	Flush Toilet	Other Toilet	Without Toilet of any Type	Unknown
LATIN AMERICA (continued)													
Paraguay	Total	1982	578714	110827	110827	-	467887	-	561830	151873	409957	16884	-
			100	19.2	19.2	-	80.8	-	97.1	26.2	70.8	2.9	-
Paraguay	Urban	1982	265422	87150	87150	-	178272	-	258099	136147	121952	7323	-
			100	32.8	32.8	-	67.2	-	97.2	51.3	45.9	2.8	-
Paraguay	Rural	1982	313292	23677	23677	-	289615	-	303731	15726	288005	9561	-
			100	7.6	7.6	-	92.4	-	96.9	5.0	91.9	3.1	-
Peru	Total	1990	3971000	1329947	1028992	300955	2641053	-	1751003	1390283	360720	2219997	-
			100	33.5	25.9	7.6	66.5	-	44.1	35.0	9.1	55.9	-
Peru	Urban	1990	2707000	1329947	1028992	300955	1377053	-	1636183	1390283	245900	1070817	-
			100	49.1	38.0	11.1	50.9	-	60.4	51.4	9.1	39.6	-
Peru	Rural	1990	1264000	-	-	-	1264000	-	114820	-	114820	1149180	-
			100	-	-	-	100.0	-	9.1	-	9.1	90.9	-
Turks & Caicos Isl.	Total	1990	2022	...	...	...	...	...	1967	1085	882	55	-
			100	...	...	...	...	...	97.3	53.7	43.6	2.7	-
NORTHERN AMERICA													
Bermuda	Total	1991	22061	21963	21757	206	98	-	...	...	...	...	...
			100	99.6	98.6	0.9	0.4	-	...	...	...	...	...
Canada	Total	1991	9872936	9860674	...	...	12262	-	9837237	9822878	14359	35699	-
			100	99.9	...	...	0.1	-	99.6	99.5	0.1	0.4	-
Canada	Urban	1991	8232429	8230488	...	...	1941	-	8211120	8200517	10603	21309	-
			100	100.0	...	...	-	-	99.7	99.6	0.1	0.3	-
Canada	Rural	1991	1640507	1630186	...	...	10321	-	1626117	1622361	3756	14390	-
			100	99.4	...	...	0.6	-	99.1	98.9	0.2	0.9	-
OCEANIA													
American Samoa	Total	1990	6959	6692	4883	1809	267	-	6736	6498	238	223	-
			100	96.2	70.2	26.0	3.8	-	96.8	93.4	3.4	3.2	-
American Samoa	Urban	1990	2378	2313	1844	469	65	-	2337	2283	54	41	-
			100	97.3	77.5	19.7	2.7	-	98.3	96.0	2.3	1.7	-
American Samoa	Rural	1990	4581	4379	3039	1340	202	-	4399	4215	184	182	-
			100	95.6	66.3	29.3	4.4	-	96.0	92.0	4.0	4.0	-
Fiji	Total	1986	124098	91501	...	...	32015	582	...	...	...	...	...
			100	73.7	...	...	25.8	0.5	...	...	...	...	...
Fiji	Urban	1986	49579	45930	...	...	3369	280	...	...	...	...	...
			100	92.6	...	...	6.8	0.6	...	...	...	...	...
Fiji	Rural	1986	74519	45571	...	...	28646	302	...	...	...	...	...
			100	61.2	...	...	38.4	0.4	...	...	...	...	...
French Polynesia	Total	1988	39513	38703	...	...	810	-	38631	...	...	882	-
			100	98.0	...	...	2.1	-	97.8	...	...	2.2	-
New Caledonia	Total [2]	1989	40266	36298	...	...	3968	-	35269	...	...	4997	-
			100	90.1	...	...	9.9	-	87.6	...	...	12.4	-
New Caledonia	Urban [2]	1989	22427	22237	...	...	190	-	22289	...	...	138	-
			100	99.2	...	...	0.8	-	99.4	...	...	0.6	-
New Caledonia	Rural [2]	1989	17839	14061	...	...	3778	-	12980	...	...	4859	-
			100	78.8	...	...	21.2	-	72.8	...	...	27.2	-
Tonga	Total [2]	1986	15091	11100	...	...	3785	206	14719	...	...	103	269
			100	73.6	...	...	25.1	1.4	97.5	...	...	0.7	1.8
Tonga	Urban [2]	1986	3233	3009	...	...	185	39	3159	...	...	9	64
			100	93.1	...	...	5.7	1.2	97.7	...	...	0.3	2.0
Tonga	Rural [2]	1986	11858	8091	...	...	3600	167	11559	...	...	94	205
			100	68.2	...	...	30.4	1.4	97.5	...	...	0.8	1.7
Vanuatu	Total	1989	28252	9874	4114	5760	17897	481	25346	4425	20921	2378	520
			100	34.9	14.6	20.4	63.3	1.7	89.7	15.7	74.1	8.4	1.8
Vanuatu	Urban	1989	5480	4577	2839	1738	757	146	5317	3467	1850	6	147
			100	83.5	51.8	31.7	13.8	2.7	97.0	63.3	33.8	0.1	2.7
Vanuatu	Rural	1989	22772	5297	1275	4022	17140	335	20029	958	19071	2372	373
			100	23.3	5.6	17.7	75.3	1.5	88.0	4.2	83.7	10.4	1.6
Wallis & Futuna Isl.	Total	1990	2348	2246	734	1512	102	-	1290	...	...	1058	-
			100	95.7	31.3	64.4	4.3	-	54.9	...	...	45.1	-

Source: United Nations, Human Settlements Statistics Questionnaire 1992.

Housing units with piped water, i.e. water provided within the housing unit by pipe from community-wide systems or from individual installations such as pressure tanks and pumps. The category with piped water includes water supply described above **inside** housing unit or **outside** housing unit but within 100 meters from the door. Housing units with piped water outside and beyond 100 metres are considered as **without piped water**.

With toilet of any type refers to housing units with an installation arranged for humans to discharge their wastes. **Flush** toilet is an installation described above but connected with piped water and from which the wastes are flushed by water. If there are no such facilities (i.e. flushing wastes by piped water) and it is still an installation, that refers to **other toilet**. If a housing unit does not have a toilet of any of these types, it is referred to as **without toilet of any type**.

For additional information and definitions of the terms: **'Housing Unit'** and **'Occupied Housing Unit'**, refer to technical notes of tables 8 and 12.

TABLE 15 *(continued)*

Occupied Housing Units by Water and Toilet Facilities, Number and Percentage, Selected Countries

Notes:

1. Data are from the Population and Housing Census 1987.
2. Data refer to households in housing units.
3. Data are presented in percentages.
4. Data refer to households having piped water inside unit and households provided with water from public taps.
5. Data refer to the Government controlled area only.
6. Figures exclude Assam and some areas where 1981 Census could not be conducted. Also, all figures refer to households, not housing units.
7. For piped water outside housing unit, there is no restriction of distance.
8. Data refer to housing units with septic tank.
9. Data refer to housing units without septic tank.
10. Data refer to other types of water supply system.
11. Data refer to buildings.
12. Data as received by the UN. However the sum of the individual categories differs from the total.
13. Data include housing units without flush toilet.
14. Data refer to the territory prior to 3 October 1990, i.e., they relate to the former Federal Republic of Germany.
15. Privately-owned houses in rural areas are excluded.
16. Including 15,565 dwellings (housing units) with no information on densely/sparsely populated areas.
17. Data refer to conventional dwellings only.
18. Including conventional dwellings with unknown equipment.
19. Data refer to both occupied and vacant conventional dwellings.
20. Data refer to principal residences only. According to census definitions, principal residences refer to the housing unit occupied by one or more persons for the most part of the year. Secondary residence is a housing unit occupied seasonally and is not considered a usual residence.
21. Data do not include facilities in privately-owned units in rural areas.
22. Water supply system—Inside housing unit—with connection to the public network.
23. Outside housing unit but within 100 meters—with connection to the air compressed water tank.
24. Data refer to occupied units with permanent residents. Excluded are huts and natural shelters.
25. Data refer to housing units with piped water outside the units disregarding how far it is.
26. Data are estimated on the basis of 2.5% sample.
27. Data don't include 11,763 "refugee" housing units which do not meet characteristics of a housing unit, also 136,341 housing units not occupied were excluded.
28. Data include housing units with toilets (74,325) which are unknown whether they have water connections.

TABLE 16

Occupied Housing Units by Water and Toilet Facilities, Number and Percentage, Selected Cities

| | | | Total Occupied Housing Units | Water Supply System | | | | | Toilet Installation | | | | |
| | | | | With Piped Water | | | Without Piped Water | Unknown | With Toilet of any Type | | | Without Toilet of any Type | Unknown |
				Total	Inside	Outside			Total	Flush Toilet	Other Toilet		
AFRICA													
Ethiopia	Addis Ababa	1984	259555	134467	10171	124296	120423	4665	180065	31023	149042	75856	3634
			100	51.8	3.9	47.9	46.4	1.8	69.4	12.0	57.4	29.2	1.4
Ethiopia	Asmara	1984	55502	25411	1680	23731	28815	1276	28206	15831	12375	26681	615
			100	45.8	3.0	42.8	51.9	2.3	50.8	28.5	22.3	48.1	1.1
Ethiopia	Dire Dawa	1984	21665	5313	423	4890	15854	498	14464	1667	12797	6892	309
			100	24.5	2.0	22.6	73.2	2.3	66.8	7.7	59.1	31.8	1.4
Ethiopia	Nazret	1984	14568	5777	194	5583	7992	799	9113	1289	7824	5272	183
			100	39.7	1.3	38.3	54.9	5.5	62.6	8.8	53.7	36.2	1.3
Malawi	Blantyre-Limbe [1]	1986	20541	18027	2244	15783	2514	...	18638	2921	15717	1903	...
			100	87.8	10.9	76.8	12.2	...	90.7	14.2	76.5	9.3	...
Malawi	Lilongwe [1]	1986	8201	6019	1555	4464	2182	...	7795	2151	5644	406	...
			100	73.4	19.0	54.4	26.6	...	95.0	26.2	68.8	5.0	...
Malawi	Mzuzu [1]	1986	5197	3189	570	2619	2008	...	4223	754	3469	974	...
			100	61.4	11.0	50.4	38.6	...	81.3	14.5	66.8	18.7	...
Malawi	Zomba [1]	1986	4550	3145	426	2719	1405	...	4107	1126	2981	443	...
			100	69.1	9.4	59.8	30.9	...	90.3	24.7	65.5	9.7	...
Mali	Bamako [2]	1987	105394	30920	22087	8833	71121	3353	11265	7399	3866	91461	2668
			100	29.3	21.0	8.4	67.5	3.2	10.7	7.0	3.7	86.8	2.5
Mali	Mopti [2]	1987	6683	5534	4309	1225	691	458	...	...	...	...	...
			100	82.8	64.5	18.3	10.3	6.9	...	...	...	...	...
Mali	Segou [2]	1987	8516	2028	1641	387	6351	137	...	...	...	...	...
			100	23.8	19.3	4.5	74.6	1.6	...	...	...	...	...
Mali	Sikasso [2]	1987	11543	2606	1958	648	8776	161	...	...	...	...	...
			100	22.6	17.0	5.6	76.0	1.4	...	...	...	...	...
Mauritius	Beau Bassin-Rose Hill	1990	20466	20357	16805	3552	109	-	20449	17163	3286	17	-
			100	99.5	82.1	17.4	0.5	-	99.9	83.9	16.1	0.1	-
Mauritius	Curepipe	1990	14850	14507	12270	2237	342	1	14812	12953	1859	37	1
			100	97.7	82.6	15.1	2.3	-	99.7	87.2	12.5	0.2	-
Mauritius	Port-Louis	1990	28604	27926	14891	13035	673	5	28432	24136	4296	171	1
			100	97.6	52.1	45.6	2.4	-	99.4	84.4	15.0	0.6	-
Mauritius	Quatre-Bornes	1990	14802	14634	11561	3073	165	3	14790	11859	2931	12	-
			100	98.9	78.1	20.8	1.1	-	99.9	80.1	19.8	0.1	-
South Africa	Cape Town	1992	495000	454000	...	...	...	...	...	...	...	...	...
			100	91.7	...	...	...	...	...	...	...	...	...
South Africa	Pretoria	1991	127680	127680	127680	-	-	-	127680	127680	-	-	-
			100	100.0	100.0	-	-	-	100.0	100.0	-	-	-
Tunisia	Tunis [2]	1989	168464	... [3]	158795	8778	...	891	161982	89468	72514	5016	1466
			100	...	94.3	5.2	...	0.5	96.2	53.1	43.0	3.0	0.9
ASIA													
Cyprus	Larnaca [4]	1982	13096	13084	12975	109	...	12	13077	11976	1101	...	19
			100	99.9	99.1	0.8	...	0.1	99.9	91.4	8.4	...	0.1
Cyprus	Limassol [4]	1982	29716	29674	29340	334	...	42	29667	28373	1294	...	49
			100	99.9	98.7	1.1	...	0.1	99.8	95.5	4.4	...	0.2
Cyprus	Nicosia [4]	1982	41542	41472	40984	488	...	70	41478	40297	1181	...	64
			100	99.8	98.7	1.2	...	0.2	99.8	97.0	2.8	...	0.2
Cyprus	Paphos [4]	1982	5822	5804	5443	361	...	18	5805	5029	776	...	17
			100	99.7	93.5	6.2	...	0.3	99.7	86.4	13.3	...	0.3
Indonesia	Jakarta	1990	1740214	...	...	...	...	...	...	...	...	...	...
			100	...	...	...	...	...	...	...	...	...	...
Iraq	Baghdad	1987	419876	...	...	...	...	...	416789	...	...	2484	603
			100	...	...	...	...	...	99.3	...	...	0.6	0.1
Iraq	Basra	1987	92005	...	...	...	...	...	88805	...	...	2689	511
			100	...	...	...	...	...	96.5	...	...	2.9	0.6
Iraq	Kirkuk	1987	69273	...	...	...	...	...	67221	...	...	1773	279
			100	...	...	...	...	...	97.0	...	...	2.6	0.4
Iraq	Mosul	1987	165963	...	...	...	...	...	141360	...	...	22984	1619
			100	...	...	...	...	...	85.2	...	...	13.8	1.0
Israel	Haifa	1983	80270	...	...	...	...	...	[5] 99.9	[5] 99.9	...	...	...
			100	...	...	...	...	...			...	...	...
Israel	Jerusalem	1983	108625	...	...	...	...	...	[5] 99.9	[5] 99.9	...	...	...
			100	...	...	...	...	...			...	...	...
Israel	Tel Aviv-Yafo	1983	128245	...	...	...	...	...	[5] 99.9	[5] 99.9	...	...	...
			100	...	...	...	...	...			...	...	...
Japan	Osaka	1988	963380	...	...	...	...	...	956440	954760	1680	...	...
			100	...	...	...	...	...	99.3	99.1	0.2	...	...
Japan	Sapporo	1988	572850	...	...	...	...	...	571060	557060	14000	...	...
			100	...	...	...	...	...	99.7	97.2	2.4	...	...
Japan	Tokyo	1988	3112590	...	...	...	...	...	2948330	2873540	74790	...	...
			100	...	...	...	...	...	94.7	92.3	2.4	...	...
Japan	Yokohama	1988	1001800	...	...	...	...	...	988320	924840	63480	...	...
			100	...	...	...	...	...	98.7	92.3	6.3	...	...

TABLE 16 (continued)

Occupied Housing Units by Water and Toilet Facilities, Number and Percentage, Selected Cities

			Total Occupied Housing Units	Water Supply System With Piped Water			Without Piped Water	Unknown	Toilet Installation With Toilet of any Type			Without Toilet of any Type	Unknown
				Total	Inside	Outside			Total	Flush Toilet	Other Toilet		
ASIA (continued)													
Pakistan	Faisalabad	1981	209768	73863	63361	10502	135905	-	...	...	...	...	...
			100	35.2	30.2	5.0	64.8	-	...	...	...	...	...
Pakistan	Islamabad	1981	36973	26269	23255	3014	10704	-	...	...	...	...	...
			100	71.0	62.9	8.2	29.0	-	...	...	...	...	...
Pakistan	Karachi	1981	811850	743583	373222	370361	68267	-	...	...	...	...	...
			100	91.6	46.0	45.6	8.4	-	...	...	...	...	...
Pakistan	Lahore	1981	447509	338658	288845	49813	108851	-	...	...	...	...	...
			100	75.7	64.5	11.1	24.3	-	...	...	...	...	...
Syrian Arab Rep.	Aleppo	1981	149878	133521	130036	3485	16357	-	145381	127195	18186	4493	4
			100	89.1	86.8	2.3	10.9	-	97.0	84.9	12.1	3.0	-
Syrian Arab Rep.	Damascus	1981	163575	156725	153653	3072	6847	3	161833	147653	14180	1731	11
			100	95.8	93.9	1.9	4.2	-	98.9	90.3	8.7	1.1	-
Syrian Arab Rep.	Homs	1981	50548	39562	38652	910	10986	-	48889	41311	7578	1657	2
			100	78.3	76.5	1.8	21.7	-	96.7	81.7	15.0	3.3	-
Syrian Arab Rep.	Lattakia	1981	32909	30003	29618	385	2901	5	32000	27081	4919	874	35
			100	91.2	90.0	1.2	8.8	-	97.2	82.3	14.9	2.7	0.1
Thailand	Bangkok	1980	[6] 902871	703784	629604	74180	177708	20275	880197	154218	725979	3935	17636
			100	77.9	69.7	8.2	19.7	2.2	97.5	17.1	80.4	0.4	2.0
Thailand	Chon Buri	1980	[6] 129899	35721	24928	10793	91542	2574	116498	6641	109857	11758	1581
			100	27.5	19.2	8.3	70.5	2.0	89.7	5.1	84.6	9.1	1.2
Thailand	Nakhon Si Thammarat	1980	[6] 214981	18040	11691	6349	194498	2431	111124	3306	107818	102141	1690
			100	8.4	5.4	3.0	90.5	1.1	51.7	1.5	50.2	47.5	0.8
Thailand	Songkhla	1980	[6] 158989	19110	15025	4085	137343	...	73835	4212	69623	83289	1843
			100	12.0	9.5	2.6	86.4	...	46.4	2.6	43.8	52.4	1.2
EUROPE													
Albania	Durres [7]	1989	8996	8119	...	...	739	138	8859	5262	3597	-	137
			100	90.3	...	...	8.2	1.5	98.5	58.5	40.0	-	1.5
Albania	Elbasan [7]	1989	8366	8031	...	...	271	64	8267	5505	2762	-	99
			100	96.0	...	...	3.2	0.8	98.8	65.8	33.0	-	1.2
Albania	Shkoder [7]	1989	7064	6898	...	...	110	56	7011	2817	4194	-	53
			100	97.7	...	...	1.6	0.8	99.2	39.9	59.4	-	0.8
Albania	Tirana [7]	1989	13866	13321	...	...	152	393	13536	12666	870	-	330
			100	96.1	...	...	1.1	2.8	97.6	91.3	6.3	-	2.4
Austria	Graz	1981	101941	95879	...	...	6062	-	85237	...	...	16704	-
			100	94.1	...	...	5.9	-	83.6	...	...	16.4	-
Austria	Linz	1981	78791	76233	...	...	2558	-	72002	...	...	6789	-
			100	96.8	...	...	3.2	-	91.4	...	...	8.6	-
Austria	Salzburg	1981	57221	56131	...	...	1090	-	54066	...	...	3155	-
			100	98.1	...	...	1.9	-	94.5	...	...	5.5	-
Austria	Vienna	1981	717608	668717	...	...	48891	-	583316	...	...	134292	-
			100	93.2	...	...	6.8	-	81.3	...	...	18.7	-
Bosnia & Herzegovina	Sarajevo	1981	103144	93179	...	...	...	...	...	...	...	...	...
			100	90.3	...	...	...	...	...	...	...	...	...
Channel Islands	Guernsey	1991	21215	...	...	...	...	...	21174	21174	-	41	-
			100	...	...	...	...	...	99.8	99.8	-	0.2	-
Channel Islands	Jersey	1991	27611	...	...	...	...	...	...	28033	...	...	...
			100	...	...	...	...	...	...	101.5	...	...	...
Croatia	Zagreb	1981	216364	198434	...	...	...	...	...	...	...	...	...
			100	91.7	...	...	...	...	...	...	...	...	...
Finland	Espoo	1989	66259	65084	65084	...	...	1175	64470	64470	...	...	1789
			100	98.2	98.2	...	...	1.8	97.3	97.3	...	...	2.7
Finland	Helsinki	1989	236785	235931	235931	...	...	854	234213	234213	...	...	2572
			100	99.6	99.6	...	...	0.4	98.9	98.9	...	...	1.1
Finland	Tampere	1989	78001	77327	77327	...	...	674	76564	76564	...	...	1437
			100	99.1	99.1	...	...	0.9	98.2	98.2	...	...	1.8
Finland	Turku	1989	74857	73484	73484	...	...	1373	72571	72571	...	...	2286
			100	98.2	98.2	...	...	1.8	96.9	96.9	...	...	3.1
Germany	Berlin (west)	1987	1043719	...	...	...	...	...	1043719	1030073	13646	-	-
			100	...	...	...	...	...	100.0	98.7	1.3	-	-
Germany	Bonn	1987	135489	...	...	...	...	...	135489	132382	3107	-	-
			100	...	...	...	...	...	100.0	97.7	2.3	-	-
Germany	Hamburg	1987	779605	...	...	...	...	...	779605	770954	8651	-	-
			100	...	...	...	...	...	100.0	98.9	1.1	-	-
Germany	Munich	1987	626425	...	...	...	...	...	626425	622641	3784	-	-
			100	...	...	...	...	...	100.0	99.4	0.6	-	-
Hungary	Budapest	1990	775523	773318	765690	7628	2205	-	...	752220	...	...	...
			100	99.7	98.7	1.0	0.3	-	...	97.0	...	...	...
Hungary	Debrecen	1990	73850	71762	68642	3120	2088	-	...	66587	...	...	...
			100	97.2	92.9	4.2	2.8	-	...	90.2	...	...	...
Hungary	Miskolc	1990	69463	68558	64315	4243	905	-	...	62580	...	...	...
			100	98.7	92.6	6.1	1.3	-	...	90.1	...	...	...
Hungary	Szeged	1990	64734	64210	61864	2346	524	-	...	52431	...	...	...
			100	99.2	95.6	3.6	0.8	-	...	81.0	...	...	...

TABLE 16 (continued)

Occupied Housing Units by Water and Toilet Facilities, Number and Percentage, Selected Cities

| | | | Total Occupied Housing Units | Water Supply System | | | | | Toilet Installation | | | | |
| | | | | With Piped Water | | | Without Piped Water | Unknown | With Toilet of any Type | | | Without Toilet of any Type | Unknown |
				Total	Inside	Outside			Total	Flush Toilet	Other Toilet		
EUROPE (continued)													
Ireland	Cork	1981	35729	35716	35179	537	8	5	35697	35675	22	14	18
			100	100.0	98.5	1.5	-	-	99.9	99.8	0.1	-	0.1
Ireland	Dublin	1981	150564	150505	149755	750	26	33	150429	150345	84	49	86
			100	100.0	99.5	0.5	-	-	99.9	99.9	0.1	-	0.1
Ireland	Limerick	1981	15181	15176	15022	154	5	-	15152	15118	34	24	5
			100	100.0	99.0	1.0	-	-	99.8	99.6	0.2	0.2	-
Isle of Man	Douglas	1991	8447	...	...	...	...	...	8445	8445	-	2	-
			100	...	...	...	...	...	100.0	100.0	-	-	-
Italy	Milan	1991	583104	...	...	...	...	...	...	...	...	...	...
			100	...	...	...	...	...	...	...	...	...	...
Italy	Naples	1991	306869	...	...	...	...	...	...	...	...	...	...
			100	...	...	...	...	...	...	...	...	...	...
Italy	Rome	1991	988543	...	...	...	...	...	...	...	...	...	...
			100	...	...	...	...	...	...	...	...	...	...
Italy	Turin	1991	392547	...	...	...	...	...	...	...	...	...	...
			100	...	...	...	...	...	...	...	...	...	...
Latvia	Daugavpils	1991	42800	35700	35700		...	...	...	35600	...	...	...
			100	83.4	83.4		...	...	...	83.2	...	...	...
Latvia	Liepaja	1991	36400	28400	28400		...	...	...	28400	...	...	...
			100	78.0	78.0		...	...	...	78.0	...	...	...
Latvia	Riga	1991	299500	292400	292400		...	...	...	290600	...	...	...
			100	97.6	97.6		...	...	...	97.0	...	...	...
Lithuania	Kaunas	1991	126076	...	117518		...	...	...	...	...	...	...
			100	...	93.2		...	...	...	...	...	...	...
Lithuania	Klaipeda	1991	59207	...	58066		...	...	...	...	...	...	...
			100	...	98.1		...	...	...	...	...	...	...
Lithuania	Siauliai	1991	44164	...	38832		...	...	...	...	...	...	...
			100	...	87.9		...	...	...	...	...	...	...
Lithuania	Vilnius	1991	162817	...	149194		...	...	...	...	...	...	...
			100	...	91.6		...	...	...	...	...	...	...
Netherlands	Amsterdam	1989	363740	...	...	...	...	...	355143	...	...	8299	298
			100	...	...	...	...	...	97.6	...	...	2.3	0.1
Netherlands	Hague, The	1989	200927	...	...	...	...	...	195933	...	...	4427	567
			100	...	...	...	...	...	97.5	...	...	2.2	0.3
Netherlands	Rotterdam	1989	269973	...	...	...	...	...	268105	...	...	1868	-
			100	...	...	...	...	...	99.3	...	...	0.7	-
Netherlands	Utrecht	1989	106154	...	...	...	...	...	93231	...	...	12923	-
			100	...	...	...	...	...	87.8	...	...	12.2	-
Norway	Bergen	1990	93949	...	...	...	...	...	93949	91214	2735	-	-
			100	...	...	...	...	...	100.0	97.1	2.9	-	-
Norway	Oslo	1990	244434	...	...	...	...	...	244434	235354	9080	-	-
			100	...	...	...	...	...	100.0	96.3	3.7	-	-
Norway	Stavanger	1990	42680	...	...	...	...	...	42680	42166	514	-	-
			100	...	...	...	...	...	100.0	98.8	1.2	-	-
Norway	Trondheim	1990	60407	...	...	...	...	...	60407	58604	1803	-	-
			100	...	...	...	...	...	100.0	97.0	3.0	-	-
Poland	Krakow [8]	1988	228245	223742	221387	2355	[9] 4503	-	212767	212767	-	[9] 15478	-
			100	98.0	97.0	1.0	2.0	-	93.2	93.2	-	6.8	-
Poland	Lodz [8]	1988	313764	295699	285067	10632	[9] 18065	-	244112	244112	-	[9] 69652	-
			100	94.2	90.9	3.4	5.8	-	77.8	77.8	-	22.2	-
Poland	Warsaw [8]	1988	581454	573952	568797	5155	[9] 7502	-	553923	553923	-	[9] 27531	-
			100	98.7	97.8	0.9	1.3	-	95.3	95.3	-	4.7	-
Poland	Wroclaw [8]	1988	194403	193214	190706	2508	[9] 1189	-	171888	171888	-	[9] 22515	-
			100	99.4	98.1	1.3	0.6	-	88.4	88.4	-	11.6	-
Romania	Brasov [10]	1992	107620	105333	104733	600	...	...	...	105131	...	...	...
			100	97.9	97.3	0.6	...	...	...	97.7	...	...	...
Romania	Bucarest [10]	1992	761156	710999	705494	5505	...	...	...	698684	...	...	...
			100	93.4	92.7	0.7	...	...	...	91.8	...	...	...
Romania	Constanta [10]	1992	110842	106510	105489	1021	...	...	...	102863	...	...	...
			100	96.1	95.2	0.9	...	...	...	92.8	...	...	...
Romania	Timisoara [10]	1992	121260	115073	113195	1878	...	...	...	113539	...	...	...
			100	94.9	93.3	1.5	...	...	...	93.6	...	...	...
Russian Federation	Moscow [2]	1989	2879323	2870676	...	...	...	...	...	2869118	...	...	...
			100	99.7	...	...	...	...	...	99.6	...	...	...
Russian Federation	Nizhny Novgorod [2]	1989	445184	413336	...	...	...	...	...	409473	...	...	...
			100	92.8	...	...	...	...	...	92.0	...	...	...
Russian Federation	Novosibirsk [2]	1989	409090	350557	...	...	...	...	...	346350	...	...	...
			100	85.7	...	...	...	...	...	84.7	...	...	...
Russian Federation	St. Petersburg [2]	1989	1457732	1431093	...	...	...	...	...	1429069	...	...	...
			100	98.2	...	...	...	...	...	98.0	...	...	...

TABLE 16 (continued)

Occupied Housing Units by Water and Toilet Facilities, Number and Percentage, Selected Cities

			Total Occupied Housing Units	Water Supply System				Unknown	Toilet Installation				Unknown
				With Piped Water			Without Piped Water		With Toilet of any Type			Without Toilet of any Type	
				Total	Inside	Outside			Total	Flush Toilet	Other Toilet		
EUROPE (continued)													
Switzerland	Basel	1980	87819	...	...	...	...	...	...	...	...	...	...
			100	...	...	...	...	...	...	...	...	...	
Switzerland	Berne	1980	67719	...	...	...	...	...	...	...	...	...	...
			100	...	...	...	...	...	...	...	...	...	
Switzerland	Geneva	1980	79628	...	...	...	...	...	...	...	...	...	...
			100	...	...	...	...	...	...	...	...	...	
Switzerland	Zurich	1980	176809	...	...	...	...	...	...	...	...	...	...
			100	...	...	...	...	...	...	...	...	...	
TFYR Macedonia	Skoplje	1981	116352	98119	...	...	...	...	...	...	...	...	...
			100	84.3	...	...	...	...	...	...	...	...	
Ukraine	Donetsk	1992	342100	271700	...	...	...	...	261800	...	...	...	...
			100	79.4	...	...	...	...	76.5	...	...	...	
Ukraine	Kharkov	1992	512700	440900	...	...	...	...	437900	...	...	...	...
			100	86.0	...	...	...	...	85.4	...	...	...	
Ukraine	Kiev	1992	833000	809100	...	...	...	...	809000	...	...	...	...
			100	97.1	...	...	...	...	97.1	...	...	...	
Ukraine	Odessa	1992	325800	284700	...	...	...	...	281700	...	...	...	...
			100	87.4	...	...	...	...	86.5	...	...	...	
Yugoslavia	Belgrade	1981	354747	334591	...	...	...	...	...	...	...	...	...
			100	94.3	...	...	...	...	...	...	...	...	
LATIN AMERICA													
Bolivia	Cochabamba	1988	86100	70700	51100	19600	15100	300	[6] 69900	[6] 52900	[6] 16900	[6] 16200	...
			100	82.1	59.3	22.8	17.5	0.3	81.2	61.4	19.6	18.8	
Bolivia	La Paz	1988	156500	[6] 152400	[6] 68000	[6] 84400	[6] 4100	100	107000	102400	4600	49500	-
			100	97.4	43.5	53.9	2.6	0.1	68.4	65.4	2.9	31.6	
Bolivia	Oruro	1988	38400	[6] 36900	[6] 9400	[6] 27500	[6] 1400	...	17200	14200	3000	21200	-
			100	96.1	24.5	71.6	3.6	...	44.8	37.0	7.8	55.2	
Bolivia	Santa Cruz	1988	112300	93200	28400	64800	19000	100	[6] 107000	[6] 22900	[6] 84000	[6] 5300	...
			100	83.0	25.3	57.7	16.9	0.1	95.3	20.4	74.8	4.7	
Cayman Islands	Georgetown	1989	4445	...	...	...	...	...	...	...	...	...	...
			100	...	...	...	...	...	...	...	...	...	
Colombia	Barranquilla	1985	[11] 152211	[12] 117537	...	...	...	...	...	...	...	930	...
			100	77.2	...	...	...	...	...	...	...	0.6	
Colombia	Bogota	1985	[11] 847523	[12] 813709	...	...	...	...	...	...	...	5883	...
			100	96.0	...	...	...	...	...	...	...	0.7	
Colombia	Cali	1985	[11] 253794	[12] 226310	...	...	...	...	...	...	...	1575	...
			100	89.2	...	...	...	...	...	...	...	0.6	
Colombia	Medellin	1985	[11] 275208	[12] 258220	...	...	...	...	...	...	...	2002	...
			100	93.8	...	...	...	...	...	...	...	0.7	
Cuba	Camaguey [13]	1981	62624	55390	39136	[14] 16254	7234	-	60406	35572	24834	2218	-
			100	88.4	62.5	26.0	11.6		96.5	56.8	39.7	3.5	
Cuba	Havana [13]	1981	500198	497544	447852	[14] 49692	2654	-	491923	484356	7567	8275	-
			100	99.5	89.5	9.9	0.5		98.3	96.8	1.5	1.7	
Cuba	Holguin [13]	1981	43956	27941	17717	[14] 10224	16015	-	40617	16389	24228	3339	-
			100	63.6	40.3	23.3	36.4		92.4	37.3	55.1	7.6	
Cuba	Santiago de Cuba [13]	1981	72760	69543	55418	[14] 14125	3217	-	70801	45190	25611	1959	-
			100	95.6	76.2	19.4	4.4		97.3	62.1	35.2	2.7	
Ecuador	Cuenca	1990	42417	40516	36273	4243	1901	-	40273	39602	671	2144	-
			100	95.5	85.5	10.0	4.5		94.9	93.4	1.6	5.1	
Ecuador	Guayaquil	1990	319900	193646	154547	39099	126254	-	305178	266314	38864	14722	-
			100	60.5	48.3	12.2	39.5		95.4	83.2	12.1	4.6	
Ecuador	Machala	1990	30903	19514	12939	6575	11389	-	28569	23531	5038	2334	-
			100	63.1	41.9	21.3	36.9		92.4	76.1	16.3	7.6	
Ecuador	Quito	1990	262709	223285	181115	42170	39424	-	255093	244536	10557	7616	-
			100	85.0	68.9	16.1	15.0		97.1	93.1	4.0	2.9	
Falkland Islands (Malvinas)	Stanley	1986	540	...	...	...	...	...	...	...	...	...	...
			100	...	...	...	...	...	...	...	...	...	
Guatemala	Guatemala City	1981	140917	114676	114676	-	26241	-	[2] 146200	[2] 116484	[2] 29716	[2] 6323	...
			100	81.4	81.4	-	18.6		103.7	82.7	21.1	4.5	
Guatemala	Mazatenango	1981	8152	3576	3576	-	4576	-	[2] 5255	[2] 3432	[2] 1823	[2] 2232	...
			100	43.9	43.9	-	56.1		64.5	42.1	22.4	27.4	
Guatemala	Puerto Barrios	1981	9579	5316	5316	-	4263	-	[2] 7864	[2] 4148	[2] 3716	[2] 2005	...
			100	55.5	55.5	-	44.5		82.1	43.3	38.8	20.9	
Guatemala	Quezaltenango	1981	11805	7058	7058	-	4747	-	[2] 11605	[2] 7351	[2] 4254	[2] 1913	...
			100	59.8	59.8	-	40.2		98.3	62.3	36.0	16.2	
Haiti	Port-au-Prince [15]	1986	158917	42237	9864	32373	108569	8111	149829	12601	137228	9088	...
			100	26.6	6.2	20.4	68.3	5.1	94.3	7.9	86.4	5.7	...

TABLE 16 (continued)

Occupied Housing Units by Water and Toilet Facilities, Number and Percentage, Selected Cities

			Total Occupied Housing Units	With Piped Water Total	With Piped Water Inside	With Piped Water Outside	Without Piped Water	Unknown	With Toilet of any Type Total	With Toilet of any Type Flush Toilet	With Toilet of any Type Other Toilet	Without Toilet of any Type	Unknown
LATIN AMERICA (continued)													
Honduras	Choluteca	1988	9823	8164	7841	323	1659	-	7598	2959	4639	2225	-
			100	83.1	79.8	3.3	16.9	-	77.3	30.1	47.2	22.7	-
Honduras	El Progreso	1988	10672	9695	9280	415	977	-	9990	7041	2949	682	-
			100	90.8	87.0	3.9	9.2	-	93.6	66.0	27.6	6.4	-
Honduras	San Pedro Sula	1988	54535	50841	49497	1344	3694	-	51696	41925	9771	2839	-
			100	93.2	90.8	2.5	6.8	-	94.8	76.9	17.9	5.2	-
Honduras	Tegucigalpa	1988	102573	83021	78223	4798	19552	-	93640	68557	25083	8933	-
			100	80.9	76.3	4.7	19.1	-	91.3	66.8	24.5	8.7	-
Mexico	Mexico City	1990 [16]	3120673	2876993	1996079	880914	222849	20831	[17]2815349	2114020	688112	286377	18947
			100	92.2	64.0	28.2	7.1	0.7	90.2	67.7	22.1	9.2	0.6
Panama	Colon	1990	15471	15431	...	...	40	-	15084	...	...	387	-
			100	99.7	...	...	0.3	-	97.5	...	...	2.5	-
Panama	Panama	1990	105409	105148	...	...	261	-	104455	...	...	954	-
			100	99.8	...	...	0.2	-	99.1	...	...	0.9	-
Panama	San Miguelito	1990	51645	51449	36952	14497	196	-	50642	29616	21026	1003	-
			100	99.6	71.6	28.1	0.4	-	98.1	57.3	40.7	1.9	-
Paraguay	Asuncion	1982	91526	52545	52545	-	38981	-	86466	73719	12747	5060	-
			100	57.4	57.4	-	42.6	-	94.5	80.5	13.9	5.5	-
Peru	Arequipa	1991	124975	114285	84229	30056	10690	-	87755	82463	5292	37220	-
			100	91.4	67.4	24.0	8.6	-	70.2	66.0	4.2	29.8	-
Peru	Callao	1991	111073	104329	93911	10418	6744	-	97001	92441	4560	14072	-
			100	93.9	84.5	9.4	6.1	-	87.3	83.2	4.1	12.7	-
Peru	Lima	1991	1099242	1032492	929392	103100	66750	-	959974	914850	45124	139268	-
			100	93.9	84.5	9.4	6.1	-	87.3	83.2	4.1	12.7	-
Peru	Trujillo	1991	105988	83096	72733	10363	22892	-	78214	59390	18824	27774	-
			100	78.4	68.6	9.8	21.6	-	73.8	56.0	17.8	26.2	-
NORTHERN AMERICA													
Canada	Montreal	1991	1239909	1239909	...	...	-	-	1235175	1235175	-	4734	-
			100	100.0	...	...	-	-	99.6	99.6	-	0.4	-
Canada	Ottawa	1991	266738	266738	...	...	-	-	266738	266738	-	-	-
			100	100.0	...	...	-	-	100.0	100.0	-	-	-
Canada	Toronto	1991	1316623	1316623	...	...	-	-	1312190	1307410	4780	4433	-
			100	100.0	...	...	-	-	99.7	99.3	0.4	0.3	-
Canada	Vancouver	1991	619152	619152	...	...	-	-	617880	617880	-	1272	-
			100	100.0	...	...	-	-	99.8	99.8	-	0.2	-
OCEANIA													
French Polynesia	Papeete	1988	5467	5453	...	...	14	-	5395	...	...	72	-
			100	99.7	...	...	0.3	-	98.7	...	...	1.3	-
New Caledonia	Noumea [2]	1989	18756	18621	...	...	135	-	18651	...	...	105	-
			100	99.3	...	...	0.7	-	99.4	...	...	0.6	-
Tonga	Nuku'alofa [2]	1986	3233	3009	...	...	185	39	3159	...	...	9	64
			100	93.1	...	...	5.7	1.2	97.7	...	...	0.3	2.0
Wallis & Futuna Isl.	Mata-Utu	1990	215	197	145	52	18	-	199	...	...	16	-
			100	91.6	67.4	24.2	8.4	-	92.6	...	...	7.4	-

Source: United Nations, Human Settlements Statistics Questionnaire 1992.

For additional information and definitions of the relevant terms refer to technical notes of tables 8, 12 and 15.

Notes:
1. Source: Malawi National Housing Survey 1986 (unweighted sample)
2. Data refer to households in housing units.
3. Data refer to households having piped water inside unit and households providing water from public taps.
4. Data refer to the Government controlled area only.
5. Data are presented in percentages.
6. Data as received by the UN. However the sum of the individual categories differs from the total.
7. Data refer to buildings.
8. Data refer to conventional dwellings only.
9. Including conventional dwellings with unknown equipment.
10. Data refer to both occupied and vacant conventional dwellings.
11. Data refer to private dwellings.
12. Data for running water only.
13. Data refer to occupied units with permanent residents. Excluded are huts and natural shelters.
14. Data refer to housing units with piped water outside the units disregarding how far it is.
15. Data are estimated on the basis of 2.5 % sample.
16. Data don't include 2,217 'refugee' housing units which do not meet characteristics of a housing unit, also 10,744 housing units not occupied were excluded.
17. Data include housing units with toilets (13,217) which are unknown whether they have water connections.

TABLE 17

Access to Safe Drinking Water and Sanitation Services: 1980, 1990

	Access to Safe Drinking Water (percentage of population)						Access to Sanitation Services (percentage of population)					
	Total		Urban		Rural		Total		Urban		Rural	
	1980	1990	1980	1990	1980	1990	1980	1990	1980	1990	1980	1990
WORLD TOTAL	...	...	...	...	...	...	...	...	...	...	...	...
More Developed Regions (*)	...	...	...	...	...	...	...	...	...	...	...	...
Less Developed Regions (+)	...	...	...	...	...	...	...	...	...	...	...	...
AFRICA	...	...	...	...	...	...	...	...	...	...	...	...
Algeria	...	75 (85)	...	85 (85)	...	55 (85)	59 (83*	57 (88*	95 (80*	80 (88*	40 (83*	40 (88*
Angola	21	41 (91)	85	71 (91)	10	20 (91)	19	19 (91)	40	25 (91)	15	15 (91)
Benin	20	56	26	73	15	43	24	45	48	60	4	35
Botswana	55 (80*	89	98 (80*	100	47 (80*	88	...	87	90 (83)	100	23 (80*	85
Burkina Faso	67 (83*	67	27	78 (91)	31	70	...	10 (88*	13	77 (91)	5	5 (88*
Burundi	24	57 (91)	90	99 (91)	20	54 (91)	35	49 (91)	40	71 (91)	35	47 (91)
Cameroon	32 (83*	48 (91)	46 (83*	100 (91)	24 (83*	27 (91)	...	74 (91)	100 (85)	100 (91)	...	64 (91)
Cape Verde	50	74 (88)	100	87 (88)	21	65 (88)	19	15 (88)	34	35 (88)	10	...
Central African Republic	...	24	13 (83*	19	5 (80*	26	20 (83*	46	36 (83*	45	9 (83*	46
Chad	29 (80*	57 (91)	...	25 (91)	30 (80*	70 (91)	...	...	...	...	...	...
Comoros	...	69 (91)	...	98 (91)	52 (80*	66 (91)	...	53 (91)	...	90 (91)	...	80 (91)
Congo	20 (80*	38 (88*	36	92 (88*	3	2 (88*	...	...	17 (80*	...	...	2 (88)
Côte d'Ivoire	17 (80*	76 (91)	30 (80*	70 (91)	10 (80*	81 (91)	17 (80*	60 (91)	13 (80*	59 (91)	20 (80*	62 (91)
Djibouti	45	84 (91)	50	88 (91)	20	70 (91)	39	55 (91)	43	64 (91)	20	24 (91)
Egypt	75	69 (91)	88	95	64	86	26	31 (91)	45	80	10	26
Equatorial Guinea	...	35 (91)	47 (80*	70 (91)	...	14 (91)	...	41 (91)	28 (83*	95 (91)	...	10 (91)
Ethiopia (former)	...	25 (91)	69 (83*	91 (91)	9 (83*	19 (91)	15 (83*	76 (91)	96 (83*	76 (91)	5 (83*	7 (91)
Gabon	50 (80*	50	75 (80*	90 (88*	34 (80*	50 (88*	...	57	...	...	...	...
Gambia	40 (80*	66	85	100	27 (80*	48	...	57	...	100	...	27
Ghana	47	52 (91)	72	93 (91)	33	35 (91)	27	42 (91)	47	64 (91)	17	32 (91)
Guinea	17	53 (91)	69	87 (91)	2	56 (91)	13	21 (91)	54	84 (91)	1	5 (91)
Guinea-Bissau	10	41 (91)	18	56 (91)	8	35 (91)	15	31 (91)	21	27 (91)	13	32 (91)
Kenya	26	49 (91)	85	74 (91)	15	43 (91)	30	43 (88*	89	69 (91)	19	35 (91)
Lesotho	14	47 (88*	37	59 (88*	11	45 (88*	14	22 (88*	13	14 (88*	14	23 (88*
Liberia	39 (80*	50 (88*	71 (80*	35 (91)	16	22 (91)	10 (83*	7 (88)	18	55 (91)	5	55 (91)
Libyan Arab Jamahirya	98	97 (88*	100	100 (88*	90	80 (88*	94	98 (88*	100	100 (88*	72	85 (88*
Madagascar	21	23 (91)	80	55 (91)	7	9 (91)	9	3 (91)	9	12 (91)	...	3 (91)
Malawi	41	55 (85)	77	97 (85)	37	49 (86*	83	84 (88*	100	100 (88*	81	81 (88*
Mali	6	41 (91)	37	53 (91)	...	38 (91)	13	24	79	81	...	10
Mauritania	84	66 (88*	80	67 (88*	85	65 (88*	1	15 (88)	5	34 (88*	...	13 (91)
Mauritius	99	100	100	100	98	100	94	100	100	100	90	100
Morocco	...	56	100	100	2 (80*	18	...	56 (88)	...	100	16 (83*	19 (88)
Mozambique	14 (83*	22 (88*	38 (83*	44 (88*	2 (80*	17 (88*	19 (83*	20 (88*	51 (80*	61 (88*	12 (83*	11 (88*
Namibia	...	37	...	98 (91)	...	35 (91)	...	13	...	24	...	11
Niger	33	53	41	98	32	45	7	14	36	71	3	4
Nigeria	32 (83*	36 (91)	60	81 (91)	30	30 (91)	13 (83*	35 (91)	30 (83*	40 (91)	5 (83*	30 (91)
Reunion	...	...	...	...	...	...	...	...	...	...	...	...
Rwanda	54	66 (91)	48	75 (91)	55	65 (91)	51	58 (91)	60	77 (91)	50	56 (91)
Sao Tome & Principe	32 (88)	...	...	33 (88)	45 (83*	32 (88)	...	11 (88)	...	8 (88)	15 (83*	13 (88)
Senegal	42	48 (91)	77	84 (91)	25	26 (91)	33	55 (91)	100	85 (91)	2	36 (91)
Seychelles	98 (88)	...	...	100 (88)	95 (83*	98 (88)	65 (88)	...	19 (88)	...	97 (88)	...
Sierra Leone	16	37 (91)	50	33 (91)	2	37 (91)	13	58 (91)	31	92 (91)	6	49 (91)
Somalia	31 (80*	37 (88*	60	7 (91)	20	29 (88*	18 (80*	18 (88*	48 (80*	44 (88*	5 (80*	5 (88*
South Africa	...	...	...	...	...	...	...	...	...	...	...	...
Sudan	45 (80*	48 (91)	100	55 (91)	31	43 (91)	8 (83*	75 (91)	20 (83*	89 (91)	5 (80*	65 (91)
Swaziland	...	22 (85)	...	100 (85)	...	7 (85)	...	36 (85)	62 (80*	100 (85)	...	25 (85)
Togo	42	60 (91)	70	77 (91)	31	53 (91)	14	23 (91)	24	56 (91)	10	10 (91)
Tunisia	63	99 (91)	100	100 (91)	17	99 (91)	56	96 (91)	100	98 (91)	...	94 (91)
Uganda	49 (80*	49 (91)	88 (80*	65 (91)	40 (80*	45 (91)	56 (80*	64 (91)	93 (80*	74 (91)	47 (80*	62 (91)
United Rep. of Tanzania	15 (83*	21 (91)	45	43 (91)	12 (80*	30	13 (83*	32 (91)	40	63 (91)	10	28 (91)
Western Sahara	...	...	...	...	...	...	...	...	...	...	...	...
Zaire	18 (80*	39	43 (80*	68	5 (80*	24	9 (80*	23	8 (80*	46	10 (80*	11
Zambia	46 (80*	53 (91)	65	70 (91)	32	28 (91)	52 (83*	37 (91)	100	75 (91)	48	12 (91)
Zimbabwe	31 (83*	84	100 (83*	95	10 (83*	80	35 (83*	40	100 (83*	95	15 (83*	22
ASIA	...	...	...	...	...	...	...	...	...	...	...	...
Afghanistan	10	99 (91)	28	79 (91)	8	85 (91)	...	71 (91)	5 (83*	71 (91)	...	...
Armenia	...	...	...	...	...	...	...	...	...	...	...	...
Azerbaijan	...	...	...	...	...	...	...	...	...	...	...	...
Bahrain	100 (80*	100	100 (80*	100	100 (80*	100 (86*	100 (80*	100	100 (80*	100	100 (80*	100 (86*
Bangladesh	38	84 (91)	26	82 (91)	40	81 (91)	3	31 (91)	21	63 (91)	1	26 (91)
Bhutan	8	34 (91)	50	60 (91)	5	30 (91)	...	13 (91)	...	50 (91)	...	7 (91)
Brunei Darussalam	98	98 (88)	100	100 (88)	95	95 (88)	...	99 (88)	75 (80*	100 (88)	98 (80*	98 (88)
Cambodia	...	36 (91)	...	65	...	33 (91)	...	14 (91)	...	81 (91)	...	8 (91)
China	...	79 (91)	...	87	...	81 (91)	...	85	...	100	...	95 (91)
Cyprus	100 (80*	100	100	100	100	100	100 (80*	97	100 (80*	96	100 (80*	100
Dem. People's Rep. of Korea	100 (83*	100 (86*	100 (83*	100 (86*	100 (83*	100 (86*	100 (83*	100 (86*	100 (83*	100 (86*	100 (83*	100 (86*
East Timor	...	...	...	...	...	...	...	...	...	...	...	...

TABLE 17 (continued)

Access to Safe Drinking Water and Sanitation Services: 1980, 1990

	Access to Safe Drinking Water (percentage of population)						Access to Sanitation Services (percentage of population)					
	Total		Urban		Rural		Total		Urban		Rural	
	1980	1990	1980	1990	1980	1990	1980	1990	1980	1990	1980	1990
ASIA (continued)												
Gaza Strip (Palestine)	...	...	...	...	...	...	...	...	...	...	...	...
Georgia	...	...	...	...	...	...	...	...	...	...	...	...
Hong Kong	100	100	100	100	95	96	93	87	100	90	...	50
India	41	85 (91)	77	87 (91)	31	85 (91)	6	16 (91)	27	53 (91)	1	2 (91)
Indonesia	24	51 (91)	35	68 (91)	19	43 (91)	24	44 (91)	29	64 (91)	21	36 (91)
Iran (Islamic Republic of)	52 (80*)	90 (91)	70 (80*)	98 (91)	33 (80*)	15 (91)	60 (80*)	86 (91)	90 (80*)	86 (91)	30 (80*)	35
Iraq	69 (80*)	78	92 (80*)	93	22 (80*)	41	66 (83*)	72 (88)	90 (83*)	96	15 (83*)	18 (88)
Israel	...	100 (86*)	...	100 (86*)	...	97 (86*)	...	99 (86*)	...	99 (86*)	...	95 (86*)
Japan	...	93	...	100	...	85	...	...	...	85 (88*)	...	...
Jordan	89	99	100	100	65	97	76	100	94	100	34	32 (91)
Kazakhstan	...	...	...	...	...	...	...	...	...	...	...	...
Kuwait	100 (80*)	100 (88)	100 (80*)	100 (88)	100 (80*)	100 (86*)	100 (80*)	98 (88)	100 (80*)	100 (88)	100 (80*)	100 (86*)
Kyrgyzstan	...	...	...	...	...	...	...	...	...	...	...	...
Lao People's Dem. Republic	...	36 (91)	21	54 (91)	20 (83)	33 (91)	5 (80*)	21 (91)	13 (80*)	97 (91)	4 (80*)	8 (91)
Lebanon	93 (80*)	92 (88*)	95 (80*)	95 (88*)	85 (80*)	85 (88*)	76 (80*)	...	94 (80*)	...	18 (80*)	...
Macau	100	100	100	100	100	...	99	...	100	...	60	...
Malaysia	63	78	90	96	49	66	70	94	100	94	55	94
Maldives	5	69 (91)	11	100 (91)	3	33 (91)	15	49 (91)	60	100 (91)	1	4
Mongolia	100 (83*)	80	...	100	100 (83*)	58	...	74	...	100	...	47
Myanmar	21	32 (91)	38	37 (91)	15	72	21	36 (91)	38	39 (91)	15	35 (91)
Nepal	14	42 (91)	83	67 (91)	7	39 (91)	2	6 (91)	16	52 (91)	1	3 (91)
Oman	15 (80*)	84 (91)	70 (80*)	91 (91)	10 (80*)	77 (91)	30 (83*)	71 (91)	60 (80*)	75 (91)	25 (83*)	40 (91)
Pakistan	35	56 (91)	72	80 (91)	20	45 (91)	13	24 (91)	42	55 (91)	2	10 (91)
Philippines	51	82 (91)	65	85 (91)	43	79 (91)	72	69 (91)	81	78 (91)	67	62 (91)
Qatar	92 (80*)	91 (88*)	98 (80*)	100	50 (80*)	48 (88)	...	97	70 (80*)	100	...	85
Republic of Korea	78	97 (91)	86	97 (91)	61	96 (91)	100	100 (91)	100	100 (91)	100	100 (91)
Saudi Arabia	91	95 (88)	92	100 (88*)	87	74 (88*)	76	86 (88*)	81	100 (88*)	50	30 (88*)
Singapore	100	100	100	100	100 (80*)	...	80	99	80	99	...	...
Sri Lanka	33	71 (91)	65	100 (91)	18	64 (91)	69	60 (91)	80	73 (91)	63	56 (91)
Syrian Arab Republic	71	74 (91)	98	90 (91)	54	58 (91)	45	83 (91)	74	84 (91)	28	82 (91)
Tajikistan	...	...	...	...	...	...	...	...	...	...	...	...
Thailand	63	77 (91)	65	89 (91)	63	72 (91)	46	74 (91)	64	80 (91)	41	72 (91)
Turkey	76	...	95	...	62	...	92 (83*)	...	56	...	90 (83*)	...
Turkmenistan	...	...	...	...	...	...	...	...	...	...	...	...
United Arab Emirates	93	95 (88*)	95	100 (86*)	81	100 (86*)	86	77 (88*)	93	93 (88*)	22	22 (88*)
Uzbekistan	...	...	...	...	...	...	...	...	...	...	...	...
Viet Nam	45 (83*)	24 (91)	70 (83*)	39 (91)	32	21 (91)	...	17 (91)	23	34 (91)	55	13 (91)
Yemen	...	36 (91)	...	61 (91)	...	30 (91)	...	65 (91)	...	87 (91)	...	60 (91)
EUROPE	...	...	...	...	...	...	...	...	...	...	...	...
Albania	97 (83*)	...	100 (83*)	...	95 (83*)	...	100 (83*)	...	100 (83*)	...	100 (83*)	...
Andorra	...	...	...	...	...	...	...	...	...	...	...	...
Austria	100	...	100	...	100	...	100 (83*)	...	99	...	100 (83*)	...
Belarus	...	...	100 (83*)	...	100 (83*)	...	...	...	...	...	...	...
Belgium	...	100 (86*)	...	100 (86*)	...	100 (86*)	...	100 (86*)	...	100 (86*)	...	100 (86*)
Bulgaria	...	99 (86*)	...	100 (86*)	...	96 (86*)	...	100 (86*)	...	100 (86*)	...	100 (86*)
Channel Islands	...	...	...	...	...	...	...	...	...	...	...	...
Czechoslovakia (former)	...	100 (85)	...	100 (85)	...	100 (85)	...	100 (85)	...	100 (85)	...	100 (85)
Denmark	...	100 (86*)	100	100 (86*)	100	100 (86*)	...	99 (86*)	100	99 (86*)	100	100 (86*)
Estonia	...	...	...	...	...	...	...	...	...	...	...	...
Faeroe Islands	...	...	...	...	...	...	...	...	...	...	...	...
Finland	100	98 (85)	100	100 (85)	100	99 (85)	...	100 (86*)	96	100 (86*)	67	100 (86*)
France	...	100 (85)	...	100 (85)	...	100 (85)	100 (83*)	...	100 (83*)	...	100 (83*)	...
Germany	...	100 (86*)	...	100 (86*)	...	100 (86*)	...	...	...	...	...	...
Gibraltar	...	...	...	...	...	...	...	...	...	...	...	...
Greece	98 (83*)	...	93	...	100	...	98 (83*)	...	83	...	80	...
Hungary	100	99 (85)	100	100 (85)	100	98 (85)	...	100 (85)	90	100 (85)	...	98 (85)
Iceland	100 (83*)	...	100 (83*)	...	100 (83*)	...	100 (83*)	...	100 (83*)	...	100 (83*)	...
Ireland	100 (83*)	...	100 (83*)	...	100 (83*)	...	100 (83*)	...	100 (83*)	...	100 (83*)	...
Isle of Man	...	...	...	...	...	...	...	...	...	...	...	...
Italy	100 (83*)	...	100 (83*)	...	100 (83*)	...	100 (83*)	...	100 (83*)	...	100 (83*)	...
Latvia	...	...	...	...	...	...	...	...	...	...	...	...
Liechtenstein	...	...	...	...	...	...	...	...	...	...	...	...
Lithuania	...	...	...	...	...	...	...	...	...	...	...	...
Luxembourg	...	100 (86*)	...	100 (86*)	...	100 (86*)	...	100 (86*)	...	100 (86*)	...	100 (86*)
Malta	100	...	100	...	100	...	96	...	100	...	84	...
Monaco	...	...	100	...	100 (83*)	...	...	...	...	...	...	...
Netherlands	...	100 (85)	100	100 (85)	100 (83)	99 (85)	...	100 (85)	100	100 (85)	...	100 (85)
Norway	...	100 (86*)	88	100 (86*)	100	100 (86*)	100 (83*)	...	76	...	100 (83*)	...
Poland	...	89 (85)	...	100 (85)	...	73 (85)	...	77 (85)	...	100 (85)	...	42 (85)

TABLE 17 (*continued*)

Access to Safe Drinking Water and Sanitation Services: 1980, 1990

	Access to Safe Drinking Water (percentage of population)						Access to Sanitation Services (percentage of population)					
	Total		Urban		Rural		Total		Urban		Rural	
	1980	1990	1980	1990	1980	1990	1980	1990	1980	1990	1980	1990
EUROPE (continued)												
Portugal	...	58 (85)	...	100 (85)	...	22 (85)	...	52 (85)	...	100 (85)	11 (85)	...
Republic of Moldova	...	...	...	...	...	...	...	...	...	...	...	...
Romania	95 (83*	...	100 (83*	...	90 (83*	...	97 (83*	...	100 (83*	...	95 (83*	...
Russian Federation	...	...	...	...	...	...	...	...	...	...	...	...
San Marino	...	...	100 (83*	...	100 (83*	...	...	...	100 (83*	...	100 (83*	...
Spain	...	98 (85)	100	100 (85)	68	81 (85)	...	72 (85)	81	73 (85)	79	69 (85)
Sweden	...	100 (86*	100	100 (86*	99	100 (86*	...	100 (86*	100	100 (86*	100	100 (86*
Switzerland	100	100 (86*	100	100 (86*	100	100 (86*	...	100 (86*	100	100 (86*	90	100 (86*
Ukraine	...	...	100 (83*	...	100 (83*	...	...	...	100 (83*	...	100 (83*	...
United Kingdom	...	100 (85)	100	100 (85)	99	100 (85)	100	100 (85)	100	100 (85)	100	100 (85)
Yugoslavia (former)	...	83 (86*	...	100 (86*	...	65 (86*	...	63 (86*	...	78 (86*	46 (86*	...
LATIN AMERICA	...	...	...	...	...	...	...	...	...	...	...	...
Anguilla	...	...	...	...	...	...	...	...	...	...	...	...
Antigua & Barbuda	...	...	...	...	...	...	...	...	100 (83*	...	100 (83*	...
Argentina	57	65 (88*	65	73 (88*	17	17 (88*	79	69 (88*	89	75 (88*	32	35 (88*
Aruba	...	...	...	...	...	...	...	...	...	...	...	...
Bahamas	...	94	100	98	...	75	...	81	100	98	...	2
Barbados	99 (83*	100 (91)	100	100 (91)	99 (83*	100 (91)	100 (83*	100 (91)	100 (83*	100	100 (83*	100 (91)
Belize	...	90 (91)	100	95 (91)	38 (83*	53	...	47	62	76	75	22
Bolivia	37	52 (91)	69	77 (91)	10	27 (91)	18	26 (91)	37	40 (91)	4	13 (91)
Brazil	71	87	80	95	51	61	43 (83*	71	32	84	2 (83*	32
British Virgin Islands	...	100 (91)	...	100 (91)	...	100 (91)	...	100 (91)	...	100 (91)	...	100 (91)
Cayman Islands	100	...	100	98 (85)	...	...	94	96 (85)	94	96 (85)	...	...
Chile	84	86 (88*	100	100 (91)	17	21 (88)	80	83 (88*	99	100 (91)	4 (80*	20 (91)
Colombia	92	85	100	87	79	82	65	64	100	84	4	18
Costa Rica	84	93 (91)	100	100 (91)	68	86 (91)	87	97 (91)	93	100 (91)	82	94 (91)
Cuba	...	98	99 (83)	100	...	91	...	92	...	100	...	68
Dominica	...	96 (91)	...	97 (91)	...	95 (91)	...	99 (91)	...	100 (91)	...	98 (91)
Dominican Republic	59	67	85	82	33	45	15	87	25	95	4	75
Ecuador	45	55 (91)	82	63 (91)	16	44 (91)	25	48 (91)	39	56 (91)	14	38 (91)
El Salvador	51	47 (91)	67	85 (91)	40	19 (91)	49	58 (91)	80	86 (91)	26	36 (91)
Falkland Islands (Malvinas)	...	...	...	...	...	...	...	...	...	...	...	...
French Guiana	...	...	...	...	...	...	...	...	...	...	...	...
Grenada	...	...	...	...	...	...	...	...	...	...	...	...
Guadeloupe	...	...	...	...	...	...	...	...	...	...	...	...
Guatemala	45	61	89	92	18	43	29	59	45	72	20	52 (91)
Guyana	72	65 (91)	100	90 (91)	60	51 (91)	86	93 (91)	100	90 (91)	80	89 (91)
Haiti	33	39 (91)	48	55 (91)	25 (80*	33 (91)	19 (80*	24 (91)	41 (80*	55 (91)	12 (80*	16 (91)
Honduras	44	77 (91)	50	98 (91)	40	63 (91)	35	61 (91)	49	98 (91)	26	43 (91)
Jamaica	96 (83*	100 (91)	99 (83*	100 (91)	...	100 (91)	91 (83*	89 (91)	92 (83*	100 (91)	90 (83*	80 (91)
Martinique	...	...	...	...	...	...	...	...	...	...	...	...
Mexico	56	76 (91)	64	81 (91)	43	68 (91)	37	50 (91)	51	70 (91)	12	17 (91)
Montserrat	...	45 (91)	...	100 (91)	...	27 (91)	...	84 (91)	...	100 (91)	...	...
Netherlands Antilles	...	...	...	...	...	...	...	...	...	...	...	...
Nicaragua	53	53 (91)	91	78 (91)	10	21 (91)	27 (83*	...	35	78 (91)	16 (83*	...
Panama	82	83 (88*	100	100 (88*	65	66 (88*	45	84 (91)	62	100 (88*	28	84 (91)
Paraguay	21	35 (91)	39	50 (91)	10	24 (91)	91	62 (91)	95	56 (91)	89	67 (91)
Peru	51	53	68	77 (91)	21	10 (91)	37	57	57	77 (91)	13 (83*	20 (91)
Puerto Rico	...	...	...	...	...	...	...	...	...	...	...	...
Saint Kitts & Nevis	...	100 (91)	100 (83*	100 (91)	100 (83*	100 (91)	...	100 (91)	...	98 (91)	...	100 (91)
Saint Lucia	...	...	...	...	...	...	...	...	...	...	...	...
St. Vincent & Grenadines	...	89 (91)	...	100 (91)	...	85 (91)	...	98 (91)	78 (83*	100 (91)	78 (83*	100 (91)
Suriname	83 (83*	73 (88)	100	82 (88)	96 (80*	56 (88)	98 (80*	56 (88)	100 (80*	64 (88)	96 (80*	43 (91)
Trindad & Tobago	98	97 (91)	100	99 (91)	93	91 (91)	93	79 (91)	95	99 (91)	88	98 (91)
Turks & Caicos Islands	...	69 (85)	...	87 (85)	...	68 (85)	...	...	...	...	...	88 (91)
Uruguay	80	75 (88*	96	100	2	5 (88*	59	61 (88*	59	60 (88*	60	65 (88*
US Virgin Islands	...	...	...	...	...	...	...	...	...	...	...	...
Venezuela	81	89 (88*	91	89 (88*	50	36	85	92 (88*	90	97 (88*	70	72
NORTHERN AMERICA	...	...	...	...	...	...	...	...	...	...	...	...
Bermuda	...	...	...	...	...	...	...	...	...	...	...	...
Canada	...	...	100 (83*	...	100 (83*	...	...	...	...	...	...	...
Greenland	100	...	100	...	100	...	...	...	78	...	100	...
St. Pierre & Miquelon	...	...	...	...	...	...	...	...	...	...	...	...
United States	...	...	100 (83*	...	100 (83*	...	...	...	...	...	...	...
OCEANIA	...	...	...	...	...	...	...	...	...	...	...	...
American Samoa	100	...	100	...	100	...	97	...	100	...	92	...
Australia	...	100	...	100	...	100	...	100	...	100	...	100
Cook Islands	...	100 (91)	100	100 (91)	85 (83)	100 (91)	79	100 (91)	100	100 (91)	76	100 (91)
Fiji	77	79	94	96	66	69	70	75	85	91	60	65

TABLE 17 (continued)

Access to Safe Drinking Water and Sanitation Services: 1980, 1990

	Access to Safe Drinking Water (percentage of population)						Access to Sanitation Services (percentage of population)					
	Total		Urban		Rural		Total		Urban		Rural	
	1980	1990	1980	1990	1980	1990	1980	1990	1980	1990	1980	1990
OCEANIA (continued)												
French Polynesia	...	63	...	100	...	18	...	97	...	98	...	95
Guam	100	94	100	100 (88)	100	100	...	98 (88)	100 (83)	100 (88)	100	90 (88)
Kiribati	44	73	93	91	25	63	82	64	87	91	80	49
Marshall Islands	...	74	...	100	...	45	...	74	...	100	...	45
Micronesia, Fed.States of	...	52	...	...	...	38	...	62	...	99	...	46
Nauru	...	...	...	...	...	...	...	...	...	...	...	...
New Caledonia	52	...	100	...	18	...	80	...	100	...	65	...
New Zealand	...	97	100 (83*)	100	100 (83*)	82	...	94	...	...	...	88
Niue	...	100	100 (83)	...	...	100	...	100	100 (83)	...	...	100
Northern Mariana Islands	...	92	...	100	...	...	...	98	...	100	...	71
Pacific Islands (Palau)	...	99	69	100	23	97	26	96	75	95	5	100
Papua New Guinea	16	33	55	94	10	20	14	56 (88)	96	57	3	56 (88)
Pitcairn	...	...	...	...	...	...	...	...	...	...	...	...
Samoa	95	82	97	100	94	77	84	94	86	100	83	92
Solomon Islands	27	61	91	82	20	58	17	12	82	73	10	2
Tokelau	...	...	...	...	...	...	...	...	...	...	...	...
Tonga	74	96	86	92	70	98	95	82	97	88	94	78
Tuvalu	...	100 (88)	...	99 (88)	...	100 (88)	86	78 (88)	100	79 (88)	80	77 (88)
Vanuatu	55	70 (88)	65	100 (88)	53	64 (88)	73	41 (88)	95	82 (88)	68	33 (88)
Wake Islands	...	...	...	...	...	...	...	...	...	...	...	...
Wallis & Futuna Islands	...	...	...	...	...	...	...	...	...	...	...	...
U.S.S.R (FORMER)	100 (83*	...	100 (83*	...	100 (83*	...	100 (83*	...	100 (83*	...	100 (83*	...

Sources: World Health Organization: The International Drinking Water Supply and Sanitation Decade Review of National Baseline Data (1980), The International Drinking Water Supply and Sanitation Decade Review of Mid-Decade Progress (1985), The International Drinking Water Supply and Sanitation Decade Review of Decade Progress (1988), The International Drinking Water Supply and Sanitation Decade End of decade review (1990); WHO and UNICEF, Water Supply and Sanitation Sector Monitoring Report 1993; World Health Organization, World Health Statistics 1985 & 1991; United Nations Children's Fund, The State of The World Children 1994.

Access to Safe Drinking Water: Data refer to the percentage of the population with access to an adequate amount of safe drinking water located within a convenient distance from the user's dwelling. It should be noted that the definitions of 'access', 'adequate amount', 'safe', 'convenient distance' differ among countries.

Access to Sanitation Services: Proportion of the population with access to a sanitary facility for human excreta disposal in the dwelling or located within a convenient distance from the user's dwelling. But again the definitions of 'access', 'sanitary facility', 'convenient distance' differ among countries.

Notes:
(80* - refers to the years 1980-82.
(83* - refers to the years 1983-85.
(86* - refers to the years 1986-87.
(88* - refers to the years 1988-91.

TABLE 18

Emissions from Industrial Processes, Land Use Change and Anthropogenic Sources, 1991

	Carbon Dioxide Emissions from Industrial Processes						CO₂ Emissions from Land-Use Change	Methane Emissions from Anthropogenic Sources				
	Solid	Liquid	Gas and Gas Flaring	Cement Manufacture	Total	Per Capita		Coal Mining Oil & Gas Production	Solid Waste	Wet Rice Agriculture	Livestock	Total
	(000 ton)	(000 ton)	(000 ton)	(000 ton)	(000 ton)	(ton)	(000 ton)	(000 ton)	(000 ton)	(000 ton)	(000 ton)	(000
WORLD TOTAL	8581088	9493424	4008416	593568	22672832	4.21	3400000	66000	40000	72000	76000	250000
More Developed Regions (*)	5176275	5734747	3228046	274946	14414015	12.61	22000	41108	29287	2769	25609	97929
Less Developed Regions (+)	3404813	3758677	780370	318622	8258817	1.99	3378000	24892	10713	69231	50391	152071
AFRICA	273606	255487	117363	25138	671600	1.03	640000	2600	1400	2600	9600	16000
Algeria	3558	24032	24418	3189	55194	2.16	...	690	110	...	160	960
Angola	-	1517	2774	497	4789	0.51	16000	3	24	8	120	150
Benin	-	425	-	136	561	0.11	3000	...	15	2	44	61
Botswana	2154	-	-	-	2154	1.69	3200	...	3	...	110	110
Burkina Faso	-	557	-	-	557	0.07	3400	...	7	12	200	220
Burundi	15	205	-	-	220	0.04	120	...	3	8	22	32
Cameroon	4	1920	-	-	1924	0.15	23000	...	42	5	200	250
Central African Republic	-	209	-	-	209	0.07	23000	...	12	3	98	110
Chad	-	253	-	-	253	0.04	7100	...	14	21	210	250
Congo	4	1788	173	51	2015	0.88	12000	...	8	2	4	14
Côte d'Ivoire	-	6130	-	249	6379	0.51	9900	...	11	150	49	240
Djibouti	-	359	-	-	359	0.81	...	...	3	...	14	17
Egypt	2623	56664	14905	7475	81667	1.54	...	120	130	310	290	850
Equatorial Guinea	-	121	-	-	121	0.33	2600	...	1	...	-	1
Ethiopia (former)	-	2682	-	145	2825	0.07	8000	...	54	...	1400	1400
Gabon	-	2349	3583	56	5987	5.02	47000	2	5	...	2	9
Gambia	-	198	-	-	198	0.22	94	...	2	3	16	21
Ghana	7	3111	-	337	3455	0.22	15000	...	21	8	62	91
Guinea	-	1026	-	-	1026	0.18	9800	...	13	360	68	440
Guinea-Bissau	-	205	-	-	205	0.22	1700	...	2	33	17	51
Kenya	355	3745	-	746	4847	0.18	360	...	49	8	600	660
Liberia	-	275	-	-	275	0.11	7400	...	10	36	4	49
Madagascar	40	1022	-	11	1074	0.07	20000	...	25	690	370	1100
Malawi	29	561	-	38	630	0.07	10000	...	9	17	34	61
Mali	-	425	-	10	436	0.04	8400	...	15	64	250	330
Mauritania	15	2645	-	45	2704	1.28	1	...	8	2	140	150
Mauritius	176	1041	-	-	1216	1.14	...	...	4	...	2	5
Morocco	4785	17243	73	2093	24197	0.95	...	9	100	2	220	330
Mozambique	165	821	-	40	1030	0.07	14000	...	...	...	...	...
Niger	421	594	-	14	1030	0.15	...	2	13	6	120	140
Nigeria	169	37329	52689	1745	91930	0.81	10000	77	2	330	700	1100
Rwanda	-	407	2	30	436	0.07	71	...	5	2	28	35
Senegal	-	2554	-	249	2799	0.37	4600	...	24	15	130	170
Sierra Leone	-	689	-	-	689	0.15	1800	...	11	110	14	130
Somalia	-	524	-	-	524	0.07	360	...	23	1	630	660
South Africa	241681	33276	-	3736	278695	7.18	...	1500	180	1	920	2600
Sudan	-	3320	-	84	3404	0.15	38000	...	47	1	1100	1100
Swaziland	330	-	-	-	330	0.44	...	...	2	...	27	29
Togo	-	524	-	199	722	0.18	2100	...	8	8	27	42
Tunisia	359	9801	2951	1695	14810	1.80	...	5	37	...	72	110
Uganda	-	909	-	5	912	0.04	4700	...	17	24	200	240
United Republic of Tanzania	15	1993	-	149	2158	0.07	21000	...	79	200	520	790
Zaire	931	3081	-	224	4236	0.11	280000	1	120	150	75	340
Zambia	850	1392	-	188	2429	0.29	33000	-	36	6	100	150
Zimbabwe	14905	1729	-	348	16983	1.65	4100	44	23	...	230	300
ASIA	3314509	2546227	528230	282563	6671525	2.11	920000	20200	8200	67000	25000	120000
Afghanistan	363	1711	3017	54	5148	0.29	...	37	27	85	160	310
Bangladesh	311	5910	9057	165	15444	0.15	6800	73	160	5000	960	6200
Bhutan	48	81	-	-	128	0.07	4100	...	1	21	15	37
Cambodia	-	462	-	-	462	0.01	34000	...	...	...	...	...
China	2024074	365118	30778	123411	2543380	2.20	...	14250	880	19000	5400	40000
Dem. People's Rep. of Korea	221628	13469	-	8137	243235	10.96	...	820	110	310	53	1300
India	496545	151583	30508	24915	703550	0.81	21000	1960	2300	19000	12000	35000
Indonesia	17829	91728	52861	8049	170468	0.92	330000	802	480	5100	650	7100
Iran (Islamic Republic of)	4976	144409	65501	7475	222361	3.70	...	407	260	280	640	1600
Iraq	4	487341	30449	2491	520281	27.86	...	20	290	53	130	490
Israel	10871	23200	48	1447	35566	7.29	...	-	35	...	15	50
Japan	320944	619476	106278	44449	1091147	8.79	...	132	1900	1400	280	3600
Jordan	-	9112	-	897	10010	2.42	...	...	23	...	12	35
Kuwait	-	7801	3889	149	11842	5.68	...	8	41	...	2	51
Lao People's Dem. Republic	4	249	-	-	253	0.07	36000	...	7	190	86	280
Lebanon	-	7907	-	452	8361	3.00	...	...	19	...	6	25
Malaysia	6141	41345	9970	3736	61196	3.31	110000	250	65	290	39	640
Mongolia	7581	2045	-	199	9823	4.36	...	5	10	...	260	280
Myanmar	187	2572	2015	183	4961	0.11	120000	15	86	3000	440	3600
Nepal	180	692	-	50	923	0.04	7600	...	16	560	400	980
Oman	-	4738	6464	497	11695	7.40	...	41	4	...	14	59

TABLE 18 *(continued)*

Emissions from Industrial Processes, Land Use Change and Anthropogenic Sources, 1991

	Carbon Dioxide Emissions from Industrial Processes						CO₂ Emissions from Land-Use Change	Methane Emissions from Anthropogenic Sources				
	Solid	Liquid	Gas and Gas Flaring	Cement Manufacture	Total	Per Capita		Coal Mining Oil & Gas Production	Solid Waste	Wet Rice Agriculture	Livestock	Total
	(000 ton)	(000 ton)	(000 ton)	(000 ton)	(000 ton)	(ton)	(000 ton)	(000 ton)	(000 ton)	(000 ton)	(000 ton)	(000
ASIA (continued)												
Pakistan	8424	32492	23982	3587	68487	0.55	9700	172	41	1100	1900	3200
Philippines	6298	36050	-	2242	44587	0.70	110000	...	220	1500	220	1900
Republic of Korea	96554	143940	7214	16943	264647	6.05	...	260	260	640	80	1200
Saudi Arabia	-	122707	86233	5981	214919	13.96	...	580	240	...	77	890
Singapore	44	40154	-	1096	41293	15.06	...	...	61	...	-	62
Sri Lanka	7	3961	-	199	4166	0.26	3700	...	24	460	110	600
Syrian Arab Republic	-	26700	1323	1745	29766	2.31	...	5	54	...	110	160
Thailand	15510	66113	10274	8996	100896	1.83	91000	92	110	5300	440	6000
Turkey	65084	57708	6797	12970	142555	2.49	...	26	290	25	740	1100
United Arab Emirates	-	17965	39996	1501	59459	36.49	...	370	26	...	13	410
Viet Nam	10904	7944	1577	149	20573	0.29	33000	75	120	3400	270	3900
Yemen	-	9545	-	398	9940	0.81	...	...	9	...	...	9
EUROPE	**1696520**	**1600516**	**692907**	**123816**	**4113771**	**8.20**	**...**	**6026**	**14561**	**239**	**7679**	**28429**
Albania	2832	2008	1059	348	6272	1.91	...	9	16	1	38	64
Austria	16330	31342	10171	2491	60331	7.80	...	13	87	...	150	250
Belgium	36831	41825	19987	3436	102079	10.22	...	12	190	...	...	200
Bulgaria	29579	14909	9508	2676	56675	6.30	...	1	8500	4	160	8700
Czechoslovakia (former)	137583	26124	23512	4136	191356	12.20	...	247	170	...	290	710
Denmark	31968	24941	5147	997	63054	12.24	...	41	26	...	140	210
Finland	20848	24934	5467	798	52047	10.41	...	-	58	...	78	140
France	81022	217920	62215	12956	374113	6.56	...	117	290	17	1300	1700
Germany	507548	307926	133228	20930	969630	12.13	...	980	1300	...	770	3000
Greece	29616	36204	318	6727	72866	7.18	...	2	120	8	130	270
Hungary	23490	20537	18203	1345	63574	6.05	...	164	94	6	120	380
Iceland	234	1513	-	56	1803	7.00	...	-	5	...	11	15
Ireland	14337	12714	4386	798	32236	9.23	...	24	42	...	360	420
Italy	50527	234478	97576	19931	402516	6.96	...	190	610	110	600	1500
Netherlands	30891	28671	77809	1623	138990	9.23	...	770	250	...	310	1300
Norway	3041	27949	27108	572	58672	13.74	...	300	75	...	72	450
Poland	251251	34636	16279	5994	308164	8.06	...	933	380	...	630	1900
Portugal	10516	28290	-	2984	41792	4.25	...	3	10	22	130	160
Romania	37944	44148	49457	6478	138027	5.94	...	359	170	15	510	1100
Spain	79304	113895	12939	13741	219877	5.64	...	255	590	50	520	1400
Sweden	9123	40989	894	2491	53498	6.23	...	...	70	...	100	170
Switzerland	1220	33844	4192	2590	41843	6.16	...	...	18	...	110	130
United Kingdom	251402	216084	103689	5981	577157	10.00	...	1580	1300	...	910	3800
Yugoslavia (former)	39080	34636	9766	3738	87225	3.66	...	26	190	6	240	460
LATIN AMERICA	**90578**	**679220**	**204446**	**42828**	**1017087**	**1.21**	**1750187**	**1830**	**2756**	**1044**	**16316**	**21989**
Argentina	2719	59818	51313	1994	115848	3.55	...	350	230	19	3000	3600
Belize	-	264	-	-	264	1.36	840	...	...	-	2	2
Bolivia	-	3386	2194	273	5855	0.81	140000	43	32	18	250	340
Brazil	39879	153009	9754	12956	215601	1.43	970000	62	1100	330	8300	9800
Chile	7991	20471	3165	897	32525	2.42	...	43	93	6	160	310
Colombia	16158	29418	8738	3189	57503	1.76	100000	284	140	260	910	1600
Costa Rica	-	2803	-	447	3250	1.06	12000	...	12	8	64	84
Cuba	700	32346	59	1295	34398	3.22	2800	...	65	110	190	370
Dominican Republic	-	5763	-	497	6262	0.84	4800	...	36	39	88	160
Ecuador	-	15187	1498	1096	17785	1.65	68000	2	50	43	170	270
El Salvador	-	2213	-	319	2532	0.48	290	...	20	3	45	67
Guatemala	-	3228	-	847	4074	0.44	20000	...	31	4	78	110
Guyana	-	850	-	-	850	1.06	6500	...	2	14	9	26
Haiti	-	634	-	99	733	0.11	57	...	16	9	66	91
Honduras	-	1619	-	325	1946	0.37	17000	...	19	4	89	110
Jamaica	-	4411	-	260	4672	1.91	7000	...	11	...	13	24
Mexico	20801	251061	54709	13304	339873	3.92	50000	510	540	16	1300	2400
Nicaragua	-	2004	-	70	2074	0.55	32000	...	20	19	64	100
Panama	476	2854	117	149	3594	1.47	21000	...	11	13	52	75
Paraguay	-	1616	-	163	1781	0.40	28000	...	17	3	300	320
Peru	546	16477	1135	997	19155	0.88	94000	9	130	42	230	400
Suriname	-	1993	-	25	2019	4.69	4800	...	2	37	3	42
Trindad & Tobago	-	5884	12324	219	18430	14.73	1100	87	7	1	3	98
Uruguay	-	4210	-	249	4459	1.43	...	...	22	23	440	490
Venezuela	1308	57701	59440	3158	121604	6.16	170000	440	150	23	490	1100
NORTHERN AMERICA	**-**	**-**	**1191951**	**-**	**-**	**13.73**	**22000**	**15830**	**9600**	**750**	**6740**	**32300**
Canada	94696	178078	132373	5481	410628	15.21	...	1430	1200	...	740	3300
United States	1803838	2034044	1059578	34174	4931630	19.53	22000	14400	8400	750	6000	29000

TABLE 18 (continued)

Emissions from Industrial Processes, Land Use Change and Anthropogenic Sources, 1991

	Carbon Dioxide Emissions from Industrial Processes						CO₂ Emissions from Land-Use Change	Methane Emissions from Anthropogenic Sources				
	Solid	Liquid	Gas and Gas Flaring	Cement Manufacture	Total	Per Capita		Coal Mining Oil & Gas Production	Solid Waste	Wet Rice Agriculture	Livestock	Total
	(000 ton)	(000 ton)	(000 ton)	(000 ton)	(000 ton)	(ton)	(000 ton)	(000 ton)	(000 ton)	(000 ton)	(000 ton)	(000
OCEANIA	**154562**	**89321**	**41103**	**3783**	**288767**	**11.24**	**29000**	**1900**	**630**	**66**	**3000**	**5600**
Australia	149557	76644	32258	3363	261818	15.10	...	1730	570	60	2100	4500
Fiji	48	594	-	45	689	0.95	...	...	2	6	7	15
New Zealand	4954	9669	8845	375	23842	6.96	...	90	56	...	910	1100
Papua New Guinea	4	2253	-	-	2257	0.59	29000	...	5	...	5	10
Solomon Islands	-	161	-	-	161	0.48	...	...	...	...	1	1
U.S.S.R. (FORMER)	**1105766**	**1216320**	**1195807**	**63288**	**3581179**	**12.31**	**...**	**17300**	**2600**	**320**	**7900**	**2800**

Source: World Resources Institute, *World Resources 1994-95*.

Data were compiled by the World Resources Institute. The methods were chosen to maximize the use of the available international data so as to be comparable among countries.

Data on industrial additions to the carbon dioxide flux from solid fuels, liquid fuels, gas fuels, gas flaring, and cement manufacture have been calculated from data on the net apparent consumption of fossil fuels, and from data on world cement manufacture. Emissions are calculated using global average fuel chemistry and usage. Estimates of total and per capita national emissions do not include bunker fuels used in international transport because of the difficulty of apportioning these fuels among the countries benefiting from that transport. Carbon dioxide emissions from land-use change are based on FAO estimates of deforestation and forest biomass for the world's tropical countries.

CH_4 emissions from coal mining were estimated using information on the average CH_4 content of the anthracite and bituminous coals, subbituminous coals, and lignite mined around the world. The amount of CH_4 vented in the course of oil production is estimated at 25 per cent of the amount that is flared. CH_4 emissions from municipal solid waste were calculated by multiplying the 1991 population by per capita emission coefficients. CH_4 emissions from the practice of wet rice agriculture were calculated using the area of rice production (as reported by the FAO) minus those areas devoted to dry (upland) and deepwater (floating) rice production. CH_4 emissions from domestic livestock were calculated using FAO statistics on animal populations and published estimates of CH_4 emissions from each type of animal raised.

For additional information refer to the technical notes for tables 23.1 & 23.2 of the *World Resources 1994-95*.

TABLE 19

Air Pollution in Urban Areas: 1980, 1990

| | | | Suspended Particulate Matter (mean annual values in kg/m³ and number of observations) | | | | Sulphur Dioxide | |
| | | | Total Concentrations (high-volume gravimetric or equivalent methode) | | Smoke Concentrations (smoke shade reflectance methode) | | (concentrations at selected GEMS / Air sites) | |
			1980	1990	1980	1990	1980-81	1988-89
AFRICA								
Egypt	Cairo	CCC	...	...	101 [44]	49 [171]	...	...
Egypt	Cairo	SI	...	...	130	42 [207]	...	...
Egypt	Cairo	SR	...	...	83 [17]	38 [180]	...	...
Ghana	Accra	SI	109 [21]	150 [52]	...	...	...	...
Ghana	Accra	SR	92 [18]	124 [17]	...	...	...	...
ASIA								
China	Beijing	CCC	422 [76] (81)	418 [179]	...	...	66.0 [113] *	103.0 [351]
China	Beijing	CCR	415 [79] (81)	371 [175]	...	...	98.0 [110] *	114.5 [330]
China	Beijing	SI	479 [75] (81)	430 [168]	...	...	38.0 [104] *	53.5 [336]
China	Beijing	SR	252 [62] (81)	271 [174]	...	...	6.0 [93] *	29.5 [326]
China	Guangzhou	CCC	260 [38] (81)	142 [157]	...	...	117.0 [76] *	58.5 [353]
China	Guangzhou	CCI	...	...	...	...	12.0 [55] *	135.5 [354]
China	Guangzhou	CCR	117 [39] (81)	176 [157]	...	...	66.0 [97] *	99.0 [346]
China	Guangzhou	SR	96 [24] (81)	269 [162]	...	...	140.0 [93] *	20.5 [350]
China	Guangzhou	SR	375 [38] (81)	114 [155]	...	...	...	...
China	Shanghai	CCC	205 [88] (81)	211 [167]	...	...	65.0 [85] *	69.0 [343]
China	Shanghai	CCI	330 [89] (81)	269 [166]	...	...	23.0 [88] *	55.5 [338]
China	Shanghai	CCR	235 [87] (81)	280 [163]	...	...	52.0 [87] *	104.0 [294]
China	Shanghai	SR	151 [178] (83)	161 [166]	...	...	...	...
China	Shenyang	CCC	406 [72] (81)	394 [145]	...	...	72.0 [72] *	101.5 [288]
China	Shenyang	CCI	523 [72] (81)	447 [144]	...	...	136.0 [72] *	207.5 [288]
China	Shenyang	CCR	465 [72] (81)	393 [144]	...	...	29.0 [73] *	70.0 [288]
China	Shenyang	SR	225 [72] (81)	209 [144]	...	...	27.0 [72] *	29.0 [276]
China	Xian	CCC	350 [115] (81)	444 [144]	...	...	160.0 [120] *	95.5 [286]
China	Xian	CCR	387 [120] (81)	487 [144]	...	...	108.0 [119] *	97.5 [288]
China	Xian	SI	463 [117] (81)	444 [144]	...	...	46.0 [117] *	79.5 [288]
China	Xian	SR	235 [97] (81)	361 [144]	...	...	22.0 [98] *	37.0 [252]
Hong Kong	Hong Kong	CCC	...	95 [107] (88)	49 [366]	43 [207] (84)	40.0 [731]	32.0 [208] (84-85) *
Hong Kong	Hong Kong	CCI	...	143 [103] (88)	...	...	...	...
Hong Kong	Hong Kong	CCR	...	102 [107] (88)	...	...	...	...
Hong Kong	Hong Kong	SI	...	...	25 [366]	21 [208] (84)	85.5 [731]	15.0 [208] (84-85) *
India	Bombay	CCC	142 [29]	175 [32] (85)	...	...	...	...
India	Bombay	CCC	207 [34] (81)	227 [30] (85)	...	...	...	...
India	Bombay	SR	203 [32] (81)	289 [29] (85)	...	...	...	...
India	Calcutta	CCC	462 [31]	374 [31] (85)	...	...	...	...
India	Calcutta	SI	356 [30]	405 [26] (85)	...	...	...	...
India	Calcutta	SR	393 [27]	297 [30] (85)	...	...	...	...
India	Delhi	CCC	535 [35]	439 [27] (85)	...	...	...	...
India	Delhi	CCI	453 [40]	488 [27] (85)	...	...	...	...
India	Delhi	CCR	322 [39]	294 [25] (85)	...	...	...	...
Indonesia	Jakarta	CCI	359 [21] (82)	175 [28] (85)	...	...	...	...
Indonesia	Jakarta	CCR	274 [57]	204 [43] (85)	...	...	...	...
Indonesia	Jakarta	NA	...	237 [53] (89)	...	...	...	...
Indonesia	Jakarta	SI	167 [50]	188 [51] (88)	...	...	...	...
Iran (Islamic Republic of)	Tehran	CCC	292 [80]	241 [22]	...	...	...	...
Iran (Islamic Republic of)	Tehran	CCC	...	...	175 [80]	155 [19]	169.5 [172]	211.0 [42]
Iran (Islamic Republic of)	Tehran	SI	370 [60]	277 [13]	...	...	137.5 [154]	149.0 [28]
Iran (Islamic Republic of)	Tehran	SI	...	...	222 [69]	181 [11]	...	...
Iran (Islamic Republic of)	Tehran	SR	...	...	128 [76]	56 [5]	140.0 [160]	81.5 [30]
Iran (Islamic Republic of)	Tehran	SR	291 [65]	220 [8]	...	...	...	...
Japan	Osaka	CCC	49 [361]	42 [338]	...	...	34.5 [724]	27.0 [366] *
Japan	Osaka	CCI	53 [364]	43 [304]	...	...	35.5 [719]	25.0 [366] *
Japan	Osaka	CCI	60 [362]	56 [365]	...	...	41.0 [731]	34.0 [366] *
Japan	Osaka	SR	58 [362]	54 [346] (87)	...	...	32.0 [730]	24.0 [363] *
Japan	Tokyo	CCC	59 [354]	56 [365]	...	...	42.0 [719]	19.0 [360]
Japan	Tokyo	CCI	52 [314] (84)	63 [353]	...	...	48.5 [724]	26.0 [366]
Japan	Tokyo	SR	52 [315]	49 [350]	...	...	40.0 [722]	18.0 [366]
Malaysia	Kuala Lumpur	SI	182 [137]	136 [49] (88)	...	...	...	...
Malaysia	Kuala Lumpur	SR	247 [41] (81)	121 [47] (88)	...	...	...	...
Pakistan	Lahore	SR	690 [106]	405 [64]	...	...	...	...
Thailand	Bangkok	SI	174 [79]	198 [67] (89)	...	...	...	...
Thailand	Bangkok	SR	115 [55]	115 [105] (89)	...	...	14.0 [155]	13.0 [190]
Thailand	Bangkok	SR	232 [11]	194 [109] (89)	...	...	...	...

TABLE 19 (continued)

Air Pollution in Urban Areas: 1980, 1990

			Suspended Particulate Matter (mean annual values in kg/m³ and number of observations)				Sulphur Dioxide	
			Total Concentrations (high-volume gravimetric or equivalent methode)		Smoke Concentrations (smoke shade reflectance methode)		(concentrations at selected GEMS / Air sites)	
			1980	1990	1980	1990	1980-81	1988-89
EUROPE								
Belgium	Brussels	CCC	25 [366]	24 [364] (86)	...	...	72.5 [727]	38.0 [355]
Croatia	Zagreb	CCI	122 [232]	118 [154] (86)	...	...	41.5 [731]	102.0 [698]
Croatia	Zagreb	CCC	119 [197]	130 [131]	...	...	87.5 [671]	82.5 [694]
Croatia	Zagreb	SR	130 [201]	64 [196]	...	...	41.5 [730]	44.0 [637]
Denmark	Copenhagen	CCC	...	...	23 [366]	28 [365] (86)	...	...
Denmark	Copenhagen	SI	46 [343]	55 [341] (86)	16 [366]	18 [334] (86)	...	...
Finland	Helsinki	CCC	75 [167]	87 [175] (89)	...	...	20.5 [690]	30.0 [683]
Finland	Helsinki	SI	76 [161]	60 [171] (89)	...	...	...	...
Germany	Frankfurt	CCC	25 [318]	36 [89]	...	...	70.5 [625]	26.0 [421]
Greece	Athens	CCC	218 [57]	155 [44] (86)	107 [174] (83)	91 [346] (86)	44.5 [539]	35.0 [122] (86-87) *
Greece	Athens	SI	202 [41]	136 [29] (86)	34 [175] (83)	25 [342] (86)	49.5 [262]	27.0 [130] (86-87) *
Ireland	Dublin	CCI	...	...	17 [361]	39 [364] (89)	41.5 [727]	23.0 [720]
Ireland	Dublin	CCR	...	...	49 [348]	43 [361] (89)	65.5 [722]	28.5 [704]
Ireland	Dublin	SR	...	...	19 [364]	47 [265] (89)	37.0 [725]	18.0 [578]
Luxembourg	Vianden	NA	...	...	7 [331]	3 [317] (88)	...	...
Poland	Warsaw	CCC	...	...	56 [193]	57 [143]	46.0 [367]	23.5 [574]
Poland	Warsaw	CCI	...	...	47 [205]	55 [136]	39.0 [367]	29.5 [527]
Poland	Warsaw	CCR	...	...	44 [188]	46 [103]	31.5 [305]	19.5 [409]
Poland	Wroclaw	CCC	...	...	76 [293]	86 [145]	39.0 [577]	53.0 [564]
Poland	Wroclaw	CCI	...	...	53 [291]	78 [137]	27.5 [583]	34.5 [542]
Poland	Wroclaw	CCR	...	...	51 [291]	63 [140]	31.5 [558]	40.0 [506]
Portugal	Lisbon	CCR	105 [50] (81)	138 [10]	...	...	...	...
Portugal	Lisbon	CCR	99 [128] (81)	91 [12]	...	...	...	...
Portugal	Lisbon	SR	100 [42] (82)	156 [9]	...	...	...	...
Spain	Madrid	CCC	...	...	129 [281]	104 [334]	111.5 [578]	31.5 [663]
Spain	Madrid	CCI	...	...	...	...	113.5 [310]	...
Spain	Madrid	SI	...	...	...	62 [363]	...	...
Spain	Madrid	SR	...	...	56 [330]	20 [358]	46.0 [653]	17.5 [658]
United Kingdom	Glasgow	CCC	...	...	30 [366]	20 [365] (85)	...	...
United Kingdom	Glasgow	SR	...	...	27 [366]	15 [339] (85)	...	...
United Kingdom	London	CCC	...	...	16 [366]	32 [307] (85)	55.0 [730]	42.5 [673] (84-85)
United Kingdom	London	SI	...	...	27 [346]	12 [361] (85)	56.5 [678]	33.5 [727] (84-85)
LATIN AMERICA								
Brazil	Sao Paulo	CCM	...	...	126 [361]	65 [59] (88)	127.0 [723]	50.0 [61] *
Brazil	Sao Paulo	CCR	...	...	56 [362]	50 [60] (88)	...	...
Brazil	Sao Paulo	CCR	162 [28]	100 [56] (85)	80 [365]	66 [57] (88)	120.0 [729]	55.0 [61] *
Chile	Santiago	CCC	...	...	100 [313]	75 [362] (85)	67.5 [659]	79.5 [691] (84-85)
Chile	Santiago	CCR	...	...	40 [246]	64 [359] (84)	37.0 [587]	46.0 [360] (84-85) *
Venezuela	Caracas	CCC	...	...	23 [183]	20 [273] (88)	29.5 [397]	21.0 [270]
Venezuela	Caracas	NA	77 [33] (81)	105 [57] (85)	...	...	...	...
Venezuela	Caracas	NA	132 [27] (81)	50 [57] (85)	...	...	...	...
NORTHERN AMERICA								
Canada	Hamilton	CCC	99 [56]	88 [55] (88)	...	...	30.5 [727]	24.0 [360] *
Canada	Hamilton	SR *1	112 [55]	93 [55] (88)	...	...	35.5 [696]	42.0 [259] (84-85) *
Canada	Montreal	CCC	69 [56]	59 [55] (88)	...	...	43.5 [614]	25.0 [360] (84-85)
Canada	Montreal	SR	84 [60]	59 [55] (88)	...	...	...	...
Canada	Montreal	SR	75 [49]	34 [45]	...	...	27.5 [557]	14.0 [299] (86-87) *
Canada	Toronto	CCC	59 [34] (81)	62 [48]	...	...	...	...
Canada	Toronto	SI	99 [58]	75 [59] (88)	...	...	16.0 [645]	12.0 [351] (84-85) *
Canada	Toronto	SR	76 [57]	53 [57]	...	...	20.0 [695]	8.0 [684]
Canada	Vancouver	CCC	76 [51]	40 [57]	...	...	...	...
Canada	Vancouver	CCR	62 [51]	38 [4] (86)	...	...	17.0 [614]	18.0 [335] (82-83) *
Canada	Vancouver	SI	79 [52]	58 [55] (88)	...	...	...	...
Canada	Vancouver	SR	...	29 [54]	...	...	...	...
United States	Azusa	SI	115 [57] (84)	114 [61]	...	...	...	...
United States	Birmingham	CCC	95 [290]	76 [285] (86)	...	...	...	...
United States	Birmingham	CCI	121 [290]	94 [59]	...	...	...	...
United States	Chattanooga	CCC	73 [45]	48 [59]	...	...	...	...
United States	Chattanooga	CCR	62 [43]	52 [25] (88)	...	...	...	...

TABLE 19 (continued)

Air Pollution in Urban Areas: 1980, 1990

| | | | Suspended Particulate Matter (mean annual values in kg/m³ and number of observations) | | | | Sulphur Dioxide | |
| | | | Total Concentrations (high-volume gravimetric or equivalent methode) | | Smoke Concentrations (smoke shade reflectance methode) | | (concentrations at selected GEMS / Air sites) | |
			1980	1990	1980	1990	1980-81	1988-89
United States (continued)								
United States	Chicago	CCI	129 [52]	79 [55]	...	...	...	...
United States	Chicago	CCI	95 [60] (82)	87 [60] (89)	...	...	...	...
United States	Chicago	CCR	72 [61] (82)	68 [42] (88)	...	...	...	...
United States	Houston	CCC	82 [52]	48 [18] (88)	...	...	...	...
United States	Houston	SR	93 [31]	54 [57] (86)	...	...	...	...
United States	Long Beach	SC	...	88 [61]	...	...	...	...
United States	New York City	CCI	63 [53]	67 [28]	...	...	50.5 [726]	40.0 [350] (86-87) *
United States	New York City	CCR	62 [50]	56 [61]	...	...	70.5 [725]	52.0 [364] (86-87) *
United States	New York City	SR	51 [56]	50 [58] (87)	...	...	40.0 [728]	27.0 [361] (86-87) *
OCEANIA								
Australia	Melbourne	CCC	73 [46]	...	...	...	7.5 [585]	10.0 [157] (84-85)
Australia	Sydney	CCC	118 [55]	138 [59] (85)	...	...	...	...
Australia	Sydney	SI	85 [56]	51 [54] (85)	...	...	35.0 [692]	13.0 [697] (84-85)
New Zealand	Auckland	SI	...	...	6 [331]	3 [342]	20.5 [698]	3.0 [682]
New Zealand	Christchurch	NA	...	22 [356]	...	...	...	...
New Zealand	Christchurch	SC	...	...	32 [316]	30 [210] (86)	28.0 [646]	16.0 [193] (86-87) *
New Zealand	Christchurch	SI	...	...	21 [354]	26 [212] (86)	35.5 [674]	43.0 [97] (86-87) *
New Zealand	Christchurch	SR	...	...	41 [325]	16 [184] (87)	21.0 [646]	20.5 [442] (86-87)

Source: United Nations Environment Programme, Environmental Data Reports 1991-1992 & 1993-1994.

This table is devoted to the Urban air pollution of some cities in 1980 and 1990 for some air pollutants such as Suspended Particulate Matter and Sulphur Dioxide.

Suspended Particulate Matter: Data have been grouped according to the method employed for the measurement of suspended particulate matter in air. Measurement of particles collected on a filter by the High-Volume Sampler is based on a mass or gravimetric determination. The Black Smoke Method involves drawing a known volume of air through a filter; the density or reflectivity of the resulting stain is then related to a weight of smoke particles by means of an established calibration curve. Measurements of airborne particles by the two different methods are not directly comparable.

Sulphur dioxide: Annual mean concentrations of SO_2 are based on data for two years, except where indicated. The total number of observations made during each two-year period is given in parentheses in order to provide an indication of the level of completeness of the data. Although many sites make observations on a daily basis, at some locations measurements are made less frequently, e.g. once every six days. Thus the use of the number of observations to assess data completeness must be viewed with some caution.

The number of observations made during the year are given in parentheses in order to provide an indication of the level of completeness of the data set. Although many sites make observations on a daily basis, at some locations measurements are made less frequently, for example, once every six days. As long as these measurements are made regularly throughout the year, this level of sampling will generate a representative annual mean. Thus the use of the number of observations to assess data quality must be viewed with some caution.

Notes:
The GEMS/Air site codes are as follows:

CCC = City Centre Commercial
CCI = City Centre Industrial
CCR = City Centre Residential
CCM = City Centre Mobile
SI = Suburban Industrial
SR = Suburban Residential
NA = Not Applicable, i.e., the site has not been assigned a GEMS/Air site code.

*1 Site location changed in 1985.
* Based on one year of measurements only.

TABLE 20

Energy, Transport and Transport Infrastructure

	Production Total (1000 Tera Joules)		Commercial Energy Consumption Total		Per Capita (Giga Joules)		Traditional Fuels (% of total consumption)		Density of Railway (km/1000 km²)	Density of Road Network (km/1000 km²)	Paved (%)	Motor Cars (per thousand population)
	1980	1992	1980	1992	1980	1992	1980	1992	1991	1991	1991	1991
WORLD TOTAL	271524	336531	250414	320794	56	58	6	6	...	...	...	110.1
More Developed Regions (*)	...	...	...	...	...	...	...	...	...	...	...	...
Less Developed Regions (+)	...	...	...	...	...	...	...	...	...	...	...	...
AFRICA	17113	21230	5693	8450	12	12	41	37	...	...	...	...
Algeria	2993	4626	726	1231	39	47	2	2	1.7	32	59	48.3 (90)
Angola	323	1100	31	26	4	3	70	68	2.0	59	12	17.7 (90)
Benin	...	12	5	7	1	1	88	88	5.1	87	11	7.3 (90)
Botswana	...	...	...	...	...	...	...	...	1.2	16	27	54.4
Burkina Faso	...	...	6	8	1	1	91	92	1.8 (80s)	35	17	6.5
Burundi	-	1	2	3	-	1	94	94	...	202	16	4.9
Cameroon	120	303	61	35	7	3	56	77	2.5	148	5	7.4
Cape Verde	...	...	1	2	3	5	...	...	...	323	31	9.3 (87)
Central African Republic	-	-	3	3	1	1	89	91	...	40	2	5.2 (90)
Chad	...	...	3	4	1	1	96	90	...	21	2	2.7 (87)
Comoros	...	-	1	1	3	2	...	...	...	404	72	10.2 (87)
Congo	135	364	4	23	3	10	78	49	2.3	28	11	20.0
Côte d'Ivoire	10	17	48	79	6	6	58	58	3.6	154	9	20.5 (90)
Djibouti	...	...	9	18	29	39	...	...	4.3	157	10	18.3 (87)
Egypt	1347	2370	590	1132	14	21	5	4	8.6	32	45	25.5
Equatorial Guinea	-	-	1	2	3	5	80	67	...	143	31	...
Ethiopia (former)	2	6	25	45	1	1	91	91	0.6	32	35	1.2
Gabon	386	615	25	31	23	25	32	47	1.2	32	8	26.8 (87)
Gambia	...	...	2	3	3	3	80	75	...	283	18	8.3 (89)
Ghana	23	22	44	65	4	4	61	70	3.9	154	23	8.3 (90)
Guinea	-	1	12	15	2	2	71	71	3.8	121	15 (90)	15.9
Guinea-Bissau	...	...	1	3	1	3	80	57	...	115	9	7.7 (87)
Kenya	4	20	67	84	4	3	79	82	4.6	117	15	12.6
Lesotho	...	...	...	...	...	...	...	...	0.1 (80s)	162	12	10.9 (87)
Liberia	1	1	22	4	12	1	65	92	5.0	62	39	14.1 (87)
Libyan Arab Jamahirya	3959	3217	214	494	72	101	2	1	...	45	78 (80s)	169.4 (90)
Madagascar	1	1	25	14	3	1	80	85	1.8	87	10	8.2 (87)
Malawi	1	3	10	11	2	1	92	90	6.6	112	19	¹ 4.8 (90)
Mali	-	1	6	7	1	1	87	89	0.5	12	15	3.8 (88)
Mauritania	...	-	9	39	6	18	-	-	0.6	7	11	9.7 (87)
Mauritius	-	-	9	19	9	17	59	49	...	1134	86	63.7
Morocco	29	22	187	312	9	12	6	4	4.0	140	46	¹ 40.3
Mozambique	61	1	46	15	4	1	73	91	3.9	45	15	4.6 (87)
Namibia	...	...	...	...	...	...	...	...	2.9	8	8 (80s)	...
Niger	1	5	8	14	2	2	79	77	...	16	22	6.3 (87)
Nigeria	4507	4039	322	700	4	6	68	60	3.8	121	28	3.7 (90)
Reunion	1	2	11	18	21	29	35	25	...	...	...	² 253.9
Rwanda	1	1	3	7	1	1	94	88	...	506	6	2.0 (90)
Sao Tome & Principe	...	-	...	1	...	8	...	-	...	250	42	26.1 (87)
Senegal	...	...	32	34	6	4	52	58	6.0	79	27	14.7 (87)
Seychelles	...	...	2	2	31	28	...	...	...	1079	70	78.6 (90)
Sierra Leone	...	...	8	5	2	1	90	86	1.2 (80s)	124	19	12.8 (87)
Somalia	...	...	13	13 (89)	3	2 (89)	77	86 (89)	...	34	28	1.6 (87)
South Africa	³ 2741	³ 3936	³ 2642	³ 3303	³ 81	³ 73	³ 5	³ 4	19.3 (80s)	160 (87)	29 (87)	¹ 137.6
Sudan	2	3	45	48	2	2	88	82	1.9	4	34	9.2 (87)
Swaziland	...	...	...	...	...	...	...	...	18.4	204	21	71.5 (90)
Togo	-	-	9	9	4	2	36	55	9.1	138	25	1.1 (87)
Tunisia	257	226	120	180	19	21	16	15	15.1	124	76	48.4 (87)
Uganda	2	3	10	15	1	1	96	90	4.7	122	15	2.0
United Republic of Tanzania	2	2	25	28	1	1	93	92	2.8	88	4	3.8 (90)
Western Sahara	...	...	2	3	15	12	...	...	...	...	...	...
Zaire	62	83	58	74	2	2	82	84	2.2	63	2	5.1 (87)
Zambia	47	38	67	51	12	6	56	72	2.6	52	16	⁴ 15.6 (87)
Zimbabwe	96	187	122	224	17	21	33	21	8.7	202	17	37.8
ASIA	72221	109435	46285	91197	18	28	13	10	...	1340 (88)	100 (88)	...
Afghanistan	108	9	22	23	2	1	68	71	...	29 (82)	15 (82)	3.7 (90)
Armenia	...	...	...	77	...	22	...	-	...	...	...	...
Azerbaijan	...	766	...	469	...	64	...	-	...	...	...	...
Bahrain	227	305	129	231	372	433	-	-	...	3891 (90)	75 (90)	259.0
Bangladesh	47	203	113	292	1	2	74	54	19.1 (90)	90 (89)	58 (89)	0.9
Bhutan	...	6	...	2	...	1	100	86	...	...	...	...
Brunei Darussalam	929	744	133	135	583	500	1	1	...	381 (89)	50 (89)	479.1
Cambodia	-	-	1	7	...	1	98	89	...	...	...	...
China	⁵ 18027	⁵ 30387	⁵ 16494	⁵ 28506	⁵ 17	⁵ 24	⁵ 9	⁵ 7	5.6 (90)	107	...	...
Cyprus	...	...	35	61	56	85	...	...	...	995 (88)	48 (87)	¹ 385.9
Dem. People's Rep. of Korea	1312	2560	1423	2821	80	125	4	1	70.6 (80s)	168 (80s)	2 (80s)	...
East Timor	...	...	1	...	2	...	86	...	...	...	...	...

TABLE 20 (continued)

Energy, Transport and Transport Infrastructure

	Production Total (1000 Tera Joules)		Commercial Energy Consumption Total		Per Capita (Giga Joules)		Traditional Fuels (% of total consumption)		Density of Railway (km/1000 km²)	Density of Road Network (km/1000 km²)	Paved (%)	Motor Cars (per thousand population)
	1980	1992	1980	1992	1980	1992	1980	1992	1991	1991	1991	1991
ASIA (continued)												
Gaza Strip (Palestine)	...	...	...	...	...	...	...	...	...	...	...	...
Georgia	...	16	...	208	...	38	...	1	...	...	...	109.2 (90)
Hong Kong	...	...	214	388	42	67	1	1	116.3 (90)	1470	100 (88)	63.0
India	3327	7915	4085	9021	6	10	34	24	18.9 (89)	599 (90)	[6] 49 (90)	[1] 7.8
Indonesia	3928	[7] 5767	1016	[7] 2145	7	[7] 11	52	[7] 41	3.5 (88)	140 (89)	44 (89)	16.6
Iran (Islamic Republic of)	3456	8372	1339	2998	35	49	-	1	1.4 (90)	24 (87)	66 (87)	[4] 50.7 (89)
Iraq	5615	1202	312	705	24	37	-	-	7.0 (80s)	100 (88)	81 (88)	57.5 (90)
Israel	6	1	258	491	67	96	-	-	25.6 (80s)	228 (80s)	100 (80s)	209.4 (90)
Japan	1239	3139	12744	17275	109	139	-	-	[8] 53.6 (89)	2967	67 (88)	[9] 473.3
Jordan	...	-	59	142	20	33	-	-	8.9 (80s)	67 (90)	100 (87)	[1] 51.4
Kazakhstan	...	4560	...	3174	...	186	-	-	...	...	...	...
Kuwait	3861	2403	202	233	147	118	-	-	...	240 (80s)	...	304.6 (89)
Kyrgyzstan	...	106	...	235	...	52	...	-	...	...	...	...
Lao People's Dem. Republic	3	3	6	5	2	1	85	89	...	119 (80s)	7 (80s)	...
Lebanon	3	1	74	148	28	52	3	3	21.7 (80s)	684 (80s)	80 (80s)	...
Macau	...	...	7	15	24	30	-	-	...	...	...	[1] 91.9
Malaysia	[10] 580	[10] 2133	[10] 358	[10] 992	[10] 26	[10] 53	[10] 16	[10] 8	6.3 (84)	154 (90)	68 (90)	[11] 131.6
Maldives	...	...	...	1	...	4	...	...	...	...	...	...
Mongolia	50	85	76	107	46	46	15	11	1.2 (80s)	30 (80s)	3 (80s)	...
Myanmar	83	75	63	67	2	2	72	75	4.8 (80s)	41 (80s)	12 (80s)	[1] 3.4
Nepal	1	3	6	19	-	1	96	92	0.7 (80s)	53	43 (80s)	...
Oman	598	1619	21	137	21	84	...	...	...	121 (90)	19 (90)	...
Pakistan	330	770	488	1092	6	9	27	22	11.0 (89)	140 (88)	53 (88)	[1] 8.2
Philippines	50	271	490	772	10	12	39	34	3.5 (82)	524 (88)	14 (88)	20.1 (90)
Qatar	1153	1432	192	525	780	1159	-	-	...	136 (80s)	67 (80s)	314.6 (90)
Republic of Korea	378	858	1534	4126	40	93	4	1	31.5 (89)	570 (89)	70 (89)	97.7
Saudi Arabia	21722	19756	742	2845	80	179	-	-	0.3 (90)	47 (90)	37 (86)	187.2 (90)
Singapore	...	...	263	690	109	249	-	-	59.0 (80s)	4716	95 (85)	157.3
Sri Lanka	5	10	48	78	3	4	59	54	22.1 (90)	396 (90)	41 (85)	19.1
Syrian Arab Republic	366	1193	215	502	24	38	-	-	12.1 (90)	181 (90)	94 (90)	19.5
Tajikistan	...	61	...	121	...	22	...	...	...	...	...	...
Thailand	19	635	507	1460	11	26	41	37	7.3 (87)	87 (89)	87 (89)	40.6
Turkey	422	743	936	1787	21	31	22	6	10.8 (88)	411 (88)	14 (88)	40.7
Turkmenistan	...	2569	...	467	...	121	...	...	...	...	...	...
United Arab Emirates	[12] 4040	[12] 5711	[12] 494	[12] 1276	[12] 504	[12] 764	...	...	...	187 (88)	6 (88)	...
Uzbekistan	...	1973	...	2025	...	94	...	...	...	...	...	...
Viet Nam	157	392	192	245	4	4	50	51	8.9 (80s)	261 (80s)	11 (80s)	...
Yemen	...	341	...	121	...	10	...	2	...	...	...	...
(former Dem. Rep)	...	33 (90)	29	70 (90)	16	28 (90)	6	4 (90)	...	33 (85)	19 (85)	...
(former Arab Rep)	...	354 (90)	16	46 (90)	3	5 (90)	...	...	...	187 (88)	6 (88)	...
EUROPE	37220	96018	62868	111210	130	153	1	1	...	...	...	...
Albania	146	51	91	55	33	17	15	21	19.8 (80s)	...	...	[13] 0.9 (90)
Andorra	...	...	...	...	...	...	...	...	...	...	...	...
Austria	283	256	893	950	119	122	2	3	69.5 (80s)	1336	100 (88)	[14] 484.7
Belarus	...	161	...	1537	...	149	...	1	26.9 (88)	[15] 229 (87)	...	...
Belgium	219	494	1733	2013	176	201	-	-	116.5 (88)	4656	96 (87)	435.7
Bulgaria	500	358	1387	824	154	92	1	2	38.8 (88)	330 (88)	95 (88)	161.8 (90)
Channel Islands	...	...	...	...	...	...	...	...	...	...	...	...
Czechoslovakia (former)	1947	1780 (91)	2856	2606 (91)	187	166 (91)	1	1 (91)	102.5 (88)	571	100 (88)	245.0
Denmark	13	485	789	704	154	136	...	1	57.5 (88)	1648	100 (88)	[16] 372.9
Estonia	...	153	...	248	...	157	...	4	...	...	...	166.2
Faeroe Islands	-	-	6	8	146	170	...	...	...	...	...	...
Finland	87	264	774	907	162	181	5	3	17.4 (88)	[17] 228	59 (88)	438.5
France	[18] 1474	[18] 4462	[18] 6953	[18] 9110	[18] 129	[18] 159	[18] 1	[18] 1	62.7 (88)	[19] 1469	100 (88)	486.5
Germany	...	6700	...	13854	...	173	...	...	...	1759	...	[20] 508.5
(former Fed. Rep)	4789	5399 (90)	10534	11218 (90)	171	183 (90)	-	- (90)	119.6 (80s)	2023	99 (87)	...
(former Dem. Rep)	2451	2661 (90)	3569	3474 (90)	213	214 (90)	-	- (90)	129.5 (88)	1154	...	...
Gibraltar	...	...	1	1	34	32	-	-	...	...	...	796.4 (90)
Greece	140	330	590	967	61	95	3	1	18.8 (88)	876 (87)	83 (85)	251.6
Hungary	644	574	1189	1029	111	98	2	2	84.1 (88)	1139	54 (87)	223.5
Iceland	11	24	33	47	143	181	...	...	...	107	17 (88)	530.6
Ireland	76	140	326	408	96	117	-	-	27.7 (88)	1309	94 (88)	271.8 (90)
Isle of Man	...	...	...	...	...	...	...	...	...	...	...	...
Italy	[21] 770	[21] 1174	[21] 5125	[21] 6809	[21] 91	[21] 118	[21] 1	[21] 1	64.9 (88)	1012	100 (86)	544.1
Latvia	...	13	...	254	...	95	...	8	...	...	...	154.9
Liechtenstein	...	...	...	...	...	...	...	...	...	...	...	...
Lithuania	...	164	...	457	...	122	...	2	...	...	...	171.8
Luxembourg	1	2	144	155	395	410	-	-	104.6 (88)	1962 (88)	99 (88)	[20] 584.9
Malta	...	...	14	21	38	58	...	...	...	4688 (88)	...	402.5
Monaco	...	...	...	...	...	...	...	...	...	...	100 (88)	...
Netherlands	3455	3064	2727	3164	192	209	-	-	75.8 (88)	[22] 3163	88 (88)	410.0
Norway	2423	6044	770	844	188	197	1	1	12.9 (88)	278	67 (88)	[1] 457.4
Poland	5095	3776	5180	3922	145	102	-	1	77.4 (88)	1167	61 (88)	[24] 192.4

TABLE 20 *(continued)*

Energy, Transport and Transport Infrastructure

	Production Total (1000 Tera Joules)		Commercial Energy Consumption Total		Per Capita (Giga Joules)		Traditional Fuels (% of total consumption)		Density of Railway (km/1000 km²)	Density of Road Network (km/1000 km²)	Paved (%)	Motor Cars (per thousand population)
	1980	1992	1980	1992	1980	1992	1980	1992	1991	1991	1991	1991
EUROPE (Continued)												
Portugal	32	22	329	610	34	62	1	1	39.2 (80s)	920	100 (86)	25 370.9
Republic of Moldova	...	1	...	216	...	50	...	-	...	...	...	53.1
Romania	2512	1353	2931	1847	132	79	1	2	48.1 (80s)	307 (87)	49 (87)	...
Russian Federation	...	46996	...	32128	...	216	...	2	...	...	...	...
San Marino	...	...	...	...	...	...	...	...	...	...	...	...
Spain	623	1249	2590	3562	69	91	-	1	28.1 (88)	630 (88)	56 (86)	384.8
Sweden	310	963	1304	1759	158	203	11	7	25.7 (88)	302	71 (88)	497.0
Switzerland	170	378	682	978	107	143	1	1	113.1 (80s)	1720	...	26 489.0
Ukraine	...	4961	...	9165	...	176	...	-	37.8 (88)	27 270 (87)	...	70.8
United Kingdom	8211	9019	7942	9165	142	158	-	-	69.2 (88)	1544 (88)	100 (88)	413.4
Yugoslavia (former)	838	626 (91)	1408	1212 (91)	63	51 (91)	2	1 (91)	36.5 (88)	570 (88)	58 (86)	67.0 (90)
LATIN AMERICA	...	...	...	...	...	...	...	...	...	...	...	...
Anguilla	...	...	...	...	...	...	...	...	...	...	...	...
Antigua & Barbuda	...	...	2	4	27	61	-	-	...	2648 (86)	...	359.4
Argentina	1499	2298	1445	1934	51	58	6	5	12.3 (90)	76 (86)	27 (86)	177.7 (90)
Aruba	...	...	...	9	...	145	...	...	...	...	...	...
Bahamas	...	...	34	25	162	95	-	-	...	168 (85)	73 (85)	324.2 (90)
Barbados	2	3	9	14	35	54	25	7	...	3651	99	186.7 (89)
Belize	...	...	3	4	21	20	50	50	...	131 (87)	13 (80s)	25.8
Bolivia	137	168	62	81	11	11	22	19	3.4 (92)	38 (88)	4 (88)	30.6
Brazil	1011	2424	2711	3656	22	24	43	34	3.5 (90)	175 (90)	10 (90)	88.0 (90)
British Virgin Islands	...	...	-	1	-	59	...	...	...	...	...	387.5 (90)
Cayman Islands	...	...	1	4	59	138	...	...	...	...	...	496.3
Chile	169	237	334	520	30	38	14	14	9.1	105	15	87.0
Colombia	642	1814	698	837	27	25	19	22	2.8 (90)	113 (89)	8 (89)	4 41.4 (86)
Costa Rica	8	13	37	60	16	19	35	38	10.9 (90)	696 (90)	15 (90)	1 89.0
Cuba	13	41	398	365	41	34	28	36	43.7 (89)	420 (86)	27 (86)	43.3 (88)
Dominica	-	-	-	1	-	14	...	...	...	1547 (84)	...	131.0 (90)
Dominican Republic	2	3	82	134	15	18	29	17	10.7 (80s)	362 (84)	80 (84)	28 35.5 (87)
Ecuador	449	730	166	249	21	23	28	17	3.4 (92)	152 (92)	14 (92)	36.9
El Salvador	5	19	28	63	6	12	62	41	28.6 (92)	589 (92)	14 (87)	22.6 (90)
Falkland Islands (Malvinas)	...	-	...	-	...	-	...	...	...	...	...	...
French Guiana	...	...	5	8	76	77	17	11	...	1200 (88)	40 (88)	290.6 (90)
Grenada	...	...	1	2	9	22	...	...	...	2882 (83)	...	...
Guadeloupe	...	...	7	15	22	38	22	6	...	...	...	311.6
Guatemala	10	21	57	76	8	8	55	64	10.5 (89)	120 (89)	23 (89)	20.4 (90)
Guyana	-	-	21	12	24	15	25	37	...	41 (85)	8 (80s)	41.5 (90)
Haiti	1	1	10	10	2	1	83	86	1.5 (80s)	133 (85)	17 (85)	5.5 (90)
Honduras	3	8	27	44	7	8	61	58	8.9 (89)	101 (90)	21 (90)	16.2 (90)
Jamaica	1	-	114	109	53	44	5	5	27.1 (80s)	1579 (87)	30 (80s)	45.2
Martinique	...	...	9	19	29	52	-	-	...	...	...	338.9 (90)
Mexico	5806	7942	3476	4887	50	55	5	5	13.5 (92)	125 (92)	36 (92)	127.4
Montserrat	...	...	...	1	...	91	...	...	...	...	...	...
Netherlands Antilles	...	...	29 122	30 39	29 494	30 223	...	...	...	...	...	...
Nicaragua	2	18	27	48	10	12	53	44	1.7 (92)	118 (87)	11 (87)	20.2 (90)
Panama	31 4	31 7	31 49	31 63	31 25	31 25	31 30	31 21	6.3 (92)	131 (92)	32 (92)	78.4
Paraguay	2	98	22	43	7	10	67	56	1.1 (90)	36 (85)	14 (85)	49.9
Peru	485	317	351	319	20	14	17	20	1.9	54 (89)	11 (89)	28.3
Puerto Rico	1	1	341	239	107	66	...	...	...	...	87 (86)	438.9
Saint Kitts & Nevis	...	...	1	1	19	24	50	50	...	883 (85)	44 (85)	140.5
Saint Lucia	...	...	2	14	17	102	...	...	...	1565 (88)	...	108.3 (90)
St. Vincent & Grenadines	-	-	1	1	10	9	...	...	...	2692 (87)	27 (87)	75.0
Suriname	3	16	35	23	99	53	3	4	...	56 (90)	26 (90)	1 133.8
Trinidad & Tobago	615	525	219	312	205	247	1	1	...	1009 (85)	...	164.9 (90)
Turks & Caicos Islands	...	...	...	...	...	...	...	...	...	...	...	...
Uruguay	13	29	81	76	28	24	15	28	16.9	54 (92)	2 (80s)	140.8
US Virgin Islands	...	...	128	95	1306	888	-	-	...	...	...	...
Venezuela	5684	6549	1437	1902	92	94	1	1	0.4 (90)	110 (86)	33 (86)	104.9 (90)
NORTHERN AMERICA	...	...	...	...	...	...	...	...	...	...	...	...
Bermuda	...	...	6	6	85	97	...	...	...	...	...	382.3
Canada	8232	12199	7449	8794	309	321	1	1	9.1 (80s)	93	29 (87)	1 594.8
Greenland	-	-	8	7	154	123	...	...	...	...	...	1 60.7
St. Pierre & Miquelon	...	...	1	1	167	167	...	...	...	...	...	...
United States	59954	67157	69297	80292	304	315	1	1	21.9 (88)	666	56 (87)	754.9 (90)
OCEANIA	3482	7210	3085	4519	134	164	5	5	...	...	...	...
American Samoa	...	...	6	4	188	80	...	...	...	...	...	115.4 (85)
Australia	3311	32 6695	2673	32 3804	182	32 216	4	32 4	4.6 (89)	111	50 (85)	570.6
Cook Islands	...	...	9	-	474	-	...	...	...	...	...	...
Fiji	...	1	10	11	16	15	47	52	35.2 (80s)	240 (80s)	13 (80s)	1 103.9
French Polynesia	...	-	4	9	27	43	...	...	...	...	...	...
Guam	...	...	27	21	250	151	...	...	...	...	...	651.2 (89)

TABLE 20 (continued)

Energy, Transport and Transport Infrastructure

	Production Total (1000 Tera Joules)		Commercial Energy Consumption Total		Per Capita (Giga Joules)		Traditional Fuels (% of total consumption)		Density of Railway (km/1000 km²)	Density of Road Network (km/1000 km²)	Paved (%)	Motor Cars (per thousand population)
	1980	1992	1980	1992	1980	1992	1980	1992	1991	1991	1991	1991
OCEANIA (continued)												
Kiribati	...	...	...	...	...	...	...	...	...	...	...	...
Marshall Islands	...	...	...	...	...	...	...	...	...	...	...	...
Micronesia, Fed. States of	...	...	...	...	...	...	...	...	...	...	...	...
Nauru	...	...	2	2	286	200	...	...	...	...	...	...
New Caledonia	1	1	27	24	190	139	-	-	...	...	...	434.5 [90]
New Zealand	169	510	293	601	92	174	-	-	15.8 [84]	343	55 [87]	547.5
Niue	...	...	...	...	...	...	...	...	...	...	...	...
Northern Mariana Islands	...	...	...	...	...	...	...	...	...	...	...	...
Pacific Islands (Palau)	...	-	[28] 2	[29] 3	[33] 15	[34] 14	...	...	...	...	...	...
Papua New Guinea	1	2	26	33	8	8	67	65	...	43 [82]	5 [82]	[1] 12.0 [87]
Samoa	-	-	1	2	6	13	50	33	...	735 [81]	12 [81]	36.5 [89]
Solomon Islands	...	...	1	2	4	6	67	60	...	75 [80s]	1 [80s]	...
Tonga	...	...	1	1	10	10	...	...	...	...	...	60.8
Tuvalu	...	...	...	...	...	...	...	...	...	...	...	...
Vanuatu	...	...	1	1	8	6	-	-	...	...	...	[1] 43.1
Wake Islands	...	...	1	1	500	250	...	...	...	...	...	...
Wallis & Futuna Islands	...	...	...	...	...	...	...	...	...	...	...	...
U.S.S.R. (FORMER)	56737	64994 [91]	43174	54726 [91]	163	188 [91]	2	1	6.5 [88]	[27] 71 [87]	74 [87]	[2] 59.3 [89]

Sources: United Nations, Energy Statistics Yearbooks 1983 & 1992. World Resources Institute, World Resources 1992-93 & 1994-95. International Road Federation, World Road Statistics 1984-1988. United Nations, Statistical Yearbook for Asia and The Pacific 1992. United Nations, African Statistical Yearbook 1990/91. United Nations, Statistical Yearbook for Latin America and the Caribbean 1993, United Nations, Statistical Abstract of the Region of the Economic and Social Commission for Western Asia 1981-90. United Nations, The Environment in Europe and North-America. Annotated Statistics 1992. Organization for Economic Cooperation and Development, OECD Environmental Data Compendium 1993.

Commercial Energy Production includes: solids (hard coal, lignite, peat and oil shale), liquids (crude petroleum and natural gas liquids), gas (natural gas) and electricity (primary electricity generation from hydro, nuclear, geothermal, wind, tide, wave and solar sources). Data refer to the first stage of commercial primary energy production: accordingly, for hard coal the data refer to mine production; for crude petroleum and natural gas to production at oil and gas wells etc.

Commercial Energy Consumption includes solids (consumption of primary forms of solid fuels, net imports and changes in stocks of secondary fuels), liquid (consumption of energy petroleum products, input of crude petroleum to thermal power plants), gases (consumption of natural gas, net import and changes in stocks of gasworks and coke-oven gas) and electricity (production of primary electricity and net imports of electricity). Consumption refers to 'apparent consumption' and are derived from the formula: 'production + imports – exports – bunkers +/– stock changes'.

Traditional Fuels include fuelwood, charcoal, bagasse, animal, vegetal and other wastes.
Motor Cars: refer to passenger cars and commercial vehicles. Special purpose vehicles such as two- or three-wheeled cycles and motorcycles, trams, trolley-buses, ambulances, hearses, military vehicles operated by police or other governmental security organizations are excluded.

Notes:
1. Including some special-purpose vehicles.
2. Passenger cars only.
3. Including South Africa, Botswana, Lesotho, Swaziland and Namibia.
4. Including vehicles no longer in circulation.
5. Excluding data for Taiwan Province.
6. Surfaced roads.
7. Including East Timor.
8. Japan National Railway only.
9. Excluding small vehicles.
10. Comprising Peninsular Malaysia, Sabah and Sarawak.
11. Excluding tractors.
12. Comprising the seven emirates of former Trucial Oman: Abu Dhabi, Ajiman, Dubai, Fujairah, Ras al Khaim, Sharjah and Umm al Qaiwain.
13. Commercial vehicles only.
14. Including vehicles operated by police or other governmental security organizations and farm tractors.
15. Public and departmental road suitable for motor traffic.
16. Including vehicles operated by police or other governmental security organizations; Including Faeroe Islands.
17. Urban streets are excluded.
18. Including Monaco.
19. Excluding certain rural roads (700,000 km in 1987).
20. Including farm tractors.
21. Including San Marino.
22. Excluding unsurfaced roads.
23. Including vehicles operated by police or other governmental security organizations; Excluding diplomatic corps vehicles.
24. Excluding buses and tractors, but including special lorries.
25. Excluding Madeira and Azores; Including special-purpose vehicles.
26. Including vehicles operated by police or other governmental security organizations; Excluding small vehicles.
27. All roads suitable for motor traffic.
28. Excluding jeeps.
29. Comprising Aruba, Bonaire, Curacao, Saba, St. Eustatius, the Dutch part of St. Martin.
30. Comprising Bonaire, Curacao, Saba, St. Eustatius, the Dutch part of St. Martin.
31. Including former Panama Canal Zone.
32. Including Christmas Island.
33. Comprising of Caroline, Mariana and Marshall Islands.
34. Including data for Federated States of Micronesia, Marshall Islands and Northern Mariana Islands.

TABLE 21

Social Indicators

	Housing Expenditure (% of GDP)			Telephones # / 100	School Enrolment (Gross Ratio)		Access to Health Care (%)	Population per Hospital Bed		Population in Poverty		
	1980	1985	1990	1991	Primary	Secondary	1988-1993	1975	1990	Total (%)	Rural (%)	Urban (%)
										1980-1990		
WORLD TOTAL	...	...	...	...	98 (92)	53 (92)	...	...	...	...	...	...
More Developed Regions (*)	...	...	...	...	...	...	...	...	...	...	...	...
Less Developed Regions (+)	...	...	...	...	...	...	...	...	...	...	...	...
Africa	...	...	...	...	74 (92)	30 (92)	...	...	...	...	...	...
Algeria	...	...	6	3.4	99 (92)	59 (92)	88	352 (70)	400	23	25	20
Angola	...	...	8 (89)	0.8	91 (90)	12 (90)	30	368 (70)	771	...	65	...
Benin	...	10	...	0.3	66 (91)	12 (91)	18	851 (70)	684 (80)	...	65	...
Botswana	8	5	...	2.6	116 (92)	54 (92)	89	...	...	43	55	30
Burkina Faso	...	...	15	0.2	37 (91)	8 (91)	49	1750 (70)	3392	...	90	...
Burundi	...	9	...	0.2	69 (92)	7 (92)	80	890	1476 (86)	84	85	55
Cameroon	8	11	...	0.3	101 (90)	28 (90)	41	400	393	37	40	15
Cape Verde	...	...	4 (89)	2.3	116 (90)	24 (91)	...	710 (70)	457 (80)	...	40	...
Central African Republic	...	...	11	0.2	68 (89)	12 (89)	45	542 (70)	1171	...	90	...
Chad	...	...	8	0.1	65 (91)	9 (91)	30	763 (70)	1373 (91)	54	56	30
Comoros	...	...	4	0.7	79 (91)	18 (91)	82 (82)	476 (70)	...	...	50	...
Congo	...	4	...	0.7	...	...	83	218 (70)	...	...	80	...
Côte d'Ivoire	6	3	...	0.6	69 (91)	24 (91)	30	864 (70)	1260	...	...	30
Djibouti	...	...	6 (89)	1.4	41 (93)	14 (92)	37 (80)	179 (70)	...	...	70	...
Egypt	...	6	...	3.6	101 (91)	80 (91)	99	491	536	23	25	21
Equatorial Guinea	...	...	12	0.4	...	...	...	...	...	67	70	60
Ethiopia (former)	14	12	...	1 0.3	22 (92)	11 (92)	44 (84)	3500	4141	60	63	...
Gabon	...	...	1	1.8	...	...	90	101 (70)	800 (85)	...	41	...
Gambia	...	...	8 (89)	1.6	69 (92)	20 (92)	90 (85)	...	600 (85)	...	85	...
Ghana	10 (78)	...	6	0.3	74 (91)	38 (91)	60	800	685	42	54	20
Guinea	...	...	9	0.2	42 (92)	12 (92)	80	562 (70)	1804	...	70	...
Guinea-Bissau	...	...	12	0.6	60 (88)	7 (88)	40	572 (70)	562 (80)	...	75	...
Kenya	8	8	...	0.8	95 (90)	27 (92)	77	800	623	52	55	10
Lesotho	...	...	...	0.6	106 (92)	26 (92)	80	597	...	54	55	50
Liberia	...	8 (86)	...	0.1	35 (86)	...	39	607	...	20	23	...
Libyan Arab Jamahirya	...	...	14	5.7	...	...	100 (83)	262 (70)	246	...	...	...
Madagascar	10	10	...	0.3	79 (93)	15 (93)	65	400	1140	43	50	21
Malawi	9	7	...	0.3	66 (90)	4 (90)	80	650 (70)	645	82	90	25
Mali	5	7	...	0.1	25 (91)	7 (91)	20 (80)	1400	...	54	60	27
Mauritania	...	...	...	0.4	62 (92)	15 (92)	45	2904	1278 (84)	...	80	...
Mauritius	...	14	...	6.0	106 (91)	54 (91)	100	300	300 (85)	8	12	...
Morocco	10	7	...	1.9	69 (92)	35 (92)	70	700	809	37	45	28
Mozambique	...	...	9	0.4	60 (92)	7 (92)	39	850 (70)	1280	59	65	40
Namibia	...	...	...	3.8	124 (92)	52 (92)	72	...	...	...	...	...
Niger	...	...	...	0.1	29 (90)	7 (90)	32	1974	...	...	35	...
Nigeria	7	3	...	0.2	76 (91)	23 (91)	66	1799	599	40	51	21
Reunion	...	...	...	28.5	...	...	...	121 (70)	...	...	...	...
Rwanda	...	13	...	0.2	77 (91)	10 (91)	80	805	602	85	90	30
Sao Tome & Principe	...	...	13	1.8	...	...	...	37 (70)	...	...	50	...
Senegal	12	10	...	0.6	59 (91)	17 (91)	40	775	1385	...	70	...
Seychelles	...	...	12 (89)	11.8	...	...	99 (84)	200	201 (85)	...	20	...
Sierra Leone	...	13	...	0.4	48 (90)	16 (90)	38	1103	830 (80)	...	65	...
Somalia	...	12	...	0.2	11 (85)	7 (85)	27	845	1333	60	70	...
South Africa	5	7	13	8.8	109 (92)	71 (92)	...	...	...	...	...	...
St. Helena	...	...	...	15.9	...	...	...	...	...	...	...	...
Sudan	11 (79)	13 (81)	...	0.2	51 (91)	21 (91)	51	1000	959	...	85	...
Swaziland	...	...	4	1.9	115 (92)	50 (92)	...	296 (70)	...	48	50	45
Togo	...	...	9	0.3	111 (90)	23 (90)	61	700	686	...	30	...
Tunisia	13	9	...	4.1	120 (93)	49 (92)	90	400	516	17	15	20
Uganda	...	...	12	0.2	2 80 (88)	2 14 (88)	49	607	1248	...	80	...
United Republic of Tanzania	7	7	...	0.3	68 (92)	5 (92)	76	677 (76)	938	58	60	10
Zaire	...	3	10 (89)	0.1	70 (90)	24 (87)	26	311	701	70	90	...
Zambia	6	8	...	3 0.8	92 (90)	20 (88)	75	300	...	64	80	47
Zimbabwe	6	8	...	1 1.2	119 (93)	47 (92)	85	300	1970	...	60	...
ASIA	...	...	...	...	104 (92)	49 (92)	...	...	...	...	...	...
Afghanistan	...	...	...	0.2	24 (89)	8 (89)	29	5025 (70)	4003	53	60	18
Armenia	...	...	5	17.7	...	...	...	...	114 (88)	...	...	...
Azerbaijan	...	...	5	9.0	...	...	...	...	101 (88)	...	...	...
Bahrain	...	...	...	1 19.4	93 (92)	99 (92)	100 (85)	230 (70)	...	...	...	...
Bangladesh	...	15	...	0.2	77 (90)	19 (90)	45	6467 (70)	3113	78	86	...
Bhutan	...	...	...	0.2	...	...	65	...	1400 (86)	...	90	...
Brunei Darussalam	...	...	...	14.8	113 (92)	72 (92)	96 (84)	285 (70)	319 (82)	...	...	...
Cambodia	...	...	5	0.1	...	...	53	925 (70)	476	...	...	...
China	6 (81)	...	...	0.7	121 (92)	54 (92)	90	600	388	9	13	...
Cyprus	6	7	...	39.2	4 102 (91)	4 94 (91)	100 (85)	186 (70)	...	...	9	...
Dem. People's Rep. of Korea	...	...	...	3.6	104 (87)	...	100 (84)	...	...	...	20	...
Georgia	...	...	5	10.3	...	...	...	...	90 (88)	...	...	...

TABLE 21 (continued)

Social Indicators

	Housing Expenditure (% of GDP)			Telephones # / 100	School Enrolment (Gross Ratio)		Access to Health Care (%)	Population per Hospital Bed		Population in Poverty		
	1980	1985	1990	1991	Primary	Secondary	1988 - 1993	1975	1990	Total (%)	Rural (%)	Urban (%)
											1980 - 1990	
ASIA (continued)												
Hong Kong	9	10	...	45.9	108 (91)	75 (92)	99	198	234	...	...	...
India	7	7	...	0.7	102 (92)	49 (92)	85	1700	1371	40	42	33
Indonesia	8	...	...	0.7	115 (92)	43 (92)	80	1222	1503	25	27	20
Iran (Islamic Republic of)	8 (75)	15	...	4.1	109 (92)	62 (92)	80	725 (70)	724	...	30	...
Iraq	...	...	...	3.6	89 (92)	43 (92)	93	513 (70)	603	...	30	...
Israel	12	13	...	34.9	94 (92)	86 (92)	100 (84)	200	220	...	...	...
Japan	10	11	...	[1] 45.4	102 (92)	97 (91)	...	80 (70)	64	...	...	...
Jordan	6	6	...	6.4	105 (92)	53 (92)	97	975	519	16	17	14
Kazakhstan	...	...	5	11.1	...	...	...	...	75 (88)	...	...	...
Kirgyzstan	...	...	4	7.3	...	55 (92)	...	...	85 (88)	...	...	...
Kuwait	...	...	...	16.1	60 (92)	55 (92)	100	207 (70)	...	...	...	...
Lao People's Dem. Republic	...	...	16	0.1	98 (91)	22 (91)	67	1078 (70)	399	...	85	...
Lebanon	...	...	...	11.1	111 (91)	69 (91)	95	230 (70)	...	...	15	...
Macau	...	...	...	22.3	...	...	...	182 (70)	...	...	...	...
Malaysia	5 (78)	...	...	9.9	93 (92)	60 (92)	...	299	430	16	22	8
Maldives	...	...	...	3.5	...	...	...	...	...	...	40	...
Mongolia	...	...	14	3.0	89 (91)	77 (91)	95	105 (70)	89 (80)	...	...	...
Myanmar	...	...	...	0.2	105 (90)	23 (90)	48	1176 (70)	1591	35	40	...
Nepal	...	13	...	0.3	102 (92)	36 (92)	...	7100	4010	60	61	51
Oman	...	...	11 (88)	7.6	100 (92)	64 (92)	96	...	...	...	6	...
Pakistan	13	12	...	0.9	46 (90)	21 (90)	55	1900	1769	28	29	26
Philippines	7	15	...	1.0	109 (92)	76 (92)	76	600	780	54	64	40
Qatar	...	...	...	21.9	95 (92)	88 (92)	95 (82)	181 (70)	...	...	...	...
Republic of Korea	7	6	...	33.3	102 (93)	93 (93)	100	1900	339	5	4	5
Saudi Arabia	...	...	13	8.4	78 (92)	51 (92)	97	846 (70)	377	...	...	...
Singapore	6	6	...	40.2	107 (91)	69 (91)	100	270	275	...	...	...
Sri Lanka	5	4	...	0.7	107 (92)	75 (92)	93	300	365	39	46	15
Syrian Arab Republic	8 (75)	...	...	3.9	107 (92)	48 (92)	90	1000	920	...	54	...
Tajikistan	...	...	5	4.8	...	...	...	...	96 (88)	...	...	...
Thailand	4 (75)	5	...	[5] 2.8	97 (92)	33 (90)	90	899	626	30	34	17
Turkey	...	9	...	14.3	113 (91)	51 (91)	...	500	505	...	14	...
Turkmenistan	...	...	5	6.3	...	...	...	...	92 (88)	...	...	...
United Arab Emirates	...	...	...	29.5	118 (92)	72 (92)	99	...	...	...	...	...
Uzbekistan	...	...	5	7.1	...	...	...	...	83 (88)	...	...	...
Viet Nam	...	...	5	0.1	108 (92)	33 (92)	90	...	261	54	60	...
Yemen	...	...	...	1.1	...	...	36	1155	1136	...	30	...
(former Dem. Rep)	...	...	...	...	88 (90)	21 (89)	...	...	...	...	...	...
(former Arab Rep)	...	...	...	...	76 (90)	31 (90)	...	...	...	...	...	...
EUROPE	...	...	...	...	**98 (92)**	**94 (92)**	...	...	...	...	...	...
Albania	...	4	...	1.3	101 (90)	79 (90)	...	141 (70)	246	...	...	...
Andorra	...	...	...	38.3	...	...	...	...	...	...	...	...
Austria	9	11	...	43.2	104 (92)	106 (92)	...	92 (70)	94	...	...	...
Belarus	...	...	5	16.3	...	...	...	...	74 (88)	...	...	...
Belgium	11	13	...	41.0	99 (91)	102 (91)	100 (84)	120 (70)	121	...	...	...
Bulgaria	...	...	7	24.6	90 (92)	70 (92)	100 (83)	129 (70)	104	...	...	...
Channel Islands	...	...	...	60.9	...	...	...	...	...	...	...	...
Czechoslovakia (former)	...	...	3	15.7	95 (91)	79 (91)	100 (84)	97 (70)	126	...	...	...
Denmark	13	14	...	[1] 57.7	96 (91)	110 (91)	100 (83)	103 (70)	177	...	...	...
Estonia	...	...	4	21.0	85 (92)	91 (92)	...	...	82 (88)	...	...	...
Faeroe Islands	...	...	...	50.5	...	...	...	...	...	...	...	...
Finland	9	10	...	54.4	100 (92)	124 (92)	100 (84)	77 (70)	93	...	...	...
France	10	12	...	51.1	106 (92)	102 (92)	...	139 (70)	109	...	...	...
Germany	11	13	...	42.0	94 (92)	98 (92)	100 (84)	73 (70)	118	...	...	...
(former Fed. Rep)	...	...	...	48.9 (90)	105 (89)	104 (89)	...	...	...	...	...	...
(former Dem. Rep)	...	...	...	11.7 (90)	106 (89)	79 (89)	...	...	...	...	...	...
Gibraltar	...	...	...	37.2	...	...	...	...	...	...	...	...
Greece	8	8	...	41.3	97 (89)	98 (89)	...	200	197	...	...	...
Hungary	5	6	...	10.7	89 (91)	82 (91)	100 (84)	123 (70)	99	...	...	...
Iceland	...	...	...	52.7	101 (89)	99 (89)	100 (82)	...	...	...	...	...
Ireland	6	8	...	30.0	103 (91)	103 (91)	100 (83)	79 (70)	101	...	...	...
Italy	8	10	...	40.0	95 (92)	77 (92)	100 (84)	95 (70)	133	...	...	...
Latvia	...	...	5	23.9	86 (92)	85 (92)	...	...	72 (88)	...	...	...
Liechtenstein	...	...	...	62.5	...	...	...	...	...	...	...	...
Lithuania	...	...	4	21.6	92 (92)	79 (92)	...	...	79 (88)	...	...	...
Luxembourg	12	13	...	51.1	90 (90)	75 (90)	100 (84)	86 (70)	88 (80)	...	...	...
Malta	6	5	...	39.0	110 (90)	85 (90)	100 (84)	100	...	...	...	...
Monaco	...	...	...	92.9	...	...	...	...	...	...	...	...
Netherlands	9	12	...	47.7	98 (92)	117 (92)	100 (84)	94 (70)	170	...	...	...
Norway	7	9	...	51.5	99 (92)	111 (92)	...	91 (70)	211	...	...	...
Poland	5	4	...	9.3	98 (92)	84 (92)	100 (82)	131 (70)	153	...	...	...
Portugal	12	6	...	27.3	120 (91)	81 (91)	100 (83)	193	226	...	...	...

TABLE 21 (continued)

Social Indicators

	Housing Expenditure (% of GDP)			Telephones # / 100	School Enrolment (Gross Ratio)		Access to Health Care (%)	Population per Hospital Bed		Population in Poverty		
	1980	1985	1990	1991	Primary	Secondary	1988 - 1993	1975	1990	Total (%)	Rural (%)	Urban (%)
										1980 - 1990		
EUROPE (continued)												
Republic of Moldova	...	...	5	11.3	...	...	... (84)	...	77 (88)	...	...	...
Romania	4 (75)	...	...	10.5	88 (92)	82 (92)	100 (84)	120 (70)	113	...	...	...
Russian Federation	...	...	3	15.0	...	...	...	...	73 (88)	...	...	...
San Marino	...	...	...	47.0	...	...	...	...	...	...	...	...
Spain	8	11	...	34.0	107 (91)	109 (91)	95 (85)	192 (70)	209	...	...	...
Sweden	...	14	...	68.7	101 (92)	96 (92)	100 (83)	67 (70)	161	...	...	...
Switzerland	12	12 (84)	...	60.3	105 (92)	92 (92)	100 (83)	90 (70)	93	...	...	...
Ukraine	...	...	5	15.6	...	...	...	...	75 (88)	...	...	...
United Kingdom	11	13	...	44.5	104 (90)	86 (90)	100 (85)	105 (70)	160	...	...	...
Yugoslavia (former)	5	6	...	10.5	94 (90)	80 (90)	100 (83)	200	168	...	...	...
LATIN AMERICA	...	...	...	...	106 (92)	53 (92)	...	...	...	...	...	...
Antigua & Barbuda	...	...	...	28.8	...	...	100 (85)	153 (70)	...	...	50	...
Argentina	7	...	...	9.8	107 (91)	71 (91)	71	179 (70)	216	16	20	15
Aruba	...	...	...	32.3	...	...	...	...	...	...	...	...
Bahamas	12	14	...	23.8	105 (92)	93 (92)	100 (84)	196 (70)	227 (80)	...	...	...
Barbados	...	12	...	30.2	106 (91)	87 (89)	100 (83)	98 (70)	117 (80)	15	23	...
Belize	...	...	10 (89)	10.4	...	...	...	185 (70)	301 (86)	...	65	...
Bolivia	10	...	...	2.5	85 (90)	34 (90)	67	499	828	60	86	30
Brazil	8	...	...	6.6	106 (91)	39 (91)	...	200	301	47	73	38
Cayman Islands	...	...	...	45.5	...	...	...	...	...	...	...	...
Chile	10	...	...	7.4	96 (92)	70 (92)	97	265 (70)	318	...	25	...
Colombia	9	...	...	8.0	117 (92)	61 (92)	60	451 (70)	703	42	45	40
Costa Rica	7	...	...	9.8	105 (93)	47 (93)	80	253 (70)	...	29	34	24
Cuba	...	...	...	3.2	102 (92)	84 (92)	98	217 (70)	207	...	35	...
Dominica	...	...	...	19.4	...	...	100 (85)	225 (70)	...	...	70	...
Dominican Republic	12	...	...	5.6	95 (89)	74 (86)	80	400	529	55	70	45
Ecuador	7	4	...	4.5	116 (88)	56 (87)	88	400	736	56	65	40
El Salvador	6	...	...	2.5	78 (92)	26 (92)	40	500	699	51	75	20
Falkland Islands (Malvinas)	...	...	...	29.0 (88)	...	...	...	...	...	...	...	...
French Guiana	...	...	...	32.7	...	...	...	82 (70)	...	...	...	...
Grenada	...	15	...	17.8	...	...	...	139 (70)	168 (80)	...	25	...
Guadeloupe	...	...	...	32.1	...	...	...	90 (70)	...	...	...	...
Guatemala	11	...	...	2.1	79 (91)	23 (91)	34	500	673	71	74	66
Guyana	...	...	...	2.0	112 (88)	57 (88)	89 (84)	200	300 (85)	...	60	...
Haiti	...	...	...	0.8	56 (90)	22 (90)	50	1289	1323	76	80	65
Honduras	15	16	...	1.8	105 (91)	31 (91)	66	600	993	37	55	14
Jamaica	9	11	...	4.7	106 (90)	62 (90)	90	200	293 (85)	...	80	...
Martinique	...	...	...	36.4	...	...	...	99 (70)	...	...	...	...
Mexico	6	5 (84)	...	7.0	113 (92)	56 (92)	78	760	801	30	51	23
Montserrat	...	...	...	28.4 (88)	...	...	...	...	...	...	...	...
Netherlands Antilles	...	...	...	26.9	...	...	...	...	...	...	...	...
Nicaragua	...	...	...	1.3	102 (92)	42 (92)	83	403	538	20	19	21
Panama	7	...	...	9.3	105 (91)	61 (90)	80	300	300 (85)	42	65	21
Paraguay	16	...	...	2.7	110 (92)	34 (92)	63	599	1087	35	50	19
Peru	10	...	...	2.6	119 (92)	67 (92)	75	400	708	32	75	13
Puerto Rico	...	...	...	6 28.9	...	...	...	...	...	...	...	...
Saint Kitts & Nevis	...	...	...	-	...	...	99 (85)	168 (70)	116 (80)	46	50	40
Saint Lucia	...	11	...	12.7	...	...	100 (85)	197 (70)	...	...	50	...
St. Vincent & Grenadines	...	...	12	13.9	...	...	80 (85)	200 (70)	...	...	50	...
Suriname	...	6	...	9.4	127 (88)	54 (88)	100 (85)	176 (70)	...	...	57	...
Trinidad & Tobago	...	12	...	14.1	95 (91)	79 (91)	100	201	196 (86)	...	39	...
Turks & Caicos Islands	...	...	...	17.0 (89)	...	...	...	...	...	...	...	...
Uruguay	8	...	...	14.5	108 (92)	83 (92)	82	200	221	13	29	10
US Virgin Islands	...	...	...	47.8	...	...	...	...	...	...	...	...
Venezuela	4	5	...	8.1	99 (91)	34 (91)	...	3000	365	31	58	28
NORTHERN AMERICA	...	...	...	...	104 (92)	101 (92)	...	...	...	...	...	...
Bermuda	...	...	...	62.0	...	...	...	107 (70)	...	...	...	...
Canada	11	14	...	58.6	107 (92)	107 (92)	...	101 (70)	64	...	...	...
Greenland	...	...	...	29.9	...	...	...	...	...	...	...	...
St. Pierre & Miquelon	...	...	...	54.5	...	...	...	...	...	...	...	...
United States	13	13	...	6 55.3	104 (91)	94 (91)	100 (84)	127 (70)	194	...	...	...
OCEANIA	...	...	...	...	106 (92)	71 (92)	...	...	...	...	...	...
American Samoa	...	...	...	12.2	...	...	...	...	...	...	...	...
Australia	...	14	...	3 46.4	107 (92)	83 (92)	99 (82)	83 (70)	183	...	...	...
Cook Islands	...	...	...	17.6 (90)	...	...	...	...	...	...	...	...
Fiji	8	9	...	6.2	128 (92)	60 (92)	100 (82)	300	...	...	20	...
French Polynesia	...	...	...	20.3	...	...	...	...	...	...	...	...
Guam	...	...	...	31.8	...	...	...	...	...	...	...	...

TABLE 21 *(continued)*

Social Indicators

	Housing Expenditure (% of GDP)			Telephones # / 100	School Enrolment (Gross Ratio)		Access to Health Care (%)	Population per Hospital Bed		Population in Poverty		
	1980	1985	1990	1991	Primary	Secondary	1988 - 1993	1975	1990	Total (%)	Rural (%)	Urban (%)
										1980 - 1990		
OCEANIA (continued)												
Kiribati	...	...	...	1.8	...	...	95 (84)	81 (70)	196 (80)	...	...	...
Micronesia, Federal States of	...	...	...	2.5	...	...	...	...	...	...	...	...
Nauru	...	...	...	13.1 (88)	...	...	...	...	...	...	...	...
New Caledonia	...	...	...	18.5	...	...	...	...	...	...	...	...
New Zealand	...	9	...	43.6	104 (92)	92 (92)	100 (84)	99 (70)	149	...	...	...
Papua New Guinea	6 (70)	...	...	0.9	73 (92)	13 (92)	96	202	299	73	75	10
Samoa	...	...	6	2.5	...	...	100 (84)	220 (70)	222 (80)	...	60	...
Solomon Islands	...	...	...	1.4	90 (92)	16 (92)	...	139 (70)	179 (81)	...	60	...
Tonga	...	...	...	5.2	...	...	80 (84)	386 (70)	290 (80)	...	...	...
Tuvalu	...	...	...	...	...	...	...	...	...	...	...	...
Vanuatu	...	...	...	2.0	...	...	80 (83)	93 (70)	163 (80)	...	...	...
Wallis & Futuna Islands	...	...	...	...	...	...	...	...	...	...	...	...
U.S.S.R. (FORMER)	...	...	...	...	87 (90)	94 (90)	...	...	...	...	...	...

Sources: The World Bank, Stars 2. United Nations Educational, Scientific and Cultural Organization, Statistical Yearbook 1994. United Nations, Statistical Yearbook (Thirty-ninth issue). United Nations Development Programme, Human Development Report 1994.

Housing Expenditure (as percentage of GDP): the percentage share of housing in total household consumption expenditure, reflecting actual and imputed household expenditure outlays, such as actual and imputed rents and repair and main tenancy charges, as well as fuel and power for heating, lighting, cooking, and so forth.

Primary/Secondary School Enrolment Ratio: the gross enrolment of all ages at primary/secondary levels as a percentage of children in the country's primary/secondary school age groups.

Access to Health Care: defined as the percentage of the population that can reach local health services by local transport in no more than one hour

Population in Poverty: the percentage of population whose income is not enough to afford a minimum nutritionally adequate diet plus essential non-food requirements.

Notes:
1. Telephone subscriber connections, subscriptions or subscriber lines.
2. Government maintained and aided schools only.
3. Telephone services in operation or working lines.
4. Excluding Turkish enrolment and population.
5. Main telephone stations.
6. Switched access lines.

Index